LaunchPad Featuring **LearningCurve** Quizzing

Introducing Psychology, Fourth Edition

Available February 2018 at launchpadworks.com

Each chapter in LaunchPad for *Introducing Psychology*, Fourth Edition, features a collection of activities carefully chosen to help master the major concepts. Students gain a comprehensive online study guide with opportunities for self-quizzing, exam preparation, and further exploration of topics from the textbook. Instructors can instantly assign any or all units, with students' results and analytics collected in the Gradebook.

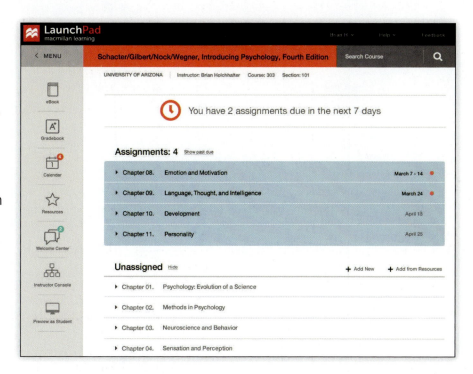

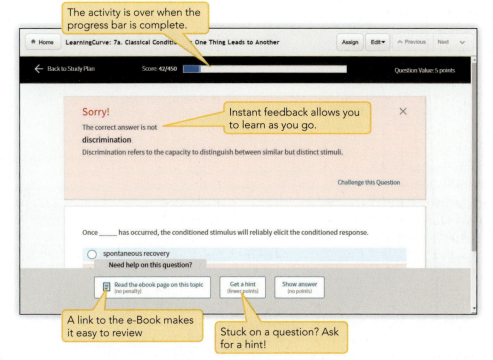

Study Smarter with LearningCurve!

LearningCurve is an adaptive study tool designed to increase your understanding and memory of the core concepts in every chapter. Based on insights from the latest learning and memory research, the LearningCurve system pairs multiple-choice and fill-in-the-blank questions with instantaneous feedback and a rich array of study tools, including videos, animations, and lab simulations. The more questions you answer correctly, the more challenging the questions become.

LearningCurve is available as part of LaunchPad for *Introducing Psychology*, Fourth Edition. To find out more or purchase access, go to launchpadworks.com

Introducing Psychology

Introducing Psychology

FOURTH EDITION

Daniel L. Schacter
Harvard University

Daniel T. Gilbert
Harvard University

Matthew K. Nock
Harvard University

Daniel M. Wegner
Harvard University

worth publishers

Macmillan Learning

New York

Vice President, Social Science and High School: Charles Linsmeier

Director of Content and Assessment, Social Sciences: Shani Fisher

Executive Program Manager: Daniel DeBonis

Senior Development Editor: Valerie Raymond

Editorial Assistant: Un Hye Kim

Senior Marketing Manager: Lindsay Johnson

Marketing Assistant: Morgan Ratner

Director of Media Editorial, Social Sciences: Noel Hohnstine

Media Editor: Stefani Wallace

Media Project Manager: Joseph Tomasso

Director, Content Management Enhancement: Tracey Kuehn

Managing Editor: Lisa Kinne

Senior Content Project Manager: Elizabeth Geller

Senior Project Manager: Matt Gervais, Lumina Datamatics, Inc.

Senior Workflow Project Supervisor: Susan Wein

Senior Workflow Project Manager: Paul Rohloff

Director of Design, Content Management: Diana Blume

Senior Design Manager and Cover Designer: Vicki Tomaselli

Text Design: Lumina Datamatics, Inc.

Photo Editor: Sheena Goldstein

Art Manager: Matt McAdams

Illustrations: Mapping Specialists, Eli Ensor, Christy Krames, Don Stewart, Todd Buck, Evelyn Pence, Jackie Heda

Composition: Lumina Datamatics, Inc.

Printing and Binding: LSC Communications

Cover: © Jason deCaires Taylor. All rights reserved, DACS/ARS 2017. Photo: Jason deCaires Taylor

Library of Congress Project Control Number: 2017954579

ISBN-13: 978-1-4641-5554-3

ISBN-10: 1-4641-5554-2

Worth Publishers

One New York Plaza

Suite 4500

New York, NY 10004-1562

www.macmillanlearning.com

We dedicate this edition to the memory of
Dan Wegner, our co-author, colleague, and friend.
Forever gone, never forgotten.

About the Authors

Daniel Schacter is William R. Kenan Jr. Professor of Psychology at Harvard University. Dan received his BA degree from the University of North Carolina at Chapel Hill. He subsequently developed a keen interest in amnesic disorders associated with various kinds of brain damage. He continued his research and education at the University of Toronto, where he received his PhD in 1981. He taught on the faculty at Toronto for the next six years before joining the psychology department at the University of Arizona in 1987. In 1991, he joined the faculty at Harvard University. His research explores the relationship between conscious and unconscious forms of memory, the nature of distortions and errors in remembering, and the ways in which we use memory to imagine future events. Many of his studies are summarized in his 1996 book, *Searching for Memory: The Brain, The Mind, and The Past*, and his 2001 book, *The Seven Sins of Memory: How the Mind Forgets and Remembers*, both winners of the American Psychological Association's William James Book Award. He has also received a number of awards for teaching and research, including the Harvard-Radcliffe Phi Beta Kappa Teaching Prize, the Award for Distinguished Scientific Contributions from the American Psychological Association, and the William James Fellow Award from the Association for Psychological Science. In 2013, he was elected to the National Academy of Sciences.

Daniel Gilbert is the Edgar Pierce Professor of Psychology at Harvard University. Dan received his BA from the University of Colorado at Denver and his PhD from Princeton University. From 1985 to 1996 he taught at the University of Texas at Austin, and in 1996 he joined the faculty of Harvard University. He has received the American Psychological Association's Distinguished Scientific Award for an Early Career Contribution to Psychology and the Diener Award for Outstanding Contributions to Social Psychology, and has won teaching awards that include the Phi Beta Kappa Teaching Prize and the Harvard College Professorship. His research focuses on how and how well people think about their emotional reactions to future events. He is the author of the international best seller *Stumbling on Happiness*, which won the Royal Society's General Prize for best popular science book of the year, he is the cowriter and host of the PBS television series *This Emotional Life*, and yes, he's also that guy in the Prudential commercials.

Matthew Nock is a Professor of Psychology at Harvard University. Matt received his BA from Boston University (1995) and his PhD from Yale University (2003), and he completed his clinical internship at Bellevue Hospital and the New York University Child Study Center (2003). He joined the faculty of Harvard University in 2003. While an undergraduate, he became very interested in the question of why people do things to intentionally harm themselves, and he has been conducting research aimed at answering this question ever since. His research is multidisciplinary in nature and involves a range of methodological approaches (e.g., epidemiologic surveys, laboratory-based experiments, and clinic-based studies) to understand better how these behaviors develop, how to predict them, and how to prevent their occurrence. He has received multiple teaching awards at Harvard and four early career awards recognizing his research, and in 2011 was named a MacArthur Fellow.

Daniel Wegner was the John Lindsley Professor of Psychology in Memory of William James at Harvard University. He received his BS in 1970 and his PhD in 1974, both from Michigan State University. He began his teaching career at Trinity University in San Antonio, Texas, before receiving his appointments at the University of Virginia in 1990 and then at Harvard University in 2000. He was a Fellow of the American Academy of Arts and Sciences and also the recipient of the William James Award from the Association for Psychological Science, the Award for Distinguished Scientific Contributions from the American Psychological Association, and the Distinguished Scientist Award from the Society of Experimental Social Psychology. His research focused on thought suppression and mental control, transactive memory in relationships and groups, and the experience of conscious will. His work on thought suppression and consciousness served as the basis of two popular books, *White Bears and Other Unwanted Thoughts* and the *Illusion of Conscious Will*, both of which were named *Choice* Outstanding Academic Books. He passed away in 2013.

Brief Contents

Contents

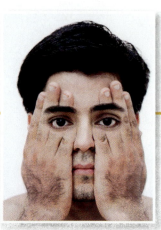

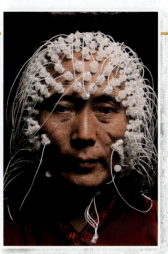

Cary Wolinsky/Aurora/Getty Images

Andrew Geiger

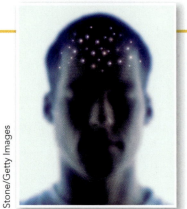

Stone/Getty Images

6 Memory   163

David Johnston/Photolibrary/Getty Images

9 Language, Thought, and Intelligence   267

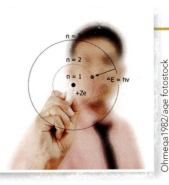

Ohmega1982/age fotostock

Tooga/The Image Bank/ Getty Images

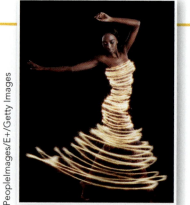

PeopleImages/E+/Getty Images

Tim Macpherson/Stone/Getty Images

Fotosearch/AGE Fotostock

easyFotostock/AGE Fotostock

Livia Fernandes - Brazil/Moment Select/Getty Images

Preface

Why are you reading this? This book doesn't really get going for another 10 pages, so why are you starting here instead of skipping ahead? Are you the kind of person who just can't stand the thought of missing something? Are you trying to justify the cost of the book by consuming every word of it? Or maybe you opened to this page out of habit or obligation? Are you starting to think that maybe you made a big mistake?

For as long as we can remember, we've been asking questions like these about ourselves, about our friends, and about anyone else who didn't run away fast enough. Our curiosity about why people think, feel, and act as they do drew each of us into our first psychology course, and although we remember being swept away by the lectures, we don't remember much about our textbooks. That's probably because those textbooks were little more than colorful encyclopedias of facts and jargon, names and dates. No wonder we sold them back to the bookstore the moment we finished our final exams.

Then we became psychology professors and did all the things psychology professors do: We taught classes, we conducted research, and we wore sweater vests long after they stopped being fashionable. We also wrote some things that people really enjoyed reading—magazine articles and popular books, for instance—and that made us wonder why no one had ever written an introductory psychology textbook that students really enjoyed reading. After all, psychology is the single most interesting subject in the known universe, so why shouldn't a psychology textbook be the single most interesting object in a student's backpack? We couldn't think of a reason, so we sat down and wrote the book that we wished our professors had given us when we were students. The first edition of *Introducing Psychology* was published in 2008, and the reaction to it was astounding. We'd never written a textbook before, so we didn't know exactly what to expect, but never in our wildest dreams did we imagine that we would *win the Pulitzer Prize*!

Which was good, because we didn't. But what actually happened was even better: We started getting e-mails from students all over the world who wanted to tell us how much they actually *liked* reading our book. They liked the content, of course, because as we already mentioned, psychology is the single most interesting subject in the known universe. But they also liked the fact that our textbook didn't *sound* like a textbook. It wasn't written in the stodgy voice of the announcer from one of those nature films that we all saw in seventh-grade biology class ("Behold the sea otter, nature's furry little scavenger"). Rather, it was written in *our* voices—the same voices we use when we talk to our students, our spouses, our kids, and our pets (which explains why the original title of Chapter 12 was "Stop Chewing My Shoes!"). We made a conscious effort to tell the *story* of psychology—to integrate topics, rather than just listing them, to illustrate ideas rather than just describing them. We realized that, because science is a complicated and serious business, some teachers might think that a science textbook should be complicated and serious, too. With all due respect, we just didn't see it that way ourselves. We thought that writing was the art of making complicated things seem simple and of making serious things seem fun. The students who sent us nice letters seemed to agree, even if the Pulitzer Prize committee didn't.

The last edition of our book was a big hit—so why have we replaced it? Because three things have changed. First, science has changed: Psychologists know all sorts of things about the mind and the brain that they didn't know just a few years ago. Second, the world has changed: When we wrote the last edition, there was no such thing as Snapchat and Donald Trump was a real estate developer. And third, we've changed: Our research has given us new perspectives on many psychological issues, and our teaching has showed us new ways to help students learn. With all of these changes happening, we thought it only fitting that our book should change as well. Plus, we really like the new cover.

Changes in the Fourth Edition

New Learning Outcomes

In preparing this new edition, we heard from teachers across the country who are increasingly being asked to describe the goals of their course and how they are assessing those goals. To aid them in their efforts, we considered how to articulate the goals of this text in a way that will aid students as well as teachers and allow them to better track their learning progress. The result is a new set of pedagogical features:

- **Learning Outcomes**, introduced at the beginning of each major section of each chapter, have been written to align with the goals of the American Psychological Association (APA). These outcomes describe the key points presented in the section and can be used to preview the material. We believe strongly that a first course in psychology is about more than just being able to recite a bunch of facts; rather, it should foster the ability to understand and draw connections among concepts. Consequently, the outcomes set the expectation that readers will not only learn about psychology but also will learn *how to think about* psychology.

- **Build to the Outcomes** questions conclude each section and provide the scaffolding necessary to reach the outcomes. Students can use them as a study guide, or instructors can use them as writing assignments. Guides for answering the questions can be found in the **Chapter Review** section at the end of each chapter.

- **Quiz questions in LearningCurve** give students an additional means of interleaved practice. This builds on what we know about learning (covered in the Learning chapter): that self-testing and mixing study tools improves understanding and retention. LearningCurve also allows instructors to track students' learning at a glance.

- The **Test Bank** allows the flexibility to create additional formative and summative assessments. This program offers a new way of setting and tracking goals consistently throughout the course.

Culture and Beyond

In the last decade, many psychologists have become interested in culture, and we've become interested in it, too. Previous editions of our book had special sections and boxes on culture. But human beings differ along many important dimensions, and culture is just one of them. Thought, feeling, and behavior are influenced by culture, but also by gender, race, religion, age, sexual orientation, and all the other individual differences that make us so diverse. So in this edition, we've expanded our focus on culture to include many of these other interesting differences as well. You'll notice this especially in two new features:

- A World of Difference is a new boxed feature that covers exciting research on a wide range of human differences, from culture to gender to social class.

- "Paired photos" are visual reminders that people across our planet differ in remarkable and consequential ways.

CULTURE AND MULTICULTURAL EXPERIENCE

THE PSYCHOLOGY OF MEN AND WOMEN

New Research

A textbook should give students a complete tour of the classics, of course, but it should also take them on a tour of the cutting edge. Psychology has a history; besides being a collection of past events, it also includes current events. We want students to realize that this young and evolving science is about them—and that it even has a place for them if they want it. So we've packed the fourth edition with information about what's happening in the field right this very minute. (Okay, well, not *this* minute because we had to write the book in the past so you could read it in the present, but you get the point.) Not only have we included more than 350 new citations but we've also featured some of the hottest new science in a box that we creatively called "Hot Science." You'll find one in almost every chapter.

Proven Strengths

Focus on Critical Thinking

Flip-flopper. Waffler. Wishy-washy. Namby-pamby. Those are just some of the inventive invectives we use to describe people who change their minds. But science is constantly uncovering new evidence that changes the way we think about old evidence, so good scientists change their minds all the time. Some of the facts that students learn in their first psychology course still will be facts a century from now, but others will require qualification or will turn out to have been just plain wrong. That's why students need not only to learn the facts but also how to *think* about facts—how to examine, question, and weigh the kinds of evidence that scientists produce. We call this *critical thinking*, and although we emphasize it throughout our textbook, we discuss it specifically in a section designed to help students understand the kinds of mistakes that human beings commonly make when they consider evidence (see "Thinking Critically About Evidence" in Chapter 2, Methods in Psychology). This section is meant to help students learn how to develop well-founded beliefs—about psychological science and about the stuff of which their lives are made.

The "Changing Minds" questions that are included at the end of every chapter are another way that we try to get students to think critically. These questions ask students to consider everyday situations in which a common misconception about human behavior might arise, and then to use psychological science to overcome that misconception. These exercises are meant to encourage students to apply what they are learning in their psychology course to their daily lives.

Changing Minds

1. One of the senators from your state is supporting a bill that would impose heavy fines on aggressive drivers who run red lights. One of your classmates thinks this is a good idea. "The textbook taught us a lot about punishment and reward. It's simple. If we punish aggressive driving, its frequency will decline." Is your classmate right? Might the new law backfire? Might another policy be more effective in promoting safe driving?

Many New "Other Voices"

Long before psychologists appeared on earth, the human nature business was dominated by poets, playwrights, pundits, philosophers, and several other groups whose names begin with *p*. Those folks are still in that business today, and they continue to have deep and original insights into how and why human beings behave as they do. So we decided to invite some of them to share their thoughts with students via a feature that we call "Other Voices." Many of the chapters have a short essay by someone who has three important qualifications: (1) They think deeply; (2) they write beautifully; and (3) they know things we don't. For example, students will find essays by leading writers such as Ted Gup, Tina Rosenberg, David Ewing Duncan, and Peter Brown; by award-winning educator Julie Lythcott-Haims; by renowned legal scholars such as Gustin Reichbach, Stephen Carter, Karen L. Daniel, and Elyn Saks; and by eminent psychologists Timothy Wilson, Henry Roediger, and Mark McDaniel. Every one of these amazing people has something important to say about human nature, and we are delighted that they've agreed to say it in these pages. Not only do these essays encourage students to think critically about a variety of topical issues, but they also demonstrate psychology's relevance and growing importance in the public forum.

CHAPTER NUMBER	OTHER VOICES
1	Is Psychology a Science? Timothy D. Wilson, pp. 8–9
5	A Judge's Plea for Pot, the Honorable Gustin L. Reichbach, p. 156
6	Memories Inside Out, Karen L. Daniel, p. 189
7	Learning at Jiffy Lube University, Peter Brown, Henry Roediger, and Mark McDaniel, p. 228
8	Should We Pay People to Vote? Stephen Carter, p. 260
9	How Science Can Build a Better You, David Ewing Duncan, p. 301
12	Ninety-One Percent of All Students Read This Box and Love It, Tina Rosenberg, p. 392
13	The Dangers of Overparenting, Julie Lythcott-Haims, p. 436
14	Successful and Schizophrenic, Elyn R. Saks, pp. 462–463
15	Diagnosis: Human, Ted Gup, p. 501

Practical Application: "The Real World" Boxes

From cells in petri dishes to rats in mazes to participants in experimental cubicles, a psychology textbook can seem like a report about things that happened in places that aren't much like the place students are sitting in right now. That's why we have included a box called "The Real World" that shows students how the facts and concepts of psychology have been or can be applied to the stuff of everyday life, from dating to studying to going on a job interview.

CHAPTER NUMBER	THE REAL WORLD
1	Improving Study Skills, p. 5
2	Oddsly Enough, p. 44
3	Brain Plasticity and Sensations in Phantom Limbs, p. 74
4	Multitasking, p. 95
5	Drugs and the Regulation of Consciousness, p. 151
6	Is Google Hurting Our Memories? p. 183

Data Visualization Activities

Is SAT performance related to family income and education level? How do concussion rates for high school sports differ? How important is a good night's sleep? The Data Visualization Activities invite readers to consider these questions as scientists by looking at real experimental data. Available in LaunchPad, each activity is based around an interactive graph that displays actual data from a published study. After reading a description of the study, students have to answer questions that test their ability to understand and reason about the data. Integrated lessons in statistical concepts further build students' quantitative-reasoning skills. The Data Visualization Activities engage students in the science of psychology and help to prepare them for later courses in statistics and research methods.

Focus on Learning Outcomes

Teaching with the APA Learning Goals and Outcomes: More Specifics

In every chapter in this book, you will see references to "Learning Outcomes." What in the world are these, you ask? In an effort to develop greater consensus on what undergraduate students should be learning in their psychology courses, the APA formed the Task Force on Undergraduate Psychology Major Competencies to provide a framework for educators. The task force published comprehensive recommendations in *The APA Guidelines for the Undergraduate Introducing Psychology Major*, with the revised version 2.0 released in August 2013. These revised guidelines present a rigorous standard for what students should gain from foundational courses and from the psychology major as a whole. They comprise five goals relating to the following:

Goal 1: Knowledge Base in Psychology

Goal 2: Scientific Inquiry and Critical Thinking

Goal 3: Ethical and Social Responsibility in a Diverse World

Goal 4: Communication

Goal 5: Professional Development

In order to make sure that you know everything that students of psychology should know, this textbook, and the people who created it—Worth Publishers—offer a wide variety of resources to support you in achieving the APA outcomes. Most important, a document showing how the content of this textbook maps onto the APA goals is available for download from the Resources area of LaunchPad at launchpadworks.com. To assist with assessment, Worth has tagged all of the items included in the Test Bank accompanying this book to the relevant outcomes. In addition, the Instructor's

Resources and LaunchPad learning system feature a variety of activities and additional content items that contribute to the APA goals. All of these resources in combination offer instructors (and their students!) a powerful set of tools for achieving their course outcomes.

Preparing for the MCAT

Is medical school a goal? If so, all the more reason to make sure to master the material in this revised edition of our textbook, because psychological science now makes up a significant portion of the material in the standardized test that students must take when applying to medical school. More specifically, from 1977 to 2014, the Medical College Admission Test (MCAT) focused only on biology, chemistry, and physics, but as of 2015, 25% of its questions now cover "Psychological, Social, and Biological Foundations of Behavior," with most of those questions concerning the psychological science taught in introductory psychology courses. According to the *Preview Guide for the MCAT 2015 Exam* (second edition), the addition of this content "recognizes the importance of socio-cultural and behavioral determinants of health and health outcomes." The psychology material in the new MCAT covers the breadth of topics in this textbook. The table below offers a sample of how the topics in this textbook's Sensation and Perception chapter correspond precisely to the topics laid out in the MCAT *Preview Guide*. A complete correlation of the MCAT psychology topics with this book's contents is available for download from the Resources area of Launch-Pad at launchpadworks.com. In addition, since the MCAT sets a global standard for assessing the ability to reason about scientific information, the Test Bank for *Introducing Psychology*, Fourth Edition, features a new set of data-based questions for each chapter that are designed to test students' quantitative reasoning. These questions are available for preview in LaunchPad.

MCAT: CATEGORIES IN SENSATION AND PERCEPTION	INTRODUCING PSYCHOLOGY, FOURTH EDITION, CORRELATIONS	
	Section Title	Page Number(s)
Content Category 6A: Sensing the Environment		
Sensory processing	Sensation and Perception	90–127
Sensation	Sensation and Perception	90–127
Thresholds	Measuring Thresholds	92–93
Weber's law	Measuring Thresholds	92–93
Signal detection theory	Signal Detection	94
Sensory adaptation	Sensory Adaptation	94–95
Sensory receptors	Sensation and Perception Are Distinct Activities	92–95
Sensory pathways	The Visual Brain	102–103
	Sensing Touch	116–117
	Sensing Pain & Receiving Pain	117–119
	Body Position, Movement, and Balance	119
	Sense of Smell & Perceiving Smell	120–122
	Sense of Taste & Perceiving Taste	122–124
Types of sensory receptors	Vision I: The Eyes and the Brain Convert Light Waves to Neural Signals	96–103
	Audition: More Than Meets the Ear	111–116

Media and Supplements

LaunchPad with LearningCurve Quizzing

A comprehensive Web resource for teaching and learning psychology, LaunchPad combines Worth Publishers' award-winning media with an innovative platform for easy navigation. For students, it is the ultimate online study guide, with rich interactive tutorials and videos, as well as an e-Book and the LearningCurve adaptive quizzing system. For instructors, LaunchPad is a full course space where class documents can be posted, quizzes easily assigned and graded, and students' progress assessed and recorded. Whether you are looking for the most effective study tools or a robust platform for an online course, LaunchPad is a powerful way to enhance your class. LaunchPad for *Introducing Psychology*, Fourth Edition, can be previewed and purchased at launchpadworks.com.

> *Introducing Psychology*, Fourth Edition, and LaunchPad can be ordered together with ISBN-10: 1-319-17043-9 / ISBN-13: 978-1-319-17043-1.

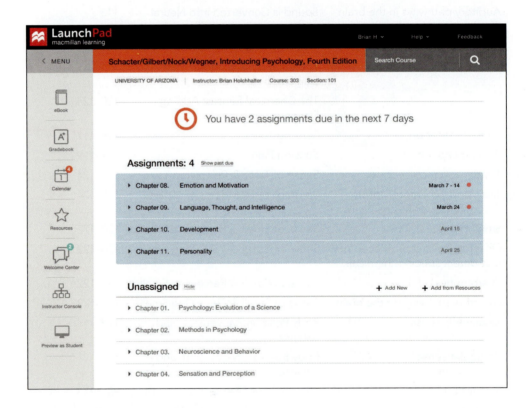

LaunchPad for *Introducing Psychology*, Fourth Edition, includes all the following resources:

- The design of the **LearningCurve** quizzing system is based on the latest findings from learning and memory research. It combines adaptive question selection, immediate and valuable feedback, and a gamelike interface to engage students in a learning experience that is unique to them. Each LearningCurve quiz is fully integrated with other resources in LaunchPad through the Personalized Study Plan, so students will be able to review using Worth's extensive library of videos and activities. And state-of-the-art question analysis reports allow instructors to track the progress of individual students as well as their class as a whole.

- **Immersive Learning Activities: Data Visualization Activities** offer students practice in understanding and reasoning about data. In each activity, students interact with a graph or visual display of data and must think like scientists to answer the accompanying questions. These activities build quantitative reasoning skills and offer a deeper understanding of how science works.

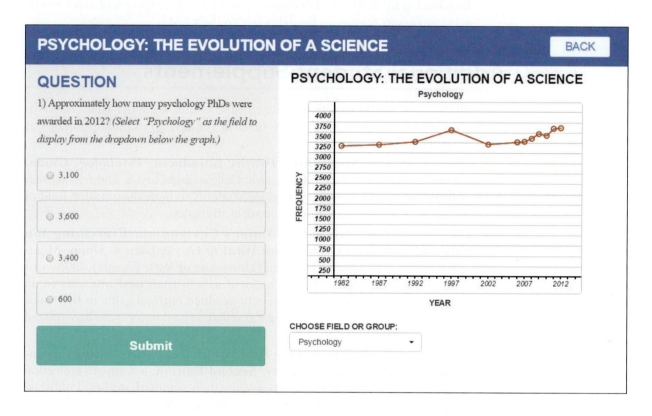

- **An interactive e-Book** allows students to highlight, bookmark, and add their own notes on the e-Book page, just as they would in a printed textbook. Google-style searching and in-text glossary definitions make the text ready for the digital age.

- **Video Activities** comprise more than 100 engaging video modules that instructors can easily assign and customize for student assessment. Videos cover classic experiments, current news footage, and cutting-edge research, all of which are sure to spark discussion and encourage critical thinking. Each activity includes a quiz to check students' understanding.

- The award-winning tutorials in **PsychSim 6.0** by Tom Ludwig (Hope College) and John Krantz (Hanover College) give students an engaging, interactive introduction to psychological phenomena, integrating demonstrations and experimental tasks. In addition, each activity includes integrated formative and summative assessment questions.

- The newly revised series of **Concept Practice** activities by Tom Ludwig (Hope College) allow students to practice their understanding of individual concepts in less than five minutes. All of the 120+ activities feature new art and assessment features to deepen students' interaction with the material.

- The *Scientific American* Newsfeed delivers weekly articles, podcasts, and news briefs on the very latest developments in psychology from the first name in popular-science journalism.

- **Deep integration** is available between LaunchPad products and most learning management systems, including Blackboard, Brightspace by D2L, Canvas, and Moodle. These deep integrations offer educators single sign-on and Gradebook sync, now with auto refresh. These best-in-class integrations offer deep linking to all Macmillan digital content at the chapter and asset levels, giving professors maximum flexibility within their LMS.

Additional Student Supplements

Macmillan offers a wide variety of texts to supplement students' first course in psychology. Find out more about these titles or request an examination copy at www.macmillanlearning.com.

- *Pursuing Human Strengths: A Positive Introducing Psychology Guide*, **Second Edition**, by Martin Bolt (Calvin College) and Dana S. Dunn (Moravian College), is a perfect way to introduce students to both the amazing field of positive psychology and their own personal strengths.

- *The Introducing Psychology Major's Companion: Everything You Need to Know to Get Where You Want to Go*, by Dana S. Dunn (Moravian College) and Jane S. Halonen (University of West Florida), helps students to declare the psychology major if it is in their best interests to do so, to learn strategies regarding how to produce optimal gains in the major experience, and to prepare for either graduate school or a psychology-related professional life.

- *Introducing Psychology and the Real World: Essays Illustrating Fundamental Contributions to Society*, **Second Edition**, is a superb collection of essays by major researchers that describe their landmark studies. Published in association with the not-for-profit FABBS Foundation, the new edition of this engaging reader includes Alan Kazdin's reflections on his research on treating children with severe aggressive behavior, Adam Grant's look at work and motivation, and Steven Hayes's research on mindfulness and acceptance and commitment therapy. A portion of all proceeds is donated to FABBS to support societies of cognitive, psychological, behavioral, and brain sciences.

- *The Critical Thinking Companion for Introductory Psychology*, **Third Edition**, by Jane S. Halonen (University of West Florida) and Cynthia Gray (Beloit College), contains a guide to critical thinking strategies as well as exercises in pattern recognition, practical problem solving, creative problem solving, scientific problem solving, psychological reasoning, and perspective taking.

- *The Worth Expert Guide to Scientific Literacy: Thinking Like a Psychological Scientist*, by Kenneth D. Keith (University of San Diego) and Bernard Beins (Ithaca College), helps students foster solid habits of scientific thought, learning to apply an empirical attitude and data-driven decision making in their lives. With this increased level of scientific literacy, students will be better able to make sense of complex scientific information and to recognize pseudoscientific claims that are not only invalid but also potentially harmful.

Take advantage of our most popular supplements!

Worth Publishers is pleased to offer cost-saving packages of *Introducing Psychology*, Fourth Edition, with our most popular supplements. Below is a list of some of the most popular combinations available for order through your local bookstore.

Introducing Psychology, 4th Ed., & LaunchPad Access Card
ISBN-10: 1-319-17043-9 / ISBN-13: 978-1-319-17043-1

Introducing Psychology, 4th Ed., & iClicker 2
ISBN-10: 1-319-15576-6 / ISBN-13: 978-1-319-15576-6

Introducing Psychology, 4th Ed., & *Pursuing Human Strengths: A Positive Introducing Psychology Guide*
ISBN-10: 1-319-15488-3 / ISBN-13: 978-1-319-15488-2

Introducing Psychology, 4th Ed., & *The Introducing Psychology Major's Companion*
ISBN-10: 1-319-15493-X / ISBN-13: 978-1-319-15493-6

Introducing Psychology, 4th Ed., & *Introducing Psychology and the Real World*
ISBN-10: 1-319-15494-8 / ISBN-13: 978-1-319-15494-3

Introducing Psychology, 4th Ed., & *The Critical Thinking Companion for Psychology*
ISBN-10: 1-319-15498-0 / ISBN-13: 978-1-319-15498-1

Introducing Psychology, 4th Ed., & *The Worth Expert Guide to Scientific Literacy* ISBN-10: 1-319-15500-6 / ISBN-13: 978-1-319-15500-1

ForeWords Custom Publishing Library

The ForeWords Library contains special chapters and other print content to supplement *Introducing Psychology*, Fourth Edition, through Macmillan's custom publishing program. ForeWords content is authored by recognized experts and can be added to a custom book at little or no cost. Current offerings include:

- **New!** *Introducing Psychology and Sustainability* by Susan Clayton of the College of Wooster
- *A Practical Guide to Study Skills* by Amy Himsel of El Camino College
- *Industrial/Organizational Introducing Psychology and Human Factors* by Paul Levy of the University of Akron and Karen Marando of Argosy University
- *The Basics of Scientific Writing in APA Style* by Pam Marek of Kennesaw State University
- And many others!

For more information, visit our Curriculum Solutions Web page at www.worthpublishers.com/psychologyforewords.

Assessment

- The **Computerized Test Bank**, powered by Diploma, includes a full assortment of test items from author Chad Galuska (College of Charleston). Each chapter features over 200 multiple-choice, true/false, and essay questions to test students at several levels of Bloom's taxonomy. All the questions are tagged to the text's learning outcomes, the book page, the chapter section, and the outcomes recommended in the 2013 APA Guidelines for the Undergraduate Psychology Major, allowing for incredible ease in finding and selecting items for a wide variety of assessments. In the new edition, the test bank items are divided into two forms with similar characteristics to make it even easier to create two different tests covering the same material at comparable levels of difficulty.

  This title also features a special set of data-based scenario questions to test advanced critical thinking skills in a manner similar to the MCAT. They pair perfectly with the Data Visualization exercises featured in LaunchPad for an incomparable introduction to scientific literacy. Adopters also have access to a special collection of integrative questions which require students to connect material from multiple chapters—a challenging addition for midterm and final exams. The accompanying Gradebook software makes it easy to record students' grades throughout a course, to sort student records, to view detailed analyses of test items, to curve tests, to generate reports, and to add weights to grades.

- The **iClicker** Classroom Response System is a versatile polling system developed by educators for educators that makes class time more efficient and interactive. iClicker allows you to ask questions and instantly record your students' responses, take attendance, and gauge students' understanding and opinions. iClicker is available at a 10% discount when packaged with *Introducing Psychology*, Fourth Edition.

Presentation

- **Lecture Slides** by Linda Lockwood (Metropolitan State University of Denver) are complimentary to adopters of *Introducing Psychology*, Fourth Edition, and are perfect for technology novices and experts alike. Fully updated to support the new edition, they include images from the text and clicker questions to spark discussion. The Lecture Slides are available to download in LaunchPad at launchpadworks.com.

- The **Instructor's Resources** by Jeffrey Henriques (University of Wisconsin–Madison) feature a variety of materials that are valuable to new and veteran teachers alike. In addition to background on the chapter reading and suggestions for in-class lectures, the manual is rich with activities to engage students in different modes of learning. The Instructor's Resources are available to download in LaunchPad at launchpadworks.com.

- The **Video Collection for Introductory Psychology** includes over 150 unique video clips to bring lectures to life. Provided complimentary to adopters of *Introducing Psychology*, Fourth Edition, this rich collection includes clinical footage, interviews, animations, and news segments that vividly illustrate topics across the psychology curriculum. Request a copy from your local Macmillan representative.

- **Macmillan Community** is an online forum where teachers can find and share favorite teaching ideas and materials, including videos, animations, images, PowerPoint slides, news stories, articles, Web links, and lecture activities. It is also the home of Worth's abundant social media content, including tweets, blog posts, webinars (featuring Daniel Schacter, Daniel Gilbert, Matthew Nock,

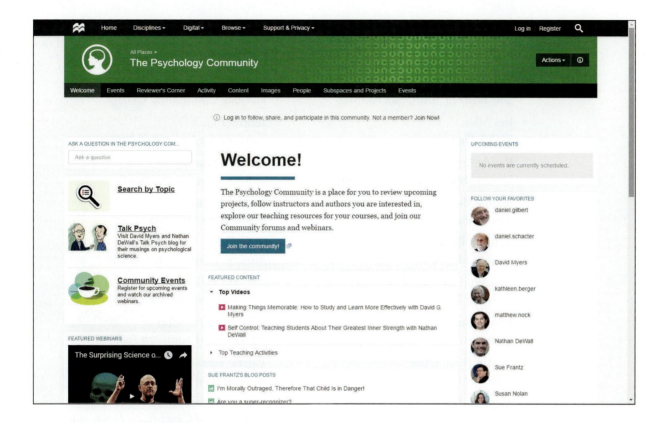

and others), and more! Browse the site and share your favorite materials for teaching psychology at https://community.macmillan.com.

Acknowledgments

Despite what you might guess by looking at our photographs, we all found women who were willing to marry us, though in some cases it required special pleading. We are grateful to our amazing wives—Susan McGlynn, Marilynn Oliphant, and Keesha Nock—who never once complained on all those long nights and weekends when we were busy writing this book instead of hanging out with them. Hey, wait a minute. You did miss us, didn't you?

Although ours are the only names on the cover, writing a textbook is a team sport, and we were lucky to have a terrific group of professionals in our dugout. We greatly appreciate the contributions of our distinguished colleagues, Martin M. Antony, Mark Baldwin, Michelle A. Butler, Patricia Csank, Denise D. Cummins, Ian J. Deary, Howard Eichenbaum, Sam Gosling, Paul Harris, Melanie Maggard, Catherine Myers, Shigehiro Oishi, Arthur S. Reber, Morgan T. Sammons, Dan Simons, Alan Swinkels, Richard M. Wenzlaff, and Steven Yantis.

We thank our core supplements authors, who provided insight into the role our book can play in the classroom and adeptly developed the materials to support it. Chad Galuska, Jeff Henriques, Melanie Maggard, Matthew Isaak, Linda Lockwood, and Richard Hullinger, we appreciate your tireless work in the classroom and the experience you brought to our book's supplements. We also appreciate the editorial, clerical, and research assistance we received from Molly Evans and Franchesca Ramirez. What would we have done without you?

We would also like to thank the faculty members who reviewed our book. These dedicated teachers showed a level of engagement we have come to expect from our best colleagues:

Eileen Achorn
University of Texas, San Antonio

Jim Allen
SUNY Geneseo

Randy Arnau
University of Southern Mississippi

Joanne Bagshaw
Montgomery College

Kathryn Becker-Blease
Oregon State University

Benjamin Bennett-Carpenter
Oakland University

Joan Bihun
University of Colorado, Denver

Kristin Biondolillo
Arkansas State University

Stephen Blessing
University of Tampa

Jeffrey Blum
Los Angeles City College

Richard Bowen
Loyola University of Chicago

Nicole Bragg
Mt. Hood Community College

Jennifer Breneiser
Valdosta State University

Christopher Brill
Old Dominion University

Michele Brumley
Idaho State University

Josh Burk
College of William and Mary

Jennifer Butler
Case Western Reserve University

Richard Cavasina
California University of Pennsylvania

Amber Chenoweth
Kent State University

Stephen Chew
Samford University

Chrisanne Christensen
Southern Arkansas University

Sheryl Civjan
Holyoke Community College

Jennifer Dale
Community College of Aurora

Jennifer Daniels
University of Connecticut

Joshua Dobias
Marywood University

Dale Doty
Monroe Community College

Vanessa Edkins
Dawson College

Julie Evey-Johnson
University of Southern Indiana

Valerie Farmer-Dugan
Illinois State University

Diane Feibel
University of Cincinnati, Raymond Walters College

Jocelyn Folk
Kent State University

Chad Galuska
College of Charleston

Afshin Gharib
Dominican University of California

Jeffrey Gibbons
Christopher Newport University

Adam Goodie
University of Georgia

John Governale
Clark College

Patricia Grace
Kaplan University Online

Stephanie Griffiths
Okanagan College

Sarah Grison
University of Illinois at Urbana–Champaign

Tom Hancock
University of Central Oklahoma

Deletha Hardin
University of Tampa

Jason Hart
Christopher Newport University

Lesley Hathorn
Metropolitan State College of Denver

Mark Hauber
Hunter College

Jacqueline Hembrook
University of New Hampshire

Allen Huffcutt
Bradley University

Mary Hughes-Stone
San Francisco State University

Mark Hurd
College of Charleston

Linda Jackson
Michigan State University

Jennifer Johnson
Rider University

Linda Johnson
Butte College

Lance Jones
Bowling Green State University

Linda Jones
Blinn College

Evan Jordan
Oklahoma State University

Katherine Judge
Cleveland State University

Don Kates
College of DuPage

Donna Kearns
University of Central Oklahoma

Martha Knight-Oakley
Warren Wilson College

Ken Koenigshofer
Chaffey College

Neil Kressel
William Patterson University

Josh Landau
York College of Pennsylvania

Fred Leavitt
California State University, East Bay

Tera Letzring
Idaho State University

Karsten Loepelmann
University of Alberta

Laura Loewen
Okanagan College

Ray Lopez
University of Texas at San Antonio

Jeffrey Love
Penn State University

Greg Loviscky
Penn State, University Park

Julianne Ludlam
University of Missouri, Columbia

Keith Maddox
Tufts University

Lynda Mae
Arizona State University at Tempe

Caitlin Mahy
University of Oregon

Gregory Manley
University of Texas at San Antonio

Karen Marsh
University of Minnesota at Duluth

Sarah Marsh
Minnesota State University

Robert Mather
University of Central Oklahoma

Wanda McCarthy
University of Cincinnati at Clermont College

Daniel McConnell
University of Central Florida

Robert McNally
Austin Community College

Dawn Melzer
Sacred Heart University

Christopher Meshanko
College of Charleston

Dennis Miller
University of Missouri

Mignon Montpetit
Miami University

Tonya Nascimento
University of West Florida

William P. Neace
Lindsey Wilson College

Todd Nelson
California State University at Stanislaus

Margaret Norwood
Community College of Aurora

Aminda O'Hare
University of Kansas

Gina A. O'Neal-Moffitt
Florida State University

Melissa Pace
Kean University

Linda Peters
Springfield Technical Community College

Brady Phelps
South Dakota State University

Raymond Phinney
Wheaton College

Claire St. Peter Pipkin
West Virginia University, Morgantown

John Pisano
Luzerne County Community College

Christy Porter
College of William and Mary

Jens Pruessner
McGill University

Douglas Pruitt
West Kentucky Community and Technical College

Elizabeth Purcell
Greenville Technical College

Gabriel Radvansky
University of Notre Dame

Celia Reaves
Monroe Community College

Diane Reddy
University of Wisconsin, Milwaukee

Cynthia Shinabarger Reed
Tarrant County College

David Reetz
Hanover College

Ann Renken
University of Southern California

Tanya Renner
Kapi'olani Community College

Anthony Robertson
Vancouver Island University

Nancy Rogers
University of Cincinnati

Wendy Rote
University of Rochester

Larry Rudiger
University of Vermont

Sharleen Sakai
Michigan State University

Matthew Sanders
Marquette University

Phillip Schatz
Saint Joseph's University

Vann Scott
Armstrong Atlantic State University

Gwendolyn Scott-Jones
Delaware State University

Colleen Seifert
University of Michigan at Ann Arbor

Keith Shafritz
Hofstra University

Wayne Shebilske
Wright State University

Elisabeth Sherwin
University of Arkansas at Little Rock

Lisa Shin
Tufts University

Robert Short
Arizona State University

Kenith Sobel
University of Central Arkansas

Genevieve Stevens
Houston Community College

Mark Stewart
American River College

Holly Straub
University of South Dakota

Mary Strobbe
San Diego Miramar College

William Struthers
Wheaton College

Donald Tellinghuisen
Calvin College

Lisa Thomassen
Indiana University

Ross Thompson
University of California, Davis

Jeremy Tost
Valdosta State University

Susan Troy
Northeast Iowa Community College

Laura Turiano
Sacred Heart University

Jeffrey Wagman
Illinois State University

Kelly Warmuth
Providence College

Alexander Williams
University of Kansas

John Wright
Washington State University

Jennifer Yanowitz
Utica College

Dean Yoshizumi
Sierra College

Keith Young
University of Kansas

We continue to be grateful to the good folks at Worth Publishers. They include vice president Charles Linsmeier, who provided guidance and encouragement at all stages of the project; our senior acquisitions editor, Dan DeBonis, who managed the project with brio; our brilliant, talented, and preternaturally cheerful senior development editor, Valerie Raymond, who not only puts up with us, but makes us sound a whole lot smarter than we actually are; our director, content management enhancement, Tracey Kuehn; and our editorial assistant Un Kim, all of whom somehow turned a manuscript into a real book; our senior design manager, Vicki Tomaselli, our art manager, Matt McAdams, and our photo editor Sheena Goldstein, all of whom worked to make our book an aesthetic delight; our media editor Stefani Wallace and director of media editorial Noel Hohnstine, who guided the development and creation of a superb supplements package; and our senior marketing manager Lindsay Johnson, who continues to be a tireless public advocate for our vision. Gracias, arigato, danke, merci, xie xie, and Way Big Thanks to all of you.

Finally, allow us to acknowledge the essential contributions of our dear friend, colleague, and co-author, Dan Wegner. Dan was diagnosed with ALS and passed away before we began work on this edition, but his brilliant ideas and beautiful words remain—in our pages and in our hearts. Ad perpetuam rei memoriam.

Daniel L. Schacter

Daniel T. Gilbert

Matthew K. Nock
Cambridge, 2017

Psychology: Evolution of a Science

A lot was happening in 1860. Abraham Lincoln had just been elected president of the United States, the Pony Express had just begun to deliver mail between Missouri and California, and a woman named Anne Kellogg had just given birth to a child who would one day grow up to invent the cornflake. But none of this mattered very much to William James, a bright, taciturn, 18-year-old who loved to paint and draw but had no idea what to do with his life. Like many young people faced with similar decisions, he chose to do something in which he had little interest but of which his family heartily approved: He decided to become a doctor. Alas, within a few months of arriving at Harvard Medical School, he found himself depressed and uninspired. So he put his medical studies on hold and took off for Europe, where he learned about a new science called *psychology* (from a combination of the Greek *psyche* [soul] and *logos* [to study]). Excited about the new discipline, James returned to America and quickly finished his medical degree. But he never practiced medicine. Instead, he became a professor at Harvard University and devoted the rest of his life to philosophy and psychology. His landmark book *The Principles of Psychology* is still widely read and remains one of the most influential books ever written on the subject (James, 1890).

A LOT HAS HAPPENED SINCE THEN. Abraham Lincoln has become the face on the penny, the Pony Express has been replaced by Snapchat, and the Kellogg Company made about $15 billion in net sales last year. If William James (1842–1910) were alive today, he would surely be amazed by these things. But he would be even more amazed by the intellectual advances that have taken place in the science that he helped create.

James wanted to learn about human nature, but he confronted a very different situation than a similarly curious student would confront today, largely because psychology did not yet exist as an independent field of study. As he famously joked, "The first lecture in psychology that I ever heard was the first I ever gave." Of course, that doesn't mean no one had ever thought about human nature before. For 2,000 years, thinkers with scraggly beards and poor dental hygiene had pondered such questions, and in fact, modern psychology acknowledges its deep roots in philosophy.

We will begin by examining some of the early attempts to develop a scientific approach to psychology by relating the mind to the brain. Next, we discuss important developments in the evolution of psychological science, including the emergence of clinical psychology, behaviorism, cognitive psychology, and social and cultural psychology. We conclude by describing how the profession of psychology has changed in important ways, and what it is that professional psychologists actually do today.

William James (1842–1910) began college as a chemistry major, then switched to anatomy, and then traveled to Europe, where he became interested in the new science of psychology. Luckily for us, he stuck with it for a while. Letters to William James from Various Correspondents and Photograph Album, 1865–1929. Ms Am 1092 (1185) #8, Houghton Library, Harvard University

Psychology's Roots: The Path to a Science of Mind

- Explain what makes psychology a science.
- Identify key steps in the early development of the field of psychology.

psychology The scientific study of mind and behavior.

mind The private inner experience of perceptions, thoughts, memories, and feelings.

behavior Observable actions of human beings and nonhuman animals.

nativism The philosophical view that certain kinds of knowledge are innate or inborn.

philosophical empiricism The view that all knowledge is acquired through experience.

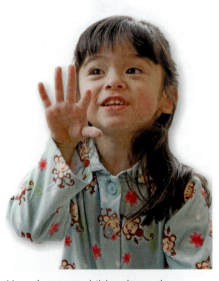

How do young children learn about the world? Plato believed that certain kinds of knowledge are innate, whereas Aristotle believed that the mind is a blank slate on which experiences are written. Geo Martinez/Feature Pics

Psychology is *the scientific study of mind and behavior.* The **mind** refers to *the private inner experience of perceptions, thoughts, memories, and feelings,* an ever-flowing stream of consciousness. **Behavior** refers to *observable actions of human beings and nonhuman animals,* the things that we do in the world, by ourselves or with others. As you will see in the chapters to come, psychology is an attempt to use scientific methods to address fundamental questions about mind and behavior such as:

- How do we experience the electrical and chemical activity in our brains as things like thoughts, feelings, and behaviors?
- How do our minds respond to, and learn from, the world around us so quickly, and in ways that ensure our survival?
- What leads the mind to function so ineffectively in some people, such as in those who experience hallucinations, dramatic mood swings, or intense urges to end their own lives?

These questions are merely the tip of the iceberg, and this textbook is a guide to exploring the rest of it. But before we don our parkas and grab our pick axes, we need to understand how the iceberg got here in the first place. To understand psychology in the 21st century, we need to become familiar with the psychology of the past.

Psychology's Ancestors: The Great Philosophers

The desire to understand ourselves is not new. Greek thinkers such as Plato (428–347 BCE) and Aristotle (384–322 BCE) were among the first to struggle with questions about how the mind works (Robinson, 1995). Greek philosophers debated many of the questions that psychologists continue to debate today. For example, are cognitive abilities and knowledge inborn, or are they acquired only through experience? Plato argued in favor of **nativism**, *the philosophical view that certain kinds of knowledge are innate or inborn.* Aristotle believed that the child's mind was a *tabula rasa* (blank slate) on which experiences were written, and he argued for **philosophical empiricism**, *the view that all knowledge is acquired through experience.*

Although few modern psychologists believe that either nativism or empiricism is entirely correct, the issue of just how much "nature" and "nurture" explain any given behavior is still a matter of controversy. In some ways, it is quite amazing that ancient philosophers were able to articulate so many of the important questions in psychology. Their ideas came from personal observations, intuition, and speculation. Although they were quite good at arguing with one another, they usually found it impossible to settle their disputes because their approach provided no means of testing their theories. As you will see in the Methods chapter, the ability to test a theory is the cornerstone of the scientific approach and the basis for reaching conclusions in modern psychology.

Linking the Mind to the Brain: The French Connection

We all know that the brain and the body are physical objects that we can see and touch and that the subjective contents of our minds—our perceptions, thoughts, and feelings—are not. Inner experience is perfectly real, but where in the world is it? The French philosopher René Descartes (1596–1650) argued that body and mind are different things—that the body is made of a material substance, whereas the mind (or soul) is made of an immaterial or spiritual substance. But if the mind and the body are different things made of different substances, how do they interact? How does the mind tell the body to put its foot forward, and when the body steps on a rusty nail, why does the mind say "ouch"? This is the problem of *dualism,* or how mental activity can be reconciled and coordinated with physical behavior.

These turned out to be difficult questions to answer, and the British philosopher Thomas Hobbes (1588–1679) argued that the reason they were difficult is that they were defective. The mind and body aren't different things, he claimed; rather, the mind *is* what the brain *does.* From Hobbes's perspective, looking for a place in the brain where the mind meets the body is like looking for the place in a television where the picture meets the flat panel display. For example, the French surgeon Paul Broca (1824–1880) worked with a patient who had suffered damage to a small part of the left side of the brain (now known as *Broca's area*). The patient was virtually unable to speak and could utter only the single syllable "tan,"—yet he understood everything that was said to him and was able to communicate using gestures. Broca had the crucial insight that damage to a specific part of the brain impaired a specific mental function, clearly demonstrating that our mental lives are the products of the physical workings of one of the body's major organs: the brain. This may seem obvious to you now, but it was a radical idea in the 19th century when most people believed, as Descartes had, that the mind and body are different things made of different substances and obeying different rules.

Structuralism: A First Step Toward the Scientific Method

In the middle of the 19th century, psychology benefited from the work of German scientists who were trained in the field of **physiology**, *the study of biological processes, especially in the human body.* Physiologists had developed methods that allowed them to measure such things as the speed of nerve impulses, and some of them had begun to use these methods to measure mental abilities. William James was drawn to the work of two such physiologists: Hermann von Helmholtz (1821–1894) and Wilhelm Wundt (1832–1920). "It seems to me that perhaps the time has come for psychology to begin to be a science," James wrote in a letter during his visit to Berlin in 1867. "Helmholtz and a man called Wundt at Heidelberg are working at it." What attracted James to the work of these two scientists?

A brilliant experimenter with a background in both physiology and physics, Helmholtz had developed a method for measuring the speed of nerve impulses. He trained his human participants to respond when he applied a **stimulus**—*sensory input from the environment*—to different parts of the leg. He recorded his participants' **reaction time**, or *the amount of time taken to respond to a specific stimulus,* after applying the stimulus. Helmholtz found that people generally took longer to respond when the toe was stimulated than when the thigh was stimulated, and the difference between these reaction times allowed him to estimate how long it took a nerve impulse to travel to the brain. These results were astonishing to 19th-century scientists because, at that time, just about everyone thought that mental processes occurred instantaneously. Helmholtz showed that this wasn't true. In so doing, he also demonstrated that reaction time could be a useful way to study the mind and the brain.

Helmholtz's research assistant, Wilhelm Wundt, went on to teach what was probably the first course in physiological psychology, at the University of Heidelberg, and he opened the first psychology laboratory in 1879 at the University of Leipzig. Wundt believed that scientific psychology should focus on analyzing **consciousness**, *a person's subjective experience of the world and the mind.* Consciousness encompasses a broad range of subjective experiences. We may be conscious of sights, sounds, tastes, smells, bodily sensations, thoughts, or feelings. As Wundt tried to figure out a way to study consciousness scientifically, he noted that chemists try to understand the structure of matter by breaking down natural substances into basic elements. His students built on this approach, which later came to be known as **structuralism**, *the analysis of the basic elements that constitute the mind.* This approach involved breaking down consciousness into elemental sensations and feelings.

This brain, now preserved in a jar in a Paris museum, belonged to a patient who was nicknamed "Tan" because it was the only word he could say. When "Tan" died in 1861, Paul Broca dissected his brain and found a lesion in the left hemisphere that he believed was responsible for the patient's loss of speech. APIC/Getty Images

physiology The study of biological processes, especially in the human body.

stimulus Sensory input from the environment.

reaction time The amount of time taken to respond to a specific stimulus.

consciousness A person's subjective experience of the world and the mind.

structuralism The analysis of the basic elements that constitute the mind.

By measuring a person's reaction times to different stimuli, Hermann von Helmholtz (1821–1894) estimated the length of time it takes a nerve impulse to travel to the brain. Hulton Archive/Getty Images

Wilhelm Wundt (1832–1920), far right, founded the first laboratory devoted exclusively to psychology. He sought to understand consciousness by breaking it down into its basic parts, including individual sensations and feelings. The Drs. Nicholas and Dorothy Cummings Center for the History of Psychology, the University of Akron

introspection The subjective observation of one's own experience.

functionalism The study of how mental processes enable people to adapt to their environments.

natural selection Charles Darwin's theory that the features of an organism that help it survive and reproduce are more likely than other features to be passed on to subsequent generations.

You don't have to look at this photo for more than a half-second to know that Vladimir Putin, the president of Russia, is not feeling very happy. William James suggested that your ability to read emotional expressions in an instant serves an important function that promotes your survival and well-being.
YURI KADOBNOV/AFP/Getty Images

Some of Wundt's studies used the method of **introspection**, *the subjective observation of one's own experience.* In a typical experiment, research participants were presented with a stimulus (usually a color or a sound) and then asked to report their introspections: perhaps describing the brightness of the color or the loudness of the tone. By analyzing the relation between feelings and perceptual sensations, Wundt and his students hoped to uncover the basic structure of conscious experience.

The influence of the structuralist approach gradually faded, due mostly to the introspective method. Science requires replicable observations; we could never determine the structure of a cell or the life span of a dust mite if every scientist who looked through a microscope saw something different. Alas, even trained observers provided conflicting introspections about their conscious experiences ("I see a cloud that looks like a duck"—"No, I think that cloud looks like a horse"), thus making it difficult for different psychologists to agree on the basic elements of conscious experience. Indeed, some psychologists had doubts about whether it was even possible to identify such elements through introspection alone. One of the most prominent skeptics was someone you've already met: a young man with a bad attitude and a useless medical degree named William James.

Functionalism: Mental Processes as Adaptations

William James agreed with Wundt on the importance of focusing on immediate experience and the usefulness of introspection as a technique (Bjork, 1983), but he disagreed with Wundt's claim that consciousness could be broken down into separate elements. James believed that consciousness was like a flowing stream that could only be understood in its entirety. So James decided to approach psychology from a different perspective entirely and developed an approach known as **functionalism**, *the study of how mental processes enable people to adapt to their environments.* In contrast to structuralism, which examined the structure of mental processes, functionalism set out to understand the functions those mental processes served. (See The Real World: Improving Study Skills for some strategies to enhance one of those functions—learning.)

James's thinking was inspired by Charles Darwin (1809–1882), who in 1859 had published a groundbreaking book entitled *On the Origin of Species by Means of Natural Selection.* In that book, Darwin proposed the principle of **natural selection:** *The features of an organism that help it survive and reproduce are more likely than other features to be passed on to subsequent generations.* James realized that, like other animals,

Improving Study Skills

Our minds don't work like video cameras, passively recording everything that happens and then faithfully storing the information. In order to retain new information, you need to take an active role in learning, by doing such things as rehearsing, interpreting, and testing yourself. These activities initially might seem difficult, but in fact they are what psychologists call *desirable difficulties* (Bjork & Bjork, 2011): Making it more difficult by actively engaging during critical phases of learning will increase your retention and ultimately result in improved performance. Here are four specific suggestions:

- **Rehearse.** One useful type of active manipulation is rehearsal: repeating to-be-learned information to yourself. For example, suppose that you want to learn the name of a person you've just met. Repeat the name to yourself right away, wait a few seconds and think of it again, wait a bit longer (maybe 30 seconds) and bring the name to mind once more, then rehearse the name again after a minute and once more after 2 or 3 minutes. This type of rehearsal improves long-term learning more than does rehearsing the name without any spacing between rehearsals (Landauer & Bjork, 1978).

You can apply this technique to names, dates, definitions, and many other kinds of information, including concepts presented in this textbook.

- **Interpret.** If we think deeply enough about what we want to remember, the act of reflection itself will virtually guarantee good memory. For example, the Changing Minds scenarios at the end of each chapter require you to reflect on and interpret the material, and to relate it to other things you already know about. A happy consequence of that activity is that you will be more likely to remember

Anxious feelings about an upcoming exam may be unpleasant, but as you've probably experienced yourself, they can motivate much-needed study.   Commercial Eye/Getty Images

the information that the questions engage you to think about.

- **Test.** Don't just look at your class notes or this textbook; test yourself on the material as often as you can. Testing yourself will alert you to when you need to study more, even when the information seems familiar. The Build to the Outcomes questions that you will encounter at the ends of sections throughout this textbook are designed to test you and thereby increase learning and retention. Be sure to use them. The LearningCurve study aid will also help you to test and learn. (See the Preface for further discussion of LearningCurve.)

- **Hit the main points.** Take some of the load off your memory by developing effective note-taking and outlining skills. Realize that you can't write down everything an instructor says, and try to focus on making detailed notes about the main ideas, facts, and people mentioned in the lecture. Later, organize your notes into an outline in a way that clearly highlights the major concepts. This will force you to reflect on the information in a way that promotes retention and will also provide you with a helpful study guide to promote self-testing and review.

people must avoid predators, locate food, and attract mates. Applying Darwin's principle of natural selection, James (1890) reasoned that the ultimate function of all psychological processes must be to help people survive and reproduce, and he suggested that psychology's mission should be to find out exactly how different psychological processes execute that function. James's arguments attracted much attention, and by the 1920s, functionalism was the dominant approach to psychology in North America.

BUILD TO THE OUTCOMES

1. What specifically do psychologists study?

2. Why were Greek philosophers unable to settle the dispute between nativism and philosophical empiricism?

3. How did Broca's study of a patient with brain damage help demonstrate the mind–brain connection?

4. How did Helmholtz's discovery about stimulus reaction time disprove previous assumptions about mental processes?

5. How did the approach of chemists influence Wundt's work?

6. What aspects of the theory of natural selection inspired James and the functionalist approach?

The Development of Clinical Psychology

LEARNING OUTCOMES

- Explain the insights that early clinicians brought to psychology.
- Outline Freud's major contributions.
- Explain how the humanist approach came to overtake Freud's ideas.

hysteria A temporary loss of cognitive or motor functions, usually as a result of emotionally upsetting experiences.

Mistakes can teach us a lot about how people think—or fail to think, as the case may be. AP Photo/Kalamazoo Gazette, Jill Mclane Baker

unconscious The part of the mind that operates outside of conscious awareness but influences conscious thoughts, feelings, and actions.

psychoanalytic theory An approach that emphasizes the importance of unconscious mental processes in shaping feelings, thoughts, and behaviors.

psychoanalysis A therapeutic approach that focuses on bringing unconscious material into conscious awareness to better understand psychological disorders.

While experimental psychologists were developing structuralism and functionalism, clinical psychologists were beginning to study people with psychological disorders, and their observations of mental disorders influenced the development of clinical psychology.

Lessons From Work With Patients

In the mid-19th century, the French physician Jean-Martin Charcot (1825–1893) became interested in patients who had developed a condition known then as **hysteria**, a *temporary loss of cognitive or motor functions, usually as a result of emotionally upsetting experiences*. Some of these patients became blind, others were paralyzed, or lost their memories, even though there was no known physical cause of their problems. However, when the patients were put into a trancelike state through the use of hypnosis (an altered state of consciousness characterized by suggestibility), their symptoms disappeared: Blind patients could see, paralyzed patients could walk, and forgetful patients could remember. After coming out of the hypnotic trance, the patients forgot what had happened under hypnosis and again showed their symptoms. Each patient behaved like two different people in the waking versus hypnotic states.

Freud Develops Psychoanalytic Theory

Charcot's striking observations made a big impression on a young physician from Vienna, Austria, named Sigmund Freud (1856–1939). Freud theorized that hysteria was caused by painful childhood experiences that the person could not remember. He suggested that these seemingly lost memories resided in the **unconscious**, which is *the part of the mind that operates outside of conscious awareness but influences conscious thoughts, feelings, and actions*. This idea led Freud to develop **psychoanalytic theory**, *an approach that emphasizes the importance of unconscious mental processes in shaping feelings, thoughts, and behaviors*. From a psychoanalytic perspective, it is important to uncover a person's early experiences and to illuminate a person's unconscious anxieties, conflicts, and desires. Psychoanalytic theory formed the basis for a therapy that Freud called **psychoanalysis**, which focuses on *bringing unconscious material into conscious awareness to better understand psychological disorders*. During psychoanalysis, patients recalled past experiences ("When I was a toddler, I was frightened by a masked man on a black horse") and related their dreams and fantasies ("Sometimes I close my eyes and imagine not having to pay for this session"). Psychoanalysts used Freud's theoretical approach to interpret what their patients said.

By the early 1900s, Freud's ideas had attracted a large number of followers in Europe. But those ideas were quite controversial in America because they suggested that understanding a person's thoughts, feelings, and behavior required a thorough exploration of the person's early sexual experiences and unconscious sexual desires. In those days, these topics were considered far too racy for discussion amongst polite people. In addition, Freud and most of his followers were trained as physicians and did not conduct psychological experiments in the laboratory or hold positions in universities, so they developed their ideas in isolation from the research-based approaches of Wundt, James, and others.

Most historians consider Freud to be one of the two or three most important thinkers of the 20th century, and the psychoanalytic movement influenced everything from literature and art to history and politics. Within psychology, psychoanalysis had its greatest impact on clinical practice, but that influence has diminished considerably over the past 40 years.

This famous psychology conference, held in 1909 at Clark University, brought together many notable figures, such as William James and Sigmund Freud. Both men are circled, with James on the left. Historical/Corbis

The Rise of Humanistic Psychology

Freud's influence diminished partly because his vision of human nature was a dark one, emphasizing limitations and problems rather than possibilities and potentials. He saw people as hostages to their forgotten childhood experiences and primitive sexual impulses, and the pessimism of his perspective frustrated those psychologists who had a more optimistic view of human nature. In the latter half of the 20th century, psychologists such as Abraham Maslow (1908–1970) and Carl Rogers (1902–1987) pioneered a new movement called **humanistic psychology**, *an approach to understanding human nature that emphasizes the positive potential of human beings.* Humanistic psychologists focused on people's highest aspirations. Rather than regarding people as prisoners of past events, humanistic psychologists viewed people as free agents who have an inherent need to develop, grow, and attain their full potential. The movement reached its peak in the 1960s, when a "hippie generation" found it quite natural to think of psychological life as a blossoming of the spirit. Humanistic therapists sought to help people realize their full potential, and they purposefully called those people *clients* rather than *patients* so that the person and his or her therapist would be on equal footing. The development of the humanistic perspective was yet another reason for the diminished influence of Freud's ideas.

Humanistic psychology offered a positive view of human nature that matched the zeitgeist of the 1960s, when open-air music festivals such as Woodstock drew massive crowds seeking peace and love. ©CBW/Alamy

humanistic psychology An approach to understanding human nature that emphasizes the positive potential of human beings.

BUILD TO THE OUTCOMES

1. What did early clinicians learn from hypnotizing patients with hysteria?
2. What are the basic ideas behind psychoanalytic theory?
3. Why are Freud's ideas less influential today?
4. What are the basic ideas behind humanistic psychology?

The Search for Objective Measurement: Behaviorism Takes Center Stage

behaviorism An approach that advocates that psychologists restrict themselves to the scientific study of objectively observable behavior.

The schools of psychological thought that had developed by the early 20th century—structuralism, functionalism, and psychoanalysis—differed substantially from each other. But they shared an important similarity: Each tried to understand the inner workings of the mind by examining conscious perceptions, thoughts, memories, and feelings or by trying to elicit previously unconscious material, all of which were reported by participants in experiments or patients in a clinical setting. In each case it proved difficult to establish with much certainty just what was going on in people's minds, due to the unreliable nature of the methodology. As the 20th century unfolded, a new approach developed as psychologists challenged the idea that psychology should focus on mental life at all. This new approach was called **behaviorism**, which *advocated that psychologists restrict themselves to the scientific study of objectively observable behavior.* (See Other Voices: Is Psychology a Science? below for a modern discussion of the

OTHER VOICES

Is Psychology a Science?

Timothy D. Wilson is a professor of psychology at the University of Virginia and the author of several popular books, including *Redirect: The Surprising New Science of Psychological Change* (2011). Photo by Jen Fariello, Courtesy Timothy D. Wilson

Nobody can dispute that you are taking a course in psychology, but are you taking a science course? Some critics maintain that psychology fails to meet accepted criteria for what constitutes a science. Timothy Wilson, a psychology professor at the University of Virginia, took on the critics by drawing from an appropriate source: the scientific literature (Wilson, 2012).

Once, during a meeting at my university, a biologist mentioned that he was the only faculty member present from a science department. When I corrected him, noting that I was from the Department of Psychology, he waved his hand dismissively, as if I were a Little Leaguer telling a member of the New York Yankees that I, too, played baseball.

There has long been snobbery in the sciences, with the "hard" ones (physics, chemistry, biology) considering themselves to be more legitimate than are the "soft" ones (psychology, sociology). It is thus no surprise that many members of the general public feel the same way. But of late, skepticism about the rigors of social science has reached absurd heights.

The U.S. House of Representatives recently voted to eliminate funding for political science research through the National Science Foundation. In the wake of that

action, an opinion writer for the *Washington Post* suggested that the House didn't go far enough. The NSF should not fund any research in the social sciences, wrote Charles Lane, because "unlike hypotheses in the hard sciences, hypotheses about society usually can't be proven or disproven by experimentation."

Lane's comments echoed ones by Gary Gutting in the Opinionator blog of the *New York Times.* "While the physical sciences produce many detailed and precise predictions," wrote Gutting, "the social sciences do not. The reason is that such predictions almost always require randomized controlled experiments, which are seldom possible when people are involved."

This is news to me and the many other social scientists who have spent their careers doing carefully controlled experiments on human behavior, inside and outside the laboratory. What makes the criticism so galling is that those who voice it, or members of their families, have undoubtedly benefited from research in the disciplines they dismiss.

Most of us know someone who has suffered from depression and sought psychotherapy. He or she probably benefited from therapies, such as cognitive behavioral therapy, that have been shown to work in randomized clinical trials.

Problems such as child abuse and teenage pregnancy take a huge toll on society. Interventions developed by research psychologists, tested with the experimental method, have been found to lower the incidence of child abuse and reduce the rate of teenage pregnancies.

Ever hear of stereotype threat? It is the double jeopardy that people face when they are at risk of confirming a negative stereotype of their group. When African American students take a difficult test, for example, they are concerned not only about how well they will do but also about the possibility that

science of psychology.) Behaviorism was a dramatic departure from previous schools of thought.

Watson and the Emergence of Behaviorism

John Broadus Watson (1878–1958) believed that private experience was too idiosyncratic and vague to be an object of scientific inquiry. Science required replicable, objective measurements of phenomena that were accessible to all observers, and the introspective methods used by structuralists and functionalists were far too subjective for that. So instead of describing conscious experiences, Watson proposed that psychologists focus entirely on the study of behavior—what people *do*, rather than what people *experience*—because behavior can be observed by anyone and it can be measured objectively.

At the time, animal behavior specialists such as Margaret Floy Washburn (1871–1939) were arguing that nonhuman animals have conscious mental experiences (Scarborough & Furumoto, 1987). Watson reacted to this claim with venom. Because we cannot ask pigeons about their private, inner experiences

In 1894, Margaret Floy Washburn (1871–1939) was the first woman to receive a PhD degree in psychology. Washburn wrote an influential book, *The Animal Mind*, and contributed to the development of psychology as a profession. The Drs. Nicholas and Dorothy Cummings Center for the History of Psychology, the University of Akron

performing poorly will reflect badly on their entire group. This added worry has been shown time and again, in carefully controlled experiments, to lower academic performance. But fortunately, experiments have also shown promising ways to reduce this threat. One intervention, for example, conducted in a middle school, reduced the achievement gap by 40%.

If you know someone who was unlucky enough to be arrested for a crime he didn't commit, he may have benefited from social psychological experiments that have resulted in fairer lineups and interrogations, making it less likely that innocent people are convicted.

An often-overlooked advantage of the experimental method is that it can demonstrate what doesn't work. Consider three popular programs that research psychologists have debunked: critical-incident stress debriefing (CISD), used to prevent posttraumatic stress disorder in first responders and others who have witnessed horrific events; the D.A.R.E. anti-drug program, used in many schools throughout America; and Scared Straight programs designed to prevent at-risk teens from engaging in criminal behavior.

All three of these programs have been shown, with well-designed experimental studies, to be ineffective or, in some cases, to make matters worse. And as a result, the programs have become less popular or have changed their methods. By discovering what doesn't work, social scientists have saved the public billions of dollars.

To be fair to the critics, social scientists have not always taken advantage of the experimental method as much as they could. Too often, for example, educational programs have been implemented widely without being adequately tested. But increasingly, educational researchers are employing better methodologies. For example, in a recent study, researchers randomly assigned teachers to a program called My Teaching Partner, which is designed to improve teaching skills, or to a control group. Students taught by the teachers who participated in the program did significantly better on achievement tests than did students taught by teachers in the control group.

Are the social sciences perfect? Of course not. Human behavior is complex, and it is not possible to conduct experiments to test all aspects of what people do or why. There are entire disciplines devoted to the experimental study of human behavior, however, in tightly controlled, ethically acceptable ways. Many people benefit from the results, including those who, in their ignorance, believe that science is limited to the study of molecules.

Wilson's examples of psychological investigations that have had beneficial effects on society are excellent, but perhaps even more important is his point that much of psychology is based on carefully controlled experimentation using randomization procedures that the critics apparently believe—mistakenly—cannot be applied to the study of human beings. The next chapter in this textbook is devoted to explaining how psychologists apply the scientific method to the study of the mind and behavior. It should come as no surprise to learn that your textbook authors believe that psychology is indeed a science. But what *kind* of science is psychology? (See the Hot Science box on page 20 for one approach to this question.) Should psychology strive to come up with general laws like those of physics or try to make precise predictions like those made by the so-called hard sciences? Should psychologists focus on laboratory experimentation or spend more effort attempting to study behavior in everyday life? What methods seem most promising to you as tools for psychological investigations? There is room for debate about what kind of science psychology is and should be; we hope that you think about these questions as you read this textbook.

Wilson, T. D. (July 12, 2012). Stop Bullying the 'Soft' Sciences. In *The Los Angeles Times* (Op Ed). Copyright 2012 Timothy D. Wilson and Sherrell J. Aston. Reproduced by permission.

(well, we can ask, but they never will tell us), Watson decided that the only way to understand how animals learn and adapt was to focus solely on their behavior, and he suggested that the study of human beings should proceed on the same basis.

Watson was influenced by the work of the Russian physiologist Ivan Pavlov (1849–1936), who noticed that the dogs who lived in his laboratory not only salivated at the sight of food, but also at the sight of the people who fed them. The feeders were not dressed in Milk Bone suits, so why should the mere sight of them trigger a basic digestive response? To answer this question, Pavlov developed a procedure in which he sounded a tone every time he fed the dogs, and after a while he observed that the dogs would salivate when they heard the tone alone. In Pavlov's experiments, the sound of the tone was a *stimulus* (sensory input from the environment) that influenced the salivation of the dogs, which was a **response:** *an action or physiological change elicited by a stimulus.* Watson and other behaviorists made these two notions the building blocks of their theories, which is why behaviorism is sometimes called *stimulus–response psychology* (or just *S-R psychology* for short).

response An action or physiological change elicited by a stimulus.

reinforcement The consequences of a behavior determine whether it will be more or less likely to occur again.

B. F. Skinner and the Development of Behaviorism

Burrhus Frederick Skinner (1904–1990) was a professor at Harvard who admired Pavlov's experiments as well as Watson's theories. But he thought something was missing. Pavlov's dogs were passive participants that stood around, listened to tones, and drooled. But in everyday life, animals don't just stand there—they do something! Animals *act* on their environments in order to find shelter, food, or mates, and Skinner wondered if he could develop behaviorist principles that would explain how they *learned* to act in those situations. To do so, he built what he called a *conditioning chamber* and what the rest of the world would come to call a *Skinner box*. The box had a lever and a food tray, and a hungry rat could get food delivered to the tray by pressing the lever. Skinner noticed that when a rat was put in the box, it would wander around, sniffing and exploring, and would eventually press the bar by accident, at which point a food pellet would drop into the tray. Once that happened, the rate at which the rat would press the bar increased dramatically and remained high until the rat was full. Skinner took this as evidence of what he called the principle of **reinforcement**, which states that *the consequences of a behavior determine whether it will be more or less likely to occur again.*

Inspired by John B. Watson's behaviorism, B. F. Skinner (1904–1990) investigated the way an animal learns by interacting with its environment. Here, he demonstrates the Skinner box, in which rats learn to press a lever to receive food: The lever press is the learned behavior, and the food is the reinforcement that increases the frequency of future lever pressing. Nina Leen/Getty Images

Real-World Application

The concept of reinforcement became the foundation of Skinner's new approach to behaviorism, and he set out to use this concept to solve everyday problems. For example, one day he was visiting his daughter's fourth-grade class when he realized that he could improve the classroom instruction by breaking each complicated task into smaller bits and then using the principle of reinforcement to teach the children each bit (Bjork, 1993). To solve a complicated math problem, for instance, students would first be asked an easy question about the simplest part of the problem. They would then be told whether the answer was right or wrong, and if they gave a correct response, they would move on to a more difficult question. (This important innovation is incorporated in modern approaches to enhancing learning, such as the LearningCurve program discussed in the Preface [p. xxx]). Skinner thought that the satisfaction of knowing they had gotten the right answer for one bit would be reinforcing and would motivate them to learn the next bit.

Real-World Overreach

If fourth graders and rats could be successfully trained, then why stop there? In a controversial series of popular books, Skinner laid out his vision of a utopian society in which behavior was controlled by the judicious application of the principle of reinforcement (Skinner, 1971, 1986). According to Skinner, people do things for which they were rewarded in the past, and their belief that they "chose" to do them is nothing more than an illusion of free will. Not surprisingly, that claim sparked an outcry from critics who believed that Skinner was giving away one of our most cherished attributes and calling for a repressive society that manipulated people for its own ends. One magazine even claimed he was advocating "the taming of mankind through a system of dog obedience schools for all" (Bjork, 1993, p. 201). Skinner, on the other hand, claimed that he was simply suggesting that an understanding of the principles by which behavior is generated could be used to improve human well-being. The controversy drew world-wide attention, and a popular magazine listed Skinner as one of the 100 most important people who had ever lived—and ranked him just 39 points below Jesus Christ (Herrnstein, 1977)!

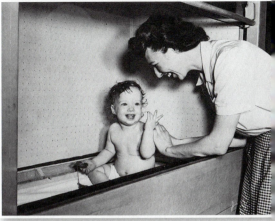

B. F. Skinner's well-publicized questioning of such cherished notions as free will led to a rumor that he had raised his own daughter in a Skinner box. This urban legend, though untrue, likely originated from the climate-controlled, glass-encased crib that he invented to protect his daughter from the cold Minnesota winter. Skinner marketed the crib under various names, including the "Air-Crib" and the "Heir Conditioner," but it failed to catch on with parents. Bettmann/Corbis

BUILD TO THE OUTCOMES

1. What shared idea behind structuralism, functionalism, and psychoanalysis did the behaviorists challenge?

2. What did Watson believe should be the goal of scientific psychology?

3. What were the results of the research done with the Skinner box?

4. Which of Skinner's claims provoked an outcry?

Return of the Mind: Psychology Expands

Behaviorism dominated psychology from the 1930s to the 1950s. As the psychologist Ulric Neisser recalled, "That was the age when it was supposed that no psychological phenomenon was real unless you could demonstrate it in a rat" (quoted in Baars, 1986, p. 275). But behaviorism wouldn't dominate the field for much longer, and Neisser himself would play an important role in developing an alternative perspective.

The Pioneers of Cognitive Psychology

Even at the height of behaviorist domination, there were a few revolutionaries whose research and writings were focused on the mental processes that behaviorism ignored or denied. For example, the German psychologist Max Wertheimer (1880–1943) focused on the study of **illusions**, which are *errors of perception, memory, or judgment in which subjective experience differs from objective reality.* In one of Wertheimer's experiments, two lights flashed quickly on a screen, one after the other.

LEARNING OUTCOMES

- Outline the research into mental processes that filled gaps left by the work of behaviorists.

- Explain how new technologies furthered the field of cognitive neuroscience.

- Describe the ideas behind evolutionary psychology.

illusions Errors of perception, memory, or judgment in which subjective experience differs from objective reality.

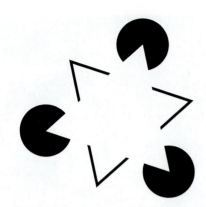

What do you see when you look at this image? Why do you see more than just random markings?

Gestalt psychology A psychological approach that emphasizes that we often perceive the whole rather than the sum of the parts.

cognitive psychology The scientific study of mental processes, including perception, thought, memory, and reasoning.

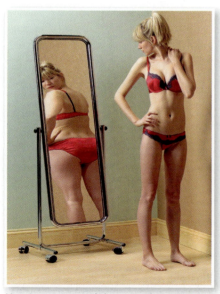

Kurt Lewin argued that people react to the world as they see it and not to the world as it is. Peter Dazeley/Getty Images

When the time between two flashes was one fifth of a second or more, observers would see two lights flashing in alternation. But when Wertheimer reduced the time between flashes to around one twentieth of a second, observers saw a single flash of light moving back and forth (Fancher, 1979; Sarris, 1989). Wertheimer argued that during perception, the mind brings the disparate elements together and combines them into a unified whole, which in German is called a *gestalt*. This and other of Wertheimer's ideas led to the development of **Gestalt psychology**, *a psychological approach that emphasizes that we often perceive the whole, rather than the sum of the parts.* According to Gestalt psychology, the mind imposes organization on what it perceives. The German psychologist Kurt Lewin (1890–1947) was strongly influenced by these ideas and argued that the best way to predict a person's behavior was to focus not on the stimulus to which the person was responding, but rather on the person's subjective interpretation, or *construal,* of the stimulus. A pinch on the cheek can be pleasant or unpleasant depending on who administers it, under what circumstances, and to which set of cheeks.

The Computer as a Model of the Human Mind

Aside from Wertheimer, Lewin, and a handful of others, most psychologists happily ignored mental processes until the 1950s, when something important happened to change their minds: The computer was invented. People and computers differ in important ways, of course, but both seem to register, store, and retrieve information, and so psychologists began to wonder whether the computer might be a good model for the human mind. Computers are physical information-processing systems, and if mental events—such as remembering, attending, thinking, believing, evaluating, feeling, and assessing—are simply words we use to describe the processing of information by the human mind, then the events that take place inside a mind are every bit as real as the events that take place inside a computer. This line of thinking led to the emergence of **cognitive psychology**, *the scientific study of mental processes, including perception, thought, memory, and reasoning.*

Cognitive psychologists began conducting experiments and devising theories to understand how the mind processed information. For example, during World War II, the military turned to psychologists to help understand how soldiers could best learn to use new technologies, such as radar. Radar operators had to pay close attention to their screens for long periods while trying to decide whether blips were friendly aircraft, enemy aircraft, or flocks of wild geese in need of a good chasing (Ashcraft, 1998; Lachman, Lachman, & Butterfield, 1979). How could radar operators be trained to make quicker and more accurate decisions? The answer to this question required that those who designed the equipment think about cognitive processes, such as perception, attention, identification, memory, and decision making. For instance, pilots can't attend to many different instruments at once and must actively move the focus of their attention from one to another (Best, 1992). In fact, the limited capacity to handle incoming information is a fundamental feature of human cognition: We can pay attention to, and briefly hold in memory, about seven (give or take two) pieces of information (Miller, 1956).

The waxing of cognitive psychology and the waning of behaviorism was due in part to the invention of the computer; but ironically, it was also due in part to the appearance of a book by B. F. Skinner called *Verbal Behavior,* which offered a behaviorist analysis of language. After it appeared, a linguist named Noam Chomsky (b. 1928) published a devastating critique, arguing that Skinner's insistence on studying only observable behavior had caused him to miss some of the most important features of language. According to Chomsky, just as a computer program contains a set of step-by-step rules for generating output, so, too, does human language rely on mental rules that allow people to understand and produce novel words and sentences. The ability of young children to generate new sentences that they have never heard before flew in the face of the behaviorist claim that children learn language by reinforcement. Chomsky provided a clever, detailed, and thoroughly cognitive account of language that could explain many of the phenomena that the behaviorist account could not (Chomsky, 1959). These and other developments during the 1950s set the stage for an explosion of cognitive studies during the 1960s.

The Brain Meets the Mind: The Rise of Cognitive Neuroscience

Although cognitive psychologists studied the "software of the mind," they had little to say about the hardware of the brain. The psychologist Karl Lashley (1890–1958) had conducted a famous series of studies in which he had trained rats to run mazes, surgically removed parts of their brains, and then measured how well they could run the maze again. Although Lashley had hoped to find the precise spot in the brain where learning occurred, he found that no single spot seemed to uniquely and reliably underlie all kinds of learning (Lashley, 1960). Although Lashley did not find a "learning area" in the brain, his efforts inspired other scientists to develop a research area called *physiological psychology*. Today, this area has grown into **behavioral neuroscience**, *an approach to psychology that links psychological processes to activities in the nervous system and to other bodily processes.* To learn about the relationship between brain and behavior, behavioral neuroscientists observe animals' responses as the animals perform specially constructed tasks, such as running through a maze to obtain food rewards. The neuroscientist can record electrical or chemical responses in the brain as the task is being performed or later remove specific parts of the brain to see how performance is affected.

Of course, experimental brain surgery cannot ethically be performed on human beings; thus, psychologists who want to study the human brain often have to rely on nature's cruel and inexact experiments. Birth defects, accidents, and illnesses often cause damage to particular brain regions, and if that damage disrupts a particular ability, then psychologists assume that the region is involved in producing the ability. For example, in the Memory chapter you'll learn about a patient whose memory was virtually eliminated by damage to a specific part of his brain, and you'll see how this tragedy provided scientists with remarkable clues about how memories are stored (Scoville & Milner, 1957). But in the late 1980s, technological breakthroughs led to the development of noninvasive brain scanning techniques that made it possible for psychologists to watch what happens inside a human brain as a person performs a task such as reading, imagining, listening, or remembering (see **FIGURE 1.1**). Brain scanning is an invaluable tool because it allows us to observe the brain in action and to see which parts are involved in which operations (see the Neuroscience and Behavior chapter). In fact, there's a name for this area of research: **Cognitive neuroscience** is the *field of study that attempts to understand the links between cognitive processes and brain activity* (Gazzaniga, 2000).

The Adaptive Mind: The Emergence of Evolutionary Psychology

Psychology's renewed interest in mental processes and its growing interest in the brain were two developments that pulled psychology away from behaviorism. A third development provided yet another tug. In the 1960s and 1970s, psychologist John Garcia and his colleagues showed that rats can learn to associate nausea

This 1950s computer was among the first generation of digital computers. How was the computer analogy helpful in the early days of cognitive psychology? Bettmann/Corbis

behavioral neuroscience An approach to psychology that links psychological processes to activities in the nervous system and other bodily processes.

cognitive neuroscience The field of study that attempts to understand the links between cognitive processes and brain activity.

Noam Chomsky (b. 1928) pointed out that even young children generate sentences they have never heard before and therefore could not possibly be learning language by reinforcement. This critique of Skinner's theory signaled the end of behaviorism's dominance in psychology and helped spark the development of cognitive psychology. Ollyy/Shutterstock

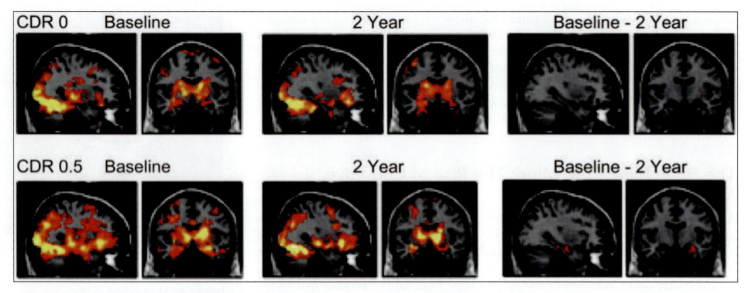

Figure 1.1 FUNCTIONAL MAGNETIC RESONANCE IMAGING (FMRI) is one of several brain imaging technologies that psychologists use to observe the living brain. These images come from a study in which elderly adults were scanned when they first entered the study ("baseline") and then again two years later. The top row shows group averaged scans from 21 participants who were judged to be cognitively normal at the start of the study. The bottom row shows scans from 30 participants who initially showed mild cognitive impairment (MCI). When the baseline scans were compared with those obtained two years later (Baseline - 2 Year on the right side of the figure), MCI participants showed significantly reduced activity in the hippocampus, a structure that is important for memory, whereas "cognitively normal" patients showed no change in hippocampal activity (O'Brien et al., 2010). Republished with permission of Wolters Kluwer Health, from *Neurology*, J.L. O'Brien et al, 74, 24, 2010 p. 1969–1976; permission conveyed through Copyright Clearance Center, Inc.

evolutionary psychology A psychological approach that explains mind and behavior in terms of the adaptive value of abilities that are preserved over time by natural selection.

with the smell of food much more quickly than they can learn to associate nausea with a flashing light (Garcia, 1981). Why should this be? In the real world of forests, sewers, and garbage cans, nausea is usually caused by spoiled food and not by lightning, and although these particular rats had been born in a laboratory and had never left their cages, millions of years of evolution had prepared their brains to learn the natural association more quickly than the artificial one.

Behaviorism said that a rat's behavior was simply the product of its learning history. But clearly, it was not only a rat's learning history but also the rat's *ancestors'* learning histories that determined how and how quickly a rat learned.

This fact gave rise to **evolutionary psychology**, which is *a field that explains mind and behavior in terms of the adaptive value of abilities that are preserved over time by natural selection*. Evolutionary psychology had its roots in Charles Darwin's theory of natural selection, which suggested that those features of an organism that help it survive and reproduce are more likely than other features to be passed on to subsequent generations. Consider, for example, how evolutionary psychology treats the emotion of jealousy. Most of us who have been in romantic relationships have experienced jealousy, if only because we noticed our partner noticing someone else. Jealousy can be

In 1925, the schoolteacher John Scopes was arrested for teaching students about Darwin's theory of evolution. Today, that theory is the centerpiece of modern biology—and of evolutionary psychology. Hulton Archive/Getty Images

a powerful, overwhelming emotion that we might wish to avoid, but according to evolutionary psychology, it exists today because it once served an adaptive function. If some of our hominid ancestors experienced jealousy and others did not, then those who experienced it might have been more likely to guard their mates and aggress against their rivals and thus may have been more likely to reproduce and pass on their "jealous genes" to the next generation (Buss, 2000, 2007; Buss & Haselton, 2005).

Of course, because we don't have a record of our ancestors' thoughts, feelings, and actions, testing ideas about the evolutionary origins of psychological phenomena can be a challenging task, but not an impossible one (Buss et al., 1998; Pinker, 1997a, 1997b). If a particular psychological feature was favored by natural selection, then it should be possible to find some evidence of this in the numbers of offspring that are produced by those who have it. Consider, for instance, the hypothesis that men tend to have deep voices because women prefer to mate with baritones, rather than with sopranos (presumably because a low voice signals the presence of testosterone, which makes a man more dominant and gives him higher status and more resources). To investigate this hypothesis, researchers studied a group of modern hunter–gatherers: the Hadza people of Tanzania. The researchers found that consistent with the evolutionary hypothesis, the pitch of a man's voice did indeed predict how many children he would have, but that the pitch of a woman's voice did not (Apicella, Feinberg, & Marlowe, 2007). This kind of study provides evidence that allows evolutionary psychologists to test their ideas. Not every evolutionary hypothesis can be tested, of course, but evolutionary psychologists are becoming increasingly inventive in their strategies.

Behaviorists explain behavior in terms of organisms learning to make particular responses that are paired with reinforcement (and to avoid responses that are paired with punishment). Evolutionary psychology focuses on how abilities are preserved over time if they contribute to an organism's ability to survive and reproduce. How might a proponent of each approach explain the fact that a rat placed in an unfamiliar environment will tend to stay in dark corners and avoid brightly lit open areas? ©Juniors Bildarchiv gmbh/Alamy

BUILD TO THE OUTCOMES

1. What is the fundamental idea behind Gestalt psychology?

2. How did the advent of computers change psychology?

3. How did Chomsky's work dispute Skinner's theory?

4. How have new technologies furthered the understanding of the relationship between the brain and behavior?

5. What evidence suggests that some traits can be inherited?

Beyond the Individual: Social and Cultural Perspectives

Although psychologists often do focus on the brain and the mind of the individual, they have not lost sight of the fact that human beings are fundamentally social animals who are part of a vast network of family, friends, teachers, and coworkers. Trying to understand people in the absence of that fact is a bit like trying to understand an ant or a bee without considering the function and influence of the colony or hive. People are the most important and most complex organisms that we ever encounter; thus, it is not surprising that our behavior is strongly influenced by their presence—or their absence. The two areas of psychology that most strongly emphasize these facts are social and cultural psychology.

LEARNING OUTCOMES

• Explain how historical events are tied to the emergence of social psychology.

• Give examples of the range of cultural psychology.

The Development of Social Psychology

social psychology The study of the causes and consequences of sociality.

Social psychology is *the study of the causes and consequences of sociality.* Social psychology emerged in the 1930s, largely in reaction to historical events. The rise of Nazism led many of Germany's most talented scientists to immigrate to America, where they began to generate theories of social behavior and do experiments to test those theories. The Holocaust had brought the problems of conformity and obedience into sharp focus, and social psychologists began examining the conditions under which people can influence each other to think and act in irrational, and sometimes inhuman, ways. For example, Solomon Asch (1907–1996) studied the circumstances under which people would do something wrong just because they had seen others do it, and Stanley Milgram (1933–1984) studied the circumstances under which people would harm another person just because an authority figure had ordered them to. A few decades later, the civil rights movement and the rising tensions between African Americans and White Americans brought new problems to the attention of social psychologists. Gordon Allport (1897–1967) initiated the scientific study of stereotyping, prejudice, and racism, while Bib Latane (b. 1937) and John Darley (b. 1938) sought to understand why people so often fail to help those in need. Social psychologists today study a much wider variety of topics (from social memory to social relationships) and use a much wider variety of techniques (from opinion polls to neuroimaging) than did their forebears, but this field of psychology remains dedicated to understanding the brain as a social organ, the mind as a social adaptation, and the individual as a social creature.

Social psychology studies how the thoughts, feelings, and behaviors of individuals can be influenced by the presence of others. Members of the Reverend Sun Myung Moon's Unification Church are often married to each other in ceremonies of 10,000 people or more; in some cases, couples don't know each other before the wedding begins. Social movements such as this have the power to sway individuals. AP Images/AHN Young-Joon

The Emergence of Cultural Psychology

cultural psychology The study of how cultures reflect and shape the psychological processes of their members.

Although all human beings have a lot in common, there is considerable diversity within the species with regard to social practices, customs, and ways of living. *Culture* refers to the values, traditions, and beliefs that are shared by a particular group of people. Although we usually think of culture in terms of nationality and ethnic groups, cultures can also be defined by age (youth culture, elderly culture), gender (female culture, transgender culture), sexual orientation (straight culture, gay culture), religion (Jewish culture, Christian culture), occupation (student culture, academic culture), and many other of the dimensions on which people differ (see A World of Difference: To Have and Have Not). **Cultural psychology** is *the study of how cultures reflect and shape the psychological processes of their members* (Shweder & Sullivan, 1993).

Anthropologists have studied culture by traveling to far-flung regions of the world and carefully observing child-rearing patterns, rituals, religious ceremonies, and the like (Mead, 1934/1968; Read, 1965). Cultural psychologists, on the other hand, bring the tools of experimental science to the study of culture as they try to determine which psychological phenomena are universal and which vary from place to place and time to time. Today, most psychologists agree that some psychological phenomena are universal, and that others are influenced by culture. You might be surprised by which are which. For example, judgments

A WORLD OF DIFFERENCE

To Have and Have Not

When we think about "other cultures," most of us imagine faraway lands filled with people eating exotic foods, wearing unusual clothes, and speaking languages we can't understand. But you don't have to board an airplane to visit a culture much different from your own because, in just about every place on earth, there are two distinctly different cultures living side by side: those who have more—more money, more education, more prestige—and those who have less (Kraus, Piff, & Keltner, 2011). In even the most egalitarian societies, people can be divided into higher and lower social classes, and as it turns out, social class is a powerful determinant of human behavior.

Consider an example. Because upper-class people have ample material resources, they don't need to depend much on others. When problems arise, upper-class people rely on their bank accounts, whereas lower-class people rely on family, friends, and neighbors with whom they must maintain good relationships. In a way, upper-class people have the *luxury* of not worrying too much about what others feel or think. Does that influence their behavior?

Indeed it does. In laboratory studies, upper-class people often prove to be less generous, less charitable, less trusting, and less helpful toward others (Piff et al., 2010), as well as more likely to lie and cheat for personal gain (Gino & Pearce, 2009; Piff et al., 2012). This "me first" orientation is easy to see outside of the laboratory, too. For example, in one study, researchers stood near the intersection of two busy streets and recorded the make, model, and year of the cars that approached, and then watched to see whether they cut off other cars and pedestrians in the intersection. As the two graphs show, the drivers of new, expensive cars were considerably more likely to zip through intersections without regard for others. Is this because being upper class makes people selfish? Or because being selfish makes people upper class? Some studies suggest that the first explanation is the right one. For example, when participants in experiments are randomly assigned to *think* of themselves as upper class—for instance, when they are asked to compare their incomes with those who have less—they also behave more selfishly (Piff et al., 2012).

Social class matters. And so do gender, race, religion, age, and most of the other dimensions on which human beings differ. Psychological science often produces conclusions about "people on average," but it is important to keep in mind that while averages are useful for understanding and predicting behavior, people actually come in nearly infinite varieties, and the things that distinguish them are often as interesting as the things that make them one. We hope to prove that to you throughout the rest of this textbook in the boxes called "A World of Difference."

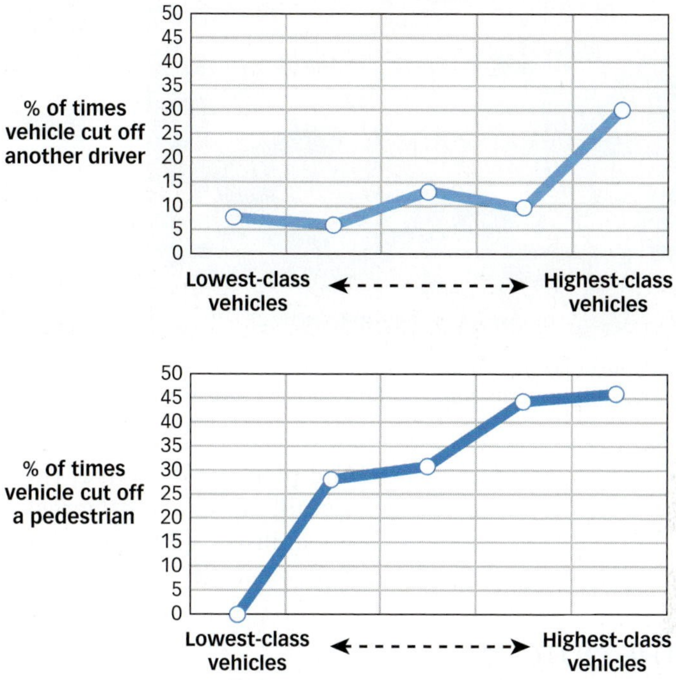

Data from Piff, P. K., Stancato, D. M., Côté, S., Mendoza-Denton, R., & Keltner, D. (2012). Higher Social Class Predicts Increased Unethical Behavior. *Proceedings of the National Academy of Sciences of the United States of America, 109*(11), 4086–91. http://doi.org/10.1073/pnas.1118373109

of facial attractiveness do not appear to be strongly influenced by culture (Cunningham et al., 1995), but the age of a person's earliest memory seems to differ dramatically across cultures (MacDonald, Uesiliana, & Hayne, 2000). The most universal phenomena are those that are closely associated with the basic biology that all human beings share, and the most culturally varied phenomena are those that are rooted in the many daily practices that differ across people

Psychologists don't necessarily have to travel the world to study the effects of culture on psychological phenomena. In big cities like New York, shown in both photos above, different subcultures live in close proximity Christian Heeb/Laif/Redux (left); Richard Levine/Agefotostock (right)

and places. Of course, the only way to determine whether a phenomenon is variable or constant across cultures is to design research to investigate these possibilities, and cultural psychologists do just that (Cole, 1996; Segall, Lonner, & Berry, 1998).

BUILD TO THE OUTCOMES

1. Why did social psychology arise as a field in response to events such as the rise of Nazism and the civil rights movement?

2. What is the scope of the study of cultural psychology?

The Profession of Psychology: Past and Present

LEARNING OUTCOMES

- Outline the evolution of the APA.
- Link the value of training in psychology to a number of careers.
- Describe psychology's importance as a field of study.

In July of 1892, William James and six other psychologists came together for a meeting at Clark University and decided that it was time to form an organization that represented psychology as a profession. On that day, the American Psychological Association (APA) was born. Today, their little club has blossomed into an organization with more than 150,000 members. Although all of the original members were employed by universities or colleges, academic psychologists make up only 20% of the membership today, and nearly 70% of current members work in clinical and health-related settings. Because the APA focused less and less on academic psychology as the years passed, in 1988 a group of academic psychologists formed the Association for Psychological

DATA VISUALIZATION

Science (APS), which focused exclusively on the needs of psychologists who carry out scientific research. Today, the APS has about 12,000 members (see Data Visualization: Understanding How to Use [or Misuse!] Data at www.launchpadworks.com).

The Growing Roles of Women and Minorities

In 1892, the APA had 31 members, and every one of them was a White man. Surveys of recent PhD recipients reveal an increasingly diverse field. In 1950, women represented only 15% of all students receiving PhDs in psychology, but by 2010 that number had grown to an astounding 70%. The proportion of racial minorities receiving PhDs in psychology grew from nearly zero in the middle of the 20th century to about 24% today. Clearly, American psychology is looking more and more like America itself.

The current involvement of women and minorities in psychology can be traced to early pioneers who blazed trails that others followed. For example, Mary Whiton Calkins (1863–1930) studied with William James and later became a professor of psychology at Wellesley College, and in 1905 she became the first woman to serve as president of the APA. Calkins wrote four books and published over 100 articles during her illustrious career (Calkins, 1930; Scarborough & Furumoto, 1987; Stevens & Gardner, 1982). The first member of a minority group to become president of the APA was Kenneth Clark (1914–2005), who was elected in 1970. Clark studied the self-image of African American children and argued that segregation of the races causes severe psychological harm. Clark's conclusions had a great influence on public policy, and his research contributed to the Supreme Court's 1954 ruling (*Brown v. Board of Education*) that outlawed segregation in public schools (Guthrie, 2000).

Mary Whiton Calkins (1863–1930), the first woman elected APA president, suffered from the sex discrimination that was common during her lifetime. Despite academic setbacks (such as Harvard University's refusal to grant a woman an official PhD), Calkins went on to a distinguished career in research and teaching at Wellesley College. Macmillan Learning

What Psychologists Do

Psychology is a very popular academic major that prepares students for a variety of careers, and most students who major in psychology do not become psychologists (see Hot Science: Psychology as a Hub Science). But what should you do if you *do* want to become a psychologist (and what should you not do if you desperately want to avoid it)? As it turns out, there are a variety of ways to become "a psychologist" because the people who call themselves psychologists can hold a variety of different degrees.

Typically, students intending to pursue careers in psychology finish college and then go to graduate school to obtain a PhD (doctor of philosophy) degree in a particular area of psychology (e.g., social, cognitive, developmental, etc.). During graduate school, students generally gain exposure to the field by taking classes and they learn to conduct research by collaborating with their professors. Although William James was able to master every area of psychology because the areas were so small during his lifetime, today a student can spend the better part of a decade and still not fully master one. After receiving a PhD, these students often go on for more specialized research training by pursuing a postdoctoral fellowship under the supervision of an established researcher. Ultimately, most of them either apply for a faculty position at a college or university or for a research position in government or industry. Academic careers usually involve a combination of teaching and research, whereas careers in government or industry are typically dedicated to research alone.

Kenneth B. Clark (1914–2005) studied the developmental effects of prejudice, discrimination, and segregation on children. In one classic study from the 1950s, he found that African American preschoolers preferred White dolls to Black ones. Clark's research was cited by the U.S. Supreme Court in its decision for the landmark *Brown v. Board of Education* case that ended school segregation. New York Times Co./Getty Images

A person earning a PhD in psychology can go on to a wide range of fields, such as these three (*from left to right*): Lynne Madden is a clinical psychologist who works with individuals and groups. Gloria Balague applies her training as a clinical psychologist to her work with athletes. Lynne Owens Mock directs a community mental health center in Chicago. ©Macmillan Learning

Psychology as a Hub Science

This chapter describes how psychology emerged as a field of study, and the Other Voices box on pages 8–9 illustrates some of the ways in which psychology is indeed a *scientific* field of study. But where does psychology stand in relation to other areas of science? That is, how big a field is it? What links does it have to other scientific disciplines? What fields (if any) are influenced by psychological science? With recent advances in computing and electronic record keeping, researchers are now able to literally create maps of science.

As an example, in an article called "Mapping the Backbone of Science," Kevin Boyack and his colleagues (2005) used data from more than 1 million articles, with more than 23 million references, published in more than 7,000 journals to create a map showing the interconnectedness of different areas of science based on how frequently journal articles from different disciplines cite each other. The results are fascinating. As shown in the figure on the right, seven major fields, or "hub sciences," emerged in the data: math, physics, chemistry, earth sciences, medicine, *psychology,* and social science. There were also smaller "subfields" that fell between the hub sciences: public health and neurology fall between psychology and medicine, statistics between psychology and math, and economics between social science and math.

Another study used data from more than 6 million citations, found in more than 6,000 journals, to create a map of citation patterns focusing on citations to articles published from 2000 to 2004 (Rosvall & Bergstrom, 2008). Psychology again emerged as a major scientific hub with strong links to neuroscience, psychiatry, education, sociology, business and marketing, medicine, and ecology and evolution. More recent and larger studies continue to support the overall structure of these maps of science (Börner et al., 2012).

Studies such as these show the relationships among different academic departments and how the scientific work of one field relates to science as a whole. They also show the reach of psychology into other disciplines and support the idea that knowledge about psychology has relevance for many related disciplines and career paths. Good thing you are taking this class!

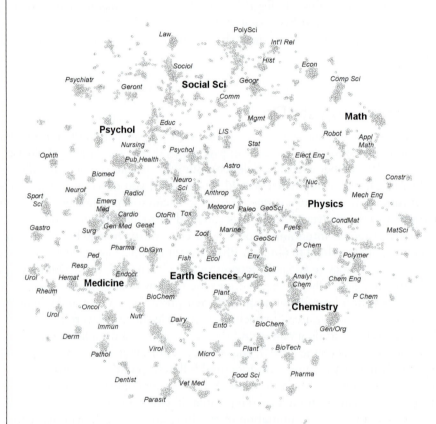

Republished with Permission of Springerverlag/Akadèmiai Diado, "Mapping the Backbone of Science," by K. W. Boyack, R. Klavans, and K. Borner, 2005, *Scientometrics,* 64, p. 364. Permission Conveyed through Copyright Clearance Center, Inc.

But most psychologists neither teach nor do research. Rather, they assess or treat people with psychological problems. Most of these *clinical psychologists* work in private practice, often in partnerships with other psychologists or with psychiatrists (who have earned an MD, or medical degree, and are allowed to prescribe medication). Other clinical psychologists work in hospitals or medical schools, some have faculty positions at universities or colleges, and some combine private practice with an academic job. Many clinical psychologists focus on specific problems or disorders, such as depression or anxiety, whereas others focus on specific populations such as children, ethnic minority groups, or older adults (see **FIGURE 1.2**). Just over 10% of APA members are *counseling psychologists,* who

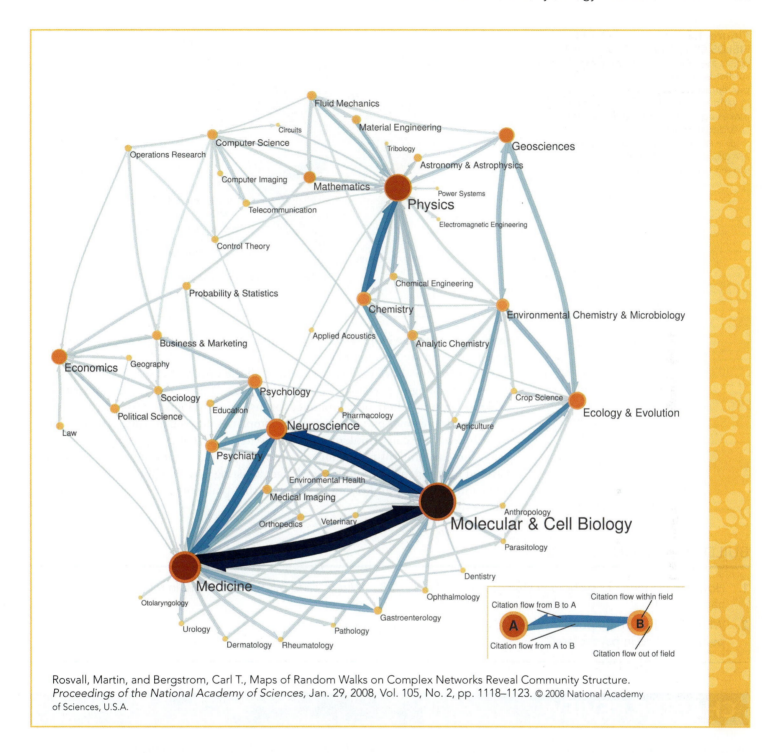

Fluid Mechanics
Circuits
Material Engineering
Computer Science
Geosciences
Operations Research
Tribology
Astronomy & Astrophysics
Computer Imaging
Mathematics
Physics
Power Systems
Telecommunication
Electromagnetic Engineering
Control Theory
Chemical Engineering
Probability & Statistics
Chemistry
Environmental Chemistry & Microbiology
Business & Marketing
Applied Acoustics
Analytic Chemistry
Economics
Geography
Psychology
Pharmacology
Crop Science
Ecology & Evolution
Sociology
Education
Neuroscience
Agriculture
Political Science
Law
Psychiatry
Environmental Health
Medical Imaging
Anthropology
Molecular & Cell Biology
Orthopedics
Veterinary
Parasitology
Dentistry
Medicine
Otolaryngology
Ophthalmology
Gastroenterology
Urology
Pathology
Dermatology
Rheumatology

Citation flow within field
Citation flow from B to A
A
Citation flow from A to B
B
Citation flow out of field

Rosvall, Martin, and Bergstrom, Carl T., Maps of Random Walks on Complex Networks Reveal Community Structure. *Proceedings of the National Academy of Sciences*, Jan. 29, 2008, Vol. 105, No. 2, pp. 1118–1123. © 2008 National Academy of Sciences, U.S.A.

assist people in dealing with work or career issues and changes or help people deal with common crises such as divorce, the loss of a job, or the death of a loved one. Counseling psychologists may have a PhD or an MA (master's degree) in counseling psychology or an MSW (master of social work).

Psychologists are also quite active in educational settings. About 5% of APA members are *school psychologists*, who offer guidance to students, parents, and teachers. A similar proportion of APA members, known as *industrial/ organizational psychologists*, focus on issues in the workplace. These psychologists typically work in business or industry and may be involved in assessing potential employees, finding ways to improve productivity, or helping staff and

Figure 1.2 THE MAJOR SUB-FIELDS OF PSYCHOLOGY Psychologists are drawn to many different subfields in psychology. Here are the percentages of people receiving PhDs in various subfields. Clinical psychology makes up over half of the doctorates awarded in psychology. Data from *Graduate Study in Psychology, 2016 Edition*. Prepared by APA Office of Graduate and Postgraduate Education and Training.

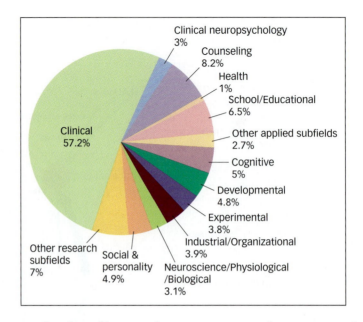

management to develop effective planning strategies for coping with change or anticipated future developments.

Of course, this brief list doesn't include all the different career paths that someone with training in psychology might take. For instance, sports psychologists help athletes improve their performance, forensic psychologists assist attorneys and courts, and consumer psychologists help companies develop and advertise new products. Indeed, we can't think of any major enterprise that *doesn't* employ psychologists. You can think of psychology as an international community of professionals devoted to advancing scientific knowledge; assisting people with psychological problems and disorders; and trying to enhance the quality of life in work, school, and other everyday settings.

BUILD TO THE OUTCOMES

1. How has the face of psychology changed as the field has evolved?

2. What are a few of the possible career choices for people trained in psychology?

3. Where does psychology stand in relation to other areas of science?

CHAPTER REVIEW

Psychology's Roots: The Path to a Science of Mind

• Psychologists use scientific methods to study mind and behavior.

• Early philosophers pondered and debated ideas about human nature, but could not provide empirical evidence to support their claims.

• Wilhelm Wundt is credited with the founding of psychology as a scientific discipline. He focused on analyzing the basic elements of consciousness, an approach that became known as structuralism.

• William James applied Darwin's theory of natural selection to the study of the mind. His functionalist approach focused on how mental processes enable people to adapt to their environments.

The Development of Clinical Psychology

• Through his work with hysteric patients, Sigmund Freud developed psychoanalysis, which emphasized the importance of unconscious influences and childhood experiences in shaping thoughts, feelings, and behaviors.

- Freud's influence waned both because his dark view of human nature fell out of step in later, more optimistic times and because his ideas were difficult to test.
- Humanistic psychologists offered a more positive view of the human condition, suggesting that people are inherently disposed toward growth and can usually reach their full potential with a little help from their friends.

The Search for Objective Measurement: Behaviorism Takes Center Stage

- Behaviorists advocated the study of observable actions and responses and held that inner mental processes were private events that could not be studied scientifically.
- John B. Watson proposed that psychologists focus on what people do, rather than on what they experience.
- Working with dogs, Ivan Pavlov studied the association between a stimulus and a response and emphasized the importance of the environment in shaping behavior.
- B. F. Skinner developed the concept of reinforcement and demonstrated that animals and humans repeat behaviors that generate pleasant results and avoid performing those that generate unpleasant results. Skinner suggested that free will is an illusion and that the principle of reinforcement can be used to benefit society.

Return of the Mind: Psychology Expands

- The emerging field of cognitive psychology, the scientific study of mental processes, undercut behaviorism's dominance.
- Noninvasive brain scanning techniques made it possible for cognitive neuroscientists to observe the brain in action, furthering attempts to link psychology and physiology.

- Evolutionary psychology focuses on the adaptive function that minds and brains serve and seeks to understand the nature and origin of psychological processes in terms of natural selection.

Beyond the Individual: Social and Cultural Perspectives

- Social psychology recognizes that people exist as part of a network of other people and examines how individuals influence and interact with each other.
- Cultural psychology is concerned with the effects of the broader culture on individuals and with similarities and differences among people in different cultures.

The Profession of Psychology: Past and Present

- The American Psychological Association (APA) now includes over 150,000 members working in clinical, academic, and applied settings. Psychologists are also represented by professional organizations such as the Association for Psychological Science (APS), which focuses on scientific psychology.
- Through the efforts of pioneers such as Mary Calkins, women have come to play an increasingly important role in the field and are now as well represented as men. Minority involvement in psychology took longer, but the pioneering work of Kenneth B. Clark and others have led to increased participation of minorities in psychology.
- Psychologists prepare for research careers through graduate and postdoctoral training and work in a variety of applied settings, including schools, clinics, and industry.

KEY CONCEPT QUIZ

1. In the 1800s, the French surgeon Paul Broca conducted research that demonstrated a connection between
   a. animals and humans.
   b. the mind and the brain.
   c. brain size and mental ability.
   d. skull indentations and psychological attributes.

2. What was the subject of the famous experiment conducted by Hermann von Helmholtz?
   a. reaction time
   b. childhood learning
   c. phrenology
   d. functions of specific brain areas

3. William James espoused _____, the study of the purpose mental processes serve in enabling people to adapt to their environment.
   a. empiricism
   b. nativism
   c. structuralism
   d. functionalism

4. The functional approach to psychology was inspired by
   a. Darwin's *On the Origin of Species by Means of Natural Selection*.
   b. James's *Principles of Psychology*.
   c. Wundt's *Principles of Physiological Psychology*.
   d. Skinner's *The Behavior of Organisms*.

5. To understand human behavior, Jean-Martin Charcot studied people
   a. who appeared to be completely healthy.
   b. with psychological disorders.
   c. with damage in particular areas of the brain.
   d. who had suffered permanent loss of cognitive and motor function.

6. Building on the work of Charcot and others, Sigmund Freud developed
   a. psychoanalytic theory.
   b. the theory of hysteria.
   c. humanistic psychology.
   d. physiological psychology.

7. The psychological theory that emphasizes the positive potential of human beings is known as
   a. structuralism.
   b. psychoanalytic theory.
   c. humanistic psychology.
   d. functionalism.

8. Behaviorism involves the study of
   a. observable actions and responses.
   b. the potential for human growth.
   c. unconscious influences and childhood experiences.
   d. human behavior and memory.

9. The experiments of Ivan Pavlov and John B. Watson centered on
   a. perception and behavior.
   b. stimulus and response.
   c. reward and punishment.
   d. conscious and unconscious behavior.

10. Who developed the concept of reinforcement?
   a. B. F. Skinner
   b. Ivan Pavlov
   c. John Watson
   d. Margaret Floy Washburn

11. The study of mental processes such as perception and memory is called
   a. behavioral determinism.
   b. Gestalt psychology.
   c. social psychology.
   d. cognitive psychology.

12. The use of scanning techniques to observe the brain in action and to see which parts are involved in which operations helped the development of
   a. evolutionary psychology.
   b. cognitive neuroscience.
   c. cultural psychology.
   d. cognitive accounts of language formation.

13. Central to evolutionary psychology is the _____ function that minds and brains serve.
   a. emotional
   b. adaptive
   c. cultural
   d. physiological

14. Social psychology differs most from other psychological approaches in its emphasis on
   a. human interaction.
   b. behavioral processes.
   c. the individual.
   d. laboratory experimentation.

15. Cultural psychology emphasizes that
   a. all psychological processes are influenced to some extent by culture.
   b. psychological processes are the same across all human beings, regardless of culture.
   c. culture shapes some but not all psychological phenomena.
   d. insights gained from studying individuals from one culture will only rarely generalize to individuals from other cultures, which have different social identities and rituals.

16. Mary Calkins
   a. studied with Wilhelm Wundt in the first psychology laboratory.
   b. did research on the self-image of African American children.
   c. was present at the first meeting of the APA.
   d. became the first woman president of the APA.

17. Kenneth Clark
   a. did research that influenced the Supreme Court decision to ban segregation in public schools.
   b. was one of the founders of the APA.
   c. was a student of William James.
   d. did research that focused on the education of African American youth.

 **LearningCurve** Don't stop now! Quizzing yourself is a powerful study tool. Go to LearningCurve at www.launchpadworks.com for more practice.

KEY TERMS

psychology (p. 2)
mind (p. 2)
behavior (p. 2)
nativism (p. 2)
philosophical empiricism (p. 2)
physiology (p. 3)
stimulus (p. 3)
reaction time (p. 3)

consciousness (p. 3)
structuralism (p. 3)
introspection (p. 4)
functionalism (p. 4)
natural selection (p. 4)
hysteria (p. 6)
unconscious (p. 6)
psychoanalytic theory (p. 6)

psychoanalysis (p. 6)
humanistic psychology (p. 7)
behaviorism (p. 8)
response (p. 10)
reinforcement (p. 10)
illusions (p. 11)
Gestalt psychology (p. 12)
cognitive psychology (p. 12)

behavioral neuroscience (p. 13)
cognitive neuroscience (p. 13)
evolutionary psychology (p. 14)
social psychology (p. 16)
cultural psychology (p. 16)

CHANGING MINDS

1. One of your classmates says that she's taking this class only because it's required for her education major. "Psychology is all about understanding mental illness and treatment. I don't know why I have to learn this stuff when I'm going to be a teacher, not a psychologist." Why should your friend reconsider her opinion? What subfields of psychology are especially important for a teacher?

2. One of your friends confesses that he really enjoys his psychology courses, but he's decided not to declare a major in psychology. "You have to get a graduate degree to do anything with a psychology major," he says, "and I don't want to stay in school for the rest of my life. I want to get out there and work in the real world." Knowing what you've read in this chapter about careers in psychology, what might you tell him?

3. On May 6, you spot a news item announcing that it's the birthday of Sigmund Freud, "the father of psychology." How accurate is it to call Freud the "father of psychology?" Having read about psychology's subfields, do you

think other people are as important or more important than Freud?

4. One of your classmates has flipped ahead in this textbook and noticed that there is going to be a lot of material—including an entire chapter—on the brain. "I don't see why we have to learn so much biology," he says. "I want to be a school counselor, not a brain surgeon. I don't need to understand the parts of the brain or chemical reactions in order to help people." How are the brain and the mind connected? In what specific ways might knowing about the brain help us to understand the mind?

5. Another classmate is very unsettled after reading about B. F. Skinner's claim that free will is an illusion. "Psychology always tries to treat human beings like lab rats, whose behavior can be manipulated," she says. "I have free will, and I decide what I'm going to do next." What would you tell your friend? Does an understanding of the basic principles of psychology allow us to predict every detail of what individual humans will do?

ANSWERS TO KEY CONCEPT QUIZ

1. b; 2. a; 3. d; 4. a; 5. b; 6. a; 7. c; 8. a; 9. b; 10. a; 11. d; 12. b; 13. b; 14. a; 15. c; 16. d; 17. a.

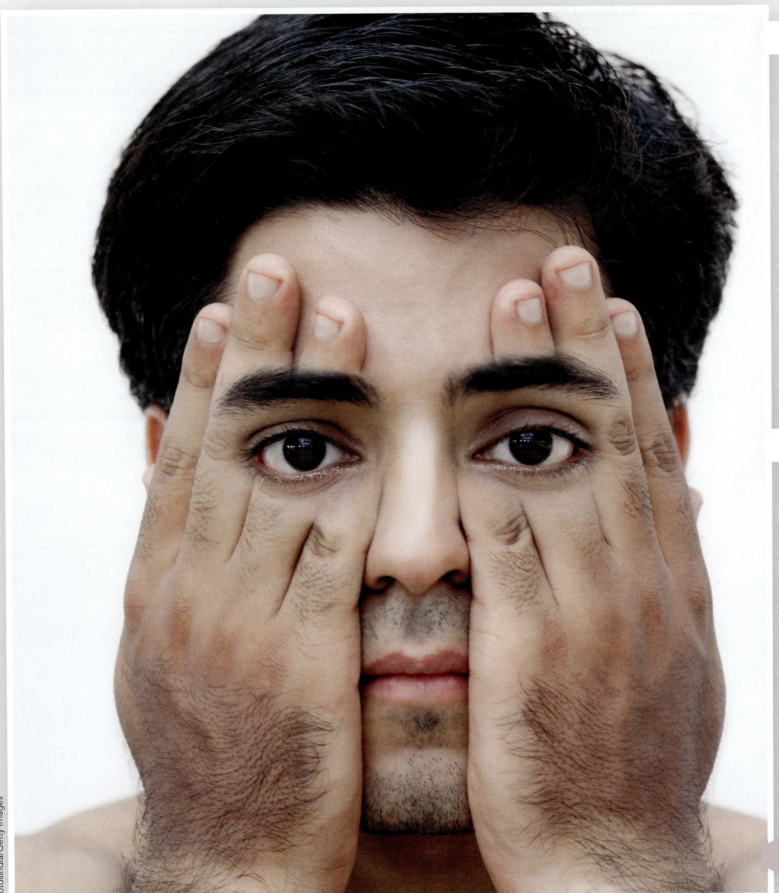

Methods in Psychology

2

You Can Heal Your Life has sold over 35 million copies. Its author, Louise Hay, suggests that everything that happens to us is a result of the thoughts we choose to think. She claims that she cured herself of cancer simply by changing her thoughts, and she says that others can learn to do the same by buying her books, CDs, and DVDs, and by attending her seminars. In a television interview, Hay explained how she knows that her technique is effective.

INTERVIEWER: How do you know what you're saying is right?

HAY: Oh, my inner ding.

INTERVIEWER: Ding?

HAY: My inner ding. It speaks to me. It feels right or it doesn't feel right. Happiness is choosing thoughts that make you feel good. It's really very simple.

INTERVIEWER: But I hear you saying that, even if there were no proof for what you believed, or even if there were scientific evidence against it, it wouldn't change.

HAY: Well, I don't believe in scientific evidence, I really don't. Science is fairly new. It hasn't been around that long. We think it's such a big deal, but it's, you know, it's just a way of looking at life.

Louise Hay says she doesn't believe in scientific evidence. But what could that possibly mean? After all, if Hay's techniques really do cure cancer, as she says, then cancer patients who practice her techniques ought to have a higher rate of remission than do those who don't. That isn't "a way of looking at life." It's just plain, old-fashioned, common sense—exactly the kind of common sense that lies at the heart of science.

Science tells us that the only way to know for sure whether a claim is true is to go out and have a look. But that sounds a lot simpler than it is. For example, exactly where would you go to have a look if you wanted to determine whether Louise Hay's claims are true? Would you go to one of her seminars and ask people in the audience whether or not they'd been healed? Would you examine the medical records of people who had and hadn't bought her books? Would you invite people to sign up for a class that teaches her techniques and then wait to see how many got cancer? All of these things sound reasonable, but in fact, none of them would answer your question. There are a few good ways to test claims like Louise Hay's and a whole lot of bad ways, and in this chapter you will learn to tell one from the other. Scientists have developed powerful tools for determining when an inner ding is right and when it is wrong. These tools have allowed human beings to learn more about themselves and their world in the last four hundred years than they learned in all the previous millennia combined.

Louise Hay says she doesn't believe in scientific evidence and instead trusts her "inner ding." Which do you trust more? Michele Asselin/Contour by Getty Images

WE'LL START BY EXAMINING THE GENERAL PRINCIPLES THAT GUIDE scientific research. Next, we'll see that the methods of psychology are meant to answer two basic questions: What do people do, and why do they do it? Psychologists answer the first question by observing and measuring, and they answer the second question by looking for relationships between the things they measure. We'll see that scientific research allows us to draw certain kinds of conclusions and not others, and we'll see that most people have problems thinking critically about scientific evidence. Finally, we'll consider the unique ethical questions that confront scientists who study people and other animals.

Empiricism: How to Know Stuff

LEARNING OUTCOMES

- Explain why direct observation is essential to an accurate understanding of nature.
- Identify the two key elements of the scientific method.

empiricism The belief that accurate knowledge can be acquired through observation.

scientific method A procedure for finding truth by using empirical evidence.

When ancient Greeks sprained their ankles, caught the flu, or accidentally set their nose hair on fire, they had to choose between two kinds of doctors: dogmatists (from *dogmatikos,* meaning "belief"), who thought that the best way to understand illness was to speculate about the body's functions, and empiricists (from *empeirikos,* meaning "experience"), who thought that the best way to understand illness was to observe sick people. The rivalry between these two schools of medicine didn't last long because the people who went to see dogmatists tended to die, which was bad for business. Today, we use the word *dogmatism* to describe people's tendency to cling to their assumptions, and the word **empiricism** to describe *the belief that accurate knowledge can be acquired through observation.* The fact that we can answer questions about the natural world by examining it may seem obvious to you, but for most of human history, people turned to authorities for the answers to difficult and important questions, and it is only in the last millennium that people have begun to trust their eyes and ears more than their elders.

The Scientific Method

Empiricism is the essential element of the **scientific method**, which is *a procedure for finding facts by using empirical evidence.* In essence, the scientific method suggests that when we have an idea about the world—about how

The astronomer Galileo Galilei (1564–1642) was excommunicated and sentenced to prison for sticking to his own observations of the solar system, rather than accepting the teachings of the Church. In 1597, he wrote to his friend and fellow astronomer Johannes Kepler (1571–1630), "What would you say of the learned here, who, replete with the pertinacity of the asp, have steadfastly refused to cast a glance through the telescope? What shall we make of this? Shall we laugh, or shall we cry?" As it turned out, the answer was *cry.* Bettmann/Corbis

bats navigate, or where the moon came from, or why people can't forget traumatic events—we should gather empirical evidence relevant to that idea and then modify the idea to fit with the evidence. Scientists usually refer to an idea of this kind as a **theory**, which is *a hypothetical explanation of a natural phenomenon*. For example, we might theorize that bats navigate by making sounds and then listening for the echo. Nice idea, but how do we determine if that theory is right?

Theories make specific predictions about what we should observe in the world if the theory is true, and what we should observe if it is not. For example, if bats really do navigate by making sounds and then listening for echoes, then we should observe that deaf bats have a really hard time navigating. That "should statement" is technically known as a **hypothesis**, which is *a falsifiable prediction made by a theory*. The word *falsifiable* is a critical part of that definition. Some theories, such as "God created the universe," do not specify what we should observe if they are true and what we should observe if they are false, and so observation cannot falsify them. What *can* observation do? Well, imagine what you would learn about the navigation-by-sound theory if you observed a few bats. If you saw the deaf bats navigating every bit as well as the hearing bats, then the navigation-by-sound theory would instantly be proved wrong. If the deaf bats navigated more poorly, would the theory be proved right? No! Although that observation would be *consistent* with the navigation-by-sound theory, it would not prove it to be true because, after all, even if you didn't see a deaf bat navigating perfectly today, it is possible that you will see one tomorrow. Theories can be disproved by observation but they can never be proved. We can become increasingly confident in a theory, but we can never be absolutely sure it is right.

The Art of Looking

An **empirical method** is *a set of rules and techniques for observation*. Unlike the behavior of molecules or galaxies, the behavior of people is easy to see, so you might expect psychology's empirical method to be relatively simple. In fact, the opposite is true, and that's because people have three qualities that make them especially difficult to study:

- *Complexity:* No molecule or galaxy or particle or machine is as complicated as the human brain. Scientists can describe the birth of a star or the death of a cell in exquisite detail, but they can barely begin to say how the 500 million interconnected neurons that constitute the brain give rise to the thoughts, feelings, and actions that are psychology's core concerns.

- *Variability:* In almost all the ways that matter, one *E. coli* bacterium is pretty much like another. But people are as varied as their fingerprints. No two individuals ever do, say, think, or feel exactly the same thing under exactly the same circumstances, which means that even when you've seen one, you've still not seen them all.

- *Reactivity:* A cesium atom oscillates at exactly the same rate, regardless of whether anyone is watching. But people often think, feel, and act one way when they are being observed and a different way when they are not. When people know they are being studied, they don't always behave as they otherwise would.

The fact that human beings are complex, variable, and reactive presents a major challenge to the scientific study of their behavior (see A World of

Classical thinkers such as Euclid and Ptolemy believed that our eyes work by emitting rays that travel to the objects we see. Ibn al-Haytham (965–1039) reasoned that, if this were true, then when we open our eyes it should take longer to see something far away than something nearby. And guess what? It doesn't. And with that single observation, a centuries-old theory vanished—in the blink of an eye. Science Source/Colorization by: Mary Martin

empirical method A set of rules and techniques for observation.

theory A hypothetical explanation of a natural phenomenon.

hypothesis A falsifiable prediction made by a theory.

People are reactive—that is, they behave differently when they know they are being observed. For example, if actress Mila Kunis had realized that a photographer was lurking nearby, she might have found a more discreet way to express her opinion of passion fruit tea. James Devaney/WireImage/Getty Images

Are Heroes and Sheroes Divided by Zeroes?

Galileo, Newton, Mendel, Darwin, Faraday, Einstein, Turing, Tesla—what do all these people have in common? First, they were all brilliant scientists. And second, they were all men. The history of science is pretty much the history of smart men having big ideas and making big discoveries. So where are all the women hiding? There are two answers to this question. The first is that, until quite recently, educational and employment opportunities for women were limited. For most of history, women were either subtly discouraged or actively prohibited from studying science—and you really can't win the Nobel Prize in Physics if they won't let you take algebra. Women, it seems, have been hiding right where men put them: in the kitchen.

Of course, another possible reason why most great scientists have been men is that men and women may have different talents, and the talents men have may be precisely the talents people need to become great scientists. Is there any truth to this suggestion? A few years ago, a group of male and female scientists got together, surveyed all the scientific evidence on sex differences in cognitive abilities, and drew a striking conclusion: Yes, they concluded, the evidence does show that men and women differ with regard to certain talents (Halpern et al., 2007). Specifically, men are more variable than women on almost every measure of quantitative ability (the ability to use numbers) and visuo-spatial ability (the ability to use images), both of which are important to success in many sciences. Being more variable means that although men and women have the same average amount of talent on these dimensions, there are more men at both the very lowest and very highest ends of the spectrum. If great scientists tend to come from the highest end of the quantitative and visuo-spatial ability spectrums, then men will naturally be overrepresented among great scientists. And indeed, recent data show that men are overrepresented in scientific fields that are "math intensive" such as geoscience, engineering, economics, mathematics, computer science, and the physical sciences, but not in other scientific fields such as biology, psychology, and sociology (Ceci et al., 2014).

So men are more variable than women on certain dimensions. But why? Is it because they are encouraged to hone their quantitative and visuo-spatial skills by parents who buy them video games instead of dolls, and by teachers who encourage them to join the math team rather than the debate team? Or is it because there is some innate difference in the structure or function of the male and female brains? Once again, an expert review of the evidence concludes that "sex differences in spatial and mathematical reasoning need not stem from biological bases, that the gap between average female and male math ability is narrowing (suggesting strong environmental influences), and that sex differences in math ability at the right tail [which is the "high" end of the ability spectrum] show variation over time and across nationalities, ethnicities, and other factors, indicating that the ratio of males to females at the right tail can and does change" (Ceci et al., p. 75). In short, no one really knows why men are more variable, but the smart money seems to be on nurture rather than nature.

We agree with the experts who concluded that "there are no single or simple answers to the complex questions about sex differences in science and mathematics" (Halpern et al., 2007, p. 75). However, we feel confident that one day in the not-too-distant future, a brilliant young psychological scientist will discover the answer to this important and complex question. We just hope she does it soon.

Difference: Are Heroes and Sheroes Divided by Zeroes?). To solve these problems, psychologists have developed two kinds of methods: *methods of observation* that allow them to figure out what people do, and *methods of explanation* that allow them to figure out why people do it. We'll examine both of these methods in the sections that follow.

BUILD TO THE OUTCOMES

1. How does empiricism differ from dogmatism?
2. What is the difference between a theory and a hypothesis?
3. Why can theories be proven wrong but not right?
4. What makes human beings especially difficult to study?

Observation: What Do People Do?

To *observe* means to use one's senses to learn about the properties of an event (e.g., a storm or a parade) or an object (e.g., an apple or a person). For example, when you observe a round, red apple, your brain is using the pattern of light that is coming into your eyes to draw an inference about the apple's identity, shape, and color. That kind of informal observation is fine for buying fruit but not for doing science. Why? First, informal observations are unstable: The same apple can appear red in the daylight and crimson at night, or spherical to one person and elliptical to another. Second, informal observations can't tell us about many of the properties that might interest us: No matter how long and hard you look at an apple, you will never be able to see its crunchiness. So instead of relying on informal observation, scientists make *measurements*. But what exactly does measurement entail?

LEARNING OUTCOMES

- Explain what measurement involves, and what properties a good definition and a good instrument must have.

- Identify some of the methods psychologists use to avoid demand characteristics and observer bias.

Measurement

Whether we want to measure the intensity of an earthquake, the distance between molecules, or the attitude of a voter, we must always do two things—*define* the property we wish to measure, and then find a way to *detect* the property we've defined.

For example, if we wanted to measure a person's happiness, we would first need to define that squishy word in some non-squishy way. An **operational definition** is *a description of a property in terms of some concrete, observable event.* We might operationally define happiness as *a person's response to the question "How happy are you?"* or as *the frequency with which a person smiles.* The most important feature of an operational definition is its **validity**, which is *how well the concrete, observable event indicates the property.* How happy people say they are and how frequently they smile are both valid ways to define happiness because, as we all know, happy people really do tend to say they are happy and they really do tend to smile a lot. Do they also eat more and spend more money? Well, maybe. But maybe not. And that's why most psychologists would probably regard a person's food consumption and credit card balance to be invalid measures of their happiness.

Once we have a valid operational definition, we need an **instrument**, which is *anything that can detect the concrete, observable event to which an operational definition refers.* To detect the frequency of smiling, for example, we might use a computer that is equipped with a camera and special software, or we might just use a human observer who is equipped with a clipboard and a pencil. A good instrument has two important features. The first is **reliability**, which is *the tendency for an instrument to produce the same measurement every time it is used to measure the same thing.* If a person smiles exactly as often on Tuesday and Wednesday, then a good smile-detector should produce the same measurements on those two days. If it doesn't, then it isn't very reliable. The second feature is **power**, which is *an instrument's ability to detect small magnitudes of a property.* If a person smiles just a teeny weeny tiny bit more often on Thursday than on Friday, then a good smile-detector should produce different measurements on those two days. If it doesn't, then it isn't very powerful (see **FIGURE 2.1**).

operational definition A description of a property in terms of some concrete, observable event.

validity The extent to which a concrete, observable event indicates the property.

instrument Anything that can detect the concrete, observable event to which an operational definition refers.

reliability The tendency for an instrument to produce the same measurement every time it is used to measure the same thing.

power An instrument's ability to detect small magnitudes of a property.

Demand Characteristics: Doing What Is Expected

Once we have an operational definition that is valid and a measuring instrument that is both reliable and powerful, are we ready to measure human behavior?

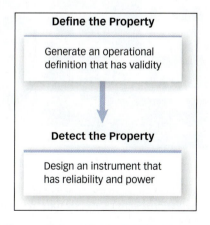

Figure 2.1 MEASUREMENT There are two steps in the measurement of a property.

demand characteristics Those aspects of an observational setting that cause people to behave as they think someone else wants or expects.

naturalistic observation A technique for gathering scientific information by unobtrusively observing people in their natural environments.

Countries that have a faster pace of life tend to have higher rates of heart disease but also greater happiness. How do researchers measure the "pace of life"? They make naturalistic observations, in this case, by measuring the average walking speed of pedestrians in different cities. By the way, the fastest pedestrians are the Irish (top) and the slowest are the Romanians (bottom) (Levine & Norenzayan, 1999). Izzet Keribar/Getty Images; Chris Ratcliffe/Bloomberg Via Getty Images

Almost, but not quite. There is still one problem to solve, which is that when people know we are measuring their behavior, they often change their behavior and start acting as they believe we want them to act or expect them to act. **Demand characteristics** are *those aspects of an observational setting that cause people to behave as they think someone else wants or expects them to*. We call these demand characteristics because they seem to "demand" or require that people say and do certain things. For instance, you couldn't very well measure a person's honesty by walking into a room, putting a ten-dollar bill on the table, saying, "This is an honesty test," and then standing there and waiting to see whether they take your money. By announcing your purpose and then standing there and watching them, you have created a situation that "demands" honesty. Even a dishonest person would be unlikely to take the money under these circumstances. So how can we avoid demand characteristics?

One way is through **naturalistic observation**, which is *a technique for gathering scientific information by unobtrusively observing people in their natural environments*. For example, by using naturalistic observation, psychologists have discovered that the biggest groups of diners leave the smallest tips in restaurants (Freeman et al., 1975) and that the hungriest shoppers buy the most impulse items at the grocery store (Gilbert, Gill, & Wilson, 2002). Each of these conclusions is the result of measurements made by psychologists who observed people who didn't know they were being observed. It seems unlikely that the diners and shoppers would have behaved the same way if they knew they were being scrutinized.

But naturalistic observation isn't always possible because some of the things psychologists want to observe just don't occur naturally. If we wanted to know whether people who have undergone sensory deprivation perform poorly on motor tasks, we would have to hang around the shopping mall for a very long time before a few dozen blindfolded people with earplugs just happened to wander by and start typing. When naturalistic observation isn't possible, there are other ways to reduce demand characteristics. For example, people are less likely to be influenced by demand characteristics when they are allowed to respond privately (e.g., by having them complete questionnaires when they are alone) or anonymously (e.g., when their names or addresses are not recorded). Another way to reduce demand characteristics is to measure behaviors that people can't control. Even if a person wanted to appear uninterested in a piece of salacious gossip or a sexy video, they couldn't stop their pupils from dilating if they were interested because…well, that's just what interested pupils do! Finally, a very common technique for reducing demand characteristics is to make sure that the people being observed don't know what the researcher expects. If a person isn't aware that a researcher is trying to show that classical music can enhance mood, they won't feel obligated to smile when they hear Bach. This is why psychologists typically don't reveal the true purpose of their observations to the people they are observing until the study is over.

Observer Bias: Seeing What Is Expected

The people being observed aren't the only ones who can make measurement tricky. Researchers can make it tricky, too! In one study, students in a psychology class were asked to measure the speed with which a rat learned to run through a maze (Rosenthal & Fode, 1963). Some students were told that their rat had been specially bred to learn slowly and others were told that their rat had been specially bred to learn quickly. In fact, all the rats were actually the same breed. And yet, those students who *thought* their rat was slow-witted reported that their rats took longer to learn the maze than did the students who *thought* their rat was a furry genius. In other words, the measurements revealed precisely what the students expected them to reveal.

Why did this happen? First, *expectations can influence observations*. It is easy to make errors when measuring the speed of a rat, and our expectations often determine the kinds of errors we make. Does putting one paw over the finish line count as learning the maze? If a rat runs a maze in 18.5 seconds, should that number be rounded up or rounded down before it is recorded in the log book? The answers to these questions may depend on how smart one thinks the rat is. The students who timed the rats probably tried to be honest, vigilant, and objective, but they could not stop their expectations from influencing their observations. Second, *expectations can influence reality*. Students who thought they were timing a brilliant rat may have unknowingly done things to help the little guy along, for example, by muttering, "Oh, no!" when their rat looked the wrong way, or by petting it more when it succeeded.

Observers' expectations, then, can have a powerful influence on both their observations and on the behavior of those whom they observe. Psychologists use many techniques to avoid these influences in their research, and one of the most common is the **double-blind observation**, which is *a technique where the true purpose is hidden from both the observer and the person being observed*. For example, if the students had not been told anything about the abilities of their rats, then they wouldn't have *had* any expectations to influence their measurements. That's why it is common practice in psychology to make sure that the research assistants who are executing a study do not themselves know what is being studied or why.

double-blind observation A technique whose true purpose is hidden from both the observer and the person being observed.

One way to avoid demand characteristics is to measure behaviors that people can't control. For example, our pupils contract when we are bored (photo 1) and dilate when we are interested (photo 2), which makes pupillary dilation a useful measure of a person's interest in what they are seeing. Thinkstock

People's expectations can cause the phenomena they expect. In 1929, investors who expected the stock market to collapse sold their stocks and thereby caused the very crisis they feared. In this photo, panicked citizens stand outside the New York Stock Exchange the day after the crash, which the *New York Times* attributed to "mob psychology." The Granger Collection, NYC. All Rights Reserved. Bettmann/Corbis

1. What property does a good operational definition have?

2. What two properties does a good measuring instrument have?

3. What techniques do psychologists use to avoid demand characteristics?

4. What techniques do psychologists use to avoid seeing what they expect to see?

Explanation: Why Do People Do What They Do?

LEARNING OUTCOMES

*   Explain what a correlation is and how it is measured.

*   Understand the essential ingredients of an experiment and explain how they allow researchers to establish the causal relationship between variables.

variable A property whose value can vary across individuals or over time.

correlation Two variables are said to "be correlated" when variations in the value of one variable are synchronized with variations in the value of the other.

You may be interested to know that happy people are healthier than are unhappy people, but you would probably be even more interested in knowing why. Does happiness make people healthier? Does being healthy make people happier? Does being rich make people both healthy and happy? These are the kinds of questions scientists usually want to answer, and they have developed some clever ways of using their measurements to do so. In this section, we'll start by examining techniques that can tell us whether two variables (such as happiness and health) are related (Correlation); then we'll examine techniques that can tell us whether they are related because one causes the other (Causation). Next, we'll see what kinds of conclusions these techniques do and don't allow us to draw. Finally, we'll discuss the difficulty that most of us have thinking critically about scientific evidence.

Correlation

"How much sleep did you get last night, and how many U.S. presidents can you recall?" If you asked a dozen college students those two questions, you might see a pattern of responses like the one shown in **TABLE 2.1**. If you study this pattern, you'll probably conclude that people who get a good night's sleep have better recall than people who don't. But how did you come to that conclusion? You came to it by doing these three things:

TABLE 2.1	Hypothetical Data Showing the Relationship Between Sleep and Recall	
Participant	Hours of Sleep	# of Presidents Recalled
A	0	11
B	0	17
C	2.7	16
D	3.1	21
E	4.4	17
F	5.5	16
G	7.6	31
H	7.9	41
I	8	40
J	8.1	35
K	8.6	38
L	9	

*   First, you measured a pair of **variables**, which are *properties whose values can vary across individuals or over time*. You measured one variable (number of hours slept) whose value could vary from *0* to *24*, and you measured a second variable (number of presidents recalled) whose value could vary from *0* to *45*.

*   Second, you measured again and again. That is, you made a *series* of measurements by putting your questions to many people and not just to one.

*   Third and last, you sat back and looked for a *pattern* in the series of measurements you made. You probably noticed that the values in the second column of Table 2.1 increase from top to bottom, and you probably noticed that the values in the third column do exactly the same thing. This relationship between the columns is called a **correlation** (as in "co-relation"), which occurs when *variations in the value of one variable are synchronized with variations in the value of the other.*

Your conclusion that "people who get a good night's sleep have better recall than people who don't" is a statement about the correlation between two variables. When two variables have a "more-is-more" relationship (e.g., *more* sleep is associated with *more* recall), we say

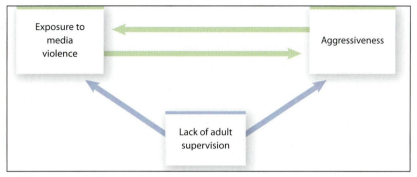

Figure 2.2 CAUSES OF CORRELATION If exposure to media violence and aggressiveness are correlated, then there are at least three possible explanations: exposure causes aggressiveness, aggressiveness causes exposure, or a third variable, such as lack of adult supervision, causes both exposure and aggressiveness, neither of which causes the other.

that they are positively correlated, and when two variables have a "more-is-less" relationship (e.g., *more* sleep is associated with *less* partying), we say they are negatively correlated. (See Appendix: Statistics for Psychology for more details on how correlations are measured.)

Causation

Natural correlations are *the correlations observed in the world around us,* and although such observations can tell us whether two variables have a relationship, they cannot tell us why. For example, many studies have found a positive correlation between the amount of violence to which a child is exposed through media such as television, movies, and video games, and the aggressiveness of the child's behavior (Anderson & Bushman, 2001; Anderson et al., 2003; Huesmann et al., 2003). The more media violence a child is exposed to, the more aggressive that child is likely to be. These two variables—exposure and aggressiveness—are positively correlated. But why?

One possibility is that *exposure causes aggressiveness*. For example, playing violent video games may teach children that aggression is fun, or is a reasonable way to solve problems, and therefore may cause them to be more aggressive in their everyday lives. Another possibility is that *aggressiveness causes exposure*. For example, aggressive children may be especially likely to play violent video games because such games allow them to behave the way they want to. A final possibility is that *a third variable causes both aggressiveness and exposure, neither of which causes the other*. For example, children who don't have much adult supervision at home may behave aggressively toward their peers and may also choose to play violent video games. If so, then the correlation between aggressiveness and exposure would be a case of **third-variable correlation**, which means that *two variables are correlated not because one causes the other but because both are caused by a third variable*. **FIGURE 2.2** shows the three possible reasons for any correlation.

Observation alone cannot tell us which of these reasons is the right one. Knowing that aggressiveness and exposure are correlated doesn't tell us whether one of these variables causes the other, or whether a third variable causes both. Luckily, there is a way to answer this

natural correlation A correlation observed in the world around us.

third-variable correlation Two variables are correlated not because one causes the other but because both are caused by a third variable.

In 1949, Dr. Benjamin Sandler noticed a correlation between the incidence of polio and ice cream consumption and concluded that sugar made children susceptible to the disease. Public health officials issued warnings. As it turned out, a third variable—warm weather—caused both an increase in disease (viruses become more active in the summer) and an increase in ice cream consumption. Bettmann/Corbis; George Marks/Getty Images

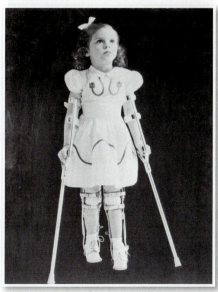

(a)   (b)

Where should you put the "sign up" button on a Web page? Developers often create two versions of their Web pages. Some visitors see one version, some see the other, and the developer measures the number of clicks that each version elicits. Developers call this "A/B testing," but scientists just call it experimentation. Macmillan Learning

experiment A technique for discovering the causal relationship between variables.

manipulation Changing a variable in order to determine its causal power.

independent variable The variable that is manipulated in an experiment.

How do you determine whether eating a dozen hot dogs will make you sick? You eat them one day, don't eat them the next day, and then see which day you barf. *That's* manipulation! By the way, in 2015, the world champion Matt Stonie ate 62 hot dogs in 10 minutes by folding them up. That's manipulation too. Bobby Bank/Wireimage/Getty Images

question. An **experiment** is *a technique for discovering the causal relationship between variables.* Unlike mere observation, experiments can tell us *why* two variables are correlated, and they can do this because they have two key features: *manipulation* and *random assignment.* Let's explore them both.

Manipulation: Making Changes in the Independent Variable

The most important thing to know about experiments is that you've been doing them all your life. For example, just imagine that you are watching a video on your laptop when all of a sudden you lose your wireless connection. You suspect that another device—say, your roommate's new television—is the cause of the problem. What would you do to test your suspicion? Observing a natural correlation wouldn't be much help. You could spend days taking careful notes about when you were and weren't connected, and when your roommate was and wasn't watching his TV. But even if you did observe a correlation between these two variables—connectivity and television usage—you still wouldn't know if your roommate's TV was *causing* your connectivity problem. After all, maybe your roommate tends to go out when the weather is good but stay home and watch television when the weather is bad, and maybe the same bad weather that makes him watch TV also interferes with the Internet connection to your house. If so, then bad weather would be the cause both of your roommate's TV usage *and* your laptop's connectivity problems.

So how *could* you test your suspicion? Well, rather than *observing* the correlation between your roommate's TV watching and your laptop's connectivity, you could try to *create* a correlation by turning the TV on and off and observing changes in your laptop's connectivity as you did so. If you found that whenever you turned the TV on your laptop fell off the network, and when you turned the TV off your laptop reconnected, then you could conclude that your roommate's television was indeed the *cause* of your problem. The technique you intuitively used is one the hallmarks of experimentation. It is called **manipulation**, which involves *changing a variable in order to determine its causal power.*

The same technique can be used to solve problems in psychology. For example, if we wanted to know *why* aggression and exposure are positively correlated, we could manipulate exposure in exactly the same way that you manipulated your roommate's television, and then measure aggressiveness in exactly the same way you measured your laptop's connectivity. We could start by inviting some children to participate in an experiment, and assigning half of them to play violent video games for an hour and assigning the other half to play nonviolent video games for an hour. Then, at the end of the hour, we could measure the children's aggressiveness, perhaps by asking them a series of questions (e.g., "Do you think it is okay to push other children out of your way? Do you think it is okay to take other children's toys away from them?") and counting how many times they say yes. If we compared the measurements across the two groups, we would essentially be computing the correlation between exposure (which was either low or high) and aggressiveness (which ranged from low to high). But because we *manipulated* exposure, rather than just measuring it, we would not have to ask whether a third variable such as lack of adult supervision might have caused the children in our experiment to have different amounts of exposure. After all, we already *know* what caused them to have different amounts of exposure: *We did!*

Experimentation involves three critical steps and several ridiculously confusing terms:

- First, we perform a manipulation. We call *the variable that is manipulated* the **independent variable** because it is under our control and therefore "independent" of what the participant does. When we manipulate an independent

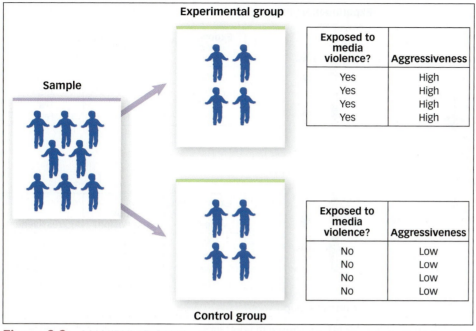

Figure 2.3 MANIPULATION The independent variable is exposure to media violence, and the dependent variable is aggressiveness. Manipulation of the independent variable results in an experimental group and a control group. When we compare the behavior of participants in these two groups, we are actually computing the correlation between the independent variable and the dependent variable.

variable (such as exposure), we create at least two groups of participants: an **experimental group**, which is *the group of participants who experience a particular manipulation,* and a **control group**, which is *the group of participants who do not experience that particular manipulation.*

- Second, having manipulated one variable (exposure), we now measure another variable (aggressiveness). We call *the variable that is measured* the **dependent variable** because its value "depends" on what the participant does.

- Third and finally, we look to see whether our manipulation of the independent variable produced changes in the dependent variable. **FIGURE 2.3** shows exactly how manipulation works.

Random Assignment: Avoiding Self-Selection

Manipulation is one of the key features of an experiment, but there is another. When we did our imaginary experiment on exposure and aggressiveness, we invited children to participate. Imagine that when they arrived at our laboratory we asked each child whether he or she preferred to play a violent or nonviolent video game, and then we let them play the game they chose. Imagine that we later measured their aggressiveness and found that the children who had played violent video games gave more aggressive responses than did those who played nonviolent video games. Would our experiment allow us to conclude that exposure to violence causes aggressiveness?

No, it would not—and the reason why not is that we made a critical mistake by allowing the children to decide which of the two groups—the experimental group or the control group—they would be in. This mistake is known as **self-selection**, which is *a problem that occurs when anything about a participant determines whether he or she will be included in the experimental or control group.* Why is self-selection a mistake? Children who prefer to play violent games are probably different in many ways from those who prefer not to. Maybe they are older or stronger or meaner.

experimental group The group of participants who are exposed to a particular manipulation, compared with the control group, in an experiment.

control group The group of participants who are not exposed to the particular manipulation, compared with the experimental group, in an experiment.

dependent variable The variable that is measured in a study.

self-selection A problem that occurs when anything about a participant determines whether he or she will be included in the experimental or control group.

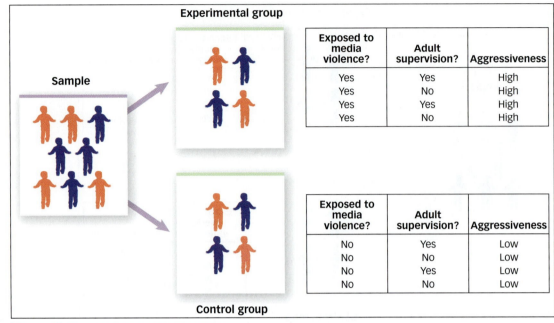

Experimental group

Exposed to media violence?	Adult supervision?	Aggressiveness
Yes	Yes	High
Yes	No	High
Yes	Yes	High
Yes	No	High

Sample

Exposed to media violence?	Adult supervision?	Aggressiveness
No	Yes	Low
No	No	Low
No	Yes	Low
No	No	Low

Control group

Figure 2.4   RANDOM ASSIGNMENT Children with adult supervision are shown in orange; those without adult supervision are shown in blue. The independent variable is exposure to media violence; the dependent variable is aggressiveness. Random assignment ensures that participants in the experimental and the control groups are, on average, equal in terms of all possible third variables.

internal validity An attribute of an experiment that allows it to establish causal relationships.

random assignment A procedure by which participants are assigned to the experimental group or control group by chance alone.

Do strawberries taste better when dipped in chocolate? If you dip the big juicy ones and don't dip the small dry ones, then you won't know if the chocolate is what made the difference. But if you randomly assign some to be dipped and others not to be dipped, and if the dipped ones taste better on average, then you will have demonstrated scientifically what every 3-year-old already knows. Robert Daly/Getty Images

Maybe they are younger or weaker or nicer. Maybe they are supervised by adults more or less often, maybe they get better or worse grades in school, maybe they have more or fewer friends. The list of possible differences goes on and on, and any one of those differences might have been responsible for the different amounts of aggressiveness the two groups displayed. A good experiment is said to have **internal validity**, which is *the attribute of an experiment that allows it to establish causal relationships*. Self-selection threatens the internal validity of an experiment, and that's a problem.

How do psychologists avoid this problem? They use **random assignment**, which is a *procedure by which participants are assigned to the experimental group or the control group by chance alone*. For example, when a child showed up to participate in our experiment we could have flipped a coin. If the coin came up heads, we could have assigned the child to play violent video games; and if the coin came up tails, we could have assigned the child to play nonviolent video games. What would have happened if we'd done this? As **FIGURE 2.4** shows, the first thing that would have happened is that about half the children would have been assigned to the experimental group and about half would have been assigned to the control group. The second thing that would have happened—and this is the really *important* thing—is that the experimental group and the control group would have had roughly equal numbers of kids with adult supervision and roughly equal numbers kids without adult supervision. They would have had roughly equal numbers of mean kids and nice kids, of kids who get good grades and bad grades, of kids who have many friends and few friends, and so on. In other words, the children in the two groups would have been *the same on average* in terms of age, niceness, academic performance, popularity, and every other variable in the known universe except for one: exposure. And because exposure would have been the *one and only* difference between the two groups of children, we could be confident that it was the one and only *cause* of the differences in aggressiveness that we observed (see Hot Science: Is Science Gender Biased?).

Is Science Gender Biased?

Women are often discouraged from pursuing scientific careers because they notice that many scientific disciplines are dominated by men, and that makes them worry that they may experience discrimination when it comes time to find a job. Is that worry well founded? Traditionally, scientists who have investigated gender discrimination in hiring have examined natural correlations to see if a larger percentage of men than women are hired, promoted, or given a raise. But, as you know from reading this chapter, natural correlations can never provide clear evidence of causation. If the psychology department at a major university hires a smaller percentage of female than male applicants, that could be due to gender discrimination. But it could also be due to the fact that the female applicants got their degrees at less prestigious universities, or published fewer scientific papers, or were just less aggressive in pestering the faculty for an interview. Correlations just can't answer this important question.

But experiments can. In a recent study, nearly a thousand professors from science departments at several hundred universities and colleges in the United States were shown descriptions of several applicants who were applying for a professorship, and were asked to rank the applicants from the most to least hireable (Williams

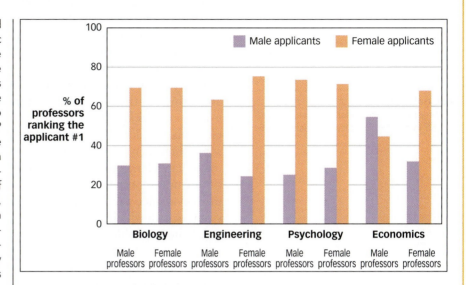

and Ceci, 2015). What the professors were not told was that the researchers had manipulated the applicants' genders so that some professors saw an applicant referred to as "he" and other professors saw the same applicant referred to as "she." Because the professors were randomly assigned to condition, and because the only thing that differed between those conditions was the gender of otherwise identical applicants, the experimenters were able to determine whether professors were gender biased. And indeed they were—but not in the way you might think. Results showed that both male and female professors tended to favor female applicants.

Of course, experiments are not miniature versions of the real world, so isn't it possible that in real hiring situations, real professors would show the opposite bias? It is possible, of course, but the data suggest that it probably isn't true. "Research on actual hiring shows female Ph.D.s are disproportionately less likely to apply for tenure-track positions, but if they do apply, they are more likely to be hired, sometimes by a 2:1 ratio" (Williams & Ceci, 2015, p. 5365). Although no research can ever answer a question like this once and for all, it appears that now is a very good time for women to choose a career in science.

Drawing Conclusions: What Do Measurements Tell Us?

So now you know how to design an internally valid experiment to study the effects of exposure to violent video games on aggressiveness. If that experiment revealed differences between the aggressiveness of children in the experimental and control groups, what should we conclude? You may be tempted to say, "We should conclude that exposure to violence causes aggressiveness." That's almost right, but not quite. The right conclusion is this: "Exposure to violence *as we defined it* causes aggressiveness *as we defined it* in the people *whom we studied*." Notice those phrases in italics. Each one of them corresponds to an important restriction on the kinds of conclusions we can draw from any experiment, so let's consider each in turn.

Representative Variables

Before we did our imaginary experiment, we had to come up with operational definitions of "exposure to media violence" and of "aggressiveness." Ours were pretty good ones, but they weren't the only possibilities, and if we had defined these variables differently, we might have gotten different results. What would have happened if we had defined exposure as "watching two hours of gory axe murders"? What about "watching 10 minutes of high school football"? What would have happened if we had defined aggressiveness as "asking for something without saying please"? How about "punching another child in the face"? The way we define these variables would probably have a big impact on the experiment's results—so which of these is the *right* way to define them?

One answer is that we should always define variables in an experiment as they are defined in the real world. **External validity** is *an attribute of an experiment in which variables have been defined in a normal, typical, or realistic way.* It seems pretty clear that the kind of aggressive behavior that concerns teachers and parents lies somewhere between a failure of manners and a physical assault, and that the kind of media violence to which children are typically exposed lies somewhere between torture and sports. If the goal of an experiment is to determine whether the kinds of media violence to which children are typically exposed causes the kinds of aggressiveness with which societies are typically concerned, then external validity is essential. When variables are defined in an experiment as they typically are in the real world, we say that the variables are *representative* of the real world.

external validity An attribute of an experiment in which variables have been defined in a normal, typical, or realistic way.

External validity sounds like such a good idea that you may be surprised to learn that most psychology experiments are externally *in*valid—and that most psychologists don't mind. The reason for this is that psychologists are rarely trying to learn about the real world by creating tiny replicas of it in their laboratories. Rather, they are usually trying to learn about the real world by using experiments to test hypotheses derived from theories, and externally invalid experiments can often do that quite nicely (Mook, 1983).

To see how, consider an example from physics. Physicists have a theory stating that heat is the result of the rapid movement of molecules. This theory gives rise to a hypothesis, namely, that when the molecules that constitute an object are slowed, the object should become cooler. Now imagine that a physicist tested this hypothesis by performing an experiment in which a laser was used to slow the movement of the molecules in a rubber ball, whose temperature was then measured. Would you criticize this experiment by saying, "Sorry, but your experiment teaches us nothing about the real world because in the real world, no one actually uses lasers to slow the movement of the molecules in rubber balls"? Let's hope not. The physicist's theory (molecular motion causes heat) led to a hypothesis about *what would happen in the laboratory* (slowing the molecules in a rubber ball should cool it), and the events that the physicist manipulated and measured in the laboratory tested the hypothesis. Similarly, a well-thought-out theory about the causal relationship between exposure to media violence and aggressiveness should lead to hypotheses about how children in a laboratory will behave after playing a violent video game, and so their behavior after playing the game tests the hypothesis. If children who play *Bloodborne* are more likely to say that it is permissible to shove other people out of the way, then any theory that claims that media violence cannot influence aggressiveness has just been proved wrong.

In short, theories allow us to generate hypotheses about what can, must, or will happen under particular circumstances, and experiments are usually meant to create those circumstances, test the hypotheses, and thereby provide evidence for or against the theories that generated them. Experiments are not usually meant to be miniature versions of everyday life, and thus external invalidity is not necessarily a problem.

Representative People

Our imaginary experiment on exposure and aggressiveness would allow us to conclude that exposure *as we defined it* caused aggression *as we defined it* in the people *whom we studied*. That last phrase names another important restriction on the kinds of conclusions we can draw from experiments.

Does piercing make a person more or less attractive? The answer, of course, depends entirely on your operational definition of *piercing*. AP Photo/Keystone, Tipress/Samuel Golay; Dinodia Photos/Alamy Stock Photo

Who are the people whom psychologists study? Psychologists rarely observe an entire **population**, which is *a complete collection of people*, such as the population of human beings (about 7 billion), the population of Californians (about 38 million), or the population of people with Down syndrome (about 1 million). Rather, they observe a **sample**, which is *a partial collection of people drawn from a population*. In some cases, that sample is as small as 1. We can learn a lot about memory by studying individuals like Rajveer Meena, who memorized the first 70,000 digits of pi, or about intelligence and creativity by studying individuals like Tanishq Abraham, who graduated from college at the age of 11 and began consulting in the aerospace industry. When psychologists study individuals they are using the **case method**, which is *a procedure for gathering scientific information by studying a single person*. Of course, most of the psychological studies you will read about in this book included samples of ten, a hundred, a thousand, or a few thousand people. So how do psychologists decide which people to include in their samples?

Tanishq Abraham graduated from college in 2015 at the age of 11. He told reporters, "I want to become a doctor, but I also want to become a medical researcher, and also the President of the United States." We see no reason why he shouldn't be all three. Renee C. Byer/Newscom/Zuma Press/Sacramento, CA/USA

One way is by **random sampling**, which is *a technique for choosing participants that ensures that every member of a population has an equal chance of being included in the sample*. When we randomly sample participants from a population, the sample is said to be *representative* of the population. This allows us to *generalize* from the sample to the population—that is, to conclude that what we observed in our sample would also have been observed if we had measured the entire population. Random sampling sounds like such a good idea that you might be surprised to learn that most psychological studies involve nonrandom samples. Indeed, virtually every participant in every psychology experiment you will ever read about was a volunteer, and most were college students who were significantly younger, smarter, healthier, wealthier, and Whiter than the average earthling. About 96% of the people whom psychologists study come from countries that have just 12% of the world's population, and 70% come from the United States alone (Henrich, Heine, & Norenzayan, 2010). This is because most psychology experiments are conducted by professors and graduate students at colleges and universities in the Western Hemisphere, and as much as they might *like* to sample the population of the planet randomly, the practical truth is that they are pretty much stuck studying the folks who volunteer for their studies. So how can we learn *anything* from psychology experiments? Isn't the failure to sample randomly a fatal flaw? No, it's not, and there are three reasons why.

population A complete collection of people.

sample A partial collection of people drawn from a population.

case method A procedure for gathering scientific information by studying a single person.

random sampling A technique for choosing participants that ensures that every member of a population has an equal chance of being included in the sample.

Nonrandom sampling can lead to errors. In the presidential election of 1948, the *Chicago Tribune* mistakenly predicted that Thomas Dewey would beat Harry Truman. Why? Because polling was done by telephone, and Dewey Republicans were more likely to have telephones than were Truman Democrats. In the presidential election of 2004, exit polls mistakenly predicted that John Kerry would beat George Bush. Why? Because polling was done by soliciting voters as they left the polls, and Kerry supporters were more willing to stop and talk. Ullstein Bild/The Granger Collection , NYC. All Rights Reserved.Pete Marovich/Newscom/Zuma Press/Washington/District of Columbia/U.S.

This mouse died after drinking the green stuff. Want to drink the green stuff? Why not? You're not a mouse, are you? David J. Green—Animals/Alamy Stock Photo

direct replication An experiment that uses the same procedures as a previous experiment but with a new sample.

1. Sometimes the similarity of a sample and a population doesn't matter. If one pig flew over the Statue of Liberty just one time, it would instantly disprove the traditional theory of porcine locomotion. It wouldn't matter if all pigs flew or if any other pigs flew. If one did, then that's enough. An experimental result can be illuminating even when the sample isn't typical of the population.

2. When the ability to generalize an experimental result *is* important, psychologists can perform a **direct replication**, which is *an experiment that uses the same procedures as a previous experiment but with a new sample*. For example, after measuring how a nonrandomly selected group of American children behaved after playing violent video games, we could replicate our experiment with Japanese children, or with American teenagers, or with deaf adults. If the results of our study were replicated in these other samples, then we would be more confident (but never completely confident) that the results describe a basic human tendency. If the results were not replicated, then we would learn something potentially interesting about the influence of culture or age or ability on aggressiveness. Replicating research with new samples drawn from different populations is a win–win strategy: No matter what happens, we stand to gain new knowledge.

3. Sometimes the similarity of the sample and the population is a reasonable starting assumption. For example, few of us would be willing to take an experimental medicine if a nonrandom sample of seven participants took it and died. Indeed, we would probably refuse the medicine even if the seven participants were mice. Although these nonrandomly sampled participants were different from us in many ways (including tails and whiskers), most of us would be willing to generalize from their experience to ours because we know that even mice share enough of our basic biology to make it a good bet that what harms them can harm us too. By this same reasoning, if a psychology experiment demonstrated that some American children behaved aggressively after playing violent video games, we might ask whether there is a compelling reason to suspect that Ecuadorian college students or middle-aged Australians would be any different. If the answer was yes, then experiments would provide a way for us to investigate that possibility.

BUILD TO THE OUTCOMES

1. What are the steps to take to determine whether or not two variables are correlated?

2. What are the three possible reasons for two variables to be correlated?

3. What are the key ingredients for an experiment?

4. How do manipulation and random assignment solve the third-variable problem?

5. Why is self-selection a problem?

6. What is the difference between a dependent and independent variable?

7. What is the difference between internal validity and external validity?

8. What is the difference between a population and a sample?

Thinking Critically About Evidence

LEARNING OUTCOMES

• Identify the two psychological tendencies that make critical thinking so difficult.

• Describe the two steps people can take to help them think critically.

Experiments generate evidence. But interpreting that evidence requires *critical thinking*, which involves asking tough questions about whether we have interpreted the evidence in an unbiased way, and about whether the evidence tells not just the truth, but the *whole* truth (see Data Visualization: Does SAT performance correlate with income and education level? at www.launchpadworks.com). Research suggests that most people have trouble doing both of these things, and that educational programs designed to teach or improve critical thinking skills are not particularly effective (Willingham, 2007). Why do people have so much trouble thinking critically?

We See What We Expect

One problem is that our preexisting beliefs color our view of new evidence, causing us to see what we expect to see. That's why evidence so often seems to confirm what we believed all along. For instance, participants in one study (Darley & Gross, 1983) learned about a little girl named Hannah. One group of participants was told that Hannah came from an affluent family, and another group was told that Hannah came from a poor family. All participants were then shown a video of Hannah taking a reading test, and were then asked to rate Hannah's performance. Although the video was exactly the same for all participants, those who believed that Hannah was affluent rated her performance more positively than did those who believed that Hannah was poor. What's more, both groups of participants defended their conclusions by citing evidence from the video! Experiments like this one suggest that when we consider evidence, what we see depends on what we *expected* to see. In addition, people tend to surround themselves with others who believe what they believe, which means that our friends and families are much more likely to validate our beliefs than to challenge them. Studies also show that when given the opportunity to search for evidence, people preferentially search for evidence that confirms their beliefs (Hart et al., 2009). When people find evidence that confirms their beliefs, they tend to stop looking, but when they find evidence that does the opposite, they keep searching for more evidence (Kunda, 1990).

The first rule of critical thinking is to doubt your own conclusions—but that's hard to do when everyone tells you you're right! Recent research shows that Facebook users create "echo chambers" by sharing stories and links only with friends who already share their points of view (Del Vicario et al., 2016). David J. Green/Alamy Stock Photo

Because it is so easy to see what we expect to see, the first rule of critical thinking is simply this: *Doubt your own conclusions*. One of the best ways to doubt yourself is to find people who doubt you and then listen carefully to what they have to say. That's why scientists go out of their way to expose themselves to criticism by sending their papers to colleagues who are likely to disagree with them or by presenting their findings to an audience of critics. They do this not because it is so much fun to be critiqued but because it helps them achieve a more balanced view of their own conclusions.

We Consider What We See and Ignore What We Don't

The evidence we see is important, but so is the evidence we don't see. And yet, studies suggest that one of the greatest threats to critical thinking is that people often fail to consider missing information. For example, participants in a study were randomly assigned to play one of two roles in a game (Ross, Amabile, & Steinmetz, 1977). The "quizmasters" were asked to make up a series of difficult questions, and the "contestants" were asked to answer them. If you give this a quick try, you will discover that it's very easy to generate questions that you can answer but that most other people cannot. Think of the last city you visited, give a friend the name of the hotel you stayed in, and ask your friend to name the street it's on. Unless you have extremely well-traveled friends, he or she probably won't know. So participants who were cast in the role of quizmaster asked lots of clever-sounding questions, and participants who were cast in the role of contestant gave lots of wrong answers.

Ever since I began using your product, I haven't had a single unwanted thought about white bears. Thank you so much for this amazing discovery. It has really changed my life!

Mr. Ferb Kushman
Lansing, MI

The second rule of critical thinking is to consider what you don't see. Businesses often provide testimonials from satisfied customers, but where are all the dissatisfied customers, and what might they have to say? Daniel Gilbert

Now comes the interesting part. Quizmasters and contestants played this game while another participant—the observer—watched. After the game was over, the observer was asked to make some guesses about what the players were like in their everyday lives. The results were clear: Observers consistently concluded that the quizmaster was a more knowledgeable person than the contestant! Observers *saw* the quizmaster asking sharp questions and *saw* the contestant saying, "Um, gosh, I don't know," and observers considered the evidence they saw. What they failed to consider was the evidence they did *not* see. Specifically, they failed to consider what would have happened if the person who had been assigned to play the role of quizmaster had instead been assigned to play the role of contestant, and vice versa. If that had happened, then surely the contestant would have been the one asking clever questions and the quiz-master would have been the one struggling to answer them. Bottom line? If the first rule of critical thinking is to doubt what you see, then the second rule is to *consider what you don't see*. To practice these and other critical thinking skills, check out the Changing Minds questions in the review section at the conclusion of each chapter.

The Skeptical Stance

Winston Churchill once said that democracy is the worst form of government except for all the others. Similarly, science is not an infallible method for learning about the world; it's just a whole lot less fallible than are the other methods. Science is a human enterprise, and humans make mistakes: They see what they expect to see, and they rarely consider what they can't see at all.

What makes science different from most other human enterprises is that science actively seeks to discover and remedy its own biases and errors. Scientists are constantly striving to make their observations more accurate and their reasoning more rigorous, and they invite anyone and everyone to examine their evidence and challenge their conclusions. Thus, science is the ultimate democracy—one of the

Oddsly Enough

A recent Gallup survey found that 53% of college graduates believe in extrasensory perception, or ESP. Very few psychologists share that belief. What makes them such a skeptical lot is their understanding of the laws of probability.

The Nobel laureate Luis Alvarez was reading the newspaper one day, and a particular story got him thinking about an old college friend whom he hadn't seen in years. A few minutes later, he turned the page and was shocked to see the very same friend's obituary. But before concluding that he had an acute case of ESP, Alvarez decided to use probability theory to determine just how amazing this coincidence really was.

First, he estimated the number of friends an average person has, and then he estimated how often an average person thinks about each of those friends. With these estimates in hand, he did a few simple calculations and determined the likelihood that someone would think about a friend five minutes before learning about that friend's death. The odds were astonishing. In a country the size of the United States, for example, Alvarez predicted that this amazing coincidence should happen to 10 people every day (Alvarez, 1965).

Another Nobel laureate disagreed. He put the number closer to 80 people a day (Charpak & Broch, 2004)!

"In 10 years there are 5 million minutes," says the statistics professor Irving Jack. "That means each person has plenty of opportunity to have some remarkable coincidences in his life" (quoted in Neimark, 2004). For example, 250 million Americans dream for about two hours every night (that's a half billion hours of dreaming!), so it isn't surprising that two people sometimes have the same dream, or that we sometimes dream about something that actually happens the next day. As the mathematics professor John Allen Paulos (quoted in Neimark, 2004) put it, "In reality, the most astonishingly incredible coincidence imaginable would be the complete absence of all coincidence."

If all of this seems surprising to you, then you are not alone. Research

"Idaho! What a coincidence—I'm from Idaho."

Michael Maslin ©The New Yorker Collection/www.cartoonbank.com

shows that people routinely underestimate the likelihood of coincidences happening by chance (Diaconis & Mosteller, 1989; Falk & McGregor, 1983; Hintzman, Asher, & Stern, 1978). If you want to profit from this fact, assemble a group of 24 or more people and bet anyone that at least 2 of the people share a birthday. The odds are in your favor, and the bigger the group, the better the odds. In fact, in a group of 35, the odds are 85%. Happy fleecing!

only institutions in the world in which the lowliest nobody can triumph over the most celebrated someone. When an unknown Swiss patent clerk named Albert Einstein challenged the greatest physicists of his day, he didn't have a famous name, a fancy degree, powerful friends, or a fat wallet. He just had evidence. And he prevailed for one reason: His evidence was right.

So think of the remaining chapters in this textbook as a report from the field—a description of the work that psychological scientists have done as they stumble toward knowledge. These chapters tell the story of the men and women who have put their faith in the scientific method and used it to pry loose small pieces of the truth about who we are, how we work, and what we are all doing here together on the third stone from the sun. Read it with interest, but also with skepticism. Some of the things we are about to tell you simply aren't true; we just don't yet know which things they are. We hope you will think critically about what you read here—and everywhere else. (See The Real World: Oddsly Enough.)

BUILD TO THE OUTCOMES

1. What two human tendencies are enemies of critical thinking?

2. What does it mean to say, "If you want to be happy, take your friend to lunch; if you want to be right, take your enemy"?

3. What makes science different from most other human enterprises?

The Ethics of Science: What's Right?

Somewhere along the way, someone probably told you that it isn't nice to treat people like objects. And yet, it may seem that psychologists do just that by creating situations that cause people to feel fearful or sad, to do things that are embarrassing or immoral, and to learn things about themselves and others that they might not really want to know. Don't be fooled by appearances. The fact is that psychologists go to great lengths to protect the well-being of their research participants, and they are bound by a code of ethics that is as detailed and demanding as the professional codes that bind physicians, lawyers, and accountants. That code requires that psychologists show respect for people, for animals, and for the truth. Let's examine each of these obligations in turn.

LEARNING OUTCOMES
- Identify the things that ethical research must always respect.
- Identify the ways in which psychologists ensure that their research respects people.
- Identify the ways in which psychologists ensure that their research respects truth.

Respecting People

During World War II, Nazi doctors performed truly barbaric experiments on human subjects, such as removing organs or submerging people in ice water just to see how long it would take them to die. After the war ended, the international community developed the Nuremberg Code of 1947 and then the Declaration of Helsinki in 1964, which spelled out rules for the ethical treatment of human subjects. Unfortunately, not everyone obeyed them. For example, from 1932 until 1972, the U.S. Public Health Service conducted the infamous Tuskegee experiment, in which 399 African American men with syphilis were denied treatment so that researchers could observe the progression of the disease. As one journalist noted, the government "used human beings as laboratory animals in a long and inefficient study of how long it takes syphilis to kill someone" (Coontz, 2008).

In 1979, the U.S. Department of Health, Education and Welfare released what came to be known as the Belmont Report, which described three basic principles

The man at this bar is upset. He just saw another man slip a drug into a woman's drink and he is alerting the bartender. What he doesn't know is that all the people at the bar are actors and that he is being filmed for the television show *What Would You Do?* Was it ethical for ABC to put this man in such a stressful situation without his consent? And how did the men who didn't alert the bartender feel when they turned on their televisions months later and were confronted by their own shameful behavior?

informed consent A written agreement to participate in a study made by an adult who has been informed of all the risks that participation may entail.

that all research involving human subjects must follow. First, research must show *respect for persons* and their right to make decisions for and about themselves without undue influence or coercion. Second, research must be *beneficent,* which means that it must attempt to maximize benefits and reduce risks to the participant. Third, research must be *just,* which means that it must distribute benefits and risks equally to participants without prejudice toward particular individuals or groups.

The specific ethical code that psychologists follow incorporates these basic principles and expands them. (You can find the American Psychological Association's *Ethical Principles of Psychologists and Code of Conduct* [2002] at http://www.apa.org/ethics/code/index.aspx.) Here are a few of the most important rules that govern the conduct of psychological research:

- *Informed consent:* Participants may not take part in a psychological study unless they have given **informed consent**, which is *a written agreement to participate in a study made by an adult who has been informed of all the risks that participation may entail.* This doesn't mean that the person must know everything about the study (e.g., the hypothesis), but it does mean that the person must know about anything that might potentially be harmful or painful. If people cannot give informed consent (e.g., because they are minors or are mentally incapable), then informed consent must be obtained from their legal guardians. And even after people give informed consent, they always have the right to withdraw from the study at any time without penalty.

- *Freedom from coercion:* Psychologists may not coerce participation. Coercion not only means physical and psychological coercion but monetary coercion as well. It is unethical to offer people large amounts of money to persuade them to do something that they might otherwise decline to do.

- *Protection from harm:* Psychologists must take every possible precaution to protect their research participants from physical or psychological harm. If there are two equally effective ways to study something, the psychologist must use the safer method.

- *Risk-benefit analysis:* Although participants may be asked to accept small risks, such as a minor shock or a small embarrassment, they may not even be *asked* to accept large risks, such as severe pain, psychological trauma, or any risk that is greater than the risks they would ordinarily take in their everyday lives. Even when participants are asked to take small risks, the psychologist must first demonstrate that these risks are outweighed by the social benefits of the new knowledge that might be gained from the study.

- *Deception:* Psychologists may use deception only when it is justified by the study's scientific, educational, or applied value and when alternative procedures are not feasible. They may never deceive participants about any aspect of a study that could cause them physical or psychological harm or pain.

- *Debriefing:* If a participant is deceived in any way before or during a study, the psychologist must provide a **debriefing**, which is *a verbal description of the true nature and purpose of a study.*

- *Confidentiality:* Psychologists are obligated to keep private and personal information obtained during a study confidential.

debriefing A verbal description of the true nature and purpose of a study.

These are just some of the rules that psychologists must follow. But how are those rules enforced? Almost all psychology studies are done by psychologists who work at colleges and universities that have institutional review boards (IRBs) that are composed of instructors and researchers, university staff, and laypeople from the community (e.g., business leaders or members of the clergy). If the research is federally funded, then the law requires that the IRB include at least one nonscientist and one person who is not affiliated with the institution. A psychologist may conduct a study only after the IRB has reviewed and approved it. The code of ethics and the procedure for approval are so strict that many studies simply cannot be performed anywhere, by anyone, at any time, because doing so would require unethical experiments that violate basic human rights.

Respecting Animals

Not all research participants have human rights because not all research participants are human. Some are chimpanzees, rats, pigeons, or other nonhuman animals. The American Psychological Association's code specifically describes the special rights of these nonhuman participants, and some of the more important ones are these:

- All procedures involving animals must be supervised by psychologists who are trained in research methods and experienced in the care of laboratory animals and who are responsible for ensuring appropriate consideration of the animals' comfort, health, and humane treatment.

- Psychologists must make reasonable efforts to minimize the discomfort, infection, illness, and pain of animals.

- Psychologists may use a procedure that subjects an animal to pain, stress, or privation only when an alternative procedure is unavailable and when the procedure is justified by the scientific, educational, or applied value of the study.

- Psychologists must perform all surgical procedures under appropriate anesthesia and must minimize an animal's pain during and after surgery.

That's good—but is it good enough? Some people don't think so (Singer, 1975). They believe it is unethical to use nonhuman animals in research, and they believe that nonhuman animals should have the same fundamental rights as humans. But most Americans consider it morally acceptable to use nonhuman animals in research and say they would reject a governmental ban on such research (Kiefer, 2004; Moore, 2003). Science is not in the business of resolving moral controversies, and every individual must draw his or her own conclusions about this issue. But whatever position

Some people consider it unethical to use animals for clothing or research. Others see an important distinction between these two purposes. Paul McErlane/Reuters/Corbis

you take, it is important to note that only a small percentage of psychological studies involve animals, and only a small percentage of those studies cause animals pain or harm. Psychologists mainly study people, and when they do study animals, they mainly study their behavior.

Respecting Truth

Institutional review boards ensure that data are collected ethically. But once the data are collected, who ensures that they are ethically analyzed and reported? No one does. Psychology, like all sciences, works on the honor system. You may find that a bit odd. After all, we don't use the honor system in stores ("Take the television set home and pay us next time you're in the neighborhood"), banks ("I don't need to look up your account, just tell me how much money you want to withdraw"), or courtrooms ("If you say you're innocent, well then, that's good enough for me"), so why would we expect it to work in science? Are scientists more honest than everyone else?

Definitely! Okay, we just made that up. But the honor system doesn't depend on scientists being especially honest, but on the fact that science is a community enterprise. When scientists claim to have discovered something important, other scientists don't just applaud. They start studying it, too. When the physicist Jan Hendrik Schön announced in 2001 that he had produced a molecular-scale transistor, other physicists were deeply impressed—that is, until they tried to replicate his work and discovered that Schön had fabricated his data (Agin, 2007). Schön lost his job, and his doctoral degree was revoked, but the important point is that such frauds can't last long because one scientist's conclusion is the next scientist's research question. This doesn't mean that all frauds are uncovered swiftly: The psychologist Diederik Stapel lied, cheated, and made up his data for decades before people became suspicious enough to investigate (Levelt Committee, Noort Committee, Drenth Committee, 2012). But it does mean that the *important* frauds are uncovered eventually. The psychologist who fraudulently claims to have shown that chimps are smarter than goldfish may never get caught because no one is likely to follow up on such an obvious finding, but the psychologist who fraudulently claims to have shown the opposite will soon have a lot of explaining to do.

What exactly are psychologists on their honor to do? At least three things. First, when they write reports of their studies and publish them in scientific journals, psychologists are obligated to report truthfully on what they did and what they found. They can't fabricate results (e.g., by claiming to have performed studies that they never really performed) or fudge results (e.g., by changing records of data that were actually collected), and they can't mislead by omission (e.g., by reporting only the results that confirm their hypothesis and saying nothing about the results that don't). Second, psychologists are obligated to share credit fairly by including as co-authors of their reports the other people who contributed to the work, and by mentioning in their reports the other scientists who have done related work. And third, psychologists are obligated to share their data with other scientists who seek to verify their findings through reanalysis of the data. The fact that anyone can check up on anyone else is part of why the honor system works as well as it does.

BUILD TO THE OUTCOMES

1. What is an institutional review board (IRB)?

2. What is informed consent?

3. What is debriefing?

4. What steps must psychologists take to protect nonhuman subjects?

5. What three things must psychologists do when they report the results of their research?

6. How does science uncover fraud?

CHAPTER REVIEW

Empiricism: How to Know Stuff

- Empiricism is the belief that the best way to understand the world is to observe it firsthand. It is only in the last few centuries that people have begun systematically collecting and evaluating evidence to test the accuracy of their beliefs about the world.
- The scientific method involves (a) developing a theory that gives rise to a falsifiable hypothesis; and then (b) making observations that test that hypothesis. Although tests can prove theories false, they cannot prove them true.
- The methods of psychology are special because human beings are more complex, variable, and reactive than almost anything else that scientists study.

Observation: What Do People Do?

- Measurement involves (a) defining a property in terms of some concrete, observable event, and then (b) using an instrument to detect the event to which the definition refers.
- A good definition is valid, meaning that the observable event does a good job of indicating the property being measured.
- A good instrument is both reliable (it produces the same measurement every time it is used to measure the same thing) and powerful (it can detect small magnitudes of the property).
- Demand characteristics are aspects of an observational setting that cause people to behave as they think someone else wants or expects them to. Psychologists try to reduce or eliminate demand characteristics by observing participants when they don't know they are being observed, by giving participants privacy and anonymity, by measuring uncontrollable behavior, and by keeping both participants and researchers "blind" to the hypothesis being tested.

Explanation: Why Do People Do What They Do?

- To determine whether two variables are related, we can measure each variable many times and then compare the patterns of variation within each series of measurements. If the patterns are synchronized, then the variables are said to be correlated.

- When we observe a natural correlation between two variables, we still don't know whether one caused the other, or whether both were caused by a third variable.
- Experiments allow psychologists to know why two variables are correlated. They involve manipulating an independent variable, randomly assigning participants to the experimental and control groups that this manipulation creates, and measuring a dependent variable. These measurements are then compared across groups.
- An internally valid experiment can establish that changes in an independent variable caused changes in a dependent variable as they were operationally defined and among the particular participants who were studied. An externally valid experiment operationalizes these variables in "realistic" ways.

Thinking Critically About Evidence

- Thinking critically about evidence is difficult because people have a natural tendency to see what they expect to see, and to consider what they see but not what they don't.
- To practice critical thinking, doubt your own conclusions and consider what you don't see.
- One of the things that makes science so different from most other human enterprises is that scientists actively seek to discover and remedy their own biases and errors.

The Ethics of Science: What's Right?

- Institutional review boards ensure that the rights of human beings who participate in scientific research are based on the principles of respect for persons, beneficence, and justice.
- Psychologists are obligated to uphold these principles by getting informed consent from participants, not coercing participation, protecting participants from harm, weighing benefits against risks, avoiding deception, and keeping information confidential.
- Psychologists are obligated to respect the rights of animals and treat them humanely. Very little psychological research requires harming animals. Most people are in favor of using animals in scientific research.
- Psychologists are obligated to tell the truth about their studies, to share credit appropriately, and to grant others access to their data.

KEY CONCEPT QUIZ

1. The belief that accurate knowledge can be acquired through observation is
   a. not very new.
   b. dogmatism.
   c. empiricism.
   d. wrong.

2. Which of the following is the best definition of a hypothesis?
   a. empirical evidence
   b. a scientific investigation
   c. a falsifiable prediction
   d. a theoretical idea

3. If a measure produces the same results every time it is used to measure the same thing, it is said to have
   a. validity.
   b. reliability.
   c. power.
   d. concreteness.

4. Aspects of an observational setting that cause people to behave as they think someone else wants them to or expects them to are called
   a. observer biases.
   b. reactive conditions.
   c. natural habitats.
   d. demand characteristics.

5. In a double-blind observation
   a. the participants know what is being measured.
   b. people are observed in their natural environments.
   c. the hypothesis is hidden from both the observer and the participant.
   d. the researcher and participant never see each other.

6. When two variables (A and B) are correlated, we can be sure that
   a. A caused B.
   b. B caused A.
   c. a third variable caused both A and B.
   d. variations in the value of A are synchronized with variations in the value of B.

7. A researcher administers a questionnaire concerning attitudes toward global warming to men and women who range in age from 18 to 75 and who live in either the United States or Canada. The dependent variable in the study is the _____ of the participants.
   a. age
   b. gender
   c. attitude toward global warming
   d. geographic location

8. The attribute of an experiment that allows it to establish causal relationships is called
   a. external validity.
   b. internal validity.
   c. random assignment.
   d. self-selection.

9. An experiment that operationally defines variables in a realistic way is said to be
   a. externally valid.
   b. controlled.
   c. operationally defined.
   d. randomly sampled.

10. When people find evidence that confirms their beliefs, they often
   a. tend to stop looking for further evidence.
   b. seek further evidence that will disconfirm their beliefs.
   c. question the evidence.
   d. doubt their own beliefs.

11. What are psychologists ethically required to do when reporting research results?
   a. report findings truthfully
   b. share credit for research
   c. make data available for further research
   d. all of the above

 **LearningCurve**   Don't stop now! Quizzing yourself is a powerful study tool. Go to LearningCurve at www.launchpadworks.com for more practice.

KEY TERMS

empiricism (p. 28)	power (p. 31)	manipulation (p. 36)	population (p. 41)
scientific method (p. 28)	demand characteristics (p. 32)	independent variable (p. 36)	sample (p. 41)
theory (p. 29)	naturalistic observation (p. 32)	experimental group (p. 37)	case method (p. 41)
hypothesis (p. 29)	double-blind observation (p. 33)	control group (p. 37)	random sampling (p. 41)
empirical method (p. 29)	variable (p. 34)	dependent variable (p. 37)	direct replication (p. 42)
operational definition (p. 31)	correlation (p. 34)	self-selection (p. 37)	informed consent (p. 46)
validity (p. 31)	natural correlation (p. 35)	internal validity (p. 38)	debriefing (p. 46)
instrument (p. 31)	third-variable correlation (p. 35)	random assignment (p. 38)	
reliability (p. 31)	experiment (p. 36)	external validity (p. 40)	

CHANGING MINDS

1. Back in Psychology: Evolution of a Science, you read about B. F. Skinner, who studied the principle of reinforcement, which states that the consequences of a behavior determine whether it will be more or less likely to occur in the future. So, for example, a rat's rate of lever pressing will increase if it receives food reinforcement after each

lever press. When you tell a classmate about this principle, she only shrugs. "That's obvious. Anyone who's ever owned a dog knows how to train animals. If you ask me, psychology is just common sense. You don't have to conduct scientific experiments to test things that everyone already knows are true." How would you explain the value of studying something that seems like "common sense"?

2. You're watching TV with a friend when a news program reports that a research study has found that people in Europe who work shorter hours are happier than those who work longer hours, but in the United States people who work longer hours are happier (Okulicz-Kozaryn, 2011). "That's an interesting experiment," he says. You point out that the news only said it was a research study, not an experiment. What would have to be true for it to be an experiment? Why aren't all research studies experiments? What can you *not* learn from this study that you *could* learn from an experiment?

3. After the first exam, your professor says she's noticed a strong positive correlation between the location of students' seats and their exam scores: "The closer students sit to the front of the room, the higher their scores on the exam," she says. After class, your friend suggests that the two of you should sit up front for the rest of the semester to improve your grades. Having read about correlation and causation, should you be skeptical? What are some possible reasons for the correlation between seating position and good grades? Could you design an experiment to test whether sitting up front actually causes good grades?

4. A classmate in your criminal justice class suggests that mental illness is a major cause of violent crimes in the United States. As evidence, he mentions a highly publicized murder trial in which the convicted suspect was diagnosed with schizophrenia. What scientific evidence would he need to support this claim?

5. You ask your friend if he wants to go to the gym with you. "No," he says, "I never exercise." You tell him that regular exercise has all kinds of health benefits, including greatly reducing the risk of heart disease. "I don't believe that," he replies. "I had an uncle who got up at 6 a.m. every day of his life to go jogging, and he still died of a heart attack at age 53." What would you tell your friend? Does his uncle's case prove that exercise really doesn't protect against heart disease after all?

ANSWERS TO KEY CONCEPT QUIZ

1. c; 2. c; 3. b; 4. d; 5. c; 6. a; 7. c; 8. b; 9. a; 10. a; 11. d.

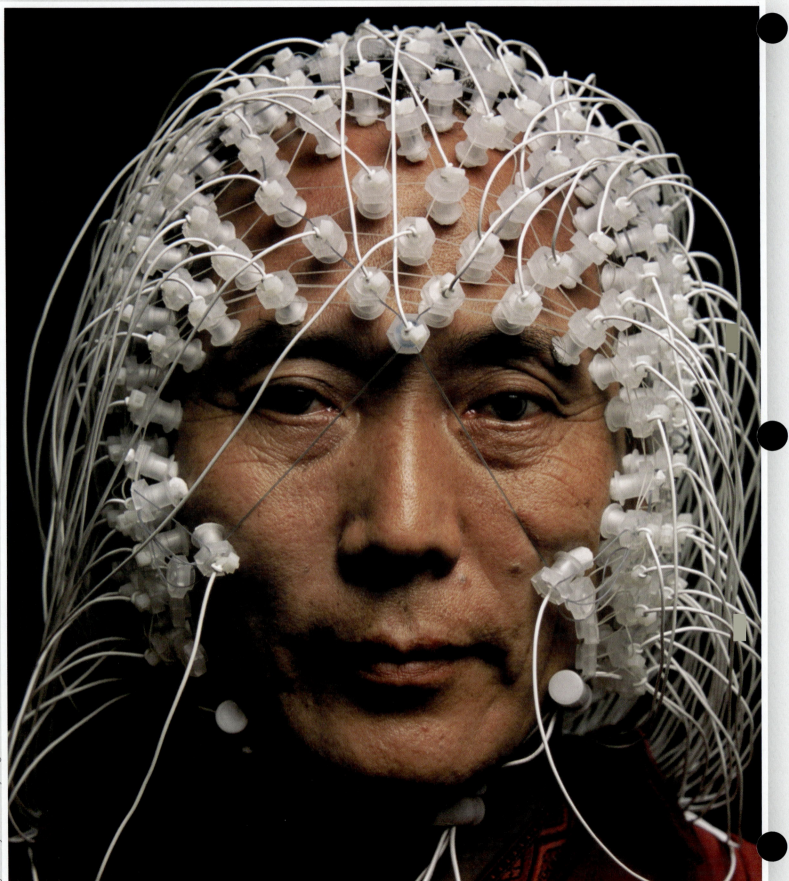

Neuroscience and Behavior

3

R ay Easterling and Dave Duerson came from different times and places, but both loved football and played the position of defensive back well enough to make it all the way to the National Football League—Easterling for the Atlanta Falcons during the 1970s and Duerson for the Chicago Bears in the 1980s. Unfortunately, the parallels between Easterling and Duerson continued into their retirement years. Both men suffered from significant cognitive decline and depression, and both ended up taking their own lives: Duerson in 2011, Easterling in 2012. Postmortem analyses of their brains revealed the presence of a condition known as *chronic traumatic encephalopathy (CTE),* a form of progressive brain damage that has been linked to repeated concussions (Montenigro et al., 2015). Duerson and Easterling are just two of many former NFL players who have been diagnosed with CTE, including the Hall of Famer and former *Monday Night Football* broadcaster Frank Gifford, whose death in August 2015 focused national attention on the problem. CTE has also been observed after repeated head injuries in boxing, wrestling, hockey, and rugby (Costanza et al., 2011; Daneshvar et al., 2011; Lahkan & Kirchgessner, 2012; McKee et al., 2012).

In December 2015, attention to CTE was further heightened by the release of the movie *Concussion,* which focuses on the story of Bennet Omalu (played by Will Smith), the pathologist who first uncovered evidence for CTE in the brain of an NFL player. Although statements in the movie imply that CTE has caused the decline and death of former NFL players, scientists are still actively debating the nature and consequences of CTE (Castellani, Perry, & Iverson, 2015). However, we do know that CTE is associated with symptoms including inability to concentrate, memory loss, irritability, and depression, usually beginning within a decade after repeated concussions and worsening with time (McKee et al., 2009; Montenigro et al., 2015). Fortunately, growing awareness of CTE is leading professional sports organizations, as well as colleges, schools, and others

 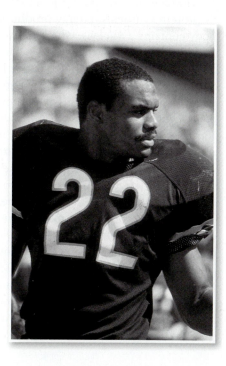

Ray Easterling (left) and Dave Duerson (right) had similarly outstanding NFL careers and similarly troubled retirements, perhaps associated with brain damage. Uncredited/AP Images
Michael J. Minardi/Getty Images

 involved in youth sports, to take steps to address the problem (see Data Visualization: Which sports have the highest rates of concussion? at www.launchpadworks.com).

The symptoms of CTE are reminders that our psychological, emotional, and social well-being depend critically on the health and integrity of the brain. The more we know about the brain, and the more people who know it, the better our chances of finding solutions to problems such as CTE.

IN THIS CHAPTER, WE'LL CONSIDER HOW THE BRAIN WORKS, what happens when it doesn't, and how both states of affairs determine behavior. First, we'll introduce you to the basic unit of information processing in the brain, the neuron. Neurons are the starting point of all behavior, thought, and emotion. Next, we'll consider the anatomy of the central nervous system, focusing especially on the brain, including its overall organization, its key structures that perform different functions, and its evolutionary development. Finally, we'll discuss methods that allow us to study both damaged and healthy brains.

Neurons: The Origin of Behavior

LEARNING OUTCOMES

- Explain the function of neurons.
- Outline the components of the neuron.
- Describe the functions of the three major types of neurons.

neurons Cells in the nervous system that communicate with one another to perform information-processing tasks.

cell body (or soma) The part of a neuron that coordinates information-processing tasks and keeps the cell alive.

dendrite The part of a neuron that receives information from other neurons and relays it to the cell body.

axon The part of a neuron that carries information to other neurons, muscles, or glands.

synapse The junction or region between the axon of one neuron and the dendrites or cell body of another.

myelin sheath An insulating layer of fatty material.

glial cells Support cells found in the nervous system.

An estimated 1 billion people watch the final game of World Cup soccer every four years. That's a whole lot of people, but to put it in perspective, it's still only a little over 14% of the estimated 7 billion people currently living on earth. But a really, really big number is inside your skull right now: There are approximately *100 billion* nerve cells in your brain that perform a variety of tasks to allow you to function as a human being. All of your thoughts, feelings, and behaviors spring from cells in the brain that take in information and produce some kind of output trillions of times a day. These cells are **neurons**, *cells in the nervous system that communicate with each other to perform information-processing tasks.*

Components of the Neuron

Neurons are complex structures composed of three basic parts: the cell body, the dendrites, and the axon (see **FIGURE 3.1**). Like cells in all organs of the body, neurons have a **cell body** (also called the *soma*), the largest component of the neuron, *which coordinates the information-processing tasks and keeps the cell alive.* Functions such as protein synthesis, energy production, and metabolism take place here. The cell body contains a *nucleus*, which houses chromosomes that contain your DNA, or the genetic blueprint of who you are. The cell body is surrounded by a porous cell membrane that allows some molecules to flow into and out of the cell.

Unlike other cells in the body, neurons have two types of specialized extensions that allow them to communicate: dendrites and axons. **Dendrites** *receive information from other neurons and relay it to the cell body.* The term *dendrite* comes from the Greek word for "tree"; indeed, most neurons have many dendrites that look like tree branches. The **axon** *carries information to other neurons, muscles, or glands.* Axons can be very long, even stretching up to a meter from the base of the spinal cord down to the big toe.

The dendrites and axons of neurons do not actually touch each other. There's a small gap between the axon of one neuron and the dendrites or cell body of another. This gap is part of the **synapse**, *the junction or region between the axon of one neuron and the dendrites or cell body of another* (see Figure 3.1). Many of the 100 billion neurons in your brain have a few thousand synaptic junctions, so it should come as no shock that most adults have 100 to 500 trillion synapses. As you'll read shortly, the transmission of information across the synapse is fundamental to communication between neurons, a process that allows us to think, feel, and behave.

In many neurons, the axon is covered by a **myelin sheath**, *an insulating layer of fatty material.* The myelin sheath is composed of **glial cells** (named for the Greek

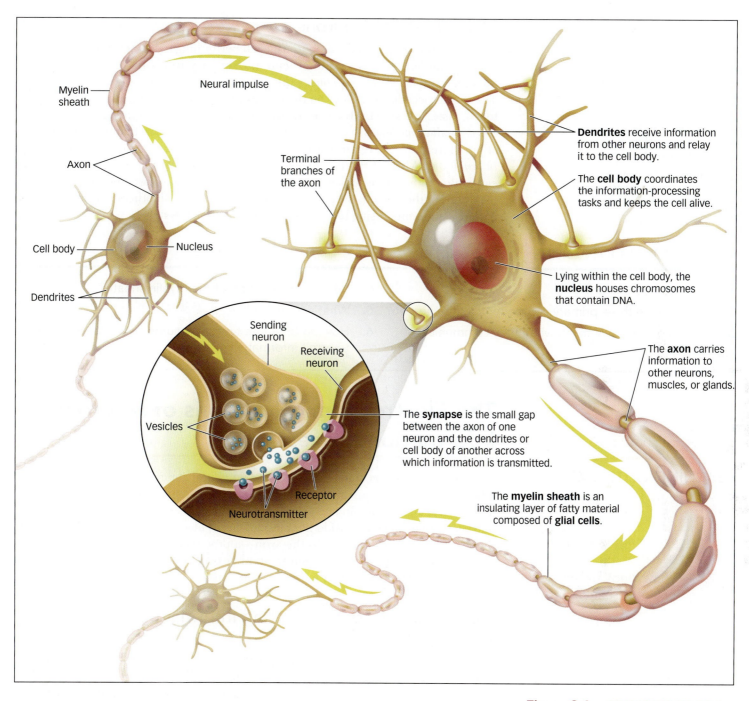

Myelin sheath

Neural impulse

Axon

Cell body

Nucleus

Dendrites

Terminal branches of the axon

Dendrites receive information from other neurons and relay it to the cell body.

The **cell body** coordinates the information-processing tasks and keeps the cell alive.

Lying within the cell body, the **nucleus** houses chromosomes that contain DNA.

The **axon** carries information to other neurons, muscles, or glands.

Sending neuron

Receiving neuron

Vesicles

Neurotransmitter

Receptor

The **synapse** is the small gap between the axon of one neuron and the dendrites or cell body of another across which information is transmitted.

The **myelin sheath** is an insulating layer of fatty material composed of **glial cells**.

Figure 3.1 COMPONENTS OF A NEURON A neuron is made up of three parts: a cell body, dendrites, and an axon. Notice that neurons do not actually touch one another: There is a small synaptic space between them across which information is transmitted.

word for "glue"), which are *support cells found in the nervous system*. Although there are 100 billion neurons busily processing information in your brain, there are 10 to 50 times that many glial cells serving a variety of functions. Some glial cells digest parts of dead neurons, others provide physical and nutritional support for neurons, and others form myelin to help the axon carry information more efficiently. An axon insulated with myelin can more efficiently transmit signals to other neurons, organs, or muscles. In fact, *demyelinating diseases*, such as multiple sclerosis, cause the myelin sheath to deteriorate, slowing the transmission of information from one neuron to another (Schwartz & Westbrook, 2000). This slowdown leads to a variety of problems, including loss of feeling in the limbs, partial blindness, and difficulties in coordinated movement and cognition (Butler, Corboy, & Filley, 2009).

Major Types of Neurons

There are three major types of neurons, each performing a distinct function: sensory neurons, motor neurons, and interneurons. **Sensory neurons** *receive information from the external world and convey this information to the brain via the spinal cord.* They have specialized endings on their dendrites that receive signals for light, sound, touch, taste, and smell. **Motor neurons** *carry signals from the spinal cord to the muscles to produce movement.* These neurons often have long axons that reach to muscles at our extremities. **Interneurons** *connect sensory neurons, motor neurons, or other interneurons.* Most of the nervous system is composed of the interneurons. Some carry information from sensory neurons into the nervous system, others carry information from the nervous system to motor neurons, and still others perform a variety of information-processing functions within the nervous system.

sensory neurons Neurons that receive information from the external world and convey this information to the brain via the spinal cord.

motor neurons Neurons that carry signals from the spinal cord to the muscles to produce movement.

interneurons Neurons that connect sensory neurons, motor neurons, or other interneurons.

BUILD TO THE OUTCOMES

1. What do neurons do?
2. What are the three primary components of the neuron?
3. Do neurons actually touch when they communicate? Explain.
4. What is the function of the myelin sheath?
5. What are glial cells?
6. How do the three types of neurons work together to transmit information?

The Electrochemical Actions of Neurons: Information Processing

LEARNING OUTCOMES

- Describe how an electric signal moves across a neuron.
- Outline the steps in synaptic transmission.
- Explain how drugs are able to mimic neurotransmitters.

Our thoughts, feelings, and actions depend on neural communication, but how does it happen? The communication of information between neurons happens in the form of electrical signals within and between neurons. This occurs in two stages. First, information has to travel inside the neuron, via an electrical signal that travels from the dendrites to the cell body to the axon—a process called *conduction*. Then, the signal has to pass from one neuron to another over the synapse—a process called *transmission*. Let's look at both in more detail.

Electric Signaling: Conducting Information Within a Neuron

The neuron's cell membrane has small pores that act as channels to allow small electrically charged molecules, called *ions*, to flow in and out of the cell. It is this flow of ions across the neuron's cell membrane that creates the conduction of an electric signal within the neuron. How does it happen?

The Resting Potential: The Origin of the Neuron's Electrical Properties

resting potential The difference in electric charge between the inside and outside of a neuron's cell membrane.

Neurons have a natural electric charge called the **resting potential**, *the difference in electric charge between the inside and outside of a neuron's cell membrane* (Kandel, 2000). The resting potential is about −70 millivolts (for comparison, a 9-volt battery has 9,000 millivolts). The resting potential is caused by the difference in concentrations of ions inside and outside the neuron's cell membrane (see **FIGURE 3.2a**). Ions can carry a positive (+) or a negative (−) charge. In the resting state, there is a high concentration of positively charged potassium ions (K^+), as well as larger, negatively charged protein ions (A^-), *inside* the neuron's cell membrane compared to outside

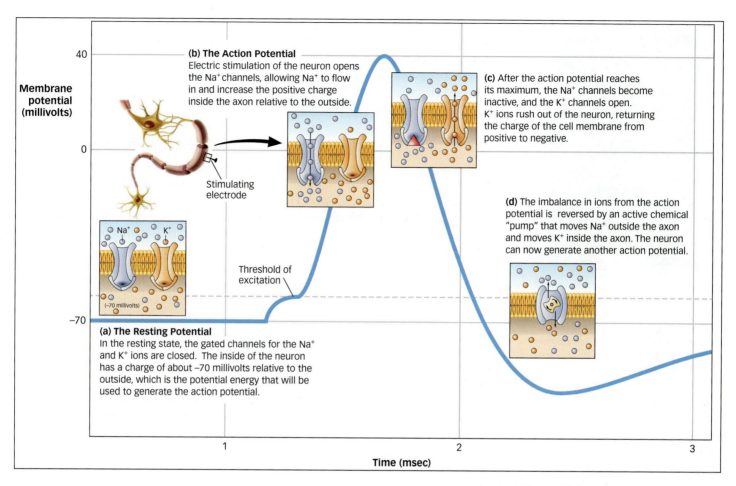

Membrane potential (millivolts)

40

0

−70

(b) The Action Potential
Electric stimulation of the neuron opens the Na⁺ channels, allowing Na⁺ to flow in and increase the positive charge inside the axon relative to the outside.

(c) After the action potential reaches its maximum, the Na⁺ channels become inactive, and the K⁺ channels open. K⁺ ions rush out of the neuron, returning the charge of the cell membrane from positive to negative.

Stimulating electrode

Na⁺   K⁺

(−70 millivolts)

Threshold of excitation

(d) The imbalance in ions from the action potential is reversed by an active chemical "pump" that moves Na⁺ outside the axon and moves K⁺ inside the axon. The neuron can now generate another action potential.

(a) The Resting Potential
In the resting state, the gated channels for the Na⁺ and K⁺ ions are closed. The inside of the neuron has a charge of about −70 millivolts relative to the outside, which is the potential energy that will be used to generate the action potential.

1   2   3

Time (msec)

it. By contrast, there is a high concentration of positively charged sodium ions (Na⁺) and negatively charged chloride ions (Cl⁻) *outside* the neuron's cell membrane. As a result, during the resting potential, the inside of the cell membrane is negatively charged relative to the outside.

Normally, ions from the area of higher concentration move to the area of lower concentration until the concentrations are equal—or in equilibrium—but special channels in the cell membrane restrict the movement of the ions in and out of the cell. An active chemical "pump" in the cell membrane helps maintain the high concentration of K⁺ ions inside by pushing Na⁺ ions out of the cell and pulling K⁺ ions into the cell. As a result, during the resting potential, excess K⁺ ions are built up inside the cell, ready to rush out, and excess Na⁺ ions outside the cell are ready to rush in. Special channels in the cell membrane, specific to the K⁺ and Na⁺ ions, are closed during the resting potential, allowing the inside of the neuron to maintain the electrical charge of −70 millivolts relative to the outside. Like the Hoover Dam, which holds back the Colorado River until the floodgates are released, these channels in the cell membrane hold back the ions, building potential energy that can be released as an electrical impulse in a small fraction of a second.

The Action Potential: Sending Signals Across the Neuron

The neuron maintains its resting potential most of the time. But biologists Alan Hodgkin and Andrew Huxley noticed that they could produce a signal by stimulating the axon with a brief electric shock, which resulted in the conduction of an electrical impulse down the length of the axon (Hausser, 2000; Hodgkin & Huxley, 1939). This electric impulse is called an **action potential,** *an electric signal that is conducted along the length of a neuron's axon to a synapse.*

Figure 3.2   THE RESTING AND ACTION POTENTIALS Neurons have a natural electric charge called a resting potential. Electric stimulation causes an action potential.

action potential An electric signal that is conducted along a neuron's axon to a synapse.

Like the flow of electricity when you turn on a light, the action potential is all or none. Either the switch is turned on or the room remains dark. Similarly, either the electrical stimulation in the neuron reaches the threshold to fire an action potential, or it remains at the resting potential. Guelphite/iSTOCK/Getty Images

refractory period The time following an action potential during which a new action potential cannot be initiated.

The action potential occurs only when the electric shock reaches a certain level, or *threshold*. The action potential is *all or none*: Electric stimulation below the threshold fails to produce an action potential, whereas electric stimulation at or above the threshold always produces the action potential. The action potential always occurs with exactly the same characteristics and at the same magnitude, regardless of whether the stimulus is at or above the threshold.

Membrane Channels Change to Allow in Positively Charged Ions

The action potential occurs when there is a change in the state of the axon's membrane channels. Remember, during the resting potential, the special channels for the K+ and Na+ ions are closed. However, when an electric charge is raised to the threshold value, the sodium-specific channels open up like the floodgate of a dam, and the Na+ ions rush into the cell (see **FIGURE 3.2b**). In less than one millisecond, the rapid influx of Na+ ions raises the charge of the inside membrane from negative (−70 millivolts) to positive (+40 millivolts).

At this point, two events restore the negative charge of the resting potential. First, the Na+ channels inactivate themselves for several milliseconds, blocking the flow of Na+ ions. During this inactivation time, the neuron is said to be in a **refractory period**, *the time following an action potential during which a new action potential cannot be initiated.* In the second event, channels specific to the K+ ions open, allowing the excess K+ ions inside the cell to escape (see **FIGURE 3.2c**). The rapid exit of the positively charged K+ ions returns the electrical charge of the membrane to a negative state, after which the K+ channels close. Ion pumps continue to push Na+ ions out of the cell and bring in additional K+ ions. Along with other special channels, they return the concentrations of ions to the resting potential (see **FIGURE 3.2d**). The entire process is so fast that some neurons fire more than 100 times in a single second.

The Action Potential Moves Across the Neuron in a Domino Effect

So far, we've described how the action potential occurs at one point in the neuron. But how does this electric charge move down the axon? It's a domino effect. When an action potential is generated at the beginning of the axon, it spreads a short distance along the axon's length, which generates an action potential at a nearby location on the axon, and so on, thus conducting the charge down the length of the axon.

The myelin sheath facilitates the conduction of the action potential. Myelin doesn't cover the entire axon; rather, it clumps around the axon with little break points between clumps, looking kind of like sausage links. These breakpoints are called the *nodes of Ranvier*, after the French pathologist Louis-Antoine Ranvier, who discovered them (see **FIGURE 3.3**). When an electric current passes down the length of a myelinated axon, the charge seems to "jump" from node to node, rather than having to traverse the entire axon (Poliak & Peles, 2003). This process is called *saltatory conduction*, and it helps speed the flow of information down the axon.

Figure 3.3   MYELIN AND NODES OF RANVIER Myelin is formed by a type of glial cell. It wraps around a neuron's axon to speed the movement of the action potential along the length of the axon. Breaks in the myelin sheath are called the nodes of Ranvier. The electric impulse jumps from node to node, thereby speeding the conduction of information down the axon.

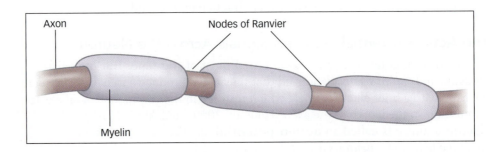

Chemical Signaling: Transmission Between Neurons

When the action potential reaches the end of an axon, you might think that it stops there. After all, the synaptic space between neurons means that the axon of one neuron and the neighboring neuron's dendrites do not actually touch one another. However, the electric charge of the action potential takes a form that can cross the relatively small synaptic gap by relying on a bit of chemistry.

Axons usually end in **terminal buttons**, *knoblike structures that branch out from an axon.* A terminal button is filled with tiny *vesicles*, or "bags," that contain **neurotransmitters**, *chemicals that transmit information across the synapse to a receiving neuron's dendrites.* The dendrites of the receiving neuron contain **receptors**, *parts of the cell membrane that receive neurotransmitters and either initiate or prevent a new electric signal.*

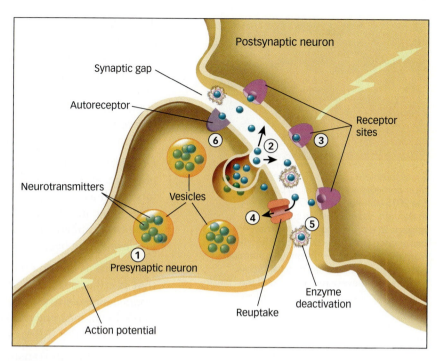

Figure 3.4 SYNAPTIC TRANSMISSION (1) The action potential travels down the axon of the presynaptic neuron and (2) stimulates the release of neurotransmitters from vesicles. (3) The neurotransmitters are released into the synapse, where they float to bind with receptor sites on a dendrite of a postsynaptic neuron, initiating a new action potential. The neurotransmitters are cleared out of the synapse by (4) reuptake into the sending neuron, (5) being broken down by enzymes in the synapse, or (6) binding to autoreceptors on the sending neuron.

Inside the sending neuron, or *presynaptic* neuron, the action potential travels down the length of the axon to the terminal buttons, where it stimulates the release of neurotransmitters from vesicles into the synapse. These neurotransmitters float across the synapse and bind to receptor sites on a nearby dendrite of the receiving neuron, or *postsynaptic neuron*. A new electric signal is initiated in that neuron, which may generate an action potential in the postsynaptic neuron in turn. This electrochemical action, called *synaptic transmission* (see **FIGURE 3.4**), allows neurons to communicate with each other and ultimately underlies your thoughts, emotions, and behavior.

Neurotransmitters and receptor sites act like a lock-and-key system. Just as a particular key will only fit in a particular lock, so too will only some neurotransmitters bind to specific receptor sites on a dendrite. The molecular structure of the neurotransmitter must "fit" the molecular structure of the receptor site.

What happens to the neurotransmitters left in the synapse after the chemical message is relayed to the postsynaptic neuron? Something must make neurotransmitters stop acting on neurons; otherwise, there'd be no end to the signals that they send. Neurotransmitters leave the synapse through three processes (see Figure 3.4). First, neurotransmitters can be reabsorbed by the terminal buttons of the presynaptic neuron's axon, in a process called *reuptake*. Second, neurotransmitters can be destroyed by enzymes in the synapse in a process called *enzyme deactivation*. Third, neurotransmitters can bind to certain receptor sites called *autoreceptors* on the presynaptic neurons. Autoreceptors detect how much of a neurotransmitter has been released into a synapse and signal the presynaptic neuron to stop releasing the neurotransmitter when an excess is present.

terminal buttons Knoblike structures that branch out from an axon.

neurotransmitters Chemicals that transmit information across the synapse to a receiving neuron's dendrites.

receptors Parts of the cell membrane that receive the neurotransmitter and initiate or prevent a new electric signal.

Types and Functions of Neurotransmitters

You might wonder how many types of neurotransmitters are floating across synapses in your brain right now. Today, we know that some 60 chemicals play a role in transmitting information throughout the brain and body and differentially affect thought, feeling, and behavior, but a few major classes seem particularly important. We'll summarize those here, and you'll meet some of these neurotransmitters again in later chapters.

Swiss triathlete Daniela Ryf greets fans after completing the running portion of the 2015 Ironman World Championship in Bahrain. When athletes such as Ryf engage in extreme sports, they may experience the subjective highs that result from the release of endorphins—chemical messengers acting in emotion and pain centers that elevate mood and dull the experience of pain. Hasan Jamali/AP Images

agonists Drugs that increase the action of a neurotransmitter.

antagonists Drugs that block the function of a neurotransmitter.

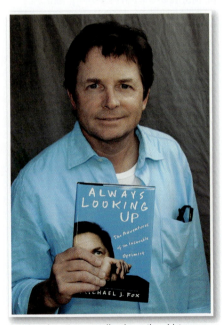

Michael J. Fox vividly described his struggles with Parkinson's disease in his 2009 memoir. Fox's visibility has increased public awareness of the disease and spurred greater efforts toward finding a cure. David Livingston/Getty Images Entertainment/Getty Images

- *Acetylcholine (ACh)* is a neurotransmitter involved in a number of functions, including voluntary motor control. Acetylcholine is found in neurons of the brain and in the synapses where axons connect to muscles and body organs, such as the heart. Acetylcholine contributes to the regulation of attention, learning, sleeping, dreaming, and memory (Gais & Born, 2004; Hasselmo, 2006; Wrenn et al., 2006). Alzheimer's disease, a medical condition involving severe memory impairments (Salmon & Bondi, 2009), is associated with the deterioration of ACh-producing neurons.

- *Dopamine* is a neurotransmitter that regulates motor behavior, motivation, pleasure, and emotional arousal. Because of its role in basic motivated behaviors, such as seeking pleasure or associating actions with rewards, dopamine plays a role in drug addiction (Baler & Volkow, 2006). High levels of dopamine have been linked to schizophrenia (Winterer & Weinberger, 2004), whereas low levels have been linked to Parkinson's disease.

- *Glutamate* is the major excitatory neurotransmitter in the brain, meaning that it enhances the transmission of information between neurons. *GABA* (*gamma-aminobutyric acid*), in contrast, is the primary inhibitory neurotransmitter in the brain, meaning that it tends to stop the firing of neurons. Too much glutamate, or too little GABA, can cause neurons to become overactive, causing seizures.

- Two related neurotransmitters influence mood and arousal: norepinephrine and serotonin. *Norepinephrine* is particularly involved in states of vigilance, or a heightened awareness of dangers in the environment (Ressler & Nemeroff, 1999). *Serotonin* is involved in the regulation of sleep and wakefulness, eating, and aggressive behavior (Dayan & Huys, 2009; Kroeze & Roth, 1998). Because both neurotransmitters affect mood and arousal, low levels of each have been implicated in mood disorders (Tamminga et al., 2002).

- *Endorphins* are chemicals that act within the pain pathways and emotion centers of the brain (Keefe et al., 2001). Endorphins help dull the experience of pain and elevate moods. The "runner's high" experienced by many athletes as they push their bodies to painful limits of endurance can be explained by the release of endorphins in the brain (Boecker et al., 2008).

Each of these neurotransmitters affects thought, feeling, and behavior in different ways, so normal functioning involves a delicate balance of each. Even a slight imbalance—too much of one neurotransmitter or not enough of another—can dramatically affect behavior. People who smoke, drink alcohol, or take drugs, legal or not, are altering the balance of neurotransmitters in their brains.

How Drugs Mimic Neurotransmitters

Many drugs that affect the nervous system operate by increasing, interfering with, or mimicking the manufacture or function of neurotransmitters (Cooper, Bloom, & Roth, 2003; Sarter, 2006). **Agonists** are *drugs that increase the action of a neurotransmitter*. **Antagonists** are *drugs that block the function of a neurotransmitter*. Some drugs alter a step in the production or release of the neurotransmitter, whereas others have a chemical structure so similar to a neurotransmitter that the drug is able to bind to that neuron's receptor. If, by binding to a receptor, a drug activates the neurotransmitter, it is an agonist; if it blocks the action of the neurotransmitter, it is an antagonist (see **FIGURE 3.5**).

For example, the drug L-dopa was developed to treat Parkinson's disease, a movement disorder characterized by tremors and difficulty initiating movement, caused by the loss of neurons that use the neurotransmitter dopamine. Dopamine is created in neurons by a modification of a common molecule called L-dopa. Ingesting L-dopa will spur the surviving neurons to produce more dopamine. The use of L-dopa has been reasonably successful in the alleviation of Parkinson's disease symptoms (Muenter & Tyce, 1971; Schapira et al., 2009).

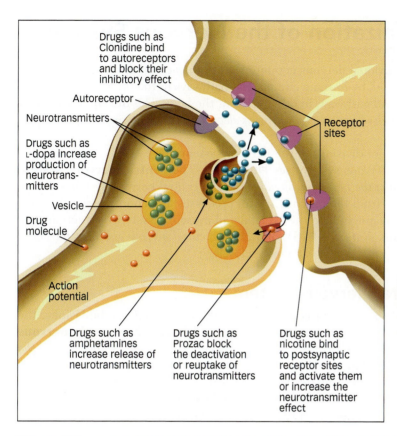

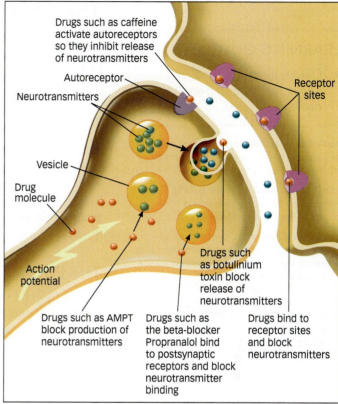

Figure 3.5   THE ACTIONS OF AGONIST AND ANTAGONIST DRUGS Agonist and antagonist drugs can enhance or interfere with synaptic transmission by affecting the production of neurotransmitters, the release of neurotransmitters, the autoreceptors, reuptake, the postsynaptic receptors, and the synapse itself.

As another example, *amphetamine* is a drug that stimulates the release of norepinephrine and dopamine. In addition, both amphetamine and *cocaine* prevent the reuptake of norepinephrine and dopamine. The combination of increased release of norepinephrine and dopamine and prevention of their reuptake floods the synapse with those neurotransmitters, resulting in increased activation of their receptors. Both of these drugs therefore are strong agonists, although their psychological effects differ somewhat because of subtle distinctions in where and how they act on the brain. Norepinephrine and dopamine play a critical role in mood control, such that increases in either neurotransmitter result in euphoria, wakefulness, and a burst of energy. However, norepinephrine also increases heart rate. An overdose of amphetamine or cocaine can cause the heart to contract so rapidly that heartbeats do not last long enough to pump blood effectively, leading to fainting and sometimes death.

Other drugs that mimic neurotransmitters, such as antianxiety and antidepression drugs, will be discussed later, in the Treatment of Psychological Disorders chapter.

BUILD TO THE OUTCOMES

1. What difference between the inside and outside of the neuron's cell membrane creates the resting potential?

2. How does the neuron's membrane change over the course of an action potential?

3. What is the importance of the "pump" in the last stage of the action potential?

4. What is the role of neurotransmitters in neural communication?

5. Choose two neurotransmitters and compare and contrast their functions.

6. Is L-dopa an agonist for dopamine or an antagonist? Explain.

The Organization of the Nervous System

nervous system An interacting network of neurons that conveys electrochemical information throughout the body.

central nervous system (CNS) The part of the nervous system that is composed of the brain and spinal cord.

peripheral nervous system (PNS) The part of the nervous system that connects the central nervous system to the body's organs and muscles.

somatic nervous system A set of nerves that conveys information between voluntary muscles and the central nervous system.

We've seen how individual neurons communicate with each other. What's the bigger picture? Neurons work by forming circuits and pathways in the brain, which in turn influence circuits and pathways in other areas of the body. The **nervous system** is *an interacting network of neurons that conveys electrochemical information throughout the body.*

There are two major divisions of the nervous system: the central nervous system and the peripheral nervous system (see **FIGURE 3.6**). The **central nervous system (CNS)** is *composed of the brain and spinal cord.* The central nervous system receives sensory information from the external world, processes and coordinates this information, and sends commands to the skeletal and muscular systems for action. The **peripheral nervous system (PNS)** *connects the central nervous system to the body's organs and muscles.* Let's look at each more closely.

The Peripheral Nervous System

The peripheral nervous system is itself composed of two major subdivisions, the somatic nervous system and the autonomic nervous system. The **somatic nervous system** is *a set of nerves that conveys information between voluntary muscles and the central nervous system.* Humans have conscious control over this system and use it to perceive, think, and coordinate their behaviors. For example, reaching for your morning cup of coffee involves the elegantly orchestrated activities of the somatic nervous system: Information from the receptors in your eyes travels to your brain,

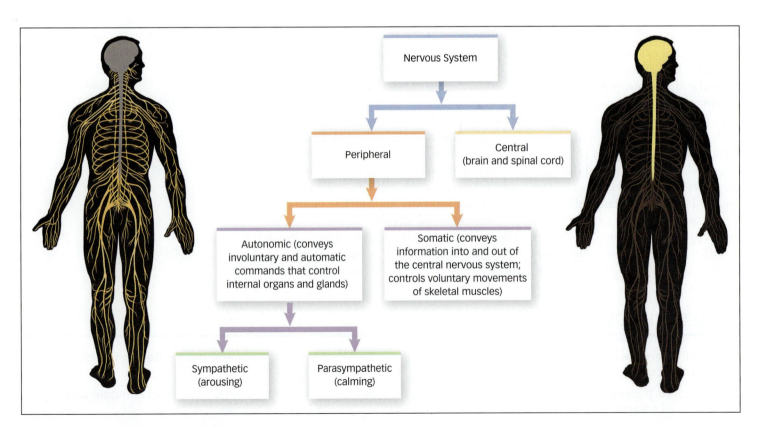

Figure 3.6 THE HUMAN NERVOUS SYSTEM The nervous system is organized into the peripheral and central nervous systems. The peripheral nervous system is further divided into the autonomic and somatic nervous systems.

registering that a cup is on the table; signals from your brain travel to the muscles in your arm and hand; feedback from those muscles tells your brain that the cup has been grasped; and so on.

In contrast, the **autonomic nervous system (ANS)** is *a set of nerves that carries involuntary and automatic commands that control blood vessels, body organs, and glands.* As suggested by its name, this system works on its own to regulate bodily systems, largely outside of conscious control. The ANS has two major subdivisions, the sympathetic nervous system and the parasympathetic nervous system. Each exerts a different type of control on the body.

The **sympathetic nervous system** is *a set of nerves that prepares the body for action in challenging or threatening situations*, and the **parasympathetic nervous system** *helps the body return to a normal resting state* (see **FIGURE 3.7**). For example, imagine that you are walking alone late at night and are frightened by footsteps behind you in a dark alley. Your sympathetic nervous system kicks into action at this point: It dilates your pupils to let in more light, increases your heart rate and respiration to pump more oxygen to your muscles, diverts blood flow to your brain and muscles, and activates sweat glands to cool your body. To conserve energy, the sympathetic nervous system inhibits salivation and bowel movements, suppresses the body's immune responses, and suppresses responses to pain and injury. The sum total of these fast, automatic responses is that they increase the likelihood that you can escape. When you're far away from your would-be attacker, your body doesn't need to remain on red alert. Now the parasympathetic

autonomic nervous system (ANS) A set of nerves that carries involuntary and automatic commands that control blood vessels, body organs, and glands.

sympathetic nervous system A set of nerves that prepares the body for action in challenging or threatening situations.

parasympathetic nervous system A set of nerves that helps the body return to a normal resting state.

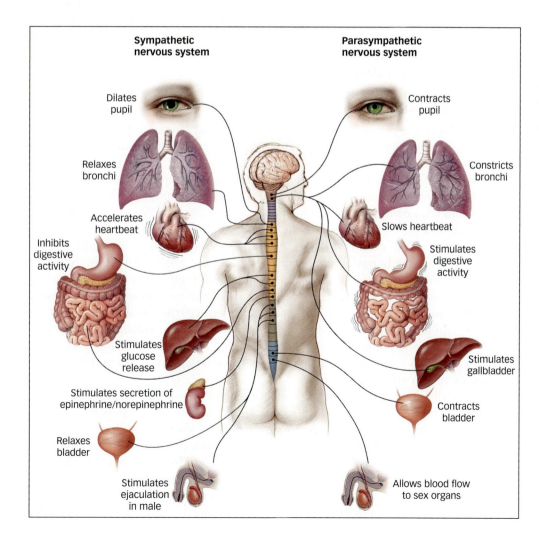

Figure 3.7 SYMPATHETIC AND PARASYMPATHETIC SYSTEMS The autonomic nervous system is composed of two subsystems: the sympathetic system, which serves several aspects of arousal, and the parasympathetic nervous system, which returns the body to its normal resting state.

spinal reflexes Simple pathways in the nervous system that rapidly generate muscle contractions.

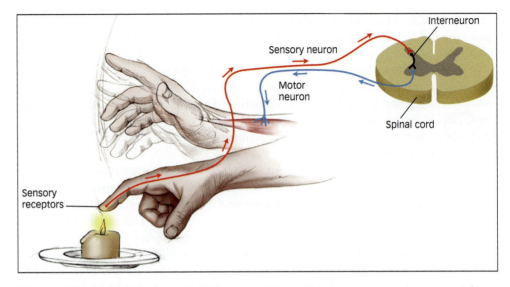

Figure 3.8   THE PAIN WITHDRAWAL REFLEX Many actions of the central nervous system don't require the brain's input. For example, withdrawing from pain is a reflexive activity controlled by the spinal cord. Painful sensations (such as the heat of fire) travel directly to the spinal cord via sensory neurons, which then issue an immediate command to motor neurons to retract the hand.

nervous system kicks in to reverse the effects of the sympathetic nervous system and return your body to its normal state. The parasympathetic nervous system generally mirrors the connections of the sympathetic nervous system. For example, the parasympathetic nervous system constricts your pupils, slows your heart rate and respiration, diverts blood flow to your digestive system, and decreases activity in your sweat glands.

The Central Nervous System

Compared with the many divisions of the peripheral nervous system, the central nervous system may seem simple. After all, it has only two elements: the brain and the spinal cord. But those two elements are ultimately responsible for most of what we do as humans. The brain supports the most complex perceptual, motor, emotional, and cognitive functions of the nervous system. The spinal cord branches down from the brain to relay commands to the body.

The spinal cord often seems like the brain's poor relation: The brain gets all the glory, and the spinal cord just hangs around, carrying out the brain's orders. But for some very basic behaviors, the spinal cord doesn't need input from the brain at all. Connections between the sensory inputs and motor neurons in the spinal cord mediate **spinal reflexes**, *simple pathways in the nervous system that rapidly generate muscle contractions.* If you touch a hot stove, the sensory neurons that register pain send inputs directly into the spinal cord (see **FIGURE 3.8**). Through just a few synaptic connections within the spinal cord, interneurons relay these sensory inputs to motor neurons that connect to your arm muscles and direct you to quickly retract your hand.

More elaborate tasks require the collaboration of the spinal cord and the brain. The peripheral nervous system sends messages from sensory neurons through the spinal cord into the brain. The brain sends commands for voluntary movement through the spinal cord to motor neurons, whose axons project out to skeletal muscles. Damage to the spinal cord severs the connection from the brain to the sensory and motor neurons that are essential to sensory perception and movement. The location of the spinal injury often determines the extent of the abilities that are lost. As you can see in **FIGURE 3.9**, different regions of the spinal cord control

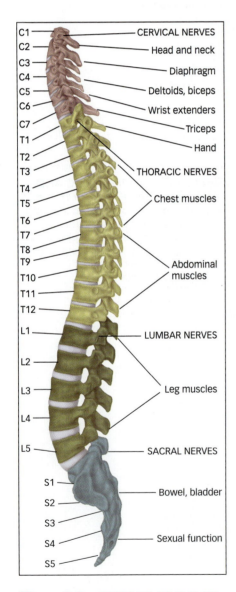

Figure 3.9   REGIONS OF THE SPINAL CORD The spinal cord is divided into four main sections; each controls different parts of the body. Damage higher on the spinal cord usually means greater impairment.

different systems of the body. Individuals with damage at a particular level of the spinal cord lose sensations of touch and pain in body parts below the level of the injury, as well as a loss of motor control of the muscles in the same areas. A spinal injury higher up the cord usually predicts a much poorer prognosis, such as quadriplegia (loss of sensation and motor control over all limbs), breathing through a respirator, and lifelong immobility. On a brighter note, researchers are making progress in understanding the nature of spinal cord injuries and how to treat them by focusing on how the brain changes in response to injury (Blesch & Tuszynski, 2009; Dunlop, 2008), a process that is closely related to the concept of brain plasticity that we will examine later in this chapter. Progress in constructing brain-machine interfaces could also improve the lives of people who have suffered paralysis from spinal cord injuries (see Hot Science: The Power of Thought: Brain-Machine Interfaces).

→ HOT SCIENCE

The Power of Thought: Brain–Machine Interfaces

In the wildly popular James Cameron movie *Avatar*, the paraplegic marine Jake Sully's brain is able to control, via computer, the actions of an avatar body. Though this scenario is seemingly far-fetched, scientists are bringing this type of science-fiction fantasy closer to reality.

Experiments with monkeys provided initial evidence that the brain can control mechanical devices through thoughts alone (Carmena et al., 2003). Researchers trained monkeys to obtain juice reward by moving a joystick that controlled a cursor on a computer screen. Meanwhile, they recorded neural activity in each monkey's motor cortex and fed the patterns into a computer program that learned which patterns of activity corresponded to different joystick movements. Then, they disconnected the joystick, and instead fed signals extracted from the monkey's motor cortex directly into the computer program, which used that information to control the cursor. With just a few days of practice, the monkeys learned to adjust their motor cortex activity patterns to hit the targets successfully. In effect, the monkeys were controlling the cursor with their thoughts.

These findings raised the possibility that cortical recordings and state-of-the-art computer programs could be developed into a kind of neuroprosthesis to help people with brain or spinal injuries. For example, Hochberg et al. (2012) worked with two patients who had suffered paralysis resulting in the loss of use of all limbs. Signals from a small population of neurons in each individual's motor cortex were decoded by a computer program and used to guide a robotic arm. Both participants learned to perform the task with relatively high levels of accuracy and speed. Using signals decoded from her motor cortex, the female patient was even able to use the robotic arm to drink her coffee (see photo)!

These results are exciting, and researchers continue to develop new ways to improve brain–machine interfaces. One recent study used a computer program that decodes brain signals generated when an individual judges that the action being carried out by a robotic arm attempting to touch a target is correct or erroneous (Iturrate et al., 2015). The researchers recorded EEG activity from the scalp in healthy young volunteers as they attempted to control the robotic arm, extracting specific signals that arise when people are aware that they have made a correct response or an error. After a relatively brief training period of about 25 minutes, participants were successful in guiding the robot arm to specific targets.

Although these studies do not quite take us all the way to the world envisioned in *Avatar*, they provide clear evidence that what we once thought of as pure science fiction is well on its way to becoming science fact.

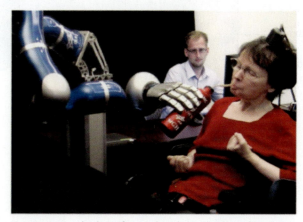

A participant drinking from a bottle using the robotic arm.
Reach and grasp by people with tetraplegia using a neurally controlled robotic arm. Hochberg, et al. *Nature 485*, 372–375 (17 May 2012) ©2012 Macmillan Publishers Limited

BUILD TO THE OUTCOMES

1. What is the neuron's role in the body's nervous system?

2. What are the components of the central nervous system?

3. What are the two divisions of the peripheral nervous system?

4. What triggers the increase in your heart rate when you feel threatened?

5. What important functions does the spinal cord perform on its own?

Structure of the Brain

LEARNING OUTCOMES

• Differentiate the functions of the major divisions of the brain.

• Describe the main glands of the endocrine system.

• Explain the functions of the cerebral cortex according to organization across hemispheres, within hemispheres, and within specific lobes.

• Define brain plasticity.

Right now, your neurons and glial cells are busy humming away, giving you potentially brilliant ideas, consciousness, and feelings. But which neurons in which parts of the brain control which functions? To answer that question, neuroscientists had to find a way of describing the brain. It can be helpful to talk about areas of the brain from "bottom to top," noting how the different regions are specialized for different kinds of tasks. In general, simpler functions are performed at the "lower" levels of the brain, whereas more complex functions are performed at successively "higher" levels (see **FIGURE 3.10a**). The brain can also be approached in a "side-by-side" fashion: Although each side of the brain is roughly analogous, one half of the brain specializes in some tasks that the other half doesn't. Although these divisions make it easier to understand areas of the brain and their functions, keep in mind that none of these structures or areas in the brain can act alone: They are all part of one big, interacting, interdependent whole.

Let's look first at the divisions of the brain, and the responsibilities of each part, moving from the bottom to the top. Using this view, we can divide the brain into three parts: the hindbrain, the midbrain, and the forebrain (see Figure 3.10a).

Figure 3.10   STRUCTURE OF THE BRAIN

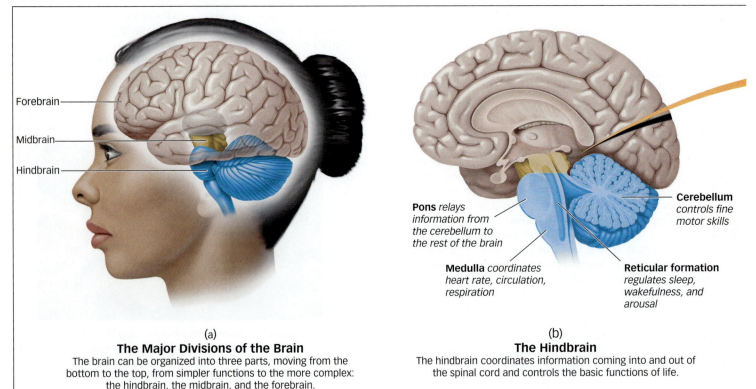

Forebrain

Midbrain

Hindbrain

Pons *relays information from the cerebellum to the rest of the brain*

Medulla *coordinates heart rate, circulation, respiration*

Cerebellum *controls fine motor skills*

Reticular formation *regulates sleep, wakefulness, and arousal*

(a)
The Major Divisions of the Brain
The brain can be organized into three parts, moving from the bottom to the top, from simpler functions to the more complex: the hindbrain, the midbrain, and the forebrain.

(b)
The Hindbrain
The hindbrain coordinates information coming into and out of the spinal cord and controls the basic functions of life.

The Hindbrain

If you follow the spinal cord from your tailbone to where it enters your skull, you'll find it difficult to determine where your spinal cord ends and your brain begins. That's because the spinal cord is continuous with the **hindbrain**, *an area of the brain that coordinates information coming into and out of the spinal cord*. The hindbrain looks like a stalk on which the rest of the brain sits, and it controls the most basic functions of life: respiration, alertness, and motor skills. The structures that make up the hindbrain include the medulla, the reticular formation, the cerebellum, and the pons (see **FIGURE 3.10b**).

The **medulla** is *an extension of the spinal cord into the skull that coordinates heart rate, circulation, and respiration*. Beginning inside the medulla and extending upward is a small cluster of neurons called the **reticular formation**, which *regulates sleep, wakefulness, and levels of arousal*. In one early experiment, researchers stimulated the reticular formation of a sleeping cat. This caused the animal to awaken almost instantaneously and remain alert. Conversely, severing the connections between the reticular formation and the rest of the brain caused the animal to lapse into an irreversible coma (Moruzzi & Magoun, 1949). The reticular formation maintains the same delicate balance between alertness and unconsciousness in humans. In fact, many general anesthetics work by reducing activity in the reticular formation, rendering the patient unconscious.

Behind the medulla is the **cerebellum**, *a large structure of the hindbrain that controls fine motor skills*. (*Cerebellum* is Latin for "little brain," and this structure does look like a small replica of the brain.) The cerebellum orchestrates the proper sequence of movements when we ride a bike, play the piano, or maintain balance while walking and running. It contributes to the fine-tuning of behavior: smoothing our actions to allow their graceful execution rather than initiating the actions (Smetacek, 2002). The initiation of behavior involves other areas of the brain; as you'll recall, different brain systems interact and are interdependent with each other.

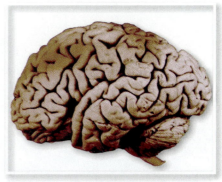

The human brain weighs only 3 pounds and isn't much to look at, but its accomplishments are staggering.
Science Source

hindbrain The area of the brain that coordinates information coming into and out of the spinal cord.

medulla An extension of the spinal cord into the skull that coordinates heart rate, circulation, and respiration.

reticular formation A brain structure that regulates sleep, wakefulness, and levels of arousal.

cerebellum A large structure of the hindbrain that controls fine motor skills.

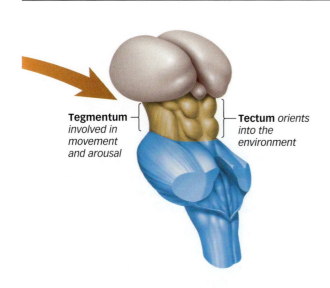

Tegmentum *involved in movement and arousal*

Tectum *orients into the environment*

(c)
The Midbrain
The midbrain is important for orientation and movement.

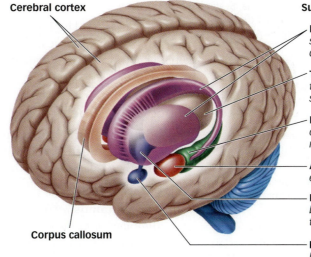

Cerebral cortex

Corpus callosum

Subcortical structures:

Basal ganglia *a set of subcortical structures that directs intentional movements*

Thalamus *receives and transmits information from the senses to the cerebral cortex*

Hippocampus *critical for creating and integrating new memories*

Amygdala *plays a role in emotional processes*

Hypothalamus *regulates body temperature, hunger, thirst, and sexual behavior*

Pituitary gland *releases hormones that direct many other glands*

(d)
The Forebrain
The forebrain is the highest level of the brain and is critical for complex cognitive, emotional, sensory, and motor functions. The forebrain is divided into two parts: the cerebral cortex and the underlying subcortical structures. The cerebral cortex, the outermost layer of the brain, is divided into two hemispheres, connected by the corpus callosum (see Figure 3.13).

The high-wire artist Freddy Nock relied on his cerebellum to coordinate the movements necessary to walk on the rope of the Corvatsch cable car from more than 10,000 feet over sea level down to the base station in Silvaplana, Switzerland, on January 29, 2011. Nock set a new mark that day for the Guinness World Records. ARNO BALZARINI/Keystone/Ap Images

The last major area of the hindbrain is the **pons**, *a structure that relays information from the cerebellum to the rest of the brain*. (*Pons* means "bridge" in Latin.) Although the detailed functions of the pons remain poorly understood, it essentially acts as a relay station or bridge between the cerebellum and other structures in the brain.

The Midbrain

Sitting on top of the hindbrain is the *midbrain*, which is relatively small in humans. As you can see in **FIGURE 3.10c**, the midbrain contains two main structures: the *tectum* and the *tegmentum*. These structures help orient an organism in the environment and guide movement toward or away from stimuli. For example, when you're studying in a quiet room and you hear a *click* behind and to the right of you, your body will swivel and orient to the direction of the sound; this is your tectum in action.

The midbrain may be relatively small, but it's important. In fact, you could survive if you had only a hindbrain and a midbrain. The structures in the hindbrain would take care of all the bodily functions necessary to sustain life, and the structures in the midbrain would orient you toward or away from pleasurable or threatening stimuli in the environment. But this wouldn't be much of a life. To understand where the abilities that make us fully human come from, we need to consider the last division of the brain.

The Forebrain

When you appreciate the beauty of a poem, plan to go skiing next winter, or notice the faint glimmer of sadness on a loved one's face, you are enlisting the forebrain. The *forebrain* is the highest level of the brain—literally and figuratively—and controls complex cognitive, emotional, sensory, and motor functions. The forebrain itself is divided into two main sections: the subcortical structures and the cerebral cortex. You'll read about the cerebral cortex in more detail in the next section. First, let's examine the subcortical structures.

Subcortical Structures

The **subcortical structures** are *areas of the forebrain housed under the cerebral cortex near the center of the brain* (see **FIGURE 3.10d**). These subcortical structures, including the thalamus, hypothalamus, hippocampus, amgydala, and basal ganglia, each play an important role in relaying information throughout the brain.

- The **thalamus** *relays and filters information from the senses and transmits the information to the cerebral cortex*. The thalamus receives inputs from all the major senses, except smell, filters this sensory information, giving more weight to some inputs and less weight to others, and then relaying the information on to a variety of locations in the brain. The thalamus also closes the pathways of incoming sensations during sleep, providing a valuable function in *not* allowing information to pass to the rest of the brain.

- The **hypothalamus,** located below the thalamus (*hypo-* is Greek for "under"), *regulates body temperature, hunger, thirst, and sexual behavior*. Lesions to some

pons A brain structure that relays information from the cerebellum to the rest of the brain.

subcortical structures Areas of the forebrain housed under the cerebral cortex near the center of the brain.

thalamus A subcortical structure that relays and filters information from the senses and transmits the information to the cerebral cortex.

hypothalamus A subcortical structure that regulates body temperature, hunger, thirst, and sexual behavior.

areas of the hypothalamus result in overeating, whereas lesions to other areas leave an animal with no desire for food at all (Berthoud & Morrison, 2008).

- The **hippocampus** (from Latin for "sea horse," due to its shape) *is critical for creating new memories and integrating them into a network of knowledge so that they can be stored indefinitely in other parts of the cerebral cortex.* Individuals with damage to the hippocampus can acquire new information and keep it in awareness for a few seconds, but as soon as they are distracted, they forget the information and the experience that produced it (Scoville & Milner, 1957; Squire, 2009). For example, people with damage to the hippocampus cannot recall a conversation they have just had.

- The **amygdala** (from Latin for "almond," also due to its shape), *located at the tip of each horn of the hippocampus, plays a central role in many emotional processes, particularly the formation of emotional memories* (Aggleton, 1992). When we are in emotionally arousing situations, the amygdala stimulates the hippocampus to remember many details surrounding the situation (Kensinger & Schacter, 2005). For example, people who lived through the terrorist attacks of September 11, 2001, remember vivid details about where they were when they heard the news, even years later (Hirst et al., 2009, 2015).

- The **basal ganglia** are *a set of subcortical structures that directs intentional movements.* The basal ganglia receive input from the cerebral cortex and send outputs to the motor centers in the brain stem (Nelson & Kreitzer, 2015). People who suffer from Parkinson's disease typically show symptoms of uncontrollable shaking and sudden jerks of the limbs and are unable to initiate a sequence of movements to achieve a specific goal. This happens because the dopamine-producing neurons in the substantia nigra (found in the tegmentum of the midbrain) have become damaged (Dauer & Przedborski, 2003). The undersupply of dopamine then affects the basal ganglia, which in turn leads to the visible behavioral symptoms of Parkinson's.

The Endocrine System

One way in which these subcortical structures affect behavior is by interacting with the **endocrine system**, *a network of glands that produce and secrete into the bloodstream chemical messages known as hormones, which influence a wide variety of basic functions, including metabolism, growth, and sexual development.* Some of the main glands in the endocrine system are shown in **FIGURE 3.11**, including the thyroid, which regulates bodily functions such as body temperature and heart rate; the adrenals, which regulate stress responses; the pancreas, which controls digestion; and the pineal, which secretes melatonin, influencing the sleep/wake cycle. The endocrine system also includes sexual reproductive glands: the ovaries in females, which make the hormone *estrogen*, and the testes in males, which make the hormone *testosterone*. The overall functioning of the endocrine system is orchestrated by the **pituitary gland**, *the "master gland" of the body's hormone-producing system, which releases hormones that direct the functions of many other glands in the body.*

The hypothalamus sends hormonal signals to the pituitary gland, which in turn signals other glands to control stress, digestive activities, and reproductive processes. For example, when we sense a threat, sensory neurons send signals to the hypothalamus, which stimulates the release of adrenocorticotropic hormone (ACTH) from the pituitary gland. ACTH, in turn, stimulates the adrenal glands to release hormones that activate the sympathetic nervous system (Selye & Fortier, 1950). As you read earlier in this chapter, the sympathetic nervous system prepares the body either to meet the threat head on or to flee from the situation.

A haunted house is designed to stimulate your amygdala, but only a little. sumnersgraphicsinc/iStock/Getty Images

hippocampus A structure critical for creating new memories and integrating them into a network of knowledge so that they can be stored indefinitely in other parts of the cerebral cortex.

amygdala A brain structure that plays a central role in many emotional processes, particularly the formation of emotional memories.

basal ganglia A set of subcortical structures that directs intentional movements.

endocrine system A network of glands that produce and secrete into the bloodstream chemical messages known as hormones, which influence a wide variety of basic functions, including metabolism, growth, and sexual development.

pituitary gland The "master gland" of the body's hormone-producing system, which releases hormones that direct the functions of many other glands in the body.

Figure 3.11 MAJOR GLANDS OF THE ENDOCRINE SYSTEM The endocrine system is a network of glands that works with the nervous system and impacts many basic functions by releasing hormones into the bloodstream.

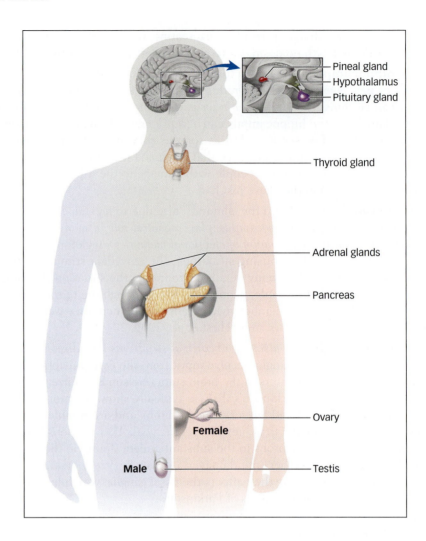

Crumpling a newspaper allows the same amount of surface area to fit into a much smaller space, just as the wrinkles and folds in the cortex allow a great deal of brain power to fit inside the human skull. Donna Ranieri

cerebral cortex The outermost layer of the brain, visible to the naked eye and divided into two hemispheres.

corpus callosum A thick band of nerve fibers that connects large areas of the cerebral cortex on each side of the brain and supports communication of information across the hemispheres.

The Cerebral Cortex

Our tour of the brain has taken us from the very small (neurons) to the somewhat bigger (major divisions of the brain) to the very large: the **cerebral cortex**, *the outermost layer of the brain*. The cortex is the highest level of the brain, and it is responsible for the most complex aspects of perception, emotion, movement, and thought (Fuster, 2003). It sits over the rest of the brain, like a mushroom cap shielding the underside and stem, and it is the wrinkled surface you see when looking at the brain with the naked eye.

The cerebral cortex occupies roughly the area of a newspaper page. Fitting that much cortex into a human skull is a tough task. But if you crumple a sheet of newspaper, you'll see that the same surface area now fits compactly into a much smaller space. The cortex, with its wrinkles and folds, holds a lot of brainpower in a relatively small package that fits comfortably inside the human skull (see **FIGURE 3.12**). The functions of the cerebral cortex can be understood at three levels: the separation of the cortex into two hemispheres, the functions of each hemisphere, and the role of specific cortical areas.

1. Organization Across Hemispheres. The first level of organization divides the cortex into the left and right hemispheres. The two hemispheres are more or less symmetrical in their appearance and, to some extent, in their functions. However, each hemisphere controls the functions of the opposite side of the body. This is called *contralateral control*, meaning that your right cerebral hemisphere perceives stimuli from and controls movements on the left side of your body, whereas your left cerebral hemisphere perceives stimuli from and controls movement on the right side of your body. The cerebral hemispheres are connected to each other by bundles of axons. The largest of these bundles is the **corpus callosum**, which *connects large areas of the cerebral cortex on each side of the brain and supports communication of information across the hemispheres* (see **FIGURE 3.13**). This means that information received in the right hemisphere, for example, can pass across the corpus callosum to the left hemisphere.

2. *Organization Within Hemispheres.* The second level of organization in the cerebral cortex distinguishes the functions of the different regions within each hemisphere of the brain. Each hemisphere of the cerebral cortex is divided into four areas, or *lobes*: From back to front, these are the occipital lobe, the parietal lobe, the temporal lobe, and the frontal lobe, as shown in Figure 3.12.

The **occipital lobe**, located at the back of the cerebral cortex, *processes visual information.* Sensory receptors in the eyes send information to the thalamus, which in turn sends information to the primary areas of the occipital lobe, where simple features of the stimulus are extracted, such as the location and orientation of an object's edges (see the Sensation and Perception chapter for more details). These features are then processed still further, leading to comprehension of what's being seen. Damage to the primary visual areas of the occipital lobe can leave a person with partial or complete blindness. Information still enters the eyes, but without the ability to process and make sense of the information at the level of the cerebral cortex, the information is as good as lost (Zeki, 2001).

The **parietal lobe**, located in front of the occipital lobe, carries out functions that include *processing information about touch.* The parietal lobe contains the *somatosensory cortex,* a strip of brain tissue running from the top of the brain down to the sides (see **FIGURE 3.14**). Within each hemisphere, the somatosensory cortex represents the skin areas on the contralateral surface of the body. Each part of the somatosensory cortex maps onto a particular part of the body. If a body area is more sensitive, a larger part of the somatosensory cortex is devoted to it. For example, the part of the somatosensory cortex that corresponds to the lips and tongue is larger than the area corresponding to the feet. The somatosensory cortex can be illustrated as a distorted figure, called a *homunculus* ("little man"), in which the body parts are rendered according to how much of the somatosensory cortex is devoted to them (Penfield & Rasmussen, 1950). Directly in front of the somatosensory cortex, in the frontal lobe, is a parallel strip of brain tissue called the *motor cortex.* As in the somatosensory cortex, different parts of the motor cortex correspond to different body parts. The motor cortex initiates voluntary movements and sends messages to the basal ganglia, cerebellum, and spinal cord. The motor and somatosensory cortices, then, are like sending and receiving areas of the cerebral cortex, taking in information and sending out commands.

The **temporal lobe**, located on the lower side of each hemisphere, is *responsible for hearing and language.* The *primary auditory cortex* in the temporal lobe is analogous to the somatosensory cortex in the parietal lobe and the primary visual areas of the occipital lobe: It receives sensory information from the ears based on the frequencies of sounds (Recanzone & Sutter, 2008). Secondary areas of the temporal lobe then process the information into meaningful units, such as speech and words. The temporal lobe also houses the visual association areas that interpret the meaning of visual stimuli and help us recognize common objects in the environment (Martin, 2007).

The **frontal lobe**, which sits behind the forehead, has *specialized areas for movement, abstract thinking, planning, memory, and judgment.* As you just read, it contains the motor cortex, which coordinates movements of muscle groups throughout

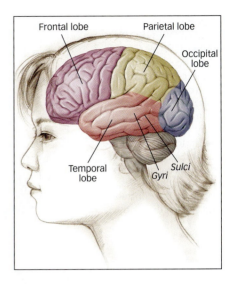

Figure 3.12   CEREBRAL CORTEX AND LOBES The four major lobes of the cerebral cortex are the occipital lobe, the parietal lobe, the temporal lobe, and the frontal lobe. The smooth surfaces of the cortex are called gyri, and the indentations are called sulci.

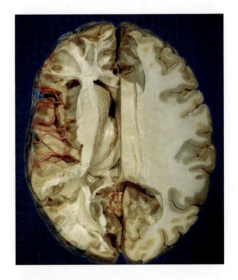

Figure 3.13   CEREBRAL HEMISPHERES The corpus callosum connects the two hemispheres of the brain and supports communication between them. VideoSurgery/Science Source

occipital lobe A region of the cerebral cortex that processes visual information.

parietal lobe A region of the cerebral cortex whose functions include processing information about touch.

temporal lobe A region of the cerebral cortex responsible for hearing and language.

frontal lobe The region of the cerebral cortex that has specialized areas for movement, abstract thinking, planning, memory, and judgment.

Figure 3.14
SOMATOSENSORY AND MOTOR CORTICES The motor cortex, a strip of brain tissue in the frontal lobe, controls movement on the contralateral side of the body. Directly behind the motor cortex, in the parietal lobe, lies the somatosensory cortex, which encodes sensation from the contralateral side of the body.

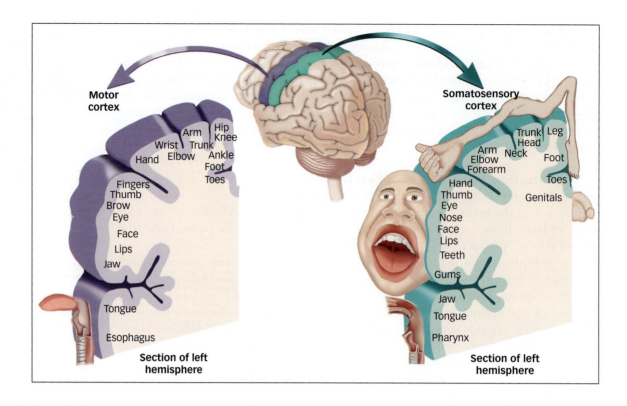

the body. Other areas in the frontal lobe coordinate thought processes that help us manipulate information and retrieve memories, which we can use to plan our behaviors and interact socially with others. In short, the frontal cortex allows us to do the kind of thinking, imagining, planning, and anticipating that sets humans apart from most other species (Schoenemann, Sheenan, & Glotzer, 2005; Stuss & Benson, 1986; Suddendorf & Corballis, 2007).

3. Organization Within Specific Lobes. The third level of organization in the cerebral cortex involves the representation of information within specific lobes in the cortex. A hierarchy of processing stages from primary areas handles fine details of information all the way up to **association areas**, which are *composed of neurons that help provide sense and meaning to information registered in the cortex.* For example, neurons in the primary visual cortex are highly specialized: Some detect features of the environment that are in a horizontal orientation, others detect movement, and still others process information about human versus nonhuman forms. Secondary areas interpret the information extracted by these primary areas (shape, motion, etc.) to make sense of what's being perceived; in this case, perhaps a large cat leaping toward your face. Similarly, neurons in the primary auditory cortex register sound frequencies, but it's the association areas of the temporal lobe that allow you to turn those noises into the meaning of your friend screaming, "Look out for the cat!" Association areas, then, help stitch together the threads of information in the various parts of the cortex to produce a meaningful understanding of what's being registered in the brain.

A striking example of this property of association areas comes from the discovery of the mirror-neuron system. **Mirror neurons** are *active when an animal performs a behavior, such as reaching for or manipulating an object, and are also activated when another animal observes that animal performing the same behavior.* Mirror neurons are found in the frontal lobe (near the motor cortex) and in the parietal lobe (Rizzolatti & Craighero, 2004; Rizzolatti & Sinigaglia, 2010). Neuroimaging studies with humans

association areas Areas of the cerebral cortex that are composed of neurons that help provide sense and meaning to information registered in the cortex.

mirror neurons Neurons that are active when an animal performs a behavior, such as reaching for or manipulating an object, and are also activated when another animal observes that animal performing the same behavior.

have shown that mirror neurons are active when people watch someone perform a behavior, such as grasping in midair, and seem to be related to recognizing the goal someone has in carrying out an action and the outcome of the action (Hamilton & Grafton, 2006, 2008; Iacoboni, 2009; Rizzolatti & Sinigaglia, 2010). In the Learning chapter we'll find out more about the role of mirror neurons in learning.

Finally, neurons in the association areas are usually less specialized and more flexible than neurons in the primary areas. Thus, they can be shaped by learning and experience to do their job more effectively. This kind of shaping of neurons by environmental forces allows the brain flexibility, or plasticity, our next topic.

Brain Plasticity

The cerebral cortex may seem to be a fixed structure, one big sheet of neurons designed to help us make sense of our external world. Remarkably, though, sensory cortices are not fixed. They can adapt to changes in sensory inputs, a quality researchers call *plasticity* (i.e., the ability to be molded). As an example, if you lose your middle finger in an accident, the part of the somatosensory area that represents that finger is initially unresponsive (Kaas, 1991). After all, there's no longer any sensory input going from that location to that part of the brain. You might expect the left middle-finger neurons of the somatosensory cortex to wither away. However, over time, that area in the somatosensory cortex becomes responsive to stimulation of the fingers *adjacent* to the missing finger. The brain is plastic: Functions that were assigned to certain areas of the brain may be capable of being reassigned to other areas of the brain to accommodate changing input from the environment (Feldman, 2009). This suggests that sensory inputs "compete" for representation in each cortical area. (See the Real World: Brain Plasticity and Sensations in Phantom Limbs for a striking example of phantom limbs.)

Plasticity is also related to a question you might not expect to find in a psychology textbook: How much exercise have you been getting lately? A large number of studies in rats and other nonhuman animals indicate that physical exercise can increase the number of synapses and even promote the development of new neurons in the hippocampus (Hillman, Erickson, & Kramer, 2008; van Praag, 2009). Recent studies with people have begun to document beneficial effects of cardiovascular exercise on aspects of brain function and cognitive performance (Colcombe et al., 2004, 2006; Prakash et al., 2015). It should be clear by now that the plasticity of the brain is not just an interesting theoretical idea; it has potentially important applications to everyday life (Bryck & Fisher, 2012).

When one animal observes another engaging in a particular behavior, some of the same neurons become active in the observer as well as in the animal exhibiting the behavior. These mirror neurons seem to play an important role in social behavior. DAVID LONGSTREATH/ AP Images

Keith Jarrett is a virtuoso who has been playing piano for more than 60 years. Compared with those of a novice, the brain regions that control Jarrett's fingers are relatively *less* active when he plays. Jacques Munch/AFP/Getty Images

BUILD TO THE OUTCOMES

1. Which part of the brain controls the basic functions of life, such as respiration?

2. Which part of the brain helps with orientation to the environment?

3. Which area of the brain is associated with emotional memories?

4. What is the main function of the pituitary gland?

5. Why is the part of the somatosensory cortex relating to the lips bigger than the area corresponding to the feet?

6. What types of thinking occur in the frontal lobe?

7. Give examples of research that proves that the brain is able to change because of a person's life experience.

Brain Plasticity and Sensations in Phantom Limbs

Long after a limb is amputated, many patients continue to experience sensations where the missing limb would be, a phenomenon called *phantom limb syndrome*. Some even report feeling pain in their phantom limbs (Ramachandran & Brang, 2015). Why does this happen? Some evidence suggests that phantom limb syndrome may arise in part because of plasticity in the brain.

Researchers stimulated the skin surface in various regions around the face, torso, and arms while monitoring brain activity in amputees (Ramachandran & Blakeslee, 1998; Ramachandran, Brang, & McGeoch, 2010; Ramachandran, Rodgers-Ramachandran, & Stewart, 1992). Stimulating areas of the face and upper arm activated an area in the somatosensory cortex that previously would have been activated by a now-missing hand. The face and arm were represented in the somatosensory cortex in an area adjacent to where the person's hand—now amputated—would have been represented. Stimulating the face or arm produced phantom limb sensations in the amputees; they reported "feeling" a sensation in their missing limbs.

Brain plasticity can explain these results (Pascual-Leone et al., 2005). The somatosensory areas for the face and upper arm were larger in amputees and indeed had taken over the part of the cortex normally representing the missing hand.

This idea has practical implications for dealing with the pain that can result from phantom limbs (Ramachandran & Altschuler, 2009). Researchers have used a "mirror box" to teach patients a new mapping to increase voluntary control over their phantom limbs. For example, a patient would place his intact right hand and phantom left hand in the mirror box such that when looking at the mir-

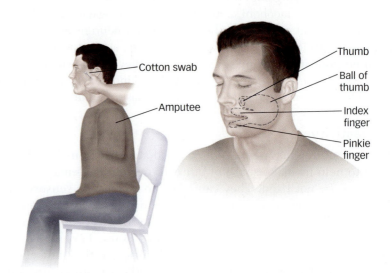

MAPPING SENSATIONS IN PHANTOM LIMBS (a) Researchers lightly touch an amputee's face with a cotton swab, eliciting sensations in the "missing" hand. (b) Touching different parts of the cheek can even result in sensations in particular fingers or the thumb of the missing hand.

ror, he sees his right hand reflected on the left—where he has placed his phantom hand—creating the illusion that the phantom has been restored. The phantom hand thus appears to respond to motor commands given by the patient, and with practice, the patient can become better at "moving" the phantom in response to voluntary commands. As a result, when feeling the excruciating pain associated with a clenched phantom hand, the patient can now voluntarily unclench the hand and reduce the pain. This therapeutic approach based on brain plasticity has been applied successfully to a variety of patient populations (Ramachandran & Altschuler, 2009). In one of the most striking applications, researchers used mirror box

therapy with survivors of the destructive 2010 earthquake in Haiti who were experiencing phantom limb pain after amputation of lower limbs (Miller, Seckel, & Ramachandran, 2012). Seventeen of the 18 amputees in that study reported a significant reduction in experienced pain following mirror box therapy.

A mirror box creates the illusion that the phantom limb has been restored. Republished with permission of V. S. Ramachandran et al., 2009. The use of visual feedback, in particular mirror visual feedback, in restoring brain function. *Brain* 2009: *132* (7); 1693–1719, p. 1693. Permission conveyed through Copyright Clearance Center, Inc.

The Development and Evolution of Nervous Systems

Far from being a single, elegant machine, the human brain is instead a system comprising many distinct components that have been added at different times during the course of evolution. The human species has retained what worked best in earlier versions of the brain, then added bits and pieces to get us to our present state through evolution.

To understand the central nervous system, it is helpful to consider two aspects of its development. Prenatal development (growth from conception to birth) reveals how the nervous system develops and changes within each member of a species. Evolutionary development reveals how the nervous system in humans evolved and adapted from other species.

LEARNING OUTCOMES

- Explain the stages of development of the embryonic brain.
- Explain the progression of the human brain's evolution.
- Give examples of the influence of genetics and the environment to human behavior.

Prenatal Development of the Central Nervous System

The nervous system is the first major bodily system to take form in an embryo (Moore, 1977). It begins to develop within the third week after fertilization, when the embryo is still in the shape of a sphere. Initially, a ridge forms on one side of the sphere and then builds up at its edges to become a deep groove. The ridges fold together and fuse to enclose the groove, forming a structure called the *neural tube*. The tail end of the neural tube will remain a tube, and as the embryo grows larger, it forms the basis of the spinal cord. The tube expands at the opposite end, so that by the fourth week the three basic levels of the brain are visible. During the fifth week, the forebrain and hindbrain further differentiate into subdivisions. During the seventh week and later, the forebrain expands considerably to form the cerebral hemispheres.

As the embryonic brain continues to grow, each subdivision folds onto the next one and begins to form the structures easily visible in the adult brain (see **FIGURE 3.15**). The hindbrain forms the cerebellum and medulla, the midbrain forms the tectum and the tegmentum, and the forebrain subdivides further, separating the thalamus and hypothalamus from the cerebral hemispheres. In about half the time it takes you to complete a 15-week semester, the basic structures of the brain are in place and rapidly developing.

Evolutionary Development of the Central Nervous System

The central nervous system evolved from the very basic ones found in simple animals to the elaborate nervous system in humans today. Even the simplest animals have sensory neurons and motor neurons for responding to the environment (Shepherd, 1988). For example, single-celled protozoa have molecules

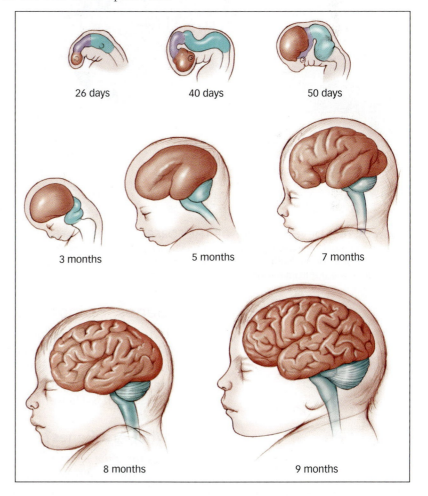

26 days　　40 days　　50 days

3 months　　5 months　　7 months

8 months　　9 months

Figure 3.15　PRENATAL BRAIN DEVELOPMENT The more primitive parts of the brain, the hindbrain and midbrain, develop first, followed by successively higher levels. The cerebral cortex undergoes most of its development late in pregnancy.

Flatworms don't have much of a brain, but then again, they don't need much of a brain. The rudimentary brain areas found in simple invertebrates eventually evolved into the complex brain structures found in humans. blickwinkel/Hecker/Alamy

in their cell membrane that are sensitive to food in the water. Those molecules trigger the movement of tiny threads called *cilia*, which help propel the protozoa toward the food source. The first neurons appeared in invertebrates, such as jellyfish; the sensory neurons in the jellyfish's tentacles can feel the touch of a potentially dangerous predator, which prompts the jellyfish to swim to safety. If you're a jellyfish, this simple neural system is sufficient to keep you alive. The first central nervous system worthy of the name, though, appeared in flatworms. The flatworm has a collection of neurons in the head—a primitive kind of brain—that includes sensory neurons for vision and taste and motor neurons that control feeding behavior. Emerging from the brain is a pair of tracts that form a spinal cord.

During the course of evolution, a major split in the organization of the nervous system occurred between invertebrate animals (those without a spinal column) and vertebrate animals (those with a spinal column). In all vertebrates, the central nervous system is organized into a hierarchy: The lower levels of the brain and spinal cord execute simpler functions, while the higher levels of the nervous system perform more complex functions. As you saw earlier, in humans, reflexes are accomplished in the spinal cord. At the next level, the midbrain executes the more complex task of orienting toward an important stimulus in the environment. Finally, a more complex task, such as imagining what your life will be like 20 years from now, is performed in the forebrain (Addis, Wong, & Schacter, 2007; Schacter et al., 2012; Szpunar, Watson, & McDermott, 2007).

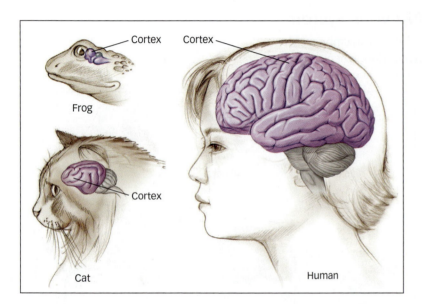

The forebrain undergoes further evolutionary advances in vertebrates. In lower vertebrate species such as amphibians (frogs and newts), the forebrain consists only of small clusters of neurons at the end of the neural tube. In higher vertebrates, including reptiles, birds, and mammals, the forebrain is much larger, and it evolves in two different patterns. Reptiles and birds have almost no cerebral cortex. By contrast, mammals have a highly developed cerebral cortex consisting of multiple areas that serve a broad range of higher mental functions. This forebrain development has reached its peak—so far—in humans (**FIGURE 3.16**).

Figure 3.16 DEVELOPMENT OF THE FOREBRAIN Reptiles and birds have almost no cerebral cortex. Mammals such as rats and cats do have a cerebral cortex, but their frontal lobes are proportionally much smaller than are the frontal lobes of humans and other primates.

Genes, Epigenetics, and the Environment

Is it genetics (nature) or the environment (nurture) that reigns supreme in directing a person's behavior? The emerging picture from current research is that both nature *and* nurture play a role in directing behavior, and the focus has shifted to examining the interaction of the two rather than the absolute contributions of either alone (Gottesman & Hanson, 2005; Rutter & Silberg, 2002; Zhang & Meaney, 2010).

What Are Genes?

gene The major unit of hereditary transmission.

chromosomes The DNA is configured in a double helix; the chromosomes aren't.

A **gene** is *the major unit of hereditary transmission*. Genes are sections on a strand of DNA (deoxyribonucleic acid) that code for the protein molecules that affect traits, such as eye color. Genes are organized into large threads called **chromosomes**, *strands of DNA wound around each other in a double-helix configuration* (see **FIGURE 3.17**). Chromosomes come in pairs, and humans have 23 pairs each. These pairs of chromosomes are similar but not identical: You inherit one of each pair from your father and one from your mother.

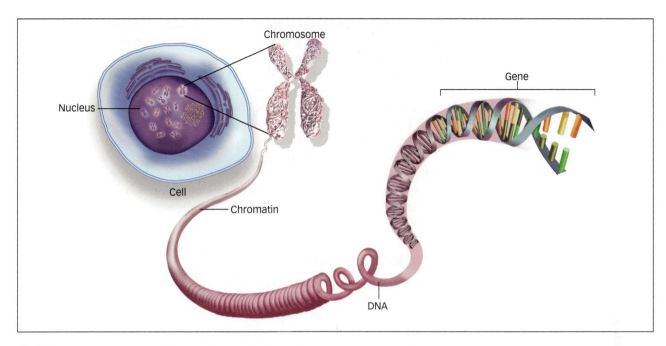

Figure 3.17 GENES The cell nucleus houses chromosomes, which are made up of double-helix strands of DNA. Most cells in our bodies have 23 pairs of chromosomes. Genes are segments on the strand of DNA.

As a species, we share about 99% of the same DNA (and almost as much with other apes), but a portion of DNA varies across individuals. Children share half their genes with each parent, a quarter of their genes with their grandparents, an eighth of their genes with cousins, and so on. The probability of sharing genes is called *degree of relatedness*. The most genetically related people are *monozygotic twins* (also called *identical twins*), who develop from the splitting of a single fertilized egg and therefore share 100% of their genes. *Dizygotic twins* (*fraternal twins*) develop from two separate fertilized eggs and share 50% of their genes, the same as any two siblings born separately.

Many researchers have tried to determine the relative influence of genetics on behavior. One way to do this is to compare a trait shown by monozygotic twins with that same trait among dizygotic twins. This type of research usually enlists twins who were raised in the same household, so that the impact of their environment (their socioeconomic status, access to education, parental child-rearing practices,

Monozygotic twins (left) share 100% of their genes in common, whereas dizygotic twins (right) share 50% of their genes, the same as other siblings. Studies of monozygotic and dizygotic twins help researchers estimate the relative contributions of genes and environmental influences on behavior. Paul Avis/ Stockbyte/Getty Images; JBphoto1/Alamy

environmental stressors) remains relatively constant. Finding that monozygotic twins have a higher presence of a specific trait suggests a genetic influence (Boomsma, Busjahn, & Peltonen, 2002).

For example, the likelihood that the dizygotic twin of a person who has schizophrenia (a mental disorder we'll discuss in greater detail in the Psychological Disorders chapter) will *also* develop schizophrenia is 27%. However, this statistic rises to 50% for monozygotic twins. That sounds scarily high—until you realize that the remaining 50% of monozygotic twins of people with schizophrenia will *not* develop the disorder. That means environmental influences must play a role too. In short, genetics can contribute to the development, likelihood, or onset of a variety of traits. But a more complete picture of genetic influences on behavior must always take the environmental context into consideration. Genes express themselves within an environment, not in isolation.

A Role for Epigenetics

epigenetics The study of environmental influences that determine whether or not genes are expressed, or the degree to which they are expressed, without altering the basic DNA sequences that constitute the genes themselves.

The idea that genes are expressed within an environment is central to an important and rapidly growing area of research known as **epigenetics**: *the study of environmental influences that determine whether or not genes are expressed, or the degree to which they are expressed, without altering the basic DNA sequences that constitute the genes themselves.* To understand how epigenetic influences work, it is useful to think about DNA as analogous to a script for a play or a movie. The biologist Nessa Carey (2012) offers the example of Shakespeare's *Romeo and Juliet*, which has been made into several movies—but the directors of each film used Shakespeare's script in different ways, and the actors in each film gave different performances. Thus, the final products were considerably different from one another, even though Shakespeare's original play still exists.

HOT SCIENCE

Epigenetics and the Persisting Effects of Early Experiences

An exciting series of studies show that epigenetic processes play a critical role in the long-lasting effects of early life experiences. Much of this work has come from the laboratory of Michael Meaney and his colleagues at McGill University.

Back in the early 1990s, Meaney's lab found that there are notable differences in the mothering styles of rats (Francis et al., 1999; Liu et al., 1997). Some mothers spend a lot of time licking and grooming their young pups ("high-grooming" mothers), which rat pups greatly enjoy, whereas others spend little time doing so ("low-grooming" mothers). The researchers found that pups of "high-grooming" mothers are much less fearful as adults when placed in stressful situations than are the adult pups of "low-grooming" mothers, and they also showed lower levels of

several stress-related hormones. In other words, these pups grow up to become "chilled out" adults, apparently due to epigenetically determined increases in the expression of genes controlling responses to stress hormones, resulting in a corresponding ability to respond more calmly to stress (Weaver et al., 2004).

But can early life experiences affect adult behavior in humans, too? Meaney's group examined samples taken from the brains of 24 men who had committed suicide around the age of 35 (McGowan et al., 2009). Twelve of those men had a history of childhood abuse, and 12 did not. Strikingly, the researchers found evidence for epigenetic changes in the 12 men who had suffered childhood abuse and committed suicide, compared with the 12 men who had not been abused. And the specific epigenetic changes were very similar

Rodent pups raised by mothers who spend a lot of time licking and grooming them are less fearful as adults in stressful situations. Juniors Bildarchiv GmbH/R211/Alamy

to those observed in adult rats that had been raised by "low-grooming" mothers.

These and related studies suggest a broad role for epigenetic influences in understanding the effects of early experiences on subsequent development and behavior (Meaney & Ferguson-Smith, 2010).

Similarly, epigenetics provides a way for the environment to influence gene expression—without altering the underlying DNA code. Epigenetics play a role in several important functions, including learning and memory (Bredy et al., 2007; Day & Sweatt, 2011; Levenson & Sweatt, 2005) and responses to stress (Zhang & Meaney, 2010). For example, studies of nurses working in high-stress versus low-stress environments found differences between the two groups in gene expression in the participants' DNA (Alasaari et al., 2012). Other studies have shown a link between gene expression and early life experience, with differences observed between individuals who grew up in relatively affluent households and others who grew up in poverty, even when controlling for such factors as current socioeconomic status (Borghol et al., 2012; Lam et al., 2012). These observations fit well with an important line of research described in Hot Science: Epigenetics and the Persisting Effects of Early Experiences, showing that gene expression plays a key role in the long-lasting effects of early experiences for both rats and humans. In short, genes set the range of possibilities that can be observed in a population, but the characteristics of any individual within that range are determined by environmental factors and experience.

"The title of my science project is 'My Little Brother: Nature or Nurture.'"

Michael Shaw/The New Yorker Collection/Cartoonbank.Com

BUILD TO THE OUTCOMES

1. Which of the major parts of the brain develop first?
2. What is the structural difference between the brain of a reptile or bird and the brain of a mammal?
3. Why do dizygotic twins share 50% of their genes, just as do siblings born separately?
4. What do epigenetic studies suggest about how early life experiences may influence whether genes are expressed?

Investigating the Brain

So far, you've read a great deal about the nervous system: how it's organized, how it works, what its components are, and what those components do. But *how* do we know all of this? Anatomists can dissect a human brain and identify its structures, but they cannot determine which structures play a role in producing which behaviors by dissecting a nonliving brain.

Scientists use a variety of methods to understand how the brain affects behavior. Let's consider three of the main ones: studying people with brain damage; studying the brain's electrical activity; and using brain imaging to study brain structure and watch the brain in action.

Studying the Damaged Brain

To understand the normal operation of a process better, it is instructive to understand what happens when that process fails. Much research in neuroscience correlates the loss of specific perceptual, motor, emotional, or cognitive functions with specific areas of brain damage (Andrewes, 2001; Kolb & Whishaw, 2003). By studying these instances, neuroscientists can theorize about the functions those brain areas normally perform.

LEARNING OUTCOME

- Identify the three main ways that researchers study the human brain.

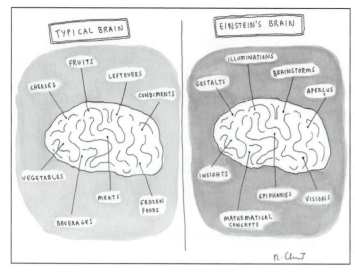

Roz Chast/The New Yorker Collection/Cartoonbank.Com

The Emotional Functions of the Frontal Lobes

As you've already seen, the human frontal lobes are a remarkable evolutionary achievement. However, psychology's first glimpse at some functions of the frontal lobes came from a rather unremarkable fellow. He was so unremarkable, in fact, that a single event in his life defined his place in the annals of psychology's history (Macmillan, 2000). Phineas Gage was a muscular 25-year-old railroad worker. On September 13, 1848, in Cavendish, Vermont, he was packing an explosive charge into a crevice in a rock when the powder exploded, driving a 3-foot, 13-pound iron rod through his head at high speed (Harlow, 1848). As **FIGURE 3.18** shows, the rod entered through his lower left jaw and exited through the middle top of his head. Incredibly, Gage lived to tell the tale. But his personality underwent a significant change.

Before the accident, Gage had been mild mannered, quiet, conscientious, and a hard worker. After the accident, however, he became irritable, irresponsible, indecisive, and given to profanity. The sad decline of Gage's personality and emotional life nonetheless provided an unexpected benefit to psychology. His case study was the first to allow researchers to investigate the hypothesis that the frontal lobe is involved in emotion regulation, planning, and decision making.

The Distinct Roles of the Left and Right Hemispheres

You'll recall that the cerebral cortex is divided into two hemispheres, although typically the two hemispheres act as one integrated unit. Sometimes, though, disorders can threaten the ability of the brain to function, and the only way to stop them is with radical methods. This is sometimes the case for people who suffer from severe, intractable epilepsy. Seizures that begin in one hemisphere cross the corpus callosum (the thick band of nerve fibers that allows the two hemispheres to communicate) to the opposite hemisphere and start a feedback loop that results in a kind of firestorm in the brain. To alleviate the severity of the seizures, surgeons can sever the corpus callosum in an operation called a *split-brain procedure*. As a result, a seizure that starts in one hemisphere cannot cross to the other side. This procedure helps people with epilepsy but also produces some unusual, if not unpredictable, behaviors.

Normally, any information that initially enters the left hemisphere is also registered in the right hemisphere and vice versa: The information comes in and travels across the corpus callosum, and both hemispheres understand what's going on (see **FIGURE 3.19**). But in a person with a split brain, information entering one hemisphere stays there. The Nobel laureate Roger Sperry (1913–1994) and his colleagues studied split-brain patients, showing that the hemispheres are specialized for different kinds of tasks. For example, language processing is largely a left-hemisphere activity. So imagine that some information came into the left hemisphere of a person with a split

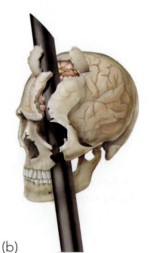

(a)   (b)

Figure 3.18   **PHINEAS GAGE** (a) Phineas Gage's traumatic accident allowed researchers to investigate the functions of the frontal lobe and its connections with emotion centers in the subcortical structures. (b) The likely path of the metal rod through Gage's skull is reconstructed here. Warren Anatomical Museum in the Francis A. Countway Library of Medicine. Gift of Jack and Beverly Wilgus

brain, and she was asked to describe verbally what it was. No problem: The left hemisphere has the information, it's the "speaking" hemisphere, and so she should have no difficulty verbally describing what she saw. But this person's right hemisphere has no clue what the object was because that information was received in the left hemisphere and was unable to travel to the right hemisphere! So even though she saw the object and could verbally describe it, she would be unable to use the right hemisphere to perform other tasks regarding that object, such as correctly selecting it from a group with her left hand (see Figure 3.19).

These split-brain studies reveal that the two hemispheres perform different functions and can work together seamlessly as long as the corpus callosum is intact. Without a way to transmit information from one hemisphere to the other, information remains in the hemisphere it initially entered, and we become acutely aware of the different functions of each hemisphere. Of course, a person with a split brain can adapt to this by simply moving her eyes a little so that the same information independently enters both hemispheres. Split-brain studies have continued over the past few decades and continue to play an important role in shaping our understanding of how the brain works (Gazzaniga, 2006).

Studying the Brain's Electrical Activity

A second approach to studying the link between brain structures and behavior involves recording the pattern of electrical activity of neurons. An **electroencephalograph (EEG)** is *a device used to record electrical activity in the brain.* Typically, electrodes are placed on the outside of the head, and even though the source of electrical activity in synapses and action potentials is far removed from these wires, the EEG can amplify the electric signals several thousand times. This provides a visual record of the underlying electrical activity, as shown in **FIGURE 3.20**. Using this technique, researchers can determine the amount of brain activity during different states of consciousness. For example, as you'll read in the Consciousness chapter, the brain shows distinctive patterns of electrical activity when awake versus asleep; in fact, different brain-wave patterns are even associated with different stages of sleep. EEG recordings allow researchers to make these fundamental discoveries about the nature of sleep and wakefulness (Dement, 1978). The EEG can also be used to examine the brain's electrical activity when awake individuals engage in a variety of psychological functions, such as perceiving, learning, and remembering.

A different approach to recording electrical activity resulted in a more refined understanding of the brain's division of responsibilities, even at a cellular level. The Nobel laureates David Hubel and Torsten Wiesel inserted electrodes into the occipital lobes of anesthetized cats and observed the patterns of action potentials of individual neurons (Hubel, 1988). They discovered that neurons in the primary

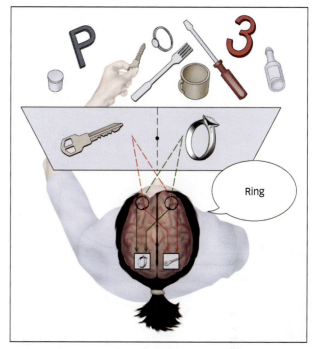

Figure 3.19   SPLIT-BRAIN EXPERIMENT When a person with a split brain is presented with the picture of a ring on the right and that of a key on the left side of a screen, she can verbalize *ring* but not *key* because the left hemisphere "sees" the ring and language is usually located in the left hemisphere. She would be able to choose a key with her left hand from a set of objects behind a screen. She would not, however, be able to pick out a ring with her left hand because what the left hemisphere "sees" is not communicated to the left side of her body.

electroencephalograph (EEG) A device used to record electrical activity in the brain.

Figure 3.20   EEG The electroencephalograph (EEG) records electrical activity in the brain. Many states of consciousness, such as wakefulness and stages of sleep, are characterized by particular types of brain waves. AJphoto/ Science Source

visual cortex are activated whenever a contrast between light and dark occurs in part of the visual field, such as a thick line of light against a dark background. They then found that each neuron responded vigorously only when presented with a contrasting edge at a particular orientation. Since then, many studies have shown that neurons in the primary visual cortex respond to particular features of visual stimuli, such as contrast, shape, and color (Zeki, 1993).

These neurons in the visual cortex are known as *feature detectors* because they selectively respond to certain aspects of a visual image. For example, some neurons fire only when detecting a vertical line in the middle of the visual field, other neurons fire when a line at a 45° angle is perceived, and still others in response to wider lines, horizontal lines, lines in the periphery of the visual field, and so on (Livingstone & Hubel, 1988). The discovery of this specialized function for neurons was a huge leap forward in our understanding of how the visual cortex works. Feature detectors identify basic dimensions of a stimulus ("slanted line . . . other slanted line . . . horizontal line"); those dimensions are then combined during a later stage of visual processing to allow recognition and perception of a stimulus ("Oh, it's a letter *A*").

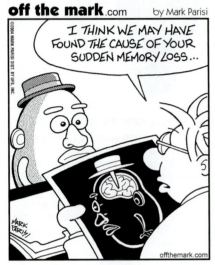

© Mark Parisi/Atlantic Feature Syndicate

Using Brain Imaging to Study Structure and to Watch the Brain in Action

The third major way that neuroscientists can peer into the workings of the human brain involves *neuroimaging techniques* that use advanced technology to create images of the living, healthy brain (Posner & Raichle, 1994; Raichle & Mintun, 2006). *Structural brain imaging* provides information about the basic structure of the brain and allows clinicians or researchers to see abnormalities in brain structure. *Functional brain imaging*, in contrast, provides information about the activity of the brain while people perform various kinds of cognitive or motor tasks.

Structural Brain Imaging

One of the first neuroimaging techniques developed was the *computerized axial tomography (CT) scan*. In a CT scan, a scanner rotates a device around a person's head and takes a series of X-ray photographs from different angles. Computer programs then combine these images to provide views from any angle. CT scans show different densities of tissue in the brain. For example, the higher-density skull looks white on a CT scan, the cortex shows up as gray, and the least dense fluid-filled ventricles in the brain look dark (see **FIGURE 3.21**).

Magnetic resonance imaging (MRI) uses a strong magnetic field to line up the nuclei of specific molecules in the brain tissue. Brief but powerful pulses of radio waves cause the nuclei to rotate out of alignment. When a pulse ends, the nuclei snap back in line with the magnetic field and give off a small amount of energy in the process. Different molecules have unique energy signatures when they snap back in line with the magnetic field, so these signatures can be used to reveal brain structures with different molecular compositions. MRI produces pictures of soft tissue at a better resolution than a CT scan, as you can see in Figure 3.21. Both CT and MRI scans give psychologists a clearer picture of the structure of the brain and can help localize brain damage (as when someone suffers a stroke), but they reveal nothing about the functions of the brain.

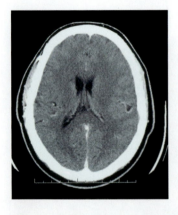 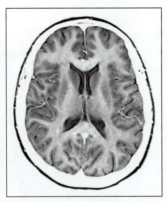

Figure 3.21 STRUCTURAL IMAGING TECHNIQUES (CT AND MRI) CT (left) and MRI (right) scans are used to provide information about the structure of the brain. Each scan shown here provides a snapshot of a single slice in the brain. Note that the MRI scan provides a clearer, higher-resolution image than does the CT scan. Southern Illinois University/Science Source/Getty Images Neil Borden/Medical Body Scans/Science Source

Diffusion tensor imaging (DTI) is a relatively recently developed type of MRI that is used to visualize white matter pathways, which are fiber bundles that connect both nearby and distant brain regions to each other. DTI measures the rate and direction of diffusion or movement of water molecules along white matter pathways. Scientists can use measures based on the rate and direction of diffusion to assess the integrity of a white matter pathway, which is very useful in cases of neurological and psychological disorders (Thomason & Thompson, 2011). DTI is a critical tool in mapping the connectivity of the human brain and plays a central role in an ambitious undertaking known as the Human Connectome Project. This is a collaborative effort funded by the National Institutes of Health beginning in 2009 that aims to provide a complete map of the connectivity of neural pathways in the brain: the human connectome (Toga et al., 2012). Researchers have already made available some of their results at their Web site (www.humanconnectomeproject.org), which include fascinating colorful images of some of the connection pathways they have discovered.

DTI allows researchers to visualize white matter pathways in the brain, the fiber bundles that play an important role by connecting brain regions to one another. Laboratory of Neuro Imaging at UCLA and Martinos Center for Biomedical Imaging at Massachusetts General Hospital, Human Connectome Project Funded by National Institute of Health © 2013 LONI. All Rights Reserved

Functional Brain Imaging

Functional brain imaging techniques show researchers much more than just the structure of the brain by allowing us to watch the brain in action. These techniques rely on the fact that activated brain areas demand more energy for their neurons to work. This energy is supplied through increased blood flow to the activated areas. Functional imaging techniques can detect such changes in blood flow. In *positron emission tomography (PET)*, a harmless radioactive substance is injected into a person's bloodstream. Then the brain is scanned by radiation detectors as the person performs perceptual or cognitive tasks, such as reading or speaking. Areas of the brain that are activated during these tasks demand more energy and greater blood flow, resulting in a higher amount of the radioactivity in that region. The radiation detectors record the level of radioactivity in each region, producing a computerized image of the activated areas (see **FIGURE 3.22**).

For psychologists, the most widely used functional brain imaging technique nowadays is *functional magnetic resonance imaging (fMRI)*, which detects the difference between oxygenated hemoglobin and deoxygenated hemoglobin when exposed to magnetic pulses. Hemoglobin is the molecule in the blood that carries oxygen to our tissues, including the brain. When active neurons demand more energy and blood flow, oxygenated hemoglobin concentrates in the active areas; fMRI detects the oxygenated hemoglobin and provides a picture of the level of activation in each brain area (see Figure 3.22). Just as MRI was a major advance over CT scans, *functional MRI* is a similar leap in our ability to record the brain's activity during behavior.

Both fMRI and PET produce images that show activity in the brain while the person performs certain tasks. For example, when people look at faces, fMRI reveals

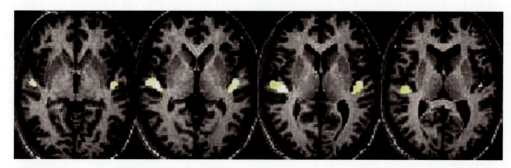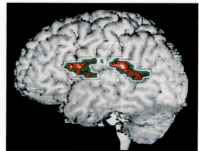

Figure 3.22 FUNCTIONAL IMAGING TECHNIQUES (PET AND FMRI) PET and fMRI scans provide information about the function of the brain by revealing which brain areas become more or less active in different conditions. The PET scan (*directly above*) shows areas in the left hemisphere that become active when people hold in mind a string of letters for a few seconds. The yellow areas in the fMRI scans (*all views to the left*) indicate activity in the auditory cortex of a person listening to music. ©WDCN/Univ. College London/Science Source; Pr. Michel Zanca/ISM/Phototake

strong activity in a region located near the border of the temporal and occipital lobes called the *fusiform gyrus* (Kanwisher, McDermott, & Chun, 1997). When this structure is damaged, people experience problems with recognizing faces—even faces of friends and family they've known for years—although they don't have problems with their eyes and can recognize visual objects other than faces (Mestry et al., 2012). On the other hand, when people perform a task that engages emotional processing (e.g., looking at sad pictures), researchers observe significant activation in the amygdala, which you learned earlier is linked with emotional arousal (McGaugh, 2015; Phelps, 2006). There is also increased activation in parts of the frontal lobe that are involved in emotional regulation—in fact, in the same areas that were most likely damaged in the case of Phineas Gage (Dolcos, 2014; Wang et al., 2005).

Both fMRI and PET have proven very useful, but fMRI has a couple of advantages over PET. First, fMRI does not require any exposure to a radioactive substance. Second, fMRI can localize changes in brain activity across briefer periods than PET, which makes it more useful for analyzing psychological processes that occur extremely quickly, such as reading a word or recognizing a face.

Functional MRI can also be used to explore the relationship of brain regions with each other, using a recently developed technique referred to as *resting state functional connectivity*. As implied by the name, this technique does not require participants to perform a task; they simply rest quietly while fMRI measurements are made. Functional connectivity measures the extent to which spontaneous activity in different brain regions is correlated over time; brain regions whose activity is highly correlated are thought to be functionally connected with each other (Lee, Smyser, & Shimony, 2013). Functional connectivity measures have been used extensively in recent years to identify brain *networks*, that is, sets of brain regions that are closely connected to each other (Yeo et al., 2011). For example, functional connectivity helped to identify the *default network* (Gusnard & Raichle, 2001; Raichle, 2015), a group of interconnected regions in the frontal, temporal, and parietal lobes that is involved in internally focused cognitive activities, such as remembering past events, imagining future events, daydreaming, and mind wandering (Andrews-Hanna, 2012; Buckner, Andrews-Hanna, & Schacter, 2008; see the chapters on Memory and Consciousness). Functional connectivity, along with DTI (which measures structural connectivity), will contribute important information to the map of the human connectome. Advances in understanding brain connectivity may also enhance our ability to predict and characterize the clinical course of brain disorders, such as Alzheimer's disease (Fornito, Zalesky, & Breakspear, 2015).

Transcranial Magnetic Stimulation

We noted earlier that scientists have learned a lot about the brain by studying the behavior of people with brain injuries. But although brain damage may be related to particular patterns of behavior, that relationship may or may not be causal. Experimentation is the premier method for establishing causal relationships between variables, but scientists cannot ethically cause brain damage in human beings just to see what behaviors might be affected. Functional neuroimaging techniques such as fMRI don't help on this point because they do not provide information about when a particular pattern of brain activity causes a particular behavior.

Happily, scientists have discovered a way to mimic brain damage with a benign technique called *transcranial magnetic stimulation (TMS)* (Barker, Jalinous, & Freeston, 1985; Hallett, 2000). TMS delivers a magnetic pulse that passes through the skull and deactivates neurons in the cerebral cortex for a short period. Researchers can direct TMS pulses to particular brain regions (essentially turning them off) and then measure temporary changes in the way a person moves, sees, thinks, remembers, speaks, or feels. By manipulating the state of the brain, scientists can perform experiments that establish causal relationships.

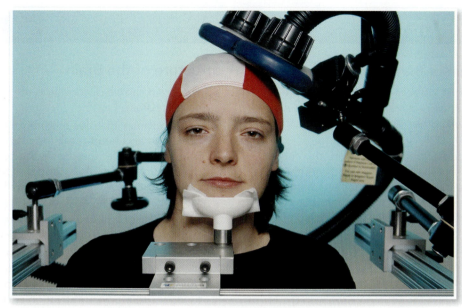

Transcranial magnetic stimulation (TMS) activates and deactivates regions of the brain with a magnetic pulse, temporarily mimicking brain damage. ASTIER/BSIP SA/Alamy

For example, in an early study using TMS, scientists discovered that magnetic stimulation of the visual cortex temporarily impairs a person's ability to detect the motion of an object without impairing the person's ability to recognize that object (Beckers & Zeki, 1995). This intriguing discovery suggests that motion perception and object recognition are accomplished by different parts of the brain, but moreover, it establishes that activity in the visual cortex *causes* motion perception. More recent research has revealed that applying TMS to the specific part of the visual cortex responsible for motion perception also impairs the accuracy with which people localize and reach for moving objects (Maus et al., 2013; Schenk et al., 2005) or for stationary objects when there is motion in the background of a visual scene (Whitney et al., 2007). These findings indicate that the visual motion area plays a crucial role in guiding actions when we're responding to motion in the visual environment.

Scientists have also begun to combine TMS with fMRI, allowing them to localize precisely where in the brain TMS is having its effect (Parkin, Ekhtiari, & Walsh, 2015). Hopefully, the picture of human brain activity that emerges from these new methods can help to dispel myths about the brain that remain popular even today, such as the misguided belief that we only use 10% of our brain (Chabris & Simons, 2012).

In the Methods in Psychology chapter, you learned about the difference between correlation and causation, and that, even if two events are correlated, it does not necessarily mean that one causes the other. Suppose a researcher designs an experiment in which participants view words on a screen and are asked to pronounce each word aloud while the researcher uses fMRI to examine brain activity. First, what areas of the brain would you expect to show activity on fMRI while participants complete this task? Second, can the researcher now safely conclude that those brain areas are required for humans to perform word pronunciation? Courtesy Vicki Gillis, Colorado State University

BUILD TO THE OUTCOMES

1. How have brain disorders been central to the study of specific areas of the brain?

2. What role does the corpus callosum play in behavior?

3. How does the EEG record electrical activity in the brain?

4. Compare what can be learned from structural brain imaging with results from functional brain imaging.

5. What does an fMRI track in an active brain?

CHAPTER REVIEW

Neurons: The Origin of Behavior

- Neurons are the building blocks of the nervous system: They process information received from the outside world, communicate with each other, and send messages to the body's muscles and organs.
- Neurons are composed of three major parts: the cell body, dendrites, and the axon. The cell body contains the nucleus, which houses the organism's genetic material. Dendrites receive sensory signals from other neurons and transmit this information to the cell body. The axon carries signals from the cell body to other neurons or to muscles and organs in the body.
- Neurons are separated by a small gap, or synapse, across which signals are transmitted from one neuron to another.
- Glial cells provide support for neurons, usually in the form of the myelin sheath, which coats the axon to facilitate the transmission of information.

The Electrochemical Actions of Neurons: Information Processing

- The neuron's resting potential is due to differences in the concentration of ions inside and outside the cell membrane.
- If electric signals within a neuron reach a threshold, this initiates an action potential, an all-or-none signal that moves down the entire length of the axon.
- Communication between neurons takes place when an action potential triggers release of neurotransmitters from the terminal buttons of the sending neuron's axon, which travel across the synapse to bind with receptors in the receiving neuron's dendrite.
- Some of the major neurotransmitters are acetylcholine (ACh), dopamine, glutamate, GABA, norepinephrine, serotonin, and endorphins. Drugs can affect behavior by facilitating or blocking the action of neurotransmitters.

The Organization of the Nervous System

- The nervous system is divided into the peripheral and the central nervous systems. The central nervous system is composed of the spinal cord and the brain.
- The peripheral nervous system connects the central nervous system with the rest of the body. It is itself divided into the somatic nervous system, which conveys information into and out of the central nervous system, and the autonomic nervous system, which automatically controls the body's organs.
- The autonomic nervous system is further divided into the sympathetic nervous system, which prepares the body for action in threatening situations, and the parasympathetic nervous system, which returns the body to its normal state.
- The spinal cord can control some basic behaviors such as spinal reflexes without input from the brain.

Structure of the Brain

- The brain can be divided into the hindbrain, midbrain, and forebrain.
- The hindbrain includes the medulla (which coordinates breathing and heart rate), the reticular formation (which regulates sleep and arousal), the cerebellum (which coordinates fine motor skills), and the pons (which communicates information from the cerebellum to the cortex).
- The structures of the midbrain, the tectum and tegmentum, coordinate functions such as orientation to the environment and movement and arousal toward sensory stimuli.
- The forebrain houses subcortical structures, such as the thalamus, hypothalamus, hippocampus, amygdala, and basal ganglia; all these structures perform a variety of functions related to motivation and emotion.
- The endocrine system is a network of glands that works with the nervous system and impacts many basic functions by releasing hormones into the bloodstream.
- The forebrain also houses the cerebral cortex, which supports functions such as thinking, planning, judging, perceiving, and behaving purposefully and voluntarily.

The Development and Evolution of Nervous Systems

- The nervous system is the first system that forms in an embryo, starting as a neural tube, then expanding to form the structures of the hindbrain, midbrain, and forebrain.
- Nervous systems evolved from simple collections of sensory and motor neurons in simple animals, such as flatworms, to elaborate centralized nervous systems found in mammals. Whereas reptiles and birds have almost no cerebral cortex, mammals have a highly developed cerebral cortex.
- Both genes and the environment work together to influence behavior. Genes set the range of variation in populations within a given environment, but they do not predict individual characteristics; experience and other environmental factors play a crucial role as well.
- Epigenetics refers to the study of environmental influences that determine whether or not genes are expressed, without altering the basic DNA sequences that constitute the genes themselves. Epigenetic influences play a critical role in persisting effects of early experiences in rats and humans.

Investigating the Brain

- The brain can be investigated by observing how perceptual, motor, intellectual, and emotional capacities are disrupted following damage to particular areas of the brain.
- Scientists can examine the patterns of electrical activity in large brain areas using the electroencephalograph (EEG), or by single-cell recordings taken from specific neurons.
- Structural imaging techniques such as CT and MRI allow scientists to view the structures of the brain.

- Functional imaging techniques such as fMRI and PET allow scientists to scan the brain as people perform different perceptual or intellectual tasks. Correlating energy consumption in particular brain areas with specific events suggests that those brain areas are involved in specific types of processing.

KEY CONCEPT QUIZ

1. Which of the following is NOT a function of a neuron?
   a. processing information
   b. communicating with other neurons
   c. nutritional provision
   d. sending messages to body organs and muscles

2. Signals from other neurons are received and relayed to the cell body by
   a. the nucleus.
   b. dendrites.
   c. axons.
   d. glands.

3. Signals are transmitted from one neuron to another
   a. across a synapse.
   b. through a glial cell.
   c. by the myelin sheath.
   d. in the cell body.

4. Which type of neuron receives information from the external world and conveys this information to the brain via the spinal cord?
   a. a sensory neuron
   b. a motor neuron
   c. an interneuron
   d. an axon

5. An electric signal that is conducted along the length of a neuron's axon to the synapse is called a(n)
   a. resting potential.
   b. action potential.
   c. node of Ranvier.
   d. ion.

6. The chemicals that transmit information across the synapse to a receiving neuron's dendrites are called
   a. vesicles.
   b. terminal buttons.
   c. postsynaptic neurons.
   d. neurotransmitters.

7. The _____ nervous system automatically controls the organs of the body.
   a. autonomic
   b. parasympathetic
   c. sympathetic
   d. somatic

8. When you feel threatened, your _____ nervous system prepares you to either fight or run away.
   a. central
   b. somatic
   c. sympathetic
   d. parasympathetic

9. Which part of the hindbrain coordinates fine motor skills?
   a. the medulla
   b. the cerebellum
   c. the pons
   d. the tegmentum

10. What part of the brain is involved in movement and arousal?
   a. the hindbrain
   b. the midbrain
   c. the forebrain
   d. the reticular formation

11. The _____ regulates body temperature, hunger, thirst, and sexual behavior.
   a. cerebral cortex
   b. pituitary gland
   c. hypothalamus
   d. hippocampus

12. What explains the apparent beneficial effects of cardiovascular exercise on aspects of brain function and cognitive performance?
   a. the different sizes of the somatosensory cortices
   b. the position of the cerebral cortex
   c. specialization of association areas
   d. neuron plasticity

13. During the course of embryonic brain growth, the _____ undergoes the greatest development.
   a. cerebral cortex
   b. cerebellum
   c. tectum
   d. thalamus

14. The first true central nervous system appeared in
   a. flatworms.
   b. jellyfish.
   c. protozoa.
   d. early primates.

15. Genes set the _____ in populations within a given environment.
   a. individual characteristics
   b. range of variation
   c. environmental possibilities
   d. behavioral standards

16. Identifying the brain areas that are involved in specific types of motor, cognitive, or emotional processing is best achieved through
   a. recording patterns of electrical activity.
   b. observing psychological disorders.
   c. psychosurgery.
   d. brain imaging.

17. Split-brain studies have revealed that
   a. neurons in the primary visual cortex represent features of visual stimuli such as contrast, shape, and color.
   b. the two hemispheres perform different functions but can work together by means of the corpus callosum.
   c. when people perform a task that involves emotional processing, the amygdala is activated.
   d. brain locations for vision, touch, and hearing are separate.

18. Researchers can observe relationships between energy consumption in certain brain areas and specific cognitive and behavioral events using
   a. functional brain imaging.
   b. electroencephalography.
   c. inserting electrodes into individual cells.
   d. CT scans.

 **LearningCurve**   Don't stop now! Quizzing yourself is a powerful study tool. Go to LearningCurve at www.launchpadworks.com for more practice.

KEY TERMS

neurons (p. 54)
cell body (or soma) (p. 54)
dendrite (p. 54)
axon (p. 54)
synapse (p. 54)
myelin sheath (p. 54)
glial cells (p. 54)
sensory neurons (p. 56)
motor neurons (p. 56)
interneurons (p. 56)
resting potential (p. 56)
action potential (p. 57)
refractory period (p. 58)
terminal buttons (p. 59)

neurotransmitters (p. 59)
receptors (p. 59)
agonists (p. 60)
antagonists (p. 60)
nervous system (p. 62)
central nervous system (CNS) (p. 62)
peripheral nervous system (PNS) (p. 62)
somatic nervous system (p. 62)
autonomic nervous system (ANS) (p. 63)
sympathetic nervous system (p. 63)
parasympathetic nervous system (p. 63)

spinal reflexes (p. 64)
hindbrain (p. 67)
medulla (p. 67)
reticular formation (p. 67)
cerebellum (p. 67)
pons (p. 68)
subcortical structures (p. 68)
thalamus (p. 68)
hypothalamus (p. 68)
hippocampus (p. 69)
amygdala (p. 69)
basal ganglia (p. 69)
endocrine system (p. 69)
pituitary gland (p. 69)

cerebral cortex (p.70)
corpus callosum (p. 70)
occipital lobe (p. 71)
parietal lobe (p. 71)
temporal lobe (p. 71)
frontal lobe (p. 71)
association areas (p. 72)
mirror neurons (p. 72)
gene (p. 76)
chromosomes (p. 76)
epigenetics (p. 78)
electroencephalograph (EEG) (p. 81)

CHANGING MINDS

1. While watching late-night TV, you come across an infomercial for all-natural BrainGro. "It's a well-known fact that most people use only 10% of their brain," the spokesman promises. "But with BrainGro, you can increase that number from 10% to 99%!" Why should you be skeptical of the claim that we use only 10% of our brains? What would happen if a drug actually increased neuronal activity tenfold?

2. Your friend has been feeling depressed and has gone to a psychiatrist for help. "He prescribed a medication that's supposed to increase serotonin in my brain," she says. "But my feelings depend on me, not on a bunch of chemicals in my head." What examples could you give your friend to convince her that hormones and neurotransmitters really do influence our cognition, mood, and behavior?

3. A classmate has read the section in this chapter about the evolution of the central nervous system. "Evolution is just a theory," he says. "Not everyone believes in it. And even if it's true that we're all descended from monkeys, that doesn't have anything to do with the psychology of humans alive today." What is your friend misunderstanding about evolution? How would you explain to him the relevance of evolution to modern psychology?

4. A news program reports on a study (Hölzel et al., 2011) in which people who practiced meditation for about 30 minutes a day for 8 weeks showed changes in their brains, including increases in the size of the hippocampus and the amygdala. You tell a friend, who's skeptical. "The brain doesn't change like that," he says. "Basically, the brain you're born with is the brain you're stuck with for the rest of your life." Why is your friend's statement wrong? What are several specific ways in which the brain does change over time?

5. A friend of yours announces that he's figured out why he's bad at math. "I read it in a book," he says. "Left-brained people are analytical and logical, but right-brained people are creative and artistic. I'm an art major, so I must be right-brained, and that's why I'm not good at math." Why is your friend's view too simplistic?

ANSWERS TO KEY CONCEPT QUIZ

1. c; 2. b; 3. a; 4. a; 5. b; 6. d; 7. a; 8. c; 9. b; 10. a; 11. c; 12. d; 13. a; 14. a; 15. b; 16. d; 17. b; 18. a.

Sensation and Perception

4

In the 1930s, a young architect and designer named Donald Deskey helped to create the box design for Procter & Gamble's revolutionary new laundry detergent, Tide, the first one made with synthetic compounds rather than plain old soap (Hine, 1995). Although extremely familiar to us today, in 1946 the bold, blue "Tide" emblazoned on bull's-eye rings of yellow and orange marked the first use of eye-catching Day-Glo colors on a commercial product, and this mix of type and graphics was unlike any product design that anyone had seen before. This product would be impossible to miss on the shelves of a store, and as admirers of the design observed, "it was the box itself that most dynamically conveyed the new product's extraordinary power" (Dyer, Dalzell, & Olegario, 2004). Tide went to market in 1949, and Procter & Gamble never looked back.

Nowadays, we're used to seeing advertisements that feature exciting, provocative, or even sexual images to sell products. The notion is that the sight and sound of exciting things will be associated with what might be an otherwise drab product. This form of advertising is known as *sensory branding* (Lindstrom, 2005). Sensory branding often enlists sound, smell, taste, and touch as well as vision. That new-car smell you anticipate while you take a test drive? It's a manufactured fragrance sprayed inside the car, carefully tested to evoke positive feelings among potential buyers. Singapore Airlines, which frequently has been rated the "world's best airline," has actually patented the smell of its airplane cabins. (It's called Stefan Floridian Waters.) Companies today, just like Procter & Gamble back in 1946, recognize the power of sensation and perception to shape human experience and behavior.

IN THIS CHAPTER, WE'LL EXPLORE KEY INSIGHTS into the nature of sensation and perception. We'll look at how physical energy in the world around us is encoded by our senses, sent to the brain, and enters our conscious awareness. Vision is predominant among our senses; correspondingly, we'll devote a fair amount of space to understanding how the visual system works. Then we'll discuss how we perceive sound waves as words or music or noise, followed by the body senses, emphasizing touch, pain, and balance. We'll end with the chemical senses of smell and taste, which together allow you to savor the foods you eat. But before doing any of that, we will provide a foundation for examining all of the sensory systems by reviewing how psychologists measure sensation and perception in the first place.

Donald Deskey recognized the power of perception back in 1946, when he grabbed the attention of consumers by using eye-catching colors and a striking design on the first box of Tide. The Photo Works

Sensation and Perception Are Distinct Activities

LEARNING OUTCOMES

- Explain the interrelationship of sensation and perception.
- Describe the basic process of transduction.
- Give examples of how sensation and perception are measured.

sensation Simple stimulation of a sense organ.

perception The organization, identification, and interpretation of a sensation in order to form a mental representation.

transduction The process that occurs when many sensors in the body convert physical signals from the environment into encoded neural signals sent to the central nervous system.

psychophysics Methods that measure the strength of a stimulus and the observer's sensitivity to that stimulus.

absolute threshold The minimal intensity needed to just barely detect a stimulus in 50% of trials.

You can enjoy a tempting ice cream sundae, even if you do not know that its sweet taste depends on a complex process of transduction, in which molecules dissolved in saliva are converted to neural signals processed by the brain. © iStockphoto.com/fotoflare

Sensation is *simple stimulation of a sense organ*. It is the basic registration of light, sound, pressure, odor, or taste as parts of your body interact with the physical world. After a sensation registers in your central nervous system, **perception** takes place at the level of your brain: *the organization, identification, and interpretation of a sensation in order to form a mental representation*. For example, your eyes are coursing across these sentences right now. The sensory receptors in your eyeballs are registering different patterns of light reflecting off the page. Your brain is integrating and processing that light information into the meaningful perception of words. Your eyes—the sensory organs—aren't really seeing words; they're simply encoding different lines and curves on a page. Your brain—the perceptual organ—is transforming those lines and curves into a coherent mental representation of words and concepts.

Sensory receptors communicate with **transduction**, which occurs *when many sensors in the body convert physical signals from the environment into encoded neural signals sent to the central nervous system*. In vision, light reflected from surfaces provides the eyes with information about the shape, color, and position of objects. In audition, vibrations (from vocal cords or a guitar string, perhaps) cause changes in air pressure that propagate through space to a listener's ears. In touch, the pressure of a surface against the skin signals its shape, texture, and temperature. In taste and smell, molecules dispersed in the air or dissolved in saliva reveal the identity of substances that we may or may not want to eat. In each case, physical energy from the world is converted to neural energy inside the central nervous system.

Psychophysics

Knowing that perception takes place in the brain, you might wonder if two people see the same colors in the sunset when looking at the evening sky. It's intriguing to consider the possibility that our basic perceptions of sights or sounds might differ fundamentally from those of other people. How can we measure such a thing objectively? Measuring the physical energy of a stimulus, such as the wavelength of a color, is easy enough: You can probably buy the necessary instruments online to do that yourself. But how do you quantify a person's private, subjective *perception* of that light?

In the mid-1800s, the German scientist and philosopher Gustav Fechner (1801–1887) developed a new approach to measuring sensation and perception called **psychophysics:** *methods that measure the strength of a stimulus and the observer's sensitivity to that stimulus* (Fechner, 1860/1966). In a typical psychophysics experiment, researchers ask people to make a simple judgment—whether or not they saw a flash of light, for example. The psychophysicist then relates the measured stimulus, such as the brightness of the light flash, to each observer's yes-or-no response.

Measuring Thresholds

Psychophysicists begin the measurement process with a single sensory signal to determine precisely how much physical energy is required for an observer to become aware of a sensation. The simplest quantitative measurement in psychophysics is the **absolute threshold,** *the minimal intensity needed to just barely detect a stimulus in*

50% of the trials. **TABLE 4.1** lists the approximate sensory thresholds for each of the five senses.

To measure the absolute threshold for detecting a sound, for example, an observer sits in a soundproof room wearing headphones linked to a computer. The experimenter presents a pure tone (the sort of sound made by striking a tuning fork), using the computer to vary the loudness or the length of time each tone lasts and recording how often the observer reports hearing that tone under each condition. The outcome of such an experiment is graphed in **FIGURE 4.1**. Notice from the shape of the curve that the transition from *not hearing* to *hearing* is gradual, rather than abrupt. (Want to know more about reading data distribution results? See Data Visualization: Finding the Best Way to Describe Experimental Data at www.launchpadworks.com.)

DATA VISUALIZATION

If we repeat this experiment for many different tones, we can observe and record the thresholds for tones ranging from very low to very high pitch. It turns out that people tend to be most sensitive to the range of tones corresponding to human conversation. If the tone is low enough, such as the lowest note on a pipe organ, most humans cannot hear it at all; we can only feel it. If the tone is high enough, we likewise cannot hear it, but dogs and many other animals can.

The absolute threshold is useful for assessing how sensitive we are to faint stimuli, but the human perceptual system is better at detecting *changes* in stimulation than the simple onset or offset of stimulation. When parents hear their infant's cry, it's useful to be able to differentiate the "I'm hungry" cry from the "I'm cranky" cry from the "something is biting my toes" cry. The **just noticeable difference (JND)** is *the minimal change in a stimulus that can just barely be detected*.

The JND is not a fixed quantity; rather, it depends on the intensity of the stimuli being measured. This relationship was first noticed by the German physiologist Ernst Weber (Watson, 1978) and is now called **Weber's law:** *The just noticeable difference of a stimulus is a constant proportion despite variations in intensity.* As an example, if you picked up a 1-ounce envelope, then a 2-ounce envelope, you'd probably notice the difference between them. But if you picked up a 20-pound package and then a 20-pound, 1-ounce package, you'd probably detect no difference at all between them.

TABLE 4.1	**Approximate Sensory Threshold**
Sense	**Absolute Threshold**
Vision	A candle flame 30 miles away on a clear, dark night
Hearing	A clock's tick 20 feet away when all is quiet
Touch	A fly's wing falling on the cheek from 1 centimeter away
Smell	A single drop of perfume diffused through an area equivalent to the volume of six rooms
Taste	A teaspoon of sugar dissolved in two gallons of water

Janos Miseta/ FeaturePics

Kateryna Moiseyenko/ Shutterstock

Antagain/Stock/ Getty Images

Marco Andras Est/ Orange Stock/ AGE Fotostock

foodfolio/Alamy

Research from Galanter (1962).

just noticeable difference (JND) The minimal change in a stimulus that can just barely be detected.

Weber's law States that the just noticeable difference of a stimulus is a constant proportion despite variations in intensity.

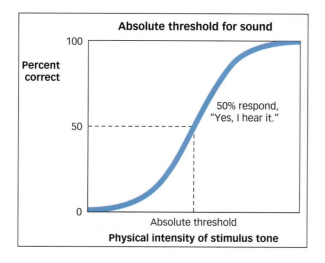

Absolute threshold for sound

100

Percent correct

50

0

50% respond, "Yes, I hear it."

Absolute threshold

Physical intensity of stimulus tone

Figure 4.1 ABSOLUTE THRESHOLD Absolute threshold is the point where the increasing intensity of the stimulus enables an observer to detect it on 50% of the trials. As its intensity gradually increases, we detect the stimulation more frequently.

Crowds of people such as this one at New York City's Thanksgiving Day Parade present our visual system with a challenging signal detection task. blickwinkel/Vockel/Alamy

signal detection theory Holds that the response to a stimulus depends on both a person's sensitivity to the stimulus in the presence of noise and the person's response criterion.

sensory adaptation The process whereby sensitivity to prolonged stimulation tends to decline over time as an organism adapts to current conditions.

Signal Detection

Measuring absolute and difference thresholds requires a critical assumption: that a threshold exists! But humans don't suddenly and rapidly switch between perceiving and not perceiving; in fact, the very same physical stimulus, such as a dim light or a quiet tone, presented on several different occasions, may be perceived by the same person on some occasions but not on others. Remember, an absolute threshold is operationalized as perceiving the stimulus 50% of the time, which means that the other 50% of the time it might go undetected.

Our accurate perception of a sensory stimulus, then, can be somewhat haphazard. Whether in the psychophysics lab or out in the world, sensory signals face a lot of competition, or *noise*, which refers to all the other stimuli coming from the internal and external environment. Memories, moods, and motives intertwine with what you are seeing, hearing, and smelling at any given time. This internal "noise" competes with your ability to detect a stimulus with perfect, focused attention. Other sights, sounds, and smells in the world at large also compete for attention. As a consequence of noise, you may not perceive everything that you sense, and you may even perceive things that you haven't sensed.

An approach to psychophysics called **signal detection theory** holds that *the response to a stimulus depends both on a person's sensitivity to the stimulus in the presence of noise and on a person's decision criterion.* That is, observers consider the sensory evidence evoked by the stimulus and compare it with an internal decision criterion (Green & Swets, 1966; Macmillan & Creelman, 2005). If the sensory evidence exceeds the criterion, the observer responds by saying, "Yes, I detected the stimulus," and if it falls short of the criterion, the observer responds by saying, "No, I did not detect the stimulus."

Signal detection theory has practical applications at home, school, and work, and even while driving. For example, a radiologist may have to decide whether a mammogram shows that a woman has breast cancer. The radiologist knows that certain features, such as a mass of a particular size and shape, are associated with the presence of cancer. But noncancerous features can have a very similar appearance to cancerous ones. The radiologist may decide on a strictly liberal criterion and check every possible case of cancer with a biopsy. This decision strategy minimizes the possibility of missing a true cancer but leads to many unnecessary biopsies. A strictly conservative criterion will cut down on unnecessary biopsies but will miss some treatable cancers. These different types of errors have to be weighed against each other in setting the decision criterion. For an example of a common everyday task that can interfere with signal detection, see The Real World: Multitasking.

Sensory Adaptation

When you walk into a bakery, the aroma of freshly baked bread overwhelms you, but after a few minutes, the smell fades. If you dive into cold water, the temperature is shocking at first, but after a few minutes you get used to it. When you wake up in the middle of the night for a drink of water, the bathroom light blinds you, but after a few minutes, you no longer squint. These are all examples of **sensory adaptation**, whereby *sensitivity to prolonged stimulation tends to decline over time as an organism adapts to current conditions.*

Sensory adaptation is a useful process for most organisms. Imagine what your sensory and perceptual world would be like without it. (If you had to be constantly aware of how your tongue feels while it is resting in your mouth, you'd be driven to distraction.) Our sensory systems respond more strongly to changes in stimulation than to constant stimulation. A stimulus that doesn't change usually

According to the theory of natural selection, inherited characteristics that provide a survival advantage tend to spread throughout the population across generations. Why might sensory adaptation have evolved? What survival benefits might it confer to a small animal trying to avoid predators? To a predator trying to hunt prey? Clement Philippe/Arterra Picture Library/Alamy

→ Multitasking

By one estimate, using a cell phone while driving makes having an accident four times more likely (McEvoy et al., 2005). In response to statistics such as this, state legislatures are passing laws that restrict, and sometimes ban, using mobile phones while driving. You might think that's a fine idea . . . for everyone else on the road. But surely *you* can manage to punch in a number on a phone, carry on a conversation, or maybe even text-message while simultaneously driving in a safe and courteous manner. Right? In a word, *wrong*.

Talking on a cell phone while driving demands that you juggle two independent sources of sensory input—vision and audition—at the same time. This is problematic because research has found that, when attention is directed to audition, activity in visual areas decreases, as shown in the figure to the right (Shomstein & Yantis, 2004). This kind of *multitasking* creates problems when you need to react suddenly while driving. Researchers have tested experienced drivers in a highly realistic driving simulator, measuring their response times to brake lights and stop signs while they listened to the radio or carried on phone conversations about a political issue, among other tasks

(Strayer, Drews, & Johnston, 2003). These experienced drivers reacted significantly more slowly during phone conversations than during the other tasks. This is because a phone conversation requires memory retrieval, deliberation, and planning what to say and often carries an emotional stake in the conversation topic. Tasks such as listening to the radio require far less attention.

Whether the phone was handheld or hands free made little difference, and similar results have been obtained in field studies of actual driving (Horrey & Wickens, 2006). This suggests that laws requiring drivers to use hands-free phones may have little effect on reducing accidents. The situation is even worse when text messaging is involved: Compared with a no-texting control condition, when either sending or receiving a text message in the simulator, drivers spent dramatically less time looking at the road, had a much harder time staying in their lane, missed numerous lane changes, and had greater difficulty maintaining an appropriate distance behind the car ahead of them (Hosking, Young, & Regan, 2009). A recent review concluded

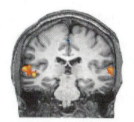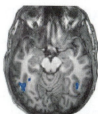

Participants received fMRI scans as they performed tasks that required them to shift their attention between visual and auditory information. When participants focused on auditory information, (a) a region in the superior (upper) temporal lobe involved in auditory processing showed increased activity (yellow/orange) (b) a visual region, the fusiform gyrus, showed decreased activity (blue). Shomstein and Yantis, 2004, Control of Attention Shifts between Vision and Audition in Human Cortex, *The Journal of Neuroscience*, 24 November 2004, *24*(47): 10702-10706; doi: 10.1523/JNEUROSCI.2939-04.2004. Permission conveyed through Copyright Clearance Center.

that the impairing effect of texting while driving is comparable with that of alcohol consumption and greater than that of smoking marijuana (Pascual-Ferrá, Liu, & Beatty, 2012).

So how well do we multitask in several thousand pounds of metal hurtling down the highway? Unless you have two heads with one brain each—one to talk and one to concentrate on driving—you would do well to keep your eyes on the road and not on the phone.

doesn't require any action; your car probably emits a certain hum all the time that you've gotten used to. But a change in stimulation often signals a need for action. If your car starts making different kinds of noises, you're not only more likely to notice them but you're also more likely to do something about it.

BUILD TO THE OUTCOMES

1. What is the difference between sensation and perception?

2. By what process do sensory inputs, such as light and sound waves, become messages sent to the brain?

3. Why isn't it enough for a psychophysicist to measure only the strength of a stimulus?

4. What is an absolute threshold?

5. What is the importance of proportion to the measurement of just noticeable difference?

6. What are the benefits of sensory adaptation?

Vision I: The Eyes and the Brain Convert Light Waves to Neural Signals

visual acuity The ability to see fine detail.

You might be proud of your 20/20 vision, even if it is corrected by glasses or contact lenses. 20/20 refers to a measurement of **visual acuity**, *the ability to see fine detail*: It is the smallest line of letters that a typical person can read from a distance of 20 feet. But hawks, eagles, and other raptors have much greater visual acuity than humans: in many cases, the equivalent of 20/2 vision (meaning that what the normal human can just see from 2 feet away can be seen by these birds at a distance of 20 feet away). Your sophisticated visual system has evolved to transduce visual energy in the world into neural signals in the brain. Understanding vision, then, starts with understanding light.

Sensing Light

Visible light is simply that portion of the electromagnetic spectrum that we can see, and it is an extremely small slice (see **FIGURE 4.2**). You can think about light as waves of energy. Like ocean waves, light waves vary in height and in the distance between their peaks, or *wavelengths*. There are three properties of light waves, each of which has a physical dimension that produces a corresponding psychological dimension (see **TABLE 4.2**): The *length* of a light wave determines its hue, or what humans perceive as color. The intensity, or *amplitude*, of a light wave—how high the peaks are—determines what we perceive as the brightness of light. *Purity* is the number of distinct wavelengths that make up the light. Purity corresponds to what humans perceive as saturation, or the richness of colors.

Figure 4.2 ELECTROMAGNETIC SPECTRUM The sliver of light waves visible to humans as a rainbow of colors from violet-blue to red is bounded on the short end by ultraviolet rays, which honeybees can see, and on the long end by infrared waves, on which night-vision equipment operates. Light waves are minute, but the scale along the bottom of this chart offers a glimpse of their varying lengths, measured in nanometers (nm; 1 nm = 1 billionth of a meter).

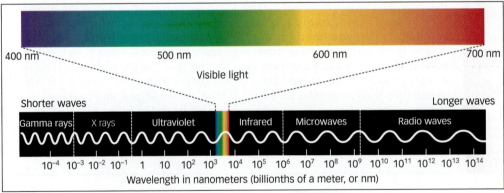

TABLE 4.2	Properties of Light Waves	
Physical Dimension		**Psychological Dimension**
Length	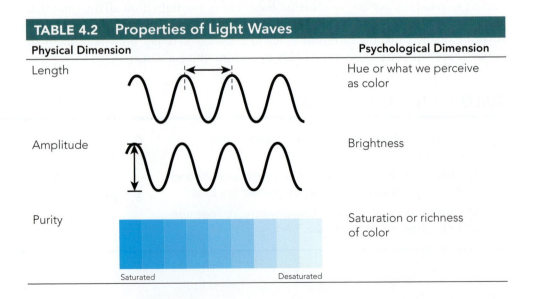	Hue or what we perceive as color
Amplitude		Brightness
Purity		Saturation or richness of color

The Eye Detects and Focuses Light

Eyes have evolved as specialized organs to detect light. **FIGURE 4.3a** shows the human eye in cross-section. Light that reaches the eyes passes first through a clear, smooth outer tissue called the *cornea*, which bends the light wave and sends it through the *pupil*, a hole in the colored part of the eye. This colored part is the *iris*, which is a translucent, doughnut-shaped muscle that controls the size of the pupil and hence the amount of light that can enter the eye.

Immediately behind the iris, muscles inside the eye control the shape of the *lens* to bend the light again and focus it onto the **retina**, *a layer of light-sensitive tissue lining the back of the eyeball*. The muscles change the shape of the lens to focus objects at different distances, making the lens flatter for objects that are far away or rounder for nearby objects. This change is called **accommodation**, *the process by which the eye maintains a clear image on the retina*. **FIGURE 4.3b** shows how accommodation works.

If your eyeballs are a little too long, images are focused in front of the retina, leading to nearsightedness (*myopia*). If the eyeball is too short, images are focused behind the retina, and the result is farsightedness (*hyperopia*). Eyeglasses, contact lenses, and surgical procedures can correct either condition. For example, eyeglasses and contacts both provide an additional lens to help focus light more appropriately, and procedures such as LASIK physically reshape the eye's cornea.

Light Is Converted Into Neural Impulses in the Retina

How does a wavelength of light become a meaningful image? The retina is the interface between the world of light outside the body and the world of vision inside the central nervous system. Two types of *photoreceptor cells* in the retina contain light-sensitive pigments that transduce light into neural impulses. **Cones** *detect color, operate under normal daylight conditions, and allow us to focus on fine detail.* **Rods** *become active under low-light conditions for night vision* (see **FIGURE 4.3c**).

Rods are much more sensitive photoreceptors than cones, but this sensitivity comes at a cost. Because all rods contain the same photopigment, they provide no information about color and sense only shades of gray. Think about this the next time you wake up in the middle of the night and make your way to the bathroom for a drink of water. Using only the moonlight from the window to light your way, do you see the room in shades of gray? About 120 million rods are distributed more or less evenly around each retina except in the very center, the **fovea**, *an area of the retina where vision is the clearest and there are no rods at all*. The absence of rods in the fovea decreases the sharpness of vision in reduced light.

In contrast to rods, each retina contains only about 6 million cones, which are densely packed in the fovea and much more sparsely distributed over the rest of the retina, as you can see in Figure 4.3c. This distribution of cones directly affects visual acuity and explains why objects off to the side, in your *peripheral vision*, aren't so clear. The light reflecting from those peripheral objects is less likely to land in the fovea, making the resulting image less sharp.

retina A layer of light-sensitive tissue lining the back of the eyeball.

accommodation The process whereby the eye maintains a clear image on the retina.

cones Photoreceptors that detect color, operate under normal daylight conditions, and allow us to focus on fine detail.

rods Photoreceptors that become active under low-light conditions for night vision.

fovea An area of the retina where vision is the clearest and there are no rods at all.

The full-color image on the top is what you'd see if your rods and cones are fully at work. The grayscale image on the bottom is what you'd see if only your rods are functioning. Mike Sonnenberg/iStockphoto/Getty Images

The image on the left was taken at a higher resolution than was the image on the right. The difference in quality is analogous to light falling on the fovea, rather than on the periphery of the retina. BackyardProduction/Thinkstock/iStock/Getty Images

a. The Eye Captures Light Waves Reflected From an Object's Surface

Light reflected from an object's surface enters the eyes via the transparent **cornea**, bending to pass through the **pupil** at the center of the colored **iris**.

Cornea

Pupil

Iris

Lens

Retina

Fovea

Behind the iris, the thickness and shape of the **lens** adjust to focus light on the **retina**, where the image appears upside down and backward. Vision is clearest at the **fovea**.

b. Muscles Change the Shape of the Lens to Focus Objects at Different Distances, a Process Called Accommodation

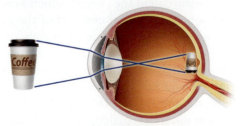

People with **normal vision** focus the image on the retina at the back of the eye, both for near and far objects.

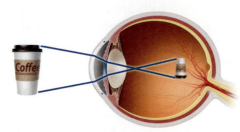

Nearsighted people see clearly what's nearby, but distant objects are blurry because light from them is focused in front of the retina.

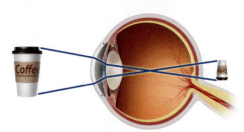

For **farsighted** people, distant objects are clear, but those nearby are blurry because their point of focus falls beyond the surface of the retina.

Figure 4.3 THE EYE TRANSDUCES LIGHT WAVES INTO NEURAL ENERGY

blind spot A location in the visual field that produces no sensation on the retina.

As seen in Figure 4.3c, the photoreceptor cells (rods and cones) form the inner-most layer of the retina. Above them, the *bipolar cells* collect neural signals from the rods and cones and transmit them to *retinal ganglion cells (RGCs)*. The axons of RGCs form the *optic nerve*, which leaves the eye through a hole in the retina. Because it contains neither rods nor cones and therefore has no mechanism for sens-ing light, this hole in the retina creates a **blind spot**, *a location in the visual field that produces no sensation on the retina.* Try the demonstration in **FIGURE 4.4** to find the blind spot in each of your own eyes.

The Optic Nerve Carries Neural Impulses to the Brain

Half of the axons in the optic nerve that leave each eye come from retinal gan-glion cells (RGCs) that code information in the right visual field, whereas the other half code information in the left visual field. These two nerve bundles link to the left and right hemispheres of the brain, respectively (see **FIGURE 4.3d**). The optic nerve travels from each eye to the *lateral geniculate nucleus (LGN)*, located in the thalamus. As you will recall from the Neuroscience and Behavior chapter, the thala-mus receives inputs from all of the senses except smell. From there, the visual signal travels to the back of the brain, to a location called **area V1**, the *part of the occipital lobe that contains the primary visual cortex.*

area V1 The part of the occipital lobe that contains the primary visual cortex.

c. The Retina Is the Interface Between the Eye and the Brain

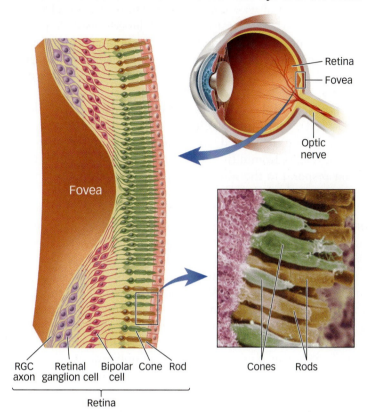

RGC axon | Retinal ganglion cell | Bipolar cell | Cone | Rod

Cones   Rods

Retina

The surface of the retina is composed of photoreceptor cells, the rods and cones, beneath a layer of transparent neurons, the bipolar and retinal ganglion cells (RGCs), connected in sequence. The axon of a retinal ganglion cell joins with all other RGC axons to form the **optic nerve**. The optic nerve creates the blind spot.

The **fovea**, the area of greatest visual acuity, is where most color-sensitive cones are concentrated, allowing us to see fine detail as well as color. Rods, the predominant photoreceptors activated in low-light conditions, are distributed everywhere else on the retina.

d. The Optic Nerve Carries the Neural Energy Into the Brain

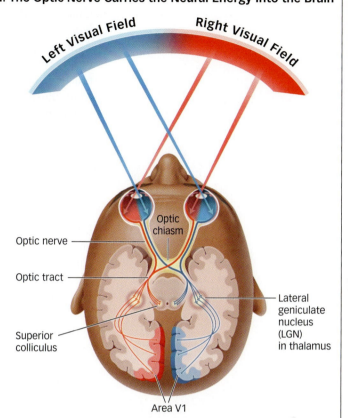

Objects in the right visual field stimulate the left half of each retina, and objects in the left visual field stimulate the right half of each retina. Just before the optic nerves enter the brain at the optic chiasm, about half the nerve fibers from each eye cross. The left half of each optic nerve (representing the right visual field) runs through the brain's left hemisphere via the thalamus, and the right half of each optic nerve (representing the left visual field) travels this route through the right hemisphere. So, information from the right visual field ends up in the left hemisphere and information from the left visual field ends up in the right hemisphere.

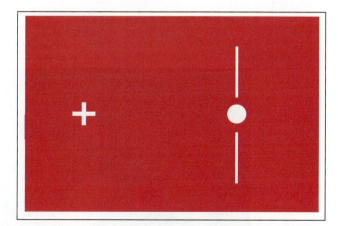

Figure 4.4 BLIND SPOT DEMONSTRATION To find your blind spot, close your left eye and stare at the cross with your right eye. Hold this book 6 to 12 inches (15 to 30 centimeters) away from your eyes and move it slowly toward and away from you until the dot disappears. The dot is now in your blind spot and not visible. At this point, the vertical lines may appear as one continuous line because the visual system fills in the area occupied by the missing dot. To test your left eye's blind spot, turn the book upside down and repeat the experiment with your right eye closed.

Perceiving Color

Color is nothing but our perception of wavelengths along the spectrum of visible light (see Figure 4.2). We perceive the shortest visible wavelengths as deep purple. As wavelengths become longer, the color we perceive changes gradually and continuously to blue, then green, yellow, orange, and, with the longest visible wavelengths, red. This rainbow of hues and accompanying wavelengths is called the *visible spectrum*, illustrated in **FIGURE 4.5**.

Cones come in three types; each type is especially sensitive to either long-wavelength (perceived as red), medium-wavelength (perceived as green), or short-wavelength (perceived as blue) light. Red, green, and blue are the primary colors of light; color perception results from different combinations of the three basic elements in the retina that respond to the wavelengths corresponding to the three primary colors of light. For example, lighting designers add primary colors of light together, as when they shine red and green spotlights on a surface to create a yellow light, as shown in **FIGURE 4.6**. Notice that, in the center of the figure, where the red, green, and blue lights overlap, the surface looks white. This demonstrates that a white surface actually reflects all visible wavelengths of light. Another example of how color perception depends critically on lighting conditions comes from the Internet phenomenon known as "The Dress," discussed in A World of Difference: The Dress.

A genetic disorder in which one of the cone types is missing—and, in some very rare cases, two or all three—causes a *color deficiency*. This trait is sex linked, affecting men much more often than it does women. Color deficiency is often referred to as *color blindness*, but in fact, people missing only one type of cone can still distinguish many colors, just not as many as someone who has the full

Figure 4.5 SEEING IN COLOR We perceive a spectrum of color because objects selectively absorb some wavelengths of light and reflect others. Color perception corresponds to the summed activity of the three types of cones. Each type is most sensitive to a narrow range of wavelengths in the visible spectrum— short (bluish light), medium (greenish light), or long (reddish light). Rods, represented by the white curve, are most sensitive to the medium wavelengths of visible light but do not contribute to color perception.

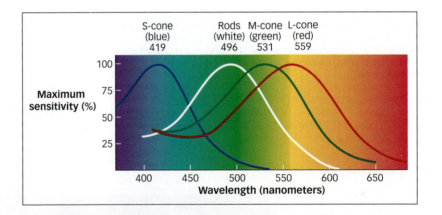

Figure 4.6 COLOR MIXING The millions of shades of color that humans can perceive are products not only of a light's wavelength but also of the mixture of wavelengths a stimulus absorbs or reflects. Colored spotlights work by causing the surface to reflect light of a particular wavelength, which stimulates cones that sense red, blue, or green light. When all visible wavelengths are present, we see white. Fritz Goro/The LIFE Picture Collection/Getty Images

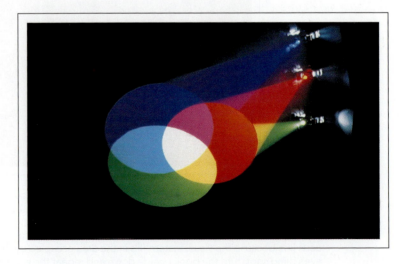

A WORLD OF DIFFERENCE

The Dress

On February 25, 2015, a Tumblr user posted a picture of a dress—and triggered a firestorm on social media. The user explained that her friends were divided on the color of the dress—some saw it as white and gold, others as blue and black. Who was right? Over the next two days, the post attracted over 400,000 notes on Tumblr. Friends and families across the globe nearly came to blows, with people typically insisting that their perception was the correct one and failing to believe that others could see it differently. In photos of the dress under different lighting conditions posted by the online retailer that sold it, the dress was unambiguously blue and black.

Vision scientists have begun to grapple with the mystery of the dress, and though we don't yet fully understand why people see its color so differently, we do have some clues and hypotheses. Researchers suggest that perception of the dress's color is heavily influenced by how people perceive the lighting of the room where the photo was taken; the lighting is highly ambiguous and thus subject to different interpretations (Lafer-Sousa, Hermann, & Conway, 2015; Gegenfurtner, Bloj & Toscani 2015; Winkler et al., 2015). Daylight has "cool" (bluish) components and "warm" (yellowish) components. If you

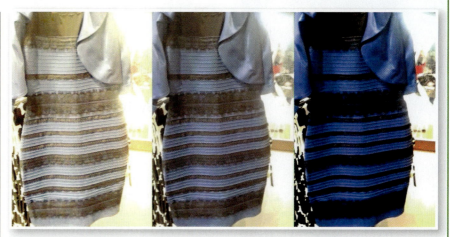

What colors do you see in the dress?

perceive the lighting in the room as "cool" and "bluish," then your visual system assigns the bluishness of the dress to the lighting, and you end up seeing the dress as white/gold. But if you perceive the room lighting as "warm" and "yellowish," your visual system attributes blue to the dress and you see blue/black. In a result consistent with this idea, changing the illumination of the room had the predicted effects on perception of the dress's color (Lafer-Sousa et al., 2015).

Still, this hypothesis just raises the question of why some people see the lighting of the room as "cool," and others see it as "warm." Though we don't have a definitive answer, Lafer-Sousa and colleagues (2015)

suggest that people who experience more daylight ("larks") may be more likely to perceive lighting as "cool" (because the sky is blue) and thus perceive the dress as white/gold, whereas "night owls" may be more likely to perceive lighting as "warm" and thus perceive the dress as blue/black. But more evidence is needed to evaluate this hypothesis.

Though still not fully understood, "the dress" highlights an important lesson: The colors we perceive are not simply inherent properties of an object, but instead represent our visual system's best guess about color on the basis of complex patterns of incoming sensory data as well as our past experiences.

complement of three cone types. You can create a kind of temporary color deficiency by exploiting the idea of sensory adaptation. Staring too long at one color fatigues the cones that respond to that color, producing a form of sensory adaptation that results in a *color afterimage*. To demonstrate this effect for yourself, follow these instructions for **FIGURE 4.7**:

- Stare at the small cross between the two color patches for about 1 minute. Try to keep your eyes as still as possible.

- After a minute, look at the lower cross. You should see a vivid color aftereffect that lasts for a minute or more. Pay particular attention to the colors in the afterimage.

Were you puzzled that the red patch produces a green afterimage and the green patch produces a red afterimage? When you view a color—let's say, green—the cones that respond most strongly to green become fatigued over time. Now, when you stare at a white or gray patch, which reflects all the colors equally, the green-sensitive

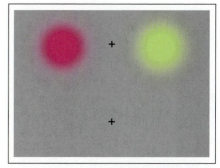

Figure 4.7 COLOR AFTERIMAGE DEMONSTRATION Follow the accompanying instructions in the text, and sensory adaptation will do the rest. When the afterimage fades, you can get back to reading the chapter.

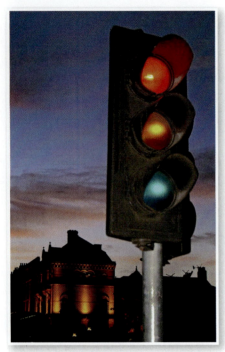

Many people (including about 5% of all males) inherit conditions in which either the red or the green photoreceptors do not transduce light properly. Such people have difficulty distinguishing hues that to typical individuals appear as red or green. Unfortunately, in the United States, traffic signals use red and green lights to indicate whether cars should stop or go through an intersection. Why do drivers with red–green blindness not risk auto accidents every time they approach an intersection? age fotostock/Superstock

cones respond only weakly compared with the still-fresh red-sensitive cones, which fire strongly. The result? You perceive the patch as tinted red.

The Visual Brain

The optic nerve carries the neural impulses to area V1 in the brain, as we've seen (Figure 4.3d). Here, the information is systematically mapped into a representation of the visual scene.

Neural Systems for Perceiving Shape

One of the most important functions of vision involves perceiving the shapes of objects; our day-to-day lives would be a mess if we couldn't reliably distinguish between a doughnut and a stalk of celery. Perceiving shape depends on the location and orientation of an object's edges. As you read in the Neuroscience and Behavior chapter, neurons in the visual cortex selectively respond to bars and edges in specific orientations in space (Hubel & Wiesel, 1962, 1998). In effect, area V1 contains populations of neurons, each "tuned" to respond to edges oriented at each position in the visual field. This means that some neurons fire when we perceive an object in a vertical orientation, other neurons fire when we perceive an object in a horizontal orientation, still other neurons fire when we perceive objects in a diagonal orientation of 45°, and so on (see **FIGURE 4.8**). The outcome of the coordinated response of all these feature detectors contributes to a sophisticated visual system that can detect where a doughnut ends and a celery stalk begins.

Pathways for What, Where, and How

Two functionally distinct pathways, or *visual streams*, project from the occipital cortex to visual areas in other parts of the brain (see **FIGURE 4.9**). One pathway, the *ventral* (below) *stream*, travels across the occipital lobe into the lower levels of the temporal lobes and includes brain areas that represent an object's shape and identity—in other words, what it is, essentially a "what" pathway (Kravitz et al., 2013; Ungerleider & Mishkin, 1982). The other pathway, the *dorsal* (above) *stream*, travels up from the occipital lobe to the parietal lobes (including some of the middle and upper levels of the temporal lobes), connecting with brain areas that identify the location and motion of an object—in other words, where it is (Kravitz et al., 2011). Because the dorsal stream allows us to perceive spatial relations,

Figure 4.8 SINGLE-NEURON FEATURE DETECTORS Area V1 contains neurons that respond to specific orientations of edges. Here, a single neuron's responses are recorded (*left*) as the monkey views bars at different orientations (*right*). This neuron fires continuously when the bar is pointing to the right at 45°, less often when it is vertical, and not at all when it is pointing to the left at 45°. Fritz Goro/The LIFE Picture Collection/Getty Images

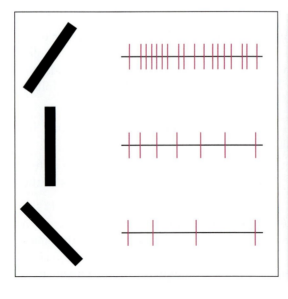

researchers originally dubbed it the "where" pathway (Ungerleider & Mishkin, 1982). Neuroscientists later argued that because the dorsal stream is crucial for guiding movements, such as aiming, reaching, or tracking with the eyes, the "where" pathway should more appropriately be called the "how" pathway (Milner & Goodale, 1995).

Some of the most dramatic evidence for the existence of these two pathways comes from studying patients with brain injuries. For example, a woman known as D.F. suffered permanent damage to a large region of the lateral occipital cortex, an area in the ventral stream (Goodale et al., 1991). Her ability to recognize objects by sight was greatly impaired, although her ability to recognize objects by touch was normal. This suggests that her *visual representation* of objects, but not her *memory* for objects, was damaged. D.F.'s brain damage belongs to a category called **visual form agnosia**, *the inability to recognize objects by sight* (Goodale & Milner, 1992, 2004). Conversely, other patients with brain damage to the parietal lobe, a section of the dorsal stream, have difficulty using vision to guide their reaching and grasping movements (Perenin & Vighetto, 1988). However, their ventral streams are intact, meaning they recognize what objects are. We can conclude from these two patterns of impairment that the ventral and dorsal visual streams are functionally distinct; it is possible for one to be damaged, whereas the other remains intact.

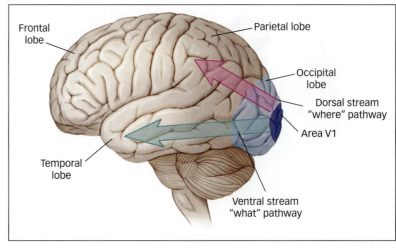

Figure 4.9   VISUAL STREAMING The ventral pathway courses from the occipital visual regions into the lower temporal lobe and enables us to identify what we see. The dorsal pathway travels from the occipital lobe through the upper regions of the temporal lobe into the parietal regions and allows us to locate objects, to track their movements, and to move in relation to them.

visual form agnosia The inability to recognize objects by sight.

BUILD TO THE OUTCOMES

1. What are the physical and psychological dimensions of the properties of light waves?

2. What is the importance of the process of accommodation in the eye?

3. What is the function of the photoreceptor cells (rods and cones)?

4. What is the relationship between the right and left eyes, and the right and left visual fields?

5. Why does color perception depend on combinations of three primary colors of light?

6. What happens when the cones in your eyes become fatigued?

7. What are the main jobs of the main and dorsal streams?

Vision II: Recognizing What We Perceive

Our journey into the visual system has already revealed how it accomplishes some pretty astonishing feats. But the system needs to do much more in order for us to be able to interact effectively with our visual worlds. Let's now consider how the system links together individual visual features into whole objects, allows us to recognize what those objects are, organizes objects into visual scenes, and detects motion and change in those scenes. Along the way, we'll see that studying visual errors and illusions provides key insights into how these processes work.

LEARNING OUTCOMES

- List the factors that allow us to recognize objects by sight.

- Describe the visual cues essential for depth perception.

- Discuss how we perceive motion and change.

We correctly combine features into unified objects, so we see the man is wearing a gray shirt and the woman is wearing a red shirt. Thomas Barwick/Iconica/Getty Images

binding problem How the brain links features together so that we see unified objects in our visual world, rather than free-floating or miscombined features.

illusory conjunction A perceptual mistake whereby the brain incorrectly combines features from multiple objects.

feature-integration theory The idea that focused attention is not required to detect the individual features that make up a stimulus but is required to bind those individual features together.

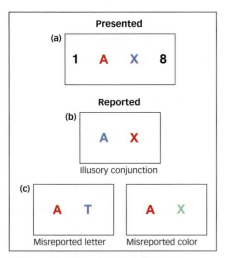

Figure 4.10 ILLUSORY CONJUNCTIONS Illusory conjunctions occur when features such as color and shape are combined incorrectly. For example, when participants are shown a red *A* and a blue *X*, they sometimes report seeing a blue *A* and a red *X*. Other kinds of errors, such as a misreported letter (e.g., reporting *T* when no *T* was presented) or misreported color (reporting green when no green was presented) occur rarely, indicating that illusory conjunctions are not the result of guessing (based on Robertson, 2003).

Attention: The "Glue" That Binds Individual Features Into a Whole

Specialized feature detectors in different parts of the visual system analyze each of the multiple features of a visible object: orientation, color, size, shape, and so forth. Ultimately, though, these different features must somehow be integrated into a single, unified perception of an object (Nassi & Callaway, 2009). What allows us to perceive so easily and correctly that the young man in the photo is wearing a gray shirt and the young woman is wearing a red shirt? Why don't we see free-floating patches of gray and red? These questions refer to what researchers call the **binding problem** in perception, *how the brain links features together so that we see unified objects in our visual world, rather than free-floating or miscombined features* (Treisman, 1998, 2006).

Illusory Conjunctions: Perceptual Mistakes

In everyday life, we correctly combine features into unified objects so automatically and effortlessly that it may be difficult to appreciate that binding is ever a problem at all. However, researchers have discovered errors in binding that reveal important clues about how the process works. One such error is known as an **illusory conjunction**, *a perceptual mistake whereby the brain incorrectly combines features from multiple objects.* In one study, researchers briefly showed study participants visual displays in which black digits flanked colored letters, such as a red *A* and a blue *X*, and instructed the participants first to report the black digits and then to the colored letters (Treisman & Schmidt, 1982). Participants frequently reported illusory conjunctions, claiming to have seen, for example, a blue *A* or a red *X* (see **FIGURE 4.10a and b**). These illusory conjunctions were not just the result of guessing; they occurred more frequently than other kinds of errors, such as reporting a letter or color that was not present in the display (see **FIGURE 4.10c**).

Why do illusory conjunctions occur? Psychologist Anne Treisman and her colleagues have tried to explain them by proposing a **feature-integration theory** (Treisman, 1998, 2006; Treisman & Gelade, 1980; Treisman & Schmidt, 1982), which holds that *focused attention is not required to detect the individual features that make up a stimulus, such as the color, shape, size, and location of letters, but is required to bind those individual features together.* From this perspective, attention provides the "glue" necessary to bind features together, and illusory conjunctions occur when it is difficult for participants to pay full attention to the features that need to be glued together. For example, in the experiments we just considered, participants were required to process the digits that flanked the colored letters, thereby reducing attention to the letters and allowing illusory conjunctions to occur. When experimental conditions are changed so that participants can pay full attention to the colored letters, and they are able to correctly bind their features together, illusory conjunctions disappear (Treisman, 1998; Treisman & Schmidt, 1982).

The Role of the Parietal Lobe

The binding process makes use of feature information processed by structures within the ventral visual stream, the "what" pathway (Seymour et al., 2010; see Figure 4.9). But because binding involves linking together features that appear at a particular spatial location, it also depends critically on the parietal lobe in the dorsal stream, the "where" pathway (Robertson, 1999). For example, Treisman and others studied a man known as R.M., who had suffered strokes that destroyed both his left and right parietal lobes. Although many aspects of his visual function were intact, he had severe problems attending to spatially distinct objects. When presented with stimuli such as those in **FIGURE 4.10**, R.M. perceived an abnormally large number of illusory conjunctions, even when he was given as much as 10 seconds to look at the displays (Friedman-Hill, Robertson, & Treisman, 1995; Robertson, 2003).

Recognizing Objects by Sight

Take a quick look at the letters in the accompanying illustration. Even though they're quite different from each other, you probably effortlessly recognized all of them as examples of the letter *G*. Now consider the same kind of demonstration but using your best friend's face. Suppose one day your friend gets a dramatic new haircut—or adds glasses, hair dye, or a nose ring. Even though your friend now looks strikingly different, you still recognize that person with ease. Just like the variability in *G*s, you somehow are able to extract the underlying features of the face that allow you to accurately identify your friend.

This thought exercise may seem trivial, but it's no small perceptual feat. If the visual system were somehow stumped each time a minor variation occurred in an object being perceived, the inefficiency of it all would be overwhelming. We'd have to process information effortfully just to perceive our friend as the same person from one meeting to another, not to mention laboring through the process of knowing when a *G* is really a *G*. In general, though, object recognition proceeds fairly smoothly, in large part due to the operation of the feature detectors we discussed earlier.

How do feature detectors help the visual system accurately perceive an object in different circumstances, such as your friend's face? Some researchers argue for a *modular view*, that specialized brain areas, or modules, detect and represent faces or houses or even body parts. Using fMRI to examine visual processing in healthy young adults, researchers found a subregion in the temporal lobe that responds most strongly to faces, rather than other types of objects, whereas a nearby area responds most strongly to buildings and landscapes (Kanwisher, McDermott, & Chun, 1997). This view suggests we have not only feature detectors to aid in visual perception but also "face detectors," "building detectors," and possibly other types of neurons specialized for particular types of object perception (Downing et al., 2006; Kanwisher & Yovel, 2006). Other researchers argue for a more *distributed representation* of object categories. In this view, it is the pattern of activity across multiple brain regions that identifies any viewed object, including faces (Haxby et al., 2001). Each of these views explains some data better than the other one, and researchers continue to debate their relative merits (Duchaine & Yovel, 2015).

Principles of Perceptual Organization

Before object recognition can even kick in, the visual system must perform another important task: grouping the image regions that belong together into a representation of an object. The idea that we tend to perceive a unified, whole object rather than a collection of separate parts is the foundation of Gestalt psychology, which you read about in the Psychology: Evolution of a Science chapter. Gestalt *perceptual grouping rules* govern how the features and regions of things fit together (Koffka, 1935). Here's a sampling:

- *Simplicity:* When confronted with two or more possible interpretations of an object's shape, the visual system tends to select the simplest or most likely interpretation. In **FIGURE 4.11a**, we see an arrow, rather than two separate shapes: a triangle sitting atop a rectangle.
- *Closure:* We tend to fill in missing elements of a visual scene, allowing us to perceive edges that are separated by gaps as belonging to complete objects. In **FIGURE 4.11b**, we see an arrow despite the gaps.

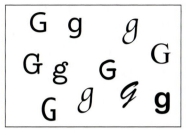

With only a quick glance, you recognize all these letters as *G*, but their varying sizes, shapes, angles, and orientations ought to make this recognition task difficult. What is it about the process of object recognition that allows us to perform this task effortlessly?

Our visual systems allow us to identify people as the same individuals even when they change such features as hairstyle and skin color. Despite the extreme changes in these two photos, you can probably tell that they both portray Johnny Depp. Jun Sato/Wireimage/Getty Images Warner Bros; The Kobal Collection/Art Resource

Figure 4.11 PERCEPTUAL GROUPING RULES Principles first identified by Gestalt psychologists and now supported by experimental evidence demonstrate that the brain is predisposed to impose order on incoming sensations.

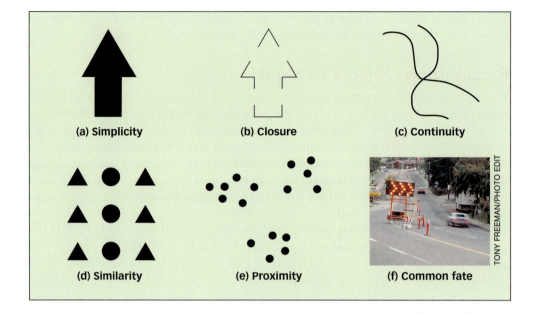

(a) Simplicity   (b) Closure   (c) Continuity

(d) Similarity   (e) Proximity   (f) Common fate

TONY FREEMAN/PHOTO EDIT

- *Continuity:* We tend to group together edges or contours that have the same orientation. In **FIGURE 4.11c**, we perceive two crossing lines instead of two V shapes.

- *Similarity:* Regions that are similar in color, lightness, shape, or texture are perceived as belonging to the same object. In **FIGURE 4.11d**, we perceive three columns—a column of circles flanked by two columns of triangles.

- *Proximity:* Objects that are close together tend to be grouped together. In **FIGURE 4.11e**, we perceive three groups or "clumps" of 5 or 6 dots each, not just 16 dots.

- *Common fate:* Elements of a visual image that move together are perceived as parts of a single moving object. In **FIGURE 4.11f**, the series of flashing lights in the road sign are perceived as a moving arrowhead.

Separating Figure From Ground

Perceptual grouping is a powerful aid to our ability to recognize objects by sight. Grouping involves visually separating an object from its surroundings. In Gestalt terms, this means identifying a *figure* apart from the (back) *ground* in which it resides. For example, you perceive the words on this page as figural: They stand out from the ground of the sheet of paper on which they're printed. Similarly, you perceive your instructor as the figure against the backdrop of all the other elements in your classroom. You certainly can perceive these elements differently, of course: The words *and* the paper are all part of a thing called *a page,* and your instructor *and* the classroom can all be perceived as *your learning environment.* Typically, though, our perceptual systems focus attention on some objects as distinct from their environments.

Size provides one clue to what's figure and what's ground: Smaller regions are likely to be figures, such as tiny letters on a big sheet of paper. Another critical step toward object recognition is *edge assignment.* When we see an edge, or boundary, between figure and ground, it helps define the object's shape, and the background continues behind the edge. Sometimes, though, it's not easy to tell which is which.

A famous illusion called the *Rubin vase* capitalizes on this ambiguity. You can view **FIGURE 4.12** in two ways, either as a vase on a black background or as a pair of silhouettes facing each other. Your visual system settles on one or the other interpretation and fluctuates between them every few seconds. This happens because the edge

Figure 4.12 AMBIGUOUS EDGES Here's how Rubin's classic reversible figure–ground illusion works: Fix your eyes on the center of the image. Your perception will alternate between a vase and facing silhouettes, even as the sensory stimulation remains constant.

that would normally separate figure from ground is really part of neither: It equally defines the contours of the vase and the contours of the faces. Evidence from fMRIs shows, quite nicely, that when people are seeing the Rubin image as faces, there is greater activity in the face-selective region of the temporal lobe we discussed earlier than when they are seeing it as a vase (Hasson et al., 2001).

Perceiving Depth and Size

Objects in the world are arranged in three dimensions—length, width, and depth—but the retinal image contains only two dimensions, length and width. How does the brain process a flat, 2-D retinal image so that we perceive the depth of an object and how far away it is? The answer lies in a collection of *depth cues* that change as you move through space.

Monocular Depth Cues

Monocular depth cues are *aspects of a scene that yield information about depth when viewed with only one eye.* These cues rely on the relationship between distance and size. Even with one eye closed, the retinal image of an object you've focused on grows smaller as that object moves farther away, and larger as it moves closer. Our brains routinely use these differences in retinal image size, or *relative size*, to perceive distance. Most adults, for example, fall within a familiar range of heights (perhaps 5–7 feet tall), so retinal image size alone is usually a reliable cue to how far away they are. Our visual system automatically corrects for size differences and attributes them to differences in distance. **FIGURE 4.13** demonstrates how strong this effect is.

In addition to relative size and familiar size, there are several more monocular depth cues, such as:

- *Linear perspective*: Parallel lines seem to converge as they recede into the distance (see **FIGURE 4.14a**).
- *Texture gradient*: The size of the elements on a patterned surface grows smaller as the surface recedes (see **FIGURE 4.14b**).
- *Interposition*: When one object partly blocks another, the blocking object is closer than the blocked object (see **FIGURE 4.14c**).
- *Relative height in the image*: Objects that are closer to you are lower in your visual field, whereas faraway objects are higher (see **FIGURE 4.14d**).

monocular depth cues Aspects of a scene that yield information about depth when viewed with only one eye.

Figure 4.13   FAMILIAR SIZE AND RELATIVE SIZE When you view images of people, such as the people in the left-hand photo, or of things you know well, the object you perceive as smaller appears farther away. With a little image manipulation, you can see in the right-hand photo that the relative size difference projected on your retinas is far greater than you perceive. The image of the person in the blue vest is exactly the same size in both photos. The Photo Works

Figure 4.14 PICTORIAL DEPTH CUES Visual artists rely on a variety of monocular cues to make their work come to life. You can rely on cues in an image such as linear perspective (a), texture gradient (b), interposition (c), and relative height (d) to infer distance, depth, and position, even if you're wearing an eye patch. (a) Dc Productions/Exactostock-1598/Superstock (b) Age Fotostock/Superstock (c) NP-e07/Istock/Getty Images Plus (d) Rob Blakers/Lonely Planet Images/Getty Images

(a) (b)

(c) (d)

binocular disparity The difference in the retinal images of the two eyes that provides information about depth.

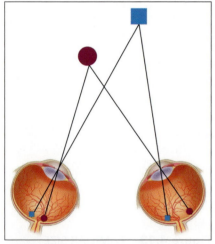

Figure 4.15 BINOCULAR DISPARITY We see the world in three dimensions because our eyes are a distance apart, so the image of an object falls on a slightly different place on the retina of each eye. In this two-object scene, the images of the square and the circle fall on different points of the retina in each eye. The disparity in the positions of the circle's retinal images provides a compelling cue to depth.

Binocular Depth Cues

We can also obtain depth information through **binocular disparity**, *the difference in the retinal images of the two eyes that provides information about depth.* Because our eyes are slightly separated, each registers a slightly different view of the world. Your brain computes the disparity between the two retinal images to perceive how far away objects are, as shown in **FIGURE 4.15**. Viewed from above in the figure, the images of the more distant square and the closer circle each fall at different points on each retina. The View-Master toy and 3-D movies both work by exploiting binocular disparity to evoke a vivid sense of depth.

Illusions of Depth and Size

We all are vulnerable to *illusions*, which, as you'll remember from the Psychology: (Evolution of a Science) chapter, are errors of perception, memory, or judgment in which subjective experience differs from objective reality (Wade, 2005). A famous illusion that makes use of a variety of depth cues is the *Ames room*, which is trapezoidal in shape rather than square (see **FIGURE 4.16a**). A person standing in one corner of an Ames room is physically twice as far away from the viewer as a person standing in the other corner. But when viewed with one eye through the small peephole placed in one wall, the Ames room looks square because the shapes of the windows and the flooring tiles are carefully crafted to *look* square from the viewing port (Ittelson, 1952). The visual system perceives the far wall as perpendicular to the line of sight so that people standing at different positions along that wall appear to be at the same distance, and the viewer's judgments of their sizes are based directly on retinal image size. As a result, a person standing in the right corner appears to be much larger than a person standing in the left corner (see **FIGURE 4.16b**).

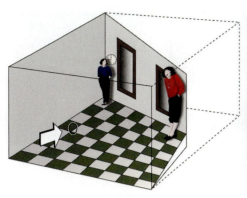 

Figure 4.16 THE AMAZING AMES ROOM (a) A diagram showing the actual proportions of the Ames room reveals its secrets. The sides of the room form a trapezoid with parallel sides but a back wall that's way off square. The uneven floor makes the room's height in the far back corner shorter than the other. (b) Looking into the Ames room through the viewing port with only one eye, the observer infers a normal size–distance relationship—that both people are the same distance away. But the different image sizes they project on the retina leads the viewer to conclude, from the monocular cue of familiar size, that one person is very small and the other is very large. Phil Schermeister/Corbis

Perceiving Motion and Change

You should now have a good sense of how we see what and where objects are, a process made substantially easier when the objects stay in one place. But in real life, of course, objects change position over time. Understanding how we perceive motion and why we sometimes fail to perceive change can bring us closer to appreciating how visual perception works in everyday life.

Motion Perception

To sense motion, the visual system must encode information about both space and time. The simplest case to consider is an observer who does not move trying to perceive an object that does.

As an object moves across a stationary observer's visual field, it first stimulates one location on the retina, and then a little later it stimulates another location on the retina. Neural circuits in the brain can detect this change in position over time and respond to specific speeds and directions of motion (Emerson, Bergen, & Adelson, 1992). A region in the middle of the temporal lobe referred to as *MT* (part of the dorsal stream we discussed earlier) is specialized for the visual perception of motion (Born & Bradley, 2005; Newsome & Paré, 1988), and brain damage in this area causes a deficit in normal motion perception (Zihl, von Cramon, & Mai, 1983).

Of course, in the real world, rarely are you a stationary observer. As you move around, your head and eyes move all the time, and motion perception is not so simple. The motion-perception system must take into account the position and movement of your eyes, and ultimately of your head and body, in order to perceive the motions of objects correctly and allow you to approach or avoid them. The brain accomplishes this by monitoring your eye and head movements and "subtracting" them from the motion in the retinal image.

The movement of objects in the world is not the only event that can evoke the perception of motion. The successively flashing lights of a Las Vegas casino sign can evoke a strong sense of motion because people perceive a series of flashing lights as a whole, moving object (see 4.11f). This *perception of movement as a result of alternating signals appearing in rapid succession in different locations* is called **apparent motion**. Video technology and animation depend on apparent motion. Motion pictures flash 24 still frames per second (fps). A slower rate would produce a much choppier sense of motion; a faster rate would be a waste of resources because we would not perceive the motion as any smoother than it appears at 24 fps.

Change Blindness and Inattentional Blindness

Motion involves a change in an object's position over time, but objects in the visual environment can change in ways that do not involve motion (Rensink,

The View-Master has been a popular toy for decades. It is based on the principle of binocular disparity: Two images taken from slightly different angles produce a stereoscopic effect. Masterfile NMPFT/SSPL/ The Image Works

apparent motion The perception of movement as a result of alternating signals appearing in rapid succession in different locations.

Figure 4.17   CHANGE BLINDNESS The white-haired man was giving directions to one experimenter (a), who disappeared behind the moving door (b), only to be replaced by another experimenter (c). Like many other people, the man failed to detect a seemingly obvious change. Research From Simons, D. J., & Levin, D. T. (1998). Failure to detect changes to people during a real-world interaction. *Psychonomic Bulletin & Review, 5*(4), 644–649.

change blindness Failure to detect changes to the visual details of a scene.

inattentional blindness A failure to perceive objects that are not the focus of attention.

2002). You might walk by the same clothing store window every day and notice when a new suit or dress is on display or register surprise when you see a friend's new haircut. Intuitively, we feel that we can easily detect changes to our visual environment. However, our comfortable intuitions have been challenged by experimental demonstrations of **change blindness**, which occurs *when people fail to detect changes to the visual details of a scene* (Rensink, 2002; Simons & Rensink, 2005). One study dramatically illustrated this idea by having an experimenter ask a person on a college campus for directions (Simons & Levin, 1998). While they were talking, two men walked between them, holding a door that hid a second experimenter (see **FIGURE 4.17**). Behind the door, the two experimenters traded places so that, when the men carrying the door moved on, a different person was asking for directions than the one who had been there just a second or two earlier. In a remarkable finding, only 7 of 15 participants reported noticing this change.

Although surprising, these findings once again illustrate the importance of focused attention for visual perception. Just as focused attention is critical for binding together the features of objects, it is also necessary for detecting changes to objects and scenes (Rensink, 2002; Simons & Rensink, 2005). Change blindness is most likely to occur when people fail to focus attention on the changed object (even though the visual system registers the object) and is least likely to occur for items that draw attention to themselves (Rensink, O'Regan, & Clark, 1997).

The role of focused attention in conscious visual experience is also dramatically illustrated by the closely related phenomenon of **inattentional blindness**, *a failure to perceive objects that are not the focus of attention*. We've already seen that using cell phones has negative effects on driving (see The Real World: Multitasking). In another study, researchers asked whether cell phone use contributes to inattentional blindness in everyday life (Hyman et al., 2010). They recruited a clown to ride a unicycle in the middle of a large square in the middle of a college campus. The researchers asked 151 students who had just walked through the square whether they saw the clown. Seventy-five percent of the students who were using cell phones failed to notice the clown, compared with less than 50% who were not using cell phones. Using cell phones draws on focused attention, resulting in increased inattentional blindness and emphasizing again that our conscious experience of our visual environment is restricted to those features or objects selected by focused attention. In some extreme cases, conscious visual experience may reflect what we expect to see, rather than what exists in the external world.

College students who were using their cell phones while walking through campus failed to notice the unicycling clown more frequently than did students who were not using their cell phones. Republished with permission Hyman et al, Did you see the Unicycling Clown? Inattentional Blindness while Walking and Talking on a Cell Phone, Ira E. Hyman Jr, S. Matthew Boss, Breanne M. Wise, Kira E. McKenzie and Jenna M. Caggiano, *Applied Cognitive Psychology* 2009, *V. 24*, Pages 597–607. Wiley Interscience; permission conveyed through Copyright Clearance Center.

BUILD TO THE OUTCOMES

1. How does the study of illusory conjunctions help us understand the role of attention in feature binding?

2. How do we recognize our friends, even when they're hidden behind sunglasses?

3. What are the perceptual grouping rules for vision?

4. How do monocular depth cues help us with depth perception?

5. What role does binocular disparity have in perceiving depth?

6. How can flashing lights on a casino sign give the impression of movement?

7. How can a failure of focused attention explain change blindness?

Audition: More Than Meets the Ear

Vision is based on the spatial pattern of light waves on the retina. The sense of hearing, by contrast, is all about *sound waves*: changes in air pressure unfolding over time. Plenty of things produce sound waves: the collision of a tree hitting the forest floor, the vibration of vocal cords during a stirring speech, the resonance of a bass guitar string during a thrash metal concert. Understanding auditory experience requires understanding how we transform changes in air pressure into perceived sounds.

Sensing Sound

Striking a tuning fork produces a *pure tone,* a simple sound wave that first increases air pressure and then creates a relative vacuum. This cycle repeats hundreds or thousands of times per second as sound waves travel outward in all directions from the source. Just as there are three dimensions of light waves corresponding to three dimensions of visual perception, so, too, there are three physical dimensions of a sound wave. Frequency, amplitude, and complexity determine what we hear as the pitch, loudness, and quality of a sound (see **TABLE 4.3**).

LEARNING OUTCOMES

*   Relate the properties of a sound wave to how sound is perceived.

*   Describe how the ear converts sound waves into neural impulses.

*   Discuss how we perceive pitch.

*   Compare the two main causes of hearing loss.

TABLE 4.3	Properties of Sound Waves	

Frequency
Corresponds to our perception of pitch.

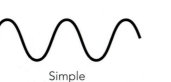

Low frequency
(low-pitched sound)

High frequency
(high-pitched sound)

Amplitude
Corresponds to our perception of loudness.

High amplitude
(loud sound)

Low amplitude
(soft sound)

Complexity
Corresponds to our perception of timbre.

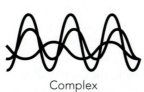

Simple
(pure tone)

Complex
(mix of frequencies)

- The *frequency* of the sound wave, or its wavelength, depends on how often the peak in air pressure passes the ear or a microphone, measured in cycles per second, or hertz (Hz). Changes in the physical frequency of a sound wave are perceived by humans as changes in **pitch**, *how high or low a sound is.*

- The *amplitude* of a sound wave refers to its height, relative to the threshold for human hearing (which is set at zero decibels, or dBs). Amplitude corresponds to **loudness**, or *a sound's intensity.* The rustling of leaves in a soft breeze is about 20 dB, normal conversation is measured at about 40 dB, shouting produces 70 dB, a Slayer concert is about 130 dB, and the sound of the space shuttle taking off 1 mile away registers at 160 dB or more.

- Differences in the *complexity* of sound waves, or their mix of frequencies, correspond to **timbre**, *a listener's experience of sound quality or resonance.* Timbre (pronounced "TAM-ber") offers us information about the nature of sound. The same note played at the same loudness produces a perceptually different experience, depending on whether it was played on a flute or a trumpet, due to timbre.

pitch How high or low a sound is.

loudness A sound's intensity.

timbre A listener's experience of sound quality or resonance.

Most sounds—such as voices, music, the sound of wind in trees, the screech of brakes, the purring of a cat—are composed of not one, but many different frequency components. Although you perceive the mixture (the cat's purr, for example, not the 206 Hz component in the purr), the first thing the ear does to a sound is to break it down—to analyze it—into its separate component frequencies. The psychological attributes of pitch, loudness, and timbre are then built up by the brain from the separate frequency components that are represented in the inner ear, just as visual perceptions are built up from the spatial pattern of activity on the retina. The focus in our discussion of hearing, then, is on how the auditory system encodes and represents sound frequency (Kubovy, 1981).

"The ringing in your ears—I think I can help."

Leo Cullum/The New Yorker Collection/
Cartoonbank.com

Having Two Ears Helps Us Localize Sound Sources

Just as the different positions of our eyes give us stereoscopic vision, the placement of our ears on opposite sides of the head gives us stereophonic hearing. The sound arriving at the ear closer to the sound source is louder than the sound in the farther ear, mainly because the listener's head partially blocks sound energy. This loudness difference decreases as the sound source moves from a position directly to one side (maximal difference) to straight ahead (no difference).

Another clue to a sound's location arises from timing: Sound waves arrive a little sooner at the near ear than at the far ear. The timing difference can be as brief as a few microseconds, but together with the intensity difference, it is sufficient to allow us to perceive the location of a sound. When the sound source is ambiguous, you may find yourself turning your head from side to side to localize it. By doing this, you are changing the relative intensity and timing of sound waves arriving in your ears and collecting better information about the likely source of the sound.

The Outer Ear Funnels Sound Waves to the Middle Ear

The human ear is divided into three distinct parts, as shown in **FIGURE 4.18**. The *outer ear* collects sound waves and funnels them toward the *middle ear*, which transmits the vibrations to the *inner ear*, where they are transduced into neural impulses.

The outer ear consists of the visible part on the outside of the head (called the *pinna*); the auditory canal; and the eardrum, an airtight flap of skin that vibrates in response to sound waves gathered by the pinna and channeled into the canal. The middle ear, a tiny, air-filled chamber behind the eardrum, contains the three smallest bones in the body, called *ossicles*. Named for their appearance as hammer, anvil, and stirrup, the ossicles fit together into a lever that mechanically transmits and intensifies vibrations from the eardrum to the inner ear.

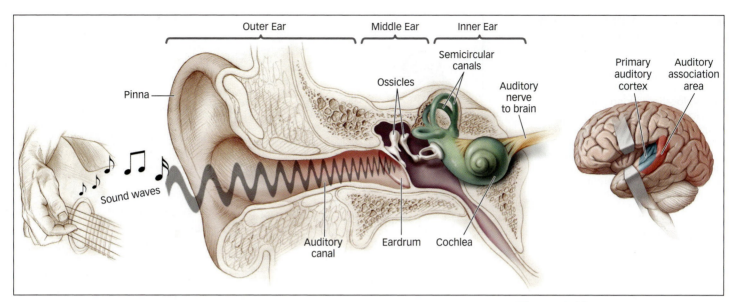

Figure 4.18 **ANATOMY OF THE HUMAN EAR** The pinna funnels sound waves into the auditory canal, causing the eardrum to vibrate at a rate that corresponds to the sound's constituent frequencies. In the middle ear, the ossicles pick up the eardrum vibrations, amplify them, and pass them along, causing the vibration of a membrane at the surface of the fluid-filled cochlea in the inner ear. Here, fluid carries the wave energy to the auditory receptors that transduce it into electrochemical activity, exciting the neurons that form the auditory nerve, leading to the brain.

Sound Is Converted Into Neural Impulses in the Inner Ear

The inner ear contains the spiral-shaped **cochlea** (Latin for "snail"), *a fluid-filled tube that is the organ of auditory transduction*. The cochlea is divided along its length by the **basilar membrane**, *a structure in the inner ear that undulates when vibrations from the ossicles reach the cochlear fluid* (see **FIGURE 4.19**). Its wavelike movement stimulates thousands of tiny **hair cells**, *specialized auditory receptor neurons embedded in the basilar membrane*. The hair cells then release neurotransmitter molecules, initiating neural signals in the auditory nerve that travels to the brain. These signals encode sound-wave frequency in two ways, one for high frequencies and one for low frequencies.

- The **place code**, used mainly for high frequencies, refers to *the process by which different frequencies stimulate neural signals at specific places along the basilar membrane*. When the frequency is low, the wide, floppy tip (*apex*) of the basilar membrane moves the most; when the frequency is high, the narrow, stiff end (*base*) of the membrane moves the most (see Figure 4.19). The movement of the basilar membrane causes hair cells to bend, initiating a neural signal in the auditory nerve. Axons fire the strongest in the hair cells along the area of the basilar membrane that moves the most, and the brain uses information about which axons are the most active to help determine the pitch you hear.

- A **temporal code** *registers relatively low frequencies (up to about 5000 Hz) via the firing rate of action potentials entering the auditory nerve*. Action potentials from the hair cells are synchronized in time with the peaks of the incoming sound waves (Johnson, 1980). If you imagine the rhythmic *boom-boom-boom* of a bass drum, you can probably also imagine the *fire-fire-fire* of action potentials corresponding to the beats. This process provides the brain with very precise information about pitch that supplements the information provided by the place code.

The Auditory Nerve Carries the Neural Impulses to the Brain

From the inner ear, action potentials in the auditory nerve travel to the thalamus and ultimately to an area of the cerebral cortex called **area A1**, *a portion of the temporal lobe that contains the primary auditory cortex* (see **FIGURE 4.20**). Neurons in area A1 respond well to simple tones, and successive auditory areas in the brain process

cochlea A fluid-filled tube that is the organ of auditory transduction.

basilar membrane A structure in the inner ear that undulates when vibrations from the ossicles reach the cochlear fluid.

hair cells Specialized auditory receptor neurons embedded in the basilar membrane.

place code The process by which different frequencies stimulate neural signals at specific places along the basilar membrane, from which the brain determines pitch.

temporal code The process whereby the cochlea registers low frequencies via the firing rate of action potentials entering the auditory nerve.

area A1 A portion of the temporal lobe that contains the primary auditory cortex.

Figure 4.19 AUDITORY TRANS-
DUCTION Inside the cochlea (shown
here as though it were uncoiling), the
basilar membrane undulates in response
to wave energy in the cochlear fluid.
Waves of differing frequencies ripple
varying locations along the membrane,
from low frequencies at its tip to high
frequencies at the base, and bend the
embedded hair cell receptors at those
locations. The hair cell motion generates impulses in the auditory neurons,
whose axons form the auditory nerve that
emerges from the cochlea.

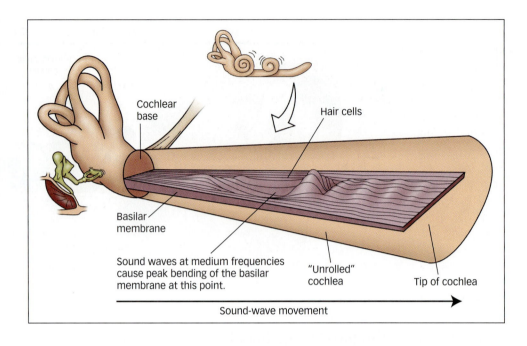

Figure 4.20 PRIMARY AUDITORY
CORTEX Area A1 is folded into the temporal lobe beneath the lateral fissure in
each hemisphere. The left hemisphere
auditory areas govern speech in most
people. The area A1 cortex has a topo-
graphic organization (inset), with lower frequencies mapping toward the front of the
brain and higher frequencies toward
the back, mirroring the organization of
the basilar membrane along the cochlea
(see FIGURE 4.19).

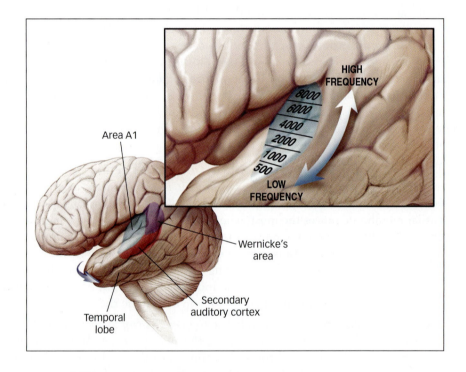

sounds of increasing complexity (see Figure 4.20, inset; Rauschecker & Scott, 2009;
Schreiner, Read, & Sutter, 2000; Schreiner & Winer, 2007). For most of us, the auditory areas in the left hemisphere analyze sounds related to language, whereas those
in the right hemisphere specialize in rhythmic sounds and music. There is also evidence that the auditory cortex is composed of two distinct streams, roughly analogous to the dorsal and ventral streams of the visual system. Spatial ("where") auditory
features, which allow you to locate the source of a sound in space, are handled by
areas toward the back (caudal) part of the auditory cortex. Nonspatial ("what") features, which allow you to identify the sound, are handled by areas in the lower (ventral) part of the auditory cortex (Recanzone & Sutter, 2008).

Hearing Loss

Hearing loss has two main causes. *Conductive hearing loss* arises because the eardrum or ossicles are damaged to the point that they cannot conduct sound waves effectively to the cochlea. In many cases, medication or surgery can correct the problem. Sound amplification from a hearing aid also can improve hearing through conduction via the bones around the ear directly to the cochlea.

Sensorineural hearing loss is caused by damage to the cochlea, the hair cells, or the auditory nerve, and it happens to almost all of us as we age. Sensorineural hearing loss can be heightened in people regularly exposed to high noise levels (such as rock musicians or jet mechanics). Simply amplifying the sound does not help because the hair cells can no longer transduce sound waves. In these cases, a *cochlear implant* may offer some relief.

A cochlear implant is an electronic device that replaces the function of the hair cells (Waltzman, 2006). The external parts of the device include a microphone and a speech processor, about the size of a USB key, worn behind the ear, and a small, flat, external transmitter that sits on the scalp behind the ear. The implanted parts include a receiver just inside the skull and a thin wire containing electrodes inserted into the cochlea to stimulate the auditory nerve. Sound picked up by the microphone is transformed into electric signals by the speech processor, which is essentially a small computer. The signal is transmitted to the implanted receiver, which activates

A cochlear implant works when a microphone picks up sounds and sends them to a small speech-processing computer worn on the user's belt or behind the ear. The electric signals from the speech processor are transmitted to an implanted receiver, which sends the signals via electrodes to the cochlea, where the signals directly stimulate the auditory nerve. AP Photo/Rochester Post-Bulletin, Jerry Olson

---

HOT SCIENCE →

Music Training: Worth the Time

Did you learn to play an instrument when you were younger? If so, there's good news for your brain. Compared with nonmusicians, musicians have greater plasticity in the motor cortex (Rosenkranz, Williamon, & Rothwell, 2007) and increased gray matter in motor and auditory brain regions (Gaser & Schlaug, 2003; Hannon & Trainor, 2007). But musical training also extends to auditory processing in nonmusical domains (Kraus & Chandrasekaran, 2010). Musicians, for example, show enhanced brain responses when listening to speech compared with nonmusicians (Parbery-Clark et al., 2012). Musicians also exhibit an improved ability to detect speech when it is presented in a noisy background (Parbery-Clark, Skoe, & Kraus, 2009; Parbery-Clark et al., 2011)

Remembering to be careful not to confuse correlation with causation, you may ask: Do differences between musicians and nonmusicians reflect the effects of musical training? Or do they reflect individual differences, perhaps genetic ones, that

Deni_M/Thinkstock/iStock/Getty Images

lead some people to become musicians in the first place? Maybe people blessed with enhanced brain responses to musical or other auditory stimuli decide to become musicians *because* of their natural abilities. Several experiments support a causal role for musical training. One study demonstrated

structural brain differences in auditory and motor areas of elementary schoolchildren after 15 months of musical training (learning to play piano), compared with children who did not receive musical training (Hyde et al., 2009). Another study compared two groups of 8-year-old children, one group with 6 months of musical training and the other with 6 months of painting training. Musical training produced changes in the brain's electrical responses to musical and speech stimuli, and those changes were correlated with enhanced performance on both musical and speech perception tasks (Moreno et al., 2009).

We don't yet know all the reasons that musical training has such broad effects on auditory processing, but one likely contributor is that learning to play an instrument demands attention to precise details of sounds (Kraus & Chandrasekaran, 2010). Future studies will no doubt pinpoint additional factors, but the research to date leaves little room for doubt that your hours of practice were indeed worth the time.

the electrodes in the cochlea. Cochlear implants are now in routine use and can improve hearing to the point that the wearer can understand speech.

Marked hearing loss is commonly experienced by people as they grow older but is rare in an infant. However, infants who have not yet learned to speak are especially vulnerable because they may miss the critical period for language learning (see the Learning chapter). Without auditory feedback during this time, normal speech is nearly impossible to achieve, but early use of cochlear implants has been associated with improved speech and language skills in deaf children (Hay-McCutcheon et al., 2008). Efforts are under way to introduce cochlear implants to children as young as 12 months old or even younger to maximize their chances of normal language development (DesJardin, Eisenberg, & Hodapp, 2006; Holman et al., 2013). (For research on the importance of music and brain development, see Hot Science: Music Training: Worth the Time.)

BUILD TO THE OUTCOMES

1. What are the three properties of sound waves?

2. Why does one note sound so different on a flute and on a trumpet?

3. How do we determine the location of a sound?

4. What are the roles of the outer, middle, and inner parts of the ear in audition?

5. How do hair cells in the ear enable us to hear?

6. How does the frequency of a sound wave relate to what we hear?

7. In which type of hearing loss does sound amplification help?

8. What causes different types of hearing loss?

The Body Senses: More Than Skin Deep

LEARNING OUTCOMES

- Describe how touch receptors transmit messages to the brain.
- Discuss why pain is both a physical and psychological perception.
- Explain how we use various senses to keep our balance.

haptic perception The active exploration of the environment by touching and grasping objects with our hands.

Vision and audition provide information about the world at a distance. By responding to light and sound energy in the environment, these "distance" senses allow us to identify and locate the objects and people around us. In comparison, the body senses, also called *somatosenses* (*soma* from the Greek for "body"), are up close and personal. **Haptic perception** is the *active exploration of the environment by touching and grasping objects with our hands*. We use sensory receptors in our muscles, tendons, and joints as well as a variety of receptors in our skin to get a feel for the world around us (see **FIGURE 4.21**).

Sensing Touch

Touch begins with the transduction of skin sensations into neural signals. Receptors located under the skin's surface enable us to sense pain, pressure, texture, pattern, or vibration against the skin (see Figure 4.21). The receptive fields of these specialized cells work together to provide a rich tactile (from Latin, "to touch") experience when you explore an object by feeling it or attempting to grasp it. In addition, *thermoreceptors*, nerve fibers that sense cold and warmth, respond when your skin temperature changes. All these sensations blend seamlessly together in perception, of course, but detailed physiological studies have successfully isolated the parts of the touch system (Hollins, 2010; Johnson, 2002).

There are three important principles regarding the neural representation of the body's surface. First, the left half of the body is represented in the right half of the brain and vice versa. Second, just as more of the visual brain is devoted to foveal

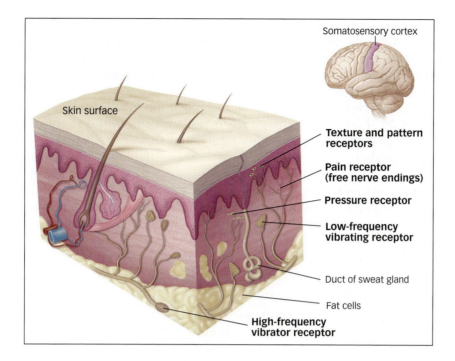

Skin surface

Somatosensory cortex

Texture and pattern receptors

Pain receptor (free nerve endings)

Pressure receptor

Low-frequency vibrating receptor

Duct of sweat gland

Fat cells

High-frequency vibrator receptor

Figure 4.21   TOUCH RECEPTORS Specialized sensory neurons form distinct groups of haptic receptors that detect pressure, temperature, and vibrations against the skin; their long axons enter the brain via the spinal or cranial nerves. Pain receptors populate all body tissues that feel pain; they are distributed around bones and within muscles and internal organs as well as under the skin surface. Sensory signals on the body travel to the somatosensory cortex.

This rather unimposing geodesic dome sits on the floor of the Exploratorium, a world-renowned science museum in San Francisco. Called the Tactile Dome, it was created in 1971 to create an environment in which only haptic perception could be used. The inside of the dome is pitch black; visitors must crawl, wiggle, slide, and otherwise navigate the unfamiliar terrain using only their sense of touch. How would you feel being in that environment for an hour or so?
© Exploratorium, www.exploratorium.edu

vision, where acuity is greatest, more of the tactile brain is devoted to parts of the skin surface where sensitivity to small spatial differences is greatest. Regions such as the fingertips and lips are very good at discriminating fine spatial detail, whereas areas such as the lower back are quite poor at that task. Refer back to Figure 3.14 in the Neuroscience and Behavior chapter; you'll recall that different locations on the body project sensory signals to different locations in the somatosensory cortex in the parietal lobe. Third, there is mounting evidence for a distinction between "what" and "where" pathways in touch analogous to similar distinctions we've already considered for vision and audition. The "what" system for touch provides information about the properties of surfaces and objects; the "where" system provides information about a location in external space that is being touched or a location on the body that is being stimulated (Lederman & Klatzky, 2009). Evidence from fMRI suggests that the "what" and "where" touch pathways involve areas in the lower and upper parts of the parietal lobe, respectively (Reed, Klatzky, & Halgren, 2005).

Touch information can have a powerful effect on our decisions and judgments. For example, recent research has shown that merely touching an object that we don't already own can increase our feeling of ownership and lead us to value the object more highly than when we view it but don't touch it (Peck & Shu, 2009); the longer we touch an object, the more highly we value it (Wolf, Arkes, & Muhanna, 2008). You might keep this "mere touch" effect in mind next time you are in a shop and considering buying an expensive item. Retailers are probably aware of this effect: During the 2003 holiday shopping season, the office of the Illinois state attorney general warned shoppers to be cautious in stores that encouraged them to touch the merchandise (Peck & Shu, 2009).

Sensing Pain

Although pain is arguably the least pleasant of sensations, this aspect of touch is among the most important for survival: Pain indicates damage or potential damage to the body. Without the ability to feel pain, we might ignore infections,

Be warned about your next shopping trip: Touching the merchandise can lead you to value it more highly than just looking at it. CKDJ/Corbis

broken bones, or serious burns. Children born with congenital insensitivity to pain, a rare inherited disorder that specifically impairs pain perception, often mutilate themselves (e.g., biting into their tongues or gouging their skin while scratching) and are at increased risk of dying during childhood (Nagasako, Oaklander, & Dworkin, 2003).

Tissue damage is transduced by pain receptors, the free nerve endings shown in Figure 4.21. Fast-acting *A-delta fibers* transmit the initial sharp pain one might feel right away from a sudden injury, and slower *C fibers* transmit the longer-lasting, duller pain that persists after the initial injury. If you were running barefoot outside and stubbed your toe against a rock, you would first feel a sudden stinging pain transmitted by A-delta fibers that would die down quickly, only to be replaced by the throbbing but longer-lasting pain carried by C fibers. Both the A-delta and C fibers are impaired in cases of congenital insensitivity to pain.

Perceiving Pain

Neural signals for perceiving pain travel to the brain via two pathways that evoke distinct psychological experiences (Treede et al., 1999). One pain pathway sends signals to the somatosensory cortex, identifying where the pain is occurring and what sort of pain it is (sharp, burning, dull). The second pain pathway sends signals to the motivational and emotional centers of the brain, such as the hypothalamus and amygdala, and to the frontal lobe. This is the aspect of pain that is unpleasant and motivates us to escape from or relieve the pain.

Pain typically feels as if it comes from the site of the tissue damage that caused it. If you burn your finger, you will perceive the pain as originating there. But we have pain receptors in many areas besides the skin: around bones and within muscles and internal organs as well. When pain originates internally, in a body organ, for example, we actually feel it on the surface of the body. This kind of **referred pain** occurs when *sensory information from internal and external areas converges on the same nerve cells in the spinal cord*. One common example is a heart attack: Victims often feel pain radiating from the left arm, rather than from inside the chest.

One influential account of pain perception is known as **gate-control theory of pain**, which holds that *signals arriving from pain receptors in the body can be stopped, or gated, by interneurons in the spinal cord via feedback from two directions* (Melzack & Wall, 1965). Pain can be gated by the skin receptors, for example, by rubbing the affected area. Rubbing your stubbed toe activates neurons that "close the gate" to stop pain signals from traveling to the brain. Pain can also be gated from the brain by modulating the activity of pain-transmission neurons. This neural feedback is elicited not by the pain itself but rather by activity in a region of the midbrain called the *periaqueductal gray (PAG)*. Under extreme conditions, such as high stress, naturally occurring endorphins can activate the PAG to send inhibitory signals to neurons in the spinal cord that then suppress pain signals to the brain, thereby modulating the experience of pain. The PAG also responds to the action of opiate drugs, such as morphine.

Although some details of the gate-control theory of pain have been challenged, a key concept underlying the theory—that perception is a two-way street—has broad implications. The senses feed information such as pain sensations to the brain, a pattern that perceptual psychologists term *bottom-up control*. The brain processes these sensory data into perceptual information at successive levels to support movement, object recognition, and eventually more complex cognitive

referred pain Feeling of pain when sensory information from internal and external areas converges on the same nerve cells in the spinal cord.

gate-control theory of pain A theory of pain perception based on the idea that signals arriving from pain receptors in the body can be stopped, or *gated*, by interneurons in the spinal cord via feedback from two directions.

tasks, such as memory and planning. But there is ample evidence that the brain exerts plenty of control over what we sense as well. Visual illusions and the gestalt principles of filling in, shaping up, and rounding out what isn't really there provide some examples. This kind of *top-down control* also explains how the brain influences the experience of touch and pain (Kucyi & Davis, 2015; Wager & Atlas, 2013).

Body Position, Movement, and Balance

It may sound odd, but one aspect of sensation and perception is knowing where parts of your body are at any given moment. Your body needs some way to sense its position in physical space other than moving your eyes constantly to see the location of your limbs. Sensations related to position, movement, and balance depend on stimulation produced within our bodies. Receptors in the muscles, tendons, and joints signal the position of the body in space, whereas information about balance and head movement originates in the inner ear.

Sensory receptors provide the information we need to perceive the position and movement of our limbs, head, and body. These receptors also provide feedback about whether we are performing a desired movement correctly and how resistance from held objects may be influencing the movement. For example, when you swing a baseball bat, the weight of the bat affects how your muscles move your arm as well as the change in sensation when the bat hits the ball.

Maintaining balance depends primarily on the **vestibular system**, *the three fluid-filled semicircular canals and adjacent organs located next to the cochlea in each inner ear* (see Figure 4.18). The semicircular canals are arranged in three perpendicular orientations and studded with hair cells that detect movement of the fluid when the head moves or accelerates. The bending of the hair cells generates activity in the vestibular nerve that is then conveyed to the brain. This detected motion enables us to maintain our balance, or the position of our bodies relative to gravity (Lackner & DiZio, 2005).

Vision also helps us keep our balance. If you see that you are swaying relative to a vertical orientation, such as the contours of a room, you move your legs and feet to keep from falling over. Psychologists have experimented with this visual aspect of balance by placing people in rooms that can be tilted forward and backward (Bertenthal, Rose, & Bai, 1997; Lee & Aronson, 1974). If the room tilts enough, people—particularly small children—will topple over as they try to compensate for what their visual system is telling them. When a mismatch between the information provided by visual cues and vestibular feedback occurs, motion sickness can result. Remember this discrepancy the next time you try reading in the back seat of a moving car!

Hitting a ball with a bat or racquet provides feedback about where your arms and body are in space, as well as how the resistance of these objects affects your movement and balance. Successful athletes, such as Serena Williams, have particularly well-developed body senses.   RICK RYCROFT/AP Images

vestibular system The three fluid-filled semicircular canals and adjacent organs located next to the cochlea in the inner ear.

BUILD TO THE OUTCOMES

1. What is the difference between the "distance" senses and the somatosenses?

2. What is the role of the various parts of the skin in touch and pain?

3. Why does rubbing an injured area sometimes help alleviate pain?

4. What is the vestibular system?

5. Why is it so hard to stand on one foot with your eyes closed?

The Chemical Senses: Adding Flavor

LEARNING OUTCOMES

- Describe how odorant molecules are converted into neural impulses in the roof of the nose.

- Explain the importance of smell in personal and social experiences.

- Describe how taste sensations are converted into neural impulses by the tongue.

Somatosensation is all about physical changes in or on the body: Vision and audition sense energetic states of the world—light and sound waves—and touch is activated by physical changes in or on the body surface. The last set of senses we'll consider share a chemical basis to combine aspects of distance and proximity. The chemical senses of *olfaction* (smell) and *gustation* (taste) respond to the molecular structure of substances floating into the nasal cavity as you inhale or dissolving in saliva. Smell and taste combine to produce the perceptual experience we call *flavor*.

Sense of Smell

Olfaction is the least understood sense and the only one directly connected to the forebrain, with pathways into the frontal lobe, amygdala, and other forebrain structures. (Recall from the Neuroscience and Behavior chapter that the other senses connect first to the thalamus.) This mapping indicates that smell has a close relationship with areas involved in emotional and social behavior. Smell seems to have evolved in animals as a signaling sense for the familiar: a friendly creature, an edible food, or a sexually receptive mate.

Countless substances release odors into the air, and some of their *odorant molecules* make their way into our noses, drifting in on the air we breathe. Situated along the top of the nasal cavity shown in **FIGURE 4.22** is a mucous membrane called the *olfactory epithelium*, which contains about 10 million **olfactory receptor neurons (ORNs)**,

olfactory receptor neurons (ORNs) Receptor cells that initiate the sense of smell.

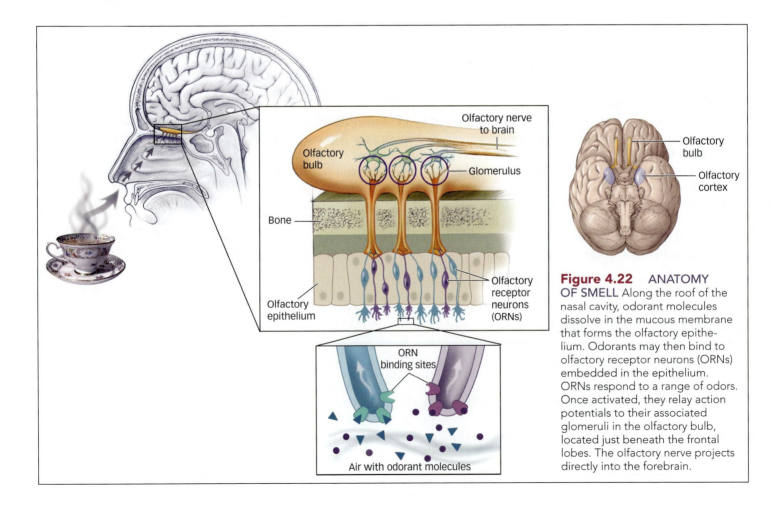

Figure 4.22 ANATOMY OF SMELL Along the roof of the nasal cavity, odorant molecules dissolve in the mucous membrane that forms the olfactory epithelium. Odorants may then bind to olfactory receptor neurons (ORNs) embedded in the epithelium. ORNs respond to a range of odors. Once activated, they relay action potentials to their associated glomeruli in the olfactory bulb, located just beneath the frontal lobes. The olfactory nerve projects directly into the forebrain.

receptor cells that initiate the sense of smell. Odorant molecules bind to sites on these specialized receptors, and if enough bindings occur, the ORNs send neural impulses into the olfactory nerve (Dalton, 2003).

Each olfactory neuron has receptors that bind to some odorants but not to others, as if the receptor is a lock and the odorant is the key (see Figure 4.22). Groups of ORNs send their axons from the olfactory epithelium into the **olfactory bulb**, *a brain structure located above the nasal cavity beneath the frontal lobes.* Humans possess about 350 different ORN types that permit us to discriminate among some 10,000 different odorants through the unique patterns of neural activity each odorant evokes. This setup is similar to our ability to see a vast range of colors through only a small number of retinal receptor cell types or to feel a range of skin sensations through only a handful of touch-receptor cell types.

olfactory bulb A brain structure located above the nasal cavity beneath the frontal lobes.

Perceiving Smell

The olfactory bulb sends outputs to various centers in the brain, including the parts that are responsible for controlling basic drives, emotions, and memories. Odor perception includes both information about the identity of an odor, which involves relating olfactory inputs to information stored in memory (Stevenson & Boakes, 2003), as well as our emotional response to whether it is pleasant or unpleasant (Khan et al., 2007). The relationship between smell and emotion explains why smells can have immediate, strongly positive or negative effects on us. If the slightest whiff of an apple pie baking brings back fond memories of childhood, or if the unexpected sniff of vomit mentally returns you to a particularly bad party you once attended, you've got the idea.

Our experience of smell is determined not only by bottom-up influences, such as odorant molecules binding to sites on ORNs, but also by top-down influences, such as our previous experiences with an odor (Gottfried, 2008; Rolls, 2015). Consistent with this idea, people rate the identical odor as more pleasant when it is paired with an appealing verbal label such as *cheddar cheese* rather than an unappealing one such as *body odor* (de Araujo et al., 2005; Herz & von Clef, 2001). fMRI evidence indicates that brain regions involved in coding the pleasantness of an experience, such as the orbitofrontal cortex, respond more strongly to the identical odor when people think it is cheddar cheese than when they think it is a body odor (de Araujo et al., 2005).

Smell may also play a role in social behavior. Humans and other animals can detect odors from **pheromones**, *biochemical odorants emitted by other members of its species that can affect the animal's behavior or physiology.* Parents can distinguish the smell of their own children from that of other people's children. An infant can identify the smell of its mother's breast as opposed to the smell of other mothers. Pheromones also play a role in reproductive behavior in insects and in several mammalian species, including mice, dogs, and primates (Brennan & Zufall, 2006). Research in humans has demonstrated no consistent tendency for people to prefer the odors of people of the opposite sex over other pleasant odors. Recent research, however, has provided a link between sexual orientation and responses to odors. Researchers used positron emission tomography (PET) scans to study the brain's response to two odors, one related to testosterone, which is produced in men's sweat, and the other related to estrogen, which is found in women's urine. The testosterone-based odor activated the hypothalamus (a part of the brain that controls sexual behavior) in heterosexual women but not in heterosexual men, whereas the estrogen-based odor activated the hypothalamus in heterosexual men but not in heterosexual women. Strikingly, homosexual men responded to the two chemicals in the same way as did heterosexual women did (Savic, Berglund,

Taste and smell both contribute to what we perceive as flavor. This is why smelling the bouquet of a wine is an essential part of the wine-tasting ritual. The experience of wine tasting is also influenced by cognitive factors, such as knowledge of a wine's price. Adam Gregor/Shutterstock

pheromones Biochemical odorants emitted by other members of its species that can affect an animal's behavior or physiology.

Figure 4.23   SMELL AND SOCIAL BEHAVIOR In a PET study, heterosexual women, homosexual men, and heterosexual men were scanned as they were presented with each of several odors. During the presentation of a testosterone-based odor (referred to in the figure as AND), there was significant activation in the hypothalamus for heterosexual women (*left*) and homosexual men (*center*) but not for (*right*) heterosexual men (Savic et al., 2005). Ivanka Savic, HA Berglund, and Per Lindstrom. *PNAS* 2005 *102*(20) 7356–7361. National Academy of Sciences, USA.

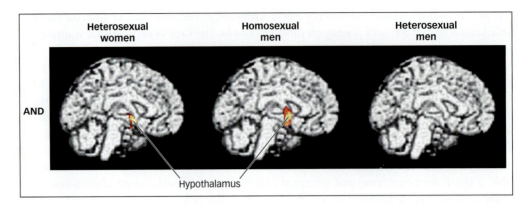

& Lindstrom, 2005; see **FIGURE 4.23**). Other common odors unrelated to sexual arousal were processed similarly by all three groups. Taken together, the two studies suggest that some human pheromones are related to sexual orientation.

Sense of Taste

One of the primary responsibilities of the chemical sense of taste is identifying things that are poisonous. Some aspects of taste perception are genetic, such as an aversion to extreme bitterness, and some are learned, such as an aversion to a particular food that once caused nausea. In either case, the direct contact between the tongue and possible foods allows us to anticipate whether something will be harmful or palatable.

The tongue is covered with thousands of small bumps, called *papillae,* which are easily visible to the naked eye. Within each papilla are hundreds of **taste buds**, *the organs of taste transduction* (see **FIGURE 4.24**). The mouth contains 5,000 to 10,000 taste buds fairly evenly distributed over the tongue, the roof of the mouth, and the upper throat (Bartoshuk & Beauchamp, 1994; Halpern, 2002). Each taste bud contains 50 to 100 taste receptor cells. Taste perception fades with age (Methven et al., 2012): On average, people lose half their taste receptors

taste buds The organs of taste transduction.

Figure 4.24   A TASTE BUD (a) Taste buds stud the bumps (papillae) on the tongue, shown here, as well as the back, sides, and roof of the mouth. (b) Each taste bud contains a range of receptor cells that respond to varying chemical components of foods called tastants. (c) Tastant molecules dissolve in saliva and stimulate the microvilli that form the tips of the taste receptor cells. Each taste bud contacts the branch of a cranial nerve at its base.

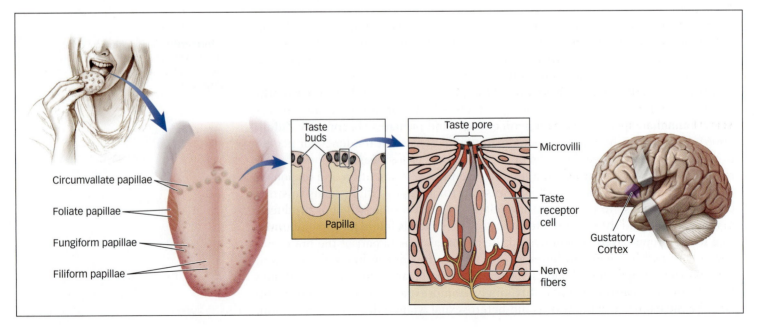

by the time they turn 20. This may help to explain why young children seem to be "fussy eaters" since their greater number of taste buds brings with it a greater range of taste sensations.

The taste system contains just five main types of taste receptors, corresponding to five primary taste sensations: salt, sour, bitter, sweet, and *umami* (savory). The first four are quite familiar, but *umami* may not be. In fact, perception researchers are still debating its existence. The umami receptor was discovered by Japanese scientists who attributed it to the tastes evoked by foods containing a high concentration of protein, such as meats and cheeses (Yamaguchi, 1998). If you're a meat eater and you savor the feel of a steak topped with butter or a cheeseburger as it sits in your mouth, you've got an idea of the umami sensation. The food additive *monosodium glutamate (MSG)*, which is often used to flavor Asian foods, particularly activates umami receptors. Some people develop headaches or allergic reactions after eating MSG.

Perceiving Taste

Of course, the variety of taste experiences greatly exceeds the five basic receptors discussed here. Any food molecules dissolved in saliva evoke specific, combined patterns of activity in the five taste receptor types. Although we often think of taste as the primary source of flavor, in fact, taste and smell collaborate to produce this complex perception. Odorants from substances outside your mouth enter the nasal cavity via the nostrils, and odorants in the mouth enter through the back of the throat. You can easily demonstrate the contribution of smell to flavor by tasting a few different foods while holding your nose, preventing the olfactory system from detecting their odors. If you have a head cold, you probably already know how this turns out. Your favorite spicy burrito or zesty pasta probably tastes as bland as can be.

Taste experiences also vary widely across individuals. About 50% of people report a mildly bitter taste in caffeine, saccharine, certain green vegetables, and other substances, whereas roughly 25% report no bitter taste. Members of the first group are called *tasters*; members of the second group are called *nontasters*. The remaining 25% of people are *supertasters*, who report that such substances, especially dark green vegetables, are extremely bitter, to the point of being inedible (Bartoshuk, 2000). Children start out as tasters or supertasters, which could help explain their early tendency toward fussiness in food preference. There is evidence that genetic factors contribute to individual differences in taste perception (Kim et al., 2003), but much remains to be learned about the specific genes that are involved (Hayes et al., 2008; Reed, 2008).

Cognitive factors can also have a strong effect on taste perception. In one study, participants drank different wines or a control solution, while undergoing fMRI scan (Plassman et al., 2008). The participants were told that they should rate how much they liked each wine. Unbeknownst to the participants, some wines were presented twice: once at their actual price, and once at a marked-up or marked-down price. Results revealed that participants reported liking the same wine better when it was accompanied by a high price than a low price. For the fMRI analysis, the researchers focused on the activity of the medial orbitofrontal cortex (mOFC), a part of the brain located deep inside the frontal lobe that is known to be involved in coding the pleasantness of an experience (Kuhn & Gallinat, 2012). There was greater mOFC activity for a wine presented with a high price than when the same wine was presented with a low price. These results demonstrate clearly that taste experience and associated neural activity can be affected by cognitive influences such as price knowledge.

Fussy eater? Or just too many taste buds? Our taste perception declines with age: We lose about half of our taste receptors by the time we're 20 years old. That can make childhood a time of either savory delight or sensory overload of taste.
Leslie Banks/istockphoto

"We would like to be genetically modified to taste like Brussels sprouts."

Sam Gross/The New Yorker Collection/
Cartoonbank.com

BUILD TO THE OUTCOMES

1. How do the chemical senses differ from the other senses?

2. What is the role of the various parts of the nose in smell?

3. How do taste and smell contribute to flavor?

4. What is the relationship between smell and emotion?

5. How does smell contribute to social behavior?

6. What are the five main types of taste receptors?

7. What are tasters, nontasters, and supertasters?

CHAPTER REVIEW

Sensation and Perception Are Distinct Activities

- Sensation is the simple stimulation of a sense organ, whereas perception organizes, identifies, and interprets sensation at the level of the brain.

- The process of transduction converts physical signals from the environment into neural signals carried by sensory neurons into the central nervous system.

- Psychophysics is an approach to studying perception that measures the strength of a stimulus and an observer's sensitivity to that stimulus. An observer's absolute threshold is the smallest intensity needed to just barely detect a stimulus; the just noticeable difference (JND) is the smallest change in a stimulus that can just barely be detected.

- Sensory adaptation occurs because sensitivity to lengthy stimulation tends to decline over time.

Vision I: The Eyes and the Brain Convert Light Waves to Neural Signals

- Light travels in waves that pass through several layers in the eye to reach the retina.

- Two types of photoreceptor cells in the retina transduce light into neural impulses: cones, which operate under normal daylight conditions and sense color; and rods, which are active under low-light conditions for night vision.

- Information encoded by the retina travels to the brain along the optic nerve, which connects to the lateral geniculate nucleus in the thalamus and then to the primary visual cortex, area V1, in the occipital lobe.

- Two pathways project from the occipital lobe to visual areas in other parts of the brain. The ventral stream travels to areas in the temporal lobes that represent an object's shape and identity. The dorsal stream travels to areas in the parietal lobes that identify the location and motion of an object.

Vision II: Recognizing What We Perceive

- Illusory conjunctions occur when features from separate objects are mistakenly combined. The parietal lobe is important for attention and contributes to feature binding.

- The principle of perceptual constancy holds that even as sensory signals change, perception remains consistent.

- Gestalt principles of perceptual grouping, such as simplicity, closure, and continuity, govern how the features and regions of things fit together.

- Depth perception depends on three types of cues: monocular cues, such as familiar size and linear perspective; binocular cues, such as retinal disparity; and motion-based cues, which are based on the movement of the head over time.

- To sense motion, the visual system encodes information about both space and time.

- Change blindness and inattentional blindness occur when we fail to notice visible and even salient features of our environment, emphasizing that our conscious visual experience depends on focused attention.

Audition: More Than Meets the Ear

- Perceiving sound depends on three physical dimensions of a sound wave: frequency (which determines pitch), amplitude (which determines loudness), and differences in the mix of frequencies (which determines sound quality or timbre).

- Auditory pitch perception begins in the outer ear, which funnels sound waves toward the middle ear, which in turn sends the vibrations to the inner ear, which contains the cochlea.

- Action potentials from the inner ear travel along an auditory pathway through the thalamus to the primary auditory cortex (area A1) in the temporal lobe.

- Auditory perception depends on both a place code and a temporal code. Our ability to localize sound sources depends critically on the placement of our ears on opposite sides of the head.

- Some hearing loss can be overcome with hearing aids that amplify sound. When hair cells are damaged, a cochlear implant is a possible solution.

The Body Senses: More Than Skin Deep

- Sensory receptors on the body send neural signals to locations in the somatosensory cortex, a part of the parietal lobe, which the brain translates as the sensation of touch.
- The experience of pain depends on signals that travel to the somatosensory cortex to indicate the location and type of pain, and to the emotional centers of the brain, which result in unpleasant feelings.
- Balance and acceleration depend primarily on the vestibular system but are also influenced by vision.

The Chemical Senses: Adding Flavor

- Our experience of smell, or olfaction, is associated with odorant molecules binding to sites on specialized olfactory receptors. The olfactory bulb sends signals to parts of the brain that control drives, emotions, and memories.
- Smell is also involved in social behavior, as illustrated by pheromones, which are related to reproductive behavior and sexual responses in several species.
- Sensations of taste depend on taste buds, which are distributed across the tongue, the roof of the mouth, and the upper throat and on taste receptors that correspond to the five primary taste sensations of salt, sour, bitter, sweet, and umami.

KEY CONCEPT QUIZ

1. Sensation involves _____, whereas perception involves _____.
   a. organization; coordination
   b. stimulation; interpretation
   c. identification; translation
   d. comprehension; information

2. What process converts physical signals from the environment into neural signals carried by sensory neurons into the central nervous system?
   a. representation
   b. identification
   c. propagation
   d. transduction

3. The smallest intensity needed to just barely detect a stimulus is called
   a. proportional magnitude.
   b. the absolute threshold.
   c. the just noticeable difference.
   d. Weber's law.

4. The world of light outside the body is linked to the world of vision inside the central nervous system by the
   a. cornea.
   b. lens.
   c. retina.
   d. optic nerve.

5. Light striking the retina, causing a specific pattern of response in the three cone types, leads to our ability to see
   a. motion.
   b. colors.
   c. depth.
   d. shadows.

6. Which part of the brain is the location of the primary visual cortex, where encoded information is systematically mapped into a representation of the visual scene?
   a. the thalamus
   b. the lateral geniculate nucleus
   c. the fovea
   d. area V1

7. Our ability to combine visual details so that we perceive unified objects is explained by
   a. feature-integration theory.
   b. illusory conjunction.
   c. synesthesia.
   d. ventral and dorsal streaming.

8. The idea that specialized brain areas represent particular classes of objects is
   a. the modular view.
   b. attentional processing.
   c. distributed representation.
   d. neuron response.

9. What kind of cues are relative size and linear perspective?
   a. motion-based
   b. binocular
   c. monocular
   d. template

10. What does the frequency of a sound wave determine?
    a. pitch
    b. loudness
    c. sound quality
    d. timbre

11. The placement of our ears on opposite sides of the head is crucial to our ability to
    a. localize sound sources.
    b. determine pitch.
    c. judge intensity.
    d. recognize complexity.

12. The place code works best for encoding
    a. high intensities.
    b. low intensities.
    c. high frequencies.
    d. low frequencies.

13. Which part of the body occupies the greatest area in the somatosensory cortex?

    a. the calves

    b. the lips

    c. the lower back

    d. the hips

14. The location and type of pain we experience is indicated by signals sent to

    a. the amygdala.

    b. the spinal cord.

    c. pain receptors.

    d. the somatosensory cortex.

15. What factor best explains why smells can have immediate and powerful effects?

    a. the involvement in smell of brain centers for emotions and memories

    b. the vast number of olfactory receptor neurons we have

    c. our ability to detect odors from pheromones

    d. the fact that different odorant molecules produce varied patterns of activity

16. People lose about half their taste buds by the time they are

    a. 20.

    b. 40.

    c. 60.

    d. 80.

 **LearningCurve**   Don't stop now! Quizzing yourself is a powerful study tool. Go to LearningCurve at www.launchpadworks.com for more practice.

KEY TERMS

sensation (p. 92)

perception (p. 92)

transduction (p. 92)

psychophysics (p. 92)

absolute threshold (p. 92)

just noticeable difference (JND) (p. 93)

Weber's law (p. 93)

signal detection theory (p. 94)

sensory adaptation (p. 94)

visual acuity (p. 96)

retina (p. 97)

accommodation (p. 97)

cones (p. 97)

rods (p. 97)

fovea (p. 97)

blind spot (p. 98)

area V1 (p. 98)

visual form agnosia (p. 103)

binding problem (p. 104)

illusory conjunction (p. 104)

feature-integration theory (p. 104)

monocular depth cues (p. 107)

binocular disparity (p. 108)

apparent motion (p. 109)

change blindness (p. 110)

inattentional blindness (p. 110)

pitch (p. 112)

loudness (p. 112)

timbre (p. 112)

cochlea (p. 113)

basilar membrane (p. 113)

hair cells (p. 113)

place code (p. 113)

temporal code (p. 113)

area A1 (p. 113)

haptic perception (p. 116)

referred pain (p. 118)

gate-control theory of pain (p. 118)

vestibular system (p. 119)

olfactory receptor neurons (ORNs) (p. 120)

olfactory bulb (p. 121)

pheromones (p. 121)

taste buds (p. 122)

CHANGING MINDS

1. A friend of yours is taking a class in medical ethics. "We discussed a tough case today," she says. "It has to do with a patient who's been in a vegetative state for several years, and the family has to decide whether to take him off life support. The doctors say he has no awareness of himself or his environment, and he is never expected to recover. But when light is shone in his eyes, his pupils contract. That shows he can sense light, so he has to have some ability to perceive his surroundings, doesn't he?" Without knowing any of the details of this particular case, how would you explain to your friend that a patient might be able to sense light but not perceive it? What other examples from the chapter could you use to illustrate the difference between sensation and perception?

2. In your philosophy class, the professor discusses the proposition that "perception is reality." From the point of view of philosophy, reality is the state of things that actually exists, whereas perception is how they appear to the observer. What does psychophysics have to say about this issue? What are three ways in which sensory transduction can alter perception, causing perceptions that may differ from absolute reality?

3. A friend comes across the story of an American soldier, Sergeant Leroy Petry, who received the Medal of Honor for saving the lives of two of his men. The soldiers were in a firefight in Afghanistan when a live grenade landed at their feet; Petry picked up the grenade and tried to toss it away from the others, but it exploded, destroying his right hand. According to the news report, Petry didn't initially feel any pain; instead, he set about applying a tourniquet to his own arm while continuing to shout orders to his men as the firefight continued. "That's amazingly heroic," your friend says, "but that bit about not feeling the pain—that's crazy. He must just be so tough that he kept going despite the pain." What would you tell your friend? How can the perception of pain be altered?

ANSWERS TO KEY CONCEPT QUIZ

1. b; 2. d; 3. b; 4. c; 5. b; 6. d; 7. a; 8. a; 9. c; 10. a; 11. a; 12. c; 13. b; 14. d; 15. a; 16. a.

Consciousness

5

Unconsciousness is something you don't really appreciate until you need it. Belle Riskin needed it one day on an operating table, when she awoke just as doctors were pushing a breathing tube down her throat. She felt she was choking, but she couldn't see, breathe, scream, or move. Unable even to blink an eye, she couldn't signal to the surgeons that she was conscious. "I was terrified," she explained later. "I knew I was conscious, that something was going on during the surgery. I had just enough awareness to know I was being intubated" (Groves, 2004).

How could this happen? Anesthesia for surgery is supposed to leave the patient unconscious, "feeling no pain," and yet in this case—and in about 1 in every 20,000 surgical procedures (Pandit et al., 2014)—the patient regains consciousness at some point. The problem arises because muscle-relaxing drugs are used to keep the patient from moving involuntarily during the operation. But when the drugs that are given to induce unconsciousness fail to do their job, the patient with extremely relaxed muscles is unable to show or tell doctors that there is a problem.

Fortunately, new methods of monitoring wakefulness by measuring the electrical activity of the brain are being developed. One system uses sensors attached to the patient's head and gives readings on a scale from 0 (*no electrical activity in the brain*) to 100 (*fully alert*), providing a kind of "consciousness meter." Anesthesiologists using this index deliver anesthetics to keep the patient in the recommended range of 40 to 60 for general anesthesia during surgery; they have found that this system reduces postsurgical reports of consciousness and memory of the surgical experience (Myles et al., 2004). One of these devices in the operating room might have helped Belle Riskin settle into the unconsciousness she so sorely needed.

MOST OF THE TIME, OF COURSE, CONSCIOUSNESS IS SOMETHING we cherish. **Consciousness** is *a person's subjective experience of the world and the mind.* Although you might think of consciousness as simply "being awake," the defining feature of consciousness is *experience*, which you have when you're awake or when you're having a vivid dream. Conscious experience is essential to what it means to be human. The anesthesiologist's dilemma in trying to monitor Belle Riskin's consciousness is a stark reminder, though, that it is impossible for one person to experience another's consciousness. Your consciousness is utterly private, a world of personal experience that only you can know.

How can this private world be studied? We'll begin by examining consciousness directly, trying to understand what it is like and how it compares with the mind's *unconscious* processes. Then we'll examine altered states of consciousness: sleep and dreams, intoxication with alcohol and other drugs, and hypnosis. Like the traveler who learns the meaning of *home* by roaming far away, we can learn the meaning of *consciousness* by exploring its exotic variations.

consciousness A person's subjective experience of the world and the mind.

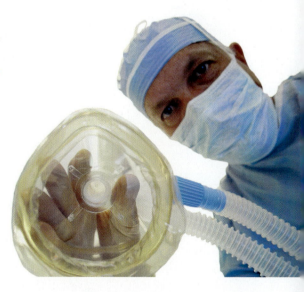

When it's time for surgery, it's great to be unconscious. Masterfile

The Mysteries of Consciousness

phenomenology The study of how things seem to the conscious person.

What does it feel like to be you right now? It probably feels as though you are somewhere inside your head, looking out at the world through your eyes. If you shut your eyes, you may be able to imagine things in your mind, even though all the while thoughts and feelings come and go, passing through your imagination. But where are "you," really? Psychologists want to include **phenomenology**, *how things seem to the conscious person*, in their understanding of mind and behavior. But the theater in your mind doesn't have seating for more than one, making it difficult to share what's on your mental screen with your friends, a researcher, or even yourself in precisely the same way a second time. Let's look at two of the more vexing mysteries of consciousness: the problem of other minds and the mind–body problem.

The Problem of Other Minds

problem of other minds The fundamental difficulty we have in perceiving the consciousness of others.

One great mystery of consciousness is called the **problem of other minds**, *the fundamental difficulty we have in perceiving the consciousness of others.* How do you know that anyone else is conscious? They tell you that they are conscious, of course, and are often willing to describe in depth how they feel, how they think, and what they are experiencing. But perhaps they are just *saying* these things. There is no clear way to distinguish a conscious person from someone who might do and say all the same things as a conscious person but who is *not* conscious.

Even the consciousness meter used by anesthesiologists falls short. It certainly doesn't give the anesthesiologist any special insight into what it is like to be the patient on the operating table; it only predicts whether patients will *say* they were conscious. We simply lack the ability to directly perceive the consciousness of others. In short, *you* are the only thing in the universe you will ever truly know what it is like to be.

The problem of other minds also means there is no way that you can tell if another person's experience is at all like yours. Although you know what the color red looks like to you, for instance, you cannot know whether it looks the same to other people, or how their experience differs from yours. Of course, most people have come to trust each other in describing their inner lives, reaching the general assumption that other human minds are pretty much like their own. But they don't know this for a fact.

How do people perceive other minds? Researchers asked people to compare the minds of 13 different targets, such as a baby, chimp, robot, man, and woman, on 18 different mental capacities, such as feeling pain, pleasure, hunger, and consciousness (Gray, Gray, & Wegner, 2007). The researchers found that people judge minds according to two dimensions: the capacity for *experience* (such as the ability to feel pain, pleasure, hunger, consciousness, anger, or fear) and the capacity for *agency* (such as the ability for self-control, planning, memory, or thought). As shown in **FIGURE 5.1**, respondents rated some targets as having little experience or agency (dead woman), others as having experiences but little agency (baby), and yet others as having both experience and agency (adult humans). Still others were perceived to have agency without experiences (robot). People appreciate that minds both have experiences and lead us to perform actions.

As you'll remember from the Methods chapter, the scientific method requires that any observation made by one scientist should, in principle, be available for observation by any other scientist. But if other minds aren't observable, how can consciousness be a topic of scientific study? One radical solution is to eliminate consciousness from psychology entirely and follow the other sciences into total objectivity by renouncing the study of *anything* mental. This was the solution offered by behaviorism, and it turned out to have its own shortcomings, as you saw in

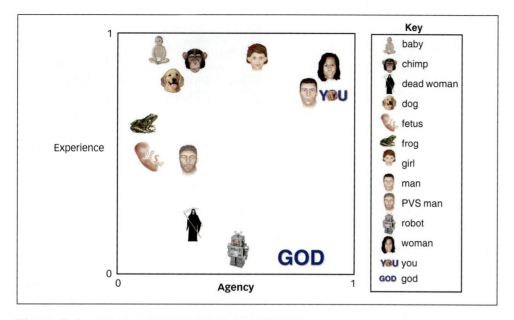

Figure 5.1 DIMENSIONS OF MIND PERCEPTION When participants judged the mental capacities of different targets, they seemed to base decisions on two dimensions of mind perception: the capacity for experience (such as abilities to feel pain or pleasure) and in the capacity for agency (such as abilities to plan or exert self-control) (Gray et al., 2007). They perceived normal adult humans (male, female, or "you," the respondent) to have minds on both dimensions, whereas other targets were perceived to have reduced experience or agency. The man in a persistent vegetative state ("PVS man"), for example, was judged to have only some experience and very little agency. Macmillan Learning

Psychology: Evolution of a Science. Despite the problem of other minds, modern psychology has embraced the study of consciousness. The astonishing richness of mental life simply cannot be ignored.

The Mind–Body Problem

Another mystery of consciousness is the **mind–body problem**, *the issue of how the mind is related to the brain and body.* The French philosopher and mathematician René Descartes (1596–1650) is famous for proposing, among other things, that the human body is a machine made of physical matter but that the human mind or soul is a separate entity made of a "thinking substance." We now know that "the mind is what the brain does" (Minsky, 1986, p. 287).

But Descartes was right in pointing out the difficulty of reconciling the physical body with the mind. Most psychologists assume that mental events are intimately tied to brain events, such that every thought, perception, or feeling is associated with a particular pattern of activation of neurons in the brain (see Neuroscience and Behavior). Thinking about a particular person, for instance, occurs with a unique array of neural connections and activations. If the neurons repeat that pattern, then you must be thinking of the same person.

One telling set of studies, however, suggests that the brain's activities *precede* the activities of the conscious mind. Electrical activity in the brains of volunteers was measured using sensors on their scalps as they repeatedly decided when to move a hand (Libet, 1985). Participants were also asked to indicate exactly when they consciously chose to move by reporting the position of a dot moving rapidly around the face of a clock just at the point of the decision (**FIGURE 5.2a**). As a rule, the brain begins to show electrical activity around half a second before a voluntary action. This makes sense because brain activity certainly seems to be necessary to get an action started. But, as shown in **FIGURE 5.2b**, the electrical activity starts even before

mind–body problem The issue of how the mind is related to the brain and body.

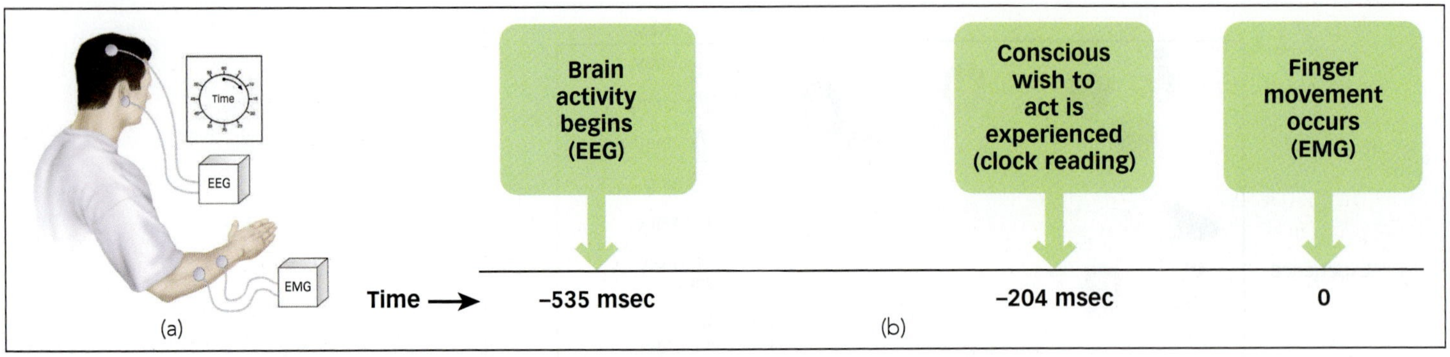

Figure 5.2   THE TIMING OF CONSCIOUS WILL (a) Participants were asked to move fingers at will while watching a dot move around the face of a clock to mark the moment at which the action was consciously willed. Meanwhile, EEG sensors timed the onset of brain activation and EMG sensors timed the muscle movement. (b) The experiment showed that brain activity (EEG) precedes the willed movement of the finger (EMG) but also precedes the reported time of consciously willing the finger to move (Libet, 1985).

the person's conscious decision to move. Although your personal intuition is that you *think* of an action and *then* do it, these experiments suggest that your brain is getting started before *either* the thinking or the doing, preparing the way for both thought and action. Quite simply, it may appear to us that our minds are leading our brains and bodies, but the order of events may be the other way around (Haggard & Tsakiris, 2009; Wegner, 2002).

BUILD TO THE OUTCOMES

1. How do people perceive other minds?

2. How does the capacity for experience differ from the capacity for agency?

3. Which comes first: brain activity or conscious thinking?

The Nature of Consciousness

LEARNING OUTCOMES

- Describe the four basic properties of consciousness.

- Compare the three levels of consciousness.

- Explain why we can't always control our conscious thoughts.

How would you describe your own consciousness? Research suggests that consciousness has four basic properties (intentionality, unity, selectivity, and transience); that it occurs on different levels; and that it includes a range of different contents.

Four Basic Properties

Researchers have identified four basic properties of consciousness, based on people's reports of conscious experience.

1. Consciousness has *intentionality*, which is the quality of being directed toward an object. Consciousness is always *about* something. Despite all the lush detail you see in your mind's eye, the kaleidoscope of sights and sounds and feelings and thoughts, the object of your consciousness at any one moment is focused on just a small part of all of this.

2. Consciousness has *unity*, which is the ability to integrate information from all of the body's senses into one coherent whole (see **FIGURE 5.3**). As you read this book, your five senses are taking in a great deal of information. Your eyes are scanning lots of black squiggles on a page (or screen) while also sensing an enormous array of shapes and colors in your periphery; your hands are gripping a heavy book (or computer); your butt may sense

Figure 5.3   BELLOTTO'S *DRESDEN* AND CLOSEUP (*left*) The people on the bridge in the distance look very finely detailed in *View of Dresden with the Frauenkirche* by Bernardo Bellotto (1720–1780). However, when you examine the detail closely (*right*), you discover that the people are made of brushstrokes merely *suggesting* people. Consciousness produces a similar impression of "filling in" detail even in areas that are peripheral (Dennett, 1991). Dresden from Right Bank of Elbe Upstream from Bridge of Augustus, Circa 1750, by Bernardo Bellotto, Known as Canaletto (1721–1780), Oil on Canvas, 50X84 CM, Detail / De Agostini Picture Library/ A. Dagli Orti / Bridgeman Images

pressure from gravity pulling you against a chair; and you may be listening to music while smelling the odor of your roommate's dirty laundry. Your brain—amazingly—integrates all of this information into the experience of one unified consciousness.

3. Consciousness has *selectivity*, the capacity to include some objects but not others. While binding the many sensations around you into a coherent whole, your mind must make decisions about which pieces of information to include and which to exclude. The conscious system is most inclined to select information of special interest to the person. For example, in what has come to be known as the **cocktail-party phenomenon**, *people tune in one message, even while they filter out others nearby.* Perhaps you have noticed how abruptly your attention is diverted from whatever conversation you are having when someone else within earshot at the party mentions your name.

4. Consciousness has *transience*, or the tendency to change. William James, whom you met way back in Psychology: Evolution of a Science, famously described consciousness as a "stream" (James, 1890)—whirling, chaotic, and constantly changing. The stream of consciousness may flow in this way partly because of the limited capacity of the conscious mind. We humans can hold only so much information in mind, so when we select more information, some of what is currently there must disappear. As a result, our focus of attention keeps changing. The stream of consciousness flows so inevitably that it even changes our perspective when we view a constant object such as a Necker cube (see **FIGURE 5.4**).

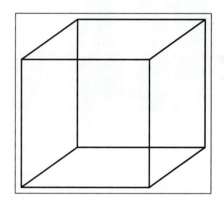

Figure 5.4   THE NECKER CUBE
This cube has the property of reversible perspective in that you can bring one or the other of its two square faces to the front in your mind's eye. Although it may take a while to reverse the figure at first, once people have learned to do it, they can reverse it regularly, about once every 3 seconds (Gomez et al., 1995). The stream of consciousness flows even when the target is a constant object.

cocktail-party phenomenon
A phenomenon in which people tune in one message, even while they filter out others nearby.

Levels of Consciousness

Consciousness can also be understood as having levels, ranging from minimal consciousness to full consciousness to self-consciousness. These levels of consciousness are not a matter of overall brain activity, and so they would probably all register as "conscious" on that wakefulness meter for surgery patients you read about at the beginning of this chapter. Instead, the levels of consciousness involve different qualities of awareness of the world and of the self.

minimal consciousness A low-level kind of sensory awareness and responsiveness that occurs when the mind inputs sensations and may output behavior.

1. **Minimal consciousness** is *a low-level kind of sensory awareness and responsiveness that occurs when the mind inputs sensations and may output behavior* (Armstrong, 1980). This kind of sensory awareness and responsiveness could even happen when someone pokes you while you're asleep and you turn over. Something seems to register in your mind, at least in the sense that you experience it, but you may not think at all about having had the experience. It could be that animals or, for that matter, even plants can have this minimal level of consciousness. But because of the problem of other minds and the notorious reluctance of animals and plants to talk to us, we can't know for sure that they *experience* the things that make them respond.

full consciousness A level of consciousness in which you know and are able to report your mental state.

2. **Full consciousness** occurs when you *know and are able to report your mental state*. Being fully conscious means that you are aware of having a mental state while you are experiencing the mental state itself. Have you ever been driving a car and suddenly realized that you don't remember the past 15 minutes of driving? Chances are that you were not unconscious, but instead minimally conscious. When you are completely aware and thinking about your driving, you have moved into the realm of full consciousness. Full consciousness involves not only thinking about things but also thinking about the fact that you are thinking about things (Jaynes, 1976; see Hot Science: The Mind Wanders).

self-consciousness A distinct level of consciousness in which the person's attention is drawn to the self as an object.

3. **Self-consciousness** is yet another *distinct level of consciousness in which the person's attention is drawn to the self as an object* (Morin, 2006). Most people report experiencing such self-consciousness when they are embarrassed, when they find themselves the focus of attention in a group or a camera, or when they are deeply introspective about their thoughts, feelings, or personal qualities. Looking in a mirror, for example, is all it takes to make people evaluate themselves—not just their looks but also about whether they are good or bad in other ways. People go out of their way to avoid mirrors when they've done something of which they are ashamed (Duval & Wicklund, 1972). However, because it makes people self-critical, the self-consciousness that results when people see their own mirror images can make them briefly more helpful, more cooperative, and less aggressive (Gibbons, 1990).

Full consciousness involves a consciousness of oneself, such as thinking about the act of driving while driving a car. How is this different from self-consciousness? Photomondo/Photodisc/Getty Images

Most animals don't appear to have self-consciousness. However, chimpanzees sometimes behave in ways that suggest they recognize themselves in a mirror. To examine this, researchers painted an odorless red dye over the eyebrow of an anesthetized chimp and then watched when the awakened chimp was presented with a mirror (Gallup, 1977). If the chimp interpreted the mirror image as a representation of some other chimp with an unusual approach to cosmetics, we would expect it just to look at the mirror or perhaps to reach toward it. But the chimp reached toward its *own eye* as it looked into the mirror, suggesting that it recognized the image as a reflection of itself. A few other animals, such as orangutans (Gallup, 1997), possibly dolphins (Reiss & Marino, 2001), and maybe even elephants (Plotnik, de Waal, & Reiss, 2006) and magpies (Prior, Schwartz, & Güntürkün, 2008) recognize their own mirror images. Dogs, cats, crows, monkeys, and gorillas have been tested, too, but don't seem to know they are looking at themselves. Even humans don't have self-recognition right away. Infants don't recognize themselves in mirrors until they've reached about 18 months of age (Lewis & Brooks-Gunn, 1979). The experience of self-consciousness, as measured by self-recognition in mirrors, is limited to a few animals and to humans only after a certain stage of development.

A chimpanzee tried to wipe off the red dye on its eyebrow in the Gallup experiment. This suggests that some animals recognize themselves in the mirror. The Povinelli Group LLC

The Mind Wanders

Yes, the mind wanders. You've no doubt had experiences of reading and suddenly realizing that you have not even been processing what you've read. Even while your eyes are dutifully following the lines of print, at some point you begin to think about something else—and only later catch yourself thinking, where was I? Or, why did I come into this room?

Mind wandering, or the experience of "stimulus-independent thoughts," occurs most often when we are engaged in repetitive, undemanding tasks (Buckner, Andrews-Hanna, & Schacter, 2008). This happens a lot. One study revealed that we engage in mind wandering during nearly half of our daily activities (46.9%), regardless of what we are doing (Killingsworth & Gilbert, 2010; see the figure). Indeed, mind wandering occurred at least 30% of the time in every activity recorded. (The one exception is making love, during which it is apparently rare to have stimulus-independent thoughts.) Although the mind often wanders, this study found that people are significantly less happy when mind wandering compared to when they are thinking about what they are currently doing.

More than that, recent research suggests that many people seriously dislike being alone with their thoughts. In a series of studies, research participants were asked to simply sit alone and think for 6 to 15 minutes (Wilson et al., 2014). Approximately half (49%) reported that they did not enjoy sitting alone with their thoughts. In fact, in one of the studies, 67% of men and 25% of women elected to self-administer electric shocks, rather than sitting quietly alone with their thoughts. It is not clear why sitting alone with one's thoughts is so aversive for some people (that's a question for a future study). Our advice is to keep your mind busy by continuing to read this textbook!

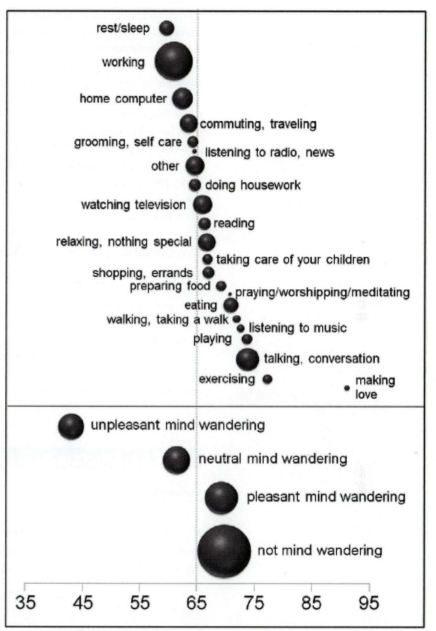

This figure shows data from Killingsworth and Gilbert's (2010) experiment in which people reported on their level of happiness (from 0–100, shown on the x-axis) while engaged in various activities. The size of the bubbles represents the frequency of occurrence. Activities from top to bottom show those associated with the least happiness (rest/sleep) to the most happiness (making love). The bottom part of the figure shows how happy people are while mind wandering—and that they are less happy when mind wandering than not mind wandering. Republished with permission of *Science* from A wandering mind is an unhappy mind, Matthew A. Killingsworth and Daniel T. Gilbert, *330* (932) 2010. Permission conveyed through Copyright Clearance Center.

Conscious Contents

What's on your mind? For that matter, what's on everybody's mind? One way to learn what is on people's minds is to ask them, and much research has called on people simply to *think aloud*. A more systematic approach is the *experience-sampling technique*, in which people are asked to report their conscious experiences at particular times. Equipped with electronic beepers or called on cell phones, for example, participants are asked to record their current thoughts when asked at random times throughout the day (Bolger, Davis, & Rafaeli, 2003).

Experience-sampling studies show that consciousness is dominated by the immediate environment—what we see, feel, hear, taste, and smell. Much of consciousness beyond engaging with one's environment turns to the person's *current concerns*, or what the person is thinking about repeatedly (Klinger, 1975). **TABLE 5.1** shows the results of a study in which 175 college students were asked to report their current concerns (Goetzman, Hughes, & Klinger, 1994). Keep in mind that these concerns are ones the students didn't mind reporting to psychologists; their private preoccupations may have been different and probably far more interesting.

Daydreams: The Brain Is Always Active

Current concerns do not seem all that concerning, however, during *daydreaming*, a state of consciousness in which a seemingly purposeless flow of thoughts comes to mind. When thoughts drift along this way, it may seem as if you are just wasting time. The brain, however, is active, even when it has no specific task at hand. Daydreaming was examined in an fMRI study of people resting in the scanner (Mason et al., 2007). Usually, people in brain-scanning studies don't have time to daydream much because they are kept busy with mental tasks—scans cost money and researchers want to get as much data as possible for their bucks. But when

TABLE 5.1 What's on Your Mind? College Students' Current Concerns		
Current Concern Category	**Example**	**Frequency of Students Who Mentioned the Concern**
Health	Diet and exercise	85%
Household	Clean room	52%
Religion	Attend church more	51%
Education	Go to graduate school	43%
Friends	Make new friends	42%
Family	Gain better relations with immediate family	40%
Social activities	Gain acceptance into a campus organization	34%
Employment	Get a summer job	33%
Roommate	Change attitude or behavior of roommate	29%
Dating	Desire to date a certain person	24%
Sexual intimacy	Abstaining from sex	16%
Government	Change government policy	14%
Finances	Pay rent or bills	8%

Data from: Goetzman, E. S., Hughes, T., & Klinger, E. (1994). *Current concerns of college students in a midwestern sample.* University of Minnesota, Morris.

people are *not* busy, they still show a widespread pattern of activation in many areas of the brain—now known as the *default network* (Gusnard & Raichle, 2001) (see **FIGURE 5.5**). The areas of the default network are known to be involved in thinking about social life, about the self, and about the past and future—all the usual haunts of the daydreaming mind (Mitchell, 2006).

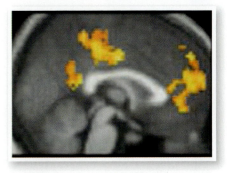

Figure 5.5 THE DEFAULT NETWORK ACTIVATED DURING DAYDREAMING An fMRI scan shows that many areas, known as the default network, are active when the person is not given a specific mental task to perform during the scan (Mason et al., 2007). Republished with permission of *Science* from Wondering minds: The default network and stimulus-independent thought. Mason, Norton, Van Horn, Wegner, Grafton, Macrae, Vol. 315, January 19, 2007, pp. 393–395. Permission conveyed through Copyright Clearance Center.

Efforts to Suppress Current Concerns Can Backfire

The current concerns that populate consciousness can sometimes get the upper hand, transforming daydreams or everyday thoughts into rumination and worry. When this happens, people may exert **mental control**, *the attempt to change conscious states of mind.* For example, someone troubled by a recurring worry about the future ("What if I can't get a decent job when I graduate?") might choose to try *not* to think about this because it causes too much anxiety and uncertainty. Whenever this thought comes to mind, the person engages in **thought suppression**, the *conscious avoidance of a thought.* This may seem like a perfectly sensible strategy because it eliminates the worry and allows the person to move on to think about something else.

Or does it? Daniel Wegner and his colleagues (1987) asked research participants to try *not* to think about a white bear for 5 minutes while they recorded all their thoughts aloud into a tape recorder. In addition, participants were asked to ring a bell if the white bear came to mind. On average, participants mentioned the white bear or rang the bell (indicating the thought) more than once per minute. Thought suppression simply didn't work and instead produced a flurry of returns of the unwanted thought. What's more, when some research participants later were specifically asked to change tasks and deliberately *think* about a white bear, they became oddly preoccupied with it. A graph of their bell rings in **FIGURE 5.6** shows that for these participants, the white bear came to mind far more often than it did for people who had only been asked to think about the bear from the outset, with no prior suppression. This **rebound effect of thought suppression**, *the tendency of a thought to return to consciousness with greater frequency following suppression,* suggests that the act of trying to suppress a thought may itself cause that thought to return to consciousness in a robust way.

mental control The attempt to change conscious states of mind.

thought suppression The conscious avoidance of a thought.

rebound effect of thought suppression The tendency of a thought to return to consciousness with greater frequency following suppression.

ironic processes of mental control A mental process can produce ironic errors because monitoring for errors can itself produce them.

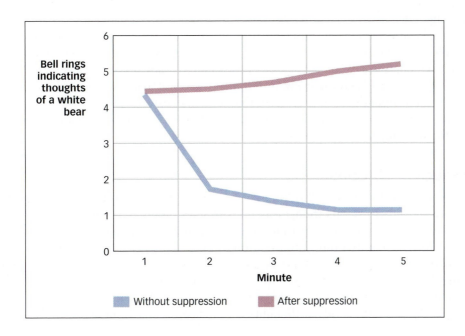

Figure 5.6 REBOUND EFFECT Research participants were first asked to try not to think about a white bear, and to ring a bell whenever it came to mind. Compared with those who were simply asked to think about a bear without prior suppression, those people who *first* suppressed the thought showed a rebound of increased thinking (Wegner et al., 1987).

Go ahead, look away from this book for a minute and try not to think about a white bear. Larry Williams/Corbis

Processes Outside of Consciousness Can Stymie Attempts at Conscious Control

As with thought suppression, other attempts to steer consciousness in any direction can result in mental states that are precisely the opposite of those desired. These ironic effects seem most likely to occur when the person is distracted or under stress. People who are distracted while they are trying to get into a good mood, for example, tend to become sad (Wegner, Erber, & Zanakos, 1993), and those who are distracted while trying to relax actually become more anxious than those who are not trying to relax (Wegner, Broome, & Blumberg, 1997). Likewise, an attempt not to overshoot a golf putt, undertaken during distraction, often yields the unwanted overshot (Wegner, Ansfield, & Pilloff, 1998).

The theory of **ironic processes of mental control** proposes that such *ironic errors occur because the mental process that monitors errors can itself produce them* (Wegner, 1994a, 2009). The irony about the attempt not to think of a white bear, for instance, is that a small part of the unconscious mind is *searching* for the white bear.

BUILD TO THE OUTCOMES

1. How does your mind know which information to allow into consciousness and which to filter out?

2. Which characteristic of full consciousness distinguishes it from minimal consciousness?

3. When do people go out of their way to avoid mirrors?

4. Which animals are also aware of their own reflection in a mirror?

5. What part of the brain is active during daydreaming?

6. Is consciously trying to suppress a worrisome thought an effective strategy?

The Unconscious Mind

LEARNING OUTCOMES

• Compare Freud's conception of the unconscious with the modern view.

There are no conscious steps between hearing an easy problem (what's four plus five?) and thinking of the answer—unless you have to count on your fingers. Fuse/Corbis/Getty Images

dynamic unconscious An active system encompassing a lifetime of hidden memories, the person's deepest instincts and desires, and the person's inner struggle to control these forces.

Many mental processes are unconscious, in the sense that they occur without our experience of them. For example, think for a moment about the mental processes involved in simple addition. What happens in consciousness between hearing a problem (what's four plus five?) and thinking of the answer (nine)? Probably nothing—the answer just appears in the mind. But this is a piece of calculation that must take at least a bit of thinking. After all, at a very young age, you may have had to solve such problems by counting on your fingers. Now that you don't have to do that anymore (please tell me you don't have to do that anymore), the answer seems to pop into your head automatically, by virtue of a process that doesn't require you to be aware of any underlying steps and, for that matter, doesn't even *allow* you to be aware of the steps. The automatic processes operating outside of your conscious awareness are the workings of your unconscious mind.

Freudian Unconscious

As you read in Psychology: Evolution of a Science, Sigmund Freud's psychoanalytic theory viewed conscious thought as the surface of a much deeper mind made up of unconscious processes—but far more than just a collection of hidden processes. Freud described a **dynamic unconscious**—*an active system encompassing a lifetime of hidden memories, the person's deepest instincts and desires, and the person's inner struggle to control these forces.* The dynamic unconscious might contain hidden sexual thoughts about one's parents, for example, or destructive urges aimed at a helpless infant—the kinds of thoughts people keep secret from others and may not even acknowledge to themselves. According to Freud's theory, the unconscious is a force to be held in check by **repression**, *a mental process that removes unacceptable thoughts and memories from consciousness and keeps them in the unconscious.* Without repression, a person might think, do, or say every unconscious impulse or animal urge, no matter how selfish or immoral. With repression, these desires are held in the recesses of the dynamic unconscious.

Freud looked for evidence of the unconscious mind in speech errors and lapses of consciousness, or what are commonly called *Freudian slips.* Forgetting the name of someone you dislike, for example, is a slip that seems to have special meaning. Freud believed that errors are not random and instead have meanings that may have been created by the unconscious mind, even though the person consciously disavows them. For example, while running for president, Hillary Clinton—the wife of former president Bill Clinton—was proposing that former prisoners should not have to check a box when applying for jobs indicating that they had been to prison. She slipped, however, and said that "former presidents [she meant 'prisoners'] won't have to declare their criminal history at the very start of the hiring process." Oops.

Did Secretary Clinton's slip mean anything? Many of the meaningful errors Freud attributed to the dynamic unconscious were not predicted in advance and so seem to depend on clever after-the-fact interpretations. Suggesting a pattern to a series of random events is not the same as scientifically predicting and explaining when and why an event should happen. Anyone can offer a reasonable, compelling explanation for an event after it has already happened, but the true work of science is to offer testable hypotheses that are evaluated based on reliable evidence.

A Modern View of the Cognitive Unconscious

Modern psychologists share Freud's interest in the impact of unconscious mental processes on consciousness and on behavior. However, rather than seeing Freud's vision of the unconscious as a teeming menagerie of animal urges and repressed thoughts, the current study of the unconscious mind views it as a rapid, automatic information processor that influences our thoughts, feelings, and behaviors. The **cognitive unconscious** includes *all the mental processes that give rise to a person's thoughts, choices, emotions, and behavior, even though they are not experienced by the person.*

Our Brains Are Wired for Both Fast and Slow Thinking

Modern views of cognition propose that we have two different types of minds wired into our one little brain. **Dual process theories** suggest that we have *two different systems in our brains for processing information: one dedicated to fast, automatic, and unconscious processing, and the other dedicated to slow, effortful, and conscious processing* (Kahneman, 2011). The fast, automatic system is at work when you effortlessly engage in activities such as reading these words, solving problems such as $2 + 2 =$ __, and walking down the street avoiding people, cars, and other obstacles. You use the slow, effortful system when you rationally and intentionally work to complete a task, such as answering this chapter's quiz questions, solving problems such as $245 \times 32 =$ __, and placing an order at a restaurant.

This dual process perspective is in some ways consistent with Freud's idea of the split between the unconscious and the conscious mind. However, dual process theories do not incorporate all of Freud's beliefs about hidden urges, defense mechanisms, and the like. Instead, they simply propose that we have these two different ways of processing information that draw on different neural pathways. Dual process theories have been used to understand the workings of different cognitive processes such as attention, learning, and memory (for example, see the discussions of implicit and explicit learning and memory in later chapters on these topics), and continue to guide thinking and research in many different areas of psychology.

repression A mental process that removes unacceptable thoughts and memories from consciousness and keeps them in the unconscious.

While campaigning for the presidency, Hillary Clinton accidentally mixed up the words "president" and "prisoner" when talking about people having to talk about their past criminal behavior. This is a textbook example of a Freudian slip, which is why we put it you know where. Cheryl Senter/AP Images

cognitive unconscious All the mental processes that give rise to a person's thoughts, choices, emotions, and behavior, even though they are not experienced by the person.

dual process theories Theories that suggest that we have two different systems in our brains for processing information: one dedicated to fast, automatic, and unconscious processing, and the other dedicated to slow, effortful, and conscious processing.

subliminal perception Thought or behavior that is influenced by stimuli that a person cannot consciously report perceiving.

Behavior Can Be Influenced by Factors Outside of Consciousness

One example of the cognitive unconscious at work occurs when a person's thoughts or behaviors are changed by exposure to information outside of consciousness. This happens in **subliminal perception**, when *thought or behavior is influenced by stimuli that a person cannot consciously report perceiving.* In one classic study, college students completed a survey that called for them to make sentences with various words (Bargh, Chen, & Burrows, 1996). The students were not informed that most of the words were commonly associated with aging (*Florida, gray, wrinkled*), and even afterward they didn't report being aware of this trend. In this case, the "aging" idea wasn't presented subliminally, just not very noticeably. As these research participants left the experiment, they were clocked as they walked down the hall. Compared with those not exposed to the aging-related words, these participants walked more slowly! Just as with subliminal perception, a passing exposure to ideas can influence actions without conscious awareness.

BUILD TO THE OUTCOMES

1. According to Freud, what is the source of unconscious errors in speech?

2. What do dual process theories suggest are the two systems in our brains for processing information?

3. How can a person's thoughts or behaviors be changed by exposure to information outside of consciousness?

Sleep and Dreaming: Good Night, Mind

LEARNING OUTCOMES

- Describe the stages of sleep.
- Identify the types of sleep disorders.
- Compare the two leading theories of why we dream.

altered state of consciousness A form of experience that departs significantly from the normal subjective experience of the world and the mind.

Dreamers, by Albert Joseph Moore (1879/1882) Although their bodies are in the same room, their minds are probably worlds apart. Moore, Albert Joseph/Birmingham Museums and Art Gallery/The Bridgeman Art Library

Sleep can produce a state of unconsciousness in which the mind and brain apparently turn off the functions that create experience: The theater in your mind is closed. But this is an oversimplification, because the theater actually seems to reopen during the night for special shows of bizarre cult films—in other words, dreams. Dream consciousness involves a transformation of experience that is so radical it is commonly considered an **altered state of consciousness**: *a form of experience that departs significantly from the normal subjective experience of the world and the mind.* Such altered states can be accompanied by changes in thinking, disturbances in the sense of time, feelings of the loss of control, changes in emotional expression, alterations in body image and sense of self, perceptual distortions, and changes in meaning or significance (Ludwig, 1966). Sleep and dreams provide two unique perspectives on consciousness: a view of the mind without consciousness and a view of consciousness in an altered state.

Sleep

Consider a typical night. As you begin to fall asleep, the busy, task-oriented thoughts of the waking mind are replaced by wandering thoughts and images and odd juxtapositions, some of them almost dreamlike. This presleep consciousness is called the *hypnagogic state.* On some rare nights, you might experience a *hypnic jerk,* a sudden quiver or sensation of dropping, as though missing a step on a staircase. No one is quite sure why these happen. Eventually, your presence of mind goes away entirely. Time and experience stop, you are unconscious, and in fact there seems to be no "you" there to have experiences. But then come dreams, whole vistas of a vivid and surrealistic consciousness. More patches of unconsciousness may occur, with more dreams here and there. And finally, the glimmerings of waking consciousness return again in a foggy and imprecise form as you enter postsleep consciousness (the *hypnopompic state*) and then awake, often with bad hair.

Sleep Cycle

The sequence of events that occurs during a night of sleep is part of one of the major rhythms of human life, the cycle of sleep and waking. This **circadian rhythm** is *a naturally occurring 24-hour cycle*, from the Latin *circa* (about) and *dies* (day). Even people sequestered in underground buildings without clocks who are allowed to sleep when they want tend to have a rest–activity cycle of about 25.1 hours (Aschoff, 1965). This slight deviation from 24 hours is not easily explained (Lavie, 2001), but it seems to underlie the tendency many people have to want to stay up a little later each night and wake up a little later each day. We're 25.1-hour people living in a 24-hour world.

The sleep cycle is far more than a simple on–off routine, however, as many bodily and psychological processes ebb and flow in this rhythm. EEG (electroencephalograph) recordings reveal a regular pattern of changes in electrical activity in the brain accompanying the circadian cycle. During waking, these changes involve alternation between high-frequency activity (*beta waves*) during alertness and lower-frequency activity (*alpha waves*) during relaxation.

The largest changes in EEG occur during sleep. These changes show a regular pattern over the course of the night corresponding to five sleep stages (see **FIGURE 5.7**). In the first stage of sleep, the EEG moves to frequency patterns even lower than alpha waves (*theta waves*). In the second stage of sleep, these patterns are interrupted by short bursts of activity called *sleep spindles* and *K complexes*, and the

circadian rhythm A naturally occurring 24-hour cycle.

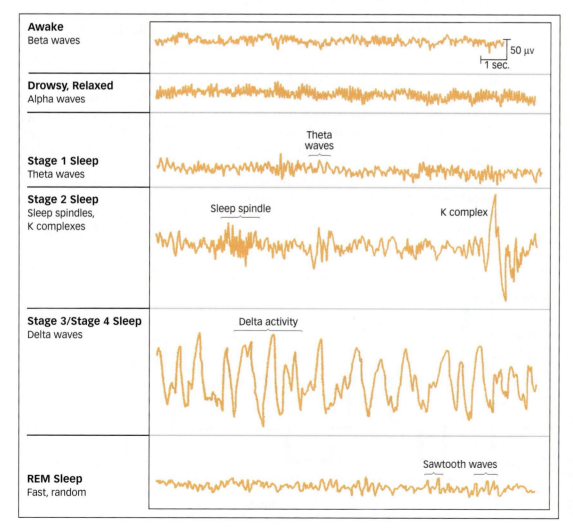

Figure 5.7 EEG PATTERNS DURING THE STAGES OF SLEEP The waking brain shows high-frequency beta wave activity, which changes during drowsiness and relaxation to lower-frequency alpha waves. Stage 1 sleep shows lower-frequency theta waves, whereas stage 2 includes irregular patterns called sleep spindles and K complexes. Stages 3 and 4 are marked by the lowest frequencies, delta waves. During REM sleep, EEG patterns return to higher-frequency sawtooth waves that resemble the beta waves of waking.

REM sleep A stage of sleep characterized by rapid eye movements and a high level of brain activity.

Psychologists learn about what happens when we sleep by recording eye movement, EEG, and other measurements from research volunteers while they sleep in sleep laboratories such as this one. Ronald Frommann/laif/Redux

sleeper becomes somewhat more difficult to awaken. The deepest stages of sleep are stages 3 and 4, known as slow-wave sleep, in which the EEG patterns show activity called *delta waves.*

During the fifth sleep stage, **REM sleep**, *a stage of sleep characterized by rapid eye movements and a high level of brain activity,* EEG patterns become high-frequency sawtooth waves, similar to beta waves, suggesting that the mind at this time is as active as it is during waking (see Figure 5.7). Sleepers wakened during REM periods reported having dreams much more often than those wakened during non-REM periods (Aserinsky & Kleitman, 1953). During REM sleep, the pulse quickens, blood pressure rises, and there are telltale signs of sexual arousal. At the same time, measurements of muscle movements indicate that the sleeper is very still, except for a rapid side-to-side movement of the eyes. (Watch someone sleeping and you may be able to see the REMs through their closed eyelids. But be careful doing this with strangers down at the bus station.) Although many people believe that they don't dream much (if at all), some 80% of people awakened during REM sleep report dreams. If you've ever wondered whether dreams actually take place in an instant or whether they take as long to happen as the events they portray might take, the analysis of REM sleep offers an answer. The sleep researchers William Dement and Nathaniel Kleitman (1957) woke volunteers either 5 minutes or 15 minutes after the onset of REM sleep and asked them to judge, on the basis of the events in the remembered dream, how long they had been dreaming. Sleepers in 92 of 111 cases were correct, suggesting that dreaming occurs in "real time." The discovery of REM sleep has offered many insights into dreaming, but not all dreams occur in REM periods. Some dreams are also reported in other sleep stages, but not as many—and the dreams that occur at those times are described as less wild than REM dreams and more like normal thinking.

Putting EEG and REM data together produces a picture of how a typical night's sleep progresses through cycles of sleep stages (see **FIGURE 5.8**). In the first hour of the night, you fall all the way from waking to the fourth and deepest stage of sleep, the stage marked by delta waves. You then return to lighter sleep stages, eventually reaching REM and dreamland. Note that, although REM sleep is lighter than that of lower stages, it is deep enough that you may be difficult to awaken. You then continue to cycle between REM and slow-wave sleep stages every 90 minutes or so throughout the night. Periods of REM last longer as the night goes on, with the deeper slow-wave stages 3 and 4 disappearing halfway through the night. Although you're either unconscious or dream-conscious at the time, your brain and mind cycle through a remarkable array of different states each time you have a night's sleep.

Figure 5.8 STAGES OF SLEEP DURING THE NIGHT
Over the course of the typical night, sleep cycles into deeper stages early on and then more shallow stages later. REM periods become longer in later cycles, and the deeper slow-wave sleep of stages 3 and 4 disappears halfway through the night.

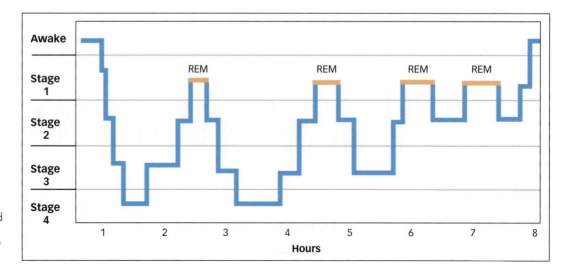

Sleep Needs and Deprivation

How much do people sleep? The answer depends on the age of the sleeper (Dement, 1999). Newborns will sleep 6 to 8 times in 24 hours, often totaling more than 16 hours. Their napping cycle gets consolidated into "sleeping through the night," usually sometime between 9 and 18 months. The typical 6-year-old child might need 11 or 12 hours of sleep, and the average adult needs about 7 to 7.5 hours per night. With aging,  people can get along with a bit less sleep than that. Over a whole lifetime, we get about 1 hour of sleep for every 2 hours we are awake (see Data Visualization: How Does Sleep Affect You? at www.launchpadworks.com). This is a lot of sleeping. Could we tolerate less? For a 1965 science project, 17-year-old Randy Gardner stayed up for 264 hours and 12 minutes. When Randy finally did go to sleep, he slept only 14 hours and 40 minutes and awakened essentially recovered (Dement, 1978).

Feats such as this one suggest that sleep might be expendable. This is the theory behind the classic all-nighter that you may have tried just before a rough exam. But it turns out that this theory is mistaken. When people learning a difficult perceptual task are then kept up all night, their learning of the task is wiped out (Stickgold et al., 2000). It is as though memories normally deteriorate unless sleep occurs to help keep them in place (see Hot Science: Sleep on It, p. 173 in the Memory chapter). Studying all night may help you cram for the exam, but it won't make the material stick, which pretty much defeats the whole purpose.

Sleep turns out to be a necessity rather than a luxury in other ways as well. At the extreme, sleep loss can be fatal. When rats are forced to break Randy Gardner's human waking record and stay awake even longer, they have trouble regulating their body temperature and lose weight although they eat much more than normal. Their bodily systems break down and they die, on average, in 21 days (Rechsthaffen et al., 1983). Even for healthy young humans, a few hours of sleep deprivation each night can have a cumulative detrimental effect: reducing mental acuity and reaction time, increasing irritability and depression, and increasing the risk of accidents and injury (Coren, 1997).

Some researchers have deprived people of different sleep stages selectively by waking them whenever certain stages are detected. Memory problems and excessive aggression are observed in both humans and rats after only a few days of being wakened whenever REM activity starts (Ellman et al., 1991). Such REM deprivation causes a rebound of more REM sleep the next night (Brunner et al., 1990). Deprivation from slow-wave sleep (in stages 3 and 4), in turn, has more physical effects, with just a few nights of deprivation leaving people feeling tired, fatigued, and hypersensitive to muscle and bone pain (Lentz et al., 1999).

It's clearly dangerous to neglect the need for sleep. But why would we have such a need in the first place? All animals appear to sleep, although the amount of sleep required varies quite a bit (see **FIGURE 5.9**). Giraffes sleep less than 2 hours daily, whereas brown bats snooze for almost 20 hours. These variations in sleep needs, and the very existence of a need, are hard to explain. Sleep is, after all, potentially costly in the course of evolution. The sleeping animal is easy prey, so the habit of sleep would not seem to have developed so widely across species unless it had significant benefits that made up for this vulnerability. Theories of sleep have not yet determined why the brain and body have evolved to need these recurring episodes of unconsciousness.

Sleep Disorders

In answer to the question "Did you sleep well?" the comedian Stephen Wright said, "No, I made a couple of mistakes." Sleeping well is something everyone would love to do, but for many people, sleep disorders are deeply troubling. The most common disorders that plague sleep include insomnia, sleep apnea, and somnambulism.

Sleep following learning is essential for memory consolidation. Sleep during class, on the other hand, not so much. Sonda Dawes/The Image Works

Roz Chast/The New Yorker Collection/www. cartoonbank.com

Figure 5.9 COMPARISON OF SLEEP ACROSS SPECIES All animals and insects seem to require sleep, although in differing amounts. Next time you oversleep and someone accuses you of "sleeping like a baby," you might tell them instead that you were sleeping like a tiger, or a brown bat. Ljerka Ilic/Hermera/Thinkstock

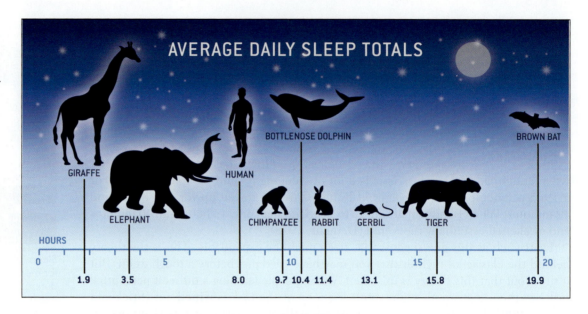

AVERAGE DAILY SLEEP TOTALS

GIRAFFE — ELEPHANT — HUMAN — BOTTLENOSE DOLPHIN — CHIMPANZEE — RABBIT — GERBIL — TIGER — BROWN BAT

HOURS

0 — 5 — 10 — 15 — 20

1.9 3.5 8.0 9.7 10.4 11.4 13.1 15.8 19.9

insomnia Difficulty in falling asleep or staying asleep.

sleep apnea A disorder in which the person stops breathing for brief periods while asleep.

somnambulism (or sleepwalking) Occurs when a person arises and walks around while asleep.

Insomnia, *difficulty in falling asleep or staying asleep*, is perhaps the most common sleep disorder. About 30 to 48% of people report symptoms of insomnia, and 6% of people meet criteria for a diagnosis of insomnia, which involves persistent and impairing sleep problems (Bootzin & Epstein, 2011; Ohayon, 2002). Insomnia has many potential causes. In some instances, it results from lifestyle choices such as working night shifts (self-induced insomnia), whereas in other cases, it occurs in response to depression, anxiety, or some other condition (secondary insomnia). In still other cases, there are no obvious causal factors (primary insomnia). Regardless of type, insomnia can be exacerbated by worrying about insomnia (Borkevec, 1982). No doubt you've experienced some nights when sleeping was a high priority, such as before a class presentation or an important interview, and you've found that you were unable to fall asleep. The desire to sleep initiates an ironic process of mental control—a heightened sensitivity to signs of sleeplessness—and this sensitivity interferes with sleep. Although sedatives can be useful for brief sleep problems associated with emotional events, their long-term use is not effective. Most sleeping pills are addictive, and even in short-term use, sedatives can reduce the proportion of time spent in REM and slow-wave sleep (Qureshi & Lee-Chiong, 2004), robbing people of dreams and their deepest sleep stages. As a result, the quality of sleep achieved with pills may not be as high as without them, and people may experience side effects such as grogginess and irritability during the day.

Sleep apnea is *a disorder in which the person stops breathing for brief periods while asleep.* A person with apnea usually snores because apnea involves an involuntary obstruction of the breathing passage. When episodes of apnea occur for over 10 seconds at a time and recur many times during the night, they may cause many awakenings and sleep loss or insomnia. Apnea occurs most often in middle-aged, overweight men (Punjabi, 2008) and may go undiagnosed because it is not easy for the sleeper to notice. Bed partners may be the ones who finally get tired of the snoring and noisy gasping for air when the sleeper's breathing restarts, or the sleeper may eventually seek treatment because of excessive sleepiness during the day. Therapies involving weight loss, drugs, sleep masks that push air into the nasal passage, or surgery may solve the problem.

Somnambulism (or sleepwalking), occurs when *a person arises and walks around while asleep.* Sleepwalking is more common in children, peaking between the ages of 4 and 8 years, with 15 to 40% of children experiencing at least one episode (Bhargava, 2011). Sleepwalking tends to happen early in the night, usually during slow-wave sleep. Sleepwalkers may awaken during their walk or return to bed without waking, in which case they will probably not remember the episode in the morning. The sleepwalker's eyes are usually open in a glassy stare. Walking with hands outstretched is uncommon except in cartoons. Sleepwalking is problematic only in that sleepwalkers sometimes engage in strange or unwise behaviors such as leaving the house while still sleeping, and they can trip over furniture or fall down stairs. Contrary to popular belief, it is safe to wake sleepwalkers or lead them back to bed.

Other sleep disorders are less common. **Narcolepsy** is *a disorder in which sudden sleep attacks occur in the middle of waking activities.* Narcolepsy is often accompanied by unrelenting excessive sleepiness and uncontrollable sleep attacks lasting from 30 seconds to 30 minutes. This disorder appears to have a genetic basis because it runs in families, and can be treated effectively with medication. **Sleep paralysis** is *the experience of waking up unable to move.* This eerie experience usually happens as you are awakening from REM sleep but before you have regained motor control. This period typically lasts only a few seconds or minutes and can be accompanied by hypnopompic (when awakening) or hypnagogic (when falling asleep) hallucinations in which dream content may appear to occur in the waking world. **Night terrors (or sleep terrors)** are *abrupt awakenings with panic and intense emotional arousal.* These terrors, which occur most often in children and in only about 2% of adults (Ohayon, Guilleminault, & Priest, 1999), happen most often in non-REM sleep early in the sleep cycle and do not usually have dream content the sleeper can report.

To sum up, a lot happens when we close our eyes for the night. Humans follow a pretty regular sleep cycle, going through the five stages of sleep during the night. Disruptions to that cycle, either from sleep deprivation or sleep disorders, can produce consequences for waking consciousness. But something else happens during a night's sleep that affects our consciousness, both while asleep and when we wake up.

Dreams

The pioneering sleep researcher William C. Dement (1959) said, "Dreaming permits each and every one of us to be quietly and safely insane every night of our lives." Indeed, dreams do seem to have a touch of insanity about them. Even more bizarre is the fact that we are the writers, producers, and directors of the crazy things we experience. Just what are these experiences, and how can they be explained?

Dream Consciousness

Dreams depart dramatically from reality. You may dream of being naked in public, of falling from a great height, of sleeping through an important appointment, or of being chased (Holloway, 2001). These things don't happen much in reality unless you're having a terrible, horrible, no good, very bad day. The quality of consciousness in dreaming is also altered significantly from waking consciousness. Five major characteristics of dream consciousness distinguish it from the waking state (Hobson, 1988).

1. We intensely feel *emotion*, whether it is bliss or terror or love or awe.
2. Dream *thought* is illogical: The continuities of time, place, and person don't apply. You may find you are in one place and then another, for example, without any travel in between—or people may change identity from one dream scene to the next.
3. *Sensation* is fully formed and meaningful; visual sensation is predominant, and you may also deeply experience sound, touch, and movement (although pain is very uncommon).

Sleepwalkers in cartoons have their arms outstretched and eyes closed, but that's just for cartoons. A real-life sleepwalker usually walks normally with eyes open, sometimes with a glassy look. esthAlto/Matthieu Spohn/ PhotoAlto Agency RF Collections/Getty Images

narcolepsy A disorder in which sudden sleep attacks occur in the middle of waking activities.

sleep paralysis The experience of waking up unable to move.

night terrors (or sleep terrors) Abrupt awakenings with panic and intense emotional arousal.

Dreams often are quite intense, vivid, and illogical. This can lead to very cool experiences, such as that depicted in this scene from the movie *Inception.* Warner Bros/The Kobal Collection/Art Resource

***The Nightmare*, by Henry Fuseli (1790).** Fuseli depicts not only a mare in this painting but also an incubus—an imp perched on the dreamer's chest that is traditionally associated with especially horrifying nightmares. Goethe House and Museum/Snark/Art Resource, NY

4. Dreaming occurs with *uncritical acceptance*, as though the images and events are perfectly normal rather than bizarre.

5. We have *difficulty remembering* the dream after it is over. People often remember dreams only if they are awakened during the dream and may lose recall for the dream within just a few minutes of waking.

Not all of our dreams are fantastic and surreal, however. We often dream about mundane topics that reflect prior waking experiences or "day residue." Current conscious concerns pop up (Nikles et al., 1998), along with images from the recent past. For instance, after a fun day at the beach with your roommates, your dream that night might include cameo appearances by bouncing beach balls or a flock of seagulls. The content of dreams takes snapshots from the day, rather than retelling the stories of what you have done or seen. This means that dreams often come without clear plots or story lines, so they may not make a lot of sense.

Some of the most memorable dreams are nightmares, and these frightening dreams can wake up the dreamer (Levin & Nielsen, 2009). One set of daily dream logs from college undergraduates suggested that the average student has about 24 nightmares per year (Wood & Bootzin, 1990), although some people may have them as often as every night. Children have more nightmares than do adults, and people who have experienced traumatic events are inclined to have nightmares that relive those events.

Dream Theories

Dreams are puzzles that cry out to be solved. The search for dream meaning goes all the way back to biblical figures, who interpreted dreams and looked for prophecies in them. In the Old Testament, the prophet Daniel (a favorite of three of the authors of this book) curried favor with King Nebuchadnezzar of Babylon by interpreting the king's dream. Unfortunately, the meaning of dreams is usually far from obvious.

In the first psychological theory of dreams, Freud (1900/1965) proposed that dreams are confusing and obscure because the dynamic unconscious creates them precisely *to be* confusing and obscure. According to Freud's theory, dreams represent wishes, and some of these wishes are so unacceptable, taboo, and anxiety producing that the mind can express them only in disguised form. For example, a dream about a tree burning down in the park across the street from where a friend once lived might represent a camouflaged wish for the death of the friend. In this case, wishing for the death of a friend is unacceptable, so it is disguised as a tree on fire. The problem with Freud's approach is that any dream has an infinite number of potential interpretations. Finding the correct one is a matter of guesswork—and of convincing the dreamer that one interpretation is superior to the others.

Although dreams may not represent elaborately hidden wishes, there is evidence that they do feature the return of suppressed thoughts. Researchers asked volunteers to think of a personal acquaintance and then to spend five minutes before going to bed writing down whatever came to mind (Wegner, Wenzlaff, & Kozak, 2004). Some participants were asked to suppress thoughts of this person as they wrote, others were asked to focus on thoughts of the person, and yet others were asked just to write freely about anything. The next morning, participants wrote dream reports. Overall, all participants mentioned dreaming more about the person they had named than about other people. But they most often dreamed of the person they named if they were in the group that had been assigned to suppress thoughts of the person the night before. This finding suggests that Freud was right to suspect that dreams harbor unwanted thoughts. Perhaps this is why actors dream of forgetting their lines, travelers dream of getting lost, and football players dream of fumbling the ball.

Another key theory of dreaming is the **activation–synthesis model** (Hobson & McCarley, 1977), which proposes that *dreams are produced when the brain attempts to make sense of random neural activity that occurs during sleep.* During waking consciousness, the mind is devoted to interpreting lots of information that arrives through the senses. You figure out that the odd noise you're hearing during class is your cell phone vibrating, for example, or that the strange smell must be from burned popcorn. In the dream state, the mind doesn't have access to external sensations, but it keeps on doing what it usually does: interpreting information. Because that information now comes from neural activations that occur without the continuity provided by the perception of reality, the brain's interpretive mechanisms can run free. This might be why, for example, a person in a dream can sometimes change into someone else. No actual person is being perceived to help the mind keep a stable view. In the mind's effort to perceive and give meaning to brain activation, the person you view in a dream about a grocery store might seem to be a clerk but then change to be your favorite teacher when the dream scene moves to your school. The great interest people have in interpreting their dreams the next morning may be an extension of the interpretive activity they've been doing all night.

The Freudian theory and the activation–synthesis theory differ in the significance they place on the meaning of dreams. In Freud's theory, dreams begin with meaning, whereas in the activation–synthesis theory, dreams begin randomly—but meaning can be added as the mind lends interpretations in the process of dreaming. Dream research has not yet sorted out whether one of these theories or yet another might be the best account of the meaning of dreams.

The Dreaming Brain

What happens in the brain when we dream? Several fMRI studies show that brain changes during REM sleep correspond clearly with alterations of consciousness that occur in dreaming. **FIGURE 5.10** shows some of the patterns of activation and deactivation found in the dreaming brain (Nir & Tononi, 2010; Schwartz & Maquet, 2002). Many dreams have emotional content: dangerous people lurking, the occasional monster, some minor worries, and that major exam you've forgotten about until you walk into class. And, as it turns out, the amygdala, which is involved in responses to threatening or stressful events, is quite active during REM sleep. However, even though the typical dream is a visual wonderland, the areas of the brain responsible for visual perception are *not* activated during dreaming. Instead, the visual association areas in the occipital lobe that are responsible for

Freud theorized that dreams represent unacceptable wishes that the mind can only express in disguised form. The activation–synthesis model proposes that dreams are produced when the mind attempts to make sense of random neural activity that occurs during sleep. Suppose that a man is expecting a visit from his mother-in-law; the night before her arrival, he dreams that a bus is driven through the living room window of his house. How might Freud have interpreted such a dream? How might the activation–synthesis model interpret such a dream? Barbara L. Salisbury/The Washington Times/Landov

activation–synthesis model The theory that dreams are produced when the brain attempts to make sense of random neural activity that occurs during sleep.

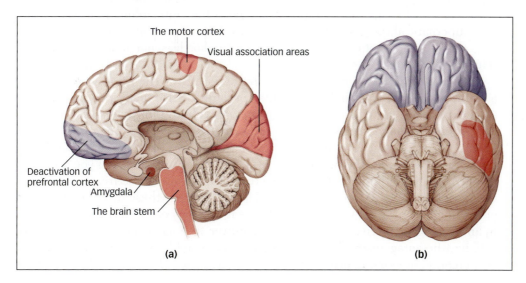

The motor cortex

Visual association areas

Deactivation of prefrontal cortex

Amygdala

The brain stem

(a) **(b)**

Figure 5.10 BRAIN ACTIVATION AND DEACTIVATION DURING REM SLEEP Brain areas shaded red are activated during REM sleep; those shaded blue are deactivated. (a) The medial view shows activation of the amygdala, the visual association areas, the motor cortex, and the brain stem and deactivation of the prefrontal cortex. (b) The ventral view shows activation of other visual association areas and deactivation of the prefrontal cortex (Schwartz & Maquet, 2002).

visual imagery *do* show activation (Braun et al., 1998). Your brain is smart enough to realize that it's not really seeing bizarre images but acts instead as though it's imagining bizarre images. Meanwhile, the prefrontal cortex—usually associated with planning and executing actions—shows *less* arousal during REM sleep than it usually does during waking consciousness. Perhaps this is why dreams often seem to be unplanned and rambling.

Another odd fact of dreaming is that, although the eyes are moving rapidly, the body is otherwise very still. During REM sleep, the motor cortex is activated, but spinal neurons running through the brain stem inhibit the expression of this motor activation (Lai & Siegal, 1999). This turns out to be a useful property of brain activation in dreaming; otherwise, you might get up and act out every dream! People who are moving during sleep are probably not dreaming. The brain specifically inhibits movement during dreams, perhaps to keep us from hurting ourselves.

BUILD TO THE OUTCOMES

1. What do EEG recordings tell us about sleep?

2. What are the stages in a typical night's sleep?

3. What is the relationship between sleep and learning?

4. What are some problems caused by sleeping pills?

5. Is it safe to wake a sleepwalker?

6. What distinguishes dream consciousness from the waking state?

7. According to Freud, what do dreams represent?

8. What does the activation–synthesis model propose about the link between the brain and dreams?

9. What do fMRI studies tell us about why dreams don't have coherent story lines?

Drugs and Consciousness: Artificial Inspiration

LEARNING OUTCOMES

- Explain the dangers of addiction.

- Identify categories of psychoactive drugs and their effects on the body.

psychoactive drugs Chemicals that influence consciousness or behavior by altering the brain's chemical message system.

The author of the dystopian novel *Brave New World*, Aldous Huxley (1932), once wrote of his experiences with the drug mescaline. *The Doors of Perception* described "a world where everything shone with the Inner Light, and was infinite in its significance. The legs, for example, of a chair—how miraculous their tubularity, how supernatural their polished smoothness! I spent several minutes—or was it several centuries?—not merely gazing at those bamboo legs, but actually *being* them" (Huxley, 1954, p. 22).

Being the legs of a chair? This probably is better than being the seat of a chair, but it still sounds like an odd experience. Still, many people seek out such experiences, often through using drugs. **Psychoactive drugs** are *chemicals that influence consciousness or behavior by altering the brain's chemical message system.* You read about several such drugs in the Neuroscience and Behavior chapter when we explored the brain's system of neurotransmitters. And you will read about them in a different light when we turn to their role in the treatment of psychological disorders in the Treatment chapter. Whether these drugs are used for entertainment, for treatment, or for other reasons, they each exert their influence by increasing the activity of a neurotransmitter (the agonists) or decreasing its activity (the antagonists). Like Huxley, who perceived himself becoming the legs of a chair, people using drugs can have experiences unlike any they might find in normal waking consciousness or even in dreams. To understand these altered states, let's explore how people use and abuse drugs, and examine the major categories of psychoactive drugs.

Drug Use and Abuse

Why do children sometimes spin around until they get dizzy and fall down? There is something strangely attractive about states of consciousness that depart from the norm, and people throughout history have sought out these altered states by dancing, fasting, chanting, meditating, and ingesting a bizarre assortment of chemicals to intoxicate themselves (Tart, 1969). People pursue altered consciousness even when there are costs, from the nausea that accompanies dizziness to the life-wrecking obsession with a drug that can come with addiction. In this regard, the pursuit of altered consciousness can be a fatal attraction.

In one study researchers allowed rats to administer cocaine to themselves intravenously by pressing a lever (Bozarth & Wise, 1985). Over the course of the 30-day study, the rats not only continued to self-administer at a high rate but also occasionally binged to the point of giving themselves convulsions. They stopped grooming themselves and eating until they lost on average almost a third of their body weight. About 90% of the rats died by the end of the study. Rats are not tiny little humans, of course, so such research is not a firm basis for understanding human responses to cocaine. But these results do make it clear that cocaine is addictive and that the consequences of such addiction can be dire.

Other laboratory studies show that animals will work to obtain not only cocaine but also alcohol, amphetamines, barbiturates, caffeine, opiates (such as morphine and heroin), nicotine, phencyclidine (PCP), MDMA (Ecstasy), and THC (tetrahydrocannabinol, the active ingredient in marijuana).

Dangers of Addiction

People usually do not become addicted to a psychoactive drug the first time they use it. They may experiment a few times, then try again, and eventually find that their tendency to use the drug increases over time. Three primary factors are influential:

1. **Drug tolerance** is *the tendency for larger drug doses to be required over time to achieve the same effect.* Physicians who prescribe morphine to control pain in their patients are faced with tolerance problems because steadily greater amounts of the drug may be needed to dampen the same pain. With increased tolerance comes the danger of drug overdose; recreational users find they need to use more and more of a drug to produce the same high. But then, if a new batch of heroin or cocaine is more concentrated than usual, the "normal" amount the user takes to achieve the same high can be fatal.

2. *Physical dependence* is the pain, convulsions, hallucinations, or other unpleasant symptoms that accompany withdrawal from drug use. People who suffer from physical dependence may seek to continue drug use to avoid becoming physically ill. A common example is the "caffeine headache" some people complain of when they haven't had their daily jolt of java.

3. *Psychological dependence* is a strong desire to return to the drug even when physical withdrawal symptoms are gone. Drugs can create an emotional need over time that continues to prey on the mind, particularly in circumstances that are reminders of the drug. Some ex-smokers report longing wistfully for an after-dinner smoke, for example, even years after they've successfully quit the habit.

The psychological and social problems stemming from drug addiction are immense. For many people, drug addiction becomes a way of life, and for some,

Why do kids enjoy spinning around until they get so dizzy that they fall down? Even when we are young, there seems to be something enjoyable about altering states of consciousness. Matthew Nock

drug tolerance The tendency for larger doses of a drug to be required over time to achieve the same effect.

Many soldiers serving in Vietnam became addicted to heroin while there. Robins and colleagues (1980) found that, after returning home to the United States, the vast majority left their drug habit behind and were no longer addicted. Bettmann/Corbis

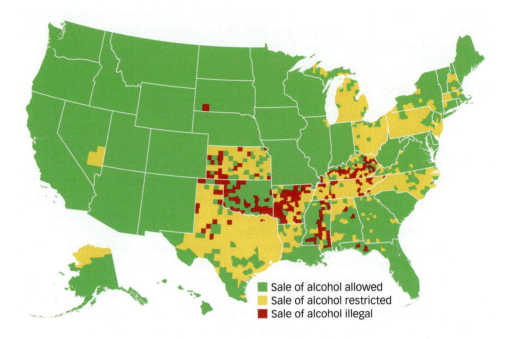

Sale of alcohol allowed
Sale of alcohol restricted
Sale of alcohol illegal

The production, sale, and transportation of alcohol was made illegal in the United States in 1920. This period of "prohibition" ended in 1933 due to social and economic pressures. Although most U.S. counties allow the sale of alcohol (shown on the map in green), there are still many counties where there are laws restricting alcohol sales (shown in yellow) and even some "dry" counties where selling alcohol is illegal (shown in red). Why might the prohibition of alcohol have failed nationally? SZ Photo/Scherl/Sueddeutsche Zeitung Photo/Alamy

it is a cause of death. Like the cocaine-addicted rats in the study noted earlier (Bozarth & Wise, 1985), some people become so attached to a drug that their lives are ruled by it. But a life of addiction is not the only possible end point of drug use. In fact, one study found that 64% of a sample of people who had a history of cigarette smoking had quit successfully, although many had to try again and again to achieve success (Schachter, 1982). Large-scale studies consistently show that approximately 75% of those with substance use disorders overcome their addiction (Heyman, 2009).

What's Considered "Addictive" Can Change

It may not be accurate to view all recreational drug use under the umbrella of "addiction." Many people would not call the repeated use of caffeine an addiction, and some do not label the use of alcohol, tobacco, or marijuana in this way. In other times and places, however, each of these has been considered a terrifying addiction worthy of prohibition and public censure. In the early 17th century, for example, tobacco use was punishable by death in Germany, by castration in Russia, and by decapitation in China (Corti, 1931). By contrast, cocaine, heroin, marijuana, and amphetamines have each been popular and even recommended as medicines at several points throughout history, each without any stigma of addiction attached (Inciardi, 2001).

Societies react differently at different times, with some uses of drugs ignored, other uses encouraged, others simply taxed, and yet others subjected to intense prohibition (see the Real World: Drugs and the Regulation of Consciousness). Rather than viewing *all* drug use as a problem, we need to consider the costs and benefits of such use and to establish ways to help people choose behaviors that are informed by this knowledge (Parrott et al., 2005).

Types of Psychoactive Drugs

Four in five North Americans use caffeine in some form every day, but not all psychoactive drugs are this familiar. To learn how both the well-known and lesser-known drugs influence the mind, let's consider five broad categories of drugs:

→ Drugs and the Regulation of Consciousness

Everyone has an opinion about drug use. Is consciousness something that governments should be able to legislate? Or should people be free to choose their own conscious states?

Many people suggest that we should answer these questions by considering the costs of drug addiction, both to the addict and to the society that must "carry" unproductive people, pay for their welfare, and often even take care of their children. Drug users appear to be troublemakers and criminals, responsible for drug-related shootings, knifings, and robberies. Widespread anger about the drug problem surfaced in the form of the War on Drugs, a federal government program born in the 1970s that focused on drug use as a criminal offense and attempted to stop drug use through the imprisonment of users.

Drug use did not stop, though, and instead, prisons filled with people arrested for drug use. From 1990 to 2007, the number of drug offenders in state and federal prisons nearly doubled, from 179,070 to 348,736 (Bureau of Justice Statistics, 2008)—not because of an increase in drug use but because of the increasing use of imprisonment for drug offenses. The drug war seemed to be causing more harm than it was preventing.

What can be done? The policy of the Obama administration was to wind down the war and instead adopt a *harm reduction approach*, focusing on reducing the harm such behaviors have on people's lives (Marlatt & Witkiewitz, 2010). Harm reduction promotes tactics such as eliminating criminal penalties for some drug use or providing intravenous drug users with sterile syringes to help them avoid contracting HIV and other infections from shared needles (Des Jarlais et al., 2009). A harm reduction idea for alcoholics, in turn, is not to condemn their drinking behavior but to allow moderate drinking while minimizing the harmful effects of heavy drinking (Marlatt & Witkiewitz, 2010). Harm reduction strategies do not always find public support because they challenge the popular idea that the solution to drug and alcohol problems must always be prohibition: stopping use entirely.

There appears to be increasing support for the idea that people should be free to decide whether they want to use substances to alter their consciousness, especially when use of the substance carries a medical benefit, such as decreased nausea, decreased insomnia, and increased appetite. Since 1996, 18 states and the District of Columbia have enacted laws to legalize the use of marijuana for medical purposes. In 2012, Colorado and Washington became the first two states to legalize marijuana for purely recreational purposes, followed shortly thereafter by Oregon and the District of Columbia. Indeed, whereas only 12% of U.S. citizens in 1969 believed that marijuana should be legal, by 2015 that number had risen to 58% (Gallup, 2015).

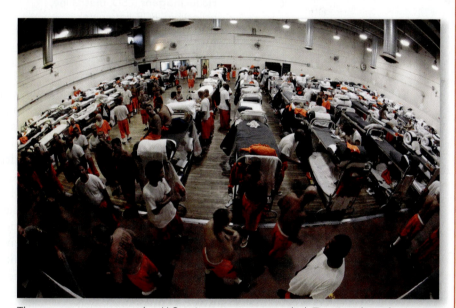

There are many reasons that U.S. prisons are overcrowded. Treating drug abuse as a crime that requires imprisonment is one of the reasons. REUTERS/Lucy Nicholson/Corbis

depressants, stimulants, narcotics, hallucinogens, and marijuana. **TABLE 5.2** summarizes what is known about the potential dangers of these different types of drugs.

Depressants

Depressants are *substances that reduce the activity of the central nervous system.* Depressants have a sedative or calming effect, tend to induce sleep in high doses, and can arrest breathing in extremely high doses. Depressants can produce both physical and psychological dependence.

depressants Substances that reduce the activity of the central nervous system.

TABLE 5.2 Dangers of Drugs

Drug	Dangers		
	Overdose (Can taking too much cause death or injury?)	Physical Dependence (Will stopping use make you sick?)	Psychological Dependence (Will you crave it when you stop using it?)
Depressants			
Alcohol	X	X	X
Benzodiazepines/Barbiturates	X	X	X
Toxic inhalants	X	X	X
Stimulants			
Amphetamines	X	X	X
MDMA (Ecstasy)	X		?
Nicotine	X	X	X
Cocaine	X	X	X
Narcotics (opium, heroin, morphine, methadone, codeine)	X	X	X
Hallucinogens (LSD, mescaline, psilocybin, PCP, ketamine)	X		?
Marijuana		?	?

The most commonly used depressant is *alcohol*, the "king of the depressants," with its worldwide use beginning in prehistory, its easy availability in most cultures, and its widespread acceptance as a socially approved substance. Fifty-two percent of Americans over 12 years of age report having had a drink in the past month, and 24% have binged on alcohol (over five drinks in succession) in that time. Young adults (ages 18–25) have even higher rates, with 62% reporting a drink the previous month and 42% reporting a binge (National Center for Health Statistics, 2012).

Alcohol's initial effects, euphoria and reduced anxiety, feel pretty positive. As alcohol is consumed in greater quantities, drunkenness results, bringing slowed reactions, slurred speech, poor judgment, and other reductions in the effectiveness of thought and action. The exact way in which alcohol influences neural mechanisms is still not understood, but like other depressants, alcohol increases activity of the neurotransmitter GABA (De Witte, 1996). As you read in the Neuroscience and Behavior chapter, GABA normally inhibits the transmission of neural impulses, and so one effect of alcohol is to stop the firing of other neurons. But there are many contradictions. Some people using alcohol become loud and aggressive, others become emotional and weepy, others become sullen, and still others turn giddy—and the same person can experience each of these effects in different circumstances. How can one drug do this? Two theories have been offered to account for these variable effects: *expectancy theory* and *alcohol myopia*.

expectancy theory The idea that alcohol effects can be produced by people's expectations of how alcohol will influence them in particular situations.

1. **Expectancy theory** suggests that *alcohol effects can be produced by people's expectations of how alcohol will influence them in particular situations* (Marlatt & Rohsenow, 1980). So, for instance, if you've watched friends or family drink at weddings and notice that this often produces hilarity and gregariousness, you could well experience these effects yourself should you drink alcohol on a similarly festive occasion. Seeing people getting drunk and fighting in bars, in turn, might lead to aggression after drinking. Evidence for expectancy theory has been obtained in studies where

participants are given drinks containing alcohol or a substitute liquid (adjusted for scent and color). Some people in each group are led to believe they had alcohol and others are led to believe they did not. These experiments often show that the belief that one has had alcohol can influence behavior as strongly as the ingestion of alcohol itself (Goldman, Brown, & Christiansen, 1987).

2. The theory of **alcohol myopia** proposes that *alcohol hampers attention, leading people to respond in simple ways to complex situations* (Steele & Josephs, 1990). This theory recognizes that life is filled with complicated pushes and pulls, and our behavior is often a balancing act. Imagine that you are really attracted to someone who is dating your friend. Do you make your feelings known or focus on your friendship? The myopia theory holds that when you drink alcohol, your fine judgment is impaired. It becomes hard to appreciate the subtlety of these different options, and the inappropriate response is to veer full tilt one way or the other.

Which theory, expectancy theory or alcohol myopia, views a person's response to alcohol as being (at least partially) learned? Lise Gagne/E+/Getty Images

alcohol myopia A condition that results when alcohol hampers attention, leading people to respond in simple ways to complex situations.

Both the expectancy and myopia theories suggest that people using alcohol will often go to extremes (Cooper, 2006). In fact, drinking is a major contributing factor to social problems that result from extreme behavior. Drinking while driving is a major cause of auto accidents. Twenty-two percent of drivers involved in fatal car crashes in 2009 had a blood alcohol level of .08% or higher (U.S. Census Bureau, 2012). Alcohol also has been linked to increased aggression toward others, including sexual violence and intimate partner violence (Crane et al., 2015).

Compared with alcohol, the other depressants are much less popular but still are widely used and abused. *Barbiturates* such as Seconal or Nembutal are prescribed as sleep aids and as anesthetics before surgery. *Benzodiazepines* such as Valium and Xanax are prescribed to treat anxiety or sleep problems. Physical dependence is possible because withdrawal from long-term use can produce severe symptoms (including convulsions), and psychological dependence is common as well. Finally, *toxic inhalants* are easily accessible, even to children, in the vapors of household products such as glue, hair spray, nail polish remover, or gasoline. Sniffing or "huffing" vapors from these products can promote temporary effects that resemble drunkenness, but overdoses can be lethal, and continued use holds the potential for permanent neurological damage (Howard et al., 2011).

Stimulants

Stimulants are *substances that excite the central nervous system, heightening arousal and activity levels.* They include caffeine, amphetamines, Ecstasy, cocaine, and nicotine, and they sometimes have a legitimate pharmaceutical purpose. Amphetamines (also called *speed*), for example, were originally prepared for medicinal uses and as diet drugs; however, amphetamines such as Methedrine and Dexedrine are widely abused, causing insomnia, aggression, and paranoia with long-term use. Stimulants increase the levels of dopamine and norepinephrine in the brain, increasing alertness and energy in the user, often producing a euphoric sense of confidence and a kind of agitated motivation to get things done. Stimulants produce physical and psychological dependence, and their withdrawal symptoms involve depressive effects such as fatigue and negative emotions.

stimulants Substances that excite the central nervous system, heightening arousal and activity levels.

Ecstasy (also known as MDMA, "X," or "E") is an amphetamine derivative. Ecstasy can make users feel empathic and close to those around them, but it has unpleasant side effects, such as interfering with the regulation of body temperature, making users highly susceptible to heat stroke and exhaustion. Although Ecstasy is not so likely as some other drugs to cause physical or psychological dependence, it nonetheless can lead to some dependence. What's more, the impurities sometimes found in street pills are also dangerous (Parrott, 2001). Ecstasy's potentially toxic effect on serotonin neurons in the human brain is under debate, although mounting evidence from animal and human studies suggests that sustained use is associated

People will often endure significant inconveniences to maintain their addictions. Angel Franco/The New York Times/Redux Pictures

with damage to serotonergic neurons and potentially associated problems with mood, attention and memory, and impulse control (Kish et al., 2010; Urban et al., 2012).

Cocaine is derived from leaves of the coca plant, which has been cultivated by indigenous peoples of the Andes for millennia and chewed as a medication. Yes, the urban legend is true: Coca-Cola contained cocaine until 1903 and still may use coca leaves (with cocaine removed) as a flavoring—although the company's not telling. (Pepsi-Cola never contained cocaine and is probably made from something brown.) Sigmund Freud tried cocaine and wrote effusively about it for a while. Cocaine (usually snorted) and crack cocaine (smoked) produce exhilaration and euphoria and are seriously addictive, both for humans and the rats you read about earlier in this chapter. Withdrawal takes the form of an unpleasant crash, and dangerous side effects of cocaine use include both psychological problems such as insomnia, depression, aggression, and paranoia, as well as physical problems such as death from a heart attack or hyperthermia (Marzuk et al., 1998). Although cocaine has enjoyed popularity as a party drug, its extraordinary potential to create dependence and potentially lethal side effects should be taken very seriously.

Nicotine is something of a puzzle. This is a drug with almost nothing to recommend it to the newcomer. It usually involves inhaling smoke that doesn't smell that great, and there's not much in the way of a high either—at best, some dizziness or a queasy feeling. So why do people use it? Tobacco use is motivated far more by the unpleasantness of quitting than by the pleasantness of using. The positive effects people report from smoking—relaxation and improved concentration, for example—come chiefly from relief from withdrawal symptoms (Baker, Brandon, & Chassin, 2004). The best approach to nicotine is to never get started.

Narcotics

narcotics (or opiates) Highly addictive drugs derived from opium that relieve pain.

Opium, which comes from poppy seeds, and its derivatives heroin, morphine, methadone, and codeine (as well as prescription drugs such as Demerol and OxyContin), are known as **narcotics (or opiates)**, *highly addictive drugs derived from opium that relieve pain.* Narcotics induce a feeling of well-being and relaxation that is enjoyable but can also induce stupor and lethargy. The addictive properties of narcotics are powerful, and long-term use produces both tolerance and dependence. Because these drugs are often administered with hypodermic syringes, they also introduce the danger of diseases such as HIV when users share syringes. Unfortunately, these drugs are especially alluring because they mimic the brain's own internal relaxation and well-being system.

The brain produces endogenous opioids or endorphins, which are neuropeptides closely related to opiates. As you learned in the Neuroscience and Behavior chapter, endorphins play a role in how the brain copes internally with pain and stress. These substances reduce the experience of pain naturally. When you exercise for a while and start to feel your muscles burning, for example, you may also find that a time comes when the pain eases—sometimes even *during* exercise. Endorphins are secreted in the pituitary gland and other brain sites as a response to injury or exertion, creating a kind of natural remedy, sometimes referred to as "runner's high" that subsequently reduces pain and increases feelings of well-being. When people use narcotics, the brain's endorphin receptors are artificially flooded, however, reducing receptor effectiveness and possibly also depressing the production of endorphins. When external administration of narcotics stops, withdrawal symptoms are likely to occur.

Hallucinogens

hallucinogens Drugs that alter sensation and perception and often cause visual and auditory hallucinations.

The drugs that produce the most extreme alterations of consciousness are the **hallucinogens**, *drugs that alter sensation and perception and often cause visual and auditory hallucinations.* These include LSD (lysergic acid diethylamide, or acid), mescaline, psilocybin, PCP (phencyclidine), and ketamine (an animal anesthetic). Some of these drugs are derived from plants (mescaline from peyote cactus, psilocybin or "shrooms" from mushrooms) and have been used by people since ancient times. For example, the ingestion of peyote plays a prominent role in some Native American religious practices. The other hallucinogens are largely synthetic.

These drugs produce profound changes in perception. Sensations may seem unusually intense, stationary objects may seem to move or change, patterns or colors may appear, and these perceptions may be accompanied by exaggerated emotions ranging from blissful transcendence to abject terror. These are the "I've-become-the-legs-of-a-chair!" drugs. But the effects of hallucinogens are dramatic and unpredictable, creating a psychological roller-coaster ride that some people find intriguing and others find deeply disturbing. Hallucinogens are the main class of drugs that animals won't work to self-administer, so it is not surprising that in humans these drugs are unlikely to be addictive. Hallucinogens do not induce significant tolerance or dependence, and overdose deaths are rare. Although hallucinogens still enjoy a marginal popularity with people interested in experimenting with their perceptions, they have been more a cultural trend than a dangerous attraction.

Marijuana

Marijuana (or cannabis) is *the leaves and buds of the hemp plant, which contain a psychoactive drug called tetrahydrocannabinol (THC)*. When smoked or eaten, either as is or in concentrated form as *hashish*, this drug produces an intoxication that is mildly hallucinogenic. Users describe the experience as euphoric, with heightened senses of sight and sound and the perception of a rush of ideas. Marijuana affects judgment and short-term memory and impairs motor skills and coordination—making driving a car or operating heavy equipment a poor choice during its use. ("Dude, where's my bulldozer?") Researchers have found that receptors in the brain that respond to THC (Stephens, 1999) are normally activated by a neurotransmitter called *anandamide* that is naturally produced in the brain (Wiley, 1999). Anandamide is involved in the regulation of mood, memory, appetite, and pain perception and has been found temporarily to stimulate overeating in laboratory animals, much as marijuana does in humans (Williams & Kirkham, 1999). Some chemicals found in dark chocolate also mimic anandamide, although very weakly, perhaps accounting for the well-being some people claim they enjoy after a "dose" of chocolate.

The addiction potential of marijuana is not strong because tolerance does not seem to develop and physical withdrawal symptoms are minimal. Psychological dependence is possible, however, and some people do become chronic users. Marijuana use has been widespread throughout the world throughout recorded history, both as a medicine for pain and/or nausea and as a recreational drug, but its use remains controversial. Marijuana abuse and dependence have been linked with increased risk of depression, anxiety, and other forms of psychopathology. Many people also are concerned that marijuana (along with alcohol and tobacco) is a **gateway drug**, *a drug whose use increases the risk of the subsequent use of more harmful drugs*. The gateway theory has gained mixed support, with recent studies challenging this theory and suggesting that early-onset drug use in general, regardless of type of drug, increases the risk of later drug problems (Degenhardt et al., 2010).

Despite the federal laws against the use of marijuana, approximately 42% of adults in the United States have reported using it at some point in their lives—a rate much higher than that observed in most other countries (Degenhardt et al., 2008). Perhaps due to the perceived acceptability of marijuana among the general public, several states recently have taken steps to permit the sale of marijuana for medical purposes, to decriminalize possession of marijuana (so violators pay a fine rather than going to jail), or to legalize its sale and possession outright. The debate about the legal status of marijuana will likely take years to resolve. In the meantime, depending on where you live, the greatest risk of marijuana use may be incarceration (see The Real World: Drugs and the Regulation of Consciousness and Other Voices: A Judge's Plea for Pot).

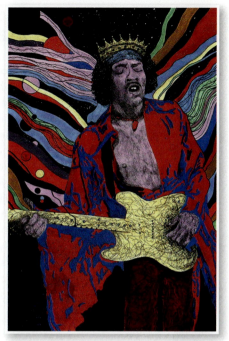

Psychedelic art and music of the 1960s were inspired by some visual and auditory effects of drugs such as LSD. Andrew Herygers Creative/Superstock

marijuana (or cannabis) The leaves and buds of the hemp plant, which contain a psychoactive drug called tetrahydrocannabinol (THC).

gateway drug A drug whose use increases the risk of the subsequent use of more harmful drugs.

A Judge's Plea for Pot

The Honorable Gustin L. Reichbach served as a New York State Supreme Court Justice from 1999 until 2012. He died of pancreatic cancer in July 2012. Rick Kopstein

Should all drugs be illegal? Where should we draw the line between acceptable chemical alteration of one's own consciousness and criminal or pathological behavior? Let's take a specific example—think for a minute about where you stand on the legalization of marijuana. The Honorable Gustin L. Reichbach (2012, p. A27), a New York State Supreme Court Justice, recently wrote a strongly worded piece (slightly condensed here) on this issue, although his position surprised many people.

Three and a half years ago, on my 62nd birthday, doctors discovered a mass on my pancreas. It turned out to be Stage 3 pancreatic cancer. I was told I would be dead in four to six months. Today I am in that rare coterie of people who have survived this long with the disease. But I did not foresee that after having dedicated myself for 40 years to a life of the law, including more than two decades as a New York State judge, my quest for ameliorative and palliative care would lead me to marijuana.

My survival has demanded an enormous price, including months of chemotherapy, radiation hell and brutal surgery. For about a year, my cancer disappeared, only to return. About a month ago, I started a new and even more debilitating course of treatment. Every other week, after receiving an IV booster of chemotherapy drugs that takes three hours, I wear a pump that slowly injects more of the drugs over the next 48 hours.

Nausea and pain are constant companions. One struggles to eat enough to stave off the dramatic weight loss that is part of this disease. Eating, one of the great pleasures of life, has now become a daily battle, with each forkful a small victory. Every drug prescribed to treat one problem leads to one or two more drugs to offset its side effects. Pain medication leads to loss of appetite and constipation. Anti-nausea medication raises glucose levels, a serious problem for me with my pancreas so compromised. Sleep, which might bring respite from the miseries of the day, becomes increasingly elusive.

Inhaled marijuana is the only medicine that gives me some relief from nausea, stimulates my appetite, and makes it easier to fall asleep. The oral synthetic substitute, Marinol, prescribed by my doctors, was useless. Rather than watch the agony of my suffering, friends have chosen, at some personal risk, to provide the substance. I find a few puffs of marijuana before dinner gives me ammunition in the battle to eat. A few more puffs at bedtime permits desperately needed sleep.

This is not a law-and-order issue; it is a medical and a human rights issue. Being treated at Memorial Sloan Kettering Cancer Center, I am receiving the absolute gold standard of medical care. But doctors cannot be expected to do what the law prohibits, even when they know it is in the best interests of their patients. When palliative care is understood as a fundamental human and medical right, marijuana for medical use should be beyond controversy. . .

Cancer is a nonpartisan disease, so ubiquitous that it's impossible to imagine that there are legislators whose families have not also been touched by this scourge. It is to help all who have been affected by cancer, and those who will come after, that I now speak. Given my position as a sitting judge still hearing cases, well-meaning friends question the wisdom of my coming out on this issue. But I recognize that fellow cancer sufferers may be unable, for a host of reasons, to give voice to our plight. It is another heartbreaking aporia in the world of cancer that the one drug that gives relief without deleterious side effects remains classified as a narcotic with no medicinal value.

Because criminalizing an effective medical technique affects the fair administration of justice, I feel obliged to speak out as both a judge and a cancer patient suffering with a fatal disease. . . . Medical science has not yet found a cure, but it is barbaric to deny us access to one substance that has proved to ameliorate our suffering.

How should we decide which consciousness-altering substances are OK for members of our society to use, and which should be made illegal? What criteria would you propose? Should this decision be based on negative health consequences associated with use of the substance? What weight should be given to positive consequences, such as those described by Justice Reichbach? Research described in this chapter tested, and failed to support, the gateway theory of drug use. If you had the opportunity to design and conduct a study to answer a key question in this area, what would you do?

Gustin L. Reichbach, "A Judge's Plea for Pot," New York Times, July 17, 2012. Reprinted by permission of Ellen Meyers and the Hope Reichbach Fund, www.hopeforbrooklyn.com

BUILD TO THE OUTCOMES

1. What is the risk associated with increased tolerance to a drug?

2. Identify both physical and psychological drug withdrawal problems.

3. Why do people experience being drunk differently?

4. Do stimulants create dependency?

5. What are some of the dangerous side effects of cocaine use?

6. Why are narcotics especially alluring?

7. What are the effects of hallucinogens?

8. What are the risks of marijuana use?

Hypnosis: Open to Suggestion

When you think of hypnosis, you may envision people completely under the power of a stage hypnotist, who is ordering them to dance like a chicken or perhaps "regress" to early childhood and talk in childlike voices. But many common beliefs about hypnosis are false. **Hypnosis** refers to *a social interaction in which one person (the hypnotist) makes suggestions that lead to a change in another person's (the subject's) subjective experience of the world* (Kirsch et al., 2011). The essence of hypnosis is in leading people to expect that certain things will happen to them that are outside their conscious will (Wegner, 2002).

Induction and Susceptibility

To induce hypnosis, a hypnotist may ask the person to be hypnotized to sit quietly and focus on some item, such as a spot on the wall (or a swinging pocket watch), and then make suggestions to the person about what effects hypnosis will have (e.g., "your eyelids are slowly closing" or "your arms are getting heavy"). Even without hypnosis, some suggested behaviors might commonly happen just because a person is concentrating on them—just thinking about their eyelids slowly closing, for instance, may make many people shut their eyes briefly or at least blink. In hypnosis, however, suggestions may be made—and followed by people in a susceptible state of mind—for very unusual behavior that most people would not normally do, such as flapping their arms and making loud clucking sounds.

Not everyone is equally hypnotizable. Some highly suggestible people are very easily hypnotized, most people are only moderately influenced, and some people are entirely unaffected by attempts at hypnosis. One of the best indicators of a person's susceptibility is the person's own judgment. So if you think you might be hypnotizable, you may well be (Hilgard, 1965). People with active, vivid imaginations, or who are easily absorbed in activities such as watching a movie, are also somewhat more likely to be good candidates for hypnosis (Sheehan, 1979; Tellegen & Atkinson, 1974).

Hypnotic Effects

From watching stage hypnotism, you might think that the major effect of hypnosis is making people do peculiar things. So what do we actually know to be true about hypnosis? Some impressive demonstrations suggest that real changes occur in those under hypnosis. At the 1849 festivities for Prince Albert of England's birthday, for example, a hypnotized guest was asked to ignore any loud noises and then didn't even flinch when a pistol was fired near his face. Other stage hypnotists claim that their volunteers can perform feats of superhuman strength under hypnosis, such as becoming "stiff as a board" and lying unsupported with shoulders on one chair and feet on another while the hypnotist stands on the hypnotized person's body.

Studies have demonstrated that hypnosis can undermine memory, but with important limitations. People susceptible to hypnosis can be led to experience **posthypnotic amnesia**, *the failure to retrieve memories following hypnotic suggestions to forget*. In one study, a researcher taught a hypnotized person the populations of some remote cities, for example, and then suggested that the participant forget the study session; after the session, the person was quite surprised at being able to give the census figures correctly (Hilgard, 1986). Asked how he knew the answers, the individual decided he might have learned them from a TV program. Such amnesia can then be reversed in subsequent hypnosis.

Some important research has found that only memories that were lost under hypnosis can be retrieved through hypnosis. The false claim that hypnosis helps people to unearth memories that they are not able to retrieve in normal consciousness seems to have surfaced because hypnotized people often make up memories to satisfy the hypnotist's suggestions. For example, Paul Ingram, a sheriff's deputy accused of sexual

hypnosis A social interaction in which one person (the hypnotist) makes suggestions that lead to a change in another person's (the subject's) subjective experience of the world.

posthypnotic amnesia The failure to retrieve memories following hypnotic suggestions to forget.

Stage hypnotists often perform an induction on the whole audience and then bring some of the more susceptible members on stage for further demonstrations. Photographer: Menelaos Prokos (www.athousandclicks.com) Hypnotist: Eric Walden (https://www.facebook.com/hypnotisteric)

abuse by his daughters in the 1980s, was asked by interrogators in session after session to relax and imagine having committed the crimes. He emerged from these sessions having confessed to dozens of horrendous acts of "satanic ritual abuse." These confessions were called into question, however, when the independent investigator used the same technique to ask Ingram about an imaginary crime, something of which Ingram had never been accused. Ingram produced a three-page handwritten confession, complete with dialogue (Ofshe, 1992). Still, prosecutors in the case accepted Ingram's guilty plea, and he was only released in 2003 after a public outcry and years of work on his defense. After a person claims to remember something, even under hypnosis, it is difficult to convince others that the memory was false (Loftus & Ketchum, 1994).

hypnotic analgesia The reduction of pain through hypnosis in people who are susceptible to hypnosis.

Hypnosis can lead to measurable physical and behavioral changes in the body. One well-established effect is **hypnotic analgesia**, *the reduction of pain through hypnosis in people who are susceptible to hypnosis.* For example, one study (see **FIGURE 5.11**) found that, for pain induced in volunteers in the laboratory, hypnosis was more effective than were morphine, diazepam (Valium), aspirin, acupuncture, or placebos (Stern et al., 1977). For people who are hypnotically susceptible, hypnosis can be used to control pain in surgeries and dental procedures, in some cases more effectively than does any form of anesthesia (Druckman & Bjork, 1994; Kihlstrom, 1985).

Hypnosis also has been shown to enable people to control mental processes previously believed to be beyond conscious control. For instance, the Stroop task (Stroop, 1935) is a classic psychological test in which a person is asked to name the color of words on a page (appearing in ink that is red, blue, green, etc.). It turns out that people are significantly slower, and make more errors, when naming ink colors that don't match the content of the word (e.g., when the word "green" is written in red ink) than if the content is neutral or congruent (e.g., if the word "desk" or "red" is written in red ink). This effect is present no matter how hard we try. In an amazing result, the effect is completely eliminated when highly suggestible people are hypnotized and told to respond to all words the same way (Raz et al., 2002). It is important, though, that follow-up studies have revealed that hypnotic induction is not required to eliminate the Stroop effect. It turns out that simply suggesting to highly suggestible people that they should respond to all words the same way has the same effect as hypnosis (Lifshitz et al., 2013). This suggests that hypnotic effects may result when highly suggestible people comply with the suggestions of others.

Nevertheless, people under hypnotic suggestion are not merely telling the hypnotist what he or she wants to hear. Instead, they seem to be experiencing what they have been asked to experience. Under hypnotic suggestion, for example, regions of the brain responsible for color vision are activated in highly hypnotizable people when they are asked to perceive color, even when they are really shown gray stimuli (Kosslyn et al., 2000). While engaged in the Stroop task, people who can eliminate the Stroop

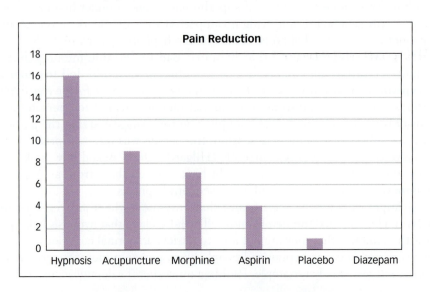

Figure 5.11 HYPNOTIC ANALGESIA The degree of pain reduction reported by people using different techniques for the treatment of laboratory-induced pain. Hypnosis wins (Stern et al., 1977).

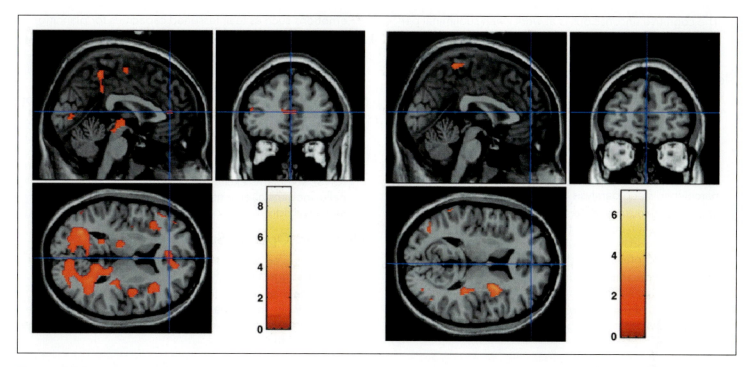

Figure 5.12   BRAIN ACTIVITY DURING HYPNOSIS (a) Researchers found that the anterior cingulate cortex (shown in the crosshairs), a part of the brain involved in conflict monitoring, is activated in all people when viewing incongruent trials during the Stroop task (for instance, when the word *red* appears in blue type). (b) However, under hypnosis, when instructed to ignore the content of the words and just name the font color, highly suggestible people do not show increased activation in this brain region during incongruent trials (Raz et al., 2005). Amire Raz, Jin Fan, and Michael Posner. Hypnotic suggestion reduces conflict in the human brain. *PNAS*, July 12, 2005, *Vol. 102*, No. 28. Copyright 2005, National Academy of Sciences, USA.

effect under suggestion show decreased activity in the anterior cingulate cortex (ACC), the part of the brain involved in conflict monitoring (**FIGURE 5.12**; Raz, Fan, & Posner 2005), consistent with the lack of conflict perceived between the color name and ink. Overall, hypnotic suggestion appears to change the subjective perception of those experiencing it, as reflected by changes in their self-report, behavior, and brain activity.

BUILD TO THE OUTCOMES

1. What factors make someone more easily hypnotizable?

2. What type of memory can be retrieved through hypnosis?

3. Can hypnosis be as effective for pain relief as anesthesia?

4. How does hypnosis change the brain activity of someone engaged in the Stroop task?

CHAPTER REVIEW

The Mysteries of Consciousness

- People judge mind perception according to the capacities for experience and agency.
- Research suggests that mental activity happens first, preparing the way for both conscious thought and action.

The Nature of Consciousness

- Consciousness has four basic properties: intentionality, unity, selectivity, and transience.
- Consciousness can also be understood in terms of three levels: minimal consciousness, full consciousness, and self-consciousness.

- Conscious contents can include current concerns, daydreams, and unwanted thoughts. Efforts to suppress a thought—such as of a white bear—may backfire as the mind searches for thoughts of that white bear to suppress.

The Unconscious Mind

- Unconscious processes are sometimes understood as expressions of the Freudian dynamic unconscious, but they are more commonly viewed as processes of the cognitive unconscious that create our conscious thought and behavior.
- Dual process theories suggest there are two systems in our brains for processing information: fast, automatic, and unconscious; and slow, effortful, and conscious.

- The cognitive unconscious is at work when subliminal perception and unconscious processes influence thought or behavior without the person's awareness.

Sleep and Dreaming: Good Night, Mind

- During a night's sleep, the brain passes in and out of five stages of sleep; most dreaming occurs in the REM sleep stage.
- Being deprived of sleep and dreams has psychological and physical costs. Sleep can be disrupted through disorders that include insomnia, sleep apnea, somnambulism, narcolepsy, sleep paralysis, and night terrors.
- Dream consciousness differs from the waking state in that: We feel emotion intensely, thought is illogical, sensation is fully formed and meaningful; images and events occur with uncritical acceptance; and dreams are difficult to remember.
- Theories of dreaming include Freud's psychoanalytic theory and the activation–synthesis model.
- fMRI studies of the brain while dreaming reveal activations associated with visual imagery, increased sensitivity to emotions such as fear, lessened capacities for planning, and the prevention of motor movement.

Drugs and Consciousness: Artificial Inspiration

- Psychoactive drugs influence consciousness by altering the brain's chemical messaging system and intensifying or dulling the effects of neurotransmitters.
- Drug tolerance can result in overdose, and physical and psychological dependence can lead to addiction.
- Depressants reduce activity of the central nervous system (CNS); stimulants excite the CNS; narcotics relieve pain; hallucinogens alter sensation and perception; and marijuana is mildly hallucinogenic.

Hypnosis: Open to Suggestion

- Hypnosis is an altered state of consciousness characterized by suggestibility.
- Although many claims for hypnosis overstate its effects, hypnosis can create the experience that one's actions are occurring involuntarily, create analgesia, and even change brain activations.

KEY CONCEPT QUIZ

1. Which of the following is NOT a basic property of consciousness?
   a. intentionality
   b. disunity
   c. selectivity
   d. transience

2. Currently, unconscious processes are understood as
   a. a concentrated pattern of thought suppression.
   b. a hidden system of memories, instincts, and desires.
   c. a blank slate.
   d. unexperienced mental processes that give rise to thoughts and behavior.

3. The _____ unconscious is at work when subliminal and unconscious processes influence thought and behavior.
   a. minimal
   b. repressive
   c. dynamic
   d. cognitive

4. The cycle of sleep and waking is one of the major patterns of human life called
   a. the circadian rhythm.
   b. the sleep stages.
   c. the altered state of consciousness.
   d. subliminal perception.

5. Sleep needs _____ over the life span.
   a. decrease
   b. increase
   c. fluctuate
   d. remain the same

6. During dreaming, the dreamer _____ changes in emotion, thought, and sensation.
   a. is skeptical of
   b. is completely unconscious of
   c. uncritically accepts
   d. views objectively

7. Which explanation of dreams proposes that they are produced when the mind attempts to make sense of random neural activity that occurs in the brain during sleep?
   a. Freud's psychoanalytic theory
   b. the activation–synthesis model
   c. the cognitive unconscious model
   d. the manifest content framework

8. fMRI studies of the dreaming brain do NOT reveal
   a. increased sensitivity to emotions.
   b. activations associated with visual activity.
   c. increased capacity for planning.
   d. prevention of movement.

9. Psychoactive drugs influence consciousness by altering the effects of
   a. agonists.
   b. neurotransmitters.
   c. amphetamines.
   d. spinal neurons.

10. Tolerance for drugs involves
    a. larger doses being required over time to achieve the same effect.
    b. openness to new experiences.
    c. the initial attraction of drug use.
    d. the decrease of the painful symptoms that accompany withdrawal.

11. Drugs that heighten arousal and activity levels by affecting the central nervous system are
   a. depressants.
   b. stimulants.
   c. narcotics.
   d. hallucinogens.

12. Alcohol expectancy refers to
   a. alcohol's initial effects of euphoria and reduced anxiety.
   b. the widespread acceptance of alcohol as a socially approved substance.
   c. alcohol leading people to respond in simple ways to complex situations.

   d. people's beliefs about how alcohol will influence them in particular situations.

13. Hypnosis has been proven to have a(n)
   a. effect on physical strength.
   b. positive effect on memory retrieval.
   c. analgesic effect.
   d. age-regression effect.

14. Which individual is LEAST likely to be a good candidate for hypnosis?
   a. Jake, who spends lots of time watching movies
   b. Ava, who is convinced she is easily hypnotizable
   c. Evan, who has an active, vivid imagination
   d. Isabel, who loves to play sports

 **LearningCurve**   **Don't stop now! Quizzing yourself is a powerful study tool. Go to LearningCurve at www.launchpadworks.com for more practice.**

KEY TERMS

consciousness (p. 129)
phenomenology (p. 130)
problem of other minds (p. 130)
mind–body problem (p. 131)
cocktail-party phenomenon (p. 133)
minimal consciousness (p. 134)
full consciousness (p. 134)
self-consciousness (p. 134)
mental control (p. 137)
thought suppression (p. 137)
rebound effect of thought suppression (p. 137)

ironic processes of mental control (p. 137)
dynamic unconscious (p. 138)
repression (p. 139)
cognitive unconscious (p. 139)
dual process theories (p. 139)
subliminal perception (p. 140)
altered state of consciousness (p. 140)
circadian rhythm (p. 141)
REM sleep (p. 142)
insomnia (p. 144)

sleep apnea (p. 144)
somnambulism (or sleepwalking) (p. 144)
narcolepsy (p. 145)
sleep paralysis (p. 145)
night terrors (or sleep terrors) (p. 145)
activation–synthesis model (p. 147)
psychoactive drugs (p. 148)
drug tolerance (p. 149)
depressants (p. 151)

expectancy theory (p. 152)
alcohol myopia (p. 153)
stimulants (p. 153)
narcotics (or opiates) (p. 154)
hallucinogens (p. 154)
marijuana (or cannabis) (p. 155)
gateway drug (p. 155)
hypnosis (p. 157)
posthypnotic amnesia (p. 157)
hypnotic analgesia (p. 158)

CHANGING MINDS

1. "I had a really weird dream last night," your friend tells you. "I dreamed that I was trying to fly like a bird, but I kept flying into clotheslines. I looked it up online, and dreams where you're struggling to fly mean that there is someone in your life who's standing in your way and preventing you from moving forward. I suppose that has to be my boyfriend, so maybe I'd better break up with him." Applying what you've read in this chapter, what would you tell your friend about the reliability of dream interpretation?

2. During an early-morning class, you notice your friend yawning, and you ask if he slept well the night before. "On weekdays, I'm in class all day, and I work the night shift," he says. "So I don't sleep much during the week. But I figure it's okay because I make up for it by sleeping late on Saturday mornings." Is it realistic for your friend

to assume that he can balance regular sleep deprivation with rebound sleep on the weekends?

3. You and a friend are watching the 2010 movie *Inception*, starring Leonardo DiCaprio as a corporate spy. DiCaprio's character is hired by a businessman named Saito to plant an idea in the unconscious mind of a competitor while he sleeps. According to the plan, when the competitor awakens, he'll be compelled to act on the idea, to the secret benefit of Saito's company. "It's a cool idea," your friend says, "but it's pure science fiction. There's no such thing as an unconscious mind, and no way that unconscious ideas could influence the way you act when you're conscious." What would you tell your friend? What evidence do we have that the unconscious mind exists and can influence conscious behavior?

ANSWERS TO KEY CONCEPT QUIZ

1. b; 2. d; 3. d; 4. a; 5. a; 6. c; 7. b; 8. c; 9. b; 10. a; 11. b; 12. d; 13. c; 14. d.

Memory

6

Jill Price was 12 years old when she began to suspect that she possessed an unusually good memory. While she was studying for a seventh-grade science final on May 30, her mind drifted and she became aware that she could recall vividly everything she had been doing on May 30 of the previous year.

Remembering specifics of events that occurred a year ago may not seem so extraordinary—you can probably recall what you did for your last birthday or where you spent last Thanksgiving. But can you recall the details of what you did exactly 1 year ago today? Probably not, but Jill Price can.

Now in her early 50s, Jill can recall clearly and in great detail what has happened to her *every single day since early 1980* (Price & Davis, 2008). This is not just Jill's subjective impression. Memory researchers asked Jill what she had been doing on various randomly chosen dates, and they checked Jill's recall against her personal diary. Again, Jill answered quickly and accurately: *July 1, 1986?*—"Tuesday. Went with (friend's name) to (restaurant name)." October 3, 1987?—"That was a Saturday. Hung out at the apartment all weekend, wearing a sling—hurt my elbow." (Parker, Cahill & McGaugh, 2006, pp. 39–40).

Jill's memory is a gift we'd all love to have—right? Not necessarily. Here's what Jill has to say about her ability: "Most have called it a gift but I call it a burden. I run my entire life through my head every day and it drives me crazy!!!" (E. S. Parker et al., 2006, p. 35).

THE EASE WITH WHICH SOMEONE SUCH AS JILL CAN INSTANTLY REMEMBER HER PAST shouldn't blind us to appreciating how complex that act of remembering really is. Because memory is so remarkably complex, it is also remarkably fragile (Schacter, 1996). We all have had the experience of forgetting something we desperately wanted to remember or of remembering something that never really happened. Why does memory serve us so well in some situations and play such cruel tricks on us in other cases? Is there just one kind of memory, or are there many? These are among the questions that psychologists have asked and answered, and they're the topics of this chapter. We'll start by answering the fundamental question: What is memory?

Jill Price can accurately remember just about everything that has happened to her during the past 30 years, as confirmed by her diary, but Jill's extraordinary memory is more of a curse than a blessing. Dan Tuffs/Contributor, Getty Images

What Is Memory?

memory The ability to store and retrieve information over time.

Memory is *the ability to store and retrieve information over time.* Even though few of us possess the extraordinary memory abilities of Jill Price, each of us has a unique identity that is intricately tied to the things we have thought, felt, done, and experienced. Memories are the residue of those events, the enduring changes that experience makes in our brains. If an experience passes without leaving a trace, it might just as well not have happened. But as Jill's story suggests, remembering all that has happened is not necessarily a good thing, either—a point we'll explore more fully later in this chapter.

encoding The process of transforming what we perceive, think, or feel into an enduring memory.

storage The process of maintaining information in memory over time.

retrieval The process of bringing to mind information that has been previously encoded and stored.

As you've seen in other chapters, the mind's mistakes provide key insights into its fundamental operation, and there is no better illustration of this than in the realm of memory. In this chapter, we'll explore the three key functions of memory: **encoding**, *the process of transforming what we perceive, think, or feel into an enduring memory;* **storage**, *the process of maintaining information in memory over time*; and **retrieval**, *the process of bringing to mind information that has been previously encoded and stored.*

Encoding: Transforming Perceptions Into Memories

LEARNING OUTCOMES

- Explain how memory is a construction and not a recording of new information.
- Describe the three main ways that information is encoded into the brain.
- Give reasons that we remember survival-related information so well.

Bubbles P., a professional gambler with no formal education who spent most of his time shooting craps at local clubs or playing high-stakes poker, had no difficulty rattling off 20 numbers, in either forward or backward order, after just a single glance (Ceci, DeSimone, & Johnson, 1992). Most people can listen to a list of numbers and then repeat them from memory—as long as the list is no more than about seven items long. (Try it for yourself using **FIGURE 6.1**.)

How did Bubbles accomplish his astounding feats of memory? For at least 2,000 years, people have thought of memory as a recording device that makes exact copies of the information that comes in through our senses, and then stores those copies for later use. This idea is simple and intuitive. It is also completely incorrect. We make memories by combining information we *already* have in our brains with new information that comes in through our senses. Memories are *constructed*, not recorded, and encoding is the process by which we transform what we perceive, think, or feel into an enduring memory. Let's look at three types of encoding processes—semantic encoding, visual imagery encoding, and organizational encoding—and then consider the possible survival value of encoding for our ancestors.

2 8
6 9 1
0 4 7 3
8 7 4 5 4
9 0 2 4 8 1
5 7 4 2 2 9 6
6 4 7 1 9 3 0 4
3 5 6 7 1 8 4 8 5
1 0 2 8 8 3 4 7 2 9
4 7 2 0 8 2 7 4 2 6 4
7 3 1 0 9 3 4 3 5 1 3 8

Figure 6.1 DIGIT MEMORY TEST How many digits can you remember? Start on the first row and cover the rows below it with a piece of paper. Study the numbers in the row for 1 second and then cover that row back up again. After a couple of seconds, try to repeat the numbers. Then uncover the row to see if you were correct. If so, continue down to the next row, using the same instructions, until you can't recall all the numbers in a row. The number of digits in the last row you can remember correctly is your digit span. Bubbles P. could remember 20 random numbers, or about five rows deep. How did you do?

Semantic Encoding

Memories are a combination of old and new information, so the nature of any particular memory depends as much on the old information already in our memories as it does on the new information coming in through our senses. In other words, how we remember something depends on how we think about it at the time. For example, as a professional gambler, Bubbles found numbers unusually meaningful, so when he saw a string of digits, he tended to think about their meanings. However, when Bubbles was tested with materials other than numbers—faces, words, objects, or locations—his memory performance was no better than average. Most of us, unlike Bubbles, can't remember 20 digits, but we can remember 20 experiences (a favorite camping trip, a 16th birthday party, a first day at college, etc.). One reason is that we often think about the meaning behind our experiences, so we semantically encode them without even trying (Craik & Tulving, 1975). **Semantic encoding** is *the process of relating new information in a meaningful way to knowledge that is already stored in memory* (Brown & Craik, 2000).

So what's going on in the brain when this type of information processing occurs? Studies reveal that semantic encoding is uniquely associated with increased activity in the lower left part of the frontal lobe and the inner part of the left temporal lobe (**FIGURE 6.2a**; Demb et al., 1995; Kapur et al., 1994; Wagner et al., 1998). In fact, the amount of activity in each of these two regions during encoding is directly related to whether people later remember an item. The more activity there is in these areas, the more likely the person will remember the information.

Have you ever wondered why you can remember 20 experiences (your favorite camping trip, your 16th birthday party, your first day at college, etc.) but not 20 digits? One reason is that we often think about the meaning behind our experiences, so we semantically encode them without even trying (Craik & Tulving, 1975). eppicphotography/iStockphoto/Thinkstock

semantic encoding The process of relating new information in a meaningful way to knowledge that is already stored in memory.

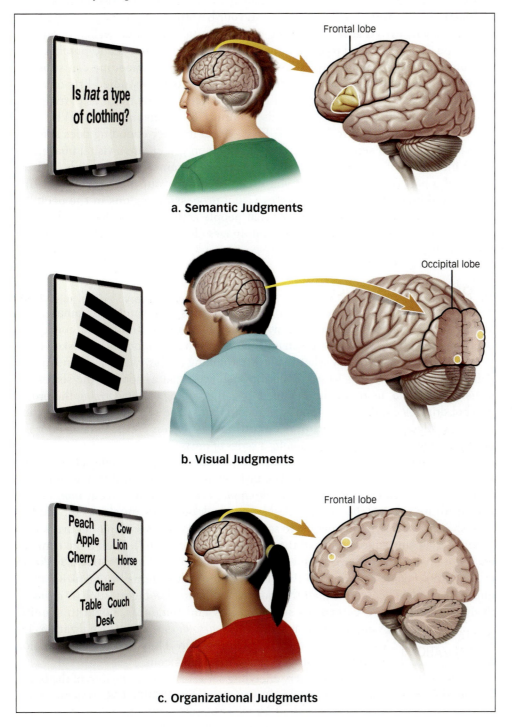

a. Semantic Judgments

b. Visual Judgments

c. Organizational Judgments

Figure 6.2 BRAIN ACTIVITY DURING DIFFERENT TYPES OF JUDGMENTS fMRI studies reveal that different parts of the brain are active during different types of judgments: (a) During semantic encoding, the lower left frontal lobe is active; (b) during visual imagery encoding, the occipital lobe is active; and (c) during organizational encoding, the upper left frontal lobe is active.

Visual Imagery Encoding

In Ancient Athens, the Greek poet Simonides had just left a banquet when the ceiling collapsed and killed all the people inside. Simonides was able to name every one of the dead simply by visualizing each chair around the banquet table and recalling the person who had been sitting there. Simonides wasn't the first, but he was among the most proficient, to use **visual imagery encoding**, *the process of storing new information by converting it into mental pictures.*

visual imagery encoding The process of storing new information by converting it into mental pictures.

If you wanted to use Simonides' method to create an enduring memory, you could simply convert the information that you wanted to remember into a visual image and then store it in a familiar location. For instance, if you were going to the grocery store and wanted to remember to buy Coke, popcorn, and cheese dip, you could use the rooms in your house as locations and imagine your living room flooded in Coke, your bedroom pillows stuffed with popcorn, and your bathtub as a greasy pond of cheese dip. When you arrived at the store, you could then take a mental walk around your house and "look" into each room to remember the items you needed to purchase.

How might you use visual encoding to help store a new fact, such as the date of a friend's birthday that falls on, say, November 24th? Radius Images/Alamy

Numerous experiments have shown that visual imagery encoding can substantially improve memory. In one experiment, participants who studied lists of words by creating visual images of them later recalled twice as many items as participants who just mentally repeated the words (Schnorr & Atkinson, 1969). Why does visual imagery encoding work so well? First, visual imagery encoding does some of the same things that semantic encoding does: When you create a visual image, you relate incoming information to knowledge already in memory. For example, a visual image of a parked car might help you create a link to your memory of your first kiss. Visual imagery encoding activates visual processing regions in the occipital lobe (see **FIGURE 6.2b**), which suggests that people actually enlist the visual system when forming memories based on mental images (Kosslyn et al., 1993; Pearson & Kosslyn, 2015).

Organizational Encoding

Have you ever ordered dinner with a group of friends and watched in amazement as your server took the order without writing anything down? To find out how this is done, one researcher wired servers in a restaurant with microphones and asked them to think aloud, that is, to say what they were thinking as they walked around all day doing their jobs (Stevens, 1988). Recordings showed that as soon as the server left a customer's table, he or she immediately began *grouping* or *categorizing* the orders into hot drinks, cold drinks, hot foods, and cold foods. The servers remembered their orders by relying on **organizational encoding**, *the process of categorizing information according to the relationships among a series of items.*

Ever wonder how a server remembers who ordered the pizza and who ordered the fries without writing anything down? Some have figured out how to use organizational encoding. Efrain Padro/Alamy Stock Photo

organizational encoding The process of categorizing information according to the relationships among a series of items.

For example, suppose you had to memorize the words *peach, cow, chair, apple, table, cherry, lion, couch, horse, desk.* The task seems difficult, but if you organize the items into three categories—fruit (*peach, apple, cherry*), animals (*cow, lion, horse*), and furniture (*chair, table, couch, desk*)—the task becomes much easier. Studies have shown that instructing people to sort items into categories is an effective way to enhance their subsequent recall of those items (Mandler, 1967). Even more complex organizational schemes have been used, such as the hierarchy in **FIGURE 6.3** (Bower et al., 1969). People can improve their recall of individual items by organizing them into multiple-level categories, all the way from a general category such as *animals*, through intermediate categories such as *birds* and *songbirds*, down to specific examples such as *wren* and *sparrow*. (see Data Visualization: Do Men and Women Differ in the Way They Remember Location Information? at www.launchpadworks.com.)

DATA VISUALIZATION

Just as semantic and visual imagery encoding activates distinct regions of the brain, so, too, does organizational encoding. As you can see in **FIGURE 6.2C**, organizational

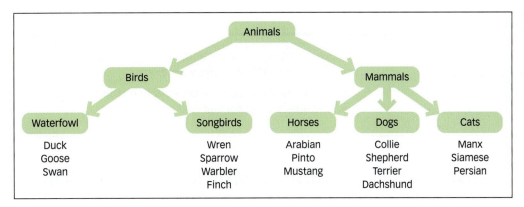

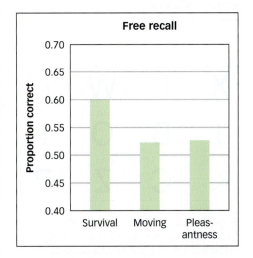

Duck, Goose, Swan under Waterfowl; Wren, Sparrow, Warbler, Finch under Songbirds; Arabian, Pinto, Mustang under Horses; Collie, Shepherd, Terrier, Dachshund under Dogs; Manx, Siamese, Persian under Cats.

Figure 6.3 ORGANIZING WORDS INTO A HIERARCHY Organizing words into conceptual groups and relating them to each other—as in this example of a hierarchy—makes it easier to reconstruct the items from memory later (Bower et al., 1969). Keeping track of the 17 items in this example can be facilitated by remembering the hierarchical groupings under which they fall.

encoding activates the upper surface of the left frontal lobe (Fletcher, Shallice, & Dolan, 1998; Savage et al., 2001). Different types of encoding strategies appear to rely on the activation of different areas of the brain.

Encoding of Survival-Related Information

Encoding new information is critical to many aspects of everyday life—prospects for attaining your degree would be pretty slim without this ability. According to the evolutionary perspective, which is based on Darwin's principle of natural selection, features of an organism that help it survive and reproduce are more likely than other features to be passed on to subsequent generations (see the Psychology: Evolution of a Science chapter). Therefore, memory mechanisms that help us to survive and reproduce should be preserved by natural selection. Our memory systems should be built in a way that allows us to remember especially well encoded information that is relevant to our survival, such as sources of food and water and the location of predators.

To test this idea, researchers gave participants three different encoding tasks (Nairne, Thompson, & Pandeirada, 2007). In the first task, a survival-encoding condition, participants were asked to imagine that they were stranded in the grasslands of a foreign land. They were told that over the next few months they would need supplies of food and water and also need to protect themselves from predators. The researchers then showed participants randomly chosen words (e.g., *stone, meadow, chair*) and asked them to rate on a 1–5 scale how relevant each item would be to survival in the hypothetical situation. In a second task, a moving-encoding condition, a second group of participants was asked to imagine that they were planning to move to a new home in a foreign land, and to rate on a 1–5 scale how useful each item might be in helping them to set up a new home. In the third task, the pleasantness-encoding condition, a third group was shown the same words and asked to rate on a 1–5 scale the pleasantness of each word. The findings, displayed in **FIGURE 6.4**, show that participants recalled more words after the survival-encoding task than after either the moving or pleasantness tasks. Exactly what about survival encoding produces such high levels of memory?

Survival encoding draws on elements of semantic, visual imagery, and organizational encoding (Burns, Hwang, & Burns, 2011). Also, survival encoding encourages participants to think in detail about the goals they want to achieve and thus engage in extensive planning, which in turn benefits memory (Bell, Roer, & Buchner, 2015). Of course, planning for the future is itself critical for our long-term survival, so these findings are still broadly consistent with the evolutionary perspective that memory is built to enhance our chances of survival (Klein, Robertson, & Delton, 2011; Schacter, 2012; Suddendorf & Corballis, 2007).

Figure 6.4 SURVIVAL ENCODING ENHANCES LATER RECALL People recall more words after survival-encoding tasks than after moving- or pleasantness-encoding tasks (Nairne et al., 2007). Explain this from an evolutionary perspective.

1. Why is memory a "construction," not a recording?

2. What do we consider when making a semantic judgment?

3. What two factors make visual imagery effective?

4. How might you use organizational encoding to remember material before an exam?

5. What is the evolutionary perspective on encoding survival-related information?

Storage: Maintaining Memories Over Time

LEARNING OUTCOMES

- Distinguish sensory memory from short-term memory.

- Describe the elements of the model of working memory.

- Explain the interrelationship between memory and the hippocampus.

- Summarize the role of the neural synapse in long-term memory storage.

sensory memory A type of storage that holds sensory information for a few seconds or less.

iconic memory A fast-decaying store of visual information.

echoic memory A fast-decaying store of auditory information.

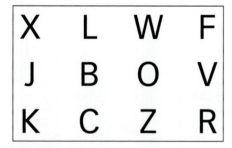

Figure 6.5 ICONIC MEMORY TEST When a grid of letters is flashed on screen for only 1/20th of a second, it is difficult to recall individual letters. But if prompted to remember a particular row immediately after the grid is shown, research participants will do so with high accuracy—indicating that although iconic memory stores the whole grid, the information fades away too quickly for a person to recall everything (Sperling, 1960).

Encoding is the process of turning perceptions into memories; storage is the process of maintaining information in memory over time. There are three major kinds of memory storage: sensory, short-term, and long-term. As these names suggest, the three kinds of storage are distinguished primarily by the amount of time over which a memory is retained.

Sensory Storage

Sensory memory is *a type of storage that holds sensory information for a few seconds or less*. In a classic experiment, participants viewed three rows of four letters each, as shown in **FIGURE 6.5**. The researcher flashed the letters on a screen for just 1/20th of a second. When asked to remember all 12 of the letters they had just seen, participants recalled fewer than half (Sperling, 1960). There were two possible explanations for this: Either people simply couldn't encode all the letters in such a brief period of time, or else people encoded the letters but forgot them while trying to recall everything they had seen.

To test the two ideas, the researcher relied on a clever trick. Just after the letters disappeared from the screen, a tone sounded that cued the participants to report the letters in a particular row. A *high* tone cued participants to report the contents of the top row, a *medium* tone cued participants to report the contents of the middle row, and a *low* tone cued participants to report the contents of the bottom row. When asked to report only a single row, people recalled almost all of the letters in that row! Because the tone sounded after the letters disappeared from the screen, and participants had no way of knowing which of the three rows would be cued, the researcher inferred that virtually all the letters had been encoded. In fact, if the tone was substantially delayed, participants couldn't perform the task because the information had slipped away from their sensory memories. Like the afterimage of a flashlight, the 12 letters flashed on a screen are visual icons, a lingering trace stored in memory for a very short period.

Because we have more than one sense, we have more than one kind of sensory memory. **Iconic memory** is *a fast-decaying store of visual information*. A similar storage area serves as a temporary warehouse for sounds. **Echoic memory** is *a fast-decaying store of auditory information*. When you have difficulty understanding what someone has just said, you probably find yourself replaying the last few words—listening to them echo in your "mind's ear," so to speak. When you do that, you are accessing information that is being held in your echoic memory store. The hallmark of both the iconic and echoic memory stores is that they hold information for a very short time. Iconic memories usually decay in about 1 second or less, and echoic memories usually decay in about 5 seconds (Darwin, Turvey, & Crowder, 1972). These two sensory memory stores are a bit like doughnut shops: The products come in, they sit briefly on the shelf, and then they are discarded. If you want one, you have to grab it fast. But how to grab it? If information from sensory memory is quickly lost, how do we recall it at all? The key is attention, and that brings us to short-term memory (see **FIGURE 6.6**).

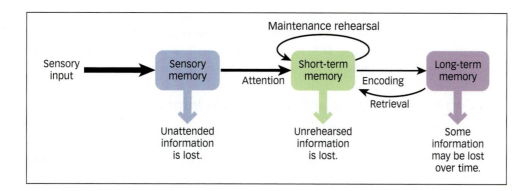

Figure 6.6   THE FLOW OF INFORMATION THROUGH THE MEMORY SYSTEM Information moves through several stages of memory as it gets encoded, stored, and made available for later retrieval.

Short-Term Storage and Working Memory

A second kind of memory storage is **short-term memory**, which *holds nonsensory information for more than a few seconds but less than a minute.* For example, if someone tells you a telephone number and you pay attention to what they say, you can usually repeat it back with ease—but you will quickly lose the information as soon as your attention focuses on anything else. In one study, research participants were given consonant strings to remember, such as DBX and HLM. After seeing each string, participants were asked to count backward from 100 by 3 for varying amounts of time and were then asked to recall the strings (Peterson & Peterson, 1959). As shown in **FIGURE 6.7**, memory for the consonant strings declined rapidly, from approximately 80% after a 3-second delay to less than 20% after a 20-second delay. These results suggest that information can be held in the short-term memory store for about 15 to 20 seconds.

short-term memory A type of storage that holds nonsensory information for more than a few seconds but less than a minute.

Rehearsal and "Chunking" Strengthen Memory

What if 15 to 20 seconds isn't enough time? What if we need the information for a while longer? We can use a trick that allows us to get around the natural limitations of our short-term memories. **Rehearsal** is *the process of keeping information in short-term memory by mentally repeating it.* If someone gives you a telephone number and you can't immediately enter it into your cell phone or write it down, you say it over and over to yourself until you can. Each time you repeat the number, you are reentering it into short-term memory, giving it another 15 to 20 seconds of shelf life.

rehearsal The process of keeping information in short-term memory by mentally repeating it.

Rehearsal can play a role in the *serial position effect,* which refers to the observation that the first few and last few items in a series are more likely to be recalled than the items in the middle. Enhanced recall of the first few items in, say, a list of words is called the *primacy effect.* It occurs because these items receive more rehearsals than subsequent items in the middle of the list and thus are more likely to be encoded into long-term storage. Enhanced recall of the last few items is called the *recency effect* and can result from rehearsing items that are still in short-term storage (Atkinson & Shiffrin, 1968). Consistent with this interpretation, classic studies showed that the recency effect—but not the primacy effect—is eliminated when participants count backward by threes after the final list item is presented, which prevents them from relying on short-term storage to rehearse the last few items (Glanzer & Cunitz, 1966). However, both primacy and recency effects can be observed in situations that involve only long-term storage, such as recalling details of opera performances over a period of 25 years (Sehulster, 1989) or recalling the order of the seven Harry Potter books (Kelley, Neath, & Surprenant, 2013).

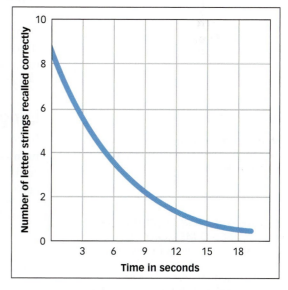

Figure 6.7   THE DECLINE OF SHORT-TERM MEMORY Short-term memory fades quickly without rehearsal. On a test for memory of three-letter strings, research participants were highly accurate when tested a few seconds after exposure to each string, but after 15 seconds, people barely recalled the strings at all (Peterson & Peterson, 1959).

Short-term memory is limited in how *long* it can hold information and also is limited in how *much* information it can hold. Most people can keep approximately seven items in short-term memory, but if they put more new items in, then old items begin to fall out (Miller, 1956). Those items can be numbers, letters, or even words or ideas. One way to

chunking Combining small pieces of information into larger clusters or chunks that are more easily held in short-term memory.

increase storage is **chunking**, which involves *combining small pieces of information into larger clusters or chunks that are more easily held in short-term memory.* Waitresses who use organizational encoding (see p. 165) to organize customer orders into groups are essentially chunking the information, giving themselves less to remember.

Working Memory Stores and Manipulates Information

Short-term memory was originally conceived of as a kind of "place" where information is kept for a limited amount of time. More recently, researchers developed and refined a more dynamic model of a limited-capacity memory system, **working memory**, which refers to *active maintenance of information in short-term storage* (Baddeley & Hitch, 1974). As illustrated in **FIGURE 6.8**, working memory includes two subsystems that store and manipulate information (*the visuo-spatial sketchpad* for visual images and *the phonological loop* for verbal information), an *episodic buffer* that integrates visual and verbal information from these two subsystems, and a *central executive* that coordinates the subsystems and the episodic buffer (Baddeley, 2001; Baddeley, Allen, & Hitch, 2011). If you wanted to keep the arrangement of pieces on a chessboard in mind as you contemplated your next move, you'd be relying on working memory to hold the visual representation of the positions of the pieces and to control mental manipulation of the possible moves. Brain imaging studies indicate that the central executive component of working memory depends on regions within the frontal lobe that are important for controlling and manipulating information on a wide range of cognitive tasks (Baddeley, 2001; D'Esposito & Postle, 2015).

working memory A type of short-term storage that actively maintains information.

Research Is Examining the Link Between Working Memory Training and Cognitive Functioning

Can working memory skills be trained, and can such training enhance cognitive functioning? Some studies suggest yes. In one study, elementary school students trained on several working memory tasks (about 35 minutes/day for several weeks) showed improvement on other working memory tasks (Holmes, Gathercole, & Dunning, 2009). However, other studies find that working memory training improves performance on the working memory task that was trained—but not other cognitive tasks (Redick et al., 2013). More research will be needed to determine whether working memory training produces any general improvements in cognitive performance (Au et al., 2015; Redick, 2015; Shipstead, Redick, & Engle, 2012).

Long-Term Storage

In contrast to the time-limited sensory and short-term storage stores, **long-term memory** is *a type of storage that holds information for hours, days, weeks, or years.* In contrast to both sensory and short-term storage, long-term memory has no known capacity limits (see Figure 6.6). For example, most people can recall 10,000 to

long-term memory A type of storage that holds information for hours, days, weeks, or years.

Figure 6.8 A REFINED MODEL OF WORKING MEMORY The working memory system consists of a central executive that controls the flow of information through the system, a visuo-spatial sketchpad and phonological loop that temporarily hold visual/spatial images and verbal/auditory information, respectively, and an episodic buffer that integrates the various kinds of information that are maintained by the visuo-spatial sketchpad and phonological loop. Baddeley et al. (2011). Binding in visual working memory: The role of the episodic buffer. *Neuropsychologia, 49*, 1393–1400.

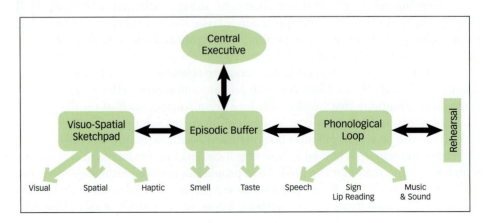

15,000 words in their native language, tens of thousands of facts (the capital of France is Paris, and 3 × 3 = 9), and an untold number of personal experiences. Just think of all the song lyrics you can recite by heart, and you'll understand that you've got a lot of information tucked away in your long-term memory!

The Hippocampus as Index: Linking Pieces Into One Memory

Where is long-term memory located in the brain? The clues to answering this question come from individuals who are unable to store long-term memories. In 1953, a young man, known then by the initials HM, suffered from intractable epilepsy (Scoville & Milner, 1957). In a desperate attempt to stop the seizures, HM's doctors removed parts of his temporal lobes, including the hippocampus and some surrounding regions (**FIGURE 6.9**). After the operation, HM could converse easily, use and understand language, and perform well on intelligence tests, but he could not remember anything that happened to him after the operation. HM could repeat a telephone number with no difficulty, suggesting that his short-term memory store was just fine (Corkin, 2002, 2013; Hilts, 1995; Squire, 2009). But after information left the short-term store, it was gone forever. For example, he would often forget that he had just eaten a meal or fail to recognize the hospital staff who helped him on a daily basis. Studies of HM and others have shown that the hippocampal region of the brain is critical for putting new information into the long-term store (Clark & Maguire, 2016; Smith et al., 2013). When this region is damaged, individuals suffer from a condition known as **anterograde amnesia**, which is *the inability to transfer new information from the short-term store into the long-term store.*

Some individuals with amnesia also suffer from **retrograde amnesia**, which is *the inability to retrieve information that was acquired before a particular date, usually the date of an injury or surgery.* The fact that HM had much worse anterograde than retrograde amnesia suggests that the hippocampal region is not the site of long-term memory. Indeed, research has shown that different aspects of a single memory—its sights, sounds, smells, emotional content—are stored in different places in the cortex (Damasio, 1989; Schacter, 1996; Squire & Kandel, 1999). Some psychologists have argued that the hippocampal region acts as a kind of "index" that links together all of these otherwise separate bits and pieces so that we remember them as one memory (Schacter, 1996; Squire, 1992; Teyler & DiScenna, 1986). Recent fMRI studies support this "index view." The evidence shows that activity in the hippocampus relates to retrieving as a holistic unit the separate elements that an episode comprises, such as a person, location, and an object, which were initially encoded by distinct regions in the cortex (Horner et al., 2015).

anterograde amnesia The inability to transfer new information from the short-term store into the long-term store.

retrograde amnesia The inability to retrieve information that was acquired before a particular date, usually the date of an injury or surgery.

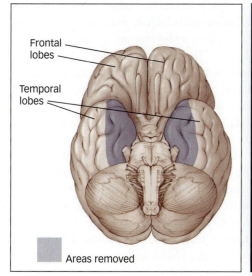

Frontal lobes

Temporal lobes

Areas removed

Figure 6.9 THE HIPPOCAMPUS PATIENT Henry Molaison (right), better known to the world as patient HM, had his hippocampus and adjacent structures of the medial temporal lobe (indicated by the shaded area) surgically removed to stop his epileptic seizures (left). As a result, he could not remember things that happened after the surgery. HM participated in countless memory experiments, and in so doing made fundamental contributions to our understanding of memory and the brain (Corkin, 2013). 2016 Macmillan Learning

Over time, however, the hippocampal index may become less necessary. You can think of the hippocampal region index as a printed recipe. The first time you make a pie, you need the recipe to help you retrieve all the ingredients and then mix them together in the right amounts. As you bake more and more pies, though, you don't need to rely on the printed recipe anymore. Similarly, although the hippocampal region index is critical when a new memory is first formed, it may become less important as the memory ages. Scientists are still debating the extent to which the hippocampal region helps us to remember details of our old memories (Bayley, et al., 2005; Kirwan et al., 2008; Moscovitch et al., 2016; Squire & Wixted, 2011; Winocur, Moscovitch, & Bontempi, 2010). However, the notion of the hippocampus as an index explains why people such as HM cannot make new memories and why they can remember many old ones.

Consolidation Stabilizes Memories

consolidation The process by which memories become stable in the brain.

The idea that the hippocampus becomes less important over time for maintaining memories is closely related to the concept of **consolidation**, *the process by which memories become stable in the brain* (McGaugh, 2000, 2015). Shortly after encoding, memories exist in a fragile state in which they can be disrupted easily; once consolidation has occurred, they are more resistant to disruption. One type of consolidation operates over seconds or minutes. For example, when someone experiences a head injury in a car crash and later cannot recall what happened during the few seconds or minutes before the crash—but can recall other events normally—the head injury probably prevented consolidation of short-term memory into long-term memory. Another type of consolidation occurs over much longer periods of time—days, weeks, months, and years—and likely involves transfer of information from the hippocampus to more permanent storage sites in the cortex. The operation of this longer-term consolidation process is why patients like HM can recall memories from childhood relatively normally, but are impaired when recalling experiences that occurred just a few years prior to the time they became amnesic (Kirwan et al., 2008; Squire & Wixted, 2011).

How does a memory become consolidated? The act of recalling a memory, thinking about it, and talking about it with others probably contributes to consolidation (Moscovitch et al., 2006). As explained in Hot Science: Sleep on It, mounting evidence gathered during the past decade indicates that sleep plays an important role in memory consolidation.

reconsolidation The process whereby memories can become vulnerable to disruption when they are recalled, thus requiring them to be consolidated again.

Recalled Memories May Be Disrupted During Reconsolidation

Many researchers have long believed that a fully consolidated memory becomes a permanent fixture in the brain, more difficult to get rid of than a computer virus. But another line of research that has developed rapidly in recent years suggests that things are not so simple. Through a process called **reconsolidation**, even seemingly consolidated *memories can become vulnerable to disruption when they are recalled, thus requiring them to be consolidated again* (Dudai, 2012; Nader & Hardt, 2009). Evidence for reconsolidation mainly comes from experiments with rats showing that when animals are cued to retrieve a new memory that was acquired a day earlier, giving the animal a drug (or an electrical shock) that prevents initial consolidation will cause forgetting (Nader, Shafe, & LeDoux, 2000; Sara, 2000). In fact, each time they are retrieved, memories become vulnerable to disruption and have to be reconsolidated.

Might it be possible one day to eliminate or modify painful memories by disrupting reconsolidation? Recent research suggests it could be. When a traumatic event was reactivated in traumatized individuals who had been given a drug to reduce anxiety, there was a subsequent reduction in traumatic symptoms (Brunet et al., 2008, 2011). Related work using fMRI indicates that disrupting

The Boston Marathon bombings in April 2013 produced detailed and disturbing memories in people at or near the site of the bombings. However, research shows that the amount of detail in these memories can be reduced by interfering with their reconsolidation. AP Photo/MetroWest Daily News, Ken McGagh

HOT SCIENCE

Sleep on It

Thinking about pulling an all-nighter before your next big test? Here's a reason to reconsider: Our minds don't simply shut off when we sleep (see the Consciousness chapter). In fact, sleep may be as important to our memories as wakefulness.

Nearly a century ago, Jenkins and Dallenbach (1924) reported that recall of recently learned information is greater immediately after sleeping than after the same amount of time spent awake. They argued that being asleep passively protects us from encountering information that interferes with our ability to remember. As is explained by retroactive interference (p. 185), that's a valid argument. However, during the past decade, evidence has accumulated that sleep does more than simply protect us from waking interference (Diekelman & Born, 2010; Ellenbogen, Payne, & Stickgold, 2006; Vorster & Born, 2015). Sleep selectively enhances the consolidation of memories that reflect the meaning or gist of an experience (Payne et al., 2009), as well as emotionally important memories (Payne et al., 2008, 2015), suggesting that sleep helps us to remember what's important and to discard what's trivial.

This idea is reinforced by evidence that shows that the beneficial effects of sleep on subsequent memory are observed only when people expect to be tested. In one study (van Dongen et al., 2012), participants studied pictures of either buildings or furniture that were each associated with a particular location on a slide (see at right). Soon after, participants received a memory test for the picture–location associations. They were then instructed that they would be retested 14 hours later for either the building pictures or the furniture pictures (the relevant category) and would not be retested on the other type of picture (the irrelevant category). Half of the participants were tested after sleep (initial learning was in the afternoon for these individuals) and half after remaining awake (initial learning was in the morning for these individuals). On the retest, there was less forgetting for the relevant than for the irrelevant categories in the sleep group, but there was no such difference in the awake group. Furthermore, participants who slept longer retained more of the relevant but not the irrelevant information.

So when you find yourself nodding off after hours of studying for your exam, the science is on the side of a good night's sleep.

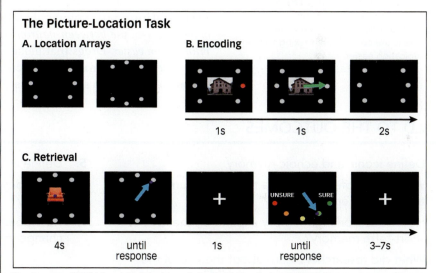

Van Dongen, EV, Thielen, J-W, Takashima, A, Barth, M, Fernández, G (2012) Sleep supports selective retention of associative memories based on relevance for future utilization. *PLoS ONE* 7(8): e43426. doi:10.1371/journal.pone.0043426. © van Dongen et al.

reconsolidation can seemingly eliminate a fear memory in a part of the brain called the *amygdala*, which we will learn, later in this chapter, plays a key role in emotional memory (Agren et al., 2012). Reconsolidation thus appears to be a key memory process with many important implications.

Memories, Neurons, and Synapses

We've already discussed parts of the brain that are related to memory storage, but we haven't said much about how or where memories are stored. Much of what we know about the neurological basis of long-term memory comes from studies of the sea slug *Aplysia*, which has an extremely simple nervous system consisting of only 20,000 neurons (compared with roughly 100 billion in the human brain). When an experimenter stimulates *Aplysia*'s tail with a mild electric shock, the slug immediately withdraws its gill, and if the experimenter does it again a moment later,

By studying the sea slug *Aplysia californica's* extremely simple nervous system, researchers were able to determine that long-term memory storage depends on the growth of new synaptic connections between neurons. Donna Ikenberry/Art Directors/Alamy Stock PHoto

long-term potentiation (LTP) A process whereby repeated communication across the synapse between neurons strengthens the connection, making further communication easier.

Aplysia withdraws its gill even more quickly. If the experimenter comes back an hour later and shocks *Aplysia*, the withdrawal of the gill happens as slowly as it did the first time, as if *Aplysia* can't "remember" what happened an hour earlier (Abel et al., 1995). But if the experimenter shocks *Aplysia* over and over, it does develop an enduring "memory" that can last for days or even weeks. Research suggests that this long-term storage involves the growth of new synaptic connections between neurons (Abel et al., 1995; Kandel, 2006; Squire & Kandel, 1999). You'll recall from the Neuroscience and Behavior chapter that neurons communicate by sending neurotransmitters across the synapse, the small space between the axon of one neuron and the dendrite of another. Learning in *Aplysia* is based on changes involving the synapses for both short-term storage (enhanced neurotransmitter release) and long-term storage (growth of new synapses).

If you're something more complex than a slug—say, a chimpanzee or your roommate—a similar process of synaptic strengthening happens in the hippocampus, which we've seen is an area crucial for storing new long-term memories. In the early 1970s, researchers applied a brief electrical stimulus to a neural pathway in a rat's hippocampus (Bliss & Lømo, 1973). They found that the electrical current produced a stronger connection between synapses that lay along the pathway and that the strengthening lasted for hours or even weeks. They called this effect **long-term potentiation** (more commonly known as **LTP**), *a process whereby communication across the synapse between neurons strengthens the connection, making further communication easier.* Drugs that block LTP can turn rats into rodent versions of patient HM: The animals have great difficulty remembering where they've been recently and become easily lost in a maze (Bliss, 1999; Morris et al., 1986).

BUILD TO THE OUTCOMES

1. Define iconic and echoic memory.

2. Why is it helpful to repeat a telephone number you're trying to remember?

3. How does working memory expand on the idea of short-term memory?

4. What did researchers learn about the role of the hippocampus and memory from HM?

5. Define anterograde and retrograde amnesia.

6. How does the process of recalling a memory affect its stability?

7. How does building a memory produce a physical change in the nervous system?

Retrieval: Bringing Memories to Mind

LEARNING OUTCOMES

• Explain the encoding specificity principle.

• Explain how memories can be changed by the act of retrieval.

• Describe the difference in brain activity when trying versus successfully recalling information.

retrieval cue External information that is associated with stored information and helps bring it to mind.

There is something fiendishly frustrating about piggy banks. You can put money in them, you can shake them around to assure yourself that the money is there, but you can't easily get the money out. If memories were like pennies in a piggy bank, stored but inaccessible, what would be the point of saving them in the first place? Retrieval is the process of bringing to mind information that has been previously encoded and stored, and it is perhaps the most important of all memory processes (Roediger, 2000; Schacter, 2001a).

Retrieval Cues: Reinstating the Past

One of the best ways to retrieve information from *inside* your head is to encounter information *outside* your head that is somehow connected to it. The information outside your head is called a **retrieval cue**, *external information that is associated with* *stored information and helps bring it to mind.* Retrieval cues can be incredibly effective. How many times have you said something such as, "I *know* who played Amy Schumer's boyfriend in *Trainwreck*, but I just can't remember his name," only to have a friend give you a hint ("He was on *Saturday Night Live* for years"), which instantly brings the answer to mind ("Bill Hader!")? Such incidents suggest that information is sometimes *available* in memory, even when it is momentarily *inaccessible*, and that retrieval cues help us bring inaccessible information to mind.

External Context Provides Cues

Hints are one kind of retrieval cue, but they are not the only kind. The **encoding specificity principle** states that *a retrieval cue can serve as an effective reminder when it helps re-create the specific way in which information was initially encoded* (Tulving & Thomson, 1973). External contexts often make powerful retrieval cues (Hockley, 2008). For example, in one study divers learned some words on land and some other words underwater; they recalled the words best when they were tested in the same dry or wet environment in which they had initially learned them because the environment itself was a retrieval cue (Godden & Baddeley, 1975). Similarly, recovering alcoholics often experience a renewed urge to drink when visiting places in which they once drank, because those places are retrieval cues.

Inner States Also Provide Cues

Retrieval cues need not be external contexts—they can also be inner states. **State-dependent retrieval** is *the process whereby information tends to be better recalled when the person is in the same state during encoding and retrieval.* For example, retrieving information when you are in a sad or happy mood increases the likelihood that you will retrieve sad or happy episodes (Eich, 1995). This is part of the reason it is so hard to "look on the bright side" when you're feeling low. If the person's state at the time of retrieval matches the person's state at the time of encoding, the state itself is a retrieval cue. It is a bridge that connects the moment at which we experience something to the moment at which we remember it. Retrieval cues can even be thoughts themselves, as when one thought calls to mind another, related thought (Anderson et al., 1976).

Matching Encoding and Retrieval Contexts Improves Recall

The encoding specificity principle makes some unusual predictions. For example, making semantic judgments about a word usually produces a more durable memory for the word than does making rhyme judgments. Suppose you were shown a cue card of the word *brain* and asked to think of a word that rhymes, while your friend was shown the same card and asked to think about what *brain* means. The next day, if we simply asked you both, "Hey, what was that word you saw yesterday?" we would expect your friend to remember it better. However, if instead we asked you both, "What was that word that rhymed with *train*?" the retrieval cue would match your encoding context better than your friend's, and we would expect you to remember it better than your friend did (Fisher & Craik, 1977). The principle of **transfer-appropriate processing** is *the idea that memory is likely to transfer from one situation to another when the encoding and retrieval contexts of the situations match* (Morris, Bransford, & Franks, 1977; Roediger, Weldon, & Challis, 1989).

Consequences of Retrieval

Human memory differs substantially from computer memory. Simply retrieving a file from my computer doesn't have any effect on the likelihood that the file will open again in the future. Not so with human memory. Retrieval doesn't merely

Retrieval cues are hints that help bring stored information to mind. How does this explain the fact that most students prefer multiple-choice exams to fill-in-the-blank exams? AP Photo/Pocono Record, Adam Richins

encoding specificity principle The idea that a retrieval cue can be an effective reminder when it helps re-create the specific way in which information was initially encoded.

state-dependent retrieval The process whereby information tends to be better recalled when the person is in the same state during encoding and retrieval.

transfer-appropriate processing The process whereby memory is more likely to transfer from one situation to another when the encoding and retrieval contexts of the situations match.

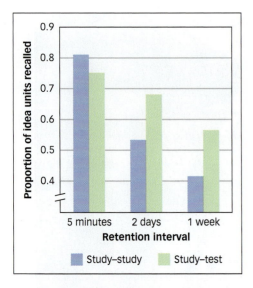

Figure 6.10 MEMORY TESTING BENEFITS LONG-TERM RETENTION With a 5-minute retention interval, the study–study condition results in slightly higher recall. But with longer retention intervals of 2 days and 1 week, the study–test condition yields much higher levels of recall than does the study–study condition (Roediger & Karpicke, 2006).

retrieval-induced forgetting A process by which retrieving an item from long-term memory impairs subsequent recall of related items.

provide a readout of what is in memory; it also changes the state of the memory system in important ways.

Retrieval Can Improve Subsequent Memory

The simple act of retrieval can strengthen a retrieved memory, making it easier to remember that information at a later time (Bjork, 1975). For example, in one experiment, participants studied brief stories and then either studied them again or were given a test that required retrieving the stories (Roediger & Karpicke, 2006). Participants were then given a final recall test for the stories either 5 minutes, 2 days, or 1 week later. As shown in **FIGURE 6.10**, at the 5-minute delay, studying the stories twice resulted in slightly higher recall than did studying paired with retrieval (testing). But the opposite occurred at the 2-day and 1-week delays: Retrieval produced much higher levels of recall than did an extra study exposure. A subsequent experiment using foreign vocabulary items also revealed that retrieval of the items produced a much bigger benefit on a delayed vocabulary test than did further study (Karpicke & Roediger, 2008). The benefits of testing on subsequent retention occur not only in adults but also in grade school children (Jaeger, Eisenkraemer, & Stein, 2015). These findings have potentially important implications for learning in educational contexts (Karpicke, 2012), which we will explore further in the Learning chapter.

Retrieval Can Also Impair Subsequent Memory

As much as retrieval can help memory, that's not always the case. **Retrieval-induced forgetting** is *a process by which retrieving an item from long-term memory impairs subsequent recall of related items* (Anderson, 2003; Anderson, Bjork, & Bjork, 1994; Murayama et al., 2014). For example, when a speaker selectively talks about some aspects of memories shared with a listener and doesn't mention related information, both the speaker and the listener later have a harder time remembering the omitted events (Cuc, Koppel, & Hirst, 2007; Hirst & Echterhoff, 2012). Retrieval-induced forgetting can even affect eyewitness memory. When witnesses to a staged crime are questioned about some details of the crime scene, their ability to later recall related details that they were not asked about is impaired, compared with that of witnesses who initially were not questioned at all (MacLeod, 2002; Shaw, Bjork, & Handal, 1995). These findings suggest that initial interviews with eyewitnesses should be as complete as possible in order to avoid potential retrieval-induced forgetting of significant details that are not probed during an interview (MacLeod & Saunders, 2008).

Retrieval Can Change Subsequent Memory

In addition to improving and impairing subsequent memory, the act of retrieval also can change what we remember from an experience. In one experiment, participants went on a tour of a museum, where they viewed designated exhibits, each of which contained several different stops (St. Jacques & Schacter, 2013). The participants each wore a camera that, every 15 seconds, automatically took pictures of what was in front of them. Two days later, the participants visited the memory laboratory (in a separate building) for a "reactivation session." Memories of some of the stops were reactivated showing participants photos and asking them to rate how vividly they reexperienced what had happened at each stop. The participants were also shown novel photos of *unvisited* stops within the exhibit, and asked to judge how closely these novel photos were related to the photos of the stops that they had actually seen in that exhibit. Two days after the reactivation session, the participants were given a memory test.

Participants sometimes incorrectly remembered that the stop shown in a novel photo had been part of the original tour. Most important, participants who tended to make this mistake also tended to have more vivid recollections during the reactivation session. In other words, retrieving and vividly reexperiencing memories of what participants actually did see at the museum led them to incorporate into their memory information that was not part of their original experience. This finding may be related to the phenomenon of reconsolidation that we discussed earlier (p. 172), where reactivating a memory temporarily makes it vulnerable to disruption and change. At the very least, this finding reinforces the idea that retrieving a memory involves far more than a simple readout of information. Cultural influences on retrieval of early childhood memories, which have been linked with cultural differences in how frequently people retrieve past experiences, make a similar point.

Separating the Components of Retrieval

Before leaving the topic of retrieval, let's look at how the process actually works. There is reason to believe that *trying* to recall an incident and *successfully* recalling one are fundamentally different processes that occur in different parts of the brain (Moscovitch, 1994; Schacter, 1996). For example, regions in the left frontal lobe show heightened activity when people *try* to retrieve information that was presented to them earlier (Oztekin, Curtis, & McElree, 2009; Tulving et al., 1994). This activity may reflect the mental effort of struggling to dredge up the past event (Lepage et al., 2000). However, *successfully* remembering a past experience tends to be accompanied by activity in the hippocampal region (see **FIGURE 6.11**; Eldridge et al., 2000; Giovanello, Schnyer, & Verfaellie, 2004; Schacter, Alpert, et al., 1996). Furthermore, successful recall also activates parts of the brain that play a role in processing the sensory features of an experience. For instance, recall of previously heard sounds is accompanied by activity in the auditory cortex (the upper part of the temporal lobe), whereas recall of previously seen pictures is accompanied by activity in the visual cortex (in the occipital lobe; Wheeler, Petersen, & Buckner, 2000). Although retrieval may seem like a single process, brain studies suggest that separately identifiable processes are at work.

This finding sheds some light on the phenomenon we just discussed: retrieval-induced forgetting. Recent fMRI evidence indicates that during memory retrieval, regions within the frontal lobe that are involved in retrieval effort play a role in suppressing competitors (Benoit & Anderson, 2012; Kuhl et al., 2007; Wimber et al., 2009). When hippocampal activity during retrieval practice signals successful recall of an unwanted competitor, frontal lobe mechanisms are recruited that help to suppress the competitor. Once the competitor is suppressed, the frontal lobe no longer has to work as hard at controlling retrieval, ultimately making it easier to recall the target item (Kuhl et al., 2007). In addition, successful suppression of an unwanted

As part of a recent experiment, participants wore cameras that took pictures every 15 seconds as they toured a museum. Daniel Schacter

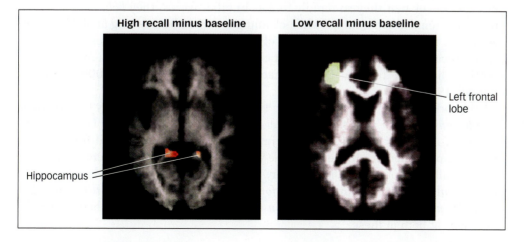

High recall minus baseline   Low recall minus baseline

Left frontal lobe

Hippocampus

Figure 6.11 PET SCANS OF SUCCESSFUL AND UNSUCCESSFUL RECALL When people successfully remembered words they saw earlier in an experiment (achieving high levels of recall on a test), the hippocampus showed increased activity. When people tried but failed to recall words they had seen earlier (achieving low levels of recall on a test), the left frontal lobe showed increased activity. Schacter DL, Alpert NM, Savage CR, Rauch SL, Albert MS. Conscious recollection and the human hippocampal formation: Evidence from positron emission tomography. *Proc Natl Acad Sci USA* 1996; 93: 321–325.

memory causes reduced activity in the hippocampus (Anderson et al., 2004). These findings make sense once we understand the specific roles played by particular brain regions in the retrieval process.

BUILD TO THE OUTCOMES

1. Why are external contexts powerful retrieval cues?
2. How does mood affect memory?
3. Should students spend more time testing themselves on material (retrieval), or studying it over and over?
4. How can retrieval-induced forgetting occur during conversations?
5. How is it possible to remember something you've never seen?
6. How is brain activity different when you are trying to recall versus successfully recalling?

Forms of Long-Term Memory: More Than One Kind

LEARNING OUTCOMES

- Distinguish between explicit and implicit memory.
- Give examples of both semantic and episodic memories.
- Describe the pros and cons of collaborative memory.

explicit memory The act of consciously or intentionally retrieving past experiences.

implicit memory The influence of past experiences on later behavior and performance, even without an effort to remember them or an awareness of the recollection.

In 1977, the neurologist Oliver Sacks interviewed a young man named Greg who had a tumor in his brain that wiped out his ability to remember day-to-day events. One thing Greg could remember was his life during the 1960s, especially attending rock concerts by his favorite band, the Grateful Dead. Greg's memories of those concerts stuck with him over the following years, when he was living in a long-term care hospital. In 1991, Dr. Sacks took Greg to a Dead concert at New York's Madison Square Garden, wondering whether such a momentous event might jolt his memory into action. "That was fantastic," Greg told Dr. Sacks as they left the concert. "I will always remember it. I had the time of my life." But when Dr. Sacks saw Greg the next morning and asked him whether he recalled the previous night's concert, Greg drew a blank: "No, I've never been to the Garden" (Sacks, 1995, pp. 76–77).

Although Greg was unable to make new memories, some of the new things that happened to him seemed to leave a mark. For example, Greg did not recall learning that his father had died, but he did seem sad and withdrawn for years after hearing the news. Similarly, HM could not make new memories after his surgery, but if he played a game in which he had to track a moving target, his performance gradually improved with each round (Milner, 1962). Greg could not consciously remember hearing about his father's death, and HM could not consciously remember playing the tracking game, but both showed clear signs of having been permanently changed by experiences that they so rapidly forgot. In other words, they *behaved* as though they were remembering things while claiming to remember nothing at all. This suggests that there must be several kinds of memory, some that are accessible to conscious recall, and some that we cannot consciously access (Eichenbaum & Cohen, 2001; Schacter & Tulving, 1994; Schacter, Wagner, & Buckner, 2000; Squire & Kandel, 1999).

Memories can be broken down into two types. **Explicit memory** occurs *when people consciously or intentionally retrieve past experiences.* Recalling last summer's vacation, incidents from a novel you just read, or facts you studied for a test all involve explicit memory. Indeed, anytime you start a sentence with "I remember . . . ," you are talking about an explicit memory. **Implicit memory** occurs when *past experiences influence later behavior and performance, even without an effort to remember them or an awareness of the recollection* (Graf & Schacter, 1985; Schacter, 1987). Let's look at both of these.

Implicit Memory

Implicit memories are not consciously recalled, but their presence is "implied" by our actions. Greg's persistent sadness after his father's death, even though he had no conscious knowledge of the event, is an example of implicit memory. So is HM's improved performance on a tracking task that he didn't consciously remember doing.

The ability to ride a bike or tie your shoelaces or play the guitar are other examples of implicit memory. You may know how to do these things, but you probably can't describe how to do them. Such knowledge reflects a particular kind of implicit memory called **procedural memory**, which refers to *the gradual acquisition of skills as a result of practice, or "knowing how" to do things.* The fact that people who have amnesia can acquire new procedural memories suggests that the hippocampal structures that are usually damaged in these individuals may be necessary for explicit memory, but they aren't needed for implicit procedural memory. In fact, it appears that brain regions outside the hippocampal area (including areas in the motor cortex) are involved in procedural memory. The Learning chapter discusses this evidence further, and you will also see that procedural memory is crucial for learning various kinds of motor, perceptual, and cognitive skills.

Priming Makes Some Information More Accessible

Not all implicit memories are procedural or "how to" memories. For example, **priming** refers to *an enhanced ability to think of a stimulus, such as a word or object, as a result of a recent exposure to the stimulus* (Tulving & Schacter, 1990). In one experiment, college students were asked to study a long list of words, including items such as *avocado, mystery, climate, octopus,* and *assassin* (Tulving, Schacter, & Stark, 1982). Later, explicit memory was tested by showing participants some of these words along with new ones they hadn't seen and asking them which words were on the list. To test implicit memory, participants received word fragments and were asked to come up with a word that fitted the fragment. Try the test yourself:

c h – – – – n k   o – t – p – –   – o g – y – – –   – l – m – t e

You probably had difficulty coming up with the answers for the first and third fragments (*chipmunk, bogeyman*) but had little trouble coming up with answers for the second and fourth (*octopus, climate*). Seeing *octopus* and *climate* on the original list made those words more accessible later, during the fill-in-the-blanks test. Just as priming a pump makes water flow more easily, priming the memory system makes some information more accessible. In the fill-in-the-blanks experiment, people showed priming for studied words, even when they failed to remember consciously that they had seen them earlier.

A truly stunning example of this point comes from a study in which participants first studied black-and-white line drawings depicting everyday objects (Mitchell, 2006). Later, the participants were shown fragmented versions of the drawings that were difficult to identify; some of them depicted objects that they had studied earlier in the experiment, whereas others depicted new objects that they had not studied. Participants correctly identified more fragmented drawings of studied than new objects, and identified more studied objects than did participants in a control group who had never seen the pictures—a clear demonstration of priming (see **FIGURE 6.12**). Here's the stunning part: The fragmented drawing test was given 17 years after presentation of the study list! By that time, participants had little or no explicit memory of having seen the drawings, and some had no recollection that they had ever participated in the experiment! These observations confirm that priming is an example of implicit memory, and also that priming can persist over very long periods of time.

Guitarists such as Jack White rely heavily on procedural memory to acquire and use the skills they need to play their music at a high level. David Wolff - Patrick/ WireImage/Getty Images

procedural memory The gradual acquisition of skills as a result of practice, or "knowing how" to do things.

priming An enhanced ability to think of a stimulus, such as a word or object, as a result of a recent exposure to that stimulus.

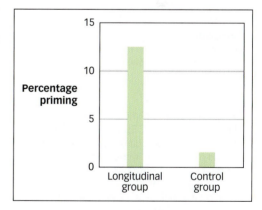

Figure 6.12 LONG-TERM PRIMING OF VISUAL OBJECTS Participants who viewed drawings of common objects, and 17 years later were given a test in which they tried to identify the objects from fragmented drawings (longitudinal group), showed a strong priming effect. In contrast, participants who had not seen the drawings 17 years earlier (control group) showed nonsignificant priming (Mitchell, 2006).

Procedural Memory and Priming Do Not Rely on the Hippocampus

Because priming is an example of implicit memory, not explicit memory, you'd expect amnesic individuals such as HM and Greg to show priming. In fact, many experiments have shown that amnesic individuals can show substantial priming effects—often as great as healthy, nonamnesic individuals—even though they have no explicit memory for the items they studied. Priming, like procedural memory, does not require the hippocampal structures that are damaged in cases of amnesia (Schacter & Curran, 2000).

If the hippocampal region isn't required for procedural memory and priming, which parts of the brain are involved? When research participants are shown the word stem *mot____* or *tab____* and are asked to provide the first word that comes to mind, parts of the occipital lobe involved in visual processing and parts of the frontal lobe involved in word retrieval become active. But if people perform the same task after being primed by seeing *motel* and *table*, there's less activity in these same regions (Buckner et al., 1995; Schott et al., 2005). Priming seems to make it easier for parts of the cortex that are involved in perceiving a word or object to identify the item after a recent exposure to it (Schacter, Dobbins, & Schnyer, 2004; Wiggs & Martin, 1998). This suggests that the brain saves a bit of processing time after priming (see **FIGURE 6.13**).

Explicit Memory: Semantic and Episodic

Consider these two questions: (1) Why do Americans celebrate on July 4? and (2) What is the most spectacular Fourth of July celebration you've ever seen? Every American knows the answer to the first question (we celebrate the signing of the Declaration of Independence on July 4, 1776), but we all have our own answers to the second. Both of these are explicit memories, consciously or intentionally retrieved from past experiences. But the first one requires you to dredge up a fact that every American schoolchild knows and that is not part of your personal autobiography, and the second requires you to revisit a particular time and place—or episode—from your personal past. These memories are called *semantic* and *episodic* memories, respectively (Tulving, 1972, 1983, 1998). **Semantic memory** is *a network of associated facts and concepts that make up our general knowledge of the world*. **Episodic memory** is *the collection of past personal experiences that occurred at a particular time and place*.

semantic memory A network of associated facts and concepts that make up our general knowledge of the world.

episodic memory The collection of past personal experiences that occurred at a particular time and place.

Figure 6.13 PRIMED AND UNPRIMED PROCESSING OF STIMULI Priming is associated with reduced levels of activation in the cortex on a number of different tasks. In each pair of fMRIs, the images on the upper left within each pair (A, C) show brain regions in the frontal lobe (A) and occipital/temporal lobe (C) that are active during an unprimed task (in this case, providing a word response to a visual word cue). The images on the lower right within each pair (B, D) show reduced activity in the same regions during the primed version of the same task. Republished with permission of Schacter & Buckner from Priming and the brain, *Neuron*, 20, 185–195. Elsevier Figure 1. (1998). Permission conveyed through Copyright Clearance Center, Inc.

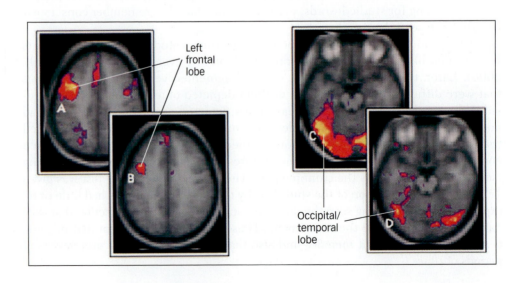

Left frontal lobe

Occipital/temporal lobe

These new Americans are taking the Oath of Allegiance after passing a citizenship test that would have required them to use their semantic memories. EPA/Jim Lo Scalzo/Newscom

Episodic memory is special because it is the only form of memory that allows us to engage in mental time travel, projecting ourselves into the past and revisiting events that have happened to us. This ability allows us to connect our pasts and our presents and construct a cohesive story of our lives. People who have amnesia can usually travel back in time and revisit episodes that occurred before they became amnesic, but they are unable to revisit episodes that happened later. For example, Greg couldn't travel back to any time after 1969 because that's when he stopped being able to create new episodic memories. But can people with amnesia create new semantic memories?

Researchers have studied three young adults who suffered damage to the hippocampus during birth as a result of difficult deliveries that interrupted oxygen supply to the brain (Brandt et al., 2009; Vargha-Khadem et al., 1997). Their parents noticed that the children could not recall what happened during a typical day, had to be constantly reminded of appointments, and often became lost and disoriented. In view of their hippocampal damage, you might also expect that these children would perform poorly in school. Remarkably, however, all three children learned to read, write, and spell; developed normal vocabularies; and acquired other kinds of semantic knowledge that allowed them to perform well in school. On the basis of this evidence, researchers have concluded that the hippocampus is not necessary for acquiring new *semantic* memories.

Episodic Memory and Imagining the Future

We've already seen that episodic memory allows us to travel backward in time, but it turns out that episodic memory also plays a role in allowing us to travel forward in time. An amnesic man known by the initials K.C. provided an early clue. K.C. could not recollect any specific episodes from his past, and when he was asked to imagine a future episode—such as what he might do tomorrow—he reported a complete "blank" (Tulving, 1985). Consistent with this observation, more recent findings from individuals with hippocampal amnesia reveal that some of them have difficulty imagining new experiences, such as sunbathing on a sandy beach (Hassabis et al., 2007), or events that might happen in their everyday lives (Race, Keane, & Verfaellie, 2011). Consistent with these findings, neuroimaging studies reveal that a network of brain regions known to be involved in episodic memory—including the hippocampus—show similarly increased activity when people remember the past and imagine the future (Addis, Wong, & Schacter, 2007; Okuda et al., 2003; Schacter et al., 2012; Szpunar, Watson, & McDermott, 2007; see **FIGURE 6.14**).

Taken together, these observations strongly suggest that we rely heavily on episodic memory to envision our personal futures (Schacter, Addis, & Buckner, 2008; Szpunar, 2010). Episodic memory is well suited to the task because it is a flexible system that allows us to recombine elements of past experience in new ways, so that we can mentally try out different versions of what might happen (Schacter, 2012; Schacter & Addis, 2007; Suddendorf & Corballis, 2007). For example, when you imagine having a difficult conversation with a friend that will take place in a couple of days, you can draw on past experiences to envision different ways in which the conversation might unfold, and hopefully avoid saying things that, based on past experience, are likely to make the situation worse. As we'll discuss later, however, this flexibility of episodic memory might also be responsible for some kinds of memory errors (see p. 193).

Collaborative Memory: Social Influences on Remembering

So far, we've focused mainly on memory in individuals functioning on their own. But remembering also serves important social functions, which is why we get together with family to talk about old times, or share our memories with our friends by posting our vacation photos on Facebook. Sharing memories with others can strengthen them (Hirst & Echterhoff, 2012), but we've already seen that talking about some aspects of a memory, but omitting other related events, can also produce retrieval-induced forgetting (see p. 176; Coman, Manier, & Hirst, 2009; Cuc et al., 2007). Psychologists have become increasingly interested in how people remember in groups, which is now referred to as *collaborative memory* (Rajaram, 2011).

In a typical collaborative memory experiment, participants first encode a set of target materials, such as a list of words, on their own (just as in the traditional memory experiments that we've already considered). At the time of retrieval, participants work together in small groups (usually two or three participants) to try to remember the target items. The number of items recalled by this group can then be compared with the number of items recalled by individuals who are trying to recall items on their own, without any help from others. The collaborative group typically recalls more target items than any individual (Hirst & Echterhoff, 2012; Weldon, 2001), suggesting that collaboration benefits memory. For example, Tim might recall an item that Emily forgot, and Eric might remember items that neither Tim nor Emily recalled, so the sum total of the group will exceed what any one person can recall.

Figure 6.14 REMEMBERING THE PAST AND IMAGINING THE FUTURE DEPEND ON A COMMON NETWORK OF BRAIN REGIONS A common brain network is activated when people remember episodes that actually occurred in their personal pasts and when they imagine episodes that might occur in their personal futures. This network includes the hippocampus, a part of the medial temporal lobe that plays an important role in episodic memory (Schacter, Addis, & Buckner, 2007).

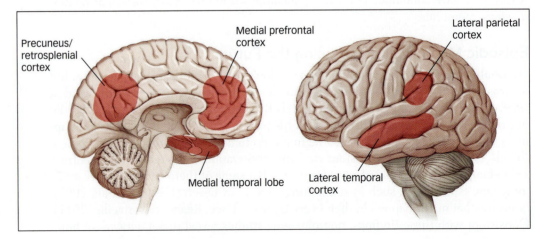

But things get really interesting when we compare the performance of the collaborative group with the performance of several individuals recalling target items on their own. For example, let's assume that after studying a list of eight words, Tim recalls items 1, 2, and 8, Emily recalls items 1, 4, and 7, and Eric recalls items 1, 5, 6, and 8—in total, seven of the eight items that were presented. (Nobody recalled item 3.) The surprising finding is that, when they remember together as a group, Tim, Emily, and Eric will typically come up with fewer total items than when they remember on their own (Basden et al., 1997; Hirst & Echterhoff, 2012; Rajaram, 2011; Rajaram & Pereira-Pasarin, 2010; Weldon, 2001). This negative effect of group recall on memory is known as *collaborative inhibition*: The same number of individuals working together recall fewer items than they would on their own.

What's going on here? One possibility is that, when recalling items together, the retrieval strategies used by some members of the group disrupt those used by others (Basden et al., 1997; Hirst & Echterhoff, 2012; Rajaram, 2011). For example, suppose that Tim goes first and recalls items in the order that they were presented. This retrieval strategy may be disruptive to Emily, who prefers to recall the last item first and then work backward through the list. Interesting recent research indicates that the negative effects of collaborative inhibition on memory persist even when individual members of a group later try to recall studied items on their own, without the disruption of retrieval strategies by other group members (Barber,

Remembering as a collaborative group leads to greater recall than any single member of the group would achieve, but less than that produced by a group of individuals remembering on their own. Blend Images/Hill Street Studios/Alamy

---

Is Google Hurting Our Memories?

Take some time to try to answer a simple question before returning to reading this box: What country has a national flag that is not rectangular? Now let's discuss what went through your mind as you searched for an answer. (The correct one is Nepal.) There probably was a time not too long ago when most people would have tried to conjure up images of national flags or take a mental world tour, but recent research conducted in the lab of one of your textbook authors indicates that, nowadays, most of us think about computers and Google searches when confronted with questions of this kind (Sparrow, Liu, & Wegner, 2011).

Further, after people were given difficult general-knowledge questions, they were slower to name the color in which a computer-related word (e.g., Google, Internet, Yahoo) was printed than the color in which a noncomputer-related word (e.g., Nike, table, Yoplait) was printed (Sparrow et al., 2011). This suggests that after being given difficult questions, these people were thinking about things related to computers,

which interfered with their ability to name the color in which the word was printed. The researchers concluded that we are now so used to searching for information on Google when we don't immediately know the answer to a question that we immediately think of computers, rather than searching our memories. This result raises troubling questions: Is reliance on computers and the Internet having an adverse effect on human memory? If we rely on Google for answers, are we unknowingly making our memories obsolete?

In fact, participants had a harder time remembering bits of trivia

What does your computer remember for you? HA Photos/Alamy

("An ostrich's eye is bigger than its brain") that they typed into a computer when they were told that the computer would save their answers than when they were told that the answers would be erased (Sparrow et al., 2011). But people often were able to remember where they saved the answers even when they did not remember the information itself. People seemed to be using the computer in an efficient way to help remember facts while relying on their own memories to recall where those facts could be found. This suggests that people may be adapting their memories to the demands of new technology, relying on computers in a way that is similar to how we sometimes rely on other people (friends, family members, or colleagues) to remember things that we may not remember ourselves. This is similar to what we discussed as collaborative memory, and just as collaborative remembering with other people has both helpful and harmful effects, so does collaborative remembering with our computers.

Harris, & Rajaram, 2015). So, next time you are sharing memories of a past activity with friends, you will be shaping your memories for both better and worse. (Can you rely on your computer for collaborative remembering? See The Real World: Is Google Hurting Our Memories?)

BUILD TO THE OUTCOMES

1. What is the type of memory in which you just "know how" to do something?

2. How does priming make memory more efficient?

3. What form of memory is like a time machine to our past?

4. How does episodic memory help us imagine our futures?

5. Why does a collaborative group typically recall fewer items than the same individuals, working independently?

Memory Failures: The Seven "Sins" of Memory

LEARNING OUTCOMES

- Identify each of the memory "sins."

- Describe possible benefits of each of the memory "sins."

You probably haven't given much thought to breathing today, and the reason is that from the moment you woke up, you've been doing it effortlessly and well. But the moment breathing fails, you are reminded of just how important it is. Memory is like that. Every time we see, think, notice, imagine, or wonder, we are drawing on our ability to use information stored in our brains, but it isn't until this ability fails that we become acutely aware of just how much we should treasure it. Such memory errors—the seven "sins" of memory—cast illumination on how memory normally operates and how often it operates well (Schacter, 1999, 2001b). We'll discuss each of the seven "sins" in detail below.

1. Transience

transience Forgetting what occurs with the passage of time.

On March 6, 2007, I. Lewis "Scooter" Libby, the former chief of staff to Vice President Dick Cheney, was convicted of perjury during an FBI investigation into whether members of the Bush administration had unlawfully disclosed the identity of a CIA agent to the media. According to Libby's defense team, any misstatements he might have made in response to FBI questioning were the result of faulty memory, not an intention to deceive. How could Libby forget such important events? Research has shown that memories can and do degrade with time. The culprit here is **transience**: *forgetting what occurs with the passage of time.*

Transience occurs during the storage phase of memory, after an experience has been encoded and before it is retrieved. This was first illustrated in the late 1870s by Hermann Ebbinghaus, a German philosopher who measured his own memory for lists of nonsense syllables at different delays after studying them (Ebbinghaus, 1885/1964). Ebbinghaus charted his recall of nonsense syllables over time, creating the forgetting curve shown in **FIGURE 6.15**. Ebbinghaus noted a rapid drop-off in retention during the first few tests, followed by a slower rate of forgetting on later tests—a general pattern confirmed by many subsequent memory researchers (Wixted & Ebbensen, 1991). So, for example, when English-speakers were tested for memory of Spanish vocabulary acquired during high school or college courses 1 to 50 years previously, there was a rapid drop-off in memory during the first 3 years after the students' last class, followed by tiny losses in later years (Bahrick, 1984, 2000). In all these studies, memories didn't fade at a constant rate as time passed;

I. Lewis "Scooter" Libby was convicted of perjury and obstructing justice, but he claimed that forgetting and related memory problems were responsible for any misstatements he made. Alex Wong/Getty Images

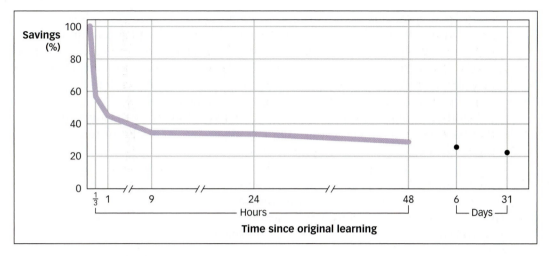

Figure 6.15 THE CURVE OF FORGETTING Hermann Ebbinghaus measured his retention at various delay intervals after he studied lists of nonsense syllables. He measured retention in percent savings, that is, the percentage of time he needed to relearn the list compared with the time he needed to learn it initially.

most forgetting happened soon after an event occurred, with increasingly less forgetting as more time passed.

Another way that memories can be distorted is by interference from other memories. For example, if you carry out the same activities at work each day, by the time Friday rolls around, it may be difficult to remember what you did on Monday because later activities blend in with earlier ones. This is an example of **retroactive interference**, *situations in which later learning impairs memory for information acquired earlier* (Postman & Underwood, 1973). **Proactive interference**, in contrast, refers to *situations in which earlier learning impairs memory for information acquired later*. If you use the same parking lot each day at work or at school, you've probably gone out to find your car and then stood there confused by the memories of having parked it on previous days.

retroactive interference Situations in which information learned later impairs memory for information acquired earlier.

proactive interference Situations in which information learned earlier impairs memory for information acquired later.

2. Absentmindedness

The great cellist Yo-Yo Ma put his treasured $2.5 million instrument in the trunk of a taxicab in Manhattan. He rode to his destination, paid the driver and left the cab, forgetting his cello. Minutes later, Ma realized what he had done and called the police. Fortunately, they tracked down the taxi and recovered the instrument (Finkelstein, 1999). But how had the celebrated cellist forgotten about something so important that had occurred only 10 minutes earlier? Transience is not a likely culprit. As soon as Mr. Ma realized what he'd done with his instrument, he recalled where he had put it. This information had not disappeared from his memory (which is why he was able to tell the police where the cello was). Instead, Yo-Yo Ma was a victim of **absentmindedness**, *a lapse in attention that results in memory failure*.

What makes people absentminded? One common cause is lack of attention. Attention plays a vital role in encoding information into long-term memory. Without proper attention, material is much less likely to be stored properly and recalled later. For example, in one study, participants listened to lists of 15 words for a later memory test (Craik et al., 1996). They were allowed to pay full attention to some of the lists, but while they heard other lists, they simultaneously performed another task that required them to press keys to indicate where an asterisk was appearing and disappearing. On a later test, participants recalled far fewer words from the list they had heard while their attention was divided.

What happens in the brain when attention is divided? As we saw earlier, greater activity in the lower left frontal region during encoding is associated with better memory. But participants show less activity in the lower left frontal lobe when their attention is divided (Shallice et al., 1994). Dividing attention, then, prevents the

absentmindedness A lapse in attention that results in memory failure.

Talking on a cell phone while driving is a common occurrence of divided attention in everyday life; texting is even worse. This can be dangerous, and an increasing number of states have banned the practice. Christina Kennedy/fStop/Getty Images

lower left frontal lobe from playing its normal role in semantic encoding, and the result is absentminded forgetting. Divided attention also leads to less hippocampal involvement in encoding (Kensinger, Clarke, & Corkin, 2003; Uncapher & Rugg, 2008). Given the importance of the hippocampus to episodic memory, this finding may help to explain why absentminded forgetting is sometimes so extreme, as when we forget where we put our keys or glasses only moments earlier.

Another common cause of absentmindedness is forgetting to carry out actions that we plan to do in the future. On any given day, you need to remember the times and places that your classes meet, you need to remember with whom and where you are having lunch, you need to remember which grocery items to pick up for dinner, and you need to remember which page of this book you were on when you fell asleep. In other words, you have to remember to remember, and this is called **prospective memory**, *remembering to do things in the future* (Einstein & McDaniel, 1990, 2005). Failures of prospective memory are a major source of absentmindedness.

3. Blocking

Have you ever tried to recall the name of a famous movie actor or a book you've read—and felt that the answer was on the tip of your tongue, rolling around in your head *somewhere* but just out of reach at the moment? This tip-of-the-tongue experience is a classic example of **blocking**, *a failure to retrieve information that is available in memory, even though you are trying to produce it*. The sought-after information has been encoded and stored, it has not faded from memory, and you aren't forgetting to retrieve it. Rather, you are experiencing a full-blown retrieval failure, which makes this memory breakdown especially frustrating. Researchers have described the tip-of-the-tongue state, in particular, as "a mild torment, something like [being] on the brink of a sneeze" (Brown & McNeill, 1966, p. 326).

Blocking occurs especially often for the names of people and places (Cohen, 1990; Semenza, 2009; Valentine, Brennen, & Brédart, 1996). Why? Because their links to related concepts and knowledge are weaker than for common names. That somebody's last name is Baker doesn't tell us much about the person, but saying that he *is* a baker does. To illustrate this point, researchers showed people pictures of cartoon and comic strip characters, some with descriptive names that highlight key features of the character (e.g., Grumpy, Snow White, Scrooge) and others with arbitrary names (e.g., Aladdin, Mary Poppins, Pinocchio). Even though the two types of names were equally familiar to participants in the experiment, they blocked less often on the descriptive names than on the arbitrary names (Brédart & Valentine, 1998).

Although it's frustrating when it occurs, blocking is a relatively infrequent event for most of us. However, it occurs more often as we grow older, and it is a very common complaint among people in their 60s and 70s (Burke et al., 1991; Schwartz, 2002). Even more striking, some individuals with brain damage live in a nearly perpetual tip-of-the-tongue state (Semenza, 2009). One such individual could recall the names of only 2 of 40 famous people when she saw their photographs, compared with 25 of 40 for healthy volunteers in the control group (Semenza & Zettin, 1989). Yet she could still recall correctly the occupations of 32 of these people—the same number as healthy people could recall. This case and similar ones have given researchers important clues about what parts of the brain are involved in retrieving proper names. Name blocking usually results from damage to parts of the left temporal lobe on the surface of the cortex, most often as a result of a stroke. This idea is supported by studies that show strong activation of regions within the temporal lobe when people recall proper names (Damasio et al., 1996; Gorno-Tempini et al., 1998).

---

prospective memory Remembering to do things in the future.

blocking A failure to retrieve information that is available in memory, even though you are trying to produce it.

Suppose that, mentally consumed with planning for a psychology test the next day, you place your keys in an unusual spot and later forget where you put them. Is this more likely to reflect the memory "sin" of transience, absentmindedness, or blocking? stillfx/AgeFotostock

4. Memory Misattribution

Shortly after the devastating 1995 bombing of the federal building in Oklahoma City, police set about searching for two suspects they called John Doe 1 and John Doe 2. John Doe 1 turned out to be Timothy McVeigh, who was quickly apprehended and later convicted of the crime and sentenced to death. John Doe 2, who had supposedly accompanied McVeigh when he rented a van from Elliott's Body Shop two days before the bombing, was never found. In fact, John Doe 2 had never existed; he was a product of the memory of Tom Kessinger, a mechanic at Elliott's Body Shop who was present when McVeigh rented the van. The day after, two other men had also rented a van in Kessinger's presence. The first man, like McVeigh, was tall and fair. The second man was shorter and stockier, was dark-haired, wore a blue and white cap, and had a tattoo beneath his left sleeve—a match to the description of John Doe 2. Tom Kessinger had confused his recollections of men he had seen on separate days in the same place. He was a victim of **memory misattribution**, *assigning a recollection or an idea to the wrong source* (see **FIGURE 6.16**).

Part of memory is knowing where our memories came from. This is known as **source memory**, *recall of when, where, and how information was acquired* (Johnson, Hashtroudi, & Lindsay, 1993; Mitchell & Johnson, 2009; Schacter, Harbluk, & McLachlan, 1984). People sometimes correctly recall a fact they learned earlier or accurately recognize a person or object they have seen before but misattribute the source of this knowledge—just as happened to Tom Kessinger (Davies, 1988). Such misattribution could be the cause of déjà vu experiences, when you suddenly feel that you have been in a situation before even though you can't recall any details. A present situation that is similar to a past experience may trigger a general sense of familiarity that is mistakenly attributed to having been in the exact situation previously (Brown, 2004; Reed, 1988).

Individuals with damage to the frontal lobes are especially prone to memory misattribution errors (Schacter et al., 1984; Shimamura & Squire, 1987). This is probably because the frontal lobes play a significant role in effortful retrieval processes, which are required to dredge up the correct source of a memory. But we are all vulnerable to memory misattribution. Take the following test and there is a good chance that you will experience it for yourself. First, study the two lists of words presented in **TABLE 6.1** by reading each word for about 1 second. When you are done, return to this paragraph for more instructions, but don't look back at the table! Now try to recognize which of the following words appeared on the list you just studied: *taste, bread, needle, king, sweet, thread*. If you think that *taste* and *thread* were on the lists you studied, you're right. And if you think that *bread* and *king* weren't on those lists, you're also right. But if you think that *needle* or *sweet* appeared on the lists, you're dead wrong.

memory misattribution Assigning a recollection or an idea to the wrong source.

source memory Recall of when, where, and how information was acquired.

TABLE 6.1	
False Recognition	
sour	thread
candy	pin
sugar	eye
bitter	sewing
good	sharp
taste	point
tooth	prick
nice	thimble
honey	haystack
soda	pain
chocolate	hurt
heart	injection
cake	syringe
tart	cloth
pie	knitting

Figure 6.16 MEMORY MISATTRIBUTION In 1995, the Murrah Federal Building in Oklahoma City was bombed in an act of terrorism. The police sketch (right) shows John Doe 2, who originally was thought to have been the culprit Timothy McVeigh's partner in the bombing. It was later determined that the witness had confused his memories of different men whom he had encountered on different days. AP Photo/David Glass; FBI/The Oklahoman/AP Photo

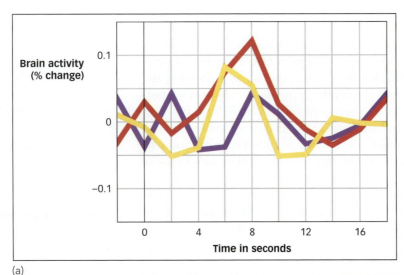

(a)

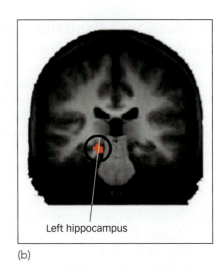

Left hippocampus

(b)

Figure 6.17 HIPPOCAMPAL ACTIVITY DURING TRUE AND FALSE RECOGNITION Many brain regions show similar activation during true and false recognition, including the hippocampus. The figure shows results from an fMRI study of true and false recognition of visual shapes (Slotnick & Schacter, 2004). (a) A plot showing the activity level in the strength of the fMRI signal from the hippocampus over time. This shows that, after a few seconds, there is comparable activation for true recognition of previously studied shapes (red line) and false recognition of similar shapes that were not presented (yellow line). Both true and false recognition show increased hippocampal activity compared with correct classification of unrelated shapes as new (purple line). (b) A region of the left hippocampus. Reprinted by permission from Macmillan Publishers Ltd. Slotnick & Schacter, A sensory signature that distinguishes true from false memories. *Nature Neuroscience*, 2004, 7(61), p. 669.

Most people make exactly the same mistake, claiming with confidence that they saw *needle* and *sweet* on the list. This mistaken feeling of familiarity, called *false recognition*, occurs because all the words in the lists are associated with *needle* or *sweet*. Seeing each word in the study list activates related words. Because *needle* and *sweet* are related to all of the associates, they become more activated than other words—so highly activated that only minutes later, people swear that they actually studied the words (Deese, 1959; Gallo, 2006, 2010; Roediger & McDermott, 1995, 2000). In fact, brain scanning studies using PET and fMRI show that many of the same brain regions are active during false recognition and true recognition, including the hippocampus (Cabeza et al., 2001; Schacter, Reiman, et al., 1996; see **FIGURE 6.17**).

When people experience a strong sense of familiarity about a person, object, or event but lack specific recollections, a potentially dangerous recipe for memory misattribution is in place, both in the laboratory and also in real-world situations involving eyewitness memory. However, false recognition can be reduced (Schacter, Israel, & Racine, 1999). For example, when participants are given a choice between an object that they actually saw (e.g., a car) and a visually similar new object (a different car that looks like the one they saw), they almost always choose the car that they actually saw and thus avoid making a false recognition error (Guerin et al., 2012a, 2012b). Understanding this point may be a key to reducing the dangerous consequences of misattribution in eyewitness testimony (see Other Voices: Memories Inside Out).

5. Suggestibility

On October 4, 1992, an El Al cargo plane crashed into an apartment building in a southern suburb of Amsterdam, killing 39 residents and all 4 members of the airline crew. The disaster dominated news in the Netherlands for days as people

Memories Inside Out

Karen L. Daniel is the director of the Center on Wrongful Convictions at Northwestern University School of Law. Jasmin Shah Photography

There's a good chance that sometime during the summer of 2015 you saw and enjoyed the hit Pixar movie *Inside Out*, which portrays the emotional struggles of the 11-year-old Riley after her family moves to a new home by drawing on psychological research that distinguishes among basic emotions (see the chapter on Emotion and Motivation, pp. 236–267). The movie also delved into Riley's memories and provided some realistic insights into how memories can be used to regulate emotions. But as Karen Daniel points out in an opinion piece published when the movie opened, the film's depiction of memory ignored some key findings and ideas from psychological research on memory, with potentially serious consequences:

Let me begin by saying that I love, love, love Pixar movies. Like many adults, I began watching them as part of my parental duties. There was a time when I could recite all the dialogue from *Monsters Inc.* and the first two *Toy Story* films.

It was thus with great anticipation that I tuned in to a radio interview of Pete Docter, the director of the latest Pixar release, *Inside Out*. What a fabulous idea: animating the emotions inside the mind of an 11-year-old child named Riley who is undergoing a major life transition. Docter explained that he researched many aspects of psychology to make the film accurate. When it came to human memory, however, Docter departed from science for the sake of the story line.

As shown in a trailer for *Inside Out*, Riley's memories are portrayed as mini-animations safely preserved inside little globes, which can be pulled out and replayed exactly the way they happened. The character Joy explains that certain of these globes contain "core memories" that form the basis of Riley's personality. This representation of memory is essential to the plot but is not true, as Docter candidly admitted.

I couldn't help but cringe. Given the wide appeal of Pixar movies, a new generation may grow up internalizing the profoundly false notion that memory works like a video recording and that perfect memories of events can be recalled at will. In reality, memory is fallible, malleable, and subject to suggestion and distortion. Docter noted that learning this was a revelation to him, even though he chose not to depict memory that way in *Inside Out*.

One may ask, "Who cares? It's just a movie." In the world of criminal justice, it matters a great deal. One of the most critical moments in a criminal trial is when a victim or witness points at the defendant and declares, "I will never forget that face." The witness usually professes complete certainty, and the prosecutor highlights this as proof of the defendant's guilt—even though experts tell us courtroom certainty does not necessarily correlate to accuracy.

In fact, mistaken identification is a leading cause of conviction of the innocent. Myriad factors that are not necessarily obvious to the average person can affect the reliability of an eyewitness identification, such as distractions at the time of the event, lapse of time, post-event discussions with police, and limitations inherent in cross-racial identifications. Expert witnesses can help explain these factors, but most judges exclude expert testimony on the ground [sic] that eyewitness identifications are a matter of "common sense" and expert assistance is not necessary. (The Illinois Supreme Court is now reviewing a case that challenges this approach.)

Which brings us back to *Inside Out*. Absent the input of an expert, jurors are left to draw on personal experiences in evaluating testimony. Today's children (and their parents) may become tomorrow's jurors who believe, incorrectly, that memories are stored intact, and that witnesses can simply compare the pictures within their little memory globes to the person sitting at the defendant's table. Docter explained that this comports with most people's sense of how memory works—which is why relying on "common sense" in criminal trials falls short.

We can never entirely eliminate human error from the justice system, but overconfidence in witnesses and misunderstanding by factfinders leads to many wrongful convictions. Let's enjoy Pixar's new film, but when we return from the movie theater, let's ensure that those charged with deciding guilt or innocence in the courtroom are armed with scientific information about eyewitness identifications rather than with the snow globe concept of memory.

As Daniel and the text point out, faulty eyewitness memories are frequently at work in wrongful convictions. It would be unfortunate if the naive view of memory communicated by *Inside Out* has a lasting influence on any prospective jurors. On a more encouraging note, there are signs that some of the important findings regarding memory's fallibility, such as the seven sins of memory that you learned about in this chapter, are being communicated to participants in the legal system. For example, in 2014 the National Academy of Sciences published a report written by a distinguished committee composed of experts in both psychology and law titled *Identifying the Culprit: Assessing Eyewitness Identification*, which is intended to convey the findings of psychological research on eyewitness memory to participants in the legal system. Though no doubt many more people saw *Inside Out* than will read this important report, it seems likely that accurate characterizations of memory research such as those contained in the National Academy of Sciences' report will ultimately be more influential in the courtroom than the entertaining though misleading depictions of Riley's memory globes.

Daniel, K. (2015, June 16). Pixar movie teaches future jurors wrong lesson on memory. *Chicago Sun-Times.*

In 1992, an El Al cargo plane crashed into an apartment building in a suburb of Amsterdam. When Dutch psychologists asked students if they had seen the television film of the plane crashing, a majority said they had. In fact, no such footage exists (Crombag et al., 1996). Albert Overbeek/AP Photo

suggestibility The tendency to incorporate misleading information from external sources into personal recollections.

viewed footage of the crash scene and read about the catastrophe. Ten months later, Dutch psychologists asked university students: "Did you see the television film of the moment the plane hit the apartment building?" Fifty-five percent answered yes (Crombag, Wagenaar, & Van Koppen, 1996). All of this might seem perfectly normal except for one key fact: There was no television film of the moment when the plane actually crashed. The researchers had asked a suggestive question that implied that television film of the crash had been shown. Respondents may have viewed television film of the postcrash scene, and they may have read, imagined, or talked about what might have happened when the plane hit the building, but they most definitely did not see it. **Suggestibility** is the *tendency to incorporate misleading information from external sources into personal recollections.*

If misleading details can be implanted in people's memories, is it also possible to suggest entire episodes that never occurred? The answer seems to be yes (Loftus, 1993, 2003). In one study, the research participant, a teenager named Chris, was asked by his older brother, Jim, to try to remember the time Chris had been lost in a shopping mall at age 5. He initially recalled nothing, but after several days, Chris produced a detailed recollection of the event. He recalled that he "felt so scared I would never see my family again" and remembered that a kindly old man wearing a flannel shirt found him crying (Loftus, 1993, p. 532). But according to Jim and other family members, Chris was never lost in a shopping mall. Of 24 participants in a larger study on implanted memories, approximately 25% falsely remembered being lost as a child in a shopping mall or in a similar public place (Loftus & Pickrell, 1995).

People develop false memories in response to suggestions for some of the same reasons memory misattribution occurs. We do not store all the details of our experiences in memory, making us vulnerable to accepting suggestions about what might have happened or should have happened. In addition, visual imagery plays an important role in constructing false memories (Goff & Roediger, 1998). Asking people to imagine an event like spilling punch all over the bride's parents at a wedding increases the likelihood that they will develop a false memory of it (Hyman & Pentland, 1996). Social pressure can enhance suggestibility, as in cases where people falsely confess to crimes that they did not commit after repeated interrogations by authority figures such as police who are convinced of their guilt and press for a confession (Kassin, 2015). In some instances, these wrongly accused individuals develop false memories of the crime (Kassin, 2007).

All of these factors were operating in a recent study that provides some of the most dramatic evidence for suggested false memories. Consider the following question: Did you ever commit a crime when you were between the ages of 11 and 14 years old? Assuming that you did not, do you think that you could ever be convinced that you did? Shaw and Porter (2015) asked college students about an experience that actually occurred between ages 11 and 14, and also about a crime that they supposedly committed during those years (theft, assault, or assault with a weapon). Although none of the students had actually committed any crimes, during three separate interviews the experimenters required them repeatedly to imagine that they did. The researchers also applied social pressure techniques, such as telling students that their parents or caregivers said they had committed the crime, and stating that most people can retrieve seemingly lost memories if they try hard enough. In a remarkable finding, by the end of the third interview 70% of the students developed a false memory of having committed the crime! A similar percentage of students in a separate group exposed to the same suggestive procedures developed noncriminal false memories of emotional events that they repeatedly imagined (an animal attack, losing a lot of money, or an accident resulting in injury).

Studies such as the one by Shaw and Porter (2015) can help us to understand the key role played by suggestibility in a controversy that arose during the 1980s and

1990s concerning the accuracy of childhood memories that people recalled during psychotherapy. One highly publicized example involved a woman named Diana Halbrooks (Schacter, 1996). After a few months in psychotherapy, she began recalling disturbing incidents from her childhood, for example, that her mother had tried to kill her and that her father had abused her sexually. Although her parents denied that these events had ever occurred, her therapist encouraged her to believe in the reality of her memories. Eventually, Diana Halbrooks stopped therapy and came to realize that the "memories" she had recovered were inaccurate.

How happy do you think you'd be if the candidate you supported won an election? Do you think you'd accurately remember your level of happiness if you recalled it several months later? Chances are good that bias in the memory process would alter your recollection of your previous happiness. Indeed, 4 months after they heard the outcome of the 2000 presidential election, Bush supporters overestimated how happy they were, whereas Gore supporters underestimated how happy they were. PAUL J. RICHARDS/AFP/Getty Images; DOUG MILLS/AP Images

How could this happen? A number of the techniques used by psychotherapists to try to pull up forgotten childhood memories are clearly suggestive (Poole et al., 1995). In an important finding, recent studies show that memories that people remember spontaneously on their own are corroborated by other people at about the same rate as the memories of individuals who never forgot their abuse, whereas memories recovered in response to suggestive therapeutic techniques are virtually never corroborated by others (McNally & Geraerts, 2009).

6. Bias

In 2000, the outcome of a very close presidential race between George W. Bush and Al Gore was decided by the Supreme Court 5 weeks after the election had taken place. The day after the election (when the result was still in doubt), supporters of Bush and Gore were asked to predict how happy they would be after the outcome of the election was determined (Wilson, Meyers, & Gilbert, 2003). These same respondents reported how happy they felt with the outcome on the day after Al Gore conceded. And 4 months later, the participants recalled how happy they had been right after the election was decided.

Bush supporters, who eventually enjoyed a positive result (their candidate took office), were understandably happy the day after the Supreme Court's decision. However, their retrospective accounts *over*estimated how happy they were at the time. Conversely, Gore supporters were not pleased with the outcome. But when polled 4 months after the election was decided, Gore supporters *under*estimated how happy they actually were at the time of the result. In both groups, recollections of happiness were at odds with existing reports of their actual happiness at the time (Wilson et al., 2003).

These results illustrate the problem of **bias**, *the distorting influences of present knowledge, beliefs, and feelings on recollection of previous experiences.* Sometimes, what people remember from their pasts says less about what actually happened than about what they think, feel, or believe now. Researchers have also found that our current moods can bias our recall of past experiences (Bower, 1981; Buchanan, 2007; Eich, 1995). So in addition to helping you recall actual sad memories (as you saw earlier in this chapter), a sad mood can also bias your recollections of experiences that may not have been so sad.

Sometimes, we exaggerate differences between what we feel or believe now and what we felt or believed in the past. For example, most of us would like to believe that our romantic attachments grow stronger over time. In one study, dating couples were asked, once a year for 4 years, to assess the present quality of their relationships and to recall how they felt in past years (Sprecher, 1999). Couples who stayed together for the 4 years recalled that the strength of their love had increased since they last reported on it. Yet their actual ratings at the time did not show any increases in love and attachment. In an objective sense, the couples did not love each other more today than yesterday. But they did from the subjective perspective of memory. People were remembering the past as they wanted it to be rather than the way it was.

bias The distorting influences of present knowledge, beliefs, and feelings on recollection of previous experiences.

7. Persistence

The artist Melinda Stickney-Gibson awoke in her apartment to the smell of smoke. She jumped out of bed and saw black plumes rising through cracks in the floor. Raging flames had engulfed the entire building, and she had no chance to escape, except by jumping from her third-floor window. Although she survived the fire and the fall, Melinda became overwhelmed by memories of the fire. When she sat down in front of a blank canvas to start a new painting, her memories of that awful night intruded. Her paintings, which were previously bright, colorful abstractions, became dark meditations that included only black, orange, and ochre—the colors of the fire (Schacter, 1996).

Melinda Stickney-Gibson's experiences illustrate memory's seventh and most deadly sin, **persistence**: *the intrusive recollection of events that we wish we could forget*. Melinda's experience is far from unique; persistence frequently occurs after disturbing or traumatic incidents, such as the fire that destroyed her home. Although being able to recall memories quickly is usually considered a good thing, in the case of persistence, that ability mutates into an unwelcome burden.

Intrusive memories are undesirable consequences of emotional experiences because emotional experiences generally lead to more vivid and enduring recollections than nonemotional experiences do. One line of evidence comes from the study of **flashbulb memories**, which are *detailed recollections of when and where we heard about shocking events* (Brown & Kulik, 1977). For example, most Americans can recall exactly where they were and how they heard about the September 11, 2001, terrorist attacks on the World Trade Center and the Pentagon—almost as if a mental flashbulb had gone off automatically and recorded the event in long-lasting and vivid detail (Kvavilashvili et al., 2009). Several studies have shown that flashbulb memories are not always entirely accurate, but they are generally better remembered than are mundane news events from the same time (Larsen, 1992; Neisser & Harsch, 1992). Enhanced retention of flashbulb memories is partly attributable to

persistence The intrusive recollection of events that we wish we could forget.

flashbulb memories Detailed recollections of when and where we heard about shocking events.

Some events are so emotionally charged—such as President Kennedy's assassination and the terrorist attack on the World Trade Center—that we form unusually detailed memories of when and where we heard about them. These flashbulb memories generally persist much longer than memories for more ordinary events. Corbis; Kathy Willens/AP Images

the emotional arousal elicited by events such as the 9/11 terrorist attacks, and partly attributable to the fact that we tend to talk and think a lot about these experiences. Recall that semantic encoding enhances memory: When we talk about flashbulb experiences, we elaborate on them and thus further increase the memorability of those aspects of the experience that we discuss (Hirst et al., 2009, 2015).

Why do our brains succumb to persistence? A key player in the brain's response to emotional events is a small, almond-shaped structure called the *amygdala*, shown in **FIGURE 6.18.** The amygdala influences hormonal systems that kick into high gear when we experience an arousing event; these stress-related hormones, such as adrenaline and cortisol, mobilize the body in the face of threat—and they also enhance memory for the experience. When research participants watch a slide show including emotional events (such as photos of a child being hit by a car) and neutral events (such as a mother walking her child to school), the participants later remember the arousing event better than they do the mundane ones, and a higher level of activity in the amygdala while watching the emotional events predicts better recall of those events on a later test (Cahill et al., 1996; Kensinger & Schacter, 2005, 2006). When people are given a drug that interferes with the amygdala-mediated release of stress hormones, their memory for the emotional sections is no better than is their memory for the mundane sections (Lonegran et al., 2013). Similarly, patients with amygdala damage remember the emotional material no better than the mundane information (Cahill & McGaugh, 1998).

In many cases, there are clear benefits to forming strong memories for highly emotional events, particularly those that are life threatening. In the case of persistence, though, such memories may be too strong—strong enough to interfere with other aspects of daily life.

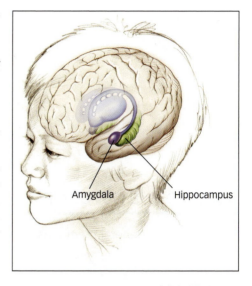

Figure 6.18 THE AMYGDALA'S INFLUENCE ON MEMORY The amygdala, located next to the hippocampus, responds strongly to emotional events. Individuals with amygdala damage are unable to remember emotional events any better than nonemotional ones (Cahill & McGaugh, 1998).

Are the Seven "Sins" Vices or Virtues?

You may have concluded that evolution has burdened us with an extremely inefficient memory system that is so prone to error that it often jeopardizes our well-being. Not so. The seven sins are the price we pay for the many benefits that memory provides, the occasional result of the normally efficient operation of the human memory system (Schacter, 2001b).

Consider transience, for example. Wouldn't it be great to remember all the details of every incident in your life, no matter how much time had passed? Not according to Jill Price (see the chapter opener), who has this ability and says it drives her crazy. If we didn't gradually forget information over time, our minds would be cluttered with details that we no longer need, such as an old phone number (Bjork, 2011; Bjork & Bjork, 1988; Norby, 2015). Memory, in essence, makes a bet that when we haven't used information recently, we probably won't need it in the future. We win this bet more often than we lose it, making transience an adaptive property of memory.

Similarly, absentmindedness and blocking can be frustrating, but they are side effects of our memory's usually successful attempt to sort through incoming information, preserving details that are worthy of attention and recall, and discarding those that are less worthy.

Memory misattribution and suggestibility both occur because we often fail to recall the details of exactly when and where we saw a face or learned a fact. Our memories carefully record such details only when we think we may need them later, and most of the time we are better off for it. Furthermore, we often use memories to anticipate possible future events. As discussed earlier, memory is flexible, allowing us to recombine elements of past experience in new ways, so that we can mentally try out different versions of what might happen. But this very flexibility—a strength of memory—may sometimes produce misattribution errors in which elements of past experience are miscombined (Schacter & Addis, 2007; Schacter, Guerin, & St. Jacques, 2011).

Bias skews our memories so that we depict ourselves in an overly favorable light, but it can produce the benefit of contributing to our overall sense of contentment, leading to greater psychological well-being (Taylor, 1989). Although persistence can cause us to be haunted by traumas that we'd be better off forgetting, overall, it is probably adaptive to remember threatening or traumatic events that could pose a threat to survival.

Although each of the seven sins can cause trouble in our lives, each has an adaptive side as well. You can think of the seven sins as costs we pay for benefits that allow memory to work as well as it does most of the time.

BUILD TO THE OUTCOMES

1. How might general memories come to distort specific memories?

2. How is memory affected for someone whose attention is divided?

3. Why is Snow White's name easier to remember than Mary Poppins's?

4. What can explain a déjà vu experience?

5. How can eyewitnesses be misled?

6. How does your current outlook color your memory of a past event?

7. How does emotional trauma affect memory?

8. How are we better off with imperfect memories?

CHAPTER REVIEW

Encoding: Transforming Perceptions Into Memories

- Memory is the ability to store and retrieve information over time.

- Memories are constructed when new information is combined with information we already have in our brains.

- Encoding is the process of transforming the information received through our senses into a lasting memory. There are three types of encoding: semantic encoding is characterized by relating new information to previous knowledge in a meaningful way; visual imagery encoding also relates new information to previous knowledge but features both a visual and a verbal placeholder; and organizational encoding is a process of finding relationships between items to make them easier to retrieve.

- Encoding information with respect to its survival value is a particularly effective method for increasing subsequent recall, perhaps because our memory systems have evolved in a way that allows us to remember especially well information that is relevant to our survival.

Storage: Maintaining Memories Over Time

- Sensory memory holds information for a second or two. "Rehearsal" helps keep memories in short-term storage, and "chunking" combines information into a single, meaningful item.

- Working memory is the active maintenance of information in short-term storage, where information is retained for about 15 to 20 seconds.

- The hippocampus functions as an index to put information into long-term memory, but it appears not to be the site of long-term memory storage.

- The act of recalling, thinking, and talking about a memory leads to consolidation. However, when memories are retrieved, they may also become vulnerable to disruption.

- Memory storage depends on changes in synapses, and long-term potentiation (LTP) increases synaptic connections.

Retrieval: Bringing Memories to Mind

- Whether we remember a past experience depends on whether retrieval cues are available to trigger recall. Retrieval cues are effective when they are given in the same context as when we encoded an experience. Moods and inner states can become retrieval cues.

- Retrieving information from memory can improve subsequent memory of the retrieved information, but it can also suppress memory for related information that is not retrieved.

- Neuroimaging studies suggest that trying to remember activates the left frontal lobe, whereas successful recovery of stored information activates the hippocampus.

Forms of Long-Term Memory: More Than One Kind

- Long-term memory consists of implicit memory, the unconscious influence of past experiences on later behavior and performance, and explicit memory, the act of consciously or intentionally retrieving past experiences.

- Implicit memory in turn includes procedural memory, the acquisition of skills as a result of practice, and priming, a change in the ability to recognize or identify an object or a word as the result of past exposure to it.

- Episodic memory is the collection of personal experiences from a particular time and place; it allows us both to recollect the past and imagine the future. Semantic memory is a networked, general, impersonal knowledge of facts, associations, and concepts.

- Collaborative memory refers to remembering in groups. Collaborative remembering can both impair memory and enhance it by exposing people to new information and helping to correct errors.

Memory Failures: The Seven "Sins" of Memory

- Memory's mistakes can be classified into seven "sins," which are the costs we pay for benefits that allow memory to work as well as it does most of the time.

- Some of these "sins" reflect inability to store or retrieve information we want. *Transience* is reflected by a rapid decline in memory followed by more gradual forgetting. *Absentmindedness* results from failures of attention, shallow encoding, and the influence of automatic behaviors. *Blocking* occurs when stored information is temporarily inaccessible, as when information is on the tip of the tongue. In contrast, *persistence* reflects the fact that emotional arousal generally leads to enhanced memory, whether we want to remember an experience or not.

- Other "sins" reflect errors in memory content. *Memory misattribution* happens when we experience a sense of familiarity but don't recall, or mistakenly recall, the specifics of when and where an experience occurred. *Suggestibility* gives rise to implanted memories of small details or entire episodes. *Bias* reflects the influence of current knowledge, beliefs, and feelings on memory or past experiences.

KEY CONCEPT QUIZ

1. Encoding is the process
   a. by which we transform what we perceive, think, or feel into an enduring memory.
   b. of maintaining information in memory over time.
   c. of bringing to mind information that has been previously stored.
   d. through which we recall information previously learned but forgotten.

2. What is the process of relating new information in a meaningful way to knowledge that is already in memory?
   a. spontaneous encoding
   b. organization encoding
   c. semantic encoding
   d. visual imagery encoding

3. Our human ancestors depended on the encoding of
   a. organizational information.
   b. reproductive mechanisms.
   c. survival-related information.
   d. pleasantness conditions.

4. What kind of memory storage holds information for a second or two?
   a. retrograde memory
   b. working memory
   c. short-term memory
   d. sensory memory

5. The process by which memories become stable in the brain is called
   a. consolidation.
   b. long-term memory.
   c. iconic memory.
   d. hippocampal indexing.

6. Long-term potentiation occurs through
   a. the interruption of communication between neurons.
   b. the strengthening of synaptic connections.
   c. the reconsolidation of disrupted memories.
   d. sleep.

7. The increased likelihood of recalling a sad memory when you are in a sad mood is an illustration of
   a. the encoding specificity principle.
   b. state-dependent retrieval.
   c. transfer-appropriate processing.
   d. memory accessibility.

8. Neuroimaging studies suggest that trying to remember activates the
   a. left frontal lobe.
   b. hippocampal region.
   c. occipital lobe.
   d. upper temporal lobe.

9. The act of consciously or intentionally retrieving past experiences is
   a. priming.
   b. procedural memory.
   c. implicit memory.
   d. explicit memory.

10. People who have amnesia are able to retain all of the following except
    a. explicit memory.
    b. implicit memory.
    c. procedural memory.
    d. priming.

11. Remembering a family reunion that you attended as a child illustrates

   a. semantic memory.
   b. procedural memory.
   c. episodic memory.
   d. perceptual priming.

12. The rapid decline in memory, followed by more gradual forgetting, is reflected by

   a. chunking.
   b. blocking.
   c. absentmindedness.
   d. transience.

13. Eyewitness misidentification or false recognition is most likely a result of

   a. memory misattribution.
   b. suggestibility.
   c. bias.
   d. retroactive interference.

14. The fact that emotional arousal generally leads to enhanced memory is supported by

   a. bias.
   b. persistence.
   c. proactive interference.
   d. source memory.

 **LearningCurve**   Don't stop now! Quizzing yourself is a powerful study tool. Go to LearningCurve at www.launchpadworks.com for more practice.

KEY TERMS

memory (p. 164)
encoding (p. 164)
storage (p. 164)
retrieval (p. 164)
semantic encoding (p. 165)
visual imagery encoding (p. 166)
organizational encoding (p. 166)
sensory memory (p. 168)
iconic memory (p. 168)
echoic memory (p. 168)
short-term memory (p. 169)
rehearsal (p. 169)

chunking (p. 170)
working memory (p. 170)
long-term memory (p. 170)
anterograde amnesia (p. 171)
retrograde amnesia (p. 171)
consolidation (p. 172)
reconsolidation (p. 172)
long-term potentiation (LTP) (p. 174)
retrieval cue (p. 174)
encoding specificity principle (p. 175)

state-dependent retrieval (p. 175)
transfer-appropriate processing (p. 175)
retrieval-induced forgetting (p. 176)
explicit memory (p. 178)
implicit memory (p. 178)
procedural memory (p. 179)
priming (p. 179)
semantic memory (p. 180)
episodic memory (p. 180)
transience (p. 184)
retroactive interference (p. 185)

proactive interference (p. 185)
absentmindedness (p. 185)
prospective memory (p. 186)
blocking (p. 186)
memory misattribution (p. 187)
source memory (p. 187)
suggestibility (p. 190)
bias (p. 191)
persistence (p. 192)
flashbulb memories (p. 192)

CHANGING MINDS

1. A friend of yours lost her father to cancer when she was a very young child. "I really wish I remembered him better," she says. "I know all the memories are locked in my head. I'm thinking of trying hypnotism to unlock some of those memories." You explain that we don't, in fact, have stored memories of everything that ever happened to us locked in our heads. What examples could you give of ways in which memories can be lost over time?

2. Another friend of yours has a very vivid memory of sitting with his parents in the living room on September 11, 2001, watching live TV as the Twin Towers fell during the terrorist attacks. "I remember my mother was crying," he says, "and that scared me more than the pictures on the TV." Later, he goes home for a visit and discusses the

events of 9/11 with his mother—and is stunned when she assures him that he was actually in school on the morning of the attacks and was only sent home at lunchtime, after the towers had fallen. "I don't understand," he tells you afterward. "I think she must be confused, because I have a perfect memory of that morning." Assuming your friend's mother is recalling events correctly, how would you explain to your friend the ways in which his snapshot memory could be wrong? What memory "sin" might be at work?

3. You ask one of your psychology classmates if she wants to form a study group to prepare for an upcoming exam. "No offense," she says, "but I can study the material best by just reading the chapter eight or nine times, and I can do that without a study group." What's wrong with your classmate's study plan? In what ways might the members of a study group help each other learn more effectively?

4. You and a friend go to a party on campus where you meet a lot of new people. After the party, your friend says, "I liked a lot of the people we met, but I'll never remember all their names. Some people just have a good memory, and some don't, and there's nothing I can do about it." What advice could you give your friend to help him remember the names of people he meets at the next party?

5. A friend of yours who is taking a criminal justice class reads about a case in which the conviction of an accused murderer was later overturned on the basis of DNA evidence. "It's a travesty of justice," she says. "An eyewitness clearly identified the man by picking him out of a lineup and then identified him again in court during the trial. No results from a chemistry lab should count more than eyewitness testimony." What is your friend failing to appreciate about eyewitness testimony? What "sin" of memory could lead an eyewitness to honestly believe she is identifying the correct man when she is actually making a false identification?

ANSWERS TO KEY CONCEPT QUIZ

1. a; 2. c; 3. c; 4. d; 5. a; 6. b; 7. b; 8. a; 9. d; 10. a; 11. c; 12. d; 13. a; 14. b.

Learning

7

Jennifer, a 45-year-old career military nurse, served 19 months abroad during the Iraq War, including 4 months in a hospital near Baghdad, where she witnessed many horrifying events including numerous deaths and serious casualties. Jennifer worked 12- to 14-hour shifts, trying to avoid incoming fire while tending to some of the most gruesomely wounded cases.

This repetitive trauma took a toll on Jennifer. Even after returning home, Jennifer thought about her war experiences repeatedly, and they profoundly influenced her reactions to many aspects of everyday life. The previously innocent sound of a helicopter approaching, which in Iraq signaled that new wounded bodies were about to arrive, now created in Jennifer heightened feelings of fear and anxiety. She regularly awoke from nightmares concerning her Iraq experiences. Jennifer was "forever changed" by her Iraq experiences (Feczer & Bjorklund, 2009). And that is one reason why Jennifer's story is a compelling, though disturbing, introduction to the topic of learning.

Much of what happened to Jennifer after she returned home reflects the operation of a kind of learning based on association. Sights, sounds, and smells in Iraq had become associated with negative emotions in a way that created an enduring bond, so that encountering similar sights, sounds, and smells at home elicited similarly intense negative feelings.

LEARNING IS A COLLECTION OF DIFFERENT TECHNIQUES, procedures, and outcomes that produce changes in an organism's behavior. In this chapter, we'll discuss the development and basic psychological principles behind major approaches to learning, such as classical conditioning and operant conditioning, learning that occurs when we simply watch others, and learning that can occur entirely outside of awareness. We'll conclude with a discussion of learning in a context that should matter a lot to you: the classroom.

During the 4 months that she served at a prison hospital near Baghdad during the Iraq War, Jennifer learned to associate the sound of an arriving helicopter with wounded soldiers. That learned association had a long-lasting influence on her. JOHN MOORE/AP Images

What Is Learning?

LEARNING OUTCOMES

- Define learning.
- Identify how even the simplest organisms appear to learn.

learning The acquisition, from experience, of new knowledge, skills, or responses that results in a relatively permanent change in the state of the learner.

habituation A general process in which repeated or prolonged exposure to a stimulus results in a gradual reduction in responding.

sensitization A simple form of learning that occurs when presentation of a stimulus leads to an increased response to a later stimulus.

How might psychologists use the concept of habituation to explain the fact that today's action movies tend, like *Avengers: Age of Ultron*, to show much more graphic violence than movies of the 1980s, which in turn tended to show more graphic violence than movies of the 1950s? Marvel/Walt Disney Pictures/The Kobal Collection

Despite the many different kinds of learning that psychologists have discovered, there is a basic principle at the core of all of them. **Learning** involves *the acquisition, from experience, of new knowledge, skills, or responses that results in a relatively permanent change in the state of the learner.* This definition emphasizes these key ideas: Learning is based on experience, learning produces changes in the organism, and these changes are relatively permanent.

Think about Jennifer's time in Iraq and you'll see all of these elements: Experiences such as the association between the sound of an approaching helicopter and the arrival of wounded soldiers changed the way Jennifer responded to certain situations in a way that lasted for years.

Learning can also occur in much simpler, nonassociative forms. You are probably familiar with the phenomenon of **habituation**, *a general process in which repeated or prolonged exposure to a stimulus results in a gradual reduction in responding.* If you've ever lived near a busy highway, you probably noticed the sound of traffic when you first moved in. You probably also noticed that, after a while, you ignored the sounds of automobiles in your vicinity. This welcome reduction in responding reflects the operation of habituation.

Habituation occurs even in the simplest organisms, such as the sea slug *Aplysia*, which you met in the Memory chapter. When lightly touched, the sea slug initially withdraws its gill, but the response gradually weakens after repeated light touches. In addition, *Aplysia* also exhibits another simple form of learning known as **sensitization**, which occurs when *presentation of a stimulus leads to an increased response to a later stimulus.* For example, after receiving a strong shock, *Aplysia* shows an increased gill-withdrawal response to a light touch. In a similar manner, people whose houses have been broken into may later become hypersensitive to late-night sounds that wouldn't have bothered them previously.

Although these simple kinds of learning are important, in this chapter we'll focus on more complex kinds of learning that psychologists have studied intensively. As you'll recall from the Psychology: Evolution of a Science chapter, the behaviorists insisted on measuring only observable, quantifiable behavior and dismissed mental activity as irrelevant and unknowable. Behaviorists argued that learning's "permanent change in experience" could be demonstrated equally well in almost any organism: rats, dogs, pigeons, mice, pigs, or humans. But there are also some important cognitive considerations (i.e., elements of mental activity) in order to understand the learning process.

BUILD TO THE OUTCOMES

1. What are the key ideas that support the definition of learning?

2. How do habituation and sensitization occur?

Classical Conditioning: One Thing Leads to Another

The American psychologist John B. Watson kick-started the behaviorist movement, arguing that psychologists should "never use the terms *consciousness, mental states, mind, content, introspectively verifiable, imagery,* and the like" (Watson, 1913, p. 166). Watson's firebrand stance was fueled in large part by the work of a Russian physiologist, Ivan Pavlov (1849–1936).

Pavlov studied the digestive processes of laboratory animals by surgically implanting test tubes into the cheeks of dogs to measure their salivary responses to different kinds of foods. Serendipitously, his explorations into spit and drool revealed a form of learning, which came to be called classical conditioning. **Classical conditioning** occurs when *a neutral stimulus produces a response after being paired with a stimulus that naturally produces a response.* Pavlov showed that dogs learned to salivate to a neutral stimulus such as a bell or a tone, after the dogs had associated that stimulus with another stimulus that naturally evokes salivation, such as food. Pavlov appreciated the significance of his discovery and embarked on a systematic investigation of the mechanisms of classical conditioning. Let's take a closer look at some of these principles. (As The Real World: Understanding Drug Overdoses shows, these principles help explain how drug overdoses occur.)

LEARNING OUTCOMES

- Describe the process of classical conditioning.
- Explain how cognitive, neural, and evolutionary aspects influence our understanding of classical conditioning.

classical conditioning A type of learning that occurs when a neutral stimulus produces a response after being paired with a stimulus that naturally produces a response.

→ THE REAL WORLD

Understanding Drug Overdoses

All too often, police are confronted with a perplexing problem: the sudden death of heroin addicts from a drug overdose. The victims are often experienced drug users; the dose taken is usually not larger than what they usually take; and the deaths tend to occur in unusual settings.

Classical conditioning provides some insight into how these deaths occur. First, when classical conditioning takes place, the CS is more than a simple bell or tone: It also includes the overall *context* within which the conditioning takes place. When the drug is injected, the entire setting (the drug paraphernalia, the room, the lighting, the addict's usual companions) functions as the CS. Second, many CRs are compensatory reactions to the US. Heroin, for example, slows down a person's breathing rate, so the body responds with a compensatory reaction that speeds up breathing in order to maintain a state of balance. Over time, these protective physiological responses become part of the CR, and like all CRs, they occur in the presence of the CS—but prior to US—in this case,

the administration of the drug. These compensatory physiological reactions are also what make drug abusers take increasingly larger doses to achieve the same effect. Ultimately, these reactions produce *drug tolerance*, discussed in the Consciousness chapter.

These principles of classical conditioning help explain why taking drugs in a new environment can be fatal for a longtime drug user. If an addict injects the usual dose in a setting that is sufficiently novel or where he or she has never taken heroin before, the CS is now altered, so that the physiological compensatory CR that usually has a protective function may not occur (Siegel et al., 2000). As a result, the addict's usual dose becomes an overdose, and death often results.

Understanding these principles has led to treatments for drug addicts. For example, the brain's compensatory response to a drug, when elicited by the familiar contextual cues ordinarily associated with drug taking that constitute the CS, can be experienced by the addict as withdrawal symptoms. In *cue exposure therapies,*

an addict is exposed to drug-related cues without being given the usual dose of the drug itself, eventually resulting in extinction of the association between the contextual cues and the compensatory CR. After such treatment, encountering familiar drug-related cues will no longer result in the CR, thereby making it easier for a recovering addict to remain abstinent (Siegel, 2005).

Although drug dens and crack houses may be considered blights, it is often safer for addicts to use drugs there. The environment becomes part of the addict's CS, so it is ironic that busting crack houses may contribute to more deaths from drug overdoses when addicts are pushed to use drugs in new situations. CHRIS GARDNER/AP Images

The Basic Principles of Classical Conditioning

Pavlov's basic experimental setup involved cradling dogs in a harness to administer the foods and to measure the salivary response, as shown in **FIGURE 7.1**. He noticed that dogs that had previously been in the experiment began to produce a kind of "anticipatory" salivary response as soon as they were put in the harness, before any food was presented. Pavlov and his colleagues regarded these responses as annoyances at first because they interfered with collecting naturally occurring salivary secretions.

In reality, the dogs were exhibiting classical conditioning. When the dogs were initially presented with a plate of food, they began to salivate. No surprise here. Pavlov called the presentation of food an **unconditioned stimulus (US)**, *something that reliably produces a naturally occurring reaction in an organism* (see **FIGURE 7.2a**). He called the dogs' salivation an **unconditioned response (UR)**, *a reflexive reaction that is reliably produced by an unconditioned stimulus.*

Then Pavlov paired the presentation of food with a stimulus such as the ringing of a bell or the flash of a light (Pavlov, 1927). Each of these stimuli was a **conditioned stimulus (CS)**, *a previously neutral stimulus that produces a reliable response in an organism after being paired with a US*. After multiple pairings of CS and US, the animal learned to associate food with the sound, and eventually the bell itself was sufficient to produce a response, or salivation (**FIGURE 7.2b**). Pavlov called this salivation a **conditioned response (CR)**, *a reaction that resembles an unconditioned response but is produced by a conditioned stimulus*. In this example, the dogs' salivation (CR) was eventually prompted by the sound of the bell (CS) alone because the sound of the bell and the food (US) had been associated so often in the past (see **FIGURE 7.2c**).

Consider your own dog (or cat). Does your dog always know when dinner's coming, preparing just short of pulling up a chair and tucking a napkin into her collar? It's as though she has one eye on the clock every day, waiting for the dinner hour. Alas, your dog is no clock-watching wonder hound. Instead, for her the presentation of food (the US) has become associated with a complex CS—your getting up, moving into the kitchen, opening the cabinet, working the can opener—such that the CS alone signals to your dog that food is on the way and therefore initiates the CR of her getting ready to eat.

After conditioning has been established, a phenomenon called **second-order conditioning** can be demonstrated: *a type of learning where a CS is paired with a stimulus that became associated with the US in an earlier procedure*. For example, in an early study, Pavlov repeatedly paired a new CS, a black square, with the now reliable tone. After a number of training trials, his dogs produced a salivary response to the black square, even though the square itself had never been directly

unconditioned stimulus (US) Something that reliably produces a naturally occurring reaction in an organism.

unconditioned response (UR) A reflexive reaction that is reliably produced by an unconditioned stimulus.

conditioned stimulus (CS) A previously neutral stimulus that produces a reliable response in an organism after being paired with a US.

conditioned response (CR) A reaction that resembles an unconditioned response but is produced by a conditioned stimulus.

second-order conditioning A type of learning where a CS is paired with a stimulus that became associated with the US in an earlier procedure.

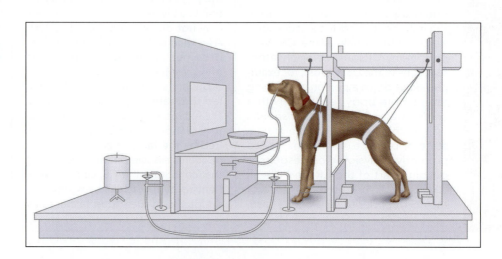

Figure 7.1 PAVLOV'S APPARATUS Pavlov's apparatus for experiments on salivation serendipitously became the setup for studies on classical conditioning. Using a bell or a tuning fork, Pavlov presented auditory stimuli to the dogs. Visual stimuli could be presented on the screen.

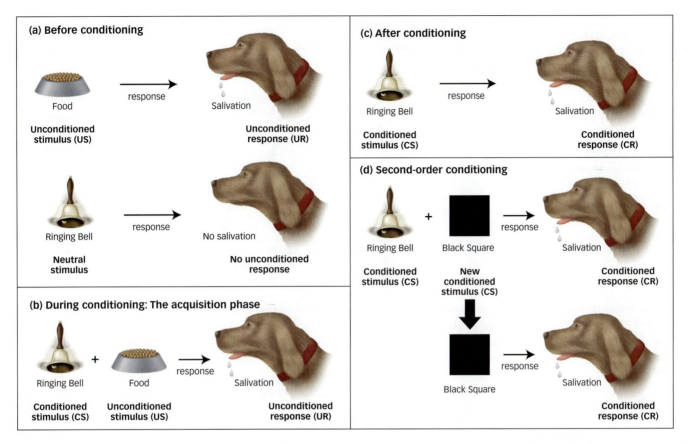

Figure 7.2 THE ELEMENTS OF CLASSICAL CONDITIONING (a) Before conditioning, the dog salivates in response to food, the unconditioned stimulus (US), but not to a ringing bell. (b) During conditioning, the food is paired with the ringing bell, which becomes a conditioned stimulus (CS). (c) After conditioning, the ringing bell, now a conditioned stimulus (CS), can produce salivation. (d) In second-order conditioning, the ringing bell can be used to condition a new stimulus, such as a black square.

acquisition The phase of classical conditioning when the CS and US are presented together.

associated with the food (see **FIGURE 7.2d**). Second-order conditioning helps explain why some people desire money to the point that they hoard it and value it even more than the objects it purchases. Money is initially used to purchase objects that produce gratifying outcomes, such as an expensive car. Although money is not directly associated with the thrill of driving a new sports car, through second-order conditioning, money can become linked with this type of desirable reward.

Acquisition, Extinction, and Spontaneous Recovery

Remember when you first got your dog? Chances are she didn't seem too smart, especially the way she stared at you vacantly as you went into the kitchen, not anticipating that food was on the way. That's because learning through classical conditioning requires some period of association between the CS and US. This is called **acquisition**, *the phase of classical conditioning when the CS and US are presented together.*

During the initial phase of the acquisition period of classical conditioning, responding typically starts low, rises rapidly, and then slowly tapers off, as shown on the left side of the first panel in **FIGURE 7.3**. Pavlov's dogs gradually increased salivation over several trials of pairing a tone with the presentation of food, and similarly, your dog eventually learned to associate your kitchen preparations with the subsequent appearance of food. After learning has been established, the CS by itself will reliably elicit the CR.

After Pavlov and his colleagues had explored the process of acquisition, they wondered what would happen if they continued to present the CS (tone) but stopped presenting the US (food). As shown on the right side of the first panel in Figure 7.3, behavior declines abruptly and continues to drop until eventually the

"I THINK MOM'S USING THE CAN OPENER."

Dennis the menace: North America Syndicate, Inc.

Figure 7.3 ACQUISITION, EXTINCTION, AND SPONTANEOUS RECOVERY In classical conditioning, the CS is originally neutral and elicits no specific response. After several trials pairing the CS with the US, the CS alone comes to elicit the salivary response (the CR). Learning tends to take place fairly rapidly and then levels off as stable responding develops. In extinction, the CR diminishes quickly until it no longer occurs. A rest period, however, is typically followed by spontaneous recovery of the CR. In fact, a well-learned CR may show spontaneous recovery after more than one rest period even without any additional learning trials.

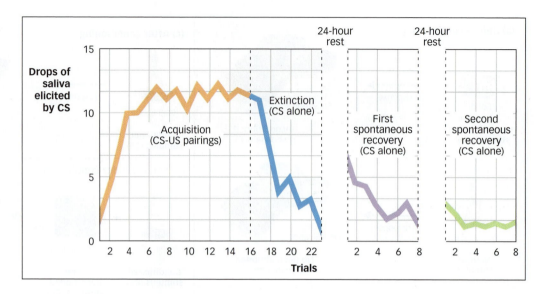

extinction The gradual elimination of a learned response that occurs when the CS is repeatedly presented without the US.

dog ceases to salivate to the sound of the tone. This process is called **extinction**, *the gradual elimination of a learned response that occurs when the CS is repeatedly presented without the US.* In effect, the conditioned response is "extinguished" and no longer observed. Having established that he could produce learning through conditioning and then extinguish it, Pavlov wondered if this elimination of conditioned behavior was permanent. Is a single session of extinction sufficient to knock out the CR completely? Or is there some residual change in the dog's behavior such that the CR might reappear?

To explore this question, Pavlov extinguished the classically conditioned salivation response, and then allowed the dogs to have a short rest period. When the dogs were brought back to the lab and presented with the CS again, they displayed **spontaneous recovery**, *the tendency of a learned behavior to recover from extinction after a rest period.* This phenomenon is shown in the middle panel in Figure 7.3. Notice that this recovery takes place even though there have not been any additional associations between the CS and US. Some spontaneous recovery even takes place after a second period of rest (see the right-hand panel in Figure 7.3). Clearly, extinction does not completely erase learning.

spontaneous recovery The tendency of a learned behavior to recover from extinction after a rest period.

Generalization and Discrimination

Do you think your dog will be stumped, unable to anticipate the presentation of her food, if you get a new can opener? Will you need to establish a whole new round of conditioning with this modified CS?

Probably not. It wouldn't be very adaptive for an organism if each little change in the CS–US pairing required an extensive regimen of new learning. Rather, the phenomenon of **generalization** tends to take place: *The CR is observed, even though the CS is slightly different from the CS used during acquisition.* This means that the conditioning generalizes to stimuli that are similar to the CS used during the original training.

generalization The CR is observed, even though the CS is slightly different from the CS used during acquisition.

As you might expect, the more the new stimulus changes, the less conditioned responding is observed. If you replaced a manual can opener with an electric can opener, your dog would probably show a much weaker conditioned response (Pearce, 1987; Rescorla, 2006). Such diminished responding to the new stimulus indicates **discrimination**, *the capacity to distinguish between similar but distinct stimuli.* Generalization and discrimination are two sides of the same coin. The more organisms show one, the less they show the other, and training can modify the balance between the two.

discrimination The capacity to distinguish between similar but distinct stimuli.

Conditioned Emotional Responses: The Case of Little Albert

The behaviorist John B. Watson and his followers thought that it was possible to develop general explanations of pretty much *any* behavior of *any* organism based on classical conditioning principles. As a step in that direction, Watson embarked on a controversial study with his research assistant Rosalie Rayner (Watson & Rayner, 1920), to see if a healthy, well-developed child could be classically conditioned to experience a strong emotional reaction—namely, fear. To find out, Watson and Rayner enlisted the assistance of 9-month-old "Little Albert" (Watson & Rayner, 1920).

Watson presented Little Albert with a variety of stimuli: a white rat, a dog, a rabbit, various masks, and a burning newspaper. Albert reacted in most cases with curiosity or indifference, and he showed no fear of any of the items. Watson also established that something *could* make Albert afraid. While Albert was watching Rayner, Watson unexpectedly struck a large steel bar with a hammer, producing a loud noise. Predictably, this caused Albert to cry, tremble, and be generally displeased.

Watson and Rayner then led Little Albert through the acquisition phase of classical conditioning. Albert was presented with a white rat. As soon as he reached out to touch it, the steel bar was struck. This pairing occurred again and again over several trials. Eventually, the sight of the rat alone caused Albert to recoil in terror. In this situation, a US (the loud sound) was paired with a CS (the rat) until the CS all by itself was sufficient to produce the CR (a fearful reaction). Little Albert also showed stimulus generalization. The sight of a white rabbit, a seal-fur coat, and a Santa Claus mask produced the same kinds of fear reactions in the infant.

This study was controversial in its cavalier treatment of a young child. Modern ethical guidelines that govern the treatment of research participants make sure that this kind of study could not be conducted today. So, what was Watson's goal in all this? First, he wanted to show that a relatively complex reaction could be conditioned using Pavlovian techniques. Second, he wanted to show that emotional responses such as fear and anxiety could be produced by classical conditioning and therefore need not be the product of deeper unconscious processes. Instead, Watson proposed that fears could be learned, just like any other behavior. Third, Watson wanted to confirm that conditioning could be applied to humans as well as to other animals.

The kind of conditioned fear responses that were at work in Little Albert's case were also important in the chapter-opening case of Jennifer, who experienced fear and anxiety when hearing the previously innocent sound of an approaching helicopter as a result of her experiences in Iraq. Indeed, a therapy that has proven effective in dealing with such trauma-induced fears is based directly on principles of classical conditioning: Individuals are repeatedly exposed to conditioned stimuli associated with their trauma in a safe setting in an attempt to extinguish the conditioned fear response (Bouton, 1988; Rothbaum & Schwartz, 2002). However, conditioned emotional responses are not limited to fear and anxiety responses. The warm and fuzzy feelings that envelop you when hearing a song on the radio that you used to listen to with a former boyfriend or girlfriend are a type of conditioned emotional response.

A Deeper Understanding of Classical Conditioning

As a form of learning, classical conditioning has a simple set of principles and applications to real-life situations. It offers a good deal of utility for psychologists who seek to understand the mechanisms underlying learning. Since Pavlov's day, classical conditioning has been subjected to deep scrutiny in order to understand exactly how, when, and why it works. Let's examine three areas that give us a closer look at the mechanisms of classical conditioning: the cognitive, neural, and evolutionary elements.

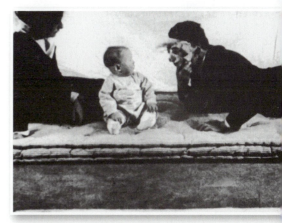

John Watson and Rosalie Rayner show Little Albert an unusual bunny mask. Why isn't the mere presence of these experimenters a conditioned stimulus in itself? Watson & Rayner, 1920

What response do you think the advertisers of Budweiser are looking for when they feature Clydesdale horses in an ad? Kyle Ericson/AP Images

The Cognitive Elements of Classical Conditioning

Curiously, although Pavlov's dogs salivated when their feeders approached (see the Psychology: Evolution of a Science chapter), they did not salivate when Pavlov himself did. Eventually someone was bound to ask an important question: *Why not?* After all, Pavlov also delivered the food to the dogs, so why didn't he become a CS?

Somehow, Pavlov's dogs were sensitive to the fact that Pavlov was not a *reliable* indicator of the arrival of food. Pavlov was linked with the arrival of food, but he was also linked with other activities that had nothing to do with food, including checking on the apparatus, bringing the dog from the kennel to the laboratory, and standing around and talking with his assistants.

Robert Rescorla and Allan Wagner (1972) were the first to theorize that classical conditioning occurs when an animal has learned to set up an *expectation*. The sound of a bell, because of its systematic pairing with food, set up this cognitive state for the laboratory dogs; Pavlov, because of the lack of any reliable link with food, did not. The Rescorla–Wagner model introduced a cognitive component that accounted for a variety of classical conditioning phenomena that were difficult to understand from a simple behaviorist point of view. For example, the model predicted that conditioning would be easier when the CS was an *unfamiliar* event than when it was familiar. The reason is that familiar events, being familiar, already have expectations associated with them, making new conditioning difficult. In short, classical conditioning might appear to be a primitive process, but it is actually quite sophisticated and incorporates a significant cognitive element.

The Neural Elements of Classical Conditioning

Pavlov saw his research as providing insights into how the brain works. Recent research has clarified some of what Pavlov hoped to understand about conditioning and the brain.

Richard Thompson and his colleagues focused on classical conditioning of eyeblink responses in rabbits, where the CS (a tone) is immediately followed by the US (a puff of air), which elicits a reflexive eyeblink response. After many CS–US pairings, the eyeblink response occurs in response to the CS alone. Thompson and colleagues showed convincingly that the cerebellum is critical for the occurrence of eyeblink conditioning (Thompson, 2005). Studies of people with lesions to the cerebellum supported these findings by demonstrating impaired eyeblink conditioning (Daum et al., 1993). Rounding out the picture, more recent neuroimaging findings in healthy young adults show activation in the cerebellum during eyeblink conditioning (Cheng et al., 2008). As you learned in the Neuroscience and Behavior chapter, the cerebellum is part of the hindbrain and plays an important role in motor skills and learning.

Also in the Neuroscience and Behavior chapter, you saw that the amygdala plays an important role in the experience of emotion, including fear and anxiety. So it should come as no surprise that the amygdala, particularly an area known as the *central nucleus*, is also critical for emotional conditioning. Normal rats, trained that a tone (CS) predicts a mild electric shock (US), show a defensive reaction (CR) known as *freezing*, in which they crouch down and sit motionless. If connections linking the amygdala to the midbrain are disrupted, the rat does not exhibit the behavioral freezing response. If the connections between the amygdala and the hypothalamus are severed, the autonomic responses associated with fear cease (LeDoux et al., 1988). Hence, the action of the amygdala is an essential element in fear conditioning, and its links with other areas of the brain are responsible for producing specific features of conditioning (Bentz & Schiller, 2015). The amygdala is involved in fear conditioning in people as well as in rats and other animals (Olsson & Phelps, 2007; Phelps & LeDoux, 2005).

The Evolutionary Elements of Classical Conditioning

Evolutionary mechanisms also play an important role in classical conditioning. As you learned in the Psychology: Evolution of a Science chapter, evolution and natural selection go hand in hand with adaptiveness: Behaviors that are adaptive allow an organism to survive and thrive in its environment.

Under certain conditions, people may develop food aversions. This serving of hummus looks inviting and probably tastes delicious, but at least one psychologist avoids it like the plague. Paul Cowan/Shutterstock

Consider this example: A psychology professor visited Southern California, and his hosts took him to lunch at a Middle Eastern restaurant. Suffering from a case of bad hummus, he was up all night long, and developed a lifelong aversion to hummus. The hummus was the CS, a bacterium or some other source of toxicity was the US, and the resulting nausea was the UR. The UR (the nausea) became linked to the once-neutral CS (the hummus) and became a CR (an aversion to hummus). This aversion was cemented with a single acquisition trial. Usually it takes several pairings of a CS and US to establish learning.

The speed of this learning makes sense from an evolutionary perspective. Any species that forages or consumes a variety of foods needs to develop a mechanism by which it can learn to avoid any food that once made it ill. To have adaptive value, this learning must be very rapid—occurring in perhaps one or two trials. If learning takes more trials than this, the animal could die from eating a toxic substance. Also, learned aversions should occur more often with novel foods than familiar ones. It is not adaptive for an animal to develop an aversion to everything it has eaten on the particular day it got sick. Our psychologist friend didn't develop an aversion to the Coke he drank with lunch or the scrambled eggs he had for breakfast that day; however, the sight and smell of hummus do make him uneasy.

Classical conditioning of food aversions has been studied in rats, using USs (such as injection or radiation) that cause nausea and vomiting (Garcia & Koelling, 1966). The researchers found weak or no conditioning when the CS was a visual, auditory, or tactile stimulus, but a strong food aversion developed with stimuli that had a distinct taste and smell. On the other hand, the taste and smell stimuli that produce food aversions in rats do not work with most species of birds, which depend primarily on visual cues for finding food and are relatively insensitive to taste and smell. However, it is relatively easy to produce a food aversion in birds using an unfamiliar visual stimulus as the CS, such as a brightly colored food (Wilcoxon, Dragoin, & Kral, 1971). Studies such as these suggest that evolution has provided each species with a kind of **biological preparedness**, *a propensity for learning particular kinds of associations over others*, so that some behaviors are relatively easy to condition in some species but not others (Domjan, 2005).

This research had an interesting application. It led to the development of a technique for dealing with an unanticipated side effect of radiation and chemotherapy: Cancer patients who experience nausea from their treatments often develop aversions to foods they ate before the therapy. Broberg and Bernstein (1987) reasoned that, if the findings with rats generalized to humans, a simple technique should minimize the negative consequences of this effect. They gave their patients an unusual food (coconut- or root-beer-flavored candy) at the end of the last meal before undergoing treatment. Sure enough, the conditioned food aversions that the patients developed were overwhelmingly for one of the unusual flavors and not for any of the other foods in the meal. Other than any root beer or coconut fanatics among the sample, patients were spared developing aversions to common foods that they were more likely to eat.

Rats can be difficult to poison because of learned taste aversions, which are an evolutionarily adaptive element of classical conditioning. Here, a worker tries his best in the sewers of Paris. Roger Viollet/ Getty Images

biological preparedness A propensity for learning particular kinds of associations over others.

BUILD TO THE OUTCOMES

1. Why do some dogs seem to know when it's dinnertime?

2. If both an unconditioned and conditioned stimulus can produce the same effect, what is the difference?

3. What is second-order conditioning?

4. How does a conditioned behavior change when the unconditioned stimulus is removed?

5. Why are generalization and discrimination "two sides of the same coin"?

6. Why did Albert fear the rat?

7. How does the role of expectation in conditioning challenge behaviorist ideas?

8. What is the role of the amygdala in fear conditioning?

9. How has cancer patients' discomfort been eased by our understanding of food aversions?

Operant Conditioning: Reinforcements From the Environment

operant conditioning A type of learning in which the consequences of an organism's behavior determine whether it will repeat that behavior in the future.

The study of classical conditioning is the study of behaviors that are *reactive*. Most animals don't voluntarily salivate or feel spasms of anxiety; rather, they exhibit these responses involuntarily during the conditioning process. But we also engage in voluntary behaviors in order to obtain rewards and avoid punishment. **Operant conditioning** is *a type of learning in which the consequences of an organism's behavior determine whether it will repeat that behavior in the future.* The study of operant conditioning is the exploration of behaviors that are *active*.

The Development of Operant Conditioning: The Law of Effect

The study of how active behavior affects the environment began at about the same time as classical conditioning. In the 1890s, Edward L. Thorndike (1874–1949) examined *instrumental behaviors*, that is, behavior that required an organism to *do* something, solve a problem, or otherwise manipulate elements of its environment (Thorndike, 1898). Some of Thorndike's experiments used a puzzle box, which was a wooden crate with a door that would open when a concealed lever was moved in the right way (see **FIGURE 7.4**). A hungry cat placed in a puzzle box would try various behaviors to get out—scratching at the door, meowing loudly, sniffing the inside of the box, putting its paw through the openings—but only one behavior opened the door and led to food: tripping the lever in just the right way. After this happened, Thorndike placed the cat back in the box for another round.

law of effect The principle that behaviors that are followed by a "satisfying state of affairs" tend to be repeated, and those that produce an "unpleasant state of affairs" are less likely to be repeated.

Over time, the ineffective behaviors became less and less frequent, and the one instrumental behavior (going right for the latch) became more frequent (see **FIGURE 7.5**). From these observations, Thorndike developed the **law of effect**, *the principle that behaviors that are followed by a "satisfying state of affairs" tend to be repeated, and those that produce an "unpleasant state of affairs" are less likely to be repeated.*

Figure 7.4 THORNDIKE'S PUZZLE BOX In Thorndike's original experiments, food was placed just outside the door of the puzzle box, where the cat could see it. If the cat triggered the appropriate lever, it would open the door and the cat could get out.

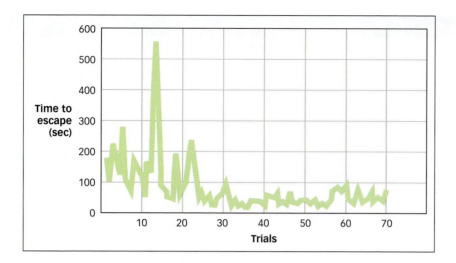

Such learning is very different from classical conditioning. Remember that in classical conditioning experiments, the US occurred on every training trial, no matter what the animal did. Pavlov delivered food to the dog whether it salivated or not. But in Thorndike's work, the behavior of the animal determined what happened next. If the behavior was "correct" (i.e., the animal triggered the latch), the animal was rewarded with food. Incorrect behaviors produced no results, and the animal was stuck in the box until it performed the correct behavior. Although different from classical conditioning, Thorndike's work resonated with most behaviorists at the time: It was still observable, quantifiable, and free from explanations involving the mind (Galef, 1998).

B. F. Skinner: The Role of Reinforcement and Punishment

Several decades after Thorndike's work, B. F. Skinner (1904–1990) coined the term **operant behavior** to refer to *behavior that an organism performs that has some impact on the environment*. In Skinner's system, all of these emitted behaviors "operated" on the environment in some manner, and the environment responded by providing events that either strengthened those behaviors (i.e., they *reinforced* them) or made them less likely to occur (i.e., they *punished* them). Skinner's elegantly simple observation was that most organisms do *not* behave like a dog in a harness, passively waiting to receive food no matter what the circumstances. Rather, most organisms are like cats in a box, actively engaging the environment in which they find themselves to reap rewards (Skinner, 1938, 1953). In order to study operant behavior scientifically, Skinner developed the *operant conditioning chamber*, or *Skinner box*, as it is commonly called (shown in **FIGURE 7.6**), which allows a researcher to study the behavior of small organisms in a controlled environment.

Skinner's approach to the study of learning focused on *reinforcement* and *punishment*. These terms, which have commonsense connotations, have particular meanings in psychology, in terms of their effects on behavior. Therefore, a **reinforcer** is *any stimulus or event that increases the likelihood of the behavior that led to it*, whereas a **punisher** is *any stimulus or event that decreases the likelihood of the behavior that led to it*.

Whether a particular stimulus acts as a reinforcer or a punisher depends in part on whether it increases or decreases the likelihood of a behavior. Presenting food is usually reinforcing and produces an increase in the behavior that led to it; removing food is often punishing and leads to a decrease in the behavior. Turning on an electric shock is typically punishing (and decreases the behavior that led to it); turning it off is rewarding (and increases the behavior that led to it).

operant behavior Behavior that an organism performs that has some impact on the environment.

reinforcer Any stimulus or event that increases the likelihood of the behavior that led to it.

punisher Any stimulus or event that decreases the likelihood of the behavior that led to it.

Figure 7.6 SKINNER BOX This is a typical Skinner box, or operant conditioning chamber. A rat, pigeon, or other suitably sized animal is placed in this environment and observed during learning trials that apply operant conditioning principles. Science Source

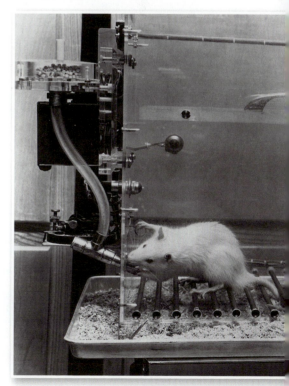

TABLE 7.1	Reinforcement and Punishment	
	Increases the Likelihood of Behavior	**Decreases the Likelihood of Behavior**
Stimulus is presented	Positive reinforcement	Positive punishment
Stimulus is removed	Negative reinforcement	Negative punishment

To keep these possibilities distinct, Skinner used the term *positive* for situations in which a stimulus was presented and *negative* for situations in which it was removed. Consequently, as shown in **TABLE 7.1**, there is *positive reinforcement* (a stimulus is presented that increases the likelihood of a behavior) and *negative reinforcement* (a stimulus is removed that increases the likelihood of a behavior), as well as *positive punishment* (a stimulus is administered that reduces the likelihood of a behavior) and *negative punishment* (a stimulus is removed that decreases the likelihood of a behavior). Here, the words *positive* and *negative* mean, respectively, something that is *added* or something that is *taken away*, but do not mean "good" or "bad" as they do in everyday speech.

These distinctions can be confusing at first; after all, "negative reinforcement" and "punishment" both sound like they should be "bad" and produce the same type of behavior. However, negative reinforcement, for example, does not involve administering something that decreases the likelihood of a behavior; it's the *removal* of something, such as a shock, that increases the likelihood of a behavior.

Reinforcement is generally more effective than punishment in promoting learning. There are many reasons for this (Gershoff, 2002), but there is one main reason that stands out: Punishment signals that an unacceptable behavior has occurred, but it doesn't specify what should be done instead. Spanking a young child for starting to run into a busy street certainly stops the behavior, but it doesn't promote any kind of learning about the *desired* behavior.

Primary and Secondary Reinforcement and Punishment

Reinforcers and punishers often gain their functions from basic biological mechanisms. A pigeon that pecks at a target in a Skinner box is usually reinforced with food pellets, just as an animal that learns to escape a mild electric shock has avoided the punishment of tingly paws. Food, comfort, shelter, and warmth are examples of *primary reinforcers* because they help satisfy biological needs. However, the vast majority of reinforcers or punishers in our daily lives have little to do with biology: Verbal approval, a bronze trophy, or money all serve powerful reinforcing functions, yet none of them taste very good or help keep you warm at night.

These *secondary reinforcers* derive their effectiveness from their associations with primary reinforcers through classical conditioning. For example, money starts out as a neutral CS that, through its association with primary USs such as acquiring food or shelter, takes on a conditioned emotional element. Flashing lights, originally a neutral CS, acquire powerful negative elements through association with a speeding ticket and a fine.

Immediate Versus Delayed Reinforcement and Punishment

A key determinant of the effectiveness of a reinforcer is the amount of time between the occurrence of a behavior and the reinforcer: The more time elapses, the less effective the reinforcer (Lattal, 2010; Renner, 1964). This was dramatically illustrated in experiments where food reinforcers were given at varying times after a rat pressed the lever (Dickinson, Watt, & Griffiths, 1992). Delaying reinforcement by even a few seconds led to a reduction in the number of times the rat subsequently

Negative reinforcement involves the removal of something unpleasant from the environment. When Daddy stops the car, he gets a reward: His little monster stops screaming. However, from the perspective of the child, this is positive reinforcement. The child's tantrum results in something positive added to the environment—stopping for a snack. Michelle Selesnick/Moment/ Getty Images

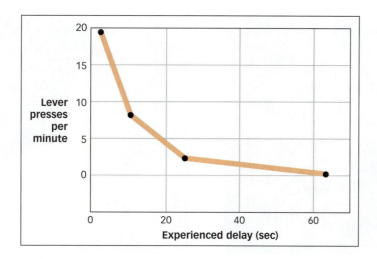

Figure 7.7 DELAY OF REINFORCE-MENT Rats pressed a lever in order to obtain a food reward. Researchers varied the amount of time between the lever press and the delivery of food reinforcement. The number of lever presses declined substantially with longer delays.

pressed the lever, and extending the delay to a minute rendered the food reinforcer completely ineffective (see **FIGURE 7.7**). The most likely explanation for this effect is that delaying the reinforcer made it difficult for the rats to figure out exactly what behavior they needed to perform in order to obtain it. In the same way, parents who wish to use a piece of candy to reinforce their children for playing quietly should provide the candy while the child is still playing quietly; waiting until later, when the child may be engaging in other behaviors—perhaps making a racket with pots and pans—will make it more difficult for the child to link the reinforcer with the behavior of playing quietly (Powell et al., 2009). Similar considerations apply to punishment: As a general rule, the longer the delay between a behavior and the administration of punishment, the less effective the punishment will be in suppressing the targeted behavior (Kamin, 1959; Lerman & Vorndran, 2002).

The greater potency of immediate versus delayed reinforcers may help us to appreciate why it can be difficult to engage in behaviors that have long-term benefits. The smoker who desperately wants to quit smoking will be reinforced immediately by the feeling of relaxation that results from lighting up, but may have to wait years to be reinforced with better health that results from quitting; the dieter who sincerely wants to lose weight may easily succumb to the temptation of a chocolate sundae that provides reinforcement now, rather than waiting weeks or months for the reinforcement (looking and feeling better) that would be associated with losing weight.

Suppose that you are the mayor of a suburban town, and you want to institute some new policies to decrease the number of drivers who speed on residential streets. How might you use punishment to decrease the undesirable behavior (speeding)? How might you use reinforcement to increase the desirable behavior (safe driving)? Thinking about the principles of operant conditioning you read about in this section, which approach do you think might be most fruitful? Eden Breitz/Alamy

The Basic Principles of Operant Conditioning

After establishing how reinforcement and punishment produced learned behavior, Skinner and other scientists began to expand the parameters of operant conditioning. Let's look at some of these basic principles of operant conditioning.

Discrimination and Generalization

Operant conditioning shows both discrimination and generalization effects similar to those we saw with classical conditioning. For example, in one study, researchers presented either a painting by the French impressionist Monet or a cubist painting by Picasso (Watanabe, Sakamoto, & Wakita, 1995). Participants in the experiment were reinforced only if they responded when the appropriate painting was presented. After training, the participants discriminated appropriately; those trained with the Monet painting responded when other paintings by Monet were presented, but not when other paintings by Picasso were shown; those trained with a Picasso painting showed the opposite behavior. What's more, the participants showed that they could generalize *across* painters as long as they were from the same artistic tradition. Those trained with

In research on stimulus control, participants trained with Picasso paintings, such as the one on the top, responded to other paintings by Picasso or even to paintings by other cubists. Participants trained with Monet paintings, such as the one at the bottom, responded to other paintings by Monet or by other French impressionists. An interesting detail: The participants in this study were pigeons. © 2016 Estate of Pablo Picasso/ Artists Rights Picasso, Pablo (1881–1973) © ARS, NY The Weeping Woman (Femme en pleurs). 1937. Oil on canvas, 60.8 × 50.0 cm. Tate Gallery, London/Art Resource, NY; Tate Gallery, London/ Art Resource, NY

Monet responded appropriately when shown other impressionist paintings, and the Picasso-trained participants responded to other cubist artwork, despite never having seen those paintings before. These results are particularly striking because the research participants were pigeons that were trained to key-peck to these various works of art.

Extinction

As in classical conditioning, operant behavior undergoes extinction when the reinforcements stop. Pigeons cease pecking at a key if food is no longer presented following that behavior. You wouldn't put more money into a vending machine if it failed to give you its promised candy bar or soda. On the surface, extinction of operant behavior looks like that of classical conditioning.

However, there is an important difference. In classical conditioning, the US occurs on every trial, no matter what the organism does. In operant conditioning, the reinforcements occur only when the proper response has been made, and they don't always occur even then. Not every trip into the forest produces nuts for a squirrel, auto salespeople don't sell to everyone who takes a test drive, and researchers run many experiments that do not work out and never get published. Yet these behaviors don't weaken and gradually extinguish. So, extinction is a bit more complicated in operant conditioning than in classical conditioning because it depends, in part, on how often reinforcement is received. In fact, this principle is an important cornerstone of operant conditioning that we'll examine next.

Schedules of Reinforcement

One day, Skinner was laboriously hand-rolling ground food pellets to reinforce the rats in his experiments. It occurred to him that perhaps he could save time and effort by not giving his rats a pellet for every bar press but instead delivering food on some intermittent schedule. The results of this hunch were dramatic. Not only did the rats continue bar pressing, but they also shifted the rate and pattern of bar pressing depending on the timing and frequency of the presentation of the reinforcers (Skinner, 1979). Unlike in classical conditioning, where the sheer *number* of learning trials was important, in operant conditioning the *pattern* with which reinforcements appeared was crucial. Skinner explored dozens of what came to be known as *schedules of reinforcement* (Ferster & Skinner, 1957; see **FIGURE 7.8**). We'll consider some of the most important next.

fixed-interval schedule (FI) An operant conditioning principle whereby reinforcers are presented at fixed time periods, provided that the appropriate response is made.

Students cramming for an exam often show the same kind of behavior as pigeons being reinforced under a fixed-interval schedule. Jupiterimages, Brand X Pictures/Stockbyte/Getty Images

Radio station promotions and giveaways often follow a variable-interval schedule of reinforcement. © Richard Hutchings/ PhotoEdit

Interval Schedules. Under a **fixed-interval schedule (FI)**, *reinforcers are presented at fixed time periods, provided that the appropriate response is made.* For

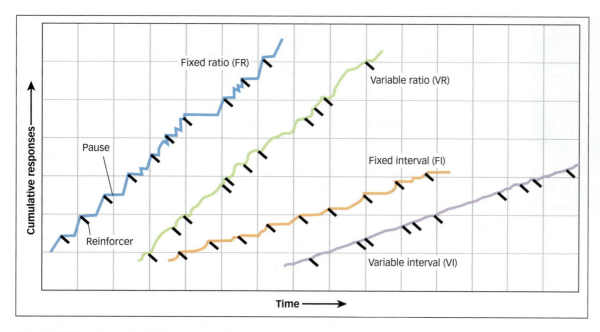

Figure 7.8 REINFORCEMENT SCHEDULES Different schedules of reinforcement produce different rates of response. These lines represent the number of responses that occur under each type of reinforcement. The black slash marks indicate when reinforcement was administered. Notice that ratio schedules tend to produce higher rates of responding than do interval schedules, as shown by the steeper lines for fixed-ratio and variable-ratio reinforcement.

example, on a 2-minute fixed-interval schedule, a response will be reinforced, but only after 2 minutes have expired since the last reinforcement. Rats and pigeons in Skinner boxes produce predictable patterns of behavior under these schedules. They show little responding right after the presentation of the reinforcement, but as the next time interval draws to a close, they show a burst of responding. Many undergraduates behave exactly like this. They do relatively little work until just before the upcoming exam, then engage in a burst of reading and studying.

Under a **variable-interval schedule (VI)**, *a behavior is reinforced on the basis of an average time that has expired since the last reinforcement*. For example, on a 2-minute variable-interval schedule, responses will be reinforced every 2 minutes *on average*. Variable-interval schedules typically produce steady, consistent responding because the time until the next reinforcement is less predictable. One example of a VI schedule in real life might be radio promotional giveaways. The reinforcement—say, a ticket to a rock concert—might occur *on average* once an hour across the span of the broadcasting day, but it might come early in the 10 o'clock hour, later in the 11 o'clock hour, immediately into the 12 o'clock hour, and so on.

Both fixed-interval schedules and variable-interval schedules tend to produce slow, methodical responding because the reinforcements follow a time scale that is independent of how many responses occur. It doesn't matter if a rat on a fixed-interval schedule presses a bar 1 time during a 2-minute period or 100 times: The reinforcing food pellet won't drop out of the chute until 2 minutes have elapsed, regardless of the number of responses.

Ratio Schedules. Under a **fixed-ratio schedule (FR)**, *reinforcement is delivered after a specific number of responses have been made.*One schedule might present reinforcement after every fourth response, and a different schedule might present reinforcement after every 20 responses; the special case of presenting reinforcement after each response is called *continuous reinforcement.* There are many situations in which people are reinforced on a fixed-ratio schedule: Book clubs often give you a

variable-interval schedule (VI) An operant conditioning principle whereby behavior is reinforced on the basis of an average time that has expired since the last reinforcement.

fixed-ratio schedule (FR) An operant conditioning principle whereby reinforcement is delivered after a specific number of responses have been made.

These pieceworkers in a textile factory get paid according to a fixed-ratio schedule: They receive payment after sewing some set number of shirts. Jeff Holt/ Bloomberg via Getty Images

Slot machines in casinos pay out following a variable-ratio schedule. This helps explain why some gamblers feel incredibly lucky, whereas others (like this chap) can't believe they can play a machine for so long without winning a thing. Stockbroker/MBI/Alamy

variable-ratio schedule (VR) An operant conditioning principle whereby the delivery of reinforcement is based on a particular average number of responses.

intermittent reinforcement An operant conditioning principle whereby only some of the responses made are followed by reinforcement.

intermittent reinforcement effect The fact that operant behaviors that are maintained under intermittent reinforcement schedules resist extinction better than do those maintained under continuous reinforcement.

shaping Learning that results from the reinforcement of successive steps to a final desired behavior.

Imagine that you own an insurance company, and you want to encourage your salespeople to sell as many policies as possible. You decide to give them bonuses according to the number of policies they sell. How might you set up a system of bonuses using an FR schedule? Using a VR schedule? Which system do you think would encourage your salespeople to work harder, in terms of making more sales? Elenathewise/iStock/Getty Images

freebie after a set number of regular purchases; pieceworkers get paid after making a fixed number of products; and some credit card companies return to their customers a percentage of the amount charged. When a fixed-ratio schedule is operating, it is possible, in principle, to know exactly when the next reinforcer is due. A laundry pieceworker on a 10-response, fixed-ratio schedule who has just washed and ironed the ninth shirt knows that payment is coming after the next shirt is done.

Under a **variable-ratio schedule (VR)**, *the delivery of reinforcement is based on a particular average number of responses*. For example, slot machines in a modern casino pay off on variable-ratio schedules. A casino might advertise that its machines pay off on "every 100 pulls on average," but one player might hit a jackpot after 3 pulls on a slot machine, whereas another player might not hit a jackpot until after 80 pulls.

It should come as no surprise that variable-ratio schedules produce slightly higher rates of responding than fixed-ratio schedules, primarily because the organism never knows when the next reinforcement is going to appear. What's more, the higher the ratio, the higher the response rate tends to be: A 20-response variable-ratio schedule will produce considerably more responding than a 2-response variable-ratio schedule.

When schedules of reinforcement provide **intermittent reinforcement**, *whereby only some of the responses made are followed by reinforcement*, they produce behavior that is much more resistant to extinction than does a continuous reinforcement schedule. One way to think about this effect is to recognize that the more irregular and intermittent a schedule is, the more difficult it becomes for an organism to detect when it has actually been placed on extinction. For example, if you've just put a dollar into a soda machine that, unknown to you, is broken, no soda comes out. Because you're used to getting your sodas on a continuous reinforcement schedule—one dollar produces one soda—this abrupt change in the environment is easy to notice, and you are unlikely to put additional money into the machine: You'd quickly show extinction. However, if you've put your dollar into a slot machine that, unknown to you, is broken, do you stop after one or two plays? Almost certainly not. If you're a regular slot player, you're used to going for many plays in a row without winning anything, so it's difficult to tell that anything is out of the ordinary. The **intermittent reinforcement effect** refers to *the fact that operant behaviors that are maintained under intermittent reinforcement schedules resist extinction better than do those maintained under continuous reinforcement*. In one extreme case, Skinner gradually extended a variable-ratio schedule until he managed to get a pigeon to make an astonishing 10,000 pecks at an illuminated key for one food reinforcer! Behavior maintained under a schedule like this is virtually immune to extinction.

Shaping Through Successive Approximations

Have you ever been to SeaWorld and wondered how the dolphins learn to jump up in the air, twist around, splash back down, do a somersault, and then jump through a hoop, all in one smooth motion? Well, they don't. At least, not all at once. Rather, elements of their behavior are shaped over time until the final product looks like one smooth motion.

Behavior rarely occurs in fixed frameworks where a stimulus is presented and then an organism has to engage in some activity or another. Most of our behaviors are the result of **shaping**, *learning that results from the reinforcement of successive steps to a final desired behavior*. The outcomes of one set of behaviors shape the next set of behaviors, whose outcomes shape the next set of behaviors, and so on.

Skinner noted that if you put a rat in a Skinner box and wait for it to press the bar, you could end up waiting a very long time: Bar pressing just isn't very high in a rat's natural hierarchy of responses. However, it is relatively easy to shape bar pressing.

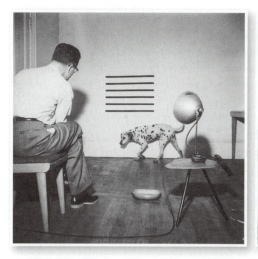

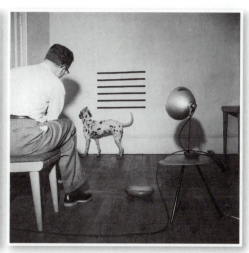
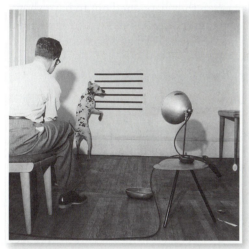
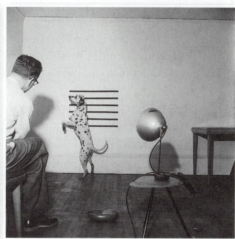
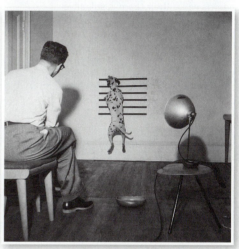

B. F. Skinner shaping a dog named Agnes. In the span of 20 minutes, Skinner was able to use reinforcement of successive approximations to shape Agnes's behavior. The result was a pretty neat trick: Agnes wandered in, stood on her hind legs, and jumped. Look Magazine Photograph Collection, Library of Congress, Prints & Photographs Division, [Reproduction Number e.g., LC-L9-60-8812, frame 8]

Wait until the rat turns in the direction of the bar, and then deliver a food reward. This will reinforce turning toward the bar, making such a movement more likely. Now wait for the rat to take a step toward the bar before delivering food; this will reinforce moving toward the bar. After the rat walks closer to the bar, wait until it touches the bar before presenting the food. Notice that none of these behaviors is the final desired behavior (reliably pressing the bar). Rather, each behavior is a *successive approximation* to the final product, or a behavior that gets incrementally closer to the overall desired behavior. In the dolphin example—and indeed, in many instances of animal training in which relatively simple animals seem to perform astoundingly complex behaviors—you can think through how each smaller behavior is reinforced until the overall sequence of behavior is performed reliably.

Superstitious Behavior

Everything we've discussed so far suggests that one of the keys to establishing reliable operant behavior is the correlation between an organism's response and the occurrence of reinforcement. As you read in the Methods in Psychology chapter, however, just because two things are correlated (i.e., they tend to occur together in time and space) doesn't imply that there is causality (i.e., the presence of one reliably causes the other to occur).

Skinner (1948) designed an experiment that illustrates this distinction. He put several pigeons in Skinner boxes, set the food dispenser to deliver food every

People believe in many superstitions and engage in all kinds of superstitious behaviors. Players in the National Hockey League do not shave their beards while their team is still alive in the playoffs, and this superstitious behavior was even adopted by a female fan of the Los Angeles Kings during the 2012 NHL playoffs. Skinner thought superstitions resulted from the unintended reinforcement of inconsequential behavior. AP Photo/Jae C. Hong

15 seconds, and left the birds to their own devices. Later, he returned and found the birds engaging in odd, idiosyncratic behaviors, such as pecking aimlessly in a corner or turning in circles. He referred to these behaviors as "superstitious" and offered a behaviorist analysis of their occurrence. A pigeon that just happened to have pecked randomly in the corner when the food showed up had connected the delivery of food to that behavior. Because this pecking behavior was reinforced by the delivery of food, the pigeon was likely to repeat it. Now pecking in the corner was more likely to occur, and it was more likely to be reinforced 15 seconds later when the food appeared again. Skinner's pigeons acted as though there was a causal relationship between their behaviors and the appearance of food when it was merely an accidental correlation.

Although some researchers questioned Skinner's characterization of these behaviors as superstitious (Staddon & Simmelhag, 1971), later studies have shown that people, like pigeons, often behave as though there's a correlation between their responses and reward when in fact the connection is merely accidental (Bloom et al., 2007; Mellon, 2009; Ono, 1987; Wagner & Morris, 1987). For example, baseball players who enjoy several home runs on a day when they happened not to have showered are likely to continue that tradition, laboring under the belief that the accidental correlation between poor personal hygiene and a good day at bat is somehow causal. This "stench causes home runs" hypothesis is just one of many examples of human superstitions (Gilbert et al., 2000; Radford & Radford, 1949).

A Deeper Understanding of Operant Conditioning

To behaviorists such as Watson and Skinner, an organism behaved in a certain way in response to stimuli in the environment, not because the animal in question wanted, wished, or willed anything. However, some research on operant conditioning digs deeper into the underlying mechanisms that produce the familiar outcomes of reinforcement. Let's examine three elements that expand our view of operant conditioning: the cognitive, neural, and evolutionary elements of operant conditioning.

The Cognitive Elements of Operant Conditioning

Edward Chace Tolman (1886–1959) argued that there was more to learning than just knowing the circumstances in the environment (the properties of the stimulus) and being able to observe a particular outcome (the reinforced response). Instead, Tolman proposed that the conditioning experience produced knowledge or a belief that, in this particular situation, a specific reward will appear if a specific response is made. Tolman's ideas may remind you of the Rescorla–Wagner model of classical conditioning. In both Rescorla's and Tolman's theories, the stimulus does not directly evoke a response; rather, it establishes an internal cognitive state that then produces the behavior.

During the 1930s and 1940s, Tolman and his students conducted studies that focused on *latent learning* and *cognitive maps*, two phenomena that strongly suggest that simple S–R interpretations of operant learning behavior are inadequate.

latent learning A process in which something is learned, but it is not manifested as a behavioral change until sometime in the future.

Latent Learning and Cognitive Maps. **Latent learning** occurs when *something is learned, but it is not manifested as a behavioral change until sometime in the future.* For example, Tolman gave three groups of rats access to a complex maze every day for over 2 weeks. The control group never received any reinforcement—they were simply allowed to run around the maze. In **FIGURE 7.9** you can see that over the 2 weeks of the study, the control group (in green) got a little better at finding their way through the maze, but not by much. A second group of rats received regular reinforcements; when they reached the goal box, they found a small food reward there. Not surprisingly, these rats showed clear learning, as can be seen in blue in Figure 7.9. A third group was treated exactly like the control group for the first 10 days and then rewarded for the last 7 days. This group's behavior (in orange) was quite striking. For the first 10 days, they behaved like the rats in the control group. However, during the final 7 days, they behaved a lot like the rats in the second group,

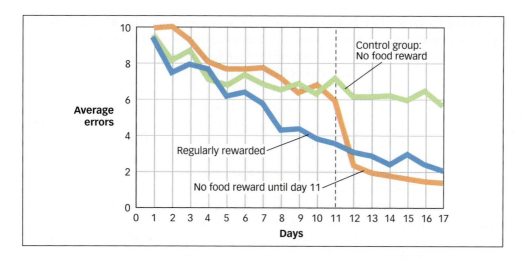

Figure 7.9 LATENT LEARNING
Rats in a control group that never received any reinforcement (green curve) improved at finding their way through the maze over 17 days, but not by much. Rats that received regular reinforcements (blue curve) showed fairly clear learning; their error rate decreased steadily over time. Rats in the latent learning group (orange curve) were treated exactly like the control group rats for the first 10 days and then like the regularly rewarded group for the last 7 days. Their dramatic improvement on day 12 shows that these rats had learned a lot about the maze and the location of the goal box, even though they had never received reinforcements. Notice, also, that on the last 7 days, these latent learners actually seem to make fewer errors than their regularly rewarded counterparts.

which had been reinforced every day. Clearly, the rats in this third group had learned a lot about the maze and the location of the goal box during those first 10 days even though they had not received any reinforcements for their behavior. In other words, they showed evidence of latent learning.

Because latent learning occurs without any obvious reinforcement, Tolman's findings posed a direct challenge to the then-dominant behaviorist position that all learning required some form of reinforcement (Tolman & Honzik, 1930a). In fact, Tolman thought that the rats had developed a mental picture of the maze, which he called a **cognitive map**, *a mental representation of the physical features of the environment* (Tolman & Honzik, 1930b; Tolman, Ritchie, & Kalish, 1946). Support for this idea was obtained in a clever experiment, where Tolman trained rats in a maze, and then changed the maze—while keeping the start and goal locations in the same spot (**FIGURE 7.10**). Behaviorists would predict that the rats, finding the familiar route blocked, would be stymied. However, faced with the blocked path, the rats instead quickly navigated a new and efficient pathway to the food. This behavior suggested that the rats had formed a sophisticated cognitive map of their environment, and could use that map after the conditions had changed. Tolman's experiments strongly suggest that there is a cognitive component, even in rats, to operant learning.

cognitive map A mental representation of the physical features of the environment.

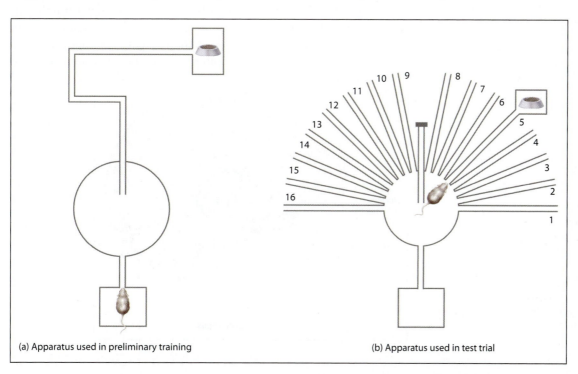

(a) Apparatus used in preliminary training

(b) Apparatus used in test trial

Figure 7.10
COGNITIVE MAPS (a) Rats trained to run from a start box to a goal box in the maze on the left mastered the task quite readily. When those rats were then placed in the maze on the right (b), in which the main straight-away had been blocked, they did something unusual. Rather than simply backtracking and trying the next closest runway (i.e., one of those labeled 8 or 9 in the figure), which would be predicted by stimulus generalization, the rats typically chose runway 5, which led most directly to where the goal box had been during their training. The rats had formed a cognitive map of their environment and knew where they needed to end up spatially, relative to where they began.

Learning to Trust: For Better or Worse. Cognitive factors also played a key role in an experiment examining learning and brain activity (using fMRI) in people who played a "trust" game with a fictional partner (Delgado, Frank, & Phelps, 2005). On each trial, a participant could either keep a $1 reward or transfer the reward to a partner, who would receive $3. The partner could then either keep the $3 or share half of it with the participant. When playing with a partner who was willing to share the reward, the participant would be better off transferring the money, but when playing with a partner who did not share, the participant would be better off keeping the reward in the first place. Participants in such experiments typically find out who is trustworthy on the basis of trial-and-error learning during the game, transferring more money to partners who reinforce them by sharing.

In the study by Delgado and colleagues, participants were given detailed descriptions of their partners that portrayed the partners as either trustworthy, neutral, or suspect. Even though during the game all three partners shared equally often, the participants' cognitions about their partners had powerful effects. Participants transferred more money to the trustworthy partner than to the others, essentially ignoring the trial-by-trial feedback that would ordinarily shape their playing behavior, thus reducing the amount of reward they received. Highlighting the power of the cognitive effect, signals in a part of the brain that ordinarily distinguishes between positive and negative feedback were evident only when participants played with the neutral partner; these feedback signals were absent when participants played with the trustworthy partner and reduced when participants played with the suspect partner.

The Neural Elements of Operant Conditioning

The first hint of how specific brain structures might contribute to the process of reinforcement came from James Olds and his associates, who inserted tiny electrodes into different parts of a rat's brain and allowed the animal to control electric stimulation of its own brain by pressing a bar. They discovered that some brain areas produced what appeared to be intensely positive experiences: The rats would press the bar repeatedly to stimulate these structures, sometimes ignoring food, water, and other life-sustaining necessities for hours on end simply to receive stimulation directly in the brain. Olds and colleagues called these parts of the brain *pleasure centers* (Olds, 1956; see **FIGURE 7.11**).

In the years since these early studies, researchers have identified a number of structures and pathways in the brain that deliver rewards through stimulation (Wise, 1989, 2005). The neurons in the *medial forebrain bundle*, a pathway that meanders its way from the midbrain through the *hypothalamus* into the *nucleus accumbens*, are

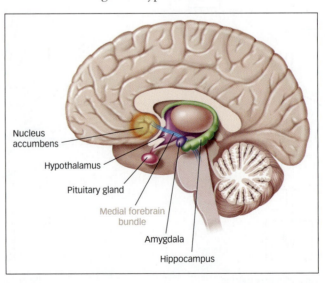

Figure 7.11 PLEASURE CENTERS IN THE BRAIN The nucleus accumbens, medial forebrain bundle, and hypothalamus are all major pleasure centers in the brain.

the most susceptible to stimulation that produces pleasure. This is not surprising, because psychologists have identified this bundle of cells as crucial to behaviors that clearly involve pleasure, such as eating, drinking, and engaging in sexual activity. Second, the neurons all along this pathway and especially those in the nucleus accumbens itself are all *dopaminergic* (i.e., they secrete the neurotransmitter *dopamine*). Remember from the Neuroscience and Behavior chapter that higher levels of dopamine in the brain are usually associated with positive emotions. During recent years, several competing hypotheses about the precise role of dopamine have emerged, including the idea that dopamine is more closely linked with the expectation of reward than with reward itself (Fiorillo, Newsome, & Schultz, 2008; Schultz, 2006, 2007), or that dopamine is more closely associated with wanting or even craving something, rather than simply liking it (Berridge, 2007). Whichever view turns out to be correct, researchers have found good support for a reward center in which dopamine plays a key role.

The Evolutionary Elements of Operant Conditioning

As you'll recall, classical conditioning has an adaptive value that has been fine-tuned by evolution. Not surprisingly, operant conditioning does too. Several behaviorists who were using simple T mazes such as the one shown in **FIGURE 7.12** to study learning in rats discovered that if a rat found food in one arm of the maze on the first trial of the day, it typically ran down the *other* arm on the very next trial. A staunch behaviorist wouldn't expect the rats to behave this way. According to operant conditioning, prior reinforcement in one arm should *increase* the likelihood of their turning in that same direction next time, not reduce it.

What was puzzling from a behaviorist perspective makes sense when viewed from an evolutionary perspective. Rats are foragers, and like all foraging species, they have evolved a highly adaptive strategy for survival. They move around in their environment, looking for food. If they find it somewhere, they eat it (or store it) and then go look somewhere else for more. So if the rat just found food in the *right* arm of a T maze, the obvious place to look next time is the *left* arm. The rat knows that there isn't any more food in the right arm because it just ate the food it found there!

Two of Skinner's former students, Keller Breland and Marian Breland, were among the first researchers to discover that it wasn't just rats in T mazes that presented a problem for behaviorists (Breland & Breland, 1961). The Brelands, who made a career out of training animals for commercials and movies, often used pigs because pigs are surprisingly good at learning all sorts of tricks. However, they discovered that it was extremely difficult to teach a pig the simple task of dropping coins in a box. Instead of depositing the coins, the pigs persisted in

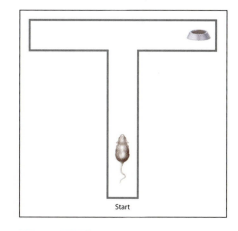

Figure 7.12 A SIMPLE T MAZE
When rats find food in the right arm of a typical T maze, on the next trial, they will often run to the left arm of the maze. This contradicts basic principles of operant conditioning: If the behavior of running to the right arm is reinforced, it should be more likely to occur again in the future. What explains this behavior?

by KAZ -Larry Katzman/CartoonStock.com

The misbehavior of organisms: Pigs are biologically predisposed to root out their food, just as raccoons are predisposed to wash their food. Trying to train either species to behave differently can prove to be an exercise in futility. John Wilkinson/Ecoscene/Corbis; Millard H. Sharp/Science Source

rooting with them as if they were digging them up in soil, tossing them in the air with their snouts and pushing them around. The Brelands tried to train raccoons at the same task, with different but equally dismal results. The raccoons spent their time rubbing the coins between their paws instead of dropping them in the box. Having learned the association between the coins and food, the animals began to treat the coins as stand-ins for food. Pigs are biologically predisposed to root out their food, and raccoons have evolved to clean their food by rubbing it with their paws. That is exactly what each species of animal did with the coins. The Brelands' work shows that all species, including humans, are biologically predisposed to learn some things more readily than others and to respond to stimuli in ways that are consistent with their evolutionary history (Gallistel, 2000).

BUILD TO THE OUTCOMES

1. What is the law of effect?

2. What do "positive" and "negative" mean in operant conditioning?

3. Why is reinforcement more constructive than punishment in learning desired behavior?

4. What are primary and secondary reinforcers?

5. How does the concept of delayed reinforcement relate to difficulties with quitting smoking?

6. How is the concept of extinction different in operant conditioning than it is in classical conditioning?

7. How does a radio station use scheduled reinforcements to keep you listening?

8. How do ratio schedules work to keep you spending your money?

9. How can operant conditioning produce complex behaviors?

10. What are cognitive maps? Why are they a challenge to behaviorism?

11. How do specific brain structures contribute to the process of reinforcement?

12. What explains a rat's behavior in a T maze?

Observational Learning: Look at Me

LEARNING OUTCOMES

- Explain the social, cultural, and evolutionary aspects of observational learning.

- Compare evidence of observational learning in animals raised among humans with that in animals raised in the wild.

- Explain the neural elements of observational learning.

observational learning A process by which an organism learns from watching the actions of others.

Four-year-old Rodney and his 2-year-old sister Margie had always been told to keep away from the stove. Being a mischievous imp, however, Rodney decided one day to place his hand over a burner until the singeing of his flesh led him to recoil, shrieking in pain. Rodney was more scared than hurt, really—and no one hearing this story doubts that he learned something important that day. But little Margie, who stood by, watching these events unfold, *also* learned the same lesson. Rodney's story is a behaviorist's textbook example: The administration of punishment led to a learned change in his behavior. But how can we explain Margie's learning? She received neither punishment nor reinforcement and yet it's arguable that she's just as likely to keep her hands away from stoves in the future as Rodney is.

Margie's is a case of **observational learning**, in which *an organism learns by watching the actions of others*. In all societies, appropriate social behavior is passed on from generation to generation, not only through deliberate training of the young but also through young people observing the patterns of behaviors of their elders and each other (Flynn & Whiten, 2008). Tasks such as using chopsticks or operating a TV's remote control are more easily acquired if we watch these activities being carried out before we try them ourselves. Even complex motor tasks, such as performing surgery, are learned in part through extensive observation and imitation of models. And anyone who is about to undergo surgery is grateful for observational learning. Just the thought of a generation of surgeons acquiring their surgical techniques through the trial-and-error methods that Thorndike studied, or the shaping of successive approximations that captivated Skinner, would make any of us very nervous.

Observational Learning in Humans

In a series of studies that have become landmarks in psychology, Albert Bandura and his colleagues investigated the parameters of observational learning (Bandura, Ross, & Ross, 1961). The researchers escorted individual preschoolers into a play area filled with toys that 4-year-olds typically like. An adult *model*—someone whose behavior might be a guide for others—then entered the room and started playing with a Bobo doll, which is a large, inflatable plastic toy with a weighted bottom that allows it to bounce back upright when knocked down. The adult played quietly for a bit but then started aggressing toward the Bobo doll, knocking it down, jumping on it, and kicking it around the room. When the children who observed these actions were later allowed to play with a variety of toys, including a child-size Bobo doll, they were more than twice as likely to interact with it in an aggressive manner as a group of children who hadn't observed the aggressive model (see **FIGURE 7.13**).

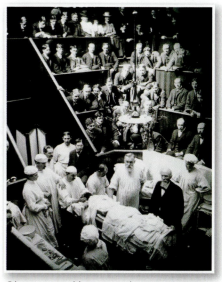

Observational learning plays an important role in surgical training, as illustrated by the medical students observing the famed German surgeon Vincenz Czerny (beard and white gown) perform stomach surgery in 1907 at a San Francisco hospital. Stanley B. Burns, MD & The Burns Archive N.Y./Science Source

Figure 7.13 **BEATING UP BOBO** Children who were exposed to an adult model who behaved aggressively toward a Bobo doll were likely to behave aggressively toward it themselves. This behavior occurred in the absence of any direct reinforcement. Observational learning was responsible for producing the children's behaviors. © Albert Bandura, Dept. of Psychology, Stanford University

Coaches rely on observational learning when they demonstrate techniques to athletes. Robert F. Bukaty/AP Images

The children in these studies also showed that they were sensitive to the consequences of the actions they observed. When they saw the adult models being punished for behaving aggressively, the children showed considerably less aggression. When the children observed a model being rewarded and praised for aggressive behavior, they displayed an increase in aggression (Bandura, Ross, & Ross, 1963). The observational learning seen in Bandura's studies has implications for social learning and cultural transmission of behaviors, norms, and values (Bandura, 1977, 1994).

Observational learning is important in many domains of everyday life. Sports provide a good example. Coaches in just about all sports rely on observational learning when they demonstrate critical techniques and skills to players, and athletes also have numerous opportunities to observe other athletes perform. Studies of athletes in both team and individual sports indicate that all rely heavily on observational learning to improve their performance (Wesch, Law, & Hall, 2007). In fact, observational learning sometimes results in just as much learning as practicing the task itself (Heyes & Foster, 2002; Mattar & Gribble, 2005; Vinter & Perruchet, 2002).

Observational Learning in Animals

Humans aren't the only creatures capable of learning through observing. In one study, for example, pigeons watched other pigeons get reinforced for either pecking at the feeder or stepping on a bar. When placed in the box later, the pigeons tended to use whatever technique they had observed other pigeons using earlier (Zentall, Sutton, & Sherburne, 1996).

One of the most important questions about observational learning in animals concerns whether monkeys and chimpanzees can learn to use tools by observing tool use in others, the way young children can. In one study, chimpanzees observed a model (the experimenter) use a metal bar shaped like a T to pull items of food toward them (Tomasello et al., 1987). Compared with a group that did not observe any tool use, these chimpanzees showed more learning when later performing the task themselves. But in a later experiment (Nagell, Olguin, & Tomasello, 1993), some chimpanzees saw the model use a rake in its normal position (with the teeth pointed toward the ground) to drag a food reward into reach; this method was rather inefficient because the teeth were widely spaced, and the food sometimes slipped between them. Other monkeys saw the model use the rake with the teeth pointed up so that the flat edge of the rake touched the ground—a more effective procedure for capturing the food. Although both groups of chimpanzees later used the tool to obtain food, the chimpanzees who observed the more efficient "teeth up" procedure did not use it any more often than did those who observed the less efficient "teeth down" procedure. By contrast, 2-year-old children exposed to the same conditions used the rake in the exact same way that they had seen the model use it. The chimpanzees seemed only to be learning that the tool could be used to obtain food, whereas the children learned something specific about how to use the tool.

The chimpanzees in these studies had been raised by their mothers in the wild. However, the researchers also showed that chimpanzees raised in a more human-like environment showed more specific observational learning—and performed similarly to human children on the raking task (Tomasello, Savage-Rumbaugh, & Kruger, 1993). This finding led Tomasello et al. (1993) to suggest that being raised in a human culture has a profound effect on the cognitive abilities of chimpanzees, especially their ability to understand the intentions of others when performing tasks such as using tools, which in turn increases their observational learning capacities.

More recent research has found something similar in capuchin monkeys, who are known for their tool use in the wild, such as employing branches or stone hammers to crack open nuts (Boinski, Quatrone, & Swartz, 2000; Fragaszy et al., 2004) or using stones to dig up buried roots (Moura & Lee, 2004). In one study, a model demonstrated two ways of using a screwdriver to gain access to a food reward hidden in a box (Fredman & Whiten, 2008). Some monkeys observed the model poke through a hole in the center of the box, whereas others watched him pry open the lid at the rim of the box (see **FIGURE 7.14**). Both mother-reared and human-reared monkeys showed evidence of observational learning, but the human-reared monkeys carried out the exact action they had observed more often than did the mother-reared monkeys.

Although this evidence implies that there is a cultural influence on the cognitive processes that support observational learning, more work is needed to understand the exact nature of those processes (Bering, 2004; Mesoudi et al., 2015; Tomasello & Call, 2004).

Neural Elements of Observational Learning

Observational learning involves a neural component as well. As you read in the Neuroscience and Behavior chapter, *mirror neurons* are a type of cell found in the frontal and parietal lobes of primates (including humans). Mirror neurons fire when an animal performs an action, as when a monkey reaches for a food item (**FIGURE 7.15**). Mirror neurons also fire when an animal watches someone *else* perform the same specific task (Rizzolatti & Craighero, 2004). For example, monkeys' mirror neurons fire when they observe humans grasping for a piece of food, either to eat it or to place it in a container (Fogassi et al., 2005). Although the exact functions of mirror neurons continue to be debated (Hickok, 2009), it seems likely that mirror neurons contribute to observational learning.

Mirror neurons exist in humans too. Studies of observational learning in healthy adults have shown that watching someone else perform a task engages some of the same brain regions that are activated when people actually perform the task themselves. In one study, participants practiced some dance sequences, and watched music videos of other dance sequences (Cross et al., 2009). The participants were then given fMRI scans while viewing videos of sequences that they had previously danced or watched. Results showed that viewing the previously danced or watched sequences caused activity in brain regions considered part of the mirror neuron system. A surprise dancing test given to participants after the conclusion of scanning showed that performance was better on sequences previously watched than on untrained sequences, demonstrating significant observational learning, but was best of all on the previously danced sequences (Cross et al., 2009). So, although watching *Dancing with the Stars* might indeed improve your dancing skills, practicing on the dance floor should help even more.

Figure 7.14   OBSERVATIONAL LEARNING Monkeys who had been reared in the wild by their mothers or by human families watched a model either (*top*) poke a screwdriver through a hole in the center of a box to obtain a food reward or (*bottom*) pry open the lid. Both groups showed some evidence of observational learning, but the human-reared monkeys were more likely to carry out the exact action they had watched.

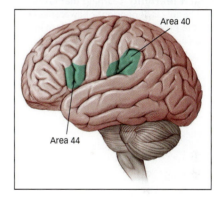

Figure 7.15   MIRROR NEURON SYSTEM Regions in the frontal lobe (area 44) and parietal lobe (area 40) are thought to be part of the mirror neuron system in humans.

Observing skilled dancers, such as this energetic pair in *Dancing with the Stars*, engages many of the same brain regions as does actual dance practice and can produce significant learning. Adam Taylor/ABC via Getty Images

1. What is observational learning?

2. Why might a younger sibling appear to learn faster than a firstborn?

3. What did the Bobo doll experiment show about children and aggressive behavior?

4. What are the cognitive differences between chimpanzees raised among humans and those raised in the wild?

5. What do mirror neurons do?

Implicit Learning: Under the Radar

LEARNING OUTCOMES

- Explain why language studies led to studies of implicit learning.

- Outline the ways that implicit and explicit learning differ.

implicit learning Learning that takes place largely independent of awareness of both the process and the products of information acquisition.

Most people are attuned to linguistic, social, emotional, or sensorimotor events in the world around them—so much so that they gradually build up internal representations of those patterns that they acquired without explicit awareness. This process is often called **implicit learning**, or *learning that takes place largely independent of awareness of both the process and the products of information acquisition*. Because it occurs without our awareness, implicit learning is knowledge that sneaks in "under the radar."

Some forms of learning start out explicitly but become more implicit over time. When you first learned to drive a car, for example, you probably devoted a lot of attention to the many movements and sequences that you needed to carry out simultaneously. ("Step lightly on the accelerator while you push the turn indicator, and look in the rearview mirror while you turn the steering wheel.") That complex interplay of motions is now probably quite effortless and automatic for you. Explicit learning has become implicit over time. These distinctions in learning might remind you of similar distinctions in memory, and for good reason. In the Memory chapter, you read about the differences between *implicit* and *explicit* memories. Do implicit and explicit learning mirror implicit and explicit memory? It's not that simple, but it is true that learning and memory are inextricably linked. Learning produces memories, and conversely, the existence of memories implies that knowledge was acquired, that experience was registered and recorded in the brain, or that learning has taken place.

Cognitive Approaches to Implicit Learning

Most children, by the time they are 6 or 7 years old, are linguistically and socially fairly sophisticated. Yet most children have very little explicit awareness of when or how they learned a particular course of action, and may not even be able to state the general principle underlying their behavior. Yet most kids have learned not to eat with their feet, to listen when they are spoken to, and not to kick the dog.

To investigate implicit learning in the laboratory, in early studies, researchers asked participants to memorize 15- or 20-letter strings. The letter strings, which at first glance look like nonsense syllables, were actually formed using a complex set of rules called an *artificial grammar* (see **FIGURE 7.16**). Participants were not told anything about the rules, but with experience, they gradually developed a vague, intuitive sense of the "correctness" of particular letter groupings and could get 60–70% correct—even though they were unable to provide much in the way of explicit awareness of the rules and regularities that they were using. The experience is similar to coming across a sentence with a grammatical error. You are immediately aware that something is wrong, and you can certainly make the sentence grammatical, but unless you are a trained linguist, you'll probably find it difficult to articulate which rules of English grammar were violated.

Other studies of implicit learning have used a *serial reaction time* task (Nissen & Bullemer, 1987). Here, research participants are presented with five small boxes on

Grammatical Strings	Nongrammatical Strings
VXJJ	VXTJJ
XXVT	XVTVVJ
VJTVXJ	VJTTVTV
VJTVTV	VJTXXVJ
XXXXVX	XXXVTJJ

Figure 7.16 ARTIFICIAL GRAMMAR AND IMPLICIT LEARNING These are examples of letter strings formed by an artificial grammar. Research participants are exposed to the rules of the grammar and are later tested on new letter strings. Participants show reliable accuracy at distinguishing the valid, grammatical strings from the invalid, nongrammatical strings—even though they usually can't explicitly state the rule they are following when making such judgments. Using an artificial grammar is one way of studying implicit learning (Reber, 1996).

a computer screen. Each box lights up briefly, and when it does, the participant is asked to press the button that is just underneath that box as quickly as possible. Like the artificial grammar task, the sequence of lights appears to be random, but in fact it follows a pattern. Research participants eventually get faster with practice as they learn to anticipate which box is most likely to light up next. But if asked, they are generally unaware that there is a pattern to the lights.

Implicit learning is remarkably resistant to various disorders that are known to affect explicit learning. For example, profoundly amnesic patients not only show normal implicit memories but also display virtually normal implicit learning of artificial grammar (Knowlton, Ramus, & Squire, 1992), even though they have essentially no explicit memory of having been in the learning phase of the experiment! Perhaps even more striking, recent evidence indicates that at least one form of implicit learning is *enhanced* in autistic adults (see A World of Difference: Implicit Learning in Autism Spectrum Disorder). In contrast, dyslexic children

Ten years ago, no one knew how to type using their thumbs; now just about all teenagers do it automatically. Mary Altaffer/AP Images

Implicit Learning in Autism Spectrum Disorder

People with autism spectrum disorder (ASD) have communication problems and engage in repetitive and restricted behaviors. But they also have some intriguing strengths, such as normal or even superior visuo-spatial abilities (Caron et al., 2006). This pattern is clearest in situations where the task is to focus on parts or local details of a visual display, as opposed to the "big picture" of how all the parts fit together (Happé & Frith, 2006; Rondan & Deruelle, 2004).

In one study (Roser et al., 2015), control participants and participants with ASD viewed a nine-box grid containing visual shapes, as in the figure to the right. Unknown to the participants, the grid contained pairs of shapes that always appeared in particular spatial relationships: shapes 1 and 2 always side by side; shapes 3 and 4 always diagonally apart; and shape 5 always above shape 6 (see top row). The shapes could appear in different positions in different grids, but they always appeared in the same spatial relationship to one another (see bottom row). During the learning phase of the experiment, participants were shown hundreds of grids and were instructed simply to look at the shapes in the grids.

Next, participants were asked whether they had noticed any regularity in the spatial arrangement of the shapes. Almost all of the participants said "no" to these questions, indicating very little explicit learning of the spatial relationships.

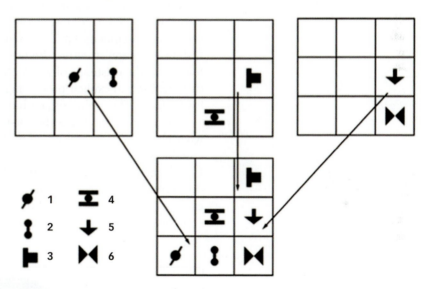

Right hemisphere dominance in visual statistical learning by Roser, M. E., Fiser, J., Aslin, R. N., & Gazzaniga, M. S. (2011). *Journal of Cognitive Neuroscience, 23,* 1091. ©2011, by the MIT Press. http://www.mitpressjournals.org/doi/abs/10.1162/jocn.2010.21508#.VzDmi9dLR28. Reprinted by permission of MIT Press Journals.

Then, the participants were shown grids that contained pairs of shapes, some in the same spatial relationship as during the learning phase, and others in a different spatial relationship. On this test, all participants showed evidence of implicit learning, that is, they tended to choose grids that had the shapes depicted in the correct spatial relationships. But strikingly, adults with ASD performed at a significantly higher level than control participants.

Roser and colleagues (2015) suggest that adults with ASD outperformed adults without ASD because when they viewed the grids during the learning phase of the experiment, they naturally focused more on the local relationships between individual pairs of objects, rather than taking in the entire display; thus, they implicitly learned more about the recurring spatial relationships of the object pairs. An intriguing question for future research concerns whether spared or enhanced capacities for implicit learning could be exploited to help individuals with ASD in everyday life.

who fail to acquire reading skills despite normal intelligence and good educational opportunities exhibit deficits in implicit learning of artificial grammars (Pavlidou, Williams, & Kelly, 2009) and motor and spatial sequences on the serial reaction time task (Bennett et al., 2008; Orban, Lungu, & Doyon, 2008; Stoodley et al., 2008). These findings suggest that problems with implicit learning play an important role in developmental dyslexia and need to be taken into account in the development of remedial programs (Stoodley et al., 2008).

Implicit and Explicit Learning Use Distinct Neural Pathways

The fact that individuals suffering amnesia show intact implicit learning strongly suggests that the brain structures that underlie implicit learning are distinct from those that underlie explicit learning. As we learned in the Memory chapter, amnesic individuals are characterized by lesions to the hippocampus and nearby structures in the medial temporal lobe; thus, researchers have concluded that these regions are not necessary for implicit learning (Bayley, Frascino, & Squire, 2005).

For example, in one study, participants saw a series of dot patterns, each of which looked like an array of stars in the night sky (Reber et al., 2003). Actually, all the stimuli were constructed to conform to an underlying prototypical dot pattern. The dots, however, varied so much that it was virtually impossible for a viewer to guess that they all had this common structure. Before the experiment began, half of the participants were told about the existence of the prototype; in other words, they were given instructions that encouraged explicit processing. The others were given standard implicit learning instructions: They were told nothing other than to attend to the dot patterns.

The participants were then asked to categorize new dot patterns, according to whether or not they conformed to the prototype. Interestingly, both groups performed equally well on this task, correctly classifying about 65% of the new dot patterns. However, brain scans revealed that the two groups made these decisions using very different parts of their brains (see **FIGURE 7.17**). Participants who were given the explicit instructions showed *increased* brain activity in the prefrontal cortex, parietal cortex, hippocampus, and a variety of other areas known to be associated with

Figure 7.17 IMPLICIT AND EXPLICIT LEARNING ACTIVATE DIFFERENT BRAIN AREAS Research participants were scanned with fMRI while engaged in either implicit or explicit learning about the categorization of dot patterns. The occipital region (in blue) showed decreased brain activity after implicit learning. The areas in yellow, orange, and red showed increased brain activity during explicit learning, including the left temporal lobe (*far left*), the right frontal lobe (*second from left and second from right*), and the parietal lobe (*second from right and far right*; Reber et al., 2003). © Reber, P. J., Gitelman, D. R., Parrish, T. B., & Mesulam, M. M. (2003). Dissociating explicit and implicit category knowledge with fMRI. *Journal of Cognitive Neuroscience, 15*, 574–583. Permission conveyed through Copyright Clearance Center, Inc.

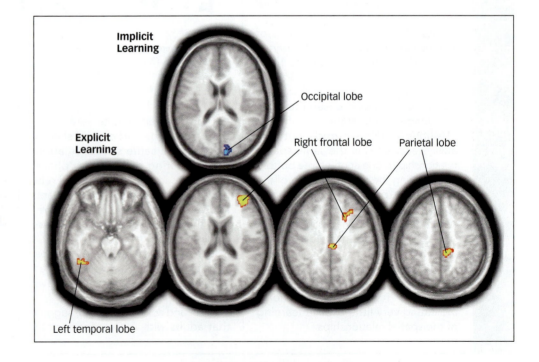

the processing of explicit memories. Those given the implicit instructions showed *decreased* brain activation primarily in the occipital region, which is involved in visual processing. This finding suggests that participants recruited distinct brain structures in different ways, depending on whether they were approaching the task using explicit or implicit learning.

BUILD TO THE OUTCOMES

1. What is the difference between implicit and explicit learning?

2. How are learning and memory linked?

3. How can you learn something without being aware of it?

4. Why are tasks learned implicitly difficult to explain to others?

5. What technology shows that implicit and explicit learning are associated with separate structures of the brain?

Learning in the Classroom

In this chapter, we've considered several different types of learning. Yet it may seem strange to you that we haven't discussed the kind of learning to which you are currently devoting much of your life: learning in educational settings such as the classroom. Way back in the first chapter of this book (Psychology: Evolution of a Science), we reviewed some techniques that we think are useful for studying the material in this course and others (see The Real World: Improving Study Skills, p. 5). But we didn't say much about the actual research that supports these suggestions. Let's consider some recent research about learning techniques, and then turn to the equally important topic of exerting control over learning processes.

LEARNING OUTCOMES

- Explain why distributed practice and practice testing are effective study techniques.

- Describe how judgments of learning (JOLs) impact learning.

Techniques for Learning

Students use a wide variety of study techniques in attempts to improve their learning, including highlighting and underlining, rereading, summarizing, and visual imagery mnemonics (Annis & Annis, 1982; Wade, Trathen, & Schraw, 1990). How effective are such techniques? A comprehensive analysis of research concerning 10 learning techniques (Dunlosky et al., 2013) evaluated the overall usefulness of each technique and classified it as high, moderate, or low utility (**TABLE 7.2**).

Despite their popularity, highlighting, rereading, summarizing, and visual imagery mnemonics all received a low utility assessment. That doesn't mean that these techniques have no value whatsoever for improving learning, but it does suggest that students could better spend their time using other approaches—a reason that none of these techniques appeared in the Improving Study Skills box. The

TABLE 7.2 Effectiveness of Study Techniques		
High Effectiveness	**Moderate Effectiveness**	**Low Effectiveness**
Practice testing	Elaborative interrogation	Summarization
Distributed practice	Self-explanation	Highlighting/Underlining
	Interleaved practice	Keyword mnemonic
		Imagery for text
		Rereading

Learning at Jiffy Lube University

Peter C. Brown is a writer in St. Paul, Minnesota. **Henry L. Roediger III** and **Mark A. McDaniel** are both professors of psychology at Washington University in St. Louis. Peter C. Brown

The study techniques we reviewed in this chapter on learning in the classroom can help to improve academic performance. But these techniques also have broader applications outside the classroom, in situations where people need to acquire new knowledge and skills. One of the most important everyday applications of learning techniques involves training to perform a job. In an excellent 2014 book called *Make It Stick: The Science of Successful Learning*, which elaborates on several of the key techniques and ideas we have discussed in this section, the writer Peter C. Brown and the cognitive psychologists Henry L. Roediger III and Mark A. McDaniel tell the story of Jiffy Lube University. This is an educational program where the well-known service-garage business has incorporated practice testing, distributed practice, and other learning techniques to aid the training of employees:

If you don't expect innovations in training to spring from your local service garage, Jiffy Lube may surprise you. An integrated suite of educational course under the felicitous name Jiffy Lube University is helping the company's franchises win customers, reduce employee turnover, broaden their service offerings, and boost sales.

Jiffy Lube is a network of more than two thousand service centers in the United States and Canada that provide oil changes, tire rotation, and other automotive services. Although the company is a subsidiary of Shell Oil Company, every outlet is owned and operated by an independent franchisee, who hires employees to serve customers.

The rapid-oil-change business, like most others, has had to adjust to changes in the marketplace and advances in technology. Synthetic lubricants have made oil changes less frequent, and because cars have become more complicated, garage employees need higher levels of training to understand diagnostic codes and provide appropriate services.

No employee may work on a customer's car until he or she has been certified as proficient. For this, they enter Jiffy Lube University, a Web-based learning platform. Certification starts with interactive e-learning, with frequent quizzing and feedback to learn what a particular job entails and how it's to be performed. When employees score 80 percent or better on an exam, they are eligible to begin training on the job, practicing new skills by following a written guide that breaks each service activity into its component steps. The steps may number as many as thirty and are performed as part of a team, often involving call and response (for example, between a technician working from the top side of an engine and another underneath). A supervisor coaches the employee and rates his or her performance on each step. When the technician demonstrates mastery, certification is recorded in his or her permanent file, signed by the supervisor. Technicians must recertify every two years to keep their mastery up to snuff and adapt to operational and technical changes. Higher-level jobs for advanced services like brake repair or running engine diagnostics are trained in the same manner.

The e-learning and on-the-job training are active learning strategies that incorporate various forms of quizzing, feedback, and spaced and interleaved practice. All progress is displayed by computer on a virtual "dashboard" that provides an individualized learning plan, enabling an employee to track his or her performance, focus on skills that need to be raised, and monitor his or her progress against the company's completion schedule. Jiffy Lube employees are typically eighteen to twenty-five years old and filing for their first jobs. As a technician is certified in one job, he or she begins training in another, until he or she has trained in all store positions, including management.

Ken Barber, Jiffy Lube International's manager of learning and development, says training has to be engaging in order to hold employees' attention. At the time we spoke, Barber was putting the finishing touches on a computer-based simulation game for company managers called "A Day in the Life of a Store Manager." The service center manager is confronted with various challenges and is required to select among a range of possible strategies for resolving them. The manager's choices determine how the game unfolds, providing feedback and the opportunity to strive for better outcomes, sharpening decision-making skill.

In the six years since Jiffy Lube University was launched, it has received many accolades from the training profession and earned accreditation by the American Council on Education. Employees who progress through training in all job certifications can enroll at a postsecondary institution with seven hours of college credit under their belts. Since the program's beginning, employee turnover has dropped and customer satisfaction has increased.

"For most employees of a Jiffy Lube franchisee, this is a way into the workforce, and the training curriculum helps them to grow and expand their knowledge," Barber says. "It helps them find a path to success."

From the results thus far, Jiffy Lube University appears to be a big success. It is notable that in addition to incorporating learning techniques that we've described in this chapter, Jiffy Lube University combines e-learning based on a Web platform with actual on-the-job training. The use of e-learning, also referred to as online learning, has expanded rapidly in recent years, and debates about its effectiveness have been spirited (Brooks, 2012; Koller, 2011). Jiffy Lube's successful combination of e-learning and live learning fits with earlier evidence indicating that combining these two formats may be especially effective (Means et al., 2010). And Jiffy Lube isn't the only company to make use of effective learning techniques. Brown, Roediger, and McDaniel also summarize successful training programs developed by Farmers Insurance, Andersen Windows and Doors, and other companies. So, after you complete your studies and enter the workforce, don't be surprised if you find yourself applying practice testing, distributed practice, and related study techniques and principles that promote effective learning.

Peter C. Brown, Henry L. Roediger III, and Mark A. McDaniel, *Make it stick: The science of successful learning* (Cambridge, MA: Harvard University Press), 245–246.

Improving Study Skills box did highlight the two strategies that received high utility assessments, including distributed practice ("Rehearse") and practice testing ("Test"). Let's take a deeper look at these now (see Other Voices: Learning at Jiffy Lube University).

Distributed Practice

Cramming for exams (neglecting to study for an extended period of time and then studying intensively just before an exam; Vacha & McBride, 1993) is a common occurrence in educational life. Surveys of undergraduates indicate that about 25–50% of students rely on cramming (McIntyre & Munson, 2008). Although cramming is better than not studying at all, when students cram for an exam, they repeatedly study the information to be learned with little or no time between repetitions, a procedure known as *massed practice*. Such students are thus denying themselves the benefits of *distributed practice*, which involves spreading out study activities so that more time intervenes between repetitions of the information to be learned. (Students who rely on cramming are also inviting some of the health and performance problems associated with procrastination that we will address in the Stress and Health chapter.)

The benefits of distributed practice have been observed in numerous studies, and have been demonstrated not only in undergraduates but also in children, older adults, and individuals with memory problems due to brain damage (Dunlosky et al., 2013). A review of 254 separate studies involving more than 14,000 participants concluded that on average, participants retained 47% of studied information after distributed practice compared with 37% after massed practice (Cepeda et al., 2006). Distributed practice can also improve long-term retention of actual classroom learning in student populations, including eighth-graders and college students (Rohrer, 2015).

Despite all the evidence indicating that distributed practice is an effective learning strategy, we still don't fully understand why that is so. One promising idea is that when we engage in massed practice, retrieving recently studied information is relatively easy, whereas during distributed practice, it is more difficult to retrieve information that we studied less recently. More difficult retrievals benefit subsequent learning more than easy retrievals, in line with the idea of "desirable difficulties" (Bjork & Bjork, 2011) introduced in the Improving Study Skills box. Whatever the explanation for the effects of distributed practice, there is no denying its benefits for students.

Researchers have also discovered some novel benefits of the closely related technique of *interleaved practice*, a practice schedule that mixes different kinds of problems or materials within a single study session. Interleaved practice may be particularly effective for learning mathematics. Researchers presented some seventh-grade students with problems in the traditional blocked form: similar problems that all required the same solution. They presented other students with problems in interleaved form: a mixture of different kinds of problems that each required distinct strategies. The interleaved practice group scored higher than the blocked practice group on surprise tests given 1 day or 30 days after the conclusion of practice (Rohrer, Dedrick, & Sterschic, 2015). The researchers suggested that interleaved practice was more effective because it requires students to choose a strategy according to the nature of individual problems (as students must do on a test), whereas during blocked practice,

Studying well in advance of an exam so that you can take breaks and distribute study time will generally produce a better outcome than cramming at the last minute. Age Fotostock/Superstock

students could repeatedly apply the same strategy without having to select among possible strategies.

Practice Testing

Practice testing, like distributed practice, has proven useful across a wide range of materials, including learning of stories, facts, vocabulary, and lectures (Dunlosky et al., 2013; Karpicke & Aue, 2015; see also the Learning-Curve system associated with this text, which uses practice testing). As you learned in the Memory chapter, practice testing is effective, in part, because actively retrieving an item from memory during a test improves subsequent retention of that item more efficiently than simply studying it again (Roediger & Karpicke, 2006). Yet when asked about their preferred study strategies, students indicated by a wide margin that they prefer rereading materials to testing themselves (Karpicke, 2012). The benefits of testing tend to be greatest when the test is difficult and requires considerable retrieval effort (Pyc & Rawson, 2009), also consistent with the desirable difficulties hypothesis (Bjork & Bjork, 2011). Not only does testing increase verbatim learning of the exact material that is tested but it also enhances the *transfer* of learning from one situation to another (Carpenter, 2012). For example, if you are given practice tests with short-answer questions, such testing improves later performance on both short-answer and multiple-choice questions more than restudying (Kang, McDermott, & Roediger, 2007). Testing also improves the ability to draw conclusions from the studied material, which is an important part of learning and often critical to performing well in the classroom (Karpicke & Blunt, 2011). Also important, studies of students' performance in actual classrooms reveal benefits of practice testing that are similar to those observed in the laboratory (McDaniel et al., 2013; McDermott et al., 2014).

Testing Aids Attention

Recent research conducted in the laboratory of one of your textbook authors highlights yet another benefit of testing: Including brief tests during a lecture can improve learning by reducing the mind's tendency to wander (Szpunar, Khan, & Schacter, 2013). How often have you found your mind wandering—thinking about your evening plans, recalling a scene from a movie, or texting a friend—in the midst of a lecture that you know that you ought to be attending to carefully? It's probably happened more than once. Research indicates that students' minds wander frequently during classroom lectures (Bunce, Flens, & Neiles, 2011; Lindquist & McLean, 2011; Wilson & Korn, 2007). Such mind wandering impairs learning of the lecture material (Risko et al., 2012). In the study by Szpunar and colleagues (2013), participants watched a videotaped statistics lecture that was divided into four segments. All of the participants were told that they might or might not be tested after each segment; they were also encouraged to take notes during the lectures. However, some participants ("tested group") received brief tests on each segment, while others ("nontested group") did not receive a test until after the final segment. A third group of participants ("restudy group") were shown, but not tested on, the same material as the tested group.

At random times during the lectures, participants in all groups were asked about whether they were paying attention to the lecture or whether their minds were wandering off to other topics. Participants in the nontested and restudy groups indicated that they were mind wandering in response to about 40% of the inquiries, but the incidence of mind wandering was cut in half, to about 20%, in the tested group. Participants in the tested group took significantly more notes during the lectures and retained significantly more information from the lecture on a final test than did participants in the other two groups, who performed similarly on this test. Participants in the tested group were also less anxious about the final test than those in the other groups. These results indicate that part of the value of testing comes from encouraging people to sustain attention to a lecture in a way that discourages task-irrelevant activities such as mind wandering and encourages task-relevant activities such as note taking. Because these benefits of testing were observed in response to a videotaped lecture, they apply most directly to online learning, where taped lectures are the norm (Breslow et al., 2013; Schacter & Szpunar, 2015), but there is every reason to believe that the results would apply to live classroom lectures as well, especially in light of the evidence we just discussed that practice testing enhances classroom performance.

Control of Learning

It's the night before the final exam in your introductory psychology course. You've put in a lot of time reviewing your course notes and the material in this textbook, and you feel that you have learned most of it pretty well. Now you've got to decide whether to devote the precious remaining minutes to studying psychological disorders or social psychology. How do you make that decision? An important part of learning involves assessing how well we know something and how much more time we need to devote to studying it.

Recent research has shown that people's judgments about what they have learned, which psychologists refer to as *judgments of learning* (JOLs), play a critical role in guiding further study and learning: People typically devote more time to studying items that they judge they have not learned well (Metcalfe & Finn, 2008; Son & Metcalfe, 2000).

Unfortunately, JOLs are often inaccurate (Castel, McCabe, & Roediger, 2007). For example, after you read and reread a chapter or article in preparation for a test, the material will likely feel quite familiar, and that feeling may convince you that you've learned the material well enough that you don't need to study it further. However, the feeling of familiarity can be misleading: It may be the result of a low-level process such as perceptual priming (see the Memory chapter) and not the kind of learning that will be required to perform well on an exam (Bjork & Bjork, 2011). One way to avoid being fooled by misleading subjective impressions is to test yourself from time to time

 when studying for an exam, and carefully compare your responses to the actual answers (see also Data Visualization: Do People Differ in How They Learn? at www.launchpadworks.com).

So, if you are preparing for the final exam in this course and need to decide whether to devote more time to studying psychological disorders or social psychology, try to exert control over your learning by testing yourself on material from those two chapters; you can use the results of those tests to help you decide which chapter requires further work. Heed the conclusion from researchers (Bjork, Dunlosky, and Kornell, 2013) that becoming a more sophisticated and effective learner requires understanding: (1) key features of learning and memory; (2) effective learning techniques; (3) how to monitor and control one's own learning; and (4) biases that can undermine judgments of learning.

BUILD TO THE OUTCOMES

1. What are the most and least effective study techniques?
2. What are the benefits of distributed practice?
3. Why does a difficult practice test have the greatest benefit?
4. How does taking practice tests help focus a wandering mind?
5. In what ways can JOLs be misleading?

CHAPTER REVIEW

What Is Learning?

- Learning involves the acquisition of new knowledge, skills, and responses. It is based on experience and produces a change in the organism, and that change is relatively permanent.
- Even the simplest organisms exhibit simple forms of learning known as habituation and sensitization.

Classical Conditioning: One Thing Leads to Another

- Classical conditioning pairs a neutral stimulus (a conditioned stimulus or CS) with a meaningful event (an unconditioned stimulus or US): eventually the CS, all by itself, elicits a response called a conditioned response (CR).
- Behaviorists viewed classical conditioning as a form of learning in which no higher-level functions, such as thinking or awareness, needed to be invoked to understand behavior.
- Later researchers showed, however, that classical conditioning involves setting up expectations, is sensitive to the degree to which the CS is a genuine predictor of the US, and can involve some degree of cognition.
- The cerebellum plays an important role in eyeblink conditioning, whereas the amygdala is important for fear conditioning.
- Each species is biologically predisposed to acquire particular CS–US associations based on its evolutionary history, showing that classical conditioning is a sophisticated mechanism that evolved because it has adaptive value.

Operant Conditioning: Reinforcements From the Environment

- Operant conditioning is a process by which reinforcements increase the likelihood of behavior and punishments decrease the likelihood of behavior.

- The behaviorists tried to explain operant conditioning without considering cognitive, neural, or evolutionary mechanisms. However, as with classical conditioning, this approach turned out to be incomplete.
- Operant conditioning has clear cognitive components: Organisms behave as though they have expectations about the outcomes of their actions and adjust their actions accordingly. Cognitive influences can sometimes override the trial-by-trial feedback that usually influences learning.
- The associative mechanisms that underlie operant conditioning have their roots in evolutionary biology. Some things are relatively easy to learn, whereas others are difficult; the history of the species is usually the best clue as to which will be which.

Observational Learning: Look at Me

- Observational learning is an important process by which species gather information about the world around them.
- Chimpanzees and monkeys can benefit from observational learning.
- The mirror neuron system becomes active during observational learning, and many of the same brain regions are active during both observation and performance of a skill.

Implicit Learning: Under the Radar

- Implicit learning is a process that detects, learns, and stores patterns without the application of explicit awareness by the learner.
- Implicit learning can produce simple behaviors such as habituation, but also complex behaviors, such as language use or socialization.
- Neuroimaging studies indicate that implicit and explicit learning recruit different brain structures, sometimes in different ways.

Learning in the Classroom

- Research on learning techniques indicates that some popular study methods, such as highlighting, underlining, and rereading, have low utility, whereas other techniques, such as practice testing and distributed practice, have high utility.

- Practice testing improves retention and transfer of learning and can also enhance learning and reduce mind wandering during lectures.
- Judgments of learning play a causal role in determining what material to study, but they can be misleading.

KEY CONCEPT QUIZ

1. In classical conditioning, a conditioned stimulus is paired with an unconditioned stimulus to produce
  a. a neutral stimulus.
  b. a conditioned response.
  c. an unconditioned response.
  d. another conditioned stimulus.

2. What occurs when a conditioned stimulus is no longer paired with an unconditioned stimulus?
  a. generalization
  b. spontaneous recovery
  c. extinction
  d. acquisition

3. What did Watson and Rayner seek to demonstrate about behaviorism through the Little Albert experiment?
  a. Conditioning involves a degree of cognition.
  b. Classical conditioning has an evolutionary component.
  c. Behaviorism alone cannot explain human behavior.
  d. Even sophisticated behaviors such as emotion are subject to classical conditioning.

4. Which part of the brain is involved in the classical conditioning of fear?
  a. the amygdala
  b. the cerebellum
  c. the hippocampus
  d. the hypothalamus

5. After having a bad experience with a particular type of food, people can develop a lifelong aversion to that food. This suggests that conditioning has a(n) _____ aspect.
  a. cognitive
  b. evolutionary
  c. neural
  d. behavioral

6. Which of the following is NOT an accurate statement concerning operant conditioning?
  a. Actions and outcomes are critical to operant conditioning.
  b. Operant conditioning involves the reinforcement of behavior.
  c. Complex behaviors cannot be accounted for by operant conditioning.
  d. Operant conditioning has roots in evolutionary behavior.

7. Which of the following mechanisms has/have no role in Skinner's approach to behavior?
  a. cognitive
  b. neural
  c. evolutionary
  d. all of the above

8. Latent learning provides evidence for a cognitive element in operant conditioning because it
  a. occurs without any obvious reinforcement.
  b. requires both positive and negative reinforcement.
  c. points toward the operation of a neural reward center.
  d. depends on a stimulus–response relationship.

9. Which statement is true of observational learning?
  a. Although humans learn by observing others, nonhuman animals seem to lack this capability.
  b. If a child sees an adult engaging in a certain behavior, the child is more likely to imitate the behavior.
  c. Humans learn complex behaviors more readily by trial and error than by observation.
  d. Observational learning is limited to transmission of information between individuals of the same species.

10. What kind of learning takes place largely independent of awareness of both the process and the products of information acquisition?
  a. latent learning
  b. implicit learning
  c. observational learning
  d. conscious learning

11. Which of the following statements about implicit learning is inaccurate?
  a. Some forms of learning start out explicitly but become more implicit over time.
  b. Implicit learning occurs even in the simplest organisms.
  c. People with amnesia tend to be severely impaired at implicit learning tasks.
  d. Children learn language and social conduct largely through implicit learning.

12. Responding to implicit instructions results in decreased brain activation in which part of the brain?
  a. the hippocampus
  b. the parietal cortex

c. the prefrontal cortex

d. the occipital region

13. Which study strategy has been shown to be the most effective?

a. highlighting text

b. rereading

c. summarizing

d. taking practice tests

14. Which of the following statements is true about judgments of learning (JOL)?

a. People are generally good judges of how well they have learned new material.

b. The feeling of familiarity with material is usually an indicator of whether the material is learned.

c. Based on JOLs, people generally spend more time studying material they feel they know well.

d. JOLs have a causal influence on learning.

15. Part of the value of self-testing as a study aid comes from:

a. increasing feeling of familiarity with the material.

b. helping to sustain attention during initial learning.

c. passive re-exposure to the material.

d. decreasing the need to take careful notes during the lecture.

 **LearningCurve** Don't stop now! Quizzing yourself is a powerful study tool. Go to LearningCurve at www.launchpadworks.com for more practice.

KEY TERMS

learning (p. 200)

habituation (p. 200)

sensitization (p. 200)

classical conditioning (p. 201)

unconditioned stimulus (US) (p. 202)

unconditioned response (UR) (p. 202)

conditioned stimulus (CS) (p. 202)

conditioned response (CR) (p. 202)

second-order conditioning (p. 202)

acquisition (p. 203)

extinction (p. 204)

spontaneous recovery (p. 204)

generalization (p. 204)

discrimination (p. 204)

biological preparedness (p. 207)

operant conditioning (p. 208)

law of effect (p. 208)

operant behavior (p. 209)

reinforcer (p. 209)

punisher (p. 209)

fixed-interval schedule (FI) (p. 212)

variable-interval schedule (VI) (p. 213)

fixed-ratio schedule (FR) (p. 213)

variable-ratio schedule (VR) (p. 214)

intermittent reinforcement (p. 214)

intermittent reinforcement effect (p. 214)

shaping (p. 214)

latent learning (p. 216)

cognitive map (p. 217)

observational learning (p. 220)

implicit learning (p. 224)

CHANGING MINDS

1. A friend is taking a class in childhood education. "Back in the old days," she says, "teachers used physical punishment, but of course that's not allowed anymore. Now, a good teacher should only use reinforcement. When children behave, teachers should provide positive reinforcement, like praise. When children misbehave, teachers should provide negative reinforcement, like scolding or withholding privileges." What is your friend misunderstanding about reinforcement? Can you give better examples of how negative reinforcement could be applied productively in an elementary school classroom?

2. A friend of your family is trying to train her daughter to make her bed every morning. You suggest trying positive reinforcement. A month later, the woman reports back to you. "It's not working very well," she says. "Every time she makes her bed, I put a gold star on the calendar, and at the end of the week, if there are seven gold stars, I give Vicky a reward—a piece of licorice. But so far, she's earned the licorice only twice." How could you explain why the desired behavior—bed making—might not increase as a result of this reinforcement procedure?

3. While studying for the psych exam, you ask your study partner to provide a definition of classical conditioning. "In classical conditioning," she says, "there's a stimulus, the CS, that predicts an upcoming event, the US. Usually, it's something bad, like an electric shock, nausea, or a frightening, loud noise. The learner makes a response, the CR, in order to prevent the US. Sometimes, the US is good, like food for Pavlov's dogs, and then the learner makes the response in order to earn the US." What's wrong with this definition?

4. One of your classmates announces that he liked the last chapter (on memory) better than he did the current chapter on learning. "I want to be a psychiatrist," he says,

"so I mostly care about human learning. Conditioning might be a really powerful way to train animals to push levers or perform tricks, but it really doesn't have much relevance to how humans learn things." How similar is learning in humans and other animals? What real-world examples can you provide to show that conditioning does occur in humans?

ANSWERS TO KEY CONCEPT QUIZ

1. b; 2. c; 3. d; 4. a; 5. b; 6. c; 7. d; 8. a; 9. b; 10. b; 11. c; 12. d; 13. d; 14. d; 15. b.

Emotion and Motivation

Leonardo is 5 years old and cute as a button. He can do many of the things that other 5-year-olds can do: solve puzzles, build towers of blocks, and play guessing games with grown-ups. But unlike other 5-year-olds, Leonardo has never been proud of his abilities, angry with his mother, or bored with his lessons. That's because Leonardo has a condition that makes him unable to experience emotions of any kind. He has never felt joy or sorrow, delight or despair, shame, envy, annoyance, excitement, gratitude, or regret. He has never laughed or cried.

As you might expect, Leonardo's condition has had a profound impact on his life. For example, because he doesn't experience emotions, he isn't motivated to do the things that bring most children pleasure, such as eating cookies or playing hide-and-seek. Leonardo's mother has spent years teaching him how to make the facial expressions that indicate different emotions, and how to detect those expressions in others. So Leonardo knows that when his mother smiles lovingly at him, he is supposed to smile lovingly back, and his mother is proud of him for learning that trick. But she is also keenly aware that, despite what his face may suggest, he doesn't actually *feel* any love for her at all.

But she doesn't mind, because even though Leonardo cannot return her affection, Dr. Cynthia Breazeal still thinks of him as one of the most wonderful robots she's ever designed (Breazeal, 2009).

A typical 5-year-old can experience emotions such as pride, anger, and boredom. Alex Cao/Photodisc/ Getty Images

Leonardo and his "mom," MIT Professor Cynthia Breazeal. Sam Ogden/Science Source Sam Ogden/Science Source

YES, LEONARDO IS A ROBOT—A MACHINE WITH A FURRY FACE. He can see and hear, remember and reason. But despite his adorable smile and knowing wink, he cannot feel a thing, and that makes him infinitely different from us. Our ability to love and to hate, to be amused and annoyed, to feel elated and devastated, is an essential element of our humanity. But what exactly are these things we call feelings? And why are they so essential? In this chapter, we will explore these questions. We'll start by discussing the nature of emotions and seeing how they relate to the states of our bodies and our brains. Next, we'll see how people express their emotions, and how they use those expressions to communicate with each other. Finally, we'll examine the essential role that emotions play in motivation—how they inform us, and how they compel us to do everything from making war to making love.

Emotional Experience: The Feeling Machine

LEARNING OUTCOMES

- Understand how and why psychologists have "mapped" the emotional landscape.

- Explain the roles that the body and brain play in producing emotional experience.

- Explain how people do and should regulate their emotions.

Leonardo doesn't know what love feels like and there's no way to teach him because trying to describe the feeling of love to someone who has never experienced it is a bit like trying to describe the color green to someone who was born blind. We could tell Leonardo what causes the feeling ("It happens whenever I see Marilynn"), and we could tell him about its consequences ("I breathe hard and say goofy stuff"). In the end, however, these descriptions would miss the point because the essential feature of love—like the essential feature of all emotions—is the *experience*. It *feels* like something to love someone, and what it feels like is love's defining attribute (Heavey, Hurlburt, & Lefforge, 2012).

What Is Emotion?

How can we scientifically study something whose defining attribute defies description? Even though people can't easily say what their emotional experiences feel like, they *can* say how similar one experience is to another ("Love is more like happiness than like anger"), and simply by asking people to rate the similarity of dozens of emotional experiences, psychologists have been able to create a map of emotional experience. How have they managed to do that?

It is almost impossible not to feel something when you look at this photograph, but it is almost impossible to say exactly what you are feeling. Stephen Morton/AP Images

If you handed your friend a list of the distances between a half dozen U.S. cities and then asked her to draw a map in which each city was exactly the right distance from every other city, your friend would be forced to draw a map that looked just like the United States (see **FIGURE 8.1**). Why? Because this is the one and only map that allows every city to appear at precisely the right distance from every other. If you don't believe it, just try moving Chicago.

When people rate the similarity of emotional experiences, they are essentially describing the "distance" between them, and psychologists can use these distances

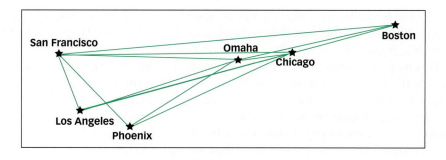

Figure 8.1 FROM DISTANCES TO MAPS Knowing the distances between things—like cities, for example—allows us to draw a map that reveals the dimensions on which they vary.

to draw a map of the emotional landscape. That map is shown in **FIGURE 8.2**. It is the one and only map that allows every emotional experience to be plotted precisely the right distance from every other.

What good is a map of the emotional landscape? Maps don't just show us how close things are to each other (which is something we already knew); they also reveal the *dimensions* on which those things vary. For example, the map in Figure 8.1 shows that cities vary on exactly two dimensions that we call longitude (the east-west dimension) and latitude (the north-south dimension). Now look at Figure 8.2. That map shows that emotional experiences also vary on two dimensions—a dimension called *valence* (how positive or negative the experience is) and a dimension called *arousal* (how active or passive the experience is). Decades of research have shown

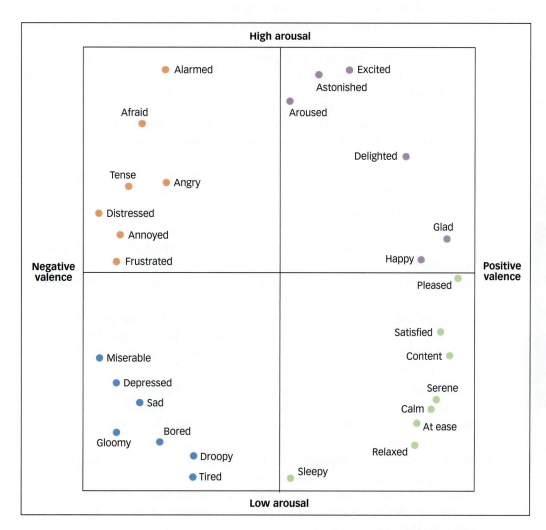

Figure 8.2 TWO DIMENSIONS OF EMOTION Just as the locations of cities vary on two dimensions called longitude and latitude, emotions vary on two dimensions called valence and arousal.

that all the emotional experiences that human beings have can be described by their unique location on this two-dimensional map (Russell, 1980; Watson & Tellegen, 1985; Yik, Russell, & Steiger, 2011).

This map can also help us say what an emotion is. Any definition of emotion must include the fact that emotional experiences have different amounts of positivity and negativity and different amounts of physiological arousal. With these facts in mind, we can define **emotion** as *a positive or negative experience that is associated with a particular pattern of physiological activity*. As you are about to see, the first step in understanding emotion involves understanding how the "experience" part of this definition and the "physiological activity" part of this definition are related.

emotion A positive or negative experience that is associated with a particular pattern of physiological activity.

The Emotional Body

You may think that if you walked into your kitchen right now and saw a bear nosing through the trash, you would feel afraid. Then your muscles would tense and your heart would start to pound. And then your legs would do everything legs can do to get your butt out of the kitchen. That's how it *feels* to be afraid. But more than a century ago, psychologists began to suspect that these particular responses don't actually happen in this particular order.

Early Theories

In the late 19th century, William James suggested that your feeling of fear does not cause your body to respond, but rather, it's the other way around: You first see the bear, and then your heart starts pounding and your leg muscles contract, and *then* you experience fear, which is nothing more or less than your perception of your body's response. The psychologist Carl Lange suggested something similar at about the same time, so this idea became known as the **James–Lange theory** of emotion, which states that *a stimulus triggers activity in the body, which in turn produces an emotional experience in the mind*. According to this theory, our emotional experiences are the consequence and not the cause of our body's reactions to events in the world. Such as bears.

James–Lange theory The theory that a stimulus triggers activity in the body, which in turn produces an emotional experience in the brain.

Not everyone thought this theory made sense. The physiologists Walter Cannon and Philip Bard argued that the James–Lange theory had four major problems:

1. Emotional experiences sometimes happen more rapidly than bodily responses do. For example, people typically feel embarrassed within a few seconds of noticing that their pants have fallen off in public, and yet the bodily response known as blushing takes a full 15 to 30 seconds to occur. So how could the feeling of embarrassment be the "perception of blushing" if blushing only happens after we feel embarrassed?

2. People are not always aware of their bodily responses. For example, most people cannot tell when their hearts start beating faster. If people can't detect changes in their bodies, and if emotions are nothing more than the perception of bodily changes, then why do they experience emotions at all?

3. All sorts of utterly unemotional events can cause the body to respond. When the room gets hot, for example, the heart starts to beat faster. If fear is just the perception of a rapid heartbeat, then why don't people feel afraid when they are in a warm room?

4. There are far fewer unique physiological patterns of bodily activity than there are unique emotional experiences. That means that several different emotional experiences must be associated with the same pattern of bodily activity. So how do people who are in a particular physiological state decide which of several emotions they are experiencing?

Did the Duchess of Cambridge just make her husband, Prince William, blush by embarrassing him, or did she embarrass him by making him blush? The experience of embarrassment precedes blushing by up to 30 seconds, so it is unlikely that blushing is the cause of the emotional experience. Andrew Milligan - WPA Pool/Getty Images

As you can probably tell, Cannon and Bard didn't think much of the James–Lange theory, but they seem to have liked the hyphen. The **Cannon–Bard theory** of emotion states that *a stimulus simultaneously triggers activity in the body and emotional experience in the mind* (Bard, 1934; Cannon, 1929). According to this theory, the bear in your kitchen makes your heart race *and* it makes you feel afraid. But those two things happen independently and simultaneously—the first is not the cause of the second.

Cannon–Bard theory The theory that a stimulus simultaneously triggers activity in the body and emotional experience in the brain.

Modern Theories

Modern psychologists generally agree that both the James–Lange and Cannon–Bard theories made good points, but that neither got it right. In the early 1960s, the psychologists Stanley Schachter and Jerome Singer argued that James and Lange were right to suggest that our experience of emotion is based on our perception of our bodily reactions, but that Cannon and Bard were right to claim that we do not have nearly enough unique bodily reactions to account for the wide variety of emotions that we experience (Schachter & Singer, 1962). So Schachter and Singer developed a new theory that took the best bits of the two theories that came before it, as well as the hyphen (see **FIGURE 8.3**). Their **two-factor theory of emotion** states that *a stimulus triggers a general state of arousal in the body, which the mind then interprets as a specific emotion.*

two-factor theory of emotion A theory that suggests that a stimulus triggers a general state of arousal in the body, which the mind then interprets as a specific emotion.

According to this theory, when you see a bear in your kitchen, your body becomes aroused—your heart pounds, your muscles tense, and you start breathing hard. Your mind notices all this activity and immediately starts looking around for an explanation. And what does it see? A bear! Having noticed both a thumping heart and a growling grizzly, your mind comes to the logical conclusion that you must be afraid. According to the two-factor theory, when you find yourself physiologically aroused in the presence of something that really ought to scare you, you interpret that arousal as *fear*. But if you had precisely the same bodily response in the presence of something that really ought to delight you, such as a pair of skydiving kittens or a mile-high stack of pancakes, then you might call that arousal *excitement*. The two-factor theory suggests that people have just one bodily reaction to all emotional stimuli, but they interpret that reaction differently on different occasions—and that is what gives rise to the experience of different emotions.

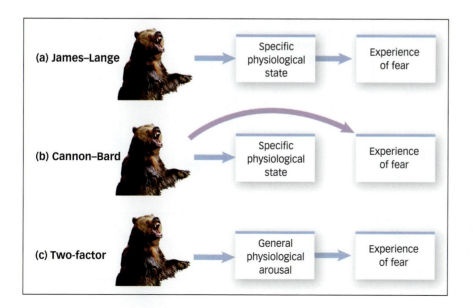

Figure 8.3 THEORIES OF EMOTION Different theories make different claims about the origins of emotion. (a) The James–Lange theory suggests that stimuli trigger specific physiological states that are then experienced as emotions. (b) The Cannon–Bard theory suggests that stimuli trigger both specific physiological states and emotional experiences independently. (c) The two-factor theory suggests that stimuli trigger general physiological arousal whose cause the brain interprets, and this interpretation leads to emotional experience.
Jim Zuckerman/Corbis

The fact that people can mistake physical arousal for romantic attraction may help explain why so many first dates involve roller coasters. Olive/PHOTOINKE/Alamy Stock Photo

How has the two-factor theory fared in the last half century? One of the theory's key claims has fared quite well: People do indeed make inferences about the causes of their physiological arousal, and those inferences determine their emotional experiences (Lindquist & Barrett, 2008). For instance, participants in one study (Schachter & Singer, 1962) were injected with epinephrine, which causes physiological arousal, and were then exposed to either a goofy or a nasty confederate. Just as the two-factor theory predicted, when the confederate acted goofy, participants concluded that they were feeling *happy*, but when the confederate acted nasty, participants concluded that they were feeling *angry*. Research has shown that when people are aroused in other ways—for example, by riding an exercise bike in the laboratory—they subsequently find attractive people more attractive, annoying people more annoying, and funny cartoons funnier, as if they were interpreting their exercise-induced arousal as attraction, annoyance, or amusement (Byrne et al., 1975; Dutton & Aron, 1974; Zillmann, Katcher, & Milavsky, 1972).

On the other hand, research has not been so kind to the two-factor theory's claim that different emotional experiences are merely different interpretations of a single bodily state called "arousal." When researchers measure people's physiological reactions as they experience different emotions, they find that anger, fear, and sadness produce a higher heart rate than disgust does; that fear and disgust produced higher galvanic skin response (sweating) than sadness or anger do; and that anger produces a larger increase in finger temperature than fear does (Ekman, Levenson, & Friesen, 1983; Levenson, Ekman, & Friesen, 1990; Levenson et al., 1991, 1992; see **FIGURE 8.4**). This does not mean that every emotion has its own individual "physiological fingerprint" (Clark-Polner, Johnson, & Barrett, 2016; Siegel et al., 2015), but it does mean that the bodily responses associated with different emotions are not always identical—a finding that is at odds with the two-factor theory.

A lot has changed since the days of William James, Walter Cannon, and Stanley Schachter. The relationship between the mind and the body, and the way they work together to produce emotional experience, has turned out to be much more complicated than any of their models suggested. We know this because new technologies have given us access to something that previous generations of psychologists could merely imagine: the emotional brain.

Figure 8.4 THE PHYSIOLOGY OF EMOTION Contrary to the claims of the two-factor theory, different emotions do seem to have different underlying patterns of physiological arousal. (a) Anger, fear, and sadness all produce higher heart rates than do happiness, surprise, and disgust. (b) Anger produces a much greater increase in finger temperature than does any other emotion.

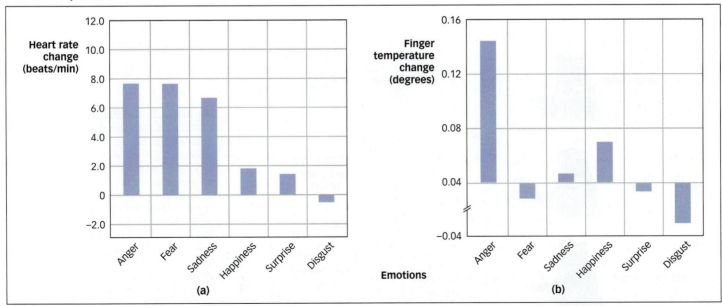

The Emotional Brain

In the late 1930s, two researchers made an accidental discovery (Klüver & Bucy, 1937). A few days after performing brain surgery on a monkey named Aurora, they noticed that she was acting strangely. First, she would eat just about anything and have sex with just about anyone—as though she could no longer distinguish between good and bad food, or between good and bad mates. Second, she was absolutely fearless and unflappable, remaining perfectly calm when she was handled by researchers or even when confronted by snakes, both of which monkeys generally don't much like. What had happened to Aurora?

The Fast and Slow Pathways

As it turned out, during the surgery, the researchers had accidentally damaged a structure in Aurora's brain called the *amygdala*. Subsequent studies have confirmed that the amygdala plays a special role in producing emotions such as fear (Cunningham & Brosch, 2012; LaBar & Phelps, 1998; van Stegeren et al., 1998; see **FIGURE 8.5**). An **appraisal** is *an evaluation of the emotion-relevant aspects of a stimulus* (Arnold, 1960; Ellsworth & Scherer, 2003; Lazarus, 1984; Roseman, 1984; Roseman & Smith, 2001; Scherer, 1999, 2001), and it appears that the amygdala's primary function is to make appraisals. In a sense, the amygdala is an extremely fast and sensitive detector whose primary job is to decide whether a stimulus is or is not a threat (Whalen et al., 1998).

Information is transmitted to the amygdala via both a "fast pathway" (which goes from the thalamus directly to the amygdala) and a "slow pathway" (which goes from the thalamus to the cortex and *then* to the amygdala; LeDoux, 2000), as **FIGURE 8.6** shows. When you see a bear, the information about the bear goes from your eye to your thalamus and then to your cortex, which uses all the information at its disposal to conduct a full-scale investigation of the stimulus in order to determine the stimulus's identity ("Seems to be an animal, probably a mammal, maybe a member of the genus *Ursus*. . . ."). While this is happening, the thalamus has also sent the information directly to your amygdala, which uses it to answer a much simpler question: Is this a threat? If your amygdala's answer to that question is yes, then it initiates the processes that produce the bodily reactions that—when your cortex is finally done with all that investigating—you will call *fear*.

The tourist and the tiger have something in common: Each has an amygdala that is working at lightning speed to decide whether the other is a threat. Let's hope the tourist's is working a little faster. DAVID LONGSTREATH/AP Images

appraisal An evaluation of the emotion-relevant aspects of a stimulus.

Figure 8.5 EMOTION RECOGNITION AND THE AMYGDALA Facial expressions of emotion were morphed into a continuum that ran from happiness to surprise to fear to sadness to disgust to anger and back to happiness. When this sequence was shown to a patient with amygdala damage, she could recognize happiness, sadness, and surprise about as accurately as healthy people could, but her recognition of anger, disgust, and fear was impaired (Calder et al., 1996). Calder, A. J., Young, A. W. Rowland, D., Perrett, D. I., Hodges, J. R., & Etcoff, N. L. (1996). Facial emotion recognition after bilateral amygdala damage: Differently severe impairment of fear. *Cognitive Neuropsychology 13*, 699–745. (Figure 1, pp. 713–714; Figure 2a, pp. 718–719. Taylor & Francis Group: www.tandfonline.com

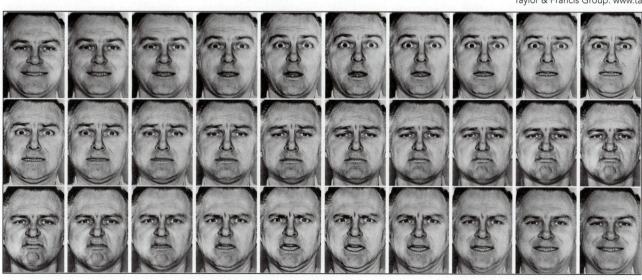

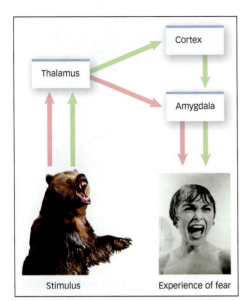

Stimulus   Experience of fear

Figure 8.6 THE FAST AND SLOW PATHWAYS OF FEAR Information about a stimulus takes two routes simultaneously through the brain: the "fast pathway" (shown in pink), which runs from the thalamus directly to the amygdala, and the "slow pathway" (shown in green), which runs from the thalamus to the cortex and then to the amygdala. Because the amygdala receives information from the thalamus before it receives information from the cortex, a person can be afraid of something before he or she knows what it is. Jim Zuckerman/Corbis; Paramount Pictures/The Kobal Collection

emotion regulation The strategies people use to influence their own emotional experiences.

reappraisal Changing one's emotional experience by changing the way one thinks about the emotion-eliciting stimulus.

Emotion regulation can be difficult. In 2011, the city of Portland, Oregon, flushed 8 million gallons of drinking water simply because a man was seen urinating into this reservoir. Although the minuscule amount of urine posed no health threat, it made people feel disgusted—and the inability to regulate that emotion cost the citizens of Portland nearly $30,000. Rick Bowmer/AP Images

That's how we get scared. So how do we stop? As Figure 8.6 shows, your amygdala receives information directly from your thalamus via the fast pathway, but it also receives information from your cortex via the slow pathway. Once the cortex has finished its full-scale investigation of the stimulus, this connection allows it send a signal to the amygdala telling it to reduce its activity. In a sense, the amygdala's job is to hit the emotional gas pedal and the cortex's job is to hit the brakes. That's why adults who have cortical damage, and children (whose cortices are not well developed), often have trouble inhibiting their emotional responses (Cohen et al., 2016; Stuss & Benson, 1986).

The Regulation of Emotion

You may or may not care about hedgehogs, earwax, or the War of 1812, but if you are human, you almost certainly care about what you are feeling. **Emotion regulation** refers to *the strategies people use to influence their own emotional experience*. Nine out of 10 people report that they attempt to regulate their emotional experience at least once a day (Gross, 1998), and they describe more than a thousand different strategies for doing so (Parkinson & Totterdell, 1999).

Some of these strategies are behavioral (e.g., avoiding situations that trigger unwanted emotions) and some are cognitive (e.g., recruiting memories that trigger the desired emotion; Webb, Miles, & Sheeran, 2012), but regardless of how they work, people seem to have a poor understanding of which are most effective (Heiy & Cheavens, 2014). For example, most people think that *suppression*, which involves inhibiting the outward signs of an emotion, is an effective way to regulate it. But they are wrong (Gross, 2002; Kalokerinos, Greenaway, & Denson, 2015). On the other hand, most people think that *affect labeling*, which involves putting one's feelings into words, will have little or no impact on their emotions. But in fact, affect labeling is an effective way to reduce the intensity of emotional states (Lieberman et al., 2011).

Research also suggests that one of the best strategies for emotion regulation is **reappraisal**, which involves *changing one's emotional experience by changing the way one thinks about the emotion-eliciting stimulus* (Ochsner et al., 2009). For example, in one study, participants' brains were scanned as they saw photos that induced negative emotions, such as a photo of a woman crying during a funeral. Some participants were then asked to reappraise the picture, for example, by imagining that the woman in the photo was at a wedding, rather than at a funeral. The results showed that when participants initially saw the photo their amygdalae were activated, but when they reappraised the picture, their cortices were activated and moments later their amygdalae were deactivated (Ochsner et al., 2002). In other words, participants were able to downregulate the activity of their own amygdalae simply by thinking about the photo in a different way.

Reappraisal is a skill. Like most skills, it can be learned (Denny & Ochsner, 2014), and like most skills, some people are naturally better at it than are others (Malooly, Genet, & Siemer, 2013). People who are especially good at reappraisal tend to be both mentally and physically healthier (Davidson, Putnam, & Larson, 2000; Gross & Muñoz, 1995) and to have better relationships (Bloch, Haase, & Levenson, 2014). This should not be surprising, given that reappraisal is one of the skills that therapists commonly try to teach people who are dealing with emotional problems (Jamieson, Nock, & Mendes, 2013). On the other hand, this skill has a dark side: People who are good at changing how they see things in order to feel better about the things they see can be less compassionate toward those who are suffering (Cameron & Payne, 2011).

BUILD TO THE OUTCOMES

1. What are the two dimensions on which emotions vary?

2. How did the Cannon–Bard theory challenge the James–Lange theory?

3. How did the two-factor theory build on earlier theories?

4. How do the amygdala and cortex interact to produce emotion?

5. What are the best ways to regulate emotion?

Emotional Communication: Msgs w/o Wrds

Leonardo the robot may not be able to feel, but he sure can smile. And wink. And nod. Indeed, people who interact with Leonardo find it hard to think of him as a machine precisely because Leonardo *expresses* emotions that he doesn't actually have. An **emotional expression** is *an observable sign of an emotional state*, and although robots can be taught to exhibit emotional expressions, human beings do so quite naturally.

Emotional states express themselves in the intonation of our speech, the direction of our gaze, and even the rhythm of our gait. But no part of our body is more exquisitely designed for communicating our emotional state than is our face. Underneath the face lie 43 muscles that are capable of creating more than 10,000 unique configurations (Ekman, 1965), and a few of these combinations are reliably associated with specific emotional states (Davidson et al., 1990; Mehu & Scherer, 2015). For example, when we feel happy, our *zygomatic major* (a muscle that pulls our lip corners up) and our *obicularis oculi* (a muscle that crinkles the outside edges of our eyes) produce a unique facial expression that we call a smile (Ekman & Friesen, 1982; Frank, Ekman, & Friesen, 1993; Steiner, 1986).

Communicative Expression

Why are our emotions written all over our faces? In 1872, Charles Darwin published *The Expression of the Emotions in Man and Animals*, in which he speculated about the evolutionary significance of emotional expression. Darwin noticed that human and nonhuman animals share certain postures and facial expressions, and he suggested that they were meant to communicate information about internal states. It isn't hard to see how such communications might be useful (Shariff & Tracy, 2011; Tracy, Randles, & Steckler, 2015). For example, if a dominant animal can bare his teeth and communicate the message "I am angry," and if a subordinate animal can lower his head and communicate the message "I am afraid," then the two can establish a pecking order without any actual pecking. In this sense, emotional expressions are a bit like the words of a nonverbal language.

The Universality of Expression

Of course, language works only when everybody speaks the same one, and that's what led Darwin to advance the **universality hypothesis**, which suggests that *emotional expressions have the same meaning for everyone*. In other words, every human being naturally expresses happiness with a smile, and every human being naturally understands that a smile signifies happiness.

Evidence suggests that Darwin was mainly right. For example, people who have never seen a human face make the same facial expressions as those who have. Congenitally blind people smile when they are happy (Galati, Scherer, & Ricci-Bitt, 1997; Matsumoto & Willingham, 2009), and 2-day-old infants make a disgust face

LEARNING OUTCOMES

-   Describe evidence for the universality hypothesis.

-   Explain the facial feedback hypothesis.

-   Describe how people use emotional expressions to deceive and how they detect such deception.

emotional expression An observable sign of an emotional state.

universality hypothesis The theory that emotional expressions have the same meaning for everyone.

According to Charles Darwin (1872/1998), both human and nonhuman animals use facial expressions to communicate information about their internal states. William H. Calvin/WilliamCalvin.org; Andreas Gebert/dpa/Newscom

Nobuyuki Tsujii (*middle*) won the prestigious Van Cliburn International Piano Competition. Although he was born blind and has never seen a facial expression, winning a million-dollar prize immediately gave rise to a million-dollar smile. Victor Trevino

facial feedback hypothesis The suggestion that emotional expressions can cause the emotional experiences they signify.

Figure 8.7 TWO EMOTIONS, ONE EXPRESSION Without any context, it is difficult to know if this man is feeling sorrow or joy. Reuters/Fayaz Aziz

when bitter chemicals are put in their mouths (Steiner, 1973, 1979). Not only are people good at identifying the emotional expressions of members of cultures with which they are familiar (Ekman & Friesen, 1971; Elfenbein & Ambady, 2002; Frank & Stennet, 2001; Haidt & Keltner, 1999), but they are also good at identifying the emotional expressions of members of cultures they have never seen before. In the 1950s, researchers showed photographs of Westerners expressing anger, disgust, fear, happiness, sadness, and surprise to members of the South Fore, a people who lived a Stone Age existence in the highlands of Papua New Guinea and who at that point had had little contact with the modern world. Researchers asked these participants to match each photograph to a word (such as "happy" or "afraid") and found that the South Fore made matches that were essentially the same as those made by Americans (cf. Gendron, 2014). Most psychologists believe that facial displays of *anger, disgust, fear, happiness,* and *sadness* are universal (Ekman, 2016), and that displays of *embarrassment, surprise, amusement, guilt, shame,* and *pride* may be universal as well (Keltner, 1995; Keltner & Buswell, 1996; Keltner & Haidt, 1999; Keltner & Harker, 1998; Tracy et al., 2013).

The Cause and Effect of Expression

Of course, just as a word (*cat*) can have more than one meaning ("a small domesticated carnivorous mammal" or "a woman given to spiteful gossip"), so too can a facial expression. Is the man in **FIGURE 8.7** feeling joy or sorrow? It is hard to tell because these two emotions often produce the same facial expression. So how do we tell them apart? Research suggests that one answer is *context*. When a man says, "My cat ate a mouse," the context of the sentence suggests that he is referring to his pet and not his wife. Similarly, the context in which a facial expression occurs often tells us what that expression means (Aviezer et al., 2008; Barrett, Mesquita, & Gendron, 2011; Kayyal, Widen, & Russell, 2015; Meeren, Heijnsbergen, & de Gelder, 2005). It may be difficult to tell what the man in Figure 8.7 is feeling, but if you turn to **FIGURE 8.11** on page 249 and see his face in context, you will have no trouble identifying his emotion. Indeed, when you return to this page, you may wonder how you could *ever* have thought he was feeling the opposite emotion.

Our emotional experiences cause our emotional expressions, but it also works the other way around. The **facial feedback hypothesis** (Adelmann & Zajonc, 1989; Izard, 1971; Tomkins, 1981) suggests that *emotional expressions can cause the emotional experiences they signify.* For instance, some studies suggest that people feel happier when they are asked to make the sound of a long *e* or to hold a pencil in their teeth (both of which cause contraction of the zygomatic major) than when they are asked to make the sound of a long *u* or to hold a pencil in their lips (Rummer et al., 2014; Strack, Martin, & Stepper, 1988; Zajonc, 1989; cf. Wagenmakers, 2016). Similarly, when people are instructed to arch their brows they find facts more surprising, and when instructed to wrinkle their noses they find odors less pleasant (Lewis, 2012). These things happen because facial expressions and emotional states become strongly associated with each other over time (Ding! Remember Pavlov?), and eventually each can bring about the other (see **FIGURE 8.8**). These effects are not limited to the face. For example, people feel more assertive when instructed to make a fist (Schubert & Koole, 2009) and more confident when instructed to stand with their legs apart (Carney, Cuddy, & Yap, 2010). They even rate others as more hostile when instructed to extend their middle fingers (Chandler & Schwarz, 2009).

The fact that emotional expressions can cause the emotional experiences they signify may explain why people are so good at recognizing the emotional expressions of others. When people interact, they unconsciously mimic their interaction partner's body postures and facial expressions (Chartrand & Bargh, 1999; Dimberg, 1982). When our interaction partners smile, we smile too (Foroni & Semin, 2009). Because facial expressions and body postures can cause people to experience the emotions they signify, mimicking an interaction partner's expressions can cause people to *feel* what their partners are feeling, which makes it easier for them to identify their partner's emotions.

For the same reason, people find it difficult to identify other people's emotions when they are unable to make facial expressions of their own, for example, if their facial muscles are paralyzed with Botox (Niedenthal et al., 2005). People also find it difficult to identify other people's emotions when they are unable to *experience* emotions of their own (Hussey & Safford, 2009; Pitcher et al., 2008). For example, some people with amygdala damage don't feel fear and anger, and as a result, they are typically poor at recognizing the expressions of those emotions in others (Adolphs, Russell, & Tranel, 1999).

Deceptive Expression

Our emotional expressions can communicate our true feelings—or not. When a stranger makes a snarky remark about our taste in music, we may express our contempt with an arched brow and a reinforcing hand gesture; but when our grandmother makes the same remark, we swallow hard and fake a smile. Our knowledge that it is permissible to show contempt for a stranger but not for a grandparent is a **display rule**, which is *a norm for the appropriate expression of emotion* (Ekman, 1972; Ekman & Friesen, 1968).

People in different cultures use different display rules. For example, in one study, Japanese and American college students watched an unpleasant video of car accidents and amputations (Ekman, 1972; Friesen, 1972). When the students didn't know that the experimenters were observing them, Japanese and American students showed similar facial expressions of disgust, but when they knew they were being observed, the Japanese students masked their disgust with pleasant expressions, but the American students did not. In many Eastern cultures it is considered rude to display negative emotions in the presence of a respected person, and so members of these cultures tend to mask or neutralize their expressions. The fact that different cultures have different display rules may be one of the reasons that people are generally better at recognizing the facial expressions of members of their own cultures (Elfenbein & Ambady, 2002; see A World of Difference: Say Cheese).

Of course, our attempts to obey our culture's display rules don't always work out. Anyone who has ever watched the loser of a beauty pageant congratulate the winner knows that voices, bodies, and faces often betray a person's true emotional state. Even when people smile bravely to mask their disappointment, for example, their faces tend to express small bursts of disappointment that last just 1/5 to 1/25 of a second (Porter & ten Brinke, 2008)—so fast that they are almost impossible to detect with the naked eye. In addition, some facial muscles tend to resist conscious control. For example, people can easily control the *zygomatic major* muscles that raise the corners of their mouths, but not the *obicularis oculi* muscles that crinkle the corners of their eyes. That's why smiles are not necessarily sincere expressions of happiness but eye crinkles are (see **FIGURE 8.9**).

Our emotions don't just leak on our faces. They leak all over the place. Research shows that many aspects of our verbal and nonverbal behavior are altered when we tell a lie (DePaulo et al., 2003). For example, liars tend to speak more slowly, take longer to respond to questions, and respond in less detail than do people who are telling the truth. Liars are also less fluent, less engaging, more uncertain, tenser, and less pleasant than truth-tellers. Oddly enough, one of the telltale signs of a liar is that his or her performances tend to be just a little too good. A liar's speech will often lack the small imperfections that a truth-teller's speech contains, such as superfluous details ("I noticed that the robber was wearing the same shoes that I saw on sale last week at Bloomingdale's and I found myself wondering what he paid for them"), spontaneous

Figure 8.8 THE FACIAL FEEDBACK HYPOTHESIS When Jonathan Kalb, a theater professor at Hunter College, contracted Bell's palsy in 2002, part of his face became paralyzed, and he lost the ability to smile. "For the past thirteen years, my smile has been an incoherent tug-of-war between a grin on one side and a frown on the other: an expression of joy spliced to an expression of horror. . . . The worst effect of my damaged smile is that it can dampen my experience of joy. . . . my brain doesn't receive the same feedback messages that normal people receive from their smiles, which reinforce their happy feelings as well as relaying them. I've been devastated by the loss" (Kalb, 2015). Jonathan Kalb

display rule A norm for the appropriate expression of emotion.

Figure 8.9 DARN THOSE RELIABLE MUSCLES! If you want to know which of the two contestants in the 1986 Miss America pageant just won the crown, check out their eyes. Only one of the women has the telltale "corner crinkles" that signify genuine happiness, and that's the one on the right. But don't feel too bad for the one on the left. That loser is named Halle Berry, and she went on to become a seriously famous movie star. RAUL DEMOLINA/AP Images

A WORLD OF DIFFERENCE

Say Cheese

Americans come from such a wide range of cultures that one of the few things they share is a need for hyphenation. African Americans, Asian Americans, European Americans, and many other kinds of Americans live and work side by side, making the United States one of the most culturally diverse nations on earth. But diversity creates challenges, and one of those is communication. Different cultures have different display rules and different ways of nonverbally expressing emotions, which suggests that Americans with different backgrounds should have trouble "reading" their neighbors. And yet, they don't seem to. How come?

To find out, researchers analyzed data from 92 scientific papers that had measured the accuracy with which people from 82 different cultures could recognize the emotional expressions of people from other cultures (Wood, Rychlowska, & Niendenthal, 2016). First, the researchers used historical, genetic, and sociological data to compute the cultural diversity of each of the 82 cultures. Nations such as Brazil and the United States scored high in diversity, whereas nations such as Japan and Ethiopia scored low (see the map above). Second, they computed how easily the facial expressions of people from each of these cultures could be recognized by people from other cultures. When they compared these two measures, they found a positive correlation (see the graph to the right). The more diverse a culture is, the more easily the facial expressions of its members can be understood by members of other cultures.

The researchers suggest that in nations with little cultural diversity, people can communicate with subtle expressions—a slightly raised eyebrow or the fleeting flare of a nostril—because everyone knows and follows the same display rules. But in diverse nations, people of different backgrounds follow different sets of rules, so to communicate with each other they have learned to use expressions that are so perfectly clear that they can be accurately recognized by any human on the planet. This fact may help explain a common stereotype about Americans: the big, toothy American smile. While many people around the world believe that the broad "American smile" is an indicator of our optimism, our phoniness, or our naiveté, it may instead be a clever solution to a knotty communication problem that results from our diversity. In a land where every face speaks a different language, it has to learn to shout.

The diversity of cultures: Darker colors indicate greater cultural diversity.

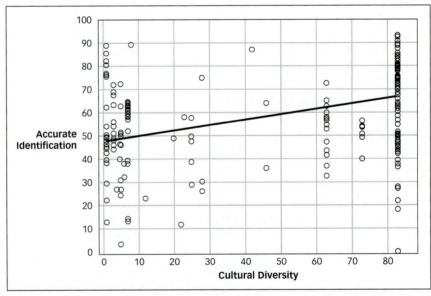

Diversity and accuracy: Each circle in this figure represents a study in which participants judged emotional expression in faces of people from a different culture. In general, participants were more accurate in judging emotional expression of faces from highly diverse cultures.

correction ("He was six feet tall . . . well, no, actually more like six-two"), and expressions of self-doubt ("I think he had blue eyes, but I'm really not sure").

Given the reliable differences between sincere and insincere expressions and between truth-tellers and liars, you might think that people would be quite good at distinguishing between them. In fact, under most circumstances, people don't perform much better than chance (DePaulo, Stone, & Lassiter, 1985; Ekman, 1992; Zuckerman, DePaulo, & Rosenthal, 1981; Zuckerman & Driver, 1985). One reason for this is that people have a strong bias toward believing that others are expressing sincere emotions or telling the truth (Gilbert, 1991). A second reason is that people don't know what to look for when they try to detect insincerity and dishonesty (Vrij et al., 2011). For instance, people think that fast talking is a sign of lying when it actually isn't. Indeed, the correlation between a person's ability to detect lies and the person's confidence in that ability is essentially zero (DePaulo et al., 1997).

When people can't do something well, such as adding 87-digit numbers or picking up 10-ton rocks, they typically turn the job over to a machine. Can machines detect lies better than we can? The answer is yes, but that's not saying very much. The most widely used lie detection machine is the *polygraph*, which measures a variety of physiological responses that are associated with stress, which people often feel when they are afraid of being caught in a lie. A polygraph can detect lies with better-than-chance accuracy, but its error rate is still too high to make it a useful lie detector. In short, neither people nor machines are particularly good at lie detection, which is probably why lying remains such a popular human sport (see **FIGURE 8.10**).

The Canadian prime minister Justin Trudeau wipes away tears after delivering an emotional speech. Crying is very difficult to control and thus provides reliable information about the intensity of a person's emotions. REUTERS/Chris Wattie

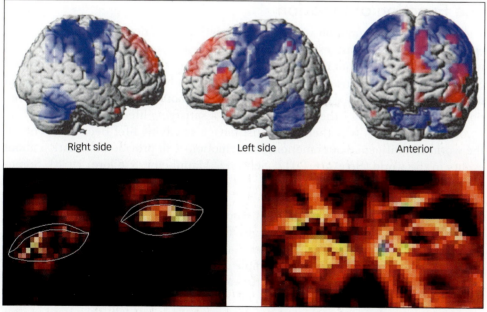

Right side   Left side   Anterior

Figure 8.10 LIE DETECTION MACHINES Some researchers hope to replace the polygraph with machines that measure changes in blood flow in the brain and the face. As the top panel shows, some areas of the brain are more active when people tell lies than when they tell the truth (shown in red), and some are more active when people tell the truth than when they tell lies (shown in blue; Langleben et al., 2005). The bottom panel shows images taken by a thermal camera that detects the heat caused by blood flow to different parts of the face. The images show a person's face before (*left*) and after (*right*) telling a lie (Pavlidis, Eberhardt, & Levine, 2002). Although neither of these new lie-detection techniques is yet extremely accurate, that could soon change. Republished with permission of Langleben, D. D., Loughead, J. W., Bilker, W. B., Ruparel, K., Childress, A. R., Busch, S. I., Gur, R. C. From (2005). Telling truth from lie in individual subjects with fast event-related fMRI. *Human Brain Mapping, 26*, pp. 262–272. Permission conveyed through Copyright Clearance Center, Inc. Republished with permission of Pavlidis, Eberhardt, and Levine, 2002. From Seeing through the face of deception. *Nature, 415* (35). Permission conveyed through Copyright Clearance Center, Inc.

Figure 8.11 WHAT DO YOU THINK NOW? This Pakistani man is being led away from the scene of the suicide bombing that killed his father. Now can you see the pain and sorrow in his face? Is it hard to imagine how this expression could ever have been mistaken for joy? Reuters/Fayaz Aziz

BUILD TO THE OUTCOMES

1. What evidence suggests that facial expressions of emotion are universal?

2. How do emotional expressions cause emotional experiences?

3. What are display rules?

4. What features distinguish between sincere and insincere facial expressions?

5. What is the problem with lie-detecting machines?

Motivation: Being Moved

LEARNING OUTCOMES

*   Identify the two basic functions of emotion.

*   Explain the concepts of instinct and drive.

motivation The psychological cause of an action.

hedonic principle The claim that people are motivated to experience pleasure and avoid pain.

When we try to make a decision, we often ask how we "feel" about it. If we couldn't feel, then we wouldn't know which alternative to choose. Without emotions, Rihanna would probably just stand there until someone came along and gave her a Grammy for Best Orange Stiletto. © MWP/ZUMAPRESS.com

Leonardo is a robot, so he does what he is programmed to do and nothing more. Because he doesn't have wants and urges—doesn't crave friendship or desire chocolate or hate homework—he doesn't initiate his own behavior. He can learn but he cannot yearn, and therefore he isn't *motivated* to act in the same way we are. A **motivation** is *the psychological cause of an action*, and it is no coincidence that the words *emotion* and *motivation* share a common linguistic root that means "to move." Unlike robots, human beings act because their emotions move them, and they do this in two ways. First, emotions provide people with *information* about the world, and second, emotions are the *objectives* toward which people strive. Let's examine each of these in turn.

The Function of Emotion

The first function of emotion is to provide us with information about the world. For example, some studies suggest that people report being more satisfied with their lives when they are asked about them on a sunny day, rather than on a rainy day (Schwarz & Clore, 1983; cf. Simonsohn, 2015). Why might that happen? Because people tend to feel happier on sunny days, and they take their emotional experience as information about the quality of their lives. After all, a satisfying life makes you happy, so if you feel happy . . . why then, you must have a satisfying life! Because events in the world can influence our emotions, our emotions can provide information about events in the world (Schwarz, 2012; Schwarz, Mannheim, & Clore, 1988). Sometimes that information leads us astray, but more often than not it is quite useful (Mikels et al., 2011; Pham, Lee, & Stephen, 2012).

Indeed, without the information that emotions provide, we would be utterly lost (Lerner et al., 2015). When a neurologist was asked to see a patient who had an unusual form of brain damage, he asked the patient to choose between two dates for an appointment. It sounds like a simple decision, but for the next half hour, the patient enumerated reasons for and against each of the two possible dates, completely unable to decide in favor of one option or the other (Damasio, 1994). The patient was unable to make a simple decision—not because he couldn't think but because he couldn't feel. His brain injury had left him unable to experience emotion, so when he entertained one option ("If I come next Tuesday, I'll have to cancel my lunch with Fred"), he didn't feel any better or any worse than when he entertained another ("If I come next Wednesday, I'll have to get up early to catch the bus"). And because he *felt* nothing when he thought about each option, he couldn't decide which was best.

If the first function of emotion is to provide us with information about the world, then the second function is to tell us what to do with that information. The **hedonic principle** is *the claim that people are motivated to experience pleasure and avoid pain.* According to the hedonic principle, our emotional experience can be thought of as a gauge that ranges from bad to good, and our primary motivation—perhaps even our *sole* motivation—is to keep the needle on the gauge as close to *good* as possible. Even when we voluntarily do things that tilt the needle in the opposite direction, such as letting the dentist drill our teeth or waking up early for a boring class, we are doing these things because we believe that they will nudge the needle toward *good* in the future and keep it there longer.

Instincts and Drives

If our primary motivation is to keep the needle on *good*, then which things push the needle in that direction and which things push it away? And exactly how do they do the pushing? The answers to such questions lie in two concepts that have played unusually important roles in the history of psychology: *instincts* and *drives*.

Instincts

When a newborn baby is given a drop of sugar water, it smiles, and when it is given a check for $10,000, it acts like it couldn't care less. By the time the baby goes to college, these responses pretty much reverse. It seems clear that nature endows us with certain motivations and that experience endows us with others. William James (1890) called the natural tendency to seek a particular goal an *instinct*, and he argued that nature hardwired people, penguins, parrots, and puppies to want certain things without being taught to want them, and to execute the behaviors that produce these things without ever thinking about it.

By 1930, the term "instinct" had fallen out of fashion. Behaviorists rejected the concept of instinct on two grounds. First, they believed that behavior should be explained by the external stimuli that evoke it and not by the hypothetical internal states on which it presumably depends, and instincts seemed to be just the sort of unnecessary "mind blather" that John Watson and the behaviorists forbade. The second reason that behaviorists rejected the concept of instinct was that instincts are inherited, and behaviorists believed that complex behaviors were learned, not hardwired. So what did the behaviorists replace instincts with?

Drives

Although Watson's younger followers agreed in principle with his ban on mind blather, they also realized that certain phenomena were difficult to explain without some reference to an organism's internal state. For example, if all behavior is a response to an external stimulus, then why does a rat that is sitting still in its cage at 9:00 a.m. start wandering around and looking for food by noon? Nothing in the cage has changed, so why has the rat's behavior changed? The obvious answer is that the rat is responding to something inside itself, which meant that Watson's young followers (the "new behaviorists" as they called themselves) were forced to look inside the rat to explain its wandering. But how could they do that without talking about the "thoughts" and "feelings" that Watson had forbidden them to mention?

They did it by talking about **drives**, which are *internal states caused by physiological needs*. Bodies, it seems, are a bit like thermostats. When a thermostat detects that the room is too cold, it sends a signal that initiates corrective actions, such as turning on a furnace. Similarly, when bodies detect that they are underfed, they send signals that initiate corrective actions such as eating. To survive, an organism needs to maintain precise levels of nutrition, warmth, and so on. When these levels deviate too much from the optimum, the brain sends a signal to the organism to take corrective action. That signal is called a drive, and **drive-reduction theory** is *a theory suggesting that organisms are motivated to reduce their drives*. According to this theory, it isn't food per se that organisms find rewarding; it is the reduction of the drive for food. A reinforcement, then, is any "substance or commodity in the environment that satisfies a need, i.e., that reduces a drive" (Hull, 1943, p. 131).

All animals are born with instincts. In the annual running of the bulls in Pamplona, Spain, no one has to teach the bulls to chase the runners, and no one has to teach the runners to flee. AP Photo/ Lalo R. Villar

drive An internal state caused by physiological needs.

drive-reduction theory A theory suggesting that organisms are motivated to reduce their drives.

BUILD TO THE OUTCOMES

1. How are emotions and motivations related?

2. How do emotions help people make decisions?

3. What is the hedonic principle?

4. Why did psychologists abandon the concept of instinct?

5. What is drive-reduction theory?

Wanting: The Body's Desires

LEARNING OUTCOMES

*   Explain Maslow's hierarchy of needs.

*   Describe the biological signals that turn hunger on and off.

*   Identify the common eating disorders.

*   Describe the biological mechanisms underlying sexual interest and activity.

Although the words *instinct* and *drive* are no longer widely used in psychology, both concepts have something to teach us. The concept of instinct reminds us that nature endows organisms with a tendency to seek certain things, and the concept of drive reminds us that this seeking is initiated by an internal state.

Abraham Maslow (1954) attempted to organize the list of these states—which he called *needs*—in a meaningful way (see **FIGURE 8.12**). He noticed that some needs (such as the need to eat) must be satisfied before other less pressing needs (such as the need to have friends). So Maslow built a "hierarchy of needs" that had the most pressing ones at the bottom and the least pressing ones at the top. Maslow suggested that, as a rule, people are more likely to experience a need when the needs below it are met. So when people are hungry or thirsty or exhausted, for example, they are less likely to seek intellectual fulfillment or moral clarity (see **FIGURE 8.13**). According to Maslow, our most pressing needs are those we share with other animals, such as the need to eat and mate. Let's explore these two needs in detail.

Hunger

Animals convert matter into energy by eating, and they are driven to do this by an internal state called *hunger*. But what is hunger and where does it come from? At every moment, your body is sending signals to your brain about its current energy state. If your body needs energy, it sends an *orexigenic* signal to your brain telling it to switch the experience of hunger on, and if your body has sufficient energy it sends an *anorexigenic* signal to your brain telling it to switch the experience of hunger off (Gropp et al., 2005). No one knows precisely what these signals are or how they are sent and received, but research has identified a few candidates. For example, *ghrelin* is a hormone that is produced in the stomach and appears to be one of the orexigenic signals that tells the brain to switch hunger on (Inui, 2001; Nakazato et al., 2001). When people are injected with ghrelin, they become intensely hungry and eat about 30% more than usual (Wren et al., 2001). *Leptin* is a chemical secreted by fat cells, and it is an anorexigenic signal that tells the brain to switch hunger off. It seems to do this by making food less rewarding (Farooqi et al., 2007). People who are born with a leptin deficiency have trouble controlling their appetites (Montague et al., 1997).

Some researchers think the idea that chemicals turn hunger on and off is far too simple. They argue that there is no general state called *hunger*, but rather that there are many different hungers, each of which is a response to a unique nutritional deficit and each of which is switched on by a unique chemical messenger (Rozin & Kalat, 1971). For example, rats that are deprived of protein will seek proteins while turning down fats and carbohydrates, suggesting that they are experiencing a specific "protein hunger" and not a general hunger (Rozin, 1968).

We do not know whether hunger is one signal or many, but we do know that the primary receiver of these signals is the hypothalamus. Different parts of the hypothalamus receive different signals. The *lateral hypothalamus* receives orexigenic

Figure 8.12 MASLOW'S HIERARCHY OF NEEDS The psychologist Abraham Maslow believed that needs form a hierarchy, with physiological needs at the bottom and self-actualization needs at the top.

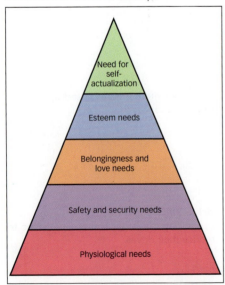

Need for self-actualization

Esteem needs

Belongingness and love needs

Safety and security needs

Physiological needs

signals, and when it is destroyed, animals sitting in a cage full of food will starve themselves to death. The *ventromedial hypothalamus* receives anorexigenic signals, and when it is destroyed, animals will gorge themselves to the point of illness and obesity (Miller, 1960; Steinbaum & Miller, 1965). These two structures were once thought to be the "hunger center" and the "satiety center" of the brain, but this view turned out to be far too simple (Woods et al., 1998). Hypothalamic structures clearly play an important role in turning hunger on and off, but the precise way in which they execute these functions remains poorly understood (Stellar & Stellar, 1985).

Eating Disorders

Feelings of hunger tell most of us when to start and stop eating. But for the 10 to 30 million Americans who have eating disorders, eating is a much more complicated affair (Hoek & van Hoeken, 2003). Let's take a quick look at some of the better-known disorders.

Binge eating disorder (or BED) is *an eating disorder characterized by recurrent and uncontrolled episodes of consuming a large number of calories in a short time.* People with BED quickly consume large quantities of food over a period of just a few hours, often at night. They often report feeling a lack of control over their own behavior—a sense that they "just can't stop eating."

Bulimia nervosa is *an eating disorder characterized by binge eating followed by compensatory behavior.* People with bulimia also binge, but then they take actions to compensate for their eating, such as fasting, excessive exercising, taking diuretics or laxatives, or even inducing vomiting to purge the food from their bodies. People with BED or bulimia are caught in a cycle: They eat to ease negative emotions such as sadness and anxiety, but then concern about weight gain leads them to experience negative emotions such as guilt and self-loathing (Sherry & Hall, 2009; cf. Haedt-Matt & Keel, 2011).

Anorexia nervosa is *an eating disorder characterized by an intense fear of being overweight and a severe restriction of food intake.* People with anorexia tend to have a distorted body image that leads them to believe they are overweight when they may actually be emaciated. They tend to be high-achieving perfectionists who see their severe control of eating as a triumph of will over impulse. Anorexia is often fatal, leading people to literally starve themselves to death.

What causes these eating disorders? Their origins appear to be genetic (Zerwas & Bulik, 2011), experiential (Inniss, Steiger, & Bruce, 2011), and psychological (Klump et al., 2004), but they may be cultural as well (Hogan & Strasburger, 2008). For example, women with anorexia typically believe that thinness equals beauty, and it isn't hard to understand why. The average American woman is 5 feet, 4 inches tall and weighs 140 pounds, but the average American fashion model is 5 feet, 11 inches tall and weighs 117 pounds. So perhaps it is not surprising that most college-age women report wanting to be thinner than they are (Rozin, Trachtenberg, & Cohen, 2001), and nearly 20% report being *embarrassed* to be seen buying chocolate (Rozin, Bauer, & Catanese, 2003). But anorexia is not just "vanity run amok" (Striegel-Moore & Bulik, 2007). Most researchers believe that there are biological and genetic components to this illness as well. For example, although anorexia primarily affects women, men have a sharply increased risk of becoming anorexic if they have a female twin who has the disorder (Procopio & Marriott, 2007), suggesting that anorexia may have something to do with prenatal exposure to female hormones.

Obesity

Bulimia and anorexia are serious problems that affect about 0.01% of the population (Hoek, 2006). But the most pervasive eating-related problem in the US is obesity, which is defined as having a body mass index (BMI) of 30 or greater. **TABLE 8.1** allows you to compute your BMI, and the odds are that you won't like what you learn.

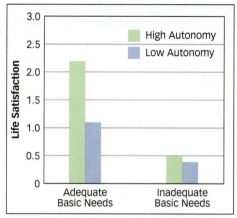

Figure 8.13 WHEN DO HIGHER NEEDS MATTER? A study of 77,000 people in the world's 51 poorest nations (Martin & Hill, 2012) showed that, if people have their basic needs adequately met, then autonomy (i.e., freedom to make their own decisions) increases their satisfaction with their lives. But when people do not have their basic needs adequately met, autonomy makes little difference.

binge eating disorder An eating disorder characterized by recurrent and uncontrolled episodes of eating a large number of calories in a short time.

bulimia nervosa An eating disorder characterized by binge eating followed by compensatory behavior.

anorexia nervosa An eating disorder characterized by an intense fear of being overweight and a severe restriction of food intake.

Bar Refaeli is Israel's best-known supermodel. In 2012, Israel enacted a law banning models whose body mass index is under 18.5 from appearing in advertisements. So a 5-foot, 8-inch model must weigh at least 119 pounds. Victor Chavez/WireImage/Getty Images

TABLE 8.1　Body Mass Index Table

BMI	Normal						Overweight					Obesity										Extreme														
	19	20	21	22	23	24	25	26	27	28	29	30	31	32	33	34	35	36	37	38	39	40	41	42	43	44	45	46	47	48	49	50	51	52	53	54
Height (Inches)	Body Weight (pounds)																																			
58	91	96	100	105	110	115	119	124	129	134	138	143	148	153	158	162	167	172	177	181	186	191	196	201	205	210	215	220	224	229	234	239	244	248	253	258
59	94	99	104	109	114	119	124	128	133	138	143	148	153	158	163	169	173	178	183	188	193	198	203	308	212	217	222	227	232	237	242	247	252	257	262	267
60	97	102	107	112	116	123	128	133	138	143	148	153	156	163	168	174	179	184	189	194	199	204	209	215	220	225	230	235	240	245	250	256	261	266	271	278
61	100	108	111	116	122	127	132	137	143	148	153	156	164	169	174	180	186	190	195	201	206	211	217	222	227	232	238	243	248	254	259	264	269	275	280	285
62	104	109	115	120	126	131	138	142	147	153	158	164	169	175	180	186	191	196	202	207	213	218	224	229	235	240	248	251	258	262	267	273	278	264	289	295
63	107	113	118	124	130	135	141	148	152	158	163	169	175	180	188	191	197	203	208	214	220	225	231	237	242	248	254	260	265	270	278	282	287	293	299	304
64	110	118	122	128	134	140	145	151	157	163	169	174	180	188	192	197	204	209	215	221	227	232	238	244	250	258	262	267	273	279	285	291	298	302	308	314
65	114	120	128	132	138	144	150	156	162	168	174	180	186	192	193	204	210	218	222	228	234	240	246	252	258	264	270	278	282	288	294	300	308	312	318	324
66	118	124	130	138	142	148	155	161	167	173	179	186	192	198	204	210	216	223	229	235	241	247	253	260	266	272	278	284	291	297	303	309	315	322	328	334
67	121	127	134	140	146	153	159	166	172	178	185	191	198	204	211	217	223	230	238	242	249	256	261	268	274	280	287	293	299	308	312	319	325	331	338	344
68	125	131	138	144	151	158	164	171	177	184	190	197	203	210	216	223	230	236	243	249	256	262	269	278	282	289	295	302	303	315	322	328	335	341	348	354
69	128	135	142	149	155	162	169	178	182	189	195	203	209	218	223	230	236	243	250	257	263	270	277	284	291	297	304	311	318	324	331	338	345	351	358	365
70	132	139	146	153	160	167	174	181	188	195	202	209	216	222	229	236	243	250	257	264	271	278	285	292	299	308	313	320	327	334	341	348	355	362	369	378
71	138	143	150	157	166	172	179	186	193	200	208	215	222	229	235	243	250	257	265	272	279	288	293	301	308	315	322	329	338	343	351	358	365	372	379	388
72	140	147	154	162	169	177	184	191	199	208	213	221	228	235	242	250	258	265	272	279	287	294	302	309	316	324	331	338	346	353	361	368	375	383	390	397
73	144	151	159	166	174	182	189	197	204	212	219	227	236	242	250	257	266	272	280	288	295	302	310	318	326	333	340	348	355	363	371	378	388	393	401	408
74	148	155	163	171	179	188	194	202	210	218	225	233	241	249	258	264	272	280	287	295	303	311	319	328	334	342	350	358	365	373	381	389	398	404	412	420
75	152	160	166	178	184	192	200	208	216	224	232	240	248	256	264	272	279	287	295	303	311	319	327	335	343	351	359	367	375	383	391	399	407	415	423	431
76	158	164	172	180	189	197	205	213	221	230	238	246	254	263	271	279	287	295	304	312	320	328	338	344	353	361	369	377	385	394	402	410	418	428	436	443

Information from: National Institutes of Health, 1998, *Clinical guidelines on the identification, evaluation, and treatment of overweight and obesity in adults: The evidence report*. This and other information about overweight and obesity can be found at https://www.nhlbi.nih.gov/health/educational/lose_wt/BMI/bmi_tbl.htm.

 **DATA VISUALIZATION**　In the last 15 years, Americans have collectively gained more than a billion pounds (Kolbert, 2009; see Data Visualization: Have BMI and Food Consumption Trends Changed Over Time? at www.launchpadworks.com). The average American man is now 17 pounds heavier and the average American woman is now 19 pounds heavier than they were in the 1970s. The proportion of overweight children has doubled, the proportion of overweight teens has tripled, and a full 40% of American women are now too heavy to enlist in the military. In 2012, only one state (Colorado) had an obesity rate *lower* than 20% (see **FIGURE 8.14**).

Every year, obesity-related illnesses cost the United States about $150 billion (Finkelstein et al., 2009) and upward of about 300,000 lives (Mokdad et al., 2003). Obese people tend to have lower psychological well-being, lower self-esteem, and lower quality of life and are viewed negatively by others (Gallup, 2014; Hebl & Heatherton, 1997; Kolotkin, Meter, & Williams, 2001; Sutin, Stephan, & Terracciano, 2015). Obese women earn about 7% less than do their nonobese counterparts (Lempert, 2007), and the stigma of obesity is so powerful that average-weight people are viewed negatively if they have a relationship with someone who is obese (Hebl & Mannix, 2003). All of this is true, but sad. As one scientist noted, we need "a war on obesity, not the obese" (Friedman, 2003).

Obesity is highly heritable (Allison et al., 1996) and may have a genetic component. Some studies suggest that toxins in the environment can disrupt the functioning of the endocrine system and predispose people to obesity (Grün & Blumberg, 2006; Newbold et al., 2005), whereas other studies suggest that obesity can be caused by a dearth of "good bacteria" in the gut (Liou et al., 2013). Whatever the cause, obese

Times have changed. Although modern ads promise to help young women lose weight, ads from the 1960s promised to help them gain it.
Cardboard America

people are often leptin-resistant (i.e., their brains do not respond to the chemical signal that tells the brain to shut hunger off), and even leptin injections don't seem to help (Friedman & Halaas, 1998; Heymsfield et al., 1999). But in most cases, the cause of obesity isn't much of a mystery: We simply eat too much. We eat when we are hungry, but we also eat when we are sad or anxious, or when everyone else is eating (Herman, Roth, & Polivy, 2003). Sometimes we eat simply because the clock tells us to, which is why people with amnesia will happily eat a second lunch shortly after finishing an unremembered first one (Rozin et al., 1998; see The Real World: A Feast for the Eyes). Why does this happen? After all, most of us don't breathe ourselves sick or sleep ourselves sick, so why do we eat ourselves sick?

Blame evolution. Hundreds of thousands of years ago, the main food-related problem facing our ancestors was starvation, and so humans evolved two strategies to avoid it. First, we developed a strong attraction to foods that provide large amounts

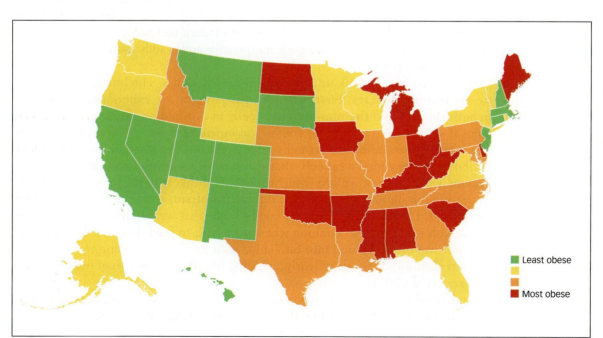

Figure 8.14 THE GEOGRAPHY OF OBESITY As this 2014 map shows, obesity is a problem everywhere in the United States, but ironically, it is most prevalent in the nation's . . . um, midsection.

Least obese

Most obese

A Feast for the Eyes

In 1923, a reporter for the *New York Times* asked the British mountaineer George Leigh Mallory why he wanted to climb Mount Everest. Mallory replied, "Because it's there."

Apparently, that's also the reason why we eat. Brian Wansink and colleagues (2005) wondered whether the amount of food people eat is influenced by the amount of food they see in front of them. So they invited participants to their laboratory, sat them down in front of a large bowl of tomato soup, and told them to eat as much as they wanted. In one condition of the study, a server came to the table and refilled each participant's bowl whenever it got down to about a quarter full. In another condition, unbeknownst to the participants, the bottom of the bowl was connected by a long tube to a large vat of soup, so whenever a participant ate from the bowl, it would slowly and almost imperceptibly refill itself.

What the researchers found was sobering. Participants who unknowingly ate from a "bottomless bowl" consumed a whopping 73% more soup than those who ate from normal bowls—and yet, they didn't think they had consumed more and they didn't report feeling any fuller.

It seems that we find it easier to keep track of *what* we are eating than *how much*, and this can cause us to overeat even when we are trying our best to do just the opposite. For instance, one study showed that diners at an Italian restaurant often chose to eat butter on their bread rather than dipping it in olive oil because they thought that doing so would reduce the number of calories per slice. And they were right. What they didn't realize, however, is that they would unconsciously compensate for this reduction in calories by eating 23% more bread during the meal (Wansink & Linder, 2003).

The researcher Brian Wansink and his bottomless soup bowl. Bob Fila/Chicago Tribune/Newscom

This and other research suggests that one of the best ways to reduce our waists is simply to count our bites.

---

of energy per bite (in other words, foods that are calorie rich), which is why most of us prefer cheeseburgers and milkshakes to spinach and tea. Second, we developed an ability to store excess food energy in the form of fat, which enabled us to eat more than we needed when food was plentiful and then live off our reserves when food was scarce. These two adaptations allowed us to survive in a world in which calorie-rich food was scarce, but we don't live in that world anymore. Instead, we live in a world in which the calorie bombs of modern technology—from chocolate cupcakes to sausage pizzas—are both inexpensive and readily available (Simpson & Raubenheimer, 2014).

It is all too easy to bulk up and so hard to slim down. The human body resists weight loss in two ways. First, when we gain weight, we experience an increase in both the size and the number of fat cells in our bodies (usually in our abdomens if we are male and in our thighs and buttocks if we are female). When we lose weight, the size of our fat cells decreases, but the number does not. Once our bodies have added a fat cell, that cell is with us pretty much forever. It may become smaller when we lose weight, but it is unlikely to die. Second, our bodies respond to dieting by decreasing our **metabolism**, which is *the rate at which energy is used by the body*. When our bodies sense that we are living through a famine (which is what they conclude when we refuse to feed them), they find more efficient ways to turn food into fat. This was a great trick for our ancestors, but it is a real nuisance for us. Clearly, avoiding obesity is easier than overcoming it (Casazza et al., 2013).

And avoiding it is exactly what some psychologists are trying to help people do by using small interventions that have a big impact. For instance, one study

metabolism The rate at which energy is used by the body.

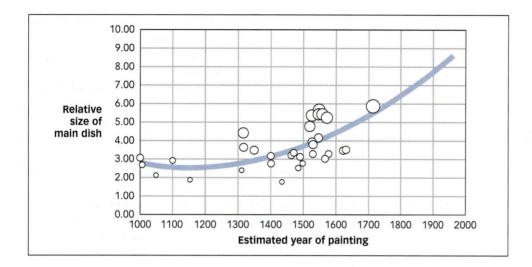

One reason that obesity rates are rising is that "normal portions" keep getting larger. When researchers analyzed 52 depictions of *The Last Supper* that were painted between the years 1000 and 1800, they found that the average plate size had increased by 66% (Wansink & Wansink, 2010). Scala/Art Resource, NY

showed that people ate fewer Pringles when every seventh chip had been colored red, simply because the color coding allowed them to keep track of how much they were eating (Geier, Wansink, & Rozin, 2012). In another study, people ate 22% less pasta with tomato sauce when they used a white plate instead of a red plate, simply because the white plate provided a stark contrast that allowed them to see what they were eating (van Ittersum & Wansink, 2012). These studies and many others show that small "nudges" can make big differences to our waistlines.

Sexual Desire

Food motivates us because we die without it. Although sex is not essential to our individual survival, it is essential to the survival of our DNA, and that's why evolution has wired sexual desire into almost everybody's brain.

The hormone *dihydroepiandosterone* (DHEA) seems to be involved in the initial onset of sexual desire. Both boys and girls begin producing this slow-acting hormone at about the age of 6, which may explain why boys and girls both experience their initial sexual interest at about the age of 10. Two other hormones have more gender-specific effects. Both males and females produce *testosterone* and *estrogen*, but males produce more of the former and females produce more of the latter. As you will learn in the Development chapter, these two hormones are largely responsible for the physical and psychological changes that characterize puberty. But are they also responsible for sexual desire in adults?

The answer is yes—as long as those adults are rats. Testosterone increases the sexual desire of male rats by acting on a particular area of the hypothalamus, and estrogen increases the sexual desire of female rats by acting on a different area of the hypothalamus. Lesions to these areas reduce sexual motivation in the respective sexes.

The story for human beings is far more interesting. The females of most mammalian species (e.g., dogs, cats, and rats) have little or no interest in sex except when their estrogen levels are high, which happens when they are ovulating, or "in estrus." In other words, estrogen regulates both ovulation and sexual interest in these mammals. But female humans can be interested in sex at any time. Although the level of estrogen in a woman's body changes dramatically over the course of her monthly menstrual cycle, studies suggest that sexual desire changes little.

The red coloration on the female gelada's chest (*top*) indicates that she is in estrus and amenable to sex. The sexual interest of a female human being (*bottom*) is not limited to a particular time in her monthly cycle and is not so easily gauged. Michael Nichols/National Geographic/Getty Images; Jupiterimages/Stockbyte/Getty Images

If estrogen is not the hormonal basis of a woman's sex drive, then what is? Two pieces of evidence suggest that the answer is testosterone—the same hormone that drives male sexuality. First, men naturally have more testosterone than women do, and they generally have stronger sex drives. Men are more likely than are women to think about sex, have sexual fantasies, seek sex and sexual variety (whether positions or partners), masturbate, want sex at an early point in a relationship, sacrifice other things for sex, have permissive attitudes toward sex, and complain about low sex drive in their partners (Baumeister, Cantanese, & Vohs, 2001). Second, when women are given testosterone, their sex drives increase. These facts suggest that testosterone may be the hormonal basis of sexual motivation in both men and women.

Men and women may have different levels of sexual drive, but their physiological responses during sex are fairly similar. Although men are more likely than women to report having sex for purely physical reasons, **TABLE 8.2** shows that men and women don't differ dramatically in their most frequent reasons. We will have much more to say about sexual attraction and relationships in the Social Psychology chapter.

TABLE 8.2   Reasons for Sex

Top Ten Reasons Why Men and Women Report Having Sex

	Women	Men
1	I was attracted to the person.	I was attracted to the person.
2	I wanted to experience the physical pleasure.	It feels good.
3	It feels good.	I wanted to experience the physical pleasure.
4	I wanted to show my affection to the person.	It's fun.
5	I wanted to express my love for the person.	I wanted to show my affection to the person.
6	I was sexually aroused and wanted the release.	I was sexually aroused and wanted the release.
7	I was "horny."	I was "horny."
8	It's fun.	I wanted to express my love for the person.
9	I realized I was in love.	I wanted to achieve an orgasm.
10	I was "in the heat of the moment."	I wanted to please my partner.

Information from: Meston & Buss, 2007.

BUILD TO THE OUTCOMES

1. Why do some motivations take precedence over others?

2. What purpose does hunger serve?

3. What causes BED, bulimia, and anorexia?

4. What causes obesity?

5. Why is dieting so difficult and ineffective?

6. Which hormones regulate sexual interest in men and women?

7. Why do people have sex?

Wanting: The Mind's Desires

Survival and reproduction are every animal's first order of business, so it is no surprise that we are strongly motivated by food and sex. But humans are motivated by other things, too. Yes, we crave kisses of both the chocolate and romantic variety, but we also crave friendship and respect, security and certainty, wisdom and meaning, and a whole lot more. Our psychological motivations can be every bit as powerful as our biological motivations, but they differ in two important ways.

First, although we share our biological motivations with most other animals, our psychological motivations appear to be unique. Chimps and rabbits and robins and turtles are all motivated to have sex, but only human beings seem motivated to imbue the act with deeper meaning. Second, although our biological motivations are of a few basic kinds—food, sex, oxygen, sleep, and a handful of other things—our psychological motivations are so numerous and varied that no psychologist has ever been able to make a complete list of them (Hofmann, Vohs, & Baumeister, 2012). Nonetheless, even if you looked at an incomplete list, you'd quickly notice that psychological motivations vary on three key dimensions: extrinsic versus intrinsic, conscious versus unconscious, and approach versus avoidance. Let's examine each of these dimensions.

Intrinsic Versus Extrinsic

Eating a potato chip and taking a psychology exam are different in many ways. One makes you chubby and the other makes you crabby, one requires that you move your lips and the other requires that you don't, and so on. But one of the most important differences between these activities is that the exam is a means to an end and the potato chip is an end in itself. An **intrinsic motivation** is *a motivation to take actions that are themselves rewarding*. When we eat a potato chip because it tastes good, exercise because it feels good, or listen to music because it sounds good, we are intrinsically motivated. These activities don't *have* a payoff because they *are* a payoff. Conversely, an **extrinsic motivation** is *a motivation to take actions that lead to reward*. When we floss our teeth so we can avoid gum disease, when we work hard for money so we can pay our rent, and when we take an exam so we can get a college degree (which allows us to earn more money and buy more dental floss), we are extrinsically motivated. None of these things is a source of pleasure in and of itself, but all can increase pleasure in the long run.

Extrinsic Motivation

Extrinsic motivation gets a bad rap. Americans tend to believe that people should "follow their hearts" and "do what they love," and we feel sorry for students who choose courses just to please their parents and for parents who choose jobs just to earn a pile of money. But our ability to engage in behaviors that are unrewarding in the present because we believe they will bring greater rewards in the future is one of our species' most significant talents, and no other species can do it quite as well as we can (Gilbert, 2006). In research studies of how well people can put off pleasure or "delay gratification" (Ayduk et al., 2007; Mischel et al., 2004) participants may get a choice between getting something they want right now (e.g., a scoop of ice cream today) or getting more of what they want later (e.g., two scoops of ice cream tomorrow). Studies show that 4-year-old children who can delay gratification are judged to be more intelligent and socially competent 10 years later and have higher SAT scores when they enter college (Mischel, Shoda, & Rodriguez, 1989). In fact, the ability to delay gratification is a better predictor of a child's grades in school than is the child's IQ (Duckworth & Seligman, 2005). Apparently, there is something to be said for extrinsic motivation (see Other Voices: Should We Pay People to Vote?).

intrinsic motivation A motivation to take actions that are themselves rewarding.

extrinsic motivation A motivation to take actions that lead to reward.

LEARNING OUTCOMES

- Explain the advantages of intrinsic and extrinsic motivations.

- Explain how rewards and threats can backfire.

- Explain when people become conscious of their motivations.

- Explain how we know that avoidance motivation is more powerful than approach motivation.

Mohamed Bouazizi was a fruit seller. In 2010, he set himself on fire to protest his treatment by the Tunisian government, and his dramatic suicide ignited the revolution that came to be known as the "Arab Spring." Clearly, psychological needs—such as the need for justice—can be even more powerful than biological needs. FETHI BELAID/AFP/Getty Images

Should We Pay People to Vote?

Stephen L. Carter is the William Nelson Cromwell Professor of Law at Yale University. His novels include *The Emperor of Ocean Park*, and his nonfiction books include *The Violence of Peace: America's Wars in the Age of Obama.* Jeff Malet/Newscom/Jeff Malet Photography/Washington/DC/United States of America

Some people think that citizens of democracies should vote because they *want* to, that they should be proud to exercise a right for which others have fought and died. But some people think that voting is too important to be voluntary, and they have called for making it compulsory in America, as it is in many other nations. Stephen Carter, a law professor and novelist, has a different idea. Instead of either leaving citizens to their own devices or forcing them to vote, why not just pay them?

President Barack Obama recently mooted the idea of making voting mandatory, as a means of increasing turnout. It's true that U.S. citizens are less likely to go to the polls than those of many (not all) other democracies. Nevertheless, with all due respect to the president, I don't much like his idea. And if getting more people to the polls is the goal, I have a better suggestion.

Let me spell out my biases. I'm a happy nonvoter. More to the point, I find that I am more at peace when I don't bother following electoral politics than when I do. Staying away from the polls helps me to focus on my work, to take a relaxed attitude toward life, even to be a better husband and father than I otherwise might. So naturally I'm distressed at the thought that my government would even consider using coercion to disturb my peace of mind.

This isn't apathy. And it's not that I'm uninformed. But given that my vote can't possibly make any difference to the outcome, I'm hard-pressed to come up with a reason to go to the polls. . . .

Still, the debate over whether voting should be compulsory has a great deal of academic currency. Supporters often argue that those who are staying away from the polls tend to be political outsiders whose views policy rarely reflects. Others contend that low information voters, if required to go to the polls, might be transformed into high information voters. President Obama put the case that mandatory voting could reduce the influence of money in politics.

These seemingly strong arguments have equally strong rejoinders. For example, as the law professor Ilya Somin has pointed out, forcing low-information voters to the polls might actually heighten the influence of money in politics—at least if, as I suspect, low-information voters tend to watch a lot of television.

As to the claim that the outsiders who stay away from the polls would make a crucial policy difference, the philosopher Jason Brennan offers a sharp riposte: "The argument seems to presume that voter[s] vote for their self-interest. But we have overwhelming empirical evidence, drawn from hundreds of studies, that they don't vote their self-interest. Instead, they vote altruistically, for what they perceive to be in the national interest."

You won't be surprised to learn that I'm with the dissenters. . . . If I'd rather spend Election Day reading a good book, I think my government should let me.

Besides, if increasing turnout is really so important, why signal that fact by punishing people who don't go to the polls? Maybe we'd do better to reward them instead. If voting is such an unadorned good, let's pay people to show up. Surely paying people to do a good thing isn't a bad thing.

Social scientists have understood for some time that cash payments alter people's incentives, sometimes drastically. For example, paying people money to quit smoking greatly enhances the chances of success. Paying students to keep a certain grade-point average seems to make a difference. Paying teenage girls not to get pregnant greatly decreases the chance that they'll get pregnant.

These are all behavioral changes we want to encourage. Why not treat voting the same way? It's likely to work. An experiment conducted by Fordham political scientist Costas Panagopoulos found that paying cash rewards of $25 raised turnout in a municipal election from 14.9 percent to 19.2 percent—no small increase. . . .

I've long been mystified by our bipartisan national determination to achieve what we think is best by punishing people who won't go along. Rewards for good behavior are better than punishments for bad. They force us to discover how much we really value what we claim to want. If increasing turnout is really as important as supporters say, let's give nonvoters a real incentive to go the polls: cash.

Most of us think it is perfectly fine to pay someone to paint our house or wash our car, but not to give us their kidney or tell us they love us. Some things should just be intrinsically motivated. So what about voting? Would paying citizens be an effective way to get them to vote? Even if it is, might there be unanticipated consequences of turning an intrinsically motivated behavior into an extrinsically motivated one?

Adapted from Stephen L. Carter, Want more voters? Pay them, *Bloomberg View*, April 2, 2015. https://www.bloomberg.com/view/articles/2015-04-02/want-more-voters-pay-them

Intrinsic Motivation

There is a lot to be said for intrinsic motivation, too (Patall, Cooper, & Robinson, 2008). People work harder when they are intrinsically motivated, they enjoy what they do more, and they do it more creatively. Both kinds of motivation have advantages, which is why many of us try to build lives in which we are both intrinsically and extrinsically motivated by the same activity—lives in which we are paid the big bucks for doing exactly what we like to do best. Who hasn't fantasized about becoming an artist or an athlete or Beyoncé's personal party planner? Alas, research suggests that it is difficult to get paid for doing what you love and still end up loving what you do because rewards can undermine intrinsic motivation (Deci, Koestner, & Ryan, 1999; Henderlong & Lepper, 2002). For example, in one study, college students who were intrinsically motivated to complete a puzzle either were paid to complete it or completed it for free. Those who received money were less likely to play with the puzzle later on (Deci, 1971; see also Lepper, Greene & Nisbett, 1973). It appears that under some circumstances, then, people interpret rewards as information about the goodness of an activity ("If they had to pay me to do that puzzle, it couldn't have been a very fun one"), which means that rewards can sometimes undermine intrinsic motivation.

Just as the promise of a reward can undermine intrinsic motivation, the threat of punishment can create it. In one study, children who had no intrinsic motivation to play with a toy suddenly gained one when the experimenter threatened to punish them if they touched the toy (Aronson, 1963). And when a group of day care centers got fed up with parents who picked up their children late, some instituted a small financial penalty for tardiness. As **FIGURE 8.15** shows, the financial penalty did not decrease tardiness—it *increased* it (Gneezy & Rustichini, 2000). Why? Because most parents were intrinsically motivated to pick up their kids on time. But when the day care centers started punishing them for their tardiness, the parents became *extrinsically* motivated to pick up their children on time—and because the price of tardiness wasn't particularly high, they decided to pay a small financial penalty in order to leave their children in day care for an extra hour. When threats and rewards change intrinsic motivation into extrinsic motivation, unexpected consequences can follow.

Conscious Versus Unconscious

When prizewinning artists and scientists are asked to explain how they achieved greatness, they typically say things such as, "I wanted to liberate color from form" or "I wanted to cure diabetes." They almost never say things such as, "I wanted to exceed my father's accomplishments, thereby proving to my mother that I was worthy of her love." Prizewinners can articulate their **conscious motivations**, which are *motivations of which people are aware*, but by definition they have trouble articulating their **unconscious motivations**, which are *motivations of which people are not aware* (Aarts, Custers, & Marien, 2008; Bargh et al., 2001; Hassin, Bargh, & Zimerman, 2009).

For example, people vary in their **need for achievement**, which is *the motivation to solve worthwhile problems* (McClelland et al., 1953). This basic motivation is unconscious, but it can be primed in much the same way that thoughts and feelings can be primed. For example, when words such as *achievement* are presented on a computer screen so rapidly that people cannot consciously perceive them, those people will work especially hard to solve a puzzle (Bargh et al., 2001) and will feel especially unhappy if they fail (Chartrand & Kay, 2006).

conscious motivations Motivations of which people are aware.

unconscious motivations Motivations of which people are not aware.

need for achievement The motivation to solve worthwhile problems.

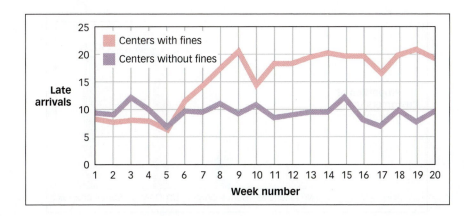

Figure 8.15 WHEN THREATS BACKFIRE Threats can cause behaviors that were once intrinsically motivated to become extrinsically motivated. Day care centers that instituted fines for late-arriving parents saw an increase in the number of parents who arrived late.

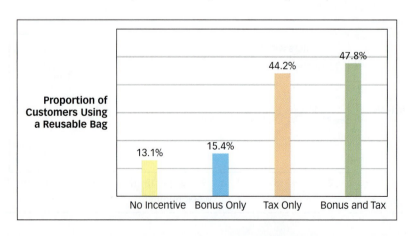

Michael Phelps is clearly high—in need for achievement, that is—which is one of the reasons he remains the most decorated Olympic athlete of all time, with 23 gold, 3 silver, and 2 bronze medals.
AP Photo/The Canadian Press, Ryan Remiorz

approach motivation The motivation to experience a positive outcome.

avoidance motivation The motivation to avoid experiencing a negative outcome.

loss aversion The tendency to care more about avoiding losses than about achieving equal-size gains.

What determines whether we are conscious of our motivations? Most actions have more than one motivation, and the ease or difficulty of performing the action sometimes determines which of these motivations we will be aware of (Vallacher & Wegner, 1985, 1987). When actions are easy (e.g., screwing in a lightbulb), we are aware of our most *general motivations* (e.g., to be helpful), but when actions are difficult (e.g., wrestling with a lightbulb that is stuck in its socket), we become aware of our more *specific motivations* (e.g., to get the threads aligned). For example, participants in one experiment drank coffee either from a normal mug or from a mug that had a heavy weight attached to the bottom, which made the mug difficult to manipulate. When asked what they were doing, those who were drinking from the normal mug explained that they were "satisfying needs," whereas those who were drinking from the weighted mug explained that they were "swallowing" (Wegner et al., 1984). The ease with which we can execute an action is one of many factors that determine the motivations of which we are conscious.

Approach Versus Avoidance

The poet James Thurber (1956) wrote: "All men should strive to learn before they die / What they are running from, and to, and why." As these lines remind us, the hedonic principle describes two distinct motivations: one that makes us "run to" pleasure and another that makes us "run from" pain. Psychologists—being a bit less poetic and a lot more precise—call these **approach motivation**, which is *the motivation to experience positive outcomes*, and **avoidance motivation**, which is *the motivation to avoid experiencing negative outcomes*. Pleasure and pain may be two sides of the same coin, but they *are* two sides. Pleasure is not just the lack of pain, and pain is not just the lack of pleasure. They are distinct experiences that are associated with different regions of the brain (Davidson et al., 1990; Gray, 1990).

Research suggests that, all else being equal, avoidance motivation tends to be stronger than approach motivation. This is easy to illustrate: Would you bet on a coin flip that will pay you $100 if it comes up heads but will require you to pay $80 if it comes up tails? Mathematically speaking, this should be an extremely attractive wager because the potential gain is larger than the equally likely potential loss. And yet most people refuse a bet such as this because they expect the pain of losing $80 will be stronger than the pleasure of winning $100. **Loss aversion** is *the tendency to care more about avoiding losses than about achieving equal-size gains* (Kahneman & Tversky, 1979, 1984), and its effects can be dramatic. Grocery stores in the Washington, DC, area tried to motivate their customers to reuse their shopping bags by giving them a bonus whenever they did (a financial gain), or by taxing them whenever they didn't (a financial loss), or by doing neither or both of these things. As **FIGURE 8.16** shows, the prospect of losing money had a large impact on shoppers' behavior, but the prospect of gaining the same amount of money had no impact at all (Homonoff, 2013).

So what is the one thing that virtually every human being wants to avoid? Death, of course. All animals strive to stay alive, but only human beings know that all that striving is

Figure 8.16 THE POWER OF LOSS
Avoidance motivation is typically more powerful than approach motivation. Shoppers in the Washington, DC, area were highly motivated to reuse their bags to avoid a 5-cent tax but were entirely unmotivated to reuse their bags to get a 5-cent bonus (Homonoff, 2013).

ultimately in vain because, no matter what you do, eventually you will die. Some psychologists have suggested that this knowledge creates a uniquely human "existential terror" that much of human behavior is an attempt to manage. **Terror management theory** is *a theory about how people respond to knowledge of their own mortality*, and it suggests that one of the ways that people cope with existential terror is by developing a *cultural worldview*, which is a shared set of beliefs about what is good and right and true (Greenberg, Solomon, & Arndt, 2008; Solomon, Greenberg, & Pyszczynski, 2004). These beliefs allow people to see themselves as more than mortal animals because they inhabit a world of meaning in which they can achieve symbolic immortality (e.g., by leaving a great legacy or having children) and perhaps even literal immortality (e.g., by being pious and earning a spot in the afterlife). According to this theory, a cultural worldview is a kind of shield that buffers people against the overwhelming anxiety that certain knowledge of their own deaths elicits. Studies show that when people are reminded of death (often in very subtle ways, such as by flashing the word *death* for just a few milliseconds on a computer monitor, or by stopping people on a street corner that happens to be near a graveyard), they are more likely to praise and reward those who share their cultural worldviews, derogate and punish those who don't, value their spouses and defend their countries, feel disgusted by "animalistic" behaviors such as breast-feeding, and so on. All of these responses are presumably ways of shoring up their cultural worldviews, thereby protecting themselves from the existential terror that reminders of mortality create.

terror management theory The theory about how people respond to knowledge of their own mortality.

BUILD TO THE OUTCOMES

1. What are intrinsic and extrinsic motivations?

2. Why do rewards sometimes backfire?

3. How does the threat of punishment affect intrinsic motivation?

4. What makes people conscious of their motivations?

5. What is loss aversion?

CHAPTER REVIEW

8

Emotional Experience: The Feeling Machine

- Emotional experiences have two underlying dimensions: arousal and valence.
- The James–Lange theory suggests that a stimulus triggers a specific bodily reaction that produces an emotional experience; the Cannon–Bard theory suggests that a stimulus triggers both a specific bodily reaction and an emotional experience at the same time; and the two-factor theory suggests that a stimulus triggers general bodily arousal, which people then interpret as a specific emotion.
- Information about a stimulus is sent simultaneously to the amygdala (which makes a quick appraisal of the stimulus) and the cortex (which does a slower and more comprehensive analysis of the stimulus).
- People use many strategies to regulate their emotions. Reappraisal involves changing the way one thinks about an emotional event, and it is one of the most effective but underutilized ways to regulate emotion.

Emotional Communication: Msgs w/o Wrds

- The voice, the body, and the face all communicate information about a person's emotional state. Research suggests that some emotional expressions may be universal.

- Emotions cause expressions, but expressions can also cause emotions.
- People follow display rules that tell them when and how to express emotion. Different cultures have different display rules, but the same basic techniques.
- There are reliable differences between honest and dishonest expressions, both verbal and nonverbal, but people are generally quite poor at telling them apart. The polygraph does a better job than most humans, but its error rate is troublingly high.

Motivation: Being Moved

- Emotions motivate us by providing information about the world and by serving as goals.
- William James called the natural tendency to pursue a particular goal an *instinct*.
- The behaviorists suggested that physiological needs produce internal states called *drives* that organisms are motivated to reduce.

Wanting: The Body's Desires

- Biological motivations generally take precedence over psychological motivations in the "hierarchy of needs."

- Hunger is the result of complex physiological processes by which the body informs the brain about its current energy state.
- Eating disorders and obesity have genetic, experiential, psychological, and cultural origins, and all are difficult to overcome.
- Men and women have sex drives that are regulated by testosterone and engage in sex for mostly the same reasons.

Wanting: The Mind's Desires

- Intrinsic motivations can be undermined by extrinsic rewards and punishments.
- People tend to be conscious of their most general motivations and become conscious of their specific motivations only when they encounter difficulty carrying out their actions.
- The fact that avoidance motivations generally are more powerful than approach motivations leads to loss aversion. The ultimate loss is death, and people develop cultural worldviews to protect themselves against the anxiety that foreknowledge of death elicits.

KEY CONCEPT QUIZ

1. Emotions can be described by their location on the two dimensions of
  a. motivation and scaling.
  b. arousal and valence.
  c. stimulus and reaction.
  d. pain and pleasure.

2. Which theorists claimed that a stimulus simultaneously causes both an emotional experience and a physiological reaction?
  a. Cannon and Bard
  b. James and Lange
  c. Schacter and Singer
  d. Maslow and Hull

3. Which brain structure is most directly involved in the rapid appraisal of whether a stimulus is good or bad?
  a. the cortex
  b. the lateral hypothalamus
  c. the amygdala
  d. the ventromedial hypothalamus

4. Through _____, we change an emotional experience by changing the meaning of the emotion-eliciting stimulus.
  a. deactivation
  b. appraisal
  c. valence
  d. reappraisal

5. Which statement does NOT provide any support for the universality hypothesis?
  a. Congenitally blind people make the facial expressions associated with the basic emotions.
  b. Infants only days old react to bitter tastes with expressions of disgust.
  c. Robots have been engineered to exhibit emotional expressions.
  d. Researchers have discovered that isolated people living a Stone Age existence with little contact with the outside world recognize the emotional expressions of Westerners.

6. _____ is the idea that emotional expressions can cause emotional experiences.
  a. A display rule
  b. Expressional deception
  c. The universality hypothesis
  d. The facial feedback hypothesis

7. Which statement is inaccurate?
  a. Certain facial muscles are reliably engaged by sincere facial expressions.
  b. Even when people smile bravely to mask disappointment, their faces tend to express small bursts of disappointment.
  c. Studies show that human lie detection ability is extremely good.
  d. Polygraph machines detect lies at a rate better than chance, but their error rate is still quite high.

8. The hedonic principle states that
  a. emotions provide people with information.
  b. people are motivated to experience pleasure and avoid pain.
  c. people use their moods as information about the likelihood of succeeding at a task.
  d. motivations are acquired solely through experience.

9. According to the early psychologists, an unlearned tendency to seek a particular goal is called a(n)
  a. instinct.
  b. drive.
  c. motivation.
  d. corrective action.

10. According to Maslow, our most basic needs are
  a. self-actualization and self-esteem.
  b. biological.
  c. unimportant until other needs are met.
  d. belongingness and love.

11. Which of the following is NOT a dimension on which psychological motivations vary?
  a. intrinsic–extrinsic
  b. conscious–unconscious
  c. avoid–approach
  d. appraisal–reappraisal

12. Which of the following activities is most likely the result of extrinsic motivation?
  a. completing a crossword puzzle
  b. pursuing a career as a musician
  c. having ice cream for dessert
  d. flossing one's teeth

13. Which statement is true?

    a. Men and women engage in sex for many of the same reasons.

    b. Boys and girls experience initial sexual interest at very different ages.

    c. The physiological responses of men and women during sex differ dramatically.

    d. The human male sex drive is regulated by testosterone, whereas the human female sex drive is regulated by estrogen.

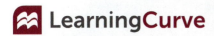 **LearningCurve**   **Don't stop now! Quizzing yourself is a powerful study tool. Go to LearningCurve at www.launchpadworks.com for more practice.**

KEY TERMS

emotion (p. 240)

James–Lange theory (p. 240)

Cannon–Bard theory (p. 241)

two-factor theory of emotion (p. 241)

appraisal (p. 243)

emotion regulation (p. 244)

reappraisal (p. 244)

emotional expression (p. 245)

universality hypothesis (p. 245)

facial feedback hypothesis (p. 246)

display rule (p. 247)

motivation (p. 250)

hedonic principle (p. 250)

drive (p. 251)

drive-reduction theory (p. 251)

binge eating disorder (p. 253)

bulimia nervosa (p. 253)

anorexia nervosa (p. 253)

metabolism (p. 256)

intrinsic motivation (p. 259)

extrinsic motivation (p. 259)

conscious motivations (p. 261)

unconscious motivations (p. 261)

need for achievement (p. 261)

approach motivation (p. 262)

avoidance motivation (p. 262)

loss aversion (p. 262)

terror management theory (p. 263)

CHANGING MINDS

1. A friend is nearing graduation and has received a few job offers. "I went on the first interview," she says, "and I really liked the company, but I know you shouldn't go with your first impressions on difficult decisions. You should be completely rational and not let your emotions get in the way." Are emotions always barriers to rational decision making? In what ways can emotions help guide our decisions?

2. While watching TV, you and a friend hear about a celebrity who punched a fan in a restaurant. "I just lost it," the celebrity said. "I saw what I was doing, but I just couldn't control myself." According to the TV report, the celebrity was sentenced to anger management classes. "I'm not excusing the violence," your friend says, "but I'm not sure anger management classes are any use either. You can't control your emotions; you just feel them." What example could you give your friend of ways in which people can control their emotions?

3. One of your friends has just been dumped by her boyfriend, and she's devastated. She's spent days in her room, refusing to go out. You and your roommate decide to keep a close eye on her during this tough time. "Negative emotions are so destructive," your roommate says. "We'd all be better off without them." What would you tell your roommate? In what ways are negative emotions critical for our survival and success?

4. A friend is majoring in education. "We learned today about several cities, including New York and Chicago, that tried giving cash rewards to students who passed their classes or did well on achievement tests. That's bribing kids to get good grades, and as soon as you stop paying them, they'll stop studying." Your friend is assuming that extrinsic motivation undermines intrinsic motivation. In what ways is the picture more complicated?

5. One of your friends is a gym rat who spends all his free time working out and is very proud of his ripped abs. His roommate, though, is very overweight. "I keep telling him to diet and exercise," your friend says, "but he never loses any weight. If he just had a little more willpower, he could succeed." What would you tell your friend? When an individual has difficulty losing weight, what factors may contribute to this difficulty?

ANSWERS TO KEY CONCEPT QUIZ

1. b; 2. a; 3. c; 4. d; 5. c; 6. d; 7. c; 8. b; 9. a; 10. b; 11. d; 12. d; 13. a.

Language, Thought, and Intelligence

9

An English boy named Christopher showed an amazing talent for languages. By the age of 6, he had learned French from his sister's schoolbooks; he acquired Greek from a textbook in only 3 months. His talent was so prodigious that grown-up Christopher could converse fluently in 16 languages. When tested on English–French translations, he scored as well as a native French-speaker. Presented with a made-up language, he figured out the complex rules easily, even though advanced language students found them virtually impossible to decipher (Smith & Tsimpli, 1995).

If you've concluded that Christopher is extremely smart, perhaps even a genius, you're wrong. His scores on standard intelligence tests are far below normal. He fails simple cognitive tests that 4-year-old children pass with ease, and he cannot even learn the rules for simple games like tic-tac-toe. Despite his dazzling talent, Christopher lives in a halfway house because he does not have the cognitive capacity to make decisions, reason, or solve problems in a way that would allow him to live independently.

CHRISTOPHER'S STRENGTHS AND WEAKNESSES offer compelling evidence that cognition is composed of distinct abilities. People who learn languages with lightning speed are not necessarily gifted at decision making or problem solving. People who excel at reasoning may have no special ability to master languages. In this chapter, you will learn about several key higher cognitive functions: acquiring and using language, forming concepts and categories, and making decisions—the components of intelligence itself. You'll also learn about where intelligence comes from, how it's measured, and whether it can be improved.

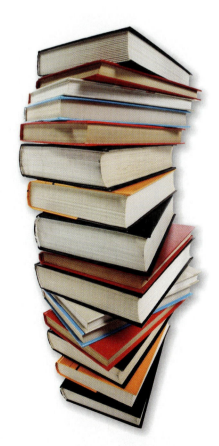

Christopher absorbed languages quickly from textbooks, yet he completely failed simple tests of other cognitive abilities. zoom-zoom/iStock/Getty Images

Language and Communication: From Rules to Meaning

LEARNING OUTCOMES

- Describe the basic characteristics of language.
- Explain the milestones of language development.
- Compare the theories of language development.
- Describe the language centers of the brain.

language A system for communicating with others using signals that are combined according to rules of grammar and that convey meaning.

grammar A set of rules that specify how the units of language can be combined to produce meaningful messages.

Most social species have systems of communication that allow them to transmit messages to each other. Honeybees communicate the location of food sources by means of a "waggle dance" that indicates both the direction and distance of the food source from the hive (Kirchner & Towne, 1994; Von Frisch, 1974). Vervet monkeys have three different warning calls that uniquely signal the presence of their main predators: a leopard, an eagle, and a snake (Cheney & Seyfarth, 1990). A leopard call provokes them to climb into a tree; an eagle call makes them look up into the sky. Each different warning call conveys a particular meaning and functions like a word in a simple language.

Language is *a system for communicating with others using signals that are combined according to rules of grammar and that convey meaning.* **Grammar** is *a set of rules that specify how the units of language can be combined to produce meaningful messages.* The complex structure of human language distinguishes it from simpler signaling systems used by other species; it allows us to express a wide range of ideas and concepts including intangible concepts, such as *unicorn* or *democracy.*

The Complex Structure of Human Language

Compared with other forms of communication, human language is a relatively recent evolutionary phenomenon, emerging as a spoken system no more than 1 to 3 million years ago and as a written system as recently as 6,000 years ago. There are approximately 4,000 human languages, which linguists have grouped into about 50 language families (Nadasdy, 1995). Despite their differences, all of these languages share a

Honeybees communicate with each other about the location of food by doing a waggle dance that indicates the direction and distance of food from the hive. Media Bakery

basic structure involving a set of sounds and rules for combining those sounds to produce meanings.

Basic Characteristics

The smallest units of sound that are recognizable as speech, rather than as random noise, are called **phonemes**. These building blocks of spoken language differ in how they are produced. For example, when you say *ba*, your vocal cords start to vibrate as soon as you begin the sound, but when you say *pa*, there is a 60-millisecond lag between the time you start the *p* sound and the time your vocal cords start to vibrate.

Every language has **phonological rules** that *indicate how phonemes can be combined to produce speech sounds.* For example, the initial sound *ts* is acceptable in German but not in English. Typically, people learn these phonological rules without instruction, and if the rules are violated, the resulting speech sounds so odd that we describe it as speaking with an accent.

Phonemes are combined to make **morphemes**, *the smallest meaningful units of language* (see **FIGURE 9.1**). For example, your brain recognizes the *p* sound you make at the beginning of *pat* as a speech *sound*, but it carries no particular meaning. The morpheme *pat*, on the other hand, is recognized as an element of speech that carries meaning. **Morphological rules** *indicate how morphemes can be combined to form words.* Some morphemes—content morphemes and function morphemes—can stand alone as words. *Content morphemes* refer to things and events (e.g., "cat," "dog," "take"). *Function morphemes* serve grammatical functions, such as tying sentences together ("and," "or," "but") or indicating time ("when"). About half of the morphemes in human languages are function morphemes, and it is the function morphemes that make human language grammatically complex enough to permit us to express abstract ideas.

Words can be combined and recombined to form an infinite number of new sentences, which are governed by **syntactical rules**, *a set of rules that indicate how words can be combined to form phrases and sentences.* A simple syntactical rule in English is that every sentence must contain one or more nouns (see **FIGURE 9.2**). A sentence also must contain one or more verbs, which may be combined with adverbs or articles to create verb phrases. So the utterance "dogs bark" is a full sentence, but "the big gray dog over by the building" is not.

phoneme The smallest unit of sound that is recognizable as speech, rather than as random noise.

phonological rules A set of rules that indicate how phonemes can be combined to produce speech sounds.

morphemes The smallest meaningful units of language.

morphological rules A set of rules that indicate how morphemes can be combined to form words.

syntactical rules A set of rules that indicate how words can be combined to form phrases and sentences.

Figure 9.1 UNITS OF LANGUAGE A sentence—the largest unit of language—can be broken down into progressively smaller units: phrases, morphemes, and phonemes. In all languages, phonemes and morphemes form words, which can be combined into phrases and ultimately into sentences.

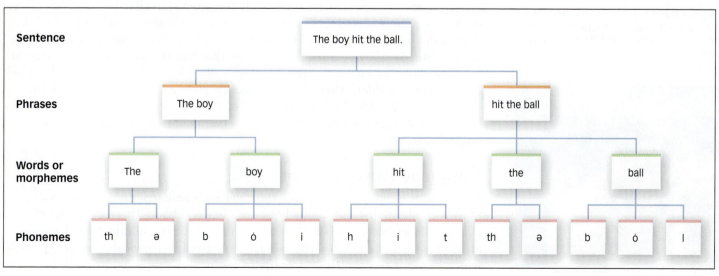

Figure 9.2 SYNTACTICAL RULES Syntactical rules indicate how words can be combined to form sentences. Every sentence must contain one or more nouns, which can be combined with adjectives or articles to create a noun phrase. A sentence also must contain one or more verbs, which can be combined with noun phrases, adverbs, or articles to create a verb phrase.

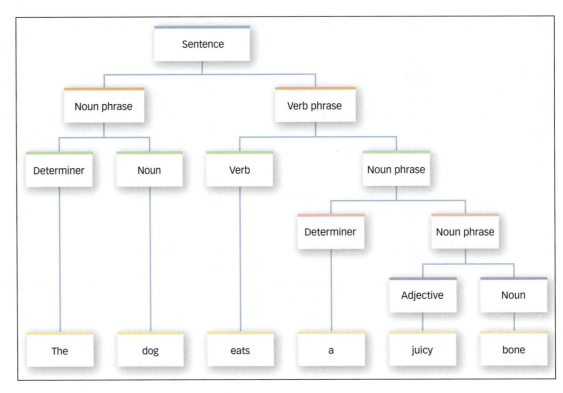

deep structure The meaning of a sentence.

surface structure How a sentence is worded.

Why are we able to communicate effectively when we quickly forget the surface structure of sentences? Why might this be an evolutionary benefit? Mihaela Ninic/Alamy

Meaning: Deep Structure Versus Surface Structure

Language usually conveys meaning quite well, but everyday experience shows us that misunderstandings can occur. These errors sometimes result from differences between the deep structure of sentences and their surface structure (Chomsky, 1957). **Deep structure** refers to *the meaning of a sentence*. **Surface structure** refers to *how a sentence is worded*. "The dog chased the cat" and "The cat was chased by the dog" mean the same thing (they have the same deep structure), even though on the surface their structures are different.

To generate a sentence, you begin with a deep structure (the meaning of the sentence) and create a surface structure (the particular words) to convey that meaning. When you comprehend a sentence, you do the reverse, processing the surface structure in order to extract the deep structure. After the deep structure is extracted, the surface structure is usually forgotten (Jarvella, 1970, 1971). In one study, researchers played tape-recorded stories to volunteers and then asked them to pick the sentences they had heard (Sachs, 1967). Participants frequently confused sentences they heard with sentences that had the same deep structure but a different surface structure. For example, if they heard the sentence "He struck John on the shoulder," they often mistakenly claimed they had heard "John was struck on the shoulder by him." In contrast, they rarely misidentified "John struck him on the shoulder" because this sentence has a different deep structure from the original sentence.

Language Development

Language is a complex cognitive skill, yet we can carry on complex conversations with playmates and family before we begin school. Three characteristics of language development are worth bearing in mind. First, children learn language at an astonishingly rapid rate. The average 1-year-old has a vocabulary of 10 words, which expands to over *10,000* words in the next 4 years, requiring the child to learn, on average, about 6 or 7 new words *every day*. Second, children make few errors while learning to speak, and as we'll see shortly, the errors they do make usually result from applying, but overgeneralizing, grammatical rules they've learned. Third, at every stage of language development, children's *passive mastery* of language (ability to understand) develops faster than their *active mastery* (ability to speak). At every stage of language development, children understand language better than they speak.

Distinguishing Speech Sounds

At birth, infants can distinguish all the sounds that occur in all human languages. Within the first 6 months of life, they lose this ability, and, like their parents, can only distinguish among the contrasting sounds in the language they hear being spoken around them. For example, two distinct sounds in English are the *l* sound and the *r* sound, as in *lead* and *read*. These sounds are not distinguished in Japanese; instead, the *l* and *r* sounds fall within the same phoneme. Japanese adults cannot hear the difference between these two phonemes, but American adults can distinguish between them easily—and so can Japanese infants.

In one study, researchers constructed a tape of a voice saying "la-la-la" or "ra-ra-ra" repeatedly (Eimas et al., 1971). They rigged a pacifier so that whenever an infant sucked on it, a tape player that broadcast the "la-la" tape was activated. When the "la-la" sound began playing in response to their sucking, the infants were delighted and kept sucking on the pacifier to keep the "la-la" sound playing. After a while, they began to lose interest, and sucking frequency declined to about half of its initial rate. At this point, the experimenters switched the tape so that "ra-ra" was repeatedly played. The Japanese infants began sucking again with vigor, indicating that they could hear the difference between the old, boring "la" sound and the new, interesting "ra" sound.

Infants can distinguish among speech sounds, but they cannot produce them reliably, relying mostly on cries, laughs, and other vocalizations to communicate. Between the ages of about 4 and 6 months, they begin to babble speech sounds. Babbling involves combinations of vowels and consonants that sound like real syllables but are meaningless. Regardless of the language they hear spoken, all infants go through the same babbling sequence. For example, *d* and *t* appear in infant babbling before *m* and *n*. Even deaf infants babble sounds they've never heard, and they do so in the same order as hearing infants do (Ollers & Eilers, 1988). This is evidence that infants aren't simply imitating the sounds they hear and suggests that babbling is a natural part of the language development process.

In order for vocal babbling to continue, however, infants must be able to hear themselves. In fact, delayed babbling or the cessation of babbling merits testing for possible hearing difficulties. Babbling problems can lead to speech impairments, but they do not necessarily prevent language acquisition. Deaf infants whose parents communicate using American Sign Language (ASL) begin to babble with their hands at the same age that hearing children begin to babble vocally—between 4 and 6 months (Petitto & Marentette, 1991).

Language Milestones

At about 10 to 12 months of age, infants begin to utter (or sign) their first words. By 18 months, they can say about 50 words and can understand several times more than that. Toddlers generally learn nouns before verbs, and the nouns they learn first are names for everyday, concrete objects (e.g., chair, table, milk) (see **TABLE 9.1**). At about this time, their vocabularies undergo explosive growth. By the time the average child begins school, a vocabulary of 10,000 words is not unusual. (These averages

In this videotaped test, the infant watches an animated toy animal while a single speech sound is repeated. After a few repetitions, the sound changes and then the display changes, and then they both change again. If the infant switches her attention when the sound changes, she is anticipating the new display, which demonstrates that she can discriminate between the sounds. Courtesy Dr. Patricia K. Kuhl, UW Institute for Learning and Brain Sciences

Deaf infants who learn sign language from their parents start babbling with sign language syllables that are the fundamental components of ASL. Christina Kennedy/Alamy

TABLE 9.1	Language Milestones
Average Age	**Language Milestones**
0–4 months	Can tell the difference between speech sounds (phonemes); cooing, especially in response to speech
4–6 months	Babbles consonants
6–10 months	Understands some words and simple requests
10–12 months	Begins to use single words
12–18 months	Vocabulary of 30–50 words (simple nouns, adjectives, and action words)
18–24 months	Two-word phrases ordered according to syntactic rules; vocabulary of 50–200 words; understands rules
24–36 months	Vocabulary of about 1,000 words; production of phrases and incomplete sentences
36–60 months	Vocabulary grows to more than 10,000 words; production of full sentences; mastery of grammatical morphemes (such as -ed for past tense) and function words (such as the, and, but); can form questions and negations

fast mapping The process whereby children can map a word onto an underlying concept after only a single exposure.

telegraphic speech Speech that is devoid of function morphemes and consists mostly of content words.

may differ for children in low- and high-income families, as discussed in A World of Difference: Exploring the 30-Million-Word Gap). By fifth grade, the average child knows the meanings of 40,000 words. By college, the average student's vocabulary is about 200,000 words. **Fast mapping**, *the process whereby children map a word onto an underlying concept after only a single exposure*, enables them to learn at this rapid pace (Kan & Kohnert, 2008; Mervis & Bertrand, 1994). This astonishingly easy process contrasts dramatically with the effort required later to learn other concepts and skills, such as arithmetic or writing.

Around 24 months, children begin to form two-word sentences, such as "more milk" or "throw ball." Such sentences are referred to as **telegraphic speech** because they are *devoid of function morphemes and consist mostly of content words*. Yet despite the absence of function words, these two-word sentences tend to be grammatical; the words are ordered in a manner consistent with the syntactical rules of the language children are learning to speak. So, for example, toddlers will say "throw ball" rather than "ball throw" when they want you to throw the ball to them and "more milk" rather than "milk more" when they want you to give them more milk. With these seemingly primitive expressions, 2-year-olds show that they have already acquired an appreciation of the syntactical rules of the language they are learning.

The Emergence of Grammatical Rules

If you listen to average 2- or 3-year-old children speaking, you may notice that they use the correct past-tense versions of common verbs, as in the expressions "I ran" and "you ate." By the age of 4 or 5, the same children will be using incorrect forms of these verbs, saying such things as "I runned" or "you eated," forms most children are unlikely ever to have heard (Prasada & Pinker, 1993). The reason is that very young children memorize the particular sounds (i.e., words) that express what they want to communicate. But as children acquire the grammatical rules of their language, they tend to *overgeneralize*. For example, if a child overgeneralizes the rule that past tense is indicated by -ed, then *run* becomes *runned*, or even *ranned*, instead of *ran*.

These errors show that language acquisition is not simply a matter of imitating adult speech. Instead, children acquire grammatical rules by listening to the speech around them and using those rules to create verbal forms they've never heard. They manage this without explicit awareness of the grammatical rules they've learned.

Exploring the 30-Million-Word Gap

For over 2½ years, psychologists Betty Hart and Todd Risley observed the language development of 1- to 2-year-old children in 42 families at different levels of socioeconomic status (SES), ranging from families on welfare (low SES) to working class (middle SES) and professional (high SES; Hart & Risley, 1995). The results were stunning: By the time they reached age 3, the children in high-SES families were exposed to millions more words than were the children in lower-SES families, which came to be known as the "30-million-word gap." The researchers also found that these early language differences were highly predictive of how these children performed as third graders on various language and cognitive tests. (For further discussion of the effects of SES on various aspects of intellectual function, see later in this chapter.)

What exactly is it that produces these troubling lags in low-SES children? Research suggests that the *quality* of early communications makes an important contribution. One study (Hirsh-Pasek et al., 2015) focused on 24-month-old children from low-SES families, using video records of mother-child interactions while they played with items from three different boxes (a storybook, toy stove/cooking accessories, and a dollhouse). The researchers assessed the quantity of words used during these interactions and also the quality of the communications, such as how coordinated the mother-child interactions were (e.g., taking turns), and how often they were jointly engaged in a task (e.g., when playing with the dollhouse, the child produced the word "baby" with a gesture indicating sleep, and the mother placed the figure on the bed). A year later, the researchers assessed language performance in the children. The *quantity* of words mattered: More words from the mother during the play session predicted better language performance by the child later. But the *quality* of communication during the play task was an even stronger predictor of language performance a year later. The findings thus suggest that, to counter some of the negative consequences associated with the 30-million-word gap, it will be important to take into account and improve the quality of communications between parents and children in low-SES families.

Quantity and quality of communication between a parent and a child is an essential factor in language development. Esthermm/Moment Open/Getty Images

In fact, few children or adults can articulate the grammatical rules of their native language, yet the speech they produce obeys these rules.

By about 3 years of age, children begin to generate complete simple sentences that include function words (e.g., "Give me *the* ball" and "That belongs *to* me"). The sentences increase in complexity over the next 2 years. By the time children are 4 to 5 years of age, many aspects of the language acquisition process are complete. As children continue to mature, their language skills become more refined, with added appreciation of subtler communicative uses of language, such as humor, sarcasm, or irony.

Language Development and Cognitive Development

Language development typically unfolds as a sequence of steps in which children achieve one milestone before moving on to the next. Nearly all infants begin with one-word utterances before progressing to telegraphic speech and then to simple sentences that include function morphemes. This orderly progression could result from general cognitive development that is unrelated to experience with a specific language (Shore, 1986; Wexler, 1999). For example, perhaps infants begin with one- and then two-word utterances because their short-term memories are so limited that initially they can hold in mind only a word or two; additional cognitive development might be necessary before they have the capacity to put together a simple sentence. Alternatively, the orderly progression might depend on experience with a specific language, reflecting a child's emerging knowledge of that language (Bates & Goodman, 1997; Gillette et al., 1999).

Chinese preschoolers who are adopted by English-speaking parents progress through the same sequence of linguistic milestones as do infants born into English-speaking families, suggesting that these milestones reflect experience with English, rather than general cognitive development. Marvin Joseph/ Washington Post/Getty Images

To tease apart these possibilities, researchers examined the acquisition of English by internationally adopted children who did not know any English prior to adoption (Snedeker, Geren, & Shafto, 2007, 2012). If the orderly sequence of milestones that characterizes the acquisition of English by infants is a by-product of general cognitive development, then different patterns should be observed in older internationally adopted children, who are more advanced cognitively than infants. However, if the milestones of language development are critically dependent on experience with a specific language—English—then language learning in older adopted children should show the same orderly progression as seen in infants. The main result was clear cut: Language acquisition in preschool-age adopted children showed the same orderly progression of milestones that characterizes infants. These children began with one-word utterances before moving on to simple word combinations. Furthermore, their vocabulary, just like that of infants, was initially dominated by nouns, and they produced few function morphemes. These results indicate that some of the key milestones of language development depend on experience with the specific language—in this case, English.

Theories of Language Development

We know a good deal about how language develops, but what underlies the process? The language acquisition process has been the subject of considerable controversy and (at times) angry exchanges among scientists coming from three different approaches: behaviorist, nativist, and interactionist.

Behaviorist Explanations

According to B. F. Skinner's behaviorist explanation of language learning, we learn to talk in the same way we learn any other skill: through reinforcement, shaping, extinction, and the other basic principles of operant conditioning that you read about in the Learning chapter (Skinner, 1957). As infants mature, they begin to vocalize. Those vocalizations that are not reinforced gradually diminish, and those that are reinforced remain in the developing child's repertoire. So, for example, when an infant gurgles "prah," most parents are pretty indifferent. However, "da-da" is likely to be reinforced with smiles, whoops, and cackles of "Goooood baaaaby!" by doting parents. Maturing children also imitate the speech patterns they hear. Then parents or other adults shape the children's speech patterns by reinforcing those that are grammatical and ignoring or punishing those that are ungrammatical. "I no want milk" is likely to be squelched by parental clucks and titters, whereas "No milk for me, thanks" will probably be reinforced.

The behaviorist explanation is attractive because it offers a simple account of language development, but this theory cannot account for three fundamental characteristics of language development (Chomsky, 1986; Pinker, 1994; Pinker & Bloom, 1990).

1. Parents don't spend much time teaching their children to speak grammatically. So, for example, when a child says, "Nobody like me," his or her mother will respond with something like "Why do you think that?" rather than "Now, listen carefully and repeat after me: Nobody likes me" (Brown & Hanlon, 1970).

2. Children generate sentences that they've never heard before. This shows that children don't just imitate, they learn the rules for generating sentences.

3. As you read earlier in this chapter, the errors children make when learning to speak tend to be overgeneralizations of grammatical rules. The behaviorist explanation would not predict these overgeneralizations if children were learning through trial and error or simply imitating what they hear.

Nativist Explanations

In a blistering reply to Skinner's behaviorist approach, linguist Noam Chomsky (1957, 1959) argued that language-learning capacities are built into the human brain. This **nativist theory** holds that *language development is best explained as an innate, biological capacity*, separate from general intelligence. According to the nativist view, language processes naturally emerge as the infant matures, provided the infant receives adequate input to maintain the acquisition process.

The story of Christopher, whom you met earlier in the chapter, is consistent with the nativist view of language development: His genius for language acquisition, despite his low overall intelligence, indicates that language capacity can be distinct from other mental capacities. Other individuals show the opposite pattern: Some people with normal or nearly normal intelligence can find certain aspects of human language difficult or impossible to learn. This condition is known as **genetic dysphasia**, *a syndrome characterized by an inability to learn the grammatical structure of language, despite having otherwise normal intelligence.*

For example, when asked to describe what she did over the weekend, one child wrote, "On Saturday I watch TV." Her teacher corrected the sentence to "On Saturday, I watch*ed* TV," drawing attention to the *-ed* rule for describing past events. The following week, the child was asked to write another account of what she did over the weekend. She wrote, "On Saturday I wash myself and I watched TV and I went to bed." Notice that, although she had memorized the past-tense forms *watched* and *went*, she could not generalize the rule to form the past tense of another word (*washed*).

Also consistent with the nativist view is evidence that language can be acquired only during a restricted period of development. This was dramatically illustrated by the tragic case of Genie (Curtiss, 1977). At the age of 20 months, Genie was tied to a chair by her parents and kept in virtual isolation. Her father forbade Genie's mother and brother to speak to her, and he himself only growled and barked at her. She remained in this brutal state until the age of 13 when her mother finally sought help for Genie. Genie's life improved substantially, and she received years of language instruction, but it was too late. Her language skills remained extremely primitive. She developed a basic vocabulary and could communicate her ideas, but she could not grasp the grammatical rules of English.

Less dramatic evidence for a restricted period in human language learning comes from studies of language acquisition in immigrants. In one study, researchers found that the proficiency with which immigrants spoke English depended not on how long they'd lived in the United States but on their age at immigration—with those who had arrived as children being more proficient than those who arrived after puberty (Johnson & Newport, 1989). More recent work using fMRI shows that acquiring a second language early in childhood (between 1 and 5 years of age) results in very different representation of that language in the brain than does acquiring that language much later (after 9 years of age; Bloch et al., 2009).

Interactionist Explanations

Nativist theories are often criticized because they do not explain *how* language develops; they merely explain why. The interactionist approach holds that, although infants are born with an innate ability to acquire language, social interactions also play a crucial role in language. Interactionists point out that parents tailor their verbal interactions with children in ways that simplify the language acquisition process: They speak slowly, enunciate clearly, and use simpler sentences than they do when speaking with adults (Bruner, 1983; Farrar, 1990).

Further evidence of the interaction of biology and experience comes from a fascinating study of deaf children's creation of a new language (Senghas, Kita, &

"GOT IDEA. TALK BETTER. COMBINE WORDS. MAKE SENTENCES."

© Sidney Harris/ScienceCartoonsPlus.com

nativist theory The view that language development is best explained as an innate, biological capacity.

genetic dysphasia A syndrome characterized by an inability to learn the grammatical structure of language, despite having otherwise normal intelligence.

Immigrants who learn English as a second language are more proficient if they start to learn English before puberty, rather than after. Spencer Grant/PhotoEdit

How does the evolution of the Nicaraguan deaf children's sign language support the interactionist explanation of language development? Susan Meiselas/ Magnum

Ozyurek, 2004). Prior to about 1980, deaf children in Nicaragua stayed at home and usually had little contact with other deaf individuals. In 1981, some deaf children began to attend a new vocational school. At first, the school did not teach a formal sign language, and none of the children had learned to sign at home, but the children gradually began to communicate using hand signals that they invented. Initially, the gestures were simple, but over the past 30 years, their sign language has developed considerably, and now it contains many of the same features as more mature languages, including signs to describe complex concepts (Pyers et al., 2010). These acts of creation nicely illustrate the interplay of nativism (the predisposition to use language) and experience (growing up in an insulated deaf culture).

Language Development and the Brain

aphasia Difficulty in producing or comprehending language.

Figure 9.3 BROCA'S AND WERNICKE'S AREAS Neuroscientists study people with brain damage in order to better understand how the brain normally operates. When Broca's area is damaged, people have a hard time producing sentences. When Wernicke's area is damaged, people can produce sentences, but they tend to be meaningless.

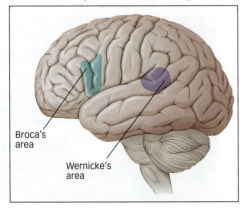

Broca's area

Wernicke's area

In early infancy, language processing is distributed across many areas of the brain. But language processing gradually becomes more and more concentrated in two areas, Broca's area and Wernicke's area. *Broca's area* is located in the left frontal cortex and is involved in the production of the sequential patterns in vocal and sign languages (see **FIGURE 9.3**). *Wernicke's area*, located in the left temporal cortex, is involved in language comprehension (whether spoken or signed). Together, Broca's area and Wernicke's area are sometimes referred to as the language centers of the brain; damage to them results in a serious condition called **aphasia**, *difficulty in producing or comprehending language.* As you saw in the Psychology: Evolution of a Science chapter, patients with damage to Broca's area understand language relatively well, although they have increasing comprehension difficulty as grammatical structures get more complex. But their real struggle is with speech production. Typically, they speak in short, staccato phrases that consist mostly of content morphemes: "Ah, Monday, uh, Casey park. Two, uh, friends, and, uh, 30 minutes." On the other hand, patients with damage to Wernicke's area can produce grammatical speech, but it tends to be meaningless: "Feel very well. In other words, I used to be able to work cigarettes. I don't know how. Things I couldn't hear from are here."

As important as Broca's and Wernicke's areas are for language, they are not the entire story. A number of neuroimaging studies have revealed evidence of right-hemisphere activation during language tasks, and individuals with damage to the right hemisphere sometimes have subtle problems with language.

Brain changes also appear to account for the fact that children who are fluent in two languages score higher than monolingual children on several measures of

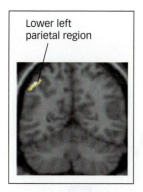

Lower left parietal region

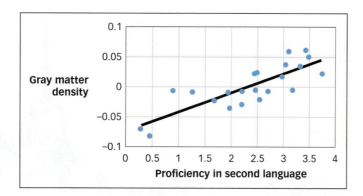

Figure 9.4 BILINGUALISM ALTERS BRAIN STRUCTURE Learning a second language early in life increases the density of gray matter in the brain. (a) A view of the lower left parietal region, which has denser gray matter in bilingual relative to monolingual individuals. (b) As proficiency in a second language increases, so does the density of gray matter in the lower parietal region. People who acquired a second language earlier in life were also found to have denser gray matter in this region. Interestingly, this area corresponds to the same area that is activated during verbal fluency tasks (Mechelli et al., 2004). Reprinted by permission from Macmillan Publishers Ltd: Structural plasticity in the bilingual brain, Mechelli, et al., 2004 *NATURE* 431, 157, Fig.1A.; Data from © Mechelli et al., Structural Plasticity in the Bilingual Brain, 2004. *NATURE*, 431, 157, Fig. 1A.

cognitive functioning, including executive control capacities such as the ability to prioritize information and flexibly focus attention (Bialystok, 1999, 2009; Bialystok, Craik, & Luk, 2012). The idea here is that bilingual individuals benefit from exerting executive control in their daily lives when they attempt to suppress the language that they don't want to use. Research shows that learning a second language produces lasting changes in the brain (Mechelli et al., 2004; Stein et al., 2009). For example, the gray matter in a part of the left parietal lobe that is involved in language is denser in bilingual than in monolingual individuals, and the increased density is most pronounced in those who are most proficient in using their second language (Mechelli et al., 2004; see **FIGURE 9.4**).

BUILD TO THE OUTCOMES

1. What are language and grammar?

2. What is a distinction between human language and animal communication?

3. Is the meaning of a sentence more memorable than how the sentence is worded?

4. What language ability do infants have that adults do not?

5. What are the language milestones?

6. How do children learn and use grammatical rules?

7. What is the role of cognitive development in acquiring language?

8. How do behaviorists, nativists, and interactionists explain language development?

9. What are Broca's and Wernicke's areas?

10. How does bilingualism influence brain structure?

Concepts and Categories: How We Think

A 69-year-old man known by the initials JB went for a neurological assessment because he was having difficulty understanding the meaning of words, even though he still performed well on many other perceptual and cognitive tasks. Over the next few years, his color language deteriorated dramatically; he had great difficulty naming colors and could not even match objects with their typical colors (e.g., strawberry and red, banana and yellow). Yet he could still classify colors normally, sorting color patches into groups of green, yellow, red, and blue in the exact same manner that healthy participants did. JB retained an intact concept of colors despite the decline of his language ability—a finding that suggests that we need to look at factors in addition to language in order to understand concepts (Haslam et al., 2007).

LEARNING OUTCOMES

- Identify why concepts are fundamental to our ability to think.

- Compare the family resemblance, prototype, and exemplar theories of concepts.

- Describe the involvement of the brain in organizing and processing concepts.

concept A mental representation that groups or categorizes shared features of related objects, events, or other stimuli.

family resemblance theory The concept that members of a category have features that appear to be characteristic of category members but may not be possessed by every member.

prototype The "best" or "most typical" member of a category.

"Attention, everyone! I'd like to introduce the newest member of our family."

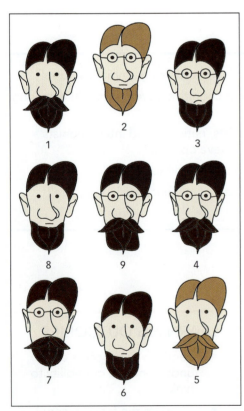

Figure 9.5 FAMILY RESEMBLANCE THEORY The family resemblance here is unmistakable, even though no two Smith brothers share all the family features. The prototype is brother 9. He has it all: brown hair, large ears, large nose, mustache, and glasses.

A **concept** is *a mental representation that groups or categorizes shared features of related objects, events, or other stimuli.* Our category for *chair* may be something like "sturdy, flat-bottomed thing you can sit on." Our category for *bird* may be something like "small, winged, beaked creature that flies." We form these categories in large part by noticing similarities among objects and events that we experience in everyday life. Concepts are fundamental to our ability to think and make sense of the world.

Psychological Theories of Concepts and Categories

What is your definition of *dog*? Can you come up with a rule of "dogship" that includes all dogs and excludes all non-dogs? Most people can't, but they still use the term *dog* intelligently, easily classifying objects as dogs or non-dogs. Three theories seek to explain how people perform these acts of categorization.

1. **Family resemblance theory** focuses on *features that appear to be characteristic of category members but may not be possessed by every member* (Rosch, 1973, 1975; Rosch & Mervis, 1975; Wittgenstein, 1953/1999). For example, you and your brother may have your mother's eyes, although you and your sister may have your father's high cheekbones. There is a strong family resemblance among you, your parents, and your siblings despite the fact that there is no necessarily defining feature that you all have in common. Similarly, many members of the *bird* category have feathers and wings, so these are the characteristic features. Anything that has these features is likely to be classified as a bird because of this "family resemblance" to other members of the *bird* category (see **FIGURE 9.5**).

2. **Prototype theory** is based on *the "best" or "most typical" member of a category.* A prototype possesses most (or all) of the most characteristic features of the category. For North Americans, the prototype of the *bird* category would be something like a wren: a small animal with feathers and wings that flies through the air, lays eggs, and migrates (see **FIGURE 9.6**). People make category judgments by comparing new instances with the category's prototype. According to *prototype theory*, if your prototypical bird is a robin, then a canary would be considered a better example of a bird than would an ostrich, because a canary has more features in common with a robin than an ostrich does.

Properties	Generic bird	Wren	Blue heron	Golden eagle	Domestic goose	Penguin
Flies regularly	✔	✔	✔	✔		
Sings	✔	✔	✔			
Lays eggs	✔	✔	✔	✔	✔	✔
Is small	✔	✔				
Nests in trees	✔	✔				

Figure 9.6 CRITICAL FEATURES OF A CATEGORY We tend to think of a generic bird as possessing a number of critical features, but not every bird possesses all of those features. In North America, a wren is a better example of a bird than is a penguin or an ostrich.

3. **Exemplar theory** holds that *we make category judgments by comparing a new instance with stored memories for other instances of the category* (Medin & Schaffer, 1978). Imagine that you're out walking in the woods, and from the corner of your eye you spot a four-legged animal that might be a wolf but that reminds you of your cousin's German shepherd. You figure it must be a dog and continue to enjoy your walk, rather than fleeing in a panic. You probably categorized this new animal as a dog because it bore a striking resemblance to other dogs you've encountered; in other words, it was a good example (or an *exemplar*) of the category *dog*. Exemplar theory does a better job than prototype theory of accounting for certain aspects of categorization, especially in that we recall not only what a *prototypical* dog looks like but also what *specific* dogs look like. **FIGURE 9.7** on page 280 illustrates the difference between prototype theory and exemplar theory.

exemplar theory A theory of categorization that argues that we make category judgments by comparing a new instance with stored memories of other instances of the category.

Concepts, Categories, and the Brain

Researchers using neuroimaging techniques have concluded that we use both prototypes and exemplars when forming concepts and categories. The visual cortex is involved in forming prototypes, whereas the prefrontal cortex and basal ganglia are involved in learning exemplars (Ashby & Ell, 2001; Ashby & O'Brien, 2005).

"Don't panic. It's only a prototype."

Robert Mankoff/The New Yorker Collection/ Cartoonbank.com

Figure 9.7 PROTOTYPE THEORY AND EXEMPLAR THEORY According to prototype theory, we classify new objects by comparing them to the "prototype" (or most typical) member of a category. According to exemplar theory, we classify new objects by comparing them with all category members. GK Hart/Vikki Hart/Stone/Getty Images; age fotostock/Superstock; imageBRO-KER/Alamy; Pixtal/Pixtal/Superstock; Juniors Bildarchiv/F237/Alamy; otsphoto/Shutterstock

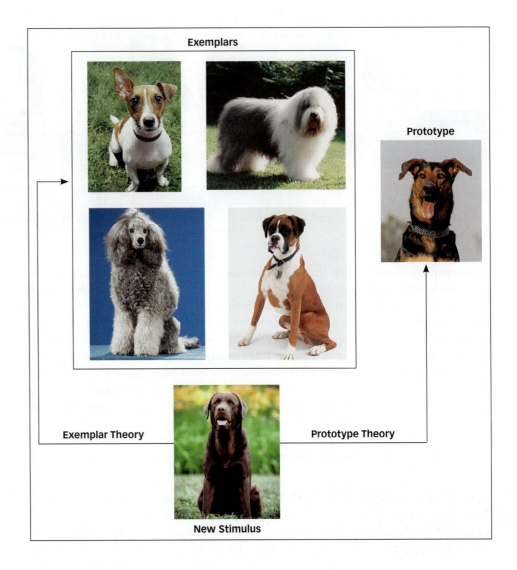

This evidence suggests that exemplar-based learning involves analysis and decision making (prefrontal cortex), whereas prototype formation is a more holistic process involving image processing (visual cortex).

Some of the most striking evidence linking concepts and categories with the brain comes from patients with brain damage. For example, one patient could not recognize a variety of human-made objects or retrieve any information about them, but his knowledge of living things and foods was perfectly normal (Warrington & McCarthy, 1983). Other patients exhibit the reverse pattern: They can recognize information about human-made objects but not living things and foods (Martin & Caramazza, 2003; Warrington & Shallice, 1984). Such unusual cases became the basis for a syndrome called **category-specific deficit**, *an inability to recognize objects that belong to a particular category, although the ability to recognize objects outside the category is undisturbed.*

The type of category-specific deficit suffered depends on where the brain is damaged. Damage to the front part of the left temporal lobe results in difficulty identifying humans; damage to the lower left temporal lobe results in difficulty identifying animals; damage to the region where the temporal lobe meets the occipital and parietal lobes impairs the ability to retrieve names of tools (Damasio et al., 1996). Similarly, when healthy people undertake the same task, imaging studies have demonstrated that the same regions of the brain are more active during naming of tools than during naming of animals and vice versa, as shown in **FIGURE 9.8** (Martin, 2007; Martin & Chao, 2001).

category-specific deficit A neurological syndrome that is characterized by an inability to recognize objects that belong to a particular category, although the ability to recognize objects outside the category is undisturbed.

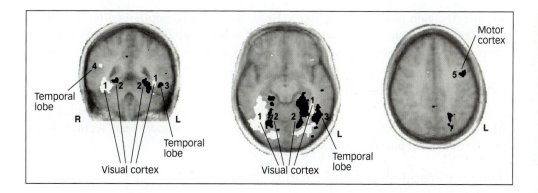

Figure 9.8 BRAIN AREAS INVOLVED IN CATEGORY-SPECIFIC PROCESSING Participants were asked to silently name pictures of animals and tools while they underwent fMRI scanning. The fMRIs revealed greater activity in areas of the visual cortex (white) when participants named animals, while other areas in visual cortex, temporal lobe, and motor cortex (black) showed greater activity when participants named tools. Note that the images are left/right reversed. Republished with permission of Alex Martin and Linda Chao, from *Current Opinions Neurobiology* 2001, 11:194–20; permission conveyed through Copyright Clearance Center, Inc.

How do particular brain regions develop category preferences for objects such as tools or animals? In one fMRI study, blind and sighted individuals each heard a series of words referring to animals and tools (Mahon et al., 2009). In both groups, category-preferential regions in the visual cortex and temporal lobe responded to animals and tools in much the same manner as shown in Figure 9.8. These results provide compelling evidence that category-specific organization of visual regions does not depend on an individual's visual experience. The simplest explanation may be that category-specific brain organization is innately determined (Bedny & Saxe, 2012; Mahon et al., 2009).

BUILD TO THE OUTCOMES

1. What are concepts?

2. Why are concepts useful to us?

3. How do the family resemblance, prototype, and exemplar theories differ?

4. How do prototypes and exemplars relate to each other?

5. What evidence suggests that the brain is "prewired" to organize perceptual and sensory inputs?

6. What is the role of vision in category-specific organization?

Decision Making: Rational and Otherwise

We use categories and concepts to guide the hundreds of decisions and judgments we make during the course of an average day. Some decisions are easy (what to wear; what to eat for breakfast; whether to walk or drive to class) and some are more difficult (which car to buy, which apartment to rent, and even which job to take after graduation). Some decisions are based on sound judgments. Others are not.

The Rational Ideal

Economists contend that if we are rational and are free to make our own decisions, we will behave as predicted by **rational choice theory**: *We make decisions by determining how likely something is to happen, judging the value of the outcome, and then multiplying the two* (Edwards, 1955). This means that our judgments will vary depending on the value we assign to the possible outcomes. Suppose, for example, that you were asked to choose between a 10% chance of gaining $500 and a 20% chance of gaining $2,000. The rational person would choose the second alternative because the expected payoff is $400 ($2,000 × 20%), whereas the first offers

LEARNING OUTCOMES

- Explain why people sometimes fail to make rational decisions.

- Describe the role of the brain in decision making.

rational choice theory The classical view that we make decisions by determining how likely something is to happen, judging the value of the outcome, and then multiplying the two.

People don't always make rational choices. When a lottery jackpot is larger than usual, more people will buy lottery tickets, thinking that they might well win big. However, more people buying lottery tickets reduces the likelihood of any one person winning the lottery. Ironically, people have a better chance at winning a lottery with a relatively small jackpot. Santa Rosa Press Democrat/ZUMAPRESS.com/Alamy

an expected gain of only $50 ($500 × 10%). Selecting the option with the highest expected value seems very straightforward. But how well does this theory describe decision making in our everyday lives? In many cases, the answer is not very well.

The Irrational Reality

Is the ability to classify new events and objects into categories always a useful skill? Alas, no. The same principles that allow cognition to occur easily and accurately can pop up to bedevil our decision making.

Judging Frequencies and Probabilities

Consider the following list of words:

> *block table block pen telephone block disk glass table block*
> *telephone block watch table candy*

You probably noticed that the words *block* and *table* occur more frequently than the other words do. In fact, studies have shown that people are quite good at estimating *frequency*, or the number of times something will happen. In contrast, we perform poorly on tasks that require us to think in terms of *probabilities*, or the likelihood that something will happen.

In one experiment, 100 physicians were asked to predict the incidence of breast cancer among women whose mammograms showed possible evidence of breast cancer. The physicians were told to take into consideration the rarity of breast cancer (1% of the population at the time the study was done) and radiologists' record in diagnosing the condition (correctly recognized only 79% of the time and falsely diagnosed almost 10% of the time). Of the 100 physicians, 95 estimated the probability that cancer was present to be about 75%! The correct answer was 8% (Eddy, 1982). But dramatically different results were obtained when the study was repeated using *frequency* information instead of *probability* information. Stating the problem as "10 out of every 1,000 women actually have breast cancer" instead of "1% of women actually have breast cancer" led 46% of the physicians to derive the right answer (Hoffrage & Gigerenzer, 1998). This finding suggests, at a minimum, that when seeking advice (even from a highly skilled decision maker), make sure your problem is described using frequencies, rather than probabilities.

availability bias The concept that items that are more readily available in memory are judged as having occurred more frequently.

Availability Bias

Take a look at the list of names in **FIGURE 9.9**. Now look away from the figure and estimate the number of male names and female names you saw. Did you notice that some of the women on the list are famous and none of the men are? Was your estimate off because you thought the list contained more women's than men's names (Tversky & Kahneman, 1973, 1974)? People typically fall prey to **availability bias**: *Items that are more readily available in memory are judged as having occurred more frequently.*

The availability bias affects our estimates because memory strength and frequency of occurrence are directly related. Frequently occurring items are remembered more easily than *in*frequently occurring items, so you naturally conclude that items for which you have better memory must also have been more frequent. Unfortunately, better memory in this case was not due to greater *frequency*, but to greater *familiarity*.

Jennifer Aniston	Robert Kingston
Judy Smith	Gilbert Chapman
Frank Carson	Gwyneth Paltrow
Elizabeth Taylor	Martin Mitchell
Daniel Hunt	Thomas Hughes
Henry Vaughan	Michael Drayton
Agatha Christie	Julia Roberts
Arthur Hutchinson	Hillary Clinton
Jennifer Lopez	Jack Lindsay
Allen Nevins	Richard Gilder
Jane Austen	George Nathan
Joseph Litton	Britney Spears

Figure 9.9 AVAILABILITY BIAS
Looking at this list of names, estimate the number of women's and men's names.

The Conjunction Fallacy

Consider the following description:

> Linda is 31 years old, single, outspoken, and very bright. In college, she majored in philosophy. As a student, she was deeply concerned with issues of discrimination and social justice and also participated in antinuclear demonstrations.

Which state of affairs is more probable?

    a. Linda is a bank teller.

    b. Linda is a bank teller and is active in the feminist movement.

In one study, 89% of participants rated option b as more probable than option a (Tversky & Kahneman, 1983).

    This situation is called the **conjunction fallacy** because *people think that two events are more likely to occur together than is either individual event.* Actually, the reverse is true: The probability of two or more events occurring simultaneously (in conjunction) is always *less* than the probability of either event occurring alone, as you can see in **FIGURE 9.10**.

Representativeness Heuristic

Think about the following situation:

    A panel of psychologists wrote descriptions of 100 people, including 70 engineers and 30 lawyers. You will be shown a random selection of these descriptions. Read each and then pause and decide if it is more likely that the person is an engineer or a lawyer.

    1. Jack enjoys reading books on social and political issues. During the interview, he displayed particular skill at argument.

    2. Tom is a loner who enjoys working on mathematical puzzles during his spare time. During the interview, his speech remained fairly abstract and his emotions were well controlled.

    3. Harry is a bright man and an avid racquetball player. During the interview, he asked many insightful questions and was very well spoken.

    Research participants were shown a series of descriptions like these; the majority thought Jack was more likely to be a lawyer, and Tom more likely to be an engineer. Harry's description doesn't sound like a lawyer's or an engineer's, so most people said he was *equally likely* to hold either occupation (Kahneman & Tversky, 1973). But remember that the pool of descriptions contains more than twice as many engineers as lawyers, so based on this proportion it is far *more* likely that Harry is an engineer. People seem to ignore information about *base rate* and instead base their judgments on similarities to categories. Researchers call this the **representativeness heuristic**: *making a probability judgment by comparing an object or event with a prototype of the object or event* (Kahneman & Tversky, 1973).

Framing Effects

If people are told that a particular drug has a 70% effectiveness rate, they're usually pretty impressed. Tell them instead that a drug has a 30% failure rate, and they typically perceive it as risky and potentially harmful. Notice that the information is the same: A 70% effectiveness rate means that 30% of the time, it's ineffective. The way the information is presented, however, leads to substantially different conclusions (Tversky & Kahneman, 1981). This is called the **framing effect**, which occurs when *people give different answers to the same problem, depending on how the problem is phrased (or framed).*

    One of the most striking framing effects is the **sunk-cost fallacy**, which occurs when *people make decisions about a current situation on the basis of what they have previously invested in the situation.* Imagine waiting in line for 3 hours, paying $100 for a ticket to see your favorite band, and waking on the day of the outdoor concert to find that it's bitterly cold and rainy. If you go, you'll feel miserable. But you go anyway, reasoning that the $100 you paid for the ticket and the time you spent in line will have been wasted if you stay home.

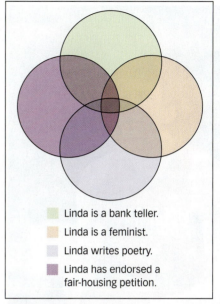

Linda is a bank teller.

Linda is a feminist.

Linda writes poetry.

Linda has endorsed a fair-housing petition.

Figure 9.10 THE CONJUNCTION FALLACY People often think that with each additional bit of information, the probability that all the facts are simultaneously true of a person increases. In fact, the probability decreases dramatically. Notice how the intersection of all these possibilities is much smaller than the area of any one possibility alone.

conjunction fallacy When people think that two events are more likely to occur together than is either individual event.

representativeness heuristic A mental shortcut that involves making a probability judgment by comparing an object or event with a prototype of the object or event.

framing effects A bias whereby people give different answers to the same problem, depending on how the problem is phrased (or framed).

sunk-cost fallacy A framing effect in which people make decisions about a current situation on the basis of what they have previously invested in the situation.

Worth the cost? Sports teams sometimes try to justify their investment in an expensive player who is underperforming, an example of a sunk-cost effect. Ömer Aşik is a highly paid basketball player, but his recent performance has not lived up to his salary. Joe Robbins/Getty Images

prospect theory The theory that people choose to take on risk when evaluating potential losses and avoid risks when evaluating potential gains.

optimism bias A bias whereby people believe that, compared with other people, they are more likely to experience positive events and less likely to experience negative events in the future.

Notice that you have two choices: (1) Stay comfortably at home; or (2) endure many uncomfortable hours in the rain. The $100 is gone in either case: It's a sunk cost, irretrievable at the moment of your decision. But because you invested time and money, you feel obligated to follow through, even though it's something you no longer want.

Even the National Basketball Association (NBA) is guilty of a sunk-cost fallacy. Coaches should play their most productive players and keep them on the team longer, but they don't. The most *expensive* players are given more time on court and are kept on the team longer than cheaper players, even if the costly players are not performing up to par (Staw & Hoang, 1995). Coaches act to justify their team's investment in an expensive player, rather than recognize the loss. Framing effects can be costly!

Another kind of framing effect occurs when information is presented in terms of losses instead of in terms of savings. For example, imagine that you're renting a new apartment and, as part of a promotion, you're given a choice between a $300 rebate on your first month's rent or spinning a wheel that offers an 80% chance of getting a $400 rebate. Which would you choose? If you're like most people, you'll choose the sure $300 over the risky $400.

But suppose that the lease offers you a choice of penalty for damaging the apartment: either $300, or spin a wheel that offers an 80% chance of a $400 fine. Now which would you choose? Most people will choose to gamble by spinning the wheel, taking the chance of avoiding the fine altogether, even though the odds are they'll wind up paying more than the sure $300.

Prospect theory states that *people choose to take on risk when evaluating potential losses and avoid risks when evaluating potential gains* (Tversky & Kahneman, 1992). This asymmetry in risk preferences shows that we are willing to take on risk if we think it will ward off a loss, but we're risk-averse if we expect to lose some benefits.

Optimism Bias

In addition to the biases we've just considered, human decision making often reflects the effects of **optimism bias**: *People believe that, compared with other people, they are more likely to experience positive events and less likely to experience negative events in the future* (Sharot, 2011). For example, compared with others, people believe that they are more likely to own their own homes and live a long life, and that they are less likely to have a heart attack or a drinking problem (Weinstein, 1980). Although optimism about the future is often a good thing for our mental and physical health—optimistic individuals are usually well adjusted psychologically and are able to handle stress well (Nes & Sergerstrom, 2006)—too much optimism can be detrimental because it may prevent us from taking the necessary steps to achieve our goals.

Decision Making and the Brain

A man identified as Elliot was a successful businessman, husband, and father prior to developing a brain tumor. After surgery, his intellectual abilities seemed intact, but he was unable to differentiate between important and unimportant activities and would spend hours at mundane tasks. He lost his job and got involved in several risky financial ventures that bankrupted him. He had no difficulty discussing what had happened, but his descriptions were so detached and dispassionate that it seemed as though his abstract intellectual functions had become dissociated from his social and emotional abilities.

Research confirms that this interpretation of Elliot's downfall is right on track. In one study, researchers looked at how healthy volunteers differed from people with prefrontal lobe damage on a gambling task that involves risky decision making

(Bechara et al., 1994, 1997). Participants were allowed to choose cards one at a time from any of four decks; each card specified an amount of play money won or lost. Unbeknownst to the participants, two of the decks usually provided large payoffs or large losses (the "risky" decks), whereas the other two provided smaller payoffs and losses (the "safe" decks). Early on, participants chose from each deck equally, but healthy participants gradually shifted to choosing primarily from the safer decks. In contrast, patients with prefrontal damage continued to select equally from the risky and safe decks, leading most to eventually go bankrupt in the game. This performance mirrors Elliot's real-life problems. The healthy participants' galvanic skin responses (GSRs) also jumped dramatically when they were thinking about choosing a card from the risky deck—an anticipatory emotional reaction (Bechara et al., 1997). The participants with prefrontal damage didn't show these anticipatory feelings when they were thinking about selecting a card from the risky deck. Apparently, their emotional reactions did not guide their thinking, so they continued to make risky decisions, as shown in **FIGURE 9.11**.

The risky decision making by participants with prefrontal damage seems to grow out of insensitivity to the future consequences of their behavior (Naqvi, Shiv, & Bechara, 2006). Unable to think beyond immediate consequences, they cannot shift their choices in response to a rising rate of losses or a declining rate of rewards (Bechara, Tranel, & Damasio, 2000). Interestingly, substance-dependent individuals, such as alcoholics, binge eaters, and cocaine addicts, act the same way. Most perform as poorly on the gambling task as do individuals with prefrontal damage (Bechara et al., 2001; Johnson, Xiao, et al., 2008). These findings have potentially important implications for such everyday issues as road safety. In one study, people who had been convicted of driving while impaired with alcohol (DWI) were tested on the gambling task. Offenders who performed poorly on the gambling task were

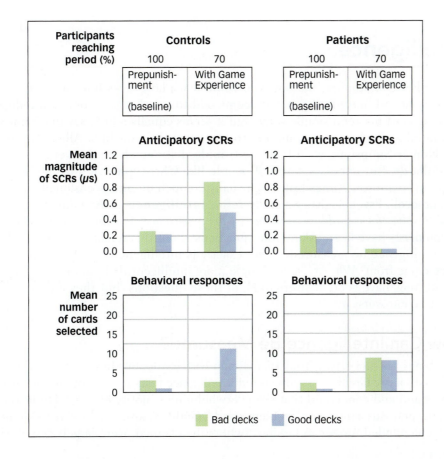

Figure 9.11 THE NEUROSCIENCE OF RISKY DECISION MAKING In a study of risky decision making, participants played a game in which they selected a card from one of four decks. Two of the decks were made up of riskier cards that provided large payoffs or large losses. The other two contained safer cards with much smaller payoffs and losses. At the beginning of the game, both groups chose cards from all four decks with equal frequency. Over the course of the game, healthy participants avoided the riskier decks and showed large emotional responses (SCRs, or skin conductance responses) when they considered choosing a card from a riskier deck. Participants with prefrontal brain damage, on the other hand, continued to choose cards from all four decks with equal frequency and showed no evidence of emotional learning and eventually went bankrupt (data from Bechara et al., 1997).

much more likely to commit repeated DWI offenses than those who performed well on the gambling task (Bouchard, Brown, & Nadeau, 2012). Related work has documented gambling-task impairments in binge eaters, another group in which there is an insensitivity to the future consequences of behavior (Danner et al., 2012).

Neuroimaging studies of healthy individuals show that, during the gambling task, an area in the prefrontal cortex is activated when participants make risky decisions as compared with safe decisions. Indeed, the activated region is in the part of the prefrontal cortex that is typically damaged in participants who perform poorly on the gambling task, and greater activation in this region is correlated with better task performance in healthy individuals (Fukui et al., 2005; Lawrence et al., 2009). Taken together, the neuroimaging and lesion studies show clearly that aspects of risky decision making depend critically on the contributions of the prefrontal cortex.

BUILD TO THE OUTCOMES

1. What is the importance of rational choices in decision making?

2. Why is a better decision more likely when we consider frequency, rather than the likelihood that something will happen?

3. How are memory strength and frequency of occurrence related?

4. How can more information sometimes lead people to wrong conclusions?

5. What can cause people to ignore the base rate of an event?

6. How does framing a problem differently influence one's answer?

7. Why will most people take more risks to avoid losses than to make gains?

8. What role does the prefrontal cortex play in risky behavior?

Intelligence

LEARNING OUTCOMES

- Explain how and why intelligence tests were developed.

- Explain why intelligence matters.

- Describe the kinds of intelligence that IQ tests do and do not measure.

intelligence The ability to use one's mind to solve novel problems and learn from experience.

Remember Christopher, the boy who could learn languages but not tic-tac-toe? Would you call him intelligent? It seems odd to say that someone is intelligent when he can't master a simple game, but it seems equally odd to say that someone is unintelligent when he can master 16 languages. In a world of Albert Einsteins and Homer Simpsons, we'd have no trouble distinguishing the geniuses from the dullards. But ours is a world of people like Christopher and people like us: people who are sometimes brilliant, usually competent, and occasionally dimmer than broccoli. Psychologists generally define **intelligence** as *the ability to use one's mind to solve novel problems and learn from experience*. For more than a century, psychologists have been asking four questions about this remarkable ability: *How* can intelligence be measured? *What* exactly is intelligence? *Where* does intelligence come from? *Why* are some people more intelligent than others? As you will see, we now have good answers to all of these questions, but they did not come without controversy.

How Can Intelligence Be Measured?

Few things are more dangerous than a man with a mission. In the 1920s, the psychologist Henry Goddard administered intelligence tests to arriving immigrants at Ellis Island and concluded that the overwhelming majority of Jews, Hungarians, Italians, and Russians were "feebleminded." Goddard also used his tests to identify feebleminded American families (whom, he claimed, were largely responsible

MEANS PROPOSED FOR CUTTING OFF THE SUPPLY OF HUMAN DEFECTIVES AND DEGENERATES

I. LIFE SEGREGATION

II. STERILIZATION

III. RESTRICTIVE MARRIAGE

IV. EUGENIC EDUCATION

V. SYSTEM OF MATINGS

VI. GENERAL ENVIRONMENTAL

VII. POLYGAMY

VIII. EUTHANASIA

IX. NEO-MALTHUSIAN DOCTRINE

X. LAISSEZ-FAIRE

Which of these remedies shall be applied? Shall one, two, several or all be made to operate.

What are the limitations and possibilities of each remedy?

Shall one class of the socially unfit be treated with one remedy and another with a different one?

Shall the specifically selected remedy be applied to the class or to the individual?

What are the principles and the limits of compromise between conservation and elimination in cases of individuals bearing a germ-plasm with a mixture of the determiners for both defective and sterling traits.

What are the criteria for the identification of individuals bearing defective germ-plasm.

What can be hoped from the application of some definite elimination program?

What practical difficulties stand in the way? How can they be overcome?

During the early 20th century, laws required the involuntary sterilization of people with low intelligence. These laws were widely supported, and the U.S. Supreme Court upheld their constitutionality. As Chief Justice Oliver Wendell Holmes declared in 1927, "Three generations of imbeciles are enough." The Harry H. Laughlin Papers, Truman State University

for the nation's social problems) and suggested that the government should segregate them in isolated colonies and "take away from these people the power of procreation" (Goddard, 1913, p. 107). The United States subsequently passed laws restricting the immigration of people from southern and eastern Europe, and the majority of U.S. states passed laws requiring the sterilization of "mental defectives."

From Goddard's day to our own, intelligence tests have been used to rationalize prejudice and discrimination against people of different races, religions, and nationalities. This is especially ironic because those tests were originally developed for the noblest of purposes: to help underprivileged children succeed in school. At the end of the 19th century, France instituted a sweeping set of social reforms that for the first time required all boys and girls between the ages of 6 and 13 to attend school. The problem was that not all children of the same age were equally prepared to learn. The French psychologist Alfred Binet thought that schools should use

 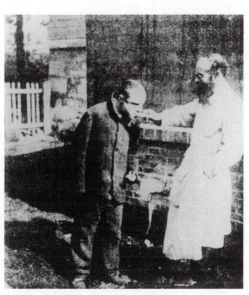

Alfred Binet (1857–1911; *left*) and Théodore Simon (1872–1961; *right*) developed the first intelligence test to identify children who needed remedial education. Corbis; The Drs. Nicholas and Dorothy Cummings Center for the History of Psychology, The University of Akron

In 2012, 4-year-old Heidi Hankins became one of the youngest people ever admitted to Mensa, an organization for people with unusually high IQs. Heidi's IQ is 159—about the same as Albert Einstein's. Solent News/Rex Features/AP Images

intelligence quotient (or IQ) A statistic obtained by dividing an adult's test score by the average adult's test score and then multiplying the quotient by 100.

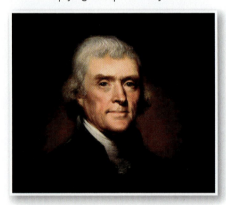

Intelligence is a good predictor of success. Thomas Jefferson is considered the most intelligent of all U.S presidents, and Calvin Coolidge is considered the least intelligent (Simonton, 2006). Jefferson gave us the Declaration of Independence and Coolidge gave us the Great Depression. John Parrot/Stocktrek Images/Getty Images; Stock Montage / Getty Images

objective methods to assess each child's ability to learn, and so he and his student, Théodore Simon, created a series of tasks that the most able children could perform well and that the least able children could not. These tasks included solving logic problems, remembering words, copying pictures, distinguishing edible and inedible foods, making rhymes, and answering questions such as "Before deciding something important, what should you do?"

One of the best things about Binet and Simon's tasks is that psychologists could use them to estimate each student's "mental level" simply by computing the average score of many students in different age groups, and then finding the age group whose average score best matched the score of the particular student. For example, a 10-year-old child whose score was about the same as the average score of all 8-year-olds was said to have the mental level of an 8-year-old. However, psychologists quickly realized that comparing mental age with chronological age works well for kids, but doesn't work very well for adults because adults of different ages don't have remarkably different intellectual capacities. To solve this problem, psychologists began to compute what is now known as the **intelligence quotient** (or **IQ**), which is *a statistic obtained by dividing an adult's test score by the average adult's test score and then multiplying the quotient by 100.* Instead of comparing a person's mental age with her physical age, the IQ score compares her performance with the performance of others. An adult who scores the same as the average adult has an IQ of 100.

The Intelligence Test

Most modern intelligence tests have their roots in the test that Binet and Simon developed more than a century ago. The most widely used modern intelligence tests are the *Wechsler Adult Intelligence Scale* (WAIS) and the *Wechsler Intelligence Scale for Children* (WISC), which are named after their originator, psychologist David Wechsler. Like Binet and Simon's original test, the WAIS and the WISC measure intelligence by asking people to answer questions and solve problems, to see similarities and differences between ideas and objects, to define words, to recall general knowledge, and so forth. Some sample problems from the WAIS are shown in **TABLE 9.2**.

Decades of research show that a person's performance on tests like the WAIS predict an astonishing number of important life outcomes (Deary, Batty, Pattie, & Gale, 2008; Der, Batty, & Deary, 2009; Gottfredson & Deary, 2004; Leon et al., 2009; Richards et al., 2009; Rushton & Templer, 2009; Whalley & Deary, 2001). For example, one study that compared siblings who had significantly different IQs found that the less intelligent sibling earned roughly half of what the more intelligent sibling earned over the course of their lifetimes (Murray, 2002; see **FIGURE 9.12**). In part, this is because intelligent people are more patient, better at calculating risk, and better at predicting how other people will act and how they should respond (Burks et al., 2009). But the main reason that intelligent people earn more money than their less intelligent counterparts (or siblings!) is that they get more education (Deary et al., 2005; Nyborg & Jensen, 2001) and perform better in school (Roth et al., 2015).

Intelligent people aren't just wealthier; they are healthier as well. Researchers who have followed millions of people over decades have found a strong correlation between intelligence and health (Calvin et al., 2011; Wraw et al., 2015). Intelligent people are less likely to smoke and drink alcohol and are more likely to exercise and eat well (Batty et al., 2007; Ciarrochi, Heaven, & Skinner, 2012; Weiser et al., 2010). Not surprisingly, they also live longer (Calvin et al., 2010; Deary, Weiss, & Batty, 2011; Jokela et al., 2009). The bottom line is that intelligence matters for almost everything people value.

TABLE 9.2 The Tests and Core Subtests of the Wechsler Adult Intelligence Scale IV

WAIS-IV Test	Core Subtest	Questions and Tasks
Verbal Comprehension Test	Vocabulary	The test taker is asked to tell the examiner what certain words mean. For example: *chair* (easy), *hesitant* (medium), and *presumptuous* (hard).
	Similarities	The test taker is asked what 19 pairs of words have in common. For example: In what way are an apple and a pear alike? In what way are a painting and a symphony alike?
	Information	The test taker is asked several general knowledge questions. These cover people, places, and events. For example: How many days are in a week? What is the capital of France? Name three oceans. Who wrote *The Inferno*?
Perceptual Reasoning Test	Block Design	The test taker is shown 2-D patterns made up of red and white squares and triangles and is asked to reproduce these patterns using cubes with red and white faces.
	Matrix Reasoning	The test taker is asked to add a missing element to a pattern so that it progresses logically. For example: Which of the four symbols at the bottom goes in the empty cell of the table?
	Visual Puzzles	The test taker is asked to complete visual puzzles like this one: "Which three of these pictures go together to make this puzzle?"
Working Memory Test	Digit Span	The test taker is asked to repeat a sequence of numbers. Sequences run from two to nine numbers in length. In the second part of this test, the sequences must be repeated in reversed order. An easy example is to repeat 3-7-4. A harder one is 3-9-1-7-4-5-3-9.
	Arithmetic	The test taker is asked to solve arithmetic problems, progressing from easy to difficult ones.
Processing Speed Test	Symbol Search	The test taker is asked to indicate whether one of a pair of abstract symbols is contained in a list of abstract symbols. There are many of these lists, and the test taker does as many as he or she can in 2 minutes.
	Coding	The test taker is asked to write down the number that corresponds to a code for a given symbol (e.g., a cross, a circle, and an upside-down T) and does as many as he or she can in 90 seconds.

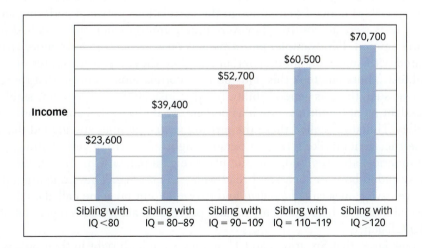

Figure 9.12 INCOME AND INTELLIGENCE AMONG SIBLINGS This graph shows the average annual salary of a person who has an IQ of 90–109 (shown in pink) and of his or her siblings who have higher or lower IQs (shown in blue).

What Is Intelligence?

Many people assume that Michael Jordan is some guy who works in Nike's Extremely Expensive Shoe Department. But in fact, during the 1990s, Michael Jordan won the National Basketball Association's Most Valuable Player award five times, led the Chicago Bulls to six league championships, and had the highest regular-season

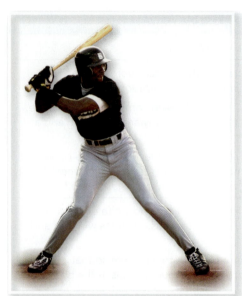

Michael Jordan was an extraordinary basketball player and a mediocre baseball player. So was he or wasn't he a great athlete? Sports Illustrated/Getty Images

The psychologist Angela Duckworth received a so-called genius award from the MacArthur Foundation for her research on how traits other than intelligence enable people to succeed. Spearman's notion of *g* suggests that because she's *really* good at psychology, she's probably *pretty* good at most other things too. Charles Sykes/NBC/NBCU Photo Bank via Getty Images

two-factor theory of intelligence Spearman's theory suggesting that a person's performance on a test is due to a combination of general ability and skills that are specific to the test.

scoring average in the history of the game. ESPN named him the greatest athlete of the century. So when Jordan quit professional basketball in 1993 to join professional baseball, he was as surprised as anyone to find that he was truly awful. One of his teammates lamented that Jordan "couldn't hit a curveball with an ironing board," and a major-league manager called him "a disgrace to the game" (Wulf, 1994). Apparently, basketball and baseball require different abilities that are not necessarily possessed by the same individual. And yet, if basketball and baseball require different abilities, then what does it mean to say that someone is the greatest athlete of the century? Is *athleticism* a meaningless abstraction? Or does it actually refer to a real ability?

The science of intelligence has grappled with a similar question for more than a hundred years. Intelligence test scores predict important outcomes, from academic success to wealth and longevity, but is that because they measure a real ability? Or is intelligence just a meaningless abstraction? If there really is a single, general ability called *intelligence* that enables people to perform a variety of intelligent behaviors, then those who have this ability should do well at just about everything, and those who lack it should do well at just about nothing. In other words, if intelligence is a single, general ability, then there should be a very strong positive correlation between people's performances on many kinds of tests.

This is precisely the hypothesis that the psychologist Charles Spearman (1904) set out to examine. He began by measuring how well school-age children could discriminate small differences in color, auditory pitch, and weight, and he then computed the correlation between these scores and the children's grades in different academic subjects. Spearman discovered that performances on these different tests were positively correlated, which is to say that children who performed well on one test (e.g., distinguishing the musical notes C# and D) tended to perform well on other tests (e.g., solving algebraic equations). But he also discovered that performances on different tests were not *perfectly* correlated. In other words, the child who had the very highest score on one test didn't necessarily have the very highest score on *every test*. Spearman combined these two facts into his **two-factor theory of intelligence**, which suggests that *a person's performance on a test is due to a combination of general ability and skills that are specific to the test*. Spearman referred to general ability as *g* and to specific ability as *s*.

As sensible as Spearman's theory was, not everyone agreed with it. Louis Thurstone (1938) noticed that although the correlations between performances on different tests were all *positive*, they were much *stronger* when the tests had something in common. For example, performances on a verbal test were more strongly correlated with scores on another verbal test than they were with scores on a perceptual test. Thurstone took this "clustering of correlations" to mean that there was actually no such thing as general ability, but that instead there were a few stable and independent mental abilities—such as perceptual ability, verbal ability, and numerical ability. Thurstone called these the *primary mental abilities* and argued that they were neither general like *g* (e.g., a person might have strong verbal abilities and weak numerical abilities), nor specific like *s* (e.g., a person who had strong verbal abilities tended both to speak and read well). In essence, Thurstone argued that just as we have games called *baseball* and *basketball* but no game called *athletics*, so we have abilities such as verbal ability and perceptual ability but no general ability called intelligence.

We now know that Spearman and Thurstone were both right in their own way. A massive re-analysis of almost every scientific study of intelligence conducted since 1900 shows that people's performances are best described by a three-level hierarchy (see **FIGURE 9.13**) with a *general factor* (much like Spearman's *g*) at the top, *specific factors* (much like Spearman's *s*) at the bottom, and a set of factors called *group*

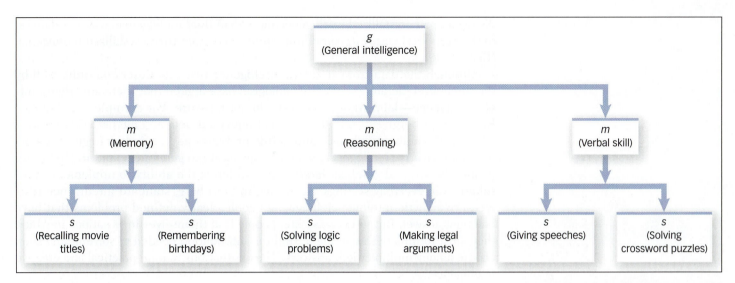

Figure 9.13 A THREE-LEVEL HIER-ARCHY Most intelligence test data are best described by a three-level hierarchy with general intelligence (*g*) at the top, specific abilities (*s*) at the bottom, and a small number of middle-level abilities (*m*) (sometimes called group factors) in the middle.

factors (much like Thurstone's *primary mental abilities*) in the middle (Carroll, 1993; Gustafsson, 1984). This hierarchy suggests that people have a very general ability called intelligence, which is made up of eight middle-level abilities, which are made up of a nearly infinite set of specific abilities that are unique to particular tasks. The eight middle-level abilities are *memory and learning, visual perception, auditory perception, retrieval ability, cognitive speediness, processing speed, crystallized intelligence,* and *fluid intelligence* (Carroll, 1993).

Although most of these abilities are self-explanatory, the last two are not (Horn & Cattell, 1966). **Crystallized intelligence** refers to *the ability to apply knowledge that was acquired through experience,* and it is generally measured with tests of vocabulary and factual information. **Fluid intelligence** refers to *the ability to solve and reason about novel problems,* and it is generally measured with tests that present people with abstract problems in new domains that must be solved under time pressure (see **FIGURE 9.14**). Problems that require crystallized or fluid intelligence appear to activate different regions of the brain. For example, both autism and Alzheimer's

crystallized intelligence The ability to apply knowledge that was acquired through experience.

fluid intelligence The ability to solve and reason about novel problems.

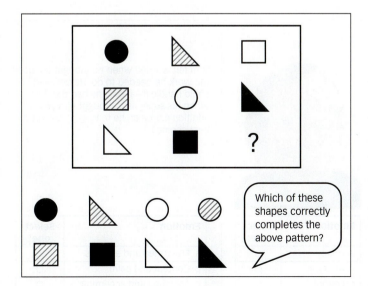

Figure 9.14 MEASURING FLUID INTELLIGENCE Problems like this one from Raven's Progressive Matrices Test (Raven, Raven, & Court, 2004) measure fluid intelligence, rather than crystallized intelligence. Raven's Progressive Matrices (Standard, Sets A-E) (SPM). Copyright © 1998, 1976, 1958, 1938 NCS Pearson, Inc. Reproduced with permission. All rights reserved. "Ravens" is a trademark, in the United States and/or other countries, of Pearson Education, Inc. or its affiliates(s).

disease impair crystallized intelligence more than fluid intelligence, whereas damage to the prefrontal cortex impairs fluid intelligence more than crystalized intelligence (Blair, 2006).

Although the data from standard intelligence tests are described quite well by the three-level hierarchy, some psychologists have argued that there are other kinds of intelligence—kinds that these tests do not measure. For example, psychologist Robert Sternberg (1999, 2006) has distinguished between *analytic intelligence*, which is the ability to identify and define problems and to find strategies for solving them; *creative intelligence*, which is the ability to generate solutions that other people do not; and *practical intelligence*, which is the ability to implement these solutions in everyday settings. According to Sternberg, standard intelligence tests measure analytic intelligence by giving people clearly defined problems that have one right answer. But in everyday life, people find themselves in situations in which they must formulate the problem, find the information needed to solve it, and then choose among multiple right answers. These situations require practical and creative intelligence.

Another kind of intelligence that standard tests don't measure is **emotional intelligence**, *the ability to reason about emotions and to use emotions to enhance reasoning* (Mayer, Roberts, & Barsade, 2008; Salovey & Grewal, 2005). Emotionally intelligent people know what kinds of emotions a particular event will trigger; they can identify, describe, and manage their emotions; and they can identify other people's emotions from facial expressions and tones of voice. Emotionally intelligent people have better social skills and more friends (Eisenberg et al., 2000; Mestre et al., 2006; Schultz, Izard, & Bear, 2004), they are judged to be more competent in their interactions (Brackett et al., 2006), and they have better romantic relationships (Brackett, Warner, & Bosco, 2005) and workplace relationships (Elfenbein et al., 2007; Lopes et al., 2006). (See The Real World: Look Smart.) Given all this, it isn't surprising that emotionally intelligent people tend to be happier (Brackett & Mayer, 2003; Brackett et al., 2006), healthier (Mikolajczak et al., 2015) and more satisfied with their lives (Ciarrochi, Chan, & Caputi, 2000; Mayer, Caruso, & Salovey, 1999).

emotional intelligence The ability to reason about emotions and to use emotions to enhance reasoning.

Two items from a test of emotional intelligence. Item 1 measures the accuracy with which a person can read emotional expressions (*left*). Item 2 measures the ability to predict emotional responses to events (*right*). The correct answer on both items is (a). Photo courtesy Daniel Gilbert. Test: Research from Mayer et al., 2008

1.

Emotion	Select one:
a. Happy	○
b. Angry	○
c. Fearful	○
d. Sad	○

2.

Tom felt worried when he thought about all the work he needed to do. He believed he could handle it—if only he had the time. When his supervisor brought him an additional project, he felt _____. (Select the best choice.)

Emotion	Select one:
a. Frustrated and anxious	○
b. Content and calm	○
c. Ashamed and accepting	○
d. Sad and guilty	○

Look Smart

Your interview is in 30 minutes. You've checked your hair twice, eaten your weight in breath mints, combed your résumé for typos, and rehearsed your answers to all the standard questions. Now you have to dazzle them with your intelligence. Because intelligence is one of the most valued of all human traits, we often try to make others think we're smart (regardless of whether that's true). So we make clever jokes and drop the names of some of the longer books we've read in the hope that prospective employers, prospective dates, prospective customers, and prospective in-laws will be appropriately impressed.

But are we doing the right things? If so, are we getting the credit we deserve? Research shows that ordinary people are, in fact, reasonably good judges of other people's intelligence (Borkenau & Liebler, 1995). For example, observers can look at a pair of photographs and reliably determine which of the two people in them is smarter (Zebrowitz et al., 2002). When observers watch 1-minute videotapes of people engaged in social interactions, they can accurately estimate which person has the highest IQ—even if they see the videos without sound (Murphy, Hall, & Colvin, 2003).

People base their judgments of intelligence on a wide range of cues, from physical features (being tall and attractive) to dress (being well groomed and wearing glasses) to behavior (walking and talking quickly). And yet none of these cues is actually a reliable indicator of a person's intelligence. The reason that people are such good judges of intelligence is that, in addition to all these useless cues, they also take into account one very useful cue: eye contact. Intelligent people hold the gaze of their conversation partners both when they are speaking and when they are listening. Observers seem to know this, which is what enables them to estimate a person's intelligence accurately, despite their mythical beliefs about the informational value of spectacles and neckties (Murphy et al., 2003). All of this is especially true when the observers are women (who tend to be better judges of intelligence) and the people being observed are men (whose intelligence tends to be easier to judge).

The bottom line? Breath mints are fine and a little gel on the cowlick certainly can't hurt, but when you get to the interview, don't forget to stare.

Wahad Mehood is interviewing for a job as a petroleum engineer with EPC Global. Studies show that when a job candidate holds an interviewer's gaze, the interviewer is more likely to consider the candidate to be intelligent. And the interviewer is right! TIM JOHNSON/AP Images

BUILD TO THE OUTCOMES

1. Why were intelligence tests originally developed?
2. What is an intelligence quotient (IQ)?
3. What important life outcomes do intelligence test scores predict?
4. What was the debate between Spearman and Thurstone and how was it resolved?
5. What are fluid and crystallized intelligences?
6. What is emotional intelligence?

Where Does Intelligence Come From?

No one is born knowing calculus, and no one has to be taught how to blink. Some things are learned, others are not. But almost all of the really *interesting* things about people are a joint product of the experiences they have had and the characteristics with which they were born. Intelligence is one of those really interesting things, and it is influenced both by nature and by nurture. Let's examine them in turn.

Nature: Genetic Influences on Intelligence

Smart parents seem to have smart kids. But the fact that intelligence appears to "run in families" isn't very good evidence of genetic influence because although family members often share genes, they also share experiences. Parents and children

LEARNING OUTCOMES

- Describe the influence of genes on intelligence.
- Explain how environmental factors influence intelligence.

Tamara Rabi and Adriana Scott were 20 years old when they met in a McDonald's parking lot in New York. "I'm just standing there looking at her," Adriana recalled. "It was a shock. I saw me" (Gootman, 2003). The two soon discovered that they were identical twins who had been separated at birth and adopted by different families. © Angel Franco/*The New York Times*/Redux

fraternal twins (or dizygotic twins) Twins who develop from two different eggs that were fertilized by two different sperm.

identical twins (or monozygotic twins) Twins who develop from the splitting of a single egg that was fertilized by a single sperm.

typically live in the same house and eat the same foods. Siblings often go to the same schools, watch the same TV shows and movies, and have many of the same friends. Family members may have similar levels of intelligence because they share genes, because they share environments, or both. If we want to study the influence of genes and environments separately, we need to study the intelligence of people who share genes but not environments; people who share environments but not genes; and people who share both.

Luckily for psychologists, different kinds of siblings have different degrees of genetic relatedness. Two siblings who have the same biological parents but different birthdays will share on average about 50% of their genes. Twins are siblings who share a birthday and they come in two kinds: **Fraternal twins** (or **dizygotic twins**) are *twins who develop from two different eggs that were fertilized by two different sperm*, and **identical twins** (or **monozygotic twins**) are *twins who develop from the splitting of a single egg that was fertilized by a single sperm.* Fraternal twins are merely siblings who happened to share a womb, and like all siblings, they share on average about 50% of their genes. But identical twins are the result of a single fertilized egg that then divided in two, so they are genetic duplicates who share 100% of their genes.

These different degrees of genetic relatedness allow psychologists to assess the influence that genes have on intelligence, and that influence turns out to be quite powerful. For example, the intelligence test scores of identical twins are about as highly correlated with each other as are the intelligence tests scores of a single individual who has taken the test twice. Large correlations are observed even between identical twins who were adopted at birth by different families and raised in different households. Indeed, identical twins who are raised apart have more similar IQs than do fraternal twins who are raised together! All of this suggests that people who share genes tend to have similar IQs, and the more genes they share, the more similar their IQs tend to be.

Nurture: Environmental Influences on Intelligence

Intelligence is influenced by genes, but it is also influenced by the environment and changes over time. For example, as **FIGURE 9.15** shows, intelligence changes over the life span, increasing between adolescence and middle age, and declining in old age (Kaufman, 2001; Owens, 1966; Salthouse, 1996a, 2000; Schaie, 1996, 2005; Schwartzman, Gold, & Andres, 1987). Intelligence also changes over generations. The *Flynn effect* refers to the fact that the average IQ score today is roughly 30 points higher than it was a century ago (Dickens & Flynn, 2001; Flynn, 2012; cf. Lynn, 2013). This means that the average person today is smarter than 95% of the people who were alive in 1900!

One of the environmental factors that most strongly influences intelligence is the material wealth of the family in which a person is raised—what scientists call *socioeconomic status* (SES). Studies suggest that being raised in a high-SES family,

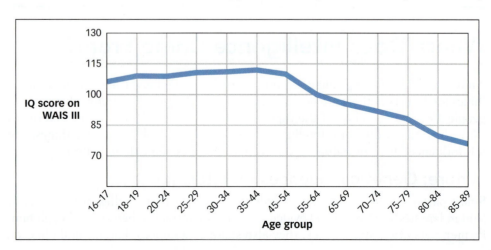

Figure 9.15 Intelligence Changes Over the Lifespan Information from Kaufman, 2001

rather than a low-SES family, is worth between 12 and 18 IQ points (Nisbett, 2009; van IJzendoorn, Juffer, & Klein Poelhuis, 2005). Low-SES children have poorer nutrition and medical care, they experience greater daily stress, and they are more likely to be exposed to environmental toxins such as air pollution and lead—all of which can impair brain development (Chen, Cohen, & Miller, 2010; Evans, 2004; Hackman & Farah, 2008). Furthermore, intellectual stimulation increases intelligence (Nelson et al., 2007), and research shows that high-SES parents are more likely to provide it (Nisbett, 2009). For instance, high-SES parents are more likely to read to their children and to connect what they are reading to the outside world ("Billy has a rubber ducky. Who do you know who has a rubber ducky?"; Heath, 1983; Lareau, 2003). When high-SES parents talk to their children, they tend to ask stimulating questions ("Do you think a ducky likes to eat grass?"), whereas low-SES parents tend to give instructions ("Please put your ducky away"; Hart & Risley, 1995). By the age of 3, the average high-SES child has heard 30 million different words, whereas the average low-SES child has heard only 10 million different words. As a result, the high-SES child knows 50% more words than his or her low-SES counterpart. Clearly, poverty is the enemy of intelligence (Evans & Kim, 2012).

And education is its friend. The correlation between the amount of formal education a person receives and his or her intelligence is quite large (Ceci, 1991; Neisser et al., 1996). One reason for this is that smart people tend to stay in school, but the other reason is that school makes people smarter (Ceci & Williams, 1997). When schooling is delayed because of war, political strife, or the simple lack of qualified teachers, children show a measurable decline in intelligence (Nisbett, 2009). Does this mean that anyone can become a genius just by showing up for class? Unfortunately, not. Although education increases intelligence, its impact tends to be small (Protzko, 2015, 2016). For example, prekindergarten programs for low-SES children tend to raise their IQs, but the effects fade once these children leave their intellectually enriched environments and go to elementary school. So far, very few educational interventions have been shown to produce large and long-lasting increases in intelligence. That doesn't mean education is unimportant. In terms of just about every important outcome—from health to wealth to happiness—the difference between an illiterate person with an IQ of 100 and a literate person with an IQ of 101 is much larger than a single IQ point would suggest.

To encourage low-SES parents to talk more to their children, the city of Providence, Rhode Island, created a program called "Providence Talks." Once a month, a child wears a small recording device for the day, which allows a computer to calculate how many words she spoke, how many were spoken by adults in her vicinity, and how many conversational exchanges she experienced. A caseworker then visits her parent and provides a progress report. Katherine Taylor/*The New York Times*/Redux Pictures

The Nature–Nurture Distinction

Although nature and nurture both influence intelligence, that shouldn't lead you to think of genes and environments as two separate ingredients that are somehow blended together like flour and sugar in a recipe for IQ. Even the distinction between them is murky. For example, a gene that made someone sociable might lead her to have good relationships with peers, which might lead her to stay in school longer, which might lead her to become smarter—but would we call such a gene a "sociability gene" or an "intelligence gene" (Posthuma & de Geus, 2006)? Would we attribute that person's intelligence to her genes or to the environment that her genes enabled her to create? As these questions suggest, genes and environments are not independent influences on intelligence. Rather, they interact in complex ways that scientists are just beginning to understand (see Data Visualization: How Do Nature and Nurture Influence Intelligence? at www.launchpadworks.com).

DATA VISUALIZATION

BUILD TO THE OUTCOMES

1. What do twin studies teach us about the influence of genes and environments on intelligence?

2. What are the most important environmental influences on intelligence?

3. What makes the nature–nurture distinction murky?

Who Is Most Intelligent?

LEARNING OUTCOMES

- Describe myths about the intellectually gifted and the intellectually disabled.

- Explain what is and is not known about between-group differences in intelligence.

- Identify ways that intelligence can be enhanced.

Individual Differences in Intelligence

The average IQ is 100, and 68% of us have IQs between 85 and 115 (see **FIGURE 9.16**). But some people are *intellectually gifted* (they have very high IQs) and some are *intellectually disabled* (they have very low IQs that impair their ability to carry out the tasks of daily life). Those who live at the very high and very low ends of the intelligence continuum have something in common: They are more likely to be male than female. Males and females have the same average IQ, but the distribution of males' IQ scores is wider and more variable than is the distribution of females' IQ scores, which means that there are more males than females at both the very top and the very bottom of the IQ range (Hedges & Nowell, 1995; Lakin, 2013; Wai, Putallaz, & Makel, 2012). Some of this difference is due to the different ways in which boys and girls are socialized, and whether any of this difference is due to innate biological differences between males and females remains a hotly debated issue in psychology (Ceci, Williams, & Barnett, 2009; Nisbett et al., 2012; Spelke, 2005).

Those of us who occupy the large middle of the intelligence spectrum often have two misconceptions about those who live at the extremes. First, although movies often portray the "tortured genius" as a person who is brilliant, creative, misunderstood, despondent, and more than a little bit weird, the fact is that people with very high intelligence tend to be *less* susceptible to mental illness than people with very low intelligence (Dekker & Koot, 2003; Didden et al., 2012; Walker et al., 2002). Indeed, gifted children tend to be just as well-adjusted as their peers (Garland & Zigler, 1999; Neihart, 1999). Second, gifted children are rarely gifted in all departments and instead tend to have gifts in a single domain such as math, language, or music. More than 95% of gifted children show a sharp disparity between their mathematical and verbal abilities (Achter, Lubinski, & Benbow, 1996). Because gifted children tend to be "single gifted," they also tend to be single minded, displaying a "rage to master" the domain in which they excel. Indeed, some research suggests that the one thing that most clearly distinguishes gifted children from their less gifted peers is the sheer amount of time they spend engaged in their domain of excellence (Ericsson & Charness, 1999).

On the other end of the intelligence spectrum are people with intellectual disabilities, which is defined by an IQ of less than 70. About 70% of people with IQs in this range are male. Two of the most common causes of intellectual disability are *Down syndrome* (caused by the presence of a third copy of chromosome 21) and *fetal alcohol syndrome* (caused by a mother's excessive alcohol use during pregnancy). These intellectual disabilities are quite general, and people who have them typically show impaired performance on most or all cognitive tasks. Perhaps the greatest myth about the intellectually disabled is that they are unhappy. A recent survey of

The artist Vincent van Gogh was the iconic "tortured genius." But data suggest that low intelligence, not high intelligence, is most strongly associated with mental illness. *Lee Foster/Alamy*

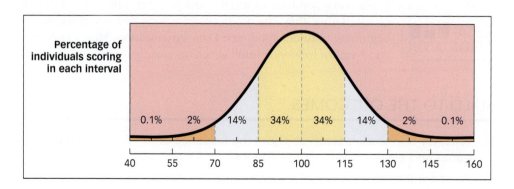

Figure 9.16 THE NORMAL CURVE OF INTELLIGENCE IQ scores produce a normal curve. This graph shows the percentage of people who score in each range of IQ.

Percentage of individuals scoring in each interval

0.1%   2%   14%   34%   34%   14%   2%   0.1%

40   55   70   85   100   115   130   145   160

The artist Judith Scott, who died in 2005, had Down syndrome. Her remarkable textile sculptures have been the subjects of articles, books, and films, and can be seen in galleries and museums all over the world. Vicente Franco

people with Down syndrome revealed that more than 96% are happy with their lives, like who they are, and like how they look (Skotko, Levine, & Goldstein, 2011). People with intellectual disabilities face many challenges, and being misunderstood is one of the most difficult.

Group Differences in Intelligence

In the early 1900s, Professor Lewis Terman of Stanford University improved on Binet and Simon's work and produced the intelligence test now known as the Stanford–Binet Intelligence Scale. Among the things his test revealed was that Whites performed better than did non-Whites. "Are the inferior races really inferior, or are they merely unfortunate in their lack of opportunity to learn?" he asked, and then answered unequivocally: "Their dullness seems to be racial, or at least inherent in the family stocks from which they come" (Terman, 1916, pp. 91–92).

A century later, these sentences make most of us cringe. But exactly which parts are cringe-worthy? Terman was making three independent claims: (1) intelligence is influenced by genes; (2) members of some racial groups score better than others on intelligence tests; and (3) the reason members of some racial groups score better than others on intelligence tests is due to differences in their genes. Virtually all modern scientists agree that Terman's first two claims are true: Intelligence *is* influenced by genes, and some groups *do* perform better than others on intelligence tests. But Terman's third claim—that differences in genes are the *reason* why some groups outperform others—is not a fact. It is a provocative conjecture that has been the subject of both passionate and acrimonious debate. What does science have to tell us about it?

Before answering that question, let's be clear about one thing: Between-group differences in intelligence are not inherently troubling. No one is troubled by the possibility that this year's winners of the Nobel Prize are on average more intelligent than this year's winners of the Super Bowl, or that people who graduate from college are on average more intelligent than people who do not. On the other hand, most

Women tend to perform better than men on tests of verbal ability, so you won't be surprised to learn that actress Hedy Lamarr spoke beautifully in dozens of hit movies of the 1940s. But women tend to perform more poorly than men on tests of mathematical ability, so you might be surprised to learn that in her spare time, Lamarr designed torpedo guidance systems for the U.S. Navy and invented (and patented!) the "spread spectrum" technology that is used today in Wi-Fi, Bluetooth, and cellphones. By the way, her co-star Clark Gable invented the pencil mustache, which today is used approximately never. Archive Photos/Moviepix/Getty Images

of us *are* troubled by the possibility that people of one gender, race, or nationality may be more intelligent than people of another because intelligence is a valuable commodity, and it doesn't seem fair for a few groups to corner the market by accidents of birth or geography.

But fair or not, they do. Whites routinely outscore Blacks on standard intelligence tests (Neisser et al., 1996; Nisbett et al., 2012). Women routinely outscore men on tests that require rapid access to and use of semantic information, production and comprehension of complex prose, fine motor skills, and perceptual speed of verbal intelligence. Men routinely outscore women on tests that require transformations in visual or spatial memory, certain motor skills, spatiotemporal responding, and fluid reasoning in abstract mathematical and scientific domains (Halpern et al., 2007; Nisbett et al., 2012). Indeed, group differences in performance on intelligence tests "are among the most thoroughly documented findings in psychology" (Suzuki & Valencia, 1997, p. 1104). The question is not whether, but why?

Some people suggest that intelligence tests are culturally biased. And indeed, the earliest intelligence tests did ask questions whose answers were more likely to be known by members of one group (usually White Europeans) than by members of another. For example, when Binet and Simon asked students, "When anyone has offended you and asks you to excuse him, what ought you to do?" they were looking for answers such as "accept the apology graciously." Answers such as "demand three goats" would have been counted as wrong. But intelligence tests have come a long way in a century, and one would have to look hard to find questions on a modern intelligence test that have the same blatant cultural bias that Binet and Simon's tests did (Suzuki & Valencia, 1997). It is very unlikely that the differences between the average scores of different groups is due entirely—or even largely—to a cultural bias in IQ tests.

These high school juniors in South Carolina are taking the SAT. When people are asked about their race or gender before taking a test, their performance can be affected. Why? MARY ANN CHASTAIN/AP Images

But even when test *questions* are unbiased, testing *situations* may not be. For example, studies show that African American students (but not European American students) perform more poorly on tests if they are asked to report their race at the top of the answer sheet, presumably because doing so leads them to feel anxious about confirming racial stereotypes (Steele & Aronson, 1995), and anxiety naturally interferes with test performance (Reeve, Heggestad, & Lievens, 2009). **Stereotype threat** is *the fear of confirming the negative beliefs that others may hold* (Aronson & Steele, 2004; Schmader, Johns, & Forbes, 2008; Walton & Spencer, 2009), and it can exert a powerful influence on people's test performance. When Asian American women are reminded of their gender, they perform unusually poorly on tests of mathematical skill, presumably because they are aware of stereotypes suggesting that women can't do math. But when the same women are instead reminded of their ethnicity, they perform unusually well on such tests, presumably because they are aware of stereotypes suggesting that Asians are especially good at math (Shih, Pittinsky, & Ambady, 1999). Findings such as these remind us that the situations in which intelligence tests are administered can affect members of different groups differently and may cause group differences in performance that do not reflect group differences in actual intelligence.

Although biases in the testing situation may explain some of the between-group differences in intelligence test scores, the major cause of these differences is the environment. African American children have lower birth weights, poorer diets, higher rates of chronic illness, and poorer medical care. They attend worse schools and are three times more likely than are European American children to live in single-parent households (Acevedo-Garcia et al., 2007; National Center for Health Statistics, 2016). Given the vast differences between the SES of European Americans and African Americans, it isn't surprising that African Americans score on average 10 points lower on IQ tests than do European Americans. Do genes play any role in producing this difference? So far, there is no compelling evidence to support this hypothesis (Nisbett, 2009). Although the absence of evidence is not evidence of an absence, the majority of modern psychologists currently believe that between-group differences in intelligence are caused by between-group differences in the environment, and not by between-group differences in genes.

stereotype threat The fear of confirming the negative beliefs that others may hold.

Improving Intelligence

Given how strongly environment affects intelligence, what can average parents do to raise their child's IQ? Research suggests four specific ways parents can make their children smarter (Protzko, Aronson, & Blair, 2013):

1. Supplementing the diets of pregnant women and neonates with long-chain polyunsaturated fatty acids (substances found in breast milk) appears to raise children's IQ by about 4 points.

2. Enrolling low-SES infants in so-called early educational interventions tends to raise their IQ by about 6 points (though enrolling them at a younger age seems to be no better than enrolling them at an older age).

3. Reading to children in an interactive manner raises their IQ by about 6 points (and in this case, the earlier the parent starts reading the better).

4. Sending children to preschool raises their IQ by about 6 points.

cognitive enhancers Drugs that improve the psychological processes that underlie intelligent performance.

There are also some things parents can do to make themselves smarter. Research suggests that training for long periods of time with complex "mental exercises" can produce improvements in fluid intelligence, in both children and adults (e.g., Mackey et al., 2011; Tranter and Koutstaal, 2007) and may even slow cognitive decline among the elderly (Salthouse, 2015). But improving intelligence does not always take work. **Cognitive enhancers** are *drugs that improve the psychological processes that underlie intelligent performance.* For example, stimulants such as Ritalin (methylphenidate) and Adderall (mixed amphetamine salts) can enhance cognitive performance by improving people's ability to focus their attention, manipulate information in working memory, and flexibly control their responses (Sahakian & Morein-Zamir, 2007). These drugs can have damaging side effects and can lead to abuse, but their effects on cognitive performance are clear.

In the near future, cognitive enhancement may not be achieved with chemicals that temporarily alter the brain's function, but rather, with techniques that permanently alter its structure. By manipulating the genes that guide hippocampal development, for instance, scientists have created a strain of "smart mice" that have extraordinary memory and learning abilities, leading the researchers to conclude that "genetic enhancement of mental and cognitive attributes such as intelligence and memory in mammals is feasible" (Tang et al., 1999, p. 64). And new "gene-editing" techniques such as CRISPR-Cas9 may allow animals to pass these genetic modifications to their young. Although no one has yet developed a safe and powerful "smart pill" or a gene-editing technique that enhances intelligence in mammals, many experts believe that both of these things will happen in the next few years (Farah et al., 2004; Rose, 2002; Turner & Sahakian, 2006).

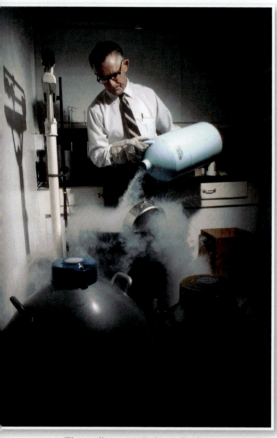

The millionaire Robert Graham opened the Repository for Germinal Choice in 1980 to collect sperm from Nobel laureates and mathematical prodigies and allow healthy young women to be inseminated with it. His "genius factory" produced more than 200 children but closed after his death in 1999. No records survived, so no one knows if his experiment was a success. Paul Harris/Getty Images

At that point, we will have some tough choices to make because there is no bright line between technological enhancements and the more traditional kinds. If Adderall and "mental exercise" both enhance cognition by altering the way the brain functions, then what is the difference between them? Some think the answer is more ethical than biological: Both drugs and memory-training games can enhance fluid intelligence, but one requires hard work and commitment, whereas the other requires only a prescription. Do we want to live in a world in which a highly prized human ability such as intelligence can be purchased, rather than being earned by hard work or endowed by nature? That's a question we will all soon be asking, and we will need a whole lot of intelligence to answer it (see Other Voices: How Science Can Build a Better You).

How Science Can Build a Better You

David Ewing Duncan is an award-winning author and journalist whose most recent book is *When I'm 164: The New Science of Radical Life Extension, and What Happens If It Succeeds.* Chris Hardy Photograpy

Intelligence is a highly prized commodity that buys people a lot of the good things in life. It can be increased by a solid education and a healthy diet, and everyone is in favor of those things. But it can also be increased by drugs—and there is little doubt that in the near future it will be increased by other even more powerful technologies. Is this a bad idea or a moral imperative? How will we decide who gets to use these technologies and who gets left behind? The author David Ewing Duncan thinks these are critically important questions that we must answer now—*before* the "Age of Enhancement" begins.

Over the last couple of years during talks and lectures, I have asked thousands of people a hypothetical question that goes like this: "If I could offer you a pill that allowed your child to increase his or her memory by 25 percent, would you give it to them?"

The show of hands in this informal poll has been overwhelming, with 80 percent or more voting no.

Then I asked a follow-up question. "What if this pill was safe and increased your kid's grades from a B average to an A average?" People tittered nervously, looked around to see how others were voting as nearly half said yes. (Many didn't vote at all.)

"And what if all of the other kids are taking the pill?" I asked. The tittering stopped and nearly everyone voted yes.

No pill now exists that can boost memory by 25 percent. Yet neuroscientists tell me that pharmaceutical companies are testing compounds in early stage human trials that may enable patients with dementia and other memory-stealing diseases to have better recall. No one knows if these will work to improve healthy people, but it's possible that one will work in the future.

More intriguing is the notion that a supermemory or attention pill might be used someday by those with critical jobs like pilots, surgeons, police officers—or the chief executive of the United States. In fact, we may demand that they use them, said the bioethicist Thomas H. Murray. "It might actually be immoral for a surgeon not to take a drug that was safe and steadied his hand," said Mr. Murray, the former president of the Hastings Center, a bioethics research group. "That would be like using a scalpel that wasn't sterile.". . .

For years, scientists have been manipulating genes in animals to make improvements in neural performance, strength and agility, among other augmentations. Directly altering human DNA using "gene therapy" in humans remains dangerous and fraught with ethical challenges. But it may be possible to develop drugs that alter enzymes and other proteins associated with genes for, say, speed and endurance or dopamine levels in the brain connected to improved neural performance.

Synthetic biologists contend that re-engineering cells and DNA may one day allow us to eliminate diseases; a few believe we will be able to build tailor-made people. Others are convinced that stem cells might one day be used to grow fresh brain, heart or liver cells to augment or improve cells in these and other organs.

Not all enhancements are high-tech or invasive. Neuroscientists are seeing boosts from neuro-feedback and video games designed to teach and develop cognition and from meditation and improvements in diet, exercise and sleep. "We may see a convergence of several of these technologies," said the neurologist Adam Gazzaley of the University of California at San Francisco. He is developing brain-boosting games with developers and engineers who once worked for Lucas Arts, founded by the "Star Wars" director George Lucas. . . .

Ethical challenges for the coming Age of Enhancement include, besides basic safety questions, the issue of who would get the enhancements, how much they would cost, and who would gain an advantage over others by using them. In a society that is already seeing a widening gap between the very rich and the rest of us, the question of a democracy of equals could face a critical test if the well-off also could afford a physical, genetic or bionic advantage. It also may challenge what it means to be human.

Still, the enhancements are coming, and they will be hard to resist. The real issue is what we do with them once they become irresistible.

David Ewing Duncan sees a brave new world on the not-too-distant horizon. The possibility of using technology to increase human intelligence is very exciting because intelligence can bring great rewards to those who have it, as well as to those around them. But how wisely will we seize this opportunity? Will all of humankind reap the harvest and become brighter, more peaceful, and more productive? Or will we end up with a Master Class of highly intelligent people who run the world for their own benefit? We will probably know the answer to this question in your lifetime.

BUILD TO THE OUTCOMES

1. What are the most common misconceptions about the intellectually gifted and the intellectually disabled?

2. What one thing most clearly distinguishes gifted children from others?

3. How can the testing situation affect a person's performance on an IQ test?

4. What is the current best guess about the cause(s) of between-group differences in intelligence?

5. How can intelligence be enhanced? What ethical questions are raised?

CHAPTER REVIEW

Language and Communication: From Rules to Meaning

- Human language is characterized by a complex organization—from phonemes to morphemes to phrases and finally to sentences.

- Children can distinguish between all contrasting sounds of human language but lose that ability within the first 6 months.

- Children acquire grammatical rules in development, even without being taught explicitly.

- The behaviorist explanation for language learning is based on operant conditioning, whereas nativists hold that humans are biologically predisposed to process language. Interactionists explain language learning as both a biological and a social process.

- Our abilities to produce and comprehend language depend on distinct regions of the brain, with Broca's area critical for language production and Wernicke's area critical for comprehension. Gray matter in the part of the brain involved in language is denser in bilingual individuals.

Concepts and Categories: How We Think

- We organize knowledge about objects, events, or other stimuli by creating concepts, prototypes, and exemplars.

- We acquire concepts using three theories: family resemblance theory, which states that items in the same category tend to share certain features; prototype theory, which uses the most typical member of a category to assess new items; and exemplar theory, which states that we compare new items with stored memories of other members of the category.

- The brain organizes concepts into distinct categories, such as living things and human-made things. Visual experience is not necessary for the development of such categories.

Decision Making: Rational and Otherwise

- Human decision making often departs from a completely rational process. The mistakes that accompany this departure tell us a lot about how the human mind works.

- When people are asked to make probability judgments, they will turn the problem into something they know how to solve, such as judging memory strength, judging similarity to prototypes, or estimating frequencies. This can lead to errors of judgment.

- Because we feel that avoiding losses is more important than achieving gains, framing effects can affect our choices. Emotional information also strongly influences our decision making, even when we are not aware of it. Although this influence can lead us astray, it often is crucial for making decisions in everyday life.

- The prefrontal cortex plays an important role in decision making, and patients with prefrontal damage make more risky decisions than do non-brain-damaged individuals.

Intelligence

- *Intelligence* is the ability to use one's mind to solve novel problems and learn from experience. Binet and Simon developed a test that was meant to measure a child's natural aptitude for learning independent of previous experience.

- Intelligence tests produce a score known as an *intelligence quotient*, which is the deviation of an adult's test score from the average adult's test score.

- People who score well on one test of mental ability tend to score well on others, which suggests that each person has a particular level of general intelligence (*g*), but they don't *always* score well on others, which suggests that different people have different specific abilities (*s*). Research reveals that between *g* and *s* are eight *middle-level abilities*.

- Practical intelligence and emotional intelligence are just two of the kinds of intelligence that traditional tests do not measure.

Where Does Intelligence Come From?

- Both genes and environments can influence intelligence.

- SES has a powerful influence on IQ and education has a moderate influence on IQ.

Who Is Most Intelligent?

- Intelligence is correlated with mental health, and gifted children are as well adjusted as their peers. Despite what some people believe, people with intellectual disabilities are not necessarily unhappy.
- Some groups outscore others on intelligence tests because (a) testing situations can impair the performance of some groups more than others, and (b) low-SES environments have an adverse impact on intelligence.
- There is no compelling evidence to suggest that group differences on intelligence tests are due to the genetic differences between the groups.
- Human intelligence can be increased by a variety of means, from preschool to mental exercise to pharmaceuticals. Some of these methods carry greater risks and raise more difficult ethical questions than others.

KEY CONCEPT QUIZ

1. The combining of words to form phrases and sentences is governed by _____ rules.
   a. phonological
   b. morphological
   c. structural
   d. syntactical

2. Language development as an innate, biological capacity is explained by
   a. fast mapping.
   b. behaviorism.
   c. nativist theory.
   d. interactionist explanations.

3. Damage to the brain region called Broca's area results in
   a. failure to comprehend language.
   b. difficulty in producing grammatical speech.
   c. the reintroduction of infant babbling.
   d. difficulties in writing.

4. The "most typical" member of a category is a(n)
   a. prototype.
   b. exemplar.
   c. concept.
   d. definition.

5. Which theory of how we form concepts is based on our judgment of features that appear to be characteristic of category members but may not be possessed by every member?
   a. prototype theory
   b. family resemblance theory
   c. exemplar theory
   d. heuristic theory

6. People give different answers to the same problem, depending on how the problem is phrased, because of
   a. the availability bias.
   b. the conjunction fallacy.
   c. the representativeness heuristic.
   d. framing effects.

7. Intelligence tests
   a. were first developed to help children who lagged behind their peers.
   b. were developed to measure aptitude, rather than educational achievement.
   c. have been used for detestable ends.
   d. all of the above.

8. Intelligence tests have been shown to be predictors of
   a. academic performance.
   b. mental health.
   c. physical health.
   d. all of the above.

9. People who score well on one test of mental ability usually score well on others, suggesting that
   a. tests of mental ability are perfectly correlated.
   b. intelligence cannot be measured meaningfully.
   c. there is a general ability called intelligence.
   d. intelligence is genetic.

10. Most scientists now believe that intelligence is best described
   a. as a set of group factors.
   b. by a two-factor framework.
   c. as a single, general ability.
   d. by a three-level hierarchy.

11. Standard intelligence tests typically measure
   a. analytic intelligence.
   b. practical intelligence.
   c. creative intelligence.
   d. all of the above.

12. Intelligence is influenced by
   a. genes alone.
   b. genes and environment.
   c. environment alone.
   d. neither genes nor environment.

13. Intelligence changes
   a. over the life span and across generations.
   b. over the life span but not across generations.
   c. across generations but not over the life span.
   d. neither across generations nor over the life span.

14. A person's socioeconomic status has a(n) _____ effect on intelligence.
   a. powerful
   b. negligible
   c. unsubstantiated
   d. unknown

15. On which of the following statements does broad agreement exist among scientists?

    a. Differences in the intelligence test scores of different ethnic groups are clearly due to genetic differences between those groups.

    b. Differences in the intelligence test scores of different ethnic groups are caused in part by factors such as low birth weight and poor diet, which are more prevalent in some groups than in others.

    c. Differences in the intelligence test scores of different ethnic groups always reflect real differences in intelligence.

    d. Genes that are strongly associated with intelligence have been found to be more prevalent in some ethnic groups than in others.

 **LearningCurve**   Don't stop now! Quizzing yourself is a powerful study tool. Go to LearningCurve at www.launchpadworks.com for more practice.

KEY TERMS

language (p. 268)

grammar (p. 268)

phoneme (p. 269)

phonological rules (p. 269)

morphemes (p. 269)

morphological rules (p. 269)

syntactical rules (p. 269)

deep structure (p. 270)

surface structure (p. 270)

fast mapping (p. 272)

telegraphic speech (p. 272)

nativist theory (p. 275)

genetic dysphasia (p. 275)

aphasia (p. 276)

concept (p. 278)

family resemblance theory (p. 278)

prototype (p. 278)

exemplar theory (p. 279)

category-specific deficit (p. 280)

rational choice theory (p. 281)

availability bias (p. 282)

conjunction fallacy (p. 283)

representativeness heuristic (p. 283)

framing effects (p. 283)

sunk-cost fallacy (p. 283)

prospect theory (p. 284)

optimism bias (p. 284)

intelligence (p. 286)

intelligence quotient (or IQ) (p. 288)

two-factor theory of intelligence (p. 290)

crystallized intelligence (p. 291)

fluid intelligence (p. 291)

emotional intelligence (p. 292)

fraternal twins (or dizygotic twins) (p. 294)

identical twins (or monozygotic twins) (p. 294)

stereotype threat (p. 299)

cognitive enhancers (p. 300)

CHANGING MINDS

1. You mention to a friend that you've just learned that the primary language we learn can shape the way that we think. Your friend says that people are people everywhere and that this can't be true. What evidence could you describe to support your point?

2. In September 2011, *Wired* magazine ran an article discussing the fourth-down decisions of NFL coaches. On fourth down, a coach can choose to play aggressively and go for a first down (or even a touchdown), or the coach can settle for a punt or a field goal, which are safer options but result in fewer points than a touchdown. Statistically, the riskier play results in greater point gain, on average, than does playing it safe. But in reality, coaches choose the safer plays over 90% of the time. Reading this article, one of your friends is incredulous. "Coaches aren't stupid, and they want to win," he says. "Why would they always make the wrong decision?" Your friend is assuming that humans are rational decision makers. In what ways is your friend wrong? What might be causing the football coaches to make irrational decisions?

3. In biology class, the topic turns to genetics. The professor describes how scientists used gene editing to make a smarter mouse. Your classmate turns to you. "I knew it," she said. "There's a 'smart gene' after all. Some people have it, and some people don't, and that's why some people are intelligent, and some people aren't." What would you tell her about the role genetics plays in intelligence and about the way in which genes affect it?

4. One of your friends tells you about his sister. "We're very competitive," he says. "But she's smarter. We both took IQ tests when we were kids, and she scored 104, but I only scored 102." What would you tell your friend about the relationship between IQ scores and intelligence?

5. A new survey shows that in mathematics departments all over the country, tenured male professors outnumber tenured female professors by about 9 to 1. One of your friends says, "But it's a fact—girls just don't do as well as boys at math, so it's not surprising that fewer girls choose math-related careers." Thinking about what you've read in this chapter about group differences in intelligence, how might you explain this fact to your friend?

6. One of your cousins has a young son, and she's very proud of the boy's accomplishments. "He's very smart," she says. "I know this because he has a great memory: He gets 100% on all his vocabulary tests." What kind of intelligence do vocabulary tests measure? Although these skills are important for intelligence, what other abilities contribute to an individual's overall intelligence?

ANSWERS TO KEY CONCEPT QUIZ

1. d; 2. c; 3. b; 4. a; 5. b; 6. d; 7. d; 8. d; 9. c; 10. d; 11. a; 12. b; 13. a; 14. a; 15. b.

Development

10

H is mother called him Adi and showered him with affection, but his father was not so kind. As his sister later recalled, Adi "got his sound thrashing every day." Although his father wanted him to become a civil servant, Adi's true love was art, and his mother quietly encouraged that gentle interest. Adi was just 18 years old when his mother was diagnosed with terminal cancer. He was heartbroken when she died, but he had little time for grieving. As he later wrote, "Poverty and hard reality compelled me to make a quick decision. I was faced with the problem of somehow making my own living." Adi decided to defy his father's wishes and make his living as an artist. But when he applied to art school, he was flatly rejected. So, mother-less, homeless, and penniless, Adi wandered the streets for years, sleeping on park benches, living in shelters, and eating in soup kitchens, all the while trying desper-ately to sell his sketches and watercolors. What became of him?

In just 10 years, Adi achieved a degree of fame that few artists ever dream of. Today, art collectors all over the world compete at auctions to buy his paintings, which rarely come up for sale. The largest collection of his work, however, is not in the hands of any private citizen or museum. Rather, it is owned by the U.S. government, which keeps the collection under lock and key, in a windowless room in Washington, DC, where few people have ever been allowed to visit. Marylou Gjernes, the long-time curator of the government's collection, once remarked, "I often looked at them and wondered, 'What if? What if he had been accepted into art school? Would World War II have happened?'" Why would the curator ask such a question? Because the artist's mother called him Adi, but the rest of us know him as Adolf Hitler.

Adi painted in many styles, including the precise and well-structured watercolor shown here. In 2013, one of his paintings sold at auction for $ 40,000. INTERFOTO/Alamy

developmental psychology The study of continuity and change across the life span.

WHY IS IT SO DIFFICULT TO IMAGINE ONE OF THE GREATEST mass murderers of the 20th century as a gentle child who loved to draw, as a compassionate adolescent who cared for his ailing mother, or as a dedicated young adult who endured cold and hunger for the sake of his art? After all, *you* didn't begin as the person you are today, and odds are that you aren't yet in finished form. From birth to infancy, from childhood to adolescence, from young adulthood to old age, human beings change over time. Their development includes both dramatic transformations and striking consistencies in the way they look, think, feel, and act. **Developmental psychology** is *the study of continuity and change across the life span*, and in the last century, developmental psychologists have discovered some truly amazing things about this metamorphosis.

The story starts where people do: at conception. First, we'll examine the 9-month period between conception and birth and see how prenatal events set the stage for everything to come. Then we'll examine infancy and childhood, the period during which children must learn how to think about the world and their relationship to it, to understand and bond with others, and to tell the difference between right and wrong. Next, we'll examine a relatively new invention called adolescence, which is the stage at which children become both independent and sexual creatures. Finally, we'll examine adulthood, the stage at which people typically leave their parents, find mates, and have children of their own.

From infancy to childhood to adolescence to adulthood, people exhibit both continuity and change.
Courtesy of Daniel Gilbert

Prenatality: A Womb with a View

LEARNING OUTCOMES

• Describe the three prenatal stages of development.

• Explain how the prenatal environment influences the fetus's development.

You probably calculate your age by counting your birthdays, but the fact is that on the day you were born, you were already 9 months old. The *prenatal stage* of development ends with birth and begins 9 months earlier when about 200 million sperm set out on a pilgrimage from a woman's vagina, through her uterus, and to her fallopian tubes. Many are called, but few are chosen. Some of the sperm don't swim vigorously enough to make any progress, and others get stuck in a kind of spermatozoidal traffic jam. Of those that do manage to make their way through the uterus, many sperm take the wrong turn and end up in the fallopian tube that does not contain an egg. When all is said and done, only one out of every million sperm manages to get close enough to an egg to release enzymes that erode the egg's protective outer coating. The moment the first sperm does this, the egg releases a chemical that seals its coating back up and keeps all the other sperm from entering. After triumphing over 199,999,999 of its fellow travelers, this single successful sperm sheds its tail and fertilizes the egg. About 12 hours later, the egg merges with the nuclei of the sperm, and the prenatal development of a unique human being begins.

Prenatal Development

A **zygote** is *a fertilized egg that contains chromosomes from both an egg and a sperm*, and from the first moment of its existence, the zygote has one thing in common with the person it will soon become: sex. Each human sperm and each human egg contain 23 *chromosomes*. One of these chromosomes (the 23rd) comes in two varieties known as X and Y. An egg's 23rd chromosome is always of the X variety, but a sperm's 23rd chromosome can be of either the X or Y variety. If the egg is fertilized by a sperm whose 23rd chromosome is Y, then the zygote is a male (also called an XY). If the egg is fertilized by a sperm whose 23rd chromosome is an X, then the zygote is a female (also called an XX).

The **germinal stage** is *the 2-week period that begins at conception*. During this stage, the one-celled zygote divides into two cells that then divide into four cells that then divide into eight, and so on. By the time an infant is born, its body contains trillions of cells, each of which came from the original zygote, and each of which contains exactly one set of 23 chromosomes from the sperm and one set of 23 chromosomes from the egg. During the germinal stage, the zygote migrates down the fallopian tube and implants itself in the wall of the uterus. This too is a difficult journey, and about half of zygotes do not complete it, either because they are defective or because they implant themselves in an inhospitable part of the uterus. Male zygotes are especially unlikely to complete this journey, but no one understands why (though several comedians have suggested it's because male zygotes are unwilling to stop and ask for directions).

The moment the zygote successfully implants itself in the uterine wall, it loses its old name and earns a new one: *embryo*. The **embryonic stage** is *a period that starts around the 2nd week after conception and lasts until about the 8th week* (see **FIGURE 10.1**). During this stage, the implanted embryo continues to divide, and its cells begin to differentiate. Although it is only an inch long, the embryo already has arms, legs, and a beating heart. It also has the beginnings of female reproductive organs, and if it is a male embryo, it begins to produce a hormone called testosterone which masculinizes those organs.

The embryo doesn't have a lot of time to get used to its new name because at about 9 weeks it is called a *fetus*. The **fetal stage** is *a period that lasts from about the 9th week after conception until birth*. The fetus has a skeleton and muscles that make it capable of movement. It develops a layer of insulating fat beneath its skin, and its digestive and respiratory systems mature. During the fetal stage, brain cells begin to generate axons and dendrites (which allow them to communicate with other brain cells). They also begin to undergo a process (described in the Neuroscience

This electron micrograph shows several human sperm, one of which is fertilizing an egg. Contrary to what many people think, fertilization does not happen right away. It typically happens 1 to 2 days after intercourse but can happen as much as 5 days later. Eye of Science/Science Source

zygote A fertilized egg that contains chromosomes from both a sperm and an egg.

germinal stage The 2-week period of prenatal development that begins at conception.

embryonic stage The period of prenatal development that lasts from the 2nd week until about the 8th week.

fetal stage The period of prenatal development that lasts from the 9th week after conception until birth.

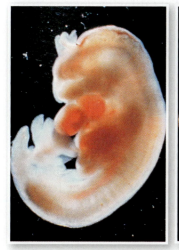
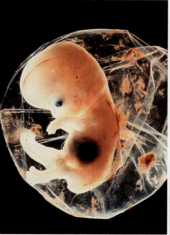
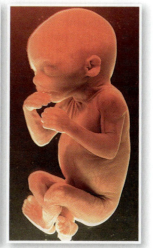

Figure 10.1 Human beings undergo amazing changes during the 9 months of prenatal development. These images show an embryo at 30 days (about the size of a poppy seed), an embryo at 8 to 9 weeks (about the size of an olive), and a fetus at 5 months (about the size of a pomegranate). Claude Edelmann/Science Source; Biophoto Associates/Science Source; James Stevenson/Science Source

This chimp and boy share a deep interest in dirt, bugs, and leaves. But one big difference between them is that the chimp was born with an almost adult-size brain, whereas the boy was born with a brain that ultimately will nearly quadruple in size. Karen Huntt/Corbis

myelination The formation of a fatty sheath around the axons of a neuron.

teratogen Any substance that passes from mother to unborn child and impairs development.

fetal alcohol syndrome (FAS) A developmental disorder that stems from heavy alcohol use by the mother during pregnancy.

This child has some of the telltale facial features associated with fetal alcohol syndrome (FAS): short eye openings, a flat midface, a flat ridge under the nose, a thin upper lip, and an underdeveloped jaw. Rick's Photography/Shutterstock

and Behavior chapter) known as **myelination**, which is *the formation of a fatty sheath around the axons of a neuron.* Just as plastic sheathing insulates a wire, myelin insulates a brain cell and prevents the leakage of neural signals that travel along the axon. Myelination starts during the fetal stage, but it doesn't end until adulthood.

The human brain grows rapidly during the fetal period, but unlike the brains of other primates, it does not come close to achieving its adult size. A newborn chimpanzee's brain is nearly 60% of its adult size, but a newborn human's brain is only 25% of its adult size, which is to say that 75% of a human's brain development occurs after birth. Why are humans born with such underdeveloped brains? First, humans have really big heads, and if a newborn baby's head were 60% of its adult size (as a newborn chimp's head is), then the baby could never pass through its mother's birth canal. Second, one of our species' greatest talents is its ability to adapt to a wide range of novel environments that differ in climate, social structure, and so on. So, rather than arriving in the world with a highly developed brain that may or may not meet the requirements of its environment, human beings arrive with underdeveloped brains that do much of their developing *within* the very environments in which they ultimately must function, thereby gaining the unique capacities that each environment requires.

Prenatal Environment

The word *environment* probably makes you think of green fields and blue skies. But the womb is also an environment, and it has a powerful impact on development (Coe & Lubach, 2008; Glynn & Sandman, 2011; Wadhwa, Sandman, & Garite, 2001). For example, a woman's bloodstream is physically connected to the bloodstream of her unborn child, and therefore the foods she eats can affect it. Studies show that infants tend to like the foods and spices that their mothers ate while the infants were in the womb (Mennella, Johnson, & Beauchamp, 1995). More importantly, the children of women who don't receive enough nutrition during pregnancy are at increased risk for a variety of illnesses, such as schizophrenia and antisocial personality disorder (Neugebauer, Hoek, & Susser, 1999; Susser, Brown, & Matte, 1999). Indeed, almost anything a woman eats, drinks, inhales, injects, sniffs, snorts, or rubs on her skin can enter the unborn child's bloodstream. A **teratogen** is *any substance that passes from mother to unborn child and impairs development.* Teratogens include the mercury in fish, the lead in water, and the paint dust in air.

But the most common teratogens can be purchased at a convenience store. **Fetal alcohol syndrome (FAS)** is *a developmental disorder that stems from heavy alcohol use by the mother during pregnancy,* and children with FAS have a variety of brain abnormalities and cognitive deficits (Carmichael Olson et al., 1997; Streissguth et al., 1999). Some studies suggest that light drinking does not harm the fetus, but there is little consensus about how much drinking is light (Warren & Hewitt, 2009). On the other hand, everyone agrees that "none" is a perfectly safe amount. Tobacco is the other common teratogen. Mothers who smoke during pregnancy have babies that are smaller (Horta et al., 1997) and more likely to have perceptual and attentional problems in childhood (Espy et al., 2011; Fried & Watkinson, 2000). Even secondhand smoke can lead to reduced birth weight and deficits in attention and learning (Makin, Fried, & Watkinson, 1991; Windham, Eaton, & Hopkins, 1999).

The prenatal environment is rich with chemicals that affect the unborn child, but it is also rich with auditory information. Wombs are dark because only the brightest light can filter through the mother's abdomen, but they are not quiet. The fetus can hear its mother's heartbeat, the gastrointestinal sounds associated with her digestion, and her voice. Newborns will suck a nipple more vigorously when they hear the sound of their mother's voice than when they hear the voice of a female stranger

(Querleu et al., 1984), demonstrating that even at birth they are already more familiar with the former. Newborns who listen to strangers speaking two languages will suck more vigorously when they hear words from their mother's native language—unless their mother happens to be bilingual, in which case they suck equally vigorously to both languages (Byers-Heinlein, Burns, & Werker, 2010). What unborn children hear in the womb even influences the sounds they make at birth: French newborns cry with a rising melody and German newborns with a falling melody, mimicking the cadence of their mother's native tongue (Mampe et al., 2009). Clearly, the fetus is listening.

BUILD TO THE OUTCOMES

1. What are the three prenatal stages?

2. Why are human beings born with underdeveloped brains?

3. How does the uterine environment affect the unborn child?

4. What are teratogens?

5. What can a fetus hear?

Infancy and Childhood: Doing and Thinking

Newborns appear to be capable of little more than sleeping, squalling, and squirming, but in the last two decades, researchers have discovered that they are much more sophisticated than they appear. **Infancy** is *the stage of development that begins at birth and lasts between 18 and 24 months*, and as you will see, a lot more happens during this stage than meets the untrained eye.

Perceptual Development

New parents like to stand around the crib and make goofy faces at the baby because they think the baby will be amused. But newborns have a fairly limited range of vision: The amount of detail that a newborn can see at a distance of 20 feet is roughly equivalent to the amount of detail that an adult can see at 600 feet (Banks & Salapatek, 1983), which is to say that infants are missing a whole lot of the cribside shenanigans. On the other hand, newborns can see things that are 8 to 12 inches away, which happens to be roughly the distance between a mother's face and her nursing infant's eyes. How do psychologists know what a newborn can and can't see? Experiments! For example, in one study, newborns were repeatedly shown a circle with diagonal stripes. The newborns stared a lot at first, and then less and less on each subsequent presentation. You'll recall from the Learning chapter that *habituation* is the tendency for organisms to respond less intensely to a stimulus each time it is presented, and infants habituate just as mice do. But when the researchers rotated the circle 90°, the newborns started staring at it again, indicating that they had noticed the change in the circle's orientation (Slater, Morison, & Somers, 1988).

Newborns are especially attentive to social stimuli (Biro et al., 2014). For example, in one study, researchers stood close to some newborns while sticking out their tongues and stood close to other newborns while pursing their lips. Newborns in the first group stuck out their own tongues more often than those in the second group did, and newborns in the second group pursed their lips more often than those in the first group did (Meltzoff & Moore, 1977). Indeed, newborns have been shown to mimic facial expressions in their very first *hour* of life (Reissland, 1988) and to mimic speech sounds as early as 12 weeks (Kuhl & Meltzoff, 1996).

LEARNING OUTCOMES

- Describe the evidence for visual perception in newborns.

- Explain the two rules of motor development.

- Explain the stages of Piaget's theory of cognitive development.

- Explain egocentrism and theory of mind.

- Describe the key skills that allow infants to learn from others.

infancy The stage of development that begins at birth and lasts between 18 and 24 months.

Infants mimic the facial expressions of adults—and vice versa, of course!
tonphotographe.com/Shutterstock

Motor skills develop through practice. In just 1 hour in a playroom, the average 12- to 19-month-old infant takes 2,368 steps, travels 0.4 miles, and falls 17 times (Adolph et al., 2012). *Kayte Deioma/Photo Edit*

motor development The emergence of the ability to execute physical action.

motor reflexes Specific motor responses that are triggered by specific patterns of sensory stimulation.

cephalocaudal rule The "top-to-bottom" rule that describes the tendency for motor skills to emerge in sequence from the head to the feet.

proximodistal rule The "inside-to-outside" rule that describes the tendency for motor skills to emerge in sequence from the center to the periphery.

Motor Development

Infants can use their eyes and ears right away, but they have to spend a considerable amount of time learning how to use their other parts. **Motor development** is *the emergence of the ability to execute physical actions* such as reaching, grasping, crawling, and walking. Infants are born with a small set of **motor reflexes**, which are *specific motor responses that are triggered by specific patterns of sensory stimulation*. For example, the *rooting reflex* causes infants to move their mouths toward any object that touches their cheek, and the *sucking reflex* causes them to suck any object that enters their mouth. Together, these two reflexes allow newborn infants to find their mother's nipple and begin feeding—a behavior so vitally important that nature took no chances and hard-wired it into every one of us. Interestingly, these and other reflexes that are present at birth seem to disappear in the first few months as infants learn to execute more sophisticated motor behavior.

The development of these more sophisticated behaviors tends to obey two general rules. The first is the **cephalocaudal rule** (or the "top-to-bottom" rule), which describes *the tendency for motor skills to emerge in sequence from the head to the feet*. Infants tend to gain control over their heads first, their arms and trunks next, and their legs last. A young infant who is placed on her stomach may lift her head and her chest by using her arms for support, but she typically has little control over her legs. The second rule is the **proximodistal rule** (or the "inside-to-outside" rule), which describes *the tendency for motor skills to emerge in sequence from the center to the periphery*. Infants learn to control their trunks before their elbows and knees, which they learn to control before their hands and feet (see **FIGURE 10.2**). Although motor skills develop in an orderly sequence, they do not develop on a strict timetable. Rather, the timing of these skills is influenced by many factors, such as the infant's incentive for reaching, body weight, muscular development, and general level of activity.

Figure 10.2 MOTOR DEVELOPMENT Infants learn to control their bodies from head to feet and from center to periphery. These skills do not emerge on a strict timetable, but they do emerge in a fairly strict sequence.

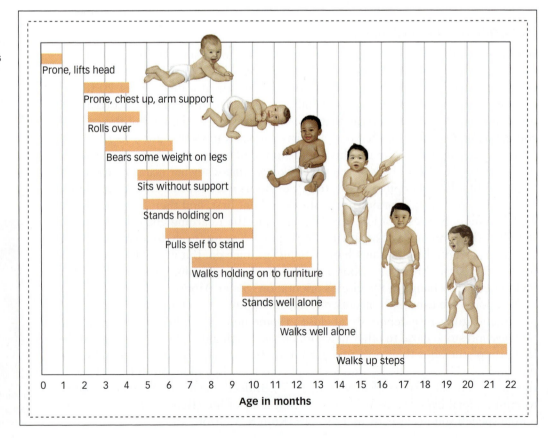

Cognitive Development

So infants can hear and see and move their bodies. But can they think? In the first half of the 20th century, a Swiss biologist named Jean Piaget became interested in this question. **Cognitive development** is *the process by which infants and children gain the ability to think and understand.* Piaget suggested that during this process, infants and children learn how the physical world works, how their own minds work, and how other people's minds work. Let's see how they achieve these essential understandings.

Discovering the World

Piaget (1954) suggested that cognitive development occurs in four discrete stages: the *sensorimotor* stage, the *preoperational* stage, the *concrete operational* stage, and the *formal operational* stage (see **TABLE 10.1**). The **sensorimotor stage** is *a stage of cognitive development that begins at birth and lasts through infancy.* As the word *sensorimotor* suggests, infants at this stage are mainly busy using their ability to *sense* and their ability to *move* to acquire information about the world.

By actively exploring their environments with their eyes, mouths, and fingers, infants begin to construct **schemas**, which are *theories about the way the world works.* As every scientist knows, the good thing about theories is that they allow us to predict what will happen next. If an infant learns that tugging at a stuffed animal brings the toy closer, then that observation is incorporated into the infant's theory about how physical objects behave ("Things come closer if I pull them"), and the infant can later use that theory when she wants a different object to come closer, such as a rattle or a ball. Piaget called this **assimilation**, which happens when *infants apply their schemas in novel situations.* Of course, if the infant applies this theory to the family cat, the cat is likely to sprint in the opposite direction. Infants' theories about the world are occasionally disconfirmed by experience, which causes infants to take special notice (Stahl & Feigenson, 2015) and to adjust their theories ("Inanimate things come closer when I pull them, but animate things just hiss and run"). Piaget called this **accommodation**, which happens when *infants revise their schemas in light of new information.*

Piaget suggested that infants are surprisingly clueless about some of the most basic properties of the physical world and must acquire information about those properties through experience. For example, when you put your shoes in the closet, you know that they are still there even after you close the closet door, and you would be kind of surprised if you opened the door a moment later and found the closet

Jean Piaget (1896–1980) was the father of modern developmental psychology, as well as the last man who actually looked cool wearing a beret. Farrell Grehan/Corbis

cognitive development The process by which infants and children gain the ability to think and understand.

sensorimotor stage A stage of cognitive development that begins at birth and lasts through infancy, during which infants acquire information about the world by sensing it and moving around within it.

schemas Theories about the way the world works.

assimilation The process by which infants apply their schemas in novel situations.

accommodation The process by which infants revise their schemas in light of new information.

TABLE 10.1 Piaget's Four Stages of Cognitive Development	
Stage	**Characteristic**
Sensorimotor (Birth–2 years)	Infant experiences world through movement and senses, develops schemas, begins to act intentionally, and shows evidence of understanding object permanence.
Preoperational (2–6 years)	Child acquires motor skills but does not understand conservation of physical properties. Child begins this stage by thinking egocentrically but ends with a basic understanding of other minds.
Concrete operational (6–11 years)	Child can think logically about physical objects and events and understands conservation of physical properties.
Formal operational (11 years and up)	Child can think logically about abstract propositions and hypotheticals.

During the sensorimotor stage, infants explore with their hands and mouths, learning important lessons about the physical world such as, "If you smear enough jelly on your face, someone will probably take your picture." Michael Hagedorn/Corbis

object permanence The fact that objects continue to exist even when they are not visible.

empty. But according to Piaget, this wouldn't surprise an infant because infants do not have a theory of **object permanence**, which refers to *the fact that objects exist even when they are not visible*. Piaget noted that in the first few months of life, infants act as though objects stop existing the moment they are out of sight.

But in the last few decades, researchers have shown that infants know more about object permanence than Piaget suspected. For instance, in one study, infants were shown a miniature drawbridge that flipped up and down (see **FIGURE 10.3**). Once the infants got used to this, they watched as a solid box was placed behind the drawbridge—in the path of the drawbridge, but out of the infant's sight. Some infants then saw a *possible* event: The drawbridge began to flip and then it suddenly stopped, as if its motion was being impeded by the unseen solid box. Other infants saw an *impossible* event: The drawbridge began to flip—and then it didn't stop, as if its motion was unimpeded by the unseen solid box. Four-month-old infants stared longer at the impossible event than at the possible event, suggesting that they were puzzled by it (Baillargeon, Spelke, & Wasserman, 1985). Of course, the only thing that made the impossible event impossible was the fact that an unseen box should have—but didn't—impede the motion of the drawbridge. Studies such as these suggest that infants acquire a theory of object permanence much earlier than Piaget suspected (Shinskey & Munakata, 2005; Wang & Baillargeon, 2008).

Discovering the Mind

childhood The stage of development that begins at about 18 to 24 months and lasts until adolescence, which begins between 11 and 14 years.

preoperational stage The stage of cognitive development that begins at about 2 years and ends at about 6 years, during which children develop a preliminary understanding of the physical world.

concrete operational stage The stage of cognitive development that begins at about 6 years and ends at about 11 years, during which children learn how various actions, or *operations*, can affect or transform *concrete* objects.

The long period following infancy is called **childhood**, which is *the period that begins at about 18 to 24 months and lasts until about 11 to 14 years*. According to Piaget, children enter childhood at the **preoperational stage**, which is *the stage of cognitive development that begins at about 2 years and ends at about 6 years, during which children develop a preliminary understanding of the physical world*. They exit childhood at the **concrete operational stage**, which is *the stage of cognitive development that begins at about 6 years and ends at about 11 years, during which children learn how actions, or operations, can transform the concrete objects of the physical world*.

The difference between these stages is nicely illustrated by one of Piaget's clever experiments in which he showed children a row of cups and asked them to place an egg in each. Preoperational children were able to do this, and afterward they readily agreed that there were just as many eggs as there were cups. Then Piaget removed

  Initial Event  Possible Event  Impossible Event

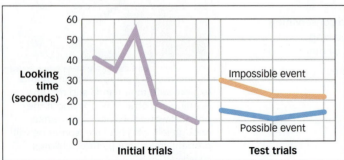

Figure 10.3 THE IMPOSSIBLE EVENT (a) During the initial trials, infants watch a drawbridge flip back and forth with nothing in its path. During the test trials, a box is placed behind the drawbridge, and the infants are shown either a possible event (in which the motion of the drawbridge is impeded) or an impossible event (in which the motion of the drawbridge is not impeded). (b) The graph shows the infants' looking times during the initial trials and the test trials. During the test trials, their interest was reawakened by the impossible event but not by the possible event (Baillargeon, Spelke, & Wasserman, 1985).

the eggs and spread them out in a long line that extended beyond the row of cups. Preoperational children incorrectly claimed that there were now more eggs than cups, pointing out that the row of eggs was longer than the row of cups and hence there must be more of them. Concrete operational children, on the other hand, correctly reported that the number of eggs did not change when they were spread out in a longer line. They understood that *quantity* is a property of a set of concrete objects that does not change when an operation such as *spreading out* alters the set's appearance (Piaget, 1954). Piaget called the child's insight **conservation**, which is *the notion that the quantitative properties of an object are invariant despite changes in the object's appearance.*

Why don't preoperational children grasp the notion of conservation? Adults naturally distinguish between appearances and realities, between the way things look and the way things are. We know that a wagon can *be* red but *look* gray at dusk, and that a highway can *be* dry but *look* wet in the heat. Visual illusions delight us precisely because we know that they look one way when they are really another. But preoperational children don't make this distinction. They assume that when something *looks* gray or wet it must *be* gray or wet. As they move from the preoperational to the concrete operational stage, they come to realize that the way the world *appears* and the way the world *is* are sometimes very different things.

Once children have this epiphany, they can understand that when a ball of clay is rolled, stretched, or flattened, it is still the same amount of clay despite the fact that it looks larger in one form than in another. They can understand that when water is poured from a short, wide beaker into a tall, thin cylinder, it is still the same amount of water despite the fact that the water level in the cylinder is higher. In short, they understand that certain operations—such as squishing, pouring, and spreading out—can change what an object *looks* like without changing what the object *is* like.

Children learn to solve physical problems at the concrete operational stage, and they learn to solve nonphysical problems at the **formal operational stage**, which is *the final stage of cognitive development that begins around the age of 11, during which children learn to reason about abstract concepts.* Childhood ends when formal operations begin, and people are able to reason systematically about abstract concepts such as *liberty* and *love* and about hypotheticals and counterfactuals—about events that have not yet happened, and about events that might have happened but didn't. There are no concrete objects in the world to which words such as *liberating* or *loving* refer, and yet people at the formal operational stage can think and reason about such concepts in the same way that a concrete operational child can think and reason about squishing and folding. The ability to generate, consider, reason about, or mentally "operate on" abstract objects is the hallmark of formal operations.

Discovering Other Minds

As children develop, they discover their own minds. But they also discover the minds of others. Because preoperational children don't fully grasp the fact that they have minds that mentally represent objects, they also don't fully grasp the fact that other people have minds that may mentally represent the same objects in different ways. That's why preoperational children mistakenly expect others to see the world as they do. **Egocentrism** is *the failure to understand that the world appears different to different people.*

Egocentrism is a hallmark of the preoperational stage. For example, 3-year-old children generally don't realize that other people don't know what they know. This fact has been demonstrated in studies using *the false-belief task* (Wimmer & Perner, 1983). In the standard version of this task, children see a puppet named Maxi deposit some chocolate in a cupboard and then leave the room. A second puppet arrives a moment later, finds the chocolate, and moves it to a different

When preoperational children are shown two equal-size glasses filled with equal amounts of liquid, they correctly say that neither glass "has more." But when the contents of one glass are poured into a taller, thinner glass, they incorrectly say that the taller glass now "has more." Concrete operational children don't make this mistake because they recognize that operations such as pouring change the appearance of the liquid but not its actual volume. Macmillan Learning/ Photo by Bianca Moscatelli

conservation The notion that the quantitative properties of an object are invariant despite changes in the object's appearance.

formal operational stage The final stage of cognitive development that begins around the age of 11, during which children learn to reason about abstract concepts.

egocentrism The failure to understand that the world appears different to different people.

People who reach the formal operational stage can reason about abstract concepts such as freedom and justice. These two protesters are taking part in a demonstration in front of the White House, calling for the closing of the U.S. military prison at Guantánamo Bay, Cuba. Jacquelyn Martin/AP Images

When small children are told to hide, they sometimes cover their eyes. Because they can't see you, they assume that you can't see them (Russell, Gee, & Bullard, 2012). *Courtesy of Daniel Gilbert*

theory of mind The understanding that the mind produces representations of the world and that these representations guide behavior.

People with autism often have an unusual ability to concentrate on small details, words, and numbers for extended periods of time. Thorkil Sonne (*right*) started a company called Specialisterne.com, which places people with autism—such as his son Lars (*left*)—at jobs that they can do better than more "neurotypical" people can. *Joachim Ladefoged/VII*

cupboard. The children are then asked where Maxi will look for the chocolate when he returns: in the first cupboard, where he initially put it, or in the second cupboard, where the children know it currently is? Most 5-year-olds realize that Maxi will search the first cupboard because Maxi did not see what the children saw, namely, that the chocolate was moved. But 3-year-olds typically claim that Maxi will look in the second cupboard—because that's where *the children* know the chocolate is, and they assume that what they know, everyone knows! Children are able to give the right answer in the false-belief task somewhere between the ages of 4 to 6 (Callaghan et al., 2005), and children in some cultures are able to give it earlier than children in others (Liu et al., 2008).

On the other hand, even very young children who do not yet fully understand that others have different perceptions or beliefs do seem to understand that other people have different desires. For example, a 2-year-old who likes dogs can understand that other children don't like dogs and can correctly predict that other children will avoid dogs that the child herself would approach. When 18-month-old toddlers see an adult express disgust while eating a food that the toddlers enjoy, they hand the adult a different food, as if they understand that different people have different tastes (Repacholi & Gopnik, 1997).

Eventually, the vast majority of children ultimately come to understand that they and others have minds and that these minds represent the world in different ways. Once children understand these things, they are said to have acquired a **theory of mind**, which is *the understanding that the mind produces representations of the world and that these representations guide behavior*. The age at which most children acquire a theory of mind appears to be influenced by a variety of factors, such as the number of siblings the child has, the frequency with which the child engages in pretend play, whether the child has an imaginary companion, the socioeconomic status of the child's family, and even culture (see A World of Difference: That's the Dumbest Thing I Never Heard!). But of all the factors researchers have studied, language seems to be the most important (Astington & Baird, 2005). Children's language skills are an excellent predictor of how well they perform on false-belief tasks (Happé, 1995).

Language—and especially language about thoughts and feelings—is an important tool for helping children make sense of their own and others' minds (Harris, de Rosnay, & Pons, 2005). This fact also helps explain why deaf children whose parents do not know sign language are slow to acquire a theory of mind (DeVilliers, 2005; Peterson & Siegal, 1999; Peterson et al., 2016; Pyers & Senghas, 2009). Another group of people who are slow to acquire a theory of mind are children with *autism*, a disorder we'll cover in more depth in the Disorders chapter. Although children with autism are typically normal on most intellectual dimensions—and sometimes far better than normal—they have difficulty understanding the inner lives of other people (Dawson et al., 2007; Peterson et al., 2016). They do not seem to understand that other people can have false beliefs (Baron-Cohen, Leslie, & Frith, 1985; Senju et al., 2009), and they have special trouble understanding belief-based emotions such as embarrassment and shame (Baron-Cohen, 1991; Heerey, Keltner, & Capps, 2003).

Cognitive development is a strange and complex journey, and Piaget's ideas about it were nothing short of groundbreaking. Many of his ideas have held up quite well, but in the last few decades, psychologists have discovered two ways in which Piaget got it wrong. First, Piaget thought that children graduated from one stage to another in the same way that they graduated from kindergarten to first grade. But modern psychologists see development as a more fluid, continuous, and less steplike progression. In a sense, cognitive development is more like the gradual change of seasons than it is like graduation day. Second, children acquire many abilities much earlier than Piaget realized (Gopnik, 2012). Every year, clever researchers find new ways

That's the Dumbest Thing I Never Heard!

Everyone sees the world a bit differently. As children develop, they acquire a theory of mind, and one component of that theory is the realization that other people may believe things that the child doesn't, and may not believe things that the child does.

Piaget thought children came to this realization in the course of their social interactions, where they inevitably encountered disagreement. A child says, "That dog is mean," and his father replies, "No, he's very nice." A playmate says, "My house is red," and another responds, "You're nuts. It's blue!" All of the disagreeable talk that children hear eventually leads them to understand that different people have different beliefs about the world.

Although being disagreeable is a popular pastime in Western societies, not all cultures appreciate a good shouting match as much as Americans do. For instance, many Eastern cultures encourage respect for one's elders and family harmony and encourage people to avoid arguments and conflicts. In these cultures, if a person doesn't have something agreeable to say, they often say nothing at all. Thus, children who grow up in these cultures do not normally hear people challenging each other's beliefs—so how do they come to understand that different people *have* different beliefs?

The answer seems to be: s-l-o-w-l-y! For example, in one study, 77% of Australian preschoolers understood that different people have different beliefs, but only 47% of Iranian preschoolers understood the same (Shahaeian et al., 2011). Were the Iranian children just slow learners? Nope. In fact, they were just as likely as the Australian children to have acquired other components of a theory of mind—for example, the realization that different people *like* different things—and they were even *more* likely than the Australian children to realize that people know what they see and not what they don't. It just takes them a bit longer to understand that people have different beliefs presumably because they are exposed to fewer debates about them. The pattern seen in Australia is also seen in the United States, and the pattern seen in Iran is also seen in China, suggesting that this is a stable difference between Western and Eastern cultures (Wellman et al., 2006).

In the end, of course, everyone comes to realize that human beings don't always see eye to eye. But people who live in places where they are encouraged to speak their minds and

When parents debate the best way to get a bike into a car, their children learn that people have different beliefs. For example, Mom believes that Dad should shut up, and Dad doesn't believe that. Yet. PhotoAlto/Laurence Mouton/ Getty Images

debate their differences in public seem to figure that out a bit earlier than most. At least that's what research suggests. Do you agree? Well, why not? What's the matter with you anyway?

of testing infants and children, and every year, textbook authors must lower the age at which cognitive milestones are achieved. Don't be too surprised if in the coming years, someone discovers that zygotes can do algebra.

Discovering Our Cultures

Piaget saw the child as a lone scientist who went out into the world and made observations, developed theories, and then revised those theories in light of new observations. But scientists rarely go it alone. Rather, they receive training from more experienced scientists, inherit the theories and methods of their forebears, and seek each other's opinions. According to the Russian psychologist Lev Vygotsky, children do the same thing. Vygotsky believed that cognitive development was largely the result of the child's interaction with members of his or her own culture, rather than his or her interaction with concrete objects (Vygotsky, 1978).

For example, in both English and Chinese, the numbers beyond 20 are named by a decade (twenty) that is followed by a digit (one), and their names follow a

As Vygotsky pointed out, children are not lone explorers who discover the world for themselves but members of families, communities, and societies that teach them much of what they need to know. Daniel Gilbert

Figure 10.4 JOINT ATTENTION
Joint attention allows children to learn from others. When a 12-month-old infant interacts with an adult (a) who then looks at an object (b), the infant will typically look at the same object (c) (Meltzoff et al., 2009) Republished with permission of A. N. Meltzoff, P. K. Kuhl, T. J. Senjowski, & J. Movellan. Foundations for a new science of learning. Published in *Science*, 2009, Vol. 325, July 17, pp. 284–288; permission conveyed through Copyright Clearance Center

logical pattern (twenty-one, twenty-two, twenty-three, etc.). In Chinese, the numbers from 11 to 19 are constructed the same way (ten-one, ten-two, ten-three . . .). But in English, the names of the numbers between 11 and 19 either reverse the order of the decade and the digit (sixteen, seventeen) or are just plain arbitrary (eleven, twelve). The difference in the regularity of these two systems makes a big difference to the children who must learn them. The fact that 12 is a 10 plus a 2 is obvious to the Chinese child, who actually calls the number "ten-two," but not so obvious to the English-speaking child, who calls it "twelve." In one study, children from many countries were asked to hand an experimenter a certain number of bricks. Some of the bricks were single, and some were glued together in strips of 10. When Asian children were asked to hand the experimenter 26 bricks, they tended to hand over two strips of 10 plus six singles. Non-Asian children used the clumsier strategy of counting out 26 single bricks (Miura et al., 1994). Results such as these suggest that the regularity of the counting system that children inherit can promote or discourage their discovery of basic mathematical facts (Gordon, 2004; Imbo & LeFevre, 2009).

Human children can take advantage of the accumulated wisdom of their species because unlike most animals, they have three essential skills that allow them to learn from others (Meltzoff et al., 2009; Striano & Reid, 2006):

1. *Joint attention* is the ability to focus on what another person is focused on. If an adult turns her head to the left, young infants (3 months) and older infants (9 months) will look to the left. But if the adult first closes her eyes and then looks to the left, the young infant will look to the left, but the older infant will not (Brooks & Meltzoff, 2002). This suggests that younger infants are following the adult's head movements, but that older infants are following her gaze (see **FIGURE 10.4**). They are trying to see what they think she is seeing.

2. *Imitation* is the tendency to do what an adult does, or means to do. Infants naturally mimic adults (Jones, 2007). But very early on, infants begin to mimic adults' *intentions* rather than their actions per se. When an 18-month-old sees an adult's hand slip as the adult tries to pull the lid off a jar, the infant won't copy the slip, but will instead perform the *intended* action of removing the lid (Meltzoff, 1995, 2007; Yu & Kushnir, 2014).

3. *Social referencing* is the ability to use another person's reactions as information about how we should think (Kim, Walden, & Knieps, 2010; Walden & Ogan, 1988). An infant who approaches a new toy will often stop and look back to examine her mother's face for cues about whether Mom thinks the toy is or isn't dangerous.

Joint attention ("I see what you see"), imitation ("I do what you do"), and social referencing ("I think what you think") are three of the basic abilities that allow infants to learn from other members of their species (Heyes, 2016).

BUILD TO THE OUTCOMES

1. Why are infants born with reflexes?

2. What happens at each of Piaget's stages of cognitive development?

3. What does the false-belief task demonstrate?

4. Which children have special difficulty acquiring a theory of mind?

5. How does culture affect cognitive development?

6. What are the three of the basic abilities that allow infants to learn from others?

Infancy and Childhood: Caring and Belonging

Unlike baby turtles, baby humans cannot survive without their caregivers. But what exactly do caregivers provide? Some obvious answers are warmth, safety, and food, and those obvious answers are right. But caregivers also provide something that is far less obvious but every bit as essential to an infant's development.

Social Development

During World War II, psychologists studied infants who were living in orphanages while awaiting adoption. Although these children were warm, safe, and well fed, many were developmentally impaired, both physically and psychologically (Spitz, 1949). A few years later, the psychologists (Harry Harlow 1958; Harlow & Harlow, 1965) discovered that infant rhesus monkeys that were warm, safe, and well fed, but that were not allowed any social contact for the first 6 months of their lives, developed a variety of behavioral abnormalities. They compulsively rocked back and forth while biting themselves, and if they were introduced to other monkeys, they avoided them entirely. These socially isolated monkeys turned out to be incapable of communicating with or learning from others of their kind, and when the females matured

LEARNING OUTCOMES

*   Describe attachment and its four styles.

*   Compare Piaget's and Kohlberg's theories of moral development.

*   Explain the moral intuitionist perspective.

Harlow's monkeys preferred the comfort and warmth of a soft cloth mother (*left*) to the wire mother (*right*), even when the wire mother was associated with food.   Photo Researchers, Inc.

Like hatchlings, human infants need to stay close to their mothers to survive. Unlike hatchlings, human infants know how to get their mothers to come to them, rather than the other way around. John St. Germain/Alamy; Peter Burian/Corbis

attachment The emotional bond that forms between newborns and their primary caregivers.

and became mothers, they ignored, rejected, and sometimes even attacked their own infants. Harlow also discovered that when socially isolated monkeys were put in a cage with two "artificial mothers"—one that was made of wire and dispensed food and one that was made of cloth and dispensed no food—they spent most of their time clinging to the soft cloth mother despite the fact that the wire mother was the source of their nourishment. Clearly, these infants required something more from their caregivers than mere sustenance. But what? The answer is: attachment.

Becoming Attached

Few things are cuter than a string of ducklings following their mother. But how do they know who their mother is? In a series of studies, the biologist Konrad Lorenz discovered that ducklings don't actually know who their mothers are at all. Rather, new hatchlings just faithfully follow the first moving object they see after they are born—even if that object is a human being or a tennis ball. Lorenz (1952) theorized that nature designed birds so that the first moving object they saw was *imprinted* on their brains as "the thing I must always stay near."

Psychiatrist John Bowlby was fascinated by Lorenz's work, as well as by Harlow's studies of rhesus monkeys reared in isolation and the work on children reared in orphanages, and he sought to understand how human infants form attachments to their caregivers (Bowlby, 1969, 1973, 1980). Bowlby began by noting that from the moment they are born, ducks waddle after their mothers and monkeys cling to their mothers' furry chests, because the newborns of both species must stay close to their caregivers to survive. Human infants, he suggested, have a similar need, but because they are much less physically developed than ducks or monkeys, they can neither waddle nor cling. What they can do is smile and cry. When an infant cries, gurgles, coos, makes eye contact, or smiles, most adults reflexively move toward the infant. Smiles and cries are signals to which human adults normally respond.

According to Bowlby, infants initially send these signals to anyone within visual or auditory range, and they keep a "mental tally" of who responds most often and most promptly to their signals. Then, at about 6 months, they begin to target the best and fastest responder, also known as the *primary caregiver*. This person quickly becomes the emotional center of the infant's universe. Infants feel secure in the primary caregiver's presence and will happily crawl around, exploring their environments. But if their primary caregiver gets too far away, infants begin to feel insecure, and they take action to decrease the distance between themselves and their primary caregiver, perhaps by crawling toward their caregiver or perhaps by crying until their caregiver moves toward them. Bowlby believed that all of this happens because evolution has equipped human infants with a social reflex that is every bit as basic as the physical reflexes that cause them to suck and to grasp. Human infants, Bowlby suggested, are predisposed to form an **attachment**—that is, *an emotional bond*—with a primary caregiver.

The nature of these attachments vary, and infants tend to show one of four basic *attachment styles* (Ainsworth et al., 1978), which can be inferred by watching how the infants respond when their caregivers leave them alone for a few minutes and then return:

1. *Secure attachment.* When the caregiver leaves, the infant may or may not be distressed. When she returns, the nondistressed infant acknowledges her with a glance or greeting, and the distressed infant goes to her and is calmed by her presence.

2. *Avoidant attachment.* When the caregiver leaves, the infant is not distressed, and when she returns, the infant does not acknowledge her.

3. *Ambivalent attachment.* When the caregiver leaves, the infant is distressed, and when she returns, the infant rebuffs her, refusing any attempt at calming while arching his or her back and squirming to get away.

4. *Disorganized attachment.* These infants show no consistent pattern of response to their caregiver's leaving and returning.

Most American infants (about 60%) display a secure attachment style, which is the most common style all over the world (van IJzendoorn & Kroonenberg, 1988). However, attachment styles do vary across cultures. For example, German children are more likely to have avoidant than ambivalent attachment styles, whereas Japanese children are more likely to have ambivalent than avoidant attachment styles (Takahashi, 1986).

Attachment Styles

Children's attachment styles are determined in part by their **temperament**, or *characteristic pattern of emotional reactivity* (Thomas & Chess, 1977). Whether measured by parents' reports or by physiological indices such as heart rate or cerebral blood flow, very young children vary in their tendency toward fearfulness, irritability, positive affect, and other emotional traits (Rothbart & Bates, 1998). To some extent, these temperamental differences among infants reflect innate biological differences (Baker et al., 2013). But for the most part, attachment style is determined by an infant's social interactions with his or her caregiver. Mothers of securely attached infants tend to be especially sensitive to signs of their child's emotional state, especially good at detecting their infant's "request" for reassurance, and especially responsive to that request (Ainsworth et al., 1978; De Wolff & van IJzendoorn, 1997). In contrast, mothers of infants with an ambivalent attachment style tend to respond inconsistently, only sometimes attending to their infants when they show signs of distress.

As a result of all their interactions, infants develop an **internal working model of relationships**, which is *a set of beliefs about the self, the primary caregiver, and the relationship between them* (Bretherton & Munholland, 1999). Specifically, infants with a secure attachment style act as though they are certain that their primary caregiver will respond when they feel insecure, and infants with an avoidant attachment style act as though they are certain that their primary caregiver will *not* respond. Infants with an ambivalent attachment style act as though they are uncertain about whether their primary caregiver will respond. Infants with a disorganized attachment style seem to be confused about their caregivers, which has led some psychologists to speculate that this style primarily characterizes children who have been abused (Carolson, 1998; Cicchetti & Toth, 1998).

Differences in how caregivers respond are due in large part to differences in their ability to read their infants' emotional states. Mothers who think of their infants as unique individuals with emotional lives and not just as creatures with urgent physical needs are more likely to have infants who are securely attached (Meins, 2003; Meins et al., 2001). Although such data are merely correlational, there is reason to suspect that a mother's sensitivity and responsiveness are a *cause* of the infant's attachment style. For instance, researchers studied a group of young mothers whose 6-month-old infants were particularly irritable or difficult. Half the mothers participated in a training program designed to sensitize them to their infants' emotional signals and to encourage them to be more responsive. A year or two later, those infants whose mothers had received the training were considerably more likely to have a secure attachment style than were those whose mothers did not receive the training (van den Boom, 1994, 1995).

An infant's attachment style has consequences for the person he or she will become. Children who were securely attached as infants do better than children who were not securely attached on a wide variety of measures, from their academic achievement (Jacobson & Hoffman, 1997) and cognitive functioning (Bernier et al., 2015) to their psychological well-being (Madigan et al., 2013) and social relationships (McElwain, Booth-LaForce, & Wu, 2011; Schneider, Atkinson, & Tardif, 2001; Simpson, Collins, & Salvatore, 2011; Sroufe, Egeland, & Kruetzer, 1990;

temperament A characteristic pattern of emotional reactivity.

internal working model of relationships A set of beliefs about the self, the primary caregiver, and the relationship between them.

Does spending time in day care impair the attachment process? A massive long-term study by the National Institute for Child Health and Human Development showed that attachment style is strongly influenced by maternal sensitivity and responsiveness, but that the quality, amount, stability, or type of day care a child experiences is not in and of itself a cause of poor attachment (Friedman & Boyle, 2008). David Grossman/Alamy

According to Piaget, young children do not realize that moral rules can vary across persons and cultures. For instance, most Americans think it is immoral to eat a dog, but most Vietnamese disagree. HOANG DINH NAM/AFP/Getty Images

Steele et al., 1999; Vondra et al., 2001). Similarly, securely attached infants become more successful adults. Some research suggests that adults continue to apply the working models they developed as infants to their relationships with teachers, friends, and lovers (Waters et al., 2015).

Moral Development

From the moment of birth, human beings can make one distinction quickly and well, and that's the distinction between pleasure and pain. Over the next few years, they begin to notice that their pleasures ("Throwing food is fun") are often someone else's pains ("Throwing food makes Mom mad"), which is a bit of a problem because infants need these other people to survive. So they start to learn how to balance their needs and the needs of those around them, and they do this in part by developing a distinction between *right* and *wrong*.

Knowing What's Right

How do children think about right and wrong? Just as Piaget identified four stages of cognitive development, he also identified three ways in which children's moral thinking shifts as they grow and develop (Piaget, 1932/1965).

1. Children's moral thinking tends to shift *from realism to relativism*. Very young children regard moral rules as real, inviolable truths about the world. For the young child, right and wrong are like day and night: They exist in the world and do not depend on what people think or say. That's why young children generally don't think that a bad action (such as hitting someone) can ever be good, even if everyone agreed to allow it. As they mature, children begin to realize that some moral rules (e.g., wives should obey their husbands) are inventions and not discoveries and that people can therefore agree to adopt them, change them, or abandon them entirely.

2. Children's moral thinking tends to shift *from prescriptions to principles*. Young children think of moral rules as guidelines for specific actions in specific situations. ("Each child can play with the iPad for 5 minutes and must then pass it to the child sitting to his or her left.") As they mature, children come to see that rules are expressions of more general principles, such as fairness and equity, which means that specific rules can be abandoned or modified when they fail to uphold the general principle. ("If Jason missed his turn with the iPad, then he should get two turns now.")

3. Children's moral thinking tends to shift *from outcomes to intentions*. For the young child, an unintentional action that causes great harm ("Josh accidentally broke Dad's iPad") seems "more wrong" than does an intentional action that causes slight harm ("Josh got mad and broke Dad's pencil") because young children tend to judge the morality of an action by its outcome, rather than by the actor's intentions. As they mature, children begin to see that the morality of an action is critically dependent on the actor's state of mind.

Psychologist Lawrence Kohlberg used Piaget's insights as the basis of a detailed theory of the development of moral reasoning (Kohlberg, 1963, 1986). Kohlberg (1958) based his theory on people's responses to a series of "moral dilemmas." For example, people learned about a woman who was dying of cancer but could not afford to pay for the drug that might save her life. So her husband stole the drug from a local pharmacy. People were asked whether the husband's actions were right or wrong, and were asked to explain why. People's answers suggested to Kohlberg that moral reasoning develops in three stages:

1. Most children are at the **preconventional stage**, which is *a stage of moral development in which the morality of an action is primarily determined by its*

preconventional stage A stage of moral development in which the morality of an action is primarily determined by its consequences for the actor.

consequences for the actor. Immoral actions are simply those for which one is punished. For example, children at this stage often base their moral judgment of the husband on the relative costs of one decision ("It would be bad if he got blamed for his wife's death") and another ("It would be bad if he went to jail for stealing").

2. Around adolescence, most people move to the **conventional stage**, which is *a stage of moral development in which the morality of an action is primarily determined by the extent to which it conforms to social rules*. Immoral actions are those for which one is condemned by others. People at this stage argue that the husband must weigh the dishonor he will bring on himself and his family by stealing (i.e., breaking a law) against the guilt he will feel if he allows his wife to die (i.e., failing to fulfill a familial obligation).

3. Finally, most adults move to the **postconventional stage**, which is *a stage of moral development in which the morality of an action is determined by a set of general principles that reflect core values*, such as the right to life, liberty, and the pursuit of happiness. When a behavior violates these principles, it is immoral, and if a law requires these principles to be violated, then it should be disobeyed. For a person who has reached the postconventional stage, a woman's life is always more important than a pharmacy's profits. Thus, stealing the drug is not only a moral behavior, it is a moral obligation.

Research supports Kohlberg's general claim that moral reasoning shifts from an emphasis on punishment to an emphasis on social rules and finally to an emphasis on ethical principles (Walker, 1988). But research also suggests that these stages are not quite so discrete as Kohlberg thought. For instance, a single person might apply preconventional, conventional, and postconventional thinking in different circumstances, which suggests that the developing person does not "reach a stage" so much as he "acquires a skill" that he may or may not use on a particular occasion. Others have criticized Kohlberg's theory on the grounds that it doesn't apply well to different societies. For example, some non-Western societies value obedience and community over liberty and individuality; thus, the moral reasoning of people in those societies may *appear* to reflect a conventional devotion to social norms when it *actually* reflects a postconventional consideration of ethical principles.

Feeling What's Right

Moral dilemmas don't just make us think; they also make us *feel*. Consider this one:

> You are standing on a bridge. Below you can see a runaway trolley hurtling down the track toward five people who will be killed if it remains on its present course. You are sure that you can save these people by flipping a lever that will switch the trolley onto a different track, where it will kill just one person instead of five. Is it morally permissible to divert the trolley and prevent five deaths at the cost of one?

Now consider a slightly different version of this problem:

> You and a large man are standing on a bridge. Below you can see a runaway trolley hurtling down the track toward five people who will be killed if it remains on its present course. You are sure that you can save these people by pushing the large man onto the track, where his body will be caught up in the trolley's wheels and stop it before it kills the five people. Is it morally permissible to push the large man and prevent five deaths at the cost of one?

These scenarios are illustrated in **FIGURE 10.5**. If you are like most people, you concluded that it is morally permissible to pull a switch but not to push a man

During World War II, many Albanian Muslims shielded their Jewish neighbors from the Nazis. "There was no government conspiracy; no underground railroad; no organized resistance of any kind. Only individual Albanians, acting alone, to save the lives of people whose lives were in immediate danger," wrote Norman Gershman, who photographed Muslims such as Baba Haxhi Dede Reshatbardhi (pictured) who saved so many Jewish lives. Godong/Newscom/Robert Harding Picture Library

conventional stage A stage of moral development in which the morality of an action is primarily determined by the extent to which it conforms to social rules.

postconventional stage A stage of moral development in which the morality of an action is determined by a set of general principles that reflect core values.

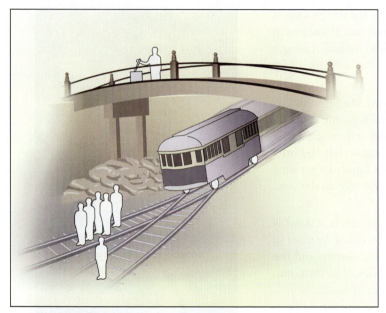 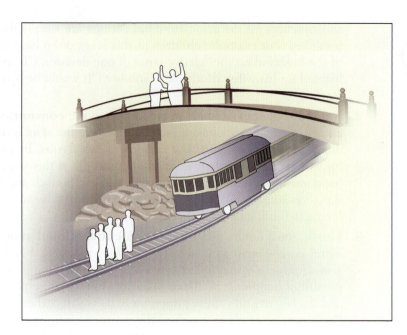

Figure 10.5 THE TROLLEY PROBLEM Why does it seem okay to trade one life for five lives by pulling a switch, but not by pushing a man from a bridge? Research suggests that the scenario shown in (b) elicits a more negative emotional response than does the scenario shown in (a), and this emotional response may be the basis for our moral intuitions.

Most people are upset by the suffering of others, and research suggests that even young children have this response, which may be the basis of their emerging morality. JGI/Jamie Grill/Getty Images

(Greene et al., 2001). In both cases you had to decide whether to sacrifice one human life in order to save five, and in one case you said yes and in another you said no. How can moral reasoning lead to such different conclusions? It can't, and the odds are that you didn't reach these conclusions by moral reasoning at all. Rather, you simply had a strong negative emotional reaction to the thought of pushing another human being into the path of an oncoming trolley and watching him get sliced and diced, and that reaction instantly led you to conclude that pushing him was wrong. Sure, you may have come up with a few good arguments to support this conclusion ("What if he turned around and bit me?" or "I'd hate to get spleen on my new shoes"), but those arguments probably followed rather than preceded your conclusion (Greene, 2013).

The way people respond to cases such as these has convinced some psychologists that moral judgments are the consequences—and not the causes—of emotional reactions (Haidt, 2001; Ongley & Malti, 2014). According to this *moral intuitionist* perspective, we have evolved to react emotionally to a small family of events that are particularly relevant to reproduction and survival, and we have developed the distinction between right and wrong as a way of labeling and explaining these emotional reactions (Hamlin, Wynn, & Bloom, 2007). The moral intuitionist perspective suggests that we consider it immoral to push someone onto the tracks simply because the idea of watching someone suffer makes us feel bad (Greene et al., 2001).

And indeed, other people's suffering seems to have precisely this effect. In fact, watching someone suffer activates the very same brain regions that are activated when we suffer ourselves (Carr et al., 2003; see the discussion of mirror neurons in the Neuroscience and Behavior chapter). In one study, women received a shock or watched their romantic partners receive a shock on different parts of their bodies. The regions of the women's brains that processed information about the location of the shock were activated only when the women experienced the shock themselves, but the regions that processed emotional information were activated whether the women received the shock or observed it (Singer et al., 2004). The fact that we can actually *feel* another person's suffering may explain why even a small child who is incapable of sophisticated moral reasoning still considers it wrong when someone hurts someone else, especially when the person being hurt is similar to the child (Hamlin et al., 2013). Indeed, even very young children say that hitting is wrong, even when an adult instructs someone to do it (Laupa & Turiel, 1986). It appears that from a very early age, other people's suffering can become our suffering, and this leads us to conclude that the actions that caused the suffering are immoral.

BUILD TO THE OUTCOMES

1. How is attachment assessed?

2. How do caregivers influence an infant's attachment style?

3. According to Piaget, what three shifts characterize moral development?

4. What are Kohlberg's three stages of moral development?

5. Do moral judgments come before or after emotional reactions?

6. What happens when we see others suffer?

Adolescence: Minding the Gap

Between childhood and adulthood is an extended developmental stage that may not qualify for a "hood" of its own, but that is clearly distinct from the stages that come before and after. **Adolescence** is *the period of development that begins with the onset of sexual maturity (about 11 to 14 years of age) and lasts until the beginning of adulthood (about 18 to 21 years of age).* Unlike the transition from embryo to fetus, or from infant to child, this transition is sudden and clearly marked. In just 3 or 4 years, the average adolescent gains about 40 pounds and grows about 10 inches. For girls, all this growing starts at about the age of 10 and ends at about the age of 15.5. For boys it starts at about the age of 12 and ends at about the age of 17.5.

The beginning of this growth spurt signals **puberty**, which is *the onset of bodily changes associated with sexual maturity.* These changes involve the **primary sex characteristics**, which are *bodily structures that are directly involved in reproduction.*

LEARNING OUTCOMES

- Explain why the protraction of adolescence matters.

- Describe the determinants of sexual orientation and behavior.

- Explain how adolescents are influenced by their peers.

adolescence The period of development that begins with the onset of sexual maturity (about 11 to 14 years of age) and lasts until the beginning of adulthood (about 18 to 21 years of age).

puberty The onset of bodily changes associated with sexual maturity.

primary sex characteristics Bodily structures that are directly involved in reproduction.

Adolescents are often described as gawky because different parts of their faces and bodies mature at different rates. But as the musician and actor Justin Timberlake can attest, the gawkiness generally clears up. Seth Poppel/Yearbook Library; Stills Press/Alamy

Figure 10.6 YOUR BRAIN ON PUBERTY The development of neurons peaks in the frontal and parietal lobes at about age 12 (a, b) and in the temporal lobe at about age 16 (c), and continues to increase in the occipital lobe through age 20 (d).

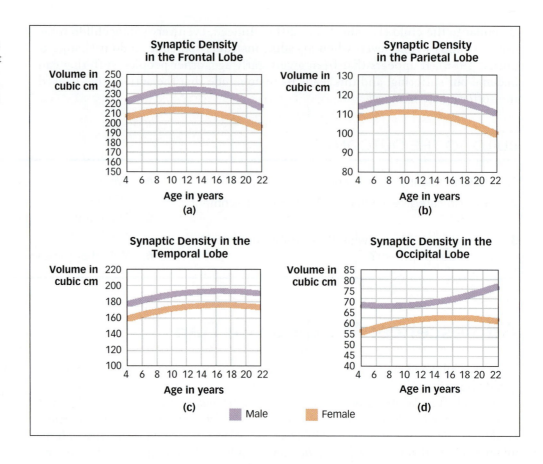

secondary sex characteristics Bodily structures that change dramatically with sexual maturity but that are not directly involved in reproduction.

The famous Leipzig Boys Choir is running out of sopranos. Boys enter the choir at the age of 9 and sing soprano until their voices change. Back in 1723, when Johann Sebastian Bach was the choirmaster, that happened at about the age of 17. Today it happens at about the age of 12. As a result, by the time a soprano learns to sing well, he isn't a soprano anymore. Wolfgang Kluge/AP Images

For example, girls begin to menstruate; boys experience enlargement of the testes, scrotum, and penis and acquire the capacity for ejaculation. These changes also involve the **secondary sex characteristics**, which are *bodily structures that change dramatically with sexual maturity but that are not directly involved in reproduction.* For example, girls' breasts become enlarged and their hips widen. Facial hair, pubic hair, underarm hair, and the lowering of the voice appear in both sexes. This pattern of changes is largely caused by increased production of estrogen in girls and testosterone in boys.

Just as the body changes during adolescence, so too does the brain. For example, there is a marked increase in the growth rate of tissue connecting different regions of the brain just before puberty (Thompson et al., 2000). Between the ages of 6 and 13, the connections between the temporal lobe (the brain region specialized for language) and the parietal lobe (the brain region specialized for understanding spatial relations) multiply rapidly and then stop—just about the time that the critical period for learning a language ends (see **FIGURE 10.6**). There is also a massive increase in number of new synapses in the prefrontal cortex before puberty, followed by a period of "synaptic pruning" after puberty, during which the connections that are not frequently used are eliminated. Clearly, the adolescent brain is a work in progress.

The Protraction of Adolescence

The age at which puberty begins varies across individuals (e.g., people tend to reach puberty at about the same age as their same-sexed parent did) and across ethnic groups (e.g., African American girls tend to reach puberty before European American girls do). It also varies across generations (Malina, Bouchard, & Beunen, 1988). During the 19th century, girls in the United States had their first menstrual periods when they were about 17 years old, but by 1960, that age had fallen to about 13 years. The average age at which American boys reach puberty has now fallen to between 9 and 10 years old (Herman-Giddens et al., 2012).

Why is puberty happening so much earlier now than it did just a few decades ago? For girls, at least, the main reason appears to be diet (Ellis & Garber, 2000). Young women have more body fat today than ever before, and body fat secretes estrogen, which hastens puberty. Some evidence suggests that puberty in girls can also be hastened by exposure to environmental toxins that mimic estrogen (Buck Louis et al., 2008), or by stress (Belsky, 2012; Belsky et al., 2015). Studies show that girls reach puberty earlier if they grow up in unpredictable households with high levels of conflict, or households without a biological father, or if they are victims of early sexual abuse (Greenspan & Deardorff, 2014).

Whatever its causes, early puberty has important psychological consequences. Just two centuries ago, the gap between childhood and adulthood was relatively brief in Western societies because people became physically mature at roughly the same time that they were ready to accept adult roles in society—that is, to marry and get a job. But today, people get married and get jobs much later, because they typically spend 3 to 10 extra years in school. Thus, although the age at which people become physically adult has decreased, the age at which they are prepared or allowed to take on adult responsibilities has increased, and so the period between childhood and adulthood has become stretched out or *protracted*.

Adolescence is often characterized as a time of internal turmoil and external recklessness, and some psychologists have speculated that the protraction of adolescence is partly to blame for its sorry reputation (Moffitt, 1993). In some sense, adolescents are adults who have temporarily been denied a place in adult society. As such, they feel especially compelled to do things to protest these restrictions and demonstrate their adulthood, such as smoking, drinking, using drugs, having sex, and committing crimes.

But the storm and stress of adolescence is neither as prevalent nor as inevitable as HBO would have us believe (Steinberg & Morris, 2001). Research suggests that the "moody adolescent" who is a victim of "raging hormones" is largely a myth. Adolescents are no moodier than children (Buchanan, Eccles, & Becker, 1992), and fluctuations in their hormone levels have a very small impact on their moods (Brooks-Gunn, Graber, & Paikoff, 1994). Although they can be more impulsive and susceptible to peer influence than adults (see **FIGURE 10.7**), they are just as capable

About 60 percent of preindustrial societies don't have a word for adolescence because there is no such stage. When a Krobo girl menstruates for the first time, older women take her into seclusion for 2 weeks and teach her about sex, birth control, and marriage. Afterward, a public ceremony is held, and the young woman who was regarded as a child just days earlier is thereafter regarded as an adult. © Robert Burch Photography

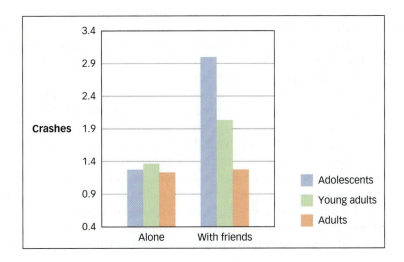

Figure 10.7 HOW DO PEERS AFFECT DECISION MAKING? Adolescents sometimes make bad decisions to impress their friends. Participants in one study played a video driving game with or without their peers in the room. The presence of peers greatly increased the number of risks taken and crashes experienced by adolescents, but had little or no effect on adults (Gardner & Steinberg, 2005).

These students (*left*) may be experimenting with reckless behavior, but they are unlikely to become reckless adults. Of course, the Vermont state trooper (*right*) who is inspecting the car in which four teens died after a night of drinking would probably like to remind them that this rule applies only to those who survive. Fuse/Corbis/Getty Images; ALDEN PELLETT/AP Images

of making wise decisions based on good information (Steinberg, 2007). The fact is that adolescence is not a terribly troubled time for most people, and most adolescents "age out" of whatever troubles they manage to get themselves into (Martin et al., 2014; Sampson & Laub, 1995).

Sexuality

Puberty can be a difficult time, but it is especially difficult for girls who reach it earlier than their peers. These girls are more likely to experience a range of negative consequences, from distress and depression to delinquency and disease (Mendle, Turkheimer, & Emery, 2007). Early bloomers don't have as much time as their peers do to develop the skills necessary to cope with adolescence (Petersen & Grockett, 1985), but because they look so mature, people expect them to act like adults. Early-blooming girls also draw the attention of older men, who may lead them into a variety of unhealthy activities (Ge, Conger, & Elder, 1996). Some research suggests that for girls, the *timing* of puberty has a greater influence on emotional and behavioral problems than does the occurrence of puberty itself (Buchanan et al., 1992). The timing of puberty does not have such consistent effects on boys: Some studies suggest that early-maturing boys do better than their peers, some suggest they do worse, and some suggest that there is no difference at all (Ge, Conger, & Elder, 2001).

Sexual Orientation: A Matter of Biology

For some adolescents, puberty is additionally complicated by the fact that they are attracted to members of the same sex. Roughly 1 to 2% of adolescents identify themselves as gay or lesbian, and about 4 to 7% report having had a same-sex relationship or attraction (Coker, Austin, & Schuster, 2010). This means that lesbian, gay, and bisexual adolescents are different from the vast majority of their peers, and they are in a minority that is often subject to the disdain and disapproval of family, friends, and community. Engaging in sexual activity with members of the same sex is illegal in 75 nations and punishable by death in 11 (Bailey et al., 2016). Although Americans are rapidly becoming more accepting of gay, lesbian, and bisexual people (see **FIGURE 10.8**), many still disapprove to varying degrees, and social disapproval naturally makes an adolescent's life difficult.

What determines whether a person's sexuality is primarily oriented toward the same or the opposite sex? For a long time, psychologists thought the answer was upbringing. For example, during the 1940s and 1950s, psychoanalytic theorists suggested that boys who grow up with domineering mothers and cold, distant fathers are less likely to identify with their fathers and are therefore more likely to be gay. But scientific research has so far failed to identify *any* aspect of parenting that has a significant impact on a child's ultimate sexual orientation (Bell, Weinberg, & Hammersmith, 1981). Indeed, researchers have not even been able to find evidence that a parent's sexual orientation has any influence on the sexual orientation of his or her child (Patterson, 2013). Although peers do have a

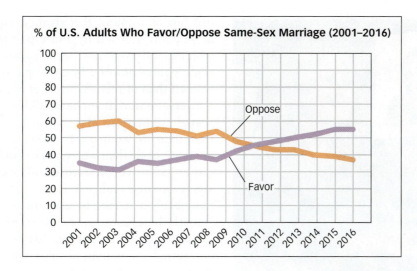

% of U.S. Adults Who Favor/Oppose Same-Sex Marriage (2001–2016)

Oppose

Favor

Figure 10.8 CHANGING ATTITUDES TOWARD SAME-SEX MARRIAGE In 1965, homosexuality was illegal in America, and most Americans thought it was a mental illness. Things have changed dramatically in the last few years, as witnessed by the striking turn-around of Americans' attitudes toward same-sex marriage. BINSAR BAKKARA/AP Images

measurable influence on both the decision to engage in sexual activity and the desire for romantic relationships, they appear to have no influence on an adolescent's sexual orientation (Brakefield et al., 2014).

So what *does* determine a person's sexual orientation? There is now considerable evidence to suggest that biology plays the major role. For instance, the brother or fraternal twin of a gay man (with whom he shares 50% of his genes) has only a 15% chance of being gay, but the identical twin of a gay man (with whom he shares 100% of his genes) has about a 50% chance of being gay (Bailey & Pillard, 1991; Gladue, 1994). A similar pattern has emerged in studies of women (Bailey et al., 1993). Further, in some ways the brains of gay and lesbian people tend to look like the brains of opposite-gendered heterosexual people (Savic & Lindstrom, 2008). For example, among straight women and gay men (both of whom are attracted to men) the left and right cerebral hemispheres tend to be about the same size, whereas among straight men and gay women (both of whom are attracted to women), the left and right cerebral hemispheres tend to be of different sizes.

Another striking piece of evidence for the role of biology is the fact that a child's behavior is a surprisingly good predictor of his or her adult sexual orientation (Bailey & Zucker, 1995). Most children go through a period in which they adamantly refuse to do anything that is stereotypically associated with the opposite gender (Halim et al., 2014). But a few children are eager to engage in what researchers call "gender nonconforming behavior," which for boys includes dressing like a girl and playing with dolls, and for girls includes dressing like a boy and engaging in rough play. These behaviors usually emerge by the time the child is 2 to 4 years old, despite the fact that parents typically discourage them (Cohen-Kettenis & Pfäfflin, 2003). As it turns out, children who engage in gender nonconforming behavior are significantly more likely to become gay, lesbian, or bisexual adults. In one study, participants who watched family videos of children were able to predict the child's ultimate sexual orientation with surprising accuracy (Rieger et al., 2008). This does not mean that every boy who likes pigtails will become a gay man or that every girl who likes pigskin will become a lesbian, but it does mean that some signs of adult sexual orientation are observable long before people begin to experience sexual attraction, around the age of 10.

It is worth noting that men and women differ in how they experience their sexual orientations. For example, a man's sexual orientation is a good predictor of his physiological arousal to erotic stimuli. For example, straight men are aroused by erotic pictures of women but not of men, and gay men are aroused by erotic pictures of men

In 2004, Massachusetts became the first U.S. state to legalize same-sex marriage, and Marcia Kadish (*left*) and Tanya McCloskey became the first couple to make use of the new law. A decade later, the Supreme Court ruled that same-sex marriage was legal in all 50 states. Dina Rudick/The Boston Globe via Getty Images

but not of women. But straight women are equally aroused by erotic pictures of women and men, and lesbians are only slightly more aroused by erotic pictures of women than of men (Chivers et al., 2004; Chivers, Seto, & Blanchard, 2007). Men's sexual orientations also appear to be less fluid than are women's. For instance, men are more likely than women to report being either exclusively heterosexual or exclusively homosexual, whereas women are more likely than men to report being either "mostly heterosexual" or bisexual (Savin-Williams & Vrangalova, 2013). Women's sexual orientations are also more likely than men's to depend on circumstances and to shift over time (Bailey et al., 2016; Baumeister, 2000).

The science of sexual orientation is still young and fraught with conflicting findings, but at least two conclusions are noncontroversial. First, sexual orientation clearly has a biological component and is not just a "lifestyle choice." This is probably why "conversion" or "reparative" therapies that attempt to transform gay, lesbian, or bisexual people into heterosexuals have proved ineffective (American Psychological Association, 2009). Second, human sexual orientation is far more complex and diverse than labels such as "straight" and "gay" seem to suggest. Physiological arousal, psychological attraction, sexual behavior, biological sex, and gender identity are different things that combine in seemingly endless variations that defy simple categorization (see The Real World: Coming to Terms). Indeed, in a recent survey of U.S. adults, the percent who identified as gay or lesbian was only slightly larger than was the percent who identified as "something else" or who said they didn't know the answer (Ward et al., 2014). Human beings are sexual creatures who still have a great deal to learn about this aspect of themselves.

Sexual Behavior: A Matter of Choice

Sexual orientation may not be a choice, but sexual behavior is—and many teenagers choose it. Although the percentage of American high school students who have had sex has been steadily declining in recent years (see **FIGURE 10.9**), it is still nearly

Figure 10.9 TEENAGERS ARE DELAYING SEX The age at which young Americans have sex for the first time has dropped considerably over the last 25 years. CDC, Youth Risk Behavior Surveillance System

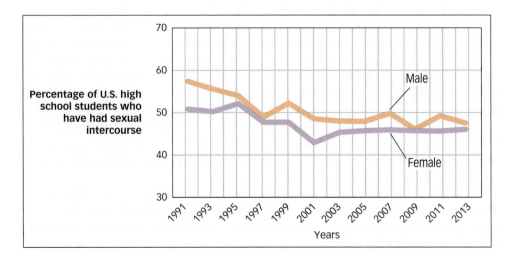

→ Coming to Terms

Sexuality is about both the body and the mind. But people's bodies are hidden beneath their clothes, and people's minds are hidden behind their eyes, so the diversity of sexuality in the real world is all too easy to miss. Understanding it requires understanding three distinct but related concepts.

Sex refers to the bodies we are born with. Most (though not all) human bodies are either male (i.e., they have XY chromosomes and a penis) or female (i.e., they have XX chromosomes and a vagina). *Gender* refers to our identities—how we see ourselves, how we want others to see us, and how it feels to be inside our own skins. Most (though not all) adults identify themselves as men or women. Last, *sexual orientation* refers to the kinds of people to whom we find ourselves attracted. Most (though not all) adults are attracted to people of the opposite sex. The table shows the terms that are typically used to refer to people who differ on these dimensions.

The term *transgender* refers to anyone whose gender and sex do not match, and the term *cisgender* refers to anyone whose gender and sex do match. Most people prefer to be described in terms of their gender rather than their sex, so both transgender and cisgender women typically prefer to be called *she,* and both cisgender and transgender men typically prefer to be called *he.* It makes sense to think of people as they think of themselves.

It also makes sense to talk about them that way. Over time, descriptors of human categories often take on pejorative connotations for the people they describe. The word *homosexual,* for example, has traditionally been used to describe people with same-sex orientations, but it is quickly becoming an unflattering way to refer to gay and lesbian people. Conversely, terms that were once pejorative are sometimes reclaimed by the people whom they were initially meant to demean. For example, in some communities, *queer* is now a positive description of anyone who is not cisgender and straight. The National Queer Arts Festival has been thriving in San Francisco since 1998, but its name would have been an unthinkable slur just 20 years earlier.

The majority of people are cisgender and straight, and all these new categories and changing terms can make them long for simpler times. But there never were simpler times—just times in which the complexity of human sexuality was a secret, hidden from our view. Those times have passed, and the full range of our diversity is now on display. For those who hope to understand it scientifically, this is a welcome change.

		SEX			
		Male		Female	
		Gender		**Gender**	
		Man	Woman	Man	Woman
Sexual Orientation Toward...	Males	Cisgender Gay Man	Transgender Straight Woman	Transgender Gay Man	Cisgender Straight Woman
	Females	Cisgender Straight Man	Transgender Lesbian	Transgender Straight Man	Cisgender Lesbian
	Males & Females	Cisgender Bisexual Man	Transgender Bisexual Woman	Transgender Bisexual Man	Cisgender Bisexual Woman

half. The problem with this is that teenagers' interest in sex typically surpasses their knowledge about it. Ignorance has consequences. Among the American high school students who report having had sexual intercourse, only 59% report using a condom during their last encounter (Kann et al., 2014). Although teen birth rates have been falling in the United States for about 20 years, they are still the highest in the developed world.

What can be done? Sex education leads teens to delay having sex for the first time, increases the likelihood they will use birth control when they do have sex, and lowers the likelihood that they will get pregnant or catch a sexually transmitted disease (Mueller, Gavin, & Kulkarni, 2008; Satcher, 2001). But despite these documented benefits, sex education in American schools is often absent, sketchy, or based on the goal of abstinence rather than harm prevention. Alas, there is little evidence to suggest that abstinence-only programs are effective (Kohler, Manhart, & Lafferty, 2008), and some studies suggest that teens who

The human papilloma virus is a sexually transmitted disease that can lead to cervical cancer. Luckily, there is a vaccine that can prevent it. Some parents worry that being vaccinated will encourage their daughters to have sex early, but studies show that young women who have been vaccinated do not have sex earlier than do those who have not been vaccinated. Blend Images/ERproductions Ltd/ Getty Images

"You're free-range when I say you're free-range."

© Charles Barsotti/The New Yorker/www.cartoonbank .com

take abstinence pledges are just as likely to have sex as are those who don't, but are less likely to use birth control (Rosenbaum, 2009). That's too bad because teenage mothers fare more poorly than teenage women without children on almost every measure of academic and economic achievement, and their children fare more poorly on most measures of educational success and emotional well-being than do the children of older mothers (Olausson et al., 2001).

From Parents to Peers

Children's views of themselves and their world are tightly tied to the views of their parents, but puberty creates a new set of needs that begins to snip away at those bonds by orienting adolescents toward peers rather than parents. Whereas children define themselves almost entirely in terms of their relationships with parents and siblings, adolescence marks a shift in emphasis from family relations to peer relations (Roisman et al., 2004).

Two things can make this shift difficult. First, children cannot choose their parents, but adolescents can choose their peers. As such, adolescents have the power to shape themselves by joining groups that will lead them to develop new values, attitudes, beliefs, and perspectives (Shin & Ryan, 2014). The responsibility this opportunity entails can be overwhelming (Tarantino et al., 2014). Second, as adolescents strive for greater autonomy, their parents naturally rebel. For instance, parents and adolescents tend to disagree about the age at which certain adult behaviors—such as staying out late or having sex—are permissible (Holmbeck & O'Donnell, 1991). Because adolescents and parents often have different ideas about who should control the adolescent's behavior, their relationships become more conflictive and less close, and their interactions become briefer and less frequent (Larson & Richards, 1991).

When adolescents pull away from their parents, they move toward their peers. Studies show that across a wide variety of cultures, historical epochs, and even species, peer relations evolve in a similar way (Dunphy, 1963; Weisfeld, 1999). Most young adolescents initially form groups or "cliques" with same-sex peers, many of whom were friends during childhood (Brown, Mory, & Kinney, 1994). Next, male cliques and female cliques begin to meet in public places, such as town squares or shopping malls, and they begin to interact—but only in groups and only in public.

After a few years, the older members of these same-sex cliques peel off and form smaller, mixed-sex cliques, which may assemble in private as well as in public, but usually assemble as a group (Molloy et al., 2014). Finally, couples (typically but not always a male and a female) peel off from the small, mixed-sex clique and begin romantic relationships.

Studies show that throughout adolescence, people spend increasing amounts of time with opposite-sex peers while maintaining the amount of time they spend with same-sex peers (Richards et al., 1998), and they accomplish this by spending less time with their parents (Larson & Richards, 1991). Although peers exert considerable influence on the adolescent's beliefs and behaviors, this influence generally occurs because adolescents like their peers and want to impress them, and not because the peers exert pressure (Smith, Chein, & Steinberg, 2014; Susman et al., 1994). In fact, as they age, adolescents show an increasing tendency to resist peer pressure (Steinberg & Monahan, 2007). Acceptance by peers is of tremendous importance to adolescents, and those who are rejected by their peers tend to be withdrawn, lonely, and depressed (Pope & Bierman, 1999). Fortunately for those of us who were seventh-grade nerds, individuals who are unpopular in early adolescence can become popular in later adolescence as their peers become less rigid and more tolerant (Kinney, 1993).

Just by looking at where and how these adolescents are standing, you can tell that they are in the early phase of peer relationship. Adrian Sherratt/Alamy

BUILD TO THE OUTCOMES

1. How does the brain change at puberty?
2. What is the importance of an earlier onset of puberty?
3. Are adolescent problems inevitable?
4. What makes adolescence especially difficult?
5. Is sexual orientation a matter of choice?
6. Why do many adolescents make unwise choices about sex?
7. How do family and peer relationships change during adolescence?

adulthood The stage of development that begins around 18 to 21 years and ends at death.

Adulthood: Change We Can't Believe In

In fewer than 7,000 days, a single-celled zygote can become a registered voter. **Adulthood** is *the stage of development that begins around 18 to 21 years and ends at death*. Because physical change slows from a gallop to a crawl, many of us think of adulthood as the destination to which the process of development finally delivers us, and that once we've arrived, our journey is pretty much complete. Nothing could be further from the truth because a whole host of physical, cognitive, and emotional changes take place between our first legal beer and our last legal breath.

LEARNING OUTCOMES

- Describe the physical and psychological changes that occur in adulthood.
- Describe the effects of children on parental happiness.

Changing Abilities

The early 20s are the peak years for health, stamina, vigor, and prowess, and because our psychology is so closely tied to our biology, these are also the years during which many of our cognitive abilities are at their sharpest. If you are a typical college student, then at this very moment you see farther, hear better, and remember more than you ever will again. Enjoy it while you can. Somewhere between the ages of 26 and 30, you will begin the slow and steady decline that will not end until you do. Just 10 or 15 years after puberty, your body will begin to break down in almost every way. Your muscles will be replaced by fat, your skin will become less elastic, your hair will thin and your bones will weaken, your sensory abilities will become less acute, and your brain cells will die at an accelerated rate. Eventually, if you are a woman, your ovaries will stop producing eggs and you will become infertile. Eventually, if you are a man, your erections will be fewer and farther between. Indeed, other than being more resistant to colds and less sensitive to pain, your elderly body just won't work as well as your youthful body does.

As these physical changes accumulate, they will begin to have measurable psychological consequences (Hartshorne & Germine, 2015; Salthouse, 2006). For instance, as your brain ages, your prefrontal cortex and its associated subcortical connections will deteriorate more quickly than the other areas of your brain (Raz, 2000), and you will experience a noticeable decline on many cognitive tasks that require effort, initiative, or strategy. Your memory will get worse overall, though some kinds will get worse than others. For instance, you will experience a greater decline in working memory (the ability to hold information "in mind") than in long-term memory (the ability to retrieve information), a greater decline in episodic memory (the ability to remember particular past events) than in semantic memory (the ability to remember general information such as the meanings of words), and a greater decline in retrieval accuracy than in recognition accuracy (see Data Visualization: Is There a Cognitive Decline With Age Regardless of Cognitive Stimulation? at www.launchpadworks.com).

Is the news all bad? Not really. Even though some of your cognitive machinery will get creakier and rustier as you age, you will learn to use it more skillfully (Bäckman & Dixon, 1992; Salthouse, 1987). Older chess players *remember* chess positions more poorly than younger players do, but they *play* just as well because they learn to search the board more efficiently (Charness, 1981). Older typists *react* more slowly than younger typists do, but they *type* just as quickly and accurately because they are better at anticipating the next word in spoken or written text (Salthouse, 1984). Older airline pilots are worse than younger pilots when it comes to keeping a list of words in short-term memory, but this age difference disappears when those words are the heading commands that pilots receive from the control tower every flight (Morrow et al., 1994). As **FIGURE 10.10** shows, performance on some cognitive tasks peaks when people are young, but performance on other tasks doesn't peak until people are in their 30s, their 40s, and even their 50s (see Hot Science: I Won't Make *That* Mistake Again!).

How do older adults compensate for age-related declines in memory and attention? As you know from the Neuroscience and Behavior chapter, young brains are highly differentiated—that is, they have different parts that do different things. But as the brain ages, it becomes *de-differentiated* (Lindenberger & Baltes, 1994). It appears that the brain is like a bunch of specialists who work independently when they are young and able, but who pull together as a team when each specialist gets older and slower (Park & McDonough, 2013). For example, when young adults try to keep verbal information in

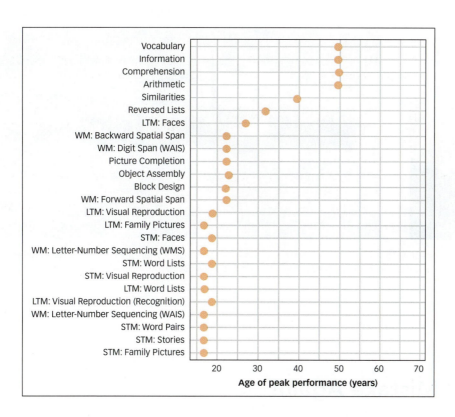

Figure 10.10 AGE-RELATED CHANGES IN COGNITIVE PERFORMANCE This chart shows the age of peak performances on a wide variety of cognitive tests, some of which measure working memory (WM), short-term memory (STM), and long-term memory (LTM). Data from Hartshorne & Germine (2015)

working memory, the left prefrontal cortex is more strongly activated than the right, and when young adults try to keep spatial information in working memory, the right prefrontal cortex is more strongly activated than the left (Smith & Jonides, 1997). But this *bilateral asymmetry* pretty much disappears in older adults, which suggests that the older brain is compensating for the declining abilities of each individual neural structure by calling on its other neural structures to help out (Cabeza, 2002; see **FIGURE 10.11**). The physical machinery breaks down as time passes, and one of the ways in which the brain rises to that challenge is by changing its division of labor.

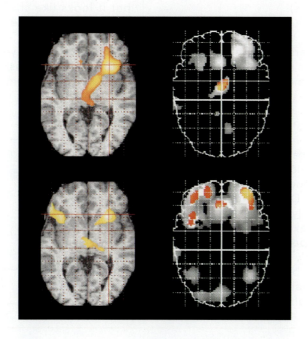

Figure 10.11 BILATERALITY IN OLDER AND YOUNGER BRAINS Across a variety of tasks, older adult brains show bilateral activation, and young adult brains show unilateral activation. One explanation for this is that older brains compensate for the declining abilities of one neural structure by calling on other neural structures for help. Roberto Cabeza, Center for Cognitive Neuroscience, Duke University. Research from Cabeza et al. (1997) and Madden et al. (1999)

One week before his 58th birthday, U.S. Airways pilot Chesley "Sully" Sullenberger made a perfect emergency landing in the Hudson River and saved the lives of everyone on board. None of the passengers wished they'd had a younger pilot. Noah Berger/AP Images; Steven Day/AP Images

I Won't Make *That* Mistake Again!

What was the name of the woman who founded the Red Cross? If you don't know, then ask your parents. Although younger adults outperform older adults on a wide variety of cognitive tasks, answering general-knowledge questions is an exception to this rule. The reason seems obvious: Older adults have had more time to accumulate facts about the world, which explains why they typically clobber their children and grandchildren when playing Trivial Pursuit. But what seems obvious may not be entirely correct. A recent study suggests that older adults don't outperform younger ones simply because they've had more time to get the facts right but because they pay closer attention when they get the facts wrong.

Researchers gave a group of young adults (24 years old on average) and a group of older adults (74 years old on average) a long series of trivia questions (Metcalfe et al., 2015). They asked the participants to answer each question and to say how confident they were in their answers. As expected, older adults got more of the trivia questions right on the very first round.

Next, the researchers gave the participants a chance to learn from their mistakes by showing them the correct answers. No matter how much they knew, all participants naturally made some *surprising mistakes* (i.e., they were wrong about answers in which they'd expressed great confidence) and some *unsurprising mistakes* (i.e., they were wrong about answers in which they'd expressed little confidence).

After the participants finished studying the right answers, the researchers asked the participants to answer all the trivia questions a second time. The y-axis in the graph shows the percentage of incorrectly answered questions from the first round that participants answered correctly in the second round. As the leftmost bars show, younger and older participants learned about the same amount from their surprising mistakes: Discovering that you were completely, totally, and utterly mistaken makes a pretty big impression on people of any age ("I was absolutely *sure* the Red Cross was founded by Florence Nightingale —and man, was I wrong!"). But as the rightmost bars show, older

adults learned much more than younger adults did from their unsurprising mistakes ("I had a vague hunch that it might be Florence Nightingale, but I guess it wasn't"). Apparently, older people pay close attention whenever they are wrong, but younger people only pay close attention when they are *surprised* to be wrong. Grandma may know more about the world than you do because she's been in it longer, but it looks like she's also better at learning from the mistakes she made along the way.

And oh by the way—the founder of the Red Cross was Clara Barton. Someday you'll remember that.

Changing Goals

One reason that Grandpa can't find his car keys is that his prefrontal cortex doesn't work as well as it used to. But another reason is that the location of car keys just isn't the sort of thing that grandfathers want to spend their precious time memorizing (Haase, Heckhausen, & Wrosch, 2013). According to *socioemotional selectivity theory* (Carstensen & Turk-Charles, 1994), younger adults are largely oriented toward the acquisition of information that will be useful to them in the future (e.g., reading restaurant reviews), whereas older adults are generally oriented toward information that brings emotional satisfaction in the present (e.g., reading detective novels). Because young people have such long futures, they invest their time attending to, thinking about, and remembering potentially useful information that may be helpful tomorrow. Because older people have much shorter futures, they spend their time attending to, thinking about, and remembering positive information that fills their emotional needs today. For example, older people perform *much* more poorly than younger people when they are asked to remember a series of unpleasant pictures (see **FIGURE 10.12**) but only *slightly* more poorly when they are asked to remember a series of pleasant pictures (Mather & Carstensen, 2003).

Indeed, compared with younger adults, older adults are generally better at sustaining positive emotions and curtailing negative ones (Isaacowitz, 2012; Isaacowitz & Blanchard-Fields, 2012; Lawton et al., 1992; Mather & Carstensen, 2005). They also experience fewer negative emotions (Carstensen et al., 2000; Charles, Reynolds, & Gatz, 2001; Mroczek & Spiro, 2005; Schilling, Wahl, & Wiegering, 2013) and are more accepting of them when they do (Shallcross et al., 2013). Given all this, you shouldn't be surprised to learn that people find late adulthood to be one of the happiest and most satisfying periods of life (see **FIGURE 10.13**).

Because having a short future orients people toward emotionally satisfying rather than profitable experiences, older adults become more selective about their interaction partners, choosing to spend time with family and a few close friends rather than with a large circle of acquaintances (Chui et al., 2014). One study monitored a group of people from the 1930s to the 1990s and found that their rate of interaction with acquaintances declined from early to middle adulthood, but their rate of interaction with spouses, parents, and siblings remained stable or increased (Carstensen, 1992). "Let's go meet some new people" isn't something that most 60-year-olds tend to say, but "Let's go hang

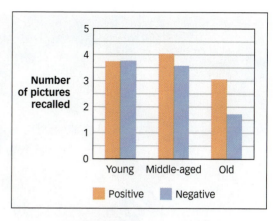

Figure 10.12 MEMORY FOR PICTURES Memory generally declines with age, but the ability to remember negative information—such as unpleasant pictures—declines much more quickly than the ability to remember positive information (Carstensen et al., 2000).

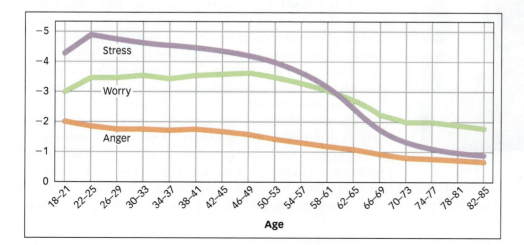

Figure 10.13 EMOTIONS AND AGE Older adults experience much lower levels of stress, worry, and anger than younger adults do (Stone et al., 2010).

As people age, they prefer to spend time with family and a few close friends rather than large circles of acquaintances. *Courtesy of Joanne Gilbert*

out with some old friends" is. It is sad but instructive to note that many of these same cognitive and emotional changes can be observed among younger people who have discovered that their futures will be short because of a terminal illness (Carstensen & Fredrickson, 1998).

Changing Roles

The psychological separation from parents that begins in adolescence usually becomes a physical separation in adulthood. In virtually all human societies, young adults leave home, get married, and have children of their own. If you are an average college-age American, then you are likely to get married at around the age of 27, have approximately 1.8 children, and consider both your partner and your children to be sources of great joy.

But do marriage and children really make us happy? Some data suggest they do. For example, married people report being happier than unmarried people—whether those unmarried people are single, widowed, divorced, or cohabiting (Dion, 2005; Johnson & Wu, 2002; Lucas & Dyrenforth, 2005). But some researchers suggest that married people are happier simply because happy people are likely to get married, and that marriage is often the consequence—and not the cause—of happiness (Lucas et al., 2003). The general consensus among scientists seems to be that both of these positions have merit: Even before marriage, people who will end up married tend to be happier than those who will never marry, but marriage does seem to confer some further happiness benefit, particularly when the members of the couple regard each other as their "best friend" (Helliwell & Grover, 2014). It is worth noting that marriage has become less popular over the last few decades in most Western nations and being single has become an increasingly attractive and satisfying option for many (DePaulo & Morris, 2006). If these trends continue, the happiness boost that marriage seems to provide may soon be a thing of the past.

Children are another story. In general, research suggests that children do not increase their parents' happiness, and may even decrease it (Stanca, 2016). For example, parents typically report lower marital satisfaction than do nonparents—and the more children they have, the less satisfaction they report (Twenge, Campbell, & Foster, 2003). Studies suggest that marital satisfaction starts out high, plummets at about the time that the children are in diapers, begins to recover, plummets again when the children are in adolescence, and returns to its premarital levels only when children leave home (see **FIGURE 10.14**). Given that mothers typically do much more child care than do fathers, it is not surprising that the negative impact of parenthood is stronger for women than for men. Women with young children are especially likely to experience role conflicts ("How am I supposed to manage being a full-time lawyer and a full-time mother?") and restrictions of freedom ("I never get to play tennis anymore").

Research suggests that marriage has a positive impact on happiness. Especially in the first five minutes. *Courtesy of Joanne Gilbert*

One study found that American women were less happy when taking care of their children than when eating, exercising, shopping, napping, or watching

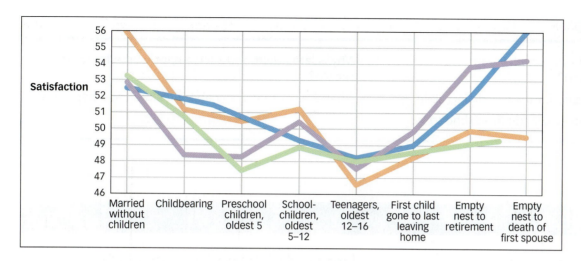

Figure 10.14 MARITAL SATISFACTION OVER THE LIFE SPAN This graph shows the results of four independent studies suggesting that marital satisfaction is highest before children are born and after they leave home (Walker, 1977).

television—and only slightly happier than when they were doing housework (Kahneman et al., 2004).

Does all of this mean that people would be happier if they didn't have children? Not necessarily. Because researchers cannot randomly assign people to be parents or nonparents, studies of the effects of parenthood are necessarily correlational. People who want children and have children may be somewhat less happy than are people who neither want them nor have them, but it is possible that people who want children would be even less happy if they didn't have them. What does seem clear is that raising children is a challenging job that people find most rewarding when they're not in the middle of doing it.

Parents tend to be less happy than nonparents. But this effect is stronger in some countries than in others, and in a few countries, parents are actually happier. In 2015, parents in Macedonia (*left*) experienced the largest "happiness penalty" and parents in Montenegro (*right*) experienced the largest "happiness premium." Bill Bachmann/Getty Images; and Witold Skrypczak/Getty Images

BUILD TO THE OUTCOMES

1. What physical and psychological changes are associated with adulthood?

2. How do adults compensate for their declining abilities?

3. How do informational goals change in adulthood?

4. Why is late adulthood such a happy time for most people?

5. What does research say about children and happiness?

CHAPTER REVIEW

Prenatality: A Womb With a View

- Developmental psychology studies continuity and change across the life span.

- The prenatal stage of development begins when a sperm fertilizes an egg, producing a zygote. The zygote develops into an embryo at 2 weeks and then into a fetus at 8 weeks.

- The fetal environment has important physical and psychological influences on the fetus. In addition to the food a pregnant woman eats, teratogens—agents that impair fetal development—can affect the fetus. The most common teratogens are tobacco and alcohol.

- In the womb, the fetus can hear sounds and become familiar with those it hears often, such as its mother's voice.

Infancy and Childhood: Doing and Thinking

- Infants have a limited range of vision, but they can see and remember objects that appear within it. They learn to control their bodies from the top down and from the center out.

- Infants slowly develop theories about how the world works. Piaget believed that these theories developed through four stages in which children learn basic facts about the world, such as the fact that objects continue to exist even when they are out of sight, and the fact that objects have enduring properties that are not changed by superficial transformations. Children also learn that their minds represent objects; hence, objects may not be as they appear, and others may not see them as the child does.

- Cognitive development also comes about through social interactions in which children are given tools for understanding that have been developed over millennia by members of their cultures.

Infancy and Childhood: Caring and Belonging

- At a very early age, human beings develop strong emotional ties to their primary caregivers. The quality of these ties is determined both by the caregiver's behavior and the child's temperament.

- Piaget concluded that children's reasoning about right and wrong is initially based on inviolable truths about the world, but as they mature, children begin to consider the actor's intentions as well as the extent to which the action obeys abstract moral principles.

- Kohlberg argued that children's reasoning about right and wrong is initially based on an action's consequences, later on how it aligns with social rules, and finally on core values.

- Moral judgments may be the consequences of our emotional reactions to the suffering of others.

Adolescence: Minding the Gap

- Adolescence is a stage of development that begins with puberty, the onset of sexual maturity of the human body. Puberty now occurs earlier than ever before, and the entrance of young people into adult society occurs later.

- Adolescents are somewhat more likely to do things that are risky or illegal, but they rarely inflict serious or enduring harm on themselves or others.

- Although most people are attracted to members of the opposite sex, some are not, and research suggests that biology plays a key role in determining a person's sexual orientation. Sex education has been shown to reduce risky sexual behavior.

- As adolescents seek to develop their adult identities, they seek increasing autonomy from their parents and become more peer oriented, forming single-sex cliques, followed by mixed-sex cliques. Finally, they pair off as couples.

Adulthood: Change We Can't Believe In

- Performance on most cognitive tasks peaks when people are in their 20s, but performance on other tasks peaks when people are in their 30s, 40s, and even 50s.
- Older people develop a variety of strategies to compensate for their cognitive declines.
- Older people are more oriented toward emotional satisfaction, which influences the way they attend to and remember information, the size and structure of their social networks, and their happiness.
- For most people, adulthood means leaving home, getting married, and having children. The responsibilities of parenthood present a significant challenge to people's happiness.

KEY CONCEPT QUIZ

1. The sequence of prenatal development is
   a. fetus, embryo, zygote.
   b. zygote, embryo, fetus.
   c. embryo, zygote, fetus.
   d. zygote, fetus, embryo.

2. Learning begins
   a. in the womb.
   b. at birth.
   c. in the newborn stage.
   d. in infancy.

3. The proximodistal rule states that
   a. motor skills emerge in sequence from the center to the periphery.
   b. motor skills emerge in sequence from the top to the bottom.
   c. motor skills such as rooting are hard-wired by nature.
   d. simple motor skills disappear as more sophisticated motor skills emerge.

4. Which statement is true of vulnerability to teratogens?
   a. Heavy alcohol use during the early stages of pregnancy will probably not damage the fetus because critical brain systems have not yet developed.
   b. Exposure of the mother to environmental poisons such as lead in the drinking water can interfere with the development of the fetus.
   c. The babies of women who smoke while pregnant may have impaired development, but exposure to second-hand smoke is okay.
   d. All of the above

5. Piaget believed that infants construct _____, which are theories about the way the world works.
   a. assimilations
   b. accommodations
   c. schemas
   d. habituations

6. Once children understand that human behavior is guided by mental representations, they are said to have acquired
   a. joint attention.
   b. a theory of mind.
   c. formal operational ability.
   d. egocentrism.

7. When infants in a new situation examine their mother's face for cues about what to do, they are demonstrating an ability known as
   a. joint attention.
   b. social referencing.
   c. imitation.
   d. All of the above

8. The capacity for attachment may be innate, but the quality of attachment is influenced by
   a. the child's temperament.
   b. the primary caregiver's ability to read the child's emotional state.
   c. the interaction between the child and the primary caregiver.
   d. All of the above

9. According to Kohlberg, each stage in the development of moral reasoning is characterized by a specific focus. What is the correct sequence of these stages?
   a. focus on consequences, focus on ethical principles, focus on social rules
   b. focus on ethical principles, focus on social rules, focus on consequences
   c. focus on consequences, focus on social rules, focus on ethical principles
   d. focus on social rules, focus on consequences, focus on ethical principles

10. Evidence indicates that American adolescents are
   a. moodier than are children.
   b. victims of raging hormones.
   c. likely to develop drinking problems.
   d. living in a protracted gap between childhood and adulthood.

11. Scientific evidence suggests that _____ play(s) a key role in determining a person's sexual orientation.
   a. personal choices
   b. parenting styles
   c. sibling relationships
   d. biology

12. Adolescents place the greatest emphasis on relationships with

 a. peers.
 b. parents.
 c. siblings.
 d. nonparental authority figures.

13. The peak years for health, stamina, vigor, and prowess are

 a. childhood.
 b. the early teens.
 c. the early 20s.
 d. the early 30s.

14. Data suggest that, for most people, the last decades of life are

 a. characterized by an increase in negative emotions.
 b. spent attending to the most useful information.
 c. extremely satisfying.
 d. a time during which they begin to interact with a much wider circle of people.

15. Which statement is true of marital satisfaction over the life span?

 a. It increases steadily.
 b. It decreases steadily.
 c. It is remarkably stable.
 d. It shows peaks and valleys, corresponding to the presence and ages of children.

 **LearningCurve**   Don't stop now! Quizzing yourself is a powerful study tool. Go to LearningCurve at www.launchpadworks.com for more practice.

KEY TERMS

developmental psychology (p. 308)
zygote (p. 309)
germinal stage (p. 309)
embryonic stage (p. 309)
fetal stage (p. 309)
myelination (p. 310)
teratogen (p. 310)
fetal alcohol syndrome (FAS) (p. 310)
infancy (p. 311)

motor development (p. 312)
motor reflexes (p. 312)
cephalocaudal rule (p. 312)
proximodistal rule (p. 312)
cognitive development (p. 313)
sensorimotor stage (p. 313)
schemas (p. 313)
assimilation (p. 313)
accommodation (p. 313)
object permanence (p. 314)

childhood (p. 314)
preoperational stage (p. 314)
concrete operational stage (p. 314)
conservation (p. 315)
formal operational stage (p. 315)
egocentrism (p. 315)
theory of mind (p. 316)
attachment (p. 320)
temperament (p. 321)

internal working model of relationships (p. 321)
preconventional stage (p. 322)
conventional stage (p. 323)
postconventional stage (p. 323)
adolescence (p. 325)
puberty (p. 325)
primary sex characteristics (p. 325)
secondary sex characteristics (p. 326)
adulthood (p. 333)

CHANGING MINDS

1. One of your friends recently got married, and she and her husband are planning to have children. You mention to your friend that once this happens she'll have to stop drinking. She scoffs. "They make it sound as though a pregnant woman who drinks alcohol is murdering her baby. Look, my mom drank wine every weekend when she was pregnant with me, and I'm just fine." What is your friend failing to understand about the effects of alcohol on prenatal development? What other teratogens might you tell her about?

2. You are at the grocery store when you spot a crying child in a stroller. The mother picks up the child and cuddles it until it stops crying. A grocery clerk is standing next to you, stocking the shelves. He leans over and says, "Now, that's bad parenting. If you pick up and cuddle a child every time it cries, you're reinforcing the behavior, and the result will be a very spoiled child." Do you agree? Does research suggest that it is generally good or generally bad for mothers to be responsive to their infants' emotional needs?

3. You and your roommate are watching a movie in which a young man tells his parents that he's gay. The parents react badly and decide that they should send him to a "camp" where he can learn to change his sexual orientation. Your roommate turns to you: "Do you know anything about this? Can people really be changed from gay to straight?" What would you tell your friend about "conversion therapy" and about the factors that determine sexual orientation?

4. One of your cousins has just turned 30 and, to his horror, has discovered a gray hair. "This is the end," he says. "Soon I'll start losing my eyesight, growing new chins, and forgetting how to use my cell phone. Aging is just one long, slow, agonizing decline." What could you tell your cousin to cheer him up? Does everything in life get worse with age?

ANSWERS TO KEY CONCEPT QUIZ

1. b; 2. a; 3. a; 4. b; 5. c; 6. b; 7. b; 8. d; 9. c; 10. d; 11. d; 12. a; 13. c; 14. c; 15. d.

Personality

11

Growing up, Stefani Joanne Angelina Germanotta seemed to have personality. As a child, she was said to have shown up at the occasional family gathering naked. Now, known as the pop star Lady Gaga, she continues the tradition of being different. Her first albums, *The Fame* and *The Fame Monster,* and the fact that she calls her fans "Little Monsters" and herself the "Mother Monster," hinted she might have issues. But she, like most of us, is not one-dimensional. Yes, her style is eccentric and seems silly to many (we're looking at you, raw meat dress), but she also is a serious supporter of humanitarian and personal causes, including equality for people who are gay, bisexual, lesbian, or transgender (as in her song "Born This Way"). Lady Gaga is one of a kind. She has personality in an important sense—she has qualities that make her psychologically different from other people.

THE FORCES THAT CREATE ANY ONE PERSONALITY ARE something of a mystery. Your personality is different from anyone else's and expresses itself pretty consistently across settings—at home, in the classroom, and elsewhere. But how and why do people differ psychologically? By studying many unique individuals, psychologists seek to gather enough information to answer these central questions of personality psychology scientifically.

Personality is *an individual's characteristic style of behaving, thinking, and feeling.* Whether Lady Gaga's quirks are real or merely put on for publicity, they certainly are hers and they show her distinct personality. In this chapter, we will explore personality, first by looking at what it is and how it is measured, and then by focusing on each of four main approaches to understanding personality: trait–biological, psychodynamic, humanistic–existential, and social–cognitive. At the end of the chapter, we discuss the psychology of self to see how our views of what we are like can shape and define our personality.

The singer Lady Gaga in her meat dress at the MTV Video Music Awards, September 2010. PA Wire/AP Images

personality An individual's characteristic style of behaving, thinking, and feeling.

Personality: What It Is and How It Is Measured

LEARNING OUTCOMES

- Explain how prior and anticipated events explain personality differences.
- Compare personality inventories and projective techniques.

Howard Stern
Ray Tamarra/Film-
magic/Getty Images

Hillary Clinton
Lawrence Jackson/AP
Images

Kim Kardashian
Steve Granitz/Wireim-
age/Getty Images

Chris Rock
Earl Gibson III/Getty
Images for ESSENCE

How would you describe each of these personalities?

If someone said, "You have no personality," how would you feel? Like a boring, grayish lump who should go out and get a personality as soon as possible? As a rule, people don't strive for a personality—one seems to develop naturally as we travel through life. As psychologists have tried to understand the process of personality development, they have pondered questions of description (*how* do people differ?), explanation (*why* do people differ?), and the more quantitative question of measurement (how can personality be *assessed*?).

Describing and Explaining Personality

As the first biologists attempted to classify all plants and animals (whether lichens or ants or fossilized lions), personality psychologists began by labeling and describing different personalities. Most personality psychologists focus on specific, psychologically meaningful individual differences, characteristics such as honesty, anxiety, or moodiness. Still, personality is often in the eye of the beholder. When one person describes another as a "conceited jerk," for example, you may wonder whether you have just learned more about the describer or the person being described. It is interesting that studies that ask acquaintances to describe each other find a high degree of similarity among any one individual's descriptions of many different people ("Jason thinks that Carlos is considerate, Renata is kind, and Jean Paul is nice to others"). In contrast, resemblance is quite low when many people describe one person ("Carlos thinks Jason is smart, Renata thinks he is competitive, and Jean Paul thinks he has a good sense of humor"; Dornbusch et al., 1965).

What leads Lady Gaga to all of her entertaining extremes? Many psychologists attempt to explain personality differences in terms of *prior events* that may have shaped an individual's personality or *anticipated events* that motivate the person to reveal particular personality characteristics. In a biological prior event, Stefani Germanotta received genes from her parents that may have led her to develop into the sort of person who loves putting on a display (and raw meat). Researchers interested in events that happen prior to our behavior study our genes, brains, and other aspects of our biological makeup, and also delve into our subconscious and into our circumstances and interpersonal surroundings. The consideration of *anticipated events* emphasizes the person's own, subjective perspective and often seems intimate and personal in its reflection of the person's inner life (hopes, fears, and aspirations).

Of course, our understanding of how the baby named Stefani Germanotta grew into the adult Lady Gaga (or of the life of any woman or man) also depends on insights into the interaction between the prior and anticipated events: We need to know how our history may shape our motivations.

Measuring Personality

Of all the things psychologists have set out to measure, personality may be one of the toughest. How do you capture the uniqueness of a person? What aspects of people's personalities are important to know about? How should we quantify them? The general personality measures can be classified broadly into personality inventories and projective techniques.

Personality Inventories Rely on Self-Reporting

To learn about an individual's personality, you could follow the person around and, clipboard in hand, record every single thing the person does, says, thinks, and feels (including how long this goes on before the person calls the police). Some observations might involve your own impressions (Day 5: seems to be getting irritable); others would involve objectively observable events that anyone could verify (Day 7: grabbed my pencil and broke it in half, then bit my hand).

Psychologists have figured out ways to obtain objective data on personality without driving their subjects to violence. The most popular technique is **self-report**, *a method in which people provide subjective information about their own thoughts, feelings, or behaviors, typically via questionnaire or interview.* Scales based on the content of self-reports have been devised to assess a whole range of personality characteristics, all the way from general tendencies such as overall happiness (Lyubomirsky, 2008; Lyubomirsky & Lepper, 1999) to specific ones such as responding rapidly to insults (Swann & Rentfrow, 2001) or complaining about poor service (Lerman, 2006).

For example, the **Minnesota Multiphasic Personality Inventory (MMPI)** is *a well-researched clinical questionnaire that is used to assess personality and psychological problems.* The MMPI was developed in 1939 and has been revised several times over the years, leading up to the current version, the MMPI–2–RF (restructured form; Ben-Porath & Tellegen, 2008). The MMPI–2–RF consists of 338 self-descriptive statements to which the respondent answers "true," "false," or "cannot say." The MMPI–2–RF measures a wide range of psychological constructs: clinical problems (e.g., antisocial behavior, thought dysfunction), somatic problems (e.g., head pain, cognitive complaints), internalizing problems (e.g., anxiety, self-doubt), externalizing problems (e.g., aggression, substance abuse), and interpersonal problems (e.g., family problems, avoidance). The MMPI–2–RF also includes *validity scales* that assess a person's attitudes toward test taking and any tendency to try to distort the results by faking answers.

Personality inventories such as the MMPI–2–RF are easy to administer: All that is needed is the test and a pencil (or a computer-based version). The respondent's scores are then calculated and compared with the average ratings of thousands of other test takers. Because no human interpretation of the responses is needed (i.e., "true" means true, "false" means false, etc.), any potential biases of the person giving the test are minimized. Of course, an accurate measurement of personality will only occur if people provide accurate responses. Although self-report test results are easy to obtain, critics of this approach highlight several limitations. One problem is that many people have a tendency to respond in a socially desirable way, such that they underreport things that are unflattering or embarrassing. Perhaps even more problematic is that there are many things we don't know about ourselves and so are unable to report! Studies show that people often are inaccurate in their self-report about what they have experienced in the past, what factors are motivating their behaviors in the present, or how they will feel or behave in the future (Wilson, 2009).

self-report A method in which a person provides subjective information about his or her own thoughts, feelings, or behaviors, typically via questionnaire or interview.

Minnesota Multiphasic Personality Inventory (MMPI) A well-researched clinical questionnaire that is used to assess personality and psychological problems.

Personality inventories ask people to report what traits they possess; however, many psychologists believe that people do not always know what's in their mind. Can we rely on people to accurately report on their personality? Spencer Grant/ PhotoEdit

Figure 11.1 SAMPLE RORSCHACH INKBLOT Test takers are shown a card such as this sample and asked, "What might this be?" What they perceive, and why they believe it looks that way, are assumed to reflect unconscious aspects of their personality. Science Source

projective tests Tests designed to reveal inner aspects of individuals' personalities by analysis of their responses to a standard series of ambiguous stimuli.

Rorschach Inkblot Test A projective technique in which respondents' inner thoughts and feelings are believed to be revealed by analysis of their responses to a set of unstructured inkblots.

Thematic Apperception Test (TAT) A projective technique in which respondents' underlying motives, concerns, and the way they see the social world are believed to be revealed through analysis of the stories they make up about ambiguous pictures of people.

Figure 11.2 SAMPLE TAT CARD Test takers are shown cards with ambiguous scenes such as this sample and are asked to tell a story about what is happening in the picture. The main themes of the story, the thoughts and feelings of the characters, and how the story develops and resolves are considered useful indices of unconscious aspects of an individual's personality (Murray, 1943). Lewis J. Merrim/Science Source

Projective Techniques Rely on Analysis of Ambiguous Information

A second, somewhat controversial, class of tools for evaluating personality designed to circumvent the limitations of self-report mentioned above, is **projective tests**, which are *tests designed to reveal inner aspects of individuals' personalities by analysis of their responses to a standard series of ambiguous stimuli.* The developers of projective tests assume that people will project personality factors that are below awareness—wishes, concerns, impulses, and ways of seeing the world—onto the ambiguous stimuli and will not censor these responses. Probably the best known is the **Rorschach Inkblot Test**, *a projective technique in which respondents' inner thoughts and feelings are believed to be revealed by analysis of their responses to a set of unstructured inkblots.* An example inkblot is shown in **FIGURE 11.1**. Responses are scored according to complicated systems (derived in part from research with people with psychological disorders) that classify what people see (Exner, 1993; Rapaport, 1946). For example, most people who look at Figure 11.1 report seeing birds or people. Someone who reports seeing something very unusual (e.g., "I see two purple tigers eating a velvet cheeseburger") may be experiencing thoughts and feelings that are very different from those of most other people.

The **Thematic Apperception Test (TAT)** is *a projective technique in which respondents' underlying motives, concerns, and the way they see the social world are believed to be revealed through analysis of the stories they make up about ambiguous pictures of people.* To get a sense of the test, look at **FIGURE 11.2**. The test administrator shows the respondent the card and asks him or her to tell a story about the picture, asking questions such as: Who is the woman shown on the card? What is happening? What will happen next? Different people tell very different stories about the images. In creating the stories, the respondent is thought to identify with the main characters and to project his or her view of others and the world onto the other details in the drawing. Thus, any details that are not obviously drawn from the picture are believed to be projected onto the story from the respondent's own desires and internal conflicts.

The value of projective tests is debated by psychologists. For example, if a respondent tells a story about an abusive father, the examiner must always add an interpretation (Was this about the respondent's actual father, or was the respondent merely trying to be funny or provocative?), and that interpretation could well be the scorer's *own* projection into the mind of the test taker. Thus, despite the rich picture of a personality and the insights into an individual's motives that these tests offer, we should understand projective tests primarily as a way in which a psychologist can get to know someone personally and intuitively (McClelland et al., 1953). When measured by rigorous scientific criteria, projective tests such as the TAT and the Rorschach have not been found to be reliable or valid in predicting behavior (Lilienfeld, Lynn, & Lohr, 2003).

Methods Utilizing Technology

Newer personality measurement methods are moving beyond both self-report inventories and projective tests (Robins, Fraley, & Krueger, 2007). High-tech methods such as wireless communication, real-time computer analysis, and automated behavior identification open the door to personality measurements that are leaps beyond following the person around with a clipboard—and can lead to surprising findings. The stereotype that women are more talkative than men, for example, was challenged by findings when 396 college students in the United States and Mexico each spent several days wearing an EAR (electronically activated recorder) that captured random snippets of their talk (Mehl et al., 2009). The result? Women and men were *equally* talkative, each averaging about 16,000 words per day. The advanced measurement of how people differ (and how they do not) is a key step in understanding personality.

Psychologists also are using social media to better understand personality traits and how people express themselves in different ways. An important advantage of this approach, as with the EAR, is that it allows psychologists to study people as they actually behave out in the world while interacting with others (versus in the lab under experimental conditions). For example, one recent study analyzed over 700 million words and phrases that 75,000 people posted on their Facebook pages and compared them to the results from personality tests given to the same people (Schwartz et al., 2013). The results revealed significant differences in how males and females express themselves, as well as differences by age and by personality. For instance, females use more words about emotions, whereas males use more words about objects and more swear words. People who post about going out and partying also score high on extraversion, people who post about being "sick of" things also score high on neuroticism, and people who post about computers and Pokémon cards also score high on introversion. As the world creates newer forms of communicating, psychologists benefit by having newer ways of studying personality.

The EAR (electronically activated recorder), shown here, recorded parts of the conversations of college men and women and found that, when measured objectively in this way, there is no difference between women and men in the amount that they talk to others (Mehl et al., 2009). Thanks to Stephanie Levitt; © Matthias Mehl, University of Arizona

BUILD TO THE OUTCOMES

1. What does it mean to say that personality is in the eye of the beholder?

2. Compare the reliability of personality inventories and projective tests.

3. What is the advantage of measurements taken with the EAR and social media?

The Trait Approach: Identifying Patterns of Behavior

Imagine writing a story about the people you know. To capture their special qualities, you might describe their traits: Keesha is *friendly*, *aggressive*, and *domineering*; Seth is *flaky*, *humorous*, and *superficial*. With a thesaurus and a free afternoon, you might even be able to describe William as *perspicacious*, *flagitious*, and *callipygian*. The trait approach to personality uses such trait terms to characterize differences among individuals. In attempting to create manageable and meaningful sets of descriptors, trait theorists face two significant challenges: narrowing down the almost infinite set of adjectives and answering the more basic question of why people have particular traits and whether those traits arise from biological or hereditary foundations.

LEARNING OUTCOMES

- Describe how the trait approach to personality has changed over time.

- Describe the traits in the Big Five Factor Model.

- Explain the biological basis for personality traits.

Traits as Behavioral Dispositions and Motives

One way to think about personality is as a combination of traits. This was the approach of Gordon Allport (1937), one of the first trait theorists, who believed people could be described in terms of traits just as an object could be described in terms of its properties. He saw a **trait** as *a relatively stable disposition to behave in a particular and consistent way.* For example, a person who keeps his books organized alphabetically in bookshelves, hangs his clothing neatly in the closet, and keeps a clear agenda in his smartphone or daily planner can be said to have the trait of *orderliness.* This trait consistently manifests itself in a variety of settings.

trait A relatively stable disposition to behave in a particular and consistent way.

The orderliness trait *describes* a person but doesn't *explain* his or her behavior. Why does the person behave in this way? A trait might provide an explanation for behavior in two basic ways: The trait may be a preexisting disposition of the person that causes the person's behavior, or it may be a motivation that guides the person's behavior. Allport saw traits as preexisting dispositions, causes of behavior that reliably trigger that behavior. The person's orderliness, for example, is an inner property of the person that will cause the person to straighten things up and be tidy in a wide array of situations. Other personality theorists suggested instead that traits reflect motives. Just as a hunger motive might explain someone's many trips to the snack bar, a need for orderliness might explain the neat closet and alphabetically organized bookshelves (Murray & Kluckhohn, 1953). Researchers examining traits as causes have used personality inventories to measure them, whereas those examining traits as motives have more often used projective tests.

The Search for Core Traits

Picking a single trait such as orderliness and studying it in depth doesn't get us very far in the search for the core of human character: the basic set of traits that defines how humans differ from each other. How have researchers tried to discover the core personality traits?

Early Research Focused on Adjectives That Describe Personality

The study of core traits began with an exploration of how personality is represented in the store of wisdom we call *language*. Generation after generation, people have described people with words, so early psychologists proposed that core traits could be discerned by finding the main themes in all the adjectives used to describe personality. In one such analysis, a painstaking count of relevant words in a dictionary of English resulted in a list of over 18,000 potential traits (Allport & Odbert, 1936)! Attempts to narrow down the list to a more manageable set depend on the idea that traits might be related in a hierarchical pattern (see **FIGURE 11.3**), with

Figure 11.3 HIERARCHICAL STRUCTURE OF TRAITS Traits may be organized in a hierarchy in which many specific behavioral tendencies are associated with a higher-order trait (Eysenck, 1990).

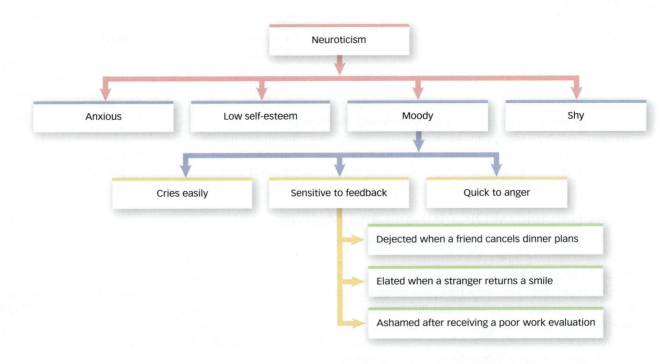

more general or abstract traits at higher levels than more specific or concrete traits. The highest-level traits are sometimes called dimensions or *factors* of personality.

But how many factors are there? Different researchers have proposed different answers. Cattell (1950) proposed a 16-factor theory of personality (way down from 18,000, but still a lot), whereas Hans Eysenck (1967) simplified things nicely with a model of personality with only two major traits (although he later expanded it to three). Eysenck identified one dimension, Extraversion, that distinguished people who are sociable and active (extraverts) from those who are more introspective and quiet (introverts). He also identified a second dimension, Neuroticism, ranging from the tendency to be very neurotic or emotionally unstable to the tendency to be more emotionally stable. The third factor he proposed was Psychoticism, which refers to the extent to which a person is impulsive or hostile. (Note that nowadays, the term *psychotic* refers to an abnormal mental state marked by detachment from reality. This is discussed further in the Disorders chapter.)

A Consensus Is Reached: The Big Five Dimensions of Personality

Today, most researchers agree that personality is best captured by 5 factors, rather than by 2, 3, 16, or 18,000 (John & Srivastava, 1999; McCrae & Costa, 1999). The **Big Five**, as they are affectionately called, are *the traits of the five-factor personality model: openness to experience, conscientiousness, extraversion, agreeableness, and neuroticism* (see **TABLE 11.1**; remember them by the initials O.C.E.A.N.). The five-factor model, which overlaps with the pioneering work of Cattell and Eysenck, is now widely preferred for several reasons. First, this set of five factors strikes the right balance between accounting for wide variation in personality while avoiding overlapping traits. Second, in a large number of studies using different kinds of data (people's descriptions of their own personalities, other people's descriptions of their personalities, interviewer checklists, and behavioral observation), the same five factors have emerged. Third, and perhaps most important, the basic five-factor structure seems to show up across a wide range of participants, including children, adults in other cultures, and even among those who use other languages, suggesting that the Big Five may be universal (John & Srivastava, 1999). It turns out that the Big Five personality traits also predict people's online behavior on social networking sites such as Facebook (see Hot Science: Personality on the Surface).

Research on the Big Five has shown that people's personalities tend to remain fairly stable through their lifetime (Caspi, Roberts, & Shiner, 2005). William James offered the opinion that "in most of us, by the age of thirty, the character has set like plaster, and will never soften again" (James, 1890, p. 121), but this turns out to be too strong a view. Some variability is typical in childhood, and though there is less in adolescence, some personality change can even occur in adulthood for some people (Srivistava et al., 2003). In general, people become slightly more conscientious in their 20s (got to keep that job!) and a bit more agreeable in their 30s (got to keep those friends!). Neuroticism decreases with age, but only among women (Srivastava et al., 2003). So enjoy the

Big Five The traits of the five-factor model: openness to experience, conscientiousness, extraversion, agreeableness, and neuroticism.

TABLE 11.1	The Big Five Factor Model	
	High on trait	**Low on trait**
Openness to experience	imaginative	down-to-earth
	variety	routine
	independent	conforming
Conscientiousness	organized	disorganized
	careful	careless
	self-disciplined	weak-willed
Extraversion	social	retiring
	fun loving	sober
	affectionate	reserved
Agreeableness	softhearted	ruthless
	trusting	suspicious
	helpful	uncooperative
Neuroticism	worried	calm
	insecure	secure
	self-pitying	self-satisfied

Personality on the Surface

When you judge someone as friend or foe, interesting or boring, how do you do it? It's nice to think that your impressions of personality are based on solid foundations. You wouldn't judge personality based on something as shallow as someone's looks, or what's on his Facebook page, would you? These criteria may seem to be flimsy bases for understanding personality, but it turns out that some remarkably accurate personality judgments can be made from exactly such superficial cues.

Studies have shown that extraverts tend to talk faster than others and to subtly mimic other people's behavior as a means of building rapport with them (Duffy & Chartrand, 2015), and people high in openness to experience are more likely to have tattoos (Swami et al., 2012). Findings such as these suggest that people can manipulate their surface identities to try to make desired impressions on others and that surface signs of personality might therefore be false or misleading. However, one recent study of people's Facebook pages, which are clearly surface expressions of personality intended for others to see, found that the personalities people project online are similar to their own scores on traditional personality tests (Schwartz et al., 2013). The signs of personality that appear on the surface may be more than skin deep.

If we go one step further, people's Facebook activity is significantly associated with their self-reported personality traits. People high in extraversion report having more Facebook friends as well as making more status updates and comments. People high in agreeableness make more comments on their friends' posts, whereas those high on sensation seeking and openness to experience report playing a lot of games. And as you might have guessed, people high on narcissism post lots of comments, as well as lots of pictures of themselves (Seidman, 2013; Wang et al., 2012).

They say you can't judge a book by its cover, but some new research suggests you can judge a person by their Facebook page. Pablo Martinez Monsivais/AP Images

 personality you have now because it may be changing soon (see also Data Visualization: Does Personality Remain Stable over Time? at www.launchpadworks.com).

Traits as Biological Building Blocks

Can we explain *why* a person has a stable set of personality traits? Many trait theorists have argued that unchangeable brain and biological processes produce the remarkable stability of traits over the life span. Brain damage certainly can produce personality change, as the classic case of Phineas Gage so vividly demonstrates (see the Neuroscience and Behavior chapter). You may recall that after the blasting accident that blew a steel rod through his frontal lobes, Gage showed a dramatic loss of social appropriateness and conscientiousness (Damasio, 1994). In fact, when someone experiences a profound change in personality, testing often reveals the presence of such brain pathologies as Alzheimer's disease, stroke, or brain tumor (Feinberg, 2001). Antidepressant medication and other pharmaceutical treatments that change brain chemistry also can trigger personality changes, making people, for example, somewhat more extraverted and less neurotic (Bagby et al., 1999; Knutson et al., 1998).

Genes, Traits, and Personality

Some of the most compelling evidence for the importance of biological factors in personality comes from genetics. Simply put, the more genes you have in common with someone, the more similar your personalities are likely to be. For example, in one review of studies involving over 24,000 twin pairs (Loehlin, 1992), identical twins (who share 100% of their genes) proved markedly more similar to each other in personality than did fraternal twins (who share on average only 50% of their genes). And identical twins reared apart in adoptive families end up at least as similar in personality as those who grew up together (McGue & Bouchard, 1998; Tellegen et al., 1988). These and other studies suggest that simply growing up in the same family does not make people very similar—but genes do.

People who share genes often have striking similarities in behavior and attitude. One study that examined 3,000 pairs of identical and fraternal twins found similar views on topics such as socialism, church authority, the death penalty, and interracial marriage (Martin et al., 1986). It is very unlikely that a specific gene is directly responsible for a complex psychological outcome such as beliefs about social or political issues. Rather, a set of genes (or, more likely, many interacting genes) may produce specific characteristics or tendencies to think in a conservative or a liberal manner. One recent study examined the DNA of 13,000 people and measured the extent to which they reported conservative versus liberal attitudes. The researchers found associations between conservatism–liberalism and chromosomal regions linked to mental flexibility, or the extent to which people change their thinking in response to shifts in their environment, which could be one of the factors influencing our views on social and political issues (Hatemi et al., 2011). Current research by psychological scientists is aimed at better understanding how variations in our genetic code may contribute to the development of personality.

Our genes influence our personality in various ways. For instance, genetic factors can affect how rigidly versus flexibly we think about things such as religion and politics. This Trump supporter probably shares the same religious and political leanings as other members of his family. George Frey/Getty Images

Gender Differences: Biology or Culture?

Do you think there is a typical female personality or a typical male personality? On a variety of personality characteristics, men and women on average seem to be far more similar in personality than they are different (Hyde, 2005). However, researchers have found some reliable differences between men and women that conform to North American stereotypes of masculine and feminine. For example, researchers have found women to be more verbally expressive, more sensitive to nonverbal cues, and more nurturing than are men. Males are more physically aggressive than females, but females engage in more relational aggression (e.g., using relationships to harm someone, such as intentionally excluding them from a social group) than do males, even from a very young age (Crick & Grotpeter, 1995; Leff, Waasdorp, & Crick, 2010; see A World of Difference: Why Do Males and Females Have Different Personality Traits?).

Many of the gender differences that exist among adults are much less pronounced during childhood. For instance, one review of over 150 previous studies that included more than 20,000 participants found gender differences in the expression of emotion, with girls showing more internalizing emotions such as sadness and anxiety, and boys showing more externalizing emotions like anger (Chaplin & Aldao, 2013). However, these differences were much more pronounced as children aged into adolescence, suggesting that cultural factors may play a role in how children learn to express their emotions. The finding that gender differences in personality do not begin to emerge until adolescence also has been reported in studies conducted across dozens of different cultures around the world, suggesting that this is a universal phenomenon (De Bolle et al., 2015).

Research has shown that there are small differences in the personalities of men versus women; however, these differences are largely absent during childhood and don't emerge until adolescence, suggesting that they may be learned based on cultural expectations. This brother and sister seem to have the same personality. Their dog looks happy though. Eric Raptosh Photography/Getty Images

A WORLD OF DIFFERENCE

Why Do Males and Females Have Different Personality Traits?

Although the gender differences in personality are quite small, they tend to get a lot of attention—and spur a lot of debate about origins. The evolutionary perspective holds that men and women have evolved different personality characteristics, in part because their reproductive success depends on different behaviors. For instance, aggressiveness in men may have an adaptive value in intimidating sexual rivals; women who are agreeable and nurturing may have evolved to protect and ensure the survival of their offspring (Campbell, 1999), as well as to secure a reliable mate and provider (Buss, 1989).

On the other hand, a social-cognitive perspective known as *social role theory* holds that personality characteristics and behavioral differences between men and women result from cultural standards and expectations: socially permissible jobs, activities, and family positions (Eagly & Wood, 1999). Because of their physical size and their freedom from childbearing, men historically have taken roles of greater power—roles that in postindustrial society don't necessarily require physical strength. These differences then snowball, with men generally taking roles that require assertiveness and aggression (e.g., executive, school principal, surgeon) and women pursuing roles that

emphasize greater supportiveness and nurturance (e.g., nurse, day care worker, teacher).

Regardless of the source of gender differences in personality, the degree to which people identify personally with masculine and feminine stereotypes may tell us about important personality differences between individuals. Sandra Bem (1974) designed a scale to assess the degree of identification with stereotypically masculine traits (such as self-reliance, independence, and assertiveness) and feminine traits (such as affection, sympathy, and kindness). Bem suggested that

Cultures differ in their appreciation of male and female characteristics, but the Hindu deity Ardhanarishwara represents the value of combining both parts of human nature. Male on one side and female on the other, this god is symbolic of the dual nature of the sacred. The only real problem with such side-by-side androgyny comes in finding clothes that fit. Ardhanarishvara, University of California, Berkeley Art Museum and Pacific Film Archive, gift of Jean and Francis Marshall, 1999.15.10. Photographed by Ben Blackwell

psychologically *androgynous* people (those who adopt the best of both worlds and identify with positive feminine traits such as kindness and positive masculine traits such as assertiveness might be better adjusted than people who identify strongly with only one sex role. So far, the data seem to support this idea. For instance, those who endorse an androgynous sex role report fewer symptoms of depression than those with a masculine or feminine role, regardless of their biological sex (Vafaei et al., 2016). This is also good news for the Hindu deity pictured above.

Another factor that may contribute to the emergence of personality differences in adolescence, however, is the emergence of differences in sex hormones during puberty. As you know from the Development chapter, a lot of things change during adolescence (e.g., more hormones, more interactions with friends, less time spent with parents), and it can be difficult to know what changes are causing what other changes. Interestingly, however, the effect of hormones on personality can be studied experimentally. One recent study followed a sample of transgender men over a 3-month period during which they were undergoing testosterone treatment (in an effort to make their bodies more masculine). Personality tests administered before and after testosterone treatment revealed that significant changes occurred, with the transgender men viewing themselves as being more masculine and their scores more closely matching those of nontransgender men (Keo-Meier et al., 2015).

Traits Are Wired in the Brain

What neurophysiological mechanisms might influence the development of personality traits? Eysenck (1967) speculated that extraversion and introversion might arise from individual differences in cortical arousal. Eysenck suggested that extraverts pursue stimulation because their *reticular formation* (the part of the brain that regulates arousal or alertness, as described in the Neuroscience and Behavior chapter) is not easily stimulated. To achieve greater cortical arousal and feel fully alert, Eysenck argued, extraverts seek out social interaction, parties, and other activities to achieve mental stimulation. In contrast, introverts may prefer reading or quiet activities because their cortex is very easily stimulated to a point higher than optimal alertness.

Behavioral and physiological research generally supports Eysenck's view. When introverts and extraverts are presented with a range of intense stimuli, introverts respond more strongly, including salivating more when a drop of lemon juice is placed on their tongues and reacting more negatively to electric shocks or loud noises (Bartol & Costello, 1976; Stelmack, 1990). This reactivity has an impact on the ability to concentrate: Extraverts tend to perform well at tasks that are done in a noisy, arousing context (such as bartending or teaching), whereas introverts are better at tasks that require concentration in tranquil contexts (such as the work of a librarian or nighttime security guard; Geen, 1984; Lieberman & Rosenthal, 2001; Matthews & Gilliland, 1999).

In a refined version of Eysenck's ideas, Jeffrey Gray (1970) proposed that the dimensions of extraversion–introversion and neuroticism reflect two basic brain systems. The *behavioral activation system (BAS)*, essentially a "go" system, activates approach behavior in response to the anticipation of reward. The extravert has a highly reactive BAS and will actively engage the environment, seeking social reinforcement and being on the go. The *behavioral inhibition system (BIS)*, a "stop" system, inhibits behavior in response to stimuli signaling punishment. The anxious or introverted person, in turn, has a highly reactive BIS and will focus on negative outcomes and be on the lookout for stop signs.

Recent brain imaging studies have suggested the core personality traits may arise from individual differences in the volume of the different brain regions associated with each trait. For instance, self-reported neuroticism is correlated with the volume of brain regions involved in sensitivity to threat; agreeableness with areas associated with processing information about the mental states of other people; conscientiousness with regions involved in self-regulation; and extraversion with areas associated with processing information about reward (DeYoung et al., 2010). Research aimed at understanding how the structure and activity of our brains can contribute to the formation of our personality traits is still in its early stages but is a growing area of the field that many believe holds great promise for helping us better understand how we each develop into the unique people that we are.

Extraverts pursue stimulation in the form of people, loud noise, and bright colors. Introverts tend to prefer softer, quieter settings. Pop quiz: Miley Cyrus—introvert or extravert? Kevin Winter/Getty Images

BUILD TO THE OUTCOMES

1. How might traits explain behavior?

2. How do psychologists identify the core personality traits?

3. What are the strengths of the five-factor model?

4. What do studies of twins tell us about personality?

5. Are there significant personality differences between the genders?

6. What neurological differences explain why extraverts pursue more stimulation that introverts?

The Psychodynamic Approach: Forces That Lie Beneath Awareness

Sigmund Freud was the first psychology theorist to be honored with his own bobblehead doll. Let's hope he's not the last. The Photo Works

psychodynamic approach An approach that regards personality as formed by needs, strivings, and desires largely operating outside of awareness—motives that also can produce emotional disorders.

id The part of the mind containing the drives present at birth; it is the source of our bodily needs, wants, desires, and impulses, particularly our sexual and aggressive drives.

superego The mental system that reflects the internalization of cultural rules, mainly learned as parents exercise their authority.

ego The component of personality, developed through contact with the external world, that enables us to deal with life's practical demands.

Rather than trying to understand personality in terms of broad theories for describing individual differences, Freud looked for personality in the details: the meanings and insights revealed by careful analysis of the tiniest blemishes in a person's thought and behavior. Working with patients who came to him with disorders that did not seem to have any physical basis, he began by interpreting the origins of their everyday mistakes and memory lapses, errors that have come to be called *Freudian slips*.

The theories of Freud and his followers (discussed in the Treatment chapter) are referred to as the **psychodynamic approach**, *an approach that regards personality as formed by needs, strivings, and desires largely operating outside of awareness—motives that can produce emotional disorders.* The real engines of personality, in this view, are forces of which we are largely unaware.

The Structure of the Mind: Id, Ego, and Superego

To explain the emotional difficulties that beset his patients, Freud proposed that the mind consists of three independent, interacting, and often conflicting systems: the id, the superego, and the ego.

The most basic system, the **id**, is *the part of the mind containing the drives present at birth; it is the source of our bodily needs, wants, desires, and impulses, particularly our sexual and aggressive drives.* The id motivates the tendency to seek immediate gratification of any impulse. If governed by the id alone, you would never be able to tolerate the buildup of hunger while waiting to be served at a restaurant but would simply grab food from tables nearby.

Opposite the id is the **superego**, *the mental system that reflects the internalization of cultural rules, mainly learned as parents exercise their authority.* The superego acts as a kind of conscience, punishing us when it finds we are doing or thinking something wrong (by producing guilt or other painful feelings) and rewarding us (with feelings of pride or self-congratulation) for living up to ideal standards.

The final system of the mind, according to psychoanalytic theory, is the **ego**, *the component of personality, developed through contact with the external world, that enables us to deal with life's practical demands.* The ego is a regulating mechanism that enables us to delay gratifying immediate needs and function effectively in the real world. It is

"I'm sorry, I'm not speaking to anyone tonight. My defense mechanisms seem to be out of order."

Joseph Mirachi/The New Yorker Collection/Cartoonbank.com

the mediator between the id and the superego. The ego helps you resist the impulse to snatch others' food and also finds the restaurant and pays the check.

Freud believed that the relative strength of the interactions among the three systems of mind (i.e., which system is usually dominant) determines an individual's basic personality structure. He believed that the dynamics among the id, superego, and ego are largely governed by *anxiety,* an unpleasant feeling that arises when unwanted thoughts or feelings occur, such as when the id seeks a gratification that the ego thinks will lead to real-world dangers or that the superego sees as leading to punishment. When the ego receives an "alert" signal in the form of anxiety, it launches into a defensive position in an attempt to ward off the anxiety. According to Freud, it does so using one of several different **defense mechanisms,** *unconscious coping mechanisms that reduce anxiety generated by threats from unacceptable impulses* (see **TABLE 11.2**). Psychodynamically oriented psychologists believe that defense

defense mechanisms Unconscious coping mechanisms that reduce anxiety generated by threats from unacceptable impulses.

TABLE 11.2	Defense Mechanisms	
Repression is the first defense the ego tries, but if it is inadequate, then other defense mechanisms may come into play.		
Defense Mechanism	**Description**	**Example**
Repression	Removing painful experiences and unacceptable impulses from the conscious mind: "motivated forgetting"	Not lashing out physically in anger; putting a bad experience out of your mind
Rationalization	Supplying a reasonable-sounding explanation for unacceptable feelings and behavior to conceal (mostly from oneself) one's underlying motives or feelings	Dropping calculus, allegedly because of poor ventilation in the classroom
Reaction formation	Unconsciously replacing threatening inner wishes and fantasies with an exaggerated version of their opposite	Being rude to someone to whom you're attracted
Projection	Attributing one's own threatening feelings, motives, or impulses to another person or group	Judging others as being dishonest because you believe that you are dishonest
Regression	Reverting to an immature behavior or earlier stage of development, a time when things felt more secure, to deal with internal conflict and perceived threat	Using baby talk, even though able to use appropriate speech, in response to distress
Displacement	Shifting unacceptable wishes or drives to a neutral or less threatening alternative	Slamming a door; yelling at someone other than the person at whom you're angry
Identification	Dealing with feelings of threat and anxiety by unconsciously taking on the characteristics of another person who seems more powerful or better able to cope	A bullied child becoming a bully
Sublimation	Channeling unacceptable sexual or aggressive drives into socially acceptable and culturally enhancing activities	Diverting anger to the football or rugby field, or other contact sport

psychosexual stages Distinct early life stages through which personality is formed as children experience sexual pleasures from specific body areas and caregivers redirect or interfere with those pleasures.

fixation A phenomenon in which a person's pleasure-seeking drives become psychologically stuck, or arrested, at a particular psychosexual stage.

oral stage The first psychosexual stage, in which experience centers on the pleasures and frustrations associated with the mouth, sucking, and being fed.

anal stage The second psychosexual stage, in which experience is dominated by the pleasures and frustrations associated with the anus, retention and expulsion of feces and urine, and toilet training.

phallic stage The third psychosexual stage, in which experience is dominated by the pleasure, conflict, and frustration associated with the phallic–genital region, as well as coping with powerful incestuous feelings of love, hate, jealousy, and conflict.

Oedipus conflict A developmental experience in which a child's conflicting feelings toward the opposite-sex parent are (usually) resolved by identifying with the same-sex parent.

latency stage The fourth psychosexual stage, in which the primary focus is on the further development of intellectual, creative, interpersonal, and athletic skills.

genital stage The fifth and final psychosexual stage, the time for the coming together of the mature adult personality with a capacity to love, work, and relate to others in a mutually satisfying and reciprocal manner.

One of the id's desires is to make a fine mess (a desire that is often frustrated early in life, perhaps during the anal stage). The famous painter Jackson Pollock found a way to make extraordinarily fine messes—behavior that at some level all of us envy. Martha Holmes/The LIFE Picture Collection/Getty Images

mechanisms help us overcome anxiety and engage effectively with the outside world and that our characteristic style of defense becomes our signature in dealing with the world—and an essential aspect of our personality.

Psychosexual Stages and the Development of Personality

Freud also proposed that a person's basic personality is formed before 6 years of age during a series of **psychosexual stages**, *distinct early life stages through which personality is formed as children experience sexual pleasures from specific body areas and caregivers redirect or interfere with those pleasures.*

Problems and conflicts encountered at any psychosexual stage, Freud believed, will influence personality in adulthood. Conflict resulting from a person's being deprived or, paradoxically, overindulged at a given stage could result in **fixation**, *a phenomenon in which a person's pleasure-seeking drives become psychologically stuck, or arrested, at a particular psychosexual stage.* Here's how he explained each stage and the effects of fixation at each stage:

- In the first year and a half of life, the infant is in the **oral stage**, *the first psychosexual stage, in which experience centers on the pleasures and frustrations associated with the mouth, sucking, and being fed.* Infants who are deprived of pleasurable feeding or indulgently overfed are believed to have a personality style in which they focus on issues related to fullness and emptiness and what they can "take in" from others.

- Between 2 and 3 years of age, the child moves on to the **anal stage**, *the second psychosexual stage, in which experience is dominated by the pleasures and frustrations associated with the anus, retention and expulsion of feces and urine, and toilet training.* Individuals who have had difficulty negotiating this conflict are believed to develop a rigid personality and remain preoccupied with issues of control.

- Between the ages of 3 and 5 years, the child is in the **phallic stage**, *the third psychosexual stage, in which experience is dominated by the pleasure, conflict, and frustration associated with the phallic–genital region, as well as coping with powerful incestuous feelings of love, hate, jealousy, and conflict.* According to Freud, children in the phallic stage experience the **Oedipus conflict**, *a developmental experience in which a child's conflicting feelings toward the opposite-sex parent are (usually) resolved by identifying with the same-sex parent.*

- Between the ages of 5 and 13, children experience the **latency stage**, *the fourth psychosexual stage, in which the primary focus is on the further development of intellectual, creative, interpersonal, and athletic skills.* Because Freud believed that the most significant aspects of personality development occur before the age of 6, simply making it to the latency period relatively undisturbed by conflicts of the earlier stages is a sign of healthy personality development.

- At puberty and thereafter, the **genital stage** is *the fifth and final psychosexual stage, representing the coming together of the mature adult personality with a capacity to love, work, and relate to others in a mutually satisfying and reciprocal manner.* Freud believed that people who are fixated in a prior stage fail to develop healthy adult sexuality and a well-adjusted adult personality.

What should we make of all this? On the one hand, the psychoanalytic theory of psychosexual stages offers an intriguing picture of early family relationships and the extent to which they allow the child to satisfy basic needs and wishes. On the other hand, critics argue that psychodynamic explanations lack any real evidence and tend to focus on provocative after-the-fact interpretation rather than testable prediction. The psychosexual stage theory offers a compelling set of story lines for interpreting lives once they have unfolded, but it has not generated clear-cut predictions supported by research.

BUILD TO THE OUTCOMES

1. According to Freud, how is personality shaped by the interaction of the id, superego, and ego?

2. What are the various defense mechanisms we use to reduce anxiety?

3. How can fixation influence adult personality?

4. What is believed to occur in each psychosexual stage?

5. Why do critics say Freud's psychosexual stages are more interpretation than explanation?

The Humanistic–Existential Approach: Personality as Choice

During the 1950s and 1960s, psychologists began to try to understand personality from a very different viewpoint. Humanistic and existential theorists turned attention to how humans make *healthy choices* that create their personalities. *Humanistic psychologists* emphasized a positive, optimistic view of human nature that highlights people's inherent goodness and their potential for personal growth. *Existentialist psychologists* focused on the individual as a responsible agent who is free to create and live his or her life while negotiating the issue of meaning and the reality of death. The *humanistic–existential approach* integrates these insights with a focus on how a personality can become optimal.

Human Needs and Self-Actualization

Humanists see the **self-actualizing tendency**, *the human motive toward realizing our inner potential*, as a major factor in personality. The pursuit of knowledge, the expression of one's creativity, the quest for spiritual enlightenment, and the desire to give to society all are examples of self-actualization. As you saw in the Emotion and Motivation chapter, the humanistic theorist Abraham Maslow (1943) proposed a *hierarchy of needs*, a model of essential human needs arranged according to their priority, in which basic physiological and safety needs must be satisfied before a person can afford to focus on higher-level psychological needs. Only when these basic needs are met can one pursue higher needs, culminating in *self-actualization*: the need to be good, to be fully alive, and to find meaning in life.

Humanist psychologists explain individual personality differences as arising from the various ways that the environment facilitates—or blocks—attempts to satisfy psychological needs. For example, someone with the inherent potential to be a great scientist, artist, parent, or teacher might never realize these talents if his or her energies and resources are instead directed toward meeting basic needs of security, belongingness, and the like. Research indicates that when people shape their lives around goals that do not match their true nature and capabilities, they are less likely to be happy than those whose lives and goals do match (Ryan & Deci, 2000).

It feels great to be doing exactly what you are capable of doing. Engagement in tasks that exactly match one's abilities creates a mental state of energized focus that

LEARNING OUTCOMES

- Describe the humanistic–existential approach to personality.

- Explain the role of self-actualization and angst in personality development.

self-actualizing tendency The human motive toward realizing our inner potential.

Decades of research have shown that growing up in a distressed neighborhood is associated with worse educational, occupational, and health outcomes. Humanistic psychologists would suggest that people in such settings must struggle to meet their basic daily needs and so do not have opportunities for self-actualization. Image Source/Getty Images

Figure 11.4 FLOW EXPERIENCE
It feels good to do things that challenge your abilities but that don't challenge them too much; this feeling between boredom and anxiety is the "flow experience" (Csikszentmihalyi, 1990).

existential approach A school of thought that regards personality as governed by an individual's ongoing choices and decisions in the context of the realities of life and death.

humanists call *flow* (see **FIGURE 11.4**; Csikszentmihalyi, 1990). Tasks that are below our abilities cause boredom, those that are too challenging cause anxiety, and those that are "just right" lead to the experience of flow. If you know how to play the piano, for example, and are playing a Chopin prelude that you know well enough that it just matches your abilities, you are likely to experience this optimal state. People report being happier at these times than at any other times. Humanists believe that such peak experiences, or states of flow, reflect the realization of one's human potential and represent the height of personality development.

Personality as Existence

Existentialists agree with humanists about many of the features of personality but focus on challenges to the human condition that are more profound than the lack of a nurturing environment. For existentialists, specific aspects of the human condition, such as awareness of our own existence and the ability to make choices about how to behave, have a double-edged quality: They bring an extraordinary richness and dignity to human life, but they also force us to confront realities that are difficult to face, such as the prospect of our own death. The **existential approach** is *a school of thought that regards personality as governed by an individual's ongoing choices and decisions in the context of the realities of life and death.*

According to the existential perspective, the difficulties we face in finding meaning in life and in accepting the responsibility of making free choices provoke a type of anxiety existentialists call *angst* (the anxiety of fully being). The human ability to consider limitless numbers of goals and actions is exhilarating, but it can also open the door to profound questions such as Why am I here? What is the meaning of my life?

Thinking about the meaning of existence also can evoke an awareness of the inevitability of death. What is the purpose of living if life as we know it will end one day? Alternatively, does life have more meaning, given that it is so temporary? Existential theorists do not suggest that people consider these profound existential issues on a day-to-day and moment-to-moment basis. Rather than ruminating about death and meaning, people typically pursue superficial answers that help them deal with the angst and dread they experience, and the defenses they construct form the basis of their personalities (Binswanger, 1958; May, 1983). Some people organize their lives around obtaining material possessions; others may immerse themselves in drugs or addictive behaviors such as compulsive Web browsing, video gaming, or television watching in order to numb the mind to existential realities.

For existentialists, a healthier solution is to face the issues head on and learn to accept and tolerate the pain of existence. Indeed, being fully human means confronting existential realities, rather than denying them or embracing comforting illusions. This requires the courage to accept the inherent anxiety and the dread of nonbeing that is part of being alive. Such courage may be bolstered by developing supportive relationships with others who can supply unconditional positive regard. Something about being loved helps take away the angst.

BUILD TO THE OUTCOMES

1. How does the humanistic–existential approach differ from the trait and psychodynamic approaches?

2. What does it mean to be self-actualized?

3. How is "flow" created?

4. What is the existential approach to personality?

5. What is angst? How is it created?

The Social–Cognitive Approach: Personalities in Situations

What is it like to be a person? The **social–cognitive approach** *views personality in terms of how the person thinks about the situations encountered in daily life and behaves in response to them.* Bringing together insights from social psychology, cognitive psychology, and learning theory, this approach emphasizes how the person experiences and interprets situations (Bandura, 1986; Mischel & Shoda, 1999; Ross & Nisbett, 1991; Wegner & Gilbert, 2000).

Researchers in social cognition believe that both the current situation and learning history are key determinants of behavior. The social–cognitive approach looks at how personality and situation interact to cause behavior, how personality contributes to the way people construct situations in their own minds, and how people's goals and expectancies influence their responses to situations.

Consistency of Personality Across Situations

At the core of the social–cognitive approach is a natural puzzle, the **person–situation controversy**, which focuses on *the question of whether behavior is caused more by personality or by situational factors.* This controversy began in earnest when Walter Mischel (1968) argued that measured personality traits often do a poor job of predicting individuals' behavior. Mischel also noted that knowing how a person will behave in one situation is not particularly helpful in predicting that person's behavior in another situation. For example, in classic studies, Hugh Hartshorne and M. A. May (1928) assessed children's honesty by examining their willingness to cheat on a test and found that such dishonesty was not consistent from one situation to another. The assessment of a child's trait of honesty in a cheating situation was of almost no use in predicting whether that child would act honestly in a different situation, such as when given the opportunity to steal money. Mischel proposed that measured traits do not predict behaviors very well because behaviors are determined more by situational factors than personality theorists were willing to acknowledge.

Is there no personality, then? Do we all just do what situations require? It turns out that information about both personality and situation are necessary to predict behavior accurately (Fleeson, 2004; Mischel, 2004). Some situations are particularly powerful, leading most everyone to behave similarly, regardless of personality (Cooper & Withey, 2009). At a funeral, almost everyone looks somber, and during an earthquake, almost everyone shakes. But in more moderate situations, personality can come forward to influence behavior (Funder, 2001). Among the children in Hartshorne and May's (1928) studies, cheating versus not cheating on a test was actually a fairly good predictor of cheating on a test later—as long as the situation was similar. Personality consistency, then, appears to be a matter of when and where a certain kind of behavior tends to be shown (see The Real World: Does Your Personality Change Depending on Who You're With?).

Personal Constructs: The Key to the Perceiver's Personality

How can we understand differences in how situations are interpreted? Recall our notion that personality often exists in the eye of the beholder. Situations may exist in the eye of the beholder as well. One person's gold mine may be another person's useless hole in the ground. George Kelly (1955) long ago realized that these differences in perspective could be used to understand the *perceiver's* personality. He

LEARNING OUTCOMES

- Describe the social–cognitive approach to personality.

- Explain how personal constructs are key to personality differences.

- Identify how one's perception of control influences behavior.

social–cognitive approach An approach that views personality in terms of how the person thinks about the situations encountered in daily life and behaves in response to them.

person–situation controversy The question of whether behavior is caused more by personality or by situational factors.

Is a student who cheats on a test more likely than are others to steal candy or lie to his grandmother? Social–cognitive research indicates that behavior in one situation does not necessarily predict behavior in a different situation. Digital Vision/Photodisc/Getty Images

Does Your Personality Change Depending on Who You're With?

Social–cognitive psychologists suggest that how you behave is influenced by both your personality and the situations you are in. For instance, you act differently when sitting in a classroom than you do when dancing at a club (unless it's a really fun class). But do your personality and behavior also change when you're talking to different people?

For most people, the answer is yes. For example, we speak and act differently when interacting with our parents ("*Hello mother, hello father*") than with our friends ("*Yo! Sup, punk?!*"). Many people change their language and personality when interacting with people from their own race or cultural group as opposed to those from other groups (e.g., Coates, 2015). And there is evidence from studies of bilingual speakers that people's personality traits shift slightly when they are speaking in one language versus another (Ramirez-Esparza et al., 2004).

Why would our personality characteristics change when we are interacting with one person versus another? One possibility is that we shift our personality and language to match the people with whom we are interacting in order to signal closeness or affiliation with them. Another possibility is that we do this to influence what other people think about us. For instance, one recent study found that people in positions of power tend to down-play their competence when interacting with subordinates in order to appear warmer and more likeable, whereas subordinates tend to conceal their warmth in order to appear more competent (Swencionis & Fiske, 2016). The authors suggest that in both situations, the participants are attempting to increase the perceived similarity between them and the person with whom they are interacting. The fact that things such as personality, similarity, and perceived competence can influence decisions about hiring and promotions (Rivera, 2012; Tews, Stafford, & Tracey, 2011) means that personality actually has a huge impact on the experiences you have in the real world.

Are two of these people taller and one shorter? Are two bareheaded, while one wears a hood? Or are two the daughters and one the mom? George Kelly held that the personal constructs we use to distinguish among people in our lives are basic elements of our own personalities. Daniel Wegner

personal constructs Dimensions people use in making sense of their experiences.

suggested that people view the social world from differing perspectives and that these different views arise through the application of **personal constructs**, *dimensions people use in making sense of their experiences*. Consider, for example, different individuals' personal constructs of a clown: One person may see him as a source of fun, another as a tragic figure, and yet another as so frightening that McDonald's must be avoided at all costs.

Kelly proposed that different personal constructs are the key to personality differences and lead people to engage in different behaviors. Taking a long break from work for a leisurely lunch might seem lazy to you. To your friend, the break might seem an ideal opportunity for catching up with friends and she might wonder why you always choose to eat at your desk. Social–cognitive theory explains different responses to situations with the idea that people experience and interpret the world in different ways.

Personal Goals and Expectancies Lead to a Characteristic Style of Behavior

Social–cognitive theories also recognize that a person's unique perspective on situations is reflected in his or her personal goals, which are often conscious. In fact, people can usually tell you their goals, whether to find a date for this weekend, get a good grade in psych, establish a fulfilling career, or just get this darn bag of chips open. These goals often reflect the tasks that are appropriate to the person's situation and, in a larger sense, fit the person's role and stage of life (Cantor, 1990; Klinger, 1977; Little, 1983; Vallacher & Wegner, 1985). For instance, common goals for adolescents include being popular, achieving greater independence from parents and family, and getting into a good college. Common goals for adults include developing a meaningful career, finding a mate, securing financial stability, and starting a family.

People translate goals into behavior in part through **outcome expectancies**, *a person's assumptions about the likely consequences of a future behavior*. Just as a laboratory rat learns that pressing a bar releases a food pellet, we learn that "if I am friendly toward people, they will be friendly in return," and "if I ask people to pull my finger, they will withdraw from me." So we learn to perform behaviors that we expect will have the outcome of moving us closer to our goals. We learn outcome expectancies through direct experience, both bitter and sweet, and through merely observing other people's actions and their consequences. Outcome expectancies combine with a person's goals to produce that person's characteristic style of behavior. We do not all want the same things from life, clearly, and our personalities largely reflect the goals we pursue and the expectancies we have about the best ways to pursue them.

People also differ in their expectancy for achieving goals. Some people feel fully in control of what happens to them in life, whereas others feel that the world doles out rewards and punishments to them irrespective of their actions. A person's **locus of control** is *the tendency to perceive the control of rewards as internal to the self or external in the environment* (Rotter, 1966). People who believe they control their own destiny are said to have an *internal* locus of control, whereas those who believe that outcomes are random, determined by luck, or controlled by other people are described as having an *external* locus of control. These beliefs translate into individual differences in emotion and behavior. For example, people with an internal locus of control tend to be less anxious, achieve more, and cope better with stress than do people with an external orientation (Lefcourt, 1982). To get a sense of your standing on this trait dimension, choose one of the options for each of the sample items from the locus-of-control scale in **TABLE 11.3**.

outcome expectancies A person's assumptions about the likely consequences of a future behavior.

locus of control A person's tendency to perceive the control of rewards as internal to the self or external in the environment.

Some days, you feel like a puppet on a string. If you have an external locus of control and believe you are at the mercy of other people, or of fate, you may feel that way most days. Asia Images/Superstock

TABLE 11.3 Rotter's Locus-of-Control Scale

For each pair of items, choose the option that most closely reflects your personal belief. Then check the answer key below to see if you have more of an internal or external locus of control.

1. a. Many of the unhappy things in people's lives are partly due to bad luck.
    b. People's misfortunes result from the mistakes they make.

2. a. I have often found that what is going to happen will happen.
    b. Trusting to fate has never turned out as well for me as making a decision to take a definite course of action.

3. a. Becoming a success is a matter of hard work; luck has little or nothing to do with it.
    b. Getting a good job depends mainly on being in the right place at the right time.

4. a. When I make plans, I am almost certain that I can make them work.
    b. It is not always wise to plan too far ahead because many things turn out to be a matter of good or bad fortune anyhow.

Source: Rotter, 1966.

Answers: A more internal locus of control would be reflected in choosing options 1b, 2b, 3a, and 4a.

BUILD TO THE OUTCOMES

1. Do researchers in social cognition think that personality arises from past experiences or from the current environment?

2. How well do measured personality traits predict behavior, according to the social–cognitive approach?

3. Does personality or the current situation predict a person's behavior?

4. What are personal constructs?

5. How do outcome expectancies and personal goals combine to form personality?

6. What is the advantage of an internal, over an external, locus of control?

The Self: Personality in the Mirror

LEARNING OUTCOMES

- Describe the features that make up the self-concept.
- Identify how self-esteem develops.
- Identify the motivations for self-esteem.

Imagine that you wake up tomorrow morning, drag yourself into the bathroom, look into the mirror, and don't recognize the face looking back at you. This was the plight of a woman, married for 30 years and the mother of two grown children, who one day began to respond to her mirror image as if it were a different person (Feinberg, 2001). She talked to and challenged the person in the mirror. When she got no response, she tried to attack it as if it were an intruder. Her husband, shaken by this bizarre behavior, brought her to the neurologist, who was gradually able to convince her that the image in the mirror was in fact herself.

Most of us are pretty familiar with the face that looks back at us from every mirror. We develop the ability to recognize ourselves in mirrors by 18 months of age (as discussed in the Consciousness chapter). Self-recognition in mirrors signals our

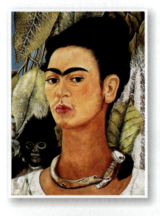

What do these self-portraits of Frida Kahlo, Vincent van Gogh, Pablo Picasso, Salvador Dali, Wanda Wulz, and Jean-Michel Basquiat reveal about each artist's self-concept? © 2013 Banco De México Diego Rivera Frida Kahlo Museums Trust, Mexico, D.F./Artists Rights Society (ARS), New York; © Albright-Knox Art Gallery/CORBIS; © Deagostini/ Superstock; © 2014 Estate of Pablo Picasso/Artists Rights Society (ARS), New York; PAINTING/Alamy; © Salvador Dalí, Fundació Gala-Salvador Dalí, Artists Rights Society (ARS), New York 2013 By permission of the Salvador Dali Estate. © Philippe Halsman/Magnum; Alinari/Art Resource, NY; © The Estate of Jean-Michel Basquiat/ADAGP, Paris/ARS, New York 2013, Banque d'Images, ADAGP/Art Resource, NY

amazing capacity for reflexive thinking, for directing attention to our own thoughts, feelings, and actions—an ability that enables us to construct ideas about our own personality. Unlike a cow, which will never know that it has a poor sense of humor, or a cat, which will never know that it is awfully friendly, humans have rich and detailed self-knowledge.

Self-Concept

If asked to describe yourself, you might mention your physical characteristics (male or female, tall or short, dark-skinned or light); your activities (listening to hip-hop, alternative rock, jazz, or classical music); your personality traits (extraverted or introverted, agreeable or independent); or your social roles (student, son or daughter, member of a hiking club, krumper). These features make up the **self-concept**, *a person's explicit knowledge of his or her own behaviors, traits, and other personal characteristics.* A person's self-concept is an organized body of knowledge that develops from social experiences and has a profound effect on a person's behavior throughout life.

self-concept A person's explicit knowledge of his or her own behaviors, traits, and other personal characteristics.

Self-Concept Organization

Our knowledge of ourselves seems to be organized naturally in two ways: as narratives about episodes in our lives and in terms of traits (as would be suggested by the distinction between episodic and semantic memory discussed in the Memory chapter).

The aspect of the self-concept that is a *self-narrative* (a story that we tell about ourselves) can be brief or very lengthy. Your life story could start with your birth and upbringing, describe a series of defining moments, and end where you are today. Self-narrative organizes the highlights (and low blows) of your life into a story in which you are the leading character and binds them together into your self-concept (McAdams, 1993; McLean, 2008).

Self-concept is also organized in terms of personality traits—whether you are considerate or smart or lazy or active. Each person finds certain unique personality traits particularly important for conceptualizing the self (Markus, 1977). One person might define herself as independent, for example, whereas another might not care much about her level of independence but instead emphasize her sense of style.

Think about your own self-narrative (what you have done) and self-concept (how you view yourself). Are there areas that don't match up? Are there things that you've done, good or bad, that are not part of your self-concept? How might you explain that? David Bathgate/Corbis

Our self-narratives and trait self-concepts don't always match up. You may think of yourself as an honest person, for example, but also recall that time you nabbed a handful of change from your parents' dresser and conveniently forgot to replace it. The traits we use to describe ourselves are generalizations, and not every episode in our life stories may fit them. In fact, research suggests that the stores of knowledge about our behaviors and traits are not very well integrated (Kihlstrom, Beer, & Klein, 2002). In people who develop amnesia, for example, memory for behaviors can be lost even though the trait self-concept remains stable (Klein, 2004). People can have a pretty strong sense of who they are, even though they may not remember a single example of when they acted that way.

Causes and Effects of Self-Concept

How do self-concepts arise, and how do they affect us? Although we can gain self-knowledge in private moments of insight, we more often arrive at our self-concepts through interacting with others. Young children in particular receive

"I don't want to be defined by who I am."

P. C. Vey/The New Yorker Collection/Cartoonbank.com

self-verification The tendency to seek evidence to confirm the self-concept.

self-esteem The extent to which an individual likes, values, and accepts the self.

plenty of feedback from their parents, teachers, siblings, and friends about their characteristics, and this helps them to form an idea of who they are. Even adults would find it difficult to hold a view of the self as "kind" or "smart" if no one else ever shared this impression. The sense of self, then, is largely developed and maintained in relationships with others.

Over the course of a lifetime, however, we become less and less impressed with what others have to say about us. All the things people have said about us accumulate after a while into what we see as a kind of consensus held by the "generalized other" (Mead, 1934). We typically adopt this general view of ourselves and hold on to it stubbornly. Just as we might argue vehemently with someone who tried to tell us a refrigerator is a pair of underpants, we are likely to defend our self-concept against anyone whose view of us departs from our own.

Because it is so stable, a major effect of the self-concept is to promote consistency in behavior across situations (Lecky, 1945). We tend to engage in **self-verification**, *the tendency to seek evidence to confirm the self-concept*, and we find it disconcerting if someone sees us quite differently from the way we see ourselves. For example, in one study, people who considered themselves submissive received feedback that they seemed very dominant and forceful (Swann, 1983). Rather than accepting this discrepant information, they went out of their way to act in an extremely submissive manner. As existential theorists emphasize, people derive a comforting sense of familiarity and stability from knowing who they are.

Self-Esteem

When you think about yourself, do you feel good and worthy? Do you like yourself? Or do you feel bad and have negative, self-critical thoughts? **Self-esteem** is *the extent to which an individual likes, values, and accepts the self*. Researchers who study self-esteem typically ask participants to fill out a self-esteem questionnaire such as the one shown in **TABLE 11.4** (Rosenberg, 1965). People who strongly agree with the

TABLE 11.4 Rosenberg Self-Esteem Scale				
Consider each statement and circle SA for strongly agree, A for agree, D for disagree, and SD for strongly disagree.				
1. On the whole, I am satisfied with myself.	SA	A	D	SD
2. At times, I think I am no good at all.	SA	A	D	SD
3. I feel that I have a number of good qualities.	SA	A	D	SD
4. I am able to do things as well as most other people.	SA	A	D	SD
5. I feel I do not have much to be proud of.	SA	A	D	SD
6. I certainly feel useless at times.	SA	A	D	SD
7. I feel that I'm a person of worth, at least on an equal plane with others.	SA	A	D	SD
8. I wish I could have more respect for myself.	SA	A	D	SD
9. All in all, I am inclined to feel that I am a failure.	SA	A	D	SD
10. I take a positive attitude toward myself.	SA	A	D	SD

Source: Rosenberg, 1965.

Scoring: For items 1, 3, 4, 7, and 10, SA = 3, A = 2, D = 1, SD = 0; for items 2, 5, 6, 8, and 9, the scoring is reversed, with SA = 0, A = 1, D = 2, SD = 3. The higher the total score, the higher one's self-esteem.

positive statements about themselves and strongly disagree with the negative statements are considered to have high self-esteem.

In general, compared with people with low self-esteem, those with high self-esteem tend to live happier and healthier lives, cope better with stress, and be more likely to persist at difficult tasks (Baumeister et al., 2003). How does this aspect of personality develop? And why does everyone—whether high or low in self-esteem—seem to *want* high self-esteem?

Sources of Self-Esteem

An important factor in determining self-esteem is whom people choose for comparison. For example, James (1890) noted that an accomplished athlete who is the second best in the world should feel pretty proud, but this athlete might not if the standard of comparison involves being best in the world. In fact, athletes in the 1992 Olympics who had won silver medals looked less happy during the medal ceremony than did those who had won bronze medals (Medvec, Madey, & Gilovich, 1995). If people see the actual self as falling short of the ideal self (the person that they would like to be), they tend to feel sad or dejected. When they become aware that the actual self is inconsistent with the self they have a duty to be, they are likely to feel anxious or agitated (Higgins, 1987).

These are the men's 1,500-meter speed-skating medalists at the 2014 Winter Olympics. From left, Denny Morrison of Canada (bronze), Zbigniew Brodka of Poland (gold), and Koen Verweij of the Netherlands (silver) pose with their medals. Notice the expression on Verweij's face compared with those of the gold- and bronze-medal winners. AP Photo/Morry Gash

Self-esteem is also affected by what kinds of domains we consider most important in our self-concept. One person's self-worth might be entirely contingent on, for example, how well she does in school, whereas another's self-worth might be based on her physical attractiveness (Crocker & Wolfe, 2001; Pelham, 1985). The first person's self-esteem might receive a big boost when she gets an A on an exam, but much less of a boost when she's complimented on her new hairstyle, and this effect might be exactly reversed in the second person.

The Desire for Self-Esteem

What's so great about self-esteem? Why do people want to see themselves in a positive light and avoid seeing themselves negatively? Three key theories on the benefits of self-esteem focus on social status, belonging, and security.

1. *Social Status.* People with high self-esteem carry themselves in a way that is similar to how high-status animals of other social species carry themselves. Dominant male gorillas, for example, appear confident and comfortable, not anxious or withdrawn. Perhaps high self-esteem in humans reflects high social status or suggests that the person is worthy of respect, and this perception triggers natural affective responses (Barkow, 1980; Maslow, 1937).

2. *Belongingness.* Evolutionary theory holds that early humans who managed to survive and pass on their genes were those able to maintain good relations with others, rather than being cast out to fend for themselves. Thus, self-esteem could be an inner gauge of how much a person feels included by others (Leary & Baumeister, 2000). According to evolutionary theory, then, we have evolved to seek out belongingness in our families, work groups, and culture, and higher self-esteem indicates that we are being accepted.

Survivor, The Bachelor, Big Brother. Why are shows in which everyone is fighting to remain a part of the group so popular today? Is it because these shows exploit the evolutionary desire to belong? (Or do people just like to see other people get kicked out of the club?) Timothy Kuratek/CBS via Getty Images

3. *Security.* Existential and psychodynamic approaches to personality suggest that the source of distress underlying negative self-esteem is ultimately the fear of death (Solomon, Greenberg, & Pyszczynski, 1991). In this view, humans find it terrifying to contemplate their own mortality, and so they try to defend against this awareness by immersing themselves in activities (such as earning money or dressing up to appear attractive) that their culture defines as meaningful and valuable. The desire for self-esteem may stem from a need to find value in ourselves as a way of escaping the anxiety associated with recognizing our mortality. The higher our self-esteem, the less anxious we feel with the knowledge that someday we will no longer exist.

Whatever the reason that low self-esteem feels so bad and high self-esteem feels so good, people are generally motivated to see themselves positively. In fact, we often process information in a biased manner in order to feel good about the self. Research on the **self-serving bias** shows that *people tend to take credit for their successes but downplay responsibility for their failures.* You may have noticed this tendency in yourself, particularly in terms of the attributions you make about exams when you get a good grade ("I studied really intensely, and I'm good at that subject") or a bad grade ("The test was ridiculously tricky, and the professor is unfair").

On the whole, most people satisfy the desire for high self-esteem and maintain a reasonably positive view of self by engaging in the self-serving bias (Miller & Ross, 1975; Shepperd, Malone, & Sweeny, 2008). In fact, if people are asked to rate themselves across a range of characteristics, they tend to see themselves as better than the average person in most domains (Alicke et al., 1995). For example, 90% of drivers describe their driving skills as better than average, and 86% of workers rate their performance on the job as above average. Even among university professors, 94% feel they are above average in teaching ability compared with other professors (Cross, 1977). These kinds of judgments simply cannot be accurate, statistically

self-serving bias People's tendency to take credit for their successes but downplay responsibility for their failures.

"I suffer from accurate self-esteem."

Ariel Molvig/The New Yorker Collection/www.cartoonbank.com

speaking, because the average of a group of people has to be the average, not better than average! This particular error may be adaptive, however. People who do not engage in this self-serving bias to boost their self-esteem tend to be more at risk for depression, anxiety, and related health problems (Taylor & Brown, 1988).

On the other hand, a few people take positive self-esteem too far—a trait called **narcissism**, *a grandiose view of the self combined with a tendency to seek admiration from and exploit others*. At its extreme, narcissism is considered a personality disorder (see the Psychological Disorders chapter). Research has documented disadvantages of an overinflated view of self, most of which arise from the need to defend that grandiose view at all costs. For example, when highly narcissistic adolescents were given reason to be ashamed of their performance on a task, their aggressiveness increased in the form of willingness to deliver loud blasts of noise to punish their opponents in a laboratory game (Thomaes et al., 2008).

narcissism A trait that reflects a grandiose view of the self combined with a tendency to seek admiration from and exploit others.

Implicit Egotism

What's your favorite letter of the alphabet? About 30% of people answer by picking what just happens to be the first letter of their first name. Could this choice indicate that some people think so highly of themselves that they base judgments of seemingly unrelated topics on how much those topics remind them of themselves?

This *name-letter effect* was discovered some years ago (Nuttin, 1985), but more recently, researchers have gone on to discover how broad the egotistic bias in preferences can be, even influencing how people choose their home cities, streets, and even occupations (Pelham, Mirenberg, & Jones, 2002). For example, when researchers examined the rolls of people moving into several southern states, they found that people named George were more likely than were those with other names to move to Georgia. The same was true for Florences (Florida), Kenneths (Kentucky), and Louises (Louisiana). You can guess where the Virginias tended to relocate. The name effect seems to work for occupations as well: Slightly more people named Dennis and Denise chose dentistry, and Lauras and Lawrences chose law, compared with other occupations. Although the biases are small, they are consistent across many tests of this hypothesis. These biases have been called expressions of *implicit egotism* because people are not typically aware that they are influenced by the wonderful sound of their own names (Pelham, Carvallo, & Jones, 2005).

Daniel Schacter

Daniel Gilbert

Matthew Nock

Daniel Wegner

Which one of your authors would be least likely to want to move to Danville? Why? Courtesy of Daniel Schacter; Courtesy of Daniel Gilbert; Matthew Nock photo courtesy of Nicolas Guevara; The family of Daniel Wegner

The self is the part of personality that the person knows and can report about. Some of the personality measures we have seen in this chapter (such as personality inventories based on self-reports) are really no different from measures of self-concept. Both depend on the person's perceptions and memories of the self's behavior and traits. But personality runs deeper than this as well. The unconscious forces identified in psychodynamic approaches provide themes for behavior and sources of mental disorder that are not accessible for self-report. The humanistic and existential approaches remind us of the profound concerns we humans face and the difficulties we may have in understanding all the forces that shape our self-views. Finally, in emphasizing how personality shapes our perceptions of social life, the social–cognitive approach brings the self back to center stage. The self, after all, is the hub of each person's social world.

BUILD TO THE OUTCOMES

1. What makes up our self-concept?
2. How does our self-narrative contribute to our self-concept?
3. Why don't traits always reflect knowledge of behavior?
4. How does self-concept influence behavior?
5. What impact does self-verification have on our behaviors?

6. What is self-esteem? Why do we want to be high in it?
7. How do comparisons with others affect self-esteem?
8. How might self-esteem have played a role in evolution?
9. Why is it possible to have too much self-esteem?

CHAPTER REVIEW

Personality: What It Is and How It Is Measured

- In psychology, *personality* refers to a person's characteristic style of behaving, thinking, and feeling. Personality differences can be studied from two points of view: *prior events*, such as biological makeup, life circumstances, and culture; and *anticipated events*, as reflected in a person's hopes, dreams, and fears.
- Personality can be measured by personality inventories which rely on self-report (such as the MMPI–2–RF), and projective techniques that rely on responses to ambiguous stimuli (such as the Rorschach Inkblot Test and the TAT). Newer, high-tech methods are proving to be even more effective.

The Trait Approach: Identifying Patterns of Behavior

- The trait approach tries to identify personality dimensions that can be used to characterize an individual's behavior. Researchers have attempted to boil down into some core personality dimensions the potentially huge array of things people do, think, and feel.
- Many personality psychologists currently focus on the Big Five personality factors: openness to experience,

conscientiousness, extraversion, agreeableness, and neuroticism.
- Twin studies indicate that the more genes you have in common with someone else, the more similar your personalities will be.
- The reticular formation, a part of the brain that regulates arousal and alertness, is more easily stimulated in introverts than in extraverts, who may need to seek out more interaction and activity to achieve mental stimulation.

The Psychodynamic Approach: Forces That Lie Beneath Awareness

- Freud believed that the personality results from forces that are largely unconscious, shaped by the interplay among id, superego, and ego.
- Defense mechanisms are techniques the mind may use to reduce anxiety generated by unacceptable impulses.
- Freud also believed that the developing person passes through a series of psychosexual stages and that failing to progress beyond one of the stages results in fixation, which is associated with corresponding personality traits.
- Critics argue that psychodynamic explanations lack real evidence and are after-the-fact interpretations.

The Humanistic–Existential Approach: Personality as Choice

- The humanistic–existential approach to personality grew out of philosophical traditions that are at odds with most of the assumptions of the trait and psychoanalytic approaches. It focuses on how people make healthy choices that form their personalities.
- Humanists see personality as directed by an inherent striving toward self-actualization and development of our unique human potentials.
- Existentialists focus on angst and the defensive response people often have to questions about the meaning of life and the inevitability of death.

The Social–Cognitive Approach: Personalities in Situations

- The social–cognitive approach focuses on personality as arising from individuals' behavior in situations.
- According to social–cognitive personality theorists, the same person may behave differently in different situations but should behave consistently in similar situations.
- Personal constructs are dimensions people use to make sense of their experiences and that reveal the perceiver's personality.

- People translate their goals into behavior through outcome expectancies.
- People who believe they control their own destiny (internal locus of control) tend to be better able to cope with stress and achieve more, compared with people who believe they are at the mercy of fate or other people (external locus of control).

The Self: Personality in the Mirror

- The self-concept is a person's knowledge of self, including both specific self-narratives and more abstract personality traits.
- People's self-concept develops through social feedback, and people often act to try to confirm these views through a process of self-verification.
- Self-esteem is a person's evaluation of self; it is derived from being accepted by others, as well as by how we evaluate ourselves by comparison to others. Theories suggest that we seek positive self-esteem to achieve perceptions of status, or belonging, or of being symbolically protected against mortality.
- People strive for positive self-views through self-serving biases and implicit egotism.

KEY CONCEPT QUIZ

1. From a psychological perspective, personality refers to
   a. a person's characteristic style of behaving, thinking, and feeling.
   b. physiological predispositions that manifest themselves psychologically.
   c. past events that have shaped a person's current behavior.
   d. choices people make in response to cultural norms.

2. Which statement is NOT a drawback of self-report measures such as the MMPI-2?
   a. People may respond in ways that put themselves in flattering light.
   b. Some people tend to always agree or always disagree with the statements on the test.
   c. Interpretation is subject to the biases of the researcher.
   d. People are unaware of some of their personality characteristics and thus cannot answer accurately.

3. Projective techniques to assess personality involve
   a. personal inventories.
   b. self-reporting.
   c. responses to ambiguous stimuli.
   d. actuarial methodology.

4. A relatively stable disposition to behave in a particular and consistent way is a
   a. motive.
   b. goal.
   c. trait.
   d. reflex.

5. Which of the following is NOT one of the Big Five personality factors?
   a. conscientiousness
   b. agreeableness
   c. neuroticism
   d. orderliness

6. Compelling evidence for the importance of biological factors in personality is best seen in studies of
   a. parenting styles.
   b. identical twins reared apart.
   c. brain damage.
   d. cross-cultural trends.

7. Which of Freud's systems of the mind would lead you to, if hungry, start grabbing food off people's plates upon entering a restaurant?
   a. the id
   b. the reality principle
   c. the ego
   d. the pleasure principle

8. After performing poorly on an exam, you drop a class, saying that you and the professor are just a poor match. According to Freud, what defense mechanism are you employing?
   a. regression
   b. rationalization
   c. projection
   d. reaction formation

9. According to Freud, a person who is preoccupied with possessions, money, issues of submission and rebellion, and concerns about cleanliness versus messiness is fixated at which psychosexual stage?
   a. the oral stage
   b. the anal stage
   c. the latency stage
   d. the genital stage

10. Humanists see personality as directed toward the goal of
    a. existentialism.
    b. self-actualization.
    c. ego control.
    d. sublimation.

11. According to the existential perspective, the difficulties we face in finding meaning in life and in accepting the responsibility for making free choices provoke a type of anxiety called
    a. angst.
    b. flow.
    c. the self-actualizing tendency.
    d. mortality salience.

12. Which of the following is NOT an emphasis of the social-cognitive approach?
    a. how personality and situation interact to cause behavior
    b. how personality contributes to the way people construct situations in their own minds
    c. how people's goals and expectancies influence their responses to situations
    d. how people confront realities, rather than embrace comforting illusions

13. According to social–cognitive theorists, _____ are the dimensions people use in making sense of their experiences.
    a. personal constructs
    b. outcome expectancies
    c. loci of control
    d. personal goals

14. Tyler has been getting poor evaluations at work. He attributes this to having a mean boss who always assigns him the hardest tasks. This suggests that Tyler has
    a. external locus of control.
    b. internal locus of control.
    c. high performance anxiety.
    d. poorly developed personal constructs.

15. What we think about ourselves is referred to as our _____, and how we feel about ourselves is referred to as our _____.
    a. self-narrative; self-verification
    b. self-concept; self-esteem
    c. self-concept; self-verification
    d. self-esteem; self-concept

16. On what do the key theories on the benefits of self-esteem focus?
    a. status
    b. belonging
    c. security
    d. all of the above

17. When people take credit for their successes but downplay responsibility for their failures, they are exhibiting
    a. narcissism.
    b. implicit egotism.
    c. the self-serving bias.
    d. the name-letter effect.

LearningCurve Don't stop now! Quizzing yourself is a powerful study tool. Go to LearningCurve at www.launchpadworks.com for more practice.

KEY TERMS

personality (p. 345)
self-report (p. 347)
Minnesota Multiphasic Personality Inventory (MMPI) (p. 347)
projective tests (p. 348)
Rorschach Inkblot Test (p. 348)
Thematic Apperception Test (TAT) (p. 348)
trait (p. 349)
Big Five (p. 351)

psychodynamic approach (p. 356)
id (p. 356)
superego (p. 356)
ego (p. 356)
defense mechanisms (p. 357)
psychosexual stages (p. 358)
fixation (p. 358)
oral stage (p. 358)
anal stage (p. 358)
phallic stage (p. 358)

Oedipus conflict (p. 358)
latency stage (p. 358)
genital stage (p. 358)
self-actualizing tendency (p. 359)
existential approach (p. 360)
social–cognitive approach (p. 361)
person–situation controversy (p. 361)
personal constructs (p. 362)
outcome expectancies (p. 363)
locus of control (p. 363)

self-concept (p. 365)
self-verification (p. 366)
self-esteem (p. 366)
self-serving bias (p. 368)
narcissism (p. 369)

CHANGING MINDS

1. A presidential candidate makes a Freudian slip on live TV, calling his mother "petty"; he corrects himself quickly and says he meant to say "pretty." The next day the video has gone viral, and the morning talk shows discuss the possibility that the candidate has an unresolved Oedipal conflict. If so, he's stuck in the phallic stage and is likely a relatively unstable person preoccupied with issues of seduction, power, and authority (which may be why he wants to be president). Your roommate knows you're taking a psychology class and asks for your opinion: "Can we really tell that a person is sexually repressed, and maybe in love with his own mother, just because he stumbled over a single word?" How would you reply? How widely are Freud's ideas about personality accepted by modern psychologists?

2. While reading a magazine, you come across an article on the nature–nurture controversy in personality. The magazine describes several adoption studies in which adopted children (who share no genes with each other but grow up in the same household) are no more like each other than are complete strangers. This suggests that family environment—and the influence of parental behavior—on personality is very weak. You show the article to a friend, who has trouble believing the results: "I always thought parents who don't show affection produce kids who have trouble forming lasting relationships." How would you explain to your friend the relationship between nature, nurture, and personality?

3. One of your friends has found an online site that offers personality testing. He takes the test and reports that the results prove he's an "intuitive," rather than a "sensing," personality, who likes to look at the big picture, rather than focus on tangible here-and-now experiences. "This explains a lot," he says, "like why I have trouble remembering details like other people's birthdays, and why it's hard for me to finish projects before the deadline." Aside from warning your friend about the dangers of self-diagnosis via Internet quizzes, what would you tell him about the relationship between personality types and behavior? How well do scores on personality tests predict a person's actual behavior?

4. One of your friends tells you that her boyfriend cheated on her, so she will never date him or anyone who has ever been unfaithful because "once a cheat, always a cheat." She goes on to explain that personality and character are stable over time, so people will always make the same decisions and repeat the same mistakes over time. What do we know about the interaction between personality and situations that might confirm or deny her statements?

ANSWERS TO KEY CONCEPT QUIZ

1. a; 2. c; 3. c; 4. c; 5. d; 6. b; 7. a; 8. b; 9. b; 10. b; 11. a; 12. d; 13. a; 14. a; 15. b; 16. d; 17. c

Social Psychology

12

John McCain, the senior senator from Arizona, and Nelson Mandela, the former president of South Africa, were different in many ways. One is a White man; one was a Black man. One is a right-wing conservative; one was a left-wing socialist. But both were victims of torture. McCain was an American navy pilot when he was shot down and captured by the North Vietnamese, and Mandela was a political activist when he was imprisoned for 27 years in South Africa. Both men experienced a variety of tortures at the hands of their captors, and both agreed about which was the worst. It has nothing to do with electric shock or waterboarding. It does not require rope or razor blades. It is a remarkably simple technique that has been used for millennia to break the body and destroy the mind. It is called solitary confinement. McCain spent two years in a cell by himself, and Mandela spent six. "It crushes your spirit and weakens your resistance more effectively than any other form of mistreatment," said McCain. "Nothing is more dehumanizing," said Mandela.

Torture often causes pain by depriving people of something they desperately need, such as oxygen, water, food, or sleep. As it turns out, the need for social interaction is just as vital. "I found solitary confinement the most forbidding aspect of prison life," Mandela wrote. "I have known men who took half a dozen lashes in preference to being locked up alone." Indeed, studies of prisoners show that extensive periods of isolation can induce symptoms of psychosis (Grassian, 2006), and even in smaller doses, social isolation takes a toll. Ordinary people who are socially isolated are more likely to become depressed, to become ill, and to die prematurely. In fact, being socially isolated is as bad for your health as being obese or smoking (Cacioppo & Patrick, 2008; Holt-Lunstad et al., 2015).

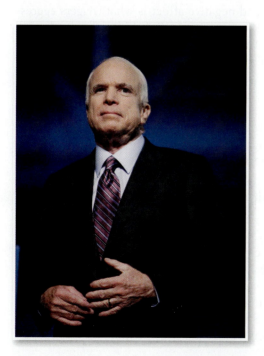

John McCain and Nelson Mandela each spent years in isolation and described it as the worst form of torture. Brooks Kraft/ Corbis; Getty Images

social psychology The study of the causes and consequences of sociality.

WHAT KIND OF ANIMAL GETS SICK OR GOES CRAZY when left alone? The social kind. Of the 8.7 million species on our planet, human beings are by far the most social. **Social psychology** is *the study of the causes and consequences of sociality*. As you'll see in the first two sections of this chapter, every animal faces the twin problems of survival and reproduction, and, sociality is how human beings solve those problems. In the third section, you'll see how social creatures like us learn to influence and control each other's behavior by appealing to each other's basic motives. Finally, in the fourth section, you'll see how we gather and use information to make judgments about each other—sometimes for better and often for worse.

The Survival Game

LEARNING OBJECTIVES

- Identify biological and cultural influences on aggression.
- Explain why cooperation is risky.
- Describe the costs and benefits of groups.
- Distinguish between apparent and genuine altruism.

aggression Behavior whose purpose is to harm another.

frustration–aggression hypothesis A principle stating that animals aggress when their goals are frustrated.

To survive, all animals must obtain resources such as food, water, and shelter. Animals often solve this problem by hurting each other or helping each other. *Hurting* and *helping* are antonyms, so you might expect them to have little in common, but as you are about to see, these disparate behaviors are actually two solutions to the same problem (Hawley, 2002).

Aggression

What is the simplest way to solve the problem of scarce resources? Take what you want and kick the stuffing out of anyone who tries to stop you. **Aggression** is *behavior whose purpose is to harm another* (Anderson & Bushman, 2002; Bushman & Huesmann, 2010), and it is a strategy used by just about every animal on the planet. Aggression is not something that animals do for sport but rather as a way of achieving their goals. The **frustration–aggression hypothesis** suggests that *animals aggress when their goals are frustrated* (Dollard et al., 1939). The chimp wants the banana (*goal*), but the pelican is about to take it (*frustration*), so the chimp threatens the pelican with its fist (*aggression*). The robber wants the money (*goal*), but the teller has it all locked up in a vault (*frustration*), so the robber threatens the teller with a gun (*aggression*).

Frustrated goals don't cause aggression directly. Rather, they induce negative affect (commonly known as *feeling bad*), and negative affect is what triggers aggression (Berkowitz, 1990). That's why rats that are given painful electric shocks will attack anything in their cage, including other animals, stuffed dolls, or even tennis balls (Kruk et al., 2004). And that's why experimental participants who are required to immerse their hands in ice water or to sit in a very hot room are more likely to blast others with noise weapons or make others eat hot chili (Anderson, 1989; Anderson, Bushman, & Groom, 1997). The idea that negative affect causes aggression may help explain why so many acts of violence—from murders to brawls—are more likely to occur on hot days when people are feeling irritated and uncomfortable (Van Lange, Rinderu, & Bushman, 2016; see **FIGURE 12.1**).

How Biology Influences Aggression

People aggress when they feel bad. But not everyone does, and no one does all the time. So who does, and when, and why? If you want to know whether someone is likely to behave aggressively and you can ask them just one question, it should be this: "Are you a man?" (Wrangham & Peterson, 1997). Violent crimes such as assault, battery, and murder are almost exclusively perpetrated by men (and especially by young men), who are responsible for about 90% of the murders and 80% of the violent crimes in the United States (Strueber, Lueck, & Roth, 2006). Although socialization practices all over the world encourage males to be more aggressive than

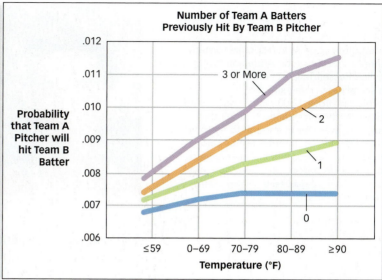

females (more on that shortly), male aggressiveness is not merely the product of playing with toy soldiers or watching football as a child. Studies show that aggression is strongly correlated with the presence of a hormone called *testosterone*, which is typically higher in men than in women, in younger men than in older men, and in violent criminals than in nonviolent criminals (Dabbs et al., 1995).

Testosterone appears to promote aggression by making people feel powerful and confident in their ability to prevail in interpersonal conflicts (Eisenegger et al., 2010; Eisenegger, Haushofer, & Fehr, 2011). Testosterone also makes people more sensitive to provocation (Ronay & Galinsky, 2011) and less sensitive to signs of retaliation. Participants in one experiment watched a face as its expression changed from neutral to threatening and were asked to respond as soon as the expression became threatening (see **FIGURE 12.2**). Participants who were given a small dose of testosterone were slower to recognize the threatening expression (van Honk & Schutter, 2007; see also Olsson et al., 2016). As you can imagine, failing to recognize that the guy you are arguing with over a parking space is getting really, really mad is a fairly good way to end up in a fight.

One of the most reliable methods for eliciting aggression in men is to challenge their status or dominance. Indeed, three quarters of all murders can be classified as "status competitions" or "contests to save face" (Daly & Wilson, 1988). Contrary to popular wisdom, it isn't men with low self-esteem who are most prone to aggression but men with unrealistically *high* self-esteem because those men are especially likely to perceive others' actions as a challenge to their own inflated sense of worth (Baumeister, Smart, & Boden, 1996). Men seem especially sensitive to these challenges when they are competing for the attention of women (Ainsworth & Maner, 2012),

Figure 12.1 HOT AND BOTHERED (a) Professional pitchers have awfully good aim, so when they hit batters with the baseball, it's safe to assume it wasn't an accident. (b) This graph shows data from nearly 60,000 major-league baseball games. As the temperature on the field increases, so does the likelihood that Team A pitchers will hit Team B batters (blue line). This effect becomes even stronger when Team A batters have previously been hit by Team B pitchers (green, orange, and purple lines), suggesting that the Team A pitcher is seeking revenge (Larrick et al., 2011). *New York Daily News/Getty Images, Data from Larrick et al., 2011*

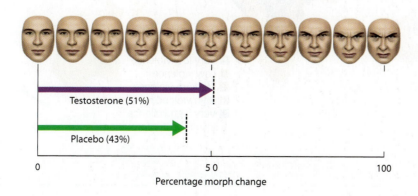

Figure 12.2 I SPY THREAT Subjects who were given testosterone needed to see a more threatening expression before they were able to recognize it as such (van Honk & Schutter, 2007). Research from Van Honk, J.; Schutter, D. J. (2007).

Men often aggress in response to status threats. In 2005, John Anderson (*right*) called Russell Tavares (*left*) a "nerd" on a social networking site. So Tavares got in his car, drove 1,300 miles, and burned down Anderson's trailer. "I didn't think anybody was stupid enough to try to kill anybody over an Internet fight," said Anderson. Tavares was later sentenced to 7 years in prison. Jerry Larson/McLennan County Sheriff's Department/AP Images; Jerry Larson/AP Images

and losing those competitions can be deadly—for women. The rate at which women in their reproductive years die at the hands of a current or former partner is about as high as the rate at which they die of cancer (Garcia-Moreno et al., 2006).

Women can be just as aggressive as men, but their aggression tends to be more focused on obtaining or protecting an actual resource rather than status. Women are much less likely than men to aggress without provocation or to aggress in ways that cause physical injury, but they are only slightly less likely than men to aggress when provoked or to aggress in ways that cause psychological injury (Bettencourt & Miller, 1996; Eagly & Steffen, 1986). Indeed, women may even be more likely than men to aggress by causing social harm, for example, by ostracizing others (Benenson et al., 2011) or by spreading malicious rumors about them (Richardson, 2014).

How Culture Influences Aggression

Figure 12.3 THE GEOGRAPHY OF VIOLENCE Some places are more violent than others. In 2016, Iceland was the least violent nation on Earth, and Syria was the most violent. Research from World Health Organization, 2004

Aggression has a biological basis, but it is also strongly influenced by culture (see **FIGURE 12.3**). For example, violent crime in the United States is far more prevalent in the South, where men are taught to react aggressively when they feel their status has been challenged (Brown, Osterman, & Barnes, 2009; Nisbett & Cohen, 1996).

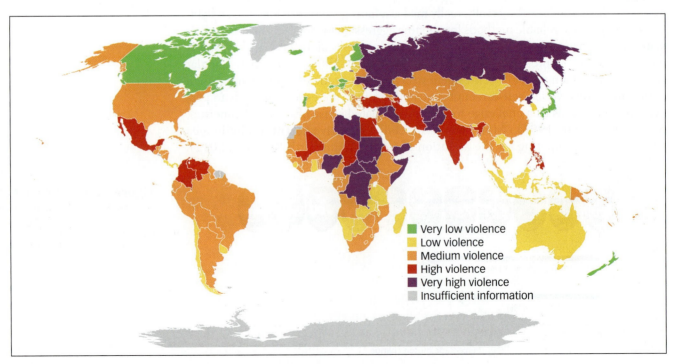

- Very low violence
- Low violence
- Medium violence
- High violence
- Very high violence
- Insufficient information

Depending on where you live, violence may be normal, or it may be unthinkable. In Iraq, where children are exposed to the brutality of extremist groups such as ISIS on a daily basis, boys stage a mock execution as part of their daily play. In India, where Jain children are taught that every form of life is sacred, a girl wears a mask at all times so that she will not harm insects or microbes by inhaling them. HADI MIZBAN/AP Images; MANISH SWARUP/AP Images

In one set of experiments, researchers insulted American volunteers from northern and southern states and found that southerners were more likely to experience a surge of testosterone and to feel that their status had been diminished by the insult (Cohen et al., 1996). When a large man walked directly toward them as they were leaving the experiment, the insulted southerners got "right up in his face" before giving way, whereas northerners just stepped aside. On the other hand, in the control condition in which participants were *not* insulted, southerners stepped aside *before* northerners did, which is to say that when they aren't being insulted, southerners are generally more polite! Clearly, culture plays an important role in determining whether our innate capacity for aggression will actually lead to aggressive behavior (Leung & Cohen, 2011).

Cooperation

Aggression may be the simplest way to solve the problem of scarce resources, but it isn't the best because when individuals work together they can often each get more resources than either could get alone. **Cooperation** is *behavior by two or more individuals that leads to mutual benefit* (Rand & Nowak, 2016), and it is one of our species' greatest achievements—right up there with language, fire, and dental floss (Axelrod, 1984; Axelrod & Hamilton, 1981; Nowak, 2006). Every roadway and supermarket, every iPad and cell phone, every ballet and surgery is the result of cooperation, and it is difficult to think of an important human achievement that could have occurred without it. (See Data Visualization: Do Humans Have a "Social Brain"? at www.launchpadworks.com) But if the benefits of cooperation are so big and so clear, then why don't we cooperate all the time?

cooperation Behavior by two or more individuals that leads to mutual benefit.

Cooperation Is Risky

Although cooperation can be beneficial, it can also be risky, and a simple game called the *prisoner's dilemma* shows how. Imagine that you and your friend Tucker have been arrested for hacking into a bank's mainframe and stealing a few million dollars. The police have found some stolen bank codes on your laptops but they don't know which of you actually did the hacking. You and Tucker are now being interrogated in separate rooms, and the detectives ask each of you to sign a statement saying that the other was the actual hacker. They explain that if you both sign, then you'll both get 2 years in prison for hacking, and if you both refuse to sign, then you'll both get 1 year in prison for possession of the stolen codes. However, if one of you signs and the other refuses, then the one who signs

Figure 12.4 THE PRISONER'S DILEMMA GAME The prisoner's dilemma game illustrates the risk of cooperation. Mutual cooperation leads to a moderate benefit to both players, but if one player cooperates and the other one doesn't, the cooperator gets no benefit and the noncooperator gets a large benefit.

	Tucker refuses to sign (i.e., he cooperates with you)	Tucker signs (i.e., he does not cooperate with you)
You refuse to sign (i.e., you cooperate with Tucker)	You both serve 1 year	You serve 3 years Tucker goes free
You sign (i.e., you do not cooperate with Tucker)	You go free Tucker serves 3 years	You both serve 2 years

Kevin Hart owns the Gator Motel in Fargo, Georgia, which he runs on an honor system: Guests arrive, stay as long as they like, and leave their payment on the dresser. If just a few people cheated, it would not affect the room rates, but if too many cheated, then prices would have to rise. How would you decide whether to pay or to cheat? Before answering this question, please notice the large dog. ELLIOTT MINOR/AP Images

group A collection of people who have something in common that distinguishes them from others.

prejudice A positive or negative evaluation of another person based on their group membership.

common knowledge effect The tendency for group discussions to focus on information that all members share.

will go free, and the one who refuses will get 3 years in prison. What should you do (other than math)? As **FIGURE 12.4** shows, it would be great if you and Tucker cooperated and agreed not to sign because you'd both get off with a very light sentence. But if you agree to cooperate and then Tucker gets sneaky and decides to sign, you'll serve a long sentence while Tucker goes free. So should you cooperate with Tucker or not? The prisoner's dilemma illustrates a basic fact about everyday life: Cooperation always requires taking the risk of benefiting someone else and *trusting* that that person will also benefit you.

How Groups Minimize the Risks of Cooperation

So how do you know whom you can trust? A **group** is *a collection of people who have something in common that distinguishes them from others.* Every one of us is a member of many groups—from families and teams to religions and nations. Although these groups are quite different, they all have one thing in common, which is that the people in them tend to be especially nice to each other. **Prejudice** is *a positive or negative evaluation of another person based solely on their group membership* (Dovidio & Gaertner, 2010). Although people are not always negatively prejudiced against members of other groups, they are almost always positively prejudiced toward members of their own groups (Brewer, 1999; DiDonato, Ullrich, & Krueger, 2011). Even when people are randomly assigned to be members of meaningless groups such as "Group 1" or "Group 2," they still favor members of their own group (Hodson & Sorrentino, 2001; Locksley, Ortiz, & Hepburn, 1980). It appears that simply knowing that "I'm one of *us* and not one of *them*" is sufficient to create in-group favoritism (Tajfel et al., 1971). Because group members can be relied on to favor each other, group membership makes cooperation less risky.

But if groups have benefits, they also have costs. For example, when groups try to make decisions, they rarely do better than the best member would have done alone—and they often do worse (Minson & Mueller, 2012). There are at least four reasons that this happens:

1. Groups usually don't capitalize fully on the expertise of their members (Hackman & Katz, 2010). For instance, groups (such as a school board) often give too little weight to the opinions of members who are experts (the professor) and too much weight to the opinions of members who happen to be high in status (the mayor) or especially talkative (the mayor).

2. The **common knowledge effect** is *the tendency for group discussions to focus on information that all members share* (Gigone & Hastie, 1993; Kerr & Tindale, 2004). What makes this a problem is that the information everyone shares (the size of the gymnasium) is often relatively unimportant, whereas the truly important information (how a school in a different district solved its budget crisis) is known to just a few.

3. A group whose members begin with moderate opinions ("We should probably just renovate the auditorium") can end up making an extreme decision ("Let's build a new high school!") simply because, in the course of discussion, each member was exposed to many different arguments in favor of a single position (Isenberg, 1986). **Group polarization** is *the tendency for groups to make decisions that are more extreme than any member would have made alone* (Myers & Lamm, 1975).

4. Group members usually care about how other members feel and are sometimes reluctant to "rock the boat" even when it needs a good rocking. **Groupthink** is *the tendency for groups to reach consensus in order to facilitate interpersonal harmony* (Janis, 1982). Harmony is important (especially if the group is a choir), but studies show that groups often sacrifice the soundness of their decisions in order to achieve it (Turner & Pratkanis, 1998).

The costs of groups go beyond making bad decisions. People in groups sometimes do truly terrible things that none of their members would do alone (Yzerbyt & Demoulin, 2010). Lynching, rioting, and gang-raping—why do human beings sometimes behave so badly when they assemble in groups? One reason is **deindividuation**, which occurs *when immersion in a group causes people to become less concerned with their personal values* (Postmes & Spears, 1998) and can lead them to do things they might not do on their own (Baumeister, Ainsworth, & Vohs, 2015). You may want to steal the Rolex you've had your eye on for weeks or plant a kiss on an attractive stranger you've had your eye on for months, but these acts conflict with your personal values, and so you refrain. But when individuals assemble in groups, their attention is drawn toward others and away from themselves, which makes them less likely to consider their personal values when they take action (Wicklund, 1975).

A second reason that people in groups sometimes behave so badly is **diffusion of responsibility**, which refers to *the tendency for individuals to feel diminished responsibility for their actions when they are surrounded by others who are acting the same way*. For example, studies of **bystander intervention**—which is *the act of helping strangers in an emergency situation*—reveal that people are less likely to help an innocent person in distress when there are many other bystanders present, simply because they assume that the other bystanders are collectively more responsible than they are (Darley & Latané, 1968; Fischer et al., 2011). If you saw a fellow student cheating on an exam, you'd probably feel more responsible for reporting the incident if you were taking the exam in a group of 3 than in a group of 3,000 because you'd have a greater share of the responsibility in the first instance than in the second (see **FIGURE 12.5**).

If groups make bad decisions and foster bad behavior, then might we be better off without them? Probably not. Not only do groups minimize the risks of cooperation, but they also contribute to our general well-being (Myers & Diener, 1995). People

group polarization The tendency for groups to make decisions that are more extreme than any member would have made alone.

groupthink The tendency for groups to reach consensus in order to facilitate interpersonal harmony.

deindividuation A phenomenon that occurs when immersion in a group causes people to become less concerned with their individual values.

diffusion of responsibility The tendency for individuals to feel diminished responsibility for their actions when they are surrounded by others who are acting the same way.

bystander intervention The act of helping strangers in an emergency situation.

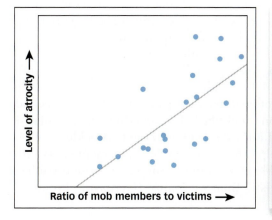

Figure 12.5 MOB SIZE AND LEVEL OF ATROCITY Groups are capable of horrible things. These two men were rescued by police just as residents of their town prepared to lynch them for stealing a car. Because larger groups provide more opportunity for diffusion of responsibility, their atrocities become more horrible as the ratio of mob members to victims becomes larger (Leader, Mullen, & Abrams, 2007). STR/AP Images

In 2013, a customer at a Tim Horton's drive-through in Winnipeg, Canada, decided to perform a random act of kindness and pay for the order of the car behind him. This caused a chain reaction of altruism as 228 consecutive cars received free orders and, in turn, decided to pay for the order of the folks in the next car. The cascade ended when a customer who received four free coffees refused to pay for the car behind him, which had ordered just three coffees. Kathy deWitt/Alamy Stock Photo

Wesley Autrey jumped onto the subway tracks to save a stranger's life. Would you have done what he did? Are you sure? Robert Kalfus/Splash News/Newscom

altruism Intentional behavior that benefits another at a cost to oneself.

kin selection The process by which evolution selects for individuals who cooperate with their relatives.

reciprocal altruism Behavior that benefits another with the expectation that those benefits will be returned in the future.

who are excluded from groups are typically anxious, lonely, depressed, and at increased risk for illness and premature death (Cacioppo & Patrick, 2008; Cohen, 1988; Leary, 1990). Groups may sometimes cause us to misjudge and misbehave, but they are also key to our cooperativeness, our health, and our happiness.

Altruism

Cooperation solves the problem of scarce resources. But is that the only reason we cooperate with others? Aren't we ever just . . . well, *nice*? **Altruism** is *intentional behavior that benefits another at a cost to oneself*, and for centuries, scientists and philosophers have argued about whether people are ever truly altruistic. That may seem like an odd argument to have. After all, people give their blood to the injured, their food to the homeless, and their time to the elderly. We volunteer, donate, contribute, and tithe. People do nice things like these all the time—so why is there any debate about whether people are altruistic?

Because behaviors that appear to be altruistic often have hidden benefits for those who do them. For example, squirrels emit alarm calls when they see a predator, which puts them at increased risk of being eaten but allows their fellow squirrels to escape. This behavior appears to be altruistic, but in fact it is not because the animals who give help are *genetically related* to the animals who receive it. When an animal promotes the survival of its relatives, it is actually promoting the survival of its own genes (Hamilton, 1964). **Kin selection** is *the process by which evolution selects for individuals who cooperate with their relatives*, and although cooperating with related individuals may look altruistic, it's actually just selfishness in disguise.

Cooperating with unrelated individuals isn't necessarily altruistic either. Male baboons will sometimes risk injury to help an unrelated male baboon win a fight, and monkeys will spend time grooming unrelated monkeys when they could be doing something else. But, as it turns out, the animal that gives favors today tends to get favors tomorrow. **Reciprocal altruism** is *behavior that benefits another with the expectation that those benefits will be returned in the future*, and despite the second word in this term, there's nothing altruistic about it (Trivers, 1972). Indeed, reciprocal altruism is merely cooperation extended over time.

The behavior of nonhuman animals provides little if any evidence of genuine altruism (cf. Bartal, Decety, & Mason, 2011). So what about us? Are we any different? Like other animals, we tend to help our kin more than we help strangers (Burnstein, Crandall, & Kitayama, 1994; Komter, 2010), and we tend to expect those we help to help us in return (Burger et al., 2009). But unlike other animals, we *do* sometimes provide benefits to complete strangers who have no chance of repaying us (Batson, 2002; Warneken & Tomasello, 2009). We hold the door for people who share precisely none of our genes, tip waiters in restaurants to which we will never return, and give advice (and sometimes parking spaces) to complete strangers. And we do much more than that. In 2007, Wesley Autrey noticed a student who was having an epileptic seizure and had fallen onto the subway track just as a train was approaching. So Autrey jumped onto the tracks and lay on top of the student, holding him down and allowing the train to pass over both of them with only an inch to spare. "I had a split-second decision to make," Autrey said. "I don't feel like I did something spectacular; I just saw someone who needed help. I did what I felt was right" (Buckley, 2007). Clearly, human beings sometimes help others even when the personal costs are potentially staggering. We are capable of genuine altruism, and some studies suggest that we are even more altruistic than we realize (Gerbasi & Prentice, 2013; Miller & Ratner, 1998).

BUILD TO THE OUTCOMES

1. How does the frustration–aggression hypothesis explain aggressive behaviors?

2. How and why does gender influence aggression?

3. What evidence suggests that culture can influence aggression?

4. What are the potential costs and benefits of cooperation?

5. How do groups lower the risks of cooperation?

6. How and why do individuals behave differently when they are in groups?

7. How can we explain selfish behaviors that appear to be altruistic?

The Mating Game

All animals must survive and reproduce. As you have seen, social behavior can be very beneficial for survival. But is it an absolute prerequisite for reproduction. The first step on the road to reproduction is finding someone who wants to travel that road with us, so let's start by seeing how humans do that.

Selectivity

With the exception of a few well-known celebrities, most people don't mate randomly. Rather, they *select* their sexual partners, and women tend to be more selective than men (Feingold, 1992; Fiore et al., 2010). When researchers arranged for an attractive person to approach opposite-sex strangers on a college campus and ask, "Would you go out with me?" they found that roughly half of the men and half of the women agreed to the request. On the other hand, when the attractive person said to the stranger, "Would you go to bed with me?" exactly *none* of the women and *three quarters* of the men agreed to the request (Clark & Hatfield, 1989). There are of course many reasons that a woman might turn down a sexual offer from a strange man under such circumstances (Conley, 2011), but research suggests that women tend to be choosier than men under most other circumstances as well (Buss & Schmitt, 1993; Schmitt et al., 2012).

Why are women choosier? One reason is biology. Men produce billions of sperm in their lifetimes, their ability to conceive a child tomorrow is not inhibited by having conceived one today, and conception has no significant physical costs. Therefore, if a man makes a "mating error" and selects a woman who does not produce healthy offspring or who won't do her part to raise them, he's lost nothing but a few minutes and a teaspoon of bodily fluid. But women produce a small number of eggs in their lifetimes, conception eliminates their ability to conceive for at least 9 months, and pregnancy produces physical changes that increase their nutritional requirements and put them at risk of illness and death. So if a woman makes a mating error, she has lost a precious egg, borne the costs of pregnancy, risked her life in childbirth, and missed at least 9 months of other reproductive opportunities. Basic biology makes sex a riskier proposition for women than for men.

But culture and personal experience also play an important role in determining how selective a person will be (Petersen & Hyde, 2010; Zentner & Mitura, 2012). For example, women are typically approached by men more often than men are approached by women (Conley et al., 2011), which means that women can afford to be more selective simply because they have a larger selection from which to choose! Another reason that women are more selective is that, in most cultures, the reputational costs of promiscuity are higher for women than for men (Eagly & Wood, 1999; Kasser & Sharma, 1999). Indeed, when the potential costs of mating errors

LEARNING OUTCOMES

- Explain the biological and cultural factors that influence selectivity in mate choice.

- Describe the situational, physical, and psychological factors that determine feelings of attraction.

- Describe the factors that cause people to get married and divorced.

Among sea horses, it is the male that carries the young, and not coincidentally, males are more selective than are females. If human males could become pregnant, how might their behavior change? Creatas/Getty Images; Dr. Paul Zahl / Science Source

Making the Move

Women are generally choosier about their romantic partners than men are, and most scientists believe this has a lot to do with differences in their reproductive biology. But it might also have something to do with the nature of the courtship dance itself.

When it comes to approaching a potential romantic partner, the person with the most interest should be most inclined to "make the first move." Of course, in most cultures, men are *expected* to make the first move. Could this *cause* men to think that they have more interest in a woman than she has in them?

To find out, researchers created two kinds of speed-dating events (Finkel & Eastwick, 2009). In the traditional event, the women stayed in their seats and the men moved around the room, stopping to spend a few minutes chatting with each woman. In the nontraditional event, the men stayed in their seats and the women moved around the room, stopping to spend a few minutes chatting with each man. When the event was over, the researchers asked each man and woman privately to indicate whether they wanted to exchange phone numbers with any of the potential partners they'd met.

The results were striking (see the accompanying figure). When men made the move (as they traditionally do), women were the choosier gender. That is, men wanted to get a lot more phone numbers than women wanted to give. But when women made the move, that difference disappeared. Apparently, approaching someone makes us eager, and being approached makes us cautious. One reason that women are so often the choosier gender may simply be that in most cultures, men are expected to make the first move. All of this suggests that if you'd like to meet the attractive person at the next table at Starbucks, you should probably avoid saying, "Can I sit with you?" and instead try saying, "Would you like to sit with me?"

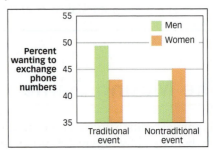

GREG GILBERT KRT/Newscom

are high for men (e.g., when they are choosing a long-term mate rather than a short-term date), they can be every bit as choosy as women (Kenrick et al., 1990). In fact, as The Real World: Making the Move box explains, relatively minor changes in the courtship ritual can actually cause men to be *choosier* than women. The point is that biology makes sex a riskier proposition for women than for men, but other factors can exaggerate, equalize, or even reverse those risks. The higher the risk, the more selective people of both sexes tend to be.

Attraction

For most of us, there is a very small number of people with whom we are willing to have sex, an even smaller number of people with whom we are willing to have children, and a staggeringly large number of people with whom we are unwilling to have either. So when we meet someone new, how do we decide which of these categories they belong in? Many things go into choosing a date, a lover, or a partner for life, but perhaps none is more important than the simple feeling we call *attraction* (Berscheid & Reis, 1998). Research suggests that this feeling is the result of situational, physical, and psychological factors.

Attraction Depends on Situational Factors

We tend to think that we select our romantic partners on the basis of their personalities, appearances, and so on—and we do. But we get to select only from the pool of people we've met, and the likelihood of meeting a potential partner naturally increases with proximity. Before you ever start ruling out potential romantic partners, geography has already ruled out more than 99.99% of the world's population for you (Festinger, Schachter, & Back, 1950). Proximity not only provides the opportunity for attraction, it also provides the motivation. When you are assigned a roommate or an office mate, you know that your day-to-day existence will be a whole lot easier if you like them than if you don't, so you go out of your way to notice their good qualities and ignore their bad ones. When research participants are told that they will later interact with another person, they immediately like that person more, even before the interaction begins (Darley & Berscheid, 1967).

Proximity breeds attraction for another reason as well. The **mere-exposure effect** is *the tendency for liking to increase with the frequency of exposure* (Bornstein, 1989; Zajonc, 1968). Every time we encounter a person, that person becomes a bit more familiar to us, and research shows that people generally prefer familiar to unfamiliar stimuli. For instance, in some experiments, geometric shapes, faces, or alphabetical characters were flashed on a computer screen so quickly that participants were unaware of having seen them. Participants were then shown some of the "old" stimuli that had been flashed across the screen as well as some "new" stimuli that had not. Although they could not reliably say which stimuli were old and which were new, they *liked* the old stimuli more than the new ones (Monahan, Murphy, & Zajonc, 2000). The fact that mere exposure leads to liking may explain why college students who were randomly assigned to seats during a brief psychology experiment were likely to be friends with the person they sat next to a full year later (Back, Schmukle, & Egloff, 2008). Although there are some circumstances under which "familiarity breeds contempt" (Norton, Frost, & Ariely, 2007), for the most part, familiarity seems to breed liking (Reis et al., 2011).

Attraction Depends on Physical Factors

Once people are in the same place at the same time, they can begin to learn about each other's personal qualities, and in most cases, the first quality they learn about is the other person's appearance. The influence of appearance on attraction is remarkably strong. For instance, one study found that a man's height and a woman's weight were among the best predictors of how many responses a personal ad received (Lynn & Shurgot, 1984), and another study found that physical attractiveness was the *only* factor that predicted the online dating choices of both women and men (Green, Buchanan, & Heuer, 1984). Beautiful people have more sex, more friends, and more fun than the rest of us do (Curran & Lippold, 1975), and they even earn about 10% more money over the course of their lives (Hamermesh & Biddle, 1994; see **FIGURE 12.6**).

So yes, it pays to be beautiful. But what exactly constitutes beauty? Although different cultures have different standards of beauty, those standards have a surprising amount in common (Cunningham et al., 1995). For example, in most cultures, male bodies are considered attractive when they are shaped like a triangle (i.e., broad shoulders with a narrow waist and hips), and female bodies are considered attractive when they are shaped like an hourglass (i.e., broad shoulders and hips with a narrow waist). People in all cultures also seem to prefer faces and bodies that are *bilaterally symmetrical*—that is, faces and bodies whose left half is a mirror image of the right half (Perilloux, Webster, & Gaulin, 2010; Perrett et al., 1999). And in every culture, straight women tend to prefer older men, and straight men tend to prefer younger

"I'm a beast, I'm an animal, I'm that monster in the mirror." Like it or not, the mirror is the place where Usher most often sees himself. As a result, he probably prefers pictures of himself that are horizontally reversed (*left*), whereas his fans probably prefer pictures of him that are not (*right*). One consequence of the mere exposure effect is that people tend to like the photographic images with which they are most familiar (Mita, Dermer, & Knight, 1977). Peter Kramer/NBC/NBC NewsWire via Getty Images

mere-exposure effect The tendency for liking to increase with the frequency of exposure.

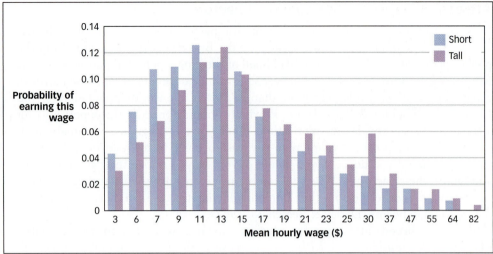

Figure 12.6 HEIGHT MATTERS The NFL quarterback Tom Brady is 6′4″ tall, and his wife, the supermodel Gisele Bundchen, is 5′10″ tall. Research shows that tall people earn $789 more per inch per year. The graph shows the average hourly wage of adult White men in the United States classified by height (Mankiew & Weinzierl, 2010). Kevin Mazur/Getty Images

women (Buss, 1989). Each of these features can be thought of as a signal—either of general health (symmetry), of the ability to bear children (female body shape and age), or of social dominance and the potential to command resources (male body shape and age). That feeling we call *attraction* may simply be nature's way of telling us that we are in the presence of a person who has what it takes to produce and protect children.

Attraction Depends on Psychological Factors

Physical appearance is assessed easily, early, and from across a crowded room (Lenton & Francesconi, 2010), and it definitely determines who draws our attention and quickens our pulse. But once people begin interacting, they move beyond appearances (Cramer, Schaefer, & Reid, 1996; Regan, 1998), which is why physical attractiveness matters less when people have known each other for a long time (Hunt, Eastwick, & Finkel, 2015). People's *inner* qualities—their personalities, points of view, attitudes, beliefs, values, ambitions, and abilities—play an important role in determining their sustained interest in each other, and there isn't much

Although standards of beauty in all cultures have a lot in common, there are some differences. For example, unlike the US, women in Mauritania are considered more beautiful when they are heavy rather than thin (left), and men in Ghana are considered more handsome when they are short rather than tall (right). SEYLLOU/AFP/Getty Images; Michael Dwyer/Alamy

mystery about the kinds of inner qualities that most people find attractive. Intelligence, ambitiousness, loyalty, trustworthiness, and kindness seem to be high on just about everybody's list (Daniel et al., 1985; Farrelly, Lazarus, & Roberts, 2007; Fletcher et al., 1999). Exactly how much of these valuable traits do we want our mates to have?

Research suggests that people are most attracted to those who are similar to them on most dimensions (Byrne, Ervin, & Lamberth, 1970; Hatfield & Rapson, 1992; Neimeyer & Mitchell, 1988). We marry people of a similar age with similar levels of education, similar religious backgrounds, similar ethnicities, similar socioeconomic statuses, and similar personalities (Botwin, Buss, & Shackelford, 1997; Buss, 1985; Caspi & Herbener, 1990). Why is similarity so attractive? First, it's easy to interact with people who are similar to us because we can instantly agree on a wide range of issues, such as what to eat, where to live, how to raise children, and how to spend our money. Second, when someone shares our attitudes and beliefs, we feel validated, and we become more confident that our attitudes and beliefs are right (Byrne & Clore, 1970). Third, because we like people who share our attitudes and beliefs, we can reasonably expect them to like us for exactly the same reason, and *being liked* is a powerful source of attraction (Aronson & Worchel, 1966; Backman & Secord, 1959; Condon & Crano, 1988).

Similarity is a very strong source of attraction. Don Tremain/Getty Images

Relationships

Most animals have relationships that end approximately thirty seconds after sex is over. But human children require years of nurturing before they can fend for themselves, and so human adults tend to do their mating and child-rearing in the context of committed, long-term relationships (Clark & Lemay, 2010). In most cultures, those relationships are signified by marriage. About 80% of all 40-year-old Americans have been married, and although marriage has become less popular over the last few decades, the best estimate is that about 75% of current 20-year-olds will eventually get married too (Wang & Parker, 2014).

Throughout history, marriage was traditionally regarded as an alliance that helped people fulfill basic needs, such as growing food, building shelter, and protecting each other from violence, but in the 20th century, people began marrying for an entirely new reason called love (Finkel et al., 2015). Psychologists distinguish two basic kinds of love: **passionate love**, which is *an experience involving feelings of euphoria, intimacy, and intense sexual attraction*, and **companionate love**, which is *an experience involving affection, trust, and concern for a partner's well-being* (Acevedo & Aron, 2009; Hatfield, 1988; Rubin, 1973; Sternberg, 1986). The ideal romantic relationship gives rise to both types of love, but the speeds, trajectories, and durations of the two experiences are markedly different (see **FIGURE 12.7**). Passionate love is what brings people together: It has a rapid onset, reaches its peak quickly, and begins to diminish within just a few months (Aron et al., 2005). Companionate love is what keeps people together: It takes some time to get started, grows slowly, and need never stop growing (Gonzaga et al., 2001).

Marriage offers benefits (such as love, sex, and financial security), but it also imposes costs (such as additional responsibility, loss of personal freedom, and the potential for interpersonal conflict), and people tend to remain in relationships only as long as they perceive a favorable ratio of costs to benefits

passionate love An experience involving feelings of euphoria, intimacy, and intense sexual attraction.

companionate love An experience involving affection, trust, and concern for a partner's well-being.

Figure 12.7 PASSIONATE AND COMPANIONATE LOVE Passionate love begins to cool within just a few months, but companionate love can grow slowly but steadily over years.

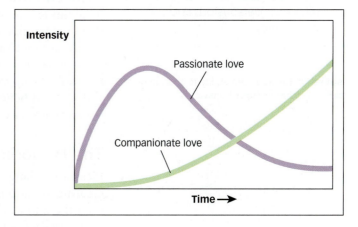

(Homans, 1961; Thibaut & Kelley, 1959). More than a third of Americans who are currently married will eventually decide to terminate that relationship because the cost–benefit ratio of their marriage has become unfavorable. Whether a particular cost–benefit ratio seems favorable or unfavorable depends on at least two things (Le & Agnew, 2003; Lemay, 2016; Rusbult & Van Lange, 2003). First, it depends on the available alternatives—that is, on whether a person thinks he or she can "do better" with another partner. Second, it depends on how much the person has already invested in the relationship. A ratio that seems favorable to people who have been married for many years may seem unfavorable to people who have been married for just a few months, which is one of the reasons why new marriages are more likely to end than old ones are (Bramlett & Mosher, 2002; Cherlin, 1992).

BUILD TO THE OUTCOMES

1. Why are women generally more selective than men when choosing mates?

2. What situational factors play a role in attraction?

3. Why is physical appearance so important?

4. What kind of information does physical appearance convey?

5. Why is similarity such a powerful determinant of attraction?

6. What are the two basic kinds of love?

7. How do people weigh the costs and benefits of their relationships?

Controlling Others

LEARNING OUTCOMES

- Describe the hedonic motive and explain how appeals to it can backfire.

- Describe the approval motive and distinguish normative influence, conformity, and obedience.

- Describe the accuracy motive and distinguish informational influence, persuasion, and consistency.

social influence The ability to change or direct another person's behavior.

Those of us who grew up reading comics or watching cartoons have usually thought a bit about which of the standard superpowers we'd most like to have. Super strength and super speed have obvious benefits, invisibility and X-ray vision could be interesting as well as lucrative, and there's a lot to be said for flying. But when it comes down to it, the ability to control other people would probably be the most useful of all. Why get in a death match with an alien overlord or rescue orphans from a burning building when you can convince someone else to do these things for you? The things we want from life—gourmet food, interesting jobs, big houses, fancy cars—can all be given to us by others, and the things we want most—loving families, loyal friends, admiring children, appreciative employers—cannot be gotten in any other way.

Social influence is *the ability to change or direct another person's behavior* (Cialdini & Goldstein, 2004), and people have three basic motivations that make them susceptible to it (Bargh, Gollwitzer, & Oettingen, 2010; Fiske, 2010). First, people are motivated to experience pleasure and to avoid experiencing pain (the *hedonic motive*). Second, people are motivated to be accepted and to avoid being rejected (the *approval motive*). Third, people are motivated to believe what is right and to avoid believing what is wrong (the *accuracy motive*). As you will see, most attempts at social influence appeal to one or more of these motives.

The Hedonic Motive

Pleasure seeking is the most basic of all motives, and social influence often involves creating situations in which others can achieve more pleasure by doing what we want them to do than by doing something else. Parents, teachers, governments, and businesses influence our behavior by offering rewards and threatening punishments (see **FIGURE 12.8**). There's nothing mysterious about how these influence attempts

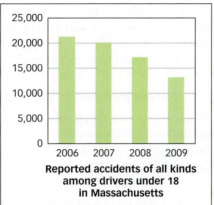

work, and they are often quite effective. When the Republic of Singapore warned its citizens that anyone caught chewing gum in public would face a year in prison and a $5,500 fine, the rest of the world was outraged; but when the outrage subsided, it was hard to ignore the fact that gum chewing in Singapore had fallen to an all-time low. A good caning will get your attention every time.

But in some instances, rewards and punishments can backfire. For example, children in one study were allowed to play with colored markers, and then some were given a "Good Player Award." When the children were given markers the next day, those who had received an award the previous day were *less* likely to play with the markers than were those who had not received an award (Lepper, Greene, & Nisbett, 1973). Why? Because children who had received an award the first day came to think of drawing as something one does to receive rewards, and if no one was going to give them an award the second day, then why the heck should they do it (Deci, Koestner, & Ryan, 1999)? Similarly, rewards and punishments can backfire simply because people resent being bribed and threatened. Researchers placed signs in two restrooms on a college campus: "Please don't write on these walls" and "Do not write on these walls under any circumstances." Two weeks later, the walls in the second restroom had more graffiti, presumably because students didn't appreciate the threatening tone of the second sign and wrote on the walls just to show that they could (Pennebaker & Sanders, 1976).

The civil rights leader Martin Luther King Jr. (1929–1968) and the suffragist and feminist Susan B. Anthony (1820–1906) are among the 50 most influential Americans who have ever lived. In what ways did these two people "change or direct" your behavior? Central Press/Getty Images; PhotoQuest/Getty Images

The Approval Motive

Other people stand between us and starvation, predation, loneliness, and all the other things that make getting shipwrecked such a bad idea. We depend on others for safety, sustenance, and solidarity, and being rejected or excluded by others is one of the most painful of all human experiences (Eisenberger, Lieberman, & Williams, 2003; Uskul & Over, 2014; Williams, 2007). We are powerfully motivated to have others accept us, like us, and approve of us (Baumeister & Leary, 1995; Leary, 2010), and that motive leaves us vulnerable to social influence.

Normative Influence: We Do What's Appropriate

norms Customary standards for behavior that are widely shared by members of a culture.

normative influence A phenomenon that occurs when another person's behavior provides information about what is appropriate.

norm of reciprocity The unwritten rule that people should benefit those who have benefited them.

When you get on an elevator you are supposed to face forward and not talk to the person next to you even if you were talking to that person before you got on the elevator, unless you are the only two people on the elevator, in which case it's okay to talk and face sideways but still not backward. Although no one ever taught you this long-winded rule, you probably picked it up somewhere along the way. The unwritten rules that govern social behavior are called **norms**, which are *customary standards for behavior that are widely shared by members of a culture* (Cialdini, 2013; Miller & Prentice, 1996). We learn norms with exceptional ease, and we obey them with exceptional fidelity, because we know that if we don't, others won't approve of us (Centola & Baronchelli, 2015). **Normative influence** occurs when *another person's behavior provides information about what is appropriate* (see **FIGURE 12.9**).

For example, every human culture has a **norm of reciprocity**, which is *the unwritten rule that people should benefit those who have benefited them* (Gouldner, 1960). When a friend buys you lunch, you return the favor; and if you don't, your friend gets miffed. Indeed, the norm of reciprocity is so strong that when researchers randomly pulled the names of strangers from a telephone directory and sent them all Christmas cards, they received Christmas cards back from most (Kunz & Woolcott, 1976). Waiters and waitresses also know about the norm of reciprocity, which is why they often give customers a piece of candy along with the bill. Studies show that customers who receive a candy feel obligated to do "a little extra" for the waiter who did "a little extra" for them (Strohmetz et al., 2002).

Have you ever wondered which big spender left the bill as a tip? In fact, the bills are often put there by the very people you are tipping because they know that the presence of paper money will suggest to you that others are leaving big tips and that it would be socially appropriate for you to do the same. By the way, the customary gratuity for someone who writes a textbook for you is 15%. But most students send more. Don Paulson Photography/Purestock/ Superstock

Conformity: We Do What Others Do

People can influence us by invoking familiar norms, such as the norm of reciprocity. But if you've ever found yourself at a fancy dinner, sneaking a peek at the person next to you in the hopes of discovering whether the little fork is supposed to be used for the shrimp or the salad, then you know that other people can influence us by

Figure 12.9 THE PERILS OF CONNECTION Other people's behavior defines what is normal, and so we tend to do the things we see others doing. Overeating is one of those things. Research shows that if someone you know becomes obese, your chances of becoming obese can increase dramatically (Christakis & Fowler, 2007). Francis Dean/Dean Pictures/The Image Works

On average, your risk of becoming obese increases by ...

. . . **57%** if someone you consider a friend becomes obese.

. . . **37%** if your spouse becomes obese.

. . . **171%** if a very close friend becomes obese.

. . . **40%** if one of your siblings becomes obese.

. . . **100%** if you are a man and your male friend becomes obese.

. . . **67%** if you are a woman and your sister becomes obese.

. . . **38%** if you are a woman and your female friend becomes obese.

. . . **44%** if you are a man and your brother becomes obese.

A perplexed participant (*center*), flanked by trained actors, is on the verge of conforming in one of Solomon Asch's line-judging experiments. © William Van-divert

defining *new* norms in ambiguous or novel situations. **Conformity** is *the tendency to do what others do simply because others are doing it*, and it results in part from normative influence.

In a classic study, the psychologist Solomon Asch had participants sit in a room with seven other people who appeared to be ordinary participants, but who were actually trained actors (Asch, 1951, 1956). An experimenter explained that the participants would be shown cards with three printed lines and their job was simply to say which of the three lines matched a "standard line" that was printed on another card (see **FIGURE 12.10**). The experimenter held up a card and then asked each person to answer in turn. The real participant was among the last to be called on. Everything went well on the first two trials, but then on the third trial, something really strange happened: The actors all began giving the same wrong answer! What did the real participants do? Although most participants gave the right answer on most trials, 75% conformed and announced the wrong answer on at least one trial. Subsequent research has shown that these participants didn't actually misperceive the length of the lines but were instead succumbing to normative influence (Asch, 1955; Nemeth & Chiles, 1988). Giving the wrong answer was apparently the "right thing to do," and so participants did it.

The behavior of others can tell us what is proper, appropriate, expected, and accepted (in other words, it can define a norm), and once a norm is defined, we feel obliged to honor it. When a Holiday Inn in Tempe, Arizona, left a variety of different "message cards" in guests' bathrooms in the hopes of convincing those guests to reuse their towels rather than laundering them every day, it discovered that the single most effective message was the one that simply read: "Seventy-five percent of our guests use their towels more than once" (Cialdini, 2005). Clearly, normative influence can be a force for good (see Other Voices: Ninety-One Percent of All Students Read This Box and Love It).

conformity The tendency to do what others do simply because others are doing it.

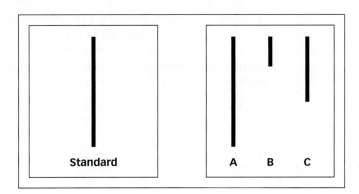

Standard

A   B   C

Figure 12.10 ASCH'S CONFORMITY STUDY If you were asked which of the lines on the right (A, B, or C) matches the standard line on the left, what would you say? Research on conformity suggests that your answer would depend, in part, on how other people in the room answered the same question. © William Vandivert

Ninety-One Percent of All Students Read This Box and Love It

Tina Rosenberg is an editorial writer for the *New York Times*. Her 1995 book *The Haunted Land: Facing Europe's Ghosts After Communism* won both the Pulitzer Prize and the National Book Award. Noah Greenberg Photography

Binge drinking is a problem on college campuses across America (Wechsler & Nelson, 2001). About half of all students report doing it, and those who do are much more likely to miss classes, fall behind in their school work, drive drunk, and have unprotected sex. So what to do? Writer Tina Rosenberg has a suggestion.

Colleges have tried a number of remedies—from education to abstinence—and none of them has worked particularly well. But lately, some schools have taken a new approach called "social norming." Although this approach is surprisingly effective, it is also controversial. Tina Rosenberg's most recent book is *Join the Club: How Peer Pressure Can Transform the World*. In the following essay, she describes both the technique and the controversy.

Like most universities, Northern Illinois University in DeKalb has a problem with heavy drinking. In the 1980s, the school was trying to cut down on student use of alcohol with the usual strategies. One campaign warned teenagers of the consequences of heavy drinking. "It was the 'don't run with a sharp stick you'll poke your eye out' theory of behavior change," said Michael Haines, who was the coordinator of the school's Health Enhancement Services. When that didn't work, Haines tried combining the scare approach with information on how to be well: "It's O.K. to drink if you don't drink too much—but if you do, bad things will happen to you."

That one failed, too. In 1989, 45 percent of students surveyed said they drank more than five drinks at parties. This percentage was slightly higher than when the campaigns began. And students thought heavy drinking was even more common; they believed that 69 percent of their peers drank that much at parties.

But by then Haines had something new to try. In 1987 he had attended a conference on alcohol in higher education sponsored by the United States Department of Education. There Wes Perkins, a professor of sociology at Hobart and William Smith Colleges, and Alan Berkowitz, a psychologist in the school's counseling center, presented a paper that they had just published on how student drinking is affected by peers. "There are decades of research on peer influence—that's nothing new," Perkins said at the meeting. What was new was their survey showing that when students were asked how much their peers drank, they grossly overestimated the amount.

If the students were responding to peer pressure, the researchers said, it was coming from imaginary peers.

The "aha!" conclusion Perkins and Berkowitz drew was this: maybe students' drinking behavior could be changed by just telling them the truth.

Haines surveyed students at Northern Illinois University and found that they also had a distorted view of how much their peers drink. He decided to try a new campaign, with the theme "most students drink moderately." The centerpiece of the campaign was a series of ads in the *Northern Star*, the campus newspaper, with pictures of students and the caption "two thirds of Northern Illinois University students (72%) drink 5 or fewer drinks when they 'party.'" . . .

Haines's staff also made posters with campus drinking facts and told students that if they had those posters on the wall when an inspector came around, they would earn $5 (35 percent of the students did have them posted when inspected). Later they made buttons for students in the fraternity and sorority system—these students drank more heavily—that said "Most of Us," and offered another $5 for being caught wearing one. The buttons were deliberately cryptic, to start a conversation.

After the first year of the social norming campaign, the perception of heavy drinking had fallen from 69 to 61 percent. Actual heavy drinking fell from 45 to 38 percent. The campaign went on for a decade, and at the end of it NIU students believed that 33 percent of their fellow students were episodic heavy drinkers, and only 25 percent really were—a decline in heavy drinking of 44 percent. . . .

Why isn't this idea more widely used? One reason is that it can be controversial. Telling college students "most of you drink moderately" is very different than saying "don't drink." (It's so different, in fact, that the National Social Norms Institute, with headquarters at the University of Virginia, gets its money from Anheuser Busch—a decision that has undercut support for the idea of social norming.) The approach angers people who lobby for a strong, unmuddied message of disapproval—even though, of course, disapproval doesn't reduce bad behavior, and social norming does.

Rosenberg's essay suggests that social norming is a powerful tool for changing behavior, but its use raises important questions. When we tell students about drinking on campus, should we tell them what's true—even if the truth is a bit ugly? Or should we tell them what's best—even if they are unlikely to do it? There are no easy or obvious answers to this question, but as a society, we have no choice but to choose.

Normative Influence at Home In 2008, the Sacramento Municipal Utility District randomly selected 35,000 of its customers and sent them electric bills like this one. The bill showed how much electricity the customer had used, and also how much electricity was used by neighbors who lived in similar-sized homes. Customers who received this "compare with the neighbors" bill reduced their electricity consumption by 2%, compared with customers who had received a traditional bill (Kaufman, 2009). Max Whittaker/The New York Times/Redux

Obedience: We Do What We're Told

In most situations, there are a few people whom we all recognize as having special authority both to define the norms and to enforce them. The guy who works at the movie theater may be some high-school fanboy with a bad haircut and a 10:00 p.m. curfew, but in the context of the theater, he is the authority. So when he asks you to put away your cell and stop texting in the middle of the movie, you do as you are asked. **Obedience** is *the tendency to do what powerful people tell us to do.*

Why do we obey powerful people? Well, yes, sometimes they have guns. But while powerful people are often capable of rewarding and punishing us, research shows that much of their influence is *normative* (Tyler, 1990). The psychologist Stanley Milgram (1963) demonstrated this in one of psychology's most infamous experiments. The participants in this experiment met a middle-aged man who was introduced as another participant but who was actually a trained actor. An experimenter in a lab coat explained that the participant would play the role of *teacher* and the actor would play the role of *learner*. The teacher and the learner would sit in different rooms, the teacher would read words to the learner over a microphone, and the learner would then repeat the words back to the teacher. If the learner made a mistake, the teacher would press a button that delivered an electric shock to the learner (see **FIGURE 12.11**). The shock-generating machine (which was totally fake) offered 30 levels of shock, ranging from 15 volts (labeled *slight shock*) to 450 volts (labeled *Danger: severe shock*).

After the learner was strapped into his chair, the experiment began. When the learner made his first mistake, the participant dutifully delivered a 15-volt shock. As the learner made more mistakes, he received more shocks. When the participant delivered the 75-volt shock, the learner cried out in pain. At 150 volts, the learner

obedience The tendency to do what powerful people tell us to do.

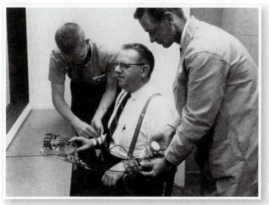

Figure 12.11 MILGRAM'S OBEDIENCE STUDIES The learner (*left*) is being hooked up to the shock generator (*right*) that was used in Stanley Milgram's obedience studies. © 1965 by Stanley Milgram; Stanley and Alexandra Milgram

screamed, "I refuse to go on. Let me out!" With every shock, the learner's screams became more agonized. Then, after receiving the 330-volt shock, the learner stopped responding altogether. Participants were naturally upset by all this and typically asked the experimenter to stop, but the experimenter simply replied, "You have no choice. You must go on." The experimenter never threatened the participant with punishment of any kind. Rather, he just stood there with his clipboard in hand and calmly instructed the participant to continue. So what did the participants do? Eighty percent of the participants continued to shock the learner even after he screamed, complained, pleaded, and then fell silent. And 62% went all the way, delivering the highest possible voltage. Although Milgram's study was conducted nearly half a century ago, a recent replication revealed about the same rate of obedience (Burger, 2009).

Would normal people electrocute a stranger just because some guy in a lab coat told them to? The answer, it seems, is *yes*—as long as *normal* means being sensitive to social norms (Zimbardo, 2007). The participants in this experiment knew that hurting others is *often* wrong but not *always* wrong: Doctors give painful injections, and teachers give painful exams. There are many situations in which it is permissible—and even desirable—to cause someone to suffer in the service of a higher goal. The experimenter's calm demeanor and persistent instruction suggested that he, and not the participants, knew what was appropriate in this particular situation, and so the participants did as ordered.

The Accuracy Motive

attitude An enduring positive or negative evaluation of an object or event.

belief An enduring piece of knowledge about an object or event.

When you are hungry, you open the refrigerator and grab an apple because you know that apples taste good and are in the refrigerator. This action, like most actions, relies on both an **attitude**, which is *an enduring positive or negative evaluation of an object or event*, and a **belief**, which is *an enduring piece of knowledge about an object or event*. In a sense, our attitudes ("Apples are good") tell us what we should do (*eat an apple*) and our beliefs ("Apples are in the fridge") tell us how to do it (*open the refrigerator and grab one*). If our attitudes or beliefs are inaccurate—that is, if we can't tell good from bad or true from false—then our actions are likely to be fruitless. Because we rely so much on our attitudes and beliefs, it isn't surprising that we are motivated to have the right ones, and that motivation leaves us vulnerable to social influence.

Informational Influence: We Do What's Right

informational influence A phenomenon that occurs when another person's behavior provides information about what is true.

If everyone in the mall suddenly ran screaming for the exit, you'd probably join them—not because you were afraid they would disapprove of you if you didn't, but because their behavior would suggest to you that there was something worth running from. **Informational influence** occurs when *another person's behavior provides information about what is true*. You can observe the power of informational influence yourself just by standing in the middle of the sidewalk, tilting back your head, and staring at the top of a tall building. Research shows that within just a few minutes, other people will stop and stare too (Milgram, Bickman, & Berkowitz, 1969). Why? They will assume that if you are looking, then there must be something worth looking at.

You are the constant target of informational influence. Advertisements that refer to soft drinks as "popular" or books as "best sellers" are reminding you that other people are buying these particular drinks and books, which suggests that they know something you don't and that you'd be wise to follow their example. Situation comedies provide laugh tracks because the producers know that when you hear other people laughing, you will mindlessly assume that something must be funny (Fein, Goethals, & Kugler, 2007; Nosanchuk & Lightstone, 1974). Bars and nightclubs make people stand in line outside, even when there is plenty of room inside, because they know that passersby will see the line and assume that the club is worth waiting for. In short, the world is full of objects and events that we know little about, and we can often cure our ignorance by paying attention to the way in which others are acting toward them. Alas, the very thing that makes us open to information leaves us open to manipulation as well.

Persuasion: Changing Behavior by Changing Minds

Persuasion occurs when *a person's attitudes or beliefs are influenced by a communication from another person* (Albarracín & Vargas, 2010; Petty & Wegener, 1998). How does it work? Candidates for political office often try to win votes by making thoughtful arguments about important issues, but they also try to win votes by standing next to popular celebrities and American flags. The first of these is called **systematic persuasion**, which is *the process by which attitudes or beliefs are changed by appeals to reason*, and the second is called **heuristic persuasion**, which is *the process by which attitudes or beliefs are changed by appeals to habit or emotion* (Chaiken, 1980; Petty & Cacioppo, 1986). (*Heuristics* are simple shortcuts or "rules of thumb.") Which form of persuasion will be more effective depends on whether the listener is willing and able to weigh evidence and analyze arguments.

In one study, students heard a speech that contained either strong or weak arguments in favor of instituting comprehensive exams at their school (Petty, Cacioppo, & Goldman, 1981). Some students were told that the speaker was a Princeton University professor, and others were told that the speaker was a high-school student—a bit of information that the students could use as a heuristic to decide whether to believe the speech. Some students were told that their university was considering implementing these exams right away, motivating them to analyze the evidence, whereas others were told that their university was considering implementing these exams in 10 years, which gave them less motivation to analyze the evidence (because they themselves would have graduated by the time the exams were given). As **FIGURE 12.12** shows, when students were motivated to analyze the evidence, they were systematically persuaded—that is, their attitudes and beliefs were strongly influenced by the strength of the arguments but influenced little by the status of the speaker.

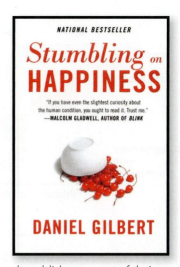

Why do publishers go out of their way to tell readers that a book is a "national bestseller"? Because publishers know that when people who are browsing books see that others have bought one, they become more inclined to buy it too.

persuasion A phenomenon that occurs when a person's attitudes or beliefs are influenced by a communication from another person.

systematic persuasion The process by which attitudes or beliefs are changed by appeals to reason.

heuristic persuasion The process by which attitudes or beliefs are changed by appeals to habit or emotion.

Does Kim Kardashian know more about toilet paper than you do? Probably not. So why do advertisers hire celebrities like her to endorse their products? (If the phrase "heuristic persuasion" doesn't come to mind, go back and reread this section.) WENN Ltd/Alamy Stock Photo

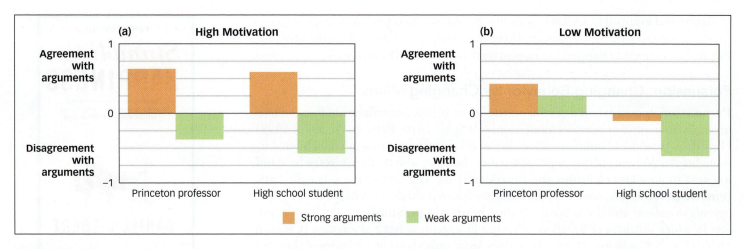

Figure 12.12 SYSTEMATIC AND HEURISTIC PERSUASION (a) *Systematic persuasion.* When students were motivated to analyze arguments because they would be personally affected by them, their attitudes were influenced by the strength of the arguments (strong arguments were more persuasive than weak arguments) but not by the status of the communicator (the Princeton professor was not more persuasive than the high school student). (b) *Heuristic persuasion.* When students were not motivated to analyze arguments because they would not be personally affected by them, their attitudes were influenced by the status of the communicator (the Princeton professor was more persuasive than the high school student) but not by the strength of the arguments (strong arguments were no more persuasive than weak arguments; Petty, Cacioppo, & Goldman, 1981).

foot-in-the-door technique A technique that involves making a small request and following it with a larger request.

cognitive dissonance An unpleasant state that arises when a person recognizes the inconsistency of his or her actions, attitudes, or beliefs.

But when students were not motivated to analyze the evidence, they were heuristically persuaded—that is, their attitudes and beliefs were strongly influenced by the status of the speaker but influenced little by the strength of the arguments.

Consistency: Changing Minds by Changing Behavior

If a friend told you that rabbits had just staged a coup in Antarctica and were halting all carrot exports, you probably wouldn't turn on CNN. You'd know right away that your friend was either joking or really, really gullible because the statement is logically inconsistent with other things that you know are true—for example, that rabbits do not foment revolution and that Antarctica does not export carrots. People evaluate the accuracy of new beliefs by assessing their *consistency* with old beliefs. Although this is not a foolproof method for determining whether something is true, it provides a pretty good approximation. We are motivated to be accurate, and because consistency is a rough measure of accuracy, we are motivated to be consistent as well (Cialdini, Trost, & Newsom, 1995).

That motivation leaves us vulnerable to social influence. For example, the **foot-in-the-door** technique involves *making a small request and then following it with a larger request* (Burger, 1999). In one study (Freedman & Fraser, 1966), experimenters went to a neighborhood and knocked on doors to see if they could convince homeowners to agree to have a big ugly "Drive Carefully" sign installed in their front yards. One group of homeowners was simply asked to install the sign, and only 17% said yes. A second group of homeowners was first asked to sign a petition urging the state legislature to promote safe driving (which almost all agreed to do) and was *then* asked to install the ugly sign. And 55% said yes! Why would homeowners be more likely to grant two requests than one?

Just imagine how the homeowners in the second group felt. They had just signed a petition stating that they thought safe driving was important, yet they knew they didn't want to install an ugly sign in their front yards. As they wrestled with this inconsistency, they probably began to experience **cognitive dissonance**, which is *an unpleasant state that arises when a person recognizes the inconsistency of his or her actions, attitudes, or beliefs* (Festinger, 1957). When people experience cognitive dissonance, they naturally try to alleviate it, and one way to do this is to put your money where your mouth is—that is, to act in ways that are consistent with your beliefs (Aronson, 1969; Cooper & Fazio, 1984; Harmon-Jones, Harmon-Jones, & Levy, 2015). Agreeing to install a yard sign was just such an action. Indeed, one of the best ways to get people to take an action is to first get them to express an attitude with which that action is consistent. If hotel guests are subtly induced at check-in to call themselves "Friends of the Earth," they are 25% more likely to reuse their towels during their stay (Baca-Motes et al., 2013).

We are motivated to be consistent, but inevitably there are times when we just can't—for example, when we tell a friend that her new hairstyle is "daring" when it actually resembles a wet skunk after an unfortunate encounter with a snow blower. Why don't we experience cognitive dissonance under such circumstances and come to believe our own lies? Because whereas telling a friend that her hairstyle is daring is inconsistent with the belief that her hairstyle is hideous, it is perfectly consistent with the belief that one should be nice to one's friends. When small inconsistencies are *justified* by large consistencies, cognitive dissonance is reduced.

For example, participants in one study were asked to perform a dull task that involved turning knobs one way, then the other way, and then back again. After the participants were sufficiently bored, the experimenter explained that he desperately needed a few more people to volunteer for the study, and he asked the participants to go find another person, and tell that person that the knob-turning task was great fun. The experimenter offered some participants $1 to tell this lie, and he offered other participants $20. All participants agreed to tell the lie, and after they did so, they were asked to report their true enjoyment of the knob-turning task. The results showed that participants liked the task *more* when they were paid $1 than $20 to lie about it (Festinger & Carlsmith, 1959). Why? Because the belief *this knob-turning task is dull* was inconsistent with the belief *I recommended the task to that person in the hallway*, but the latter belief was perfectly consistent with the belief that *$20 is a lot of money*. For some participants, the large payment justified the lie, so only those people who received the small payment experienced cognitive dissonance. As such, only the participants who received $1 felt the need to restore consistency by changing their beliefs about the enjoyableness of the task (see **FIGURE 12.13**).

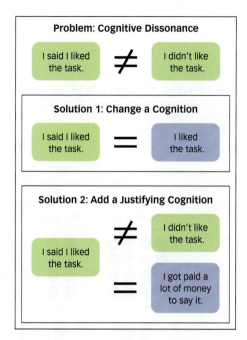

Figure 12.13 ALLEVIATING COGNITIVE DISSONANCE Telling a lie can produce an uncomfortable feeling known as cognitive dissonance. One way to reduce that dissonance is to justify having told the lie.

BUILD TO THE OUTCOMES

1. What are the three basic motives that social influence involves?

2. Why do attempts to influence others with rewards and punishments sometimes backfire?

3. How can the norm of reciprocity be used to influence people?

4. Why do people sometimes do what they see others doing?

5. When and why do people obey authority?

6. What is the difference between normative and informational influence?

7. When is it more effective to engage in systematic persuasion rather than heuristic persuasion?

8. Why does the accuracy motive lead to a desire for consistency?

9. What is cognitive dissonance? How do people alleviate it?

Understanding Others

Of the many objects you encounter on a daily basis, other human beings are the single most important. **Social cognition** is *the processes by which people come to understand others*, and your brain is doing it all day long. Whether you know it or not, your brain is constantly making inferences about other people's thoughts and feelings, beliefs and desires, abilities and aspirations, intentions, needs, and characters. It bases these inferences on two kinds of information: the categories to which people belong, and the things people do and say.

Stereotyping: Drawing Inferences from Categories

You'll recall from the Language, Thought, and Intelligence chapter that categorization is the process by which people identify a stimulus as a member of a class of related stimuli. Once we have identified a novel stimulus as a member of a

LEARNING OUTCOMES

- Explain how stereotypes cause people to draw inaccurate conclusions about others.

- Explain why stereotypes are so difficult to overcome.

- Explain what an attribution is and what kinds of errors attributions entail.

social cognition The processes by which people come to understand others.

category ("That's a textbook"), we can then use our knowledge of the category to make educated guesses about the properties of the novel stimulus ("It's probably expensive") and act accordingly ("I think I'll download it illegally").

What we do with textbooks we also do with people. No, not the illegal downloading part. The educated guessing part. **Stereotyping** is *the process by which people draw inferences about others based on their knowledge of the categories to which others belong.* The moment we categorize a person as an adult, a male, a baseball player, and a Russian, we can use our knowledge of those categories to make some educated guesses about him—for example, that he shaves his face but not his legs, that he understands the infield fly rule, and that he knows more about Vladimir Putin than we do. When we offer children candy instead of beer or ask gas-station attendants for directions instead of financial advice, we are making inferences about people whom we have never met before based solely on their category membership. As these examples suggest, stereotyping is a very helpful process (Allport, 1954). And yet, ever since the word was coined by the journalist Walter Lippmann in 1936, it has had a distasteful connotation. Why? Because stereotyping is a helpful process that can often produce harmful results, and it does so because stereotypes tend to have four properties: They can be inaccurate, overused, self-perpetuating, and unconscious and automatic. Let's examine each of them.

stereotyping The process by which people draw inferences about others based on their knowledge of the categories to which others belong.

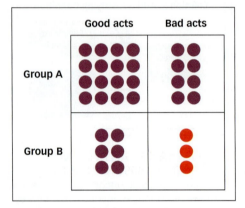

Figure 12.14 SEEING CORRELATIONS THAT AREN'T REALLY THERE Group A and Group B each perform two thirds good acts and one third bad acts. However, Group B and bad acts are both rare, leading people to notice and remember their co-occurrence, which leads them to perceive a correlation between group membership and behavior that isn't really there.

Stereotypes can be inaccurate. Shlomo Koenig does not fit most people's stereotype of a police officer or a rabbi, but he is both. GINO DOMENICO/AP Images

1. Stereotypes Can Be Inaccurate

Much of what we think we know about human categories is stuff we picked up from watching television, listening to pop songs, or just hearing people talk at the bus stop. These are not particularly authoritative sources, so not surprisingly, much of what we believe about human categories is just plain wrong. But inaccurate beliefs about human categories can also be produced by direct observation of their members. For example, research participants in one study were shown a long series of positive and negative behaviors and were told that each behavior had been performed by a member of one of two groups: Group A or Group B (see **FIGURE 12.14**). The behaviors were carefully arranged so that each group behaved negatively exactly one third of the time. However, there were more positive than negative behaviors in the series, and there were more members of Group A than of Group B. Thus, negative behaviors were rarer than positive behaviors, and Group B members were rarer than Group A members. After seeing the behaviors, participants correctly reported that Group A had behaved negatively one third of the time. However, they incorrectly reported that Group B had behaved negatively more than *half* the time (Hamilton & Gifford, 1976).

Why did this happen? Bad behavior was rare, and being a member of Group B was rare. Thus, participants were especially likely to notice when the two co-occurred ("Aha! There's one of those unusual Group B people doing an unusually awful thing again"). These findings help explain why members of majority groups tend to overestimate the number of crimes (which are relatively rare events) committed by members of minority groups (who are relatively rare people, hence the word *m-i-n-o-r-i-t-y*). The point here is that even when we directly observe people, we can end up with inaccurate beliefs about the groups to which they belong.

2. Stereotypes Can Be Overused

Because all thumbtacks are pretty much alike, our stereotypes about thumbtacks (small, cheap, painful when chewed) are quite useful. We will rarely be mistaken if we generalize from one thumbtack to another. But human categories are so variable that our stereotypes may offer only the vaguest of clues about the individuals who populate those categories. You probably believe that men have greater upper body strength than women do, and this belief is right *on average*. But the upper body strength of individuals *within* each of these categories is so varied that you cannot easily predict how much weight a particular person can lift simply by knowing that person's gender. The inherent variability of human categories makes stereotypes much less useful than they seem.

Alas, we don't always recognize this because the mere act of categorizing a stimulus tends to warp our perceptions of that category's variability. For instance, participants in some studies were shown a series of lines of different lengths (see **FIGURE 12.15**; McGarty & Turner, 1992; Tajfel & Wilkes, 1963). For one group of participants, the longest lines were labeled *Group A* and the shortest lines were labeled *Group B*, as they are on the right side of Figure 12.15. For the second group of participants, the lines were shown without these category labels, as they are on the left side of Figure 12.15. Interestingly, those participants who saw the category labels *overestimated* the similarity of the lines that shared a label and *underestimated* the similarity of lines that did not. What's true of lines is true of people as well. The mere act of categorizing people as Blacks or Whites, Jews or Gentiles, artists or accountants, can cause us to underestimate the variability within those categories ("All artists are wacky") and to overestimate the variability between them ("Artists are much wackier than accountants"). When we underestimate the variability of a human category, we naturally overestimate how useful our stereotypes about it will be (Park & Hastie, 1987; Rubin & Badea, 2012).

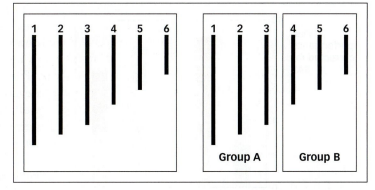

Figure 12.15 HOW CATEGORIZATION WARPS PERCEPTION People who see the lines on the right tend to *overestimate the similarity* of lines 1 and 3 and *underestimate the similarity* of lines 3 and 4. Simply labeling lines 1–3 *Group A* and lines 4–6 *Group B* causes the lines within a group to seem more similar to each other than they really are and the lines in different groups to seem more different from each other than they really are.

3. Stereotypes Can Be Self-Perpetuating

When we meet a truck driver who likes ballet more than football or a senior citizen who likes Drake more than Bach, why don't we simply abandon our stereotypes of these groups? The answer is that stereotypes tend to be self-perpetuating. Like viruses and parasites, once they take up residence inside us, they resist even our most concerted efforts to eradicate them.

One reason is **self-fulfilling prophecy**: *the tendency for people to behave as they are expected to behave*. When people know that observers have a negative stereotype about them, they may experience **stereotype threat**, which is *the fear of confirming the negative beliefs that others may hold* (Aronson & Steele, 2004; Schmader, Johns, & Forbes, 2008; Walton & Spencer, 2009). Ironically, this fear may cause them to behave in ways that confirm the very stereotype that threatened them. In one study (Steele & Aronson, 1995), African American and

self-fulfilling prophecy The tendency for people to behave as they are expected to behave.

stereotype threat The fear of confirming the negative beliefs that others may hold.

The former First Lady of the United States, Michelle Obama, understands the nature of stereotype threat. "That's a burden that President Obama and I proudly carry every single day in the White House, because we know that everything we do and say can either confirm the myths about folks like us— or it can change those myths" (Baker, 2015). Chip Somodevilla/Getty Images

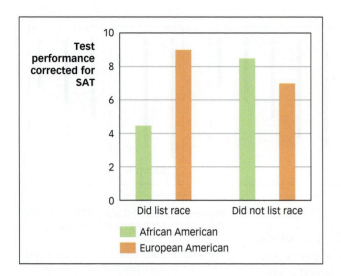

Figure 12.16 STEREOTYPE THREAT When asked to indicate their race before taking an exam, African American students performed below their academic level (as determined by their SAT scores), but European American students did not.

perceptual confirmation The tendency for people to see what they expect to see.

White students took a test, and half the students in each group were asked to list their race at the top of the exam. When students were not asked to list their race, they performed at their academic level, but when students were asked to list their race, African American students became anxious about confirming a negative stereotype of their group, which caused them to perform well below their academic level (see **FIGURE 12.16**). Stereotypes perpetuate themselves in part by causing the stereotyped individual to behave in ways that confirm the stereotype.

Another reason stereotypes persist is that, even when people do *not* confirm stereotypes, observers often think they have. **Perceptual confirmation** is *the tendency for people to see what they expect to see*, and this tendency helps perpetuate stereotypes. In one study, participants listened to a radio broadcast of a college basketball game and were asked to evaluate the performance of one of the players. Although all participants heard the same prerecorded game, some were led to believe that the player was African American, and others were led to believe that the player was White. Participants' stereotypes led them to expect different performances from athletes of different ethnic origins—and the participants perceived just what they expected. Those who believed the player was African American thought he had demonstrated greater athletic ability but less intelligence than did those who thought he was White (Stone, Perry, & Darley, 1997). Stereotypes perpetuate themselves in part by biasing our perception of individuals, leading us to believe that those individuals have confirmed our stereotypes even when they have not (Fiske, 1998).

4. Stereotyping Can Be Unconscious and Automatic

If we recognize that our stereotypes are inaccurate and self-perpetuating, then why don't we just make a firm resolution to stop using them? The answer is that stereotyping often happens *unconsciously* (which means that we don't always know we are doing it) and *automatically* (which means that we often cannot avoid doing it even when we try; Banaji & Heiphetz, 2010; Greenwald, McGhee, & Schwartz, 1998; Greenwald & Nosek, 2001).

For example, in one study, participants played a video game in which photos of Black or White men holding either guns or cameras were briefly flashed on the screen. Participants earned money by shooting men with guns and lost money by shooting men with cameras. Participants made two kinds of mistakes: They tended to shoot Black men holding cameras and tended not to shoot White men holding guns (Correll et al., 2002). Although the photos appeared on the screen so quickly that participants did not have enough time to consciously consider their stereotypes, those stereotypes worked unconsciously, causing them to mistake a camera for a gun when it was in the hands of a Black man and a gun for a camera when it was in the hands of a White man (Correll et al., 2015). It is instructive to note that Black participants were just as likely to make this pattern of errors as were White participants. Why did these errors happen?

Stereotypes comprise all the information about human categories that we have absorbed over the years from friends and uncles, books and blogs, jokes and movies, and late-night television. When we see Black men holding guns in rap videos, our minds associate these two things, and although we realize that we are watching art and not news, our brains make and remember the association. We cannot later *decide* that we just won't be influenced by it any more than we can *decide* that we just won't be influenced by our knowledge of English or the smell of French fries.

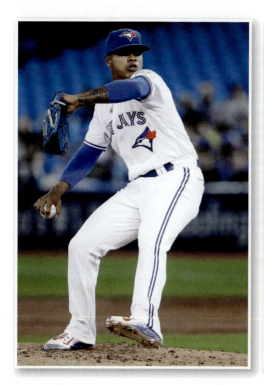

Major League Baseball umpires try to be objective, but when they mistakenly call a strike, it benefits the pitcher's team. A recent study showed that umpires are 10% less likely to make this "helpful error" when the pitcher is African American than when he is European American (Kim & King, 2014). Because stereotypes are automatic, they can influence the judgments of even those who work hard not to apply them. Carlos Osorio/Toronto Star via Getty Images; Thearon W. Henderson/ Getty Images

Are the Consequences of Stereotyping Inevitable?

Although stereotyping is unconscious and automatic, that does not mean that its undesirable consequences—bias and prejudice—are inevitable (Blair, 2002; Kawakami et al., 2000; Milne & Grafman, 2001; Rudman, Ashmore, & Gary, 2001). For instance, police officers who receive special training before playing the camera-or-gun video game described earlier do not show the same biases that ordinary people do (Correll et al., 2007). Like ordinary people, they take a few milliseconds longer to decide not to shoot a Black man than a White man, indicating that their stereotypes are unconsciously and automatically influencing their perception. But unlike ordinary people, they don't actually *shoot* Black men more often than they shoot White men, indicating that they have learned how to keep those stereotypes from influencing their behavior (Phills et al., 2011; Todd et al., 2011).

So what's the best way to reduce unconscious stereotyping? In 2014, a team of psychologists held a contest in which they invited researchers to submit techniques for reducing unconscious stereotyping of Blacks and then tested each of the techniques against the other. As **FIGURE 12.17** shows, about half the techniques had some effect, and these tended to be techniques that exposed Whites to examples of Blacks who defy their stereotypes. For example, the most effective technique asked participants to imagine in gory detail that they were being assaulted by a White man and then to imagine being rescued by a Black man. The least effective techniques were those that simply encouraged people to feel compassion toward or take the perspective of a Black person (see Hot Science: Through Other Eyes). One troubling finding was that many of the failed techniques look a lot like the techniques that are often used in schools, businesses, and other organizations, which often implement stereotyping-reduction programs without actually testing them (Paluck & Green, 2009). Eliminating the prejudice that stereotyping can produce in everyday settings is a worthwhile goal, but science suggests that it is not one we are yet close to achieving.

The Implicit Association Test measures how easily people can learn to associate two things (Greenwald, McGhee, & Schwartz, 1998). Studies using the test show that 70% of White Americans find it easier to associate White faces with positive concepts, such as "peace," and Black faces with negative concepts, such as "bomb," than the other way around. Surprisingly, 40% of African Americans show this same pattern. You can take the IAT yourself at https://implicit.harvard.edu/implicit/ ColorBlind Images/Blend Images/Alamy; Radius Images/Alamy

Figure 12.17 STEREOTYPE CONTEST Results of a study that compared 18 techniques for reducing unconscious stereotyping of Blacks by Whites (data from Lai et al., 2014). ColorBlind Images / Blend Images / Alamy

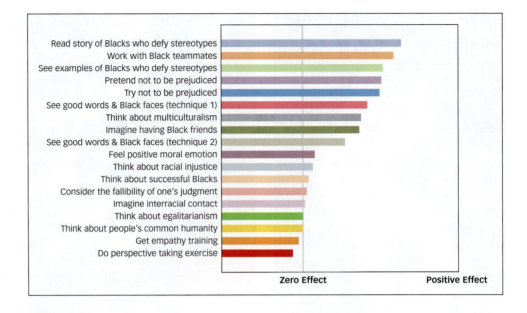

Read story of Blacks who defy stereotypes
Work with Black teammates
See examples of Blacks who defy stereotypes
Pretend not to be prejudiced
Try not to be prejudiced
See good words & Black faces (technique 1)
Think about multiculturalism
Imagine having Black friends
See good words & Black faces (technique 2)
Feel positive moral emotion
Think about racial injustice
Think about successful Blacks
Consider the fallibility of one's judgment
Imagine interracial contact
Think about egalitarianism
Think about people's common humanity
Get empathy training
Do perspective taking exercise

Zero Effect · Positive Effect

Through Other Eyes

You may have heard the adage that you can never really understand what it's like to be someone else unless you "walk a mile in that person's shoes." To explore this idea, researchers gave sighted people the opportunity to experience blindness (Silverman, Gwinn & van Boven, 2015). Participants reported to the laboratory, were blindfolded, and were then asked to perform a variety of ordinary tasks ranging from filling a glass with water to finding the stairwell in a hallway.

Wearing the blindfold did make participants feel more empathetic, friendly, and warm toward blind people. But it also had a side effect:, participants thought that blind people were much less competent and capable—less able to get around a city, to cook, to own their own business, to teach school or become an accountant, and so on. In other words, walking in a blind person's shoes for a few minutes led participants to conclude that walking was pretty much impossible.

But it isn't. Most blind people are perfectly capable of performing ordinary tasks, such as pouring water and finding a stairwell, and perfectly capable of performing jobs from

schoolteacher to accountant. Blindness is a disability to which people adapt extraordinarily well over time, and although there are a few things that blind people can't do as well as sighted people can (e.g., drive), there are other things they can do even better (e.g., hear). Participants in this study had enough time to experience blindness but not enough time to adapt to it. And yet, being blindfolded for a few minutes led them to mistakenly believe that they understood what a lifetime of blindness was like. Rather than becoming more

accurate about what it is like to have this particular disability, they became less accurate.

All of us are forever trapped inside our own skins. We can never really know what another person's experience of the world is like, and well-meaning exercises that are designed to expand our horizons can actually do the opposite. If we listen carefully to people, we can gain some appreciation of their perspectives. But we should not be fooled into thinking that we have ever seen the world through someone else's eyes.

Paul Scruggs is blind, but that doesn't prevent him from working as a machine operator in a factory that makes military uniforms. You could probably run this machine with your eyes closed—but not in the first hour of trying. Jay Mallin/Bloomberg via Getty Images

HOT SCIENCE

Attribution: Drawing Inferences from Actions

In 1963, Dr. Martin Luther King Jr. gave a speech in which he described his vision for America: "I have a dream that my four children will one day live in a nation where they will not be judged by the color of their skin but by the content of their character." Research on stereotyping demonstrates that Dr. King's concern was well justified. We do judge others by the color of their skin—as well as by their gender, nationality, religion, age, and occupation—and in so doing, we sometimes make consequential mistakes. But are we any better at judging people by the content of their character? If we could somehow turn off our stereotypes and treat each person as a unique individual, would we judge them more accurately?

Not necessarily. Treating people as individuals means judging them by their own words and deeds. This is more difficult than it sounds because the relationship between what a person *is* and what a person *says or does* is not always straightforward. An honest person may lie to save a friend from embarrassment, and a dishonest person may tell the truth to bolster her credibility. Happy people have some weepy moments, polite people can be rude in traffic, and people who despise us can be flattering when they need a favor. In short, people's behavior sometimes tells us about the kinds of people they are, but sometimes it simply tells us about the kinds of situations they happen to be in. To understand people, we need to know not only *what* they did but also *why* they did it. Is the batter who hit the home run a talented slugger, or was the wind blowing in just the right direction at just the right time? Is the politician who gave the pro-life speech really opposed to abortion, or was she just trying to win the conservative vote?

When we answer questions such as these, we are making **attributions**, which are *inferences about the causes of people's behavior* (Epley & Waytz, 2010; Gilbert, 1998). We make *situational attributions* when we decide that a person's behavior was caused by some temporary aspect of the situation in which it happened ("He was lucky that the wind carried the ball into the stands"), and we make *dispositional attributions* when we decide that a person's behavior was caused by a relatively enduring tendency to think, feel, or act in a particular way ("He's got a great eye and a powerful swing"). Research shows that this decision is quite difficult and that people often make the wrong one. Specifically, people are prone to **correspondence bias**, which is *the tendency to make a dispositional attribution when we should instead make a situational attribution* (Gilbert & Malone, 1995; Jones & Harris, 1967; Ross, 1977). This bias is so common and so basic that it is often called the *fundamental attribution error*.

For example, volunteers in one experiment observed a trivia game in which a quizmaster made up a list of unusual questions, while a contestant tried to answer those questions. The quizmasters tended to ask tricky questions based on their own idiosyncratic knowledge, and contestants were generally unable to answer them. After watching the game, the observers were asked to decide how knowledgeable the quizmaster and the contestant were. Although the quizmasters had asked good questions and the contestants had given bad answers, it should have been clear to the observers that all this asking and answering was a product of the roles they had been assigned to play and that the contestant would have asked equally good questions and the quizmaster would have given equally bad answers had their roles been reversed. And yet observers tended to rate the quizmaster as more knowledgeable than the contestant (Ross, Amabile, & Steinmetz, 1977) and were more likely to choose the quizmaster as their own partner in an upcoming game (Quattrone, 1982). Even when we know that a successful athlete had a home-field advantage or that a successful entrepreneur had family connections, we tend to attribute their success to talent and tenacity.

The correspondence bias is stronger in some circumstances than in others. For example, we seem to be more prone to correspondence bias when judging other people's behavior than when judging our own. The **actor–observer effect**

"I think success is all perspiration. You make your own luck," said Robert Herjavec, a successful businessman and a judge on *Shark Tank*. But research on the correspondence bias suggests that it is dangerously easy to credit success to intelligence and tenacity, and to blame failure on stupidity and laziness. John Lamparski/WireImage/Getty Images

attribution An inference about the cause of a person's behavior.

correspondence bias The tendency to make a dispositional attribution when we should instead make a situational attribution.

actor–observer effect The tendency to make situational attributions for our own behaviors while making dispositional attributions for the identical behavior of others.

is *the tendency to make situational attributions for our own behaviors while making dispositional attributions for the identical behavior of others* (Jones & Nisbett, 1972). When college students are asked to explain why they and their friends chose their majors, they tend to explain their own choices in terms of situations ("I chose economics because my parents told me I have to support myself as soon as I'm done with college") and their friends' choices in terms of dispositions ("Leah chose economics because she's materialistic"; Nisbett et al., 1973). The actor–observer effect occurs because people typically have more information about the situations that caused their own behavior than about the situations that caused other people's behavior. We will always remember getting the please-major-in-something-practical lecture from our parents, but we weren't at Leah's house to see her get the same lecture. Indeed, when people are shown videotapes of their conversations that allow them to see themselves from their partner's point of view, they tend to make dispositional attributions for their own behavior and situational attributions for their partner's (Storms, 1973; Taylor & Fiske, 1975).

BUILD TO THE OUTCOMES

1. Where do stereotypes come from? What purpose do they serve?
2. When are stereotypes most and least likely to be useful?
3. Why do stereotypes sometimes seem more accurate than they really are?
4. Why is it difficult not to use stereotypes?
5. Why do people tend to make dispositional attributions, even when they should not?

CHAPTER REVIEW

The Survival Game

- Survival and reproduction require scarce resources; aggression and cooperation are two ways to acquire those resources.
- Aggression often results from negative affect. The likelihood that people will aggress when they experience negative affect is determined both by biological and cultural factors.
- Cooperation can be beneficial, but it also is risky. One strategy for reducing those risks is to form groups whose members show in-group favoritism.
- Groups can be beneficial, but they also have costs. They make poor decisions because they overemphasize information that all members share, and they allow people to behave unethically by causing them to lose focus on their personal values.
- Many behaviors that appear to be altruistic have hidden benefits for the person who performs them, but there is no doubt that humans sometimes do exhibit genuine altruism.

The Mating Game

- Both biology and culture tend to make the costs of reproduction higher for women than for men, which is one reason that women tend to be choosier when selecting potential mates.
- Attraction is determined by situational factors (such as proximity), physical factors (such as symmetry), and psychological factors (such as similarity).
- People weigh the costs and benefits of their relationships and are least likely to end them when they believe no better alternatives are available and/or when they have invested a lot of time in the relationship.

Controlling Others

- People are motivated to experience pleasure and avoid pain (the hedonic motive) and thus can be influenced by rewards and punishments. These influence attempts can sometimes backfire by changing how people think about their own behavior or by making them feel as though they are being manipulated.

- People are motivated to attain the approval of others (the approval motive) and thus can be influenced by social norms, such as the norm of reciprocity. People often look to the behavior of others to determine what kinds of behavior are normative, and they tend to obey authorities even when they should not.
- People are motivated to know what is true (the accuracy motive).
- People can be persuaded by appeals to reason or emotion. Each is effective under different circumstances.
- People feel bad when they notice inconsistency among their attitudes, beliefs, and actions, and they will often change one of these things in order to achieve consistency.

Understanding Others

- We make inferences about others based on the categories to which they belong (stereotyping). This sometimes leads us to misjudge others because stereotypes are often inaccurate, overused, self-perpetuating, unconscious, and automatic.
- Some techniques may reduce stereotyping, but so far, none has proved powerful and long-lasting.
- We sometimes make mistakes when drawing inferences about people from their behaviors. We tend to attribute those behaviors to the person's dispositions even when we should attribute them to the person's situation.

KEY CONCEPT QUIZ

1. Why are acts of aggression—from violent crime to athletic brawls—more likely to occur on hot days when people are feeling irritated and uncomfortable?
   a. frustration
   b. negative affect
   c. resource scarcity
   d. the prisoner's dilemma

2. What is the single best predictor of aggression?
   a. temperament
   b. age
   c. gender
   d. status

3. The prisoner's dilemma game illustrates
   a. in-group favoritism.
   b. the diffusion of responsibility.
   c. group polarization.
   d. the benefits and costs of cooperation.

4. Which of the following is NOT a downside of being in a group?
   a. Groups are positively prejudiced toward other members and tend to discriminate in their favor.
   b. Groups often show prejudice and discrimination toward nonmembers.
   c. Groups sometimes make poor decisions.
   d. Groups may take extreme actions an individual member would not take alone.

5. Which of the following best describes reciprocal altruism?
   a. the ultimatum game
   b. diminished responsibility in groups
   c. cooperation extended over time
   d. cooperation with relatives

6. Which of the following is NOT an explanation for increased selectivity by women in choosing a mate?
   a. Sex is potentially more costly for women than for men.
   b. Communal styles of child-rearing argue for increased selectivity.
   c. The reputational costs of sex are historically much higher for women than for men.
   d. Pregnancy increases women's nutritional requirements and puts them at risk of illness and death.

7. Which of the following is a situational factor that influences attraction?
   a. proximity
   b. similarity
   c. appearance
   d. personality

8. The _____ motive explains the fact that people prefer to experience pleasure rather than pain.
   a. altruistic
   b. accuracy
   c. approval
   d. hedonic

9. The tendency to do what authorities tell us to do is known as
   a. persuasion.
   b. obedience.
   c. conformity.
   d. the self-fulfilling prophecy.

10. What is the process by which people come to understand others?
    a. heuristic processing
    b. reciprocal altruism
    c. social cognition
    d. cognitive dissonance

11. A common occupational stereotype is that lawyers are manipulative. Most people who subscribe to this stereotype
   a. believe that the stereotype applies to *all* lawyers.
   b. believe that the stereotype accurately applies to just a small percentage of lawyers.
   c. believe that lawyers are more likely than others to have this characteristic.
   d. would not be likely to misperceive lawyers when they actually meet.

12. The tendency to make a dispositional attribution even when a person's behavior was caused by the situation is referred to as
   a. comparison leveling.
   b. stereotyping.
   c. covariation.
   d. correspondence bias.

 **LearningCurve** Don't stop now! Quizzing yourself is a powerful study tool. Go to LearningCurve at www.launchpadworks.com for more practice.

KEY TERMS

social psychology (p. 376)
aggression (p. 376)
frustration–aggression hypothesis (p. 376)
cooperation (p. 379)
group (p. 380)
prejudice (p. 380)
common knowledge effect (p. 380)
group polarization (p. 381)
groupthink (p. 381)
deindividuation (p. 381)

diffusion of responsibility (p. 381)
bystander intervention (p. 381)
altruism (p. 382)
kin selection (p. 382)
reciprocal altruism (p. 382)
mere-exposure effect (p. 385)
passionate love (p. 387)
companionate love (p. 387)
social influence (p. 388)
norms (p. 390)

normative influence (p. 390)
norm of reciprocity (p. 390)
conformity (p. 391)
obedience (p. 393)
attitude (p. 394)
belief (p. 394)
informational influence (p. 394)
persuasion (p. 395)
systematic persuasion (p. 395)
heuristic persuasion (p. 395)

foot-in-the-door technique (p. 396)
cognitive dissonance (p. 396)
social cognition (p. 397)
stereotyping (p. 398)
self-fulfilling prophecy (p. 399)
stereotype threat (p. 399)
perceptual confirmation (p. 400)
attribution (p. 403)
correspondence bias (p. 403)
actor–observer effect (p. 403)

CHANGING MINDS

1. One of the senators from your state is supporting a bill that would impose heavy fines on aggressive drivers who run red lights. One of your classmates thinks this is a good idea. "The textbook taught us a lot about punishment and reward. It's simple. If we punish aggressive driving, its frequency will decline." Is your classmate right? Might the new law backfire? Might another policy be more effective in promoting safe driving?

2. One of your friends is outgoing, funny, and a star athlete on the women's basketball team. She has started to date a man who is introverted and prefers playing computer games to attending parties. You tease her about the contrast in personalities, and she replies, "Well, opposites attract." Is she right?

3. A large law firm is found guilty of discriminatory hiring practices. Your friend reads about the case and scoffs,

"People are always so quick to claim racism. Sure, there are still a few racists out there, but if you do surveys and ask people what they think about people of other races, they generally say they feel fine about them." What would you tell your friend?

4. One of your friends has a very unique fashion sense and always wears a neon orange tracksuit with a battered fedora. "Most people follow the crowd," he explains. "I don't. I'm an individual, and I make my own choices, without influence from anyone else." Could he be right? What examples might you provide for or against your friend's claim?

5. A classmate learns about the Milgram (1963) study, in which participants were willing to obey orders to administer painful electric shocks to a learner who begged them to stop. "Some people are such sheep!" she says.

"I know that I wouldn't behave like that." Is she right? What evidence would you give her to support or oppose her claim?

6. Your family gathers for a holiday dinner, and your cousin Wendy brings her fiancée, Amanda. It's the first time Amanda has met the whole family, and she seems nervous. She talks too much, laughs too loud, and rubs everyone the wrong way. Later, an uncle says to you, "It's hard to imagine Wendy wanting to spend the rest of her life married to someone so annoying." How can you explain to your uncle that you think he has fallen prey to the correspondence bias?

ANSWERS TO KEY CONCEPT QUIZ

1. b; 2. c; 3. d; 4. a; 5. c; 6. b; 7. a; 8. d; 9. b; 10. c; 11. c; 12. d.

Stress and Health

13

"I have a knife to your neck. Don't make a sound. Get out of bed and come with me or I will kill you and your family." These are the words that awoke 14-year-old Elizabeth Smart in the middle of the night of June 5, 2002. Fearing for her life, and the lives of her family, she kept quiet and left with her abductor, Brian David Mitchell, a man Elizabeth's parents had hired previously to do some roof work on their home. Mitchell and his wife held Elizabeth in captivity for nine months, during which time Mitchell repeatedly raped her and threatened to kill her and her entire family. Mitchell, his wife, and Smart were spotted walking down the street by a couple who recognized them from a recent episode of the television show *America's Most Wanted* and called the police. Mitchell and his wife were apprehended, and Elizabeth was returned to her family.

Elizabeth suffered under unimaginable circumstances for a prolonged period of time in one of the most stressful situations possible. Fortunately, she is now safe and sound, happily married, and working as an activist. She endured life-threatening stressors for months, and those experiences undoubtedly affected her in ways that will last her entire lifetime. Yet, despite the very difficult hand she was dealt, she appears to have bounced back and to be leading a happy, productive, and rewarding life. Hers is a story of both stress and health.

This smiling young face is that of Elizabeth Smart, who, between the times of these two photographs, was kidnapped, raped, and tortured for nearly a year. Stressful life events often affect us in ways that cannot be seen from the outside. Fortunately, there are things that we can do in response to even the most stressful of life events that can get us smiling again. SLCPD UPI Photo Service/Newscom/United Press International (UPI)/Washington, D.C., USA; Michael Loccisano/Getty Images

stressors Specific events or chronic pressures that place demands on a person or threaten the person's well-being.

stress The physical and psychological response to internal or external stressors.

health psychology The subfield of psychology concerned with ways psychological factors influence the causes and treatment of physical illness and the maintenance of health.

FORTUNATELY, VERY FEW OF US WILL EVER HAVE TO ENDURE the type of stress that Elizabeth Smart lived through. But life has its **stressors**, *specific events or chronic pressures that place demands on a person or threaten the person's well-being.* Although such stressors rarely involve threats of death, they do have both immediate and cumulative effects that can influence health.

In this chapter, we'll look at what psychologists and physicians have learned about the kinds of life events that produce **stress**, *the physical and psychological response to internal or external stressors;* typical responses to such stressors; and ways to manage stress. Stress has such a profound influence on health that we consider stress and health together in this chapter. And because sickness and health are not merely features of the physical body, we then consider the more general topic of **health psychology**, *the subfield of psychology concerned with ways psychological factors influence the causes and treatment of physical illness and the maintenance of health.* You will see how perceptions of illness can affect its course and how health-promoting behaviors can improve the quality of people's lives.

Sources of Stress: What Gets to You

LEARNING OUTCOMES

- Compare the impact of stressful events and chronic stress.
- Identify the importance of perceived control.

A natural catastrophe, such as a hurricane, earthquake, or volcanic eruption, is an obvious source of stress. But for most of us, stressors are personal events that affect the comfortable pattern of our lives and little annoyances that bug us day after day. Let's look at the life events that can cause stress, chronic sources of stress, and the relationship between lack of perceived control and the impact of stressors.

Stressful Events

People often seem to get sick after major life events. In fact, simply adding up the stress ratings of each life change experienced is a significant indicator of a person's likelihood of future illness (Miller, 1996). Someone who becomes divorced, loses a job, and has a friend die all in the same year, for example, is more likely to get sick than is someone who escapes the year with only a divorce.

A checklist adapted for the life events of college students (and sporting the snappy acronym CUSS, for College Undergraduate Stress Scale) is shown in **TABLE 13.1**. To assess your stressful events, check off any events that have happened to you in the past year and sum your point total. In a large sample of students in an introductory psychology class, the average was 1,247 points, ranging from 182 to 2,571 (Renner & Mackin, 1998).

Looking at the list, you may wonder why positive events, such as getting married, are included. Compared with negative events, positive events produce less psychological distress and fewer physical symptoms (McFarlane et al., 1980). However, positive events often require readjustment and preparedness that many people find extremely stressful (e.g., Brown & McGill, 1989), so these events are included in computing life-change scores.

As the movie *Bridesmaids* showcased perfectly, although weddings are positive events, they can also be stressful due to the often overwhelming amount of planning and decision making involved (and occasionally because of the difficulties in managing the interactions of friends and family). Universal Pictures/The Kobal Collection/Hanover, Suzanne

TABLE 13.1	College Undergraduate Stress Scale			
Event	**Stress Rating**	**Event**	**Stress Rating**	
Being raped	100	Talking in front of class	72	
Finding out that you are HIV positive	100	Lack of sleep	69	
Being accused of rape	98	Change in housing situation (hassles, moves)	69	
Death of a close friend	97	Competing or performing in public	69	
Death of a close family member	96	Getting in a physical fight	66	
Contracting a sexually transmitted disease (other than AIDS)	94	Difficulties with a roommate	66	
		Job changes (applying, new job, work hassles)	65	
Concerns about being pregnant	91	Declaring a major or concerns about future plans	65	
Finals week	90	A class you hate	62	
Concerns about your partner being pregnant	90	Drinking or use of drugs	61	
Oversleeping for an exam	89	Confrontations with professors	60	
Flunking a class	89	Starting a new semester	58	
Having a boyfriend or girlfriend cheat on you	85	Going on a first date	57	
Ending a steady dating relationship	85	Registration	55	
Serious illness in a close friend or family member	85	Maintaining a steady dating relationship	55	
Financial difficulties	84	Commuting to campus or work or both	54	
Writing a major term paper	83	Peer pressures	53	
Being caught cheating on a test	83	Being away from home for the first time	53	
Drunk driving	82	Getting sick	52	
Sense of overload in school or work	82	Concerns about your appearance	52	
Two exams in one day	80	Getting straight A's	51	
Cheating on your boyfriend or girlfriend	77	A difficult class that you love	48	
Getting married	76	Making new friends; getting along with friends	47	
Negative consequences of drinking or drug use	75	Fraternity or sorority rush	47	
Depression or crisis in your best friend	73	Falling asleep in class	40	
Difficulties with parents	73	Attending an athletic event	20	

Note: To compute your personal life change score, sum the stress ratings for all events that have happened to you in the last year.

Information from: Renner & Mackin (1998).

Chronic Stressors

Life would be simpler if an occasional stressful event such as a wedding or a lost job were the only pressure we faced. At least each event would be limited in scope, with a beginning, a middle, and, ideally, an end. But unfortunately, life brings with it continued exposure to **chronic stressors**, *sources of stress that occur continuously or repeatedly*. Strained relationships, discrimination, bullying, overwork, money troubles—small stressors that may be easy to ignore if they happen only occasionally—can accumulate to produce distress and illness. People who report being affected by daily hassles also report more psychological symptoms (LaPierre et al., 2012) and physical symptoms (Piazza et al., 2013), and these effects often have a greater and longer-lasting impact than do major life events.

Many chronic stressors are linked to social relationships. For instance, as described in the Social Psychology chapter, people often form different social groups based on race, culture, interests, popularity, and so on. Being outside the ingroup

chronic stressors Sources of stress that occur continuously or repeatedly.

City life can be fun, but the higher levels of noise, crowding, and violence can also be sources of chronic stress.

Chaoss/Shutterstock

can be stressful. Being actively targeted by members of the ingroup can be even more stressful, especially if this happens repeatedly over time (see A World of Difference: Can Discrimination Cause Stress and Illness?). Chronic stressors also can be linked to particular environments. For example, features of city life—noise, traffic, crowding, pollution, and even the threat of violence—provide particularly insistent sources of chronic stress (Evans, 2006). Rural areas have their own chronic stressors, of course, especially isolation and lack of access to amenities such as health care. The realization that chronic stressors are linked to environments has spawned the subfield of *environmental psychology*, the scientific study of environmental effects on behavior and health.

Perceived Control Over Stressful Events

What do catastrophes, stressful life changes, and daily hassles have in common? Right off the bat, of course, their threat to the person or the status quo is easy to see. Stressors challenge you to *do something*—to take some action to eliminate or overcome the stressors.

Paradoxically, events are most stressful when there is *nothing to do*—no way to deal with the challenge. Expecting that you will have control over what happens to you is associated with effectiveness in dealing with stress. The researchers David Glass and Jerome Singer (1972), in classic studies of *perceived control*, looked at the

Can Discrimination Cause Stress and Illness?

Have you ever been discriminated against because of your race, gender, sexual orientation, or some other characteristic? If so, then you know that this can be a pretty stressful experience. But what exactly does it *do* to people?

Recent research has shown that there are a number of ways that discrimination can lead to elevated stress and negative health outcomes. People from socially disadvantaged groups who experience higher levels of stress as a result of discrimination engage more frequently in maladaptive behaviors (e.g., drinking, smoking, and overeating) in efforts to cope with stress. They also can experience difficulties in their interactions with health care professionals (e.g., clinician biases, patient suspiciousness about treatment; Major, Mendes, & Dovidio, 2013).

Together, these factors may help to explain why members of socially disadvantaged groups have significantly higher rates of health problems than do members of socially advantaged groups (Penner et al., 2010).

One study exposed Black and White participants to social rejection by a person of the same race or by a person of a different race to test whether there is something particularly harmful about discrimination, compared with social rejection in general (Jamieson, Koslov, et al., 2013). To test this, the researchers had participants deliver a speech to two confederates in different rooms via a video chat program, after which the confederates provided negative feedback about the participant's speech. The confederates were not seen by the participant but were represented by computer avatars that either matched the

participant's race or did not. The results showed that, whereas being rejected by people of your own race was associated with greater displays of shame and physiological changes associated with an avoidance state (increased cortisol), being rejected by members of a different race was associated with displays of anger, greater vigilance for danger, physiological changes (i.e., higher cardiac output and lower vascular resistance), and higher risk taking.

Studies such as this one help to explain some of the health disparities that currently exist across different social groups. The results suggest that discrimination can lead to physiological, cognitive, and behavioral changes that in the short term prepare a person for action, but in the long term could lead to negative health outcomes.

aftereffects of loud noise on people who could or could not control it. Participants were asked to solve puzzles and proofread in a quiet room or in a room filled with loud noise. Glass and Singer found that bursts of such noise hurt people's performance on the tasks after the noise was over. However, this dramatic decline in performance did not occur among participants who were told during the noise period that they could stop the noise just by pushing a button. They didn't actually take this option, but just having access to the "panic button" shielded them from the detrimental effects of the noise.

Subsequent studies have found that a lack of perceived control underlies other stressors, too. The stressful effects of crowding, for example, appear to stem from the feeling that you can't control getting away from the crowded conditions (Evans & Stecker, 2004). Being jammed into a crowded dormitory room may be easier to handle, after all, the moment you realize you could take a walk and get away from it all.

Some stressful life events, such as those associated with drunk driving, are within our power to control. We gain control when we give away the car keys to a designated driver. Kwame Zikomo/Purestock/Alamy

BUILD TO THE OUTCOMES

1. Which of the events on the stress rating scale relate to you? Do any of the ratings surprise you?

2. How can positive events be stressful?

3. Give examples of chronic stressors.

4. What are some examples of environmental factors that cause chronic stress?

5. What makes events most stressful?

Stress Reactions: All Shook Up

It was a regular Tuesday morning in New York City. College students were sitting in their morning classes. People were arriving at work and the streets were beginning to fill with shoppers and tourists. Then, at 8:46 a.m., American Airlines Flight 11 crashed into the North Tower of the World Trade Center. People watched in horror. How could this have happened? This seemed like a terrible accident. Then at 9:03 a.m., United Airlines Flight 175 crashed into the South Tower of the World Trade Center. There were then reports of a plane crashing into the Pentagon. And another somewhere in Pennsylvania. America was under attack, and no one knew what would happen next on this terrifying morning of September 11, 2001. The terrorist attacks on the World Trade Center were an enormous stressor that had a lasting impact on many people, physically and psychologically. People living in close proximity to the World Trade Center (within 1.5 miles) on 9/11 were found to have less gray matter in the amygdala, hippocampus, insula, anterior cingulate, and medial prefrontal cortex than did those living more than 200 miles away during the attacks, suggesting that the stress associated with the attacks may have reduced the size of these parts of the brain that play an important role in emotion, memory, and decision making (Ganzel et al., 2008). Children who watched more television coverage of 9/11 had higher symptoms of posttraumatic stress disorder than did children who watched less coverage (Otto et al., 2007). Stress can produce changes in every system of the body and mind, stimulating both physical reactions and psychological reactions. Let's consider each in turn.

LEARNING OUTCOMES

- Explain physical responses to stress.
- Identify possible psychological responses to stress.

The threat of death or injury, such as many in New York City experienced at the time of the 9/11 attacks, can cause significant and lasting physical and psychological stress reactions. Photo by Spencer Platt/Getty Images

Physical Reactions

fight-or-flight response An emotional and physiological reaction to an emergency that increases readiness for action.

The **fight-or-flight response** is *an emotional and physiological reaction to an emergency that increases readiness for action* (Cannon, 1929). The mind asks, "Should I stay and fight? Or should I flee this situation?" And the body prepares to react.

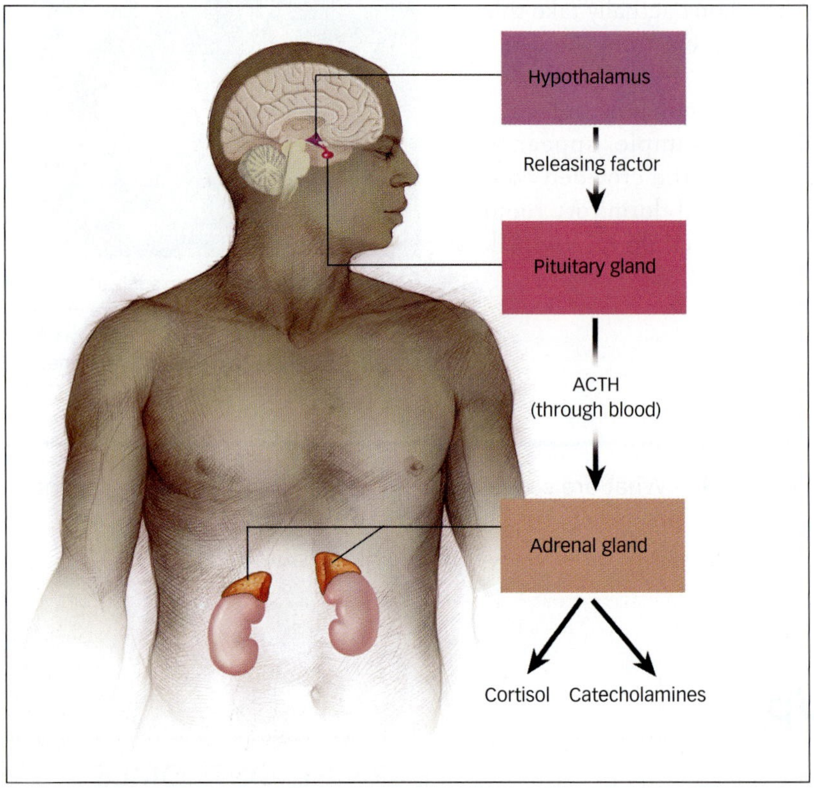

Brain activation in response to threat occurs in the hypothalamus, initiating a cascade of bodily responses that include stimulation of the nearby pituitary gland, which in turn stimulates the adrenal glands atop the kidneys (see **FIGURE 13.1**). This pathway is sometimes called the HPA (hypothalamic–pituitary–adrenocortical) axis. The adrenal glands release hormones, including *catecholamines* (epinephrine and norepinephrine), which increase sympathetic nervous system activation (and therefore increase heart rate, blood pressure, and respiration rate) and decrease parasympathetic activation (see the Neuroscience and Behavior chapter). The increased respiration and blood pressure make more oxygen available to the muscles to energize attack or to initiate escape. The adrenal glands also release *cortisol*, a hormone that increases the concentration of glucose in the blood to make fuel available to the muscles. Everything is prepared for a full-tilt response to the threat.

Figure 13.1 HPA AXIS Just a few seconds after a fearful stimulus is perceived, the hypothalamus activates the pituitary gland, which in turn activates the adrenal glands to release catecholamines and cortisol, which energize the fight-or-flight response.

general adaptation syndrome (GAS) A three-stage physiological response that appears, regardless of the stressor that is encountered.

General Adaptation Syndrome

What might have happened if the terrorist attacks of 9/11 were spaced out over a period of days or weeks? In the 1930s, Canadian physician Hans Selye subjected rats to heat, cold, infection, trauma, hemorrhage, and other prolonged stressors and found that the stressed-out rats developed physiological responses that included enlargement of the adrenal cortex, shrinking of the lymph glands, and ulceration of the stomach. Noting that many different kinds of stressors caused similar patterns of physiological change, he called the reaction the **general adaptation syndrome (GAS)**, which he defined as *a three-stage physiological stress response that appears, regardless of the stressor that is encountered.*

The three stages of the GAS are shown in **FIGURE 13.2**. First comes the *alarm phase*, equivalent to the fight-or-flight response, in which the body rapidly mobilizes its resources to respond to the threat. Next, in the *resistance phase*, the body tries to adapt and cope with the stressor by shutting down unnecessary processes such as digestion, growth, and sex drive. If the GAS continues long enough, the *exhaustion phase* sets in: The body's resistance collapses, creating damage that can include susceptibility to infection, tumor growth, aging, irreversible organ damage, or death.

Stress Negatively Affects Health and Speeds Aging

As people age, the body slowly begins to break down. (Just ask any of the authors of this textbook.) Interestingly, recent research has revealed that stress significantly accelerates the aging process. Elizabeth Smart's parents noted that, on

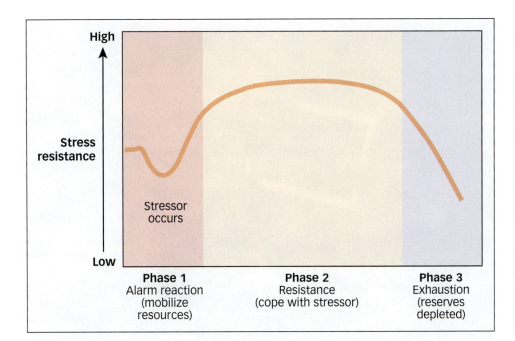

Figure 13.2 SELYE'S THREE PHASES OF STRESS RESPONSE In Selye's theory, resistance to stress builds over time, but then can only last so long before exhaustion sets in.

being reunited with her after 9 months of separation, they almost did not recognize her because she appeared to have aged so much (Smart, Smart, & Morton, 2003). More generally, people exposed to chronic stress, whether due to their relationships or jobs, or something else, experience actual wear and tear on their bodies and accelerated aging. Take a look at the pictures of three of the past presidents before and after their terms as president of the United States (arguably, one of the most stressful jobs in the world). As you can see, they appear to have aged much more than the 4 to 8 years that passed between their first and second photographs.

Understanding this process requires knowing a little bit about how aging occurs. The cells in our bodies are constantly dividing, and as part of this process, our chromosomes are repeatedly copied so that our genetic information is carried into the new cells. Each time a cell divides, the tips of the chromosomes (called *telomeres*) become slightly shorter. Over time, if the telomeres become too short, cells can no longer divide properly. The recent discovery of the function of telomeres, and their relation to aging and disease, has been one of the most exciting advances in science in the past several decades.

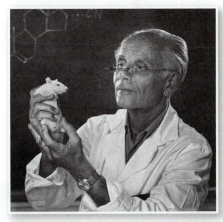

Hans Selye with a rat. Given all the stress under which Selye put rats, this one looks surprisingly calm. Yousuf Karsh/Julie Grahame

Chronic stress can actually speed the aging process. Just look at how much each of our last three presidents aged while in office. College can be stressful, too, but hopefully not so much so that you have gray hair by graduation. Jüschke/Ullstein Bild via Getty Images Tim Sloan/AFP/Getty Images Stephen Jaffe/AFP/Getty Images Yuri Gripas-Pool/Getty Images Alex Wong/Getty Images Max Mumby/Indigo/Getty Images

Dr. Elizabeth Blackburn was awarded a Nobel Prize in 2009 for her groundbreaking discoveries on the functions of telomeres (shown here in yellow). Nathan Devery/Science Source Thor Swift/*The New York Times*/Redux Pictures

immune system A complex response system that protects the body from bacteria, viruses, and other foreign substances.

Interestingly, social stressors can play an important role in this process. People exposed to chronic stress have shorter telomere length (Epel et al., 2004). Laboratory studies suggest that increased cortisol can lead to shortened telomeres, which in turn can lead to accelerated aging and increased risk of a wide range of diseases including cancer, cardiovascular disease, diabetes, and depression (Blackburn, Epel & Lin, 2015). The good news is that activities such as exercise and meditation seem to prevent chronic stress from shortening telomere length, providing a potential explanation of how these activities may convey health benefits such as longer life and lower risk of disease (Epel et al., 2009; Puterman et al., 2010) (see Hot Science: Stress, Health, and Money).

Chronic Stress Affects the Immune Response

The **immune system** is *a complex response system that protects the body from bacteria, viruses, and other foreign substances.* The immune system is remarkably responsive to psychological influences. Stressors can cause hormones known as *glucocorticoids* (such as cortisol) to flood the brain (described in the Neuroscience and Behavior chapter), wearing down the immune system and making it less able to fight invaders (Webster Marketon, & Glaser, 2008). For example, in one study, medical student volunteers agreed to receive small wounds to the roof of the mouth. These wounds healed more slowly during exam periods than during summer vacation (Marucha, Kiecolt-Glaser, & Favagehi, 1998).

Chris Rock's joke that "rich 50 is like poor 35!" matches up with data suggesting that wealthier people tend to be healthier and younger looking than are poorer people. Andrew Toth/Film Magic/Getty Images

The effect of stress on immune response may help to explain why social status is related to health. The stress of living life at the bottom levels of society may increase the risk of infection by weakening the immune system. People who perceive themselves as low in social status are more likely to suffer from respiratory infections, for example, than those who do not bear this social burden— and the same holds true for low-status male monkeys (Cohen, 1999).

Stress, Health, and Money

HOT SCIENCE

There has always been a general assumption that money will bring happiness. But does it? A recent study of 450,000 showed that, as your income increases, your self-reported happiness indeed goes up, and stress goes down (Kahneman & Deaton, 2010). But only up until a point. And that point is approximately $75,000 (which is about the 66th percentile). Beyond that point, higher income is not associated with happiness or stress. In other words: If you are already among the richest one-third of people, more money won't make you happier or less stressed—but for everyone else, less money is associated with less happiness and more stress. People with higher incomes also live significantly longer than do those with lower incomes (Chetty et al., 2016), with the wealthiest 1% of men living 15 years longer on average than the poorest 1%, as shown in the figure. Women live longer than do men on average, but the richest 1% of women still live an average of 10 years longer than do the poorest 1%.

Lower income contributes to increased rates of sickness and death through many pathways. The greater levels of stress among those with less money can shorten telomeres, compromise immune functioning, and increase the risk of heart disease and other illnesses (as described in this chapter). Recent research also suggests that economic stress contributes to climbing rates of death due to drugs, alcohol, and suicide among certain subgroups in the United States (Case & Deaton, 2015).

But income is not destiny, and even among the poorest in society, behavioral and environmental factors can make a huge difference. For instance, the poorest 5% of people live 5 years longer in places such as New York and San Francisco than they would if they lived in Detroit (Chetty et al., 2016). Why? It turns out that poor people who live in wealthier cities (e.g., New York and San Francisco) also engage in healthier behaviors and, in addition, may benefit from better government services and policies.

Recent research has taught us a great deal about the associations between stress, health, and money, but we still have a lot to learn about the full nature of these associations and about how we can use psychological science to mitigate stress and increase health among all members of society.

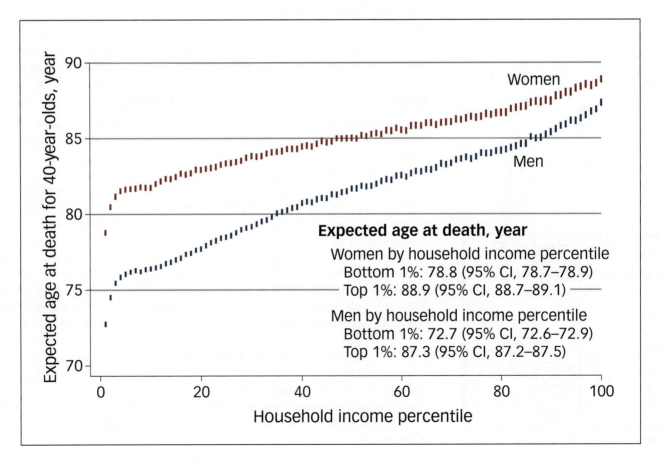

Data from Chetty et al. (2016). *Journal of the American Medical Association.*

Stress Affects Cardiovascular Health

The heart and circulatory system also are sensitive to stress. Chronic stress also is a major contributor to coronary heart disease (Silvani et al., 2016) because prolonged stress-activated arousal of the sympathetic nervous system raises blood pressure and gradually damages the blood vessels. The damaged vessels accumulate plaque, in a process known as *atherosclerosis*, and the more plaque, the greater the likelihood of coronary heart disease. In one study, men who exhibited elevated blood pressure in response to stress and who reported that their work environment was especially stressful showed progressive atherosclerosis of a major artery in the neck during the 4-year study (Everson et al., 1997).

During the 1950s, researchers conducted a revolutionary study that demonstrated a link between work-related stress and coronary heart disease (Friedman & Rosenman, 1974). They interviewed and tested 3,000 healthy middle-aged men and then tracked their subsequent cardiovascular health. Some of the men displayed a **Type A behavior pattern**, *a tendency toward easily aroused hostility, impatience, a sense of time urgency, and competitive achievement strivings*. Other men displayed a less driven behavior pattern (sometimes called *Type B*). The Type A men were identified by their answers to questions in the interview (agreeing that they walk and talk fast, work late, set goals for themselves, work hard to win, and easily get frustrated and angry at others), and also by the pushy and impatient way in which they answered the questions. In the decade that followed, men who had been classified as Type A were more likely to have heart attacks compared with the Type B men.

Type A behavior pattern The tendency toward easily aroused hostility, impatience, a sense of time urgency, and competitive achievement strivings.

Psychological Reactions

The body's response to stress is intertwined with responses of the mind. Perhaps the first thing the mind does is try to sort things out—to interpret whether an event is threatening or not—and if it is, whether something can be done about it.

Stress Interpretation Is a Two-Step Process

The interpretation of a stimulus as stressful or not is called *primary appraisal* (Lazarus & Folkman, 1984). Primary appraisal allows you to realize that a small, dark spot on your shirt is a stressor (spider!) or that a 70-mile-per-hour drop from a great height in a small car full of screaming people may not be (roller coaster!).

The next step in interpretation is *secondary appraisal*, determining whether the stressor is something you can handle or not; that is, whether you have control over the event (Lazarus & Folkman, 1984). Interestingly, the body responds differently depending on whether the stressor is perceived as a *threat* (a stressor you believe you might *not* be able to overcome) or a *challenge* (a stressor you feel fairly confident you can control; Blascovich & Tomaka, 1996). The same midterm exam is seen as a challenge if you are well prepared, but a threat if you didn't study. Although both threats and challenges raise the heart rate, threats increase vascular reactivity (such as constriction of the blood vessels, which can lead to high blood pressure).

Fortunately, interpretations of stressors can change them from threats to challenges. One study (Jamieson et al., 2010) showed that instructing students to reframe their anxiety about an upcoming exam as arousal that would help them on the test actually improved test performance. Remember this technique next time you are feeling anxious about a test or presentation: Increased arousal can improve your performance!

Isabella Bannerman/www.cartoonstock.com

Chronic Stress Can Lead to Burnout

Did you ever take a class from an instructor who had lost interest in the job? The syndrome is easy to spot: The teacher looks distant and blank, almost robotic, giving predictable and humdrum lessons each day, as if it doesn't matter whether anyone is listening. Now imagine being this instructor. You decided to teach because you wanted to shape young minds. You worked hard, and for a while things were great. But one day, you looked up to see a room full of students who were bored and didn't care about anything you had to say. They updated their Facebook pages while you talked and started putting things away long before the end of class. You're happy at work only when you're not in class. When people feel this way, especially about their jobs or careers, they are suffering from **burnout,** *a state of physical, emotional, and mental exhaustion resulting from long-term involvement in an emotionally demanding situation and accompanied by lowered performance and motivation.*

Burnout is a particular problem in the helping professions (Fernandez Nievas & Thaver, 2015). Teachers, nurses, clergy, doctors, dentists, psychologists, social workers, police officers, and others who repeatedly encounter emotional turmoil on the job may only be able to work productively for a limited time. Eventually, many succumb to symptoms of burnout: overwhelming exhaustion, a deep cynicism and detachment from the job, and a sense of ineffectiveness and lack of accomplishment (Maslach, 2003). Their unhappiness can even spread to others; people with burnout tend to become disgruntled employees who revel in their coworkers' failures and ignore their coworkers' successes (Brenninkmeijer, Vanyperen, & Buunk, 2001).

What causes burnout? One theory suggests that the culprit is using your job to give meaning to your life (Pines, 1993). If you define yourself only by your career and gauge your self-worth by success at work, you risk having nothing left when work fails. For example, a teacher in danger of burnout might do well to invest time in family, hobbies, or other self-expressions. Others argue that some emotionally

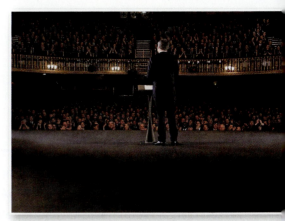

Stressed out about a class exam or presentation? Remember that interpreting that stress as a 'challenge' to be overcome rather than a 'threat' that you might not overcome actually leads to better performance. Caiaimage/Martin Barraud/Getty Images

burnout A state of physical, emotional, and mental exhaustion resulting from long-term involvement in an emotionally demanding situation and accompanied by lowered performance and motivation.

Is there anything worse than taking a horribly boring class? How about being the teacher of that class? What techniques would prevent burnout from stress in people in helping professions (teachers, doctors, nurses, etc.)? ©Stock4B Gmbh/Alamy

stressful jobs lead to burnout no matter how they are approached and that active efforts to overcome the stress before burnout occurs are important. The stress management techniques discussed in the next section may be lifesavers for people in such jobs.

BUILD TO THE OUTCOMES

1. How does the body react to a fight-or-flight situation?
2. What are the three phases of GAS?
3. What is a telomere? What do telomeres do for us?
4. How does stress affect the immune system?
5. How does chronic stress increase the chance of a heart attack?

6. What is the difference between a threat and a challenge?
7. Why is burnout a problem, especially in the helping professions?

Stress Management: Dealing with It

LEARNING OUTCOMES

- Explain techniques for coping with psychological stress.
- Identify physical activities that reduce stress.
- Define and give examples of situation management.

Most college students (92%) say they occasionally feel overwhelmed by the tasks they face, and over a third say they have dropped courses or received low grades in response to severe stress (Duenwald, 2002). No doubt you are among the lucky 8% who are entirely cool and report no stress. But just in case you're not, you may be interested in stress management techniques.

Mind Management

Stressful events are magnified in the mind. If you fear public speaking, for example, just the thought of an upcoming presentation to a group can create anxiety. And if you do break down during a presentation (going blank, for example, or blurting out something embarrassing), intrusive memories of this stressful event could echo in your mind afterward. A significant part of stress management, then, is control of the mind. Let's look at three specific strategies.

1. Repressive Coping: Holding an Artificially Positive Viewpoint

repressive coping Avoiding feelings, thoughts, or situations that are reminders of a stressor and maintaining an artificially positive viewpoint.

Controlling your thoughts is not easy, but some people do seem to be able to banish unpleasant thoughts from the mind. **Repressive coping** is characterized by *avoiding feelings, thoughts, or situations that are reminders of a stressor and maintaining an artificially positive viewpoint*. Like Elizabeth Smart, who for years after her rescue focused in interviews on what was happening in her life now, rather than repeatedly discussing her past in captivity, people often rearrange their lives in order to avoid stressful situations. It may make sense to try to avoid stressful thoughts and situations if you're the kind of person who is good at putting unpleasant thoughts and emotions out of mind (Coifman et al., 2007). For some people, however, the avoidance of unpleasant thoughts and situations is so difficult that it can turn into a grim preoccupation (Parker & McNally, 2008; Wegner & Zanakos, 1994). For those who can't avoid negative emotions effectively, it may be better to come to grips with them. This is the basic idea of rational coping.

2. Rational Coping: Working to Overcome

Rational coping involves *facing the stressor and working to overcome it.* This strategy is the opposite of repressive coping, so it may seem to be the most unpleasant and unnerving thing you could do when faced with stress. It requires approaching, rather than avoiding, a stressor in order to diminish its longer-term negative impact (Hayes, Strosahl, & Wilson, 1999).

Rational coping is a three-step process. The first step is *acceptance,* coming to realize that the stressor exists and cannot be wished away. The second step is *exposure,* attending to the stressor, thinking about it, and even seeking it out. Psychological treatment may help during the exposure step by aiding victims in confronting and thinking about what happened. Using a technique called *prolonged exposure,* rape survivors relive the traumatic event in their imaginations by recording a verbal account of the event and then listening to the recording daily. This sounds like bitter medicine indeed, but it is remarkably effective, producing significant reductions in anxiety and symptoms of posttraumatic stress disorder compared with no therapy and compared with other therapies that promote more gradual and subtle forms of exposure (Foa & McLean, 2016). The third element of rational coping is *understanding,* working to find the meaning of the stressor in your life.

3. Reframing: Changing Your Thinking

Changing the way you think is another way to cope with stressful thoughts. **Reframing** involves *finding a new or creative way to think about a stressor that reduces its threat.* If you experience anxiety at the thought of public speaking, for example, you might reframe by shifting from thinking of an audience as evaluating you to thinking of yourself as evaluating them, and this might make speech giving easier.

Reframing can take place spontaneously if people are given the opportunity to spend time thinking and writing about stressful events. For example, one series of studies found that the physical health of college students improved after they spent a few hours writing about their deepest thoughts and feelings. Compared with students who had written about something else, members of the self-disclosure group were less likely in subsequent months to visit the student health center; they also used less aspirin and achieved better grades (Pennebaker & Chung, 2007). In fact, engaging in such expressive writing was found to improve immune function (Pennebaker, Kiecolt-Glaser, & Glaser, 1988), whereas suppressing emotional topics weakened it (Petrie, Booth, & Pennebaker, 1998). The positive effect of self-disclosing writing may reflect its usefulness in reframing trauma and reducing stress.

Body Management

Stress can express itself as tension in your neck muscles, back pain, a knot in your stomach, sweaty hands, or the harried face you glimpse in the mirror. Because stress so often manifests itself through bodily symptoms, body management can reduce stress. Here are four techniques.

Terrorist attacks in Paris in November 2015 left 130 people dead and hundreds more wounded. People deal with major stressful life events such as this in different ways. Repressive copers use avoidance; rational copers use acceptance, exposure, and understanding; and reframers try to think about the situation in more positive ways. Christopher Furlong/Getty Images

rational coping Facing a stressor and working to overcome it.

reframing Finding a new or creative way to think about a stressor that reduces its threat.

This young woman is praying during a vigil held for the victim of a gang rape in New Delhi. Extremely stressful events, such as rape, are not only acute stressors but often have lasting psychological consequences. Fortunately, there are effective techniques for learning to cope with such events that can lead to improved psychological health. Reuters/Amit Dave/Newscom

Stress can affect the body, and it often shows. This guy had a stressful day of trading at the New York Stock Exchange. Looks like he could use a little body management. Andrew Burton/Getty Images

1. Meditation: Turning Inward

meditation The practice of intentional contemplation.

Meditation is *the practice of intentional contemplation.* Techniques of meditation are associated with a variety of religious traditions and are also practiced outside religious contexts. Some forms of meditation call for attempts to clear the mind of thought; others involve focusing on a single thought (e.g., thinking about a candle flame); still others involve concentration on breathing or on a *mantra* (a repetitive sound such as *om*). At a minimum, these techniques have in common a period of quiet.

Time spent meditating can be restful and revitalizing. Beyond these immediate benefits, many people also meditate in an effort to experience deeper or transformed consciousness. Whatever the reason, meditation does appear to have positive psychological effects (Hölzel et al., 2011). Many believe it does so, in part, by improving control over attention. Interestingly, experienced meditators show deactivation in the default mode network (which is associated with mind wandering; see Figure 5.5 in the Consciousness chapter) during meditation (Brewer et al., 2011). Even short-term meditation training administered to college undergraduates has been shown to improve the connectivity between parts of the brain involved in conflict monitoring and cognitive and emotional control (Tang et al., 2012). Moreover, recent research suggests that those engaging in several weeks of intensive meditation actually show lengthening of their telomeres, suggesting a slight reversal of the effects of stress and aging described above (Conklin et al., 2015). Taken together, these findings suggest that meditators may be better able to regulate their thoughts and emotions, which may translate to a better ability to manage interpersonal relations, anxiety, and a range of other activities that require conscious effort (Sedlmeier et al., 2012).

Aung San Suu Kyi, the leader of the Myanmar opposition party who was awarded the Nobel Peace Prize in 1991, endured house arrest from 1989 until 2010. She has said that daily meditation helped her through this difficult time by improving her mood, awareness, and clarity. Alison Wright/Robert Harding/Alamy

2. Relaxation: Picturing Peace

Imagine for a moment that you are scratching your chin. Don't actually do it; just think about it and notice that your body participates by moving ever so slightly, tensing and relaxing in the sequence of the imagined action. Our bodies respond to all the things we think about doing every day. These thoughts create muscle tension even when we think we're doing nothing at all.

Relaxation therapy is *a technique for reducing tension by consciously relaxing muscles of the body.* A person in relaxation therapy may be asked to relax specific muscle groups one at a time or to imagine warmth flowing through the body or to think about a relaxing situation. This activity draws on a **relaxation response**, *a condition of reduced muscle tension, cortical activity, heart rate, breathing rate, and blood pressure* (Benson, 1990). Basically, as soon as you get in a comfortable position, quiet down, and focus on something repetitive or soothing that holds your attention, you relax.

Relaxing on a regular basis can reduce symptoms of stress (Carlson & Hoyle, 1993) and even reduce blood levels of cortisol, the biochemical marker of the stress response (McKinney et al., 1997). For example, in individuals who are suffering from tension headache, relaxation reduces the tension that causes the headache; in people with cancer, relaxation makes it easier to cope with stressful treatments; in people with stress-related cardiovascular problems, relaxation can reduce the high blood pressure that puts the heart at risk (Mandle et al., 1996).

relaxation therapy A technique for reducing tension by consciously relaxing muscles of the body.

relaxation response A condition of reduced muscle tension, cortical activity, heart rate, breathing rate, and blood pressure.

3. Biofeedback: Enlisting the Help of an External Monitor

Wouldn't it be nice if, instead of having to learn to relax, you could just flip a switch and relax as fast as possible? **Biofeedback**, *the use of an external monitoring device to obtain information about a bodily function and possibly gain control over that function*, was developed with the goal of high-tech relaxation in mind. You might not be aware right now of whether your fingers are warm or cold, for example, but with an electronic thermometer displayed before you, the ability to sense your temperature might allow you (with a bit of practice) to make your hands warmer or cooler at will (e.g., Roberts & McGrady, 1996).

Biofeedback can help people control physiological functions they are not otherwise aware of. For example, you probably have no idea right now what brain-wave patterns you are producing. But people can change their brain waves from alert beta patterns to relaxed alpha patterns and back again when they are permitted to monitor their brains using the electroencephalograph or EEG (which you read about in the Neuroscience and Behavior chapter). Often, however, the use of biofeedback to produce relaxation in the brain turns out to be a bit of technological overkill and may not be much more effective than simply having the person stretch out in a hammock and hum a happy tune.

biofeedback The use of an external monitoring device to obtain information about a bodily function and possibly gain control over that function.

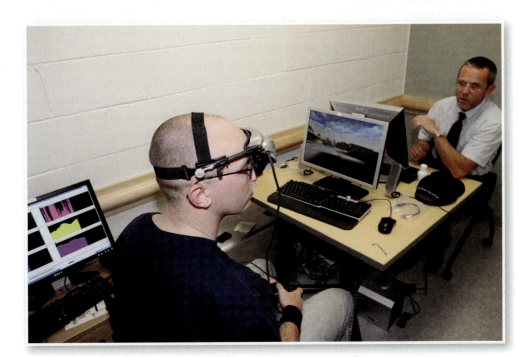

Biofeedback gives people access to visual or audio feedback showing levels of psychophysiological functions such as heart rate, breathing, brain electrical activity, or skin temperature that they would otherwise be unable to sense directly. Photo by Charles Baldwin of East Carolina University/Courtesy Dr. Carmen Russoniello

Exercise helps reduce stress—unless, as for John Stibbard, your exercise involves carrying the Olympic torch on a wobbly suspension bridge over a 70-meter gorge. Matt Dunham/AP Images

social support The aid gained through interacting with others.

4. Aerobic Exercise: Boosting Mood

Studies indicate that *aerobic exercise* (exercise that increases heart rate and oxygen intake for a sustained period) is associated with psychological well-being (Hassmen, Koivula, & Uutela, 2000). In various studies, researchers have randomly assigned people to aerobic exercise activities and no-exercise comparison groups and have found that exercise actually does promote stress relief and happiness. One review compiled data from 90 studies in which people with chronic illness were randomly assigned either to an exercise or a no-exercise condition, and found that people assigned to the aerobic exercise condition experienced a significant reduction in depressive symptoms (Herring et al., 2012). Another review found that exercise is as effective as the most effective psychological interventions for depression (Rimer et al., 2012), and that exercise even shows positive physical and mental health benefits for individuals with schizophrenia (Gorczynski & Faulkner, 2011). Pretty good effects for a simple, timeless intervention with no side effects!

The reasons for these positive effects are unclear. Researchers have suggested that the effects result from increases in the body's production of neurotransmitters such as serotonin, which can have a positive effect on mood (as discussed in the Neuroscience and Behavior chapter) or from increases in the production of endorphins (the endogenous opioids discussed in the Neuroscience and Behavior and Consciousness chapters; Jacobs, 1994). Perhaps the simplest thing you can do to improve your happiness and health, then, is to participate regularly in an aerobic activity. Pick something you find fun: Sign up for a dance class, get into a regular basketball game, or start paddling a canoe—just not all at once.

Situation Management

After you have tried to manage stress by managing your mind and managing your body, what's left to manage? Look around and you'll notice a whole world out there. Situation management involves changing your life situation as a way of reducing the impact of stress on your mind and body.

1. Social Support: "Swimming with a Buddy"

The wisdom of the National Safety Council's first rule—"Always swim with a buddy"— is obvious when you're in water over your head, but people often don't realize that the same principle applies whenever danger threatens. Other people can offer help in times of stress. **Social support** is *aid gained through interacting with others*. Good ongoing relationships with friends and family and participation in social activities and religious groups can be as healthy for you as exercising and avoiding smoking (Umberson et al., 2006). Lonely people are more likely than are others to be stressed and depressed (Baumeister & Leary, 1995), and they can be more susceptible to illness because of lower-than-normal levels of immune functioning (Kiecolt-Glaser et al., 1984).

Many first-year college students experience something of a crisis of social support. No matter how outgoing and popular they were in high school, newcomers typically find the task of developing satisfying new social relationships quite daunting. It's not surprising that research shows that students reporting the greatest feelings of isolation also show reduced immune responses to flu vaccinations (Pressman et al., 2005). Time spent getting to know people in new social situations can be an investment in your own health.

The value of social support in protecting against stress may be very different for women and men: Whereas women seek support under stress, men are less likely to do so. The fight-or-flight response to stress may be largely a male reaction, whereas the female response to stress may instead be to *tend-and-befriend* by taking care of people and bringing them together (Taylor, 2002). After a hard day at work, a man may come home frustrated and worried about his job and end up drinking a beer and

Women are more likely than are men to seek support when under stress. Chinaface/Getty Images; Image Source/ Getty Images

fuming alone. A woman under the same type of stress may be more likely to instead play with her kids or talk to friends on the phone. The tend-and-befriend response to stress may help to explain why women are healthier and have a longer life span than do men. The typical male response amplifies the unhealthy effects of stress, whereas the female response takes less of a toll on a woman's mind and body and provides social support for the people around her as well.

2. Religious Experiences: Reaping Earthly Rewards

National polls indicate that over 90% of Americans believe in God and that most who do pray at least once per day. Although many who believe in a higher power believe that their faith will be rewarded in an afterlife, it turns out that there may be some benefits here on earth as well. An enormous body of research has found associations between *religiosity* (affiliation with or engagement in the practices of a particular religion) and *spirituality* (having a belief in and engagement with some higher power, not necessarily linked to any particular religion) and positive health outcomes, including lower rates of heart disease, decreases in chronic pain, and improved psychological health (Seybold & Hill, 2001).

Why do people who endorse religiosity or spirituality have better mental and physical health? Engagement in religious or spiritual practices, such as attendance at weekly religious services, may lead to the development of a stronger and more extensive social network, which has well-known health benefits. Those who are religious or spiritual also may fare better psychologically and physically as a result of following the healthy recommendations offered in many religious or spiritual teachings. That is, they may be more likely to observe dietary restrictions, abstain from the use of drugs or alcohol, or endorse a more hopeful and optimistic perspective of daily life events, all of which can lead to more positive health outcomes (Seeman, Dubin, & Seeman, 2003; Seybold & Hill, 2001). However, many claims made by some religious groups have not been supported, such as the beneficial effects of intercessory prayer (see **FIGURE 13.3**). Psychologists are actively testing the effectiveness of

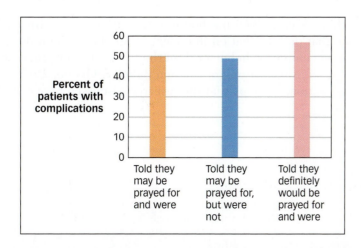

Figure 13.3 PRAY FOR ME? To test whether praying for someone in their time of need actually helped them, researchers randomly assigned patients about to undergo cardiac bypass surgery to one of three conditions: those told that they might be prayed for and were; those told that they might be prayed for and weren't; and those told that they definitely would be prayed for and were. Unfortunately, there were no differences in the presence of complications between those who were or were not prayed for. To make matters worse, those who knew they would be prayed for experienced significantly more complications than did the other two groups (Benson et al., 2006).

various religious and spiritual practices with the goal of better understanding how they might help to explain, and improve, the human condition.

3. Humor: Laughing It Off

Wouldn't it be nice to laugh at your troubles and move on? Most of us recognize that humor can defuse unpleasant situations and reduce stress. Is laughter truly the best medicine? Should we close down the hospitals and send in the clowns?

There is a kernel of truth to the theory that humor can help us cope with stress. For example, humor can reduce sensitivity to pain and distress. In one study, participants wearing an overinflated blood pressure cuff were more tolerant of the pain during a laughter-inducing comedy audiotape than during a neutral tape or guided relaxation (Cogan et al., 1987).

Humor can also reduce the time needed to calm down after a stressful event. For example, men viewing a highly stressful film about three industrial accidents were asked to narrate the film aloud, either by describing the events seriously or by making their commentary as funny as possible. Although men in both groups reported feeling tense while watching the film and showed increased levels of sympathetic nervous arousal (increased heart rate and skin conductance, decreased skin temperature), those looking for humor in the experience bounced back to normal arousal levels more quickly than did those in the serious story group (Newman & Stone, 1996).

4. Scheduling and Activating: Getting It Done

At one time or another, most of us have avoided carrying out a task or put it off to a later time. Over 70% of college students report that they engage in some form of procrastination, such as putting off writing a term paper or preparing for a test (Schouwenburg, 1995). Some procrastinators defend this practice by claiming that they tend to work best under pressure or by noting that as long as a task gets done, it doesn't matter if it is completed just before the deadline. Is there any merit to such claims? Or are they just feeble excuses for counterproductive behavior?

A study of 60 undergraduate psychology college students provided some intriguing answers (Tice & Baumeister, 1997). At the beginning of the semester, the instructor announced a due date for the term paper and told students that if they could not meet the date, they would receive an extension to a later date. About a month later, students completed a scale that measures tendencies toward procrastination. Students who scored high on the procrastination scale tended to turn in their papers late. At the end of the semester, the procrastinators reported more stress and more health symptoms than did the nonprocrastinators, and they reported more visits to the health center. The procrastinators also received lower grades on their papers and on course exams.

Although there is no proven method of eliminating procrastination, there is some evidence that procrastination in college students can be reduced by training in time management or behavioral methods that target processes that are believed to be responsible for procrastination (Glick & Orsillo, 2015). If you tend toward procrastination, we hope that the research discussed here can alert you to its pitfalls.

When Andrew Mason, CEO of the Internet company Groupon, left his position, his resignation letter read: "After four and a half intense and wonderful years as CEO of Groupon, I've decided that I'd like to spend more time with my family. Just kidding—I was fired today." He went on to add, "I am so lucky to have had the opportunity to take the company this far with all of you. I'll now take some time to decompress (FYI I'm looking for a good fat camp to lose my Groupon 40, if anyone has a suggestion), and then maybe I'll figure out how to channel this experience into something productive." This seems like a textbook case of using humor to mitigate stress, which is why we put it, um, you know where. JUSTIN LANE/European Pressphoto Agency/NEW YORK/NEW YORK/ UNITED STATES/Newscom

Are you a procrastinator? Macmillan Learning

BUILD TO THE OUTCOMES

1. When is it useful to avoid stressful thoughts? When is avoidance a problem?

2. What are the three steps in rational coping?

3. What is the difference between repressive and rational coping?

4. How has writing about stressful events been shown to be helpful?

5. What are some positive outcomes of meditation?

6. How does biofeedback work?

7. What are the benefits of exercise?

8. What are the benefits of social support?

9. Why are religiosity and spirituality associated with health benefits?

10. How does humor mitigate stress?

11. How do good study habits support good health?

The Psychology of Illness: Mind Over Matter

One of the mind's most important influences on the body's health and illness is the mind's sensitivity to bodily symptoms. Noticing what is wrong with the body can be helpful when it motivates a search for treatment, but sensitivity can also lead to further problems when it snowballs into a preoccupation with illness that itself can cause harm.

LEARNING OUTCOME

- Describe the interrelationship between the mind and body relating to illness.

Psychological Effects of Illness

Why does it feel so bad to be sick? You notice scratchiness in your throat or the start of sniffles, and you think you might be coming down with something. And in just a few short hours, you're achy all over, energy gone, no appetite, feverish, feeling dull and listless. You're sick. The question is, why does it have to be like this? As long as you're going to have to stay at home and miss out on things anyway, couldn't sickness be less of a pain?

Sickness makes you miserable for good reason. Misery is part of the *sickness response*, a coordinated, adaptive set of reactions to illness organized by the brain (Hart, 1988; Watkins & Maier, 2005). Feeling sick keeps you home, where you'll spread germs to fewer people. More important, the sickness response makes you withdraw from activity and lie still, conserving the energy for fighting illness that you'd normally expend on other behavior. Appetite loss is similarly helpful: The energy spent on digestion is conserved. Thus, the behavioral changes that accompany illness are not random side effects; they help the body fight disease.

How does the brain know it should do this? The immune response to an infection begins with one of the components of the immune response, the activation of white blood cells that "eat" microbes and also release *cytokines,* proteins that circulate through the body (Maier & Watkins, 1998). Cytokines do not enter the brain, but they activate the vagus nerve, which runs from the intestines, stomach, and chest to the brain and conveys the "I am infected" message (Goehler et al., 2000;

How much does it hurt? Pain is a psychological state that can be difficult to measure. One way to put a number on a pain is to have people judge with reference to the external expression of the internal state. Copyright 1983 Wong-Baker FACES Foundation. www.WongBakerFACES.org. Used with permission. Originally published in Whaley & Wong's *Nursing Care of Infants and Children.* Copyright Elsevier Inc.

Klarer et al., 2014). Perhaps this is why we often feel sickness in the "gut," a gnawing discomfort in the very center of the body.

Interestingly, the sickness response can be prompted without any infection at all, merely by the introduction of stress. The stressful presence of a predator's odor, for instance, can trigger the sickness response of lethargy in an animal, along with symptoms of infection such as fever and increased white blood cell count (Maier & Watkins, 2000). In humans, the connection among sickness response, immune reaction, and stress is illustrated in depression, a condition in which all the sickness machinery runs at full speed. So in addition to fatigue and malaise, depressed people show signs characteristic of infection, including high levels of cytokines circulating in the blood (Maes, 1995). Just as illness can make you feel a bit depressed, severe depression seems to recruit the brain's sickness response and make you feel ill (Watkins & Maier, 2005).

Recognizing Illness and Seeking Treatment

You probably weren't thinking about your breathing a minute ago, but now that you're reading this sentence, you notice it. Sometimes we are very attentive to our bodies. At other times, the body seems to be on "automatic," running along unnoticed until specific symptoms announce themselves or are pointed out by an annoying textbook writer.

People differ substantially in the degree to which they attend to and report bodily symptoms. People who report many physical symptoms tend to be negative in other ways as well, describing themselves as anxious, depressed, and under stress (Watson & Pennebaker, 1989). Do people with many symptom complaints truly have a lot of problems? In one study, volunteers underwent several applications of a thermal stimulus (110–120 °F) to the leg; as you might expect, some of the participants found it more painful than did others. fMRI brain scans during the painful events revealed that the anterior cingulate cortex, somatosensory cortex, and prefrontal cortex (areas known to respond to painful body stimulation) were particularly active in those participants who reported higher levels of pain experience (see **FIGURE 13.4**), suggesting that people can report accurately on the extent to which they experience pain (Coghill, McHaffie, & Yen, 2003).

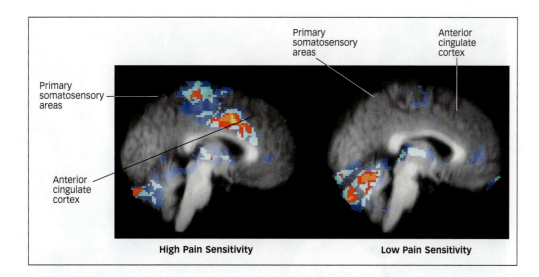

Primary somatosensory areas

Primary somatosensory areas

Anterior cingulate cortex

Anterior cingulate cortex

High Pain Sensitivity

Low Pain Sensitivity

Figure 13.4 THE BRAIN IN PAIN These fMRI scans show brain activation in high- (*left*) and low-pain-sensitive (*right*) individuals during painful stimulation. The anterior cingulate cortex and primary somatosensory areas show greater activation in high-pain-sensitive individuals. Levels of activation are highest in yellow and red, and lower in light blue and dark blue (Coghill, McHaffie, & Yen, 2003). Neural Correlates of Interindividual Differences in the Subjective Experience of Pain, Coghill, Mchaffie, & Yen. Copyright 2003 National Academy of Sciences, USA

In contrast to complainers, other people underreport symptoms and pain or ignore or deny the possibility that they are sick. Insensitivity to symptoms comes with costs: It can delay the search for treatment, sometimes with serious repercussions. In one study, 40% of patients treated for a heart attack had delayed going to the hospital for over 6 hours from the time they first noticed suspicious symptoms (Gurwitz et al., 1997). These people often waited around for hours, not calling an ambulance or their doctor, just hoping the problem would go away. This is not a good idea because many of the treatments that can reduce the damage of a heart attack are most useful when provided early. When it comes to your own health, protecting your mind from distress through the denial of illness can result in exposing your body to great danger.

Somatic Symptom Disorders

The flip side of denial is excessive sensitivity to illness, and it turns out that sensitivity also has its perils. Indeed, hypersensitivity to symptoms or to the possibility of illness underlies a variety of psychological problems and can also undermine physical health. Psychologists studying **psychosomatic illness**, *an interaction between mind and body that can produce illness*, explore ways in which mind (*psyche*) can influence body (*soma*) and vice versa. The study of mind–body interactions focuses on psychological disorders called **somatic symptom disorders**, in which *a person with at least one bodily symptom displays significant health-related anxiety, expresses disproportionate concerns about his or her symptoms, and devotes excessive time and energy to symptoms or health concerns*. These disorders will be discussed in the Psychological Disorders chapter, but their association with symptoms in the body makes them relevant to this chapter's concern with stress and health.

psychosomatic illness An interaction between mind and body that can produce illness.

somatic symptom disorders The set of psychological disorders in which a person with at least one bodily symptom displays significant health-related anxiety, expresses disproportionate concerns about his or her symptoms, and devotes excessive time and energy to the symptoms or health concerns.

On Being a Patient

Getting sick is more than a change in physical state: It can involve a transformation of identity. This change can be particularly profound with a serious illness: A kind of cloud settles over you, a feeling that you are now different, and this transformation can influence everything you feel and do in this new world of illness. You even take

Have you ever ridden on a crowded train next to a person with a hacking cough or aggressive sneeze? We are bombarded by advertisements for medicines designed to suppress symptoms of illness so that we can keep going. Is staying home with a cold socially acceptable? Or is it malingering? How does this jibe with the concept of the *sick role*? Image Source/Getty Images

sick role A socially recognized set of rights and obligations linked with illness.

on a new role in life, a **sick role**: *a socially recognized set of rights and obligations linked with illness* (Parsons, 1975). The sick person is absolved of responsibility for many everyday obligations and enjoys exemption from normal activities. For example, in addition to skipping school and homework and staying on the couch all day, a sick child can watch TV and avoid eating anything unpleasant at dinner. In return for these exemptions, the sick role also incurs obligations. The properly "sick" individual cannot appear to enjoy the illness or reveal signs of wanting to be sick and must also take care to pursue treatment to end this "undesirable" condition.

Some people feign medical or psychological symptoms to achieve something they want, a type of behavior called *malingering*. Because many symptoms of illness cannot be faked, malingering is possible only with a small number of illnesses. Faking illness is suspected when the secondary gains of illness, such as the ability to rest, to be freed from performing unpleasant tasks, or to be helped by others, outweigh the costs. Such gains can be very subtle, as when a child stays in bed because of the comfort provided by an otherwise distant parent, or they can be obvious, as when insurance benefits turn out to be a cash award for best actor. For this reason, malingering can be difficult to diagnose and treat (Bass & Halligan, 2014).

Patient–Practitioner Interaction

Medical care usually occurs through a strange interaction. On one side is a patient, often miserable, who expects to be questioned and examined and possibly prodded, pained, or given bad news. On the other side is a health care provider, who hopes to quickly obtain information from the patient by asking lots of extremely personal questions (and examining extremely personal parts of the body); to identify the problem and a potential solution; to help in some way; and to achieve all of this as efficiently as possible because more patients are waiting. It seems less like a time for healing than an occasion for major awkwardness.

One of the keys to an effective medical care interaction is physician empathy (Kelm et al., 2014). To offer successful treatment, the clinician must simultaneously

"Whoa—way too much information."
Alex Gregory/The New Yorker Collection/ www.cartoonbank.com

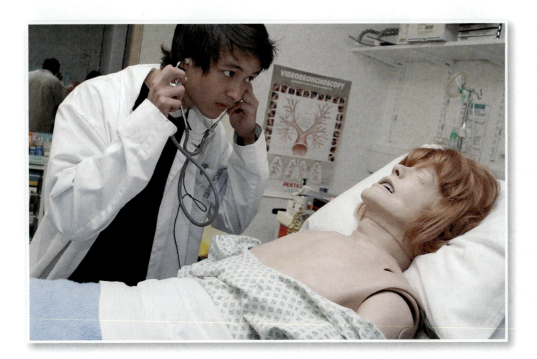

Doctor and patient have two modes of interaction, the technical and the interpersonal. Medical training with robot patients may help doctors learn the technical side of health care, but it is likely to do little to improve the interpersonal side. Dan Atkin/Alamy

understand the patient's physical state *and* psychological state. Physicians often err on the side of failing to acknowledge patients' emotions, focusing instead on technical issues of the case (Suchman et al., 1997). This is unfortunate because many patients who seek medical care do so for treatment of psychological and emotional problems (Wiegner et al., 2015). The best physician treats the patient's mind as well as the patient's body.

Another important part of the medical care interaction is motivating the patient to follow the prescribed regimen of care (Miller & Rollnick, 2012). When researchers check compliance by counting the pills remaining in a patient's bottle after a prescription has been started, they find that patients often do an astonishingly poor job of following doctors' orders (see **FIGURE 13.5**). Compliance

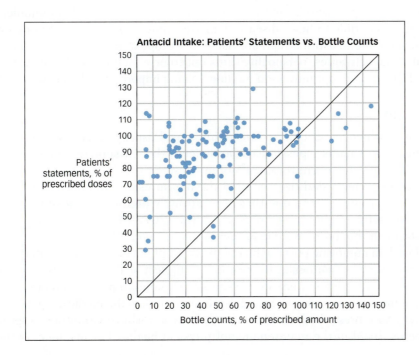

Antacid Intake: Patients' Statements vs. Bottle Counts

Patients' statements, % of prescribed doses

Bottle counts, % of prescribed amount

Figure 13.5 ANTACID INTAKE
A scatterplot of actual antacid intake measured by bottle count plotted against patients' stated intake for 116 patients. When the actual and stated intakes are the same, the point lies on the diagonal line; when stated intake is greater than actual, the point lies above the line. Most patients exaggerated their intake (Roth & Caron, 1978).

deteriorates when the treatment must be frequent, as when eye drops for glaucoma are required every few hours, or inconvenient or painful, such as drawing blood or performing injections in managing diabetes. Finally, compliance decreases as the number of treatments increases. This is a worrisome problem, especially for older patients, who may have difficulty remembering when to take which pill. Failures in medical care may stem from the failure of health care providers to recognize the psychological challenges that are involved in self-care. Helping people follow doctors' orders involves psychology, not medicine, and is an essential part of promoting health.

BUILD TO THE OUTCOMES

1. What are the physical benefits of the sickness response?

2. What is the relationship between pain and activity in the brain?

3. How can hypersensitivity to symptoms undermine health?

4. What benefits might come from being ill?

5. Why is it important that a physician express empathy?

The Psychology of Health: Feeling Good

LEARNING OUTCOME

• Explain the attitudes and behaviors that lead to good health.

Two kinds of psychological factors influence personal health: health-relevant personality traits and health behavior. Personality can influence health through relatively enduring traits that make some people particularly susceptible to health problems or stress while sparing or protecting others. The Type A behavior pattern is an example. Because personality is not typically something we choose ("I'd like a bit of that sense of humor and extraversion over there, please, but hold the whininess"), this source of health can be beyond personal control. In contrast, engaging in positive health behaviors is something anyone can do, at least in principle.

Personality and Health

Different health problems seem to plague different social groups. For example, men are more susceptible to heart disease than are women, and African Americans are more susceptible to asthma than are Asian or European Americans. Beyond these general social categories, personality turns out to be a factor in wellness, with individual differences in optimism and hardiness being important influences.

Optimism

An optimist who believes that "in uncertain times, I usually expect the best" is likely to be healthier than is a pessimist who believes that "if something can go wrong for me, it will." One recent review of dozens of studies including tens of thousands of participants concluded that, of all of the measures of psychological well-being examined, optimism is the one that most strongly predicted a positive outcome for cardiovascular health (Boehm & Kubzansky, 2012). Does just having positive thoughts about the future make it so? Unfortunately not.

Rather than improving physical health directly, optimism seems to aid in the maintenance of *psychological* health in the face of physical health problems. When sick, optimists are more likely than are pessimists to maintain positive emotions, avoid negative emotions such as anxiety and depression, stick to the medical regimens their caregivers have prescribed, and keep up their relationships with others. Optimism also seems to aid in the maintenance of physical health. For instance, optimism appears to be associated with cardiovascular health because optimistic people tend to engage in healthier behaviors such as eating a balanced diet and exercising, which decreases the risk of heart disease (Boehm et al., 2013). So being optimistic is a positive asset, but it takes more than just hope to obtain positive health benefits.

The benefits of optimism raise an important question: If the traits of optimism and pessimism are stable over time—even resistant to change—can pessimists ever hope to gain any of the advantages of optimism (Heatherton & Weinberger, 1994)? Research has shown that even die-hard pessimists can be trained to become significantly more optimistic and that this training can improve their psychosocial health outcomes. For example, pessimistic breast cancer patients who received 10 weeks of training in stress management techniques became more optimistic and were less likely than were those who received only relaxation exercises to suffer distress and fatigue during their cancer treatments (Antoni et al., 2001).

Hardiness

Some people seem to be thick-skinned, somehow able to take stress or abuse that could be devastating to others. In one study, a group of stress-resistant business executives reported high levels of stressful life events but had histories of relatively few illnesses compared with a similar group who succumbed to stress by getting sick (Kobasa, 1979). The stress-resistant group (labeled *hardy*) shared several traits, all conveniently beginning with the letter C. They showed a sense of *commitment*, an ability to become involved in life's tasks and encounters rather than just dabbling. They exhibited a belief in *control*, the expectation that their actions and words have a causal influence over their lives and environment. And they were willing to accept *challenge*, undertaking change and accepting opportunities for growth.

Can just anyone develop hardiness? In one study, participants attended 10 weekly hardiness-training sessions, in which they were encouraged to examine their stresses, develop action plans for dealing with them, explore their bodily reactions to stress, and find ways to compensate for unchangeable situations without falling into self-pity. Compared with control groups (who engaged in relaxation and meditation training or in group discussions about stress), the hardiness-training group reported greater reductions in their perceived personal stress as well as fewer symptoms of illness (Maddi, Kahn, & Maddi, 1998). Hardiness training can have similar positive effects in college students, for some even boosting their GPA (Maddi et al., 2009).

Adrianne Haslet was approximately 4 feet away from one of the bombs that exploded at the Boston Marathon in 2013. Although the explosion caused her to lose her left foot, Adrianne vowed that she would continue her career as a dancer—and she actually ran in the Boston Marathon in 2016. She is an optimist, and optimism can lead to positive health outcomes. Bill Greene/*The Boston Globe* via Getty Images

Sometimes hardiness tips over the edge into foolhardiness. Members of the Coney Island Polar Bear Club take the plunge every Sunday of winter. Kathy Willens/AP Images

Health-Promoting Behaviors and Self-Regulation

Even without changing our personalities at all, we can do certain things to be healthy. The importance of healthy eating, safe sex, and giving up smoking are common knowledge. But we don't seem to be acting on the basis of this knowledge. Sixty-nine percent of Americans over 20 are overweight or obese (National Center for Health Statistics, 2012). The prevalence of unsafe sex is difficult to estimate, but 20 million Americans contract one or more new sexually transmitted diseases (STDs) each year (Satterwhite et al., 2013). And despite endless warnings, 17% of U.S. adults still smoke cigarettes (CDC, 2015). What's going on?

Self-Regulation

self-regulation The exercise of voluntary control over the self to bring the self into line with preferred standards.

Doing what is good for you is not necessarily easy. Engaging in health-promoting behaviors involves **self-regulation**, *the exercise of voluntary control over the self to bring the self into line with preferred standards.* When you decide on a salad rather than a cheeseburger, for instance, you control your impulse and behave in a way that will help to make you the kind of person you would prefer to be—a healthy one. Self-regulation often involves putting off immediate gratification for longer-term gains.

One theory suggests that self-control is a kind of strength that can be fatigued (Baumeister, Vohs, & Tice, 2007). In other words, trying to exercise control in one area may exhaust self-control, leaving behavior in other areas unregulated. To test this theory, researchers seated hungry volunteers near a batch of fresh, hot, chocolate chip cookies. They asked some participants to leave the cookies alone but help themselves to a healthy snack of radishes, whereas others were allowed to indulge. When later challenged with an impossibly difficult figure-tracing task, the self-control group was more likely than the self-indulgent group to abandon the difficult task—behavior interpreted as evidence that they had depleted their pool of self-control (Baumeister et al., 1998). The take-home message from this experiment is that to control behavior successfully, we need to choose our battles, exercising self-control mainly on the personal weaknesses that are most harmful to health.

Nobody ever said self-control was easy. Probably the only reason you're able to keep yourself from eating this cookie is that it's just a picture of a cookie. Really. Don't eat it. Jean Sander/Featurepics

Eating Wisely

In many Western cultures, the weight of the average citizen is increasing alarmingly. One explanation is based on our evolutionary history: In order to ensure their survival, our ancestors found it useful to eat well in times of plenty to store calories for leaner times. In 21st-century postindustrial societies, however, there are no leaner times, and people can't burn all of the calories they consume (Pinel, Assanand, & Lehman, 2000). But why, then, are people in France leaner on average than Americans, even though their foods are high in fat? One reason has to do with the fact that activity level in France is higher. Another is that portion sizes in France are significantly smaller than in the United States, but at the same time, people in France take longer to finish their smaller meals (Rozin, Kabnick, et al., 2003). Right now, Americans seem to be involved in some kind of national eating contest, whereas in France people are eating less food more slowly, perhaps leading them to be more conscious of what they are eating. This, ironically, probably leads to lower French fry consumption.

Short of moving to France, what can you do? Studies indicate that dieting doesn't always work because the process of conscious self-regulation can easily be undermined by stress, causing people who are trying to control themselves to lose control by overindulging in the very behavior they had been trying to overcome (see Data Visualization: How Are Stress and Eating Habits Related? at www.launchpadworks.com). This may remind you of a general principle we discussed in the Consciousness chapter: Trying hard not to do something can often directly result in the unwanted behavior (Wegner, 1994a, 1994b). Rather than dieting, then, heading toward normal weight should involve a new

DATA VISUALIZATION

emphasis on exercise and nutrition (Prochaska & Sallis, 2004). In emphasizing what is good to eat, a person can think freely about food rather than trying to suppress thoughts about it. Self-regulation is more effective when it focuses on what to do, rather than on what *not* to do (Molden, Lee, & Higgins, 2009; Wegner & Wenzlaff, 1996).

Avoiding Sexual Risks

People put themselves at risk when they have unprotected vaginal, oral, or anal intercourse. Sexually active adolescents and adults are usually aware of such risks, not to mention the risk of unwanted pregnancy, and yet many behave in risky ways nonetheless. Why doesn't awareness translate into avoidance? Risk takers harbor an *illusion of unique invulnerability*, a systematic bias toward believing that they are less likely to fall victim to the problem than are others (Perloff & Fetzer, 1986). For example, a study of sexually active female college students found that respondents judged their own likelihood of getting pregnant in the next year as less than 10%, but estimated the average for other women at the university to be 27% (Burger & Burns, 1988).

   Unprotected sex often is the impulsive result of last-minute emotions. When thought is further blurred by alcohol or recreational drugs, people often fail to use the latex condoms that can reduce their exposure to the risks of pregnancy, HIV, and many other STDs. One approach to reducing sexual risk taking, then, is simply finding ways to help people plan ahead. Sex education programs offer adolescents just such a chance by encouraging them, at a time when they have not had much sexual experience, to think about what they might do when they need to make decisions. Although sex education is sometimes criticized as increasing adolescents' awareness of and interest in sex, the research evidence is clear: Sex education reduces the likelihood that adolescents will engage in unprotected sexual activity and benefits their health (American Psychological Association, 2005). The same holds true for adults.

Not Smoking

One in two smokers dies prematurely from smoking-related diseases such as lung cancer, heart disease, emphysema, and cancer of the mouth and throat. Although the overall rate of smoking in the United States is declining, new smokers abound, and many can't seem to stop. College students are puffing away along with everyone else, with 20% of college students currently smoking (Thompson et al., 2007). In the face of all the devastating health consequences, why don't people quit?

   Nicotine, the active ingredient in cigarettes, is addictive, so smoking is difficult to stop once the habit is established (as discussed in the Consciousness chapter). As with other forms of self-regulation, the resolve to quit smoking is fragile and seems to

One of the reasons that people in France are leaner than are people in the United States is that the average French diner spends 22 minutes to consume a fast-food meal, whereas the average American diner spends only 15 minutes. How could the length of the average meal influence an individual's body weight? Jeff Gilbert/Alamy

"Boy, I'm going to pay for this tomorrow at yoga class."

Alex Gregory/The New Yorker Collection/www.cartoonbank.com

The Dangers of Overparenting

Julie Lythcott-Haims Kristina Vetter

Many parents want to protect their children from experiencing any stress or hardship. This is only natural; we want to protect the ones we love from being hurt, and we want to ensure that they have the best life possible. But is there a downside to doing so? Julie Lythcott-Haims, who for a decade served as Stanford University's Dean of Freshman, believes that "overparenting" can cause significant harm by depriving children of opportunities to learn creativity, competence, and confidence, and to develop a true sense of who they really are. In her new book, *How to Raise an Adult*, Lythcott-Haims describes how overbearing "helicopter parenting" can backfire among college students.

I became a university dean because I'm interested in supporting humans in growing to become who they're meant to become, unfettered by circumstances or other people's expectations. I expected that the kids who would need my help would be first-generation college students or low-income kids, and these populations certainly benefited from the mentorship and support that a dean could provide. But it was my solidly middle- or upper-middle-class students who had the most bewildered looks on their faces, looks that turned to relief when Mom or Dad handled the situations, whatever it was. These parents seemed involved in their college students' lives in ways that held their kids back instead of propelling them forward.

In 2013 the news was filled with worrisome statistics about the mental health crisis on college campuses, particularly the number of students medicated for depression. Charlie Gofen, the retired chairman of the board at the Latin School of Chicago, a private school serving about 1,100 students, emailed the statistics off to a colleague at another school and asked, "Do you think parents at your school would rather their kid be depressed at Yale or happy at University of Arizona?" The colleague quickly replied, "My guess is 75 percent of the parents would rather see their kids depressed at Yale. They figure that the kid can straighten the emotional stuff out in his/her 20's, but no one can go back and get the Yale undergrad degree."

In 2013 the American College Health Association surveyed close to 100,000 college students from 153 different campuses about their health. When asked about their experiences, at some point over the past 12 months:

- 84.3 percent felt overwhelmed by all they had to do
- 60.5 percent felt very sad
- 57.0 percent felt very lonely
- 51.3 percent felt overwhelming anxiety
- 8.0 percent seriously considered suicide

You're right to be thinking *Yes, but do we know whether overparenting causes this rise in mental health problems?* The answer is that we don't have studies proving causation, but a number of recent studies show *correlation*.

In 2010, psychology professor Neil Montgomery of Keene State College in New Hampshire surveyed 300 college freshmen nationwide and found that students with helicopter parents were less open to new ideas and actions and more vulnerable, anxious, and self-conscious. "[S]tudents who were given responsibility and not constantly monitored by their parents—so-called 'free rangers'—the effects were reversed," Montgomery's study found. A 2011 study by Terri LeMoyne and Tom Buchanan at the University of Tennessee at Chattanooga looking at more than 300 students found that students with "hovering" or "helicopter" parents are more likely to be medicated for anxiety and/or depression.

When parents have tended to do the stuff of life for kids—the waking up, the transporting, the reminding about deadlines and obligations, the bill-paying, the question-asking, the decision-making, the responsibility-taking, the talking to strangers, and the confronting of authorities, kids may be in for quite a shock when parents turn them loose in the world of college or work. They will experience setbacks, which will feel to them like failure. Lurking beneath the problem of whatever thing needs to be handled is the student's inability to differentiate the self from the parent.

Here's the point—and this is so much more important than I realized until rather recently when the data started coming in: The research shows that figuring out for themselves is a critical element to people's mental health. Your kids have to be there for *themselves*. That's a harder truth to swallow when your kid is in the midst of a problem or worse, a crisis, but taking the long view, it's the best medicine for them.

Is being exposed to stressful situations necessarily a bad thing? How else will we learn how to cope with difficult situations? If we never learn to do so, we may be more likely to experience some of the bad outcomes that Lythcott-Haims writes about. So get out there, get stressed, and manage it!

OTHER VOICES

break down under stress. In the months following 9/11, for example, cigarette sales jumped 13% in Massachusetts (Phillips, 2002). And for some time after quitting, ex-smokers remain sensitive to cues in the environment: Eating or drinking, a bad mood, anxiety, or just seeing someone else smoking is enough to make them want a cigarette (Shiffman et al., 1996). The good news is that the urge diminishes, and people become less likely to relapse the longer they've been away from nicotine.

Psychological programs and techniques to help people kick the habit include nicotine replacement systems such as gum and skin patches, counseling programs, and hypnosis, but these programs are not always successful. Trying again and again in different ways is apparently the best approach (Schachter, 1982). After all, to quit smoking forever, you need to quit only one more time than you start up. But like the self-regulation of eating and sexuality, the self-regulation of smoking can require effort and thought. Keeping healthy by behaving in healthy ways is one of the great challenges of life (see Other Voices: The Dangers of Overparenting).

BUILD TO THE OUTCOMES

1. Why do optimists tend to have better health?

2. What is hardiness?

3. Why is it difficult to achieve and maintain self-control?

4. Why is exercise a more effective weight-loss choice than dieting?

5. Why does planning ahead reduce sexual risk taking?

6. To quit smoking forever, how many times do you need to quit?

CHAPTER REVIEW

Sources of Stress: What Gets to You

- Stressors are events and threats that place specific demands on a person or threaten well-being.
- Sources of stress include major life events (even happy ones), and also chronic stressors that occur repeatedly.
- Events are most stressful when we perceive that there is no way to control or deal with the challenge.

Stress Reactions: All Shook Up

- The body responds to stress with an initial fight-or-flight reaction, which activates the hypothalamic–pituitary–adrenocortical (HPA) axis and prepares the body to face the threat or run away from it.
- Chronic stress can wear down the immune system, causing susceptibility to infection, aging, tumor growth, organ damage, and death.
- The response to stress will vary depending on whether it's interpreted as something that can be overcome or not.
- If prolonged, the psychological response to stress can lead to burnout.

Stress Management: Dealing with It

- The management of stress involves strategies for influencing the mind, the body, and the situation.
- Mind management strategies include repressing stressful thoughts or avoiding the situations that produce them, rationally coping with the stressor, and reframing.

- Body management strategies involve attempting to reduce stress symptoms through meditation, relaxation, biofeedback, and aerobic exercise.
- Situation management strategies can involve seeking out social support, engaging in religious experiences, or attempting to find humor in stressful events.

The Psychology of Illness: Mind Over Matter

- The psychology of illness concerns how sensitivity to the body leads people to recognize illness and seek treatment.
- Somatic symptom disorders can stem from excessive sensitivity to physical problems.
- The sick role is a set of rights and obligations linked with illness; some people fake illness in order to accrue those rights.
- Successful health care providers interact with their patients to understand both the physical state and the psychological state.

The Psychology of Health: Feeling Good

- The connection between mind and body can be revealed through the influences of personality and self-regulation of behavior on health.
- The personality traits of optimism and hardiness are associated with reduced risk for illnesses, perhaps because people with these traits can fend off stress.
- The self-regulation of behaviors such as eating, sexuality, and smoking is difficult for many people because self-regulation is easily disrupted by stress.

KEY CONCEPT QUIZ

1. What kinds of stressors are you likely to be exposed to if you live in a dense urban area with considerable traffic, noise, and pollution?
   a. cultural stressors
   b. intermittent stressors
   c. chronic stressors
   d. positive stressors

2. In an experiment, two groups are subjected to distractions while attempting to complete a task. Those in group A are told they can quiet the distractions by pushing a button. This information is withheld from group B. Why will group A's performance at the task likely be better than group B's?
   a. Group B is working in a different environment.
   b. Group A has perceived control over a source of performance-impeding stress.
   c. Group B is less distracted than group A.
   d. The distractions affecting group B are now chronic.

3. The brain activation that occurs in response to a threat begins in the
   a. pituitary gland.
   b. hypothalamus.
   c. adrenal gland.
   d. corpus callosum.

4. According to the general adaptation syndrome, during the _____ phase, the body adapts to its high state of arousal as it tries to cope with a stressor.
   a. exhaustion
   b. alarm
   c. resistance
   d. energy

5. Which of the following statements most accurately describes the physiological response to stress?
   a. Type A behavior patterns have psychological but not physiological ramifications.
   b. The link between work-related stress and coronary heart disease is unfounded.
   c. Stressors can cause hormones to flood the brain, strengthening the immune system.
   d. The immune system is remarkably responsive to psychological influences.

6. Meditation is an altered state of consciousness that occurs
   a. with the aid of drugs.
   b. through hypnosis.
   c. naturally or through special practices.
   d. as a result of dreamlike brain activity.

7. Engaging in aerobic exercise is a way of managing stress by managing the
   a. environment.
   b. body.
   c. situation.
   d. intake of air.

8. Finding a new or creative way to think about a stressor that reduces its threat is called
   a. stress inoculation.
   b. repressive coping.
   c. reframing.
   d. rational coping.

9. The positive health outcomes associated with religiosity and spirituality are believed to be the result of all of the following except
   a. enhanced social support.
   b. engagement in healthier behavior.
   c. endorsement of hope and optimism.
   d. intercessory prayer.

10. A person who is preoccupied with minor symptoms and believes they signify a life-threatening illness is likely to be diagnosed with
   a. cytokines.
   b. repressive coping.
   c. burnout.
   d. a somatic symptom disorder.

11. Faking an illness is a violation of
   a. malingering.
   b. somatoform disorder.
   c. the sick role.
   d. the Type B pattern of behavior.

12. Which of the following describes a successful health care provider?
   a. displays empathy
   b. pays attention to both the physical and psychological states of the patient
   c. uses psychology to promote patient compliance
   d. all of the above

13. When sick, optimists are more likely than are pessimists to
   a. maintain positive emotions.
   b. become depressed.
   c. ignore their caregiver's advice.
   d. avoid contact with others.

14. Which of the following is NOT a trait associated with hardiness?
   a. a sense of commitment
   b. an aversion to criticism
   c. a belief in control
   d. a willingness to accept challenge

15. Stress _____ the self-regulation of behaviors such as eating and smoking.
   a. strengthens
   b. has no effect on
   c. disrupts
   d. normalizes

 **LearningCurve**

Don't stop now! Quizzing yourself is a powerful study tool. Go to LearningCurve at www.launchpadworks.com for more practice.

KEY TERMS

stressors (p. 410)

stress (p. 410)

health psychology (p. 410)

chronic stressors (p. 411)

fight-or-flight response (p. 414)

general adaptation syndrome (GAS) (p. 414)

immune system (p. 416)

Type A behavior pattern (p. 418)

burnout (p. 419)

repressive coping (p. 420)

rational coping (p. 421)

reframing (p. 421)

meditation (p. 422)

relaxation therapy (p. 423)

relaxation response (p. 423)

biofeedback (p. 423)

social support (p. 424)

psychosomatic illness (p. 429)

somatic symptom disorders (p. 429)

sick role (p. 430)

self-regulation (p. 434)

CHANGING MINDS

1. In 2002, researchers compared severe acne in college students during a relatively stress-free period with acne during a highly stressful exam period. After adjusting for other variables such as changes in sleep or diet, the researchers concluded that increased acne severity was strongly correlated with increased levels of stress. Learning about the study, your roommate is surprised. "Acne is a skin disease," your roommate says. "I don't see how it could have anything to do with your mental state." How would you weigh in on the role of stress in medical diseases? What other examples could you give of ways in which stress can affect health?

2. A friend of yours who is taking a heavy course load confides that he's feeling overwhelmed. "I can't take the stress," he says. "Sometimes I daydream of living on an island somewhere, where I can just lie in the sun and have

no stress at all." What would you tell your friend about stress? Is all stress bad? What would a life with no stress really be like?

3. One of your classmates spent the summer interning in a neurologist's office. "One of the most fascinating things," she says, "was the patients with psychosomatic illness. Some had seizures or partial paralysis of an arm, and there were no neurological causes—so it was all psychosomatic. The neurologist tried to refer these patients to psychiatrists, but a lot of the patients thought he was accusing them of faking their symptoms, and were very insulted." What would you tell your friend about psychosomatic illness? Could a disease that's "all in the head" really produce symptoms such as seizures or partial paralysis, or are these patients definitely faking their symptoms?

ANSWERS TO KEY CONCEPT QUIZ

1. c; 2. b; 3. b; 4. c; 5. d; 6. c; 7. b; 8. c; 9. d; 10. d; 11. c; 12. d; 13. a; 14. b; 15. c.

Psychological Disorders

14

Robin Williams was one of the funniest and most beloved comedians in history, best known for his fun and zany improvisational style. He appeared in over 100 films and television shows, including four movies released in 2014. On August 11, 2014, Williams locked himself in his bedroom and hanged himself with his belt. Why would a person who was so successful and beloved purposely end his life?

What many people did not know was that Williams suffered from major depressive disorder, a mental illness characterized by long periods of depressed mood, diminished interest in pleasurable activities, and feelings of worthlessness. He also struggled with drug- and alcohol-use disorders and, shortly before his death, he was diagnosed with Parkinson's disease and dementia, conditions associated with a progressive decline of physical and mental abilities. Many people who are suicidal say that their motivation to die is to escape from some seemingly intolerable situation, such as a long-term struggle with mental illness. That may have been the reason for Williams's suicide, although we will never know for sure.

Williams's case highlights several important facts about mental disorders. They can affect anyone, regardless of the amount of perceived happiness or success one has had. They are characterized by extreme distress and impairment, often limiting a person's ability to carry out their daily activities. But at the same time, many people suffer from them silently, unknown to those around them. And finally, in extreme cases, they can be lethal, leading to severe self-injury or death by suicide. Thus, there is a great need for us to better understand what mental disorders are and what causes them.

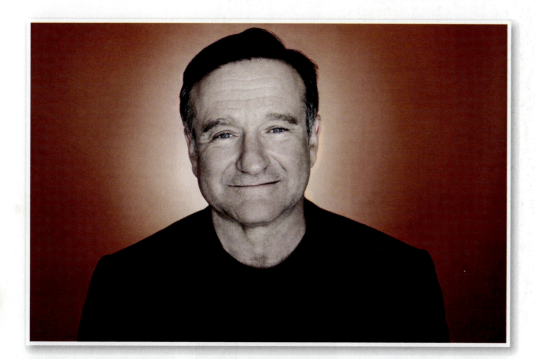

The actor and comedian Robin Williams (1951–2014) in 2009. Williams was a brilliant performer who had audiences laughing for over 40 years. In his personal life, however, he suffered with bouts of addiction, depression, and dementia, ending with his suicide in 2014. Mararten De Boer/Sagf/Contour by Getty Images

IN THIS CHAPTER, WE FIRST CONSIDER THE QUESTION, How do psychologists decide when a person's thoughts, emotions, and behaviors are "disordered" or abnormal? We'll then focus on several major forms of *mental disorder*: depressive and bipolar disorders; anxiety, obsessive-compulsive, and trauma-related disorders; schizophrenia; disorders that begin in childhood and adolescence; and self-harm behaviors. As we view each type of disorder, we will examine how they manifest and what is known about their prevalence and causes. In the next chapter, we'll discuss how these disorders are currently treated.

Defining Mental Disorders: What Is Abnormal?

LEARNING OUTCOMES

- Explain why the *DSM* has become a more credible diagnostic tool over the course of revisions to each edition.

- Identify the fundamental ideas behind the medical model, the biopsychosocial perspective, and the diathesis–stress model.

- Relate how the RDoC expands on the *DSM*.

- Explain why labeling someone with a disorder can be problematic.

mental disorder A persistent disturbance or dysfunction in behavior, thoughts, or emotions that causes significant distress or impairment.

The concept of a mental disorder seems simple at first glance, but turns out to be very complex (similar to clearly defining "consciousness," "stress," or "personality"). Any extreme variation in your thoughts, feelings, or behaviors is not a mental disorder. For instance, severe anxiety before a test, sadness after the loss of a loved one, or a night of excessive alcohol consumption is not necessarily pathological. Similarly, a persistent pattern of deviating from the norm does not qualify as a mental disorder. If it did, we would diagnose mental disorders in the most creative and visionary people—anyone whose ideas deviate from those of people around them.

So what *is* a mental disorder? Perhaps surprisingly, there is no universal agreement on a precise definition of the term *mental disorder*. However, there is general agreement that a **mental disorder** can be broadly defined as *a persistent disturbance or dysfunction in behavior, thoughts, or emotions that causes significant distress or impairment* (Stein et al., 2010; Wakefield, 2007). One way to think about mental disorders is as dysfunctions or deficits in the normal human psychological processes you have learned about throughout this textbook. People with mental disorders have problems with their perception, memory, learning, emotions, motivation, thinking, and social processes. Of course, this definition leaves many questions unanswered. What kinds of disturbances count as mental disorders? How long must they last to be considered "persistent"? And how much distress or impairment is required? These are hotly debated questions in the field.

Conceptualizing Mental Disorders

Since ancient times, there have been reports of people acting strangely or reporting bizarre thoughts or emotions. Until fairly recently, such difficulties were conceptualized as the result of religious or supernatural forces. In some cultures, psychopathology is still interpreted as possession by spirits or demons, as enchantment by a witch or shaman, or as God's punishment for wrongdoing. In many societies, including our own, people with psychological disorders have been feared and ridiculed, and often treated as criminals: punished, imprisoned, or put to death for their "crime" of deviating from the normal.

Over the past 200 years, these ways of looking at psychological abnormalities have largely been replaced in most parts of the world by a **medical model**, *an approach*

medical model An approach that conceptualizes abnormal psychological experiences as illnesses that, like physical illnesses, have biological and environmental causes, defined symptoms, and possible cures.

Although mental disorders are deviations from normal behavior, not all deviations from the norm are disordered. Indeed, people thinking differently about the world, and behaving in ways that deviated from the norm, have brought remarkable advances, such as Mickey Mouse, iPhones, and racial equality.
Lawrence Schiller/Polaris Communications/ Getty Images; Shaun Curry/AFP/Getty Images; Howard Sochurek/The LIFE Picture Collection/ Getty Images

that conceptualizes abnormal psychological experiences as illnesses that, like physical illnesses, have biological and environmental causes, defined symptoms, and possible cures. Conceptualizing abnormal thoughts and behaviors as illness suggests that a first step is to determine the nature of the problem through *diagnosis.*

In diagnosis, clinicians seek to determine the nature of a person's mental disorder by assessing *signs* (objectively observed indicators of a disorder) and *symptoms* (subjectively reported behaviors, thoughts, and emotions) that suggest an underlying illness. So, for example, just as self-reported sniffles and a cough are symptoms of a cold, Robin Williams's depressed mood can be seen as a symptom of his depressive disorder. It is important to note the differences among three related general medical and classification terms:

- A *disorder* is a common set of signs and symptoms.
- A *disease* is a known pathological process affecting the body.
- A *diagnosis* is a determination as to whether a disorder or disease is present (Kraemer, Shrout, & Rubio-Stipec, 2007).

It is important to note that knowing that a disorder is present (i.e., diagnosed) does not necessarily mean that we know the underlying disease process in the body that gives rise to the signs and symptoms of the disorder.

Viewing mental disorders as medical problems reminds us that people who are suffering deserve care and treatment, not condemnation. Nevertheless, there are some criticisms of the medical model. Some psychologists argue that it is inappropriate to use clients' subjective self-reports, rather than physical tests of pathology (as in other areas of medical diagnostics), to determine underlying illness. Others argue that the model often "medicalizes" or "pathologizes" normal human behavior. For instance, extreme sadness can be considered to be an illness called *major depressive disorder*; extreme shyness can be diagnosed as an illness called *social anxiety disorder*; and trouble concentrating in school is called *attention-deficit/hyperactivity disorder*. Although there are some valid concerns about the current method of defining and classifying mental disorders, it is a huge advance over older alternatives, such as viewing mental disorders as the product of witchcraft or as punishment for sin.

Classifying Disorders: The *DSM*

So how is the medical model used to classify the wide range of abnormal behaviors that occur among humans? Most people working in the area of mental disorders use a standardized system for classifying mental disorders called the **Diagnostic and Statistical Manual of Mental Disorders (DSM)**. The *DSM* is *a classification system that describes the symptoms used to diagnose each recognized mental disorder and indicates how the disorder can be distinguished from other, similar problems.* Each disorder is named and classified as a distinct illness. The initial version of the *DSM*, published in 1952, provided a common language for talking about disorders; however, the diagnostic criteria were quite vague. Over the decades, revised editions of the *DSM* moved from vague descriptions of disorders to very detailed lists of symptoms (or *diagnostic criteria*) that had to be present in order for a disorder to be diagnosed. For instance, in addition to being extremely sad or depressed (for at least 2 weeks), a person must have at least five of nine agreed-on symptoms of depression—for example, diminished interest in normally enjoyable activities, significant

The professional baseball player Zack Greinke was unable to play baseball in 2006, early in his professional career, due to social phobia. Fortunately, through correct diagnosis and effective treatment, he was able to return to the game and has gone on to a very successful professional career. AP Photo/Eric Christian Smith

Diagnostic and Statistical Manual of Mental Disorders (DSM) A classification system that describes the features used to diagnose each recognized mental disorder and indicates how that disorder can be distinguished from other, similar problems.

weight loss or gain, significantly increased or decreased sleep, loss of energy, feelings of worthlessness or guilt, trouble concentrating. The use of these detailed lists led to a dramatic increase in the reliability, or consistency, of diagnoses of mental disorders. Two clinicians interviewing the same individual were now much more likely to agree on what mental disorders were present, greatly increasing the credibility of the diagnostic process (and the fields of psychiatry and clinical psychology).

In May 2013, the American Psychiatric Association released the newest, fifth edition of the *DSM*, the *DSM–5*. The *DSM–5* describes 22 major categories containing more than 200 different mental disorders (see **TABLE 14.1**).

TABLE 14.1 Main *DSM–5* Categories of Mental Disorders

1. **Neurodevelopmental Disorders:** These are conditions that begin early in development and cause significant impairments in functioning, such as intellectual disability (formerly called "mental retardation"), autism spectrum disorder (ASD), and attention-deficit/hyperactivity disorder (ADHD).

2. **Schizophrenia Spectrum and Other Psychotic Disorders:** This is a group of disorders characterized by major disturbances in perception, thought, language, emotion, and behavior.

3. **Bipolar and Related Disorders:** These disorders include major fluctuations in mood—from mania to depression—and also can include psychotic experiences, which is why they are placed between the psychotic and depressive disorders in *DSM–5*.

4. **Depressive Disorders:** These are conditions characterized by extreme and persistent periods of depressed mood.

5. **Anxiety Disorders:** These are disorders characterized by excessive fear and anxiety that are extreme enough to impair a person's functioning, such as panic disorder, generalized anxiety disorder, and specific phobias.

6. **Obsessive-Compulsive and Related Disorders:** These are conditions characterized by the presence of obsessive thinking followed by compulsive behavior in response to that thinking.

7. **Trauma- and Stressor-Related Disorders:** These are disorders that develop in response to a traumatic event, such as posttraumatic stress disorder.

8. **Dissociative Disorders:** These are conditions characterized by disruptions or discontinuity in consciousness, memory, or identity, such as dissociative identity disorder (formerly called "multiple personality disorder").

9. **Somatic Symptom and Related Disorders:** These are conditions in which a person experiences bodily symptoms (e.g., pain, fatigue) associated with significant distress or impairment.

10. **Feeding and Eating Disorders:** These are problems with eating that impair health or functioning, such as anorexia nervosa and bulimia nervosa.

11. **Elimination Disorders:** These involve inappropriate elimination of urine or feces (e.g., bedwetting).

12. **Sleep–Wake Disorders:** These are problems with the sleep–wake cycle, such as insomnia, narcolepsy, and sleep apnea.

13. **Sexual Dysfunctions:** These are problems related to unsatisfactory sexual activity, such as erectile disorder and premature ejaculation.

14. **Gender Dysphoria:** This is a single disorder characterized by incongruence between a person's experienced/expressed gender and assigned gender.

15. **Disruptive, Impulse-Control, and Conduct Disorders:** These are conditions involving problems controlling emotions and behaviors, such as conduct disorder, intermittent explosive disorder, and kleptomania.

16. **Substance-Related and Addictive Disorders:** This collection of disorders involves persistent use of substances or some other behavior (e.g., gambling) despite the fact that it leads to significant problems.

17. **Neurocognitive Disorders:** These are disorders of thinking caused by conditions such as Alzheimer's disease or traumatic brain injury.

18. **Personality Disorders:** These are enduring patterns of thinking, feeling, and behaving that lead to significant life problems.

19. **Paraphilic Disorders:** These are conditions characterized by inappropriate sexual activity, such as pedophilic disorder.

20. **Other Mental Disorders:** This is a residual category for conditions that do not fit into one of the above categories but are associated with significant distress or impairment, such as an unspecified mental disorder due to a medical condition.

21. **Medication-Induced Movement Disorders and Other Adverse Effects of Medication:** These are problems with physical movement (e.g., tremors, rigidity) that are caused by medication.

22. **Other Conditions That May Be the Focus of Clinical Attention:** These include disorders related to abuse, neglect, relationship, and other problems.

Information from *DSM–5* (American Psychiatric Association, 2013).

Studies of large, representative samples of the U.S. population reveal that approximately half of Americans report experiencing at least one mental disorder during the course of their lives (Kessler, Berglund, et al., 2005). And most of those with a mental disorder (greater than 80%) report **comorbidity**, *the co-occurrence of two or more disorders in a single individual* (Gadermann et al., 2012; see also Data Visualization: Comorbidity: How Often Do Multiple Disorders Occur? at www.launchpadworks.com).

DATA VISUALIZATION

The major mental disorders seen in the United States appear in countries and cultures all around the world (see **FIGURE 14.1**; Kessler & Üstün, 2008). For instance, all over the globe, depression and anxiety are always the most common, followed by impulse-control and substance use disorders (Kessler et al., 2007). But although all countries appear to have common mental disorders, cultural context can influence how mental disorders are experienced, described, assessed, and treated. To address this issue, the *DSM–5* includes a section devoted to cultural considerations in diagnosing mental disorders that is intended to help the clinician understand how the client's culture might influence the experience, expression, and explanation of his or her mental disorder.

Causation of Disorders

The medical model of mental disorder suggests that, just as different viruses, bacteria, or genetic abnormalities cause different physical illnesses, a specifiable pattern of causes (or *etiology*) may exist for different psychological disorders. The medical model also suggests that each category of mental disorder is likely to have a common *prognosis*, a typical course over time and susceptibility to treatment and cure. Unfortunately, this basic medical model is usually an oversimplification; it is rarely useful to focus on a *single cause* that is *internal* to the person and that suggests a *single cure*.

Instead, most psychologists take an integrated **biopsychosocial perspective** that *explains mental disorders as the result of interactions among biological, psychological, and social factors* (see **FIGURE 14.2a**). Biological factors promoting mental disorders can include genetic influences, biochemical imbalances, and abnormalities in brain structure and function. Psychological factors can include maladaptive learning and coping, cognitive biases, dysfunctional attitudes, and

comorbidity The co-occurrence of two or more disorders in a single individual.

biopsychosocial perspective A view that explains mental disorders as the result of interactions among biological, psychological, and social factors.

Figure 14.1 LIFETIME PREVALENCE OF MENTAL DISORDERS AROUND THE WORLD (Data from Kessler et al., 2007)

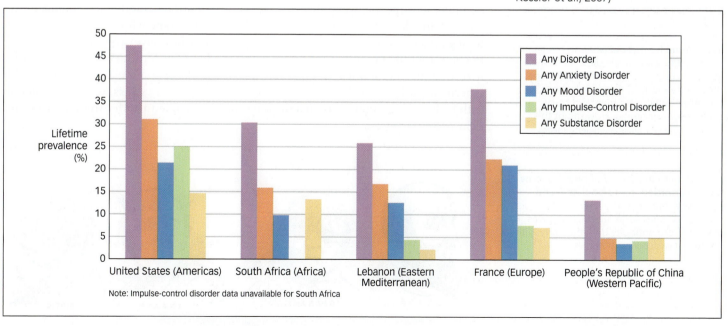

Note: Impulse-control disorder data unavailable for South Africa

Figure 14.2 PROPOSED MODELS OF HOW DISORDERS DEVELOP
(a) The biopsychosocial model suggests that biological, psychological, and social factors all interact to produce mental health or mental illness. (b) The diathesis–stress model suggests that mental illness develops when a person who has some predisposition or vulnerability to mental illness (the "diathesis") experiences a major life stressor (the "stress").

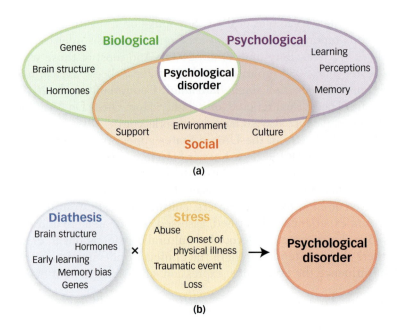

diathesis–stress model A model that suggests that a person may be predisposed to a psychological disorder that remains unexpressed until triggered by stress.

Mental disorders can be caused by biological, psychological, and environmental factors. The diathesis–stress model suggests that a person may be predisposed for a psychological disorder that remains unexpressed until triggered by stress. Suppose that identical twins (with the same genetic profile) grow up in the same household (sharing the same parents, the same basic diet, the same access to television, and so on). When they are teenagers, one twin but not the other develops a mental disorder such as schizophrenia. How might this happen? Terry Schmidbauer/Getty Images

interpersonal problems. Social factors can include poor socialization, stressful life experiences, and cultural and social inequities. The large number of interacting factors suggests that different individuals can experience a psychological disorder (e.g., depression) for different reasons. A person might fall into a depression as a result of biological causes (e.g., genetics, hormones), psychological causes (e.g., faulty beliefs, hopelessness, poor strategies for coping with loss), environmental causes (e.g., stress or loneliness), or more likely as a result of some combination of these factors. And, of course, multiple causes mean there may not be a single cure.

The observation that most mental disorders have both internal (biological/psychological) *and* external (environmental) causes has given rise to a theory known as the **diathesis–stress model**, which suggests that *a person may be predisposed to a psychological disorder that remains unexpressed until triggered by stress* (see **FIGURE 14.2b**). The diathesis is the internal predisposition, and the stress is the external trigger. For example, most people were able to cope with their strong emotional reactions to the terrorist attacks of September 11, 2001. However, for some who had a predisposition to negative emotions, the horror of the events may have overwhelmed their ability to cope, thereby precipitating a psychological disorder. Although diatheses can be inherited, it's important to remember that heritability is not destiny. A person who inherits a diathesis may never encounter the precipitating stress, whereas someone with little genetic propensity to a disorder may still come to suffer from it, given the right pattern of stress.

According to the theory of physiognomy, mental disorders could be diagnosed from facial features. This fanciful theory is now considered superstition, but it was popular from antiquity until the early 20th century. Fowler & Wells (1896)

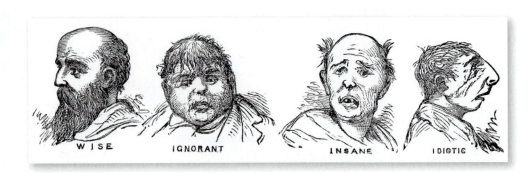

A New Approach to Understanding Mental Disorders: RDOC

Although the *DSM* and *ICD* (*International Classification of Diseases*) provide a useful framework for classifying disorders, concern has been growing that the findings from scientific research on the biopsychosocial factors that appear to cause psychopathology do not map neatly onto individual *DSM* diagnoses. Researchers at the National Institute of Mental Health (NIMH) have proposed a new framework for thinking about mental disorders, focused not on the currently defined *DSM* categories of disorders but on the more basic biological, cognitive, and behavioral processes that are believed to be the building blocks of mental disorders. This system is called the **Research Domain Criteria Project (RDoC)**, *an initiative that aims to guide the classification and understanding of mental disorders by revealing the basic processes that give rise to them*. The RDoC is not intended to immediately replace the *DSM* but to inform future revisions in the coming years (see The Real World: How Are Mental Disorders Defined and Diagnosed?).

Using the RDoC, researchers focus on biological domains such as arousal and sleep patterns; psychological domains, such as learning, attention, memory; and social domains, such as attachment and social communication (see **TABLE 14.2** for a list of domains). The RDoC approach similarly aims to shift the focus away from classifications based on surface symptoms and toward an understanding of the processes that give rise to disordered behavior. For instance, rather than studying cocaine addiction as a distinct disorder, from the RDoC perspective researchers might try to understand what causes abnormalities in "responsiveness to reward," a factor seen in those with excessive cocaine use as well as in those with other addictive behaviors. The basic idea is that some people seem to have trouble inhibiting their reward-seeking behavior, which in turn could predispose a person to develop addiction. Importantly, understanding what processes cause problems such as addiction will help us to develop more effective treatments, a topic we address in more detail in the next chapter.

You might have noticed that the list of domains in Table 14.2 looks like a slightly more detailed version of the table of contents for this textbook! The

The Research Domain Criteria (RDoC) approach may help us better understand why some people seem to have addictive personalities and have trouble limiting their engagement in pleasurable experiences. FSTOP/Superstock

Research Domain Criteria Project (RDoC) An initiative that aims to guide the classification and understanding of mental disorders by revealing the basic processes that give rise to them.

TABLE 14.2   Research Domain Criteria (RDoC)

Domains / Constructs				
Negative Valence Systems	**Positive Valence Systems**	**Cognitive Systems**	**Systems for Social Processes**	**Arousal and Regulatory Systems**
acute threat ("fear")	approach motivation	attention	affiliation and attachment	arousal
potential threat ("anxiety")	initial responsiveness to reward	perception	social communication	circadian rhythms
sustained threat	sustained responsiveness to reward	working memory	perception and understanding of self	sleep and wakefulness
loss	reward learning	declarative memory	perception and understanding of others	
frustrative nonreward	habit	language behavior cognitive (effortful) control		

Units of Analysis							
genes	molecules	cells	circuits	physiology	behavior	self-reports	paradigms

Although we label mental disorders, we should not apply those labels to people. For instance, rather than saying someone "is ADHD," we would say that the person currently meets diagnostic criteria for ADHD. Juanmonino/iStock/Getty Images

RDoC approach has an overall emphasis on neuroscience (Chapter 3), and specific focuses on abnormalities in emotional and motivational systems (Chapter 8), cognitive systems such as memory (Chapter 6), learning (Chapter 7), language and cognition (Chapter 9), social processes (Chapter 12), and stress and arousal (Chapter 13). From the RDoC perspective, mental disorders can be thought of as the result of abnormalities or dysfunctions in normal psychological processes. By learning about many of these processes in this textbook, you will likely have a good understanding of new definitions of mental disorders as they are developed in the years ahead.

Dangers of Labeling

An important complication in the diagnosis and classification of psychological disorders is the effect of labeling. Psychiatric labels can have negative consequences because many carry the baggage of negative stereotypes and stigma, such as the idea that a mental disorder is a sign of personal weakness or the idea that all psychiatric patients are dangerous. The stigma associated with mental disorders may explain why most people with diagnosable psychological disorders (approximately 60%) do not seek treatment (Kessler, Demler, et al., 2005; Wang, Berglund, et al., 2005).

Unfortunately, educating people about mental disorders does not dispel the stigma borne by those with these conditions (Phelan et al., 1997). In fact, expectations created by psychiatric labels can sometimes even compromise the judgment of mental health professionals (Garb, 1998). In a classic demonstration of this phenomenon, researchers reported to different mental hospitals complaining of "hearing voices," a symptom sometimes found in people with schizophrenia. Each was admitted to a hospital, and each promptly reported that the symptom had ceased. Even so, hospital staff were reluctant to identify these people as normal: It took an average of 19 days for these "patients" to secure their release, and even then they

---

THE REAL WORLD

How Are Mental Disorders Defined and Diagnosed?

Who decides what goes in the *DSM*? These decisions are made by consensus among leaders in the research field, who decide which disorders should be included in the new revision of the *DSM* and how they should be defined. Over the years, these decisions have been based on descriptive research reporting in which clinical symptoms tend to cluster together. However, as the currently available body of knowledge about mental disorders grows, the field is moving beyond simple descriptive diagnostic categories toward others based on underlying biopsychosocial processes, such as the Research Domain Criteria Project. Future decisions about how mental disorders are defined will likely continue to be reached by consensus among leaders in the field but will be driven more directly by research on the underlying causes of these disorders.

Who decides whether someone actually has a diagnosable disorder? Over the years, researchers have developed structured clinical interviews that convert the lists of symptoms included in the *DSM* into sets of interview questions through which the clinician (psychologist, psychiatrist, social worker) makes a determination about whether or not a given person meets the criteria for a given disorder (Nock et al., 2007). For instance, according to *DSM–5*, a person must have at least five of the nine symptoms of major depressive disorder in order to meet the criteria for this disorder. Structured clinical interviews typically include nine questions about depression (one per symptom), and if the person reports having at least five of these symptoms, the clinician may conclude that this person is suffering from major depression. Right now, diagnoses are determined primarily by client self-reporting of symptoms. With increasing attention to the underlying causes of mental disorders, many hope that in the future we will have biological and behavioral tests to help us make decisions about who has a mental illness and who does not.

1. What is a mental disorder?

2. How does the medical model explain abnormal behavior?

3. What is the first step in helping someone with a mental disorder?

4. What are the differences among disorder, disease, and diagnosis?

5. What is the *DSM*? How has it changed over time?

6. How do the biopsychosocial perspective and the diathesis–stress model explain disorders?

7. Why does assessment require looking at a number of factors?

8. What is the RDoC? How does it differ from the *DSM*?

9. Why might someone avoid seeking help for a disorder?

10. What are the dangers of labeling?

were released with the diagnosis of "schizophrenia in remission" (Rosenhan, 1973). Apparently, once hospital staff had labeled these patients as having a psychological disease, the label stuck.

These effects of labeling are particularly disturbing in light of evidence that hospitalizing people with mental disorders is seldom necessary. One set of studies in Vermont followed the lives of patients who were thought to be too dangerous to release and therefore had been kept in the back wards of institutions for years. Their release resulted in no harm to the community (Harding et al., 1987), and further studies have shown that those with a mental disorder are no more likely to be violent than those without a disorder (Elbogen & Johnson, 2009; Monahan, 1992).

Labeling may even affect how individuals view themselves; persons given such a label may come to view themselves not just as mentally disordered but as hopeless or worthless. Such a view may cause them to develop an attitude of defeat and, as a result, to fail to work toward recovery. As one small step toward counteracting such consequences, clinicians have adopted the important practice of applying labels to the disorder and not to the person with the disorder. For example, an individual might be described as "a person with schizophrenia," not as "a schizophrenic." You'll notice that we follow this convention in the text.

Anxiety Disorders: Excessive Fear, Anxiety, and Avoidance

"Okay, time for a pop quiz that will be half your grade for this class." If your instructor had actually said that, you would probably have experienced a wave of anxiety and dread. Your reaction would not be a sign that you have a mental disorder. In fact, situation-related anxiety is normal and adaptive: in this case, perhaps by reminding you to keep up with your textbook assignments so you are prepared for pop quizzes. But when anxiety is out of proportion to real threats and challenges, it is maladaptive: It can take hold of people's lives, stealing their peace of mind and undermining their ability to function normally. **Anxiety disorders** are *the class of mental disorders in which anxiety is the predominant feature.* Among the anxiety disorders recognized in the *DSM–5* are phobic disorders, panic disorder, and generalized anxiety disorder.

Phobic Disorders

Mary, a 47-year-old mother of three, sought treatment for *claustrophobia*—an intense fear of enclosed spaces. She traced her fear to her childhood, when her

LEARNING OUTCOMES

- Explain the major symptoms of anxiety disorders, including phobias, panic disorder, and GAD.

- Describe factors that contribute to phobias, panic disorder, and GAD.

anxiety disorder The class of mental disorders in which anxiety is the predominant feature.

older siblings would scare her by locking her in closets. She wanted to find a job but could not because of a terror of elevators and other confined places that, she felt, shackled her to her home (Carson, Butcher, & Mineka, 2000). Many people feel a little anxious in enclosed spaces, but Mary's fears were abnormal and dysfunctional because they were disproportionate to any actual risk and impaired her ability to carry out a normal life. The *DSM–5* describes **phobic disorders** as characterized by *marked, persistent, and excessive fear and avoidance of specific objects, activities, or situations.* An individual with a phobic disorder recognizes that the fear is irrational but cannot prevent it from interfering with everyday functioning.

A **specific phobia** is *an irrational fear of a particular object or situation that markedly interferes with an individual's ability to function.* Specific phobias fall into five categories: (1) animals (e.g., dogs, cats, rats, snakes, spiders); (2) natural environments (e.g., heights, darkness, water, storms); (3) situations (e.g., bridges, elevators, tunnels, enclosed places); (4) blood, injections, and injury; and (5) other phobias, including choking or vomiting; and in children, loud noises or costumed characters. Approximately 12% of people in the United States will develop a specific phobia during their lives (Kessler, Berglund, et al., 2005), with rates slightly higher among women than men (Kessler et al., 2012).

Social phobia involves *an irrational fear of being publicly humiliated or embarrassed.* Social phobia can be restricted to situations such as public speaking or eating in public, or it can be generalized to a variety of social situations that involve being observed or interacting with unfamiliar people. Individuals with social phobia try to avoid situations where unfamiliar people might evaluate them, and they experience intense anxiety and distress when public exposure is unavoidable. Social phobia typically emerges between early adolescence and early adulthood (Kessler, Berglund, et al., 2005). About 12% of men and 14% of women qualify for a diagnosis of social phobia at some time in their lives (Kessler et al., 2012).

Why are phobias so common? The high rates of both specific and social phobias suggest a predisposition to be fearful of certain objects and situations. Indeed, most of the situations and objects of people's phobias could pose a real threat, for example,

phobic disorders Disorders characterized by marked, persistent, and excessive fear and avoidance of specific objects, activities, or situations.

specific phobia A disorder that involves an irrational fear of a particular object or situation that markedly interferes with an individual's ability to function.

social phobia A disorder that involves an irrational fear of being publicly humiliated or embarrassed.

The preparedness theory explains why most merry-go-rounds carry children on beautiful horses. This mom might have some trouble getting her daughter to ride on a big spider or snake. Courtesy of Daniel Wegner

falling from a high place or being attacked by a vicious dog or a poisonous snake or spider. Social situations have their own dangers. A roomful of strangers could form impressions that affect your prospects for friends, jobs, or marriage. And of course, in very rare cases, they could attack or bite.

Observations such as these are the basis for the **preparedness theory** of phobias, which maintains that *people are instinctively predisposed toward certain fears* (Seligman, 1971). The preparedness theory is supported by research showing that both humans and monkeys can quickly be conditioned to have a fear response for stimuli such as snakes and spiders, but not for neutral stimuli such as flowers or toy rabbits (Cook & Mineka, 1989; Öhman, Dimberg, & Öst, 1985). Similarly, research on facial expressions has shown that people are more easily conditioned to fear angry facial expressions than other types of expressions (Öhman, 1996; Woody & Nosen, 2008). Phobias are particularly likely to form for objects that evolution has predisposed us to avoid.

Neurobiological factors may also play a role. Abnormalities in the neurotransmitters serotonin and dopamine are more common in individuals who report phobias than they are among people who don't (Stein, 1998). In addition, individuals with phobias sometimes show abnormally high levels of activity in the amygdala, an area of the brain linked with the development of emotional associations (discussed in the chapter on Emotion and Motivation and in Stein et al., 2001). Interestingly, although people with social phobia report feeling much more distressed than do those without social phobia during tasks involving social evaluation (such as giving a speech), they are actually no more physiologically aroused than others (Jamieson, Nock, & Mendes, 2013). This suggests that social phobia may be due to a person's subjective experience of the situation, rather than an abnormal physiological stress response to such situations.

This evidence does not rule out the influence of environments on the development of phobias. As the behaviorist John Watson (1924) demonstrated many years ago, phobias can be classically conditioned (see the discussion of Little Albert and the white rat in the Learning chapter). Similarly, the discomfort of a dog bite could create a conditioned association between dogs and pain, resulting in an irrational fear of all dogs. The idea that phobias are learned from emotional experiences with feared objects, however, is not a complete explanation for the occurrence of phobias. Most studies find that people with phobias are no more likely than people without phobias to recall personal experiences with the feared object that could have provided the basis for classical conditioning (Craske, 1999; McNally & Steketee, 1985). Moreover, many people are bitten by dogs, but few develop phobias. Despite its shortcomings, however, the idea that this is a matter of learning provides a useful model for therapy (see the Treatment of Psychological Disorders chapter).

Panic Disorder and Agoraphobia

Wesley, a 20-year-old college student, began having panic attacks with increasing frequency, often two or three times a day. The attacks began with a sudden wave of "intense, terrifying fear" that seemed to come out of nowhere, often accompanied by dizziness, a tightening of the chest, and the thought that he was going to pass out or possibly die. Wesley finally decided to seek help from a clinic because he had begun to avoid buses, trains, and public places for fear that he would have an attack like this and not be able to escape.

Wesley's condition, called **panic disorder**, is characterized by *the sudden occurrence of multiple psychological and physiological symptoms that contribute to a feeling of stark terror*. The acute symptoms of a panic attack typically last only

preparedness theory The idea that people are instinctively predisposed toward certain fears.

Phobias are anxiety disorders that involve excessive and persistent fear of a specific object, activity, or situation. Some phobias may be learned through classical conditioning, in which a conditioned stimulus (CS) that is paired with an anxiety-evoking unconditioned stimulus (US) itself comes to elicit a conditioned fear response (CR). Suppose your friend has a phobia of dogs that is so intense that he is afraid to go outside in case one of his neighbors' dogs barks at him. Applying the principles of classical conditioning that you studied in the Learning chapter, how might you help him overcome his fear? Matthew Nock

panic disorder A disorder characterized by the sudden occurrence of multiple psychological and physiological symptoms that contribute to a feeling of stark terror.

a few minutes and include shortness of breath, heart palpitations, sweating, dizziness, depersonalization (a feeling of being detached from one's body) or derealization (a feeling that the external world is strange or unreal), and a fear that one is going crazy or about to die. Not surprisingly, panic attacks often send people rushing to emergency rooms or their physicians' offices for what they believe are heart attacks. Unfortunately, because many of the symptoms mimic various medical disorders, a correct diagnosis may take years (Katon, 1994). According to the *DSM–5* diagnostic criteria, people should be diagnosed with panic disorder only if they experience recurrent unexpected attacks and report significant anxiety about having another attack.

A disorder that sometimes co-occurs with panic disorder is **agoraphobia**, *a specific phobia involving a fear of public places*. Many people with agoraphobia, including Wesley, are not frightened of public places in themselves; instead, they are afraid that something terrible will happen (including having panic symptoms) while they are in a public place and that they will not be able to escape or get help. In severe cases, people who have agoraphobia are unable to leave home, sometimes for years.

Approximately 22% of the U.S. population reports having had at least one panic attack (Kessler, Chiu, et al., 2006), typically during a period of intense stress (Telch, Lucas, & Nelson, 1989). An occasional episode is not sufficient for a diagnosis of panic disorder: The individual also has to experience significant dread and anxiety about having another attack. When this criterion is applied, approximately 5% of people will have diagnosable panic disorder sometime in their lives (Kessler, Berglund, et al., 2005). Panic disorder is more prevalent among women (7%) than among men (3%; Kessler et al., 2012).

The difference in responses to this chemical may be due to differing interpretations of physiological signs of anxiety; that is, people who experience panic attacks may be hypersensitive to physiological signs of anxiety, which they interpret as having disastrous consequences for their well-being. Supporting this cognitive explanation is research showing that people who are high in anxiety sensitivity (i.e., they believe that bodily arousal and other symptoms of anxiety

agoraphobia A specific phobia involving a fear of public places.

Agoraphobia, the fear of being in public because something bad is going to happen and escape will not be possible, may prevent a person from going outside at all. Lolostock/Shutterstock

can have dire consequences) have an elevated risk for experiencing panic attacks (Olatunji & Wolitzky-Taylor, 2009). Thus, panic attacks may be conceptualized as a "fear of fear" itself.

Generalized Anxiety Disorder

Gina, a 24-year-old woman, began to experience debilitating anxiety during her first year of graduate school. At first, she worried about whether she was sufficiently completing all of her assignments. Soon her concerns spread to focus on her health (did she have an undiagnosed medical problem?) as well as that of her boyfriend (he smokes cigarettes . . . is he giving himself cancer?). She worried incessantly for a year and ultimately took time off from school to get treatment for her worries, extreme agitation, fatigue, and feelings of sadness and depression.

Gina's symptoms are typical of **generalized anxiety disorder (GAD)**—called *generalized* because the unrelenting worries are not focused on any particular threat; they are, in fact, often exaggerated and irrational. GAD is *chronic excessive worry accompanied by three or more of the following symptoms: restlessness, fatigue, concentration problems, irritability, muscle tension, and sleep disturbance.* In people suffering from GAD, the uncontrollable worrying produces a sense of loss of control that can so erode self-confidence that simple decisions seem fraught with dire consequences. For example, Gina struggled to make everyday decisions as basic as which vegetables to buy at the market and how to prepare her dinner.

Approximately 6% of people in the United States suffer from GAD at some time in their lives (Kessler, Berglund, et al., 2005), with women experiencing GAD at higher rates (8%) than do men (5%; Kessler et al., 2012). Research suggests that both biological and psychological factors contribute to the risk of GAD. Biological explanations of GAD suggest that neurotransmitter imbalances may play a role in the disorder. Although the precise nature of this imbalance is not clear, *benzodiazepines* (a class of sedative drugs discussed in the Treatment of

generalized anxiety disorder (GAD) A disorder characterized by chronic excessive worry accompanied by three or more of the following symptoms: restlessness, fatigue, concentration problems, irritability, muscle tension, and sleep disturbance.

The experience of major stressful life events, such as losing a job or a home, can lead to generalized anxiety disorder, a condition characterized by chronic, excessive worry. John Henley/Getty Images

Psychological Disorders chapter; e.g., Valium, Librium) that appear to stimulate the neurotransmitter *gamma-aminobutyric acid (GABA)* can sometimes reduce the symptoms of GAD, suggesting a potential role for this neurotransmitter in the occurrence of GAD.

Psychological explanations of GAD focus on anxiety-provoking situations. The condition is especially prevalent among people who have low incomes, are living in large cities, and/or are in environments rendered unpredictable by political and economic strife. Unpredictable traumatic experiences in childhood increase the risk of developing GAD (Torgensen, 1986). Risk of GAD also increases following the experience of a loss or future perceived danger (Kendler et al., 2003). Still, many people who might be expected to develop GAD don't, supporting the diathesis–stress notion that personal vulnerability must also be a key factor in this disorder.

BUILD TO THE OUTCOMES

1. What is an anxiety disorder?

2. When is anxiety helpful? When is it harmful?

3. What is a phobic disorder? What are the different types?

4. Why might we be predisposed to certain phobias?

5. What is a panic disorder?

6. What is it about public places that many people with agoraphobia fear?

7. What is generalized anxiety disorder (GAD)? What factors contribute to it?

Obsessive-Compulsive Disorder: Persistent Thoughts and Repetitive Behaviors

LEARNING OUTCOME

- Describe the symptoms and potential causes of OCD.

You may have had an irresistible urge to go back to check whether you actually locked the door or turned off the oven, even when you're pretty sure that you did. Or you may have been unable to resist engaging in some superstitious behavior, such as not walking under a ladder or stepping on a crack. For some people, such thoughts and actions spiral out of control and become a serious problem.

Karen, a 34-year-old with four children, sought treatment after several months of experiencing intrusive, repetitive thoughts in which she imagined that one or more of her children was having a serious accident. In addition, an extensive series of protective counting rituals hampered her daily routine. For example, when grocery shopping, Karen felt that if she selected the first item (say, a box of cereal) on a shelf, something terrible would happen to her oldest child. If she selected the second item, a disaster would befall her second child, and so on for all four children. Karen's preoccupation with numbers extended to other activities: If she drank one cup of coffee, she felt compelled to drink four more to protect her children from harm. She acknowledged that her counting rituals were irrational, but she became extremely anxious when she tried to stop (Oltmanns, Neale, & Davison, 1991).

Karen's symptoms are typical of **obsessive-compulsive disorder (OCD)**, in which *repetitive, intrusive thoughts (obsessions) and ritualistic behaviors (compulsions) designed to fend off those thoughts interfere significantly with an individual's functioning.* Anxiety plays a role in this disorder because the obsessive thoughts typically produce anxiety, and the compulsive behaviors are performed to reduce it. In OCD, these obsessions and compulsions are intense, frequent, and experienced as irrational and excessive. Attempts to cope with the obsessive thoughts by trying to suppress or ignore them are of little or no benefit. In fact (as discussed in the Consciousness chapter), thought suppression can backfire, increasing the frequency and intensity of the obsessive thoughts (Wegner, 1989; Wenzlaff & Wegner, 2000). Despite anxiety's role, *DSM–5* classifies OCD separately from anxiety disorders, because researchers believe that this disorder has a distinct cause and is maintained via different neural circuitry in the brain than the anxiety disorders.

Although 28% of adults in the United States report experiencing obsessions or compulsions at some point in their lives (Ruscio et al., 2010), only 2% will develop actual OCD (Kessler, Berglund, et al., 2005). Similar to anxiety disorders, rates of OCD are higher among women than men (Kessler et al., 2012). Compulsive behavior can vary considerably in intensity and frequency. For example, fear of contamination may lead to 15 minutes of hand washing in some individuals with OCD, whereas others may need to spend hours with disinfectants and extremely hot water, scrubbing their hands until they bleed.

The obsessions that plague individuals with OCD typically derive from concerns that could pose a real threat (such as contamination or disease), which supports preparedness theory. Thinking repeatedly about whether we've left a stove burner on when we leave the house makes sense, after all, if we want to return to a house that is not "well done." The concept of preparedness places OCD in the same evolutionary context as phobias (Szechtman & Woody, 2006). However, as with phobias, fears that may have served an evolutionary purpose become distorted and maladaptive.

Researchers have not determined the biological mechanisms contributing to OCD (Friedlander & Desrocher, 2006), but one hypothesis implicates the caudate nucleus of the brain, a portion of the basal ganglia (discussed in the Neuroscience and Behavior chapter) known to be involved in the initiation of intentional actions (Rapoport, 1990). Drugs that increase the activity of the neurotransmitter serotonin in the brain can inhibit the activity of the caudate nucleus and relieve some of the symptoms of obsessive-compulsive disorder (Hansen et al., 2002). However, this finding does not indicate that overactivity of the caudate nucleus is the cause of OCD. It could also be an effect of the disorder: People with OCD often respond favorably to psychotherapy and show a corresponding reduction in activity in the caudate nucleus (Baxter et al., 1992).

obsessive-compulsive disorder (OCD) A disorder in which repetitive, intrusive thoughts (obsessions) and ritualistic behaviors (compulsions) designed to fend off those thoughts interfere significantly with an individual's functioning.

Howie Mandel is a successful comedian, but his struggle with OCD is no laughing matter. Like approximately 2% of people in the United States, Mandel struggles with extreme fears of being contaminated by germs and engages in repeated checking and cleaning behaviors that often interfere with his daily life. He has spoken publicly about his struggles with OCD and about the importance of seeking effective treatment for this condition. Charles Sykes/AP Images

BUILD TO THE OUTCOMES

1. What is obsessive-compulsive disorder (OCD)?

2. How effective is willful effort in curing OCD?

3. What factors may contribute to OCD?

Posttraumatic Stress Disorder: Distress and Avoidance After a Trauma

posttraumatic stress disorder (PTSD) A disorder characterized by chronic physiological arousal, recurrent unwanted thoughts or images of the trauma, and avoidance of things that call the traumatic event to mind.

The traumatic events of war leave many debilitated by PTSD. But PTSD does not leave any visible wounds, so it can be difficult to diagnose with certainty. Because of this, the Pentagon has decided that psychological casualties of war are not eligible for the Purple Heart—the hallowed medal given to those wounded or killed in action (Alvarez & Eckholm, 2009).
Jim Barber/Shutterstock

Figure 14.3 HIPPOCAMPAL VOLUMES OF VIETNAM VETERANS AND THEIR IDENTICAL TWINS Average hippocampal volumes for four groups of participants: (1) combat-exposed veterans who developed PTSD; (2) their combat-unexposed twins with no PTSD themselves; (3) combat-exposed veterans who never developed PTSD; and (4) their unexposed twins, also with no PTSD. Smaller hippocampal volumes were found for both the combat-exposed veterans with PTSD (group 1) and their twins (group 2), in contrast to veterans without PTSD (group 3) and their twins (group 4). This pattern of findings suggests that a smaller hippocampus may make some people susceptible to develop PTSD (Gilbertson et al., 2002).

Psychological reactions to traumatic or stressful events can lead to stressor-related disorders. For example, a person who lives through a terrifying and uncontrollable experience may develop **posttraumatic stress disorder (PTSD)**, *a disorder characterized by chronic physiological arousal, recurrent unwanted thoughts or images of the trauma, and avoidance of things that call the traumatic event to mind.*

Psychological disorders following exposure to traumatic events are perhaps nowhere more apparent than in war. Many soldiers returning from combat experience symptoms of PTSD, including flashbacks of battle, exaggerated anxiety and startle reactions. Most of these symptoms are normal, appropriate responses to horrifying events, and for most people, the symptoms subside with time. In PTSD, however, the symptoms can last much longer. For example, approximately 12% of U.S. veterans of recent operations in Iraq met the criteria for PTSD after their deployment; and the observed rates of PTSD are even higher in non-Western and developing countries (Keane, Marshall, & Taft, 2006). The effects of PTSD are now recognized not only among victims, witnesses, and perpetrators of war but also among ordinary people who are traumatized by terrible events in civilian life. About 7% of Americans will suffer from PTSD at some point in their lives (Kessler, Berglund, et al., 2005).

Not everyone who is exposed to a traumatic event develops PTSD, suggesting that people differ in their degree of sensitivity to trauma. Research using brain imaging techniques has found that those with PTSD show heightened activity in the amygdala (a region associated with the evaluation of threatening information and fear conditioning), decreased activity in the medial prefrontal cortex (a region important in the extinction of fear conditioning), and a smaller-size hippocampus (the part of the brain most linked with memory, as described in the Neuroscience and Behavior and Memory chapters; Shin, Rauch, & Pitman, 2006). Of course, an important question is whether people whose brains have these characteristics are at greater risk for PTSD if traumatized, or if these characteristics are the consequences of trauma in some people. For instance, does reduced hippocampal volume reflect a preexisting condition that makes the brain sensitive to stress? Or does the traumatic stress itself somehow kill hippocampal cells? One important study suggests that although a group of combat veterans with PTSD showed reduced hippocampal volume, so did the identical (monozygotic) twins of those men (see **FIGURE 14.3**), even though

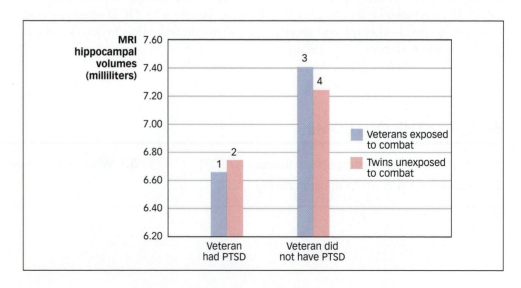

the twins had never had any combat exposure or developed PTSD (Gilbertson et al., 2002). This suggests that the veterans' reduced hippocampal volumes weren't caused by the combat exposure; instead, both these veterans and their twin brothers might have had a smaller hippocampus to begin with, a preexisting condition that made them susceptible to developing PTSD when they were later exposed to trauma.

BUILD TO THE OUTCOMES

1. What is posttraumatic stress disorder (PTSD)?

2. How might brain structure and functioning be related to susceptibility to PTSD?

Depressive and Bipolar Disorders: Extreme Highs and Lows

You're probably in a mood right now. Maybe you're happy that it's almost time to get a snack or saddened by something you heard from a friend. As you learned in the Emotion and Motivation chapter, moods are relatively long-lasting, nonspecific emotional states—and *nonspecific* means we often may have no idea what has caused a mood. Changing moods lend variety to our experiences, like different-colored lights shining on the stage as we play out our lives. However, for people like Robin Williams and others with mood disorders, moods can become so intense that they are pulled or pushed into life-threatening actions. **Mood disorders** are *mental disorders that have mood disturbance as their predominant feature*.

LEARNING OUTCOMES

- Describe the symptoms of mood disorders, including depressive and bipolar disorders.

- Identify genetic and environmental factors may be an influence in mood disorders.

mood disorders Mental disorders that have mood disturbance as their predominant feature.

Depressive Disorders

Everyone feels sad, pessimistic, and unmotivated from time to time. For most people, these periods are relatively short lived and mild, but depression is much more than typical sadness. Consider Mark, a 34-year-old man who visited his primary-care physician complaining of difficulties falling asleep and staying asleep that left him

The Blue Devils—!! George Cruikshank (1792–1878) portrayed a depressed man tormented by demons suggesting methods of suicide, harassing him as bill collectors, and forming a funeral procession. *"The Blue Devils—!!"* Published by Hannah Humphrey, 10th January 1823 (Coloured Engraving)/Cruikshank, George (1792–1878)/ Indivision Charmet/Bibliotheque Nationale, Paris, France/Bridgeman Images

major depressive disorder (or unipolar depression) A disorder characterized by a severely depressed mood and/or inability to experience pleasure that lasts 2 or more weeks and is accompanied by feelings of worthlessness, lethargy, and sleep and appetite disturbance.

seasonal affective disorder (SAD) Recurrent depressive episodes in a seasonal pattern.

Postpartum depression can cause new mothers to feel extreme sadness, guilt, and disconnection, and even to experience serious thoughts of suicide. The actress Brooke Shields wrote about her experience with postpartum depression in a popular book on this condition.
Nancy Kaszerman/ZUMA Press/Newscom

Seasonal affective disorder is not merely having the blues because of the weather. It appears to be due to reduced exposure to light in the winter months. Ragnar Th Sigurdsson/Arctic Images/Alamy; Andrey Arkusha/Shutterstock

chronically tired, so much so that he feared that maybe he had some kind of medical problem. He no longer had the energy to exercise and had gained 10 pounds over 6 months. He had lost all interest in going out with his friends. Nothing he normally enjoyed, even sexual activity, gave him pleasure anymore; he had trouble concentrating and was forgetful, irritable, impatient, and frustrated. Mark's change in mood and behavior, and the sense of hopelessness and weariness he felt, go far beyond normal sadness. Instead, depressive disorders fall outside the range of socially or culturally expected responses.

Major depressive disorder (or unipolar depression), which we refer to here simply as "depression," is characterized by *a severely depressed mood and/or inability to experience pleasure that lasts 2 or more weeks and is accompanied by feelings of worthlessness, lethargy, and sleep and appetite disturbance.* Some people experience *recurrent depressive episodes in a seasonal pattern* that is commonly known as **seasonal affective disorder (SAD)**. In most cases, SAD episodes begin in fall or winter and remit in spring, in a pattern that is due to reduced levels of light over the colder seasons (Westrin & Lam, 2007). Nevertheless, recurrent summer depressive episodes have been reported. A winter-related pattern of depression appears to be more prevalent in higher latitudes.

Approximately 18% of people in the United States meet the criteria for depression at some point in their lives (Kessler et al., 2012). On average, major depression lasts about 12 weeks (Eaton et al., 2008). However, without treatment, approximately 80% of individuals will experience at least one recurrence of the disorder (Judd, 1997; Mueller et al., 1999).

Similar to anxiety disorders, the rate of depression is much higher in women (22%) than in men (14%; Kessler et al., 2012). Socioeconomic standing has been invoked as an explanation for women's heightened risk: Their incomes are lower than those of men, and poverty could cause depression. Sex differences in hormones are another possibility: Estrogen, androgen, and progesterone influence depression; some women experience *postpartum depression* (depression following childbirth) due to changing hormone balances. It is also possible that the higher rate of depression in women reflects their greater willingness to face their depression and seek out help, leading to higher rates of diagnosis (Nolen-Hoeksema, 2008).

Neurotransmitters Play a Role, and So Does Stress

Beginning in the 1950s, researchers noticed that drugs that increased levels of the neurotransmitters norepinephrine and serotonin could sometimes reduce depression. This suggested that depression might be caused by depletion of these neurotransmitters (Schildkraut, 1965), leading to the development and widespread use of popular prescription drugs such as Prozac and Zoloft, which increase the availability of serotonin in the brain. However, reduced levels of these neurotransmitters cannot be the whole story regarding the causes of depression. For example, some studies have found *increases* in norepinephrine activity among depressed individuals (Thase & Howland, 1995). Moreover, even though antidepressant medications change neurochemical transmission in less than a day, they typically take at least 2 weeks to relieve depressive symptoms. In many cases, they are not effective in decreasing depressive symptoms. A biochemical model of depression has yet to be developed that accounts for all the evidence.

Newer biological models of depression have tried to understand depression using a diathesis–stress framework. For instance, stressful life events are much more likely to lead to depression among those with a certain genetic trait (vulnerability) related to the activity of the neurotransmitter serotonin (Caspi et al., 2003), a finding showing that nature and nurture interact to influence brain structure, function, and chemistry in depression (see **FIGURE 14.4**).

Negative Thoughts Contribute to Depression

If optimists see the world through rose-colored glasses, people who suffer from depression tend to view the world through dark gray lenses. Their negative cognitive style is remarkably consistent and, some argue, begins in childhood with experiences that create a pattern of negative self thoughts (Blatt & Homann, 1992; Gibb, Alloy, & Tierney, 2001). One of the first theorists to emphasize the role of thought in depression, Aaron T. Beck (1967), noted that his depressed patients distorted perceptions of their experiences and embraced dysfunctional attitudes that promoted and maintained negative mood states. His observations led him to develop a *cognitive model of depression*, which states that biases in how information is attended to, processed, and remembered lead to and maintain depression.

Elaborating on this initial idea, researchers proposed a theory of depression that emphasizes the role of people's negative inferences about the causes of their experiences (Abramson, Seligman, & Teasdale, 1978). **Helplessness theory**, which is a part of the cognitive model of depression, maintains that *individuals who are prone to depression automatically attribute negative experiences to causes that are internal (i.e., their own fault), stable (i.e., unlikely to change), and global (i.e., widespread).* For example, a student at risk for depression might view a bad grade on a math test as a sign of low intelligence (internal) that will never change (stable) and that will lead to failure

The cognitive model of depression is based on approaches to thinking developed by the Stoic philosophers of ancient Greece and Rome. Epictetus's famous quote, "Men are disturbed not by things, but by the principles and notions which they form concerning things," is commonly cited by cognitive theorists as a guiding principle of the cognitive model of depression. Mary Evans Picture Library/Alamy

helplessness theory The idea that individuals who are prone to depression automatically attribute negative experiences to causes that are internal (i.e., their own fault), stable (i.e., unlikely to change), and global (i.e., widespread).

Figure 14.4 GENE × ENVIRONMENT INTERACTIONS IN DEPRESSION The serotonin transporter gene comes in two variants, or *alleles*: a short allele and a long allele that is associated with more efficient serotonergic function. Stressful life experiences, such as maltreatment, are much more likely to lead to later depression in people who have inherited one, or especially two, copies of the short allele, compared with people who have inherited two copies of the long allele.

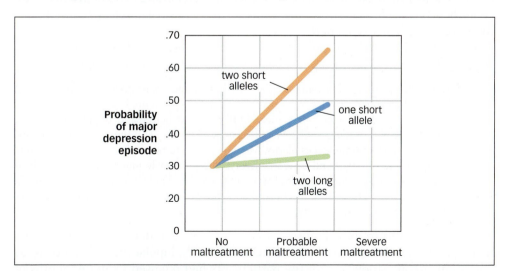

in all his or her future endeavors (global). In contrast, a student without this tendency might have the opposite response, attributing the grade to something external (poor teaching), unstable (a missed study session), and/or specific (boring subject).

More recent research suggests that people with depression may have biases that lead them to interpret neutral information negatively—seeing the world through gray glasses—coupled with better recall of negative information and trouble turning their attention away from negative information (Gotlib & Joormann, 2010). For example, a student at risk for depression who gets a bad grade on a test might interpret a well-intentioned comment from the teacher ("Good job on the test") negatively ("She's being sarcastic!"); have trouble forgetting about both the test score and the perceived negative comment; and have better memory about this test in the future ("Sure, I did well on my English exam, but don't forget about that bad math test last month"). These cognitive biases may reflect differences in brain structure and function. For instance, people with depression show abnormalities in parts of the brain involved in attention and memory, especially when presented with negative information (Disner et al., 2011). Although we don't fully understand the causes of depression, pieces of the puzzle are being discovered and put together as you read this.

Bipolar Disorder

bipolar disorder A condition characterized by cycles of abnormal, persistent high mood (mania) and low mood (depression).

Julie, a 20-year-old college sophomore, had gone 5 days without sleep and expressed bizarre thoughts and ideas. She proclaimed to friends that she did not menstruate because she was "of a third sex, a gender above the two human sexes." She claimed to be a "superwoman," capable of avoiding human sexuality and yet still able to give birth. She felt that she could save the world from nuclear destruction, and began to campaign for an elected position in the U.S. government (even though no elections were scheduled at that time). Worried that she would forget some of her thoughts, she left hundreds of notes about her ideas and activities everywhere, including on the walls and furniture of her dormitory room (Vitkus, 1999).

In addition to her manic episodes, Julie had a history of depression. The diagnostic label for this constellation of symptoms is **bipolar disorder**, *a condition characterized by cycles of abnormal, persistent high mood (mania) and low mood (depression).* The depressive phase of bipolar disorder is often clinically indistinguishable from major depression (Johnson, Cuellar, & Miller, 2009). In the manic phase, which must last at least 1 week to meet *DSM* requirements, mood can be elevated, expansive, or irritable. Other prominent symptoms include grandiosity, decreased need for sleep, talkativeness, racing thoughts, distractibility, and reckless behavior (such as compulsive gambling, sexual indiscretions, and unrestrained spending sprees). Psychotic features such as hallucinations (erroneous perceptions) and delusions (erroneous beliefs) may be present, so the disorder can be misdiagnosed as schizophrenia (described in a later section of this chapter).

Here's how Kay Redfield Jamison (1995, p. 67) described her own experience with bipolar disorder in *An Unquiet Mind: A Memoir of Moods and Madness.*

> There is a particular kind of pain, elation, loneliness, and terror involved in this kind of madness. When you're high it's tremendous. The ideas and feelings are fast and frequent like shooting stars, and you follow them until you find better and brighter ones. . . . But, somewhere, this changes. The fast ideas are far too fast, and there are far too many; overwhelming confusion replaces clarity. Memory goes. Humor and absorption on friends' faces are replaced by fear and concern. Everything previously moving with the grain is now against—you are irritable, angry, frightened, uncontrollable, and enmeshed totally in the blackest caves of the mind. You never knew those caves were there. It will never end, for madness carves its own reality.

The psychologist Kay Redfield Jamison has written several best-selling books about her own struggles with bipolar disorder. Cannarsa Basso/Luzphoto/Redux

The lifetime risk for bipolar disorder is about 2.5% and does not differ between men and women (Kessler et al., 2012). Unfortunately, bipolar disorder tends to be persistent. In one study, 24% of the participants had relapsed within 6 months of recovery from an episode, and 77% had at least one new episode within 4 years of recovery (Coryell et al., 1995).

Some researchers have suggested that people with psychotic and mood (especially bipolar) disorders have higher creativity and intellectual ability (Andreasen, 2011). In bipolar disorder, this suggestion goes, before the mania becomes too pronounced, the energy, grandiosity, and ambition that it supplies may help people achieve great things. Notable individuals thought to have had the disorder include Isaac Newton, Vincent van Gogh, Abraham Lincoln, Ernest Hemingway, Winston Churchill, and Theodore Roosevelt.

Genetics and Life Situation Play a Role

Like most other mental disorders, bipolar disorder likely arises from the interaction of multiple genes; however, these genes have been difficult to identify. Adding to the complexity, there also is evidence that common genetic risk factors are associated with bipolar disorder and schizophrenia, as well as major depression, autism spectrum disorder, and attention-deficit/hyperactivity disorder. These disorders share overlapping symptoms such as problems with mood regulation, cognitive impairments, and social withdrawal (Cross-Disorder Group of the Psychiatric Genomics Consortium, 2013). Findings like these are exciting because they help us begin to understand why we see similar symptoms in people with what we previously thought were unrelated disorders. Although some genetic links have been made, we currently lack an understanding of how different biological factors work together to cause the symptoms observed in bipolar depression and other disorders.

There is growing evidence that the epigenetic changes you learned about in the Neuroscience and Behavior chapter can help to explain how genetic risk factors influence the development of bipolar and related disorders. Remember how rat pups whose moms spent less time licking and grooming them experienced epigenetic changes that led to a poorer stress response? Epigenetic effects also seem to occur in humans who develop symptoms of mental disorders. For instance, studies examining monozygotic twin pairs (identical twins, who share 100% of their DNA) in which one develops bipolar disorder or schizophrenia and one doesn't, reveal significant epigenetic differences between the two, particularly at genetic locations known to be important in brain development and the occurrence of bipolar disorders and schizophrenia (Dempster et al., 2011; Labrie, Pai, & Petronis, 2012).

Stressful life experiences often precede manic and depressive episodes (Johnson, Cuellar, et al., 2008). One study found that severely stressed individuals took an average of three times longer to recover from an episode than did individuals not affected by stress (Johnson & Miller, 1997). Personality characteristics such as neuroticism and conscientiousness also predict increases in bipolar symptoms over time (Lozano & Johnson, 2001). Finally, people living with family members who express hostility and criticism are more likely to relapse than people with supportive families (Miklowitz & Johnson, 2006); this is true not just of those with bipolar disorder, but across a wide range of mental disorders (Hooley, 2007).

BUILD TO THE OUTCOMES

1. What is a mood disorder?

2. What is the difference between depression and sadness?

3. What are the types of depressive disorders?

4. What factors may explain why women experience higher rates of depression than men?

5. How does the diathesis–stress framework help explain depression?

6. What is helplessness theory?

7. What is bipolar disorder?

8. Why is bipolar disorder sometimes misdiagnosed as schizophrenia?

9. How does stress relate to manic-depressive episodes?

Schizophrenia and Other Psychotic Disorders: Losing the Grasp on Reality

LEARNING OUTCOMES

- Compare the negative, positive, and cognitive symptoms of schizophrenia.

- Describe the biological factors contributing to schizophrenia.

- Explain the evidence for the influence of environmental factors.

Margaret, a 39-year-old mother, believed that God was punishing her for marrying a man she did not love and bringing two children into the world. As her punishment, God had made her and her children immortal so that they would have to suffer in their unhappy home life forever—a realization that came to her one evening when she was washing dishes and saw a fork lying across a knife in the shape of a cross. A local television station was rerunning old episodes of a sitcom in which the main characters often argue and shout at each other; Margaret saw this as a sign from God that her own marital conflict would go on forever. She believed (falsely) that the pupils of her children's eyes were fixed in size and would neither dilate nor constrict—a sign of their immortality (Oltmanns et al., 1991). Margaret was suffering from the best-known, most widely studied psychotic disorder: schizophrenia. Schizophrenia is one of the most mystifying and devastating of all the mental disorders. Many people with this disorder experience a lifetime of suffering and impairment (but see Other Voices: Successful and Schizophrenic for a discussion of the fact that many with this disorder have very successful careers and fulfilling lives).

Successful and Schizophrenic

Elyn R. Saks is a law professor at the University of Southern California and the author of the memoir *The Center Cannot Hold: My Journey Through Madness.* Photo by Mikel Healey, Courtesy Elyn R. Saks

This chapter describes what we know about the characteristics and causes of mental disorders, and the next chapter describes how these disorders are commonly treated. For some of the more severe disorders, such as schizophrenia, the picture does not look good. People diagnosed with schizophrenia often are informed that it is a lifelong condition, and although current treatments show some effectiveness in decreasing the delusional thinking and hallucinations often present in those with schizophrenia, people with this disorder often are unable to hold down a full-time job, maintain healthy relationships, or achieve a high quality of life.

Elyn Saks is one such person. She received a diagnosis of schizophrenia and was informed of this prognosis. She described what happened next in a longer version of the following article, which appeared in the *New York Times.*

Thirty years ago, I was given a diagnosis of schizophrenia. My prognosis was "grave": I would never live independently, hold a job, find a loving partner, get married. My home would be a board-and-care facility, my days spent watching TV in a day room with other people debilitated by mental illness. . . .

Then I made a decision. I would write the narrative of my life. Today I am a chaired professor at the University of Southern California Gould School of Law. I have an adjunct appointment in the department of psychiatry at the medical school of the University of California, San Diego. The MacArthur Foundation gave me a genius grant.

Although I fought my diagnosis for many years, I came to accept that I have schizophrenia and will be in treatment the rest of my life. . . . What I refused to accept was my prognosis.

Conventional psychiatric thinking and its diagnostic categories say that people like me don't exist. Either I don't have schizophrenia (please tell that to the delusions crowding my mind), or I couldn't have accomplished what I have (please tell that to U.S.C.'s committee on faculty affairs). But I do, and I have. And I have undertaken research with colleagues at U.S.C. and U.C.L.A. to show that I am not alone. There are others with schizophrenia and such active symptoms as delusions and hallucinations who have significant academic and professional achievements.

Over the last few years, my colleagues . . . and I have gathered 20 research subjects with high-functioning schizophrenia in Los Angeles. They suffered from symptoms like mild delusions or hallucinatory behavior. Their average age was 40. Half were male, half female, and more than half were minorities. All had high school diplomas, and a majority either had or were working toward college or graduate degrees. They were graduate students, managers, technicians and professionals, including a doctor, lawyer, psychologist and chief executive of a nonprofit group. At the same time, most were unmarried and childless, which is consistent with their diagnoses. . . . More than three-quarters had been hospitalized between two and five times because of their illness, while three had never been admitted.

How had these people with schizophrenia managed to succeed in their studies and at such high-level jobs?

Symptoms and Types of Schizophrenia

Schizophrenia is *a psychotic disorder (psychosis is a break from reality) characterized by the profound disruption of basic psychological processes; a distorted perception of reality; altered or blunted emotion; and disturbances in thought, motivation, and behavior.* Traditionally, schizophrenia was regarded primarily as a disturbance of thought and perception, in which the sense of reality becomes severely distorted and confused. However, this condition is now understood to take different forms affecting a wide range of functions, with symptoms that are often separated into *positive, negative,* and *cognitive symptoms.* To be diagnosed with schizophrenia, the *DSM–5* requires that at least two symptoms emerge during a period of at least a month, and that signs of the disorder persist for at least 6 months.

Positive symptoms of schizophrenia include *thoughts and behaviors, such as delusions and hallucinations, not seen in those without the disorder:*

- **Hallucinations** are *false perceptual experiences that have a compelling sense of being real despite the absence of external stimulation.* These can include hearing, seeing, smelling, or having a tactile sensation of things that are not there. Among people with schizophrenia, some 65% report hearing voices repeatedly

schizophrenia A psychotic disorder characterized by the profound disruption of basic psychological processes; a distorted perception of reality; altered or blunted emotion; and disturbances in thought, motivation, and behavior.

positive symptoms Thoughts and behaviors, such as delusions and hallucinations, present in schizophrenia but not seen in those without the disorder.

hallucination A false perceptual experience that has a compelling sense of being real despite the absence of external stimulation.

We learned that, in addition to medication and therapy, all the participants had developed techniques to keep their schizophrenia at bay. For some, these techniques were cognitive. An educator with a master's degree said he had learned to face his hallucinations and ask, "What's the evidence for that? Or is it just a perception problem?" Another participant said, "I hear derogatory voices all the time. . . . You just gotta blow them off." . . .

Other techniques that our participants cited included controlling sensory inputs. For some, this meant keeping their living space simple (bare walls, no TV, only quiet music), while for others, it meant distracting music. "I'll listen to loud music if I don't want to hear things," said a participant who is a certified nurse's assistant. Still others mentioned exercise, a healthy diet, avoiding alcohol and getting enough sleep. . . .

One of the most frequently mentioned techniques that helped our research participants manage their symptoms was work. "Work has been an important part of who I am," said an educator in our group. "When you become useful to an organization and feel respected in that organization, there's a certain value in belonging there." This person works on the weekends too because of "the distraction factor." In other words, by engaging in work, the crazy stuff often recedes to the sidelines. . . .

That is why it is so distressing when doctors tell their patients not to expect or pursue fulfilling careers. Far too often, the conventional psychiatric approach to mental illness is to see clusters of symptoms that characterize people. Accordingly, many psychiatrists hold the view that treating symptoms with medication is treating mental illness. But this fails to take into account individuals' strengths and capabilities, leading mental health professionals to underestimate what their patients can hope to achieve in the world. . . . A recent New York Times Magazine article described a new company that hires high-functioning adults with autism, taking advantage of their unusual memory skills and attention to detail. . . .

An approach that looks for individual strengths, in addition to considering symptoms, could help dispel the pessimism surrounding mental illness. Finding "the wellness within the illness," as one person with schizophrenia said, should be a therapeutic goal. Doctors should urge their patients to develop relationships and engage in meaningful work. They should encourage patients to find their own repertory of techniques to manage their symptoms and aim for a quality of life as they define it. And they should provide patients with the resources—therapy, medication and support—to make these things happen.

Elyn Saks's story is amazing and inspiring. It also is quite unusual. How should we incorporate stories like hers and the people in the research study she described? Are these people outliers—simply a carefully selected collection of people who had unusually favorable outcomes? (Given that Los Angeles is such a large city, it is reasonable to think one could amass a small sample of such cases.) Or has Professor Saks touched on an important limitation to the way in which the field currently conceptualizes, classifies, and treats mental disorders? Do we focus too much on what is wrong and on how professionalized health care can treat the pathology and not enough on what inherent strengths people have that can help them overcome their challenges, function at a high level, and achieve a high quality of life? These are all questions that are testable with the methods of psychological science, and the answers may help to improve the lives of many people.

delusion A false belief, often bizarre and grandiose, that is maintained in spite of its irrationality.

disorganized speech A severe disruption of verbal communication in which ideas shift rapidly and incoherently among unrelated topics.

grossly disorganized behavior Behavior that is inappropriate for the situation or ineffective in attaining goals, often with specific motor disturbances.

negative symptoms Deficits in or disruptions of normal emotions and behaviors.

cognitive symptoms Deficits in cognitive abilities, specifically executive functioning, attention, and working memory, present in those with schizophrenia.

(Frith & Fletcher, 1995). The voices typically command, scold, suggest bizarre actions, or offer snide comments.

- **Delusions** are *false beliefs, often bizarre and grandiose, that are maintained in spite of their irrationality*. For example, an individual with schizophrenia may believe that he or she is Jesus Christ, Napoleon, Joan of Arc, or some other well-known person. Delusions of persecution are also common. Some individuals believe that the CIA, demons, extraterrestrials, or other malevolent forces are conspiring to harm them or control their minds. Given that people with schizophrenia have little or no insight into their disordered perceptual and thought processes (Karow et al., 2007), these unusual beliefs and theories may represent the patients' attempt to make sense of the tormenting delusions (Roberts, 1991).

- **Disorganized speech** is *a severe disruption of verbal communication in which ideas shift rapidly and incoherently among unrelated topics*. The abnormal speech patterns in schizophrenia reflect difficulties in organizing thoughts and focusing attention. For example, asked by her doctor, "Can you tell me the name of this place?" one patient with schizophrenia responded, "I have not been a drinker for 16 years. I am taking a mental rest after a 'carter' assignment of 'quill.' You know, a 'penwrap.' I had contracts with Warner Brothers Studios and Eugene broke phonograph records but Mike protested" (Carson et al., 2000, p. 474).

- **Grossly disorganized behavior** is *behavior that is inappropriate for the situation or ineffective in attaining goals, often with specific motor disturbances*. An individual might exhibit constant childlike silliness, improper sexual behavior (such as masturbating in public), disheveled appearance, or loud shouting or swearing. Specific motor disturbances might include strange movements, rigid posturing, odd mannerisms, bizarre grimacing, or hyperactivity.

Negative symptoms of schizophrenia are *deficits in or disruptions of normal emotions and behaviors*. They include emotional and social withdrawal; apathy; poverty of speech; and other indications of the absence or insufficiency of normal behavior, motivation, and emotion. These symptoms refer to things missing in people with schizophrenia.

Cognitive symptoms of schizophrenia are *deficits in cognitive abilities, specifically in executive functioning, attention, and working memory*. These are the least noticeable symptoms because they are much less bizarre and public than the positive and negative symptoms. However, these cognitive deficits often play a large role in preventing people with schizophrenia from achieving a high level of functioning, such as maintaining friendships and holding down a job (Green et al., 2000).

Schizophrenia occurs in about 1% of the population (Jablensky, 1997) and is slightly more common in men than in women (McGrath et al., 2008). Recent studies suggest that schizophrenia rarely develops before early adolescence (Rapoport et al., 2009). Despite its relatively low frequency, schizophrenia is the primary diagnosis for nearly 40% of all admissions to state and county mental hospitals (Rosenstein, Milazzo-Sayre, & Manderscheid, 1990). The disproportionate rate of hospitalization for schizophrenia is a testament to the devastation it causes in people's lives.

Biological Factors

Over the years, accumulating evidence for the role of biology in schizophrenia has come from studies of genetic factors, biochemical factors, and neuroanatomy. Family studies indicate that the closer a person's genetic relatedness to a person with

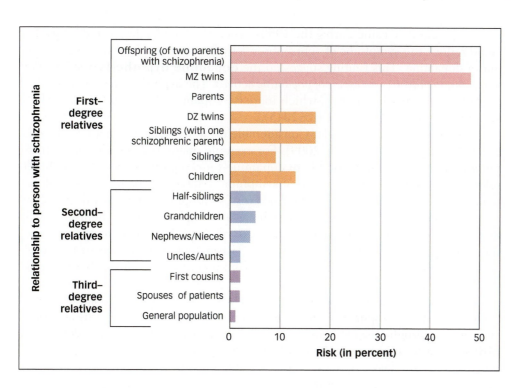

Figure 14.5 AVERAGE RISK OF DEVELOPING SCHIZOPHRENIA The risk of schizophrenia among biological relatives is greater for those with greater degrees of relatedness. An identical (MZ) twin of a person with schizophrenia has a 48% risk of developing schizophrenia, for example. Offspring of two parents with schizophrenia have a 46% risk of developing this disorder (data from Gottesman, 1991).

schizophrenia, the greater the likelihood of developing the disorder (Gottesman, 1991), as shown in **FIGURE 14.5**. Although genetics clearly have a strong predisposing role in schizophrenia, considerable evidence suggests that environmental factors also play a role (Jurewicz, Owen, & O'Donovan, 2001; Thaker, 2002; Torrey et al., 1994). For example, because approximately 70% of identical twins share the same prenatal blood supply, toxins in the mother's blood could contribute to the high concordance rate. More recent studies are contributing to a better understanding of how environmental stressors can trigger epigenetic changes that increase susceptibility to this disorder.

Those suffering from schizophrenia often experience hallucinations and delusions, unable to determine what is real and what their own minds have created. The experience of John Nash, a Nobel Prize–winning economist with schizophrenia, was depicted in the book and movie *A Beautiful Mind.* Dreamworks/Universal/The Kobal Collection/Eli Reed

dopamine hypothesis The idea that schizophrenia involves an excess of dopamine activity.

A major advance came during the 1950s, when researchers discovered drugs that could reduce the symptoms of schizophrenia by lowering levels of the neurotransmitter dopamine. This finding suggested the **dopamine hypothesis**, *the idea that schizophrenia involves an excess of dopamine activity.* The hypothesis has been invoked to explain why amphetamines, which increase dopamine levels, often exacerbate symptoms of schizophrenia (Harro, 2015).

If only things were so simple. Considerable evidence suggests that this hypothesis is inadequate (Moncrieff, 2009). For example, many individuals with schizophrenia do not respond favorably to dopamine-blocking drugs, and those who do seldom show a complete remission of symptoms. Moreover, the drugs block dopamine receptors very rapidly, yet individuals with schizophrenia typically do not show a beneficial response for weeks. Research has also implicated other neurotransmitters in schizophrenia, suggesting that the disorder may involve a complex interaction among a host of different biochemicals (Risman et al., 2008; Sawa & Snyder, 2002). In sum, the precise role of neurotransmitters in schizophrenia has yet to be determined.

Finally, neuroimaging studies provide evidence of a variety of brain abnormalities associated with schizophrenia. One study examined changes in the brains of adolescents with schizophrenia (Thompson et al., 2001). By superimposing the adolescents' MRI scans onto an image of a standardized brain, the researchers were able to detect progressive tissue loss beginning in the parietal lobe and eventually encompassing much of the brain (see **FIGURE 14.6**). All adolescents lose some gray matter over time in a kind of normal "pruning" of the brain, but in those developing schizophrenia, the loss was dramatic enough to seem pathological.

Figure 14.6 BRAIN TISSUE LOSS IN ADOLESCENT SCHIZOPHRENIA MRI scan composites reveal brain tissue loss in adolescents diagnosed with schizophrenia. Normal brains show minimal loss due to "pruning" (*top*). By contrast, scans of adolescents who recently developed schizophrenia ("early deficit" group) reveal loss in the parietal areas (*middle*); individuals at this stage may experience symptoms such as hallucinations or bizarre thoughts. Scans 5 years later reveal extensive tissue loss over much of the cortex (*bottom*); individuals at this stage are likely to suffer from delusions, disorganized speech and behavior, and negative symptoms such as social withdrawal (Thompson et al., 2001). Thompson et al. (2001), National Academy of Sciences, USA

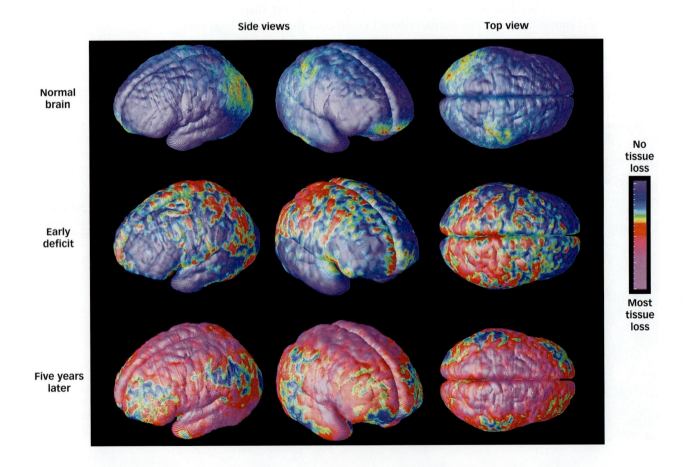

Side views   Top view

Normal brain

Early deficit

Five years later

No tissue loss

Most tissue loss

Social/Psychological Factors

With all these potential biological contributors to schizophrenia, you might think there would be few psychological or social causes of this disorder. However, several studies suggest that family environment plays a role in the development of and recovery from the condition. One large-scale study compared the risk of schizophrenia in children adopted into healthy families and those adopted into severely disturbed families (Tienari et al., 2004). (Disturbed families were defined as those with extreme conflict, lack of communication, or chaotic relationships.) Among children whose biological mothers had schizophrenia, the disturbed environment increased their likelihood of developing schizophrenia—an outcome that was not found among children who were also reared in disturbed families but whose biological mothers did *not* have schizophrenia. This finding provides support for the diathesis–stress model described earlier.

BUILD TO THE OUTCOMES

1. What is schizophrenia?
2. What are the positive, negative, and cognitive symptoms of schizophrenia?
3. What is the role of genetics in schizophrenia?
4. How do biochemical factors contribute to schizophrenia?
5. What changes appear in the brains of people with schizophrenia?
6. What environmental factors contribute to schizophrenia?

Disorders of Childhood and Adolescence

Most of the disorders described above can have their onset during childhood, adolescence, or adulthood. In fact, half of all disorders begin by age 14 and three quarters by age 24 (Kessler, Berglund, et al., 2005). But some disorders *always*, by definition, begin in childhood or adolescence, and if they don't, you are never going to have them. These include autism spectrum disorder, attention-deficit/hyperactivity disorder, conduct disorder, intellectual disability (formerly called *mental retardation*), learning disorders, communication disorders, and motor skill disorders, in addition to many others. The first three are among the most common and best known, so we will review them briefly here.

LEARNING OUTCOMES

- Describe the characteristic indications of autism.
- Define the difference between normal problems with inattention and ADHD.
- Explain why it is difficult to pin down the causes of conduct disorder.

Autism Spectrum Disorder

Marco is a 4-year-old child. Although his mother stays home with him all day and tries to talk with him and play with him, he still has not spoken a single word, and he shows little interest in trying. He spends much of his time playing with his toy trains, sometimes sitting for hours staring at spinning train wheels or pushing a single train back and forth, seeming completely in his own world, uninterested in playing with anyone else. Marco's parents have become concerned about his apparent inability to speak, lack of interest in others, and development of some peculiar mannerisms, such as flapping his arms repeatedly for no apparent reason.

Autism spectrum disorder (ASD) is *a condition beginning in early childhood in which a person shows persistent communication deficits as well as restricted and repetitive*

autism spectrum disorder (ASD) A condition beginning in early childhood in which a person shows persistent communication deficits as well as restricted and repetitive patterns of behaviors, interests, or activities.

Temple Grandin, a professor of animal sciences at Colorado State University, is living proof that people with autism spectrum disorder are able to have very successful professional careers.
Vera Anderson/WireImage/Getty Images

patterns of behaviors, interests, or activities. In *DSM–5*, ASD now subsumes multiple disorders that were considered separate in *DSM–IV*: autistic disorder, Asperger's disorder, childhood disintegrative disorder, and pervasive developmental disorder not otherwise specified (i.e., these disorders are no longer recognized in the *DSM*).

The true rate of ASD is difficult to pinpoint, especially given the recent change in diagnostic definition. Estimates from the 1960s indicated that autism was a rare diagnosis, occurring in 4 per 10,000 children. Estimates have been creeping up over time and now stand at approximately 10 to 20 per 10,000 children. If one considers the full range of disorders that now fall under the ASD umbrella in the *DSM–5*, the rate is 60 per 10,000 children (Newschaffer et al., 2007). It is unclear whether this increased rate is due to increased awareness and recognition of ASD, better screening and diagnostic tools, or to some other factor. Boys have higher rates of ASD than do girls by a ratio of about 4:1. Although the causes of ASD are not yet fully understood, a great deal of research has provided no evidence that ASD is caused by vaccinations (Mandy & Lai, 2016).

One current model suggests that ASD can be understood as an impaired capacity for *empathizing*, knowing the mental states of others, combined with a superior ability for *systematizing*, understanding the rules that organize the structure and function of objects (Baron-Cohen & Belmonte, 2005). Consistent with this model, brain imaging studies show that people with autism have decreased activity in regions associated with understanding the minds of others and greater activation in regions

HOT SCIENCE

Optimal Outcome in Autism Spectrum Disorder

When you think of the word autism, what kind of people do you imagine? If the people are adults, can they hold a job? Can they care for themselves? Many people consider autism spectrum disorder (ASD) a lifelong condition entailing significant difficulties and disabilities in their interpersonal, education, and occupational functioning. However, recent studies are helping to change this outlook.

One review suggested that 3 to 25% of children ultimately lose their ASD diagnosis over time (Helt et al., 2008). There are several potential explanations for this change. The most obvious is that some children are misdiagnosed and don't really have ASD. Perhaps they are overly shy, or quiet, or develop speech later than do other children, and this is misinterpreted as ASD. Another possibility is that children who lose their ASD diagnosis had a milder form of the disorder and/or were identified and treated earlier (Moulton et al., 2016).

The possibility of effectively treating ASD was raised in an important

study, in which children with autism were assigned either to an intensive behavioral intervention including over 40 hours per week of one-on-one behavior therapy for 2 years, or to control conditions in which they received fewer than 10 hours per week of treatment (Lovaas, 1987). Amazingly, 47% of children in the intensive behavior therapy condition obtained a normal level of intellectual and educational functioning—passing through a normal first grade class—compared with only 2% of those in the control conditions. Later studies suggested that toddlers with ASD who receive intensive, long-term behavioral treatment show significant improvements in IQ, language, and social functioning (Dawson et al., 2010), and many of these gains persist for years after treatment has ended (Estes et al., 2015).

Given that early detection and treatment can lead to such positive outcomes for those with ASD, should we be screening all young children for ASD so we can catch it early and intervene? This is an area of intense

debate. A recent report concluded that there is insufficient evidence to conclude that the benefits of universal screening outweigh the potential risks of misdiagnosis (Siu & U.S. Preventive Task Force, 2016). However, others argue that, because we have methods of effectively treating ASD in young children, we should screen all children for this disorder, so that we can maximize their chances of optimal outcomes (Dawson, 2016). Researchers and policy makers will be working actively on this issue in the years ahead.

Autism was once viewed as a condition with lifelong impairments. New research suggests that early intervention can help many of those in whom ASD is diagnosed to achieve normal levels of functioning. baona/Vetta/Getty Images

related to basic object perception (Sigman, Spence, & Wang, 2006). At the same time, some people with ASD have remarkable abilities to perceive or remember details or to master symbol systems such as mathematics or music (Happé & Vital, 2009).

Although many people with ASD experience impairments throughout their lives that prevent them from having relationships and holding down a job, others have very successful careers. The renowned behavioral scientist and author Temple Grandin (2006) was diagnosed with autism at age 3, started learning to talk late, and then suffered teasing for odd habits and "nerdy" behavior. Fortunately, she developed ways to cope and found a niche through her special talent—the ability to understand animal behavior (Sacks, 1996). She is now a professor, author, and the central character in an HBO movie based on her life. Temple Grandin's story lets us know that there are happy endings. Overall, those diagnosed with ASD as children have highly variable trajectories, with some achieving normal or better-than-normal functioning and others struggling with profound disorder (see Hot Science: Optimal Outcome in Autism Spectrum Disorder).

Attention-Deficit/Hyperactivity Disorder

Chances are you have had the experience of being distracted during a lecture or while reading one of your *other* textbooks. We all have trouble focusing from time to time. Far beyond normal distraction, **attention-deficit/hyperactivity disorder (ADHD)** is *a persistent pattern of severe problems with inattention and/ or hyperactivity or impulsiveness that cause significant impairments in functioning.* This is quite different from occasional mind wandering or bursts of activity. Children with ADHD show inattention (e.g., persistent problems with sustained attention, organization, memory, following instructions), hyperactivity–impulsiveness (e.g., persistent difficulties with remaining still, waiting for a turn, interrupting others), or both. Most children experience some of these behaviors at some point, but to meet the criteria for ADHD, a child has to have many of these behaviors for at least 6 months in at least two settings (e.g., home and school) to the point where they impair the child's ability to perform at school or get along at home. Approximately 10% of boys and 4% of girls meet criteria for ADHD (Polanczyk et al., 2007).

For a long time, ADHD was thought of as a disorder that affects only children and adolescents and that people "age out" of it. However, we now know that in many instances this disorder persists into adulthood. For example, children with ADHD may struggle with attention and concentration in the classroom, whereas adults may experience the same problems in meetings. Approximately 4% of adults meet the criteria for ADHD; they are more likely to be male, divorced, and unemployed—and most do not receive any treatment for their ADHD (Kessler, Adler, et al., 2006). Unfortunately, most people still think of ADHD as a disorder of childhood and don't realize that adults can suffer from it as well. This could be why so few adults with ADHD receive treatment and why the disorder often wreaks havoc on job performance and relationships.

Because ADHD, like most disorders, is defined by the presence of a wide range of symptoms, it is unlikely that it emerges from one single cause. Some studies suggest a strong genetic influence (Faraone et al., 2005). Brain imaging studies suggest that those with ADHD have smaller brain volumes (Castellanos et al., 2002) as well as abnormalities in brain networks associated with attention and behavioral inhibition (Makris et al., 2009). The good news is that current drug treatments for ADHD are effective and appear to decrease the risk of later psychological and academic problems (Biederman et al., 2009).

attention-deficit/hyperactivity disorder (ADHD) A persistent pattern of severe problems with inattention and/ or hyperactivity or impulsiveness that cause significant impairments in functioning.

Psychologists are attempting to identify the causes of conduct disorder in the hope of being able to decrease the harmful behaviors, such as bullying, that often accompany it. Photoalto/Laurence Mouton/Getty Images

conduct disorder A persistent pattern of deviant behavior involving aggression toward people or animals, destruction of property, deceitfulness or theft, or serious rule violations.

Conduct Disorder

Michael is an 8-year-old boy whose mother brought him into a local clinic because his behavior had been getting progressively out of control, and his parents and teachers were no longer able to control him. At home he routinely bullied his siblings, threw glasses and dishes at family members, and even punched and kicked his parents. Outside of the house, Michael had been getting into trouble for stealing from the local store and yelling at his teacher. Nothing his parents tried seemed to change his behavior.

Conduct disorder is a condition in which a child or adolescent engages in a *persistent pattern of deviant behavior involving aggression to people or animals, destruction of property, deceitfulness or theft, or serious rule violations.* Approximately 9% of people in the United States report a lifetime history of conduct disorder (12% of boys and 7% of girls; Nock et al., 2006).

Meeting the criteria for conduct disorder requires having any 3 of the 15 symptoms of conduct disorder. This means that approximately 32,000 different combinations of symptoms could lead to a diagnosis, which makes those with conduct disorder a pretty diverse group. This diversity makes it difficult to pin down the causes of conduct disorder. Researchers currently are attempting to better understand the pathways through which inherited genetic factors interact with environmental stressors (e.g., childhood adversities) to create characteristics in brain structure and function (e.g., reduced activity in brain regions associated with planning and decision making) that interact with environmental factors (e.g., affiliation with deviant peers) to lead to the behaviors that are characteristic of conduct disorder.

BUILD TO THE OUTCOMES

1. What is autism spectrum disorder (ASD)?
2. What is the relationship between ASD and empathy?
3. What is attention-deficit/hyperactivity disorder (ADHD)?
4. What are the criteria for an ADHD diagnosis?
5. What is conduct disorder?

6. How is it possible that there are 32,000 different combinations of symptoms that could lead to a diagnosis of conduct disorder? What does this say about the population of people who have been given this diagnosis?

Personality Disorders: Extreme Traits and Characteristics

LEARNING OUTCOMES

- Identify the three types of personality disorders.
- Explain the diagnostic signs of APD.

personality disorders Enduring patterns of thinking, feeling, or relating to others or controlling impulses that deviate from cultural expectations and cause distress or impaired functioning.

As discussed in the chapter on Personality, we all have one, and we all differ in our ways of behaving, thinking, and feeling. Sometimes, personality traits can become so extreme that they can be considered mental disorders. **Personality disorders** are *enduring patterns of thinking, feeling, or relating to others or controlling impulses that deviate from cultural expectations and cause distress or impaired functioning.* Personality disorders begin in adolescence or early adulthood and are relatively stable over time.

The *DSM–5* lists 10 specific personality disorders (see **TABLE 14.3**). Personality disorders have been a bit controversial for several reasons. First, critics question whether having a problematic personality is really a disorder. Given that approximately 15% of the U.S. population has a personality disorder according

TABLE 14.3 Clusters of Personality Disorders

Cluster	Personality Disorder	Characteristics
A. Odd/Eccentric	Paranoid	Distrust in others, suspicion that people have sinister motives. Apt to challenge the loyalties of friends and read hostile intentions into others' actions. Prone to anger and aggressive outbursts but otherwise emotionally cold. Often jealous, guarded, secretive, overly serious.
	Schizoid	Extreme introversion and withdrawal from relationships. Prefers to be alone, little interest in others. Humorless, distant, often absorbed with own thoughts and feelings, a daydreamer. Fearful of closeness, with poor social skills, often seen as a "loner."
	Schizotypal	Peculiar or eccentric manners of speaking or dressing. Strange beliefs. "Magical thinking," such as belief in ESP or telepathy. Difficulty forming relationships. May react oddly in conversation, not respond, or talk to self. Speech elaborate or difficult to follow. (Possibly a mild form of schizophrenia.)
B. Dramatic/Erratic	Antisocial	Impoverished moral sense or "conscience." History of deception, crime, legal problems, impulsive and aggressive or violent behavior. Little emotional empathy or remorse for hurting others. Manipulative, careless, callous. At high risk for substance abuse and alcoholism.
	Borderline	Unstable moods and intense, stormy personal relationships. Frequent mood changes and anger, unpredictable impulses. Self-mutilation or suicidal threats or gestures to get attention or manipulate others. Self-image fluctuation and a tendency to see others as "all good" or "all bad."
	Histrionic	Constant attention seeking. Grandiose language, provocative dress, exaggerated illnesses, all to gain attention. Believes that everyone loves them. Emotional, lively, overly dramatic, enthusiastic, and excessively flirtatious. Shallow and labile emotions. "Onstage."
	Narcissistic	Inflated sense of self-importance, absorbed by fantasies of self and success. Exaggerates own achievement, assumes others will recognize they are superior. Good first impressions but poor longer-term relationships. Exploitative of others.
C. Anxious/Inhibited	Avoidant	Socially anxious and uncomfortable unless they are confident of being liked. In contrast with schizoid person, yearns for social contact. Fears criticism and worries about being embarrassed in front of others. Avoids social situations due to fear of rejection.
	Dependent	Submissive, dependent, requiring excessive approval, reassurance, and advice. Clings to people and fears losing them. Lacking self-confidence. Uncomfortable when alone. May be devastated by end of close relationship or suicidal if breakup is threatened.
	Obsessive-compulsive	Conscientious, orderly, perfectionist. Excessive need to do everything "right." Inflexibly high standards and caution can interfere with their productivity. Fear of errors can make them strict and controlling. Poor expression of emotions. (Not the same as obsessive-compulsive disorder.)

Information from *DSM–5* (American Psychiatric Association, 2013).

to the *DSM*–5, perhaps it might be better just to admit that a lot of people can be difficult to interact with and leave it at that. Another question is whether personality problems correspond to "disorders" in that there are distinct *types*, or whether such problems might be better understood as extreme values on trait *dimensions* such as the Big Five traits discussed in the Personality chapter (Trull & Durrett, 2005).

One of the most thoroughly studied of all the personality disorders is **antisocial personality disorder (APD)**, *a pervasive pattern of disregard for and violation of the rights of others that begins in childhood or early adolescence and continues into adulthood.* The terms *sociopath* and *psychopath* describe people

antisocial personality disorder (APD) A pervasive pattern of disregard for and violation of the rights of others that begins in childhood or early adolescence and continues into adulthood.

Ever browse a copy of *Architectural Digest* and wonder who would live in one of those perfect homes? A person with obsessive-compulsive personality disorder might fit right in. This personality disorder (characterized by excessive perfectionism) should not be mistaken, by the way, for obsessive-compulsive disorder—the anxiety disorder in which the person suffers from repeated unwanted thoughts or actions. Takahiro Igarashi/Image Source

with APD who are especially coldhearted, manipulative, and ruthless—yet may be glib and charming (Cleckley, 1976; Hare, 1998). For example, in 1914 a man named Henri Desiré Landru began using personal ads to attract a woman "interested in matrimony," and he succeeded in seducing 10 of them. He bilked them of their savings, poisoned them, and cremated them in his stove. He recorded his murders in a notebook and maintained a marriage and a mistress all the while. The gruesome actions of serial killers such as Landru leave us frightened and wondering; however, bullies, compulsive liars, and even drivers who regularly speed through a school zone share the same shocking blindness to human pain. Many people with APD do commit crimes, and many are caught because of the frequency and flagrancy of their infractions. Among 22,790 prisoners in one study, 47% of the men and 21% of the women were diagnosed with APD (Fazel & Danesh, 2002). Statistics such as these support the notion of a "criminal personality."

Adults with an APD diagnosis typically have a history of *conduct disorder* before the age of 15. In adulthood, a diagnosis of APD is given to individuals who show three or more of a set of seven diagnostic signs: illegal behavior, deception, impulsivity, physical aggression, recklessness, irresponsibility, and a lack of remorse for wrongdoing. About 3.6% of the general population has APD, and the rate of occurrence in men is 3 times the rate in women (Grant et al., 2004).

Evidence of brain abnormalities in people with APD is also accumulating (Blair, Peschardt, & Mitchell, 2005). For example, criminal psychopaths who are shown negative emotional words such as *hate* or *corpse* exhibit less activity in the amygdala and hippocampus than do noncriminals (Kiehl et al., 2001). These two brain areas are involved in the process of fear conditioning (Patrick, Cuthbert, & Lang, 1994), so their relative inactivity in such studies suggests that psychopaths are less sensitive to fear than are other people. It might seem peaceful to go through life "without fear," but perhaps fear is useful in keeping people from the extremes of antisocial behavior.

Henri Desiré Landru (1869–1922) was a serial killer who met widows through newspaper ads. After obtaining enough information to embezzle money from them, he murdered 10 women and the son of one of the women. He was executed for serial murder in 1922. Three Lions/Hulton Archive/Getty Images

BUILD TO THE OUTCOMES

1. What are personality disorders?

2. What are the characteristics of a person with antisocial personality disorder (APD)?

3. Why do prison statistics support the idea of a "criminal personality"?

Self-Harm Behaviors: Intentionally Injuring Oneself

We all have an innate drive to keep ourselves alive. We eat when we are hungry, get out of the way of fast-moving vehicles, and go to school so we can earn a living to keep ourselves, and our families, alive (see the discussion of evolutionary psychology in the Psychology: Evolution of a Science chapter). One of the most extreme manifestations of abnormal human behavior is revealed when a person acts in direct opposition to this drive for self-preservation and engages in intentionally self-destructive behavior. Accounts of people intentionally harming themselves date back to the beginning of recorded history. However, it is only over the past several decades that we have begun to gain an understanding of why people purposely do things to hurt themselves. *DSM–5* includes two self-destructive behaviors in a special section on disorders in need of further study: suicidal behavior disorder and nonsuicidal self-injury disorder.

LEARNING OUTCOMES

- Explain the factors that increase the risk of suicide.

- Explain what is currently known to be the motivation behind nonsuicidal self-injury.

Suicidal Behavior

Tim, a 35-year-old accountant, had by all appearances been living a happy, successful life. He was married to his high school sweetheart and had two young children. Over the past several years, though, his workload had increased, and he started to experience severe job-related stress. At around the same time, he and his wife began to experience some financial problems, and his alcohol consumption increased, all of which put significant strain on the family and began to affect his work. One evening, after a heated argument with his wife, Tim went into the bathroom and swallowed a bottle full of prescription medicine in an effort to end his life. He was taken to the hospital and kept there to be treated for suicidal behavior.

Suicide, *intentional self-inflicted death*, is the tenth leading cause of death in the United States and the second leading cause of death among people 15 to 24 years old. It takes the lives of more than five times as many people as HIV/AIDS each year in the United States, and more than twice as many people as homicide (Hoyert & Xu, 2012). Approximately 80% of suicides around the world occur among men. White people are much more likely to kill themselves than members of other racial and ethnic groups, accounting for 90% of all suicides (Centers for Disease Control and Prevention, 2013). Unfortunately, we currently do not have a good understanding of why these enormous sociodemographic differences exist.

Nonfatal **suicide attempts**, in which people engage in *potentially harmful behavior with some intention of dying*, occur much more frequently than suicide deaths. In the United States, approximately 15% of adults report that they have seriously considered suicide at some point in their lives, 5% have made a plan to kill themselves, and 5% have actually made a suicide attempt. Although many more men than women die by suicide, women experience suicidal thoughts and (nonfatal) suicide attempts at significantly higher rates than do men (Nock et al., 2008). Suicidal thoughts and behaviors

suicide Intentional self-inflicted death.

suicide attempt Engagement in potentially harmful behavior with some intention of dying.

We all have an innate desire to keep ourselves alive. So why do some people purposely do things to harm themselves?
Piotr Powietrzynski/Getty Images

Figure 14.7 AGE OF ONSET OF SUICIDAL BEHAVIOR DURING ADOLESCENCE A recent survey of a nationally representative sample of U.S. adolescents shows that, although suicidal thoughts and behaviors are quite rare among children (the rate was 0.0 for ages 1–4), they increase dramatically starting at age 12 and continue to climb throughout adolescence (data from Nock et al., 2013).

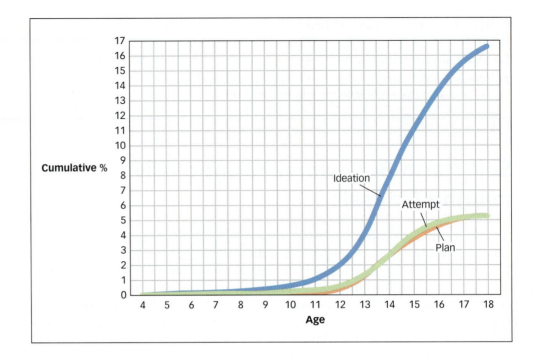

nonsuicidal self-injury (NSSI) Direct, deliberate destruction of body tissue in the absence of any intent to die.

Although in Western cultures self-injury is considered to be pathological, in some parts of the world scarification of the skin is viewed as a rite of passage into adulthood and a symbol of one's tribe, as in the case of this young man from the Republic of Benin in West Africa.
Jean-Michel Clajot/Aurora Photos

are virtually nonexistent before age 10 but increase dramatically from ages 12 to 18 (see **FIGURE 14.7**) before leveling off during early adulthood (Nock et al., 2013).

So the numbers are staggering, but *why* do people try to kill themselves? The short answer is: We do not yet know, and it's complicated. When interviewed in the hospital following their suicide attempt, most people who have tried to kill themselves report that they did so in order to escape from an intolerable state of mind or impossible situation (Boergers, Spirito, & Donaldson, 1998). Consistent with this explanation, research has documented that the risk of suicidal behavior is significantly increased if a person experiences distressing states, such as the presence of multiple mental disorders (more than 90% of people who die by suicide have at least one mental disorder); the experience of significant negative life events during childhood and adulthood (e.g., physical or sexual assault); and the presence of severe medical problems (Nock, Borges, & Ono, 2012). The search is ongoing for a more comprehensive understanding of why some people respond to negative life events with suicidal thoughts and behaviors, as well as on methods of better predicting and preventing these devastating outcomes.

Nonsuicidal Self-Injury

Louisa, an 18-year-old college student, secretly cuts her lower abdomen and upper thighs about once per week, typically when she is feeling intense anger and hatred, either toward herself or someone else. She was 14 when she started to use self-injury as a way to calm herself down. Louisa feels a little ashamed after each episode of cutting, but she doesn't know how else to calm down when she gets really upset, and so she has no plans to stop this behavior.

Louisa is engaging in a behavior called **nonsuicidal self-injury (NSSI)**, the *direct, deliberate destruction of body tissue in the absence of any intent to die.* NSSI has been reported since the beginning of recorded history; however, it is a behavior that appears to be on the rise over the past few decades. Recent studies suggest that as many as 15 to 20% of adolescents and 3 to 6% of adults report engaging in NSSI at some point in their lifetime (Muehlenkamp et al., 2012). The rates appear to be even between males and females, and for people of different races and ethnicities. Like suicidal behavior, NSSI is virtually absent during childhood, increases dramatically during adolescence, and then appears to decrease across adulthood.

In some parts of the world, cutting or scarification of the skin is socially accepted, and in some cases encouraged as a rite of passage (Favazza, 2011). In parts of the world where self-cutting is not socially encouraged, why would a person purposely hurt him- or herself if not to die? Recent studies suggest that people who engage in self-injury have very strong emotional and physiological responses to negative events, that they perceive this response as intolerable, and that NSSI serves to diminish the intensity of this response (Nock, 2009). There also is some evidence that in many instances, people engage in self-injury as a means to communicate distress or elicit help from others (Nock, 2010).

Unfortunately, like suicidal behavior, our understanding of the genetic and neurobiological influences on NSSI is limited, and there currently are no effective medications for these problems. There also is very limited evidence for behavioral interventions or prevention programs (Mann et al., 2005). So, whereas suicidal behavior and NSSI are some of the most disturbing and dangerous mental disorders, they also, unfortunately, are among the most perplexing. The field has made significant strides in our understanding of these behavior problems in recent years, but there is a long way to go before we are able to predict and prevent them accurately and effectively.

BUILD TO THE OUTCOMES

1. What factors create the distressing states that can lead to suicide?
2. What reason has been given in hospital interviews for the suicide attempt?
3. What is nonsuicidal self-injury (NSSI)?
4. How does culture play a role in the view of self-injury as pathological?
5. Why might people engage in self-injury?

CHAPTER REVIEW

Defining Mental Disorders: What Is Abnormal?

- The *DSM–5* is a classification system that defines a mental disorder as occurring when a person experiences disturbances of thought, emotion, or behavior that produce distress or impairment. The original volume provided a common language for talking about disorders, but diagnostic criteria were vague. The *DSM–5* includes detailed lists of criteria, including cultural considerations, designed to increase the validity of the process.
- The medical model conceptualizes abnormal thought and behaviors as illnesses with defined symptoms and possible cures.
- According to the biopsychosocial model, mental disorders arise from an interaction of biological, psychological, and social factors.

- The diathesis–stress model suggests that a person may be predisposed for a disorder that can be manifested if triggered by stress.
- The RDoC is a new classification system that focuses on biological, cognitive, and behavioral aspects of mental disorders.
- Psychiatric labels may create negative stereotypes and may be one reason that many people do not seek help.

Anxiety Disorders: Excessive Fear, Anxiety, and Avoidance

- People with anxiety disorders have irrational worries and fears that undermine their ability to function normally.
- Phobic disorders are characterized by excessive fear and avoidance of specific objects, activities, or situations.

The preparedness theory posits that people are instinctively predisposed toward certain fears, and heritability studies support this idea. Temperament and the influence of environment are additional factors.

- People who suffer from panic disorder experience sudden, terrifying attacks of intense anxiety. Agoraphobia can lead people to be housebound for fear of public humiliation. Panic disorder has a hereditary component, and people who experience panic attacks may be hypersensitive to physiological signs of anxiety.

- Generalized anxiety disorder (GAD) involves a chronic state of anxiety, whereas phobic disorders involve anxiety tied to a specific object or situation. Biological explanations of GAD suggest a role for neurotransmitters, but the evidence is unclear. Life situation and experience play a role as well, supporting the diathesis–stress notion.

Obsessive-Compulsive Disorder: Persistent Thoughts and Repetitive Behaviors

- People with obsessive-compulsive disorder experience recurring, anxiety-provoking thoughts that compel them to engage in ritualistic, irrational behavior.

- OCD derives from concerns that could be real, supporting the preparedness theory. Studies indicate a moderate genetic link.

Posttraumatic Stress Disorder: Distress and Avoidance After a Trauma

- In posttraumatic stress disorder (PTSD), a person experiences chronic physiological arousal, unwanted thoughts or images, and avoidance of things or situations that remind the person of a traumatic event.

- Research has identified neural correlates of PTSD.

Depressive and Bipolar Disorders: Extreme Highs and Lows

- Mood disorders are mental disorders in which a disturbance in mood is the predominant feature.

- Major depression (or unipolar depression) is characterized by a severely depressed mood lasting at least 2 weeks; symptoms include excessive self-criticism, guilt, difficulty concentrating, suicidal thoughts, sleep and appetite disturbances, and lethargy.

- Bipolar disorder is an unstable emotional condition involving extreme mood swings of depression and mania, periods of abnormally and persistently elevated, expansive, or irritable mood.

- Depression has at its roots socioeconomic, hormonal, genetic, and neural factors. Helplessness theory indicates that biases in how information is processed can lead to depression.

- Bipolar disorder likely is the result of the interaction of multiple genes. Epigenetics helps explain some of the genetic risk factors, a link to the influence of environment.

Schizophrenia and Other Psychotic Disorders: Losing the Grasp on Reality

- Schizophrenia is a severe psychological disorder involving hallucinations, disorganized thoughts and behavior, and emotional and social withdrawal.

- Positive symptoms are thoughts and behaviors *not* seen in those without the disorder; negative symptoms indicate an absence of normal behavior; cognitive symptoms are impairments in executive functioning, attention, and working memory.

- Schizophrenia affects only 1% of the population, but it accounts for a disproportionate share of psychiatric hospitalizations.

- The first drugs that reduced the availability of dopamine sometimes reduced the symptoms of schizophrenia, suggesting that the disorder involved an excess of dopamine activity, but recent research suggests that schizophrenia may involve a complex interaction among a variety of neurotransmitters.

- Brain changes are evident in people with schizophrenia, but evidence shows children whose biological mothers had schizophrenia are more likely to develop it if they are raised in an affected family.

Disorders of Childhood and Adolescence

- Autism spectrum disorder (ASD) emerges in early childhood and involves persistent communication deficits, as well as restricted and repetitive patterns of behavior, interests, or activities.

- Attention-deficit/hyperactivity disorder (ADHD) begins by age 12 and involves persistent severe problems with inattention and/or hyperactivity that cause significant impairments in functioning.

- Conduct disorder begins in childhood or adolescence and involves persistent behavior involving aggression toward people or animals, destruction of property, deceitfulness or theft, or serious rule violations.

Personality Disorders: Extreme Traits and Characteristics

- Personality disorders are enduring patterns of thinking, feeling, relating to others, or controlling impulses that cause distress or impaired functioning.

- Persons with antisocial personality disorder (APD) show a lack of moral emotions and can be manipulative, dangerous, and reckless, often hurting others and sometimes hurting themselves.

Self-Harm Behaviors: Intentionally Injuring Oneself

- Suicide is among the leading causes of death in the United States and the world. Most people who die by suicide have a mental disorder. Suicide attempts most often are motivated by an attempt to escape intolerable mental states or situations.

- Nonsuicidal self-injury (NSSI) is performed without suicidal intent; like suicidal behavior, it is most often motivated by an attempt to escape from painful mental states.

KEY CONCEPT QUIZ

1. The conception of psychological disorders as diseases that have symptoms and possible cures is referred to as
   a. the medical model.
   b. physiognomy.
   c. the root syndrome framework.
   d. a diagnostic system.

2. The *DSM–5* is best described as a
   a. medical model.
   b. classification system.
   c. set of theoretical assumptions.
   d. collection of physiological definitions.

3. *Comorbidity of disorders* refers to
   a. symptoms stemming from internal dysfunction.
   b. the relative risk of death arising from a disorder.
   c. the co-occurrence of two or more disorders in a single individual.
   d. the existence of disorders on a continuum from normal to abnormal.

4. The RDoC aims to
   a. more accurately estimate the rates of *DSM–5* disorders.
   b. shift researchers from focusing on a symptom-based classification of mental disorders to a focus on underlying processes that may lead to mental disorders.
   c. prevent the negative consequences of labeling individuals with mental disorders.
   d. help researchers better classify mental disorders based on psychodynamic symptoms.

5. Irrational worries and fears that undermine one's ability to function normally are an indication of
   a. a genetic abnormality.
   b. dysthymia.
   c. diathesis.
   d. an anxiety disorder.

6. A(n) _____ disorder involves anxiety tied to a specific object or situation.
   a. generalized anxiety
   b. environmental
   c. panic
   d. phobic

7. Agoraphobia often develops as a result of
   a. preparedness theory.
   b. obsessive-compulsive disorder.
   c. panic disorder.
   d. social phobia.

8. Kelly's fear of germs leads her to wash her hands repeatedly throughout the day, often for a half hour or more, under extremely hot water. From which disorder does Kelly suffer?
   a. panic attacks
   b. obsessive-compulsive disorder
   c. phobia
   d. generalized anxiety disorder

9. Which of the following is not a symptom of PTSD?
   a. chronic physiological arousal
   b. avoidance of things or places that might serve as reminders of the traumatic event
   c. recurrent, intrusive thoughts about the traumatic event
   d. impaired acquisition of conditioned depressive responses

10. Extreme mood swings between _____ characterize bipolar disorder.
   a. depression and mania
   b. stress and lethargy
   c. anxiety and arousal
   d. obsessions and compulsions

11. Schizophrenia is characterized by which of the following?
   a. hallucinations
   b. disorganized thoughts and behavior
   c. emotional and social withdrawal
   d. all of the above

12. Autism spectrum disorder is most often characterized by which of the following?
   a. communication deficits and restricted, repetitive behavior
   b. hallucinations and delusions
   c. suicidal thoughts
   d. schizophrenia

13. Attention-deficit/hyperactivity disorder
   a. must begin before the age of 4.
   b. never persists into adulthood.
   c. sometimes persists into adulthood.
   d. affects only boys.

14. Jim was diagnosed as having antisocial personality disorder based on the fact that he
   a. is emotionally distant, suspicious of others, and has an intense fear of rejection.
   b. avoids social interaction, has very poor social skills, and is often seen as a "loner."

   c. is very peculiar in his speech and dress and has difficulty forming relationships.
   d. is manipulative, impulsive, and shows little emotional empathy.

15. In the United States, those at highest risk for suicide are
   a. men.
   b. White people.
   c. those with a mental disorder.
   d. all of the above

 **LearningCurve**   **Don't stop now! Quizzing yourself is a powerful study tool.** Go to LearningCurve at www.launchpadworks.com for more practice.

KEY TERMS

mental disorder (p. 442)

medical model (p. 442)

Diagnostic and Statistical Manual of Mental Disorders (DSM) (p. 443)

comorbidity (p. 445)

biopsychosocial perspective (p. 445)

diathesis–stress model (p. 446)

Research Domain Criteria Project (RDoC) (p. 447)

anxiety disorder (p. 449)

phobic disorders (p. 450)

specific phobia (p. 450)

social phobia (p. 450)

preparedness theory (p. 451)

panic disorder (p. 451)

agoraphobia (p. 452)

generalized anxiety disorder (GAD) (p. 453)

obsessive-compulsive disorder (OCD) (p. 455)

posttraumatic stress disorder (PTSD) (p. 456)

mood disorders (p. 457)

major depressive disorder (or unipolar depression) (p. 458)

seasonal affective disorder (SAD) (p. 458)

helplessness theory (p. 459)

bipolar disorder (p. 460)

schizophrenia (p. 463)

positive symptoms (p. 463)

hallucination (p. 463)

delusion (p. 464)

disorganized speech (p. 464)

grossly disorganized behavior (p. 464)

negative symptoms (p. 464)

cognitive symptoms (p. 464)

dopamine hypothesis (p. 466)

autism spectrum disorder (ASD) (p. 467)

attention-deficit/hyperactivity disorder (ADHD) (p. 469)

conduct disorder (p. 470)

personality disorders (p. 470)

antisocial personality disorder (APD) (p. 471)

suicide (p. 473)

suicide attempt (p. 473)

nonsuicidal self-injury (NSSI) (p. 474)

CHANGING MINDS

1. You catch a TV interview with a celebrity who describes his difficult childhood, living with a mother who suffered from major depression. "Sometimes my mother stayed in her bed for days, not even getting up to eat," he says. "At the time, the family hushed it up. My parents were immigrants, and they came from a culture where it was considered shameful to have mental problems. You are supposed to have enough strength of will to overcome your problems, without help from anyone else. So my mother never got treatment." How might the idea of a medical model of psychiatric disorders have helped this woman and her family in the decision whether to seek treatment?

2. You're studying for your upcoming psychology exam when your roommate breezes in, saying: "I was just at the gym and I ran into Sue. She's totally schizophrenic: nice one minute, mean the next." You can't resist the opportunity to set the record straight. How does the behavior your roommate is describing differ from the symptoms of schizophrenia?

3. A friend of yours has a family member who is experiencing severe mental problems, including delusions and loss of motivation. "We went to one psychiatrist," she says, "and got a diagnosis of schizophrenia. We went for a second opinion, and the other doctor said it was probably bipolar disorder. They're both good doctors, and they're both using the same *DSM*—how can they come up with different diagnoses?"

4. After reading the chapter, one of your classmates turns to you with a sigh of relief. "I finally figured it out. I have a deadbeat brother, who always gets himself into trouble and then blames other people for his problems. Even when he gets a ticket for speeding, he never thinks it's his fault—the police were picking on him, or his passengers were urging him to go too fast. I always thought he was just a loser, but now I realize he has a personality disorder!" Do you agree with your classmate's diagnosis of his brother? How would you caution your classmate about the dangers of self-diagnosis, or diagnosis of friends and family?

ANSWERS TO KEY CONCEPT QUIZ

1. a; 2. b; 3. c; 4. b; 5. d; 6. d; 7. c; 8. b; 9. d; 10. a; 11. d; 12. a; 13. c; 14. d; 15. d.

Treatment of Psychological Disorders

"Today we're going to be touching a dead mouse I saw in the alley outside my office building," Dr. Jenkins said. "Okay, let's do it, I'm ready," Christine responded. The pair walked down to the alley and spent the next 50 minutes touching, then stroking, the dead mouse. They then went back upstairs to plan out what other disgusting things Christine was going to touch over the next 7 days before coming back for her next therapy session. This is all part of the psychological treatment of Christine's obsessive-compulsive disorder (OCD). It is an approach called *exposure and response prevention* (ERP), in which people are gradually exposed to the content of their obsessions and prevented from engaging in their compulsions. Christine's obsessions include the fear that she is going to be contaminated by germs and die of cancer; her compulsive behavior involves several hours per day of washing her body and scrubbing everything around her with alcohol wipes in order to decrease the possibility of developing cancer. After dozens and dozens of exposures, without performing the behaviors that they believe have been keeping them safe, people undergoing ERP eventually learn that their obsessive thoughts are not accurate and that they don't have to act out their compulsions. ERP can be a very scary treatment, but it has proven amazingly effective (Foa, 2010). ERP is just one of many approaches currently being used to help people to overcome the mental disorders you learned about in the last chapter.

In this chapter, we will explore the most common approaches to psychological treatment. We will examine why people need to seek psychological help in the first place, and then explore how psychotherapy for individuals is built on the major theories of the causes and cures of disorders, including psychoanalytic, humanistic, existential, behavioral, and cognitive theories. We also will consider biological approaches to treatment that focus on directly modifying brain structure and function. We'll discuss which treatments work best and also look to the future by exploring some exciting new directions in the assessment and treatment of disorders using innovative technologies.

Exposure-based treatments, in which people learn to face the source of their fear and anxiety, have proven to be an effective way to treat anxiety disorders. Keith Binns/Getty Images

Treatment: Getting Help to Those Who Need It

LEARNING OUTCOMES

- Describe reasons people with mental disorders may fail to get treatment.

- Outline different approaches to treatment.

Estimates suggest that 46.4% of people in the United States suffer from a mental disorder at some point in their lifetime (Kessler, Berglund, et al., 2005), and 26.2% suffer from at least one disorder during a given year (Kessler, Chiu, et al., 2006). The personal costs of these disorders include anguish to the sufferers as well as interference in their ability to carry on the activities of daily life. Think about Christine from the example above. Her OCD was causing major problems in her life. She had to quit her job at the local coffee shop because she was no longer able to touch money or anything else that had been touched by other people without washing it first. Her relationship with her boyfriend was in trouble because he was growing tired of her constant reassurance seeking regarding cleanliness (hers and his). She desperately wanted and needed some way to break out of this vicious cycle. She needed an effective treatment.

The personal and social burdens associated with mental disorders are enormous, and there are financial costs too. Depression is the second leading cause of all disability worldwide (Ferrari et al., 2013), and recent estimates suggest that depression-related lost work productivity costs somewhere from $30 to $50 billion per year (Kessler, 2012). If we add in similar figures for all other psychological problems, the overall costs are astronomical. In addition to the personal benefits of treatment, then, society also stands to benefit from the effective treatment of psychological disorders.

Unfortunately, only about 18% of people in the United States with a mental disorder in a given 12-month period receive treatment during the same time frame. Treatment rates are even lower elsewhere around the world, especially in low-income or developing countries (Wang et al., 2007). Even among those who do receive treatment, the average delay from onset until first receiving treatment is over a decade (Wang et al., 2004)!

Why Many People Fail to Seek Treatment

A physical symptom such as a toothache would send most people to the dentist—a trip that usually results in a successful treatment. The clear source of pain and the obvious solution make for a quick and effective response. In contrast, the path from a mental disorder to a successful treatment is often far less clear. Here are three reasons why people may fail to get treatment for mental disorders:

1. *People may not realize that they have a mental disorder that can be effectively treated.* Approximately 45% of those with a mental disorder who do not seek treatment report that they didn't think that they needed to be treated (Mojtabai et al., 2011). Although most people know what a toothache is and that it can be successfully treated, far fewer people know when they have a mental disorder and what treatments might be available.

2. *People's beliefs may keep them from getting help.* Individuals may believe that they should be able to handle things themselves. In fact, this is the primary reason that people with a mental disorder give for not seeking treatment (72.6%) and for dropping out of treatment prematurely (42.2%; Mojtabai et al., 2011). Other attitudinal barriers for not seeking treatment include perceived stigma from others.

3. *Structural barriers prevent people from physically getting to treatment.* Like finding a good lawyer or plumber, finding the right psychologist can be difficult. This confusion is understandable given the plethora of different types of treatments available (see The Real World: Types of Psychotherapists). Other structural

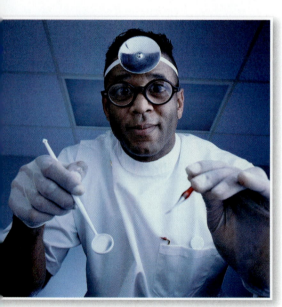

When your tooth hurts, you go to a dentist. But how do you know when to see a psychologist? The Image Bank/Getty Images

Types of Psychotherapists

Therapists have widely varying backgrounds and training, and this affects the kinds of services they offer. There are several major "flavors."

- *Psychologist* A psychologist who practices psychotherapy holds a doctorate with specialization in clinical psychology (a PhD or PsyD) and has extensive training in therapy, assessment of psychological disorders, and research. The psychologist will sometimes have a specialty, such as working with adolescents or helping people overcome sleep disorders, and will usually conduct therapy that involves talking. Psychologists must be licensed by the state.

- *Psychiatrist* A psychiatrist is a medical doctor who has completed an MD with specialized training in assessing and treating mental disorders. Psychiatrists can prescribe medications, and some also practice psychotherapy. General-practice physicians can also prescribe medications for mental disorders but they do not typically receive as much training in the diagnosis or psychological treatment of mental disorders, and they do not practice psychotherapy.

- *Clinical/psychiatric social worker* Social workers have a master's degree in social work and have training in working with people facing situations such as poverty, homelessness, or family conflict. They also receive special training to help people in these situations who have mental disorders.

- *Counselor* In some states, a counselor must have a master's degree and extensive training in therapy; other states require minimal relevant education. Counselors who work in schools usually have a master's degree and specific training in counseling in educational settings.

Some people offer therapy under made-up terms that sound professional—"mind/body healing therapist," for example, or "marital adjustment adviser." Often, these terms are simply invented to avoid licensing boards. To be safe, it is important to shop wisely for a therapist whose training and credentials reflect expertise and inspire confidence.

People you know, such as your general-practice physician, a school counselor, or a trusted friend or family member might be able to recommend a good therapist. Or you can visit the American Psychological Association Web site for referrals to licensed mental health care providers.

Before you agree to see a therapist for treatment, you should ask questions such as those below to evaluate whether the therapist's style or background is a good match for your problem:

- What type of therapy do you practice?
- What types of problems do you usually treat?
- Will our work involve "talking" therapy, medications, or both?
- How effective is this type of therapy for the type of problem I'm having?
- What are your fees for therapy? Will health insurance cover them?

Armed with the answers, you can make an informed decision about the type of service you need. The therapist's personality is also critically important. You should seek out someone who is willing and open to answer questions, and who shows general respect and empathy for you. You'll be entrusting this therapist with your mental health, and you should enter into such a relationship only if you and the therapist have good rapport.

Zigy Kaluzny/THE IMAGE BANK/Getty Image

Alina Solovyova-Vincent/Getty Images

BSIP/Universal Images Group/Getty Images

barriers include not being able to afford treatment, lack of clinician availability, inconvenience of attending treatment, and trouble finding transportation to the clinic (Mojtabai et al., 2011).

Even when people seek and find help, they sometimes do not receive the most effective treatments, which further complicates things. For starters, most of the treatment of mental disorders is not provided by mental health specialists, but by general medical practitioners (Wang et al., 2007). And even when people make it to a mental health specialist, they do not always receive the most effective treatment possible. In fact, less than 40% of those with a mental disorder receive minimally adequate treatment. Clearly, before choosing or prescribing a therapy, we need to know what kinds of treatments are available and understand which treatments are best for particular disorders.

Approaches to Treatment

Treatments can be divided broadly into two kinds: (1) psychological treatment, in which people interact with a clinician in order to change their brain and behavior; and (2) biological treatment, in which the brain is treated directly with drugs, surgery, or some other direct intervention. In some cases, both psychological *and* biological treatments are applied. Christine's OCD, for example, might be treated not only with the ERP but also with medication that mitigates her obsessive thoughts and compulsive urges. As we learn more about the biology and chemistry of the brain, approaches to mental health that begin with the brain are becoming increasingly widespread. As you'll see later in the chapter, many effective treatments combine both psychological and biological interventions (see Data Visualization: How Has the Rate of Attention-Deficit/Hyperactivity Disorder (ADHD) Diagnosis Changed Over Time? at www.launchpadworks.com).

BUILD TO THE OUTCOMES

1. What are some of the personal, social, and financial costs of mental illness?

2. What are the obstacles to treatment for the mentally ill?

3. What are the two broad types of treatment?

Psychological Treatments: Healing the Mind Through Interaction

LEARNING OUTCOMES

• Outline the aspects of each approach to psychotherapy.

• Describe the pros and cons of group treatment.

psychotherapy An interaction between a socially sanctioned clinician and someone suffering from a psychological problem, with the goal of providing support or relief from the problem.

eclectic psychotherapy A form of psychotherapy that involves drawing on techniques from different forms of therapy, depending on the client and the problem.

Psychological therapy, or **psychotherapy**, *is an interaction between a socially sanctioned clinician and someone suffering from a psychological problem, with the goal of providing support or relief from the problem.* Over 500 different forms of psychotherapy exist. A recent survey of psychotherapists asked them to describe their main theoretical orientation (Norcross & Rogan, 2013; see **FIGURE 15.1**). One out of four reported using **eclectic psychotherapy**, *a form of psychotherapy that involves drawing on techniques from different forms of therapy, depending on the client and the problem.* This approach allows therapists to apply an appropriate theoretical perspective suited to the problem at hand, rather than adhering to a single theoretical perspective for all clients and all types of problems. Nevertheless, as Figure 15.1 shows, the majority of psychotherapists use a single approach, such as psychodynamic therapy, humanistic and existential therapies, or behavioral and cognitive therapies. We'll examine each of those major approaches to psychotherapy in turn.

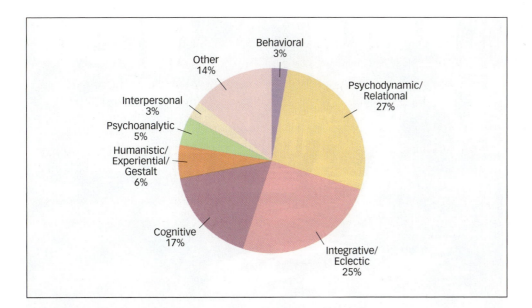

Behavioral
3%

Other
14%

Interpersonal
3%

Psychoanalytic
5%

Humanistic/
Experiential/
Gestalt
6%

Cognitive
17%

Psychodynamic/
Relational
27%

Integrative/
Eclectic
25%

Figure 15.1 APPROACHES TO PSYCHOTHERAPY IN THE 21ST CENTURY This chart shows the percentage of psychologists who have various primary psychotherapy orientations (data from Norcross & Rogan, 2013).

Psychodynamic Therapies

Psychodynamic psychotherapy has its roots in Freud's psychoanalytically oriented theory of personality. **Psychodynamic psychotherapies** *explore childhood events and encourage individuals to use this understanding to develop insight into their psychological problems.* Psychoanalysis was the first psychodynamic therapy to develop, but it has largely been replaced by modern psychodynamic therapies.

Psychoanalysis

As we saw in the Personality chapter, *psychoanalysis* assumes that people are born with aggressive and sexual urges that are repressed during childhood development through the use of defense mechanisms. Psychoanalysts encourage their clients to bring these repressed conflicts into consciousness so that the clients can understand them and reduce their unwanted influences.

Traditional psychoanalysis involves four or five sessions per week over an average of 3 to 6 years (Ursano & Silberman, 2003). During a session, the client reclines on a couch, facing away from the analyst, who asks the client to express whatever thoughts and feelings come to mind. Occasionally, the therapist may comment on some of the information the client presents but does not express his or her values and judgments. The stereotypic image you might have of psychological therapy—a person lying on a couch talking to a person sitting in a chair—springs from this approach.

The goal of psychoanalysis is for the client to understand the unconscious in a process Freud called *developing insight*. Some key techniques that psychoanalysts use to help the client develop insight include free association, in which the client reports every thought that enters the mind and the therapist looks for recurring themes, and dream analysis, in which the therapist looks for dream elements that might symbolize unconscious conflicts or wishes. Psychoanalysts also assess the client's **resistance**, or *reluctance to cooperate with treatment for fear of confronting unpleasant emotional material*. For example, the therapist might suggest that the client's problem with obsessive health worries could be traced to a childhood rivalry with her mother for her father's love and attention. The client could find the suggestion insulting and resist the interpretation, which might signal to the therapist that this is indeed an issue the client could be directed to confront in order to develop insight.

Over time, and many therapy sessions, the client and psychoanalyst often develop a close relationship. Freud believed that the development and resolution of this

In traditional psychoanalysis, the client lies on a couch, with the therapist sitting behind, out of the client's view. Antoine Devourard/Patrick Allard/Rea/Redux

psychodynamic psychotherapies Therapies that explore childhood events and encourage individuals to use this understanding to develop insight into their psychological problems.

resistance A reluctance to cooperate with treatment for fear of confronting unpleasant unconscious material.

In the movie *Good Will Hunting*, the lead character, played by Matt Damon, forms a strong bond with his therapist, played by Robin Williams. As in psychodynamic therapy, the therapist uses their relationship to help resolve the patient's inner conflict. The amazing bond that was formed between therapist and patient and the life-changing treatment delivered are the stuff of therapists' dreams (and Hollywood scripts).   Miramax/The Kobal Collection

transference An event that occurs in psychoanalysis when the analyst begins to assume a major significance in the client's life, and the client reacts to the analyst on the basis of unconscious childhood fantasies.

relationship was a key process of psychoanalysis. **Transference** occurs *when the analyst begins to assume a major significance in the client's life, and the client reacts to the analyst on the basis of unconscious childhood fantasies.* Successful psychoanalysis involves analyzing the transference so that the client understands this reaction and why it occurs.

Psychodynamic Therapy

Freud's original version of psychoanalysis is practiced by only about 5% of clinicians today (see Figure 15.1). However, many of his insights and techniques remain very influential in a broader range of psychodynamic treatments used more frequently today (about 30% of therapists today use psychodynamic therapy). One of the most common psychodynamic treatments is **interpersonal psychotherapy (IPT)**, *a form of psychotherapy that focuses on helping clients improve current relationships* (Weissman, Markowitz, & Klerman, 2000). Rather than using free association, therapists using IPT talk to clients about their interpersonal behaviors and feelings. They pay particular attention to the client's grief (an exaggerated reaction to the loss of a loved one), role disputes (conflicts with a significant other), role transitions (changes in life status, such as starting a new job, getting married, or retiring), or interpersonal deficits (lack of the necessary skills to start or maintain a relationship). The treatment assumes that, as interpersonal relations improve, symptoms will subside.

interpersonal psychotherapy (IPT) A form of psychotherapy that focuses on helping clients improve current relationships.

Modern psychodynamic psychotherapies such as IPT also differ from classical psychoanalysis in the procedures used. For starters, in modern psychodynamic therapy the therapist and client typically sit face to face. In addition, therapy is less intensive, with meetings often occurring only once a week and therapy lasting months rather than years. In contrast to classical psychoanalysis, modern psychodynamic therapists are more likely to offer support or advice in addition to interpretation (Barber et al., 2013). Therapists are also now less likely to interpret a client's statements as a sign of unconscious sexual or aggressive impulses. However, other concepts, such as transference and fostering insight into unconscious processes, remain features of most psychodynamic therapies. Freud's couch casts a long shadow.

What Is the Evidence?

Although psychodynamic therapy has been around for a long time and continues to be widely practiced, there is limited evidence for its effectiveness. However, in-depth studies that examine evidence from many prior studies find that IPT (one specific form of psychodynamic therapy) and cognitive behavioral therapy (described below) are more effective than all other treatments, especially in the case of depressive and anxiety disorders (Tolin, 2010; Watzke et al., 2012; Zhou et al., 2015). On the other hand, there is evidence that some of the aspects of psychodynamic therapy long believed to be effective may actually be harmful. For instance, research suggests that the more a therapist makes interpretations about perceived transference in the client, the worse the therapeutic alliance and the worse the clinical outcome (Henry et al., 1994).

Humanistic and Existential Therapies

Humanistic and existential therapies emerged in the middle of the 20th century, in part as a reaction to the negative views that psychoanalysis holds about human nature. Humanistic and existential therapies share the assumption that psychological problems stem from feelings of alienation and loneliness, and that those feelings can be traced to failures to reach one's potential (in the humanistic approach) or from failures to find meaning in life (in the existential approach). Although interest in these approaches peaked in the 1960s and 1970s, some therapists continue to practice these approaches today. Two well-known types are person-centered therapy (a humanistic approach) and gestalt therapy (an existential approach).

Person-Centered Therapy

Person-centered therapy (or **client-centered therapy**) *assumes that all individuals have a tendency toward growth and that this growth can be facilitated by acceptance and genuine reactions from the therapist.* Person-centered therapy assumes that each person is qualified to determine his or her own goals for therapy, such as feeling more confident or making a career decision, and even the frequency and length of therapy. In this type of nondirective treatment, the therapist tends not to provide advice or suggestions about what the client should be doing, but instead paraphrases the client's words, mirroring the client's thoughts and sentiments (e.g., "I think I hear you saying . . ."). Person-centered therapists believe that with adequate support, the client will recognize the right things to do.

Person-centered therapists should demonstrate three basic qualities. The first is *congruence*, which means ensuring that the therapist communicates the same message at all levels. For example, the therapist must communicate the same message in words, in facial expression, and in body language. Saying "I think your concerns are valid" while smirking simply will not do. The second quality is *empathy*, which is the process of trying to understand the client by seeing the world from the client's perspective, which enables the therapist to better appreciate the client's apprehensions, worries, or fears. The third quality is *unconditional positive regard*, meaning that the therapist must provide a nonjudgmental, warm, and accepting environment in which the client can feel safe expressing his or her thoughts and feelings.

The goal is not to uncover repressed conflicts, as in psychodynamic therapy, but instead to try to understand the client's experience and reflect that experience back to the client in a supportive way, encouraging the client's natural tendency toward growth. This style of therapy is reminiscent of psychoanalysis in its way of encouraging the client toward the free expression of thoughts and feelings.

person-centered therapy (or client-centered therapy) A form of psychotherapy that assumes that all individuals have a tendency toward growth and that this growth can be facilitated by acceptance and genuine reactions from the therapist.

As part of gestalt therapy, clients may be encouraged to imagine that another person is sitting across from them in a chair. The client then moves from chair to chair, role-playing what he or she would say to the imagined person and how that person would answer. Photoalto/Alamy

gestalt therapy A form of psychotherapy whose goal is helping the client become aware of his or her thoughts, behaviors, experiences, and feelings and to "own" or take responsibility for them.

behavior therapy A type of therapy that assumes that disordered behavior is learned and that symptom relief is achieved through changing overt, maladaptive behaviors into more constructive behaviors.

A behavioral psychologist might treat a temper tantrum using time-out for reinforcement, a method that is based on the behavioral principle of operant conditioning and that ensures that a child will not be rewarded for her undesired behavior. Matthew Nock

Gestalt Therapy

Gestalt therapy *has the goal of helping the client become aware of his or her thoughts, behaviors, experiences, and feelings and to "own" or take responsibility for them.* Gestalt therapists are encouraged to be enthusiastic and warm toward their clients, an approach they share with person-centered therapists. To help facilitate the client's awareness, gestalt therapists also reflect back to the client their impressions of the client.

Gestalt therapy emphasizes the experiences and behaviors that are occurring at that particular moment in the therapy session. For example, if a client is talking about something stressful that occurred during the previous week, the therapist might ask, "How do you feel now as you describe what happened to you?" Clients are also encouraged to put their feelings into action. One way to do this is the empty-chair technique, in which the client imagines that another person (e.g., a spouse, a parent, or a coworker) is in an empty chair, sitting directly across from the client. The client then moves from chair to chair, alternating from role-playing what he or she would say to the other person and how he or she imagines the other person would respond.

Behavioral and Cognitive Therapies

Unlike the talk therapies described above, behavioral and cognitive treatments emphasize actively changing a person's current thoughts and behaviors as a way to mitigate or eliminate psychopathology. In the evolution of psychological treatments, clients started out lying down in psychoanalysis, then sitting in psychodynamic and related approaches, but often stand and engage in behavior-change homework assignments in their everyday life in behavioral and cognitive therapies.

Behavior Therapy: Changing Maladaptive Behavior Patterns

Whereas Freud developed psychoanalysis as an offshoot of hypnosis and techniques that other clinicians used before him, behavior therapy was developed on the basis of laboratory findings of earlier behavioral psychologists. As you read in the Psychology: Evolution of a Science chapter, behaviorists rejected theories that were based on "invisible" mental properties that were difficult to test and impossible to observe directly. Behaviorists found psychoanalytic ideas particularly hard to test: How do you know whether a person has an unconscious conflict? Behavioral principles, in contrast, focused solely on behaviors that could be observed (e.g., avoidance of a feared object, such as refusing to get on an airplane). **Behavior therapy** *assumes that disordered behavior is learned and that symptom relief is achieved through changing overt, maladaptive behaviors into more constructive behaviors.* A variety of behavior therapy techniques have been developed for many disorders, based on the learning principles you encountered in the Learning chapter, including operant conditioning procedures (which focus on reinforcement and punishment) and classical conditioning procedures (which focus on extinction). Here are three examples of behavior therapy techniques in action:

1. ***Eliminating Unwanted Behaviors*** How would you change a 3-year-old boy's habit of throwing tantrums at the grocery store? A behavior therapist might investigate what happens immediately before and after the tantrum: Did the child get candy to "shut him up"? The study of operant conditioning shows that behavior can be influenced by its *consequences* (the reinforcing or punishing events that follow). Adjusting these might help change the behavior. Making the consequences less reinforcing (no candy!) and more punishing (a period of time-out facing the wall in the grocery store) could eliminate the problem behavior.

2. ***Promoting Desired Behaviors*** Candy and time-outs can have a strong influence on child behavior, but they work less well with adults. How might you get an individual with schizophrenia to engage in activities of daily living, or get a cocaine addict to stop using drugs? A behavior therapy technique that has proven to be quite effective in such cases is the **token economy**, which involves *giving clients "tokens" for desired behaviors, which they can later trade for rewards.* For instance, in the case of cocaine dependence, the desired behavior is not using cocaine. Programs that reward nonuse with vouchers that can be exchanged for rewards such as money, bus passes, clothes, and so on, have shown an ability to significantly reduce cocaine use (Petry, Alessi, & Rash, 2013). Similar systems are used to promote desired behaviors in classrooms, the workplace, and commercial advertising (e.g., airline and credit card rewards programs).

token economy A form of behavior therapy in which clients are given "tokens" for desired behaviors, which they can later trade for rewards.

3. ***Reducing Unwanted Emotional Responses*** One of the most powerful ways to reduce fear is by gradual exposure to the feared object or situation. **Exposure therapy** involves *confronting an emotion-arousing stimulus directly and repeatedly, ultimately leading to a decrease in the emotional response.* This technique depends on the processes of habituation and response extinction. For example, in Christine's case her clinician gradually exposed her to the content of her obsessions (dirt and germs), which became less and less distressing with repeated exposure (as she learned that no harm actually would come to her from coming into contact with the previously feared stimulus). Similarly, for clients who are afraid of social interaction and unable to function at school or work, a behavioral treatment might involve exposure first to imagined situations in which they talk briefly with one person, then talk a bit longer to a medium-sized group, and finally, give a speech to a large group. Behavioral therapists use an exposure hierarchy to accustom the client gradually to the feared object or situation. Easier situations are practiced first, and as fear decreases, the client progresses to more difficult or frightening situations (see **TABLE 15.1**). It is vitally important that clients continue to be exposed to the feared stimulus until their anxiety decreases. If they leave the situation before it does, this can reinforce their anxiety because they fail to learn that the feared stimulus is not harmful and they learn that avoiding it decreases their anxiety. So if you have a fear of, say, public speaking, best to speak to increasingly large groups of people and to not leave each situation until your anxiety decreases!

exposure therapy An approach to treatment that involves confronting an emotion-arousing stimulus directly and repeatedly, ultimately leading to a decrease in the emotional response.

Exposure therapy can also help people overcome unwanted emotional and behavioral responses through *exposure and response prevention*. Persons with OCD,

TABLE 15.1 Exposure Hierarchy for Social Phobia	
Item	**Fear (0–100)**
1. Have a party and invite everyone from work	99
2. Go to a holiday party for 1 hour without drinking	90
3. Invite Cindy to have dinner and see a movie	85
4. Go for a job interview	80
5. Ask boss for a day off work	65
6. Ask questions in a meeting at work	65
7. Eat lunch with coworkers	60
8. Talk to a stranger on the bus	50
9. Talk to cousin on the telephone for 10 minutes	40
10. Ask for directions at the gas station	35

Information from Ellis (1991).

An exposure therapy client with obsessive-compulsive disorder who fears contamination in public restrooms might be given the "homework" of visiting three such restrooms in a week, touching the toilets, and then *not* washing up. iSTOCK/Getty Images

cognitive therapy A type of therapy that helps a client identify and correct any distorted thinking about self, others, or the world.

cognitive restructuring A therapeutic approach that teaches clients to question the automatic beliefs, assumptions, and predictions that often lead to negative emotions and to replace negative thinking with more realistic and positive beliefs.

for example, might have recurrent thoughts that their hands are dirty and need washing. Washing stops the uncomfortable feelings of contamination only briefly, though, and they wash again and again in search of relief. In exposure with response prevention, they might be asked in therapy to get their hands dirty on purpose (first by touching a coin picked up from the ground, then by touching a public toilet, and later by touching a dead mouse) and leave them dirty for hours. They may need to do this only a few times to break the cycle and be freed from the obsessive ritual (Foa et al., 2007).

Cognitive Therapy: Changing Distorted Thoughts

Whereas behavior therapy focuses primarily on changing a person's behavior, **cognitive therapy** focuses on *helping a client identify and correct any distorted thinking about self, others, or the world* (Beck, 2005). For example, behaviorists might explain a phobia as the outcome of a classical conditioning experience such as being bitten by a dog; the dog bite leads to the development of a dog phobia through the association of the dog with the experience of pain. Cognitive theorists might instead emphasize the *interpretation* of the event, and focus on a person's new or strengthened belief that dogs are dangerous.

Cognitive therapies use a technique called **cognitive restructuring**, which involves *teaching clients to question the automatic beliefs, assumptions, and predictions that often lead to negative emotions and to replace negative thinking with more realistic and positive beliefs.* Specifically, clients are taught to examine the evidence for and against a particular belief or to be more accepting of outcomes that may be undesirable yet still manageable. For example, a depressed client may believe that she is stupid and will never pass her college courses—all on the basis of one poor grade. In this situation, the therapist would work with the client to examine the validity of this belief. The therapist would consider relevant evidence such as grades on previous exams, performance on other coursework, and examples of intelligence outside school. In therapy sessions, the cognitive therapist will help the client to identify evidence that supports, and fails to support, each negative thought in order to help the client generate more balanced thoughts that accurately reflect the true state of affairs. In other words, the clinician tries to remove the dark lens through which the client views the world, not with the goal of replacing it with rose-colored glasses, but instead with clear glass. Here is a brief sample transcript of what part of a cognitive therapy session might sound like.

Clinician: Last week, I asked you to keep a record of situations that made you feel very depressed, at least one per day, and the automatic thoughts that popped into your mind. Were you able to do that?

Client: Yes.

Clinician: Wonderful, I'm glad you were able to complete this assignment. Let's take a look at this together. What's the first situation that you recorded?

Client: Well . . . I went out on Friday night with my friends, which I thought would be fun and help me to feel better. But I was feeling kind of down about things and I ended up not really talking to anyone. Instead, I just sat in the corner and drank all night. I got so drunk that I passed out at the party. I woke up the next day feeling embarrassed and more depressed than ever.

Clinician: Okay, and what thoughts automatically popped into your head?

Client: My friends think I'm a loser and won't want to hang out with me anymore.

Clinician: What evidence can you think of that supports this thought?

Client: Well . . . um . . . I got really drunk, and so they *have* to think I'm a loser. I mean, who does that?

Clinician: Is there any other evidence you can think of that supports those thoughts?

Client: No.

Clinician: All right. Now let's take a moment to think about whether there is any evidence that doesn't support those thoughts. Did anything happen that suggests that your friends don't think you are a loser or that they do want to keep hanging out with you?

Client: Well . . . my friends brought me home safely and then called the next day and joked about what happened and my one friend Tommy said something like "we've all been there" and that he wants to hang out again this weekend.

Clinician: This is very interesting. So on one hand, you feel depressed and have thoughts that you are a loser and your friends don't like you. But on the other hand, you have some pretty real-world evidence that, even though you drank too much, they were still there for you and they do in fact want to hang out with you again, yes?

Client: Yeah, I guess you're right if you put it that way. I didn't think about it like that.

Clinician: So now if we were going to replace your first thoughts, which don't seem to have a lot of real-world evidence, with a more balanced thought based on the evidence, what would that new thought be?

Client: Probably something like my friends probably weren't happy about the fact that I got so drunk because then they had to take care of me, but they are my friends and were there for me and want to keep hanging out with me.

Clinician: Excellent job. I think that sounds just right based on the evidence.

In addition to cognitive restructuring techniques, which try to change a person's thoughts to be more balanced or accurate, some forms of cognitive therapy also include techniques for coping with unwanted thoughts and feelings, techniques that resemble meditation (see the Consciousness chapter). One such technique, called **mindfulness meditation**, *teaches an individual to be fully present in each moment; to be aware of his or her thoughts, feelings, and sensations; and to detect symptoms before they become a problem.* In one study, people recovering from depression were about half as likely to relapse during a 60-week assessment period if they received mindfulness meditation-based cognitive therapy than if they received treatment as usual (Teasdale, Segal, & Williams, 2000).

Cognitive Behavioral Therapy: Blending Approaches

Historically, cognitive and behavioral therapies were considered distinct systems of therapy. Today, most therapists working with anxiety and depression use *a blend of cognitive and behavioral therapeutic strategies*, often referred to as **cognitive behavioral therapy (CBT)**. In contrast with traditional behavior therapy and cognitive therapy, CBT is *problem focused*, meaning that it is undertaken for specific problems (e.g., reducing the frequency of panic attacks or returning to work after a bout of depression), and *action oriented*, meaning that the therapist tries to assist the client in selecting specific strategies to help address those problems. The client is expected to *do* things, such as engage in exposure exercises, practice behavior change skills, or use a diary to monitor relevant symptoms (e.g., the severity of depressed mood, panic attack symptoms). This is in contrast to psychodynamic or other therapies where goals may not be explicitly discussed or agreed on and the client's only necessary action is to attend the therapy session.

Cognitive behavioral therapies have been found to be effective for a number of disorders (Butler et al., 2006; see Hot Science: "Rebooting" Psychological Treatment), including unipolar depression, generalized anxiety disorder, panic disorder, social phobia, posttraumatic stress disorder, and childhood depressive and anxiety disorders.

mindfulness meditation Teaches an individual to be fully present in each moment; to be aware of his or her thoughts, feelings, and sensations; and to detect symptoms before they become a problem.

cognitive behavioral therapy (CBT) A blend of cognitive and behavioral therapeutic strategies.

How might the use of behavior-change homework improve the effectiveness of behavior therapy? © Bonnie Kamin/Photoedit

HOT SCIENCE

"Rebooting" Psychological Treatment

Modern psychological treatments often involve sophisticated interventions supported by experimental studies showing that they actually do decrease peoples' psychological suffering. However, psychological treatment is still pretty primitive in many ways. It usually involves weekly meetings in which a clinician attempts to talk a patient out of a psychological disorder—just like in Freud's day. Alan Kazdin (and his student Stacey Blase) have called for a "rebooting" of psychotherapy research and practice to take advantage of recent advances in technology (Kazdin & Blasé, 2011).

For example, cognitive bias modification (CBM) is a computerized intervention that focuses on changing how people process information. Specifically, people with social anxiety show selective attention for threatening information. (For example, when shown a series of pairs of faces, they have an automatic tendency to look at the angrier one.) In one form of CBM for social anxiety, the patient completes a computerized training program in which he or she is repeatedly shown pairs of faces, one angry and one neutral, that flash on the screen very quickly (for 500 milliseconds), after which a letter appears behind one of them and the patient's task is to name that letter. In CBM, the letter nearly always appears behind the neutral face, which over time teaches the person to ignore the angry face and attend to the neutral face, thus reducing the tendency to attend to threatening faces. A recent review of 15 experiments including over 1,000 people found that CBM was associated with a significant decrease in symptoms of social anxiety. However,

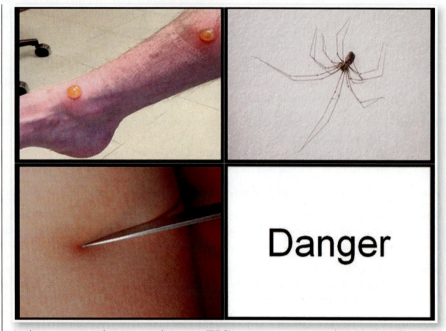

In therapeutic evaluative conditioning (TEC), patients are trained to repeatedly pair suicidal or self-injury-related images (bottom left) with aversive images (top right). Over time, people making such pairings develop an aversion to suicide/self-injury and show a decrease in these self-harm behaviors. Joseph C. Franklin

the effects were relatively small and short lasting, leading the authors to conclude that this method is not yet ready for wide-scale use (Heeren et al., 2015).

Another smartphone-based app called therapeutic evaluative conditioning (TEC) presents the user with several different images (see figure) and has them repeatedly pair suicidal or self-injury-related images with aversive images such as snakes or spiders. The idea is that, as with classical conditioning, by repeatedly pairing these images, over time people will come to associate the suicidal or self-injury-related images with the aversive feeling evoked by the pictures of snakes and spiders. In three different randomized controlled trials, people who played this

matching game for a few minutes each day for one month showed significant reductions in self-injury and suicidal behavior (Franklin et al., 2016).

The development of computer- or smartphone-based interventions has been extremely exciting; however, very few interventions using mobile technologies have data supporting their effectiveness (Larsen, Nicholas, & Christensen, 2016). So although the development of computerized approaches has opened up lots of new opportunities for intervention, it is important that psychologists carefully evaluate which ones can help improve health outcomes and which are simply fancier ways of providing ineffective treatment.

Group Treatments: Healing Multiple Minds at the Same Time

It is natural to think of psychopathology as an illness that affects only the individual. Yet each person lives in a world of other people, and interactions with others may intensify and even cause disorders. A depressed person may be lonely after moving away from friends and loved ones, or an anxious person could be worried about pressures from parents. These ideas suggest that people might be able to recover from disorders in the same way they got into them—not just as an individual effort but through social processes.

Couples and Family Therapy

When a couple is "having problems," neither individual may be suffering from any psychopathology. Rather, it may be the relationship itself that is disordered. In *couples therapy*, a married, cohabiting, or dating couple is seen together in therapy to work on problems usually arising within the relationship. For example, a couple might seek help because they are unhappy with their relationship. In this scenario, both members of the couple are expected to attend therapy sessions and the problem is seen as arising from their interaction, rather than from the problems of one half of the couple. Treatment strategies would target changes in *both* parties, focusing on ways to break their repetitive dysfunctional pattern.

Families enter therapy for many reasons, sometimes to help particular members and other times because there are problems in one or more of the relationships in the family. Anna Goldberg/Agefotostock

In some cases, therapy with even larger groups is warranted. An individual may be having a problem—say, an adolescent is abusing alcohol—but the source of the problem is the individual's relationships with family members; perhaps the mother is herself an alcoholic who subtly encourages the adolescent to drink, and the father travels and neglects the family. In this case, it could be useful for the therapist to work with the whole group at once in *family therapy*—psychotherapy involving members of a family. Family therapy can be particularly effective when adolescent children are having problems (Masten, 2004). Like in couples therapy, the problems and solutions are seen as arising from the *interactions* of these individuals, rather than simply from any one individual.

Group Therapy

Taking these ideas one step further, if individuals (or families) can benefit from talking with a psychotherapist, perhaps they can also benefit from talking with other clients who are talking with the therapist. This is **group therapy**, *a type of therapy in which multiple participants (who often do not know one another at the outset) work on their individual problems in a group atmosphere.* The therapist in group therapy serves more as a group facilitator than as a personal therapist, conducting the sessions both by talking with individuals and by encouraging them to talk with each other.

group therapy A type of therapy in which multiple participants (who often do not know each other at the outset) work on their individual problems in a group atmosphere.

Why do people choose group therapy? One advantage is that attending a group with others who have similar problems shows clients that they are not alone in their suffering. In addition, group members model appropriate behaviors for each other and share their insights about how to deal with their problems. Group therapy is often just as effective as individual therapy (e.g., Jonsson & Hougaard, 2008). So, from a societal perspective, group therapy is much more efficient.

Group therapy also has disadvantages. It may be difficult to assemble a group of individuals who have similar needs. This is particularly an issue with CBT, which tends to focus on specific problems such as depression or panic disorder. Group therapy may become a problem if one or more members undermine the treatment of other group members, for example by dominating the discussions, or making others in the group uncomfortable (e.g., attempting to date other members). Finally, clients in group therapy get less attention than they might in individual psychotherapy.

Self-Help and Support Groups

Some important types of group therapy are *self-help groups* and *support groups*, which are discussion groups that are often run by peers who have themselves

Self-help groups are a cost-effective, time-effective, and treatment-effective solution for dealing with some types of psychological problems. Many people like self-help groups, but are they effective? How could you test this?
©Richard T. Nowitz/Corbis

struggled with the same issues. The most famous self-help and support groups are Alcoholics Anonymous (AA), Gamblers Anonymous, and Al-Anon (a program for families and friends of those with alcohol problems). Other self-help groups offer support to cancer survivors or to parents of children with autism or to people with mood disorders, eating disorders, and substance abuse problems. In fact, self-help and support groups exist for just about every psychological disorder. In addition to being cost effective, self-help and support groups allow people to realize that they are not the only ones with a particular problem and give them the opportunity to offer guidance and support to each other arising from personal experiences of success.

In some cases, though, self-help and support groups can do more harm than good. Some members may be disruptive or aggressive or encourage each other to engage in behaviors that are countertherapeutic (e.g., avoiding feared situations or using alcohol to cope). People with moderate problems may be exposed to others with severe problems and may become oversensitized to symptoms that they might not otherwise have found disturbing. Because self-help and support groups are usually not led by trained therapists, mechanisms to evaluate these groups or to ensure their quality are rarely in place.

AA has more than 2 million members in the United States, with 117,000 group meetings that occur around the world (Alcoholics Anonymous, 2016). Members are encouraged to follow *12 steps* to reach the goal of lifelong abstinence from all drinking; the steps include believing in a higher power, practicing prayer and meditation, and making amends for harm to others. A few studies examining the effectiveness of AA have been conducted, and it appears that individuals who participate tend to overcome problem drinking with greater success than do those who do not participate in AA (Fiorentine, 1999; Morgenstern et al., 1997). However, several tenets of the AA philosophy are not supported by the research. We know that the general AA program is useful, but questions remain about which parts of this program are most helpful.

Considered together, the many social approaches to psychotherapy reveal how important interpersonal relationships are for each of us. It may not always be clear how psychotherapy works, whether one approach is better than another, or what particular theory best explains how problems have developed. What is clear, however, is that social interactions among people—both in individual therapy and in all the different forms of therapy in groups—can be useful in treating psychological disorders.

BUILD TO THE OUTCOMES

1. What is the basis for psychoanalysis and its key techniques?

2. In what common ways do modern psychodynamic theories differ from Freudian analysis?

3. How does a humanistic view of human nature differ from a psychodynamic view?

4. What are the characteristics of person-centered and gestalt therapies?

5. How do behavioral therapies compensate for what behaviorists saw as problems with psychoanalytic ideas?

6. What is the idea behind the concept of cognitive restructuring?

7. How is CBT both *problem focused* and *action oriented*?

8. When is group therapy the best option?

9. How do self-help and support groups differ from traditional psychotherapy?

Biological Treatments: Healing the Mind by Physically Altering the Brain

People have ingested foreign substances in an attempt to change or improve their mental state since the beginning of recorded history. Humans have been fermenting fruits and other natural substances to create alcohol since about 7000 BCE (McGovern et al., 2004). Ancient Greek physicians prescribed a substance called *theriac* to treat a wide range of ailments, including anxiety and depression; although theriac contained many ingredients (including red roses and viper's flesh), one ingredient in particular (opium) likely was responsible for its positive effects. More recently, physicians found that another substance also worked wonders as a cure for depression, headaches, indigestion, and a range of other problems. That substance was cocaine, and it has many negative side effects, which led to it falling out of favor as a sanctioned medicine (Markel, 2011). Since then, drug treatments have been developed that don't lead users to feel euphoric (as is the case with opium and cocaine). Instead, they target specific neurotransmitters in the brain that are believed to be involved in the causes of different mental disorders. These treatments are now the most common medical approach in treating psychological disorders (see **FIGURE 15.2**).

Antipsychotic Medications

Antipsychotic drugs *treat schizophrenia and related psychotic disorders*. The first antipsychotic drug was chlorpromazine (brand name Thorazine), which was originally developed back in the 1950s as a sedative. Other related medications, such as thioridazine (Mellaril) and haloperidol (Haldol), followed. Before the introduction of antipsychotic drugs, people with schizophrenia often exhibited bizarre symptoms and were sometimes so disruptive and difficult to manage that the only way to protect them (and other people) was to keep them in hospitals for people with mental disorders, which were initially called *asylums* but now are referred to as *psychiatric hospitals*. In the period following the introduction of these drugs, the number of people in psychiatric hospitals decreased by more than two thirds. Antipsychotic drugs made possible the deinstitutionalization of hundreds of thousands of people

LEARNING OUTCOMES

- Explain how antipsychotic medications affect the brain.
- Identify the risks of antianxiety medications.
- Explain how modern antidepressants affect the brain.
- Identify which herbal supplements have been proven to be effective.
- Debate pros and cons of combining psychological therapy with drug therapy.
- Identify the more extreme treatment options when psychotherapy and medications are unsuccessful.

antipsychotic drugs Medications that are used to treat schizophrenia and related psychotic disorders.

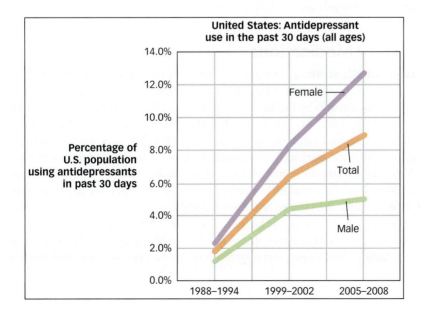

United States: Antidepressant use in the past 30 days (all ages)

Percentage of U.S. population using antidepressants in past 30 days

(Lines labeled: Female, Total, Male; x-axis: 1988–1994, 1999–2002, 2005–2008; y-axis: 0.0% to 14.0%)

Figure 15.2 ANTIDEPRESSANT USE The popularity of psychiatric medications has skyrocketed in recent years. For example, the use of antidepressant medications rose 400% from 1988 to 2008 (National Center for Health Statistics, 2012). This increase may be due to a number of factors, including the publication of data on the effectiveness of these medications, increasing efforts to disseminate them to prescribers, and enhanced efforts to market these drugs directly to consumers. The higher rates of use shown here for females may be due in part to the fact that women have higher rates of both depression and treatment use in general, compared with men.

"The drug has, however, proved more effective than traditional psychoanalysis."

Paul Noth/The New Yorker Collection/ cartoonbank.com

psychopharmacology The study of drug effects on psychological states and symptoms.

antianxiety medications Drugs that help reduce a person's experience of fear or anxiety.

If you watch television, you have seen advertisements for specific drugs. Does this direct-to-consumer advertising really work? Sure does! One study sent people posing as patients to physicians' offices asking for specific drugs and found that patient requests had a huge impact on doctors' behavior: Those asking about specific drugs were much more likely to receive a prescription than were those who did not make a request (Kravitz et al., 2005). Monkey Business/Getty Images

and gave a major boost to the field of **psychopharmacology**, *the study of drug effects on psychological states and symptoms.*

Antipsychotic medications appear to exert their effect by blocking dopamine receptors in parts of the brain. The effectiveness of schizophrenia medications led to the dopamine hypothesis (described in the Psychological Disorders chapter), suggesting that schizophrenia may be caused by excess dopamine in the synapse. Research has indeed found that dopamine overactivity in the mesolimbic pathway of the brain is related to the more bizarre positive symptoms of schizophrenia, such as hallucinations and delusions (Marangell et al., 2003).

Although antipsychotic drugs work well for positive symptoms, it turns out that negative symptoms of schizophrenia, such as emotional numbing and social withdrawal, may be related to dopamine *under*activity in the mesocortical pathways of the brain. This may help explain why antipsychotic medications do not relieve negative symptoms well. Instead of a medication that blocks dopamine receptors, negative symptoms require a medication that *increases* the amount of dopamine available at the synapse. This is a good example of how medical treatments can have broad psychological effects but do not target specific psychological symptoms.

Over the past few decades, a new class of antipsychotic drugs was introduced that includes clozapine (Clozaril), risperidone (Risperdal), and olanzepine (Zyprexa). These newer drugs are often referred to as *atypical* antipsychotics. (The older drugs are now often referred to as *conventional* or *typical* antipsychotics.) Unlike the older antipsychotic medications, these newer drugs appear to block both dopamine and serotonin receptors. Serotonin has been implicated in some of the core difficulties in schizophrenia, such as cognitive and perceptual disruptions, as well as mood disturbances, which may explain why atypical antipsychotics can provide relief for both the positive and negative symptoms of schizophrenia (Bradford, Stroup, & Lieberman, 2002).

Like most medications, antipsychotic drugs have side effects. These can include motor disturbances such as involuntary movements of the face, mouth, and extremities. In fact, people often need to take another medication to treat the unwanted side effects of the conventional antipsychotic drugs. Side effects of the newer medications tend to be different from and sometimes milder than those of the older antipsychotics. For that reason, the atypical antipsychotics are now usually the frontline treatments for schizophrenia (Meltzer, 2013).

Antianxiety Medications

Antianxiety medications are *drugs that help reduce a person's experience of fear or anxiety.* The most commonly used antianxiety medications are the benzodiazepines, a type of tranquilizer that works by facilitating the action of the neurotransmitter gamma-aminobutyric acid (GABA). As you learned in the Neuroscience and Behavior chapter, GABA inhibits certain neurons in the brain. This inhibitory action can produce a calming effect for the person. Commonly prescribed benzodiazepines include diazepam (Valium), lorazepam (Ativan), and alprazolam (Xanax). The benzodiazepines typically take effect in a matter of minutes and are effective for reducing symptoms of anxiety disorders (Roy-Byrne & Cowley, 2002).

Nonetheless, doctors are relatively cautious when prescribing benzodiazepines. One concern is that these drugs can be highly addictive. They also have side effects, including drowsiness and negative effects on coordination and memory. And benzodiazapines combined with alcohol can depress respiration, potentially causing accidental death.

Antidepressants and Mood Stabilizers

Antidepressants are *a class of drugs that help lift people's moods.* Two classes of anti-depressants were introduced in the 1950s: *monoamine oxidase inhibitors (MAOIs)* and *tricyclic antidepressants.* MAOIs prevent the enzyme monoamine oxidase from breaking down neurotransmitters such as norepinephrine, serotonin, and dopa-mine. Tricyclic antidepressants block the reuptake of norepinephrine and serotonin, thereby increasing the amount of neurotransmitter in the synaptic space between neurons. These two classes of antidepressants are used sparingly due to their side effects, which include potential dangerous increases in blood pressure, constipation, difficulty urinating, blurred vision, and racing heart (Marangell et al., 2003).

Among the most commonly used antidepressants today are the *selective serotonin reuptake inhibitors*, or SSRIs, which include drugs such as fluoxetine (Prozac), citalo-pram (Celexa), and paroxetine (Paxil). The SSRIs work by blocking the reuptake of serotonin in the brain, which makes more serotonin available in the synaptic space between neurons. The greater availability of serotonin in the synapse gives the neu-ron a better chance of "recognizing" and using this neurotransmitter in sending the desired signal. The SSRIs were developed on the basis of the hypothesis that low lev-els of serotonin are a causal factor in depression. Supporting this hypothesis, SSRIs are effective for depression, as well as for a wide range of other problems. SSRIs are called *selective* because, unlike the tricyclic antidepressants, which work on the sero-tonin and norepinephrine systems, SSRIs work more specifically on the serotonin system (see **FIGURE 15.3**).

Finally, antidepressants such as venlafaxine (Effexor) and ibupropion (Wellbutrin) offer other alternatives. Effexor is an example of a serotonin and norepinephrine reuptake inhibitor (SNRI). Whereas SSRIs act only on serotonin, SNRIs act on both serotonin and norepinephrine. Wellbutrin, in contrast, is a norepinephrine and dopa-mine reuptake inhibitor. These and other newly developed antidepressants appear to have fewer (or at least different) side effects than the tricyclic antidepressants and MAOIs.

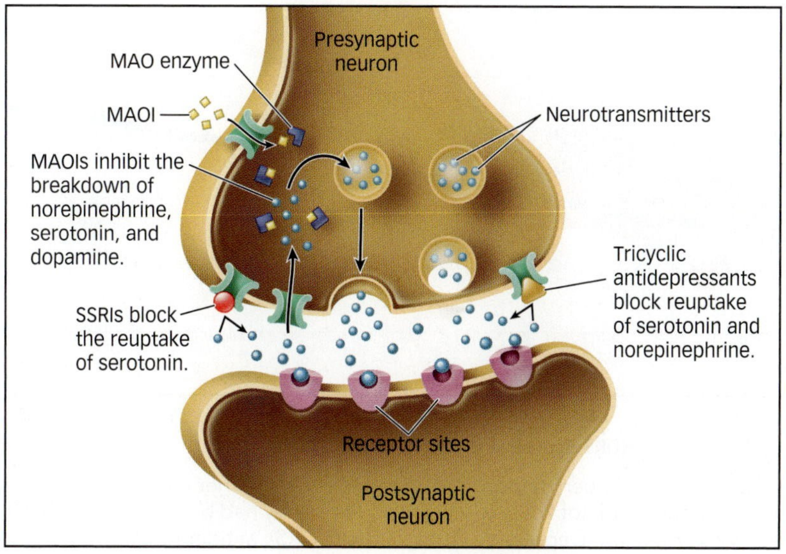

antidepressants A class of drugs that help lift people's moods.

Figure 15.3 ANTIDEPRESSANT DRUG ACTIONS Antidepressant drugs, such as MAOIs, SSRIs, and tricyclic antidepressants, act on neurotrans-mitters such as serotonin, dopamine, and norepinephrine by inhibiting their breakdown and blocking reuptake. These actions make more of the neurotransmit-ter available for release and leave more of the neurotransmitter in the synaptic gap to activate the receptor sites on the postsynaptic neuron. These drugs relieve depression and often alleviate anxiety and other disorders.

Most antidepressants can take up to a month before they start to have an effect on mood. Besides relieving symptoms of depression, almost all of the antidepressants are also used to treat anxiety disorders. However, recent research suggests that antidepressants are only slightly more effective at relieving anxiety than is a placebo (i.e., a sugar pill containing no active medicine) (Kirsch et al., 2008). (Check out A World of Difference: Differences in People's Responses to Treatment to learn more.)

A WORLD OF DIFFERENCE

Differences in People's Responses to Treatment

We are all different. We like different foods, different music, different books, and so on. It turns out that we also differ in how we respond to treatments for psychological disorders. For instance, one recent study compared symptoms of depression in 718 patients randomly assigned to receive either antidepressant medication or pill placebo (Fournier et al., 2010). Participants receiving medication showed a dramatic decrease in symptoms over the course of treatment. However, so did those taking placebo. Closer examination of the data revealed that for those with mild or moderate depression, placebo is just as effective as antidepressant medication at decreasing a person's symptoms, and it is only for people with severe depression that antidepressants seem to work better than placebo (see figure).

What predicts which kind of people will respond best to which kind of treatment? A recent study found that data collected before people are randomized to a given treatment (e.g., cognitive behavioral therapy vs. medication) could be used to predict accurately which treatment would benefit them most (DeRubeis et al., 2014). A follow-up study compared two other kinds of treatment, cognitive therapy and interpersonal psychotherapy (Huibers et al., 2015). In this study, patients who were randomly assigned to the treatment that was predicted to be more effective for them improved significantly more than those assigned to their nonoptimal treatment. Such findings suggest that, in the future, psychologists will be able to collect information from new patients in order to determine which of the many available treatments will benefit them most. This personalized, or tailored, approach to treatment is likely to lead to much better outcomes for users of psychological services in the future, and in this way is expected to make a world of difference!

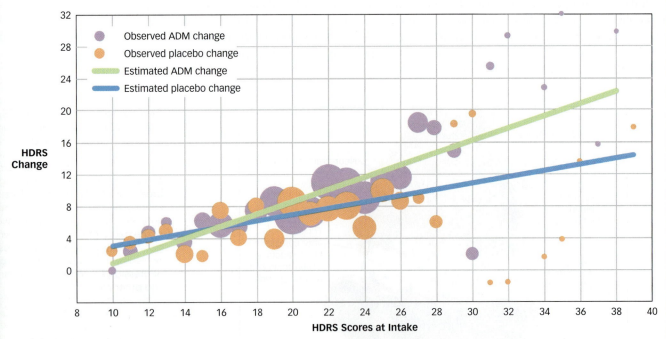

Six different studies compared depressed individuals who had been randomly assigned to receive either an antidepressant medication (ADM) or a pill placebo. Importantly, the participants did not know to which condition they had been assigned. For those with mild or moderate depression, as measured by the Hamilton Depression Rating Scale (HDRS), antidepressants did not work any better than placebo. However, patients with severe depression showed much greater improvement on antidepressants than on placebo. The circle size represents the number of people with data at each point (data from Fournier et al., 2010).

Although antidepressants are commonly used to treat major depression, they are not recommended for treating bipolar disorder because, in the process of lifting one's mood, they might actually trigger a manic episode (see the Psychological Disorders chapter). Instead, bipolar disorder is treated with *mood stabilizers*, which are medications used to suppress swings between mania and depression. Commonly used mood stabilizers include lithium and valproate.

Herbal and Natural Products

In a survey of more than 2,000 Americans, 7% of those suffering from anxiety disorders and 9% of those suffering from severe depression reported using alternative "medications" such as herbal medicines, megavitamins, or homeopathic remedies to treat these problems (Kessler et al., 2001). Major reasons people use these products are that they are easily available over the counter, are less expensive, and are perceived as "natural" alternatives to synthetic or manmade "drugs." Are herbal and natural products effective in treating mental health problems? Or are they just "snake oil"?

The answer to this question isn't simple. Herbal products are not considered medications by regulatory agencies such as the Food and Drug Administration, so they are exempt from rigorous research to establish their safety and effectiveness. There is little scientific information about herbal products, including possible interactions with other medications, side effects, appropriate dosages, how they work, or even *whether* they work—and the purity of these products often varies from brand to brand (Jordan, Cunningham, & Marles, 2010).

There is research support for the effectiveness of some herbal and natural products, but the evidence is not overwhelming (Lake, 2009). For example, some studies have shown St. John's wort has an advantage over a placebo condition for the treatment of depression (e.g., Lecrubier et al., 2002), whereas other studies show no advantage (e.g., Hypericum Depression Trial Study Group, 2002). Omega-3 fatty acids have been linked with lower rates of depression and suicide (see **FIGURE 15.4**), and several treatment studies have shown that omega-3s are superior to placebo at decreasing depression (Lewis et al., 2011; Parker et al., 2006). Overall, although herbal medications and treatments are worthy of continued research, these products should be closely monitored and used judiciously until more is known about their safety and effectiveness.

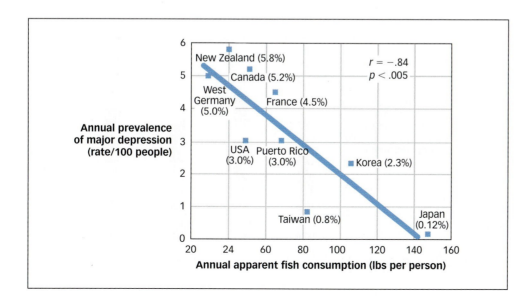

Figure 15.4 OMEGA-3 FATTY ACIDS AND DEPRESSION Recent studies have shown that consumption of omega-3 fatty acids is associated with a wide range of positive mental health outcomes. For instance, countries that consume more fish (a main dietary source of omega-3s) have significantly lower rates of depression (Hibbeln, 1998). But remember, correlation does not mean causation! It could be that some other factor explains this association. For instance, it could be that living closer to the ocean or a greater focus on health overall predicts both greater omega-3 consumption and lower rates of depression.

phototherapy A therapy that involves repeated exposure to bright light.

Photatherapy, *a therapy that involves repeated exposure to bright light*, is another natural treatment that may be helpful to people who have a seasonal pattern to their depression. This could include people suffering with seasonal affective disorder (SAD; see the Psychological Disorders chapter). Typically, people are exposed to bright light in the morning, using a lamp designed for this purpose. Phototherapy has not been as well researched as psychological treatment or medication, but the handful of studies available suggest it is about as effective as antidepressant medication in the treatment of SAD (Thaler et al., 2011).

Combining Medication and Psychotherapy

Given that psychological treatments and medications both have shown an ability to treat mental disorders effectively, some natural next questions are: Which is more effective? Is the combination of psychological and medicinal treatments better than either by itself? The answer often depends on the particular problem being considered. For example, in the cases of schizophrenia and bipolar disorder, researchers have found that medication is more effective than is psychological treatment and so is considered a necessary part of treatment. But in the case of mood and anxiety disorders, medication and psychological treatments are equally effective. One study compared cognitive behavioral therapy, imipramine (an antidepressant), and the combination of these treatments (CBT plus imipramine) with a placebo (administration of an inert medication) for the treatment of panic disorder (Barlow et al., 2000). After 12 weeks of treatment, either CBT alone or imipramine alone was found to be superior to a placebo, but the combination of treatments was not significantly more effective than was either treatment alone (see **FIGURE 15.5**). More is not always better (see Other Voices: Diagnosis: Human).

Given that both therapy and medications are effective, one question is whether they work through similar mechanisms. A study of people with social phobia examined patterns of cerebral blood flow following treatment using either citalopram (an SSRI) or CBT (Furmark et al., 2002). Participants in both groups were alerted to the possibility that they would soon have to speak in public. In both groups, those who responded to treatment showed decreased activation in the amygdala, hippocampus, and neighboring cortical areas during this challenge (see **FIGURE 15.6**). The amygdala, located next to the hippocampus (see Figure 6.18), plays a significant role in memory for emotional information. These findings suggest that both therapy and medication affect the brain in regions associated with a reaction to threat.

Figure 15.5 THE EFFECTIVENESS OF PSYCHOTHERAPY AND MEDICINE FOR PANIC DISORDER One study of CBT and medication (imipramine) for panic disorder found that the effects of CBT, medication, and treatment that combined CBT and medication were not significantly different over the short term, though all three were superior to the placebo condition (Barlow et al., 2000).

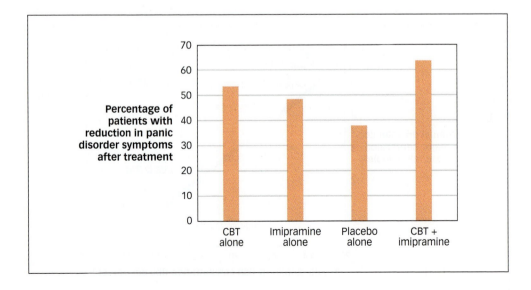

OTHER VOICES

Diagnosis: Human

Ted Gup is an author and a fellow of the Edmond J. Safra Center for Ethics at Harvard University. Susan Symones/Infinity Portrait Design

Should more people receive psychological treatment or medications? Or should fewer? On one hand, data indicate that most people with a mental disorder do not receive treatment and that untreated mental disorders are an enormous source of pain and suffering. On the other hand, some argue that we have become too quick to label normal human behavior as "disordered" and too willing to medicate any behavior, thought, or feeling that makes us uncomfortable. Ted Gup is one of these people. The following is a version of his op-ed piece that appeared in the *New York Times* on April 3, 2013, under the headline "Diagnosis: Human."

The news that 11 percent of school-age children now receive a diagnosis of attention deficit hyperactivity disorder—some 6.4 million—gave me a chill. My son David was one of those who received that diagnosis.

In his case, he was in the first grade. Indeed, there were psychiatrists who prescribed medication for him even before they met him. One psychiatrist said he would not even see him until he was medicated. For a year I refused to fill the prescription at the pharmacy. Finally, I relented. And so David went on Ritalin, then Adderall, and other drugs that were said to be helpful in combating the condition.

In another age, David might have been called "rambunctious." His battery was a little too large for his body. And so he would leap over the couch, spring to reach the ceiling and show an exuberance for life that came in brilliant microbursts.

As a 21-year-old college senior, he was found on the floor of his room, dead from a fatal mix of alcohol and drugs. The date was Oct. 18, 2011. No one made him take the heroin and alcohol, and yet I cannot help but hold myself and others to account. I had unknowingly colluded with a system that devalues talking therapy and rushes to medicate, inadvertently sending a message that self-medication, too, is perfectly acceptable.

My son was no angel (though he was to us) and he was known to trade in Adderall, to create a submarket in the drug among his classmates who were themselves all too eager to get their hands on it. What he did cannot be excused, but it should be understood. What he did was to create a market that perfectly mirrored the society in which he grew up, a culture where Big Pharma itself prospers from the off-label uses of drugs, often not tested in children and not approved for the many uses to which they are put.

And so a generation of students, raised in an environment that encourages medication, are emulating the professionals by using drugs in the classroom as performance enhancers.

And we wonder why it is that they use drugs with such abandon. As all parents learn—at times to their chagrin—our children go to school not only in the classroom but also at home, and the culture they construct for themselves as teenagers and young adults is but a tiny village imitating that to which they were introduced as children. . . .

Ours is an age in which the airwaves and media are one large drug emporium that claims to fix everything from sleep to sex. I fear that being human is itself fast becoming a condition. It's as if we are trying to contain grief, and the absolute pain of a loss like mine. We have become increasingly disassociated and estranged from the patterns of life and death, uncomfortable with the messiness of our own humanity, aging and, ultimately, mortality.

Challenge and hardship have become pathologized and monetized. Instead of enhancing our coping skills, we undermine them and seek shortcuts where there are none, eroding the resilience upon which each of us, at some point in our lives, must rely.

Have we gone too far in labeling and treatment of mental disorders? Or have we not gone far enough? On one hand, we shouldn't rush to diagnose and medicate normal behavior, but on the other hand, we must provide help to those who are suffering with a true mental disorder. One possible way forward is to ensure that people are diagnosed and treated only after a thorough evaluation by a well-trained professional. This way, we will know that a mental health professional has carefully considered whether the problems a person is having are truly disordered and in need of intervention, or just part of being human.

Figure 15.6 THE EFFECTS OF MEDICATION AND THERAPY IN THE BRAIN PET scans of individuals with social phobia showed similar reductions in activations of the amygdala–hippocampus region after they received treatment with CBT (*left*) or the SSRI citalopram (*right*) (from Furmark et al., 2002). Courtesy Tomas Furmark

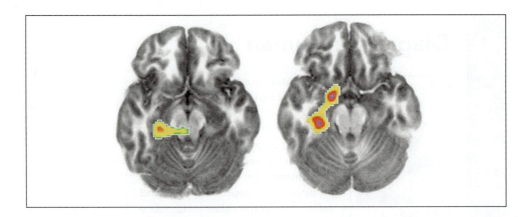

One complication in combining medication and psychotherapy is that these treatments are often provided by different people. Psychiatrists are trained in the administration of medication in medical school (and they may also provide psychological treatment), whereas psychologists provide psychological treatment but not medication. This means that the coordination of treatment often requires cooperation between psychologists and psychiatrists.

The question of whether psychologists should be licensed to prescribe medications has been a source of debate (Fox et al., 2009). Opponents argue that psychologists do not have the medical training to understand how medications interact with other drugs. Proponents argue that patient safety would not be compromised as long as rigorous training procedures were established. At present, the coordination of medication and psychological treatment usually involves a team effort of psychiatry and psychology.

Biological Treatments Beyond Medication

Medication can be an effective biological treatment, but for some people medications do not work, or side effects are intolerable. If this group of people doesn't respond to psychotherapy either, what other options do they have to achieve symptom relief? Additional avenues of help are available, but some are risky or poorly understood.

Electroconvulsive therapy (ECT), sometimes referred to as *shock therapy*, is *a treatment that involves inducing a brief seizure by delivering an electrical shock to the brain.* The shock is applied to the person's scalp for less than a second. ECT is used primarily to treat severe depression that has not responded to antidepressant medications, although it may also be useful for treating bipolar disorder (Khalid et al., 2008; Poon et al., 2012). Patients are pretreated with muscle relaxants and are under general anesthetic, so they are not conscious of the procedure. The main side effect of ECT is impaired short-term memory, which usually improves over the first month or two after the end of treatment. In addition, patients undergoing this procedure sometimes report headaches and muscle aches afterward (Marangell et al., 2003). Despite these side effects, ECT can be more effective than simulated ECT, placebo, or antidepressant drugs such as tricyclics and MAOIs (Pagnin et al., 2008).

Transcranial magnetic stimulation (TMS) is *a treatment that involves placing a powerful pulsed magnet over a person's scalp to alter neuronal activity in the brain* (see the Neuroscience and Behavior chapter). TMS is noninvasive and side effects are minimal; they include mild headache and a small risk of seizure, but TMS has no impact on memory or concentration. Daily TMS applied to the left prefrontal cortex for 4 to 6 weeks has been found to be effective in the treatment of depression in patients who have not responded to medication (Perera et al., 2016). In fact, a study comparing TMS with ECT found that both procedures were effective, with no significant differences between them (Janicak et al., 2002). Other studies have found

electroconvulsive therapy (ECT) A treatment that involves inducing a brief seizure by delivering an electrical shock to the brain.

transcranial magnetic stimulation (TMS) A treatment that involves placing a powerful pulsed magnet over a person's scalp to alter neuronal activity in the brain.

Electroconvulsive therapy (ECT) can be an effective treatment for severe depression. To reduce the side effects, it is administered under general anesthesia.
Richard Perry/*The New York Times*/Redux

that TMS can also be used to treat auditory hallucinations in schizophrenia (Aleman, Sommer, & Kahn, 2007).

In very rare cases, **psychosurgery**, *the surgical destruction of specific brain areas*, may be used to treat psychological disorders. Psychosurgery has a controversial history, beginning in the 1930s with the invention of the lobotomy by the Portuguese physician Antonio Egas Moniz (1874–1955). Lobotomies involved inserting an instrument into the brain through the patient's eye socket or through holes drilled in the side of the head. The objective was to sever connections between the frontal lobes and inner brain structures such as the thalamus, known to be involved in emotion. Although some lobotomies produced highly successful results and Moniz received the 1949 Nobel Prize for his work, significant side effects such as extreme lethargy or childlike impulsiveness detracted from these benefits. Lobotomy was used widely for years, leaving many people devastated by these permanent side effects, and because of this, for many years there was a movement challenging the awarding of the Nobel Prize to Moniz. (It was never revoked.) The development of antipsychotic drugs during the 1950s provided a safer way to treat violent individuals and brought the practice of lobotomy to an end (Swayze, 1995).

Today, psychosurgery is reserved only for extremely severe cases for which no other interventions have been effective, and the symptoms of the disorder are intolerable to the patient. Modern psychosurgery involves a very precise destruction of brain tissue in order to disrupt the brain circuits known to be involved in the generation of symptoms. For example, people suffering from OCD who fail to respond to treatment (including several trials of medications and cognitive behavioral treatment) may benefit from specific surgical procedures to destroy part of the corpus callosum (see Figure 3.13) and the cingulate gyrus (the ridge just above the corpus callosum), two brain regions known to be involved in the generation of obsessions and compulsions. Because of the relatively small number of cases of psychosurgery, there are not as many studies of these techniques as there are for other treatments. However, available studies have shown that psychosurgery typically leads to substantial improvements in both the short and long term for people with severe OCD (Csigó et al., 2010; van Vliet et al., 2013).

A final approach, called *deep brain stimulation* (DBS), combines the use of psychosurgery with the use of electrical currents (as in ECT and TMS). In DBS, a treatment pioneered only recently, a small, battery-powered device is implanted in the body to deliver electrical stimulation to specific areas of the brain known to be involved in the disorder being targeted (**FIGURE 15.7**). This technique has been

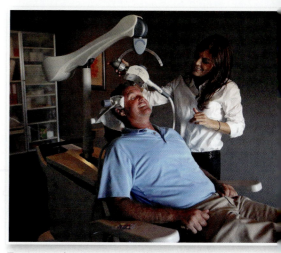

Transcranial magnetic stimulation (TMS) is an exciting new technique that allows researchers and clinicians to change brain activity using a magnetic wand—no surgery is required. Bruce R. Bennett/Corbis

psychosurgery Surgical destruction of specific brain areas.

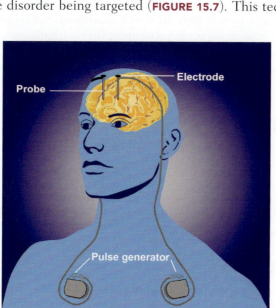

Figure 15.7 DBS Deep brain stimulation involves the insertion of battery-powered electrodes that deliver electrical pulses to specific areas of the brain believed to be causing a person's mental disorder. National Institute of Mental Health, National Institutes of Health, Department of Health and Human Services

successful for OCD treatment (Abelson et al., 2009), for treating the tremor that accompanies Parkinson's disease (Perlmutter & Mink, 2006), and some cases of severe depression that are otherwise untreatable (Mayberg et al., 2005). The early view of psychosurgery as a treatment of last resort is being replaced by a cautious hope that newer, focused treatments that target brain circuits known to be functioning abnormally in those with certain mental disorders can have beneficial effects (Ressler & Mayberg, 2007).

BUILD TO THE OUTCOMES

1. What do antipsychotic drugs do?
2. What are the advantages of the newer, atypical antipsychotic medications?
3. What are some reasons for caution when prescribing antianxiety medications?
4. How do antidepressant drugs affect neurotransmitters?
5. Why are antidepressants not prescribed for bipolar disorder?
6. Why aren't herbal and natural products given the same scrutiny given to pharmacological drugs?
7. Which herbal remedies have been proven to be effective?
8. Do therapy and medications work similarly in treating mental illness?
9. What are the benefits of ECT? The risks?
10. What is the procedure for TMS?
11. When would the use of psychosurgery be appropriate?

Treatment Effectiveness: For Better or for Worse

LEARNING OUTCOMES
- Describe treatment illusions.
- Explain research methods used in treatment studies.

Think back to Christine and the dead mouse at the beginning of this chapter. What if, instead of exposure and response prevention, Christine had been assigned psychoanalysis or psychosurgery? Could these alternatives have been just as effective (and justified) for treating her OCD? Throughout this chapter, we have explored various psychological and biological treatments that might help people with psychological disorders. But do these treatments actually work? Which ones work better than the others?

As you learned in the Methods in Psychology chapter, pinning down a specific cause for an effect can be a difficult detective exercise. The detection is made even more difficult because people may approach treatment evaluation very unscientifically, often by simply noticing an improvement (or no improvement) and reaching a conclusion based on that sole observation. Determination of a treatment's effectiveness can be misdirected by illusions that can be overcome only by careful, scientific evaluation.

Treatment Illusions

Imagine you're sick, and the doctor says, "Take a pill." You follow the doctor's orders, and you get better. To what do you attribute your improvement? If you're like most people, you reach the conclusion that the pill cured you. That's one possible explanation, but you might have fallen victim to an illusion of treatment. Such illusions can be produced by natural improvement, by placebo effects, and by reconstructive memory. Let's look more closely at each.

Natural Improvement

Natural improvement is the tendency of symptoms to return to their mean or average level. The illusion in this case happens when you conclude mistakenly that a treatment has made you better when you would have gotten better anyway. People typically turn to therapy or medication when their symptoms are at their worst. When this is the case, the client's symptoms will often improve, regardless of whether there was any treatment at all; when you're at rock bottom, there's nowhere to move but up. In most cases, for example, depression that becomes severe enough to make individuals candidates for treatment will tend to lift in several months *no matter what they do.* A person who enters therapy for depression may develop an illusion that the therapy works because the therapy coincides with the typical course of the illness and the person's natural return to health. How can we know if change was caused by the treatment or by natural improvement? As discussed in the Methods in Psychology chapter, we could do an experiment in which we assign half of the people who are depressed to receive treatment and the other half to receive no treatment, and then monitor them over time to see if the ones who got treatment actually show greater improvement. This is precisely how researchers test out different interventions, as described in more detail below.

Placebo Effects

Recovery could be produced by *nonspecific treatment effects* that are not related to the specific mechanisms by which treatment is supposed to be working. For example, simply knowing that you are getting a treatment can produce a nonspecific treatment effect. These instances include the positive influences that can be produced by a **placebo**, *an inert substance or procedure that has been applied with the expectation that it will produce a healing response.* For example, if you take a sugar pill that does not contain any painkiller for a headache thinking it is Tylenol or aspirin, this pill is a placebo. Placebos can have profound effects in the case of psychological treatments. Research shows that a large percentage of individuals with anxiety, depression, and other emotional and medical problems experience significant improvement after a placebo treatment (see A World of Difference: Differences in People's Responses to Treatment).

placebo An inert substance or procedure that has been applied with the expectation that it will produce a healing response.

Reconstructive Memory

A third treatment illusion can come about when the client's motivation to get well causes errors in *reconstructive memory* for the original symptoms. You might think that you've improved because of a treatment when in fact you're simply misremembering,

"If this doesn't help you don't worry, it's a placebo."

Peter C. Vey/The New Yorker Collection/cartooonbank.com

mistakenly believing that your symptoms before treatment were worse than they actually were. For example, a client who forms a strong expectation of success in therapy might conclude later that even a useless treatment had worked wonders by recalling past symptoms and troubles as worse than they were and thereby making the treatment seem effective.

Treatment Studies: Seeking Evidence

How can we make sure that we are using treatments that actually work and not wasting time with procedures that may be useless or even harmful? Research psychologists use the approaches covered in the Methods in Psychology chapter to create experiments that test whether treatments are effective for different mental disorders.

Treatment outcome studies are designed to evaluate whether a particular treatment works, often compared with some other treatment or a control condition. For example, to study the outcome of treatment for depression, researchers might compare the self-reported symptoms of two groups of people who were initially depressed: a group that received treatment for 6 weeks and a control group that had also been selected for the study but were assigned to a waiting list for later treatment and were simply tested 6 weeks after their selection. The treatment outcome study could determine whether this treatment had any benefit.

Researchers use a range of methods to ensure that any observed effects are not due to the treatment illusions described earlier. For example, the treatment illusions caused by natural improvement and reconstructive memory happen when people compare their symptoms before treatment with their symptoms after treatment. To avoid this, patients should be randomly assigned to a treatment (or experimental) group or a control group, which are then compared at the end of treatment. That way, natural improvement or reconstructive memory can't cause illusions of effective treatment.

But what should happen to the control group during the treatment? If they simply stay home waiting until they can get treatment later (a wait-list control group), they won't receive the placebo effects. So, ideally, a treatment should be assessed in a *double-blind experiment*, a study in which both the participant and the researcher/therapist are uninformed about which treatment the participant is receiving. In drug studies, this isn't hard to arrange because active drugs and placebos can be made to look alike to both the participants and the researchers during the study. Keeping both participants and researchers "in the dark" is much harder in the study of psychological treatments; in fact, in most cases it is not possible. Both the participant and the therapist can easily notice the differences in treatments such as psychoanalysis and behavior therapy, for example, so there's no way to keep the beliefs and expectations of both participant and therapist completely out of the picture in evaluating psychotherapy effectiveness. Nevertheless, by comparing treatments either with no treatment or with other active interventions (such as other psychological treatments or medications), researchers can determine which treatments work and which are most effective for different disorders.

Which Treatments Work According to the Evidence?

The distinguished psychologist Hans Eysenck (1916–1997) reviewed the relatively few studies of psychotherapy effectiveness available in 1957 and raised a furor among therapists by concluding that psychotherapy—particularly psychoanalysis—not only was ineffective but seemed to *impede* recovery (Eysenck, 1957). Since then, studies support a more optimistic conclusion: The typical psychotherapy client is better off than three quarters of untreated individuals (Seligman, 1995; Smith, Glass, & Miller, 1980), and strong evidence supports the effectiveness of many treatments (Nathan & Gorman, 2007). Still, some psychologists argue that

TABLE 15.2 Selected List of Specific Psychological Treatments Compared with Medication or Other Treatments

Disorder	Treatment	Results
Depression	CBT	PT = meds; PT + meds > either alone
Panic disorder	CBT	PT > meds at follow-up; PT = meds at end of treatment; both > placebo
Posttraumatic stress disorder	CBT	PT > present-centered therapy
Insomnia	CBT	PT > medication or placebo
Depression and physical health in Alzheimer's patients	Exercise and behavioral management	PT > routine medical care
Gulf War veterans' illnesses	CBT and exercise	PT > usual care or alternative treatments

Note: CBT = cognitive behavioral therapy; PT = psychological treatment; meds = medication.

Information from Barlow et al. (2013).

most psychotherapies work about equally well due to shared common factors such as contact with and empathy from a professional (Luborsky et al., 2002; Luborsky & Singer, 1975). Others have argued that some therapies are more effective than are others, especially for treating particular types of problems (Beutler, 2002; Hunsley & Di Giulio, 2002). A recent review highlighted several specific psychological treatments that have been shown to work as well as, or even better than, other available treatments, including medication (Barlow et al., 2013). **TABLE 15.2** lists several of these treatments.

Some researchers and clinicians have questioned whether treatments shown to work in well-controlled treatment studies conducted at university clinics will work in the real world. For instance, some psychologists have noted that most treatment studies reported in the literature do not have large numbers of participants who are of ethnic minority status, and so it is unclear if these treatments will work with ethnically and culturally diverse groups. One recent, comprehensive review of all available data suggests that, despite gaps in the literature, many psychological treatments work as well with ethnic minority clients as with White clients (Miranda et al., 2005).

Treatments that are shown to be effective in research studies (which often include only a small percentage of ethnic minority patients) have been found to work equally well with people of different ethnicities (Miranda et al., 2005). Mary Kate Denny/Photoedit; Wavebreak Media Ltd/Alamy Stock Photo

Even trickier than the question of establishing whether a treatment works is whether a psychotherapy or medication might actually do harm. The dangers of drug treatment should be clear to anyone who has read a magazine ad for a drug and studied the fine print with its list of side effects, potential drug interactions, and complications. Many drugs used for psychological treatment may be addictive, creating long-term dependency with serious withdrawal symptoms. The strongest critics of drug treatment claim that drugs do no more than trade one unwanted symptom for another: depression for lack of sexual interest, anxiety for intoxication, or agitation for lethargy and dulled emotion (e.g., see Breggin, 2000).

The dangers of psychotherapy are more subtle, but one is clear enough in some cases that there is actually a name for it. **Iatrogenic illness** is *a disorder or symptom that occurs as a result of a medical or psychotherapeutic treatment itself* (e.g., Boisvert & Faust, 2002). Such an illness might arise, for example, when a psychotherapist becomes convinced that a client has a disorder that in fact the client does not have. As a result, the therapist works to help the client accept that diagnosis and participate in psychotherapy to treat that disorder. Being treated for a disorder can, under certain conditions, make a person show signs of that very disorder—and so an iatrogenic illness is born. For example, there are cases of clients who have been influenced through hypnosis and repeated suggestions in therapy to "recover" memories of traumatic childhood events, when investigation reveals no evidence for these problems prior to therapy (Acocella, 1999; McNally, 2003; Ofshe & Watters, 1994).

Just as psychologists have created lists of treatments that work, they also have begun to establish lists of treatments that *harm*. The purpose of doing so is to inform other researchers, clinicians, and the public about which treatments they should avoid. Many people are under the impression that, although every psychological treatment may not be effective, some treatment is better than no treatment. However, it turns out that a number of interventions intended to help alleviate people's symptoms actually make them worse! Did your high school have a D.A.R.E. (Drug Abuse and Resistance Education) program? Have you heard of critical-incident stress debriefing (CISD), Scared Straight, and boot-camp programs? They all sound as if they might work, but careful scientific experiments have determined that people who participate in these interventions are actually worse off after doing so (see **TABLE 15.3**; Lilienfeld, 2007)!

To regulate the potentially powerful influence of therapies, psychologists hold themselves to a set of ethical standards for the treatment of people with mental disorders (American Psychological Association, 2002). Adherence to these standards is required for membership in the American Psychological Association, and state licensing boards also monitor adherence to ethical principles in therapy.

iatrogenic illness A disorder or symptom that occurs as a result of a medical or psychotherapeutic treatment itself.

TABLE 15.3 Some Psychological Treatments That Cause Harm

Type of Treatment	Potential Harm	Source of Evidence
CISD	Increased risk of PTSD	RCTs
Scared Straight	Worsening of conduct problems	RCTs
Boot-camp interventions for conduct problems	Worsening of conduct problems	Meta-analysis (review of studies)
DARE programs	Increased use of alcohol and drugs	RCTs

Note: CISD = critical-incident stress debriefing; PTSD = posttraumatic stress disorder; RCTs = randomized controlled trials.

Information from Lilienfeld (2007).

These ethical standards include (1) striving to benefit clients and taking care to do no harm; (2) establishing relationships of trust with clients; (3) promoting accuracy, honesty, and truthfulness; (4) seeking fairness in treatment and taking precautions to avoid biases; and (5) respecting the dignity and worth of all people. When people suffering from mental disorders come to psychologists for help, adhering to these guidelines is the least that psychologists can do. Ideally, in the hope of relieving this suffering, they can do much more.

BUILD TO THE OUTCOMES

1. What are three kinds of treatment illusions?
2. What is the placebo effect?
3. What methods are used in treatment outcome studies?
4. Why is a double-blind experiment so important in assessing treatment effectiveness?
5. How do psychologists know which treatments work and which might be harmful?
6. How might psychotherapy cause harm?

CHAPTER REVIEW

Treatment: Getting Help to Those Who Need It

- Mental illness is often misunderstood, and because of this, it often goes untreated as well, affecting an individual's ability to function and also causing social and financial burdens.
- Many people who suffer from mental illness do not get the help they need: They may be unaware that they have a problem, they may be uninterested in getting help for their problem, or they may face structural barriers to getting treatment.
- Treatments include psychotherapy, which focuses on the mind; medical and biological methods, which focus on the brain and body; and a combination of the two approaches.

Psychological Treatments: Healing the Mind Through Interaction

- Psychodynamic therapies, including psychoanalysis, emphasize helping clients gain insight into their unconscious conflicts.
- Humanistic approaches (e.g., person-centered therapy) and existential approaches (e.g., gestalt therapy) focus on helping people to develop a sense of personal worth.
- Behavior therapy applies learning principles to specific behavior problems. Cognitive therapy is focused on teaching people to challenge irrational thoughts. Cognitive behavioral therapy (CBT) merges these two approaches.
- Group therapies target couples, families, or groups of clients brought together for the purpose of working together to solve their problems.

Biological Treatments: Healing the Mind by Physically Altering the Brain

- Antipsychotic medications block dopamine receptors in parts of the brain, reducing dopamine activity. They are used to treat the positive symptoms of schizophrenia.
- Antianxiety medications are used to treat anxiety disorders but have the potential for abuse especially because of the development of drug tolerance.
- Antidepressants affect the level of serotonin in the brain and are used to treat depression and related disorders.
- Herbal and natural products are not considered medications by regulatory agencies and so are not subject to strict scrutiny. Although there is little scientific information on their effectiveness, some do indicate mild positive effects.
- Medications are often combined with psychotherapy. Evidence from a study on social phobia suggests that both affect the brain in regions associated with threat.
- Other biomedical treatments include electroconvulsive therapy (ECT), transcranial magnetic stimulation (TMS), and psychosurgery—this last one used in extreme cases, when other methods of treatment have been exhausted.

Treatment Effectiveness: For Better or for Worse

- Observing improvement during treatment does not necessarily mean that the treatment was effective; it might instead reflect natural improvement, nonspecific treatment effects (e.g., the placebo effect), and reconstructive memory processes.

- Treatment studies apply scientific research methods such as double-blind techniques and placebo controls to determine which treatments work.

- Some treatments for psychological disorders are more effective than are others for certain disorders, and both medication and psychotherapy have dangers that ethical practitioners must consider carefully.

KEY CONCEPT QUIZ

1. Which of the following is NOT a reason that people fail to get treatment for mental illness?
   a. People may not realize that their disorder needs to be treated.
   b. Levels of impairment for people with mental illness are comparable with or higher than those of people with chronic medical illnesses.
   c. There may be barriers to treatment, such as beliefs and circumstances that keep people from getting help.
   d. Even people who acknowledge they have a problem may not know where to look for services.

2. Which of the following statements is true?
   a. Mental illness is very rare, with only 1 person in 100 suffering from a psychological disorder.
   b. The majority of individuals with psychological disorders seek treatment.
   c. Women and men are equally likely to seek treatment for psychological disorders.
   d. Mental illness is often not taken as seriously as physical illness.

3. The most effective treatment for psychological disorders is often
   a. yoga.
   b. hypnosis.
   c. psychotherapy, medication, or a combination of the two.
   d. doing nothing since most people improve anyway.

4. Eclectic psychotherapy
   a. concentrates on the interpretation of dreams.
   b. introduces clients to strange situations.
   c. draws on techniques from different forms of therapy.
   d. focuses on the analysis of resistance.

5. The different psychodynamic therapies all share an emphasis on
   a. the influence of the collective unconscious.
   b. the importance of taking responsibility for psychological problems.
   c. combining behavioral and cognitive approaches.
   d. developing insight into the unconscious sources of psychological disorders.

6. Which type of therapy would likely work best for someone with an irrational fear of heights?
   a. psychodynamic
   b. gestalt
   c. behavioral
   d. humanistic

7. Mindfulness meditation is part of which kind of therapy?
   a. interpersonal
   b. humanistic
   c. psychodynamic
   d. cognitive

8. Which type of therapy emphasizes action on the part of the client, as well as complete transparency as to the specifics of the treatment?
   a. cognitive behavioral
   b. humanistic
   c. existential
   d. group

9. Examining the failure to reach one's potential reflects the _____ approach, whereas examining one's failure to find meaning in life reflects the _____ approach.
   a. cognitive; behavioral
   b. humanistic; existential
   c. psychodynamic; cognitive behavioral
   d. existential; humanistic

10. Antipsychotic drugs were developed to treat
   a. depression.
   b. schizophrenia.
   c. anxiety.
   d. mood disorders.

11. Atypical antipsychotic drugs
   a. act on different neurotransmitters depending on the individual.
   b. affect only the dopamine system.
   c. affect only the serotonin system.
   d. act on both the dopamine and serotonin systems.

12. Antidepressant medications have the strongest effects for people with _____ depression.
   a. no
   b. mild
   c. moderate
   d. severe

13. What do electroconvulsive therapy, transcranial magnetic stimulation, and phototherapy all have in common?
   a. They incorporate herbal remedies in their treatment regimens.
   b. They may result in the surgical destruction of certain brain areas.
   c. They are considered biological treatments beyond medication.
   d. They are typically used in conjunction with psychosurgery.

14. Which treatment illusion occurs when a client or therapist attributes the client's improvement to a feature of treatment, although that feature wasn't really the active element that caused improvement?

a. nonspecific treatment effects
b. natural improvement
c. error in reconstructive memory
d. regression to the mean

15. Current studies indicate that the typical psychotherapy client is better off than are _____ of untreated individuals.

a. one half
b. the same number
c. one fourth
d. three fourths

 **LearningCurve**   **Don't stop now! Quizzing yourself is a powerful study tool.** Go to LearningCurve at www.launchpadworks.com for more practice.

KEY TERMS

psychotherapy (p. 484)
eclectic psychotherapy (p. 484)
psychodynamic psychotherapies (p. 485)
resistance (p. 485)
transference (p. 486)
interpersonal psychotherapy (IPT) (p. 486)

person-centered therapy (or client-centered therapy) (p. 487)
gestalt therapy (p. 488)
behavior therapy (p. 488)
token economy (p. 489)
exposure therapy (p. 489)
cognitive therapy (p. 490)
cognitive restructuring (p. 490)

mindfulness meditation (p. 491)
cognitive behavioral therapy (CBT) (p. 491)
group therapy (p. 493)
antipsychotic drugs (p. 495)
psychopharmacology (p. 496)
antianxiety medications (p. 496)
antidepressants (p. 497)

phototherapy (p. 500)
electroconvulsive therapy (ECT) (p. 502)
transcranial magnetic stimulation (TMS) (p. 502)
psychosurgery (p. 503)
placebo (p. 505)
iatrogenic illness (p. 508)

CHANGING MINDS

1. One of your friends recently lost a close family member in a tragic car accident, and he's devastated. He hasn't been attending classes, and when you check up on him, you learn that he's not sleeping well or eating regularly. You want to help him but feel a little out of your depth, so you suggest he visit the campus counseling center and talk to a therapist. "Only crazy people go to therapy," he says. What could you tell your friend to dispel his assumption?

2. While you're talking to your bereaved friend, his roommate comes in. The roommate agrees with your suggestion about therapy but takes it further. "I'll give you the name of my therapist. He helped me quit smoking—he'll be able to cure your depression in no time." Why is it dangerous to assume that a good therapist can cure anyone and anything?

3. In the Methods in Psychology chapter, you read about Louise Hay, whose best-selling book, *You Can Heal Your Life*, promotes a kind of psychotherapy: teaching readers how to change their thoughts and thereby improve not only their inner lives but also their physical health. The chapter quotes Hay as saying that scientific evidence is unnecessary to validate her claims. Is there a scientific basis for the major types of psychotherapy described in this chapter? How is scientific experimentation used to assess their effectiveness?

4. In June 2009, the pop icon Michael Jackson died after receiving a fatal dose of the anesthetic propofol, which is sometimes used off label as an antianxiety drug. An autopsy confirmed that his body contained a cocktail of prescription drugs, including the benzodiazepines lorazepam and diazepam. (Jackson's cardiologist, Dr. Conrad Murray, was later convicted of involuntary manslaughter for administering the fatal dose.) Other celebrities whose deaths have been attributed to medications commonly prescribed for anxiety and depression include Prince in 2016, Heath Ledger in 2008, and Anna Nicole Smith in 2007. "These drugs are dangerous," your roommate notes. "People who have psychological problems should seek out talk therapy for their problems and stay away from the medications, even if they're prescribed by a responsible doctor." You agree that medications can be dangerous if misused, but how would you justify the use of drug treatment for serious mental disorders?

ANSWERS TO KEY CONCEPT QUIZ

1. b; 2. d; 3. c; 4. c; 5. d; 6. c; 7. d; 8. a; 9. b; 10. b; 11. d; 12. d; 13. c; 14. a; 15. d.

Essentials of Statistics for Psychological Science

Appendix

Picturing the Measurements
Describing the Measurements
Measuring Correlation
Statistical Testing

Picturing the Measurements

When psychologists collect data, they end up with a big spreadsheet full of numbers. To help them make sense of those numbers, they often use graphic representations. The most common kind of graphic representation is the **frequency distribution**, which is *a graphic representation of measurements arranged by the number of times each measurement was made*. **FIGURE A.1** shows a pair of frequency distributions that represent the hypothetical performances of a group of men and women who took a test of fine motor skills (i.e., the ability to manipulate things with their hands). Every possible test score is shown on the horizontal axis. The number of times (or the *frequency* with which) each score was observed is shown on the vertical axis. Although a frequency distribution can have any shape, a common shape is the *bell curve*, which is technically known as the *Gaussian distribution* or the **normal distribution**, which is *a mathematically defined distribution in which the frequency of measurements is highest in the middle and decreases symmetrically in both directions*. The normal distribution has a peak in the middle and trails off at both ends. It is said to be symmetrical because the left half is a mirror image of the right half.

The graph in Figure A.1 allows you to see many things easily. For instance, from the general shape of the distribution, you can see that most people have moderate motor skills and that only a few have exceptionally good or exceptionally bad motor skills. You can also see that the distribution of men's scores is displaced a bit to the left of the distribution of women's scores, which tells you that women tend to have somewhat better motor skills than men. And finally, you can see that the two distributions have a great deal of overlap, which tells you that although women tend to have better motor skills than men, there are still plenty of men who have better motor skills than plenty of women.

frequency distribution A graphical representation of measurements arranged by the number of times each measurement was made.

normal distribution A mathematically defined distribution in which the frequency of measurements is highest in the middle and decreases symmetrically in both directions.

Figure A.1 FREQUENCY DISTRIBUTIONS This graph shows how a hypothetical group of men and women scored on a test of fine motor skills. Test scores are listed along the horizontal axis, and the frequency with which each score was obtained is represented along the vertical axis.

Describing the Measurements

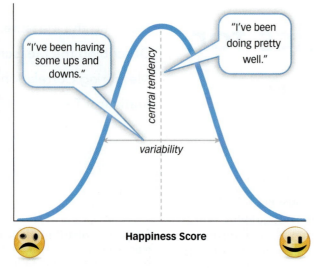

Number of days on which this score was observed

"I've been having some ups and downs."

central tendency

"I've been doing pretty well."

variability

😞 **Happiness Score** 😃

Figure A.2   TWO KINDS OF DESCRIPTIVE STATISTICS
Descriptive statistics are used to describe two important features of a frequency distribution: central tendency (where do most of the scores lie?) and variability (how much do the scores differ from one another?).

mode The value of the most frequently observed measurement.

mean The average value of all the measurements.

median The value that is in the middle—that is, greater than or equal to half the measurements and less than or equal to half the measurements.

A frequency distribution depicts every measurement and thus provides a full and complete picture of those measurements. But sometimes we just need a brief summary statement and not the complete picture. When we ask a friend how she's been doing, we want her to say something like, "I've been doing pretty well" or "I've been having some ups and downs," but not to show us a spreadsheet with hourly ratings of her happiness across 15 weeks. In psychology, brief summary statements are called *descriptive statistics* and there are two important kinds: those that describe the *central tendency* of a frequency distribution and those that describe the *variability* in a frequency distribution.

Central Tendency: Where Is the Middle?

Descriptions of *central tendency* are statements about the value of the measurements that *tend* to lie near the *center* or midpoint of the frequency distribution. When a friend says that she's been "doing pretty well," she is describing the central tendency (or approximate location of the midpoint) of the frequency distribution of her happiness over time (see **FIGURE A.2**). The three most common descriptions of central tendency are the **mode** (*the value of the most frequently observed measurement*), the **mean** (*the average value of all the measurements*), and the **median** (*the value that is in the middle, i.e., greater than or equal to half the measurements and less than or equal to half the measurements*). **FIGURE A.3** shows how each of these descriptive statistics is calculated. When you hear a descriptive statistic such as "the average American college student sleeps 8.3 hours per day," you are hearing about the central tendency of a frequency distribution (in this case, the mean).

In a normal distribution, the mean, median, and mode all have the same value, but when the distribution is not normal, these three descriptive statistics can differ. For example, imagine that you measured the net worth of 40 college professors and

- Mode = 3 because there are five 3s and only three 2s, two 1s, two 4s, one 5, one 6, and one 7.
- Mean = 3.27 because (1 + 1 + 2 + 2 + 2 + 3 + 3 + 3 + 3 + 3 + 4 + 4 + 5 + 6 + 7)/15 = 3.27
- Median = 3 because 10 scores are ≥ 3 and 10 scores are ≤ 3

Figure A.3 SOME DESCRIPTIVE STATISTICS This frequency distribution shows the scores of 15 individuals on a 7-point test. Descriptive statistics include measures of central tendency (such as the mean, median, and mode) and measures of variability (such as the range and the standard deviation).

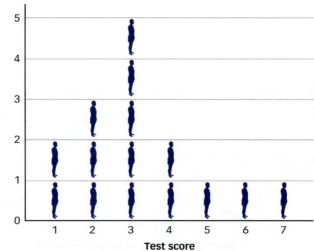

Number of people who obtained this score

Test score

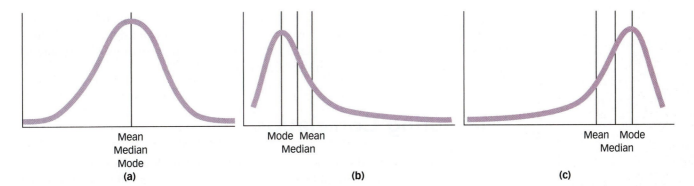

(a) (b) (c)

Figure A.4 SKEWED
DISTRIBUTIONS When a frequency
distribution is normal (a), the mean,
median, and mode are all the same,
but when it is positively skewed (b)
or negatively skewed (c), these three
measures of central tendency are quite
different.

Mark Zuckerberg. The frequency distribution of your measurements would not be normal, but *positively skewed*. As you can see in **FIGURE A.4**, the mode and the median of a positively skewed distribution are much lower than the mean because the mean is more strongly influenced by the value of a single extreme measurement (which, in case you've been sleeping for the last few years, would be the net worth of Mark Zuckerberg).

When distributions become skewed, the mean gets dragged off toward the tail, the mode stays home at the hump, and the median goes to live between the two. When distributions are skewed, a single measure of central tendency can paint a misleading picture of the measurements. For example, the average net worth of the people you measured is probably about a billion dollars each, but that statement makes the college professors sound a whole lot richer than they are. You could provide a much better description of the net worth of the people you measured if you also mentioned that the median net worth is $300,000 and that the modal net worth is $288,000. Indeed, you should always be suspicious when you hear some new fact about the "average person" but don't hear anything about the shape of the frequency distribution.

Variability: How Far From the Middle?

Whereas descriptions of central tendency are statements about the location of the measurements in a frequency distribution, descriptions of variability are statements about the extent to which the measurements differ from each other. When a friend says that she has been "having some ups and downs," she is offering a brief summary statement that describes how measurements of her happiness taken at different times tend to differ from one another. The simplest description of variability is the **range**, which is *the value of the largest measurement in a frequency distribution minus the value of the smallest measurement*. When the range is small, the measurements don't vary as much as when the range is large. The range is easy to compute, but like the mean, it can be dramatically affected by a single measurement. If you said that the net worth of people you had measured ranged from $40,000 to $14 billion, a listener might get the impression that these people were all remarkably different from each other when, in fact, they were all quite similar, save for one very rich guy from California.

Other descriptions of variability aren't quite as susceptible to this problem. For example, the **standard deviation** is *a statistic that describes the average difference between the measurements in a frequency distribution and the mean of that distribution*. In other words, on average, how far are the measurements from the center of the distribution? As **FIGURE A.5** shows, two frequency distributions can have the same mean, but very different

range The value of the largest measurement in a frequency distribution minus the value of the smallest measurement.

standard deviation A statistic that describes the average difference between the measurements in a frequency distribution and the mean of that distribution.

Figure A.5 IQS OF MEN AND WOMEN Men and women have the same average IQ, but men are more variable than women.

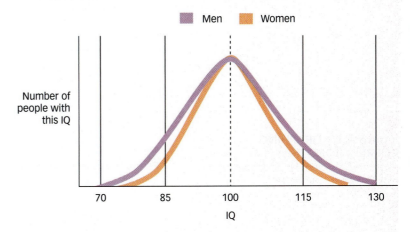

ranges and standard deviations. For example, studies show that men and women have the same mean IQ but that men have a larger range and standard deviation, which is to say that a man is more likely than a woman to be much more or much less intelligent than the average person of his or her own gender.

Measuring Correlation

correlation coefficient A mathematical measure of both the direction and strength of a correlation, which is symbolized by the letter *r*.

Most of us have learned from experience that height and weight are highly correlated. So if you were to predict that some randomly selected tall person weighed more than some randomly selected short person, you'd be right more often than you'd be wrong. But you wouldn't be right in every single instance because there are always some exceptions to the rule. *Some* tall people weigh less than *some* short people do! How often your prediction would be right would depend on the *strength* of the correlation between height and weight. If that correlation were strong, then your prediction would be right almost all of the time, and if it were weak, then your prediction would be right much less often. The **correlation coefficient** is *a mathematical measure of both the direction and strength of a correlation*, and it is symbolized by the letter *r* (as in "relationship"). The value of *r* can range from −1 to 1. What do the sign and value of *r* tells us?

- If every time the value of one variable increases by a fixed amount the value of the second variable also increases by a fixed amount, then the relationship between the variables is called a *perfect positive correlation*, and *r* = 1 (see **FIGURE A.6a**). For example, if every 1-pound increase in weight were associated with a 1-inch increase in height, then weight and height would be *perfectly positively correlated*.

- If every time the value of one variable increases by a fixed amount the value of the second variable *decreases* by a fixed amount, then the relationship between the variables is called a *perfect negative correlation*, and *r* = −1 (see **FIGURE A.6b**). For example, if every 1-pound increase in weight were associated with a 1-inch decrease in height, then height and weight would be *perfectly negatively correlated*.

- If every time the value of one variable increases by a fixed amount the value of the second variable neither increases nor decreases systematically, then the two variables are said to be *uncorrelated*, and *r* = 0 (see **FIGURE A.6c**). For example, if a 1-pound increase in weight was sometimes associated with an increase in height, sometimes associated with a decrease in height, and sometimes associated with no change in height at all, then weight and height would be uncorrelated.

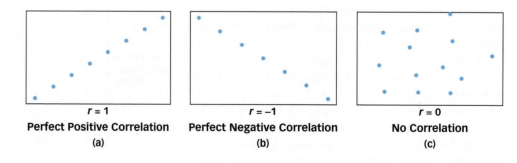

Figure A.6 GRAPHING CORRELATIONS These figures show what three different kinds of correlations look like when graphed.

r = 1
Perfect Positive Correlation
(a)

r = −1
Perfect Negative Correlation
(b)

r = 0
No Correlation
(c)

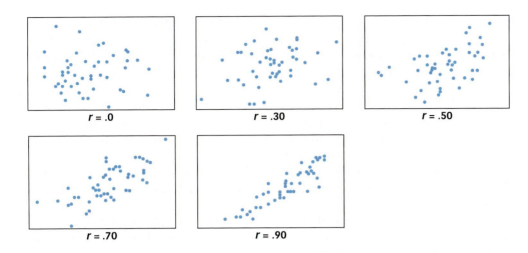

Figure A.7 POSITIVE
CORRELATIONS OF DIFFERENT
STRENGTHS These graphs illustrate
different degrees of positive correlation
between two variables. When there are
few exceptions to the rule *X* = *Y*, then
the correlation is strong, and *r* is closer
to 1. When there are many exceptions to
this rule, the correlation is weak, and *r* is
closer to 0.

Perfect correlations are extremely rare. In the real world, height and weight are indeed *positively* correlated (i.e., as one increases, the other usually increases too), but they are *imperfectly* correlated (i.e., a 1-pound increase in weight is not necessarily associated with exactly a 1-inch increase in height). We note this by giving *r* intermediate values, between 0 and 1 (for positive correlation) or between 0 and −1 (for negative correlations). In each case, the more exceptions to the rule, the closer *r* is to 0.

FIGURE A.7 shows four cases in which two variables are positively correlated but have different numbers of exceptions, and as you can see, the number of exceptions changes the value of *r* quite dramatically. Two variables can have a strong correlation (e.g., *r* = .90), a moderate correlation (e.g., *r* = .70), or a weak correlation (e.g., *r* = .30). The correlation coefficient, then, is a measure of both the *direction* and *strength* of the relationship between two variables. The sign of *r* (plus or minus) tells us the direction of the relationship, and the absolute value of *r* (between 0 and 1) tells us about the number of exceptions and hence about how confident we can be when using the correlation to make predictions.

Statistical Testing

If you flip a coin 100 times, it will come up heads roughly 50 of those times. But not exactly 50, and not every time. In fact, once in a while, it will come up heads 70 times, 80 times, or even 100 times by chance alone. This doesn't happen often, of course, but it does happen.

When we use random assignment in an experiment, we assume that people who have a particular attribute—say, high intelligence or low need for achievement—are just as likely to be assigned to the experimental group as the control group. Because the two groups have roughly equal numbers of people who have the attribute, this attribute cannot be the cause of any between-group differences we find in our dependent measure. But because random assignment is achieved by using a randomizing device such as a coin, every once in a while that coin will assign more of the people who have the attribute to one of these conditions than the other, and when this happens, we say that random assignment has failed. As you might gather from the word *fail*, that's a serious problem. When random assignment fails, we can no longer be sure that changes in our dependent variable were caused by the changes we made when we manipulated our independent variable. They may instead have been caused by that attribute, which is not equally represented in the two groups. If more of the smart people were assigned to take the smart pill, then who knows if their higher intelligence at the end of the experiment was actually caused by the pill?

How can we tell when random assignment has failed? Unfortunately, we can't ever tell for sure. But we *can* calculate the *likelihood* that random assignment failed in any particular instance. It isn't important for you to know how to do this calculation, but it is important for you to know that psychologists perform the calculation just about every time they do an experiment and that they do not accept the results of their experiments unless the calculation tells them that, if random assignment had failed, then there is less than a 5% chance that they would have seen those particular results.

When the calculations show that there is less than a 5% chance that a particular result would have occurred if random assignment had failed, then psychologists say that the result is *statistically significant*, and they report this fact by writing "$p < .05$," where p stands for *probability*. When psychologists report that $p < .05$, they are telling us that, according to their calculations, the likelihood that they would have seen the results they saw if random assignment had failed are less than 5%—and given that they *did* see those results, a failure of random assignment is unlikely to have happened.

KEY TERMS

frequency distribution (p. A-1)

normal distribution (p. A-1)

mode (p. A-2)

mean (p. A-2)

median (p. A-2)

range (p. A-3)

standard deviation (p. A-3)

correlation coefficient (p. A-4)

Glossary

absentmindedness A lapse in attention that results in memory failure.

absolute threshold The minimal intensity needed to just barely detect a stimulus in 50% of trials.

accommodation (1) The process whereby the eye maintains a clear image on the retina. (2) The process by which infants revise their schemas in light of new information.

acquisition The phase of classical conditioning when the CS and US are presented together.

action potential An electric signal that is conducted along a neuron's axon to a synapse.

activation–synthesis model The theory that dreams are produced when the brain attempts to make sense of random neural activity that occurs during sleep.

actor–observer effect The tendency to make situational attributions for our own behaviors while making dispositional attributions for the identical behavior of others.

adolescence The period of development that begins with the onset of sexual maturity (about 11 to 14 years of age) and lasts until the beginning of adulthood (about 18 to 21 years of age).

adulthood The stage of development that begins around 18 to 21 years and ends at death.

aggression Behavior whose purpose is to harm another.

agonists Drugs that increase the action of a neurotransmitter.

agoraphobia A specific phobia involving a fear of public places.

alcohol myopia A condition that results when alcohol hampers attention, leading people to respond in simple ways to complex situations.

altered state of consciousness A form of experience that departs significantly from the normal subjective experience of the world and the mind.

altruism Intentional behavior that benefits another at a cost to oneself.

amygdala A brain structure that plays a central role in many emotional processes, particularly the formation of emotional memories.

anal stage The second psychosexual stage, in which experience is dominated by the pleasures and frustrations associated with the anus, retention and expulsion of feces and urine, and toilet training.

anorexia nervosa An eating disorder characterized by an intense fear of being overweight and a severe restriction of food intake.

antagonists Drugs that block the function of a neurotransmitter.

anterograde amnesia The inability to transfer new information from the short-term store into the long-term store.

antianxiety medications Drugs that help reduce a person's experience of fear or anxiety.

antidepressants A class of drugs that help lift people's moods.

antipsychotic drugs Medications that are used to treat schizophrenia and related psychotic disorders.

antisocial personality disorder (APD) A pervasive pattern of disregard for and violation of the rights of others that begins in childhood or early adolescence and continues into adulthood.

anxiety disorder The class of mental disorders in which anxiety is the predominant feature.

aphasia Difficulty in producing or comprehending language.

apparent motion The perception of movement as a result of alternating signals appearing in rapid succession in different locations.

appraisal An evaluation of the emotion-relevant aspects of a stimulus.

approach motivation The motivation to experience a positive outcome.

area A1 A portion of the temporal lobe that contains the primary auditory cortex.

area V1 The part of the occipital lobe that contains the primary visual cortex.

assimilation The process by which infants apply their schemas in novel situations.

association areas Areas of the cerebral cortex that are composed of neurons that help provide sense and meaning to information registered in the cortex.

attachment The emotional bond that forms between newborns and their primary caregivers.

attention-deficit/hyperactivity disorder (ADHD) A persistent pattern of severe problems with inattention and/or hyperactivity or impulsiveness that cause significant impairments in functioning.

attitude An enduring positive or negative evaluation of an object or event.

attribution An inference about the cause of a person's behavior.

autism spectrum disorder (ASD) A condition beginning in early childhood in which a person shows persistent communication deficits as well as restricted and repetitive patterns of behaviors, interests, or activities.

autonomic nervous system (ANS) A set of nerves that carries involuntary and automatic commands that control blood vessels, body organs, and glands.

availability bias The concept that items that are more readily available in memory are judged as having occurred more frequently.

avoidance motivation The motivation to avoid experiencing a negative outcome.

axon The part of a neuron that carries information to other neurons, muscles, or glands.

basal ganglia A set of subcortical structures that directs intentional movements.

basilar membrane A structure in the inner ear that undulates when vibrations from the ossicles reach the cochlear fluid.

behavior Observable actions of human beings and nonhuman animals.

behavioral neuroscience An approach to psychology that links psychological processes to activities in the nervous system and other bodily processes.

behaviorism An approach that advocates that psychologists restrict themselves to the scientific study of objectively observable behavior.

behavior therapy A type of therapy that assumes that disordered behavior is learned and that symptom relief is achieved through changing overt, maladaptive behaviors into more constructive behaviors.

belief An enduring piece of knowledge about an object or event.

bias The distorting influences of present knowledge, beliefs, and feelings on recollection of previous experiences.

Big Five The traits of the five-factor model: openness to experience, conscientiousness, extraversion, agreeableness, and neuroticism.

binding problem How the brain links features together so that we see unified objects in our visual world, rather than free-floating or miscombined features.

binge eating disorder An eating disorder characterized by recurrent and uncontrolled episodes of eating a large number of calories in a short time.

binocular disparity The difference in the retinal images of the two eyes that provides information about depth.

biofeedback The use of an external monitoring device to obtain information about a bodily function and possibly gain control over that function.

biological preparedness A propensity for learning particular kinds of associations over others.

biopsychosocial perspective A view that explains mental disorders as the result of interactions among biological, psychological, and social factors.

bipolar disorder A condition characterized by cycles of abnormal, persistent high mood (mania) and low mood (depression).

blind spot A location in the visual field that produces no sensation on the retina.

blocking A failure to retrieve information that is available in memory, even though you are trying to produce it.

bulimia nervosa An eating disorder characterized by binge eating followed by compensatory behavior.

burnout A state of physical, emotional, and mental exhaustion resulting from long-term involvement in an emotionally demanding situation and accompanied by lowered performance and motivation.

bystander intervention The act of helping strangers in an emergency situation.

Cannon–Bard theory The theory that a stimulus simultaneously triggers activity in the body and emotional experience in the brain.

case method A procedure for gathering scientific information by studying a single person.

category-specific deficit A neurological syndrome that is characterized by an inability to recognize objects that belong to a particular category, although the ability to recognize objects outside the category is undisturbed.

cell body (or soma) The part of a neuron that coordinates information-processing tasks and keeps the cell alive.

central nervous system (CNS) The part of the nervous system that is composed of the brain and spinal cord.

cephalocaudal rule The "top-to-bottom" rule that describes the tendency for motor skills to emerge in sequence from the head to the feet.

cerebellum A large structure of the hindbrain that controls fine motor skills.

cerebral cortex The outermost layer of the brain, visible to the naked eye and divided into two hemispheres.

change blindness Failure to detect changes to the visual details of a scene.

childhood The stage of development that begins at about 18 to 24 months and lasts until adolescence, which begins between 11 and 14 years.

chromosomes The DNA is configured in a double helix; the chromosomes aren't.

chronic stressors Sources of stress that occur continuously or repeatedly.

chunking Combining small pieces of information into larger clusters or chunks that are more easily held in short-term memory.

circadian rhythm A naturally occurring 24-hour cycle.

classical conditioning A type of learning that occurs when a neutral stimulus produces a response after being paired with a stimulus that naturally produces a response.

cochlea A fluid-filled tube that is the organ of auditory transduction.

cocktail-party phenomenon A phenomenon in which people tune in one message, even while they filter out others nearby.

cognitive behavioral therapy (CBT) A blend of cognitive and behavioral therapeutic strategies.

cognitive development The process by which infants and children gain the ability to think and understand.

cognitive dissonance An unpleasant state that arises when a person recognizes the inconsistency of his or her actions, attitudes, or beliefs.

cognitive enhancers Drugs that improve the psychological processes that underlie intelligent performance.

cognitive map A mental representation of the physical features of the environment.

cognitive neuroscience The field of study that attempts to understand the links between cognitive processes and brain activity.

cognitive psychology The scientific study of mental processes, including perception, thought, memory, and reasoning.

cognitive restructuring A therapeutic approach that teaches clients to question the automatic beliefs, assumptions, and predictions that often lead to negative emotions and to replace negative thinking with more realistic and positive beliefs.

cognitive symptoms Deficits in cognitive abilities, specifically executive functioning, attention, and working memory, present in those with schizophrenia.

cognitive therapy A type of therapy that helps a client identify and correct any distorted thinking about self, others, or the world.

cognitive unconscious All the mental processes that give rise to a person's thoughts, choices, emotions, and behavior, even though they are not experienced by the person.

common knowledge effect The tendency for group discussions to focus on information that all members share.

comorbidity The co-occurrence of two or more disorders in a single individual.

companionate love An experience involving affection, trust, and concern for a partner's well-being.

concept A mental representation that groups or categorizes shared features of related objects, events, or other stimuli.

concrete operational stage The stage of cognitive development that begins at about 6 years and ends at about 11 years, during which children learn how various actions, or *operations*, can affect or transform *concrete* objects.

conditioned response (CR) A reaction that resembles an unconditioned response but is produced by a conditioned stimulus.

conditioned stimulus (CS) A previously neutral stimulus that produces a reliable response in an organism after being paired with a US.

conduct disorder A persistent pattern of deviant behavior involving aggression toward people or animals, destruction of property, deceitfulness or theft, or serious rule violations.

cones Photoreceptors that detect color, operate under normal daylight conditions, and allow us to focus on fine detail.

conformity The tendency to do what others do simply because others are doing it.

conjunction fallacy When people think that two events are more likely to occur together than is either individual event.

conscious motivations Motivations of which people are aware.

consciousness A person's subjective experience of the world and the mind.

conservation The notion that the quantitative properties of an object are invariant despite changes in the object's appearance.

consolidation The process by which memories become stable in the brain.

control group The group of participants who are not exposed to the particular manipulation, compared with the experimental group, in an experiment.

conventional stage A stage of moral development in which the morality of an action is primarily determined by the extent to which it conforms to social rules.

cooperation Behavior by two or more individuals that leads to mutual benefit.

corpus callosum A thick band of nerve fibers that connects large areas of the cerebral cortex on each side of the brain and supports communication of information across the hemispheres.

correlation Two variables are said to "be correlated" when variations in the value of one variable are synchronized with variations in the value of the other.

correlation coefficient A mathematical measure of both the direction and strength of a correlation, which is symbolized by the letter *r*.

correspondence bias The tendency to make a dispositional attribution when we should instead make a situational attribution.

crystallized intelligence The ability to apply knowledge that was acquired through experience.

cultural psychology The study of how cultures reflect and shape the psychological processes of their members.

debriefing A verbal description of the true nature and purpose of a study.

deep structure The meaning of a sentence.

defense mechanisms Unconscious coping mechanisms that reduce anxiety generated by threats from unacceptable impulses.

deindividuation A phenomenon that occurs when immersion in a group causes people to become less concerned with their individual values.

delusion A false belief, often bizarre and grandiose, that is maintained in spite of its irrationality.

demand characteristics Those aspects of an observational setting that cause people to behave as they think someone else wants or expects.

dendrite The part of a neuron that receives information from other neurons and relays it to the cell body.

dependent variable The variable that is measured in a study.

depressants Substances that reduce the activity of the central nervous system.

developmental psychology The study of continuity and change across the life span.

Diagnostic and Statistical Manual of Mental Disorders (DSM) A classification system that describes the features used to diagnose each recognized mental disorder and indicates how that disorder can be distinguished from other, similar problems.

diathesis–stress model A model that suggests that a person may be predisposed to a psychological disorder that remains unexpressed until triggered by stress.

diffusion of responsibility The tendency for individuals to feel diminished responsibility for their actions when they are surrounded by others who are acting the same way.

direct replication An experiment that uses the same procedures as a previous experiment but with a new sample.

discrimination The capacity to distinguish between similar but distinct stimuli.

disorganized speech A severe disruption of verbal communication in which ideas shift rapidly and incoherently among unrelated topics.

display rule A norm for the appropriate expression of emotion.

dopamine hypothesis The idea that schizophrenia involves an excess of dopamine activity.

double-blind observation A technique whose true purpose is hidden from both the observer and the person being observed.

drive An internal state caused by physiological needs.

drive-reduction theory A theory suggesting that organisms are motivated to reduce their drives.

drug tolerance The tendency for larger doses of a drug to be required over time to achieve the same effect.

dual process theories Theories that suggest that we have two different systems in our brains for processing information: one dedicated to fast, automatic, and unconscious processing, and the other dedicated to slow, effortful, and conscious processing.

dynamic unconscious An active system encompassing a lifetime of hidden memories, the person's deepest instincts and desires, and the person's inner struggle to control these forces.

echoic memory A fast-decaying store of auditory information.

eclectic psychotherapy A form of psychotherapy that involves drawing on techniques from different forms of therapy, depending on the client and the problem.

ego The component of personality, developed through contact with the external world, that enables us to deal with life's practical demands.

egocentrism The failure to understand that the world appears different to different people.

electroconvulsive therapy (ECT) A treatment that involves inducing a brief seizure by delivering an electrical shock to the brain.

electroencephalograph (EEG) A device used to record electrical activity in the brain.

embryonic stage The period of prenatal development that lasts from the 2nd week until about the 8th week.

emotion A positive or negative experience that is associated with a particular pattern of physiological activity.

emotional expression An observable sign of an emotional state.

emotional intelligence The ability to reason about emotions and to use emotions to enhance reasoning.

emotion regulation The strategies people use to influence their own emotional experiences.

empirical method A set of rules and techniques for observation.

empiricism The belief that accurate knowledge can be acquired through observation.

encoding The process of transforming what we perceive, think, or feel into an enduring memory.

encoding specificity principle The idea that a retrieval cue can be an effective reminder when it helps re-create the specific way in which information was initially encoded.

endocrine system A network of glands that produce and secrete into the bloodstream chemical messages known as hormones, which influence a wide variety of basic functions, including metabolism, growth, and sexual development.

epigenetics The study of environmental influences that determine whether or not genes are expressed, or the degree to which they are expressed, without altering the basic DNA sequences that constitute the genes themselves.

episodic memory The collection of past personal experiences that occurred at a particular time and place.

evolutionary psychology A psychological approach that explains mind and behavior in terms of the adaptive value of abilities that are preserved over time by natural selection.

exemplar theory A theory of categorization that argues that we make category judgments by comparing a new instance with stored memories of other instances of the category.

existential approach A school of thought that regards personality as governed by an individual's ongoing choices and decisions in the context of the realities of life and death.

expectancy theory The idea that alcohol effects can be produced by people's expectations of how alcohol will influence them in particular situations.

experiment A technique for discovering the causal relationship between variables.

experimental group The group of participants who are exposed to a particular manipulation, compared with the control group, in an experiment.

explicit memory The act of consciously or intentionally retrieving past experiences.

exposure therapy An approach to treatment that involves confronting an emotion-arousing stimulus directly and repeatedly, ultimately leading to a decrease in the emotional response.

external validity An attribute of an experiment in which variables have been defined in a normal, typical, or realistic way.

extinction The gradual elimination of a learned response that occurs when the CS is repeatedly presented without the US.

extrinsic motivation A motivation to take actions that lead to reward.

facial feedback hypothesis The suggestion that emotional expressions can cause the emotional experiences they signify.

family resemblance theory The concept that members of a category have features that appear to be characteristic of category members but may not be possessed by every member.

fast mapping The process whereby children can map a word onto an underlying concept after only a single exposure.

feature-integration theory The idea that focused attention is not required to detect the individual features that make up a stimulus but is required to bind those individual features together.

fetal alcohol syndrome (FAS) A developmental disorder that stems from heavy alcohol use by the mother during pregnancy.

fetal stage The period of prenatal development that lasts from the 9th week after conception until birth.

fight-or-flight response An emotional and physiological reaction to an emergency that increases readiness for action.

fixation A phenomenon in which a person's pleasure-seeking drives become psychologically stuck, or arrested, at a particular psychosexual stage.

fixed-interval schedule (FI) An operant conditioning principle whereby reinforcers are presented at fixed time periods, provided that the appropriate response is made.

fixed-ratio schedule (FR) An operant conditioning principle whereby reinforcement is delivered after a specific number of responses have been made.

flashbulb memories Detailed recollections of when and where we heard about shocking events.

fluid intelligence The ability to solve and reason about novel problems.

foot-in-the-door technique A technique that involves making a small request and following it with a larger request.

formal operational stage The final stage of cognitive development that begins around the age of 11, during which children learn to reason about abstract concepts.

fovea An area of the retina where vision is the clearest and there are no rods at all.

framing effects A bias whereby people give different answers to the same problem, depending on how the problem is phrased (or framed).

fraternal twins (or dizygotic twins) Twins who develop from two different eggs that were fertilized by two different sperm.

frequency distribution A graphical representation of measurements arranged by the number of times each measurement was made.

frontal lobe The region of the cerebral cortex that has specialized areas for movement, abstract thinking, planning, memory, and judgment.

frustration–aggression hypothesis A principle stating that animals aggress when their goals are frustrated.

full consciousness A level of consciousness in which you know and are able to report your mental state.

functionalism The study of how mental processes enable people to adapt to their environments.

gate-control theory of pain A theory of pain perception based on the idea that signals arriving from pain receptors in the body can be stopped, or *gated*, by interneurons in the spinal cord via feedback from two directions.

gateway drug A drug whose use increases the risk of the subsequent use of more harmful drugs.

general adaptation syndrome (GAS) A three-stage physiological response that appears, regardless of the stressor that is encountered.

generalization The CR is observed, even though the CS is slightly different from the CS used during acquisition.

generalized anxiety disorder (GAD) A disorder characterized by chronic excessive worry accompanied by three or more of the following symptoms: restlessness, fatigue, concentration problems, irritability, muscle tension, and sleep disturbance.

gene The major unit of hereditary transmission.

genetic dysphasia A syndrome characterized by an inability to learn the grammatical structure of language, despite having otherwise normal intelligence.

genital stage The fifth and final psychosexual stage, the time for the coming together of the mature adult personality with a capacity to love, work, and relate to others in a mutually satisfying and reciprocal manner.

germinal stage The 2-week period of prenatal development that begins at conception.

Gestalt psychology A psychological approach that emphasizes that we often perceive the whole rather than the sum of the parts.

gestalt therapy A form of psychotherapy whose goal is helping the client become aware of his or her thoughts, behaviors, experiences, and feelings and to "own" or take responsibility for them.

glial cells Support cells found in the nervous system.

grammar A set of rules that specify how the units of language can be combined to produce meaningful messages.

grossly disorganized behavior Behavior that is inappropriate for the situation or ineffective in attaining goals, often with specific motor disturbances.

group A collection of people who have something in common that distinguishes them from others.

group polarization The tendency for groups to make decisions that are more extreme than any member would have made alone.

group therapy A type of therapy in which multiple participants (who often do not know each other at the outset) work on their individual problems in a group atmosphere.

groupthink The tendency for groups to reach consensus in order to facilitate interpersonal harmony.

habituation A general process in which repeated or prolonged exposure to a stimulus results in a gradual reduction in responding.

hair cells Specialized auditory receptor neurons embedded in the basilar membrane.

hallucination A false perceptual experience that has a compelling sense of being real despite the absence of external stimulation.

hallucinogens Drugs that alter sensation and perception and often cause visual and auditory hallucinations.

haptic perception The active exploration of the environment by touching and grasping objects with our hands.

health psychology The subfield of psychology concerned with ways psychological factors influence the causes and treatment of physical illness and the maintenance of health.

hedonic principle The claim that people are motivated to experience pleasure and avoid pain.

helplessness theory The idea that individuals who are prone to depression automatically attribute negative experiences to causes that are internal (i.e., their own fault), stable (i.e., unlikely to change), and global (i.e., widespread).

heuristic persuasion The process by which attitudes or beliefs are changed by appeals to habit or emotion.

hindbrain The area of the brain that coordinates information coming into and out of the spinal cord.

hippocampus A structure critical for creating new memories and integrating them into a network of knowledge so that they can be stored indefinitely in other parts of the cerebral cortex.

humanistic psychology An approach to understanding human nature that emphasizes the positive potential of human beings.

hypnosis A social interaction in which one person (the hypnotist) makes suggestions that lead to a change in another person's (the subject's) subjective experience of the world.

hypnotic analgesia The reduction of pain through hypnosis in people who are susceptible to hypnosis.

hypothalamus A subcortical structure that regulates body temperature, hunger, thirst, and sexual behavior.

hypothesis A falsifiable prediction made by a theory.

hysteria A temporary loss of cognitive or motor functions, usually as a result of emotionally upsetting experiences.

iatrogenic illness A disorder or symptom that occurs as a result of a medical or psychotherapeutic treatment itself.

iconic memory A fast-decaying store of visual information.

id The part of the mind containing the drives present at birth; it is the source of our bodily needs, wants, desires, and impulses, particularly our sexual and aggressive drives.

identical twins (or monozygotic twins) Twins who develop from the splitting of a single egg that was fertilized by a single sperm.

illusions Errors of perception, memory, or judgment in which subjective experience differs from objective reality.

illusory conjunction A perceptual mistake whereby the brain incorrectly combines features from multiple objects.

immune system A complex response system that protects the body from bacteria, viruses, and other foreign substances.

implicit learning Learning that takes place largely independent of awareness of both the process and the products of information acquisition.

implicit memory The influence of past experiences on later behavior and performance, even without an effort to remember them or an awareness of the recollection.

inattentional blindness A failure to perceive objects that are not the focus of attention.

independent variable The variable that is manipulated in an experiment.

infancy The stage of development that begins at birth and lasts between 18 and 24 months.

informational influence A phenomenon that occurs when another person's behavior provides information about what is true.

informed consent A written agreement to participate in a study made by an adult who has been informed of all the risks that participation may entail.

insomnia Difficulty in falling asleep or staying asleep.

instrument Anything that can detect the concrete, observable event to which an operational definition refers.

intelligence The ability to use one's mind to solve novel problems and learn from experience.

intelligence quotient (or IQ) A statistic obtained by dividing an adult's test score by the average adult's test score and then multiplying the quotient by 100.

intermittent reinforcement An operant conditioning principle whereby only some of the responses made are followed by reinforcement.

intermittent reinforcement effect The fact that operant behaviors that are maintained under intermittent reinforcement schedules resist extinction better than do those maintained under continuous reinforcement.

internal validity An attribute of an experiment that allows it to establish causal relationships.

internal working model of relationships A set of beliefs about the self, the primary caregiver, and the relationship between them.

interneurons Neurons that connect sensory neurons, motor neurons, or other interneurons.

interpersonal psychotherapy (IPT) A form of psychotherapy that focuses on helping clients improve current relationships.

intrinsic motivation A motivation to take actions that are themselves rewarding.

introspection The subjective observation of one's own experience.

ironic processes of mental control A mental process can produce ironic errors because monitoring for errors can itself produce them.

James–Lange theory The theory that a stimulus triggers activity in the body, which in turn produces an emotional experience in the brain.

just noticeable difference (JND) The minimal change in a stimulus that can just barely be detected.

kin selection The process by which evolution selects for individuals who cooperate with their relatives.

language A system for communicating with others using signals that are combined according to rules of grammar and that convey meaning.

latency stage The fourth psychosexual stage, in which the primary focus is on the further development of intellectual, creative, interpersonal, and athletic skills.

latent learning A process in which something is learned, but it is not manifested as a behavioral change until sometime in the future.

law of effect The principle that behaviors that are followed by a "satisfying state of affairs" tend to be repeated, and those that produce an "unpleasant state of affairs" are less likely to be repeated.

learning The acquisition, from experience, of new knowledge, skills, or responses that results in a relatively permanent change in the state of the learner.

locus of control A person's tendency to perceive the control of rewards as internal to the self or external in the environment.

long-term memory A type of storage that holds information for hours, days, weeks, or years.

long-term potentiation (LTP) A process whereby repeated communication across the synapse between neurons strengthens the connection, making further communication easier.

loss aversion The tendency to care more about avoiding losses than about achieving equal-size gains.

loudness A sound's intensity.

major depressive disorder (or unipolar depression) A disorder characterized by a severely depressed mood and/or inability to experience pleasure that lasts 2 or more weeks and is accompanied by feelings of worthlessness, lethargy, and sleep and appetite disturbance.

manipulation Changing a variable in order to determine its causal power.

marijuana (or cannabis) The leaves and buds of the hemp plant, which contain a psychoactive drug called tetrahydrocannabinol (THC).

medical model An approach that conceptualizes abnormal psychological experiences as illnesses that, like physical illnesses, have biological and environmental causes, defined symptoms, and possible cures.

mean The average value of all the measurements.

median The value that is in the middle—that is, greater than or equal to half the measurements and less than or equal to half the measurements.

meditation The practice of intentional contemplation.

medulla An extension of the spinal cord into the skull that coordinates heart rate, circulation, and respiration.

memory The ability to store and retrieve information over time.

memory misattribution Assigning a recollection or an idea to the wrong source.

mental control The attempt to change conscious states of mind.

mental disorder A persistent disturbance or dysfunction in behavior, thoughts, or emotions that causes significant distress or impairment.

mere-exposure effect The tendency for liking to increase with the frequency of exposure.

metabolism The rate at which energy is used by the body.

mind The private inner experience of perceptions, thoughts, memories, and feelings.

mind–body problem The issue of how the mind is related to the brain and body.

mindfulness meditation Teaches an individual to be fully present in each moment; to be aware of his or her thoughts, feelings, and sensations; and to detect symptoms before they become a problem.

minimal consciousness A low-level kind of sensory awareness and responsiveness that occurs when the mind inputs sensations and may output behavior.

Minnesota Multiphasic Personality Inventory (MMPI) A well-researched clinical questionnaire that is used to assess personality and psychological problems.

mirror neurons Neurons that are active when an animal performs a behavior, such as reaching for or manipulating an object, and are also activated when another animal observes that animal performing the same behavior.

mode The value of the most frequently observed measurement.

monocular depth cues Aspects of a scene that yield information about depth when viewed with only one eye.

mood disorders Mental disorders that have mood disturbance as their predominant feature.

morphemes The smallest meaningful units of language.

morphological rules A set of rules that indicate how morphemes can be combined to form words.

motivation The psychological cause of an action.

motor development The emergence of the ability to execute physical action.

motor neurons Neurons that carry signals from the spinal cord to the muscles to produce movement.

motor reflexes Specific motor responses that are triggered by specific patterns of sensory stimulation.

myelination The formation of a fatty sheath around the axons of a neuron.

myelin sheath An insulating layer of fatty material.

narcissism A trait that reflects a grandiose view of the self combined with a tendency to seek admiration from and exploit others.

narcolepsy A disorder in which sudden sleep attacks occur in the middle of waking activities.

narcotics (or opiates) Highly addictive drugs derived from opium that relieve pain.

nativism The philosophical view that certain kinds of knowledge are innate or inborn.

nativist theory The view that language development is best explained as an innate, biological capacity.

natural correlation A correlation observed in the world around us.

naturalistic observation A technique for gathering scientific information by unobtrusively observing people in their natural environments.

natural selection Charles Darwin's theory that the features of an organism that help it survive and reproduce are more likely than other features to be passed on to subsequent generations.

need for achievement The motivation to solve worthwhile problems.

negative symptoms Deficits in or disruptions of normal emotions and behaviors (e.g., emotional and social withdrawal; apathy; poverty of speech; and other indications of the absence or insufficiency of normal behavior, motivation, and emotion) that are present in those with schizophrenia.

nervous system An interacting network of neurons that conveys electrochemical information throughout the body.

neurons Cells in the nervous system that communicate with one another to perform information-processing tasks.

neurotransmitters Chemicals that transmit information across the synapse to a receiving neuron's dendrites.

night terrors (or sleep terrors) Abrupt awakenings with panic and intense emotional arousal.

nonsuicidal self-injury (NSSI) Direct, deliberate destruction of body tissue in the absence of any intent to die.

normal distribution A mathematically defined distribution in which the frequency of measurements is highest in the middle and decreases symmetrically in both directions.

normative influence A phenomenon that occurs when another person's behavior provides information about what is appropriate.

norm of reciprocity The unwritten rule that people should benefit those who have benefited them.

norms Customary standards for behavior that are widely shared by members of a culture.

obedience The tendency to do what powerful people tell us to do.

object permanence The fact that objects continue to exist even when they are not visible.

observational learning A process by which an organism learns from watching the actions of others.

obsessive-compulsive disorder (OCD) A disorder in which repetitive, intrusive thoughts (obsessions) and ritualistic behaviors (compulsions) designed to fend off those thoughts interfere significantly with an individual's functioning.

occipital lobe A region of the cerebral cortex that processes visual information.

Oedipus conflict A developmental experience in which a child's conflicting feelings toward the opposite-sex parent are (usually) resolved by identifying with the same-sex parent.

olfactory bulb A brain structure located above the nasal cavity beneath the frontal lobes.

olfactory receptor neurons (ORNs) Receptor cells that initiate the sense of smell.

operant behavior Behavior that an organism performs that has some impact on the environment.

operant conditioning A type of learning in which the consequences of an organism's behavior determine whether it will repeat that behavior in the future.

operational definition A description of a property in terms of some concrete, observable event.

optimism bias A bias whereby people believe that, compared with other people, they are more likely to experience positive events and less likely to experience negative events in the future.

oral stage The first psychosexual stage, in which experience centers on the pleasures and frustrations associated with the mouth, sucking, and being fed.

organizational encoding The process of categorizing information according to the relationships among a series of items.

outcome expectancies A person's assumptions about the likely consequences of a future behavior.

panic disorder A disorder characterized by the sudden occurrence of multiple psychological and physiological symptoms that contribute to a feeling of stark terror.

parasympathetic nervous system A set of nerves that helps the body return to a normal resting state.

parietal lobe A region of the cerebral cortex whose functions include processing information about touch.

passionate love An experience involving feelings of euphoria, intimacy, and intense sexual attraction.

perception The organization, identification, and interpretation of a sensation in order to form a mental representation.

perceptual confirmation The tendency for people to see what they expect to see.

peripheral nervous system (PNS) The part of the nervous system that connects the central nervous system to the body's organs and muscles.

persistence The intrusive recollection of events that we wish we could forget.

personal constructs Dimensions people use in making sense of their experiences.

personality An individual's characteristic style of behaving, thinking, and feeling.

personality disorders Enduring patterns of thinking, feeling, or relating to others or controlling impulses that deviate from cultural expectations and cause distress or impaired functioning.

person-centered therapy (or client-centered therapy) A form of psychotherapy that assumes that all individuals have a tendency toward growth and that this growth can be facilitated by acceptance and genuine reactions from the therapist.

person–situation controversy The question of whether behavior is caused more by personality or by situational factors.

persuasion A phenomenon that occurs when a person's attitudes or beliefs are influenced by a communication from another person.

phallic stage The third psychosexual stage, in which experience is dominated by the pleasure, conflict, and frustration associated with the phallic–genital region, as well as coping with powerful incestuous feelings of love, hate, jealousy, and conflict.

phenomenology The study of how things seem to the conscious person.

pheromones Biochemical odorants emitted by other members of its species that can affect an animal's behavior or physiology.

phobic disorders Disorders characterized by marked, persistent, and excessive fear and avoidance of specific objects, activities, or situations.

phoneme The smallest unit of sound that is recognizable as speech, rather than as random noise.

phonological rules A set of rules that indicate how phonemes can be combined to produce speech sounds.

phototherapy A therapy that involves repeated exposure to bright light.

physiology The study of biological processes, especially in the human body.

pitch How high or low a sound is.

pituitary gland The "master gland" of the body's hormone-producing system, which releases hormones that direct the functions of many other glands in the body.

placebo An inert substance or procedure that has been applied with the expectation that it will produce a healing response.

place code The process by which different frequencies stimulate neural signals at specific places along the basilar membrane, from which the brain determines pitch.

pons A brain structure that relays information from the cerebellum to the rest of the brain.

population A complete collection of people.

positive symptoms Thoughts and behaviors, such as delusions and hallucinations, present in schizophrenia but not seen in those without the disorder.

postconventional stage A stage of moral development in which the morality of an action is determined by a set of general principles that reflect core values.

posthypnotic amnesia The failure to retrieve memories following hypnotic suggestions to forget.

posttraumatic stress disorder (PTSD) A disorder characterized by chronic physiological arousal, recurrent unwanted thoughts or images of the trauma, and avoidance of things that call the traumatic event to mind.

power An instrument's ability to detect small magnitudes of a property.

preconventional stage A stage of moral development in which the morality of an action is primarily determined by its consequences for the actor.

prejudice A positive or negative evaluation of another person based on their group membership.

preoperational stage The stage of cognitive development that begins at about 2 years and ends at about 6 years, during which children develop a preliminary understanding of the physical world.

preparedness theory The idea that people are instinctively predisposed toward certain fears.

primary sex characteristics Bodily structures that are directly involved in reproduction.

priming An enhanced ability to think of a stimulus, such as a word or object, as a result of a recent exposure to that stimulus.

proactive interference Situations in which information learned earlier impairs memory for information acquired later.

procedural memory The gradual acquisition of skills as a result of practice, or "knowing how" to do things.

projective tests Tests designed to reveal inner aspects of individuals' personalities by analysis of their responses to a standard series of ambiguous stimuli.

prospective memory Remembering to do things in the future.

prospect theory The theory that people choose to take on risk when evaluating potential losses and avoid risks when evaluating potential gains.

prototype The "best" or "most typical" member of a category.

proximodistal rule The "inside-to-outside" rule that describes the tendency for motor skills to emerge in sequence from the center to the periphery.

psychoactive drugs Chemicals that influence consciousness or behavior by altering the brain's chemical message system.

psychoanalysis A therapeutic approach that focuses on bringing unconscious material into conscious awareness to better understand psychological disorders.

psychoanalytic theory An approach that emphasizes the importance of unconscious mental processes in shaping feelings, thoughts, and behaviors.

psychodynamic approach An approach that regards personality as formed by needs, strivings, and desires largely operating outside of awareness—motives that also can produce emotional disorders.

psychodynamic psychotherapies Therapies that explore childhood events and encourage individuals to use this understanding to develop insight into their psychological problems.

psychology The scientific study of mind and behavior.

psychopharmacology The study of drug effects on psychological states and symptoms.

psychophysics Methods that measure the strength of a stimulus and the observer's sensitivity to that stimulus.

psychosexual stages Distinct early life stages through which personality is formed as children experience sexual pleasures from specific body areas and caregivers redirect or interfere with those pleasures.

psychosomatic illness An interaction between mind and body that can produce illness.

psychosurgery Surgical destruction of specific brain areas.

psychotherapy An interaction between a socially sanctioned clinician and someone suffering from a psychological problem, with the goal of providing support or relief from the problem.

puberty The onset of bodily changes associated with sexual maturity.

punisher Any stimulus or event that decreases the likelihood of the behavior that led to it.

random assignment A procedure by which participants are assigned to the experimental group or control group by chance alone.

random sampling A technique for choosing participants that ensures that every member of a population has an equal chance of being included in the sample.

range The value of the largest measurement in a frequency distribution minus the value of the smallest measurement.

rational choice theory The classical view that we make decisions by determining how likely something is to happen, judging the value of the outcome, and then multiplying the two.

rational coping Facing a stressor and working to overcome it.

reaction time The amount of time taken to respond to a specific stimulus.

reappraisal Changing one's emotional experience by changing the way one thinks about the emotion-eliciting stimulus.

rebound effect of thought suppression The tendency of a thought to return to consciousness with greater frequency following suppression.

receptors Parts of the cell membrane that receive the neurotransmitter and initiate or prevent a new electric signal.

reciprocal altruism Behavior that benefits another with the expectation that those benefits will be returned in the future.

reconsolidation The process whereby memories can become vulnerable to disruption when they are recalled, thus requiring them to be consolidated again.

referred pain Feeling of pain when sensory information from internal and external areas converges on the same nerve cells in the spinal cord.

refractory period The time following an action potential during which a new action potential cannot be initiated.

reframing Finding a new or creative way to think about a stressor that reduces its threat.

rehearsal The process of keeping information in short-term memory by mentally repeating it.

reinforcement The consequences of a behavior determine whether it will be more or less likely to occur again.

reinforcer Any stimulus or event that increases the likelihood of the behavior that led to it.

relaxation response A condition of reduced muscle tension, cortical activity, heart rate, breathing rate, and blood pressure.

relaxation therapy A technique for reducing tension by consciously relaxing muscles of the body.

reliability The tendency for an instrument to produce the same measurement every time it is used to measure the same thing.

REM sleep A stage of sleep characterized by rapid eye movements and a high level of brain activity.

representativeness heuristic A mental shortcut that involves making a probability judgment by comparing an object or event with a prototype of the object or event.

repression A mental process that removes unacceptable thoughts and memories from consciousness and keeps them in the unconscious.

repressive coping Avoiding feelings, thoughts, or situations that are reminders of a stressor and maintaining an artificially positive viewpoint.

Research Domain Criteria Project (RDoC) An initiative that aims to guide the classification and understanding of mental disorders by revealing the basic processes that give rise to them.

resistance A reluctance to cooperate with treatment for fear of confronting unpleasant unconscious material.

response An action or physiological change elicited by a stimulus.

resting potential The difference in electric charge between the inside and outside of a neuron's cell membrane.

reticular formation A brain structure that regulates sleep, wakefulness, and levels of arousal.

retina A layer of light-sensitive tissue lining the back of the eyeball.

retrieval The process of bringing to mind information that has been previously encoded and stored.

retrieval cue External information that is associated with stored information and helps bring it to mind.

retrieval-induced forgetting A process by which retrieving an item from long-term memory impairs subsequent recall of related items.

retroactive interference Situations in which information learned later impairs memory for information acquired earlier.

retrograde amnesia The inability to retrieve information that was acquired before a particular date, usually the date of an injury or surgery.

rods Photoreceptors that become active under low-light conditions for night vision.

Rorschach Inkblot Test A projective technique in which respondents' inner thoughts and feelings are believed to be revealed by analysis of their responses to a set of unstructured inkblots.

sample A partial collection of people drawn from a population.

schemas Theories about the way the world works.

schizophrenia A psychotic disorder characterized by the profound disruption of basic psychological processes; a distorted perception of reality; altered or blunted emotion; and disturbances in thought, motivation, and behavior.

scientific method A procedure for finding truth by using empirical evidence.

seasonal affective disorder (SAD) Recurrent depressive episodes in a seasonal pattern.

secondary sex characteristics Bodily structures that change dramatically with sexual maturity but that are not directly involved in reproduction.

second-order conditioning A type of learning where a CS is paired with a stimulus that became associated with the US in an earlier procedure.

self-actualizing tendency The human motive toward realizing our inner potential.

self-concept A person's explicit knowledge of his or her own behaviors, traits, and other personal characteristics.

self-consciousness A distinct level of consciousness in which the person's attention is drawn to the self as an object.

self-esteem The extent to which an individual likes, values, and accepts the self.

self-fulfilling prophecy The tendency for people to behave as they are expected to behave.

self-regulation The exercise of voluntary control over the self to bring the self into line with preferred standards.

self-report A method in which a person provides subjective information about his or her own thoughts, feelings, or behaviors, typically via questionnaire or interview.

self-selection A problem that occurs when anything about a participant determines whether he or she will be included in the experimental or control group.

self-serving bias People's tendency to take credit for their successes but downplay responsibility for their failures.

self-verification The tendency to seek evidence to confirm the self-concept.

semantic encoding The process of relating new information in a meaningful way to knowledge that is already stored in memory.

semantic memory A network of associated facts and concepts that make up our general knowledge of the world.

sensation Simple stimulation of a sense organ.

sensitization A simple form of learning that occurs when presentation of a stimulus leads to an increased response to a later stimulus.

sensorimotor stage A stage of cognitive development that begins at birth and lasts through infancy, during which infants acquire information about the world by sensing it and moving around within it.

sensory adaptation The process whereby sensitivity to prolonged stimulation tends to decline over time as an organism adapts to current conditions.

sensory memory A type of storage that holds sensory information for a few seconds or less.

sensory neurons Neurons that receive information from the external world and convey this information to the brain via the spinal cord.

shaping Learning that results from the reinforcement of successive steps to a final desired behavior.

short-term memory A type of storage that holds nonsensory information for more than a few seconds but less than a minute.

sick role A socially recognized set of rights and obligations linked with illness.

signal detection theory Holds that the response to a stimulus depends on both a person's sensitivity to the stimulus in the presence of noise and the person's response criterion.

sleep apnea A disorder in which the person stops breathing for brief periods while asleep.

sleep paralysis The experience of waking up unable to move.

social cognition The processes by which people come to understand others.

social–cognitive approach An approach that views personality in terms of how the person thinks about the situations encountered in daily life and behaves in response to them.

social influence The ability to change or direct another person's behavior.

social phobia A disorder that involves an irrational fear of being publicly humiliated or embarrassed.

social psychology The study of the causes and consequences of sociality.

social support The aid gained through interacting with others.

somatic nervous system A set of nerves that conveys information between voluntary muscles and the central nervous system.

somatic symptom disorders The set of psychological disorders in which a person with at least one bodily symptom displays significant health-related anxiety, expresses disproportionate concerns about his or her symptoms, and devotes excessive time and energy to the symptoms or health concerns.

somnambulism (or sleepwalking) Occurs when a person arises and walks around while asleep.

source memory Recall of when, where, and how information was acquired.

specific phobia A disorder that involves an irrational fear of a particular object or situation that markedly interferes with an individual's ability to function.

spinal reflexes Simple pathways in the nervous system that rapidly generate muscle contractions.

spontaneous recovery The tendency of a learned behavior to recover from extinction after a rest period.

standard deviation A statistic that describes the average difference between the measurements in a frequency distribution and the mean of that distribution.

state-dependent retrieval The process whereby information tends to be better recalled when the person is in the same state during encoding and retrieval.

stereotype threat The fear of confirming the negative beliefs that others may hold.

stereotyping The process by which people draw inferences about others based on their knowledge of the categories to which others belong.

stimulants Substances that excite the central nervous system, heightening arousal and activity levels.

stimulus Sensory input from the environment.

storage The process of maintaining information in memory over time.

stress The physical and psychological response to internal or external stressors.

stressors Specific events or chronic pressures that place demands on a person or threaten the person's well-being.

structuralism The analysis of the basic elements that constitute the mind.

subcortical structures Areas of the forebrain housed under the cerebral cortex near the center of the brain.

subliminal perception Thought or behavior that is influenced by stimuli that a person cannot consciously report perceiving.

suggestibility The tendency to incorporate misleading information from external sources into personal recollections.

suicide Intentional self-inflicted death.

suicide attempt Engagement in potentially harmful behavior with some intention of dying.

sunk-cost fallacy A framing effect in which people make decisions about a current situation on the basis of what they have previously invested in the situation.

superego The mental system that reflects the internalization of cultural rules, mainly learned as parents exercise their authority.

surface structure How a sentence is worded.

sympathetic nervous system A set of nerves that prepares the body for action in challenging or threatening situations.

synapse The junction or region between the axon of one neuron and the dendrites or cell body of another.

syntactical rules A set of rules that indicate how words can be combined to form phrases and sentences.

systematic persuasion The process by which attitudes or beliefs are changed by appeals to reason.

taste buds The organs of taste transduction.

telegraphic speech Speech that is devoid of function morphemes and consists mostly of content words.

temperament A characteristic pattern of emotional reactivity.

temporal code The process whereby the cochlea registers low frequencies via the firing rate of action potentials entering the auditory nerve.

temporal lobe A region of the cerebral cortex responsible for hearing and language.

teratogen Any substance that passes from mother to unborn child and impairs development.

terminal buttons Knoblike structures that branch out from an axon.

terror management theory The theory about how people respond to knowledge of their own mortality.

thalamus A subcortical structure that relays and filters information from the senses and transmits the information to the cerebral cortex.

Thematic Apperception Test (TAT) A projective technique in which respondents' underlying motives, concerns, and the way they see the social world are believed to be revealed through analysis of the stories they make up about ambiguous pictures of people.

theory A hypothetical explanation of a natural phenomenon.

theory of mind The understanding that the mind produces representations of the world and that these representations guide behavior.

third-variable correlation Two variables are correlated not because one causes the other but because both are caused by a third variable.

thought suppression The conscious avoidance of a thought.

timbre A listener's experience of sound quality or resonance.

token economy A form of behavior therapy in which clients are given "tokens" for desired behaviors, which they can later trade for rewards.

trait A relatively stable disposition to behave in a particular and consistent way.

transcranial magnetic stimulation (TMS) A treatment that involves placing a powerful pulsed magnet over a person's scalp to alter neuronal activity in the brain.

transduction The process that occurs when many sensors in the body convert physical signals from the environment into encoded neural signals sent to the central nervous system.

transfer-appropriate processing The process whereby memory is more likely to transfer from one situation to another when the encoding and retrieval contexts of the situations match.

transference An event that occurs in psychoanalysis when the analyst begins to assume a major significance in the client's life, and the client reacts to the analyst on the basis of unconscious childhood fantasies.

transience Forgetting what occurs with the passage of time.

two-factor theory of emotion A theory that suggests that a stimulus triggers a general state of arousal in the body, which the mind then interprets as a specific emotion.

two-factor theory of intelligence Spearman's theory suggesting that a person's performance on a test is due to a combination of general ability and skills that are specific to the test.

Type A behavior pattern The tendency toward easily aroused hostility, impatience, a sense of time urgency, and competitive achievement strivings.

unconditioned response (UR) A reflexive reaction that is reliably produced by an unconditioned stimulus.

unconditioned stimulus (US) Something that reliably produces a naturally occurring reaction in an organism.

unconscious The part of the mind that operates outside of conscious awareness but influences conscious thoughts, feelings, and actions.

unconscious motivations Motivations of which people are not aware.

universality hypothesis The theory that emotional expressions have the same meaning for everyone.

validity The extent to which a concrete, observable event indicates the property.

variable A property whose value can vary across individuals or over time.

variable-interval schedule (VI) An operant conditioning principle whereby behavior is reinforced on the basis of an average time that has expired since the last reinforcement.

variable-ratio schedule (VR) An operant conditioning principle whereby the delivery of reinforcement is based on a particular average number of responses.

vestibular system The three fluid-filled semicircular canals and adjacent organs located next to the cochlea in the inner ear.

visual acuity The ability to see fine detail.

visual form agnosia The inability to recognize objects by sight.

visual imagery encoding The process of storing new information by converting it into mental pictures.

Weber's law States that the just noticeable difference of a stimulus is a constant proportion despite variations in intensity.

working memory A type of short-term storage that actively maintains information.

zygote A fertilized egg that contains chromosomes from both a sperm and an egg.

References

Aarts, H., Custers, R., & Marien, H. (2008). Preparing and motivating behavior outside of awareness. *Science, 319,* 1639.

Abel, T., Alberini, C., Ghirardi, M., Huang, Y.-Y., Nguyen, P., & Kandel, E. R. (1995). Steps toward a molecular definition of memory consolidation. In D. L. Schacter (Ed.), *Memory distortion: How minds, brains and societies reconstruct the past* (pp. 298–328). Cambridge, MA: Harvard University Press.

Abelson, J., Curtis, G., Sagher, O., Albucher, R., Harrigan, M., Taylor, S., . . . Giordani, B. (2009). Deep brain stimulation for refractory obsessive-compulsive disorder. *Biological Psychiatry, 57,* 510–516.

Abramson, L. Y., Seligman, M. E. P., & Teasdale, J. D. (1978). Learned helplessness in humans: Critique and reformulation. *Journal of Abnormal Psychology, 87,* 49–74.

Acevedo, B. P., & Aron, A. (2009). Does a long-term relationship kill romantic love? *Review of General Psychology, 13,* 59–65.

Acevedo-Garcia, D., McArdle, N., Osypuk, T. L., Lefkowitz, B., & Krimgold, B. K. (2007). *Children left behind: How metropolitan areas are failing America's children.* Boston: Harvard School of Public Health.

Achter, J. A., Lubinski, D., & Benbow, C. P. (1996). Multipotentiality among the intellectually gifted: "It was never there and already it's vanishing." *Journal of Counseling Psychology, 43,* 65–76.

Acocella, J. (1999). *Creating hysteria: Women and multiple personality disorder.* San Francisco: Jossey-Bass.

Addis, D. R., Wong, A. T., & Schacter, D. L. (2007). Remembering the past and imagining the future: Common and distinct neural substrates during event construction and elaboration. *Neuropsychologia, 45,* 1363–1377.

Addis, D. R., Wong, A. T., & Schacter, D. L. (2008). Age-related changes in the episodic simulation of future events. *Psychological Science, 19,* 33–41.

Adelmann, P. K., & Zajonc, R. B. (1989). Facial efference and the experience of emotion. *Annual Review of Psychology, 40,* 249–280.

Adolph, K. E., Cole, W. G., Komati, M., Garciaguirre, J. S., Badaly, D., Lingeman, J. M., . . . Sotsky, R. B. (2012). How do you learn to walk? Thousands of steps and dozens of falls per day. *Psychological Science, 23*(11), 1387–1394. doi:10.1177/0956797612446346

Adolphs, R., Russell, J. A., & Tranel, D. (1999). A role for the human amygdala in recognizing emotional arousal from unpleasant stimuli. *Psychological Science, 10,* 167–171.

Aggleton, J. (Ed.). (1992). *The amygdala: Neurobiological aspects of emotion, memory and mental dysfunction.* New York: Wiley-Liss.

Agin, D. (2007). *Junk science: An overdue indictment of government, industry, and faith groups that twist science for their own gain.* New York: Macmillan.

Agren, T., Engman, J., Frick, A., Björkstrand, J., Larsson, E. M., Furmark, T., & Fredrikson, M. (2012). Disruption of reconsolidation erases a fear memory trace in the human amygdala. *Science, 337,* 1550–1552.

Ahlskog, J. E. (2011). Pathological behaviors provoked by dopamine agonist therapy of Parkinson's disease. *Physiology & Behavior, 104,* 168–172.

Ainsworth, M. D. S., Blehar, M. C., Waters, E., & Wall, S. (1978). *Patterns of attachment: A psychological study of the strange situation.* Hillsdale, NJ: Erlbaum.

Ainsworth, S. E., & Maner, J. K. (2012). Sex begets violence: Mating motives, social dominance, and physical aggression in men. *Journal of Personality and Social Psychology, 103*(5), 819–829. doi: 10.1037/a0029428

Alasaari, J. S., Lagus, M., Ollila, H. M., Toivola, A., Kivimaki, M., Vahterra, J., . . . Paunio, T. (2012). Environmental stress affects DNA methylation of a CpG rich promoter region of serotonin transporter gene in a nurse cohort. *PLoS One, 7,* e45813. doi:10.1371/journal.pone.0045813

Albarracín, D., & Vargas, P. (2010). Attitudes and persuasion: From biology to social responses to persuasive intent. In S. T. Fiske, D. T. Gilbert, & G. Lindzey (Eds.), *The handbook of social psychology* (5th ed., Vol. 1, pp. 389–422). New York: Wiley.

Alcoholics Anonymous. (2016). Estimated worldwide A.A. individual and group membership. http://www.aa.org/assets/en_US/ smf-132_en.pdf. Accessed July 5, 2016.

Aleman, A., Sommer, I. E., & Kahn, R. S. (2007). Efficacy of slow repetitive transcranial magnetic stimulation in the treatment of resistant auditory hallucinations in schizophrenia: A meta-analysis. *Journal of Clinical Psychiatry, 68,* 416–421.

Alicke, M. D., Klotz, M. L., Breitenbecher, D. L., Yurak, T. J., & Vredenburg, D. S. (1995). Personal contact, individuation, and the better-than-average effect. *Journal of Personality and Social Psychology, 68,* 804–824.

Allison, D. B., Fontaine, K. R., Manson, J. E., Stevens, J., & VanItallie, T. B. (1999). Annual deaths attributable to obesity in the United States. *Journal of the American Medical Association, 282,* 1530–1538.

Allison, D. B., Kaprio, J., Korkeila, M., Koskenvuo, M., Neale, M. C., & Hayakawa, K. (1996). The heritability of body mass index among an international sample of monozygotic twins reared apart. *International Journal of Obesity, 20*(6), 501–506.

Allport, G. W. (1937). *Personality: A psychological interpretation.* New York: Holt.

Allport, G. W. (1954). *The nature of prejudice.* Cambridge, MA: Addison-Wesley.

Allport, G. W., & Odbert, H. S. (1936). Trait-names: A psycholexical study. *Psychological Monographs, 47,* 592.

Alt, K. W., Jeunesse, C., Buitrago-Téllez, C. H., Wächter, R., Boës, E., & Pichler, S. L. (1997). Evidence for stone age cranial surgery. *Nature, 387,* 360.

Alvarez, K., & Eckholm, E. (2009, January 8). Purple heart is ruled out for traumatic stress. *New York Times,* p. A1.

Alvarez, L. W. (1965). A pseudo experience in parapsychology. *Science, 148,* 1541.

American Academy of Pediatrics. (2000, July 26). *The impact of entertainment violence on children.* Joint statement issued at a meeting of the Congressional Public Health Summit. Retrieved from http://www.aap.org/advocacy/releases/jstmtevc.htm

American Psychiatric Association. (2013). *Diagnostic and statistical manual of mental disorders* (5th ed.). Washington, DC: Author.

American Psychological Association. (2002). *Ethical principles of psychologists and code of conduct.* Washington, DC: Author. Retrieved from apa.org/code/ethics/index.aspx [includes 2010 amendments].

American Psychological Association. (2005). *Resolution in favor of empirically supported sex education and HIV prevention programs for adolescents.* Washington, DC: Author.

American Psychological Association. (2009). *Report of the American Psychological Association task force on appropriate therapeutic responses to sexual orientation.* Washington, DC: Author.

Anand, S., & Hotson, J. (2002). Transcranial magnetic stimulation: Neurophysiological applications and safety. *Brain and Cognition, 50,* 366–386.

Anderson, C. A. (1989). Temperature and aggression: Ubiquitous effects of heat on occurrence of human violence. *Psychological Bulletin, 106,* 74–96.

Anderson, C. A., Berkowitz, L., Donnerstein, E., Huesmann, L. R., Johnson, J. D., Linz, D., . . . Wartella, E. (2003). The influence of media violence on youth. *Psychological Science in the Public Interest, 4,* 81–110.

Anderson, C. A., & Bushman, B. J. (2001). Effects of violent video games on aggressive behavior, aggressive cognition, aggressive affect, physiological arousal, and prosocial behavior: A meta-analytic review of the scientific literature. *Psychological Science, 12*(5), 353–359.

Anderson, C. A., & Bushman, B. J. (2002). Human aggression. *Annual Review of Psychology, 53,* 27–51.

Anderson, C. A., Bushman, B. J., & Groom, R. W. (1997). Hot years and serious and deadly assault: Empirical tests of the heat hypothesis. *Journal of Personality and Social Psychology, 73,* 1213–1223.

Anderson, M. C. (2003). Rethinking interference theory: Executive control and the mechanisms of forgetting. *Journal of Memory and Language, 49,* 415–445.

Anderson, M. C., Bjork, R. A., & Bjork, E. L. (1994). Remembering can cause forgetting: Retrieval dynamics in long-term memory. *Journal of Experimental Psychology: Learning, Memory, and Cognition, 20,* 1063–1087.

Anderson, M. C., Ochsner, K. N., Kuhl, B., Cooper, J., Robertson, E., Gabrieli, S. W., . . . Gabrieli, J. D. E. (2004). Neural systems underlying the suppression of unwanted memories. *Science, 303,* 232–235.

Anderson, R. C., Pichert, J. W., Goetz, E. T., Schallert, D. L., Stevens, K. V., & Trollip, S. R. (1976). Instantiation of general terms. *Journal of Verbal Learning and Verbal Behavior, 15,* 667–679.

Andreasen, N. C. (2011). A journey into chaos: Creativity and the unconscious. *Mens Sana Monographs, 9,* 42–53.

Andrewes, D. (2001). *Neuropsychology: From theory to practice.* Hove, England: Psychology Press.

Andrews-Hanna, J. R. (2012). The brain's default network and its adaptive role in internal mentation. *Neuroscientist, 18,* 251–270.

Annis, L. F., & Annis, D. B. (1982). A normative study of students' reported preferred study techniques. *Literacy Research and Instruction, 21,* 201–207.

Antoni, M. H., Lehman, J. M., Kilbourn, K. M., Boyers, A. E., Culver, J. L., Alferi, S. M., . . . Carver, C. S. (2001). Cognitive-behavioral stress management intervention decreases the prevalence of depression and enhances benefit finding among women under treatment for early-stage breast cancer. *Health Psychology, 20,* 20–32.

Apicella, C. L., Feinberg, D. R., & Marlowe, F. W. (2007). Voice pitch predicts reproductive success in male hunter-gatherers. *Biology Letters, 3*(6), 682–684. doi:10.1098/rsbl.2007.0410

Arellano, D., Varona, J., & Perales, F. (2008). Generation and visualization of emotional states in virtual characters. *Computer Animation and Virtual Worlds, 19*(3–4), 259–270.

Ariyasu, H., Takaya, K., Tagami, T., Ogawa, Y., Hosoda, K., Akamizu, T., . . . Hosoda, H. (2001). Stomach is a major source of circulating ghrelin, and feeding state determines plasma ghrelin-like immunoreactivity levels in humans. *Journal of Clinical Endocrinology and Metabolism, 86,* 4753–4758.

Armstrong, D. M. (1980). *The nature of mind.* Ithaca, NY: Cornell University Press.

Arnold, M. B. (Ed.). (1960). *Emotion and personality: Psychological aspects* (Vol. 1). New York: Columbia University Press.

Aron, A., Fisher, H., Mashek, D., Strong, G., Li, H., & Brown, L. (2005). Reward, motivation, and emotion systems associated with early-stage intense romantic love. *Journal of Neurophysiology, 93,* 327–337.

Aronson, E. (1963). Effect of the severity of threat on the devaluation of forbidden behavior. *Journal of Abnormal and Social Psychology, 66,* 584–588.

Aronson, E. (1969). The theory of cognitive dissonance: A current perspective. In L. Berkowitz (Ed.), *Advances in experimental social psychology* (Vol. 4, pp. 1–34). New York and London: Academic Press.

Aronson, E., & Worchel, P. (1966). Similarity versus liking as determinants of interpersonal attractiveness. *Psychonomic Science, 5,* 157–158.

Aronson, J., & Steele, C. M. (2004). Stereotypes and the fragility of academic competence, motivation, and self-concept. In A. J. Elliot & C. S. Dweck (Eds.), *Handbook of competence and motivation* (pp. 436–456). New York: Guilford Press.

Asch, S. E. (1951). Effects of group pressure on the modification and distortion of judgments. In H. Guetzkow (Ed.), *Groups, leadership, and men* (pp. 177–190). Pittsburgh, PA: Carnegie Press.

Asch, S. E. (1955). Opinions and social pressure. *Scientific American, 193,* 31–35.

Asch, S. E. (1956). Studies of independence and conformity: 1. A minority of one against a unanimous majority. *Psychological Monographs: General and Applied, 70,* 1–70.

Aschoff, J. (1965). Circadian rhythms in man. *Science, 148,* 1427–1432.

Aserinsky, E., & Kleitman, N. (1953). Regularly occurring periods of eye motility, and concomitant phenomena, during sleep. *Science, 118,* 273–274.

Ashby, F. G., & Ell, S. W. (2001). The neurobiology of human category learning. *Trends in Cognitive Sciences, 5,* 204–210.

Ashby, F. G., & O'Brien, J. B. (2005). Category learning and multiple memory systems. *Trends in Cognitive Sciences, 9,* 83–89.

Ashcraft, M. H. (1998). *Fundamentals of cognition.* New York: Longman.

Astington, J. W., & Baird, J. (2005). *Why language matters for theory of mind.* Oxford, England: Oxford University Press.

Atkinson, R. C., & Shiffrin, R. M. (1968). Human memory: A proposed system and its control processes. In K. W. Spence & J. T. Spence (Eds.), *The psychology of learning and motivation* (Vol. 2, pp. 89–195). New York: Academic Press.

Au, J., Sheehan, E., Tsai, N., Duncan, G. J., Buschkuehl, M., & Jaeggi, S. (2015). Improving fluid intelligence with training on working memory: A meta-analysis. *Psychonomic Bulletin & Review, 22,* 366–377.

Avery, D., Holtzheimer, P., III, Fawaz, W., Russo, J., Naumeier, J., Dunner, D., . . . Roy-Byrne, P. (2009). A controlled study of repetitive transcranial magnetic stimulation in medication-resistant major depression. *Biological Psychiatry, 59,* 187–194.

Aviezer, H., Hassin, R. R., Ryan, J., Grady, C., Susskind, J., Anderson, A., . . . Bentin, S. (2008). Angry, disgusted, or afraid? Studies on the malleability of emotion perception. *Psychological Science, 19,* 724–732.

Aviezer, H., Trope, Y., & Todorov, A. (2012). Body cues, not facial expressions, discriminate between intense positive and negative emotions. *Science, 338,* 1225–1229.

Axelrod, R. (1984). *The evolution of cooperation.* New York: Basic Books.

Axelrod, R., & Hamilton, W. D. (1981). The evolution of cooperation. *Science, 211,* 1390–1396.

Ayduk, O., Shoda, Y., Cervone, D., & Downey, G. (2007). Delay of gratification in children: Contributions to social–personality psychology. In G. Downey, Y. Shoda, & C. Cervone (Eds.), *Persons in context: Building a science of the individual* (pp. 97–109). New York: Guilford Press.

Azuma, H., & Kashiwagi, K. (1987). Descriptors for an intelligent person: A Japanese study. *Japanese Psychological Research, 29,* 17–26.

Baars, B. J. (1986). *The cognitive revolution in psychology.* New York: Guilford Press.

Baca-Motes, K., Brown, A., Gneezy, A., Keenan, E. A., & Nelson, L. D. (2013). Commitment and behavior change: Evidence from the field. *Journal of Consumer Research, 39*(5), 1070–1084. doi:10.1086/667226

Back, M. D., Schmukle, S. C., & Egloff, B. (2008). Becoming friends by chance. *Psychological Science, 19,* 439–440.

Back, M. D., Stopfer, J. M., Vazire, S., Gaddis, S., Schmukle, S. C., Egloff, B., & Gosling, S. (2010). Facebook profiles reflect actual personality not self-idealization. *Psychological Science, 21,* 372–374.

Backman, C. W., & Secord, P. F. (1959). The effect of perceived liking on interpersonal attraction. *Human Relations, 12,* 379–384.

Bäckman, L., Almkvist, O., Andersson, J., Nordberg, A., Winblad, B., Reineck, R., & Långström, B. (1997). Brain activation in young and older adults during implicit and explicit retrieval. *Journal of Cognitive Neuroscience, 9,* 378–391.

Bäckman, L., & Dixon, R. A. (1992). Psychological compensation: A theoretical framework. *Psychological Bulletin, 112,* 259–283.

Baddeley, A. D. (2001). Is working memory still working? *American Psychologist, 56,* 851–864.

Baddeley, A. D., Allen, R. J., & Hitch, G. J. (2011). Binding in visual working memory: The role of the episodic buffer. *Neuropsychologia, 49,* 1393–1400.

Baddeley, A. D., & Hitch, G. J. (1974). Working memory. In S. Dornic (Ed.), *Attention and performance* (Vol. 6, pp. 647–667). Hillsdale, NJ: Erlbaum.

Bagby, R. M., Levitan, R. D., Kennedy, S. H., Levitt, A. J., & Joffe, R. T. (1999). Selective alteration of personality in response to noradrenergic and serotonergic antidepressant medication in depressed sample: Evidence of non-specificity. *Psychiatry Research, 86,* 211–216.

Bahrick, H. P. (1984). Semantic memory content in permastore: 50 years of memory for Spanish learned in school. *Journal of Experimental Psychology: General, 113,* 1–29.

Bahrick, H. P. (2000). Long-term maintenance of knowledge. In E. Tulving & F. I. M. Craik (Eds.), *The Oxford handbook of memory* (pp. 347–362). New York: Oxford University Press.

Bailey, J. M., & Pillard, R. C. (1991). A genetic study of male sexual orientation. *Archives of General Psychiatry, 48,* 1089–1096.

Bailey, J. M., Pillard, R. C., Dawood, K., Miller, M. B., Farrer, L. A., Trivedi, S., . . . Murphy, R. L. (1999). A family history study of male sexual orientation using three independent samples. *Behavior Genetics, 29,* 79–86.

Bailey, J. M., Pillard, R. C., Neale, M. C., & Agyes, Y. (1993). Heritable factors influence sexual orientation in women. *Archives of General Psychiatry, 50,* 217–223.

Bailey, J. M., Vasey, P. L., Diamond, L. M., Breedlove, S. M., Vilain, E., & Epprecht, M. (2016). Sexual orientation, controversy, and science. *Psychological Science in the Public Interest, 17*(2), 45–101. doi: 10.1177/1529100616637616

Bailey, J. M., & Zucker, K. J. (1995). Childhood sex-typed behavior and sexual orientation: A conceptual analysis and quantitative review. *Developmental Psychology, 31,* 43–55.

Baillargeon, R., Spelke, E. S., & Wasserman, S. (1985). Object permanence in 5-month-old infants. *Cognition, 20,* 191–208.

Baird, B., Smallwood, J., Mrazek, M. D., Kam, J. W. Y., Franklin, M. S., & Schooler, J. W. (2012). Inspired by distraction: Mind wandering facilitates creative incubation. *Psychological Science, 23,* 1117–1122.

Baker, D. P., Eslinger, P. J., Benavides, M., Peters, E., Dieckmann, N. F., & Leon, J. (2015). The cognitive impact of the education revolution: A possible cause of the Flynn Effect on population IQ. *Intelligence, 49,* 144–158. doi: 10.1016/j.intell.2015.01.003

Baker, E., Shelton, K. H., Baibazarova, E., Hay, D. F., & van Goozen, S. H. M. (2013). Low skin conductance activity in infancy predicts aggression in toddlers 2 years later. *Psychological Science, 24*(6), 1051–1056. doi:10.1177/0956797612465198

Baker, T. B., Brandon, T. H., & Chassin, L. (2004). Motivational influences on cigarette smoking. *Annual Review of Psychology, 55,* 463–491.

Baler, R. D., & Volkow, N. D. (2006). Drug addiction: The neurobiology of disrupted self-control. *Trends in Molecular Medicine, 12,* 559–566.

Banaji, M. R., & Heiphetz, L. (2010). Attitudes. In S. T. Fiske, D. T. Gilbert, & G. Lindzey (Eds.), *The handbook of social psychology* (5th ed., Vol. 1, pp. 348–388). New York: Wiley.

Bandura, A. (1977). *Social learning theory.* Englewood Cliffs, NJ: Prentice Hall.

Bandura, A. (1986). *Social foundations of thought and action: A social cognitive theory.* Englewood Cliffs, NJ: Prentice Hall.

Bandura, A. (1994). Social cognitive theory of mass communication. In J. Bryant & D. Zillmann (Eds.), *Media effects: Advances in theory and research* (pp. 61–90). Hillsdale, NJ: Erlbaum.

Bandura, A., Ross, D., & Ross, S. (1961). Transmission of aggression through imitation of adult models. *Journal of Abnormal and Social Psychology, 63,* 575–582.

Bandura, A., Ross, D., & Ross, S. (1963). Vicarious reinforcement and imitative learning. *Journal of Abnormal and Social Psychology, 67,* 601–607.

Banks, M. S., & Salapatek, P. (1983). Infant visual perception. In M. Haith & J. Campos (Eds.), *Handbook of child psychology: Biology and infancy* (pp. 435–572). New York: Wiley.

Barber, S. J., Harris, C. B., & Rajaram, S. (2015). Why two heads apart are better than two heads together: Multiple mechanisms underlie the collaborative inhibition effect in memory. *Journal of Experimental Psychology: Learning, Memory, and Cognition, 41,* 559–566.

Barber, J. P., Muran, J. C., McCarthy, K. S., & Keefe, J. R. (2013). Research on dynamic therapies. In M. Lambert (Ed.), *Bergin and Garfield's handbook of psychotherapy and behavior change* (6th ed., pp. 443–494). Hoboken, NJ: Wiley.

Bard, P. (1934). On emotional experience after decortication with some remarks on theoretical views. *Psychological Review, 41,* 309–329.

Bargh, J. A., Chen, M., & Burrows, L. (1996). The automaticity of social behavior: Direct effects of trait concept and stereotype activation on action. *Journal of Personality and Social Psychology, 71,* 230–244.

Bargh, J. A., Gollwitzer, P. M., Lee-Chai, A., Barndollar, K., & Trötschel, R. (2001). The automated will: Nonconscious activation and pursuit of behavioral goals. *Journal of Personality and Social Psychology, 81,* 1014–1027.

Bargh, J. A., Gollwitzer, P. M., & Oettingen, G. (2010). Motivation. In S. T. Fiske, D. T. Gilbert, & G. Lindzey (Eds.), *The handbook of social psychology* (5th ed., Vol. 1, pp. 263–311). New York: Wiley.

Barker, A. T., Jalinous, R., & Freeston, I. L. (1985). Noninvasive magnetic stimulation of the human motor cortex. *Lancet, 2,* 1106–1107.

Barkow, J. (1980). Prestige and self-esteem: A biosocial interpretation. In D. R. Omark, F. F. Stayer, & D. G. Freedman (Eds.), *Dominance relations* (pp. 319–322). New York: Garland.

Barlow, D. H., Bullis, J. R., Comer, J. S., & Ametaj, A. A. (2013). Evidence-based psychological treatments: An update and a way forward. *Annual Review of Clinical Psychology, 9,* 1–27.

Barlow, D. H., Gorman, J. M., Shear, M. K., & Woods, S. W. (2000). Cognitive-behavioral therapy, imipramine, or their combination for panic disorder: A randomized controlled trial. *Journal of the American Medical Association, 283*(19), 2529–2536.

Barnier, A. J., Levin, K., & Maher, A. (2004). Suppressing thoughts of past events: Are repressive copers good suppressors? *Cognition and Emotion, 18,* 457–477.

Baron-Cohen, S. (1991). Do people with autism understand what causes emotion? *Child Development, 62,* 385–395.

Baron-Cohen, S., & Belmonte, M. K. (2005). Autism: A window onto the development of the social and analytic brain. *Annual Review of Neuroscience, 28,* 109–126.

Baron-Cohen, S., Leslie, A., & Frith, U. (1985). Does the autistic child have a "theory of mind"? *Cognition, 21,* 37–46.

Barrett, L. F., Mesquita, B., & Gendron, M. (2011). Context in emotion perception. *Current Directions in Psychological Science, 20*(5), 286–290. doi:10.1177/0963721411422522

Bartal, I. B.-A., Decety, J., & Mason, P. (2011). Empathy and prosocial behavior in rats. *Science, 334*(6061), 1427–1430.

Bartol, C. R., & Costello, N. (1976). Extraversion as a function of temporal duration of electric shock: An exploratory study. *Perceptual and Motor Skills, 42,* 1174.

Bartoshuk, L. M. (2000). Comparing sensory experiences across individuals: Recent psychophysical advances illuminate genetic variation in taste perception. *Chemical Senses, 25,* 447–460.

Bartoshuk, L. M., & Beauchamp, G. K. (1994). Chemical senses. *Annual Review of Psychology, 45,* 419–445.

Basden, B. H., Basden, D. R., Bryner, S., & Thomas, R. L. (1997). A comparison of group and individual remembering: Does collaboration disrupt retrieval strategies? *Journal of Experimental Psychology: Learning, Memory, and Cognition, 23,* 1176–1191.

Bass, C. & Halligan, P. (2014). Factitious disorders and malingering: Challenges for clinical assessment and management. *Lancet, 383,* 1422–1432.

Bates, E., & Goodman, J. C. (1997). On the inseparability of grammar and the lexicon: Evidence from acquisition, aphasia, and real-time processing. *Language and Cognitive Processes, 12,* 507–584.

Batson, C. D. (2002). Addressing the altruism question experimentally. In S. G. Post & L. G. Underwood (Eds.), *Altruism & altruistic love: Science, philosophy, & religion in dialogue* (pp. 89–105). London: Oxford University Press.

Batty, G. D., Deary, I. J., Schoon, I., & Gale, C. R. (2007). Mental ability across childhood in relation to risk factors for premature mortality in adult life: The 1970 British Cohort Study. *Journal of Epidemiology & Community Health, 61*(11), 997–1003. doi:10.1136/jech.2006.054494

Baumeister, R. F. (2000). Gender differences in erotic plasticity: The female sex drive as socially flexible and responsive. *Psychological Bulletin, 126,* 347–374.

Baumeister, R. F., Ainsworth, S. E., & Vohs, K. D. (2015). Are groups more or less than the sum of their members? The moderating role of individual identification. *Behavioral and Brain Sciences,* 1–38. doi: 10.1017/S0140525X15000618

Baumeister, R. F., Bratslavsky, E., Muraven, M., & Tice, D. M. (1998). Ego depletion: Is the active self a limited resource? *Journal of Personality and Social Psychology, 74,* 1252–1265.

Baumeister, R. F., Campbell, J. D., Krueger, J. I., & Vohs, K. D. (2003). Does high self-esteem cause better performance, interpersonal success, happiness, or healthier lifestyles? *Psychological Science in the Public Interest, 4,* 1–44.

Baumeister, R. F., Cantanese, K. R., & Vohs, K. D. (2001). Is there a gender difference in strength of sex drive? Theoretical views, conceptual distinctions, and a review of relevant evidence. *Personality and Social Psychology Review, 5,* 242–273.

Baumeister, R. F., Heatherton, T. F., & Tice, D. M. (1995). *Losing control.* San Diego: Academic Press.

Baumeister, R. F., & Leary, M. R. (1995). The need to belong: Desire for interpersonal attachments as a fundamental human motivation. *Psychological Bulletin, 117,* 497–529.

Baumeister, R. F., Smart, L., & Boden, J. M. (1996). Relation of threatened egotism to violence and aggression: The dark side of high self-esteem. *Psychological Review, 103,* 5–33.

Baumeister, R. F., Vohs, K. D., & Tice, D. M. (2007). The strength model of self-control. *Current Directions in Psychological Science, 16,* 351–355.

Baxter, L. R., Schwartz, J. M., Bergman, K. S., Szuba, M. P., Guze, B. H., Mazziotta, J. C., Alazraki, A., . . . Munford, P. (1992). Caudate glucose metabolic rate changes with both drug behavior therapy for obsessive-compulsive disorder. *Archives of General Psychiatry, 49,* 681–689.

Bayley, P. J., Frascino, J. C., & Squire, L. R. (2005). Robust habit learning in the absence of awareness and independent of the medial temporal lobe. *Nature, 436,* 550–553.

Bayley, P. J., Gold, J. J., Hopkins, R. O., & Squire, L. R. (2005). The neuroanatomy of remote memory. *Neuron, 46,* 799–810.

Beard, C., Sawyer, A. T., & Hoffmann, S. G. (2012). Efficacy of attention bias modification using threat and appetitive stimuli: A meta-analytic review. *Behavior Therapy, 43,* 724–740.

Bechara, A., Damasio, A. R., Damasio, H., & Anderson, S. W. (1994). Insensitivity to future consequences following damage to human prefrontal cortex. *Cognition, 50,* 7–15.

Bechara, A., Damasio, H., Tranel, D., & Damasio, A. R. (1997). Deciding advantageously before knowing the advantageous strategy. *Science, 275,* 1293–1295.

Bechara, A., Dolan, S., Denburg, N., Hindes, A., & Anderson, S. W. (2001). Decision-making deficits, linked to a dysfunctional ventromedial prefrontal cortex, revealed in alcohol and stimulant abusers. *Neuropsychologia, 39,* 376–389.

Bechara, A., Tranel, D., & Damasio, H. (2000). Characterization of the decision-making deficit of patients with ventromedial prefrontal cortex lesions. *Brain, 123,* 2189–2202.

Beck, A. T. (1967). *Depression: Causes and treatment.* Philadelphia: University of Pennsylvania Press.

Beck, A. T. (2005). The current state of cognitive therapy: A 40-year retrospective. *Archives of General Psychiatry, 62,* 953–959.

Beckers, G., & Zeki, S. (1995). The consequences of inactivating areas V1 and V5 on visual motion perception. *Brain, 118,* 49–60.

Bednarczyk, R. A., Davis, R., Ault, K., Orenstein, W., & Omer, S. B. (2012). Sexual activity-related outcomes after human papillomavirus vaccination of 11- to 12-year-olds. *Pediatrics, 130*(5), 798–805. doi:10.1542/peds.2912-1516

Bedny, M., & Saxe, R. (2012). Insights into the origins of knowledge from the cognitive neuroscience of blindness. *Cognitive Neuropsychology, 29,* 56–84.

Bell, R., Roer, J. P., & Buchner, A. (2015). Adaptive memory: Thinking about function. *Journal of Experimental Psychology: Learning, Memory, & Cognition, 41,* 1038–1048.

Bell, A. P., Weinberg, M. S., & Hammersmith, S. K. (1981). *Sexual preference: Its development in men and women.* Bloomington: Indiana University Press.

Belsky, J. (2012). The development of human reproductive strategies: Progress and prospects. *Current Directions in Psychological Science, 21*(5), 310–316. doi:10.1177/0963721412453588

Belsky, J., Ruttle, P. L., Boyce, W. T., Armstrong, J. M., & Essex, M. J. (2015). Early adversity, elevated stress physiology, accelerated sexual maturation, and poor health in females. *Developmental Psychology, 51*(6), 816–822. doi: 10.1037/dev0000017

Bem, S. L. (1974). The measure of psychological androgyny. *Journal of Consulting and Clinical Psychology, 42,* 155–162.

Benenson, J. F., Markovits, H., Thompson, M. E., & Wrangham, R. W. (2011). Under threat of social exclusion, females exclude more than males. *Psychological Science, 22*(4), 538–544. doi: 10.1177/0956797611402511

Bennett, I. J., Romano, J. C., Howard, J. H., & Howard, D. V. (2008). Two forms of implicit learning in young adults with dyslexia. *Annals of the New York Academy of Sciences, 1145*, 184–198.

Benoit, R. G., & Anderson, M. C. (2012). Opposing mechanisms support the voluntary forgetting of unwanted memories. *Neuron, 76*, 450–460.

Ben-Porath, Y. S., & Tellegen, A. (2008). *Minnesota Multiphasic Personality Inventory–2–Restructured Form: Manual for administration, scoring, and interpretation.* Minneapolis: University of Minnesota Press.

Benson, H. (Ed.). (1990). *The relaxation response.* New York: Harper Torch.

Benson, H., Dusek, J. A., Sherwood, J. B., Lam, P., Bethea, C. F., Carpenter, W., . . . Hibberd, P. L. (2006). Study of the therapeutic effects of intercessory prayer (STEP) in cardiac bypass patients: A multicenter randomized trial of uncertainty and certainty of receiving intercessory prayer. *American Heart Journal, 151*, 934–942.

Bentz, D. & Schiller, D. (2015). Threat processing: Models and mechanisms. *WIREs Cognitive Science, 6*, 427–439.

Bering, J. (2004). A critical review of the "enculturation hypothesis": The effects of human rearing on great ape social cognition. *Animal Cognition, 7*, 201–212.

Berkowitz, L. (1990). On the formation and regulation of anger and aggression: A cognitive-neoassociationistic analysis. *American Psychologist, 45*, 494–503.

Bernier, A., Beauchamp, M. H., Carlson, S. M., & Lalonde, G. (2015). A secure base from which to regulate: Attachment security in toddlerhood as a predictor of executive functioning at school entry. *Developmental Psychology, 51*(9), 1177–1189. doi: 10.1037/dev0000032

Berridge, K. C. (2007). The debate over dopamine's role in reward: The case for incentive salience. *Psychopharmacology, 191*, 391–431.

Berscheid, E., Dion, K., Walster, E., & Walster, G. W. (1971). Physical attractiveness and dating choice: A test of the matching hypothesis. *Journal of Experimental Social Psychology, 7*(2), 173–189.

Berscheid, E., & Reis, H. T. (1998). Interpersonal attraction and close relationships. In D. T. Gilbert, S. T. Fiske, & G. Lindzey (Eds.), *The handbook of social psychology* (4th ed., Vol. 2, pp. 193–281). New York: McGraw-Hill.

Bertenthal, B. I., Rose, J. L., & Bai, D. L. (1997). Perception–action coupling in the development of visual control of posture. *Journal of Experimental Psychology: Human Perception & Performance, 23*, 1631–1643.

Berthoud, H.-R., & Morrison, C. (2008). The brain, appetite, and obesity. *Annual Review of Psychology, 59*, 55–92.

Best, J. B. (1992). *Cognitive psychology* (3rd ed.). New York: West Publishing.

Bettencourt, B. A., & Miller, N. (1996). Gender differences in aggression as a function of provocation: A meta-analysis. *Psychological Bulletin, 119*, 422–447.

Beutler, L. E. (2002). The dodo bird is extinct. *Clinical Psychology: Science and Practice, 9*, 30–34.

Bhargava, S. (2011). Diagnosis and management of common sleep problems in children. *Pediatrics in Review, 32*, 91.

Bialystok, E. (1999). Cognitive complexity and attentional control in the bilingual mind. *Child Development, 70*, 636–644.

Bialystok, E. (2009). Bilingualism: The good, the bad, and the indifferent. *Bilingualism: Language and Cognitive Processes, 12*, 3–11.

Bialystok, E., Craik, F. I. M., & Luk, G. (2012). Bilingualism: Consequences for mind and brain. *Trends in Cognitive Sciences, 16*, 240–250.

Biederman, J., Monuteaux, M. C., Spencer, T., Wilens, T. E., & Faraone, S. V. (2009). Do stimulants protect against psychiatric disorders in youth with ADHD? A 10-year follow-up study. *Pediatrics, 124*, 71–78.

Binet, A. (1909). *Les idées modernes sur les enfants* [Modern ideas about children]. Paris: Flammarion.

Binswanger, L. (1958). The existential analysis school of thought. In R. May (Ed.), *Existence: A new dimension in psychiatry and psychology* (pp. 191–213). New York: Basic Books.

Biro, S., Alink, L. R., van IJzendoorn, M. H., & Bakermans-Kranenburg, M. J. (2014). Infants' monitoring of social interactions: The effect of emotional cues. *Emotion, 14*(2), 263–271. doi: 10.1037/a0035589

Bjork, D. W. (1983). *The compromised scientist: William James in the development of American psychology.* New York: Columbia University Press.

Bjork, D. W. (1993). *B. F. Skinner: A life.* New York: Basic Books.

Bjork, E. L., & Bjork, R. A. (2011). Making things hard on yourself, but in a good way: Creating desirable difficulties to enhance learning. In M. A. Gernsbacher, R. W. Pewe, L. M. Hough, & J. R. Pomerantz (Eds.), *Psychology and the real world: Essays illustrating fundamental contributions to society* (pp. 56–64). New York: Worth Publishers.

Bjork, R. A. (1975). Retrieval as a memory modifier. In R. Solso (Ed.), *Information processing and cognition: The Loyola symposium* (pp. 123–144). Hillsdale, NJ: Lawrence Erlbaum Associates.

Bjork, R. A. (2011). On the symbiosis of remembering, forgetting, and learning. In A. S. Benjamin (Ed.), *Successful remembering and successful forgetting: A festschrift in honor of Robert A. Bjork* (pp. 1–22). London: Psychology Press.

Bjork, R. A., & Bjork, E. L. (1988). On the adaptive aspects of retrieval failure in autobiographical memory. In M. M. Gruneberg, P. E. Morris, & R. N. Sykes (Eds.), *Practical aspects of memory: Current research and issues* (pp. 283–288). Chichester, England: Wiley.

Bjork, R. A., Dunlosky, J., & Kornell, N. (2013). Self-regulated learning: Beliefs, techniques, and illusions. *Annual Review of Psychology, 64*, 417–444.

Blackburn, E. H., & Epel, E. S. (2012). Too toxic to ignore. *Nature, 490*, 169–171.

Blackburn, E. H., Epel, E. S., & Lin, J. (2015). Human telomere biology: A contributory and interactive factor in aging, disease risks, and protection. *Science, 350*, 1193–1198.

Blair, C. (2006). How similar are fluid cognition and general intelligence? A developmental neuroscience perspective on fluid cognition as an aspect of human cognitive ability. *Behavioral and Brain Sciences, 29*(2), 109–125 (article),125–160 (discussion). doi: 10.1017/S0140525X06009034

Blair, I. V. (2002). The malleability of automatic stereotypes and prejudice. *Personality and Social Psychology Review, 6*, 242–261.

Blair, J., Peschardt, K., & Mitchell, D. R. (2005). *Psychopath: Emotion and the brain.* Oxford, England: Blackwell.

Blascovich, J., & Tomaka, J. (1996). The biopsychosocial model of arousal regulation. In M. P. Zanna (Ed.), *Advances in experimental social psychology* (Vol. 28, pp. 1–51). San Diego: Academic Press.

Blatt, S. J., & Homann, E. (1992). Parent–child interaction in the etiology of dependent and self-critical depression. *Clinical Psychology Review, 12*, 47–91.

Blesch, A., & Tuszynski, M. H. (2009). Spinal cord injury: Plasticity, regeneration and the challenge of translational drug development. *Trends in Neurosciences, 32*, 41–47.

Bliss, T. V. P. (1999). Young receptors make smart mice. *Nature, 401*, 25–27.

Bliss, T. V. P., & Lømo, W. T. (1973). Long-lasting potentiation of synaptic transmission in the dentate area of the anesthetized rabbit following stimulation of the perforant path. *Journal of Physiology, 232*, 331–356.

Bloch, L., Haase, C. M., & Levenson, R. W. (2014). Emotion regulation predicts marital satisfaction: More than a wives' tale. *Emotion, 14*(1), 130–144. doi: 10.1037/a0034272

Bloch, C., Kaiser, A., Kuenzli, E., Zappatore, D., Haller, S., Franceschini, R., . . . Nitsch, C. (2009). The age of second language acquisition determines the variability in activation elicited by narration in three languages in Broca's and Wernicke's area. *Neuropsychologia, 47,* 625–633.

Bloom, C. M., Venard, J., Harden, M., & Seetharaman, S. (2007). Non-contingent positive and negative reinforcement schedules of supersitious behaviors. *Behavioural Process, 75,* 8–13.

Boecker, H., Sprenger, T., Spilker, M. E., Henriksen, G., Koppenhoefer, M., Wagner, K. J., . . .Tolle, T. R. (2008). The runner's high: Opioidergic mechanisms in the human brain. *Cerebral Cortex, 18,* 2523–2531.

Boehm, J. K., & Kubzansky, L. D. (2012). The heart's content: The association between positive psychological well-being and cardiovascular health. *Psychological Bulletin, 138,* 655–691.

Boehm, J. K., Williams, D. R., Rimm, E. B., Ryff, C., & Kubzansky, L. D. (2013). Relation between optimism and lipids in midlife. *American Journal of Cardiology, 111,* 1425–1431.

Boergers, J., Spirito, A., & Donaldson, D. (1998). Reasons for adolescent suicide attempts: Associations with psychological functioning. *Journal of the American Academy of Child and Adolescent Psychiatry, 37,* 1287–1293.

Bohan, J. S. (1996). *Psychology and sexual orientation: Coming to terms.* New York: Routledge.

Boinski, S., Quatrone, R. P., & Swartz, H. (2000). Substrate and tool use by brown capuchins in Suriname: Ecological contexts and cognitive bases. *American Anthropologist, 102,* 741–761.

Boisvert, C. M., & Faust, D. (2002). Iatrogenic symptoms in psychotherapy: A theoretical exploration of the potential impact of labels, language, and belief systems. *American Journal of Psychotherapy, 56,* 244–259.

Bolger, N., Davis, A., & Rafaeli, E. (2003). Diary methods: Capturing life as it is lived. *Annual Review of Psychology, 54,* 579–616.

Boomsma, D., Busjahn, A., & Peltonen, L. (2002). Classical twin studies and beyond. *Nature Reviews Genetics, 3,* 872–882.

Bootzin, R. R., & Epstein, D. R. (2011). Understanding and treating insomnia. *Annual Review of Clinical Psychology, 7,* 435–458.

Borges, G., Breslau, J., Orozco, R., Tancredi, D. J., Anderson, H., Aguilar-Gaxiola, S., & Medina-Mora, M.-E. (2011). A crossnational study on Mexico–US migration, substance use and substance use disorders. *Drug and Alcohol Dependence, 117,* 16–23.

Borghol, N., Suderman, M., McArdle, W., Racine, A., Hallett, M., Pembrey, M., . . . Szyf, M. (2012). Associations with early-life socio-economic position in adult DNA methylation. *International Journal of Epidemiology, 41,* 62–74.

Borkenau, P., & Liebler, A. (1995). Observable attributes as manifestations and cues of personality and intelligence. *Journal of Personality, 63,* 1–25.

Borkevec, T. D. (1982). Insomnia. *Journal of Consulting and Clinical Psychology, 50,* 880–895.

Born, R. T., & Bradley, D. C. (2005). Structure and function of visual area MT. *Annual Review of Neuroscience, 28,* 157–189.

Börner, K., Klavans, R., Patek, M., Zoss, A. M., Biberstine, J. R., Light, R. P., Larivière, V., & Boyack, K. W. (2012). Design and update of a classification system: The UCSD map of science. *PLoS ONE, 7,* e39464.

Bornstein, R. F. (1989). Exposure and affect: Overview and meta-analysis of research, 1968–1987. *Psychological Bulletin, 106,* 265–289.

Botwin, M. D., Buss, D. M., & Shackelford, T. K. (1997). Personality and mate preferences: Five factors in mate selection and marital satisfaction. *Journal of Personality, 65,* 107–136.

Bouchard, S. M., Brown, T. G., & Nadeau, L. (2012). Decision making capacities and affective reward anticipation in DWI recidivists compared to non-offenders: A preliminary study. *Accident Analysis and Prevention, 45,* 580–587.

Bouchard, T. J., & McGue, M. (2003). Genetic and environmental influences on human psychological differences. *Journal of Neurobiology, 54,* 4–45.

Bouton, M. E. (1988). Context and ambiguity in the extinction of emotional learning: Implications for exposure therapy. *Behaviour Research and Therapy, 26,* 137–149.

Bower, G. H. (1981). Mood and memory. *American Psychologist, 36,* 129–148.

Bower, G. H., Clark, M. C., Lesgold, A. M., & Winzenz, D. (1969). Hierarchical retrieval schemes in recall of categorical word lists. *Journal of Verbal Learning and Verbal Behavior, 8,* 323–343.

Bowlby, J. (1969). *Attachment and loss: Vol. 1. Attachment.* New York: Basic Books.

Bowlby, J. (1973). *Attachment and loss: Vol. 2. Separation.* New York: Basic Books.

Bowlby, J. (1980). *Attachment and loss: Vol. 3. Loss: Sadness and depression.* New York: Basic Books.

Boyack, K. W., Klavans, R., & Börner, K. (2005). Mapping the backbone of science. *Scientometrics, 64,* 351–374.

Boyd, R. (2008, February 7). Do people use only 10 percent of their brains? *Scientific American.* Retrieved from http://www.scientificamerican.com/article.cfm?id=people-only-use-10-percent-of-brain&page=2

Bozarth, M. A., & Wise, R. A. (1985). Toxicity associated with long-term intravenous heroin and cocaine self-administration in the rat. *Journal of the American Medical Association, 254,* 81–83.

Brackett, M. A., & Mayer, J. D. (2003). Convergent, discriminant, and incremental validity of competing measures of emotional intelligence. *Personality and Social Psychology Bulletin, 29,* 1147.

Brackett, M. A., Rivers, S. E., Shiffman, S., Lerner, N., & Salovey, P. (2006). Relating emotional abilities to social functioning: A comparison of self-report and performance measures of emotional intelligence. *Journal of Personality and Social Psychology, 91,* 780.

Brackett, M. A., Warner, R. M., & Bosco, J. (2005). Emotional intelligence and relationship quality among couples. *Personal Relationships, 12*(2), 197–212.

Bradford, D., Stroup, S., & Lieberman, J. (2002). Pharmacological treatments for schizophrenia. In P. E. Nathan & J. M. Gorman (Eds.), *A guide to treatments that work* (2nd ed., pp. 169–199). New York: Oxford University Press.

Brakefield, T. A., Mednick, S. C., Wilson, H. W., De Neve, J. E., Christakis, N. A., & Fowler, J. H. (2014). Same-sex sexual attraction does not spread in adolescent social networks. *Archives of Sexual Behavior, 43*(2), 335–344. doi: 10.1007/s10508-013-0142-9

Bramlett, M. D., & Mosher, W. D. (2002). *Cohabitation, marriage, divorce, and remarriage in the United States* (Vital and Health Statistics Series 23, No. 22). Hyattsville, MD: National Center for Health Statistics.

Brandt, K. R., Gardiner, J. M., Vargha-Khadem, F., Baddeley, A. D., & Mishkin, M. (2009). Impairment of recollection but not familiarity in a case of developmental amnesia. *Neurocase, 15,* 60–65.

Braun, A. R., Balkin, T. J., Wesensten, N. J., Gwadry, F., Carson, R. E., Varga, M., . . . Herscovitch, P. (1998). Dissociated pattern of activity in visual cortices and their projections during rapid eye movement sleep. *Science, 279,* 91–95.

Breazeal, C. (2009, December 12). The role of expression in robots that learn from people. *Philosophical Transactions of the Royal Society B, 364*(1535), 3527–3538.

Brédart, S., & Valentine, T. (1998). Descriptiveness and proper name retrieval. *Memory, 6,* 199–206.

Bredy, T. W., Wu, H., Crego, C., Zellhoefer, J., Sun, Y. E., & Barad, M. (2007). Histone modifications around individual BDNF gene promoters in prefrontal cortex are associated with extinction of conditioned fear. *Learning and Memory, 14,* 268–276.

Breggin, P. R. (1990). Brain damage, dementia, and persistent cognitive dysfunction associated with neuroleptic drugs: Evidence, etiology, implications. *Journal of Mind and Behavior, 11,* 425–463.

Breggin, P. R. (2000). *Reclaiming our children.* Cambridge, MA: Perseus Books.

Brehm, S. S. (1992). *Intimate relationships* (2nd ed.). New York: McGraw-Hill.

Breland, K., & Breland, M. (1961). The misbehavior of organisms. *American Psychologist, 16,* 681–684.

Brennan, P. A., & Zufall, F. (2006). Pheromonal communication in vertebrates. *Nature, 444,* 308–315.

Brenninkmeijer, V., Vanyperen, N. W., & Buunk, B. P. (2001). I am not a better teacher, but others are doing worse: Burnout and perceptions of superiority among teachers. *Social Psychology of Education, 4*(3–4), 259–274.

Breslau, J., Aguilar-Gaxiola, S., Borges, G., Castilla-Puentes, R. C., Kendler, K. S., Medina-Mora, M.-E., . . . Kessler, R. C. (2007). Mental disorders among English-speaking Mexican immigrants to the US compared to a national sample of Mexicans. *Psychiatry Research, 151,* 115–122.

Breslau, J., & Chang, D. F. (2006). Psychiatric disorders among foreign-born and US-born Asian-Americans in a US national survey. *Social Psychiatry & Psychiatric Epidemiology, 41,* 943–950.

Breslow, L., Pritchard, D. E., DeBoer, J., Stump, G. S., Ho, A. D., & Seaton, D. T. (2013). Studying learning in the worldwide classroom: *Research into edX's first MOOC. Research & Practice in Assessment, 8,* 13–25.

Bretherton, I., & Munholland, K. A. (1999). Internal working models in attachment relationships: A construct revisited. In J. Cassidy & P. R. Shaver (Eds.), *Handbook of attachment: Theory, research and clinical applications* (pp. 89–114). New York: Guilford Press.

Brewer, J. A., Worhunsky, P. D., Gray, J. R., Tang, Y.-Y., Weber, J., & Kober, H. (2011). Meditation experience is associated with differences in default mode network activity and connectivity. *Proceedings of the National Academy of Sciences, 108,* 20254–20259.

Brewer, M. B. (1999). The psychology of prejudice: Ingroup love or outgroup hate? *Journal of Social Issues, 55*(3), 429–444. doi: 10.1111/0022-4537.00126

Broadbent, D. E. (1958). *Perception and communication.* London: Pergamon Press.

Broberg, D. J., & Bernstein, I. L. (1987). Candy as a scapegoat in the prevention of food aversions in children receiving chemotherapy. *Cancer, 60,* 2344–2347.

Brooks, D. (2012, May 3). The campus tsunami. *New York Times.* Retreived from http://www.nytimes.com/2012/05/04/opinion/brooks-the-campus-tsunami.html

Brooks, R., & Meltzoff, A. N. (2002). The importance of eyes: How infants interpret adult looking behavior. *Developmental Psychology, 38,* 958–966.

Brooks-Gunn, J., Graber, J. A., & Paikoff, R. L. (1994). Studying links between hormones and negative affect: Models and measures. *Journal of Research on Adolescence, 4,* 469–486.

Brown, A. S. (2004). *The déjà vu experience.* New York: Psychology Press.

Brown, B. B., Mory, M., & Kinney, D. (1994). Casting crowds in a relational perspective: Caricature, channel, and context. In G. A. R. Montemayor & T. Gullotta (Eds.), *Advances in adolescent development: Personal relationships during adolescence* (Vol. 5, pp. 123–167). Newbury Park, CA: Sage.

Brown, J. D., & McGill, K. L. (1989). The cost of good fortune: When positive life events produce negative health consequences. *Journal of Personality and Social Psychology, 57,* 1103–1110.

Brown, R., & Hanlon, C. (1970). Derivational complexity and order of acquisition in child speech. In J. R. Hayes (Ed.), *Cognition and the development of language* (pp. 11–53). New York: Wiley.

Brown, R., & Kulik, J. (1977). Flashbulb memories. *Cognition, 5,* 73–99.

Brown, R., & McNeill, D. (1966). The "tip-of-the-tongue" phenomenon. *Journal of Verbal Learning and Verbal Behavior, 5,* 325–337.

Brown, R. P., Osterman, L. L., & Barnes, C. D. (2009). School violence and the culture of honor. *Psychological Science, 20*(11), 1400–1405.

Brown, S. C., & Craik, F. I. M. (2000). Encoding and retrieval of information. In E. Tulving & F. I. M. Craik (Eds.), *The Oxford handbook of memory* (pp. 93–107). New York: Oxford University Press.

Bruner, J. S. (1983). Education as social invention. *Journal of Social Issues, 39,* 129–141.

Brunet, A., Orr, S. P., Tremblay, J., Robertson, K., Nader, K., & Pitman, R. K. (2008). Effects of post-retrieval propranolol on psychophysiologic responding during subsequent script-driven traumatic imagery in posttraumatic stress disorder. *Journal of Psychiatric Research, 42,* 503–506.

Brunet, A., Poundjia, J., Tremblay, J., Bui, E., Thomas, E., Orr, S. P., . . . Pitman, R. K. (2011). Trauma reactivation under the influence of propranolol decreases posttraumatic stress symptoms and disorder. *Journal of Clinical Psychopharmacology, 31,* 547–550.

Brunner, D. P., Dijk, D. J., Tobler, I., & Borbely, A. A. (1990). Effect of partial sleep deprivation on sleep stages and EEG power spectra. *Electroencephalography and Clinical Neurophysiology, 75,* 492–499.

Bryck, R. L., & Fisher, P. A. (2012). Training the brain: Practical applications of neural plasticity from the intersection of cognitive neuroscience, developmental psychology, and prevention science. *American Psychologist, 67,* 87–100.

Buchanan, C. M., Eccles, J. S., & Becker, J. B. (1992). Are adolescents the victims of raging hormones? Evidence for activational effects of hormones on moods and behavior at adolescence. *Psychological Bulletin, 111,* 62–107.

Buchanan, T. W. (2007). Retrieval of emotional memories. *Psychological Bulletin, 133,* 761–779.

Buckholtz, J. W., & Meyer-Lindenberg, A. (2012). Psychopathology and the human connectome: Toward a transdiagnostic model of risk for mental illness. *Neuron, 74,* 990–1003.

Buck Louis, G. M., Gray, L. E., Marcus, M., Ojeda, S. R., Pescovitz, O. H., Witchel, S. F., . . . Euling, S. Y. (2008). Environmental factors and puberty timing: Expert panel research. *Pediatrics, 121*(Suppl. 3), S192–S207. doi:10.1542/peds1813E

Buckley, C. (2007, January 3). Man is rescued by stranger on subway tracks. *New York Times.* http://www.nytimes.com/2007/01/03/nyregion/03life.html

Buckner, R. L., Andrews-Hanna, J. R., & Schacter, D. L. (2008). The brain's default network: Anatomy, function, and relevance to disease. *Annals of the New York Academy of Sciences, 1124,* 1–38.

Buckner, R. L., Petersen, S. E., Ojemann, J. G., Miezin, F. M., Squire, L. R., & Raichle, M. E. (1995). Functional anatomical studies of explicit and implicit memory retrieval tasks. *The Journal of Neuroscience, 15,* 12–29.

Bunce, D. M., Flens, E. A., & Neiles, K. Y. (2011). How long can students pay attention in class? A study of student attention decline using clickers. *Journal of Chemical Education, 87,* 1438–1443.

Bureau of Justice Statistics. (2008). *Prisoners in 2007* (No. NCJ224280 by H. C. West & W. J. Sabol). Washington, DC: U.S. Department of Justice.

Burger, J. M. (1999). The foot-in-the-door compliance procedure: A multiple-process analysis and review. *Personality and Social Psychology Review, 3,* 303–325.

Burger, J. M. (2009). Replicating Milgram: Would people still obey today? *American Psychologist, 64,* 1–11.

Burger, J. M., & Burns, L. (1988). The illusion of unique invulnerability and the use of effective contraception. *Personality and Social Psychology Bulletin, 14,* 264–270.

Burger, J. M., Sanchez, J., Imberi, J. E., & Grande, L. R. (2009). The norm of reciprocity as an internalized social norm: Returning favors even when no one finds out. *Social Influence, 4*(1), 11–17.

Burke, D., MacKay, D. G., Worthley, J. S., & Wade, E. (1991). On the tip of the tongue: What causes word failure in young and older adults? *Journal of Memory and Language, 30,* 237–246.

Burks, S. V., Carpenter, J. P., Goette, L., & Rustichini, A. (2009). Cognitive skills affect economic preferences, strategic behavior, and job attachment. *Proceedings of the National Academy of Sciences, 106*(19), 7745–7750. doi: 10.1073/pnas. 0812360106

Burns, D. J., Hwang, A. J., & Burns, S. A. (2011). Adaptive memory: Determining the proximate mechanisms responsible for the memorial advantages of survival processing. *Journal of Experimental Psychology: Learning, Memory, and Cognition, 37,* 206–218.

Burnstein, E., Crandall, C., & Kitayama, S. (1994). Some neo-Darwinian decision rules for altruism: Weighing cues for inclusive fitness as a function of the biological importance of the decision. *Journal of Personality and Social Psychology, 67,* 773–789.

Bushman, B. J., & Huesmann, L. R. (2010). Aggression. In S. T. Fiske, D. T. Gilbert, & G. Lindzey (Eds.), *The handbook of social psychology* (5th ed., Vol. 2, pp. 833–863). New York: Wiley.

Buss, D. M. (1985). Human mate selection. *American Scientist, 73,* 47–51.

Buss, D. M. (1989). Sex differences in human mate preferences: Evolutionary hypotheses tested in 37 cultures. *Behavioral and Brain Sciences, 12,* 1–49.

Buss, D. M. (2000). *The dangerous passion: Why jealousy is as necessary as love and sex.* New York: Free Press.

Buss, D. M. (2007). The evolution of human mating. *Acta Psychologica Sinica, 39,* 502–512.

Buss, D. M., & Haselton, M. G. (2005). The evolution of jealousy. *Trends in Cognitive Sciences, 9,* 506–507.

Buss, D. M., Haselton, M. G., Shackelford, T. K., Bleske, A. L., & Wakefield, J. C. (1998). Adaptations, exaptations, and spandrels. *American Psychologist, 53,* 533–548.

Buss, D. M., & Schmitt, D. P. (1993). Sexual strategies theory: An evolutionary perspective on human mating. *Psychological Review, 100,* 204–232.

Butler, A. C., Chapman, J. E., Forman, E. M., & Beck, A. T. (2006). The empirical status of cognitive-behavioral therapy: A review of meta-analyses. *Clinical Psychology Review, 26,* 17–31.

Butler, M. A., Corboy, J. R., & Filley, C. M. (2009). How the conflict between American psychiatry and neurology delayed the appreciation of cognitive dysfunction in multiple sclerosis. *Neuropsychology Review, 19,* 399–410.

Byers-Heinlein, K., Burns, T. C., & Werker, J. F. (2010). The roots of bilingualism in newborns. *Psychological Science, 21*(3), 343–348. doi:10.1177/0956797609360758

Byrne, D., Allgeier, A. R., Winslow, L., & Buckman, J. (1975). The situational facilitation of interpersonal attraction: A three-factor hypothesis. *Journal of Applied Social Psychology, 5,* 1–15.

Byrne, D., & Clore, G. L. (1970). A reinforcement model of evaluative responses. *Personality: An International Journal, 1,* 103–128.

Byrne, D., Ervin, C. R., & Lamberth, J. (1970). Continuity between the experimental study of attraction and real-life computer dating. *Journal of Personality and Social Psychology, 16,* 157–165.

Byrne, D., & Nelson, D. (1965). Attraction as a linear function of proportion of positive reinforcements. *Journal of Personality and Social Psychology, 1,* 659–663.

Cabeza, R. (2002). Hemispheric asymmetry reduction in older adults: The HAROLD model. *Psychology and Aging, 17,* 85–100.

Cabeza, R., Grady, C. L., Nyberg, L., McIntosh, A. R., Tulving, E., Kapur, S., . . . Craik, F. I. M. (1997). Age-related differences in neural activity during memory encoding and retrieval: A positron emission tomography study. *The Journal of Neuroscience, 17,* 391–400.

Cabeza, R., Rao, S., Wagner, A. D., Mayer, A., & Schacter, D. L. (2001). Can medial temporal lobe regions distinguish true from false? An event-related fMRI study of veridical and illusory recognition memory. *Proceedings of the National Academy of Sciences, USA, 98,* 4805–4810.

Cacioppo, J. T., & Patrick, B. (2008). *Loneliness: Human nature and the need for social connection.* New York: Norton.

Cahill, L., Haier, R. J., Fallon, J., Alkire, M. T., Tang, C., Keator, D., . . . McGaugh, J. L. (1996). Amygdala activity at encoding correlated with long-term, free recall of emotional information. *Proceedings of the National Academy of Sciences, USA, 93,* 8016–8021.

Cahill, L., & McGaugh, J. L. (1998). Mechanisms of emotional arousal and lasting declarative memory. *Trends in Neurosciences, 21,* 294–299.

Calder, A. J., Young, A. W., Rowland, D., Perrett, D. I., Hodges, J. R., & Etcoff, N. L. (1996). Facial emotion recognition after bilateral amygdala damage: Differentially severe impairment of fear. *Cognitive Neuropsychology, 13,* 699–745.

Calkins, M. W. (Ed.). (1930). *Mary Whiton Calkins* (Vol. 1). Worcester, MA: Clark University Press.

Callaghan, T., Rochat, P., Lillard, A., Claux, M. L., Odden, H., Itakura, S., . . . Singh, S. (2005). Synchrony in the onset of mental-state reasoning: Evidence from five cultures. *Psychological Science, 16,* 378–384.

Calvin, C. M., Deary, I. J., Fenton, C., Roberts, B. A., Der, G., Leckenby, N., & Batty, G. D. (2010). Intelligence in youth and all-cause-mortality: Systematic review with meta-analysis. *International Journal of Epidemiology, 40*(3), 626–644. doi:10.1093/ije/dyq190

Calvin, C. M., Deary, I. J., Fenton, C., Roberts, B. A., Der, G., Leckenby, N., & Batty, G. D. (2011). Intelligence in youth and all-cause-mortality: Systematic review with meta-analysis. *International Journal of Epidemiology, 40*(3), 626–644.

Calzo, J. P., Antonucci, T. C., Mays, V. M., & Cochran, S. D. (2011). Retrospective recall of sexual orientation identity development among gay, lesbian, and bisexual adults. *Developmental Psychology, 47*(6), 1658–1673. doi:10.1037/a0025508

Cameron, C. D., & Payne, B. K. (2011). Escaping affect: How motivated emotion regulation creates insensitivity to mass suffering. *Journal of Personality and Social Psychology, 100*(1), 1–15.

Campbell, A. (1999). Staying alive: Evolution, culture, and women's intra-sexual aggression. *Behavioral & Brain Sciences, 22,* 203–252.

Cannon, W. B. (1929). *Bodily changes in pain, hunger, fear, and rage: An account of recent research into the function of emotional excitement* (2nd ed.). New York: Appleton-Century-Crofts.

Cantor, N. (1990). From thought to behavior: "Having" and "doing" in the study of personality and cognition. *American Psychologist, 45,* 735–750.

Caparelli, E. C. (2007). TMS & fMRI: A new neuroimaging combinational tool to study brain function. *Current Medical Imaging Review, 3,* 109–115.

Caprioli, M. (2003). Gender equality and state aggression: The impact of domestic gender equality on state first use of force. *International Interactions, 29*(3), 195–214. doi:10.1080/03050620304595

Carey, N. (2012). *The epigenetics revolution: How modern biology is rewriting our understanding of genetics, disease, and inheritance*. New York: Columbia University Press.

Carlson, C., & Hoyle, R. (1993). Efficacy of abbreviated progressive muscle relaxation training: A quantitative review of behavioral medicine research. *Journal of Consulting and Clinical Psychology, 61*, 1059–1067.

Carmena, J. M., Lebedev, M. A., Crist, R. E., O'Doherty, J. E., Santucci, D. M., Dimitrov, D. F., . . . Nicolelis, M. A. (2003). Learning to control a brain-machine interface for reaching and grasping by primates. *Public Library of Science Biology, 1*, 193–208.

Carmichael Olson, H., Streissguth, A. P., Sampson, P. D., Barr, H. M., Bookstein, F. L., & Thiede, K. (1997). Association of prenatal alcohol exposure with behavioral and learning problems in early adolescence. *Journal of the American Academy of Child & Adolescent Psychiatry, 36*(9), 1187–1194.

Carney, D. R., Cuddy, A. J. C., & Yap, A. J. (2010). Power posing: Brief nonverbal displays affect neuroendocrine levels and risk tolerance. *Psychological Science, 21*(10), 1363–1368. doi: 10.1177/0956797610383437

Carolson, E. A. (1998). A prospective longitudinal study of attachment disorganization/disorientation. *Child Development, 69*, 1107–1128.

Caron, M.-J., Mottron, L., Berthiaume, C., & Dawson, M. (2006). Cognitive mechanisms, specificity and neural underpinnings of visuospatial peaks in autism. *Brain, 129*, 1789–1802.

Carpenter, S. K. (2012). Testing enhances the transfer of learning. *Current Directions in Psychological Science, 21*, 279–283.

Carr, L., Iacoboni, M., Dubeau, M., Mazziotta, J. C., & Lenzi, G. L. (2003). Neural mechanisms of empathy in humans: A relay from neural systems for imitation to limbic areas. *Proceedings of the National Academy of Sciences, USA, 100*, 5497–5502.

Carroll, J. B. (1993). *Human cognitive abilities*. Cambridge, England: Cambridge University Press.

Carson, R. C., Butcher, J. N., & Mineka, S. (2000). *Abnormal psychology and modern life* (11th ed.). Boston: Allyn & Bacon.

Carstensen, L. L. (1992). Social and emotional patterns in adulthood: Support for socioemotional selectivity theory. *Psychology and Aging, 7*, 331–338.

Carstensen, L. L., & Fredrickson, B. L. (1998). Influence of HIV status and age on cognitive representations of others. *Health Psychology, 17*, 1–10.

Carstensen, L. L., Pasupathi, M., Mayr, U., & Nesselroade, J. R. (2000). Emotional experience in everyday life across the adult life span. *Journal of Personality and Social Psychology, 79*, 644–655.

Carstensen, L. L., & Turk-Charles, S. (1994). The salience of emotion across the adult life span. *Psychology and Aging, 9*, 259–264.

Carver, C. S. (2006). Approach, avoidance, and the self-regulation of affect and action. *Motivation and Emotion, 30*, 105–110.

Carver, C. S., & White, T. L. (1994). Behavioral inhibition, behavioral activation, and affective responses to impending reward and punishment: The BIS/BAS scales. *Journal of Personality and Social Psychology, 67*(2), 319–333.

Casazza, K., Fontaine, K. R., Astrup, A., Birch, L. L., Brown, A. W., Bohan Brown, M. M., . . . Allison, D. B. (2013). Myths, presumptions, and facts about obesity. *New England Journal of Medicine, 368*(5), 446–454.

Case, A., & Deaton, A. (2015). Rising morbidity and mortality in midlife among white non-Hispanic Americans in the 21st century. *Proceedings of the National Academy of Sciences, 112*, 15078–15083.

Caspi, A., & Herbener, E. S. (1990). Continuity and change: Assortative marriage and the consistency of personality in adulthood. *Journal of Personality and Social Psychology, 58*, 250–258.

Caspi, A., Roberts, B. W., & Shiner, R. L. (2005). Personality development: Stability and change. *Annual Review of Psychology, 56*, 453–484.

Caspi, A., Sugden, K., Moffitt, T. E., Taylor, A., Craig, I. W., Harrington, H., . . . Poulton, R. (2003). Influence of life stress on depression: Moderation by a polymorphism in the 5-HTT gene. *Science, 301*, 386–389.

Castel, A. D., McCabe, D. P., & Roediger, H. L. III. (2007). Illusions of competence and overestimation of associate memory for identical items: Evidence from judgments of learning. *Psychonomic Bulletin & Review, 14*, 107–111.

Castellani, R. J., Perry, G., & Iverson, G. L. (2015). Chronic effects of mild neurotrauma: Putting the cart before the horse? *Journal of Neuropathology & Experimental Neurology, 74*, 493–499.

Castellanos, F. X., Patti, P. L., Sharp, W., Jeffries, N. O., Greenstein, D. K., Clasen, L. S., . . . Rapoport, J. L. (2002). Developmental trajectories of brain volume abnormalities in children and adolescents with attention-deficit/hyperactivity disorder. *Journal of the American Medical Association, 288*, 1740–1748. doi: 10.1001/jama.288.14.1740

Cattell, R. B. (1950). *Personality: A systematic, theoretical, and factual study*. New York: McGraw-Hill.

Ceci, S. J. (1991). How much does schooling influence general intelligence and its cognitive components? A reassessment of the evidence. *Developmental Psychology, 27*, 703–722.

Ceci, S. J., DeSimone, M., & Johnson, S. (1992). Memory in context: A case study of "Bubbles P.," a gifted but uneven memorizer. In D. J. Herrmann, H. Weingartner, A. Searleman, & C. McEvoy (Eds.), *Memory improvement: Implications for memory theory* (pp. 169–186). New York: Springer-Verlag.

Ceci, S. J., Ginther, D. K., Kahn, S., & Williams, W. M. (2014). Women in academic science: A changing landscape. *Psychological Science in the Public Interest, 15*(3), 75–141. doi: 10.1177/1529100614541236

Ceci, S. J., & Williams, W. M. (1997). Schooling, intelligence, and income. *American Psychologist, 52*, 1051–1058.

Ceci, S. J., Williams, W. M., & Barnett, S. M. (2009). Women's underrepresentation in science: Sociocultural and biological considerations. *Psychological Bulletin, 135*(2), 218–261. doi:10.1037/a0014412

Centers for Disease Control and Prevention (CDC). (2002, June 28). Youth risk behavior surveillance. *Surveillance Summary, 51*(SS-4), 1–64. Washington, DC: Author.

Centers for Disease Control and Prevention. (2013). *Injury prevention and control: Data and statistics (WISQARS)*. Retrieved from http://www.cdc.gov/injury/wisqars/index.html

Centers for Disease Control and Prevention. (2015). Current cigarette smoking among adults—United States, 2005–2014. *Morbidity and Mortality Weekly Report, 64*, 1233–1240.

Centola, D., & Baronchelli, A. (2015). The spontaneous emergence of conventions: An experimental study of cultural evolution. *Proceedings of the National Academy of Sciences, 112*(7), 1989–1994. doi: 10.1073/pnas.1418838112

Cepeda, N. J., Pashler, H., Vul, E., Wixted, J. T., & Rohrer, D. (2006). Distributed practice in verbal recall tests: A review and quantitative synthesis. *Psychological Bulletin, 132*, 354–380.

Chabris, C., & Simons, D. (2012, November 16). Using just 10% of your brains? Think again. *Wall Street Journal Online*. Retrieved from http://online.wsj.com/article/SB100014241278873245563045781193518742 1218.html

Chaiken, S. (1980). Heuristic versus systematic information processing and the use of source versus message cues in persuasion. *Journal of Personality and Social Psychology, 39*, 752–766.

Chalmers, D. (1996). *The conscious mind: In search of a fundamental theory.* New York: Oxford University Press.

Chandler, J., & Schwarz, N. (2009). How extending your middle finger affects your perception of others: Learned movements influence concept accessibility. *Journal of Experimental Social Psychology, 45,* 123–128.

Chaplin, T. M., & Aldao, A. (2013). Gender differences in emotion expression in children: A meta-analytic review. *Psychological Bulletin, 139,* 735–765.

Charles, S. T., Reynolds, C. A., & Gatz, M. (2001). Age-related differences and change in positive and negative affect over 23 years. *Journal of Personality and Social Psychology, 80,* 136–151.

Charness, N. (1981). Aging and skilled problem solving. *Journal of Experimental Psychology: General, 110,* 21–38.

Charpak, G., & Broch, H. (2004). *Debunked! ESP, telekinesis, and other pseudoscience* (B. K. Holland, Trans.). Baltimore: Johns Hopkins University Press.

Chartrand, T. L., & Bargh, J. A. (1999). The chameleon effect: The perception-behavior link and social interaction. *Journal of Personality and Social Psychology, 76,* 893–910.

Chartrand, T. L., & Kay, A. (2006). *Mystery moods and perplexing performance: Consequences of succeeding and failing at a nonconscious goal.* Unpublished manuscript.

Chen, E., Cohen, S., & Miller, G. E. (2010). How low socioeconomic status affects 2-year hormonal trajectories in children. *Psychological Science, 21*(1), 31–37.

Cheney, D. L., & Seyfarth, R. M. (1990). *How monkeys see the world.* Chicago: University of Chicago Press.

Cheng, D. T., Disterhoft, J. F., Power, J. M., Ellis, D. A., & Desmond, J. E. (2008). Neural substrates underlying human delay and trace eyeblink conditioning. *Proceedings of the National Academy of Sciences, USA, 105,* 8108–8113.

Cherlin, A. J. (Ed.). (1992). *Marriage, divorce, remarriage* (2nd ed.). Cambridge, MA: Harvard University Press.

Chetty, R., Stepner, M., Abraham, S., Lin, S., Scuderi, B., Turner, N., . . . Cutler, D. (2016). The association between income and life expectancy in the United States, 2001–2014. *Journal of the American Medical Association, 315*(16), 1750–1766.

Chivers, M. L., Rieger, G., Latty, E., & Bailey, J. M. (2004). A sex difference in the specificity of sexual arousal. *Psychological Science, 15,* 736–744.

Chivers, M. L., Seto, M. C., & Blanchard, R. (2007). Gender and sexual orientation differences in sexual response to sexual activities versus gender of actors in sexual films. *Journal of Personality and Social Psychology, 93,* 1108–1121.

Chomsky, N. (1957). *Syntactic structures.* The Hague: Mouton.

Chomsky, N. (1959). A review of *Verbal Behavior* by B. F. Skinner. *Language, 35,* 26–58.

Chomsky, N. (1986). *Knowledge of language: Its nature, origin, and use.* New York: Praeger.

Choy, Y., Fyer, A. J., & Lipsitz, J. D. (2007). Treatment of specific phobia in adults. *Clinical Psychology Review, 27,* 266–286.

Christakis, N. A., & Fowler, J. H. (2007). The spread of obesity in a large social network over 32 years. *New England Journal of Medicine, 357*(4), 370–379.

Chui, H., Hoppmann, C. A., Gerstorf, D., Walker, R., & Luszcz, M. A. (2014). Social partners and momentary affect in the oldest-old: The presence of others benefits affect depending on who we are and who we are with. *Developmental Psychology, 50*(3), 728–740. doi: 10.1037/a0033896

Cialdini, R. B. (2005). Don't throw in the towel: Use social influence research. *American Psychological Society, 18,* 33–34.

Cialdini, R. B. (2013). The focus theory of normative conduct. In P. A. M. van Lange, A. W. Kruglanski, & E. T. Higgins (Eds.), *Handbook of theories of social psychology* (Vol. 3, pp. 295–312). New York: Sage.

Cialdini, R. B., & Goldstein, N. J. (2004). Social influence: Compliance and conformity. *Annual Review of Psychology, 55*(1), 591–621. doi: 10.1146/annurev.psych.55.090902.142015

Cialdini, R. B., Trost, M. R., & Newsom, J. T. (1995). Preference for consistency: The development of a valid measure and the discovery of surprising behavioral implications. *Journal of Personality and Social Psychology, 69,* 318–328.

Ciarrochi, J. V., Chan, A. Y., & Caputi, P. (2000). A critical evaluation of the emotional intelligence concept. *Personality & Individual Differences, 28,* 539.

Ciarrochi, J., Heaven, P. C. L., & Skinner, T. (2012). Cognitive ability and health-related behaviors during adolescence: A prospective study across five years. *Intelligence, 40*(4), 317–324. doi: 10.1016/j.intell.2012.03.003

Cicchetti, D., & Toth, S. L. (1998). Perspectives on research and practice in developmental psychopathology. In I. E. Sigel & K. A. Renninger (Eds.), *Handbook of child psychology: Vol. 4. Child psychology in practice* (5th ed., pp. 479–583). New York: Wiley.

Clark, I. A., & Maguire, E. A. (2016). Remembering preservation in hippocampal amnesia. *Annual Review of Psychology, 67,* 51–82.

Clark, M. S., & Lemay, E. P. (2010). Close relationships. In S. T. Fiske, D. T. Gilbert, & G. Lindzey (Eds.), *The handbook of social psychology* (5th ed., Vol. 2). New York: Wiley.

Clark, R. D., & Hatfield, E. (1989). Gender differences in receptivity to sexual offers. *Journal of Psychology and Human Sexuality, 2,* 39–55.

Clark-Polner, E., Johnson, T., & Barrett, L. F. (2016). Multivoxel pattern analysis does not provide evidence to support the existence of basic emotions. *Cerebral Cortex.* First published online February 29, 2016. doi: 10.1093/cercor/bhw028

Cleckley, H. M. (1976). *The mask of sanity* (5th ed.). St. Louis: Mosby.

Coates, T. (2015). *Between the world and me.* New York: Spiegel & Grau.

Coe, C. L., & Lubach, G. R. (2008). Fetal programming prenatal origins of health and illness. *Current Directions in Psychological Science, 17,* 36–41.

Cogan, R., Cogan, D., Waltz, W., & McCue, M. (1987). Effects of laughter and relaxation on discomfort thresholds. *Journal of Behavioral Medicine, 10,* 139–144.

Coghill, R. C., McHaffie, J. G., & Yen, Y. (2003). Neural correlates of individual differences in the subjective experience of pain. *Proceedings of the National Academy of Sciences, USA, 100,* 8538–8542.

Cohen, A. O., Breiner, K., Steinberg, L., Bonnie, R. J., Scott, E. S., Taylor-Thompson, K. A., . . . Casey, B. J. (2016). When is an adolescent an adult? Assessing cognitive control in emotional and nonemotional contexts. *Psychological Science, 27*(4), 549–562.

Cohen, D., Nisbett, R. E., Bowdle, B. F., & Schwarz, N. (1996). Insult, aggression, and the southern culture of honor: An "experimental ethnography." *Journal of Personality and Social Psychology, 70,* 945–960.

Cohen, G. (1990). Why is it difficult to put names to faces? *British Journal of Psychology, 81,* 287–297.

Cohen, S. (1988). Psychosocial models of the role of social support in the etiology of physical disease. *Health Psychology, 7,* 269–297.

Cohen, S. (1999). Social status and susceptibility to respiratory infections. *New York Academy of Sciences, 896,* 246–253.

Cohen, S., Frank, E., Doyle, W. J., Skoner, D. P., Rabin, B. S., & Gwaltney, J. M., Jr. (1998). Types of stressors that increase susceptibility to the common cold in healthy adults. *Health Psychology, 17,* 214–223.

Cohen-Kettenis, P. T., & Pfäfflin, F. (2003). *Transgenderism and intersexuality in childhood and adolescence: Making choices.* Thousand Oaks, CA: Sage.

Coifman, K. G., Bonanno, G. A., Ray, R. D., & Gross, J. J. (2007). Does repressive coping promote resilience? Affective-autonomic response discrepancy during bereavement. *Journal of Personality and Social Psychology, 92,* 745–758.

Coker, T. R., Austin, S. B., & Schuster, M. A. (2010). The health and health care of lesbian, gay, and bisexual adolescents. *Annual Review of Public Health, 31,* 457–477. doi: 10.1146/ annurev.publhealth.012809.103636

Colcombe, S. J., Erickson, K. I., Scalf, P. E., Kim, J. S., Prakesh, R., McAuley, E., . . . Kramer, A. F. (2006). Aerobic exercise training increases brain volume in aging humans. *Journals of Gerontology Series A: Biological Sciences and Medical Sciences, 61,* 1166–1170.

Colcombe, S. J., Kramer, A. F., Erickson, K. I., Scalf, P., McAuley, E., Cohen, N. J., . . . Elavsky, S. (2004). Cardiovascular fitness, cortical plasticity, and aging. *Proceedings of the National Academy of Sciences, USA, 101,* 3316–3321.

Cole, M. (1996). *Cultural psychology: A once and future discipline.* Cambridge, MA: Belknap Press of Harvard University Press.

Coman, A., Manier, D., & Hirst, W. (2009). Forgetting the unforgettable through conversation: Social shared retrieval-induced forgetting of September 11 memories. *Psychological Science, 20,* 627–633.

Condon, J. W., & Crano, W. D. (1988). Inferred evaluation and the relation between attitude similarity and interpersonal attraction. *Journal of Personality and Social Psychology, 54,* 789–797.

Conklin, Q., King, B., Zanesco, A., Pokorny, J., Hamidi, A., Lin, J., . . . Saron, C. (2015). Telomere lengthening after three weeks of an intensive insight meditation retreat. *Psychoneuroendocrinology, 61,* 26–27.

Conley, T. D. (2011). Perceived proposer personality characteristics and gender differences in acceptance of casual sex offers. *Journal of Personality and Social Psychology, 100*(2), 309–329. doi: 10.1037/a0022152

Conley, T. D., Moors, A. C., Matsick, J. L., Ziegler, A., & Valentine, B. A. (2011). Women, men, and the bedroom: Methodological and conceptual insights that narrow, reframe, and eliminate gender differences in sexuality. *Current Directions in Psychological Science, 20*(5), 296–300. doi: 10.1177/0963721411418467

Cook, M., & Mineka, S. (1989). Observational conditioning of fear to fear-relevant versus fear-irrelevant stimuli in rhesus monkeys. *Journal of Abnormal Psychology, 98*(4), 448–459.

Coontz, P. (2008). The responsible conduct of social research. In K. Yang & G. J. Miller (Eds.), *Handbook of research methods in public administration* (pp. 129–139). Boca Raton, FL: Taylor & Francis.

Cooper, J., & Fazio, R. H. (1984). A new look at dissonance theory. In L. Berkowitz (Ed.), *Advances in experimental social psychology* (Vol. 17, pp. 229–266). New York: Academic Press.

Cooper, J. R., Bloom, F. E., & Roth, R. H. (2003). *Biochemical basis of neuropharmacology.* New York: Oxford University Press.

Cooper, M. L. (2006). Does drinking promote risky sexual behavior? A complex answer to a simple question. *Current Directions in Psychological Science, 15,* 19–23.

Cooper, W. H., & Withey, W. J. (2009). The strong situation hypothesis. *Personality and Social Psychology Review, 13,* 62–72.

Coren, S. (1997). *Sleep thieves.* New York: Free Press.

Corkin, S. (2002). What's new with the amnesic patient HM? *Nature Reviews Neuroscience, 3,* 153–160.

Corkin, S. (2013). *Permanent present tense: The unforgettable life of the amnesic patient, H.M.* New York: Basic Books.

Correll, J., Park, B., Judd, C. M., & Wittenbrink, B. (2002). The police officer's dilemma: Using ethnicity to disambiguate potentially threatening individuals. *Journal of Personality and Social Psychology, 83,* 1314–1329.

Correll, J., Park, B., Judd, C. M., Wittenbrink, B., Sadler, M. S., & Keesee, T. (2007). Across the thin blue line: Police officers and racial bias in the decision to shoot. *Journal of Personality and Social Psychology, 92,* 1006–1023.

Correll, J., Wittenbrink, B., Crawford, M. T., & Sadler, M. S. (2015). Stereotypic vision: How stereotypes disambiguate visual stimuli. *Journal of Personality and Social Psychology, 108*(2), 219–233. doi: 10.1037/ pspa0000015

Corti, E. (1931). *A history of smoking* (P. England, Trans.). London: Harrap.

Coryell, W., Endicott, J., Maser, J. D., Mueller, T., Lavori, P., & Keller, M. (1995). The likelihood of recurrence in bipolar affective disorder: The importance of episode recency. *Journal of Affective Disorders, 33,* 201–206.

Costa, P. T., Terracciano, A., & McCrae, R. R. (2001). Gender differences in personality traits across cultures: Robust and surprising findings. *Journal of Personality and Social Psychology, 81,* 322–331.

Costanza, A., Weber, K., Gandy, S., Bouras, C., Hof, P. R., Giannakopoulos, G., & Canuto, A. (2011). Contact sport-related chronic traumatic encephalopathy in the elderly: Clinical expression and structural substrates. *Neuropathology and Applied Neurobiology, 37,* 570–584.

Cottrell, C. A., Neuberg, S. L., & Li, N. P. (2007). What do people desire in others? A sociofunctional perspective on the importance of different valued characteristics. *Journal of Personality and Social Psychology, 92,* 208–231.

Cox, B. M., Shah, M. M., Cichon, T., Tancer, M. E., Galloway, M. P., Thomas, D. M., & Perrine, S. A. (2014). Behavioral and neurochemical effects of repeated MDMA administration during late adolescence in the rat. *Progress in Neuropsychopharmacology & Biological Psychiatry, 48,* 229–235.

Coyne, J. A. (2000, April 3). Of vice and men: Review of R. Tornhill and C. Palmer, *A natural history of rape. The New Republic,* pp. 27–34.

Craik, F. I. M., Govoni, R., Naveh-Benjamin, M., & Anderson, N. D. (1996). The effects of divided attention on encoding and retrieval processes in human memory. *Journal of Experimental Psychology: General, 125,* 159–180.

Craik, F. I. M., & Tulving, E. (1975). Depth of processing and the retention of words in episodic memory. *Journal of Experimental Psychology: General, 104,* 268–294.

Cramer, R. E., Schaefer, J. T., & Reid, S. (1996). Identifying the ideal mate: More evidence for male–female convergence. *Current Psychology, 15,* 157–166.

Crane, C. A., Godleski, S. A., Przybyla, S. M., Schlauch, R. C., & Testa, M. (2015). The proximal effects of acute alcohol consumption on male-to-female aggression: A meta-analytic review of the experimental literature. *Trauma, Violence, & Abuse.* doi: 10.1177/1524838015584374

Craske, M. G. (1999). *Anxiety disorders: Psychological approaches to theory and treatment.* Boulder, CO: Westview Press.

Crick, N. R., & Grotpeter, J. K. (1995). Relational aggression, gender, and social-psychological adjustment. *Child Development, 66,* 710–722.

Crocker, J., & Wolfe, C. T. (2001). Contingencies of self-worth. *Psychological Review, 108*(3), 593–623.

Crombag, H. F. M., Wagenaar, W. A., & Van Koppen, P. J. (1996). Crashing memories and the problem of "source monitoring." *Applied Cognitive Psychology, 10,* 95–104.

Cross, E. S., Kraemer, D. J. M., Hamilton, A. F. de C., Kelley, W. M., & Grafton, S. T. (2009). Sensitivity of the action observation network to physical and observational learning. *Cerebral Cortex, 19,* 315–326.

Cross, P. (1977). Not can but will college teachers be improved? *New Directions for Higher Education, 17,* 1–15.

Cross-Disorder Group of the Psychiatric Genomics Consortium. (2013). Identification of risk loci with shared effects on five major psychiatric disorders: A genome-wide analysis. *Lancet, 381,* 1371–1379.

Csigó, K., Harsányi, A., Demeter, G., Rajkai, C., Németh, A., & Racsmány, M. (2010). Long-term follow-up of patients with obsessive-compulsive disorder treated by anterior capsulotomy: A neuropsychological study. *Journal of Affective Disorders, 126,* 198–205.

Csikszentmihalyi, M. (1990). *Flow: The psychology of optimal experience.* New York: Harper & Row.

Cuc, A., Koppel, J., & Hirst, W. (2007). Silence is not golden: A case of socially shared retrieval-induced forgetting. *Psychological Science, 18,* 727–733.

Cunningham, M. R., Roberts, A. R., Barbee, A. P., Druen, P. B., & Wu, C.-H. (1995). "Their ideas of beauty are, on the whole, the same as ours": Consistency and variability in the cross-cultural perception of female physical attractiveness. *Journal of Personality and Social Psychology, 68,* 261–279.

Cunningham, W. A., & Brosch, T. (2012). Motivational salience: Amygdala tuning from traits, needs, values, and goals. *Current Directions in Psychological Science, 21*(1), 54–59.

Curran, J. P., & Lippold, S. (1975). The effects of physical attraction and attitude similarity on attraction in dating dyads. *Journal of Personality, 43,* 528–539.

Curtiss, S. (1977). *Genie: A psycholinguistic study of a modern-day "wildchild."* New York: Academic Press.

Dabbs, J. M., Carr, T. S., Frady, R. L., & Riad, J. K. (1995). Testosterone, crime, and misbehavior among 692 male prison inmates. *Personality and Individual Differences, 18,* 627–633.

Dahger, A., & Robbins, T. W. (2009). Personality, addiction, dopamine: Insights from Parkinson's disease. *Neuron, 61,* 502–510.

Dahl, G., & Della Vigna, S. (2009). Does movie violence increase violent crime? *The Quarterly Journal of Economics, 124,* 677–734.

Dally, P. (1999). *The marriage of heaven and hell: Manic depression and the life of Virginia Woolf.* New York: St. Martin's Griffin.

Dalton, P. (2003). Olfaction. In H. Pashler & S. Yantis (Eds.), *Stevens' handbook of experimental psychology: Vol. 1. Sensation and perception* (3rd ed., pp. 691–746). New York: Wiley.

Daly, M., & Wilson, M. (1988). Evolutionary social psychology and family homicide. *Science, 242,* 519–524.

Damasio, A. R. (1989). Time-locked multiregional retroactivation: A systems-level proposal for the neural substrates of recall and recognition. *Cognition, 33,* 25–62.

Damasio, A. R. (1994). *Descartes' error: Emotion, reason, and the human brain.* New York: Putnam.

Damasio, A. R. (2005). *Descartes' error: Emotion, reason, and the human Brain.* New York: Penguin.

Damasio, A. R., Grabowski, T. J., Bechara, A., Damasio, H., Ponto, L. L. B., Parvisi, J., & Hichwa, R. D. (2000). Subcortical and cortical brain activity during the feeling of self-generated emotions. *Nature Neuroscience, 3,* 1049–1056.

Damasio, H., Grabowski, T. J., Tranel, D., Hichwa, R. D., & Damasio, A. R. (1996). A neural basis for lexical retrieval. *Nature, 380,* 499–505.

Daneshvar, D. H., Nowinski, C. J., McKee, A. C., & Cantu, R. C. (2011). The epidemiology of sport-related concussion. *Clinical Sports Medicine, 30,* 1–17.

Daniel, H. J., O'Brien, K. F., McCabe, R. B., & Quinter, V. E. (1985). Values in mate selection: A 1984 campus survey. *College Student Journal, 19,* 44–50.

Danner, U. N., Ouwehand, C., van Haastert, N. L., Homsveld, H., & de Ridder, D. T. (2012). Decision-making impairments in women with binge eating disorder in comparison with obese and normal weight women. *European Eating Disorders Review, 20,* e56–e62.

Darley, J. M., & Berscheid, E. (1967). Increased liking caused by the anticipation of interpersonal contact. *Human Relations, 10,* 29–40.

Darley, J. M., & Gross, P. H. (1983). A hypothesis-confirming bias in labeling effects. *Journal of Personality and Social Psychology, 44,* 20–33.

Darley, J. M., & Latané, B. (1968). Bystander intervention in emergencies: Diffusion of responsibility. *Journal of Personality and Social Psychology, 8,* 377–383.

Darwin, C. (1998). *The expression of the emotions in man and animals* (P. Ekman, Ed.). New York: Oxford University Press. (Original work published 1872)

Darwin, C. J., Turvey, M. T., & Crowder, R. G. (1972). An auditory analogue of the Sperling partial report procedure: Evidence for brief auditory storage. *Cognitive Psychology, 3,* 255–267.

Dauer, W., & Przedborski, S. (2003). Parkinson's disease: Mechanisms and models. *Neuron, 39,* 889–909.

Daum, I., Schugens, M. M., Ackermann, H., Lutzenberger, W., Dichgans, J., & Birbaumer, N. (1993). Classical conditioning after cerebellar lesions in humans. *Behavioral Neuroscience, 107,* 748–756.

Davidson, R. J., Ekman, P., Saron, C., Senulis, J., & Friesen, W. V. (1990). Emotional expression and brain physiology I: Approach/withdrawal and cerebral asymmetry. *Journal of Personality and Social Psychology, 58,* 330–341.

Davidson, R. J., Putnam, K. M., & Larson, C. L. (2000). Dysfunction in the neural circuitry of emotion regulation—a possible prelude to violence. *Science, 289,* 591–594.

Davies, G. (1988). Faces and places: Laboratory research on context and face recognition. In G. M. Davies & D. M. Thomson (Eds.), *Memory in context: Context in memory* (pp. 35–53). New York: Wiley.

Davis, C. (2008, March 30). Simon Cowell admits to using Botox. *People Magazine.* Retrieved from http://www.people.com/people/article/0,20181478,00.html

Davis, J. L., Senghas, A., Brandt, F., & Ochsner, K. N. (2010). The effects of BOTOX injections on emotional experience. *Emotion, 10*(3), 433–440. doi: 10.1037/a0018690

Dawson, G. (2016). Why it's important to continue universal autism screening while research fully examines its impact. *JAMA Pediatrics, 170,* 527–528.

Dawson, G., Rogers, S., Munson, J., Smith, M., Winter, J., Greenson, J., . . . Varley, J. (2010). Randomized, controlled trial of an intervention for toddlers with autism: The Early Start Denver Model. *Pediatrics, 125,* e17–e23.

Dawson, M., Soulieres, I., Gernsbacher, M. A., & Mottron, L. (2007). The level and nature of autistic intelligence. *Psychological Science, 18,* 657–662.

Day, J. J., & Sweatt, J. D. (2011). Epigenetic mechanisms in cognition. *Neuron, 70,* 813–829.

Dayan, P., & Huys, Q. J. M. (2009). Serotonin in affective control. *Annual Review of Neuroscience, 32,* 95–126.

de Araujo, I. E., Rolls, E. T., Velazco, M. I., Margot, C., & Cayeux, I. (2005). Cognitive modulation of olfactory processing. *Neuron, 46,* 671–679.

Deary, I. J. (2000). *Looking down on human intelligence: From psychometrics to the brain.* New York: Oxford University Press.

Deary, I. J., Batty, G. D., & Gale, C. R. (2008). Bright children become enlightened adults. *Psychological Science, 19*(1), 1–6.

Deary, I. J., Batty, G. D., Pattie, A., & Gale, C. R. (2008). More intelligent, more dependable children live longer: A 55-year longitudinal study of a representative sample of the Scottish nation. *Psychological Science, 19,* 874.

Deary, I. J., Der, G., & Ford, G. (2001). Reaction time and intelligence differences: A population based cohort study. *Intelligence, 29*(5), 389–399.

Deary, I. J., Taylor, M. D., Hart, C. L., Wilson, V., Smith, G. D., Blane, D., & Starr, J. M. (2005). Intergenerational social mobility and mid-life status attainment: Influences of childhood intelligence, childhood social factors, and education. *Intelligence, 33*(5), 455–472. doi: 10.1016/j.intell.2005.06.003

Deary, I. J., Weiss, A., & Batty, G. D. (2011). Intelligence and personality as predictors of illness and death: How researchers in differential psychology and chronic disease epidemiology are collaborating to understand and address health inequalities. *Psychological Science in the Public Interest, 11*(2), 53–79. doi: 10.1177/1529100610387081

Deary, I. J., Whiteman, M. C., Starr, J. M., Whalley, L. J., & Fox, H. C. (2004). The impact of childhood intelligence on later life: Following up the Scottish mental surveys of 1932 and 1947. *Journal of Personality and Social Psychology, 86,* 130–147.

De Bolle, M., De Fryut, F., McCrae, R. R., Löckenhoff, C. E., Costa, P. T. Jr., Aguilar-Valfae, M. E., . . . Terrecciano, A. (2015). The emergence of sex differences in personality traits in early adolescence: A cross-sectional, cross-cultural study. *Journal of Personality and Social Psychology, 108,* 171–185.

DeCasper, A. J., & Spence, M. J. (1986). Prenatal maternal speech influences newborns' perception of speech sounds. *Infant Behavior and Development, 9,* 133–150.

Deci, E. L. (1971). Effects of externally mediated rewards on intrinsic motivation. *Journal of Personality and Social Psychology, 18,* 105–115.

Deci, E. L., Koestner, R., & Ryan, R. M. (1999). A meta-analytic review of experiments examining the effects of extrinsic rewards on intrinsic motivation. *Psychological Bulletin, 125,* 627–668.

Deese, J. (1959). On the prediction of occurrence of particular verbal intrusions in immediate recall. *Journal of Experimental Psychology, 58,* 17–22.

Degenhardt, L., Chiu, W. T., Sampson, N., Kessler, R. C., Anthony, J. C., Angermeyer, M., . . . Wells, J. E. (2008). Toward a global view of alcohol, tobacco, cannabis, and cocaine use: Findings from the WHO World Mental Health surveys. *PLoS Medicine, 5,* e141.

Degenhardt, L., Dierker, L., Chiu, W. T., Medina-Mora, M. E., Neumark, Y., Sampson, N., . . . Kessler, R. C. (2010). Evaluating the drug use "gateway" theory using cross-national data: Consistency and associations of the order of initiation of drug use among participants in the WHO World Mental Health surveys. *Drug and Alcohol Dependence, 108,* 84–97.

Dekker, M. C., & Koot, H. M. (2003). DSM–IV disorders in children with borderline to moderate intellectual disability: I. Prevalence and impact. *Journal of the American Academy of Child and Adolescent Psychiatry, 42*(8), 915–922. doi:10.1097/01.CHI.0000046892.27264.1A

Dekker, S., Lee, N. C., Howard-Jones, P., & Jolles, J. (2012). Neuromyths in education: Prevalence and predictors of misconceptions among teachers. *Frontiers in Psychology 3:* 429. doi:10.3389/fpsyg.2012.00429

Del Vicario, M., Bessi, A., Zollo, F., Petroni, F., Scalåa, A., Caldarelli, G., . . . Quattrociocchi, W. (2016). The spreading of misinformation online. *Proceedings of the National Academy of Sciences, 113*(3), 554–559. doi: 10.1073/pnas.1517441113

Delgado, M. R., Frank, R. H., & Phelps, E. A. (2005). Perceptions of moral character modulate the neural systems of reward during the trust game. *Nature Neuroscience, 8,* 1611–1618.

Demb, J. B., Desmond, J. E., Wagner, A. D., Vaidya, C. J., Glover, G. H., & Gabrieli, J. D. E. (1995). Semantic encoding and retrieval in the left inferior prefrontal cortex: A functional MRI study of task difficulty and process specificity. *The Journal of Neuroscience, 15,* 5870–5878.

Dement, W. C. (1959, November 30). Dreams. *Newsweek.*

Dement, W. C. (1978). *Some must watch while some must sleep.* New York: Norton.

Dement, W. C. (1999). *The promise of sleep.* New York: Delacorte Press.

Dement, W. C., & Kleitman, N. (1957). The relation of eye movements during sleep to dream activity: An objective method for the study of dreaming. *Journal of Experimental Psychology, 53,* 339–346.

Dement, W. C., & Wolpert, E. (1958). Relation of eye movements, body motility, and external stimuli to dream content. *Journal of Experimental Psychology, 55,* 543–553.

Dempster, E. L., Pidsley, R., Schalkwyk, L. C., Owens, S., Georgiades, A., Kane, F., . . . Mill, J. (2011). Disease-associated epigenetic changes in monozygotic twins discordant for schizophrenia and bipolar disorder. *Human Molecular Genetics, 20,* 4786–4796.

Denison, S., Reed, C., & Xu, F. (2013). The emergence of probabilistic reasoning in very young infants: Evidence from 4.5- and 6-month-olds. *Developmental Psychology, 49*(2), 243–249. doi:10.1037/a0028278

Dennett, D. (1991). *Consciousness explained.* New York: Basic Books.

Denny, B. T., & Ochsner, K. N. (2014). Behavioral effects of longitudinal training in cognitive reappraisal. *Emotion, 14*(2), 425–433. doi: 10.1037/a0035276

Department of Transportation (U.S.), National Highway Traffic Safety Administration (NHTSA). *Traffic safety facts 2010: Alcohol-impaired driving.* Washington (DC): NHTSA; 2012 [cited 2012 Sep 28]. Available at http://www-nrd.nhtsa.dot.gov/Pubs/811606.PDF

DePaulo, B. M., Charlton, K., Cooper, H., Lindsay, J. J., & Muhlenbruck, L. (1997). The accuracy–confidence correlation in the detection of deception. *Personality and Social Psychology Review, 1,* 346–357.

DePaulo, B. M., Lindsay, J. J., Malone, B. E., Muhlenbruck, L., Charlton, K., & Cooper, H. (2003). Cues to deception. *Psychological Bulletin, 129,* 74–118.

DePaulo, B. M., & Morris, W. L. (2006). The unrecognized stereotyping and discrimination against singles. *Current Directions in Psychological Science, 15,* 251–254.

DePaulo, B. M., Stone, J. I., & Lassiter, G. D. (1985). Deceiving and detecting deceit. In B. R. Schlenker (Ed.), *The self and social life* (pp. 323–370). New York: McGraw-Hill.

Der, G., Batty, G. D., & Deary, I. J. (2009). The association between IQ in adolescence and a range of health outcomes at 40 in the 1979 U.S. national longitudinal study of youth. *Intelligence, 37*(6), 573–580.

DeRubeis, R. J., Cohen, Z. D., Forand, N. R., Fournier, J. C., Gelfand, L. A., & Lorenzo-Luaces, L. (2014). The personalized advantage index: Translating research on prediction into individualized treatment recommendations: A demonstration. *PLoS ONE, 9,* e83875.

DesJardin, J. L., Eisenberg, L. S., & Hodapp, R. M. (2006). Sound beginnings: Supporting families of young deaf children with cochlear implants. *Infants and Young Children, 19,* 179–189.

Des Jarlais, D. C., McKnight, C., Goldblatt, C., & Purchase, D. (2009). Doing harm reduction better: Syringe exchange in the United States. *Addiction, 104*(9), 1331–1446.

D'Esposito, M. & Postle, B. R. (2015). The cognitive neuroscience of working memory. *Annual Review of Psychology, 66,* 115–142.

Deutsch, M. (1949). A theory of cooperation and competition. *Human Relations, 2,* 129–152.

DeVilliers, P. (2005). The role of language in theory-of-mind development: What deaf children tell us. In J. W. Astington & J. A. Baird (Eds.), *Why language matters for theory of mind* (pp. 266–297). Oxford, England: Oxford University Press.

Dewhurst, D. L., & Cautela, J. R. (1980). A proposed reinforcement survey schedule for special needs children. *Journal of Behavior Therapy and Experimental Psychiatry, 11,* 109–112.

De Witte, P. (1996). The role of neurotransmitters in alcohol dependency. *Alcohol & Alcoholism, 31*(Suppl. 1), 13–16.

De Wolff, M., & van IJzendoorn, M. H. (1997). Sensitivity and attachment: A meta-analysis on parental antecedents of infant attachment. *Child Development, 68,* 571–591.

DeYoung, C. G., Hirsh, J. B., Shane, M. S., Papademetris, X., Rajeevan, N., & Gray, J. R. (2010). Testing predictions from personality neuroscience: Brain structure and the Big Five. *Psychological Science, 21,* 820–828.

Diaconis, P., & Mosteller, F. (1989). Methods for studying coincidences. *Journal of the American Statistical Association, 84,* 853–861.

Dickens, W. T., & Flynn, J. R. (2001). Heritability estimates versus large environmental effects: The IQ paradox resolved. *Psychological Review, 108,* 346–369.

Dickinson, A., Watt, A., & Griffiths, J. H. (1992). Free-operant acquisition with delayed reinforcement. *Quarterly Journal of Experimental Psychology Section B: Comparative and Physiological Psychology, 45,* 241–258.

Didden, R., Sigafoos, J., Lang, R., O'Reilly, M., Drieschner, K., & Lancioni, G. E. (2012). Intellectual disabilities. In P. Sturmey & M. Hersen (Eds.), *Handbook of evidence-based practice in clinical psychology.* Hoboken, NJ: Wiley. Retrieved from http://doi.wiley.com/10.1002/9781118156391.ebcp001006

DiDonato, T. E., Ullrich, J., & Krueger, J. I. (2011). Social perception as induction and inference: An integrative model of intergroup differentiation, ingroup favoritism, and differential accuracy. *Journal of Personality and Social Psychology, 100*(1), 66–83. doi: 10.1037/a0021051

Diekelmann, S., & Born, J. (2010). The memory function of sleep. *Nature Reviews Neuroscience, 11,* 114–126.

Dimberg, U. (1982). Facial reactions to facial expressions. *Psychophysiology, 19,* 643–647.

Dion, K. L. (2005). Marital status as stimulus variable and subject variable. *Psychological Inquiry, 16,* 104–110.

Disner, S. G., Beevers, C. G., Haigh, E. A., & Beck, A. T. (2011). Neural mechanisms of the cognitive model of depression. *Nature Reviews Neuroscience, 12,* 467–477.

DiTella, R., MacCulloch, R. J., & Oswald, A. J. (2003). The macroeconomics of happiness. *Review of Economics and Statistics, 85,* 809–827.

Dolcos, F. (2014). Current emotion research in cognitive neuroscience: Linking enhancing and impairing effects of emotion on cognition. *Emotion Review, 6,* 362–375.

Dollard, J., Doob, L. W., Miller, N. E., Mowrer, O. H., & Sears, R. R. (1939). *Frustration and aggression.* Oxford, England: Yale University Press.

Domjan, M. (2005). Pavlovian conditioning: A functional perspective. *Annual Review of Psychology, 56,* 179–206.

Dornbusch, S. M., Hastorf, A. H., Richardson, S. A., Muzzy, R. E., & Vreeland, R. S. (1965). The perceiver and perceived: Their relative influence on categories of interpersonal perception. *Journal of Personality and Social Psychology, 1,* 434–440.

Dovidio, J. F., & Gaertner, S. L. (2010). Intergroup bias. In S. T. Fiske, D. T. Gilbert, & G. Lindzey (Eds.), *The handbook of social psychology* (5th ed., Vol. 2, pp. 1085–1121). New York: Wiley.

Downing, P. E., Chan, A. W. Y., Peelen, M. V., Dodds, C. M., & Kanwisher, N. (2006). Domain specificity in visual cortex. *Cerebral Cortex, 16,* 1453–1461.

Dreifus, C. (2003, May 20). Living one disaster after another, and then sharing the experience. *New York Times,* p. D2.

Drigotas, S. M., & Rusbult, C. E. (1992). Should I stay or should I go? A dependence model of breakups. *Journal of Personality and Social Psychology, 62,* 62–87.

Druckman, D., & Bjork, R. A. (1994). *Learning, remembering, believing: Enhancing human performance.* Washington, DC: National Academy Press.

Duchaine, B. & Yovel, G. (2015). A revised neural framework for face processing. *Annual Review of Vision Science, 1,* 393–416.

Duckworth, A. L., & Seligman, M. E. P. (2005). Self-discipline outdoes IQ in predicting academic performance of adolescents. *Psychological Science, 16,* 939–944.

Dudai, Y. (2012). The restless engram: Consolidations never end. *Annual Review of Neuroscience, 35,* 227–247.

Duenwald, M. (2002, September 12). Students find another staple of campus life: Stress. *New York Times.* Retrieved from http://www.nytimes.com/2002/09/17/health/students-find-another-staple-of-campus-life-stress.html?pagewanted=all&src=pm

Duffy, K. A., & Chartrand, T. L. (2015). The extravert advantage: How and when extraverts build rapport with other people. *Psychological Science, 26,* 1795–1802.

Dunlop, S. A. (2008). Activity-dependent plasticity: Implications for recovery after spinal cord injury. *Trends in Neurosciences, 31,* 410–418.

Dunlosky, J., Rawson, K. A., Marsh, E. J., Nathan, M. J., & Willingham, D. T. (2013). Improving students' learning with effective learning techniques: Promising directions from cognitive and educational psychology. *Psychological Science in the Public Interest, 14*(1), 4–58.

Dunphy, D. C. (1963). The social structure of urban adolescent peer groups. *Sociometry, 26,* 230–246.

Dutton, D. G., & Aron, A. P. (1974). Some evidence for heightened sexual attraction under conditions of high anxiety. *Journal of Personality and Social Psychology, 30,* 510–517.

Duval, S., & Wicklund, R. A. (1972). *A theory of objective self awareness.* New York: Academic Press.

Dyer, D., Dalzell, F., & Olegario, F. (2004). *Rising Tide: Lessons from 165 years of brand building at Procter & Gamble.* Cambridge, MA: Harvard Business School Press.

Eacott, M. J., & Crawley, R. A. (1998). The offset of childhood amnesia: Memory for events that occurred before age 3. *Journal of Experimental Psychology: General, 127,* 22–33.

Eagly, A. H., & Steffen, V. J. (1986). Gender and aggressive behavior: A meta-analytic review of the social psychological literature. *Psychological Bulletin, 100,* 309–330.

Eagly, A. H., & Wood, W. (1999). The origins of sex differences in human behavior: Evolved dispositions versus social roles. *American Psychologist, 54,* 408–423.

Eastwick, P. W., Finkel, E. J., Mochon, D., & Ariely, D. (2007). Selective versus unselective romantic desire: Not all reciprocity is created equal. *Psychological Science, 18,* 317–319.

Eaton, W. W., Shao, H., Nestadt, G., Lee, B. H., Bienvenu, O. J., & Zandi, P. (2008). Population-based study of first onset and chronicity of major depressive disorder. *Archives of General Psychiatry, 65,* 513–520.

Ebbinghaus, H. (1964). *Memory: A contribution to experimental psychology.* New York: Dover. (Original work published 1885)

Eddy, D. M. (1982). Probabilistic reasoning in clinical medicine: Problems and opportunities. In D. Kahneman, P. Slovic, & A. Tversky (Eds.), *Judgments under uncertainty: Heuristics and biases* (pp. 249–267). New York: Cambridge University Press.

Edwards, W. (1955). The theory of decision making. *Psychological Bulletin, 51,* 201–214.

Eich, J. E. (1995). Searching for mood dependent memory. *Psychological Science, 6,* 67–75.

Eichenbaum, H., & Cohen, N. J. (2001). *From conditioning to conscious recollection: Memory systems of the brain.* New York: Oxford University Press.

Eimas, P. D., Siqueland, E. R., Jusczyk, P., & Vigorito, J. (1971). Speech perception in infants. *Science, 171,* 303–306.

Einstein, G. O., & McDaniel, M. A. (1990). Normal aging and prospective memory. *Journal of Experimental Psychology: Learning, Memory, and Cognition, 16,* 717–726.

Einstein, G. O., & McDaniel, M. A. (2005). Prospective memory: Multiple retrieval processes. *Current Direction in Psychological Science, 14,* 286–290.

Eisenberg, N., Fabes, R. A., Guthrie, I. K., & Reiser, M. (2000). Dispositional emotionality and regulation: Their role in predicting quality of social functioning. *Journal of Personality and Social Psychology, 78,* 136.

Eisenberger, N. I., Lieberman, M. D., & Williams, K. D. (2003). Does rejection hurt? An fMRI study of social exclusion. *Science, 302,* 290–292. doi: 10.1126/science.1089134

Eisenegger, C., Haushofer, J., & Fehr, E. (2011). The role of testosterone in social interaction. *Trends in Cognitive Sciences, 15*(6), 263–271. doi: 10.1016/j.tics.2011.04.008

Eisenegger, C., Naef, M., Snozzi, R., Heinrichs, M., & Fehr, E. (2010). Prejudice and truth about the effect of testosterone on human bargaining behaviour. *Nature, 463,* 356–359.

Ekman, P. (1965). Differential communication of affect by head and body cues. *Journal of Personality and Social Psychology, 2,* 726–735.

Ekman, P. (1972). Universals and cultural differences in facial expressions of emotion. In J. K. Cole (Ed.), *Nebraska Symposium on Motivation, 1971* (pp. 207–283). Lincoln: University of Nebraska Press.

Ekman, P. (1992). *Telling lies.* New York: Norton.

Ekman, P. (2016). What scientists who study emotion agree about. *Perspectives on Psychological Science, 11*(1), 31–34.

Ekman, P., & Friesen, W. V. (1968). Nonverbal behavior in psychotherapy research. In J. M. Shlien (Ed.), *Research in psychotherapy* (Vol. 3, pp. 179–216). Washington, DC: American Psychological Association.

Ekman, P., & Friesen, W. V. (1971). Constants across cultures in the face and emotion. *Journal of Personality and Social Psychology, 17,* 124–129.

Ekman, P., & Friesen, W. V. (1982). Felt, false, and miserable smiles. *Journal of Nonverbal Behavior, 6,* 238–252.

Ekman, P., Levenson, R. W., & Friesen, W. V. (1983). Autonomic nervous system activity distinguishes among emotions. *Science, 221,* 1208–1210.

Elbogen, E. B., & Johnson, S. C. (2009). The intricate link between violence and mental disorder. *Archives of General Psychiatry, 66*(2), 152–161.

Eldridge, L. L., Knowlton, B. J., Furmanski, C. S., Bookheimer, S. Y., & Engel, S. A. (2000). Remembering episodes: A selective role for the hippocampus during retrieval. *Nature Neuroscience, 3,* 1149–1152.

Elfenbein, H. A., & Ambady, N. (2002). On the universality and cultural specificity of emotion recognition: A meta-analysis. *Psychological Bulletin, 128,* 203–235.

Elfenbein, H. A., Der Foo, M. D., White, J., & Tan, H. H. (2007). Reading your counterpart: The benefit of emotion recognition accuracy for effectiveness in negotiation. *Journal of Nonverbal Behavior, 31,* 205–223.

Ellenbogen, J. M., Payne, J. D., & Stickgold, R. (2006). The role of sleep in declarative memory consolidation: Passive, permissive, or none? *Current Opinion in Neurobiology, 16,* 716–722.

Ellis, A. (1991). *Reason and emotion in psychotherapy.* New York: Carol.

Ellis, B. J., & Garber, J. (2000). Psychosocial antecedents of variation in girls' pubertal timing: Maternal depression, stepfather presence, and marital and family stress. *Child Development, 71,* 485–501.

Ellis, L., & Ames, M. A. (1987). Neurohormonal functioning in sexual orientation: A theory of homosexuality–heterosexuality. *Psychological Bulletin, 101,* 233–258.

Ellman, S. J., Spielman, A. J., Luck, D., Steiner, S. S., & Halperin, R. (1991). REM deprivation: A review. In S. J. Ellman & J. S. Antrobus (Eds.), *The mind in sleep: Psychology and psychophysiology* (2nd ed., pp. 329–376). New York: Wiley.

Ellsworth, P. C., & Scherer, K. R. (2003). Appraisal processes in emotion. In R. J. Davidson, K. R. Scherer, & H. H. Goldsmith (Eds.), *The handbook of affective science* (pp. 572–595). New York: Oxford University Press.

Emerson, R. C., Bergen, J. R., & Adelson, E. H. (1992). Directionally selective complex cells and the computation of motion energy in cat visual cortex. *Vision Research, 32,* 203–218.

Enock, P. M., & McNally, R. J. (2013). How mobile apps and other web-based interventions can transform psychological treatment and the treatment development cycle. *Behavior Therapist, 36*(3), 56, 58, 60, 62–66.

Epel, E. S., Blackburn, E. H., Lin, J., Dhabhar, F. S., Adler, N.E., Morrow, J. D., & Cawthorn, R. M. (2004). Accelerated telomere shortening in response to life stress. *Proceedings of the National Academy of Sciences, 101,* 17312–17315.

Epel, E. S., Daubenmier, J., Moskowitz, J. T., Foldman, S., & Blackburn, E. H. (2009). Can meditation slow rate of cellular aging? Cognitive stress, mindfulness, and telomerase. *Annals of the New York Academy of Sciences, 1172,* 34–53.

Epley, N., Savitsky, K., & Kachelski, R. A. (1999). What every skeptic should know about subliminal persuasion. *Skeptical Inquirer, 23,* 40–45, 58.

Epley, N., & Waytz, A. (2010). Mind perception. In S. T. Fiske, D. T. Gilbert, & G. Lindzey (Eds.), *The handbook of social psychology* (5th ed., Vol. 1, pp. 498–541). New York: Wiley.

Epstein, R. (2007a). *The case against adolescence: Rediscovering the adult in every teen.* New York: Quill Driver.

Epstein, R. (2007b). The myth of the teen brain. *Scientific American Mind, 18,* 27–31.

Ericsson, K. A., & Charness, N. (1999). Expert performance: Its structure and acquisition. In S. J. Ceci & W. M. Williams (Eds.), *The nature–nurture debate: The essential readings* (pp. 200–256). Oxford, England: Blackwell.

Espy, K. A., Fang, H., Johnson, C., Stopp, C., Wiebe, S. A., & Respass, J. (2011). Prenatal tobacco exposure: Developmental outcomes in the neonatal period. *Developmental Psychology, 47*(1), 153–169. doi:10.1037/a0020724

Estes, A., Munson, J., Rogers, S. J., Greenson, J., Winter, J., & Dawson, G. (2015). Long-term outcomes of early intervention in 6-year-old children with Autism Spectrum Disorder. *Journal of the American Academy of Child and Adolescent Psychiatry, 54,* 580–587.

Evans, G. W. (2004). The environment of childhood poverty. *American Psychologist, 59*(2), 77–92.

Evans, G. W. (2006). Child development and the physical environment. *Annual Review of Psychology, 57,* 423–451.

Evans, G. W., & Kim, P. (2012). Childhood poverty and young adults' allostatic load: The mediating role of childhood cumulative risk exposure. *Psychological Science, 23*(9), 979–983. doi:10.1177/0956797612441218

Evans, G. W., & Stecker, R. (2004). Motivational consequences of environmental stress. *Journal of Environmental Psychology, 24,* 143–165.

Everson, S. A., Lynch, J. W., Chesney, M. A., Kaplan, G. A., Goldberg, D. E., Shade, S. B., . . . Salonen, J. T. (1997). Interaction of workplace demands and cardiovascular reactivity in progression of carotid atherosclerosis: Population based study. *British Medical Journal, 314,* 553–558.

Exner, J. E. (1993). *The Rorschach: A comprehensive system: Vol. 1. Basic Foundations.* New York: Wiley.

Eysenck, H. J. (1957). The effects of psychotherapy: An evaluation. *Journal of Consulting Psychology, 16,* 319–324.

Eysenck, H. J. (1967). *The biological basis of personality.* Springfield, IL: Charles C Thomas.

Eysenck, H. J. (1990). Biological dimensions of personality. In L. A. Pervin (Ed.), *Handbook of personality: Theory and research* (pp. 244–276). New York: Guilford Press.

Falk, R., & McGregor, D. (1983). The surprisingness of coincidences. In P. Humphreys, O. Svenson, & A. Vari (Eds.), *Analysing and aiding decision processes* (pp. 489–502). New York: North Holland.

Fancher, R. E. (1979). *Pioneers in psychology.* New York: Norton.

Fantz, R. L. (1964). Visual experience in infants: Decreased attention to familiar patterns relative to novel ones. *Science, 164,* 668–670.

Farah, M. J., Illes, J., Cook-Deegan, R., Gardner, H., Kandel, E., King, P., . . . Wolpe, P. R. (2004). Neurocognitive enhancement: What can we do and what should we do? *Nature Reviews Neuroscience, 5,* 421–426.

Faraone, S. V., Perlis, R. H., Doyle, A. E., Smoller, J. W., Goralnick, J. J., Holmgren, M. A., & Sklar, P. (2005). Molecular genetics of attention-deficit/hyperactivity disorder. *Biological Psychiatry, 57,* 1313–1323.

Farooqi, I. S., Bullmore, E., Keogh, J., Gillard, J., O'Rahilly, S., & Fletcher, P. C. (2007). Leptin regulates striatal regions and human eating behavior. *Science, 317,* 1355.

Farrar, M. J. (1990). Discourse and the acquisition of grammatical morphemes. *Journal of Child Language, 17,* 607–624.

Farrelly, D., Lazarus, J., & Roberts, G. (2007). Altruists attract. *Evolutionary Psychology, 5,* 313–329.

Favazza, A. (2011). *Bodies under siege: Self-mutilation, nonsuicidal self-injury, and body modification in culture and psychiatry.* Baltimore, MD: Johns Hopkins University Press.

Fazel, S., & Danesh, J. (2002). Serious mental disorder in 23,000 prisoners: A review of 62 surveys. *Lancet, 359,* 545–550.

Fechner, G. T. (1966). *Elements of psychophysics* (H. E. Alder, Trans.). New York: Holt, Rinehart, & Winston. (Original work published 1860)

Feczer, D., & Bjorklund, P. (2009). Forever changed: Posttraumatic stress disorder in female military veterans, a case report. *Perspectives in Psychiatric Care, 45,* 278–291.

Fehr, E., & Gaechter, S. (2002). Altruistic punishment in humans. *Nature, 415,* 137–140.

Fein, D., Barton, M., Eigsti, I.-M., Kelley, E., Naigles, L., Schultz, R. T., . . . Tyson, K. (2013). Optimal outcome in individuals with a history of autism. *Journal of Child Psychology and Psychiatry, 54,* 195–205.

Fein, S., Goethals, G. R., & Kugler, M. B. (2007). Social influence on political judgments: The case of presidential debates. *Political Psychology, 28,* 165–192.

Feinberg, T. E. (2001). *Altered egos: How the brain creates the self.* New York: Oxford University Press.

Feingold, A. (1992). Gender differences in mate selection preferences: A test of the parental investment model. *Psychological Bulletin, 112,* 125–139.

Feldman, D. E. (2009). Synaptic mechanisms for plasticity in neocortex. *Annual Review of Neuroscience, 32,* 33–55.

Feldman, M. D. (2004). *Playing sick.* New York: Brunner-Routledge.

Fernandez Nievas, I. F. & Thaver, D. (2015) Work-life balance: A different scale for doctors. *Frontiers in Pediatrics, 3,* 115.

Fernyhough, C. (2012). *Pieces of light: The new science of memory.* London: Profile Books.

Ferrari, A . J., Charlson, F. J., Norman, R. E., Patten, S. B., Freedman, G., Murray, C. J. L., . . . Whiteford, H. A. (2013). Burden of depressive disorders by country, sex, age, and year: Findings from the Global Burden of Disease Study 2010. *PLoS Medicine, 10,* e1001547.

Ferster, C. B., & Skinner, B. F. (1957). *Schedules of reinforcement.* New York: Appleton-Century-Crofts.

Festinger, L. (1957). *A theory of cognitive dissonance.* Stanford, CA: Stanford University Press.

Festinger, L., & Carlsmith, J. M. (1959). Cognitive consequences of forced compliance. *Journal of Abnormal and Social Psychology, 58,* 203–210.

Festinger, L., Schachter, S., & Back, K. (1950). *Social pressures in informal groups: A study of human factors in housing.* Oxford, England: Harper & Row.

Fields, G. (2009, May 14). White House czar calls for end to "War on Drugs." *Wall Street Journal,* p. A3. Retrieved May 14, 2009, from http://online.wsj.com/article/SB124225891527617397.html

Finkel, E. J., Cheung, E. O., Emery, L. F., Carswell, K. L., & Larson, G. M. (2015). The suffocation model: Why marriage in America is becoming an all-or-nothing institution. *Current Directions in Psychological Science, 24*(3), 238–244. doi: 10.1177/0963721415569274

Finkel, E. J., & Eastwick, P. W. (2009). Arbitrary social norms influence sex differences in romantic selectivity. *Psychological Science, 20,* 1290–1295.

Finkelstein, E. A., Trogdon, J. G., Cohen, J. W., & Dietz, W. (2009). Annual medical spending attributable to obesity: Payer- and service-specific estimates. *Health Affairs, 28*(5), w822–w831.

Finkelstein, K. E. (1999, October 17). Yo-Yo Ma's lost Stradivarius is found after wild search. *New York Times,* p. 34.

Fiore, A. T., Taylor, L. S., Zhong, X., Mendelsohn, G. A., & Cheshire, C. (2010). Who's right and who writes: People, profiles, contacts, and replies in online dating. *Proceedings of Hawaii International Conferences on Systems Science, 43,* Persistent Conversation minitrack.

Fiorentine, R. (1999). After drug treatment: Are 12-step programs effective in maintaining abstinence? *American Journal of Drug and Alcohol Abuse, 25,* 93–116.

Fiorillo, C. D., Newsome, W. T., & Schultz, W. (2008). The temporal precision of reward prediction in dopamine neurons. *Nature Neuroscience, 11,* 966–973.

Fischer, P., Krueger, J. I., Greitemeyer, T., Vogrincic, C., Kastenmüller, A., Frey, D., . . . Kainbacher, M. (2011). The bystander-effect: A meta-analytic review on bystander intervention in dangerous and non-dangerous emergencies. *Psychological Bulletin, 137*(4), 517–537. doi: 10.1037/a0023304

Fisher, H. E. (1993). *Anatomy of love: The mysteries of mating, marriage, and why we stray.* New York: Fawcett.

Fisher, R. P., & Craik, F. I. M. (1977). The interaction between encoding and retrieval operations in cued recall. *Journal of Experimental Psychology: Human Learning and Perception, 3,* 153–171.

Fiske, S. T. (1998). Stereotyping, prejudice, and discrimination. In D. T. Gilbert, S. T. Fiske, & G. Lindzey (Eds.), *The handbook of social psychology* (4th ed., Vol. 2, pp. 357–411). New York: McGraw-Hill.

Fiske, S. T. (2010). *Social beings: A core motives approach to social psychology.* Hoboken, NJ: Wiley.

Fleeson, W. (2004). Moving personality beyond the person-situation debate: The challenge and opportunity of within-person variability. *Current Directions in Psychological Science, 13,* 83–87.

Fletcher, G. J. O., Simpson, J. A., Thomas, G., & Giles, L. (1999). Ideals in intimate relationships. *Journal of Personality and Social Psychology, 76,* 72–89. doi: 10.1037/0022-3514.76.1.72

Fletcher, P. C., Shallice, T., & Dolan, R. J. (1998). The functional roles of prefrontal cortex in episodic memory. I. Encoding. *Brain, 121,* 1239–1248.

Flynn, E., & Whiten, A. (2008). Cultural transmission of tool-use in young children: A diffusion chain study. *Social Development, 17,* 699–718.

Flynn, J. R. (2012). *Are we getting smarter? Rising IQ in the twenty-first century.* New York: Cambridge University Press.

Foa, E. B. (2010). Cognitive behavioral therapy of obsessive-compulsive disorder. *Dialogues in Clinical Neuroscience, 12,* 199–207.

Foa, E. B., Dancu, C. V., Hembree, E. A., Jaycox, L. H., Meadows, E. A., & Street, G. P. (1999). A comparison of exposure therapy, stress inoculation training, and their combination for reducing posttraumatic stress disorder in female assault victims. *Journal of Consulting and Clinical Psychology, 67,* 194–200.

Foa, E. B., Liebowitz, M. R., Kozak, M. J., Davies, S., Campeas, R., Franklin, M. E., . . . Tu, X. (2007). Randomized, placebo-controlled trial of exposure and ritual prevention, clomipramine, and their combination in the treatment of obsessive-compulsive disorder. *Focus, 5,* 368–380.

Foa, E. B. & McLean, C. P. (2016) The efficacy of exposure therapy for anxiety-related disorders and its underlying mechanisms: The case of OCD and PTSD. *Annual Review of Clinical Psychology, 12,* 1–28.

Fogassi, L., Ferrari, P. F., Gesierich, B., Rozzi, S., Chersi, F., & Rizzolatti, G. (2005). Parietal lobe: From action organization to intention understanding. *Science, 308,* 662–667.

Fornito, A., Zalesky, A., & Breakspear, M. (2015). The connectomics of brain disorders. *Nature Reviews Neuroscience, 16,* 159–172.

Foroni, F., & Semin, G. R. (2009). Language that puts you in touch with your bodily feelings: The multimodal responsiveness of affective expressions. *Psychological Science, 20*(8), 974–980.

Fournier, J. C., DeRubeis, R., Hollon, S. D., Dimidjian, S., Amsterdam, J. D., Shelton, R. C., & Fawcett, J. (2010). Antidepressant drug effects and depression severity. *Journal of the American Medical Association, 303,* 47–53.

Fox, R. E., DeLeon, P. H., Newman, R., Sammons, M. T., Dunivin, D. L., & Baker, D. C. (2009). Prescriptive authority and psychology: A status report. *American Psychologist, 64,* 257–268.

Fragaszy, D. M., Izar, P., Visalberghi, E., Ottoni, E. B., & de Oliveria, M. G. (2004). Wild capuchin monkeys (*Cebus libidinosus*) use anvils and stone pounding tools. *American Journal of Primatology, 64,* 359–366.

Francis, D., Diorio, J., Liu, D., & Meaney, M. J. (1999). Nongenomic transmission across generations of maternal behavior and stress responses in the rat. *Science, 286,* 1155–1158.

Frank, M. G., Ekman, P., & Friesen, W. V. (1993). Behavioral markers and recognizability of the smile of enjoyment. *Journal of Personality and Social Psychology, 64,* 83–93.

Frank, M. G., & Stennet, J. (2001). The forced-choice paradigm and the perception of facial expressions of emotion. *Journal of Personality and Social Psychology, 80,* 75–85.

Franklin, J. C., Fox, K. R., Franklin, C. R., Kleiman, E. M., Ribeiro, J. D., Jaroszewski, A. C., . . . Nock, M. K. (2016). A brief mobile app reduces nonsuicidal and suicidal self-injury: Evidence from three randomized controlled trials. *Journal of Consulting and Clinical Psychology, 84,* 544–557.

Fredman, T., & Whiten, A. (2008). Observational learning from tool using models by human-reared and mother-reared capuchin monkeys (*Cebus apella*). *Animal Cognition, 11,* 295–309.

Fredrickson, B. L. (2000). Cultivating positive emotions to optimize health and well-being. *Prevention and Treatment, 3,* Article 0001a. doi:10.1037/1522-3736.3.1.31a. Retrieved September 21, 2013 from http://psycnet.apa.org

Freedman, J. L., & Fraser, S. C. (1966). Compliance without pressure: The foot-in-the-door technique. *Journal of Personality and Social Psychology, 4,* 195–202.

Freeman, S., Walker, M. R., Borden, R., & Latané, B. (1975). Diffusion of responsibility and restaurant tipping: Cheaper by the bunch. *Personality and Social Psychology Bulletin, 1,* 584–587.

French, H. W. (1997, February 26). In the land of the small it isn't easy being tall. *New York Times.* Retrieved from http://www.nytimes.com/1997/02/26/world/in-the-land-of-the-small-it-isn-t-easy-being-tall.html

Freud, S. (1965). *The interpretation of dreams* (J. Strachey, Trans.). New York: Avon. (Original work published 1900)

Fried, P. A., & Watkinson, B. (2000). Visuoperceptual functioning differs in 9- to 12-year-olds prenatally exposed to cigarettes and marijuana. *Neurotoxicology and Teratology, 22,* 11–20.

Friedlander, L., & Desrocher, M. (2006). Neuroimaging studies of obsessive-compulsive disorder in adults and children. *Clinical Psychology Review, 26,* 32–49.

Friedman, J. M. (2003). A war on obesity, not the obese. *Science, 299*(5608), 856–858.

Friedman, J. M., & Halaas, J. L. (1998). Leptin and the regulation of body weight in mammals. *Nature, 395*(6704), 763–770.

Friedman, M., & Rosenman, R. H. (1974). *Type A behavior and your heart.* New York: Knopf.

Friedman, S. L., & Boyle, D. E. (2008). Attachment in U.S. children experiencing nonmaternal care in the early 1990s. *Attachment & Human Development, 10*(3), 225–261.

Friedman-Hill, S. R., Robertson, L. C., & Treisman, A. (1995). Parietal contributions to visual feature binding: Evidence from a patient with bilateral lesions. *Science, 269,* 853–855.

Friesen, W. V. (1972). *Cultural differences in facial expressions in a social situation: An experimental test of the concept of display rules.* Unpublished doctoral dissertation, University of California, San Francisco.

Frith, C. D., & Fletcher, P. (1995). Voices from nowhere. *Critical Quarterly, 37,* 71–83.

Frith, U. (2003). *Autism: Explaining the enigma.* Oxford, England: Blackwell.

Fukui, H., Murai, T., Fukuyama, H., Hayashi, T., & Hanakawa, T. (2005). Functional activity related to risk anticipation during performance of the Iowa gambling task. *NeuroImage, 24,* 253–259.

Funder, D. C. (2001). Personality. *Annual Review of Psychology, 52,* 197–221.

Furmark, T., Tillfors, M., Marteinsdottir, I., Fischer, H., Pissiota, A., Långström, B., & Fredrikson, M. (2002). Common changes in cerebral blood flow in patients with social phobia treated with citalopram or cognitive behavioral therapy. *Archives of General Psychiatry, 59*(5), 425–433.

Fuster, J. M. (2003). *Cortex and mind.* New York: Oxford University Press.

Gadermann, A. M., Alonso, J., Vilagut, G., Zaslavsky, A. M., & Kessler, R. C. (2012). Comorbidity and disease burden in the National Comorbidity Survey Replication (NCS-R). *Depression and Anxiety, 29,* 797–806.

Gais, S., & Born, J. (2004). Low acetylcholine during slow-wave sleep is critical for declarative memory consolidation. *Proceedings of the National Academy of Sciences, USA, 101,* 2140–2144.

Galanter, E. (1962). Contemporary psychophysics. In R. Brown, E. Galanter, E. H. Hess, & G. Mandler (Eds.), *New directions in psychology.* New York: Holt, Rinehart, & Winston.

Galati, D., Scherer, K. R., & Ricci-Bitt, P. E. (1997). Voluntary facial expression of emotion: Comparing congenitally blind with normally sighted encoders. *Journal of Personality and Social Psychology, 73,* 1363–1379.

Galef, B. (1998). Edward Thorndike: Revolutionary psychologist, ambiguous biologist. *American Psychologist, 53,* 1128–1134.

Gallistel, C. R. (2000). The replacement of general-purpose learning models with adaptively specialized learning modules. In M. S. Gazzaniga (Ed.), *The new cognitive neurosciences* (pp. 1179–1191). Cambridge, MA: MIT Press.

Gallo, D. A. (2006). *Associative illusions of memory*. New York: Psychology Press.

Gallo, D. A. (2010). False memories and fantastic beliefs: 15 years of the DRM illusion. *Memory & Cognition, 38,* 833–848.

Gallup (2014, July 10). Older Americans feel best about their physical appearance. Retrieved from http://www.gallup.com/poll/172361/older-americans-feel-best-physical-appearance.aspx

Gallup (2015, October 21). In US, 58% back legal marijuana use. Retrieved from http://www.gallup.com/poll/186260/back-legal-marijuana.aspx

Gallup, G. G. (1977). Self-recognition in primates: A comparative approach to the bidirectional properties of consciousness. *American Psychologist, 32,* 329–338.

Ganzel, B. L., Kim, P., Glover, G. H., & Temple, E. (2008). Resilience after 9/11: Multimodal neuroimaging evidence for stress-related change in the healthy adult brain. *NeuroImage, 40,* 788–795.

Garb, H. N. (1998). *Studying the clinician: Judgment research and psychological assessment.* Washington, DC: American Psychological Association.

Garcia, J. (1981). Tilting at the windmills of academe. *American Psychologist, 36,* 149–158.

Garcia, J., & Koelling, R. A. (1966). Relation of cue to consequence in avoidance learning. *Psychonomic Science, 4,* 123–124.

Garcia-Moreno, C., Jansen, H. A. F. M., Ellsberg, M., Heise, L., & Watts, C. H. (2006). Prevalence of intimate partner violence: Findings from the WHO multi-country study on women's health and domestic violence. *Lancet, 368*(9543), 1260–1269. doi: 10.1016/S0140-6736(06)69523-8

Gardner, M., & Steinberg, L. (2005). Peer influence on risk taking, risk preference, and risky decision making in adolescence and adulthood: An experimental study. *Developmental Psychology, 41*(4), 625–635. doi:10.1037/0012-1649.41.4.625

Garland, A. F., & Zigler, E. (1999). Emotional and behavioral problems among highly intellectually gifted youth. *Roeper Review, 22*(1), 41.

Garry, M., Manning, C., Loftus, E. F., & Sherman, S. J. (1996). Imagination inflation: Imagining a childhood event inflates confidence that it occurred. *Psychonomic Bulletin & Review, 3,* 208–214.

Gaser, C., & Schlaug, G. (2003). Brain structures differ between musicians and nonmusicians.*Journal of Neuroscience, 23,* 9240–9245.

Gates, F. J. (2011). *How many people are lesbian, gay, bisexual, and transgender?* Los Angeles: UCLA School of Law, Williams Institute. Retrieved from http://williamsinstitute.law.ucla.edu/wp-content/uploads/Gates-How-Many-People-LGBT-Apr-2011.pdf

Gazzaniga, M. S. (Ed.). (2000). *The new cognitive neurosciences.* Cambridge, MA: MIT Press.

Gazzaniga, M. S. (2006). Forty-five years of split brain research and still going strong. *Nature Reviews Neuroscience, 6,* 653–659.

Ge, X. J., Conger, R. D., & Elder, G. H., Jr. (1996). Coming of age too early: Pubertal influences on girls' vulnerability to psychological distress. *Child Development, 67,* 3386–3400.

Ge, X. J., Conger, R. D., & Elder, G. H., Jr. (2001). Pubertal transition, stressful life events, and the emergence of gender differences in adolescent depressive symptoms. *Developmental Psychology, 37*(3), 404–417. doi:10.1037/0012-1649.37.3.404

Geen, R. G. (1984). Preferred stimulation levels in introverts and extraverts: Effects on arousal and performance. *Journal of Personality and Social Psychology, 46,* 1303–1312.

Gegenfurtner, K. R., Bloj, M., & Toscani, M. (2015). The many colours of 'the dress'. *Current Biology, 25,* R543–R544.

Geier, A., Wansink, B., & Rozin, P. (2012). Red potato chips: Segmentation cues substantially decrease food intake. *Health Psychology, 31,* 398–401.

Gendron, M., Roberson, D., van der Vyver, J. M., & Barrett, L. F. (2014). Perceptions of emotion from facial expressions are not culturally universal: Evidence from a remote culture. *Emotion, 14,* 251–262. doi: 10.1037/a0036052

Gerbasi, M. E., & Prentice, D. A. (2013). The self- and other-interest inventory. *Journal of Personality and Social Psychology, 105*(3), 495–514. doi: 10.1037/a0033483

Gershoff, E. T. (2002). Corporal punishment by parents and associated child behaviors and experiences: A meta-analytic and theoretical review. *Psychological Bulletin, 128,* 539–579.

Gibb, B. E., Alloy, L. B., & Tierney, S. (2001). History of childhood maltreatment, negative cognitive styles, and episodes of depression in adulthood. *Cognitive Therapy and Research, 25,* 425–446.

Gibbons, F. X. (1990). Self-attention and behavior: A review and theoretical update. In M. P. Zanna (Ed.), *Advances in experimental social psychology* (Vol. 23, pp. 249–303). San Diego: Academic Press.

Giedd, J. N., Blumenthal, J., Jeffries, N. O., Castellanos, F. X., Liu, H., Zijdenbos, A., . . . Rapoport, J. L. (1999). Brain development during childhood and adolescence: A longitudinal MRI study. *Nature Neuroscience, 2,* 861–863.

Gierlach, E., Blesher, B. E., & Beutler, L. E. (2010). Cross-cultural differences in risk perceptions of disasters. *Risk Analysis, 30,* 1539–1549.

Gigerenzer, G. (1996). The psychology of good judgment: Frequency formats and simple algorithms. *Journal of Medical Decision Making, 16,* 273–280.

Gigerenzer, G., & Hoffrage, U. (1995). How to improve Bayesian reasoning without instruction: Frequency formats. *Psychological Review, 102,* 684–704.

Gigone, D., & Hastie, R. (1993). The common knowledge effect: Information sharing and group judgment. *Journal of Personality and Social Psychology, 54,* 959–974.

Gilbert, D. T. (1991). How mental systems believe. *American Psychologist, 46,* 107–119.

Gilbert, D. T. (1998). Ordinary personology. In D. T. Gilbert, S. T. Fiske, & G. Lindzey (Eds.), *The handbook of social psychology* (4th ed., Vol. 2, pp. 89–150). New York: McGraw-Hill.

Gilbert, D. T. (2006). *Stumbling on happiness.* New York: Knopf.

Gilbert, D. T., Brown, R. P., Pinel, E. C., & Wilson, T. D. (2000). The illusion of external agency. *Journal of Personality and Social Psychology, 79,* 690–700.

Gilbert, D. T., Gill, M. J., & Wilson, T. D. (2002). The future is now: Temporal correction in affective forecasting. *Organizational Behavior and Human Decision Processes, 88,* 430–444.

Gilbert, D. T., & Malone, P. S. (1995). The correspondence bias. *Psychological Bulletin, 117,* 21–38.

Gilbert, D. T., Pelham, B. W., & Krull, D. S. (1988). On cognitive busyness: When persons perceive meet persons perceived. *Journal of Personality and Social Psychology, 54,* 733–740.

Gilbert, G. M. (1951). Stereotype persistence and change among college students. *Journal of Abnormal and Social Psychology, 46,* 245–254.

Gilbertson, M. W., Shenton, M. E., Ciszewski, A., Kasai, K., Lasko, N. B., Orr, S. P., & Pitman, R. K. (2002). Smaller hippocampal volume predicts pathological vulnerability to psychological trauma. *Nature Neuroscience, 5,* 1242–1247.

Gillette, J., Gleitman, H., Gleitman, L., & Lederer, A. (1999). Human simulation of vocabulary learning. *Cognition, 73,* 135–176.

Gilovich, T. (1991). *How we know what isn't so: The fallibility of human reason in everyday life*. New York: Free Press.

Gino, F., & Pierce, L. (2009). The abundance effect: Unethical behavior in the presence of wealth. *Organizational Behavior and Human Decision Processes, 109*(2), 142–155. doi: 10.1016/j.obhdp.2009.03.003

Giovanello, K. S., Schnyer, D. M., & Verfaellie, M. (2004). A critical role for the anterior hippocampus in relational memory: Evidence from an fMRI study comparing associative and item recognition. *Hippocampus, 14*, 5–8.

Gladue, B. A. (1994). The biopsychology of sexual orientation. *Current Directions in Psychological Science, 3*, 150–154.

Glanzer, M. & Cunitz, A. R. (1966). Two storage mechanisms in free recall. *Journal of Verbal Learning and Verbal Behavior, 5*, 351–360.

Glass, D. C., & Singer, J. E. (1972). *Urban stress*. New York: Academic Press.

Glenwick, D. S., Jason, L. A., & Elman, D. (1978). Physical attractiveness and social contact in the singles bar. *Journal of Social Psychology, 105*, 311–312.

Glick, D. M., & Orsillo, S. M. (2015). An investigation of the efficacy of acceptance-based behavioral therapy for academic procrastination. *Journal of Experimental Psychology: General, 144*, 400–409.

Glynn, L. M., & Sandman, C. A. (2011). Prenatal origins of neurological development: A critical period for fetus and mother. *Current Directions in Psychological Science, 20*(6), 384–389. doi:10.1177/0963721411422056

Gneezy, U., & Rustichini, A. (2000). A fine is a price. *Journal of Legal Studies, 29*, 1–17.

Goddard, H. H. (1913). *The Kallikak family: A study in the heredity of feeble-mindedness*. New York: Macmillan.

Godden, D. R., & Baddeley, A. D. (1975). Context-dependent memory in two natural environments: On land and underwater. *British Journal of Psychology, 66*, 325–331.

Goehler, L. E., Gaykema, R. P. A., Hansen, M. K., Anderson, K., Maier, S. F., & Watkins, L. R. (2000). Vagal immune-to-brain communication: A visceral chemosensory pathway. *Autonomic Neuroscience: Basic and Clinical, 85*, 49–59.

Goetzman, E. S., Hughes, T., & Klinger, E. (1994). *Current concerns of college students in a midwestern sample*. Unpublished report, University of Minnesota, Morris.

Goff, L. M., & Roediger, H. L., III. (1998). Imagination inflation for action events—repeated imaginings lead to illusory recollections. *Memory & Cognition, 26*, 20–33.

Goldman, M. S., Brown, S. A., & Christiansen, B. A. (1987). Expectancy theory: Thinking about drinking. In H. T. Blane & K. E. Leonard (Eds.), *Psychological theories of drinking and alcoholism* (pp. 181–266). New York: Guilford Press.

Goldstein, M. H., Schwade, J. A., Briesch, J., & Syal, S. (2010). Learning while babbling: Prelinguistic object-directed vocalizations signal a readiness to learn. *Infancy, 15*, 362–391.

Gomez, C., Argandota, E. D., Solier, R. G., Angulo, J. C., & Vazquez, M. (1995). Timing and competition in networks representing ambiguous figures. *Brain and Cognition, 29*, 103–114.

Gonzaga, G. C., Keltner, D., Londahl, E. A., & Smith, M. D. (2001). Love and the commitment problem in romantic relations and friendship. *Journal of Personality and Social Psychology, 81*, 247–262.

Goodale, M. A., & Milner, A. D. (1992). Separate visual pathways for perception and action. *Trends in Neurosciences, 15*, 20–25.

Goodale, M. A., & Milner, A. D. (2004). *Sight unseen*. Oxford, England: Oxford University Press.

Goodale, M. A., Milner, A. D., Jakobson, L. S., & Carey, D. P. (1991). A neurological dissociation between perceiving objects and grasping them. *Nature, 349*, 154–156.

Goodwin, P., McGill, B., & Chandra, A. (2009). *Who marries and when? Age at first marriage in the United States, 2002* (Data Brief 19). Hyattsville, MD: National Center for Health Statistics.

Gootman, E. (2003, March 3). Separated at birth in Mexico, united at campuses on Long Island. *New York Times*, p. A25.

Gopnik, A. (2012). Scientific thinking in young children: Theoretical advances, empirical research, and policy implications. *Science, 337*(6102), 1623–1627. doi:10.1126/science.1223416

Gorczynski, P., & Faulkner, G. (2011). Exercise therapy for schizophrenia. *Cochrane Database of Systematic Reviews, 5*, CD004412.

Gordon, P. (2004). Numerical cognition without words: Evidence from Amazonia. *Science, 306*, 496–499.

Gorno-Tempini, M. L., Price, C. J., Josephs, O., Vandenberghe, R., Cappa, S. F., Kapur, N., & Frackowiak, R. S. (1998). The neural systems sustaining face and proper-name processing. *Brain, 121*, 2103–2118.

Gotlib, I. H., & Joormann, J. (2010). Cognition and depression: Current status and future directions. *Annual Review of Clinical Psychology, 6*, 285–312.

Gottesman, I. I. (1991). *Schizophrenia genesis: The origins of madness*. New York: Freeman.

Gottesman, I. I., & Hanson, D. R. (2005). Human development: Biological and genetic processes. *Annual Review of Psychology, 56*, 263–286.

Gottfredson, L. S. (1997). Mainstream science on intelligence: An editorial with 52 signatories, history, and bibliography. *Intelligence, 24*, 13–23.

Gottfredson, L. S., & Deary, I. J. (2004). Intelligence predicts health and longevity, but why? *Current Directions in Psychological Science, 13*, 1–4.

Gottfried, J. A. (2008). Perceptual and neural plasticity of odor quality coding in the human brain. *Chemosensory Perception, 1*, 127–135.

Gouldner, A. W. (1960). The norm of reciprocity. *American Sociological Review, 25*, 161–178.

Graf, P., & Schacter, D. L. (1985). Implicit and explicit memory for new associations in normal subjects and amnesic patients. *Journal of Experimental Psychology: Learning, Memory, and Cognition, 11*, 501–518.

Grandin, T. (2006). *Thinking in pictures: My life with autism* (expanded edition). Visalia, CA: Vintage.

Grant, A. M. (2008). Personal life coaching for coaches-in-training enhances goal attainment, insight, and learning. *Coaching, 1*(1), 54–70.

Grant, B. F., Hasin, D. S., Stinson, F. S., Dawson, D. A., Chou, S. P., & Ruan, W. J. (2004). Prevalence, correlates, and disability of personality disorders in the U.S.: Results from the National Epidemiologic Survey on Alcohol and Related Conditions. *Journal of Clinical Psychiatry, 65*, 948–958.

Grassian, S. (2006). Psychiatric effects of solitary confinement. *Washington University Journal of Law and Policy, 22*, 325–383.

Gray, H. M., Gray, K., & Wegner, D. M. (2007). Dimensions of mind perception. *Science, 315*, 619.

Gray, J. A. (1970). The psychophysiological basis of introversion–extraversion. *Behavior Research and Therapy, 8*, 249–266.

Gray, J. A. (1990). Brain systems that mediate both emotion and cognition. *Cognition and Emotion, 4*, 269–288.

Green, C. S., & Bavelier, D. (2007). Action video-game experience alters the spatial resolution of vision. *Psychological Science, 18*, 88–94.

Green, D. A., & Swets, J. A. (1966). *Signal detection theory and psychophysics*. New York: Wiley.

Green, M. F., Kern, R. S., Braff, D. L., & Mintz, J. (2000). Neurocognitive deficits and functional outcome in schizophrenia: Are we measuring the "right stuff"? *Schizophrenia Bulletin, 26*, 119–136.

Green, S. K., Buchanan, D. R., & Heuer, S. K. (1984). Winners, losers, and choosers: A field investigation of dating initiation. *Personality and Social Psychology Bulletin, 10*, 502–511.

Greenberg, J., Solomon, S., & Arndt, J. (2008). A basic but uniquely human motivation: Terror management. In J. Y. Shah & W. L. Gardner (Eds.), *Handbook of motivation science* (pp. 114–134). New York: Guilford Press.

Greene, J. (2013). *Moral tribes: Emotion, reason, and the gap between us and them.* New York: Penguin.

Greene, J. D., Sommerville, R. B., Nystrom, L. E., Darley, J. M., & Cohen, J. D. (2001). An fMRI investigation of emotional engagement in moral judgment. *Science, 293,* 2105–2108.

Greenspan, L., & Deardorff, J. (2014). The new puberty: *How to navigate early development in today's girls.* Emmaus, PA: Rodale Books.

Greenwald, A. G., McGhee, D. E., & Schwartz, J. L. K. (1998). Measuring individual differences in implicit cognition: The Implicit Association Test. *Journal of Personality and Social Psychology, 74,* 1464–1480.

Greenwald, A. G., & Nosek, B. A. (2001). Health of the Implicit Association Test at age 3. *Zeitschrift für Experimentelle Psychologie, 48,* 85–93.

Gropp, E., Shanabrough, M., Borok, E., Xu, A. W., Janoschek, R., Buch, T., . . . Brüning, J. C. (2005). Agouti-related peptide-expressing neurons are mandatory for feeding. *Nature Neuroscience, 8,* 1289–1291.

Gross, J. J. (1998). Antecedent- and response-focused emotion regulation: Divergent consequences for experience, expression, and physiology. *Journal of Personality and Social Psychology, 74,* 224–237.

Gross, J. J. (2002). Emotion regulation: Affective, cognitive, and social consequences. *Psychophysiology, 39,* 281–291.

Gross, J. J., & Munoz, R. F. (1995). Emotion regulation and mental health. *Clinical Psychology: Science and Practice, 2,* 151–164.

Groves, B. (2004, August 2). Unwelcome awareness. *The San Diego Union-Tribune,* p. 24.

Grün, F., & Blumberg, B. (2006). Environmental obesogens: Organotins and endocrine disruption via nuclear receptor signaling. *Endocrinology, 147,* s50–s55.

Guerin, S. A., Robbins, C. A., Gilmore, A. W., & Schacter, D. L. (2012a). Interactions between visual attention and episodic retrieval: Dissociable contributions of parietal regions during gist-based false recognition. *Neuron, 75,* 1122–1134.

Guerin, S. A., Robbins, C. A., Gilmore, A. W., & Schacter, D. L. (2012b). Retrieval failure contributes to gist-based false recognition. *Journal of Memory and Language, 66,* 68–78.

Guillery, R. W., & Sherman, S. M. (2002). Thalamic relay functions and their role in corticocortical communication: Generalizations from the visual system. *Neuron, 33,* 163–175.

Gurwitz, J. H., McLaughlin, T. J., Willison, D. J., Guadagnoli, E., Hauptman, P. J., Gao, X., & Soumerai, S. B. (1997). Delayed hospital presentation in patients who have had acute myocardial infarction. *Annals of Internal Medicine, 126,* 593–599.

Gusnard, D. A., & Raichle, M. E. (2001). Searching for a baseline: Functional imaging and the resting human brain. *Nature Reviews: Neuroscience, 2,* 685–694.

Gustafsson, J.-E. (1984). A unifying model for the structure of intellectual abilities. *Intelligence, 8,* 179–203.

Gutchess, A. H., & Schacter, D. L. (2012). The neural correlates of gist-based true and false recognition. *NeuroImage, 59,* 3418–3426.

Guthrie, R. V. (2000). Kenneth Bancroft Clark (1914–). In A. E. Kazdin (Ed.), *Encyclopedia of Psychology* (Vol. 2, p. 91). Washington, DC: American Psychological Association.

Haase, C. M., Heckhausen, J., & Wrosch, C. (2013). Developmental regulation across the life span: Toward a new synthesis. *Developmental Psychology, 49*(5), 964–972. doi:10.1037/a0029231

Hackman, D. A., & Farah, M. J. (2008). Socioeconomic status and the developing brain. *Trends in Cognitive Sciences, 13,* 65–73.

Hackman, J. R., & Katz, N. (2010). Group behavior and performance. In S. T. Fiske, D. T. Gilbert, & G. Lindzey (Eds.), *The handbook of social psychology* (5th ed., Vol. 2, pp. 1208–1251). New York: Wiley.

Haedt-Matt, A. A., & Keel, P. K. (2011). Revisiting the affect regulation model of binge eating: A meta-analysis of studies using ecological momentary assessment. *Psychological Bulletin, 137*(4), 660–681.

Haggard, P., & Tsakiris, M. (2009). The experience of agency: Feelings, judgments, and responsibility. *Current Directions in Psychological Science, 18,* 242–246.

Haidt, J. (2001). The emotional dog and its rational tail: A social intuitionist approach to moral judgment. *Psychological Review, 108,* 814–834.

Haidt, J. (2006). *The happiness hypothesis: Finding modern truth in ancient wisdom.* New York: Basic Books.

Haidt, J., & Keltner, D. (1999). Culture and facial expression: Open-ended methods find more expressions and a gradient of recognition. *Cognition and Emotion, 13,* 225–266.

Halim, M. L., Ruble, D. N., Tamis-LeMonda, C. S., Zosuls, K. M., Lurye, L. E., & Greulich, F. K. (2014). Pink frilly dresses and the avoidance of all things "girly": Children's appearance rigidity and cognitive theories of gender development. *Developmental Psychology, 50*(4), 1091–1101. doi: 10.1037/a0034906

Hallett, M. (2000). Transcranial magnetic stimulation and the human brain. *Nature, 406,* 147–150.

Halpern, B. (2002). Taste. In H. Pashler & S. Yantis (Eds.), *Stevens' handbook of experimental psychology: Vol. 1. Sensation and perception* (3rd ed., pp. 653–690). New York: Wiley.

Halpern, D. F. (1997). Sex differences in intelligence: Implications for education. *American Psychologist, 52,* 1091–1102.

Halpern, D. F., Benbow, C. P., Geary, D. C., Gur, R. C., Hyde, J. S., & Gernsbacher, M. A. (2007). The science of sex differences in science and mathematics. *Psychological Science in the Public Interest, 8,* 1–51.

Hamermesh, D. S., & Biddle, J. E. (1994). Beauty and the labor market. *American Economic Review, 84,* 1174–1195.

Hamilton, A. F., & Grafton, S. T. (2006). Goal representation in human anterior intraparietal sulcus. *The Journal of Neuroscience, 26,* 1133–1137.

Hamilton, A. F., & Grafton, S. T. (2008). Action outcomes are represented in human inferior frontoparietal cortex. *Cerebral Cortex, 18,* 1160–1168.

Hamilton, D. L., & Gifford, R. K. (1976). Illusory correlation in interpersonal perception: A cognitive basis of stereotypic judgements. *Journal of Experimental Social Psychology, 12,* 392–407.

Hamilton, W. D. (1964). The genetical evolution of social behaviour. *Journal of Theoretical Biology, 7,* 1–16.

Hamlin, J. K., Mahajan, N., Liberman, Z., & Wynn, K. (2013). Not like me = bad: Infants prefer those who harm dissimilar others. *Psychological Science, 24*(4), 589–594. doi:10.1177/0956797612457785

Hamlin, J. K., Wynn, K., & Bloom, P. (2007). Social evaluation by preverbal infants. *Nature, 450*(7169), 557–559.

Haney, C., Banks, W. C., & Zimbardo, P. G. (1973). Study of prisoners and guards in a simulated prison. *Naval Research Reviews, 9,* 1–17.

Hannon, E. E., & Trainor, L. J. (2007). Music acquisition: Effects of enculturation and formal training on development. *Trends in Cognitive Sciences, 11,* 466–472.

Hansen, E. S., Hasselbalch, S., Law, I., & Bolwig, T. G. (2002). The caudate nucleus in obsessive-compulsive disorder. Reduced metabolism following treatment with paroxetine: A PET study. *International Journal of Neuropsychopharmacology, 5,* 1–10.

Happé, F. G. E. (1995). The role of age and verbal ability in the theory of mind performance of subjects with autism. *Child Development, 66,* 843–855.

Happé, F. & Frith, U. (2006). The weak coherence account: Detail-focused cognitive style in autism spectrum disorders. *Journal of Autism and Developmental Disorders, 36,* 5–25.

Happé, F. G. E., & Vital, P. (2009). What aspects of autism predispose to talent? *Philosophical Transactions of the Royal Society B: Biological Science, 364,* 1369–1375.

Harding, C. M., Brooks, G. W., Ashikaga, T., Strauss, J. S., & Brier, A. (1987). The Vermont longitudinal study of persons with severe mental illness, II: Long-term outcome of subjects who retrospectively met DSM-III criteria for schizophrenia. *American Journal of Psychiatry, 144,* 727–735.

Hare, R. D. (1998). *Without conscience: The disturbing world of the psychopaths among us.* New York: Guilford Press.

Harlow, H. F. (1958). The nature of love. *American Psychologist, 13,* 573–685.

Harlow, H. F., & Harlow, M. L. (1965). The affectional systems. In A. M. Schrier, H. F. Harlow, & F. Stollnitz (Eds.), *Behavior of nonhuman primates* (Vol. 2, pp. 287–334). New York: Academic Press.

Harlow, J. M. (1848). Passage of an iron rod through the head. *Boston Medical and Surgical Journal, 39,* 389–393.

Harmon-Jones, E., Harmon-Jones, C., & Levy, N. (2015). An action-based model of cognitive-dissonance processes. *Current Directions in Psychological Science, 24*(3), 184–189. doi: 10.1177/0963721414566449

Harris, P. L., de Rosnay, M., & Pons, F. (2005). Language and children's understanding of mental states. *Current Directions in Psychological Science, 14,* 69–73.

Harro, J. (2015). Neuropsychiatric adverse effects of amphetamine and methamphetamine. *International Review of Neurobiology, 120,* 179–204.

Hart, B., & Risley, T. R. (1995). *Meaningful differences in the everyday experience of young American children.* Baltimore, MD: Brookes.

Hart, B. L. (1988). Biological basis of the behavior of sick animals. *Neuroscience and Biobehavioral Reviews, 12,* 123–137.

Hart, W., Albarracin, D., Eagly, A. H., Lindberg, M. J., Merrill, L., & Brechan, I. (2009). Feeling validated versus being correct: A meta-analysis of selective exposure to information. *Psychological Bulletin, 135,* 555–588.

Hartshorne, H., & May, M. (1928). *Studies in deceit.* New York: Macmillan.

Hartshorne, J. K., & Germine, L. T. (2015). When does cognitive functioning peak? The asynchronous rise and fall of different cognitive abilities across the life span. *Psychological Science, 26* (4), 433–443. doi: 10.1177/0956797614567339

Haslam, C., Wills, A. J., Haslam, S. A., Kay, J., Baron, R., & McNab, F. (2007). Does maintenance of colour categories rely on language? Evidence to the contrary from a case of semantic dementia. *Brain and Language, 103,* 251–263.

Hassabis, D., Kumaran, D., Vann, S. D., & Maguire, E. A. (2007). Patients with hippocampal amnesia cannot imagine new experiences. *Proceedings of the National Academy of Sciences, USA, 104,* 1726–1731.

Hasselmo, M. E. (2006). The role of acetylcholine in learning and memory. *Current Opinion in Neurobiology, 16,* 710–715.

Hassin, R. R., Bargh, J. A., & Zimerman, S. (2009). Automatic and flexible: The case of non-conscious goal pursuit. *Social Cognition, 27,* 20–36.

Hassmen, P., Koivula, N., & Uutela, A. (2000). Physical exercise and psychological well-being: A population study in Finland. *Preventive Medicine, 30,* 17–25.

Hasson, U., Hendler, T., Bashat, D. B., & Malach, R. (2001). Vase or face? A neural correlate of shape-selective grouping processes in the human brain. *Journal of Cognitive Neuroscience, 13,* 744–753.

Hatemi, P. K., Gillespie, N. A., Eaves, L. J., Maher, B. S., Webb, B. T., Heath, A. C., . . . Martin, N. G. (2011). A genome-wide analysis of liberal and conservative political attitudes. *The Journal of Politics, 73,* 271–285.

Hatfield, E. (1988). Passionate and companionate love. In R. J. Sternberg & M. L. Barnes (Eds.), *The psychology of love* (pp. 191–217). New Haven, CT: Yale University Press.

Hatfield, E., & Rapson, R. L. (1992). Similarity and attraction in close relationships. *Communication Monographs, 59,* 209–212.

Hausser, M. (2000). The Hodgkin-Huxley theory of the action potential. *Nature Neuroscience, 3,* 1165.

Havas, D. A., Glenberg, A. M., Gutowski, K. A., Lucarelli, M. J., & Davidson, R. J. (2010). Cosmetic use of botulinum toxin-A affects processing of emotional language. *Psychological Science, 21*(7), 895–900. doi:10.1177/0956797610374742

Hawley, P. H. (2002). Social dominance and prosocial and coercive strategies of resource control in preschoolers. *International Journal of Behavioral Development, 26,* 167–176.

Haxby, J. V., Gobbini, M. I., Furey, M. L., Ishai, A., Schouten, J. L., & Pietrini, P. (2001). Distributed and overlapping representations of faces and objects in ventral temporal cortex. *Science, 293,* 2425–2430.

Hayes, J. E., Bartoshuk, L. M., Kidd, J. R., & Duffy, V. B. (2008). Supertasting and PROP bitterness depends on more than the TAS2R38 gene. *Chemical Senses, 23,* 255–265.

Hayes, S. C., Strosahl, K., & Wilson, K. G. (1999). *Acceptance and commitment therapy: An experiential approach to behavior change.* New York: Guilford Press.

Hay-McCutcheon, M. J., Kirk, K. I., Henning, S. C., Gao, S. J., & Qi, R. (2008). Using early outcomes to predict later language ability in children with cochlear implants. *Audiology and Neuro-Otology, 13,* 370–378.

Heath, S. B. (1983). *Way with words: Language, life and work in communities and classrooms.* Cambridge, England: Cambridge University Press.

Heatherton, T. F., & Weinberger, J. L. (Eds.). (1994). *Can personality change?* Washington, DC: American Psychological Association.

Heavey, C. L., Hurlburt, R. T., & Lefforge, N. L. (2012). Toward a phenomenology of feelings. *Emotion, 12*(4), 763–777.

Hebb, D. O. (1949). *The organization of behavior.* New York: Wiley.

Hebl, M. R., & Heatherton, T. F. (1997). The stigma of obesity in women: The difference is Black and White. *Personality and Social Psychology Bulletin, 24,* 417–426.

Hebl, M. R., & Mannix, L. M. (2003). The weight of obesity in evaluating others: A mere proximity effect. *Personality and Social Psychology Bulletin, 29,* 28–38.

Hedges, L. V., & Nowell, A. (1995). Sex differences in mental test scores, variability, and numbers of high-scoring individuals. *Science, 269*(5220), 41–45.

Heeren, A., Moqoase, C., Philippot, P., & McNally, R. J. (2015). Attention bias modification for social anxiety: A systematic review and meta-analysis. *Clinical Psychology Review, 40,* 76–90.

Heerey, E. A., Keltner, D., & Capps, L. M. (2003). Making sense of self-conscious emotion: Linking theory of mind and emotion in children with autism. *Emotion, 3,* 394–400.

Heine, S. J. (2010). Cultural psychology. In S. T. Fiske, D. T. Gilbert, & G. Lindzey (Eds.), *The handbook of social psychology* (5th ed., Vol. 2, pp. 1423–1464). New York: Wiley.

Heine, S. J., & Lehman, D. R. (1995). Cultural variation in unrealistic optimism: Does the West feel more invulnerable than the East? *Journal of Peronality and Social Psychology, 68,* 595–607.

Heiy, J. E., & Cheavens, J. S. (2014). Back to basics: A naturalistic assessment of the experience and regulation of emotion. *Emotion, 14*(5), 878–891. doi: 10.1037/a0037231

Helliwell, J., & Grover, S. (2014, December). How's life at home? New evidence on marriage and the set point for happiness. NBER Working Paper No. 20794.

Helt, M., Kelley, E., Kinsbourne, M., Pandey, J., Boorstein, H., Herbert, M., & Fein, D. (2008). Can children with autism recover? If so, how? *Neuropsychology Review, 18,* 339–366.

Henderlong, J., & Lepper, M. R. (2002). The effects of praise on children's intrinsic motivation: A review and synthesis. *Psychological Bulletin, 128,* 774–795.

Henrich, J., Heine, S. J., & Norenzayan, A. (2010). Most people are not WEIRD. *Nature, 466,* 29.

Henry, W. P., Strupp, H. H., Schacht, T. E., & Gaston, L. (1994). Psychodynamic approaches. In A. E. Bergin & S. L. Garfield (Eds.), *Handbook of psychotherapy and behavior change* (pp. 467–508). New York: Wiley.

Herman, C. P., Roth, D. A., & Polivy, J. (2003). Effects of the presence of others on food intake: A normative interpretation. *Psychological Bulletin, 129,* 873–886.

Herman-Giddens, M. E., Steffes, J., Harris, D., Slora, E., Hussey, M., Dowshen, S. A., & Reiter, E. O. (2012). Secondary sexual characteristics in boys: Data from the pediatric research in office settings network. *Pediatrics, 130*(5), e1058–e1068. doi: 10.1542/peds.2011-3291

Herring, M. P., Puetz, T. W., O'Connor, P. J., & Dishman, R. K. (2012). Effect of exercise training on depressive symptoms among patients with chronic illness: A systematic review and meta-analysis of randomized controlled trials. *Archives of Internal Medicine, 172,* 101–111.

Herrnstein, R. J. (1977). The evolution of behaviorism. *American Psychologist, 32,* 593–603.

Herz, R. S., & von Clef, J. (2001). The influence of verbal labeling on the perception of odors. *Perception, 30,* 381–391.

Heyes, C. (2016). Born pupils? Natural pedagogy and cultural pedagogy. *Perspectives on Psychological Science, 11*(2), 280–295. doi: 10.1177/1745691615621276

Heyes, C. M., & Foster, C. L. (2002). Motor learning by observation: Evidence from a serial reaction time task. *Quarterly Journal of Experimental Psychology (A), 55,* 593–607.

Heyman, G. M. (2009). *Addiction: A disorder of choice.* Cambridge, MA: Harvard University Press.

Heymsfield, S. B., Greenberg, A. S., Fujioka, K., Dixon, R. M., Kushner, R., Hunt, T., . . . McCarnish, M. (1999). Recombinant leptin for weight loss in obese and lean adults: A randomized, controlled, dose-escalation trial. *Journal of the American Medical Association, 282*(16), 1568–1575.

Hibbeln, J. R. (1998). Fish consumption and major depression. *Lancet, 351,* 1213.

Hickok, G. (2009). Eight problems for the mirror neuron theory of action understanding in monkeys and humans. *Journal of Cognitive Neuroscience, 21,* 1229–1243.

Higgins, E. T. (1987). Self-discrepancy theory: A theory relating self and affect. *Psychological Review, 94,* 319–340.

Higgins, E. T. (1997). Beyond pleasure and pain. *American Psychologist, 52,* 1280–1300.

Hilgard, E. R. (1965). *Hypnotic susceptibility.* New York: Harcourt, Brace and World.

Hilgard, E. R. (1986). *Divided consciousness: Multiple controls in human thought and action.* New York: Wiley-Interscience.

Hillman, C. H., Erickson, K. I., & Kramer, A. F. (2008). Be smart, exercise your heart: Exercise effects on brain and cognition. *Nature Reviews Neuroscience, 9,* 58–65.

Hilts, P. (1995). *Memory's ghost: The strange tale of Mr. M and the nature of memory.* New York: Simon & Schuster.

Hine, T. (1995). *The total package: The evolution and secret meanings of boxes, bottles, cans, and tubes.* Boston: Little, Brown.

Hintzman, D. L., Asher, S. J., & Stern, L. D. (1978). Incidental retrieval and memory for coincidences. In M. M. Gruneberg, P. E. Morris, & R. N. Sykes (Eds.), *Practical aspects of memory* (pp. 61–68). New York: Academic Press.

Hirsh-Pasek, K., Adamson, L. B., Bakeman, R., Owen, M. T., Golinkoff., R. M., Pace, A., . . . & Suma, K. (2015). The contribution of early communication quality to low-income children's language success. *Psychological Science, 26,* 1071–1083.

Hirst, W., & Echterhoff, G. (2012). Remembering in conversations: The social sharing and reshaping of memory. *Annual Review of Psychology, 63,* 55–79.

Hirst, W., Phelps, E. A., Buckner, R. L., Budson, A. E., Cuc, A., Gabrieli, J. D. E., . . . Vaidya, C. J. (2009). Long-term memory for the terrorist attack of September 11: Flashbulb memories, event memories, and the factors that influence their retention. *Journal of Experimental Psychology: General, 138,* 161–176.

Hirst, W., Phelps, E. A., Meksin, R., Vaidya, C. J., Johnson, M. K., Mitchell, K. J., . . . Olsson, A. (2015). A ten-year follow-up of a study of memory for the attack of September 11, 2001: Flashbulb memories and memories for flashbulb events. *Journal of Experimental Psychology: General, 144,* 604–623.

Hobson, J. A. (1988). *The dreaming brain.* New York: Basic Books.

Hobson, J. A., & McCarley, R. W. (1977). The brain as a dream-state generator: An activation–synthesis hypothesis of the dream process. *American Journal of Psychiatry, 134,* 1335–1368.

Hochberg, L. R., Bacher, D., Jarosiewicz, B., Masse, N. Y., Simeral, J. D., Vogel, J. . . . Donoghue, J. P. (2012). Reach and grasp by people with tetraplegia using a neurally controlled robotic arm. *Nature, 485,* 372–377.

Hockley, W. E. (2008). The effects of environmental context on recognition memory and claims of remembering. *Journal of Experimental Psychology: Learning, Memory, and Cognition, 34,* 1412–1429.

Hodgkin, A. L., & Huxley, A. F. (1939). Action potential recorded from inside a nerve fibre. *Nature, 144,* 710–712.

Hodson, G., & Sorrentino, R. M. (2001). Just who favors the ingroup? Personality differences in reactions to uncertainty in the minimal group paradigm. *Group Dynamics, 5,* 92–101.

Hoek, H. W. (2006). Incidence, prevalence and mortality of anorexia nervosa and other eating disorders. *Current Opinion in Psychiatry, 19*(4), 389–394. doi: 10.1097/01.yco.0000228759.95237.78

Hoek, H. W., & van Hoeken, D. (2003). Review of the prevalence and incidence of eating disorders. *International Journal of Eating Disorders, 34,* 383–396.

Hoffrage, U., & Gigerenzer, G. (1998). Using natural frequencies to improve diagnostic inferences. *Academic Medicine, 73,* 538–540.

Hofmann, W., Vohs, K. D., & Baumeister, R. F. (2012). What people desire, feel conflicted about, and try to resist in everyday life. *Psychological Science, 23,* 582–588.

Hogan, M. J., & Strasburger, V. C. (2008). Body image, eating disorders, and the media. *Adolescent Medicine: State of the Art Reviews, 19*(3), 521–46, x–xi. Retrieved from http://www.ncbi.nlm.nih.gov/pubmed/19227390

Hollins, M. (2010). Somesthetic senses. *Annual Review of Psychology, 61,* 243–271.

Holloway, G. (2001). *The complete dream book: What your dreams tell about you and your life.* Naperville, IL: Sourcebooks.

Holman, M. A., Carlson, M. L., Driscoll, C. L. W., Grim, K. J., Petersson, R., Sladen, D. P., & Flick, R. P. (2013). Cochlear implantation in children 12 months of age or younger. *Otology & Neurology, 34,* 251–258.

Holmbeck, G. N., & O'Donnell, K. (1991). Discrepancies between perceptions of decision making and behavioral autonomy. In R. L. Paikoff (Ed.), *New directions for child development: Shared views in the family during adolescence* (no. 51, pp. 51–69). San Francisco: Jossey-Bass.

Holmes, J., Gathercole, S. E., & Dunning, D. L. (2009). Adaptive training leads to sustained enhancement of poor working memory in children. *Developmental Science, 12,* F9–F15.

Holt-Lunstad, J., Smith, T. B., Baker, M., Harris, T., & Stephenson, D. (2015). Loneliness and social isolation as risk factors for mortality: A meta-analytic review. *Perspectives on Psychological Science, 10*(2), 227–237. doi: 10.1177/1745691614568352

Hölzel, B. K., Carmody, J., Vangel, M., Congleton, C., Yerramsetti, S. M., Gard, T., & Lazar, S. W. (2011). Mindfulness practice leads to increases in regained gray matter density. *Psychiatry Research: Neuroimaging, 191*(1), 36–43.

Homan, K. J., Houlihan, D., Ek, K., & Wanzek, J. (2012). Cultural differences in the level of rewards between adolescents from America, Tanzania, Denmark, Honduras, Korea, and Spain. *International Journal of Psychological Studies, 4,* 264–272.

Homans, G. C. (1961). *Social behavior.* New York: Harcourt, Brace and World.

Homonoff, T. (2013, March 27). Can small incentives have large effects? The impact of taxes versus bonuses on disposable bag use. Working Papers (Princeton University. Industrial Relations Section). Retrieved from http://arks.princeton.edu/ark:/88435/dsp014q77fr47j

Hooley, J. M. (2007). Expressed emotion and relapse of psychopathology. *Annual Review of Clinical Psychology, 3,* 329–352.

Horn, J. L., & Cattell, R. B. (1966). Refinement and test of the theory of fluid and crystallized general intelligences. *Journal of Educational Psychology, 5,* 253–270.

Horner, A. J., Bisby, J. A., Bush, D., Lin, W.-J., & Burgess, N. (2015). Evidence for holistic episodic recollection via hippocampal pattern completion. *Nature Communications, 6,* 7462. doi: 10.1038/ncomms8462

Horrey, W. J., & Wickens, C. D. (2006). Examining the impact of cell phone conversation on driving using meta-analytic techniques. *Human Factors, 48,* 196–205.

Horta, B. L., Victoria, C. G., Menezes, A. M., Halpern, R., & Barros, F. C. (1997). Low birthweight, preterm births and intrauterine growth retardation in relation to maternal smoking. *Pediatrics and Perinatal Epidemiology, 11,* 140–151.

Hosking, S. G., Young, K. L., & Regan, M. A. (2009). The effects of text messaging on young drivers. *Human Factors, 51,* 582–592.

Houlihan, D., Jesse, V. C., Levine, H. D., & Sombke, C. (1991). A survey of rewards for use with teenage children. *Child & Family Behavior Therapy, 13,* 1–12.

House, J. S., Landis, K. R., & Umberson, D. (1988). Social relationships and health. *Science, 241,* 540–545.

Howard, I. P. (2002). Depth perception. In S. Yantis & H. Pashler (Eds.), *Stevens' handbook of experimental psychology: Vol. 1. Sensation and perception* (3rd ed., pp. 77–120). New York: Wiley.

Howard, M. O., Brown, S. E., Garland, E. L., Perron, B. E., & Vaughn, M. G. (2011). Inhalant use and inhalant use disorders in the United States. *Addiction Science & Clinical Practice, 6,* 18–31.

Hoyert, D. L., & Xu, J. (2012). Deaths: Preliminary data for 2011. *National Vital Statistics Reports, 61,* 1–51.

Hubel, D. H. (1988). *Eye, brain, and vision.* New York: Freeman.

Hubel, D. H., & Wiesel, T. N. (1962). Receptive fields, binocular interaction and functional architecture in the cat's visual cortex. *Journal of Physiology, 160,* 106–154.

Hubel, D. H., & Wiesel, T. N. (1998). Early exploration of the visual cortex. *Neuron, 20,* 401–412.

Huesmann, L. R., Moise-Titus, J., Podolski, C.-L., & Eron, L. D. (2003). Longitudinal relations between children's exposure to TV violence and their aggressive and violent behavior in young adulthood: 1977–1992. *Developmental Psychology, 39,* 201–221.

Huibers, M. J., Cohen, Z. D., Lemmens, L. H., Arntz, A., Peeters, F. P., Cuijpers, P., & DeRubeis, R. J. (2015). Predicting optimal outcomes in cognitive therapy or interpersonal psychotherapy for depressed individuals using the personalized advantage index approach. *PLoS ONE, 10,* e0140771.

Hull, C. L. (1943). *Principles of behavior.* New York: Appleton-Century-Crofts.

Hull, C. L. (1930). Knowledge and purpose as habit mechanisms. *Psychological Review, 37,* 511–525.

Hunsley, J., & Di Giulio, G. (2002). Dodo bird, phoenix, or urban legend? The question of psychotherapy equivalence. *Scientific Review of Mental Health Practice, 1,* 13–24.

Hunt, E. B. (2011). *Human intelligence.* New York: Cambridge University Press.

Hunt, L. L., Eastwick, P. W., & Finkel, E. J. (2015). Leveling the playing field: Longer acquaintance predicts reduced assortative mating on attractiveness. *Psychological Science, 26*(7), 1046–1053. doi: 10.1177/0956797615579273

Hunt, M. (1959). *The natural history of love.* New York: Knopf.

Hunter, J. E., & Hunter, R. F. (1984). Validity and utility of alternative predictors of job performance. *Psychological Bulletin, 96,* 72–98.

Hussey, E., & Safford, A. (2009). Perception of facial expression in somatosensory cortex supports simulationist models. *The Journal of Neuroscience, 29*(2), 301–302.

Huxley, A. (1932). *Brave new world.* London: Chatto and Windus.

Huxley, A. (1954). *The doors of perception.* New York: Harper & Row.

Hyde, J. S. (2005). The gender similarities hypothesis. *American Psychologist, 60*(6), 581–592.

Hyde, K. L., Lerch, J., Norton, A., Forgeard, M., Winner, E., Evans, A. C., & Schlaug, G. (2009). Musical training shapes structural brain development. *Journal of Neuroscience, 29,* 3019–3025.

Hyman, I. E., Jr., Boss, S. M., Wise, B. M., McKenzie, K. E., & Caggiano, J. M. (2010). Did you see the unicycling clown? Inattentional blindness while walking and talking on a cell phone. *Applied Cognitive Psychology, 24*(5), 597–607.

Hyman, I. E., Jr., & Pentland, J. (1996). The role of mental imagery in the creation of false childhood memories. *Journal of Memory and Language, 35,* 101–117.

Hypericum Depression Trial Study Group. (2002). Effect of *Hypericum perforatum* (St. John's wort) in major depressive disorder: A randomized controlled trial. *Journal of the American Medical Association, 287,* 1807–1814.

Iacoboni, M. (2009). Imitation, empathy, and mirror neurons. *Annual Review of Psychology, 60,* 653–670.

Imbo, I., & LeFevre, J.-A. (2009). Cultural differences in complex addition: Efficient Chinese versus adaptive Belgians and Canadians. *Journal of Experimental Psychology: Learning, Memory, and Cognition, 35,* 1465–1476.

Inciardi, J. A. (2001). *The war on drugs III.* New York: Allyn & Bacon.

Ingvar, M., Ambros-Ingerson, J., Davis, M., Granger, R., Kessler, M., Rogers, G. A., . . . Lynch, G. (1997). Enhancement by an ampakine of memory encoding in humans. *Experimental Neurology, 146,* 553–559.

Inniss, D., Steiger, H., & Bruce, K. (2011). Threshold and subthreshold post-traumatic stress disorder in bulimic patients: Prevalences and clinical correlates. *Eating and Weight Disorders, 16*(1), e30–6. doi: 10.1007/BF03327518

Inui, A. (2001). Ghrelin: An orexigenic and somatotrophic signal from the stomach. *Nature Reviews Neuroscience, 2,* 551–560.

Irvine, J. T. (1978). Wolof "magical thinking": Culture and conservation revisited. *Journal of Cross-Cultural Psychology, 9,* 300–310.

Isaacowitz, D. M. (2012). Mood regulation in real time: Age differences in the role of looking. *Current Directions in Psychological Science, 21*(4), 237–242. doi:10.1177/0963721412448651

Isaacowitz, D. M., & Blanchard-Fields, F. (2012). Linking process and outcome in the study of emotion and aging. *Perspectives on Psychological Science, 7*(1), 3–17. doi:10.1177/1745691611424750

Isenberg, D. J. (1986). Group polarization: A critical review and meta-analysis. *Journal of Personality and Social Psychology, 50*(6), 1141–1151. doi:10.1037/0022-3514.50.6.1141

Ittelson, W. H. (1952). *The Ames demonstrations in perception.* Princeton, NJ: Princeton University Press.

Iturrate, I., Chavarriaga, R., Montesano, L., Minguez, J., & del R. Millán, J. (2015). Teaching brain-machine interfaces as an alternative paradigm to neuroprosthetics control. *Scientific Reports, 5,* Article number: 13893. doi: 10.1038/srep13893

Izard, C. E. (1971). *The face of emotion.* New York: Appleton-Century-Crofts.

Jablensky, A. (1997). The 100-year epidemiology of schizophrenia. *Schizophrenia Research, 28,* 111–125.

Jacobs, B. L. (1994). Serotonin, motor activity, and depression-related disorders. *American Scientist, 82,* 456–463.

Jacobson, T., & Hoffman, V. (1997). Children's attachment representations: Longitudinal relations to school behavior and academic competency in middle childhood and adolescence. *Developmental Psychology, 33,* 703–710.

Jaeger, A., Eisenkraemer, R. E., & Stein, L. M. (2015). Test-enhanced learning in third-grade children. *Educational Psychology, 35,* 513–521.

James, W. (1890). *The principles of psychology.* Cambridge, MA: Harvard University Press.

Jamieson, J. P., Koslov, K., Nock, M. K., & Mendes, W. B. (2013). Experiencing discrimination increases risk-taking. *Psychological Science, 24,* 131–139.

Jamieson, J. P., Mendes, W. B., Blackstock, E., & Schmader, T. (2010). Turning the knots in your stomach into bows: Reappraising arousal improves performance on the GRE. *Journal of Experimental Social Psychology, 46,* 208–212.

Jamieson, J. P., Mendes, W. B., & Nock, M. K. (2013). Improving acute stress responses: The power of reappraisal. *Current Directions in Psychological Science, 22*(1), 51–56.

Jamieson, J. P., Nock, M. K., & Mendes, W. B. (2013). Changing the conceptualization of stress in social anxiety disorder: Affective and physiological consequences. *Clinical Psychological Science.* Advance online publication. doi:10.1177/2167702613482119

Jamison, K. R. (1995). *An unquiet mind: A memoir of moods and madness.* New York: Random House.

Janicak, P. G., Dowd, S. M., Martis, B., Alam, D., Beedle, D., Krasuski, J., . . . Viana, M. (2002). Repetitive transcranial magnetic stimulation versus electroconvulsive therapy for major depression: Preliminary results of a randomized trial. *Biological Psychiatry, 51,* 659–667.

Janis, I. L. (1982). *Groupthink: Scientific studies of policy decisions and fiascoes.* Boston: Houghton-Mifflin.

Jarvella, R. J. (1970). Effects of syntax on running memory span for connected discourse. *Psychonomic Science, 19,* 235–236.

Jarvella, R. J. (1971). Syntactic processing of connected speech. *Journal of Verbal Learning and Verbal Behavior, 10,* 409–416.

Jaynes, J. (1976). *The origin of consciousness in the breakdown of the bicameral mind.* London: Allen Lane.

Jenkins, J. G., & Dallenbach, K. M. (1924). Obliviscence during sleep and waking. *American Journal of Psychology, 35,* 605–612.

John, O. P., & Srivastava, S. (1999). The Big Five trait taxonomy: History, measurement, and theoretical perspectives. In L. A. Pervin & O. P. John (Eds.), *Handbook of personality: Theory and research* (2nd ed., pp. 102–138). New York: Guilford Press.

Johnson, C. A., Xiao, L., Palmer, P., Sun, P., Wang, Q., Wei, Y. L., . . . Bechara, A. (2008). Affective decision-making deficits, linked to dysfunctional ventromedial prefrontal cortex, revealed in 10th grade Chinese adolescent binge drinkers. *Neuropsychologia, 46,* 714–726.

Johnson, D. H. (1980). The relationship between spike rate and synchrony in responses of auditory-nerve fibers to single tones. *Journal of the Acoustical Society of America, 68,* 1115–1122.

Johnson, D. R., & Wu, J. (2002). An empirical test of crisis, social selection, and role explanations of the relationship between marital disruption and psychological distress: A pooled time-series analysis of four-wave panel data. *Journal of Marriage and the Family, 64,* 211–224.

Johnson, J. S., & Newport, E. L. (1989). Critical period effects in second language learning: The influence of maturational state on the acquisition of English as a second language. *Cognitive Psychology, 21,* 60–99.

Johnson, K. (2002). Neural basis of haptic perception. In H. Pashler & S. Yantis (Eds.), *Stevens' handbook of experimental psychology: Vol. 1. Sensation and perception* (3rd ed., pp. 537–583). New York: Wiley.

Johnson, M. K., Hashtroudi, S., & Lindsay, D. S. (1993). Source monitoring. *Psychological Bulletin, 114,* 3–28.

Johnson, S. L., Cuellar, A. K., & Miller, C. (2009). Unipolar and bipolar depression: A comparison of clinical phenomenology, biological vulnerability, and psychosocial predictors. In I. H. Gottlib & C. L. Hammen (Eds.), *Handbook of depression* (2nd ed., pp. 142–162). New York: Guilford Press.

Johnson, S. L., Cuellar, A. K., Ruggiero, C., Winnett-Perman, C., Goodnick, P., White, R., & Miller, I. (2008). Life events as predictors of mania and depression in bipolar 1 disorder. *Journal of Abnormal Psychology, 117,* 268–277.

Johnson, S. L., & Miller, I. (1997). Negative life events and time to recover from episodes of bipolar disorder. *Journal of Abnormal Psychology, 106,* 449–457.

Jokela, M., Elovainio, M., Singh-Manoux, A., & Kivimaki, M. (2009). IQ, socioeconomic status, and early death: The US National Longitudinal Survey of Youth. *Psychosomatic Medicine, 71*(3), 322–328. doi: 10.1097/PSY.0b013e31819b69f6

Jonas, E., Graupmann, V., Kayser, D. N., Zanna, M., Traut-Mattausch, E., & Frey, D. (2009). Culture, self, and the emergence of reactance: Is there a "universal" freedom? *Journal of Experimental Social Psychology, 45,* 1068–1080.

Jones, B. C., Little, A. C., Penton-Voak, I. S., Tiddeman, B. P., Burt, D. M., & Perrett, D. I. (2001). Facial symmetry and judgements of apparent health: Support for a "good genes" explanation of the attractiveness– symmetry relationship. *Evolution and Human Behavior, 22,* 417–429.

Jones, E. E., & Harris, V. A. (1967). The attribution of attitudes. *Journal of Experimental Social Psychology, 3,* 1–24.

Jones, E. E., & Nisbett, R. E. (1972). The actor and the observer: Divergent perceptions of the causes of behavior. In E. E. Jones, D. E. Kanouse, H. H. Kelley, R. E. Nisbett, S. Valins, & B. Weiner (Eds.), *Attribution: Perceiving the causes of behavior* (pp. 79–94). Morristown, NJ: General Learning Press.

Jones, S. S. (2007). Imitation in infancy. *Psychological Science, 18*(7), 593–599.

Jonsson, H., & Hougaard, E. (2008). Group cognitive behavioural therapy for obsessive-compulsive disorder: A systematic review and meta-analysis. *Acta Psychiatrica Scandinavica, 117,* 1–9.

Jordan, S. A., Cunningham, D. G., & Marles, R. J. (2010). Assessment of herbal medicinal products: Challenges and opportunities to increase the knowledge base for safety assessment. *Toxicology and Applied Pharmacology, 243,* 198–216.

Judd, L. L. (1997). The clinical course of unipolar major depressive disorders. *Archives of General Psychiatry, 54,* 989–991.

Jurewicz, I., Owen, R. J., & O'Donovan, M. C. (2001). Searching for susceptibility genes in schizophrenia. *European Neuropsychopharmacology, 11,* 395–398.

Kaas, J. H. (1991). Plasticity of sensory and motor maps in adult mammals. *Annual Review of Neuroscience, 14,* 137–167.

Kahneman, D. (2011). *Thinking fast and slow.* New York: Farrar, Straus and Giroux.

Kahneman, D., & Deaton, A. (2010). High income improves evaluation of life but not emotional well-being. *Proceedings of the National Academy of Sciences, 107,* 16489–16493.

Kahneman, D., Krueger, A. B., Schkade, D. A., Schwarz, N., & Stone, A. A. (2004). A survey method for characterizing daily life experience: The day reconstruction method. *Science, 306,* 1776–1780.

Kahneman, D., & Tversky, A. (1973). On the psychology of prediction. *Psychological Review, 80,* 237–251.

Kahneman, D., & Tversky, A. (1979). Prospect theory: An analysis of decision under risk. *Econometrica, 47,* 263–291.

Kahneman, D., & Tversky, A. (1984). Choices, values, and frames. *American Psychologist, 39,* 341–350.

Kalb. J. (2015, January 12). Give me a smile. *New Yorker.*

Kalokerinos, E. K., Greenaway, K. H., & Denson, T. F. (2015). Reappraisal but not suppression downregulates the experience of positive and negative emotion. *Emotion, 15*(3), 271–275. doi: 10.1037/emo0000025

Kamin, L. J. (1959). The delay-of-punishment gradient. *Journal of Comparative and Physiological Psychology, 52,* 434–437.

Kan, P. F., & Kohnert, K. (2008). Fast mapping by bilingual preschool children. *Journal of Child Language, 35,* 495–514.

Kandel, E. R. (2000). Nerve cells and behavior. In E. R. Kandel, G. H. Schwartz, & T. M. Jessell (Eds.), *Principles of neural science* (pp. 19–35). New York. McGraw-Hill.

Kandel, E. R. (2006). *In search of memory: The emergence of a new science of mind.* New York: Norton.

Kang, S. H. K., McDermott, K. B., & Roediger, H. L., III. (2007). Test format and corrective feedback modify the effect of testing on long-term retention. *European Journal of Cognitive Psychology, 19,* 528–558.

Kann, L., Kinchen, S., Shanklin, S. L., Flint, K. H., Hawkins, J., Harris, W. A., . . . Zaza, S. (2014). *Youth risk behavior surveillance—United States, 2013.* MMWR 2014;63(SS6304). U.S. Centers for Disease Control and Prevention. Retrieved from http://www.cdc.gov/mmwr/pdf/ss/ss6304.pdf

Kanwisher, N., McDermott, J., & Chun, M. M. (1997). The fusiform face area: A module in human extrastriate cortex specialized for face perception. *The Journal of Neuroscience, 17,* 4302–4311.

Kanwisher, N., & Yovel, G. (2006). The fusiform face area: A cortical region specialized for the perception of faces. *Philosophical Transactions of the Royal Society (B), 361,* 2109–2128.

Kaplan, R. M., & Stone, A. A. (2013). Bringing the laboratory and clinic to the community: Mobile technologies for health promotion and disease prevention. *Annual Review of Psychology, 64,* 471–498.

Kapur, S., Craik, F. I. M., Tulving, E., Wilson, A. A., Houle, S., & Brown, G. M. (1994). Neuroanatomical correlates of encoding in episodic memory: Levels of processing effects. *Proceedings of the National Academy of Sciences, USA, 91,* 2008–2011.

Karlins, M., Coffman, T. L., & Walters, G. (1969). On the fading of social stereotypes: Studies in three generations of college students. *Journal of Personality and Social Psychology, 13,* 1–16.

Karney, B. R., & Bradbury, T. N. (1995). The longitudinal course of marital quality and stability: A review of theory, methods, and research. *Psychological Bulletin, 118,* 3–34.

Karow, A., Pajonk, F. G., Reimer, J., Hirdes, F., Osterwald, C., Naber, D., & Moritz, S. (2007). The dilemma of insight into illness in schizophrenia: Self- and expert-rated insight and quality of life. *European Archives of Psychiatry and Clinical Neuroscience, 258,* 152–159.

Karpicke, J. D. (2012). Retrieval-based learning: Active retrieval promotes meaningful learning. *Current Directions in Psychological Science, 21,* 157–163.

Karpicke, J. D., & Aue, W. R. (2015). The testing effect is alive and well with complex materials. *Educational Psychology Review, 27,* 317–326.

Karpicke, J. D., & Blunt, J. R. (2011). Retrieval practice produces more learning than elaborative studying with concept mapping. *Science, 331,* 772–775.

Karpicke, J. D., & Roediger, H. L., III. (2008). The critical importance of retrieval for learning. *Science, 319,* 966–968.

Kasser, T., & Sharma, Y. S. (1999). Reproductive freedom, educational equality, and females' preference for resource-acquisition characteristics in mates. *Psychological Science, 10,* 374–377.

Kassin, S. M. (2007). Internalized false confessions. In M. Toglia, J. Read, D. Ross, & R. Lindsay (Eds.), *Handbook of eyewitness psychology: Volume 1, Memory for events* (pp. 175–192). Mahwah, NJ: Erlbaum.

Kassin, S. M. (2015). The social psychology of false confessions. *Social Issues and Policy Review, 9,* 25–51.

Katon, W. (1994). Primary care—psychiatry panic disorder management. In B. E. Wolfe & J. D. Maser (Eds.), *Treatment of panic disorder: A consensus development conference* (pp. 41–56). Washington, DC: American Psychiatric Press.

Katz, D., & Braly, K. (1933). Racial stereotypes of one hundred college students. *Journal of Abnormal and Social Psychology, 28,* 280–290.

Kaufman, A. S. (2001). WAIS-III IQs, Horn's theory, and generational changes from young adulthood to old age. *Intelligence, 29,* 131–167.

Kaufman, L. (2009, January 30). Utilities turn their customers green, with envy. *New York Times.* Retrieved from http://www.nytimes.com/2009/01/31/science/earth/31compete.html

Kawakami, K., Dovidio, J. F., Moll, J., Hermsen, S., & Russin, A. (2000). Just say no (to stereotyping): Effects of training in the negation of stereotypic associations on stereotype activation. *Journal of Personality and Social Psychology, 78,* 871–888.

Kayyal, M., Widen, S., & Russell, J. A. (2015). Context is more powerful than we think: Contextual cues override facial cues even for valence. *Emotion, 15*(3), 287–291. doi: 10.1037/ emo0000032

Kazdin, A. E., & Blasé, S. L. (2011). Rebooting psychotherapy research and practice to reduce the burden of mental illness. *Perspectives on Psychological Science, 6,* 21–37.

Keane, T. M., Marshall, A. D., & Taft, C. T. (2006). Posttraumatic stress disorder: Etiology, epidemiology, and treatment outcome. *Annual Review of Clinical Psychology, 2,* 161–197.

Keefe, F. J., Lumley, M., Anderson, T., Lynch, T., & Carson, K. L. (2001). Pain and emotion: New research directions. *Journal of Clinical Psychology, 57,* 587–607.

Kelley, H. H. (1983). Love and commitment. In H. H. Kelley, E. Berscheid, A. Christensen, & J. H. Harvey (Eds.), *Close relationships* (pp. 265–314). New York: W. H. Freeman and Company.

Kelley, M. R., Neath, I., & Surprenant, A. M. (2013). Three more semantic serial position functions and a SIMPLE explanation. *Memory & Cognition, 41,* 600–610.

Kelly, G. (1955). *The psychology of personal constructs.* New York: Norton.

Kelm, Z., Womer, J., Walter, J. K., & Feudtner, C. (2014) Interventions to cultivate physician empathy: A systematic review. *BMC Medical Education, 14,* 219.

Keltner, D. (1995). Signs of appeasement: Evidence for the distinct displays of embarrassment, amusement, and shame. *Journal of Personality and Social Psychology, 68,* 441–454.

Keltner, D., & Buswell, B. N. (1996). Evidence for the distinctness of embarrassment, shame, and guilt: A study of recalled antecedents and facial expressions of emotion. *Cognition and Emotion, 10,* 155–171.

Keltner, D., & Haidt, J. (1999). Social functions of emotions at four levels of analysis. *Cognition and Emotion, 13,* 505–521.

Keltner, D., & Harker, L. A. (1998). The forms and functions of the nonverbal signal of shame. In P. Gilbert & B. Andrews (Eds.), *Shame: Interpersonal behavior, psychopathology, and culture* (pp. 78–98). New York: Oxford University Press.

Kendler, K. S., Hettema, J. M., Butera, F., Gardner, C. O., & Prescott, C. A. (2003). Life event dimensions of loss, humiliation, entrapment, and danger in the prediction of onsets of major depression and generalized anxiety. *Archives of General Psychiatry, 60,* 789–796.

Kenrick, D. T., Sadalla, E. K., Groth, G., & Trost, M. R. (1990). Evolution, traits, and the stages of human courtship: Qualifying the parental investment model. *Journal of Personality, 58,* 97–116.

Kensinger, E. A., Clarke, R. J., & Corkin, S. (2003). What neural correlates underlie successful encoding and retrieval? A functional magnetic resonance imaging study using a divided attention paradigm. *The Journal of Neuroscience, 23,* 2407–2415.

Kensinger, E. A., & Schacter, D. L. (2005). Emotional content and reality monitoring ability: fMRI evidence for the influence of encoding processes. *Neuropsychologia, 43,* 1429–1443.

Kensinger, E. A., & Schacter, D. L. (2006). Amygdala activity is associated with the successful encoding of item, but not source, information for positive and negative stimuli. *The Journal of Neuroscience, 26,* 2564–2570.

Keo-Meier, C. L., Herman, L. I., Reisner, S. L., Pardo, S. T., Sharp, C., & Babcock, J. C. (2015). Testosterone treatment and MMPI–2 improvement in transgender men: A prospective controlled study. *Journal of Consulting and Clinical Psychology, 83,* 143–156.

Kerr, N. L., & Tindale, R. S. (2004). Group performance and decision making. *Annual Review of Psychology, 55,* 623–655. doi: 10.1146/annurev.psych.55.090902.142009

Kessler, R. C. (2012). The costs of depression. *Psychiatric Clinics of North America, 35,* 1–14.

Kessler, R. C., Adler, L., Barkley, R., Biederman, J., Connors, C. K., Demler, O., . . . Zaslavsky, A. M. (2006). The prevalence and correlates of adult ADHD in the United States: Results from the National Comorbidity Study Replication. *American Journal of Psychiatry, 163,* 716–723.

Kessler, R. C., Angermeyer, M., Anthony, J. C., deGraaf, R., Demyittenaere, K., Gasquet, I., . . . Üstün, T. B. (2007). Lifetime prevalence and age-of-onset distributions of mental disorders in the World Health Organization World Mental Health Survey Initiative. *World Psychiatry, 6,* 168–176.

Kessler, R. C., Berglund, P., Demler, M. A., Jin, R., Merikangas, K. R., & Walters, E. E. (2005). Lifetime prevalence and age-of-onset distributions of *DSM–IV* disorders in the National Comorbidity Survey replication. *Archives of General Psychiatry, 62,* 593–602.

Kessler, R. C., Chiu, W. T., Jin, R., Ruscio, A. M., Shear, K., & Walters, E. E. (2006). The epidemiology of panic attacks, panic disorder, and agoraphobia in the National Comorbidity Survey Replication. *Archives of General Psychiatry, 63,* 415–424.

Kessler, R. C., Demler, O., Frank, R. G., Olfson, M., Pincus, H. A., Walters, E. E., . . . Zaslavsky, A. M. (2005). Prevalence and treatment of mental disorders, 1990 to 2003. *New England Journal of Medicine, 352*(24), 2515–2523.

Kessler, R. C., Petukhova, M., Sampson, N. A., Zaslavsky, A. M., & Wittchen, H. U. (2012). Twelve-month and lifetime prevalence and lifetime morbid risk of anxiety and mood disorders in the United States. *International Journal of Methods in Psychiatric Research, 21*(3), 169–184.

Kessler, R. C., Soukup, J., Davis, R. B., Foster, D. F., Wilkey, S. A., Van Rompay, M. I., & Eisenberg, D. M. (2001). The use of complementary and alternative therapies to treat anxiety and depression in the United States. *American Journal of Psychiatry, 158,* 289–294.

Kessler, R. C., & Üstün, T. B. (Eds.) (2008). *The WHO Mental Health surveys: Global perspectives on the epidemiology of mental health.* Cambridge, England: Cambridge University Press.

Khalid, N., Atkins, M., Tredget, J., Giles, M., Champney-Smith, K., & Kirov, G. (2008). The effectiveness of electroconvulsive therapy in treatment-resistant depression: A naturalistic study. *The Journal of ECT, 24,* 141–145.

Khan, R. M., Luk, C.-H., Flinker, A., Aggarwal, A., Lapid, H., Haddad, R., & Sobel, N. (2007). Predicting odor pleasantness from odorant structure: Pleasantness as a reflection of the physical world. *Journal of Neuroscience, 27,* 10015–10023.

Kiecolt-Glaser, J. K., Garner, W., Speicher, C., Penn, G., & Glaser, R. (1984). Psychosocial modifiers of immunocompetence in medical students. *Psychosomatic Medicine, 46,* 7–14.

Kiefer, H. M. (2004). *Americans unruffled by animal testing.* Retrieved August 8, 2009, from http://www.gallup.com/poll/11767/Americans-Unruffled-Animal-Testing.aspx

Kiehl, K. A., Smith, A. M., Hare, R. D., Mendrek, A., Forster, B. B., Brink, J., & Liddle, P. F. (2001). Limbic abnormalities in affective processing by criminal psychopaths as revealed by functional magnetic resonance imaging. *Biological Psychiatry, 50,* 677–684.

Kihlstrom, J. F. (1985). Hypnosis. *Annual Review of Psychology, 36,* 385–418.

Kihlstrom, J. F. (1987). The cognitive unconscious. *Science, 237,* 1445–1452.

Kihlstrom, J. F., Beer, J. S., & Klein, S. B. (2002). Self and identity as memory. In M. R. Leary & J. P. Tangney (Eds.), *Handbook of self and identity* (pp. 68–90). New York: Guilford Press.

Killingsworth, M. A., & Gilbert, D. T. (2010). A wandering mind is an unhappy mind. *Science, 330,* 932.

Kim, G., Walden, T. A., & Knieps, L. J. (2010). Impact and characteristics of positive and fearful emotional messages during infant social referencing. *Infant Behavior and Development, 33,* 189–195.

Kim, J. W., & King, B. G. (2014). Seeing stars: Matthew effects and status bias in Major League Baseball umpiring. *Management Science, 60*(11), 2619–2644. doi: 10.1287/mnsc.2014.1967

Kim, K., & Smith, P. K. (1998). Childhood stress, behavioural symptoms and mother–daughter pubertal development. *Journal of Adolescence, 21,* 231–240.

Kim, U. K., Jorgenson, E., Coon, H., Leppert, M., Risch, N., & Drayna, D. (2003). Positional cloning of the human quantitive trait locus underlying taste sensitivity to phenylthiocarbamide. *Science, 299,* 1221–1225.

Kinney, D. A. (1993). From nerds to normals—the recovery of identity among adolescents from middle school to high school. *Sociology of Education, 66,* 21–40.

Kirchner, W. H., & Towne, W. F. (1994). The sensory basis of the honeybee's dance language. *Scientific American, 270*(6), 74–80.

Kirsch, I., Cardena, E., Derbyshire, S., Dienes, Z., Heap, M., Kallio, S., . . . Whalley, M. (2011). Definitions of hypnosis and hypnotizability and their relation to suggestion and suggestibility: A consensus statement. *Contemporary Hypnosis and Integrative Therapy, 28,* 107–115.

Kirsch, I., Deacon, B. J., Huedo-Medine, T. B., Scoboria, A., Moore, T. J., & Johnson, B. T. (2008). Initial severity and antidepressant benefits: A meta-analysis of data submitted to the Food and Drug Administration. *PLoS Medicine, 5*, e45.

Kirwan, C. B., Bayley, P. J., Galvan, V. V., & Squire, L. R. (2008). Detailed recollection of remote autobiographical memory after damage to the medial temporal lobe. *Proceedings of the National Academy of Sciences, USA, 105*, 2676–2680.

Kish, S. J., Lerch, J., Furukawa, Y. , Tong, J., McCluskey, T., Wilkins, D., . . . Bioleau, I. (2010). Decreased cerebral cortical serotonin transporter binding in ecstacy users: A positron emission tomography [11c] DASB and structural brain imaging study. *Brain, 133*, 1779–1797.

Kitayama, S., Duffy, S., Kawamura, T., & Larsen, J. T. (2003). Perceiving an object and its context in different cultures: A cultural look at the new look. *Psychological Science, 14*, 201–206.

Kitayama, S., & Uskul, A. K. (2011). Culture, mind, and the brain: Current evidence and future directions. *Annual Review of Psychology, 62*, 419–449.

Klarer, M., Arnold, M., Günther, L., Winter, C., Langhans, W., & Meyer, U. (2014) Gut vagal afferents differentially modulate innate anxiety and learned fear. *Journal of Neuroscience, 34*, 7067–7076.

Klein, C. T. F., & Helweg-Larsen, M. (2002). Perceived control and the optimistic bias: A meta-analytic review. *Psychology and Health, 17*, 437–446.

Klein, S. B. (2004). The cognitive neuroscience of knowing one's self. In M. Gazzaniga (Ed.), *The cognitive neurosciences* (3rd ed., pp. 1007–1089). Cambridge, MA: MIT Press.

Klein, S. B., Robertson, T. E., & Delton, A. W. (2011). The future-orientation of memory: Planning as a key component mediating the high levels of recall found with survival processing. *Memory, 19*, 121–139.

Klinger, E. (1975). Consequences of commitment to and disengagement from incentives. *Psychological Review, 82*, 1–25.

Klinger, E. (1977). *Meaning and void*. Minneapolis: University of Minnesota Press.

Klonsky, E. D. (2011). Non-suicidal self-injury in United States adults: Prevalence, sociodemographics, topography, and functions. *Psychological Medicine, 41*, 1981–1986.

Klump, K. L., & Culbert, K. M. (2007). Molecular genetic studies of eating disorders: Current status and future directions. *Current Directions in Psychological Science, 16*(1), 37–41.

Klump, K. L., Strober, M., Bulik, C. M., Thornton, L., Johnson, C., Devlin, B., . . . Kaye, W. H. (2004). Personality characteristics of women before and after recovery from an eating disorder. *Psychological Medicine, 34*(8), 1407–1418. doi: 10.1017/S0033291704002442

Klüver, H., & Bucy, P. C. (1937). "Psychic blindness" and other symptoms following bilateral temporary lobectomy in rhesus monkeys. *American Journal of Physiology, 119*, 352–353.

Knowlton, B. J., Ramus, S. J., & Squire, L. R. (1992). Intact artificial grammar learning in amnesia: Dissociation of classification learning and explicit memory for specific instances. *Psychological Science, 3*, 173–179.

Knutson, B., Wolkowitz, O. M., Cole, S. W., Chan, T., Moore, E. A., Johnson, R. C., & Reus, V. I. (1998). Selective alteration of personality and social behavior by serotonergic intervention. *American Journal of Psychiatry, 155*, 373–379.

Kobasa, S. (1979). Stressful life events, personality, and health: An inquiry into hardiness. *Journal of Personality and Social Psychology, 37*, 1–11.

Koffka, K. (1935). *Principles of Gestalt psychology*. New York: Harcourt, Brace and World.

Kohlberg, L. (1958). *The development of modes of thinking and choices in years 10 to 16*. Unpublished doctoral dissertation, University of Chicago.

Kohlberg, L. (1963). Development of children's orientation towards a moral order (Part I). Sequencing in the development of moral thought. *Vita Humana, 6*, 11–36.

Kohlberg, L. (1986). A current statement on some theoretical issues. In S. Modgil & C. Modgil (Eds.), *Lawrence Kohlberg: Concensus and controversy* (pp. 485–546). Philadelphia: Falmer.

Kohler, P. K., Manhart, L. E., & Lafferty, E. (2008). Abstinence-only and comprehensive sex education and the initiation of sexual activity and teen pregnancy. *Journal of Adolescent Health, 42*, 344–351.

Kolb, B., & Whishaw, I. Q. (2003). *Fundamentals of human neuropsychology* (5th ed.). New York: Worth Publishers.

Kolbert, E. (2009, July 20). XXXL. *The New Yorker*, pp. 73–77.

Koller, D. (2011, December 5). Death knell for the lecture: Technology as a passport to personalized education. Retrieved from http://www.nytimes.com/2011/12/06/science/daphne-koller-technology-as-a-passport-to-personalized-education.html?pageswanted=all

Kolotkin, R. L., Meter, K., & Williams, G. R. (2001). Quality of life and obesity. *Obesity Reviews, 2*, 219–229.

Komter, A. (2010). The evolutionary origins of human generosity. *International Sociology, 25*(3), 443–464.

Kosaba, S. C., Maddi, S. R., & Kahn, S. (1979). Hardiness and health: A prospective study. *Journal of Personality and Social Psychology, 42*, 168–177.

Kosslyn, S. M., Alpert, N. M., Thompson, W. L., Chabris, C. F., Rauch, S. L., & Anderson, A. K. (1993). Visual mental imagery activates topographically organized visual cortex: PET investigations. *Journal of Cognitive Neuroscience, 5*, 263–287.

Kosslyn, S. M., Thompson, W. L., Constantini-Ferrando, M. F., Alpert, N. M., & Spiegel, D. (2000). Hypnotic visual illusion alters color processing in the brain. *American Journal of Psychiatry, 157*, 1279–1284.

Kovalevskaya, S. (1978). *A Russian childhood*. New York: Springer-Verlag.

Kraemer, H. C., Shrout, P. E., & Rubio-Stipec, M. (2007). Developing the *Diagnostic and Statistical Manual–V*: What will "statistical" mean in *DSM–V*? *Social Psychiatry and Psychiatric Epidemiology, 42*, 259–267.

Krantz, D. S., & McCeney, M. K. (2002). Effects of psychological and social factors on organic disease: A critical assessment of research on coronary heart disease. *Annual Review of Psychology, 53*, 341–369.

Kraus, M. W., Piff, P. K., & Keltner, D. (2011). Social class as culture: The convergence of resources and rank in the social realm. *Current Directions in Psychological Science, 20*(4), 246–250. doi: 10.1177/0963721411414654

Kraus, N., & Chandrasekaran, B. (2010). Music training for the development of auditory skills. *Nature Reviews Neuroscience, 11*, 599–605.

Kravitz, D. J., Saleem, K. S., Baker, C. I., & Mishkin, M. (2011). A new neural framework for visuospatial processing. *Nature Reviews Neuroscience, 12*, 217–230.

Kravitz, D. J., Saleem, K. S., Baker, C. I., Ungerleider, L. G., & Mishkin, M. (2013). The ventral visual pathway: An expanded neural framework for the processing of object quality. *Trends in Cognitive Sciences, 17*, 26–49.

Kravitz, R. L., Epstein, R. M., Feldman, M. D., Franz, C. E., Azari, R., Wilkes, M. S., . . . Franks, P. (2005). Influence of patients' requests for direct-to-consumer advertised antidepressants: A randomized controlled trial. *Journal of the American Medical Association, 293*, 1995–2002.

Kreider, T. (2013, January 20). You are going to die. *New York Times*. Retrieved from http://opinionator.blogs.nytimes.com/2013/01/20/you-are-going-to-die/

Krings, T., Topper, R., Foltys, H., Erberich, S., Sparing, R., Willmes, K., & Thron, A. (2000). Cortical activation patterns during complex motor tasks in piano players and control subjects. A functional magnetic resonance imaging study. *Neuroscience Letters, 278*, 189–193.

Kristensen, P., & Bjerkedal, T. (2007). Explaining the relation between birth order and intelligence. *Science, 316*, 1717.

Kroeze, W. K., & Roth, B. L. (1998). The molecular biology of serotonin receptors: Therapeutic implications for the interface of mood and psychosis. *Biological Psychiatry, 44*, 1128–1142.

Kruk, M. R., Halasz, J., Meelis, W., & Haller, J. (2004). Fast positive feedback between the adrenocortical stress response and a brain mechanism involved in aggressive behavior. *Behavioral Neuroscience, 118,* 1062–1070.

Kubovy, M. (1981). Concurrent-pitch segregation and the theory of indispensable attributes. In M. Kubovy & J. R. Pomerantz (Eds.), *Perceptual organization* (pp. 55–96). Hillsdale, NJ: Erlbaum.

Kucyi, A., & Davis, K. D. (2015). The dynamic pain connectome. *Trends in Neurosciences, 38,* 86–95.

Kuhl, B. A., Dudukovic, N. M., Kahn, I., & Wagner, A. D. (2007). Decreased demands on cognitive control reveal the neural processing benefits of forgetting. *Nature Neuroscience, 10,* 908–917.

Kuhl, P. K., & Meltzoff, A. N. (1996). Infant vocalizations in response to speech: Vocal imitation and developmental change. *The Journal of the Acoustical Society of America, 100*(4), 2425. doi:10.1121/1.417951

Kuhn, S., & Gallinat, J. (2012). The neural correlates of subjective pleasantness. *NeuroImage, 61,* 289–294.

Kunda, Z. (1990). The case for motivated reasoning. *Psychological Bulletin, 108,* 480–498.

Kunz, P. R., & Woolcott, M. (1976). Season's greetings: From my status to yours. *Social Science Research, 5,* 269–278.

Kvavilashvili, L., Mirani, J., Schlagman, S., Foley, K., & Kornbrot, D. E. (2009). Consistency of flashbulb memories of September 11 over long delays: Implications for consolidation and wrong time slice hypotheses. *Journal of Memory and Language, 61,* 556–572.

LaBar, K. S., & Phelps, E. A. (1998). Arousal-mediated memory consolidation: Role of the medial temporal lobe in humans. *Psychological Science, 9,* 490–493.

Labrie, V., Pai, S., & Petronis, A. (2012). Epigenetics of major psychosis: Progress, problems, and perspectives. *Trends in Genetics, 28,* 427–435.

Lachman, R., Lachman, J. L., & Butterfield, E. C. (1979). *Cognitive psychology and information processing: An introduction.* Hillsdale, NJ: Erlbaum.

Lackner, J. R., & DiZio, P. (2005). Vestibular, proprioceptive, and haptic contributions to spatial orientation. *Annual Review of Psychology, 56,* 115–147.

Lafer-Sousa, R., Hermann, K. L., & Conway, B. R. Striking individual differences in color perception uncovered by "the dress" photograph. *Current Biology, 25,* R1–R2.

LaFraniere, S. (2007, July 4). In Mauritania, seeking to end an overfed ideal. *New York Times.* Retrieved from http://www.nytimes.com/2007/07/04/world/africa/04mauritania.html?pagewanted=all

Lahkan, S. E., & Kirchgessner, A. (2012, March 12). Chronic traumatic encephalopathy: The dangers of getting "dinged." *Springer Plus, 1*(2). doi:10.1186/2193-1801-1-2

Lai, C. K., Lehr, S. A., Cerruti, C., Joy-Gaba, J. A., Teachman, B. A., Koleva, S. P., . . . Hawkins, C. B. (2014). Reducing implicit racial preferences: I. A comparative investigation of 17 interventions. *Journal of Experimental Psychology. General, 143*(4), 1765–1785. doi: 10.1037/a0036260

Lai, Y., & Siegal, J. (1999). Muscle atonia in REM sleep. In B. Mallick & S. Inoue (Eds.), *Rapid eye movement sleep* (pp. 69–90). New Delhi, India: Narosa Publishing House.

Lake, J. (2009). Natural products used to treat depressed mood as monotherapies and adjuvants to antidepressants: A review of the evidence. *Psychiatric Times, 26,* 1–6.

Lakin, J. M. (2013). Sex differences in reasoning abilities: Surprising evidence that male–female ratios in the tails of the quantitative reasoning distribution have increased. *Intelligence, 41*(4), 263–274. doi:10.1016/j.intell.2013.04.004

Lam, L. L., Emberly, E., Fraser, H. B., Neumann, S. M., Chen, E., Miller, G. E., . . . Kobor, M. S. (2012). Factors underlying variable DNA methylation in a human community cohort. *Proceedings of the National Academy of Sciences, USA, 109*(Suppl. 2), 17253–17260.

Lamb, M. E., Thompson, R. A., Gardner, W., & Charnov, E. L. (1985). *Infant–mother attachment: The origins and developmental significance of individual differences in Strange Situation behavior.* Hillsdale, NJ: Erlbaum.

Landauer, T. K., & Bjork, R. A. (1978). Optimum rehearsal patterns and name learning. In M. M. Gruneberg, P. E. Morris, & R. N. Sykes (Eds.), *Practical aspects of memory* (pp. 625–632). New York: Academic Press.

Langer, E. J., & Abelson, R. P. (1974). A patient by any other name.... Clinician group difference in labeling bias. *Journal of Consulting and Clinical Psychology, 42,* 4–9.

Langleben, D. D., Loughead, J. W., Bilker, W. B., Ruparel, K., Childress, A. R., Busch, S. I., & Gur, R. C. (2005). Telling truth from lie in individual subjects with fast event-related fMRI. *Human Brain Mapping, 26,* 262–272.

Langlois, J. H., Ritter, J. M., Casey, R. J., & Sawin, D. B. (1995). Infant attractiveness predicts maternal behaviors and attitudes. *Developmental Psychology, 31,* 464–472.

LaPierre, S., Boyer, R., Desjardins, S., Dubé, M., Lorrain, D., Préville, M., & Brassard, J. (2012). Daily hassles, physical illness, and sleep problems in older adults with wishes to die. *International Psychogeriatrics, 24,* 243–252.

Lareau, A. (2003). *Unequal childhoods: Class, race, and family life.* Berkeley: University of California Press.

Larrick, R. P., Timmerman, T. A., Carton, A. M., & Abrevaya, J. (2011). Temper, temperature, and temptation: Heat-related retaliation in baseball. *Psychological Science, 22*(4), 423–428. doi:10.1177/0956797611399292

Larsen, M. E., Nicholas, J., & Christensen, H. (2016). A systematic assessment of smartphone tools for suicide prevention. *PLoS ONE, 11,* e0152285.

Larsen, S. F. (1992). Potential flashbulbs: Memories of ordinary news as baseline. In E. Winograd & U. Neisser (Eds.), *Affect and accuracy in recall: Studies of "flashbulb memories"* (pp. 32–64). New York: Cambridge University Press.

Larson, R., & Richards, M. H. (1991). Daily companionship in late childhood and early adolescence—changing developmental contexts. *Child Development, 62,* 284–300.

Lashley, K. S. (1960). In search of the engram. In F. A. Beach, D. O. Hebb, C. T. Morgan, & H. W. Nissen (Eds.), *The neuropsychology of Lashley* (pp. 478–505). New York: McGraw-Hill.

Latané, B., & Nida, S. (1981). Ten years of research on group size and helping. *Psychological Bulletin, 89*(2), 308–324.

Lattal, K. A. (2010). Delayed reinforcement of operant behavior. *Journal of the Experimental Analysis of Behavior, 93,* 129–139.

Laupa, M., & Turiel, E. (1986). Children's conceptions of adult and peer authority. *Child Development, 57,* 405–412.

Lavie, P. (2001). Sleep–wake as a biological rhythm. *Annual Review of Psychology, 52,* 277–303.

Lawrence, N. S., Jollant, F., O'Daly, O., Zelaya, F., & Phillips, M. L. (2009). Distinct roles of prefrontal cortical subregions in the Iowa Gambling Task. *Cerebral Cortex, 19,* 1134–1143.

Lawton, M. P., Kleban, M. H., Rajagopal, D., & Dean, J. (1992). The dimensions of affective experience in three age groups. *Psychology and Aging, 7,* 171–184.

Lazarus, R. S. (1984). On the primacy of cognition. *American Psychologist, 39,* 124–129.

Lazarus, R. S., & Folkman, S. (1984). *Stress, appraisal, and coping.* New York: Springer.

Leader, T., Mullen, B., & Abrams, D. (2007). Without mercy: The immediate impact of group size on lynch mob atrocity. *Personality and Social Psychology Bulletin, 33*(10), 1340–1352.

Le, B., & Agnew, C. R. (2003). Commitment and its theorized determinants: A meta–analysis of the Investment Model. *Personal Relationships, 10*(1), 37–57. doi: 10.1111/1475-6811.00035

Leary, M. R. (1990). Responses to social exclusion: Social anxiety, jealousy, loneliness, depression, and low self-esteem. *Journal of Social and Clinical Psychology, 9*, 221–229.

Leary, M. R. (2010). Affiliation, acceptance, and belonging: The pursuit of interpersonal connection. In S. T. Fiske, D. T. Gilbert, & G. Lindzey (Eds.), *The handbook of social psychology* (5th ed., Vol. 2, pp. 864–897). New York: Wiley.

Leary, M. R., & Baumeister, R. F. (2000). The nature and function of self-esteem: Sociometer theory. In M. P. Zanna (Ed.), *Advances in experimental social psychology* (Vol. 32, pp. 1–62). San Diego: Academic Press.

Leary, M. R., Britt, T. W., Cutlip, W. D., & Templeton, J. L. (1992). Social blushing. *Psychological Bulletin, 112*, 446–460.

Lecky, P. (1945). *Self-consistency: A theory of personality.* New York: Island Press.

Lecrubier, Y., Clerc, G., Didi, R., & Kieser, M. (2002). Efficacy of St. John's wort extract WS 5570 in major depression: A double-blind, placebo-controlled trial. *American Journal of Psychiatry, 159*, 1361–1366.

Lederman, S. J., & Klatzky, R. L. (2009). Haptic perception: A tutorial. *Attention, Perception, & Psychophysics, 71*, 1439–1459.

LeDoux, J. E. (2000). Emotion circuits in the brain. *Annual Review of Neuroscience, 23*, 155–184.

LeDoux, J. E., Iwata, J., Cicchetti, P., & Reis, D. J. (1988). Different projections of the central amygdaloid nucleus mediate autonomic and behavioral correlates of conditioned fear. *Journal of Neuroscience, 8*, 2517–2529.

Lee, D. N., & Aronson, E. (1974). Visual proprioceptive control of standing in human infants. *Perception & Psychophysics, 15*, 529–532.

Lee, L., Loewenstein, G., Ariely, D., Hong, J., & Young, J. (2008). If I'm not hot, are you hot or not? Physical-attractiveness evaluations and dating preferences as a function of one's own attractiveness. *Psychological Science, 19*, 669–677.

Lee, M. H., Smyser, C. D., & Shimoy, J. S. (2013). Resting-state fMRI: A review of methods and clinical applications. *American Journal of Neuroradiology, 34*, 1866–1872. doi: 10.3174/ajnr.A3263

Lefcourt, H. M. (1982). *Locus of control: Current trends in theory and research* (2nd ed.). Hillsdale, NJ: Erlbaum.

Leff, S. S., Waasdorp, T. E., & Crick, N. R. (2010). A review of existing relational aggression programs: Strengths, limitations, and future direction. *School Psychology Review, 39*, 508–535.

Lemay, E. P. (2016). The forecast model of relationship commitment. *Journal of Personality and Social Psychology, 111*(1), 34–52. doi: 10.1037/pspi0000052

Lempert, D. (2007). *Women's increasing wage penalties from being overweight and obese.* Washington, DC: U.S. Bureau of Labor Statistics.

Lenton, A. P., & Francesconi, M. (2010). How humans cognitively manage an abundance of mate options. *Psychological Science, 21*(4), 528–533. doi: 10.1177/0956797610364958

Lentz, M. J., Landis, C. A., Rothermel, J., & Shaver, J. L. (1999). Effects of selective slow wave sleep disruption on musculoskeletal pain and fatigue in middle aged women. *Journal of Rheumatology, 26*, 1586–1592.

Leon, D. A., Lawlor, D. A., Clark, H., Batty, G. D., & Macintyre, S. (2009). The association of childhood intelligence with mortality risk from adolescence to middle age: Findings from the Aberdeen children of the 1950s cohort study. *Intelligence, 37*(6), 520–528.

Lepage, M., Ghaffar, O., Nyberg, L., & Tulving, E. (2000). Prefrontal cortex and episodic memory retrieval mode. *Proceedings of the National Academy of Sciences, USA, 97*, 506–511.

Lepper, M. R., Greene, D., & Nisbett, R. E. (1973). Undermining children's intrinsic interest with extrinsic rewards: A test of the "overjustification" hypothesis. *Journal of Personality and Social Psychology, 28*, 129–137.

Lerman, D. (2006). Consumer politeness and complaining behavior. *Journal of Services Marketing, 20*, 92–100.

Lerman, D. C., & Vorndran, C. M. (2002). On the status of knowledge for using punishment: Implications for treating behavior disorders. *Journal of Applied Behavior Analysis, 35*, 4312–4464.

Lerner, J. S., Li, Y., Valdesolo, P., & Kassam, K. S. (2015). Emotion and decision making. *Annual Review of Psychology, 66*, 799–823. doi: 10.1146/annurev-psych-010213-115043

Leung, A. K.-Y., & Cohen, D. (2011). Within- and between-culture variation: Individual differences and the cultural logics of honor, face, and dignity cultures. *Journal of Personality and Social Psychology, 100*(3), 507–526. doi:10.1037/a0022151

Levelt Committee, Noort Committee, Drenth Committee. (2012, November 28). *Flawed science: The fraudulent research practices of social psychologist Diederik Stapel.* Retrieved from http://www.tilburguniversity.edu/nl/nieuws-en-agenda/finalreportLevelt.pdf

Levenson, J. M., & Sweatt, J. D. (2005). Epigenetic mechanisms in memory formation. *Nature Reviews Neuroscience, 6*, 108–118.

Levenson, R. W., Cartensen, L. L., Friesen, W. V., & Ekman, P. (1991). Emotion physiology, and expression in old age. *Psychology and Aging, 6*, 28–35.

Levenson, R. W., Ekman, P., & Friesen, W. V. (1990). Voluntary facial action generates emotion-specific autonomic nervous system activity. *Psychophysiology, 27*, 363–384.

Levenson, R. W., Ekman, P., Heider, K., & Friesen, W. V. (1992). Emotion and automatic nervous system activity in the Minangkabau of West Sumatra. *Journal of Personality and Social Psychology, 62*, 972–988.

Levin, R., & Nielsen, T. (2009). Nightmares, bad dreams, and emotion dysregulation: A review and new neurocognitive model of dreaming. *Current Directions in Psychological Science, 18*, 84–88.

Levine, R. V., & Norenzayan, A. (1999). The pace of life in 31 countries. *Journal of Cross-Cultural Psychology, 30*(2), 178–205.

Levine, R. V., Norenzayan, A., & Philbrick, K. (2001). Cross-cultural differences in helping strangers. *Journal of Cross-Cultural Psychology, 32*, 543–560.

Lewis, M., & Brooks-Gunn, J. (1979). *Social cognition and the acquisition of self.* New York: Plenum Press.

Lewis, M. B. (2012). Exploring the positive and negative implications of facial feedback. *Emotion, 12*(4), 852–859.

Lewis, M. D., Hibbeln, J. R., Johnson, J. E., Lin, Y. H., Hyun, D. Y., & Loewke, J. D. (2011). Suicide deaths of active duty U. S. military and omega-3 fatty acid status: A case control comparison. *Journal of Clinical Psychiatry, 72*, 1585–1590.

Li, R., Polat, U., Makous, W., & Bavelier, D. (2009). Enhancing the contrast sensitivity function through action video game training. *Nature Neuroscience, 12*, 549–551.

Libet, B. (1985). Unconscious cerebral initiative and the role of conscious will in voluntary action. *Behavioral and Brain Sciences, 8*, 529–566.

Liebenluft, E. (1996). Women with bipolar illness: Clinical and research issues. *American Journal of Psychiatry, 153*, 163–173.

Lieberman, M. D., Inagaki, T. K., Tabibnia, G., & Crockett, M. J. (2011). Subjective responses to emotional stimuli during labeling, reappraisal, and distraction. *Emotion, 11*, 468–480.

Lieberman, M. D., & Rosenthal, R. (2001). Why introverts can't always tell who likes them: Multitasking and nonverbal decoding. *Journal of Personality and Social Psychology, 80*, 294–310.

Lifshitz, M., Aubert Bonn, N., Fischer, A., Kashem, I. R., & Raz, A. (2013). Using suggestion to modulate automatic processes: From Stroop to McGurk and beyond. *Cortex, 49*(2), 463–473. doi:10.1016/j.cortex.2012.08.007

Lilienfeld, S. O. (2007). Psychological treatments that cause harm. *Perspectives on Psychological Science, 2,* 53–70.

Lilienfeld, S. O., Lynn, S. J., & Lohr, J. M. (Eds.) (2003). *Science and pseudoscience in clinical psychology.* New York: Guilford Press.

Lindenberger, U., & Baltes, P. B. (1994). Sensory functioning and intelligence in old age: A strong connection. *Psychology and Aging, 9*(3), 339–355. doi:10.1037/0882-7974.9.3.339

Lindquist, K., & Barrett, L. F. (2008). Constructing emotion: The experience of fear as a conceptual act. *Psychological Science, 19,* 898–903.

Lindquist, S. I., & McLean, J. P. (2011). Daydreaming and its correlates in an educational environment. *Learning and Individual Differences, 21,* 158–167.

Lindstrom, M. (2005). *Brand sense: How to build powerful brands through touch, taste, smell, sight and sound.* London: Kogan Page.

Liou, A. P., Paziuk, M., Luevano, J.-M., Machineni, S., Turnbaugh, P. J., & Kaplan, L. M. (2013). Conserved shifts in the gut microbiota due to gastric bypass reduce host weight and adiposity. *Science Translational Medicine, 5*(178), 178ra41–178ra41.

Little, B. R. (1983). Personal projects: A rationale and method for investigation. *Environment and Behavior, 15,* 273–309.

Liu, D., Diorio, J., Tannenbaum, B., Caldji, C., Francis, D., Freedman, A., . . . Meaney, M. J. (1997). Maternal care, hippocampal glucocorticoid receptors, and hypothalamic–pituitary–adrenal responses to stress. *Science, 277,* 1659–1662.

Liu, D., Wellman, H. M., Tardif, T., & Sabbagh, M. A. (2008). Theory of mind development in Chinese children: A meta-analysis of false belief understanding across cultures and languages. *Developmental Psychology, 44,* 523–531.

Livingstone, M., & Hubel, D. (1988). Segregation of form, color, movement, and depth: Anatomy, physiology, and perception. *Science, 240,* 740–749.

Locksley, A., Ortiz, V., & Hepburn, C. (1980). Social categorization and discriminatory behavior: Extinguishing the minimal intergroup discrimination effect. *Journal of Personality and Social Psychology, 39,* 773–783.

Loehlin, J. C. (1973). Blood group genes and Negro–White ability differences. *Behavior Genetics, 3*(3), 263–270.

Loehlin, J. C. (1992). *Genes and environment in personality development.* Newbury Park, CA: Sage.

Loftus, E. F. (1993). The reality of repressed memories. *American Psychologist, 48,* 518–537.

Loftus, E. F. (2003). Make-believe memories. *American Psychologist, 58,* 867–873.

Loftus, E. F., & Ketchum, K. (1994). *The myth of repressed memory.* New York: St. Martin's Press.

Loftus, E. F., & Pickrell, J. E. (1995). The formation of false memories. *Psychiatric Annals, 25,* 720–725.

Lonegran, M. H., Olivera-Figueroa, L. A., Pitman, R. K., & Brunet, A. (2013). Propranolol's effects on the consolidation and reconsolidation of long-term emotional memory in healthy participants: A meta-analyis. *Journal of Psychiatry & Neuroscience, 38,* 222–231.

Lopes, P. N., Grewal, D., Kadis, J., Gall, M., & Salovey, P. (2006). Emotional intelligence and positive work outcomes. *Psichothema, 18,* 132.

Lorenz, K. (1952). *King Solomon's ring.* New York: Crowell.

Lovaas, O. I. (1987). Behavioral treatment and normal educational and intellectual functioning in young autistic children. *Journal of Consulting and Clinical Psychology, 55,* 3–9.

Lozano, B. E., & Johnson, S. L. (2001). Can personality traits predict increases in manic and depressive symptoms? *Journal of Affective Disorders, 63,* 103–111.

Luborsky, L., Rosenthal, R., Diguer, L., Andrusyna, T. P., Berman, J. S., Levitt, J. T., . . . Krause, E. D. (2002). The dodo bird verdict is alive and well—mostly. *Clinical Psychology: Science and Practice, 9,* 2–12.

Luborsky, L., & Singer, B. (1975). Comparative studies of psychotherapies: Is it true that "everyone has won and all must have prizes"? *Archives of General Psychiatry, 32*(8), 995–1008.

Lucas, R. E., Clark, A. E., Georgellis, Y., & Diener, E. (2003). Reexamining adaptation and the set point model of happiness: Reactions to changes in marital status. *Journal of Personality and Social Psychology, 84,* 527–539.

Lucas, R. E., & Dyrenforth, P. S. (2005). The myth of marital bliss? *Psychological Inquiry, 16*(2/3), 111–115.

Ludwig, A. M. (1966). Altered states of consciousness. *Archives of General Psychiatry, 15,* 225–234.

Lynn, M., & Shurgot, B. A. (1984). Responses to lonely hearts advertisements: Effects of reported physical attractiveness, physique, and coloration. *Personality and Social Psychology Bulletin, 10,* 349–357.

Lynn, R. (2009). What has caused the Flynn effect? Secular increases in the development quotients of infants. *Intelligence, 37*(1), 16–24.

Lynn, R. (2013). Who discovered the Flynn effect? A review of early studies of the secular increase of intelligence. *Intelligence.* Advance online publication. doi:10.1016/j.intell.2013.03.008

Lyubomirsky, S. (2008). *The how of happiness: A scientific approach to getting the life you want.* New York: Penguin.

Lyubomirsky, S., & Lepper, H. S. (1999). A measure of subjective happiness: Preliminary reliability and construct validation. *Social Indicators Research, 46,* 137–155.

MacDonald, S., Uesiliana, K., & Hayne, H. (2000). Cross-cultural and gender differences in childhood amnesia. *Memory, 8,* 365–376.

Mack, A. H., Franklin, J. E., Jr., & Frances, R. J. (2003). Substance use disorders. In R. E. Hales & S. C. Yudofsky (Eds.), *The American Psychiatric Publishing textbook of clinical psychiatry* (4th ed., pp. 309–377). Washington, DC: American Psychiatric Publishing.

Mackey, A. P., Hill, S. S., Stone, S. I., & Bunge, S. A. (2011). Differential effects of reasoning and speed training in children. *Developmental Science, 14,* 582–590. doi: 10.1111/j.1467-7687.2010.01005x

MacLeod, C., & Mathews, A. (2012). Cognitive bias modification approaches to anxiety. *Annual Review of Clinical Psychology, 8,* 189–217.

MacLeod, M. D. (2002). Retrieval-induced forgetting in eyewitness memory: Forgetting as a consequence of remembering. *Applied Cognitive Psychology, 16,* 135–149.

MacLeod, M. D., & Saunders, J. (2008). Retrieval inhibition and memory distortion: Negative consequences of an adaptive process. *Current Directions in Psychological Science, 17,* 26–30.

Macmillan, M. (2000). *An odd kind of fame: Stories of Phineas Gage.* Cambridge, MA: MIT Press.

Macmillan, N. A., & Creelman, C. D. (2005). *Detection theory.* Mahwah, NJ: Erlbaum.

Madden, D. J., Turkington, T. G., Provenzale, J. M., Denny, L. L., Hawk, T. C., Gottlob, L. R., & Coleman, R. E. (1999). Adult age differences in functional neuroanatomy of verbal recognition memory. *Human Brain Mapping, 7,* 115–135.

Maddi, S. R., Harvey, R. H., Khoshaba, D. M., Fazel, M., & Resurreccion, N. (2009). Hardiness training facilitates performance in college. *The Journal of Positive Psychology, 4,* 566–577.

Maddi, S. R., Kahn, S., & Maddi, K. L. (1998). The effectiveness of hardiness training. *Consulting Psychology Journal: Practice and Research, 50,* 78–86.

Madigan, S., Atkinson, L., Laurin, K., & Benoit, D. (2013). Attachment and internalizing behavior in early childhood: A meta-analysis. *Developmental Psychology, 49*(4), 672–689. doi:10.1037/a0028793

Maes, M. (1995). Evidence for an immune response in major depression: A review and hypothesis. *Progress in Neuro-Psychopharmacology and Biological Psychiatry, 19,* 11–38.

Mahon, B. Z., Anzellotti, S., Schwarzbach, J., Zampini, M., & Caramazza, A. (2009). Category-specific organization in the human brain does not require visual experience. *Neuron, 63,* 397–405.

Mahon, B. Z., & Caramazza, A. (2009). Concepts and categories: A cognitive neuropsychological perspective. *Cognitive Neuropsychology, 60,* 27–51.

Maier, S. F., & Watkins, L. R. (1998). Cytokines for psychologists: Implications of bidirectional immune-to-brain communication for understanding behavior, mood, and cognition. *Psychological Review, 105,* 83–107.

Maier, S. F., & Watkins, L. R. (2000). The immune system as a sensory system: Implications for psychology. *Current Directions in Psychological Science, 9,* 98–102.

Major, B., Mendes, W. B., & Dovidio, J. F. (2013). Intergroup relations and health disparities: A social psychological perspective. *Health Psychology, 32,* 514–524.

Makin, J. E., Fried, P. A., & Watkinson, B. (1991). A comparison of active and passive smoking during pregnancy: Long-term effects. *Neurotoxicology and Teratology, 16,* 5–12.

Makris, N., Biederman, J., Monuteaux, M. C., & Seidman, L. J. (2009). Towards conceptualizing a neural systems-based anatomy of attention-deficit/hyperactivity disorder. *Developmental Neuroscience, 31,* 36–49.

Malina, R. M., Bouchard, C., & Beunen, G. (1988). Human growth: Selected aspects of current research on well-nourished children. *Annual Review of Anthropology, 17,* 187–219.

Malooly, A. M., Genet, J. J., & Siemer, M. (2013). Individual differences in reappraisal effectiveness: The role of affective flexibility. *Emotion, 13*(2), 302–313. doi:10.1037/a0029980

Mampe, B., Friederici, A. D., Christophe, A., & Wermke, K. (2009). Newborns' cry melody is shaped by their native language. *Current Biology, 19,* 1–4.

Mandle, C. L., Jacobs, S. C., Arcari, P. M., & Domar, A. D. (1996). The efficacy of relaxation response interventions with adult patients: A review of the literature. *Journal of Cardiovascular Nursing, 10,* 4–26.

Mandler, G. (1967). Organization and memory. In K. W. Spence & J. T. Spence (Eds.), *The psychology of learning and motivation* (Vol. 1, pp. 327–372). New York: Academic Press.

Mandy, W., & Lai, M. C. (2016). The role of the environment in the developmental psychopathology of autism spectrum condition. *Journal of Child Psychology and Psychiatry, 57,* 271–292.

Mankiw, N. G., & Weinzierl, M. (2010). The optimal taxation of height: A case study of utilitarian income redistribution. *American Economic Journal: Economic Policy, 2,* 155–176.

Mann, J. J., Apter, A., Bertolote, J., Beautrais, A., Currier, D., Haas, A., . . . Hendin, H. (2005). Suicide prevention strategies: A systematic review. *Journal of the American Medical Association, 294*(16), 2064–2074. doi:10.1001/jama.294.16.2064

Marangell, L. B., Silver, J. M., Goff, D. M., & Yudofsky, S. C. (2003). Psychopharmacology and electroconvulsive therapy. In R. E. Hales & S. C. Yudofsky (Eds.), *The American Psychiatric Publishing textbook of clinical psychiatry* (4th ed., pp. 1047–1149). Washington, DC: American Psychiatric Publishing.

Markel, H. (2011). *An anatomy of addiction: Sigmund Freud, William Halsted, and the miracle drug cocaine.* New York: Pantheon.

Markus, H. (1977). Self-schemata and processing information about the self. *Journal of Personality and Social Psychology, 35,* 63–78.

Marlatt, G. A., & Rohsenow, D. (1980). Cognitive processes in alcohol use: Expectancy and the balanced placebo design. In N. K. Mello (Ed.), *Advances in substance abuse: Behavioral and biological research* (pp. 159–199). Greenwich, CT: JAI Press.

Marlatt, G. A., & Witkiewitz, K. (2010). Update on harm reduction policy and intervention research. *Annual Review of Clinical Psychology, 6,* 591–606.

Marmot, M. G., Stansfeld, S., Patel, C., North, F., Head, J., White, L., . . . Feeney, A. (1991). Health inequalities among British civil servants: The Whitehall II study. *Lancet, 337,* 1387–1393.

Martin, A. (2007). The representation of object concepts in the brain. *Annual Review of Psychology, 58,* 25–45.

Martin, A., & Caramazza, A. (2003). Neuropsychological and neuroimaging perspectives on conceptual knowledge: An introduction. *Cognitive Neuropsychology, 20,* 195–212.

Martin, A., & Chao, L. L. (2001). Semantic memory and the brain: Structure and processes. *Current Opinion in Neurobiology, 11,* 194–201.

Martin, K. D., & Hill, R. P. (2012). Life satisfaction, self-determination, and consumption adequacy at the bottom of the pyramid. *Journal of Consumer Research, 38,* 1155–1168.

Martin, M. J., Blozis, S. A., Boeninger, D. K., Masarik, A. S., & Conger, R. D. (2014). The timing of entry into adult roles and changes in trajectories of problem behaviors during the transition to adulthood. *Developmental Psychology, 50*(11), 2473–2484. doi: 10.1037/a0037950

Martin, N. G., Eaves, L. J., Geath, A. R., Jarding, R., Feingold, L. M., & Eysenck, H. J. (1986). Transmission of social attitudes. *Proceedings of the National Academy of Sciences, USA, 83,* 4364–4368.

Martinez, G., Copen, C. E., & Abma, J. C. (2011). Teenagers in the United States: Sexual activity, contraceptive use, and childbearing, 2006–2010: National Survey of Family Growth. *Vital Health Statistics, 23*(31).

Marucha, P. T., Kiecolt-Glaser, J. K., & Favagehi, M. (1998). Mucosal wound healing is impaired by examination stress. *Psychosomatic Medicine, 60,* 362–365.

Marzuk, P. M., Tardiff, K., Leon, A. C., Hirsch, C., Portera, L., Iqbal, M. I., . . . Hartwell, N. (1998). Ambient temperature and mortality from unintentional cocaine overdose. *Journal of the American Medical Association, 279,* 1795–1800.

Maslach, C. (2003). Job burnout: New directions in research and intervention. *Current Directions in Psychological Science, 12,* 189–192.

Maslach, C., Schaufeli, W. B., & Leiter, M. P. (2001). Job burnout. *Annual Review of Psychology, 52,* 397–422.

Maslow, A. H. (1937). Dominance-feeling, behavior, and status. In R. J. Lowry (Ed.), *Dominance, self-esteem, self-actualization: Germinal papers by A. H. Maslow* (pp. 49–70). Monterey, CA: Brooks-Cole.

Maslow, A. (1943). A theory of human motivation. *Psychological Review, 50,* 370–396.

Maslow, A. H. (1954). *Motivation and personality.* New York: Harper & Row.

Mason, M. F., Magee, J. C., Kuwabara, K., & Nind, L. (2010). Specialization in relational reasoning: The efficiency, accuracy, and neural substrates of social versus nonsocial inferences. *Social Psychological and Personality Science, 1*(4), 318–326. doi:10.1177/1948550610366166

Mason, M. F., Norton, M. I., Van Horn, J. D., Wegner, D. M., Grafton, S. T., & Macrae, C. N. (2007). Wandering minds: The default network and stimulus-independent thought. *Science, 3154,* 393–395.

Masten, A. S. (2004). Family therapy as a treatment for children: A critical review of outcome research. *Family Process, 18,* 323–335.

Masuda, T., & Nisbett, R. E. (2006). Culture and change blindness. *Cognitive Science, 30,* 381–399.

Mather, M., & Carstensen, L. L. (2003). Aging and attentional biases for emotional faces. *Psychological Science, 14,* 409–415.

Mather, M., & Carstensen, L. L. (2005). Aging and motivated cognition: The positivity effect in attention and memory. *Trends in Cognitive Sciences, 9*(10), 496–502.

Matsumoto, D., & Willingham, B. (2009). Spontaneous facial expressions of emotion of congenitally and noncongenitally blind individuals. *Journal of Personality and Social Psychology, 96,* 1–10.

Mattar, A. A. G., & Gribble, P. L. (2005). Motor learning by observing. *Neuron, 46,* 153–160.

Matthews, G., & Gilliland, K. (1999). The personality theories of H. J. Eysenck and J. A. Gray: A comparative review. *Personality and Individual Differences, 26,* 583–626.

Maus, G. W., Ward, J., Nijhawan, R., & Whitney, D. (2013). The perceived position of moving objects: Transcranial magnetic stimulation of area MT+ reduces the flash-lag effect. *Cerebral Cortex, 23,* 241–247.

May, R. (1983). *The discovery of being: Writings in existential psychology.* New York: Norton.

Mayberg, H., Lozano, A., Voon, V., McNeely, H., Seminowicz, D., Hamani, C., . . . Kennedy, S. H. (2005). Deep brain stimulation for treatment-resistant depression. *Neuron, 45,* 651–660.

Mayer, J. D., Caruso, D. R., & Salovey, P. (1999). Emotional intelligence meets traditional standards for an intelligence. *Intelligence, 27,* 267.

Mayer, J. D., Roberts, R. D., & Barsade, S. G. (2008). Human abilities: Emotional intelligence. *Annual Review of Psychology, 59,* 507–536.

McAdams, D. (1993). *The stories we live by: Personal myths and the making of the self.* New York: Morrow.

McCauley, J., Ruggiero, K. J., Resnick, H. S., Conoscenti, L. M., & Kilpatrick, D. G. (2009). Forcible, drug-facilitated, and incapacitated rape in relation to substance use problems: Results from a national sample of college women. *Addictive Behaviors, 34,* 458–462.

McClelland, D. C., Atkinson, J. W., Clark, R. A., & Lowell, E. L. (1953). *The achievement motive.* New York: Appleton-Century-Crofts.

McConkey, K. M., Barnier, A. J., & Sheehan, P. W. (1998). Hypnosis and pseudomemory: Understanding the findings and their implications. In S. J. Lynn & K. M. McConkey (Eds.), *Truth in memory* (pp. 227–259). New York: Guilford Press.

McCrae, R. R., & Costa, P. T. (1990). *Personality in adulthood.* New York: Guilford Press.

McCrae, R. R., & Costa, P. T. (1999). A five-factor theory of personality. In L. A. Pervin & O. P. John (Eds.), *Handbook of personality: Theory and research* (pp. 139–153). New York: Guilford Press.

McDaniel, M. A., Thomas, R. C., Agarwal, P. K., McDermott, K. B., & Roediger, H. L. (2013). Quizzing in middle-school science: Successful transfer performance on classroom exams. *Applied Cognitive Psychology, 27,* 360–372.

McDermott, K. B., Agarwal, P. K., D'Antonio, L., Roediger, H. L., & McDaniel, M. A. (2014). Both multiple-choice and short-answer quizzes enhance later exam performance in middle and high school classes. *Journal of Experimental Psychology: Applied, 20,* 3–21.

McElwain, N. L., Booth-LaForce, C., & Wu, X. (2011). Infant–mother attachment and children's friendship quality: Maternal mental state talk as an intervening mechanism. *Developmental Psychology, 47*(5), 1295–1311. doi:10.1037/a0024094

McEvoy, S. P., Stevenson, M. R., McCartt, A. T., Woodward, M., Haworth, C., Palamara, P., & Circarelli, R. (2005). Role of mobile phones in motor vehicle crashes resulting in hospital attendance: A case-crossover study. *British Medical Journal, 331,* 428–430.

McFarlane, A. H., Norman, G. R., Streiner, D. L., Roy, R., & Scott, D. J. (1980). A longitudinal study of the influence of the psychosocial environment on health status: A preliminary report. *Journal of Health and Social Behavior, 21,* 124–133.

McGarty, C., & Turner, J. C. (1992). The effects of categorization on social judgement. *British Journal of Social Psychology, 31,* 253–268.

McGaugh, J. L. (2000). Memory: A century of consolidation. *Science, 287,* 248–251.

McGaugh, J. L. (2015). Consolidating memories. *Annual Review of Psychology, 66,* 1–24.

McGovern, P. E., Zhang, J., Tang, J., Zhang, Z., Hall, G. R., Moreau, R. A., . . . Wang, C. (2004). Fermented beverages of pre- and proto-historic China. *Proceedings of the National Academy of Sciences of the United States of America, 101,* 17593–17598.

McGowan, P. O., Sasaki, A., D., Alessio, A. D., Dymov, S., Labonté, B., Szyf, M., . . . Meaney, M. J. (2009). Epigenetic regulation of the glucocorticoid receptor in human brain associates with childhood abuse. *Nature Neuroscience, 12,* 342–348.

McGrath, J., Saha, S., Chant, D., & Welham, J. (2008). Schizophrenia: A concise overview of incidence, prevalence, and mortality. *Epidemiologic Reviews, 30,* 67–76.

McGue, M., & Bouchard, T. J. (1998). Genetic and environmental influences on human behavioral differences. *Annual Review of Neuroscience, 21,* 1–24.

McIntyre, S. H., & Munson, J. M. (2008). Exploring cramming: Student behaviors, beliefs, and learning retention in the principles of marketing course. *Journal of Marketing Education, 30,* 226–243.

McKee, A. C., Cantu, R. C., Nowinski, C. J., Hedley-Whyte, E. T., Gavett, B. E., Budson, A. E., . . . Stern, R. A. (2009). Chronic traumatic encephalopathy in athletes: Progressive tauopathy after repetitive head injury. *Journal of Neuropathology and Experimental Neurology, 68,* 709–735.

McKee, A. C., Stein, T. D., Nowinski, C. J., Stern, R. A., Daneshvar, D. H., Alvarez, V. E., . . . Cantu, R. (2012). The spectrum of disease in chronic traumatic encephalopathy. *Brain, 136*(1), 43–64. doi:10.1093/brain/aws307

McKinney, C. H., Antoni, M. H., Kumar, M., Tims, F. C., & McCabe, P. M. (1997). Effects of guided imagery and music (GIM) therapy on mood and cortisol in healthy adults. *Health Psychology, 16,* 390–400.

McLaughlin, K. A., Nandi, A., Keyes, K. M., Uddin, M., Aiello, A. E., Galea, S., & Koenen, K. C. (2012). Home foreclosure and risk of psychiatric morbidity during the recent financial crisis. *Psychological Medicine, 42,* 1441–1448.

McLean, K. C. (2008). The emergence of narrative identity. *Social and Personality Psychology Compass, 2*(4), 1685–1702.

McNally, R. J. (2003). *Remembering trauma.* Cambridge, MA: Belknap Press of Harvard University Press.

McNally, R. J., & Clancy, S. A. (2005). Sleep paralysis, sexual abuse, and space alien abduction. *Transcultural Psychiatry, 42,* 113–122.

McNally, R. J., & Geraerts, E. (2009). A new solution to the recovered memory debate. *Perspective on Psychological Science, 4,* 126–134.

McNally, R. J., & Steketee, G. S. (1985). Etiology and maintenance of severe animal phobias. *Behavioral Research and Therapy, 23,* 431–435.

McWilliams, P. (1993). *Ain't nobody's business if you do: The absurdity of consensual crimes in a free society.* Los Angeles: Prelude Press.

Mead, G. H. (1934). *Mind, self, and society.* Chicago: University of Chicago Press.

Mead, M. (1968). *Sex and temperament in three primitive societies.* New York: Dell. (Original work published 1935)

Meaney, M. J., & Ferguson-Smith, A. C. (2010). Epigenetic regulation of the neural transcriptome: The meaning of the marks. *Nature Neuroscience, 13,* 1313–1318.

Means, B., Toyama, Y., Murphy, R., Bakia, M., & Jones, K. (2010). *Evaluation of evidence based practices in online learning: Meta-analysis and review of online learning studies.* Washington, DC: U.S. Department of Education. Retrieved from https://www2.ed.gov/rschstat/eval/tech/evidence-based-practices/finalreport.pdf

Mechelli, A., Crinion, J. T., Noppeney, U., O'Doherty, J., Ashburner, J., Frackowiak, R. S., & Price, C. J. (2004). Neurolinguistics: Structural plasticity in the bilingual brain. *Nature, 431,* 757.

Medin, D. L., & Schaffer, M. M. (1978). Context theory of classification learning. *Psychological Review, 85,* 207–238.

Medvec, V. H., Madey, S. F., & Gilovich, T. (1995). When less is more: Counterfactual thinking and satisfaction among Olympic medalists. *Journal of Personality and Social Psychology, 69,* 603–610.

Meeren, H. K. M., van Heijnsbergen, C. C. R. J., & de Gelder, B. (2005). Rapid perceptual integration of facial expression and emotional body language. *Proceedings of the National Academy of Sciences, USA, 102*(45), 16518–16523.

Mehl, M. R., Vazire, S., Ramirez-Esparza, N., Slatcher, R. B., & Pennebaker, J. W. (2009). Are women really more talkative than men? *Science, 317,* 82.

Mehu, M., & Scherer, K. R. (2015). Emotion categories and dimensions in the facial communication of affect: An integrated approach. *Emotion, 15*(6), 798–811. doi: 10.1037/a0039416

Meins, E. (2003). Emotional development and attachment relationships. In A. Slater & G. Bremner (Eds.), *An introduction to developmental psychology* (pp. 141–164). Malden, MA: Blackwell.

Meins, E., Fernyhough, C., Fradley, E., & Tuckey, M. (2001). Rethinking maternal sensitivity: Mothers' comments on infants' mental processes predict security of attachment at 12 months. *Journal of Child Psychology & Psychiatry & Allied Disciplines, 42,* 637–648.

Melander, E. (2005). Gender equality and intrastate armed conflict. *International Studies Quarterly, 49*(4), 695–714. doi:10.1111/j.1468-2478.2005.00384.x

Mellon, R. C. (2009). Superstitious perception: Response-independent reinforcement and punishment as determinants of recurring eccentric interpretations. *Behaviour Research and Therapy, 47,* 868–875.

Meltzer, H. Y. (2013). Update on typical and atypical antipsychotic drugs. *Annual Review of Medicine, 64,* 393–406.

Meltzoff, A. N. (1995). Understanding the intentions of others: Reenactment of intended acts by 18-month-old children. *Developmental Psychology, 31,* 838–850.

Meltzoff, A. N. (2007). "Like me": A foundation for social cognition. *Developmental Science, 10*(1), 126–134. doi:10.1111/j.1467-7687.2007.00574x

Meltzoff, A. N., Kuhl, P. K., Movellan, J., & Sejnowski, T. J. (2009). Foundations for a new science of learning. *Science, 325,* 284–288.

Meltzoff, A. N., & Moore, M. K. (1977). Imitation of facial and manual gestures by human neonates. *Science, 198,* 75–78.

Melzack, R., & Wall, P. D. (1965). Pain mechanisms: A new theory. *Science, 150,* 971–979.

Mendle, J., Turkheimer, E., & Emery, R. E. (2007). Detrimental psychological outcomes associated with early pubertal timing in adolescent girls. *Developmental Review, 27,* 151–171.

Mennella, J. A., Johnson, A., & Beauchamp, G. K. (1995). Garlic ingestion by pregnant women alters the odor of amniotic fluid. *Chemical Senses, 20,* 207–209.

Mervis, C. B., & Bertrand, J. (1994). Acquisition of the "Novel Name" Nameless Category (N3C) principle. *Child Development, 65,* 1646–1662.

Merzenich, M. M., Recanzone, G. H., Jenkins, W. M., & Grajski, K. A. (1990). Adaptive mechanisms in cortical networks underlying cortical contributions to learning and nondeclarative memory. *Cold Spring Harbor Symposia on Quantitative Biology, 55,* 873–887.

Mesoudi, A., Chang, L., Dall, S. R. X., & Thornton, A. (2015). The evolution of individual and cultural variation in social learning. *Trends in Ecology & Evolution, 31,* 215–225.

Meston, C. M., & Buss, D. M. (2007). Why humans have sex. *Archives of Sexual Behavior, 36,* 477–507.

Mestre, J. M., Guil, R., Lopes, P. N., Salovey, P., & Gil-Olarte, P. (2006). Emotional intelligence and social and academic adaptation to school. *Psicothema, 18,* 112.

Mestry, N., Donnelly, N., Meneer, T., & McCarthy, R. A. (2012). Discriminating Thatcherised from typical faces in a case of prosopagnosia. *Neuropsychologia, 50,* 3410–3418.

Metcalfe, J., Casal-Roscum, L., Radin, A., & Friedman, D. (2015). On teaching old dogs new tricks. *Psychological Science, 26,* 1833–1842. doi: 10.1177/0956797615597912

Metcalfe, J., & Finn, B. (2008). Evidence that judgments of learning are causally related to study choice. *Psychonomic Bulletin & Review, 15,* 174–179.

Methven, L., Allen, V. J., Withers, G. A., & Gosney, M. A. (2012). Ageing and taste. *Proceedings of the Nutrition Society, 71,* 556–565.

Meyer-Bahlberg, H. F. L., Ehrhardt, A. A., Rosen, L. R., & Gruen, R. S. (1995). Prenatal estrogens and the development of homosexual orientation. *Developmental Psychology, 31,* 12–21.

Mikels, J. A., Maglio, S. J., Reed, A. E., & Kaplowitz, L. J. (2011). Should I go with my gut? Investigating the benefits of emotion-focused decision making. *Emotion, 11*(4), 743–753.

Miklowitz, D. J., & Johnson, S. L. (2006). The psychopathology and treatment of bipolar disorder. *Annual Review of Clinical Psychology, 2,* 199–235.

Mikolajczak, M., Avalosse, H., Vancorenland, S., Verniest, R., Callens, M., van Broeck, N., . . . Mierop, A. (2015). A nationally representative study of emotional competence and health. *Emotion, 15*(5), 653–667. doi: 10.1037/emo0000034

Milgram, S. (1963). Behavioral study of obedience. *Journal of Abnormal and Social Psychology, 67,* 371–378.

Milgram, S. (1974). *Obedience to authority.* New York: Harper & Row.

Milgram, S., Bickman, L., & Berkowitz, O. (1969). Note on the drawing power of crowds of different size. *Journal of Personality and Social Psychology, 13,* 79–82.

Miller, C., Seckel, E., & Ramachandran, V. S. (2012). Using mirror box therapy to treat phantom pain in Haitian earthquake victims. *Journal of Vision, 12,* article 1323. doi:10.1167/12.9.1323

Miller, D. T., & Prentice, D. A. (1996). The construction of social norms and standards. In E. T. Higgins & A. W. Kruglanski (Ed.), *Social psychology: Handbook of basic principles* (pp. 799–829). New York: Guilford Press.

Miller, D. T., & Ratner, R. K. (1998). The disparity between the actual and assumed power of self-interest. *Journal of Personality and Social Psychology, 74,* 53–62.

Miller, D. T., & Ross, M. (1975). Self-serving biases in the attribution of causality: Fact or fiction? *Psychological Bulletin, 82,* 213–225.

Miller, G. A. (1956). The magical number seven, plus or minus two: Some limits on our capacity for processing information. *Psychological Review, 63,* 81–96.

Miller, K. F., Smith, C. M., & Zhu, J. (1995). Preschool origins of cross-national differences in mathematical competence: The role of number-naming systems. *Psychological Science, 6,* 56–60.

Miller, N. E. (1960). Motivational effects of brain stimulation and drugs. *Federation Proceedings, 19,* 846–854.

Miller, T. W. (Ed.). (1996). *Theory and assessment of stressful life events.* Madison, CT: International Universities Press.

Miller, W. R., & Rollnick, S. (2012). *Motivational interviewing: Helping people change* (3rd ed.). New York: Guilford Press.

Milne, E., & Grafman, J. (2001). Ventromedial prefrontal cortex lesions in humans eliminate implicit gender stereotyping. *Journal of Neuroscience, 21,* 1–6.

Milner, A. D., & Goodale, M. A. (1995). *The visual brain in action.* Oxford, England: Oxford University Press.

Milner, B. (1962). Laterality effects in audition. In V. B. Mountcastle (Ed.), *Interhemispheric relations and cerebral dominance* (pp. 177–195). Baltimore: Johns Hopkins University Press.

Mingroni, M. A. (2007). Resolving the IQ paradox: Heterosis as a cause of the Flynn effect and other trends. *Psychological Review, 114,* 806–829.

Minsky, M. (1986). *The society of mind.* New York: Simon & Schuster.

Minson, J. A., & Mueller, J. S. (2012). The cost of collaboration: Why joint decision making exacerbates rejection of outside information. *Psychological Science, 23*(3), 219–224. doi:10.1177/0956797611429132

Miranda, J., Bernal, G., Lau, A., Kihn, L., Hwang, W. C., & LaFramboise, T. (2005). State of the science on psychological interventions for ethnic minorities. *Annual Review of Clinical Psychology, 1,* 113–142.

Mischel, W. (1968). *Personality and assessment.* New York: Wiley.

Mischel, W. (2004). Toward an integrative science of the person. *Annual Review of Psychology, 55,* 1–22.

Mischel, W., Ayduk, O., Baumeister, R. F., & Vohs, K. D. (2004). Willpower in a cognitive-affective processing system: The dynamics of delay of gratification. In *Handbook of self-regulation: Research, theory, and applications* (pp. 99–129). New York: Guilford Press.

Mischel, W., & Shoda, Y. (1999). Integrating dispositions and processing dynamics within a unified theory of personality: The cognitive affective personality system. In L. A. Pervin & O. P. John (Eds.), *Handbook of personality: Theory and research.* New York: Guilford Press.

Mischel, W., Shoda, Y., & Rodriguez, M. L. (1989). Delay of gratification in children. *Science, 244,* 933–938.

Mita, T. H., Dermer, M., & Knight, J. (1977). Reversed facial images and the mere-exposure hypothesis. *Journal of Personality and Social Psychology, 35,* 597–601.

Mitchell, J. P. (2006). Mentalizing and Marr: An information processing approach to the study of social cognition. *Brain Research, 1079,* 66–75.

Mitchell, K. J., & Johnson, M. K. (2009). Source monitoring 15 years later: What have we learned from fMRI about the neural mechanisms of source memory? *Psychological Bulletin, 135,* 638–677.

Miura, I. T., Okamoto, Y., Kim, C. C., & Chang, C. M. (1994). Comparisons of children's cognitive representation of number: China, France, Japan, Korea, Sweden and the United States. *International Journal of Behavioral Development, 17,* 401–411.

Moffitt, T. E. (1993). Adolescence-limited and life-course-persistent antisocial behavior: A developmental taxonomy. *Psychological Review, 100,* 674–701.

Mojtabai, R., Olfson, M., Sampson, N. A., Jin, R., Druss, B., Wang, P. S., . . . Kessler, R. C. (2011). Barriers to mental health treatment: Results from the National Comorbidity Survey replication. *Psychological Medicine, 41*(8), 1751–1761.

Mokdad, A. H., Ford, E. S., Bowman, B. A., Dietz, W. H., Vinicor, F., Bales, V. S., & Marks, J. S. (2003). Prevalence of obesity, diabetes, and obesity-related health risk factors, 2001. *Journal of the American Medical Association, 289*(1), 76–79. doi: 10.1001/jama.289.1.76

Molden, D., Lee, A. Y., & Higgins, E. T. (2009). Motivations for promotion and prevention. In J. Shah & W. Gardner (Eds.), *Handbook of motivation science* (pp. 169–187). New York: Guilford Press.

Molloy, L. E., Gest, S. D., Feinberg, M. E., & Osgood, D. W. (2014). Emergence of mixed-sex friendship groups during adolescence: Developmental associations with substance use and delinquency. *Developmental Psychology, 50*(11), 2449–2461. doi: 10.1037/a0037856

Monahan, J. (1992). Mental disorder and violent behavior: Perceptions and evidence. *American Psychologist, 47,* 511–521.

Monahan, J. L., Murphy, S. T., & Zajonc, R. B. (2000). Subliminal mere exposure: Specific, general, and diffuse effects. *Psychological Science, 11,* 462–466.

Moncrieff, J. (2009). A critique of the dopamine hypothesis of schizophrenia and psychosis. *Harvard Review of Psychiatry, 17,* 214–225.

Montague, C. T., Farooqi, I. S., Whitehead, J. P., Soos, M. A., Rau, H., Wareham, N. J., . . . O'Rahilly, S. (1997). Congenital leptin deficiency is associated with severe early-onset obesity in humans. *Nature, 387*(6636), 903–908.

Montenigro, P. H., Corp, D. T., Stein, T. D., Cantu, R. C., & Stern, R. A. (2015). Chronic traumatic encephalopathy: Historical origins and current perspective. *Annual Review of Clinical Psychology, 11,* 309–330.

Mook, D. G. (1983). In defense of external invalidity. *American Psychologist, 38,* 379–387.

Moon, S. M., & Illingworth, A. J. (2005). Exploring the dynamic nature of procrastination: A latent growth curve analysis of academic procrastination. *Personality and Individual Differences, 38,* 297–309.

Moore, D. W. (2003). *Public lukewarm on animal rights.* Retrieved June 22, 2010, from http://www.gallup.com/poll/8461/public-lukewarm-animal-rights.aspx

Moore, E. G. J. (1986). Family socialization and the IQ test performance of traditionally and transracially adopted Black children. *Developmental Psychology, 22,* 317–326.

Moore, K. L. (1977). *The developing human* (2nd ed.). Philadelphia: Saunders.

Moore, L. (2012, August 31). Americans' future has to be multilingual. *The Washington Diplomat.* Retrieved from http://www.washdiplomat.com/index.php?option=com_content&view=article&id=8549:op-ed-americans-future-has-to-be-multilingual&catid=1492:september-2012&Itemid=504

Moray, N. (1959). Attention in dichotic listening: Affective cues and the influence of instructions. *Quarterly Journal of Experimental Psychology, 11,* 56–60.

Moreno, S., Marques, C., Santos, A., Santos, M., Castro, S. L., & Besson, M. (2009). Musical training influences linguistic abilities in 8-year-old children: More evidence for brain plasticity. *Cerebral Cortex, 19,* 712–723.

Morewedge, C. K., & Norton, M. I. (2009). When dreaming is believing: The (motivated) interpretation of dreams. *Journal of Personality and Social Psychology, 96,* 249–264.

Morgenstern, J., Labouvie, E., McCrady, B. S., Kahler, C. W., & Frey, R. M. (1997). Affiliation with Alcoholics Anonymous after treatment: A study of its therapeutic effects and mechanisms of action. *Journal of Consulting and Clinical Psychology, 65,* 768–777.

Morin, A. (2006). Levels of consciousness and self-awareness: A comparison of various neurocognitive views. *Consciousness & Cognition, 15,* 358–371.

Morris, C. D., Bransford, J. D., & Franks, J. J. (1977). Levels of processing versus transfer-appropriate processing. *Journal of Verbal Learning and Verbal Behavior, 16,* 519–533.

Morris, R. G., Anderson, E., Lynch, G. S., & Baudry, M. (1986). Selective impairment of learning and blockade of long-term potentiation by an N-methyl-D-aspartate receptor antagonist, AP5. *Nature, 319,* 774–776.

Morrow, D., Leirer, V., Altiteri, P., & Fitzsimmons, C. (1994). When expertise reduces age differences in performance. *Psychology and Aging, 9,* 134–148.

Moruzzi, G., & Magoun, H. W. (1949). Brain stem reticular formation and activation of the EEG. *Electroencephalography and Clinical Neurophysiology, 1,* 455–473.

Moscovitch, M. (1994). Memory and working-with-memory: Evaluation of a component process model and comparisons with other models. In D. L. Schacter & E. Tulving (Eds.), *Memory systems 1994* (pp. 269–310). Cambridge, MA: MIT Press.

Moscovitch, M., Cabeza, R., Winocur, G., & Nadel, L. (2016). Episodic memory and beyond: The hippocampus and cortex in transformation. *Annual Review of Psychology, 67,* 105–134.

Moscovitch, M., Nadel, L., Winocur, G., Gilboa, A., & Rosenbaum, R. S. (2006). The cognitive neuroscience of remote episodic, semantic and spatial memory. *Current Opinion in Neurobiology, 16,* 179–190.

Moulton, E., Barton, M., Robins, D. L., Abrams, D. N., & Fein, D. (2016) Early characteristics of children with ASD who demonstrate optimal progress between age two and four. *Journal of Autism and Developmental Disorders, 46,* 2160–2173.

Moura, A. C. A. de, & Lee, P. C. (2004). Capuchin stone tool use in Caatinga dry forest. *Science, 306,* 1909.

Mroczek, D. K., & Spiro, A. (2005). Change in life satisfaction during adulthood: Findings from the Veterans Affairs Normative Aging Study. *Journal of Personality and Social Psychology, 88,* 189.

Muehlenkamp, J. J., Claes, L., Havertape, L., & Plener, P. L. (2012). International prevalence of adolescent non-suicidal self-injury and deliberate self-harm. *Child and Adolescent Psychiatry and Mental Health,* 6(10). doi:10.1156/1753-2000-6-10

Mueller, T. E., Gavin, L. E., & Kulkarni, A. (2008). The association between sex education and youth's engagement in sexual intercourse, age at first intercourse, and birth control use at first sex. *The Journal of Adolescent Health,* 42(1), 89–96.

Mueller, T. I., Leon, A. C., Keller, M. B., Solomon, D. A., Endicott, J., Coryell, W., . . . Maser, J. D. (1999). Recurrence after recovery from major depressive disorder during 15 years of observational follow-up. *American Journal of Psychiatry, 156,* 1000–1006.

Muenter, M. D., & Tyce, G. M. (1971). L-dopa therapy of Parkinson's disease: Plasma L-dopa concentration, therapeutic response, and side effects. *Mayo Clinic Proceedings, 46,* 231–239.

Munsey, C. (2008, February). Prescriptive authority in the states. *Monitor on Psychology, 39,* 60.

Murayama, K., Miyatsu, T., Buchli, D., & Storm, B. C. (2014). Forgetting as a consequence of retrieval: A meta-analytic review of retrieval-induced forgetting. *Psychological Bulletin, 140,* 1383–1409.

Murphy, N. A., Hall, J. A., & Colvin, C. R. (2003). Accurate intelligence assessments in social interactions: Mediators and gender effects. *Journal of Personality, 71,* 465–493.

Murray, C. (2002). *IQ and income inequality in a sample of sibling pairs from advantaged family backgrounds.* Paper presented at the 114th Annual Meeting of the American Economic Association.

Murray, C. J. L., & Lopez, A. D. (1996a). Evidence-based health policy—Lessons from the Global Burden of Disease study. *Science, 274,* 740–743.

Murray, C. J. L., & Lopez, A. D. (1996b). *The Global Burden of Disease: A comprehensive assessment of mortality and disability from diseases, injuries, and risk factors in 1990 and projected to 2020.* Cambridge, MA: Harvard University Press.

Murray, H. A. (1943). *Thematic Apperception Test manual.* Cambridge, MA: Harvard University Press.

Murray, H. A., & Kluckhohn, C. (1953). Outline of a conception of personality. In C. Kluckhohn, H. A. Murray, & D. M. Schneider (Eds.), *Personality in nature, society, and culture* (2nd ed., pp. 3–52). New York: Knopf.

Murray, R. M., Paparelli, A, Morrison, P. D., Marconia, A., & Di Forti, M. (2013). What can we learn about schizophrenia from studying the human model, drug-induced psychosis? *American Journal of Medical Genetics Part B, 162B,* 661–670.

Myers, D. G., & Diener, E. (1995). Who is happy? *Psychological Science,* 6, 10–19.

Myers, D. G., & Lamm, H. (1975). The polarizing effect of group discussion. *American Scientist,* 63(3), 297–303.

Myles, P. S., Leslie, K., McNell, J., Forbes, A., & Chan, M. T. V. (2004). Bispectral index monitoring to prevent awareness during anaesthesia: The B-Aware randomized controlled trial. *Lancet, 363,* 1757–1763.

Nadasdy, A. (1995). Phonetics, phonology, and applied linguistics. *Annual Review of Applied Linguistics, 15,* 68–77.

Nader, K., & Hardt, O. (2009). A single standard for memory: The case of reconsolidation. *Nature Reviews Neuroscience, 10,* 224–234.

Nader, K., Shafe, G., & LeDoux, J. E. (2000). Fear memories require protein synthesis in the amygdala for reconsolidation after retrieval. *Nature, 406,* 722–726.

Nagasako, E. M., Oaklander, A. L., & Dworkin, R. H. (2003). Congenital insensitivity to pain: An update. *Pain, 101,* 213–219.

Nagell, K., Olguin, R. S., & Tomasello, M. (1993). Processes of social learning in the tool use of chimpanzees (*Pan troglodytes*) and human children (*Homo sapiens*). *Journal of Comparative Psychology, 107,* 174–186.

Nahemow, L., & Lawton, M. P. (1975). Similarity and propinquity in friendship formation. *Journal of Personality and Social Psychology, 32,* 205–213.

Nairne, J. S., & Pandeirada, J. N. S. (2008). Adaptive memory: Remembering with a stone age brain. *Current Directions in Psychological Science, 17,* 239–243.

Nairne, J. S., Thompson, S. R., & Pandeirada, J. N. S. (2007). Adaptive memory: Survival processing enhances retention. *Journal of Experimental Psychology: Learning, Memory, and Cognition, 33,* 263–273.

Nakazato, M., Murakami, N., Date, Y., Kojima, M., Matsuo, H., Kangawa, K., & Matsukura, S. (2001). A role for ghrelin in the central regulation of feeding. *Nature, 409,* 194–198.

Naqvi, N., Shiv, B., & Bechara, A. (2006). The role of emotion in decision making: A cognitive neuroscience perspective. *Current Directions in Psychological Science, 15,* 260–264.

Nassi, J. J., & Callaway, E. M. (2009). Parallel processing strategies of the primate visual system. *Nature Reviews Neuroscience, 10,* 360–372.

Nathan, P. E., & Gorman, J. M. (2007). *A guide to treatments that work* (3rd ed.). New York: Oxford University Press.

Nathanson, C., Paulhus, D. L., & Williams, K. M. (2006). Personality and misconduct correlates of body modification and other cultural deviance markers. *Journal of Research in Personality, 40,* 779–802.

National Center for Health Statistics. (2004). *Health, United States, 2004* (with chartbook on trends in the health of Americans). Hyattsville, MD: Author.

National Center for Health Statistics. (2012). *Health, United States, 2011* (with special feature on socioeconomic status and health). Hyattsville, MD: Author.

National Center for Health Statistics. (2016). Health of Black or African American non-Hispanic population. Atlanta: Centers for Disease Control and Prevention. Retrieved from http://www.cdc.gov/nchs/fastats/black-health.htm

National Institutes of Health. (1998). *Clinical Guidelines on the Identification, Evaluation, and Treatment of Overweight and Obesity in Adults: The Evidence Report.*

Naumann, L. P., Vazire, S., Rentfrow, P. J., & Gosling, S. D. (2009). Personality judgments based on physical appearance. *Personality & Social Psychology Bulletin, 35,* 1661–1671.

Neihart, M. (1999). The impact of giftedness on psychological well-being: What does the empirical literature say? *Roeper Review,* 22(1), 10.

Neimark, J. (2004, July/August). The power of coincidence. *Psychology Today,* pp. 47–52.

Neimeyer, R. A., & Mitchell, K. A. (1988). Similarity and attraction: A longitudinal study. *Journal of Social and Personal Relationships, 5,* 131–148.

Neisser, U. (Ed.) (1998). *The rising curve: Long-term gains in IQ and related measures.* Washington, DC: American Psychological Association.

Neisser, U., Boodoo, G., Bouchard, T. J., Jr., Boykin, A. W., Brody, N., Ceci, S. J., . . . Loehlin, J. C. (1996). Intelligence: Knowns and unknowns. *American Psychologist, 51,* 77–101.

Neisser, U., & Harsch, N. (1992). Phantom flashbulbs: False recollections of hearing the news about *Challenger.* In E. Winograd & U. Neisser

(Eds.), *Affect and accuracy in recall: Studies of "flashbulb memories"* (pp. 9–31). Cambridge, England: Cambridge University Press.

Nelson, A. B., & Kreitzer, A. C. (2015). Reassessing models of basal ganglia function and dysfunction. *Annual Review of Neuroscience, 37,* 117–135.

Nelson, C. A., Zeanah, C. H., Fox, N. A., Marshall, P. J., Smyke, A. T., & Guthrie, D. (2007). Cognitive recovery in socially deprived young children: The Bucharest early intervention project. *Science, 318,* 1937–1940.

Nemeth, C., & Chiles, C. (1988). Modelling courage: The role of dissent in fostering independence. *European Journal of Social Psychology, 18,* 275–280.

Nes, L. S. & Sergerstrom, S. C. (2006). Dispositional optimism and coping: A meta-analytic review. *Personality and Social Psychology Review, 10,* 235–251.

Neugebauer, R., Hoek, H. W., & Susser, E. (1999). Prenatal exposure to wartime famine and development of antisocial personality in early adulthood. *Journal of the American Medical Association, 282,* 455–462.

Newbold, R. R., Padilla-Banks, E., Snyder, R. J., & Jefferson, W. N. (2005). Developmental exposure to estrogenic compounds and obesity. *Birth Defects Research Part A: Clinical and Molecular Teratology, 73,* 478–480.

Newman, J. P., Wolff, W. T., & Hearst, E. (1980). The feature-positive effect in adult human subjects. *Journal of Experimental Psychology: Human Learning and Memory, 6,* 630–650.

Newman, M. G., & Stone, A. A. (1996). Does humor moderate the effects of experimentally induced stress? *Annals of Behavioral Medicine, 18,* 101–109.

Newschaffer, C. J., Croen, L. A., Daniels, J., Giarelli, E., Grether, J. K., Levy, S. E., . . . Windham, G. C. (2007). The epidemiology of autism spectrum disorders. *Annual Review of Public Health, 28,* 235–258.

Newsome, W. T., & Paré, E. B. (1988). A selective impairment of motion perception following lesions of the middle temporal visual area (MT). *Journal of Neuroscience, 8,* 2201–2211.

Niedenthal, P. M., Barsalou, L. W., Winkielman, P., Krauth-Gruber, S., & Ric, F. (2005). Embodiment in attitudes, social perception, and emotion. *Personality and Social Psychology Review, 9*(3), 184–211.

Nikles, C. D., II, Brecht, D. L., Klinger, E., & Bursell, A. L. (1998). The effects of current concern- and nonconcern-related waking suggestions on nocturnal dream content. *Journal of Personality and Social Psychology, 75,* 242–255.

Nir, Y., & Tononi, G. (2010). Dreaming and the brain: From phenomenology to neurophysiology. *Trends in Cognitive Sciences, 14*(2), 88–100.

Nisbett, R. E. (2009). *Intelligence and how to get it.* New York: Norton.

Nisbett, R. E., Aronson, J., Blair, C., Dickens, W., Flynn, J., Halpern, D. F., & Turkheimer, E. (2012). Intelligence: New findings and theoretical developments. *American Psychologist, 67*(2), 130–159. doi:10.1037/a0026699

Nisbett, R. E., Caputo, C., Legant, P., & Maracek, J. (1973). Behavior as seen by the actor and as seen by the observer. *Journal of Personality and Social Psychology, 27,* 154–164.

Nisbett, R. E., & Cohen, D. (1996). *Culture of honor: The psychology of violence in the South.* Boulder, CO: Westview Press.

Nisbett, R. E., & Miyamoto, Y. (2005). The influence of culture: Holistic versus analytic perception. *Trends in Cognitive Sciences, 9,* 467–473.

Nissen, M. J., & Bullemer, P. (1987). Attentional requirements of learning: Evidence from performance measures. *Cognitive Psychology, 19,* 1–32.

Nock, M. K. (2009). Why do people hurt themselves? New insights into the nature and functions of self-injury. *Current Directions in Psychological Science, 18,* 78–83. doi:10.1111/j.1467-8721.2009.01613.x

Nock, M. K. (2010). Self-injury. *Annual Review of Clinical Psychology, 6,* 339–363. doi: 10.1146/annurev.clinpsy.121208.131258

Nock, M. K., Borges, G., Bromet, E. J., Alonso, J., Angermeyer, M., Beautrais, A., . . . Williams, D. (2008). Cross-national prevalence and risk factors for suicidal ideation, plans, and attempts. *British Journal of Psychiatry, 192,* 98–105.

Nock, M. K., Borges, G., & Ono, Y. (Eds.) (2012). *Suicide: Global perspectives from the WHO World Mental Health Surveys.* New York: Cambridge University Press.

Nock, M. K., Green, J. G., Hwang, I., McLaughlin, K. A., Sampson, N. A., Zaslavsky, A. M., & Kessler, R. C. (2013). Prevalence, correlates and treatment of lifetime suicidal behavior among adolescents: Results from the National Comorbidity Survey Replication–Adolescent Supplement (NCSA–A). *Journal of the American Medical Association Psychiatry, 70*(3), 300–310. doi:10.1001/2013.jamapsychiatry.55

Nock, M. K., Holmberg, E. G., Photos, V. I., & Michel, B. D. (2007). Structured and semi-structured interviews. In M. Hersen & J. C. Thomas (Eds.), *Handbook of clinical interviewing with children* (pp. 30–49). Thousand Oaks, CA: Sage.

Nock, M. K., Kazdin, A. E., Hiripi, E., & Kessler, R. C. (2006). Prevalence, subtypes, and correlates of *DSM–IV* conduct disorder in the National Comorbidity Survey Replication. *Psychological Medicine, 36,* 699–710.

Nolen-Hoeksema, S. (2008). Gender differences in coping with depression across the lifespan. *Depression, 3,* 81–90.

Norby, S. (2015). Why forget? On the adaptive value of memory loss. *Perspectives on Psychological Science, 10,* 551–578.

Norcross, J. C., Hedges, M., & Castle, P. H. (2002). Psychologists conducting psychotherapy in 2001: A study of the Division 29 membership. *Psychotherapy: Theory/Research/Practice/Training, 39,* 97–102.

Norcross, J. C., & Rogan, J. D. (2013). Psychologists conducting psychotherapy in 2012: Current practices and historical trends among Division 29 members. *Psychotherapy, 50,* 490–495.

Norton, M. I., Frost, J. H., & Ariely, D. (2007). Less is more: The lure of ambiguity, or why familiarity breeds contempt. *Journal of Personality and Social Psychology, 92*(1), 97–105. doi:10.1037/0022-3514.92.1.97

Nosanchuk, T. A., & Lightstone, J. (1974). Canned laughter and public and private conformity. *Journal of Personality and Social Psychology, 29,* 153–156.

Nowak, M. A. (2006). Five rules for the evolution of cooperation. *Science, 314,* 1560–1563.

Nuttin, J. M. (1985). Narcissism beyond Gestalt and awareness: The name letter effect. *European Journal of Social Psychology, 15,* 353–361.

Nyborg, H., & Jensen, A. R. (2001). Occupation and income related to psychometric g. *Intelligence, 29,* 45–55.

Oately, K., Keltner, D., & Jenkins, J. M. (2006). *Understanding emotions* (2nd ed.). Malden, MA: Blackwell.

O'Brien, J. L., O'Keefe, K. M., LaViolette, P. S., DeLuca, A. N., Blacker, D., Dickerson, B. C., & Sperling, R. A. (2010). Longitudinal fMRI in elderly reveals loss of hippocampal activation with clinical decline. *Neurology, 74,* 1969–1976.

Ochsner, K. N., Bunge, S. A., Gross, J. J., & Gabrieli, J. D. E. (2002). Rethinking feelings: An fMRI study of the cognitive regulation of emotion. *Journal of Cognitive Neuroscience, 14,* 1215–1229.

Ochsner, K. N., Ray, R. R., Hughes, B., McRae, K., Cooper, J. C., Weber, J., . . . Gross, J. J. (2009). Bottom-up and top-down processes in emotion generation: Common and distinct neural mechanisms. *Psychological Science, 20,* 1322–1331.

O'Doherty, J. P., Dayan, P., Friston, K., Critchley, H., & Dolan, R. J. (2003). Temporal difference models and reward-related learning in the human brain. *Neuron, 38,* 329–337.

Ofshe, R. J. (1992). Inadvertent hypnosis during interrogation: False confession due to dissociative state, misidentified multiple personality, and the satanic cult hypothesis. *International Journal of Clinical and Experimental Hypnosis, 40,* 125–126.

Ofshe, R., & Watters, E. (1994). *Making monsters: False memories, psychotherapy, and sexual hysteria.* New York: Scribner/Macmillan.

Ohayon, M. M. (2002). Epidemiology of insomnia: What we know and what we still need to learn. *Sleep Medicine, 6,* 97–111.

Ohayon, M. M., Guilleminault, C., & Priest, R. G. (1999). Night terrors, sleepwalking, and confusional arousals in the general population: Their frequency and relationship to other sleep and mental disorders. *Journal of Clinical Psychiatry, 60,* 268–276.

Öhman, A. (1996). Preferential preattentive processing of threat in anxiety: Preparedness and attentional biases. In R. M. Rapee (Ed.), *Current controversies in the anxiety disorders.* New York: Guilford Press.

Öhman, A., Dimberg, U., & Öst, L. G. (1985). Animal and social phobias: Biological constraints on learned fear responses. In S. Reiss & R. Bootzin (Eds.), *Theoretical issues in behavior therapy* (pp. 123–175). New York: Academic Press.

Okagaki, L., & Sternberg, R. J. (1993). Parental beliefs and children's school performance. *Child Development, 64,* 36–56.

Okuda, J., Fujii, T., Ohtake, H., Tsukiura, T., Tanji, K., Suzuki, K., . . . Yamadori, A. (2003). Thinking of the future and the past: The roles of the frontal pole and the medial temporal lobes. *NeuroImage, 19,* 1369–1380.

Okulicz-Kozaryn, A. (2011). Europeans work to live and Americans live to work (Who is happy to work more: Americans or Europeans?). *Journal of Happiness Studies, 12*(2), 225–243.

Olatunji, B. O., & Wolitzky-Taylor, K. B. (2009). Anxiety sensitivity and the anxiety disorders: A meta-analytic review and synthesis. *Psychological Bulletin, 135,* 974–999.

Olausson, P. O., Haglund, B., Weitoft, G. R., & Cnattingius, S. (2001). Teenage child-bearing and long-term socioeconomic consequences: A case study in Sweden. *Family Planning Perspectives, 33,* 70–74.

Olds, J. (1956, October). Pleasure center in the brain. *Scientific American, 195,* 105–116.

Ollers, D. K., & Eilers, R. E. (1988). The role of audition in infant babbling. *Child Development, 59,* 441–449.

Olsson, A., Kopsida, E., Sorjonen, K., & Savic, I. (2016). Testosterone and estrogen impact social evaluations and vicarious emotions: A double-blind placebo-controlled study. *Emotion, 16,* 515–523.

Olsson, A., & Phelps, E. A. (2007). Social learning of fear. *Nature Neuroscience, 10,* 1095–1102.

Oltmanns, T. F., Neale, J. M., & Davison, G. C. (1991). *Case studies in abnormal psychology* (3rd ed.). New York: Wiley.

Olton, D. S., & Samuelson, R. J. (1976). Remembrance of places passed: Spatial memory in rats. *Journal of Experimental Psychology: Animal Behavior Processes, 2,* 97–116.

Ongley, S. F., & Malti, T. (2014). The role of moral emotions in the development of children's sharing behavior. *Developmental Psychology, 50*(4), 1148–1159. doi: 10.1037/a0035191

Ono, K. (1987). Superstitious behavior in humans. *Journal of the Experimental Analysis of Behavior, 47,* 261–271.

Orban, P., Lungu, O., & Doyon, J. (2008). Motor sequence learning and developmental dyslexia. *Annals of the New York Academy of Sciences, 1145,* 151–172.

Otto, M. W., Henin, A., Hirshfeld-Becker, D. R., Pollack, M. H., Biederman, J., & Rosenbaum, J. F. (2007). Posttraumatic stress disorder symptoms following media exposure to tragic events: Impact of 9/11 on children at risk for anxiety disorders. *Journal of Anxiety Disorders, 21,* 888–902.

Overmier, J. B., & Seligman, M. E. P. (1967). Effects of inescapable shock upon subsequent escape and avoidance learning. *Journal of Comparative and Physiological Psychology, 63,* 28–33.

Owens, W. A. (1966). Age and mental abilities: A second adult follow-up. *Journal of Educational Psychology, 57,* 311–325.

Oztekin, I., Curtis, C. E., & McElree, B. (2009). The medial temporal lobe and left inferior prefrontal cortex jointly support interference resolution in verbal working memory. *Journal of Cognitive Neuroscience, 21,* 1967–1979.

Pagnin, D., de Queiroz, V., Pini, S., & Cassano, G. B. (2008). Efficacy of ECT in depression: A meta-analytic review. *Focus, 6,* 155–162.

Paivio, A. (1971). *Imagery and verbal processes.* New York: Holt, Rinehart and Winston.

Paivio, A. (1986). *Mental representations: A dual coding approach.* New York: Oxford University Press.

Paluck, B. L., & Green, D. P. (2009). Prejudice reduction: What works? A review and assessment of research and practice. *Annual Review of Psychology, 60,* 339–367.

Pandit, J. J., Andrade, J., Bogod, D. G., Hitchman, J. M., Jonker, W. R. . . . Cook, T. M. (2014). The 5th National Audit Project (NAP5) on accidental awareness during general anaesthesia: Summary of main findings and risk factors. *Anaesthesia, 69,* 1089–1101.

Parbery-Clark, A., Skoe, E., & Kraus, N. (2009). Musical experience limits the degradative effects of background noise on the neural processing of sound. *Journal of Neuroscience, 11,* 14100–14107.

Parbery-Clark, A., Strait, D. L., Anderson, S., Hittner, E., & Kraus, N. (2011). Musical experience and the aging auditory system: Implications for cognitive abilities and hearing speech in noise. *PLoS One, 6,* e18082.

Parbery-Clark, A., Tierney, A., Strait, D. L., & Kraus, N. (2012). Musicians have fine-tuned neural distinction of speech syllables. *Neuroscience, 219,* 111–119.

Park, B., & Hastie, R. (1987). Perception of variability in category development: Instance- versus abstraction-based stereotypes. *Journal of Personality and Social Psychology, 53*(4), 621–635. doi:10.1037/0022-3514.53.4.621

Park, D. C., & McDonough, I. M. (2013). The dynamic aging mind: Revelations from functional neuroimaging research. *Perspectives on Psychological Science, 8*(1), 62–67. doi:10.1177/1745691612469034

Parker, E. S., Cahill, L. S., & McGaugh, J. L. (2006). A case of unusual autobiographical remembering. *Neurocase, 12,* 35–49.

Parker, G., Gibson, N. A., Brotchie, H., Heruc, G., Rees, A. M., & Hadzi-Pavlovic, D. (2006). Omega-3 fatty acids and mood disorders. *American Journal of Psychiatry, 163,* 969–978.

Parker, H. A., & McNally, R. J. (2008). Repressive coping, emotional adjustment, and cognition in people who have lost loved ones to suicide. *Suicide and Life-Threatening Behavior, 38,* 676–687.

Parkin, B. L., Ekhtiari, H., & Walsh, V. F. (2015). Non-invasive brain stimulation in cognitive neuroscience: A primer. *Neuron, 87,* 932–945.

Parkinson, B., & Totterdell, P. (1999). Classifying affect-regulation strategies. *Cognition and Emotion, 13,* 277–303.

Parrott, A. C. (2001). Human psychopharmacology of Ecstasy (MDMA): A review of 15 years of empirical research. *Human Psychopharmacology, 16,* 557–577.

Parrott, A. C., Morinan, A., Moss, M., & Scholey, A. (2005). *Understanding drugs and behavior.* Chichester, England: Wiley.

Parsons, T. (1975). The sick role and the role of the physician reconsidered. *Milbank Memorial Fund Quarterly, Health and Society, 53*(3), 257–278.

Pascual-Ferrá, P., Liu, Y., & Beatty, M. J. (2012). A meta-analytic comparison of the effects of text messaging to substance-induced impairment on driving performance. *Communication Research Reports, 29,* 229–238.

Pascual-Leone, A., Amedi, A., Fregni, F., & Merabet, L. B. (2005). The plastic human brain cortex. *Annual Review of Neuroscience, 28,* 377–401.

Pascual-Leone, A., Houser, C. M., Reese, K., Shotland, L. I., Grafman, J., Sato, S., . . . Cohen, L. G. (1993). Safety of rapid-rate transcranial magnetic stimulation in normal volunteers. *Electroencephalography and Clinical Neurophysiology, 89,* 120–130.

Patall, E. A., Cooper, H., & Robinson, J. C. (2008). The effects of choice on intrinsic motivation and related outcomes: A meta-analysis of research findings. *Psychological Bulletin, 134*(2), 270–300.

Patrick, C. J., Cuthbert, B. N., & Lang, P. J. (1994). Emotion in the criminal psychopath: Fear image processing. *Journal of Abnormal Psychology, 103,* 523–534.

Patterson, C. J. (1995). Lesbian mothers, gay fathers, and their children. In A. R. D'Augelli & C. J. Patterson (Eds.), *Lesbian, gay and bisexual identities across the lifespan: Psychological perspectives* (pp. 262–290). New York: Oxford University Press.

Patterson, C. J. (2013). Sexual orientation and family lives. In G. W. Peterson & K. R. Bush (Eds.), *The handbook of marriage and the family.* New York: Springer.

Pavlidis, I., Eberhardt, N. L., & Levine, J. A. (2002). Human behaviour: Seeing through the face of deception. *Nature, 415,* 35.

Pavlidou, E. V., Williams, J. M., & Kelly, L. M. (2009). Artificial grammar learning in primary school children with and without developmental dyslexia. *Annals of Dyslexia, 59,* 55–77.

Pavlov, I. P. (1923a). New researches on conditioned reflexes. *Science, 58,* 359–361.

Pavlov, I. P. (1923b, July 23). Pavloff. *Time, 1*(21), 20–21.

Pavlov, I. P. (1927). *Conditioned reflexes.* Oxford, England: Oxford University Press.

Payne, J. D., Kensinger, E. A., Wamsley, E., Spreng, R. N., Alger, S., Gibler, K., . . . & Stickgold, R. (2015). Napping and the selective consolidation of negative aspects of scenes. *Emotion, 15,* 176–186.

Payne, J. D., Schacter, D. L., Propper, R., Huang, L., Wamsley, E., Tucker, M. A., . . . Stickgold, R. (2009). The role of sleep in false memory formation. *Neurobiology of Learning and Memory, 92,* 327–334.

Payne, J. D., Stickgold, R., Swanberg, K., & Kensinger, E. A. (2008). Sleep preferentially enhances memory for emotional components of scenes. *Psychological Science, 19,* 781–788.

Pearce, J. M. (1987). A model of stimulus generalization for Pavlovian conditioning. *Psychological Review, 84,* 61–73.

Pearson, J., & Kosslyn, S. M. (2015). The heterogeneity of mental representation: Ending the imagery debate. *Proceedings of the National Academy of Sciences USA, 112,* 10089–10092.

Peck, J., & Shu, S. B. (2009). The effect of mere touch on perceived ownership. *Journal of Consumer Research, 36,* 434–447.

Pelham, B. W. (1985). Self-investment and self-esteem: Evidence for a Jamesian model of self-worth. *Journal of Personality and Social Psychology, 69,* 1141–1150.

Pelham, B. W., Carvallo, M., & Jones, J. T. (2005). Implicit egotism. *Current Directions in Psychological Science, 14,* 106–110.

Pelham, B. W., Mirenberg, M. C., & Jones, J. T. (2002). Why Susie sells seashells by the seashore: Implicit egotism and major life decisions. *Journal of Personality and Social Psychology, 82,* 469–487.

Penfield, W., & Rasmussen, T. (1950). *The cerebral cortex of man: A clinical study of localization of function.* New York: Macmillan.

Pennebaker, J. W., & Chung, C. K. (2007). Expressive writing, emotional upheavals, and health. In H. Friedman & R. Silver (Eds.), *Handbook of health psychology* (pp. 263–284). New York: Oxford University Press.

Pennebaker, J. W., Kiecolt-Glaser, J. K., & Glaser, R. (1988). Disclosure of traumas and immune function: Health implications for psychotherapy. *Journal of Consulting and Clinical Psychology, 56,* 239–245.

Pennebaker, J. W., & Sanders, D. Y. (1976). American graffiti: Effects of authority and reactance arousal. *Personality and Social Psychology Bulletin, 2,* 264–267.

Penner, L. A., Albrecht, T. L., Orom, H., Coleman, D. K., & Underwood, W. (2010). Health and health care disparities. In J. F. Dovidio, M. Hewstone, P. Glick, & V. M. Esses (Eds.), *The Sage handbook of prejudice, stereotyping and discrimination* (pp. 472–489). Thousand Oaks, CA: Sage.

Perenin, M.-T., & Vighetto, A. (1988). Optic ataxia: A specific disruption in visuomotor mechanisms. I. Different aspects of the deficit in reaching for objects. *Brain, 111,* 643–674.

Perera, T., George, M. S., Grammer, G., Janicak, P. G., Pascual-Leone, A., & Wirecki, T. S. (2016). The Clinical TMS Society consensus review and treatment recommendations for TMS therapy for major depressive disorder. *Brain Stimulation, 9,* 336–346.

Perilloux, H. K., Webster, G. D., & Gaulin, S. J. C. (2010). Signals of genetic quality and maternal investment capacity: The dynamic effects of fluctuating asymmetry and waist-to-hip ratio on men's ratings of women's attractiveness. *Social Psychological and Personality Science, 1*(1), 34–42. doi: 10.1177/1948550609349514

Perkins, D. N., & Grotzer, T. A. (1997). Teaching intelligence. *American Psychologist, 52,* 1125–1133.

Perlmutter, J. S., & Mink, J. W. (2006). Deep brain stimulation. *Annual Review of Neuroscience, 29,* 229–257.

Perloff, L. S., & Fetzer, B. K. (1986). Self-other judgments and perceived vulnerability to victimization. *Journal of Personality and Social Psychology, 50,* 502–510.

Perls, F. S., Hefferkine, R., & Goodman, P. (1951). *Gestalt therapy: Excitement and growth in the human personality.* New York: Julian Press.

Perrett, D. I., Burt, D. M., Penton-Voak, I. S., Lee, K. J., Rowland, D. A., & Edwards, R. (1999). Symmetry and human facial attractiveness. *Evolution and Human Behavior, 20,* 295–307.

Perry, R. B. (1996). *The thought and character of William James.* Nashville: Vanderbilt University Press.

Pessiglione, M., Seymour, B., Flandin, G., Dolan, R. J., & Frith, C. D. (2006). Dopamine-dependent prediction errors underpin reward-seeking behavior in humans. *Nature, 442,* 1042–1045.

Petersen, A. C., & Grockett, L. (1985). Pubertal timing and grade effects on adjustment. *Journal of Youth and Adolescence, 14,* 191–206.

Petersen, J. L., & Hyde, J. S. (2010). A meta-analytic review of research on gender differences in sexuality, 1993–2007. *Psychological Bulletin, 136*(1), 21–38. doi:10.1037/a0017504

Peterson, C., & Siegal, M. (1999). Representing inner worlds: Theory of mind in autistic, deaf and normal hearing children. *Psychological Science, 10,* 126–129.

Peterson, C., Slaughter, V., Moore, C., & Wellman, H. M. (2016). Peer social skills and theory of mind in children with autism, deafness, or typical development. *Developmental Psychology, 52*(1), 46–57. doi: 10.1037/a0039833

Peterson, L. R., & Peterson, M. J. (1959). Short-term retention of individual verbal items. *Journal of Experimental Psychology, 58,* 193–198.

Petitto, L. A., & Marentette, P. F. (1991). Babbling in the manual mode: Evidence for the ontogeny of language. *Science, 251,* 1493–1496.

Petrie, K. P., Booth, R. J., & Pennebaker, J. W. (1998). The immunological effects of thought suppression. *Journal of Personality and Social Psychology, 75,* 1264–1272.

Petry, N. M., Alessi, S. M., & Rash, C. J. (2013). Contingency management treatments decrease psychiatric symptoms. *Journal of Consulting and Clinical Psychology, 81*(5), 926–931. doi:10.1037/a0032499

Petty, R. E., & Cacioppo, J. T. (1986). The elaboration likelihood model of persuasion. In L. Berkowitz (Ed.), *Advances in experimental social psychology* (Vol. 19, pp. 123–205). New York: Academic Press.

Petty, R. E., Cacioppo, J. T., & Goldman, R. (1981). Personal involvement as a determinant of argument-based persuasion. *Journal of Personality and Social Psychology, 41,* 847–855.

Petty, R. E., & Wegener, D. T. (1998). Attitude change: Multiple roles for persuasion variables. In D. T. Gilbert, S. T. Fiske, & G. Lindzey (Eds.), *The handbook of social psychology* (4th ed., Vol. 1, pp. 323–390). Boston: McGraw-Hill.

Pham, M. T., Lee, L., & Stephen, A. T. (2012). Feeling the future: The emotional oracle effect. *Journal of Consumer Research, 39*(3), 461–477.

Phelan, J., Link, B., Stueve, A., & Pescosolido, B. (1997, August). *Public conceptions of mental illness in 1950 and 1996: Has sophistication increased? Has stigma declined?* Paper presented at the American Sociological Association, Toronto, Ontario.

Phelps, E. A. (2006). Emotion and cognition: Insights from studies of the human amygdala. *Annual Review of Psychology, 24,* 27–53.

Phelps, E. A., & LeDoux, J. L. (2005). Contributions of the amygdala to emotion processing: From animal models to human behavior. *Neuron, 48,* 175–187.

Phillips, F. (2002, January 24). Jump in cigarette sales tied to Sept. 11 attacks. *Boston Globe,* p. B1.

Phills, C. E., Kawakami, K., Tabi, E., Nadolny, D., & Inzlicht, M. (2011). Mind the gap: Increasing associations between the self and Blacks with approach behaviors. *Journal of Personality and Social Psychology, 100*(2), 197–210. doi:10.1037/a0022159

Piaget, J. (1954). *The child's conception of number.* New York: Norton.

Piaget, J. (1965). *The moral judgment of the child.* New York: Free Press. (Original work published 1932)

Piazza, J. R., Charles, S. T., Sliwinski, M. J., Mogle, J., & Almeida, D. M. (2013). Affective reactivity to daily stressors and long-term risk of reporting a chronic physical health condition. *Annals of Behavioral Medicine, 45,* 110–120.

Piff, P. K., Kraus, M. W., Côté, S., Cheng, B. H., & Keltner, D. (2010). Having less, giving more: The influence of social class on prosocial behavior. *Journal of Personality and Social Psychology, 99*(5), 771–784. doi: 10.1037/a0020092

Piff, P. K., Stancato, D. M., Côté, S., Mendoza-Denton, R., & Keltner, D. (2012). Higher social class predicts increased unethical behavior. *Proceedings of the National Academy of Sciences of the United States of America, 109*(11), 4086–4091. doi: 10.1073/pnas.1118373109

Pinel, J. P. J., Assanand, S., & Lehman, D. R. (2000). Hunger, eating, and ill health. *American Psychologist, 55,* 1105–1116.

Pines, A. M. (1993). Burnout: An existential perspective. In W. B. Schaufeli, C. Maslach, & T. Marek (Eds.), *Professional burnout: Recent developments in theory and research* (pp. 33–51). Washington, DC: Taylor & Francis.

Pinker, S. (1994). *The language instinct.* New York: Morrow.

Pinker, S. (1997a). Evolutionary psychology: An exchange. *New York Review of Books, 44,* 55–58.

Pinker, S. (1997b). *How the mind works.* New York: Norton.

Pinker, S. (2003). *The blank slate: The modern denial of human nature.* New York: Viking.

Pinker, S. (2007, March 19). A history of violence. *The New Republic Online.*

Pinker, S., & Bloom, P. (1990). Natural language and natural selection. *Behavioral and Brain Sciences, 13,* 707–784.

Pitcher, D., Garrido, L., Walsh, V., & Duchaine, B. C. (2008). Transcranial magnetic stimulation disrupts the perception and embodiment of facial expressions. *Journal of Neuroscience, 28*(36), 8929–8933.

Plassman, H., O'Doherty, J., Shiv, B., & Rangel, A. (2008). Marketing actions can modulate neural representations of experienced pleasantness. *Proceedings of the National Academy of Sciences, USA, 105,* 1050–1054.

Pleis, J. R., Lucas, J. W., & Ward, B. W. (2009). Summary of health statistics for U.S. adults: National health interview survey, 2008, *Vital Health Stat 10*(242). National Center for Health Statistics.

Plotnik, J. M., de Waal, F. B. M., & Reiss, D. (2006). Self-recognition in an Asian elephant. *Proceedings of the National Academy of Sciences, USA, 103,* 17053–17057.

Polanczyk, G., de Lima, M. S., Horta, B. L., Biederman, J., & Rohde, L. A. (2007). The worldwide prevalence of ADHD: A systematic review and metaregression analysis. *American Journal of Psychiatry, 164,* 942–948.

Poliak, S., & Peles, E. (2003). The local differentiation of myelinated axons at nodes of Ranvier. *Nature Reviews Neuroscience, 4,* 968–980.

Poole, D. A., Lindsay, S. D., Memon, A., & Bull, R. (1995). Psychotherapy and the recovery of memories of childhood sexual abuse: U.S. and British practitioners' opinions, practices, and experiences. *Journal of Consulting and Clinical Psychology, 63,* 426–487.

Poon, S. H., Sim, K., Sum, M. Y., Kuswanto, C. N., & Baldessarini, R. J. (2012). Evidence-based options for treatment-resistant adult bipolar disorder patients. *Bipolar Disorders, 14,* 573–584.

Pope, A. W., & Bierman, K. L. (1999). Predicting adolescent peer problems and antisocial activities: The relative roles of aggression and dysregulation. *Developmental Psychology, 35,* 335–346.

Porter, S., & ten Brinke, L. (2008). Reading between the lies: Identifying concealed and falsified emotions in universal facial expressions. *Psychological Science, 19,* 508–514.

Posner, M. I., & Raichle, M. E. (1994). *Images of mind.* New York: W. H. Freeman and Company.

Post, R. M., Frye, M. A., Denicoff, G. S., Leverich, G. S., Dunn, R. T., Osuch, E. A., . . . Jajodia, K. (2008). Emerging trends in the treatment of rapid cycling bipolar disorder: A selected review. *Bipolar Disorders, 2,* 305–315.

Posthuma, D., & de Geus, E. J. C. (2006). Progress in the molecular-genetic study of intelligence. *Current Directions in Psychological Science, 15,* 151–155.

Postman, L., & Underwood, B. J. (1973). Critical issues in interference theory. *Memory & Cognition, 1,* 19–40.

Postmes, T., & Spears, R. (1998). Deindividuation and anti-normative behavior: A meta-analysis. *Psychological Bulletin, 123,* 238–259.

Powell, R. A., Symbaluk, D. G., MacDonald, S. E., & Honey, P. L. (2009). *Introduction to learning and behavior* (3rd ed.). Belmont, CA: Wadsworth Cengage Learning.

Prakash, R. S., Voss, M. W., Erickson, K. I., & Kramer, A. F. (2015). Moving towards a healthier brain and mind. *Annual Review of Psychology, 66,* 769–797.

Prasada, S., & Pinker, S. (1993). Generalizations of regular and irregular morphology. *Language and Cognitive Processes, 8,* 1–56.

Pratkanis, A. R. (1992). The cargo-cult science of subliminal persuasion. *Skeptical Inquirer, 16,* 260–272.

Pressman, S. D., Cohen, S., Miller, G. E., Barkin, A., Rabin, B. S., & Treanor, J. J. (2005). Loneliness, social network size, and immune response to influenza vaccination in college freshmen. *Health Psychology, 24,* 297–306.

Price, J. L., & Davis, B. (2008). *The woman who can't forget: The extraordinary story of living with the most remarkable memory known to science.* New York: Free Press.

Prior, H., Schwartz, A., & Güntürkün, O. (2008). Mirror-induced behavior in the magpie (*Pica pica*): Evidence of self-recognition. *PLoS Biology, 6,* e202.

Prochaska, J. J., & Sallis, J. F. (2004). A randomized controlled trial of single versus multiple health behavior change: Promoting physical activity and nutrition among adolescents. *Health Psychology, 23,* 314–318.

Procopio, M., & Marriott, P. (2007). Intrauterine hormonal environment and risk of developing anorexia nervosa. *Archives of General Psychiatry, 64*(12), 1402–1407.

Protzko, J. (2015). The environment in raising early intelligence: A meta-analysis of the fadeout effect. *Intelligence, 53,* 202–210. doi: 10.1016/j.intell.2015.10.006

Protzko, J. (2016). Does the raising IQ-raising g distinction explain the fadeout effect? *Intelligence, 56,* 65–71. doi: 10.1016/j.intell.2016.02.008

Protzko, J., Aronson, J., & Blair, C. (2013). How to make a young child smarter: Evidence from the database of raising intelligence. *Perspectives on Psychological Science, 8*(1), 25–40. doi:10.1177/1745691612462585

Pruitt, D. G. (1998). Social conflict. In D. T. Gilbert, S. T. Fiske, & G. Lindzey (Eds.), *The handbook of social psychology* (4th ed., Vol. 2, pp. 470–503). New York: McGraw-Hill.

Punjabi, N. M. (2008). The epidemiology of adult obstructive sleep apnea. *Proceedings of the American Thoracic Society, 5,* 136–143.

Puterman, E., Lin, J., Blackburn, E. H., O'Donovan, A., Adler, N., & Epel, E. (2010). The power of exercise: Buffering the effect of chronic stress on telomere length. *PLoS ONE, 5,* e10837.

Pyc, M. A., & Rawson, K. A. (2009). Testing the retrieval effort hypothesis: Does greater difficulty correctly recalling information lead to higher levels of memory? *Journal of Memory and Language, 60,* 437–447.

Pyers, J. E., & Senghas, A. (2009). Language promotes false-belief understanding: Evidence from learners of a new sign language. *Psychological Science, 20*(7), 805–812.

Pyers, J. E., Shusterman, A., Senghas, A., Spelke, E. S., & Emmorey, K. (2010). Evidence from an emerging sign language reveals that language supports spatial cognition. *Proceedings of the National Academy of Sciences, USA, 107,* 12116–12120.

Quattrone, G. A. (1982). Behavioral consequences of attributional bias. *Social Cognition, 1,* 358–378.

Querleu, D., Lefebvre, C., Titran, M., Renard, X., Morillon, M., & Crepin, G. (1984). Réactivité de nouveau-né de moins de deux heures de vie á la voix maternelle [Reactivity of a newborn at less than two hours of life to the mother's voice]. *Journal de Gynécologie Obstétrique et de Biologie de la Reproduction, 13,* 125–134.

Qureshi, A., & Lee-Chiong, T. (2004). Medications and their effects on sleep. *Medical Clinics of North America, 88,* 751–766.

Race, E., Keane, M. M., & Verfaellie, M. (2011). Medial temporal lobe damage causes deficits in episodic memory and episodic future thinking not attributable to deficits in narrative construction. *Journal of Neuroscience, 31,* 10262–10269.

Radford, E., & Radford, M. A. (1949). *Encyclopedia of superstitions.* New York: Philosophical Library.

Raichle, M. E. (2015). The brain's default mode network. *Annual Review of Neuroscience, 38,* 433–447.

Raichle, M. E., & Mintun, M. A. (2006). Brain work and brain imaging. *Annual Review of Neuroscience, 29,* 449–476.

Rajaram, S. (2011). Collaboration both hurts and helps memory: A cognitive perspective. *Current Directions in Psychological Science, 20,* 76–81.

Rajaram, S., & Pereira-Pasarin, L. P. (2010). Collaborative memory: Cognitive research and theory. *Perspectives on Psychological Science, 6,* 649–663.

Ramachandran, V. S., & Altschuler, E. L. (2009). The use of visual feedback, in particular mirror visual feedback, in restoring brain function. *Brain, 132,* 1693–1710.

Ramachandran, V. S., & Blakeslee, S. (1998). *Phantoms in the brain: Probing the mysteries of the human mind.* New York: Morrow.

Ramachandran, V. S., & Brang, D. (2015). Phantom touch. In T. J. Prescott, E. Ahissar, & E. Izhikevich (Eds.), *Scholarpedia of Touch* (pp. 377–386). Amsterdam: Atlantis Press.

Ramachandran, V. S., Brang, D., & McGeoch, P. D. (2010). Dynamic reorganization of referred sensations by movements of phantom limbs. *NeuroReport, 21,* 727–730.

Ramachandran, V. S., Rodgers-Ramachandran, D., & Stewart, M. (1992). Perceptual correlates of massive cortical reorganization. *Science, 258,* 1159–1160.

Ramirez-Esparza, N., Gosling, S. D., Benet-Martinez, V., & Potter, J. P. (2004). Do bilinguals have two personalities? A special case of cultural frame-switching. *Journal of Research in Personality, 40,* 99–120.

Rand, D. G., & Nowak, M. A. (2016). Human cooperation. *Trends in Cognitive Sciences, 17*(8), 413–425. doi: 10.1016/j.tics.2013.06.003

Randall, A. (2012, May 5). Black women and fat. *New York Times.* Retrieved from http://www.nytimes.com/2012/05/06/opinion/sunday/why-black-women-are-fat.html?_r=0

Rapaport, D. (1946). *Diagnostic psychological testing: The theory, statistical evaluation, and diagnostic application of a battery of tests.* Chicago: Year Book Publishers.

Rapoport, J., Chavez, A., Greenstein, D., Addington, A., & Gogtay, N. (2009). Autism-spectrum disorders and childhood onset schizophrenia: Clinical and biological contributions to a relationship revisited. *Journal of the American Academy of Child and Adolescent Psychiatry, 48,* 10–18.

Rapoport, J. L. (1990). Obsessive-compulsive disorder and basal ganglia dysfunction. *Psychological Medicine, 20,* 465–469.

Rauschecker, J. P., & Scott, S. K. (2009). Maps and streams in the auditory cortex: Nonhuman primates illuminate human speech processing. *Nature Neuroscience, 12,* 718–724.

Raven, J., Raven, J. C., & Court, J. H. (2004). *Manual for Raven's Progressive Matrices and Vocabulary Scales.* San Antonio: Harcourt Assessment.

Raz, A., Fan, J., & Posner, M. I. (2005). Hypnotic suggestion reduces conflict in the brain. *Proceedings of the National Academy of Sciences, 102,* 9978–9983.

Raz, A., Shapiro, T., Fan, J., & Posner, M. I. (2002). Hypnotic suggestion and the modulation of Stroop interference. *Archives of General Psychiatry, 59,* 1155–1161.

Raz, N. (2000). Aging of the brain and its impact on cognitive performance: Integration of structural and functional findings. In F. I. M. Craik & T. A. Salthouse (Eds.), *The handbook of aging and cognition* (pp. 1–90). Mahwah, NJ: Erlbaum.

Read, K. E. (1965). *The high valley.* London: Allen and Unwin.

Reason, J., & Mycielska, K. (1982). *Absent-minded?: The psychology of mental lapses and everyday errors.* Englewood Cliffs, NJ: Prentice-Hall.

Reber, A. S. (1996). *Implicit learning and tacit knowledge: An essay on the cognitive unconscious.* New York: Oxford University Press.

Reber, P. J., Gitelman, D. R., Parrish, T. B., & Mesulam, M. M. (2003). Dissociating explicit and implicit category knowledge with fMRI. *Journal of Cognitive Neuroscience, 15,* 574–583.

Recanzone, G. H., & Sutter, M. L. (2008). The biological basis of audition. *Annual Review of Psychology, 59,* 119–142.

Rechsthaffen, A., Gilliland, M. A., Bergmann, B. M., & Winter, J. B. (1983). Physiological correlates of prolonged sleep deprivation in rats. *Science, 221,* 182–184.

Redick, T. S. (2015). Working memory training and interpreting interactions in intelligence interventions. *Intelligence, 50,* 14–20.

Redick, T. S., Shipstead, Z., Harrison, T. L., Hicks, K. L., Fried, D. E., Hambrick, D. Z., . . . Engle, R. W. (2013). No evidence of intelligence improvement after working memory training: A randomized, placebo-controlled study. *Journal of Experimental Psychology: General, 142,* 359–379. doi:10.1037/a002908

Reed, C. L., Klatzky, R. L., & Halgren, E. (2005). What vs. where in touch: An fMRI study. *NeuroImage, 25,* 718–726.

Reed, D. R. (2008). Birth of a new breed of supertaster. *Chemical Senses, 33,* 489–491.

Reed, G. (1988). *The psychology of anomalous experience* (rev. ed.). Buffalo, NY: Prometheus Books.

Reeve, C. L., Heggestad, E. D., & Lievens, F. (2009). Modeling the impact of test anxiety and test familiarity on the criterion-related validity of cognitive ability tests. *Intelligence, 37*(1), 34–41.

Regan, P. C. (1998). What if you can't get what you want? Willingness to compromise ideal mate selection standards as a function of sex, mate value, and relationship context. *Personality and Social Psychology Bulletin, 24,* 1294–1303.

Reichbach, G. L. (2012, May 16). A judge's plea for pot [op-ed article]. *New York Times,* p. A27.

Rieger, G., Linsenmeier, J. A. W., Gygax, L., & Bailey, J. M. Sexual orientation and childhood gender nonconformity: Evidence from home videos. *Dev. Psychol. 44* (2008), pp. 46–58.

Reis, H. T., Maniaci, M. R., Caprariello, P. S., Eastwick, P. W., & Finkel, E. J. (2011). Familiarity does indeed promote attraction in live interaction. *Journal of Personality and Social Psychology, 101*(3), 557–570. doi:10.1037/a0022885

Reiss, D., & Marino, L. (2001). Mirror self-recognition in the bottlenose dolphin: A case of cognitive convergence. *Proceedings of the National Academy of Sciences, USA, 98,* 5937–5942.

Reissland, N. (1988). Neonatal imitation in the first hour of life: Observations in rural Nepal. *Developmental Psychology, 24,* 464–469.

Renner, K. E. (1964). Delay of reinforcement: A historical review. *Psychological Review, 61,* 341–361.

Renner, M. J., & Mackin, R. (1998). A life stress instrument for classroom use. *Teaching of Psychology, 25,* 46–48.

Rensink, R. A. (2002). Change detection. *Annual Review of Psychology, 53,* 245–277.

Rensink, R. A., O'Regan, J. K., & Clark, J. J. (1997). To see or not to see: The need for attention to perceive changes in scenes. *Psychological Science, 8,* 368–373.

Repacholi, B. M., & Gopnik, A. (1997). Early reasoning about desires: Evidence from 14- and 18-month-olds. *Developmental Psychology, 33,* 12–21.

Rescorla, R. A. (2006). Stimulus generalization of excitation and inhibition. *Quarterly Journal of Experimental Psychology, 59,* 53–67.

Rescorla, R. A., & Wagner, A. R. (1972). A theory of Pavlovian conditioning: Variations in effectiveness of reinforcement and nonreinforcement. In A. Black & W. F. Prokasky, Jr. (Eds.), *Classical conditioning II* (pp. 64–99). New York: Appleton-Century-Crofts.

Ressler, K. J., & Mayberg, H. S. (2007). Targeting abnormal neural circuits in mood and anxiety disorders: From the laboratory to the clinic. *Nature Neuroscience, 10,* 1116–1124.

Ressler, K. J., & Nemeroff, C. B. (1999). Role of norepinephrine in the pathophysiology and treatment of mood disorders. *Biological Psychiatry, 46,* 1219–1233.

Rice, K. G., Richardson, C. M. E., & Clark, D. (2012). Perfectionism, procrastination, and psychological distress. *Journal of Counseling Psychology, 39,* 288–302.

Richards, M., Black, S., Mishra, G., Gale, C. R., Deary, I. J., & Batty, D. G. (2009). IQ in childhood and the metabolic syndrome in middle age: Extended follow-up of the 1946 British birth cohort study. *Intelligence, 37*(6), 567–572.

Richards, M. H., Crowe, P. A., Larson, R., & Swarr, A. (1998). Developmental patterns and gender differences in the experience of peer companionship during adolescence. *Child Development, 69,* 154–163.

Richardson, D. S. (2014). Everyday aggression takes many forms. *Current Directions in Psychological Science, 23*(3), 220–224. doi: 10.1177/0963721414530143

Ridenour, T. A., & Howard, M. O. (2012). Inhalants abuse: Status of etiology and intervention. In J. C. Verster, K. Brady, M. Galanter, & P. Conrod (Eds.), *Drug abuse and addiction in medical illness: Causes, consequences, and treatment* (pp. 189–199). New York: Springer.

Rimer, J., Dwan, K., Lawlor, D. A., Greig, C. A., McMurdo, M., Morley, W., & Mead, G. E. (2012). Exercise for depression. *Cochrane Database of Systematic Reviews, 7,* CD004366.

Risko, E. F., Anderson, N., Sarwal, A., Engelhardt, M., & Kingstone, A. (2012). Every attention: Variation in mind wandering and memory in a lecture. *Applied Cognitive Psychology, 26,* 234–242.

Risman, J. E., Coyle, J. T., Green, R. W., Javitt, D. C., Benes, F. M., Heckers, S., & Grace, A. A. (2008). Circuit-based framework for understanding neurotransmitter and risk gene interactions in schizophrenia. *Trends in Neurosciences, 31,* 234–242.

Rivera, L. A. (2012) Hiring as cultural matching: The case of elite professional service firms. *American Sociological Review, 77,* 999–1022.

Rizzolatti, G., & Craighero, L. (2004). The mirror-neuron system. *Annual Review of Neuroscience, 27,* 169–192.

Rizzolatti, G., & Sinigaglia, C. (2010). The functional role of the parieto-frontal mirror circuit. *Nature Reviews Neuroscience, 11,* 264–274.

Roberts, G. A. (1991). Delusional belief and meaning in life: A preferred reality? *British Journal of Psychiatry, 159,* 20–29.

Roberts, G. A., & McGrady, A. (1996). Racial and gender effects on the relaxation response: Implications for the development of hypertension. *Biofeedback and Self-Regulation, 21,* 51–62.

Robertson, L. C. (1999). What can spatial deficits teach us about feature binding and spatial maps? *Visual Cognition, 6,* 409–430.

Robertson, L. C. (2003). Binding, spatial attention and perceptual awareness. *Nature Reviews Neuroscience, 4,* 93–102.

Robins, L. N., Helzer, J. E., Hesselbrock, M., & Wish, E. (1980). Vietnam veterans three years after Vietnam. In L. Brill & C. Winick (Eds.), *The yearbook of substance use and abuse* (Vol. 11). New York: Human Sciences Press.

Robins, R. W., Fraley, R. C., & Krueger, R. F. (Eds.). (2007). *Handbook of research methods in personality psychology.* New York: Guilford Press.

Robinson, D. N. (1995). *An intellectual history of psychology.* Madison: University of Wisconsin Press.

Roediger, H. L., III. (2000). Why retrieval is the key process to understanding human memory. In E. Tulving (Ed.), *Memory, consciousness, and the brain: The Tallinn conference* (pp. 52–75). Philadelphia: Psychology Press.

Roediger, H. L., III, & Karpicke, J. D. (2006). Test-enhanced learning: Taking memory tests improves long-term retention. *Psychological Science, 17,* 249–255.

Roediger, H. L., III, & McDermott, K. B. (1995). Creating false memories: Remembering words not presented in lists. *Journal of Experimental Psychology: Learning, Memory, and Cognition, 21,* 803–814.

Roediger, H. L., III, & McDermott, K. B. (2000). Tricks of memory. *Current Directions in Psychological Science, 9,* 123–127.

Roediger, H. L., III, Weldon, M. S., & Challis, B. H. (1989). Explaining dissociations between implicit and explicit measures of retention: A processing account. In H. L. Roediger, III, & F. I. M. Craik (Eds.), *Varieties of memory and consciousness: Essays in honor of Endel Tulving* (pp. 3–41). Hillsdale, NJ: Erlbaum.

Rogers, C. R. (1951). *Client-centered therapy: Its current practice, implications, and theory.* Boston: Houghton Mifflin.

Rohrer, D. (2015). Student instruction should be distributed over long time periods. *Educational Psychology Review, 27,* 635–643.

Rohrer, D., Dedrick, R. F., & Sterschic, S. (2015). Interleaved practice improves mathematics learning. *Journal of Educational Psychology, 107,* 900–908.

Roisman, G. I., Masten, A. S., Coatsworth, J. D., & Tellegen, A. (2004). Salient and emerging developmental tasks in the transition to adulthood. *Child Development, 75,* 123–133. doi: 10.1111/j.1467-8624.2004.00658.x

Rolls, E. T. (2015). Taste, olfactory, and food reward value processing in the human brain. *Progress in Neurobiology, 127–128*, 64–90.

Ronay, R., & Galinsky, A. D. (2011). Lex talionis: Testosterone and the law of retaliation. *Journal of Experimental Social Psychology, 47*(3), 702–705. doi: 10.1016/j.jesp.2010.11.009

Rondan, C., & Deruelle, C. (2004). Face processing in high functioning autistic adults: A look into spatial frequencies and the inversion effect. *Journal of Cognitive and Behavioral Psychotherapies, 4*, 149–164.

Rosch, E. H. (1973). Natural categories. *Cognitive Psychology, 4*, 328–350.

Rosch, E. H. (1975). Cognitive representations of semantic categories. *Journal of Experimental Psychology: General, 104*, 192–233.

Rosch, E. H., & Mervis, C. B. (1975). Family resemblances: Studies in the internal structure of categories. *Cognitive Psychology, 7*, 573–605.

Rose, S. P. R. (2002). Smart drugs: Do they work? Are they ethical? Will they be legal? *Nature Reviews Neuroscience, 3*, 975–979.

Roseman, I. J. (1984). Cognitive determinants of emotion: A structural theory. *Review of Personality and Social Psychology, 5*, 11–36.

Roseman, I. J., & Smith, C. A. (2001). Appraisal theory: Overview, assumptions, varieties and controversies. In K. R. Scherer, A. Schorr, & T. Johnstone (Eds.), *Appraisal processes in emotion: Theory, methods, research* (pp. 3–19). New York: Oxford University Press.

Rosenbaum, J. E. (2009). Patient teenagers? A comparison of the sexual behavior of virginity pledgers and matched nonpledgers. *Pediatrics, 123*(1), e110–e120.

Rosenberg, M. (1965). *Society and the adolescent self-image.* Princeton, NJ: Princeton University Press.

Rosenhan, D. (1973). On being sane in insane places. *Science, 179*, 250–258.

Rosenkranz, K., Williamon, A., & Rothwell, J. C. (2007). Motorcortical excitability and synaptic plasticity is enhanced in professional musicians. *The Journal of Neuroscience, 27*, 5200–5206.

Rosenstein, M. J., Milazzo-Sayre, L. J., & Manderscheid, R. W. (1990). Characteristics of persons using specifically inpatient, outpatient, and partial care programs in 1986. In M. A. Sonnenschein (Ed.), *Mental health in the United States* (pp. 139–172). Washington, DC: U.S. Government Printing Office.

Rosenthal, R., & Fode, K. L. (1963). The effect of experimenter bias on the performance of the albino rat. *Behavioral Science, 8*, 183–189.

Roser, M. E., Aslin, R. N., McKenzie, R., Zahra, D., & Fiser, J. (2015). Enhanced visual statistical learning in adults with autism. *Neuropsychology, 29*, 163–172.

Ross, L. (1977). The intuitive psychologist and his shortcomings: Distortions in the attribution process. *Advances in Experimental Social Psychology, 10*, 173–220.

Ross, L., Amabile, T. M., & Steinmetz, J. L. (1977). Social roles, social control, and biases in social-perception processes. *Journal of Personality and Social Psychology, 35*, 485–494.

Ross, L., Lepper, M. R., & Hubbard, M. (1975). Perseverance in self-perception and social perception: Biased attributional processing the debriefing paradigm. *Journal of Personality and Social Psychology, 32*, 880–892.

Ross, L., & Nisbett, R. E. (1991). *The person and the situation.* New York: McGraw-Hill.

Rosvall, M., & Bergstrom, C. T. (2008). Maps of random walks on complex networks reveal community structure. *Proceedings of the National Academy of Sciences, USA, 105*, 1118–1123.

Roth, B., Becker, N., Romeyke, S., Schäfer, S., Domnick, F., & Spinath, F. M. (2015). Intelligence and school grades: A meta-analysis. *Intelligence, 53*, 118–137. doi: 10.1016/j.intell.2015.09.002

Roth, H. P., & Caron, H. S. (1978). Accuracy of doctors' estimates and patients' statements on adherence to a drug regimen. *Clinical Pharmacology and Therapeutics, 23*, 361–370.

Rothbart, M. K., & Bates, J. E. (1998). Temperament. In W. Damon (Series Ed.) & N. Eisenberg (Vol. Ed.), *Handbook of child psychology: Vol. 3. Social, emotional and personality development* (5th ed., pp. 105–176). New York: Wiley.

Rothbaum, B. O., & Schwartz, A. C. (2002). Exposure therapy for posttraumatic stress disorder. *American Journal of Psychotherapy, 56*, 59–75.

Rotter, J. B. (1966). Generalized expectancies for internal versus external locus of control of reinforcement. *Psychological Monographs: General and Applied, 80*, 1–28.

Roy-Byrne, P. P., & Cowley, D. S. (2002). Pharmacological treatments for panic disorder, generalized anxiety disorder, specific phobia, and social anxiety disorder. In P. E. Nathan & J. M. Gorman (Eds.), *A guide to treatments that work* (2nd ed., pp. 337–365). New York: Oxford University Press.

Rozin, P. (1968). Are carbohydrate and protein intakes separately regulated? *Journal of Comparative and Physiological Psychology, 65*, 23–29.

Rozin, P., Bauer, R., & Catanese, D. (2003). Food and life, pleasure and worry, among American college students: Gender differences and regional similarities. *Journal of Personality and Social Psychology, 85*, 132–141.

Rozin, P., Dow, S., Moscovitch, M., & Rajaram, S. (1998). What causes humans to begin and end a meal? A role for memory for what has been eaten, as evidenced by a study of multiple meal eating in amnesic patients. *Psychological Science, 9*, 392–396.

Rozin, P., Kabnick, K., Pete, E., Fischler, C., & Shields, C. (2003). The ecology of eating: Smaller portion size in France than in the United States helps to explain the French paradox. *Psychological Science, 14*, 450–454.

Rozin, P., & Kalat, J. W. (1971). Specific hungers and poison avoidance as adaptive specializations of learning. *Psychological Review, 78*, 459–486.

Rozin, P., Trachtenberg, S., & Cohen, A. B. (2001). Stability of body image and body image dissatisfaction in American college students over about the last 15 years. *Appetite, 37*, 245–248.

Rubin, M., & Badea, C. (2012). They're all the same! . . . but for several different reasons: A review of the multicausal nature of perceived group variability. *Current Directions in Psychological Science, 21*(6), 367–372. doi:10.1177/0963721412457363

Rubin, Z. (1973). *Liking and loving.* New York: Holt, Rinehart & Winston.

Rudman, L. A., Ashmore, R. D., & Gary, M. L. (2001). "Unlearning" automatic biases: The malleability of implicit prejudice and stereotypes. *Journal of Personality and Social Psychology, 81*, 856–868.

Rummer, R., Schweppe, J., Schlegelmilch, R., & Grice, M. (2014). Mood is linked to vowel type: The role of articulatory movements. *Emotion, 14*(2), 246–250. doi: 10.1037/a0035752

Rusbult, C. E. (1983). A longitudinal test of the investment model: The development (and deterioration) of satisfaction and commitment in heterosexual involvements. *Journal of Personality and Social Psychology, 45*, 101–117.

Rusbult, C. E., & Van Lange, P. A. M. (2003). Interdependence, interaction and relationships. *Annual Review of Psychology, 54*, 351–375.

Ruscio, A. M., Stein, D. J., Chiu, W. T., Kessler, R. C. (2010). The epidemiology of obsessive-compulsive disorder in the National Comorbidity Survey Replication. *Molecular Psychiatry, 15*, 53–63.

Rushton, J. P. (1995). Asian achievement, brain size, and evolution: Comment on A. H. Yee. *Educational Psychology Review, 7,* 373–380.

Rushton, J. P., & Templer, D. I. (2009). National differences in intelligence, crime, income, and skin color. *Intelligence, 37*(4), 341–346.

Russell, B. (1945). *A history of Western philosophy.* New York: Simon & Schuster.

Russell, J., Gee, B., & Bullard, C. (2012). Why do young children hide by closing their eyes? Self-visibility and the developing concept of self. *Journal of Cognition and Development, 13*(4), 550–576. doi:10.1080/15248372.2011.594826

Russell, J. A. (1980). A circumplex model of affect. *Journal of Personality and Social Psychology, 39,* 1161–1178.

Rutledge, R. B., Lazzaro, S. C., Lau, B., Myers, C. E., Gluck, M. A., & Glimcher, P. W. (2009). Dopaminergic drugs modulate learning rates and perseveration in Parkinson's patients in a dynamic foraging task. *Journal of Neuroscience, 29,* 15104–15114.

Rutter, M., & Silberg, J. (2002). Gene–environment interplay in relation to emotional and behavioral disturbance. *Annual Review of Psychology, 53,* 463–490.

Ryan, R. M., & Deci, E. L. (2000). Self-determination theory and the facilitation of intrinsic motivation, social development, and well-being. *American Psychologist, 55,* 68–78.

Ryle, G. (1949). *The concept of mind.* Hutchinson, London.

Sachs, J. S. (1967). Recognition of semantic, syntactic, and lexical changes in sentences. *Psychonomic Bulletin & Review, 1,* 17–18.

Sacks, O. (1995). *An anthropologist on Mars.* New York: Knopf.

Sacks, O. (1996). *An anthropologist on Mars* (pbk). Visalia, CA: Vintage.

Sahakian, B., & Morein-Zamir, S. (2007). Professor's little helper. *Nature, 450*(7173), 1157–1159.

Saks, E. R. (2013, January 25). Successful and schizophrenic. *New York Times.* Retrieved from http://www.nytimes.com/2013/01/27/opinion/sunday/schizophrenic-not-stupid.html

Sallet, J., Mars, R. B., Noonan, M. P., Andersson, J. L., O'Reilly, J. X., Jbabdi, S., . . . Rushworth, M. F. S. (2011). Social network size affects neural circuits in macaques. *Science, 334*(6056), 697–700. doi:10.1126/science.1210027

Salmon, D. P., & Bondi, M. W. (2009). Neuropsychological assessment of dementia. *Annual Review of Psychology, 60,* 257–282.

Salovey, P., & Grewal, D. (2005). The science of emotional intelligence. *Current Directions in Psychological Science, 14*(6), 281–285.

Salthouse, T. A. (1984). Effects of age and skill in typing. *Journal of Experimental Psychology: General, 113,* 345–371.

Salthouse, T. A. (1987). Age, experience, and compensation. In C. Schooler & K. W. Schaie (Eds.), *Cognitive functioning and social structure over the life course* (pp. 142–150). Norwood, NJ: Ablex.

Salthouse, T. A. (1996a). General and specific mediation of adult age differences in memory. *Journal of Gerontology: Series B: Psychological Sciences and Social Sciences, 51B,* P30–P42.

Salthouse, T. A. (1996b). The processing-speed theory of adult age differences in cognition. *Psychological Review, 103,* 403–428.

Salthouse, T. A. (2000). Pressing issues in cognitive aging. In D. Park & N. Schwartz (Eds.), *Cognitive aging: A primer* (pp. 43–54). Philadelphia: Psychology Press.

Salthouse, T. A. (2006). Mental exercise and mental aging. *Perspectives on Psychological Science, 1*(1), 68–87.

Salthouse, T. A. (2015). Do cognitive interventions alter the rate of age-related cognitive change? *Intelligence, 53,* 86–91. doi: 10.1016/j.intell.2015.09.004

Sampson, R. J., & Laub, J. H. (1995). Understanding variability in lives through time: Contributions of life-course criminology. *Studies of Crime Prevention, 4,* 143–158.

Sandin, R. H., Enlund, G., Samuelsson, P., & Lenmarken, C. (2000). Awareness during anesthesia: A prospective case study. *Lancet, 355,* 707–711.

Sara, S. J. (2000). Retrieval and reconsolidation: Toward a neurobiology of remembering. *Learning & Memory, 7,* 73–84.

Sarris, V. (1989). Max Wertheimer on seen motion: Theory and evidence. *Psychological Research, 51,* 58–68.

Sarter, M. (2006). Preclinical research into cognition enhancers. *Trends in Pharmacological Sciences, 27,* 602–608.

Satcher, D. (2001). *The surgeon general's call to action to promote sexual health and responsible sexual behavior.* Washington, DC: U.S. Government Printing Office.

Satterwhite, C. L., Torrone, E., Meites, E., Dunne, E. F., Mahajan, R., Ocfernia, M. C., . . . Weinstock, H. (2013). Sexually transmitted infections among U. S. women and men: Prevalence and incidence estimates, 2008. *Sexually Transmitted Diseases, 40*(3), 187–193.

Savage, C. R., Deckersbach, T., Heckers, S., Wagner, A. D., Schacter, D. L., Alpert, N. M., . . . Rauch, S. L. (2001). Prefrontal regions supporting spontaneous and directed application of verbal learning strategies: Evidence from PET. *Brain, 124,* 219–231.

Savic, I., Berglund, H., & Lindstrom, P. (2005). Brain response to putative pheromones in homosexual men. *Proceedings of the National Academy of Sciences, USA, 102,* 7356–7361.

Savic, I., & Lindstrom, P. (2008). PET and MRI show differences in cerebral asymmetry and functional connectivity between homo- and heterosexual subjects. *Proceedings of the National Academy of Sciences, USA, 105*(27), 9403–9408.

Savin-Williams, R. C., & Vrangalova, Z. (2013). Mostly heterosexual as a distinct sexual orientation group: A systematic review of the empirical evidence. *Developmental Review, 33,* 58–88.

Sawa, A., & Snyder, S. H. (2002). Schizophrenia: Diverse approaches to a complex disease. *Science, 295,* 692–695.

Sawyer, T. F. (2000). Francis Cecil Sumner: His views and influence on African American higher education. *History of Psychology, 3*(2), 122–141.

Scarborough, E., & Furumoto, L. (1987). *Untold lives: The first generation of American women psychologists.* New York: Columbia University Press.

Scarr, S., Pakstis, A. J., Katz, S. H., & Barker, W. B. (1977). Absence of a relationship between degree of White ancestry and intellectual skills within a Black population. *Human Genetics, 39*(1), 69–86.

Schachter, S. (1982). Recidivism and self-cure of smoking and obesity. *American Psychologist, 37,* 436–444.

Schachter, S., & Singer, J. E. (1962). Cognitive, social, and physiological determinants of emotional state. *Psychological Review, 69,* 379–399.

Schacter, D. L. (1987). Implicit memory: History and current status. *Journal of Experimental Psychology: Learning, Memory, and Cognition, 13,* 501–518.

Schacter, D. L. (1996). *Searching for memory: The brain, the mind, and the past.* New York: Basic Books.

Schacter, D. L. (1999). The seven sins of memory: Insights from psychology and cognitive neuroscience. *American Psychologist, 54*(3), 182–203.

Schacter, D. L. (2001a). *Forgotten ideas, neglected pioneers: Richard Semon and the story of memory.* Philadelphia: Psychology Press.

Schacter, D. L. (2001b). *The seven sins of memory: How the mind forgets and remembers.* Boston: Houghton Mifflin.

Schacter, D. L. (2012). Adaptive constructive processes and the future of memory. *American Psychologist, 67,* 603–613.

Schacter, D. L., & Addis, D. R. (2007). The cognitive neuroscience of constructive memory: Remembering the past and imagining the future.

Philosophical Transactions of the Royal Society of London. Series B: Biological Sciences, 362, 773–786.

Schacter, D. L., Addis, D. R., & Buckner, R. L. (2007). Remembering the past to imagine the future: The prospective brain. *Nature Reviews Neuroscience, 8,* 657–661.

Schacter, D. L., Addis, D. R., & Buckner, R. L. (2008). Episodic simulation of future events: Concepts, data, and applications. *Annals of the New York Academy of Sciences, 1124,* 39–60.

Schacter, D. L., Addis, D. R., Hassabis, D., Martin, V. C., Spreng, R. N., & Szpunar, K. K. (2012). The future of memory: Remembering, imagining, and the brain. *Neuron, 16,* 582–583.

Schacter, D. L., Alpert, N. M., Savage, C. R., Rauch, S. L., & Albert, M. S. (1996). Conscious recollection and the human hippocampal formation: Evidence from positron emission tomography. *Proceedings of the National Academy of Sciences, USA, 93,* 321–325.

Schacter, D. L., & Curran, T. (2000). Memory without remembering and remembering without memory: Implicit and false memories. In M. S. Gazzaniga (Ed.), *The new cognitive neurosciences* (2nd ed., pp. 829–840). Cambridge, MA: MIT Press.

Schacter, D. L., Dobbins, I. G., & Schnyer, D. M. (2004). Specificity of priming: A cognitive neuroscience perspective. *Nature Reviews Neuroscience, 5,* 853–862.

Schacter, D. L., Gaesser, B., & Addis, D. R. (2012). Remembering the past and imagining the future in the elderly. *Gerontologist, 59*(2), 143–151. doi:10.1159/000342198

Schacter, D. L., Guerin, S. A., & St. Jacques, P. L. (2011). Memory distortion: An adaptive perspective. *Trends in Cognitive Sciences, 15,* 467–474.

Schacter, D. L., Harbluk, J. L., & McLachlan, D. R. (1984). Retrieval without recollection: An experimental analysis of source amnesia. *Journal of Verbal Learning and Verbal Behavior, 23,* 593–611.

Schacter, D. L., Israel, L., & Racine, C. A. (1999). Suppressing false recognition in younger and older adults: The distinctiveness heuristic. *Journal of Memory and Language, 40,* 1–24.

Schacter, D. L., Reiman, E., Curran, T., Yun, L. S., Bandy, D., McDermott, K. B., & Roediger, H. L., III. (1996). Neuroanatomical correlates of veridical and illusory recognition memory: Evidence from positron emission tomography. *Neuron, 17,* 267–274.

Schacter, D. L. & Szpunar, K. K. (2015). Enhancing attention and memory during video-recorded lectures. *Scholarship of Teaching and Learning in Psychology, 1,* 60–71.

Schacter, D. L., & Tulving, E. (1994). *Memory systems 1994.* Cambridge, MA: MIT Press.

Schacter, D. L., Wagner, A. D., & Buckner, R. L. (2000). Memory systems of 1999. In E. Tulving & F. I. M. Craik (Eds.), *The Oxford handbook of memory* (pp. 627–643). New York: Oxford University Press.

Schafer, R. B., & Keith, P. M. (1980). Equity and depression among married couples. *Social Psychology Quarterly, 43,* 430–435.

Schaie, K. W. (1996). *Intellectual development in adulthood: The Seattle Longitudinal Study.* New York: Cambridge University Press.

Schaie, K. W. (2005). *Developmental influences on adult intelligence: The Seattle Longitudinal Study.* New York: Oxford University Press.

Schapira, A. H. V., Emre, M., Jenner, P., & Poewe, W. (2009). Levodopa in the treatment of Parkinson's disease. *European Journal of Neurology, 16,* 982–989.

Schenk, T., Ellison, A., Rice, N., & Milner, A. D. (2005). The role of V5/MT+ in the control of catching movements: An rTMS study. *Neuropsychologia, 43,* 189–198.

Scherer, K. R. (1999). Appraisal theory. In T. Dalgleish & M. Power (Eds.), *Handbook of cognition and emotion* (pp. 637–663). New York: Wiley.

Scherer, K. R. (2001). The nature and study of appraisal: A review of the issues. In K. R. Scherer, A. Schorr, & T. Johnstone (Eds.), *Appraisal processes in emotion: Theory, methods, research* (pp. 369–391). New York: Oxford University Press.

Schildkraut, J. J. (1965). The catecholamine hypothesis of affective disorders: A review of supporting evidence. *American Journal of Psychiatry, 122,* 509–522.

Schilling, O. K., Wahl, H.-W., & Wiegering, S. (2013). Affective development in advanced old age: Analyses of terminal change in positive and negative affect. *Developmental Psychology, 49*(5), 1011–1020. doi:10.1037/a0028775

Schlegel, A., & Barry, H., III. (1991). *Adolescence: An anthropological inquiry.* New York: Free Press.

Schmader, T., Johns, M., & Forbes, C. (2008). An integrated process model of stereotype threat effects on performance. *Psychological Review, 115,* 336–356.

Schmitt, D. P., Jonason, P. K., Byerley, G. J., Flores, S. D., Illbeck, B. E., O'Leary, K. N., & Qudrat, A. (2012). A reexamination of sex differences in sexuality: New studies reveal old truths. *Current Directions in Psychological Science, 21*(2), 135–139. doi:10.1177/0963721412436808

Schmitt, D. P., Realo, A., Voracek, M., & Allik, J. (2008). Why can't a man be more like a woman? Sex differences in personality traits across 55 cultures. *Journal of Personality and Social Psychology, 94,* 168–182.

Schneider, B. H., Atkinson, L., & Tardif, C. (2001). Child–parent attachment and children's peer relations: A quantitative review. *Developmental Psychology, 37,* 86–100.

Schnorr, J. A., & Atkinson, R. C. (1969). Repetition versus imagery instructions in the short- and long-term retention of paired associates. *Psychonomic Science, 15,* 183–184.

Schoenemann, P. T., Sheenan, M. J., & Glotzer, L. D. (2005). Prefrontal white matter volume is disproportionately larger in humans than in other primates. *Nature Neuroscience, 8,* 242–252.

Schott, B. J., Henson, R. N., Richardson-Klavehn, A., Becker, C., Thoma, V., Heinze, H. J., & Duzel, E. (2005). Redefining implicit and explicit memory: The functional neuroanatomy of priming, remembering, and control of retrieval. *Proceedings of the National Academy of Sciences, USA, 102,* 1257–1262.

Schouwenburg, H. C. (1995). Academic procrastination: Theoretical notions, measurement, and research. In J. R. Ferrari, J. L. Johnson, & W. G. McCown (Eds.), *Procrastination and task avoidance: Theory, research, and treatment* (pp. 71–96). New York: Plenum Press.

Schreiner, C. E., Read, H. L., & Sutter, M. L. (2000). Modular organization of frequency integration in primary auditory cortex. *Annual Review of Neuroscience, 23,* 501–529.

Schreiner, C. E., & Winer, J. A. (2007). Auditory cortex mapmaking: Principles, projections, and plasticity. *Neuron, 56,* 356–365.

Schubert, T. W., & Koole, S. L. (2009). The embodied self: Making a fist enhances men's power-related self-conceptions. *Journal of Experimental Social Psychology, 45,* 828–834.

Schultz, D., Izard, C. E., & Bear, G. (2004). Children's emotion processing: Relations to emotionality and aggression. *Development and Psychopathology, 16*(2), 371–387.

Schultz, W. (2006). Behavioral theories and the neurophysiology of reward. *Annual Review of Psychology, 57,* 87–115.

Schultz, W. (2007). Behavioral dopamine signals. *Trends in Neurosciences, 30,* 203–210.

Schultz, W., Dayan, P., & Montague, P. R. (1997). A neural substrate of prediction and reward. *Science, 275,* 1593–1599.

Schwartz, B. L. (2002). *Tip-of-the-tongue states: Phenomenology, mechanisms, and lexical retrieval.* Mahwah, NJ: Erlbaum.

Schwartz, H. A., Eichstaedt, J. C., Kern, M. L., Dziurzynski, L., Ramones, S. M., Agrawal, M., . . . Ungar, L. H. (2013). Personality, gender, and age in the language of social media: The open-vocabulary approach. *PLoS ONE, 8*, e73791.

Schwartz, J. H., & Westbrook, G. L. (2000). The cytology of neurons. In E. R. Kandel, G. H. Schwartz, & T. M. Jessell (Eds.), *Principles of neural science* (pp. 67–104). New York: McGraw-Hill.

Schwartz, S., & Maquet, P. (2002). Sleep imaging and the neuropsychological assessment of dreams. *Trends in Cognitive Sciences, 6*, 23–30.

Schwartzman, A. E., Gold, D., & Andres, D. (1987). Stability of intelligence: A 40-year follow-up. *Canadian Journal of Psychology, 41*, 244–256.

Schwarz, N. (2012). Feelings-as-information theory. In P. A. M. Van Lange, A. W. Kruglanski, & E. T. Higgins (Eds.), *Handbook of theories of social psychology* (Vol. 1, pp. 289–308). Thousand Oaks, CA: Sage.

Schwarz, N., & Clore, G. L. (1983). Mood, misattribution, and judgments of well-being: Informative and directive functions of affective states. *Journal of Personality and Social Psychology, 45*, 513–523.

Schwarz, N., Mannheim, Z., & Clore, G. L. (1988). How do I feel about it? The informative function of affective states. In K. Fiedler & J. Forgas (Eds.), *Affect cognition and social behavior: New evidence and integrative attempts* (pp. 44–62). Toronto: C. J. Hogrefe.

Scoville, W. B., & Milner, B. (1957). Loss of recent memory after bilateral hippocampal lesions. *Journal of Neurology, Neurosurgery, and Psychiatry, 20*, 11–21.

Sedlmeier, P., Eberth, J., Schwarz, M., Zimmermann, D., Haarig, F., Jaeger, S., & Kunze, S. (2012). The psychological effects of meditation: A meta-analysis. *Psychological Bulletin, 138*, 1139–1171.

Seeman, T. E., Dubin, L. F., & Seeman, M. (2003). Religiosity/spirituality and health: A critical review of the evidence for biological pathways. *American Psychologist, 58*, 53–63.

Segall, M. H., Lonner, W. J., & Berry, J. W. (1998). Cross-cultural psychology as a scholarly discipline: On the flowering of culture in behavioral research. *American Psychologist, 53*(10), 1101–1110.

Sehulster, J. R. (1989). Content and temporal structure of autobiographical knowledge: Remembering twenty-five seasons at the Metropolitan Opera. *Memory & Cognition, 17*, 590–596.

Seidman, G. (2013). Self-presentation and belonging on Facebook: How personality influences social media use and motivations. *Personality and Individual Differences, 54*, 402–407.

Seligman, M. E. P. (1971). Phobias and preparedness. *Behavior Therapy, 2*, 307–320.

Seligman, M. E. P. (1995). The effectiveness of psychotherapy: The *Consumer Reports* study. *American Psychologist, 48*, 966–971.

Selye, H., & Fortier, C. (1950). Adaptive reaction to stress. *Psychosomatic Medicine, 12*, 149–157.

Semenza, C. (2009). The neuropsychology of proper names. *Mind & Language, 24*, 347–369.

Semenza, C., & Zettin, M. (1989). Evidence from aphasia for the role of proper names as pure referring expressions. *Nature, 342*, 678–679.

Senghas, A., Kita, S., & Ozyurek, A. (2004). Children create core properties of language: Evidence from an emerging sign language in Nicaragua. *Science, 305*, 1782.

Senior, J. (2014). *All joy and no fun: The paradox of modern parenthood.* New York: Harper-Collins.

Senju, A., Southgate, V., White, S., & Frith, U. (2009). Mindblind eyes: An absence of spontaneous theory of mind in Asperger syndrome. *Science, 325*, 883–885.

Serpell, R. (1974). Aspects of intelligence in a developing country. *African Social Research, 17*, 578–596.

Seybold, K. S., & Hill, P. C. (2001). The role of religion and spirituality in mental and physical health. *Current Directions in Psychological Science, 10*, 21–23.

Seymour, K., Clifford, C. W. G., Logothetis, N. K., & Bartels, A. (2010). Coding and binding of color and form in visual cortex. *Cerebral Cortex.* doi:10.1093/cercor/bhp265

Shahaeian, A., Peterson, C. C., Slaughter, V., & Wellman, H. M. (2011). Culture and the sequence of steps in theory of mind development. *Developmental Psychology, 47*(5), 1239–1247. doi: 10.1037/a0023899

Shallcross, A. J., Ford, B. Q, Floerke, V. A., & Mauss, I. B. (2013). Getting better with age: The relationship between age, acceptance, and negative affect. *Journal of Personality and Social Psychology, 104*(4), 734–749. doi:10.1037/a0031180

Shallice, T., Fletcher, P., Frith, C. D., Grasby, P., Frackowiak, R. S. J., & Dolan, R. J. (1994). Brain regions associated with acquisition and retrieval of verbal episodic memory. *Nature, 368*, 633–635.

Shariff, A. F., & Tracy, J. L. (2011). What are emotion expressions for? *Current Directions in Psychological Science, 20*(6), 395–399.

Sharot, T. (2011). *The optimism bias: A tour of the irrationally positive brain.* New York: Pantheon Books.

Shaw, J., & Porter, S. (2015). Constructing rich false memories of committing crime. *Psychological Science, 26*, 291–301.

Shaw, J. S., Bjork, R. A., & Handal, A. (1995). Retrieval-induced forgetting in an eyewitness paradigm. *Psychonomic Bulletin & Review, 13*, 1023–1027.

Sheehan, P. (1979). Hypnosis and the process of imagination. In E. Fromm & R. S. Shor (Eds.), *Hypnosis: Developments in research and new perspectives* (pp. 293–319). Chicago: Aldine.

Shenton, M. E., Dickey, C. C., Frumin, M., & McCarley, R. W. (2001). A review of MRI findings in schizophrenia. *Schizophrenia Research, 49*, 1–52.

Shepherd, G. M. (1988). *Neurobiology.* New York: Oxford University Press.

Shepperd, J., Malone, W., & Sweeny, K. (2008). Exploring the causes of the self-serving bias. *Social and Personality Psychology Compass, 2*(2), 895–908.

Sherry, D. F., & Schacter, D. L. (1987). The evolution of multiple memory systems. *Psychological Review, 94*, 439–454.

Sherry, S. B., & Hall, P. A. (2009). The perfectionism model of binge eating: Tests of an integrative model. *Journal of Personality and Social Psychology, 96*(3), 690–709.

Shiffman, S., Gnys, M., Richards, T. J., Paty, J. A., & Hickcox, M. (1996). Temptations to smoke after quitting: A comparison of lapsers and maintainers. *Health Psychology, 15*, 455–461.

Shih, M., Pittinsky, T. L., & Ambady, N. (1999). Stereotype susceptibility: Identity salience and shifts in quantitative performance. *Psychological Science, 10*, 80–83.

Shimamura, A. P., & Squire, L. R. (1987). A neuropsychological study of fact memory and source amnesia. *Journal of Experimental Psychology: Learning, Memory, and Cognition, 13*, 464–473.

Shin, H., & Ryan, A. M. (2014). Early adolescent friendships and academic adjustment: Examining selection and influence processes with longitudinal social network analysis. *Developmental Psychology, 50*(11), 2462–2472. doi: 10.1037/a0037922

Shin, L. M., Rauch, S. L., & Pitman, R. K. (2006). Amygdala, medial prefrontal cortex, and hippocampal function in PTSD. *Annals of the New York Academy of Science, 1071*, 67–79.

Shinskey, J. L., & Munakata, Y. (2005). Familiarity breeds searching. *Psychological Science, 16*(8), 596–600.

Shipstead, Z., Redick, T. S., & Engle, R. W. (2012). Is working memory training effective? *Psychological Bulletin, 138*, 628–654.

Shiv, B., Loewenstein, G., Bechara, A., Damasio, H., & Damasio, A. R. (2005). Investment behavior and the negative side of emotion. *Psychological Science, 16*, 435–439.

Shomstein, S., & Yantis, S. (2004). Control of attention shifts between vision and audition in human cortex. *Journal of Neuroscience, 24,* 10702–10706.

Shore, C. (1986). Combinatorial play: Conceptual development and early multiword speech. *Developmental Psychology, 22,* 184–190.

Shultz, S., & Dunbar, R. (2010). Encephalization is not a universal macroevolutionary phenomenon in mammals but is associated with sociality. *Proceedings of the National Academy of Sciences,107,* 21582–21586.

Shweder, R. A., & Sullivan, M. A. (1993). Cultural psychology: Who needs it? *Annual Review of Psychology, 44,* 497–523.

Siegel, E. H., Sands, M. K., Condon, P., Chang, Y., Dy, J., Quigley, K. S., & Barrett, L. F. (2015). Emotion fingerprints or emotion populations? A meta-analytic investigation of autonomic features of emotion categories. Unpublished manuscript.

Siegel, S. (2005). Drug tolerance, drug addiction, and drug anticipation. *Current Directions in Psychological Science, 14,* 296–300.

Siegel, S., Baptista, M. A. S., Kim, J. A., McDonald, R. V., & Weise-Kelly, L. (2000). Pavlovian psychopharmacology: The associative basis of tolerance. *Experimental and Clinical Psychopharmacology, 8,* 276–293.

Siegler, R. S. (1992). The other Alfred Binet. *Developmental Psychology, 28*(2), 179–190. doi:10.1037/0012-1649.28.2.179

Sigman, M., Spence, S. J., & Wang, T. (2006). Autism from developmental and neuropsychological perspectives. *Annual Review of Clinical Psychology, 2,* 327–355.

Silvani, A., Calandra-Buonaura, G., Dampney, R. A., & Cortelli, P. (2016). Brain-heart interactions: Physiology and clinical implications. *Philosophical Transactions of the Royal Society, A, 347* doi: 10.1098/rsta.2015.0181

Silver, N. (2013, March 26). How opinion on same-sex marriage is changing, and what it means. *New York Times.* Retrieved from http://fivethirtyeightblogs.nytimes.com/2013/03/26/how-opinion-on-same-sex-marriage-is-changing-and-what-it-means/

Silverman, A. M., Gwinn, J. D., & Van Boven, L. (2014). Stumbling in their shoes: Disability simulations reduce judged capabilities of disabled people. *Social Psychological and Personality Science, 6*(4), 464–471. doi: 10.1177/1948550614559650

Simon, R. W. (2008). The joys of parenthood reconsidered. *Contexts, 7,* 40–45.

Simons, D. J., & Levin, D. T. (1998). Failure to detect changes to people during a real-world interaction. *Psychonomic Bulletin & Review, 5,* 644–649.

Simons, D. J., & Rensink, R. A. (2005). Change blindness: Past, present, and future. *Trends in Cognitive Sciences, 9,* 16–20.

Simonton, D. K. (2006). Presidential IQ, openness, intellectual brilliance, and leadership: Estimates and correlations for 42 U.S. chief executives. *Political Psychology, 27*(4), 511–526. doi:10.1111/j.1467-9221.2006.00524.x

Simonsohn, U. (2015). Small telescopes. *Psychological Science, 26,* 559–569.

Simpson, E. L. (1974). Moral development research: A case study of scientific cultural bias. *Human Development, 17,* 81–106.

Simpson, J. A., Collins, W. A., & Salvatore, J. E. (2011). The impact of early interpersonal experience on adult romantic relationship functioning: Recent findings from the Minnesota Longitudinal Study of Risk and Adaptation. *Current Directions in Psychological Science, 20*(6), 355–359. doi:10.1177/0963721411418468

Simpson, S. J., & Raubenheimer, D. (2014). Perspective: Tricks of the trade. *Nature, 508,* S66. doi: 10.1038/508S66a

Singer, P. (1975). *Animal liberation: A new ethics for our treatment of animals.* New York: Random House.

Singer, T., Seymour, B., O'Doherty, J., Kaube, H., Dolan, R. J., & Frith, C. D. (2004). Empathy for pain involves the affective but not sensory components of pain. *Science, 303,* 1157–1162.

Siu, A. L., & U.S. Preventive Services Task Force. (2016). Screening for Autism Spectrum Disorder in young children: U.S. Preventive Services Task Force recommendation statement. *JAMA, 315,* 691–696.

Skinner, B. F. (1938). *The behavior of organisms: An experimental analysis.* New York: Appleton-Century-Crofts.

Skinner, B. F. (1948). "Superstition" in the pigeon. *Journal of Experimental Psychology, 38,* 168–172.

Skinner, B. F. (1953). *Science and human behavior.* New York: Macmillan.

Skinner, B. F. (1957). *Verbal behavior.* New York: Appleton-Century-Crofts.

Skinner, B. F. (1971). *Beyond freedom and dignity.* New York: Bantam Books.

Skinner, B. F. (1979). *The shaping of a behaviorist: Part two of an autobiography.* New York: Knopf.

Skinner, B. F. (1986). *Walden II.* Englewood Cliffs, NJ: Prentice Hall. (Original work published 1948)

Skoe, E., & Kraus, N. (2012). A little goes a long way: How the adult brain is shaped by musical training in adulthood. *Journal of Neuroscience, 32,* 11507–11510.

Skotko, B. G., Levine, S. P., & Goldstein, R. (2011). Self-perceptions from people with Down syndrome. *American Journal of Medical Genetics Part A, 155*(10), 2360–2369. doi:10.1002/ajmg.a.34235

Slater, A., Morison, V., & Somers, M. (1988). Orientation discrimination and cortical function in the human newborn. *Perception, 17,* 597–602.

Slotnick, S. D., & Schacter, D. L. (2004). A sensory signature that distinguished true from false memories. *Nature Neuroscience, 7,* 664–672.

Smart, E., Smart, L, & Morton, L. (2003). *Bringing Elizabeth home: A journey of faith and hope.* New York: Doubleday.

Smetacek, V. (2002). Balance: Mind-grasping gravity. *Nature, 415,* 481.

Smith, A. R., Chein, J., & Steinberg, L. (2014). Peers increase adolescent risk taking even when the probabilities of negative outcomes are known. *Developmental Psychology, 50*(5), 1564–1568. doi: 10.1037/a0035696

Smith, A. R., Seid, M. A., Jimanez, L. C., & Wcislo, W. T. (2010). Socially induced brain development in a facultatively eusocial sweat bee *Megalopta genalis* (Halictidae). *Proceedings of the Royal Society B: Biological Sciences.*

Smith, C. N., Frascino, J. C., Hopkins, R. O., & Squire, L. R. (2013). The nature of anterograde and retrograde impairment after damage to the medial temporal lobe. *Neuropsychologia, 51,* 2709–2714.

Smith, E. E., & Jonides, J. (1997). Working memory: A view from neuroimaging. *Cognitive Psychology, 33,* 5–42.

Smith, M. L., Glass, G. V., & Miller, T. I. (1980). *The benefits of psychotherapy.* Baltimore: Johns Hopkins University Press.

Smith, N., & Tsimpli, I.-M. (1995). *The mind of a savant.* Oxford, England: Oxford University Press.

Snedeker, J., Geren, J., & Shafto, C. (2007). Starting over: International adoption as a natural experiment in language development. *Psychological Science, 18,* 79–87.

Snedeker, J., Geren, J., & Shafto, C. (2012). Disentangling the effects of cognitive development and linguistic expertise: A longitudinal study of the acquisition of English in internationally adopted children. *Cognitive Psychology, 65,* 39–76.

Snyder, M., & Swann, W. B. (1978). Hypothesis testing processes in social interaction. *Journal of Personality and Social Psychology, 36,* 1202–1212.

Solomon, S., Greenberg, J., & Pyszczynski, T. (1991). A terror management theory of social behavior: The psychological functions of self-esteem and cultural worldviews. In M. P. Zanna (Ed.), *Advances in experimental social psychology* (Vol. 24, pp. 93–159). New York: Academic Press.

Solomon, S., Greenberg, J., & Pyszczynski, T. (2004). The cultural animal: Twenty years of terror management theory and research. In J. Greenberg, S. L. Koole, & T. Pyszczynski (Eds.), *Handbook of experimental existential psychology* (pp. 13–34). New York: Guilford Press.

Son, L. K., & Metcalfe, J. (2000). Metacognitive and control strategies in study-time allocation. *Journal of Experimental Psychology: Learning, Memory, and Cognition, 26,* 204–221.

Sparrow, B., Liu, J., & Wegner, D. M. (2011). Google effects on memory: Cognitive consequence of having information at our fingertips. *Science, 333,* 776–778.

Spearman, C. (1904). "General intelligence," objectively determined and measured. *American Journal of Psychology, 15,* 201–293.

Spelke, E. S. (2005). Sex differences in intrinsic aptitude for mathematics and science: A critical review. *The American Psychologist, 60*(9), 950–958. doi:10.1037/0003-066X.60.9.950

Spence, K. W. (1936). The nature of discrimination learning in animals. *Psychological Review, 43,* 427–449.

Spencer, L.G. (1929) *Illustrated phrenology: The science and art teaching how to read character. A manual of mental science.* London: L.N. Fowler & Company.

Sperling, G. (1960). The information available in brief visual presentations. *Psychological Monographs, 74* (Whole No. 48).

Spiro, H. M., McCrea Curnan, M. G., Peschel, E., & St. James, D. (1994). *Empathy and the practice of medicine: Beyond pills and the scalpel.* New Haven, CT: Yale University Press.

Spitz, R. A. (1949). Motherless infants. *Child Development, 20,* 145–155.

Sprecher, S. (1999). "I love you more today than yesterday": Romantic partners' perceptions of changes in love and related affect over time. *Journal of Personality and Social Psychology, 76,* 46–53.

Squire, L. R. (1992). Memory and the hippocampus: A synthesis from findings with rats, monkeys, and humans. *Psychological Review, 99,* 195–231.

Squire, L. R. (2009). The legacy of patient HM for neuroscience. *Neuron, 61,* 6–9.

Squire, L. R., & Kandel, E. R. (1999). *Memory: From mind to molecules.* New York: Scientific American Library.

Squire, L. R., Knowlton, B., & Musen, G. (1993). The structure and organization of memory. *Annual Review of Psychology, 44,* 453–495.

Squire, L. R., & Wixted, J. T. (2011). The cognitive neuroscience of memory since HM. *Annual Review of Neuroscience, 34,* 259–288.

Srivistava, S., John, O. P., Gosling, S. D., & Potter, J. (2003). Development of personality in early and middle adulthood: Set like plaster or persistent change? *Journal of Personality and Social Psychology, 84,* 1041–1053.

Sroufe, L. A., Egeland, B., & Kruetzer, T. (1990). The fate of early experience following developmental change: Longitudinal approaches to individual adaptation in childhood. *Child Development, 61,* 1363–1373.

Staddon, J. E. R., & Simmelhag, V. L. (1971). The "superstition" experiment: A reexamination of its implications for the principles of adaptive behavior. *Psychological Review, 78,* 3–43.

Stahl, A. E., & Feigenson, L. (2015). Observing the unexpected enhances infants' learning and exploration. *Science, 348*(6230), 91–94. doi: 10.1126/science.aaa3799

St. Jacques, P. L., & Schacter, D. L. (2013). Modifying memory: Selectively enhancing and updating personal memories for a museum tour by reactivating them. *Psychological Science, 24,* 537–543.

Stanca, L. (2016). The geography of well-being: Do children make us happy, where, and why? *World Happiness Report.* Retrieved from http://worldhappiness.report/

Staw, B. M., & Hoang, H. (1995). Sunk costs in the NBA: Why draft order affects playing time and survival in professional basketball. *Administrative Science Quarterly, 40,* 474–494.

Steele, C. M., & Aronson, J. (1995). Stereotype threat and the intellectual test performance of African Americans. *Journal of Personality and Social Psychology, 69,* 797–811.

Steele, C. M., & Josephs, R. A. (1990). Alcohol myopia: Its prized and dangerous effects. *American Psychologist, 45,* 921–933.

Steele, H., Steele, M., Croft, C., & Fonagy, P. (1999). Infant-mother attachment at one year predicts children's understanding of mixed emotions at six years. *Social Development, 8,* 161–178.

Stein, D. J., Phillips, K. A., Bolton, D., Fulford, K. W. M., Sadler, J. Z., & Kendler, K. S. (2010). What is a mental/psychiatric disorder? From *DSM–IV* to *DSM–V. Psychological Medicine, 40*(11), 1759–1765. doi:10.1017/S0033291709992261.

Stein, M., Federspiel, A., Koenig, T., Wirth, M., Lehmann, C., Wiest, R, . . . Dierks, T. (2009). Reduced frontal activation with increasing second language proficiency. *Neuropsychologia, 47,* 2712–2720.

Stein, M. B. (1998). Neurobiological perspectives on social phobia: From affiliation to zoology. *Biological Psychiatry, 44,* 1277–1285.

Stein, M. B., Chavira, D. A., & Jang, K. L. (2001). Bringing up bashful baby: Developmental pathways to social phobia. *Psychiatric Clinics of North America, 24,* 661–675.

Stein, Z., Susser, M., Saenger, G., & Marolla, F. (1975). *Famine and development: The Dutch hunger winter of 1944–1945.* Oxford, England: Oxford University Press.

Steinbaum, E. A., & Miller, N. E. (1965). Obesity from eating elicited by daily stimulation of hypothalamus. *American Journal of Physiology, 208,* 1–5.

Steinberg, L. (2007). Risk taking in adolescence: New perspectives from brain and behavioral science. *Current Directions in Psychological Science, 16*(2), 55–59. doi:10.1111/j.1467-8721.2007.00475x

Steinberg, L., & Monahan, K. C. (2007). Age differences in resistance to peer influence. *Developmental Psychology, 43,* 1531–1543.

Steinberg, L., & Morris, A. S. (2001). Adolescent development. *Annual Review of Psychology, 52,* 83–110.

Steiner, F. (1986). Differentiating smiles. In E. Branniger-Huber & F. Steiner (Eds.), *FACS in psychotherapy research* (pp. 139–148). Zurich: Universität Zürich, Department of Clinical Psychology.

Steiner, J. E. (1973). The gustofacial response: Observation on normal and anencephalic newborn infants. In J. F. Bosma (Ed.), *Fourth symposium on oral sensation and perception: Development in the fetus and infant* (DHEW 73–546; pp. 254–278). Bethesda, MD: U.S. Department of Heath, Education, and Welfare.

Steiner, J. E. (1979). Human facial expressions in response to taste and smell stimulation. *Advances in Child Development and Behavior, 13,* 257–295.

Stellar, J. R., & Stellar, E. (1985). *The neurobiology of motivation and reward.* New York: Springer-Verlag.

Stelmack, R. M. (1990). Biological bases of extraversion: Psychophysiological evidence. *Journal of Personality, 58,* 293–311.

Stephens, R. S. (1999). Cannabis and hallucinogens. In B. S. McCrady & E. E. Epstein (Eds.), *Addictions: A comprehensive guidebook* (pp. 121–140). New York: Oxford University Press.

Sterelny, K., & Griffiths, P. E. (1999). *Sex and death: An introduction to philosophy of biology.* Chicago: University of Chicago Press.

Stern, J. A., Brown, M., Ulett, A., & Sletten, I. (1977). A comparison of hypnosis, acupuncture, morphine, Valium, aspirin, and placebo in the management of experimentally induced pain. In W. E. Edmonston (Ed.), *Conceptual and investigative approaches to hypnosis and hypnotic*

phenomena (Vol. 296, pp. 175–193). New York: Annals of the New York Academy of Sciences.

Sternberg, R. J. (1986). A triangular theory of love. *Psychological Review, 93,* 119–135.

Sternberg, R. J. (1999). The theory of successful intelligence. *Review of General Psychology, 3*(4), 292–316. doi:10.1037/1089-2680.3.4.292

Sternberg, R. J. (2006). The Rainbow Project: Enhancing the SAT through assessments of analytical, practical, and creative skills. *Intelligence, 34*(4), 321–350. doi: 10.1016/j.intell.2006.01.002

Stevens, G., & Gardner, S. (1982). *The women of psychology* (Vol. 1). Rochester: Schenkman Books.

Stevens, J. (1988). An activity approach to practical memory. In M. M. Gruneberg, P. E. Morris, & R. N. Sykes (Eds.), *Practical aspects of memory: Current research and issues* (Vol. 1, pp. 335–341). New York: Wiley.

Stevenson, R. J., & Boakes, R. A. (2003). A mnemonic theory of odor perception. *Psychological Review, 110,* 340–364.

Stickgold, R., Hobson, J. A., Fosse, R., & Fosse, M. (2001). Sleep, learning, and dreams: Off-line memory reprocessing. *Science, 294,* 1052–1057.

Stickgold, R., Malia, A., Maguire, D., Roddenberry, D., & O'Connor, M. (2000). Replaying the game: Hypnagogic images in normals and amnesics. *Science, 290,* 350–353.

Stone, A. A., Schwartz, J. E., Broderick, J. E., & Deaton, A. (2010). A snapshot of the age distribution of psychological well-being in the United States. *Proceedings of the National Academy of Sciences, USA, 107*(22), 9985–9990. doi:10.1073/pnas.1003744107

Stone, J., Perry, Z. W., & Darley, J. M. (1997). "White men can't jump": Evidence for the perceptual confirmation of racial stereotypes following a basketball game. *Basic and Applied Social Psychology, 19,* 291–306.

Stoodley, C. J., Ray, N. J., Jack, A., & Stein, J. F. (2008). Implicit learning in control, dyslexic, and garden-variety poor readers. *Annals of the New York Academy of Sciences, 1145,* 173–183.

Storms, M. D. (1973). Videotape and the attribution process: Reversing actors' and observers' points of view. *Journal of Personality and Social Psychology, 27,* 165–175.

Strack, F., Martin, L. L., & Stepper, S. (1988). Inhibiting and facilitating conditions of the human smile: A nonobtrusive test of the facial feedback hypothesis. *Journal of Personality and Social Psychology, 54,* 768–777.

Strayer, D. L., Drews, F. A., & Johnston, W. A. (2003). Cell phone induced failures of visual attention during simulated driving. *Journal of Experimental Psychology: Applied, 9,* 23–32.

Streissguth, A. P., Barr, H. M., Bookstein, F. L., Sampson, P. D., & Carmichael Olson, H. (1999). The long-term neurocognitive consequences of prenatal alcohol exposure: A 14-year study. *Psychological Science, 10,* 186–190.

Striano, T., & Reid, V. M. (2006). Social cognition in the first year. *Trends in Cognitive Sciences, 10*(10), 471–476.

Striegel-Moore, R. H., & Bulik, C. M. (2007). Risk factors for eating disorders. *American Psychologist, 62,* 181–198.

Strohmetz, D. B., Rind, B., Fisher, R., & Lynn, M. (2002). Sweetening the till: The use of candy to increase restaurant tipping. *Journal of Applied Social Psychology, 32,* 300–309.

Stroop, J. P. (1935). Studies of interference in serial verbal reactions. *Journal of Experimental Psychology, 18,* 643–661.

Strueber, D., Lueck, M., & Roth, G. (2006). The violent brain. *Scientific American Mind, 17,* 20–27.

Stuss, D. T., & Benson, D. F. (1986). *The frontal lobes.* New York: Raven Press.

Suchman, A. L., Markakis, K., Beckman, H. B., & Frankel, R. (1997). A model of empathic communication in the medical interview. *Journal of the American Medical Association, 277,* 678–682.

Suddendorf, T., & Corballis, M. C. (2007). The evolution of foresight: What is mental time travel and is it unique to humans? *Behavioral and Brain Sciences, 30,* 299–313.

Sundet, J. M., Eriksen, W., & Tambs, K. (2008). Intelligence correlations between brothers decrease with increasing age difference: Evidence for shared environmental effects in young adults. *Psychological Science, 19,* 843–847.

Susman, S., Dent, C., McAdams, L., Stacy, A., Burton, D., & Flay, B. (1994). Group self-identification and adolescent cigarette smoking: A 1-year prospective study. *Journal of Abnormal Psychology, 103,* 576–580.

Susser, E. B., Brown, A., & Matte, T. D. (1999). Prenatal factors and adult mental and physical health. *Canadian Journal of Psychiatry, 44*(4), 326–334.

Sutin, A. R., Stephan, Y., & Terracciano, A. (2015). Weight discrimination and risk of mortality. *Psychological Science, 26*(11), 1803–1811. http://doi.org/10.1177/0956797615601103

Suzuki, L. A., & Valencia, R. R. (1997). Race-ethnicity and measured intelligence: Educational implications. *American Psychologist, 52,* 1103–1114.

Swami, V., Pietschnig, J., Bertil, B., Nader, I. W., Stieger, S., & Voracek, M. (2012) Personality differences between tattooed and non-tattooed individuals. *Psychological Reports: Mental & Physical Health, 111,* 97–106.

Swann, W. B., Jr. (1983). Self-verification: Bringing social reality into harmony with the self. In J. M. Suls & A. G. Greenwald (Ed.), *Psychological perspectives on the self* (Vol. 2, pp. 33–66). Hillsdale, NJ: Erlbaum.

Swann, W. B., Jr., & Rentfrow, P. J. (2001). Blirtatiousness: Cognitive, behavioral, and physiological consequences of rapid responding. *Journal of Personality and Social Psychology, 181*(6), 1160–1175.

Swayze, V. W., II. (1995). Frontal leukotomy and related psychosurgical procedures before antipsychotics (1935–1954): A historical overview. *American Journal of Psychiatry, 152,* 505–515.

Swencionis, J. K., & Fiske, S. T. (2016) Promote up, ingratiate down: Status comparisons drive warmth-competence tradeoffs in impression management. *Journal of Experimental Social Psychology, 64,* 27–34.

Szechtman, H., & Woody, E. Z. (2006). Obsessive-compulsive disorder as a disturbance of security motivation: Constraints on comorbidity. *Neurotoxicity Research, 10,* 103–112.

Szpunar, K. K. (2010). Episodic future thought: An emerging concept. *Perspectives on Psychological Science, 5,* 142–162.

Szpunar, K. K., Khan, N. Y., & Schacter, D. L. (2013). Interpolated memory tests reduce mind wandering and improve learning of online lectures. *Proceedings of the National Academy of Sciences, USA, 110,* 6313–6317.

Szpunar, K. K., Watson, J. M., & McDermott, K. B. (2007). Neural substrates of envisioning the future. *Proceedings of the National Academy of Sciences, USA, 104,* 642–647.

Tajfel, H., Billig, M. G., Bundy, R. P., & Flament, C. (1971). Social categorization and intergroup behaviour. *European Journal of Social Psychology, 1,* 149–178.

Tajfel, H., & Wilkes, A. L. (1963). Classification and quantitative judgement. *British Journal of Psychology, 54,* 101–114.

Takahashi, K. (1986). Examining the Strange Situation procedure with Japanese mothers and 12-month-old infants. *Developmental Psychology, 22,* 265–270.

Tamis-LeMonda, C. S., Adolph, K. E., Lobo, S. A., Karasik, L. B., Ishak, S., & Dimitropoulou, K. A. (2008). When infants take mothers' advice: 18-month-olds integrate perceptual and social information to guide motor action. *Developmental Psychology, 44,* 734–746.

Tamminga, C. A., Nemeroff, C. B., Blakely, R. D., Brady, L., Carter, C. S., Davis, K. L., . . . Suppes, T. (2002). Developing novel treatments for mood disorders: Accelerating discovery. *Biological Psychiatry, 52,* 589–609.

Tanaka, F., Cicourel, A., & Movellan, J. R. (2007). Socialization between toddlers and robots at an early childhood education center. *Proceedings of the National Academy of Sciences, USA, 104*(46), 17954–17958.

Tang, Y.-P., Shimizu, E., Dube, G. R., Rampon, C., Kerchner, G. A., Zhuo, M., . . . Tsien, J. Z. (1999). Genetic enhancement of learning and memory in mice. *Nature, 401,* 63–69.

Tang, Y. Y., Lu, Q., Fan, M., Yang, Y., & Posner, M. I. (2012). Mechanisms of white matter changes induced by meditation. *Proceedings of the National Academy of Sciences, 109,* 10570–10574.

Tarantino, N., Tully, E. C., Garcia, S. E., South, S., Iacono, W. G., & McGue, M. (2014). Genetic and environmental influences on affiliation with deviant peers during adolescence and early adulthood. *Developmental Psychology, 50*(3), 663–673. doi: 10.1037/a0034345

Tart, C. T. (Ed.). (1969). *Altered states of consciousness.* New York: Wiley.

Taylor, S. E. (1986). *Health psychology.* New York: Random House.

Taylor, S. E. (1989). *Positive illusions.* New York: Basic Books.

Taylor, S. E. (2002). *The tending instinct: How nurturing is essential to who we are and how we live.* New York: Times Books.

Taylor, S. E., & Brown, J. D. (1988). Illusion and well-being: A social psychological perspective on mental health. *Psychological Bulletin, 103,* 193–210.

Taylor, S. E., & Fiske, S. T. (1975). Point-of-view and perceptions of causality. *Journal of Personality and Social Psychology, 32,* 439–445.

Teasdale, J. D., Segal, Z. V., & Williams, J. M. G. (2000). Prevention of relapse/recurrence in major depression by mindfulness-based cognitive therapy. *Journal of Consulting and Clinical Psychology, 68,* 615–623.

Telch, M. J., Lucas, J. A., & Nelson, P. (1989). Non-clinical panic in college students: An investigation of prevalence and symptomology. *Journal of Abnormal Psychology, 98,* 300–306.

Tellegen, A., & Atkinson, G. (1974). Openness to absorbing and self-altering experiences ("absorption"), a trait related to hypnotic susceptibility. *Journal of Abnormal Psychology, 83,* 268–277.

Tellegen, A., Lykken, D. T., Bouchard, T. J., Wilcox, K., Segal, N., & Rich, A. (1988). Personality similarity in twins reared together and apart. *Journal of Personality and Social Psychology, 54,* 1031–1039.

Temerlin, M. K., & Trousdale, W. W. (1969). The social psychology of clinical diagnosis. *Psychotherapy: Theory, Research & Practice, 6,* 24–29.

Terman, L. M. (1916). *The measurement of intelligence.* Boston: Houghton Mifflin.

Tews, M. J., Stafford, K., & Tracey, J. B. (2011) What matters most? The perceived importance of ability and personality for hiring decisions. *Cornell Hospitality Quarterly, 52,* 94–101.

Teyler, T. J., & DiScenna, P. (1986). The hippocampal memory indexing theory. *Behavioral Neuroscience, 100,* 147–154.

Thaker, G. K. (2002). Current progress in schizophrenia research. Search for genes of schizophrenia: Back to defining valid phenes. *Journal of Nervous and Mental Disease, 190,* 411–412.

Thaler, K., Delivuk, M., Chapman, A., Gaynes, B. N., Kaminski, A., & Gartlehner, G. (2011). Second-generation antidepressants for seasonal affective disorder. *Cochrane Database of Systematic Reviews, CD008591.*

Thaler, R. H. (1988). The ultimatum game. *Journal of Economic Perspectives, 2,* 195–206.

Thase, M. E., & Howland, R. H. (1995). Biological processes in depression: An updated review and integration. In E. E. Beckham & W. R. Leber (Eds.), *Handbook of depression* (2nd ed., pp. 213–279). New York: Guilford Press.

Thibaut, J. W., & Kelley, H. H. (1959). *The social psychology of groups.* New Brunswick, NJ: Transaction Publishers.

Thomaes, S., Bushman, B. J., Stegge, H., & Olthof, T. (2008). Trumping shame by blasts of noise: Narcissism, self-esteem, shame, and aggression in young adolescents. *Child Development, 79*(6), 1792–1801.

Thomas, A., & Chess, S. (1977). *Temperament and development.* New York: Brunner/Mazel.

Thomason, M., & Thompson, P. M. (2011). Diffusion imaging, white matter, and psychopathology. *Annual Review of Clinical Psychology, 7,* 63–85.

Thompson, B., Coronado, G., Chen, L., Thompson, L. A., Halperin, A., Jaffe, R., . . . Zbikowski, S. M. (2007). Prevalence and characteristics of smokers at 30 Pacific Northwest colleges and universities. *Nicotine & Tobacco Research, 9,* 429–438.

Thompson, P. M., Giedd, J. N., Woods, R. P., MacDonald, D., Evans, A. C., & Toga, A. W. (2000). Growth patterns in the developing brain detected by using continuum mechanical tensor maps. *Nature, 404,* 190–193.

Thompson, P. M., Vidal, C., Giedd, J. N., Gochman, P., Blumenthal, J., Nicolson, R., . . . Rapoport, J. L. (2001). Accelerated gray matter loss in very early-onset schizophrenia. *Proceedings of the National Academy of Sciences, USA, 98,* 11650–11655.

Thompson, R. F. (2005). In search of memory traces. *Annual Review of Psychology, 56,* 1–23.

Thorndike, E. L. (1898). Animal intelligence: An experimental study of associative processes in animals. *Psychological Review Monograph Supplements, 2,* 4–160.

Thornhill, R., & Gangestad, S. W. (1993). Human facial beauty: Averageness, symmetry, and parasite resistance. *Human Nature, 4,* 237–269.

Thurber, J. (1956). *Further fables of our time.* New York: Simon & Schuster.

Thurstone, L. L. (1938). *Primary mental abilities.* Chicago: University of Chicago Press.

Tice, D. M., & Baumeister, R. F. (1997). Longitudinal study of procrastination, performance, stress, and health: The costs and benefits of dawdling. *Psychological Science, 8*(6), 454–458.

Tienari, P., Wynne, L. C., Sorri, A., Lahti, I., Läksy, K., Moring, J., . . . Wahlberg, K. E. (2004). Genotype–environment interaction in schizophrenia spectrum disorder: Long-term follow-up study of Finnish adoptees. *British Journal of Psychiatry, 184,* 216–222.

Timmerman, T. A. (2007). "It was a thought pitch": Personal, situational, and target influences on hit-by-pitch events across time. *Journal of Applied Psychology, 92,* 876–884.

Todd, A. R., Bodenhausen, G. V., Richeson, J. A., & Galinsky, A. D. (2011). Perspective taking combats automatic expressions of racial bias. *Journal of Personality and Social Psychology, 100*(6), 1027–1042. doi:10.1037/a0022308

Toga, A. W., Clark, K. A., Thompson, P. M., Shattuck, D. W., & Van Horn, J. D. (2012). Mapping the human connectome. *Neurosurgery, 71,* 1–5.

Tolin, D. F. (2010). Is cognitive-behavioral therapy more effective than other therapies? A meta-analytic review. *Clinical Psychology Review, 30,* 710–720.

Tolman, E. C., & Honzik, C. H. (1930a). "Insight" in rats. *University of California Publications in Psychology, 4,* 215–232.

Tolman, E. C., & Honzik, C. H. (1930b). Introduction and removal of reward and maze performance in rats. *University of California Publications in Psychology, 4,* 257–275.

Tolman, E. C., Ritchie, B. F., & Kalish, D. (1946). Studies in spatial learning: I: Orientation and short cut. *Journal of Experimental Psychology, 36*, 13–24.

Tomasello, M., & Call, J. (2004). The role of humans in the cognitive development of apes revisited. *Animal Cognition, 7*, 213–215.

Tomasello, M., Davis-Dasilva, M., Camak, L., & Bard, K. (1987). Observational learning of tool use by young chimpanzees. *Human Evolution, 2*, 175–183.

Tomasello, M., Savage-Rumbaugh, S., & Kruger, A. C. (1993). Imitative learning of actions on objects by children, chimpanzees, and enculturated chimpanzees. *Child Development, 64*, 1688–1705.

Tomkins, S. S. (1981). The role of facial response in the experience of emotion. *Journal of Personality and Social Psychology, 40*, 351–357.

Torgensen, S. (1986). Childhood and family characteristics in panic and generalized anxiety disorder. *American Journal of Psychiatry, 143*, 630–639.

Torrey, E. F., Bower, A. E., Taylor, E. H., & Gottesman, I. I. (1994). *Schizophrenia and manic-depressive disorder: The biological roots of mental illness as revealed by the landmark study of identical twins.* New York: Basic Books.

Tracy, J. L., Randles, D., & Steckler, C. M. (2015). The nonverbal communication of emotions. *Current Opinion in Behavioral Sciences, 3*, 25–30.

Tracy, J. L., Shariff, A. F., Zhao, W., & Henrich, J. (2013). Cross-cultural evidence that the nonverbal expression of pride is an automatic status signal. *Journal of Experimental Psychology: General, 142*(1), 163–180.

Tranter, L. J., & Koutstaal, W. (2007). Age and flexible thinking: An experimental demonstration of the beneficial effects of increased cognitively stimulating activity on fluid intelligence in healthy older adults. *Neuropsychology, Development, and Cognition. Section B, Aging, Neuropsychology and Cognition, 15*, 184–207.

Treede, R. D., Kenshalo, D. R., Gracely, R. H., & Jones, A. K. (1999). The cortical representation of pain. *Pain, 79*, 105–111.

Treisman, A. (1998). Feature binding, attention and object perception. *Philosophical Transactions of the Royal Society (B), 353*, 1295–1306.

Treisman, A. (2006). How the deployment of attention determines what we see. *Visual Cognition, 14*, 411–443.

Treisman, A., & Gelade, G. (1980). A feature integration theory of attention. *Cognitive Psychology, 12*, 97–136.

Treisman, A., & Schmidt, H. (1982). Illusory conjunctions in the perception of objects. *Cognitive Psychology, 14*, 107–141.

Trivers, R. L. (1972). Parental investment and sexual selection. In B. Campbell (Ed.), *Sexual selection and the descent of man, 1871–1971* (pp. 139–179). Chicago: Aldine.

Trompeter, S. E., Bettencourt, R., & Barrett-Connor, E. (2012). Sexual activity and satisfaction in healthy community-dwelling older women. *American Journal of Medicine, 125*(1), 37–43. doi:10.1016/j.amjmed.2011.07.036

Trull, T. J., & Durrett, C. A. (2005). Categorical and dimensional models of personality disorder. *Annual Review of Clinical Psychology, 1*, 355–380.

Tulving, E. (1972). Episodic and semantic memory. In E. Tulving & W. Donaldson (Eds.), *Organization of memory* (pp. 381–403). New York: Academic Press.

Tulving, E. (1983). *Elements of episodic memory.* Oxford, England: Clarendon Press.

Tulving, E. (1985). Memory and consciousness. *Canadian Psychologist, 25*, 1–12.

Tulving, E. (1998). Neurocognitive processes of human memory. In C. von Euler, I. Lundberg, & R. Llins (Eds.), *Basic mechanisms in cognition and language* (pp. 261–281). Amsterdam: Elsevier.

Tulving, E., Kapur, S., Craik, F. I. M., Moscovitch, M., & Houle, S. (1994). Hemispheric encoding/retrieval asymmetry in episodic memory: Positron emission tomography findings. *Proceedings of the National Academy of Sciences, USA, 91*, 2016–2020.

Tulving, E., & Schacter, D. L. (1990). Priming and human memory systems. *Science, 247*, 301–306.

Tulving, E., Schacter, D. L., & Stark, H. (1982). Priming effects in word fragment completion are independent of recognition memory. *Journal of Experimental Psychology: Learning, Memory, and Cognition, 8*, 336–342.

Tulving, E., & Thompson, D. M. (1973). Encoding specificity and retrieval processes in episodic memory. *Psychological Review, 80*, 352–373.

Turkheimer, E. (2000). Three laws of behavior genetics and what they mean. *Current Directions in Psychological Science, 9*, 160–164.

Turner, D. C., Robbins, T. W., Clark, L., Aron, A. R., Dowson, J., & Sahakian, B. J. (2003). Cognitive enhancing effects of modafinil in healthy volunteers. *Psychopharmacology, 165*, 260–269.

Turner, D. C., & Sahakian, B. J. (2006). Neuroethics of cognitive enhancement. *BioSocieties, 1*, 113–123.

Turner, M. E., & Pratkanis, A. R. (1998). Twenty-five years of groupthink theory and research: Lessons from the evaluation of a theory. *Organizational Behavior and Human Decision Processes, 73*(2–3), 105–115. doi:10.1006/obhd.1998.2756

Tversky, A., & Kahneman, D. (1973). Availability: A heuristic for judging frequency and probability. *Cognitive Psychology, 5*, 207–232.

Tversky, A., & Kahneman, D. (1974). Judgment under uncertainty: Heuristics and biases. *Science, 185*, 1124–1131.

Tversky, A., & Kahneman, D. (1981). The framing of decisions and the psychology of choice. *Science, 211*, 453–458.

Tversky, A., & Kahneman, D. (1983). Extensional versus intuitive reasoning: The conjunction fallacy in probability judgment. *Psychological Review, 90*, 293–315.

Tversky, A., & Kahneman, D. (1992). Advances in prospect theory: Cumulative representation of uncertainty. *Journal of Risk and Uncertainty, 5*, 297–323.

Twenge, J. M., Campbell, W. K., & Foster, C. A. (2003). Parenthood and marital satisfaction: A meta-analytic review. *Journal of Marriage and Family, 65*, 574–583.

Tyler, T. R. (1990). *Why people obey the law.* New Haven, CT: Yale University Press.

Umberson, D., Williams, K., Powers, D. A., Liu, H., & Needham, B. (2006). You make me sick: Marital quality and health over the life course. *Journal of Health and Social Behavior, 47*, 1–16.

Uncapher, M. R., & Rugg, M. D. (2008). Fractionation of the component processes underlying successful episodic encoding: A combined fMRI and divided-attention study. *Journal of Cognitive Neuroscience, 20*, 240–254.

Ungerleider, L. G., & Mishkin, M. (1982). Two cortical visual systems. In D. J. Ingle, M. A. Goodale, & R. J. W. Mansfield (Eds.), *Analysis of visual behavior* (pp. 549–586). Cambridge, MA: MIT Press.

Urban, N. B. L., Girgis, R. R., Talbot, P. S., Kegeles, L. S., Xu, X., Frankie, W. G., . . . Laruelle, M. (2012). Sustained recreational use of Ecstasy is associated with altered pre- and postsynaptic markers of serotonin transmission in neocortical areas: A PET study with [11c] DASB and [11c] MDL 100907. *Neuropsychopharmacology, 37*, 1465–1473.

Ursano, R. J., & Silberman, E. K. (2003). Psychoanalysis, psychoanalytic psychotherapy, and supportive psychotherapy. In R. E. Hales & S. C. Yudofsky (Eds.), *The American Psychiatric Publishing textbook of clinical psychiatry* (4th ed., pp. 1177–1203). Washington, DC: American Psychiatric Publishing.

U.S. Census Bureau. (2012). *The 2012 statistical abstract: National data book*. Washington, DC: Author.

Uskul, A. K., & Over, H. (2014). Responses to social exclusion in cultural context: Evidence from farming and herding communities. *Journal of Personality and Social Psychology, 106*(5), 752–771. doi: 10.1037/a0035810

Vacha, E., & McBride, M. (1993). Cramming: A barrier to student success, a way to beat the system, or an effective strategy? *College Student Journal, 27*, 2–11.

Vafaei, A., Ahmed, T., Falcão Freire A., Zunzunegui, M. V., & Guerra, R. O. (2016) Depression, sex and gender roles in older adult populations: The international mobility in aging studies (IMIAS). *PLoS ONE, 11*, e0146867.

Valentine, T., Brennen, T., & Brédart, S. (1996). *The cognitive psychology of proper names: On the importance of being Ernest*. London: Routledge.

Valins, S. (1966). Cognitive effects of false heart-rate feedback. *Journal of Personality and Social Psychology, 4*, 400–408.

Vallacher, R. R., & Wegner, D. M. (1985). *A theory of action identification*. Hillsdale, NJ: Erlbaum.

Vallacher, R. R., & Wegner, D. M. (1987). What do people think they're doing? Action identification and human behavior. *Psychological Review, 94*, 3–15.

van den Boom, D. C. (1994). The influence of temperament and mothering on attachment and exploration: An experimental manipulation of sensitive responsiveness among lower-class mothers with irritable infants. *Child Development, 65*, 1457–1477.

van den Boom, D. C. (1995). Do first year intervention effects endure? Follow-up during toddlerhood of a sample of Dutch irritable infants. *Child Development, 66*, 1798–1816.

Van Dongen, E. V., Thielen, J.-W., Takashima, A., Barth, M., & Fernandez, G. (2012). Sleep supports selective retention of associative memories based on relevance for future utilization. *PLoS One, 7*, e43426. doi: 10.1371/journal.pone.0043426

van Honk, J., & Schutter, D. J. L. G. (2007). Testosterone reduces conscious detection of signals serving social correction: Implications for antisocial behavior. *Psychological Science, 18*, 663–667.

van IJzendoorn, M. H., Juffer, F., & Klein Poelhuis, C. W. (2005). Adoption and cognitive development: A meta-analytic comparison of adopted and nonadopted children's IQ and school performance. *Psychological Bulletin, 131*, 301–316.

van IJzendoorn, M. H., & Kroonenberg, P. M. (1988). Cross-cultural patterns of attachment: A meta-analysis of the strange situation. *Child Development, 59*, 147–156.

van Ittersum, K., & Wansink, B. (2012). Plate size and color suggestibility: The Delboeuf illusion's bias on serving and eating behavior. *Journal of Consumer Research, 39*, 121–130.

Van Lange, P. A. M., Rinderu, M., & Bushman, B. J. (2016). Aggression and violence around the world: A model of CLimate, Aggression, and Self-control in Humans (CLASH). *Behavioral and Brain Sciences, 23*, 1–63.

van Praag, H. (2009). Exercise and the brain: Something to chew on. *Trends in Neuroscience, 32*, 283–290.

van Stegeren, A. H., Everaerd, W., Cahill, L., McGaugh, J. L., & Gooren, L. J. G. (1998). Memory for emotional events: Differential effects of centrally versus peripherally acting blocking agents. *Psychopharmacology, 138*, 305–310.

Van Vliet, I. M., van Well, E. P., Bruggeman, R., Campo, J. A., Hijman, R., Van Megen, H. J., . . . Van Rijen, P. C. (2013). An evaluation of irreversible psychosurgical treatment of patients with obsessive-compulsive disorder in the Netherlands, 2001–2008. *Journal of Nervous and Mental Disease, 201*, 226–228.

Vargha-Khadem, F., Gadian, D. G., Watkins, K. E., Connelly, A., Van Paesschen, W., & Mishkin, M. (1997). Differential effects of early hippocampal pathology on episodic and semantic memory. *Science, 277*, 376–380.

Vinter, A., & Perruchet, P. (2002). Implicit motor learning through observational training in adults and children. *Memory & Cognition, 30*, 256–261.

Vitkus, J. (1999). *Casebook in abnormal psychology* (4th ed.). New York: McGraw-Hill.

Vondra, J. I., Shaw, D. S., Swearingen, L., Cohen, M., & Owens, E. B. (2001). Attachment stability and emotional and behavioral regulation from infancy to preschool age. *Development and Psychopathology, 13*, 13–33.

Von Frisch, K. (1974). Decoding the language of the bee. *Science, 185*, 663–668.

Voon, V., Pessiglione, M., Brezing, C., Gallea, C., Fernandez, H. H., Dolan, R. J., & Hallett, M. (2011). Mechanisms underlying dopamine-mediated reward bias in compulsive behaviors. *Neuron, 65*, 135–142.

Vorster, A. P. & Born, J. (2015). Sleep and memory in mammals, birds and invertebrates. *Neuroscience and Biobehavioral Reviews, 50*, 103–119.

Vrij, A., Granhag, P. A., Mann, S., & Leal, S. (2011). Outsmarting the liars: Toward a cognitive lie detection approach. *Current Directions in Psychological Science, 20*(1), 28–32.

Vygotsky, L. S. (1978). *Mind in society: The development of higher psychological processes*. Cambridge, MA: Harvard University Press.

Wade, N. J. (2005). *Perception and illusion: Historical perspectives*. New York: Springer.

Wade, S. E., Trathen, W., & Schraw, G. (1990). An analysis of spontaneous study strategies. *Reading Research Quarterly, 25*, 147–166.

Wadhwa, P. D., Sandman, C. A., & Garite, T. J. (2001). The neurobiology of stress in human pregnancy: Implications for prematurity and development of the fetal central nervous system. *Progress in Brain Research, 133*, 131–142.

Wagenmakers, E. J. et al., (2016). Registered Replication Report. *Perspectives on Psychological Science, 11*, 917–928.

Wager, T., & Atlas, L. Y. (2013). How is pain influenced by cognition? Neuroimaging weighs in. *Perspectives on Psychological Science, 8*, 91–97.

Wagner, A. D., Schacter, D. L., Rotte, M., Koutstaal, W., Maril, A., Dale, A. M., . . . Buckner, R. L. (1998). Remembering and forgetting of verbal experiences as predicted by brain activity. *Science, 281*, 1188–1190.

Wagner, G., & Morris, E. (1987). Superstitious behavior in children. *Psychological Record, 37*, 471–488.

Wai, J., Putallaz, M., & Makel, M. C. (2012). Studying intellectual outliers: Are there sex differences, and are the smart getting smarter? *Current Directions in Psychological Science, 21*(6), 382–390. doi:10.1177/0963721412455052

Waite, L. J. (1995). Does marriage matter? *Demography, 32*, 483–507.

Wakefield, J. C. (2007). The concept of mental disorder: Diagnostic implications of the harmful dysfunction analysis. *World Psychiatry, 6*, 149–156.

Walden, T. A., & Ogan, T. A. (1988). The development of social referencing. *Child Development, 59*, 1230–1240.

Walker, C. (1977). Some variations in marital satisfaction. In R. C. J. Peel (Ed.), *Equalities and inequalities in family life* (pp. 127–139). London: Academic Press.

Walker, L. J. (1988). The development of moral reasoning. *Annals of Child Development, 55*, 677–691.

Walker, N. P., McConville, P. M., Hunter, D., Deary, I. J., & Whalley, L. J. (2002). Childhood mental ability and lifetime psychiatric contact. *Intelligence, 30*(3), 233–245. doi:10.1016/S0160-2896(01)00098-8

Walton, G. M., & Spencer, S. J. (2009). Latent ability: Grades and test scores systematically underestimate the intellectual ability of negatively stereotyped students. *Psychological Science, 20,* 1132–1139.

Waltzman, S. B. (2006). Cochlear implants: Current status. *Expert Review of Medical Devices, 3,* 647–655.

Wang, J. L., Jackson, L. A., Zhang, D. J., & Su, Z. Q. (2012). The relationships among the Big Five personality factors, self-esteem, narcissism, and sensation seeking to Chinese university students' uses of social networking sites (SNSs). *Computers in Human Behavior, 28,* 2313–2319.

Wang, L. H., McCarthy, G., Song, A. W., & LaBar, K. S. (2005). Amygdala activation to sad pictures during high-field (4 tesla) functional magnetic resonance imaging. *Emotion, 5,* 12–22.

Wang, P. S., Aguilar-Gaxiola, S., Alonso, J., Angermeyer, M. C., Borges, G., Bromet, E. J., . . . Wells, J. E. (2007). Use of mental health services for anxiety, mood, and substance disorders in 17 countries in the WHO World Mental Health Surveys. *Lancet, 370,* 841–850.

Wang, P. S., Berglund, P. A., Olfson, M., & Kessler, R. C. (2004). Delays in initial treatment contact after first onset of a mental disorder. *Health Services Research, 39,* 393–415.

Wang, P. S., Berglund, P., Olfson, M., Pincus, H. A., Wells, K. B., & Kessler, R. C. (2005). Failure and delay in initial treatment contact after first onset of mental disorders in the National Comorbidity Survey Replication. *Archives of General Psychiatry, 62*(6), 629–640.

Wang, S.-H., & Baillargeon, R. (2008). Detecting impossible changes in infancy: A three-system account. *Trends in Cognitive Sciences, 12*(1), 17–23.

Wang, W., & Parker, K. (2014). Record share of Americans have never married as values, economics and gender patterns change. Washington, DC: Pew Research Center's Social & Demographic Trends project. Retrieved from http://www.pewsocialtrends.org/2014/09/24/record-share-of-americans-have-never-married/

Wansink, B., & Linder, L. R. (2003). Interactions between forms of fat consumption and restaurant bread consumption. *International Journal of Obesity, 27,* 866–868.

Wansink, B., Painter, J. E., & North, J. (2005). Bottomless bowls: Why visual cues of portion size may influence intake. *Obesity Research, 13,* 93–100.

Wansink, B., & Wansink, C. S. (2010). The largest last supper: Depictions of food portions and plate size increased over the millennium. *International Journal of Obesity, 34,* 943–944.

Ward, B. W., Dahlhamer, J. M., Galinsky, A. M., & Joestl, S. S. (2014). Sexual orientation and health among US adults: National Health Interview Survey, 2013. *National Health Statistics Reports, 15,* 1–10.

Warneken, F., & Tomasello, M. (2009). Varieties of altruism in children and chimpanzees. *Trends in Cognitive Sciences, 13,* 397–402.

Warren, K. R., & Hewitt, B. G. (2009). Fetal alcohol spectrum disorders: When science, medicine, public policy, and laws collide. *Developmental Disabilities Research Reviews, 15,* 170–175.

Warrington, E. K., & McCarthy, R. A. (1983). Category specific access dysphasia. *Brain, 106,* 859–878.

Warrington, E. K., & Shallice, T. (1984). Category specific semantic impairments. *Brain, 107,* 829–854.

Watanabe, S., Sakamoto, J., & Wakita, M. (1995). Pigeons' discrimination of painting by Monet and Picasso. *Journal of the Experimental Analysis of Behavior, 63,* 165–174.

Waters, T. E. A., Fraley, R. C., Groh, A. M., Steele, R. D., Vaughn, B. E., Bost, K. K., . . . Roisman, G. I. (2015). The latent structure of secure base script knowledge. *Developmental Psychology, 51*(6), 823–830. doi: 10.1037/dev0000012

Watkins, L. R., & Maier, S. F. (2005). Immune regulation of central nervous system functions: From sickness responses to pathological pain. *Journal of Internal Medicine, 257,* 139–155.

Watson, D., & Pennebaker, J. W. (1989). Health complaints, stress, and distress: Exploring the central role of negative affectivity. *Psychological Review, 96,* 234–254.

Watson, D., & Tellegen, A. (1985). Toward a consensual structure of mood. *Psychological Bulletin, 98,* 219–235.

Watson, J. B. (1913). Psychology as the behaviorist views it. *Psychological Review, 20,* 158–177.

Watson, J. B. (1924). *Behaviorism.* New York: People's Institute.

Watson, J. B. (1928). *Psychological care of infant and child.* New York: Norton.

Watson, J. B., & Rayner, R. (1920). Conditioned emotional reactions. *Journal of Experimental Psychology, 3,* 1–14.

Watson, R. I. (1978). *The great psychologists.* New York: Lippincott.

Watzke, B., Rüddel, H., Jürgensen, R., Koch, U., Kristen, L., Grothgar, B., & Schulz, H. (2012). Longer term outcome of cognitive-behavioural and psychodynamic psychotherapy in routine mental health care: Randomised controlled trial. *Behaviour Research and Therapy, 50,* 580–387.

Weaver, I. C. G., Cervoni, N., Champagne, F. A., D'Alessio, A. C., Sharma, S., Seckl, J. R., . . . Meaney, M. J. (2004). Epigenetic programming by maternal behavior. *Nature Neuroscience, 7,* 847–854.

Webb, T. L., Miles, E., & Sheeran, P. (2012). Dealing with feeling: A meta-analysis of the effectiveness of strategies derived from the process model of emotion regulation. *Psychological Bulletin, 138*(4), 775–808.

Webster Marketon, J. I., & Glaser, R. (2008). Stress hormones and immune function. *Cellular Immunology, 252,* 16–26.

Wechsler, H., & Nelson, T. F. (2001). Binge drinking and the American college student: What's five drinks? *Psychology of Addictive Behaviors, 15*(4), 287–291. doi:10.1037/0893-164X.15.4.287

Wegner, D. M. (1989). *White bears and other unwanted thoughts.* New York: Viking.

Wegner, D. M. (1994a). Ironic processes of mental control. *Psychological Review, 101,* 34–52.

Wegner, D. M. (1994b). *White bears and other unwanted thoughts: Suppression, obsession, and the psychology of mental control.* New York: Guilford Press.

Wegner, D. M. (1997). Why the mind wanders. In J. D. Cohen & J. W. Schooler (Eds.), *Scientific approaches to consciousness* (pp. 295–315). Mahwah, NJ: Erlbaum.

Wegner, D. M. (2002). *The illusion of conscious will.* Cambridge, MA: MIT Press.

Wegner, D. M. (2009). How to think, say, or do precisely the worst thing for any occasion. *Science, 325,* 48–51.

Wegner, D. M., Ansfield, M., & Pilloff, D. (1998). The putt and the pendulum: Ironic effects of the mental control of action. *Psychological Science, 9,* 196–199.

Wegner, D. M., Broome, A., & Blumberg, S. J. (1997). Ironic effects of trying to relax under stress. *Behavior Research and Therapy, 35,* 11–21.

Wegner, D. M., Erber, R. E., & Zanakos, S. (1993). Ironic processes in the mental control of mood and mood-related thought. *Journal of Personality and Social Psychology, 65,* 1093–1104.

Wegner, D. M., & Gilbert, D. T. (2000). Social psychology: The science of human experience. In H. Bless & J. Forgas (Eds.), *The message within: Subjective experience in social cognition and behavior* (pp. 1–9). Philadelphia: Psychology Press.

Wegner, D. M., Schneider, D. J., Carter, S. R., & White, T. L. (1987). Paradoxical effects of thought suppression. *Journal of Personality and Social Psychology, 53,* 5–13.

Wegner, D. M., Vallacher, R. R., Macomber, G., Wood, R., & Arps, K. (1984). The emergence of action. *Journal of Personality and Social Psychology, 46,* 269–279.

Wegner, D. M., & Wenzlaff, R. M. (1996). Mental control. In E. T. Higgins & A. Kruglanski (Eds.), *Social psychology: Handbook of basic mechanisms and processes* (pp. 466–492). New York: Guilford Press.

Wegner, D. M., Wenzlaff, R. M., & Kozak, M. (2004). Dream rebound: The return of suppressed thoughts in dreams. *Psychological Science, 15,* 232–236.

Wegner, D. M., & Zanakos, S. (1994). Chronic thought suppression. *Journal of Personality, 62,* 615–640.

Weiner, R. (2012, November 7). Hickenlooper on Colorado pot vote: 'Don't break out the Cheetos.' *Washington Post.* Retrieved from http://www.washingtonpost.com/blogs/post-politics/wp/2012/11/07/hickenlooper-on-amendment-64-dont-break-out-the-cheetos/?tid=up_next.

Weinstein, N. D. (1980). Unrealistic optimism about future life events. *Journal of Personality and Social Psychology, 39,* 806–820.

Weintraub, D., Papay, K., & Siderowf, A. (2013). Screening for impulse control symptoms in patients with de novo Parkinson disease: A case-control study. *Neurology, 80,* 176–180.

Weiser, M., Zarka, S., Werbeloff, N., Kravitz, E., & Lubin, G. (2010). Cognitive test scores in male adolescent cigarette smokers compared to non-smokers: A population-based study. *Addiction, 105*(2), 358–363. doi: 10.1111/j.1360-0443.2009.02740.x

Weisfeld, G. (1999). *Evolutionary principles of human adolescence.* New York: Basic Books.

Weissman, M. M., Markowitz, J. C., & Klerman, G. L. (2000). *Comprehensive guide to interpersonal psychotherapy.* New York: Basic Books.

Weldon, M. S. (2001). Remembering as a social process. In D. L. Medin (Ed.), *The psychology of learning and motivation: Advances in research and theory* (Vol. 40, pp. 67–120). San Diego: Academic Press.

Wellman, H. M., Fang, F., Liu, D., Zhu, L., & Liu, L. (2006). Scaling theory-of-mind understandings in Chinese children. *Psychological Science, 17,* 1075–1081. doi: 10.1111/j.1467-9280.2006.01830.x

Wenzlaff, R. M., & Wegner, D. M. (2000). Thought suppression. In S. T. Fiske (Ed.), *Annual review of psychology* (Vol. 51, pp. 51–91). Palo Alto, CA: Annual Reviews.

Wesch, N. N., Law, B., & Hall, C. R. (2007). The use of observational learning by athletes. *Journal of Sport Behavior, 30,* 219–231.

Westrin, A., & Lam, R. W. (2007). Seasonal affective disorder: A clinical update. *Journal of Clinical Psychiatry, 19,* 239–246.

Wexler, K. (1999). Maturation and growth of grammar. In W. C. Ritchie & T. K. Bhatia (Eds.), *Handbook of child language acquisition* (pp. 55–110). San Diego: Academic Press.

Whalen, P. J., Rauch, S. L., Etcoff, N. L., McInerney, S. C., Lee, M. B., & Jenike, M. A. (1998). Masked presentations of emotional facial expressions modulate amygdala activity without explicit knowledge. *The Journal of Neuroscience, 18,* 411–418.

Whalley, L. J., & Deary, I. J. (2001). Longitudinal cohort study of childhood IQ and survival up to age 76. *British Medical Journal, 322,* 1–5.

Wheatley, T., & Haidt, J. (2005). Hypnotic disgust makes moral judgments more severe. *Psychological Science, 16,* 780–784.

Wheeler, M. A., Petersen, S. E., & Buckner, R. L. (2000). Memory's echo: Vivid recollection activates modality-specific cortex. *Proceedings of the National Academy of Sciences, USA, 97,* 11125–11129.

White, B. L., & Held, R. (1966). Plasticity of motor development in the human infant. In J. F. Rosenblith & W. Allinsmith (Eds.), *The cause of behavior* (pp. 60–70). Boston: Allyn & Bacon.

White, G. M., & Kirkpatrick, J. (Eds.) (1985). *Person, self, and experience: Exploring Pacific ethnopsychologies.* Berkeley: University of California Press.

Whitney, D., Ellison, A., Rice, N. J., Arnold, D., Goodale, M., Walsh, V., & Milner, D. (2007). Visually guided reaching depends on motion area MT+. *Cerebral Cortex, 17,* 2644–2649.

Whybrow, P. C. (1997). *A mood apart.* New York: Basic Books.

Wicklund, R. (1975). Objective self-awareness. In L. Berkowitz (Ed.), *Advances in experimental social psychology* (Vol. 8, pp. 233–275). New York: Academic Press.

Wiegner, L., Hange, D., Björkelund, C., & Ahlbirg, G., Jr. (2015). Prevalence of perceived stress and associations to symptoms of exhaustion, depression, and anxiety in a working age population seeking primary care: An observational study. *BMC Family Practice, 16,* 38.

Wiggs, C. L., & Martin, A. (1998). Properties and mechanisms of perceptual priming. *Current Opinion in Neurobiology, 8,* 227–233.

Wilcoxon, H. C., Dragoin, W. B., & Kral, P. A. (1971). Illness-induced aversions in rats and quail: Relative salience of visual and gustatory cues. *Science, 171,* 826–828.

Wiley, J. L. (1999). Cannabis: Discrimination of "internal bliss"? *Pharmacology, Biochemistry, & Behavior, 64,* 257–260.

Wilhelm, I., Dieckelmann, S., Molzow, I., Ayoub, A., Molle, M., & Born, J. (2011). Sleep selectively enhances memories expected to be of future relevance. *Journal of Neuroscience, 31,* 1563–1569.

Williams, C. M., & Kirkham, T. C. (1999). Anandamide induces overeating: Mediation by central cannabinoid (CB1) receptors. *Psychopharmacology, 143,* 315–317.

Williams, K. D. (2007). Ostracism. *Annual Review of Psychology, 58,* 425–452. doi: 10.1146/annurev.psych.58.110405.085641

Williams, W. M. & Ceci, S. J. (2015). National hiring experiments reveal 2:1 faculty preference for women on STEM tenure track. *Proceedings of the National Academy of Sciences, 112,* 5360–5365.

Willingham, D. T. (2007). Critical thinking: Why is it so hard to teach? *American Educator, 31*(2), 8–19.

Wilson, K., & Korn, J. H. (2007). Attention during lectures: Beyond ten minutes. *Teaching of Psychology, 34,* 85–89.

Wilson, T. D. (2002). *Strangers to ourselves: Discovering the adaptive unconscious.* Cambridge, MA: Harvard University Press.

Wilson, T. D. (2009). Know thyself. *Perspectives on Psychological Science, 4,* 384–389.

Wilson, T. D. (2011). *Redirect: The surprising new science of psychological change.* New York: Little Brown.

Wilson, T. D. (2012, July 12). Stop bullying the "soft" sciences. *Los Angeles Times.* Available from http://articles.latimes.com/2012/jul/12/opinion/la-oe-wilson-social-sciences-20120712

Wilson, T. D., Meyers, J., & Gilbert, D. T. (2003). "How happy was I, anyway?" A retrospective impact bias. *Social Cognition, 21,* 421–446.

Wilson, T. D., Reinhard, D. A., Westgate, E. C., Gilbert, D. T., Ellerbeck, N., Hahn, C., . . . Shaked, A. (2014). Just think: The challenges of the disengaged mind. *Science, 345,* 75–77.

Wimber, M., Rutschmann, R. N., Greenlee, M. W., & Bauml, K.-H. (2009). Retrieval from episodic memory: Neural mechanisms of interference resolution. *Journal of Cognitive Neuroscience, 21,* 538–549.

Wimmer, H., & Perner, J. (1983). Beliefs about beliefs: Representations and constraining function of wrong beliefs in young children's understanding of deception. *Cognition, 13,* 103–128.

Windham, G. C., Eaton, A., & Hopkins, B. (1999). Evidence for an association between environmental tobacco smoke exposure and birthweight: A meta-analysis and new data. *Pediatrics and Perinatal Epidemiology, 13,* 35–57.

Winkler, A. D., Spillmann, L., Werner, J. S., & Webster, M. A. (2015). Asymmetries in blue-yellow color perception and in the color of 'the dress.' *Current Biology, 25*, R547–R548.

Winocur, G., Moscovitch, M., & Bontempi, B. (2010). Memory formation and long-term retention in humans and animals: Convergence towards a transformation account of hippocampal–neocortical interactions. *Neuropsychologia, 48*, 2339–2356.

Winterer, G., & Weinberger, D. R. (2004). Genes, dopamine and cortical signal-to-noise ratio in schizophrenia. *Trends in Neuroscience, 27*, 683–690.

Wise, R. A. (1989). Brain dopamine and reward. *Annual Review of Psychology, 40*, 191–225.

Wise, R. A. (2005). Forebrain substrates of reward and motivation. *Journal of Comparative Neurology, 493*, 115–121.

Wittgenstein, L. (1999). *Philosophical investigations.* Upper Saddle River, NJ: Prentice Hall. (Originally published 1953)

Wixted, J. T., & Ebbensen, E. (1991). On the form of forgetting. *Psychological Science, 2*, 409–415.

Wolf, J. R., Arkes, H. R., & Muhanna, W. A. (2008). The power of touch: An examination of the effect of duration of physical contact on the valuation of objects. *Judgment and Decision Making, 3*, 476–482.

Wood, A., Rychlowska, M., & Niedenthal, P. M. (2016). Heterogeneity of long-history migration predicts emotion recognition accuracy. *Emotion, 16*(4), 413–420. doi: 1037/emo0000137

Wood, J. M., & Bootzin, R. R. (1990). Prevalence of nightmares and their independence from anxiety. *Journal of Abnormal Psychology, 99*, 64–68.

Wood, J. M., Bootzin, R. R., Rosenhan, D., Nolen-Hoeksema, S., & Jourden, F. (1992). Effects of the 1989 San Francisco earthquake on frequency and content of nightmares. *Journal of Abnormal Psychology, 101*, 219–224.

Woodley, M. A., te Nijenhuis, J., & Murphy, R. (2013). Were the Victorians cleverer than us? The decline in general intelligence estimated from a meta-analysis of the slowing of simple reaction time. *Intelligence.* Advance online publication. doi:10.1016/j.intell.2013.04.006

Woods, S. C., Seeley, R. J., Porte, D., Jr., & Schwartz, M. W. (1998). Signals that regulate food intake and energy homeostasis. *Science, 280*, 1378–1383.

Woody, S. R., & Nosen, E. (2008). Psychological models of phobic disorders and panic. In M. M. Anthony & M. B. Stein (Eds.), *Oxford handbook of anxiety and related disorders* (pp. 209–224). New York: Oxford University Press.

Wrangham, R., & Peterson, D. (1997). *Demonic males: Apes and the origin of human violence.* New York: Mariner.

Wraw, C., Deary, I. J., Gale, C. R., & Der, G. (2015). Intelligence in youth and health at age 50. *Intelligence, 53*(2015), 23–32.

Wren, A. M., Seal, L. J., Cohen, M. A., Brynes, A. E., Frost, G. S., Murphy, K. G., . . . Bloom, S. R. (2001). Ghrelin enhances appetite and increases food intake in humans. *Journal of Clinical Endocrinology and Metabolism, 86*, 5992–5995.

Wrenn, C. C., Turchi, J. N., Schlosser, S., Dreiling, J. L., Stephenson, D. A., & Crawley, J. N. (2006). Performance of galanin transgenic mice in the 5-choice serial reaction time attentional task. *Pharmacology Biochemistry and Behavior, 83*, 428–440.

Wulf, S. (1994, March 14). Err Jordan. *Sports Illustrated.*

Yamaguchi, S. (1998). Basic properties of umami and its effects in humans. *Physiology and Behavior, 49*, 833–841.

Yang, S., & Sternberg, R. J. (1997). Conceptions of intelligence in ancient Chinese philosophy. *Journal of Theoretical and Philosophical Psychology, 17*, 101–119.

Yeo, B. T. T., Krienen, F. M., Sepulcre, J., Sabuncu, M. R., Lashkari, D., Hollinshead, M., . . . Buckner, R. L. (2011). The organization of the human cerebral cortex estimated by intrinsic functional connectivity. *Journal of Neurophysiology, 106*, 1125–1165.

Yik, M., Russell, J. A., & Steiger, J. H. (2011). A 12-point circumplex structure of core affect. *Emotion, 11*(4), 705–731.

Yu, Y., & Kushnir, T. (2014). Social context effects in 2- and 4-year-olds' selective versus faithful imitation. *Developmental Psychology, 50*(3), 922–933. doi: 10.1037/a0034242

Yzerbyt, V., & Demoulin, S. (2010). Intergroup relations. In S. T. Fiske, D. T. Gilbert, & G. Lindzey (Eds.), *The handbook of social psychology* (5th ed., Vol. 2, pp. 1024–1083). New York: Wiley.

Zajonc, R. B. (1968). Attitudinal effects of mere exposure. *Journal of Personality and Social Psychology, 9*, 1–27.

Zajonc, R. B. (1989). Feeling the facial efference: Implications of the vascular theory of emotion. *Psychological Review, 96*, 395–416.

Zebrowitz, L. A., Hall, J. A., Murphy, N. A., & Rhodes, G. (2002). Looking smart and looking good: Facial cues to intelligence and their origins. *Personality and Social Psychology Bulletin, 28*, 238–249.

Zeki, S. (1993). *A vision of the brain.* London: Blackwell Scientific.

Zeki, S. (2001). Localization and globalization in conscious vision. *Annual Review of Neuroscience, 24*, 57–86.

Zentall, T. R., Sutton, J. E., & Sherburne, L. M. (1996). True imitative learning in pigeons. *Psychological Science, 7*, 343–346.

Zentner, M., & Mitura, K. (2012). Stepping out of the caveman's shadow: Nations' gender gap predicts degree of sex differentiation in mate preferences. *Psychological Science, 23*(10), 1176–1185. doi:10.1177/0956797612441004

Zernike, K. (2012, August 25). After gay son's suicide, mother finds blame in herself and in her church. *New York Times*, p. A14.

Zerwas, S., & Bulik, C. M. (2011). Genetics and epigenetics of eating disorders. *Psychiatric Annals, 41*(11), 532–538. doi: 10.3928/00485713-20111017-06

Zhang, T. Y., & Meaney, M. J. (2010). Epigenetics and the environmental regulation of the genome and its function. *Annual Review of Psychology, 61*, 439–466.

Zhou, X., Hetrick, S. E., Cuijpers, P., Qin, B., Barth, J., Whittington, C. J., . . . Xie, P. (2015). Comparative efficacy and acceptability of psychotherapies for depression in children and adolescents: A systematic review and network analysis. *World Psychiatry, 14*, 207–222.

Zihl, J., von Cramon, D., & Mai, N. (1983). Selective disturbance of movement vision after bilateral brain damage. *Brain, 106*, 313–340.

Zillmann, D., Katcher, A. H., & Milavsky, B. (1972). Excitation transfer from physical exercise to subsequent aggressive behavior. *Journal of Experimental Psychology, 8*, 247–259.

Zimbardo, P. (2007). *The Lucifer effect: Understanding how good people turn evil.* New York: Random House.

Zimprich, D., & Martin, M. (2002). Can longitudinal changes in processing speed explain longitudinal age changes in fluid intelligence? *Psychology and Aging, 17*, 690–695.

Zuckerman, M., DePaulo, B. M., & Rosenthal, R. (1981). Verbal and nonverbal communication of deception. In L. Berkowitz (Ed.), *Advances in experimental social psychology* (Vol. 14, pp. 1–59). New York: Academic Press.

Zuckerman, M., & Driver, R. E. (1985). Telling lies: Verbal and nonverbal correlates of deception. In W. Seigman & S. Feldstein (Eds.), *Multichannel integrations of nonverbal behavior* (pp. 129–147). Hillsdale, NJ: Erlbaum.

Name Index

A

Abel, T., 174
Abelson, J., 503–504
Abraham, T., 41
Abrams, D., 381
Abramson, L. Y., 459
Acevedo, B. P., 387
Acevedo-Garcia, D., 299
Achter, J. A., 296
Acocella, J., 508
Addis, D. R., 76, 182, 193
Adelmann, P. K., 246
Adelson, E. H., 109
Adler, L., 469
Adolph, K. E., 312
Adolphs, R., 247
Aggleton, J., 69
Agin, D., 48
Agnew, C. R., 388
Agren, T., 173
Ainsworth, M. D. S., 320, 321
Ainsworth, S. E., 377, 381
Alasaari, J. S., 79
Albarracín, D., 395
Albert, Prince of England, 157
Alcoholics Anonymous, 494
Aldao, A., 353
Aleman, A., 503
Alessi, S. M., 489
al-Haytham, I., 29
Alicke, M. D., 368
Allen, R. J., 170
Allison, D. B., 254
Alloy, L. B., 259
Allport, G. W., 16, 349–350, 398
Alpert, N. M., 177
Altschuler, E. L., 74
Alvarez, L., 44
Alvarez, L. W., 456
Amabile, T. M., 43, 403
Ambady, N., 247–248, 299
American Psychiatric Association, 444, 471
American Psychological Association, 18, 46–47, 330, 435, 483, 503
Anderson, C. A., 35, 177–178, 376
Anderson, J. R., 175
Anderson, M. C., 176–177
Anderson, R. E., 176
Andreasen, N. C., 461
Andres, D., 294
Andrewes, D., 79
Andrews, I., 84
Andrews-Hanna, J. R., 84, 135
Annis, D. B., 227
Annis, L. F., 227
Ansfield, M., 138
Anthony, S. B., 389
Antoni, M. H., 433
Apicella, C. L., 15

B

Baars, B. J., 11
Baca-Motes, K., 396
Bach, J. S., 32, 399
Backman, C. W., 387
Bäckman, L., 334
Baddeley, A. D., 170
Badea, C., 399
Bagby, R. M., 352
Bahrick, H. P., 184–185
Bai, D. L., 119
Bailey, J. M., 328–330
Baillargeon, R., 314
Balague, G., 19
Baler, R. D., 60
Baltes, P. B., 334
Banaji, M. R., 400
Bandura, A., 221
Banks, M. S., 311
Barber, J. P., 456, 486
Bard, P., 240–241
Bargh, J. A., 140, 246, 261, 388
Barker, A. T., 84
Barkow, J., 367
Barlow, D. H., 500, 507
Barnett, S. M., 296

Ariely, D., 385
Aristotle, 2
Arkes, H. R., 117
Armstrong, D. M., 134
Arndt, J., 263
Arnold, M. B., 243
Aron, A., 387
Aron, A. P., 242
Aronson, E., 119, 261, 387, 396
Aronson, J., 299, 300
Asch, S. E., 16, 391
Aschoff, J., 141
Ascraft, M. H., 12
Asher, S. J., 44
Ashmore, R. D., 401
Asik, O., 284
Assanand, S., 434
Astington, J. W., 316
Aston, S. J., 9
Atkinson, G., 157
Atkinson, R. C., 166
Atlas, L. Y., 119
Au, J., 170
Aue, W. R., 230
Aung San Suu Kyi, 422
Austin, S. B., 328
Autrey, W., 382
Aviezer, H., 246
Axelrod, R., 379
Ayduk, O., 259

Baronchelli, A., 390
Baron-Cohen, S., 316, 468
Barrett, L. F., 242, 246
Barsade, S. G., 292
Bartal, I. B.-A., 382
Barth, M., 173
Bartol, C. R., 355
Barton, C., 336
Bartoshuk, L. M., 122–123
Basden, B. H., 183
Basquiat, J.-M., 364
Bass, C., 430
Bates, E., 273
Bates, J. E., 321
Batson, C. D., 382
Batty, G. D., 288
Bauer, R., 253
Baumeister, R. F., 258–259, 330, 367, 377, 381, 390, 424, 426, 434
Baxter, L. R., 455
Bayley, P. J., 172, 226
Bear, G., 292
Beatty, M. J., 95
Beauchamp, G. K., 122, 310
Bechara, A., 284–285
Beck, A. T., 459, 490
Becker, J. B., 327
Beckers, G., 85
Bedny, M., 281
Beer, J. S., 365
Bell, A. P., 328
Bellotto, Bernardo, 133
Belmonte, M. K., 468
Belsky, J., 327
Bem, S. L., 354
Benbow, C. P., 296
Benenson, J. F., 378
Bennett, I. J., 226
Benoit, R. G., 177
Ben-Porath, Y. S., 347
Benson, D. F., 244
Benson, H., 423
Bentz, D., 206
Bergen, J. R., 109
Berglund, P., 445
Bergstrom, C. T., 20–21
Bering, J., 223
Berkowitz, A., 392
Berkowitz, L., 376
Bernier, A., 321
Bernstein, I. L., 207
Berridge, K. C., 219
Berry, D. S., 522
Berry, H., 247
Berry, J. W., 18
Berscheid, E., 384–385
Bertenthal, B. I., 119
Berthoud, H.-R., 68–69
Bertrand, J., 272
Bettencourt, B. A., 378

Beunen, G., 326–327
Beutler, L. E., 507
Bhargava, S., 144
Bialystok, E., 277
Bickman, L., 394
Biddle, J. E., 385
Biederman, J., 469
Bierman, K. L., 333
Bilker, J. W., 249
Binet, A., 287–288, 297–298
Binswanger, L., 360
Biro, S., 311
Bjork, R. A., 176
Bjorklund, P., 199
Blackburn, E. H., 416
Blair, C., 300
Blair, I. V., 401
Blair, J., 472
Blakeslee, S., 74
Blanchard, R., 300
Blanchard-Fields, F., 337
Blascovich, J., 418
Blatt, S. J., 459
Bliss, T. V. P., 174
Bloch, C., 275
Bloj, M., 101
Bloom, C. M., 324
Bloom, F. E., 60
Bloom, P., 216, 274
Blunt, J. R., 230
Boakes, R. A., 121
Boden, J. M., 377
Boecker, H., 60
Boehm, J. K., 432–433
Boergers, J., 474
Boinski, S., 223
Boisvert, C. M., 508
Bolger, N., 136
Bondi, M. W., 60
Bontempi, B., 172
Boomsma, D., 78
Booth, R. J., 421
Booth-LaForce, C., 321
Bootzin, R. R., 144
Borges, G., 474
Borghol, N., 79
Borkenau, P., 293
Borkevec, T. D., 144
Born, J., 60
Born, R. T., 10
Börner, K., 20
Bornstein, R. F., 385
Bosco, J., 292
Boss, S. M., 110
Botwin, M. D., 387
Bouazizi, M., 259
Bouchard, C., 326
Bouchard, S. M., 286
Bouchard, T. J., 353
Bouton, M. E., 205

Subject Index

Get the most out of *Introducing Psychology*, Fourth Edition, with LaunchPad, which combines the interactive e-Book with high-quality multimedia content and activities that give immediate feedback.

Learn more at **www.launchpadworks.com**.

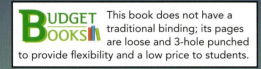

worth publishers
Macmillan Learning

macmillanlearning.com

Cover image: © Jason deCaires Taylor. All rights reserved, DACS/ARS 2017. Photo: Jason deCaires Taylor

ISBN-13: 978-1-4641-5558-1
ISBN-10: 1-4641-5558-5

90000

9 781464 155581